INTERNATIONAL YEARBOOK OF INDUSTRIAL STATISTICS
1999

INTERNATIONAL YEARBOOK OF INDUSTRIAL STATISTICS 1999

UNITED NATIONS INDUSTRIAL DEVELOPMENT ORGANIZATION
VIENNA
1999

Published by
Edward Elgar Publishing Limited
Glensanda House
Montpellier Parade
Cheltenham
Glos GL50 1UA
UK

Edward Elgar Publishing Company
6 Market Street
Northampton
Massachusetts 01060
USA

A catalogue record for this book
is available from the British Library

The description and classification of countries and territories in this publication and the arrangement of the material do not imply the expression of any opinion whatsoever on the part of the Secretariat of the United Nations Industrial Development Organization concerning the legal status of any country, territory, city or area, or of its authorities, or concerning the delimitation of its frontiers or boundaries, or regarding its economic system or degree of development. The designation "country or area" covers countries, territories, cities and areas. The designation "region, country or area" extends the preceding one by including groupings of entities designated as "country or area". Designations such as "industrialized" and "developing" countries and "newly industrialized countries" are intended for statistical convenience and do not necessarily express a judgement about the stage reached by a particular country or area in the development process.

ISBN 1 84064 051 0

Printed and bound in Great Britain by Antony Rowe Ltd, Chippenham, Wiltshire

Explanatory notes

Unless otherwise indicated, "manufacturing" includes the industry groups listed under major division 3 in the *International Standard Industrial Classification of All Economic Activities* [Statistical Papers, Series M, No.4/Rev.2 (United Nations publication, Sales No. E.68.XVII.8)]. It should be noted, however, that several countries have made a switchover from their national industrial classification schemes that were based on, or related to, Revision 2 of the International Standard Industrial Classification of All Economic Activities (ISIC) to those based on, or related to, Revision 3 of ISIC [Statistical Papers, Series M, No.4/Rev.3 (United Nations publication, Sales No. E.90.XVII.II)]. In these instances, "manufacturing" refers to table category D in that classification.

ISIC code numbers are accompanied by a descriptive title (for example in the case of Revision 2 of ISIC, ISIC 323: "Manufacture of leather and products of leather, leather substitutes and fur, except footwear and wearing apparel"). For considerations of space, however, the description is sometimes shortened (that is, ISIC 323 may be described simply as "Leather and fur products"). For both Revisions 2 and 3 of ISIC, all 3- and 4-digit codes and their corresponding descriptive titles are listed in appendix II to the introduction.

This publication contains some references to countries that no longer exist. The statistical indicators, however, generally cover most of the period when they *did* exist. On 3 October 1990, through accession of the German Democratic Republic to the Federal Republic of Germany, the two German States united to form one sovereign State: "Germany". The Union of Soviet Socialist Republics ceased to exist as of 24 December 1991. Data provided for Yugoslavia prior to 1 January 1992 refer to the Socialist Federal Republic of Yugoslavia, which was composed of six republics. Data provided for Yugoslavia after that date refer to the Federal Republic of Yugoslavia, which is composed of two republics (Serbia and Montenegro). Czechoslovakia ceased to exist on 31 December 1992. The successor States are the Czech Republic and Slovakia.

Hong Kong became the Hong Kong Special Administrative Region (SAR) of China on 1 July 1997. In the present publication, unless otherwise stated, data for China do not include data for Hong Kong SAR and for Taiwan Province of China, which are presented separately under China (Hong Kong SAR) and China (Taiwan Province).

In section 1.1, data relating to Ethiopia include the province of Eritrea, which since May 1993 has been an independent country having the same name.

Zaire was renamed the Democratic Republic of the Congo on 17 May 1997. Data for that country are presented under its new name.

In the presentation of several tables individual countries and areas are listed alphabetically, whenever appropriate, within two successive categories: industrialized countries and developing countries. Data relating to selected groups of countries are presented in part I. In addition to regional groupings, developing countries have been further classified into three income categories: developing countries with low income (less than $600 per capita gross domestic product in 1978 at current prices), those with middle income ($600–$1,320) and those with high income (more than $1,320). This group has also been arranged in four development categories: newly industrialized countries (NICs), second-generation NICs, least developed countries and other developing countries. NICs are defined as major exporters of manufactures among developing countries in the mid-1970s, with a share of manufactures in total merchandise exports exceeding 20 per cent. Second-generation NICs are developing countries with a high average annual growth rate (over 15 per cent during the period 1970–1985) and having manufactured exports exceeding $500 million in value in 1985. Countries and areas included in the groups are listed in appendix I to the introduction. Because of a lack of data, some countries could not be included in their respective groups in some tables. Taking into account the large size of its economy, China is not included in the group classified according to income level or the group classified according to development level.

Regardless of the year/period referred to, the country group European Union (EU) is related to the group consisting of the 15 countries shown under that country group in appendix I to the introduction.

In part I, references to dollars ($) are to United States dollars. National currencies have been converted to dollar equivalents by using period average exchange rates as published in *International Financial Statistics* (International Monetary Fund publication) and other sources.

Data converted to dollars by using current exchange rates are liable to be strongly influenced by fluctuations in exchange rates. Annual variations of data converted in that manner may not reflect movements in the national data.

Unless otherwise noted, average annual growth rates are calculated from the data available for each year of a given period (for example, 1980–1990), using a semi-log regression over time. Growth rates are expressed in percentages.

Periods set off by a hyphen (for instance, 1980–1990) include the beginning and end years.

Apparent arithmetical discrepancies, such as percentages that do not add up to precise totals, result from the rounding of basic data or figures known to different degrees of precision.

Three dots (...) indicate that data are not available or are not separately reported.

A dash (-) indicates that an amount is nil or negligible.

The letter "x" designates the item applicable to a country when several options exist.

To avoid ambiguity, the letters "l", "o" and "O" are not used to designate footnotes.

The following abbreviations and acronyms are used:

ASEAN	Association of South-East Asian Nations
CACM	Central American Common Market
CARICOM	Caribbean Community
CEPGL	Economic Community of the Great Lakes Countries
ECOWAS	Economic Community of West African States
EU	European Union
GDP	gross domestic product
ISIC	International Standard Industrial Classification of All Economic Activities
LAIA	Latin American Integration Association
LDCs	least developed countries
MVA	manufacturing value added
n.e.c.	not elsewhere classified
n.e.s.	not elsewhere specified
NICs	newly industrialized countries
OECD	Organisation for Economic Co-operation and Development
OECS	Organization of Eastern Caribbean States
UDEAC	Customs and Economic Union of Central Africa
UMA	Union of the Arab Maghreb
UNIDO	United Nations Industrial Development Organization
UNSD	Statistical Division of the United Nations Secretariat
VAT	value added tax

CONTENTS

PART II. COUNTRY TABLES

Statistics and Information Networks Branch

DATA AVAILABLE IN MACHINE-READABLE FORM

UNIDO maintains databases on industrial statistics, which are available on magnetic tape for mainframes or on microcomputer diskettes. New versions are published annually.

UNIDO Industrial Statistics Database, 3-Digit Level of ISIC Code

- ❑ Time series for more than 170 countries/areas compiled on nine items, including number of establishments, number of persons engaged, number of employees, number of female employees, wages and salaries paid to employees, output, value added, gross fixed capital formation and production indices.
- ❑ Data reported by country for 28 industrial branches.
- ❑ Time series on most items starting in 1963.

UNIDO Industrial Statistics Database, 4-Digit Level of ISIC Code

- ❑ Time series for more than 100 countries/areas compiled on eight items, including number of establishments, number of persons engaged, number of employees, number of female employees, wages and salaries paid to employees, output, value added and gross fixed capital formation.
- ❑ Data reported by country for up to 81 industries.
- ❑ Time series starting in 1981.

UNIDO Industrial Demand-Supply Balance Database

- ❑ Time series (starting in 1981) for more than 70 countries on output, imports, exports and apparent consumption at the 4-digit level of ISIC code (all in current US dollars).
- ❑ Data reported by country for up to 81 industries.

Further details on these three databases may be obtained from:
Statistics and Information Networks Branch, UNIDO, P.O. Box 300, A-1400 Vienna, Austria
Fax: +43-1-26026-6802 INTERNET: http://www.unido.org

INTRODUCTION

This is the fifth issue of UNIDO's annual publication, the *International Yearbook of Industrial Statistics*. The *Yearbook* succeeded the *Handbook of Industrial Statistics* which was published biennially by UNIDO up to 1992, and, at the same time, replaced the United Nations' *Industrial Statistics Yearbook,* volume I (General Industrial Statistics), which was discontinued after its 1991 edition published in 1993. These changes were in accordance with the recommendations of the United Nations Statistical Commission at its twenty-seventh session, namely that UNIDO, in collaboration with the Organisation for Economic Co-operation and Development (OECD), assumes responsibility for the collection and dissemination of world-wide general industrial statistics, effective 1994. The present *Yearbook* pertains to the manufacturing sector only.

The main purpose of the *Yearbook* is to provide statistical indicators to facilitate international comparisons relating to the manufacturing sector. The data presented were compiled bearing in mind the requirements of international comparability and the standards for this work promulgated by the United Nations. Concepts and definitions are drawn from the *International Recommendations for Industrial Statistics* [Statistical Papers, Series M, No.48/Rev.1 (United Nations publication, Sales No.E.83.XVII.8)] and the classification by industry follows Revision 2 or, for several countries, Revision 3 of ISIC.

The present *Yearbook* consists of two parts. Part I deals with the manufacturing sector as a whole (section 1.1) and with its branches (section 1.2). Statistical indicators are presented in terms of percentage distributions, cross-country averages, ratios and real growth rates that facilitate international comparison among selected country groups and/or countries. Data for manufacturing branches are arranged according to Revision 2 of ISIC at the three-digit (or major-group) level. Part II consists of a series of country/area-specific tables showing detailed data on selected basic statistics that were reported by national statistical offices. For the majority of the countries, data are presented in accordance with Revision 2 of ISIC. Several countries, however, have made a switchover from their national industrial classifications compatible with Revision 2 to those compatible with Revision 3 of ISIC. Consequently, data for those countries are presented in accordance with Revision 3 of ISIC.

Sources and methods

In section 1.1 of part I, manufacturing value added (MVA) was estimated in accordance with the national accounting concept, which represents the net contribution of the manufacturing sector to gross domestic product (GDP). The data on MVA and GDP were obtained from various national and international sources including OECD, the World Bank, the Statistical Division of the United Nations Secretariat (UNSD), the International Monetary Fund and regional development banks. These sources were supplemented with estimates generated by UNIDO. Owing to a major revision of data, there might be significant differences between the data shown in the present edition of the *Yearbook* and those shown in its previous editions. With respect to population, the information draws on the 1996 revision of the data compiled by the Population Division of the United Nations Secretariat.

The information in section 1.2 is drawn from the UNIDO Industrial Statistics Database. A large portion of the data for the years up to 1992 maintained in the database are those communicated to the United Nations by official national sources. The data for 1993 onwards, as well as additions and revisions of data referring to previous years, were reported by national statistical offices through the UNIDO General Industrial Statistics Questionnaire. With regard to figures for recent years, those referring to the member countries of OECD were compiled by that organization. New information is solicited through a questionnaire issued jointly by the two organizations.

To facilitate the comparability of the data over time and across countries, UNIDO has supplemented originally reported data with information obtained from various other sources. The latter include: industrial censuses, statistics supplied by national and international organizations, unpublished data collected in the field by UNIDO as well as estimates made by the UNIDO secretariat.*

All indicators related to value data were derived at constant 1990 prices, except for several indicators presented in tables 1.1, 1.4 and 1.11.

The indicators presented in tables 1.5 to 1.9 of section 1.2 were derived from estimates of value added at constant 1990 prices. For each country and industrial branch, these value-added estimates were generated by applying production indexes to the 1990 value-added base weights, which in turn were generated by UNIDO from various national and international sources.

---

* UNIDO's procedures for estimation are described in *"UNIDO Industrial Statistics Database — Methodological Notes"* (IRD/R.11).

Because of the increasing number of countries which have made a switchover in their reporting systems from Revision 2 to Revision 3 of ISIC, the compilation of data in accordance with Revision 2 of ISIC required considerable data estimation. Consequently, the data shown in the present edition of the *Yearbook* might not be strictly comparable with those shown in previous editions.

Users should be aware that, in section 1.2 of part I (except table 1.11), owing to a lack of relevant data, China is not included.

Except for index numbers of industrial production, the information for the countries and areas other than the OECD member countries presented in part II were compiled from (i) the 1996 edition of the UNIDO General Industrial Statistics Questionnaire completed by national statistical offices and (ii) relevant publications issued by national statistical offices. Information referring to OECD member countries is based on data compiled by OECD via questionnaire and incorporated in OECD's Information System on Industrial Statistics as well as in the UNIDO database. With respect to production indexes, data were supplied by UNSD which compiles these data regularly from national sources through the quarterly United Nations Index of Industrial Production Questionnaire.

In section 1.2 of part I and in part II, the measures generally used are census output and census value added. Thus, the costs of non-industrial services are included in value added, whereas the receipts for these services are excluded from output. For a quick reference, appendix III to this introduction provides notes on certain aspects of the data used, and it is recommended that the reader consult them when using the *Yearbook*. A detailed version appears in the individual country notes in part II, which also covers deviations from the standards applied. In general, these notes are also applicable to the estimates that supplement the officially reported data.

The co-operation of national statistical offices, OECD and UNSD in the provision of the information which is the basis of the current publication is gratefully acknowledged.

PART I. SUMMARY TABLES

Section 1.1: The manufacturing sector

Section 1.1 comprises tables 1.1 to 1.4. Table 1.1 shows the distribution of world MVA for various regions and groups of countries at constant 1990 prices as well as at current prices.

The reader should be aware that due to variation in official exchange rates the world distribution may change considerably depending on the choice of the base year.

To maintain comparability over time, composition of each group of countries was kept the same throughout the period. In this connection, EU refers to the following 15 countries: Austria, Belgium, Denmark, Finland, France, Germany, Greece, Ireland, Italy, Luxembourg, Netherlands, Portugal, Spain, Sweden and United Kingdom of Great Britain and Northern Ireland. However, due to data limitations the eastern part of Germany is excluded up to 1990.

Table 1.2 shows the shares of selected groups of developing countries in MVA and in population of all developing countries.

Table 1.3 shows real growth rates and index numbers (1990=100) of total and per-capita MVA as well as values of per-capita MVA for the latest year for individual countries and areas and for selected country groups. Data referring to country groups were based on cross-country aggregates of MVA in constant 1990 US dollars.

Table 1.4 shows the percentage shares of MVA in GDP estimated both at constant 1990 prices and at current prices. In a number of cases, consolidation of data at constant and current prices, often originating from different sources, required adjustments to the entire time series. The data are presented by individual countries and areas as well as by selected country groups. GDP has been calculated as the sum of value added of individual sectors. Data given for individual sectors may sum up to an amount different from data given for total GDP. The sources of this discrepancy are specific to each country and are rarely documented. With respect to the selected country groups, common country samples were taken for both indicators and for all reference years. Furthermore, the shares of MVA in GDP are aggregated at the level of the grouping by dividing the sum of MVA by the sum of GDP.

Section 1.2: The manufacturing branches

Section 1.2 comprises tables 1.5 to 1.11. It focuses on the branches of the manufacturing sector. Branches are defined as major ISIC (Revision 2) groups, reported in accordance with a three-digit code. The ISIC definition of manufacturing comprises 28 major groups or branches.

Table 1.5 shows the world distribution of the respective value added of selected 24 branches among selected country groups. Four branches are omitted from the table because the data are too scanty to ensure comparability between years. To derive world totals for the latest years, a number of estimates at the country level, especially for many developing countries, were generated.

Table 1.6 shows the shares of developing regions and the least developed countries in the value added of all developing countries in selected branches. Due to lack of sufficient data, estimates at the country level had to be generated to enable regional aggregation. Instead of 1996, the year 1995 has been chosen as the latest year. Nevertheless, a number of branches had to be excluded from the presentation due to data limitations.

Table 1.7 shows the world's leading producers in various industrial branches as well as the leading developing countries and areas in terms of value added. World totals exclude the countries of eastern Europe and of the former USSR. As in the case of table 1.5, data for 1996 include many estimates generated for individual countries.

Table 1.8 shows the shares of individual branches in total MVA by country grouping. In the case of developing countries the data coverage is limited but still representative; it includes 70 countries and areas which in 1990 accounted for more than 90 per cent of the MVA of all developing countries.

Table 1.9 shows real growth rates of value added of individual branches, calculated for selected country groups. The reference periods are 1980–1990 and 1990–1996. However, due to lack of comparable data, the second period is 1990–1995 or 1990–1994 in several cases.

Table 1.10 presents the share of female employees in total employment in individual branches. For some countries, employment refers to number of persons engaged instead of number of employees (see appendix III of the present introduction). Only a limited number of countries and areas have reported data on female employment at the branch level.

Table 1.11 shows, for individual countries and areas, basic indicators that are characteristic of the manufacturing branches. Average annual rates of growth refer to compound rates based on data for the initial and terminal years indicated. For the calculations of real growth rates of value added per employee and those of wage rates, value added estimates at constant 1990 prices were derived using production indexes while wages at constant 1990 prices were derived by deflating wages at current prices with consumer price indexes. Costs of input materials and utilities are calculated as output minus value added. Costs of labour refer to wages and salaries of employees only. Operating surplus is calculated as value added minus wages and salaries paid to employees.

Information concerning the following branches is excluded from table 1.11: beverages (ISIC 313); tobacco (ISIC 314); petroleum refineries (ISIC 353); and petroleum and coal products (ISIC 354). Production indicators (output, value added) for those four branches are highly sensitive to the valuation method (which may or may not include indirect taxes and subsidies). Because that method is not applied uniformly among countries, international comparison of the branches concerned is not advisable. Two more branches were excluded due to lack of sufficient data, i.e., professional and scientific equipment (ISIC 385) and other manufactures (ISIC 390).

PART II. COUNTRY TABLES

Part II comprises country/area-specific tables presenting the following selected industrial statistics: number of establishments, number of employees (or, if not reported, number of persons engaged), wages and salaries paid to employees, output, value added, gross fixed capital formation and index numbers of industrial production. All value data are presented in current national currencies. The data on these items (except gross fixed capital formation and index numbers of industrial production) relate to the last four years for which data were reported. Gross fixed capital formation refers to the last two years for which data were reported. Index numbers of industrial production refer to the period 1985-1996. When presented in accordance with Revision 2 of ISIC, production indexes for total manufacturing were derived as weighted averages across branches employing 1990 value-added base weights which were estimated by UNIDO.

Industrial classification

The classification of industrial activity set out in the tables follows either Revision 2 or Revision 3 of ISIC depending on the individual country's data reporting scheme. In either case, the employed levels of detail are the three- and four-digit levels of ISIC, or the three-digit level if no data on four-digit groups were reported. With regard to production indexes, data are arranged either in accordance with the 3-digit level of Revision 2 of ISIC or in accordance with the 2-digit level of Revision 3 of ISIC. Where information was not provided in this form, the estimates are shown in the most applicable category. Aggregates for total manufacturing are included.

It should be noted that in several cases a figure presented for a 3-digit group does not agree with the sum of data given for the corresponding 4-digit categories. As far as possible, UNIDO resolved these discrepancies with the help of available supplementary information.

Reference unit
For most countries and areas represented, the data shown relate to the activity of "establishments" in the specified industries rather than any other type of industrial unit. In a few cases, however, the concepts of "kind-of-activity unit", "local unit" or "enterprise" are found. An "establishment" is ideally a unit which engages, under a single ownership or control, in one, or predominantly one, kind of activity at a single location; for example, workshop or factory. A "kind-of-activity unit" differs from the establishment in that there is no restriction with respect to the geographical area in which a given kind of activity is carried out by a single legal entity. A "local unit", on the other hand, comprises all activities carried out under a single ownership or control at a single location and differs from the establishment-type of unit in that there is no restriction on the range of these activities.

An "enterprise" is a legal entity possessing the right to conduct business in its own name; for example, to enter into contracts, own property, incur liability for debts, and establish bank accounts. In the countries of eastern Europe and of the former USSR, the reference unit is often the enterprise and this is usually defined as the unit having a single administration with the right to conclude contracts, an independent production plan, an independent current bank account and a self-contained system of bookkeeping with independent balance sheets and profit-and-loss statements. Specific information on the character of the units covered in the tables for each country is set out in the corresponding country note.

Reference period
The statistics in the tables relate, in general, to the calendar year. It should be noted, however, that in many cases where the basic reference period of the industrial inquiry is the calendar year, returns covering proximate fiscal years may be accepted for reporting purposes and the data for these years incorporated in the calendar-year aggregates without adjustment. In a few countries, fiscal years normally used for public accounting purposes have been adopted as the basic reference periods. In the case of fiscal-year coverage, the year indicated in the tables refers to the calendar year in which the major part of the fiscal year falls. In the case of fiscal years from 1 July to 30 June, the year referred to is normally the one in which the fiscal year ends.

Concepts and definitions of the items
The United Nations standards which have been applied in preparing the tables are set out below. All values are in national currency units and are at current prices unless otherwise indicated. For countries other than the OECD member countries, deviations from these concepts and definitions are described in the respective country notes. The country notes referring to OECD member countries are based on information presented in annex I ("Sources and Definitions") of OECD's annual publication "*Industrial Structure Statistics*".

(1) Number of persons engaged and number of employees
The number of persons engaged is defined as the total number of persons who worked in or for the establishment during the reference year. However, homeworkers are excluded. The concept covers working proprietors, active business partners and unpaid family workers as well as employees. The figures reported refer normally to the average number of persons engaged during the reference year, obtained as the sum of the "average number of employees" during the year and the total number of other persons engaged measured for a single period of the year. The category "employees" is intended to include all persons engaged other than working proprietors, active business partners and unpaid family workers. In this publication, preference has been given, whenever possible, to employees over persons engaged.

(2) Wages and salaries
Estimates of wages and salaries include all payments in cash or in kind made to "employees" during the reference year in relation to work done for the establishment. Payments include: (a) direct wages and salaries; (b) remuneration for time not worked; (c) bonuses and gratuities; (d) housing allowances and family allowances paid directly by the employer; and (e) payments in kind.

Compensation of employees is equivalent to wages and salaries plus employers' contributions on behalf of their employees paid to social security, pension and insurance schemes, as well as the benefits received by employees under these schemes and severance and termination pay.

(3) Output
The measure of output normally used in the tables is the census concept which covers only activities of an industrial nature. The value of census output in the case of estimates compiled on a production basis comprises: (a) the value of all products of the establishment; (b) the net change between the beginning and the end of the reference period in the value of work in progress and stocks of goods to be shipped in the same condition as received; (c) the value of industrial work done or industrial services rendered to others; (d) the value of goods shipped in the same condition as received less the amount paid for these goods; and (e) the value of fixed assets

produced during the period by the unit for its own use. In the case of estimates compiled on a shipment basis, the net change in the value of stocks of finished goods between the beginning and the end of the reference period is also included.

Gross output is equivalent to census output plus the revenue from activities of a non-industrial nature. Valuation may be in factor values, excluding all indirect taxes falling on production and including all current subsidies received in support of production activity, or in producers' prices, including all indirect taxes and excluding all subsidies.

(4) Value added

The measure of value added normally used in the tables is the census concept, which is defined as the value of census output less the value of census input. Items covered in the latter include: (a) value of materials and supplies for production (including cost of all fuel and purchased electricity); and (b) cost of industrial services received (mainly payments for contract and commission work and repair and maintenance work). If input estimates are compiled on a "received" rather than on a "consumed" basis, the result is adjusted for the net change between the beginning and the end of the period in the value of stocks of materials, fuel and other supplies.

Total value added is the national accounting concept. It is ideally represented by the contribution of the establishments in each branch of activity to the gross domestic product. For the measure of total value added, the cost of non-industrial services is deducted and the receipts for non-industrial services are added to census value added. The estimates, whether in terms of census value added or total value added, are gross of depreciation and other provisions for capital consumption, unless otherwise stated. The valuation may be in factor costs or in producers' prices, depending on the treatment of indirect taxes and subsidies.

(5) Gross fixed capital formation

Estimates refer to the value of purchases and own-account construction of fixed assets during the reference year less the value of corresponding sales. The fixed assets covered are those (whether new or used) with a productive life of one year or more. These assets, which are intended for the use of the establishment, include fixed assets made by the establishment's own labour force for its own use. Major additions, alterations and improvements to existing assets which extend their normal economic life or raise their productivity are also included.

New fixed assets include all those that have not been previously used in the country. Thus, newly imported fixed assets are considered new whether or not used before they were imported. Used fixed assets include all those that have been previously used within the country. Transactions in fixed assets include: (a) land; (b) buildings, other construction and land improvements; (c) transport equipment; and (d) machinery and other equipment.

Assets acquired from others are valued at purchasers' prices, which cover all costs directly connected with the acquisition and installation of the items for use. In principle, assets produced on own account are also valued in this manner. However, it may frequently be necessary to value such own-account production at explicit cost, including any imputations that may be required in respect of the employed own-account labour. Assets produced by one establishment of a multi-establishment enterprise for the use of another establishment of the same enterprise should be valued by the receiving establishment as though purchased from outside the enterprise. Sales of assets should be valued at the actual amounts realized rather than at book values.

(6) Index numbers of industrial production

The indexes in the tables are compiled from national indexes which are calculated by use of the Laspeyres formula. The comparison base year is 1990. However, if different base years are used in any countries, the national indexes are converted to the comparison base year.

APPENDIX I

LIST OF COUNTRIES AND AREAS INCLUDED IN SELECTED GROUPINGS

INDUSTRIALIZED COUNTRIES

East. Europe and former USSR

Albania
Bulgaria
Czechoslovakia (former) *
Germany, eastern part
Hungary
Poland
Romania
USSR (former) **

Western Europe

Austria
Belgium
Denmark
Finland
France
Germany, western part
Greece
Iceland
Ireland
Italy
Luxembourg
Netherlands
Norway
Portugal
Spain
Sweden
Switzerland
United Kingdom

Japan

North America

Canada
United States of America

Others

Australia
Israel
New Zealand
South Africa

EU

Austria
Belgium
Denmark
Finland
France
Germany
Greece
Ireland
Italy
Luxembourg
Netherlands
Portugal
Spain
Sweden
United Kingdom

DEVELOPING COUNTRIES/AREAS

Algeria
Angola
Anguilla
Antigua and Barbuda
Argentina
Bahrain
Bangladesh
Barbados
Belize
Benin
Bermuda
Bhutan
Bolivia
Botswana
Brazil
British Virgin Islands
Brunei Darussalam
Burkina Faso
Burundi
Cambodia
Cameroon
Cape Verde
Central African Republic
Chad
Chile
China
China (Hong Kong SAR)
China (Taiwan Province)
Colombia
Comoros
Congo
Costa Rica
Côte d'Ivoire
Cuba
Cyprus
Democratic Rep. of the Congo
Djibouti
Dominica
Dominican Republic
Ecuador
Egypt
El Salvador
Equatorial Guinea
Ethiopia
Fiji
French Guiana
French Polynesia
Gabon
Gambia
Ghana
Grenada
Guadeloupe
Guatemala
Guinea
Guinea-Bissau
Guyana
Haiti
Honduras
India
Indonesia
Iran (Islamic Republic of)
Iraq
Jamaica
Jordan
Kenya
Kuwait
Lebanon
Lesotho
Liberia
Libyan Arab Jamahiriya
Madagascar
Malawi
Malaysia
Maldives
Mali
Malta
Martinique
Mauritania
Mauritius
Mexico
Mongolia
Montserrat
Morocco
Mozambique
Myanmar
Namibia
Nepal
Netherlands Antilles
New Caledonia
Nicaragua
Niger
Nigeria
Oman
Pakistan
Panama
Papua New Guinea
Paraguay
Peru
Philippines
Puerto Rico
Qatar
Republic of Korea
Réunion
Rwanda
Saint Lucia
Sao Tome and Principe
Saudi Arabia
Senegal
Seychelles
Sierra Leone
Singapore
Solomon Islands
Somalia
Sri Lanka
St. Kitts and Nevis
St. Vincent and the Grenadines
Sudan
Suriname
Swaziland
Syrian Arab Republic
Thailand
Togo
Tonga
Trinidad and Tobago
Tunisia
Turkey
Uganda
United Arab Emirates
United Republic of Tanzania
Uruguay
Vanuatu
Venezuela
Yemen
Yugoslavia (former) ***
Zambia
Zimbabwe

Depending on data availability the following countries are treated separately:

* Czech Republic and Slovakia.
** Armenia, Azerbaijan, Belarus, Estonia, Georgia, Kazakhstan, Kyrgyzstan, Latvia, Lithuania, Republic of Moldova, Russian Federation, Tajikistan, Turkmenistan, Ukraine, and Uzbekistan.
*** Bosnia and Herzegovina, Croatia, Slovenia, the former Yugoslav Republic of Macedonia, and Yugoslavia, Federal Republic of.

(continued)

APPENDIX I

LIST OF COUNTRIES AND AREAS INCLUDED IN SELECTED GROUPINGS

DEVELOPING COUNTRY GROUPINGS BY REGION, INCOME GROUP AND DEVELOPMENT GROUP

Region, country or area	Income group			Development group			
	Low income	Middle income	High income	LDCs	NICs	Second-generation NICs	Others
AFRICA							
North Africa							
Algeria		X					X
Egypt	X						X
Libyan Arab Jamahiriya			X				X
Morocco		X				X	
Sudan	X			X			
Tunisia		X				X	
Central Africa							
Angola	X			X			
Burundi	X			X			
Cameroon	X						X
Central African Republic	X			X			
Chad	X			X			
Congo		X					X
Democratic Rep. of the Congo	X			X			
Equatorial Guinea	X			X			
Gabon			X				X
Rwanda	X			X			
Sao Tome and Principe	X			X			
Western Africa (ECOWAS)							
Benin	X			X			
Burkina Faso	X			X			
Cape Verde	X			X			
Côte d'Ivoire		X					X
Gambia	X			X			
Ghana		X					X
Guinea	X			X			
Guinea-Bissau	X			X			
Liberia	X			X			
Mali	X			X			
Mauritania	X			X			
Niger	X			X			
Nigeria		X					X
Senegal	X						X
Sierra Leone	X			X			
Togo	X			X			

APPENDIX I

(continued)

LIST OF COUNTRIES AND AREAS INCLUDED IN SELECTED GROUPINGS

DEVELOPING COUNTRY GROUPINGS BY REGION, INCOME GROUP AND DEVELOPMENT GROUP

Region, country or area	Income group: Low income	Income group: Middle income	Income group: High income	Development group: LDCs	Development group: NICs	Development group: Second-generation NICs	Development group: Others
Eastern and southern Africa							
Botswana	X						X
Comoros	X			X			
Djibouti		X		X			
Ethiopia	X			X			
Kenya	X						X
Lesotho	X			X			
Madagascar	X			X			
Malawi	X			X			
Mauritius		X					X
Mozambique	X			X			
Namibia			X				X
Réunion			X				X
Seychelles			X				X
Somalia	X			X			
Swaziland	X						X
Uganda	X			X			
United Republic of Tanzania	X			X			
Zambia	X			X			
Zimbabwe	X						X
LATIN AMERICA							
Anguilla		X					X
Antigua and Barbuda		X					X
Argentina			X		X		
Barbados			X				X
Belize		X					X
Bermuda			X				X
Bolivia		X					X
Brazil			X		X		
British Virgin Islands			X				X
Chile			X				X
Colombia		X				X	
Costa Rica			X				X
Cuba		X					X
Dominica		X					X
Dominican Republic		X					X
Ecuador		X					X
El Salvador		X					X
French Guiana			X				X

APPENDIX I

(continued)

LIST OF COUNTRIES AND AREAS INCLUDED IN SELECTED GROUPINGS

DEVELOPING COUNTRY GROUPINGS BY REGION, INCOME GROUP AND DEVELOPMENT GROUP

Region, country or area	Income group			Development group			
	Low income	Middle income	High income	LDCs	NICs	Second-generation NICs	Others
Grenada	X						X
Guadeloupe			X				X
Guatemala		X					X
Guyana	X						X
Haiti	X			X			
Honduras	X						X
Jamaica		X					X
Martinique			X				X
Mexico			X		X		
Montserrat		X					X
Netherlands Antilles			X				X
Nicaragua		X					X
Panama		X					X
Paraguay		X					X
Peru		X					X
Puerto Rico			X				X
Saint Lucia		X					X
St. Kitts and Nevis		X					X
St. Vincent and the Grenadines	X						X
Suriname			X				X
Trinidad and Tobago			X				X
Uruguay			X				X
Venezuela			X				X
WEST ASIA AND EUROPE							
Bahrain			X				X
Cyprus			X				X
Iraq			X				X
Jordan		X					X
Kuwait			X				X
Lebanon		X					X
Malta			X				X
Oman			X				X
Qatar			X				X
Saudi Arabia			X				X
Syrian Arab Republic		X					X
Turkey		X				X	
United Arab Emirates			X				X
Yemen	X			X			
Yugoslavia (former) *			X		X		

Depending on data availability the following countries are treated separately:

* Bosnia and Herzegovina, Croatia, Slovenia, the former Yugoslav Republic of Macedonia, and Yugoslavia, Federal Republic of.

APPENDIX I

(continued)

LIST OF COUNTRIES AND AREAS INCLUDED IN SELECTED GROUPINGS

DEVELOPING COUNTRY GROUPINGS BY REGION, INCOME GROUP AND DEVELOPMENT GROUP

Region, country or area	Income group: Low income	Income group: Middle income	Income group: High income	Development group: LDCs	Development group: NICs	Development group: Second-generation NICs	Development group: Others
SOUTH AND EAST ASIA							
Bangladesh	X			X			
Bhutan	X			X			
Brunei Darussalam			X				X
Cambodia	X			X			
China							
China (Hong Kong SAR)			X		X		
China (Taiwan Province)			X		X		
Fiji			X				X
French Polynesia			X				X
India	X				X		
Indonesia	X					X	
Iran (Islamic Republic of)			X				X
Malaysia		X				X	
Maldives	X			X			
Mongolia		X					X
Myanmar	X			X			
Nepal	X			X			
New Caledonia			X				X
Pakistan	X						X
Papua New Guinea		X					X
Philippines	X					X	
Republic of Korea		X			X		
Singapore			X		X		
Solomon Islands	X			X			
Sri Lanka	X						X
Thailand	X					X	
Tonga	X						X
Vanuatu	X			X			

(continued)

APPENDIX I
LIST OF COUNTRIES AND AREAS INCLUDED IN SELECTED GROUPINGS

OTHER DEVELOPING COUNTRY GROUPINGS

Andean group

Bolivia
Colombia
Ecuador
Peru
Venezuela

ASEAN

Brunei Darussalam
Indonesia
Lao People's Dem. Rep. *
Malaysia
Myanmar
Philippines
Singapore
Thailand
Viet Nam *

CACM

Costa Rica
El Salvador
Guatemala
Honduras
Nicaragua

CARICOM

Antigua and Barbuda
Bahamas
Barbados
Belize
Dominica
Grenada
Guyana
Jamaica
Montserrat
Saint Lucia
St. Kitts and Nevis
St. Vincent and the Grenadines
Suriname
Trinidad and Tobago

CEPGL

Burundi
Rwanda
Democratic Rep. of the Congo

LAIA

Argentina
Bolivia
Brazil
Chile
Colombia
Ecuador
Mexico
Paraguay
Peru
Uruguay
Venezuela

UMA

Algeria
Libyan Arab Jamahiriya
Mauritania
Morocco
Tunisia

Mano River Union

Guinea
Liberia
Sierra Leone

OECS

Antigua and Barbuda
Dominica
Grenada
Montserrat
Saint Lucia
St. Kitts and Nevis
St. Vincent and the Grenadines

UDEAC

Cameroon
Central African Republic
Chad
Congo
Equatorial Guinea
Gabon

---

* Not included in any computation due to limited availability of data.

APPENDIX II

DETAILED DESCRIPTION OF INTERNATIONAL STANDARD INDUSTRIAL CLASSIFICATION OF ALL ECONOMIC ACTIVITIES (ISIC) - REVISIONS 2 AND 3

ISIC REVISION 2

ISIC		Description
3		**MANUFACTURING**
311/2		**Food manufacturing**
	3111	Slaughtering, preparing and preserving meat
	3112	Manufacture of dairy products
	3113	Canning and preserving of fruits and vegetables
	3114	Canning, preserving and processing of fish, crustacea and similar foods
	3115	Manufacture of vegetable and animal oils and fats
	3116	Grain mill products
	3117	Manufacture of bakery products
	3118	Sugar factories and refineries
	3119	Manufacture of cocoa, chocolate and sugar confectionery
	3121	Manufacture of food products not elsewhere classified
	3122	Manufacture of prepared animal feeds
313		**Beverage industries**
	3131	Distilling, rectifying and blending spirits
	3132	Wine industries
	3133	Malt liquors and malt
	3134	Soft drinks and carbonated waters industries
314	**3140**	**Tobacco manufactures**
321		**Manufacture of textiles**
	3211	Spinning, weaving and finishing textiles
	3212	Manufacture of made-up textile goods except wearing apparel
	3213	Knitting mills
	3214	Manufacture of carpets and rugs
	3215	Cordage, rope and twine industries
	3219	Manufacture of textiles not elsewhere classified
322	**3220**	**Manufacture of wearing apparel, except footwear**
323		**Manufacture of leather and products of leather, leather substitutes and fur, except footwear and wearing apparel**
	3231	Tanneries and leather finishing
	3232	Fur dressing and dyeing industries
	3233	Manufacture of products of leather and leather substitutes, except footwear and wearing apparel

ISIC REVISION 2 (continued)

ISIC		Description
324	**3240**	**Manufacture of footwear, except vulcanized or moulded rubber or plastic footwear**
331		**Manufacture of wood and wood and cork products, except furniture**
	3311	Sawmills, planing and other wood mills
	3312	Manufacture of wooden and cane containers and small cane ware
	3319	Manufacture of wood and cork products not elsewhere classified
332	**3320**	**Manufacture of furniture and fixtures, except primarily of metal**
341		**Manufacture of paper and paper products**
	3411	Manufacture of pulp, paper and paperboard
	3412	Manufacture of containers and boxes of paper and paperboard
	3419	Manufacture of pulp, paper and paperboard articles not elsewhere classified
342	**3420**	**Printing, publishing and allied industries**
351		**Manufacture of industrial chemicals**
	3511	Manufacture of basic industrial chemicals except fertilizers
	3512	Manufacture of fertilizers and pesticides
	3513	Manufacture of synthetic resins, plastic materials and man-made fibres except glass
352		**Manufacture of other chemical products**
	3521	Manufacture of paints, varnishes and lacquers
	3522	Manufacture of drugs and medicines
	3523	Manufacture of soap and cleaning preparations, perfumes, cosmetics and other toilet preparations
	3529	Manufacture of chemical products not elsewhere classified
353	**3530**	**Petroleum refineries**
354	**3540**	**Manufacture of miscellaneous products of petroleum and coal**
355		**Manufacture of rubber products**
	3551	Tyre and tube industries
	3559	Manufacture of rubber products not elsewhere classified
356	**3560**	**Manufacture of plastic products not elsewhere classified**
361	**3610**	**Manufacture of pottery, china and earthenware**
362	**3620**	**Manufacture of glass and glass products**
369		**Manufacture of other non-metallic mineral products**
	3691	Manufacture of structural clay products
	3692	Manufacture of cement, lime and plaster
	3699	Manufacture of non-metallic mineral products not elsewhere classified

ISIC REVISION 2 (continued)

ISIC		Description
371	**3710**	**Iron and steel basic industries**
372	**3720**	**Non-ferrous metal basic industries**
381		**Manufacture of fabricated metal products, except machinery and equipment**
	3811	Manufacture of cutlery, hand tools and general hardware
	3812	Manufacture of furniture and fixtures primarily of metal
	3813	Manufacture of structural metal products
	3819	Manufacture of fabricated metal products except machinery and equipment not elsewhere classified
382		**Manufacture of machinery except electrical**
	3821	Manufacture of engines and turbines
	3822	Manufacture of agricultural machinery and equipment
	3823	Manufacture of metal and wood working machinery
	3824	Manufacture of special industrial machinery and equipment except metal and wood working machinery
	3825	Manufacture of office, computing and accounting machinery
	3829	Machinery and equipment except electrical not elsewhere classified
383		**Manufacture of electrical machinery, apparatus, appliances and supplies**
	3831	Manufacture of electrical industrial machinery and apparatus
	3832	Manufacture of radio, television and communication equipment and apparatus
	3833	Manufacture of electrical appliances and housewares
	3839	Manufacture of electrical apparatus and supplies not elsewhere classified
384		**Manufacture of transport equipment**
	3841	Ship building and repairing
	3842	Manufacture of railroad equipment
	3843	Manufacture of motor vehicles
	3844	Manufacture of motorcycles and bicycles
	3845	Manufacture of aircraft
	3849	Manufacture of transport equipment not elsewhere classified
385		**Manufacture of professional and scientific, and measuring and controlling equipment not elsewhere classified, and of photographic and optical goods**
	3851	Manufacture of professional and scientific, and measuring and controlling equipment, not elsewhere classified
	3852	Manufacture of photographic and optical goods
	3853	Manufacture of watches and clocks
390		**Other manufacturing industries**
	3901	Manufacture of jewellery and related articles
	3902	Manufacture of music instruments
	3903	Manufacture of sporting and athletic goods
	3909	Manufacturing industries not elsewhere classified

ISIC REVISION 3

ISIC		Description
D		**MANUFACTURING**
151		**Production, processing and preservation of meat, fish, fruit, vegetables, oils and fats**
	1511	Production, processing and preserving of meat and meat products
	1512	Processing and preserving of fish and fish products
	1513	Processing and preserving of fruit and vegetables
	1514	Manufacture of vegetable and animal oils and fats
152	**1520**	**Manufacture of dairy products**
153		**Manufacture of grain mill products, starches and starch products, and prepared animal feeds**
	1531	Manufacture of grain mill products
	1532	Manufacture of starches and starch products
	1533	Manufacture of prepared animal feeds
154		**Manufacture of other food products**
	1541	Manufacture of bakery products
	1542	Manufacture of sugar
	1543	Manufacture of cocoa, chocolate and sugar confectionery
	1544	Manufacture of macaroni, noodles, couscous and similar farinaceous products
	1549	Manufacture of other food products n.e.c.
155		**Manufacture of beverages**
	1551	Distilling, rectifying and blending of spirits; ethyl alcohol production from fermented materials
	1552	Manufacture of wines
	1553	Manufacture of malt liquors and malt
	1554	Manufacture of soft drinks; production of mineral waters
160	**1600**	**Manufacture of tobacco products**
171		**Spinning, weaving and finishing of textiles**
	1711	Preparation and spinning of textile fibres; weaving of textiles
	1712	Finishing of textiles
172		**Manufacture of other textiles**
	1721	Manufacture of made-up textile articles, except apparel
	1722	Manufacture of carpets and rugs
	1723	Manufacture of cordage, rope, twine and netting
	1729	Manufacture of other textiles n.e.c.
173	**1730**	**Manufacture of knitted and crocheted fabrics and articles**
181	**1810**	**Manufacture of wearing apparel, except fur apparel**
182	**1820**	**Dressing and dyeing of fur; manufacture of articles of fur**

ISIC REVISION 3 (continued)

ISIC		Description
191		**Tanning and dressing of leather; manufacture of luggage, handbags, saddlery and harness**
	1911	Tanning and dressing of leather
	1912	Manufacture of luggage, handbags and the like, saddlery and harness
192	**1920**	**Manufacture of footwear**
201	**2010**	**Sawmilling and planing of wood**
202		**Manufacture of products of wood, cork, straw and plaiting materials**
	2021	Manufacture of veneer sheets; manufacture of plywood, laminboard, particle board and other panels and boards
	2022	Manufacture of builders' carpentry and joinery
	2023	Manufacture of wooden containers
	2029	Manufacture of other products of wood; manufacture of articles of cork, straw and plaiting materials
210		**Manufacture of paper and paper products**
	2101	Manufacture of pulp, paper and paperboard
	2102	Manufacture of corrugated paper and paperboard and of containers of paper and paperboard
	2109	Manufacture of other articles of paper and paperboard
221		**Publishing**
	2211	Publishing of books, brochures, musical books and other publications
	2212	Publishing of newspapers, journals and periodicals
	2213	Publishing of recorded media
	2219	Other publishing
222		**Printing and service activities related to printing**
	2221	Printing
	2222	Service activities related to printing
223	**2230**	**Reproduction of recorded media**
231	**2310**	**Manufacture of coke oven products**
232	**2320**	**Manufacture of refined petroleum products**
233	**2330**	**Processing of nuclear fuel**
241		**Manufacture of basic chemicals**
	2411	Manufacture of basic chemicals, except fertilizers and nitrogen compounds
	2412	Manufacture of fertilizers and nitrogen compounds
	2413	Manufacture of plastics in primary forms and of synthetic rubber

ISIC REVISION 3 (continued)

ISIC		Description
242		**Manufacture of other chemical products**
	2421	Manufacture of pesticides and other agro-chemical products
	2422	Manufacture of paints, varnishes and similar coatings, printing ink and mastics
	2423	Manufacture of pharmaceuticals, medicinal chemicals and botanical products
	2424	Manufacture of soap and detergents, cleaning and polishing preparations, perfumes and toilet preparations
	2429	Manufacture of other chemical products n.e.c.
243	**2430**	**Manufacture of man-made fibres**
251		**Manufacture of rubber products**
	2511	Manufacture of rubber tyres and tubes; retreading and rebuilding of rubber tyres
	2519	Manufacture of other rubber products
252	**2520**	**Manufacture of plastics products**
261	**2610**	**Manufacture of glass and glass products**
269		**Manufacture of non-metallic mineral products n.e.c.**
	2691	Manufacture of non-structural non-refractory ceramic ware
	2692	Manufacture of refractory ceramic products
	2693	Manufacture of structural non-refractory clay and ceramic products
	2694	Manufacture of cement, lime and plaster
	2695	Manufacture of articles of concrete, cement and plaster
	2696	Cutting, shaping and finishing of stone
	2699	Manufacture of other non-metallic mineral products n.e.c.
271	**2710**	**Manufacture of basic iron and steel**
272	**2720**	**Manufacture of basic precious and non-ferrous metals**
273		**Casting of metals**
	2731	Casting of iron and steel
	2732	Casting of non-ferrous metals
281		**Manufacture of structural metal products, tanks, reservoirs and steam generators**
	2811	Manufacture of structural metal products
	2812	Manufacture of tanks, reservoirs and containers of metal
	2813	Manufacture of steam generators, except central heating hot water boilers
289		**Manufacture of other fabricated metal products; metal working service activities**
	2891	Forging, pressing, stamping and roll-forming of metal; powder metallurgy
	2892	Treatment and coating of metals; general mechanical engineering on a fee or contract basis
	2893	Manufacture of cutlery, hand tools and general hardware
	2899	Manufacture of other fabricated metal products n.e.c.

ISIC REVISION 3 (continued)

ISIC		Description
291		**Manufacture of general purpose machinery**
	2911	Manufacture of engines and turbines, except aircraft, vehicle and cycle engines
	2912	Manufacture of pumps, compressors, taps and valves
	2913	Manufacture of bearings, gears, gearing and driving elements
	2914	Manufacture of ovens, furnaces and furnace burners
	2915	Manufacture of lifting and handling equipment
	2919	Manufacture of other general purpose machinery
292		**Manufacture of special purpose machinery**
	2921	Manufacture of agricultural and forestry machinery
	2922	Manufacture of machine-tools
	2923	Manufacture of machinery for metallurgy
	2924	Manufacture of machinery for mining, quarrying and construction
	2925	Manufacture of machinery for food, beverage and tobacco processing
	2926	Manufacture of machinery for textile, apparel and leather production
	2927	Manufacture of weapons and ammunition
	2929	Manufacture of other special purpose machinery
293	**2930**	**Manufacture of domestic appliances n.e.c.**
300	**3000**	**Manufacture of office, accounting and computing machinery**
311	**3110**	**Manufacture of electric motors, generators and transformers**
312	**3120**	**Manufacture of electricity distribution and control apparatus**
313	**3130**	**Manufacture of insulated wire and cable**
314	**3140**	**Manufacture of accumulators, primary cells and primary batteries**
315	**3150**	**Manufacture of electric lamps and lighting equipment**
319	**3190**	**Manufacture of other electrical equipment n.e.c.**
321	**3210**	**Manufacture of electronic valves and tubes and other electronic components**
322	**3220**	**Manufacture of television and radio transmitters and apparatus for line telephony and line telegraphy**
323	**3230**	**Manufacture of television and radio receivers, sound or video recording or reproducing apparatus, and associated goods**
331		**Manufacture of medical appliances and instruments and appliances for measuring, checking, testing, navigating and other purposes, except optical instruments**
	3311	Manufacture of medical and surgical equipment and orthopaedic appliances
	3312	Manufacture of instruments and appliances for measuring, checking, testing, navigating and other purposes, except industrial process control equipment
	3313	Manufacture of industrial process control equipment
332	**3320**	**Manufacture of optical instruments and photographic equipment**

ISIC REVISION 3 (continued)

ISIC		Description
333	**3330**	**Manufacture of watches and clocks**
341	**3410**	**Manufacture of motor vehicles**
342	**3420**	**Manufacture of bodies (coachwork) for motor vehicles; manufacture of trailers and semi-trailers**
343	**3430**	**Manufacture of parts and accessories for motor vehicles and their engines**
351		**Building and repairing of ships and boats**
	3511	Building and repairing of ships
	3512	Building and repairing of pleasure and sporting boats
352	**3520**	**Manufacture of railway and tramway locomotives and rolling stock**
353	**3530**	**Manufacture of aircraft and spacecraft**
359		**Manufacture of transport equipment n.e.c.**
	3591	Manufacture of motorcycles
	3592	Manufacture of bicycles and invalid carriages
	3599	Manufacture of other transport equipment n.e.c.
361	**3610**	**Manufacture of furniture**
369		**Manufacturing n.e.c.**
	3691	Manufacture of jewellery and related articles
	3692	Manufacture of musical instruments
	3693	Manufacture of sports goods
	3694	Manufacture of games and toys
	3699	Other manufacturing n.e.c.
371	**3710**	**Recycling of metal waste and scrap**
372	**3720**	**Recycling of non-metal waste and scrap**

APPENDIX III

DESCRIPTION OF DATA USED IN SECTION 1.2

Country or area	Value added				Output				Employment			Country or area
	Factor values	Producers' prices	Unspecified	Mixed	Factor values	Producers' prices	Unspecified	Mixed	Persons engaged	Employees	Mixed	
Albania			x		x					x		Albania
Argentina				x				x		x		Argentina
Austria		x				x				x		Austria
Azerbaijan							x			x		Azerbaijan
Bangladesh		x				x				x		Bangladesh
Belgium	x					x				x		Belgium
Bermuda										x		Bermuda
Bolivia		x				x				x		Bolivia
Brazil				x				x			x	Brazil
Bulgaria			x				x			x		Bulgaria
Cameroon		x				x				x		Cameroon
Canada		x				x				x		Canada
Chile		x				x				x		Chile
China			x				x			x		China
China (Hong Kong SAR)		x				x				x		China (Hong Kong SAR)
China (Taiwan Province)		x					x			x		China (Taiwan Province)
Colombia		x				x				x		Colombia
Costa Rica		x				x				x		Costa Rica
Croatia			x				x			x		Croatia
Cyprus		x				x				x		Cyprus
Czech Republic							x			x		Czech Republic
Denmark	x				x					x		Denmark
Ecuador		x				x				x		Ecuador
Egypt	x				x						x	Egypt
El Salvador		x						x	x			El Salvador
Ethiopia		x				x				x		Ethiopia
Finland				x				x		x		Finland
France			x				x			x		France
Gabon	x				x					x		Gabon
Germany						x			x			Germany
Ghana		x				x			x			Ghana
Honduras				x		x			x			Honduras
Hungary			x				x			x		Hungary
Iceland				x				x			x	Iceland
India	x				x					x		India
Indonesia	x					x				x		Indonesia
Israel		x				x				x		Israel
Italy			x				x			x		Italy
Jamaica		x				x				x		Jamaica
Japan			x				x				x	Japan
Jordan		x				x				x		Jordan
Kenya	x				x					x		Kenya
Kuwait		x				x				x		Kuwait
Kyrgyzstan						x			x			Kyrgyzstan
Latvia	x					x				x		Latvia
Lithuania						x				x		Lithuania
Macau		x				x				x		Macau

DESCRIPTION OF DATA USED IN SECTION 1.2

(continued)

Country or area	Value added				Output				Employment			Country or area
	Factor values	Producers' prices	Unspecified	Mixed	Factor values	Producers' prices	Unspecified	Mixed	Persons engaged	Employees	Mixed	
Malawi	X				X					X		Malawi
Malaysia	X				X					X		Malaysia
Malta		X				X				X		Malta
Mauritius		X				X					X	Mauritius
Mexico		X				X				X		Mexico
Mongolia		X				X			X			Mongolia
Morocco			X				X			X		Morocco
Mozambique							X			X		Mozambique
Namibia		X				X				X		Namibia
Nepal		X				X				X		Nepal
New Zealand		X						X		X		New Zealand
Nigeria		X				X				X		Nigeria
Norway			X				X			X		Norway
Peru		X				X			X			Peru
Philippines		X				X				X		Philippines
Puerto Rico			X				X			X		Puerto Rico
Qatar		X				X				X		Qatar
Republic of Korea		X				X				X		Republic of Korea
Republic of Moldova						X				X		Republic of Moldova
Romania			X				X			X		Romania
Russian Federation			X			X				X		Russian Federation
Senegal		X						X	X			Senegal
Singapore	X				X				X			Singapore
Slovakia			X				X		X			Slovakia
Slovenia				X				X		X		Slovenia
South Africa	X						X			X		South Africa
Spain				X				X		X		Spain
Sri Lanka		X				X			X			Sri Lanka
St. Vincent and the Grenadines										X		St. Vincent and the Grenadines
Swaziland	X				X					X		Swaziland
Sweden	X				X					X		Sweden
Switzerland		X				X			X			Switzerland
The f.Yugosl.Rep.of Macedonia			X				X			X		The f.Yugosl.Rep.of Macedonia
Thailand		X				X				X		Thailand
Tonga						X				X		Tonga
Trinidad and Tobago			X				X			X		Trinidad and Tobago
Tunisia		X				X				X		Tunisia
Turkey		X				X				X		Turkey
Ukraine					X					X		Ukraine
United Kingdom	X							X		X		United Kingdom
United States of America	X				X					X		United States of America
Uruguay				X				X			X	Uruguay
Venezuela		X				X				X		Venezuela
Yugoslavia			X				X			X		Yugoslavia
Zambia		X				X				X		Zambia
Zimbabwe	X				X					X		Zimbabwe

Part I

SUMMARY TABLES

Section 1.1

THE MANUFACTURING SECTOR

TABLE 1.1

DISTRIBUTION OF WORLD MVA, 1980-1997

Year	Industrialized countries					Developing countries								
	Eastern Europe and former USSR	Western Europe		Japan	North America	Regional groups				Development groups				
		EU a/	Other		Others	Africa	Latin America	South and East Asia	West Asia and Europe	NICs	Second-generation NICs	Least developed countries	China	Others
	Percentage share in world total MVA (at constant 1990 prices)													
1980	9.3	34.8	1.7	13.9	23.8	2.1	0.9	6.8	5.0	1.7	8.4	1.6	0.3	1.4	2.7
1985	9.6	32.2	1.5	15.7	23.8	1.9	0.9	6.0	6.5	1.9	8.4	1.8	0.3	2.0	2.8
1990	8.4	31.4	1.4	17.1	23.1	1.8	0.9	5.4	8.6	1.9	8.8	2.4	0.3	2.6	2.7
1993	4.8	31.3	1.4	17.2	23.5	1.9	0.9	5.8	11.4	1.8	9.4	3.0	0.3	4.2	3.0
1994	3.8	31.3	1.4	16.4	24.5	1.9	0.9	5.8	12.3	1.7	9.6	3.0	0.3	4.8	3.0
1995	3.6	30.5	1.4	16.3	25.3	1.8	0.9	5.5	13.0	1.7	9.5	3.2	0.3	5.2	2.9
1996 b/	3.4	29.4	1.3	16.0	26.4	1.8	0.9	5.5	13.6	1.7	9.6	3.3	0.3	5.6	2.9
1997 c/	3.2	29.0	1.3	15.8	27.0	1.8	0.9	5.3	14.0	1.7	9.7	3.3	0.3	5.9	2.7
	Percentage share in world total MVA (at current prices)													
1993	3.5	29.1	1.3	21.3	23.5	1.7	0.8	5.8	11.3	1.7	9.0	3.1	0.3	4.3	2.9
1994	3.1	29.2	1.4	21.1	24.1	1.7	0.7	6.0	11.2	1.5	9.4	3.1	0.3	3.7	2.9
1995	2.9	29.8	1.5	20.9	23.0	1.7	0.8	5.8	12.0	1.6	9.3	3.4	0.3	4.3	2.9
1996 b/	2.9	29.8	1.4	18.4	23.7	1.8	0.8	6.2	13.4	1.6	9.8	3.7	0.3	5.1	3.1

a/ Beginning 1993 including estimates for the eastern part of Germany.
b/ Provisional.
c/ Estimate.

TABLE 1.2 DISTRIBUTION OF MVA AND POPULATION AMONG SELECTED GROUPS OF DEVELOPING COUNTRIES, SELECTED YEARS

(Percentage)

Country group	MVA at constant 1990 prices						MVA at current prices				Population			
	1980	1985	1990	1994	1995	1996[a/]	1993	1994	1995	1996[a/]	1980	1985	1990	1996
Low income	14.2	15.6	18.0	17.8	18.3	18.4	16.4	17.9	18.0	18.1	46.6	47.3	47.8	48.6
Middle income	16.6	18.7	20.7	19.9	20.3	20.0	20.1	20.8	21.6	20.7	10.9	11.1	11.3	11.6
High income	59.3	52.6	45.7	39.0	36.8	35.8	41.5	42.2	38.8	38.0	11.8	11.9	12.0	12.0
China	9.9	13.1	15.6	23.3	24.6	25.8	22.0	19.1	21.6	23.2	30.7	29.7	28.9	27.8
Developing countries	100.0	100.0	100.0	100.0	100.0	100.0	100.0	100.0	100.0	100.0	100.0	100.0	100.0	100.0
Least developed countries	2.2	2.2	1.8	1.4	1.4	1.4	1.5	1.5	1.5	1.4	11.5	11.8	12.1	12.7
NICs	58.4	54.5	52.1	46.4	45.0	44.2	46.2	48.5	45.9	44.4	31.0	31.0	30.8	30.6
Second-generation NICs	10.8	11.8	14.2	14.6	15.1	15.2	15.6	16.0	16.6	16.7	11.2	11.2	11.2	11.1
China	9.9	13.1	15.6	23.3	24.6	25.8	22.0	19.1	21.6	23.2	30.7	29.7	28.9	27.8
Other developing countries	18.7	18.4	16.3	14.3	13.9	13.4	14.7	14.9	14.4	14.3	15.6	16.3	17.0	17.8
Developing countries	100.0	100.0	100.0	100.0	100.0	100.0	100.0	100.0	100.0	100.0	100.0	100.0	100.0	100.0
Africa	5.9	6.4	5.7	4.6	4.4	4.3	4.1	3.8	3.9	3.8	13.6	14.1	14.7	15.6
Latin America	47.4	38.9	32.0	28.0	26.0	25.2	29.5	30.9	28.7	28.2	11.3	11.2	11.1	11.1
South and East Asia	34.7	42.1	51.2	59.5	61.7	62.7	58.0	57.6	59.6	60.8	71.5	70.9	70.3	69.4
West Asia and Europe	12.0	12.6	11.1	7.9	7.9	7.8	8.4	7.7	7.8	7.2	3.6	3.8	3.9	3.9
Developing countries	100.0	100.0	100.0	100.0	100.0	100.0	100.0	100.0	100.0	100.0	100.0	100.0	100.0	100.0

a/ Provisional.

TABLE 1.3

ANNUAL GROWTH OF MVA, 1980-1996 AND PER-CAPITA MVA, 1996[a/]

Country group or country/area	Total MVA						Per-capita MVA						
	Growth rate (percentage)		Index (1990 = 100)				Growth rate (percentage)		Index (1990 = 100)				Value (dollars)
	1980-1990	1990-1996	1993	1994	1995	1996 b/	1980-1990	1990-1996	1993	1994	1995	1996 b/	1996 b/
Industrialized countries	2.8	1.2	96	99	104	108	2.0	0.7	94	97	101	104	3444
Eastern Europe and former USSR	2.6	-7.9	70	62	63	62	1.8	-8.1	70	61	62	61	620
EU	1.9	0.5	95	99	102	103	1.6	0.1	94	98	100	101	4421
Austria	2.7	0.8	101	104	105	106	2.5	-0.1	98	100	101	101	4741
Belgium	2.7	0.6	96	100	103	103	2.6	0.2	95	99	101	101	4128
Denmark	1.4	1.4	102	104	107	108	1.4	1.1	101	102	105	106	4328
Finland	3.4	4.9	96	108	118	122	2.9	4.4	94	106	115	119	6565
France	0.8	0.5	93	98	102	102	0.3	0.0	92	96	99	99	4477
Germany, western part	1.5	-1.2	93	95	96	96	1.4	-1.8	90	92	93	93	6718
Greece	0.5	-0.7	94	95	96	96	-0.1	-1.2	92	93	94	94	876
Ireland	4.5	...	...	...	...	...	4.3	...	...	...	...	...	...
Italy	2.9	1.2	96	101	107	106	2.8	1.1	96	101	107	105	4526
Luxembourg	4.2	0.2	96	102	103	101	3.7	-1.1	92	96	96	93	5578
Netherlands	2.3	1.9	101	106	109	110	1.8	1.2	98	103	105	106	3806
Portugal	2.3	0.3	96	97	101	102	2.2	0.4	96	98	101	103	1812
Spain	2.1	-0.7	98	102	97	96	1.7	-0.9	98	102	96	95	2704
Sweden	2.6	4.1	92	105	117	120	2.3	3.6	91	103	114	117	6163
United Kingdom	1.8	1.2	96	101	103	104	1.6	1.0	96	100	102	103	3538
Other Western Europe	1.2	1.4	100	104	106	107	0.5	0.6	97	101	102	102	6336
Iceland	0.7	0.7	97	100	101	106	-0.5	-0.3	94	96	96	100	3202
Norway	0.2	2.1	103	107	109	111	-0.2	1.7	101	105	106	108	3440
Switzerland	1.5	1.2	99	104	106	106	0.6	0.3	96	100	101	100	8197
Japan	4.8	0.5	100	99	104	107	4.2	0.3	99	98	103	106	7154
North America	3.0	5.0	101	110	120	131	2.0	4.0	98	105	114	123	4935
Canada	3.4	3.0	99	106	111	112	2.1	1.9	96	101	105	105	3358
United States of America	3.0	5.2	101	110	121	132	2.0	4.1	98	106	115	125	5109
Others	1.3	2.8	104	108	113	115	-0.7	0.8	98	100	102	102	1433
Australia	1.9	2.2	104	108	109	110	0.4	1.1	100	103	103	103	2663
Israel	2.8	7.3	124	133	144	151	1.0	3.8	112	116	122	125	3107
New Zealand	0.5	3.9	109	117	119	120	-0.3	2.7	106	111	112	112	2560
South Africa	-0.1	0.8	92	95	102	102	-2.4	-1.4	86	87	91	90	589

a/ At constant 1990 prices.
b/ Provisional.

TABLE 1.3
(continued)

ANNUAL GROWTH OF MVA, 1980-1996 AND PER-CAPITA MVA, 1996[a/]

Country group or country/area	Total MVA						Per-capita MVA						
	Growth rate (percentage)		Index (1990 = 100)				Growth rate (percentage)		Index (1990 = 100)				Value (dollars)
	1980-1990	1990-1996	1993	1994	1995	1996 b/	1980-1990	1990-1996	1993	1994	1995	1996 b/	1996 b/
Developing countries	5.1	6.9	117	127	137	147	2.9	5.1	111	119	125	133	278
excluding China	4.3	4.5	109	116	122	129	1.9	2.5	103	107	111	115	286
Algeria	3.3	-8.9	69	66	63	56	0.4	-11.0	64	60	56	48	119
Angola	-1.3	5.3	57	93	110	118	-4.0	2.0	52	82	94	98	55
Anguilla	6.6	6.0	124	128	137	147	6.6	3.5	108	112	120	128	63
Antigua and Barbuda	4.3	-2.4	87	90	86	86	3.8	-2.9	85	89	83	84	167
Argentina	-0.8	4.5	127	135	126	132	-2.2	3.1	122	128	118	122	1424
Bahrain	8.3	9.4	142	149	156	160	4.6	6.7	131	134	137	137	1877
Bangladesh	2.8	7.3	120	129	140	148	0.5	5.7	115	122	130	135	23
Barbados	-0.6	-0.9	84	90	92	93	-1.0	-1.2	83	89	90	92	423
Belize	1.3	4.5	110	116	121	127	-1.2	1.8	102	105	106	109	309
Benin	1.3	5.0	117	121	125	134	-1.8	2.0	107	108	108	113	35
Bermuda	1.2	1.1	102	102	104	107	-0.1	0.5	99	99	101	102	2719
Bhutan	12.7	10.9	138	147	170	198	10.0	9.2	133	139	158	180	25
Bolivia	-0.6	3.7	109	115	120	125	-2.6	1.2	102	104	106	108	136
Botswana	8.8	2.6	112	111	116	121	5.2	-0.0	103	100	101	104	142
Brazil	1.6	2.2	97	102	104	107	-0.3	0.7	92	96	97	99	729
British Virgin Islands	10.6	8.1	127	136	145	151	7.0	5.1	113	121	122	127	395
Brunei Darussalam	-0.3	-2.8	73	75	76	77	-3.1	-5.2	67	67	67	66	824
Burkina Faso	2.0	1.1	103	105	105	108	-0.8	-1.7	95	93	91	91	43
Burundi	5.1	-8.4	92	88	76	59	2.1	-10.3	87	82	69	52	14
Cambodia	8.0	7.8	119	128	141	160	4.7	4.9	109	114	123	135	12
Cameroon	10.4	-2.1	91	84	86	93	7.3	-4.7	83	75	75	79	136
Cape Verde	7.8	-1.8	92	91	91	91	6.0	-4.3	86	82	81	79	53
Central African Republic	4.9	-5.5	82	87	82	65	2.4	-7.6	77	79	73	57	30
Chad	6.8	-2.6	74	70	80	86	4.6	-5.2	68	63	70	74	33
Chile	3.6	6.2	123	127	135	145	1.9	4.5	117	119	125	132	639
China	10.7	16.5	161	190	216	243	9.1	15.2	155	182	204	228	258
China (Hong Kong SAR)	4.7	0.7	98	101	102	98	3.5	-0.7	94	95	95	90	1916
China (Taiwan Province)	8.4	4.6	113	119	127	132	7.0	3.7	110	115	121	125	3229
Colombia	3.5	1.4	107	109	110	107	1.4	-0.4	101	101	100	95	235
Comoros	3.1	3.4	117	118	119	121	-0.1	0.2	106	104	102	100	22
Congo	6.9	-1.9	93	78	92	95	3.8	-4.8	85	69	79	79	83
Costa Rica	3.0	4.3	120	124	128	123	0.1	1.9	111	112	114	107	385
Côte d'Ivoire	3.0	1.6	103	104	104	112	-0.5	-1.5	93	91	89	93	124
Cuba	4.4	-3.3	67	72	77	83	3.4	-3.9	66	70	74	80	348
Cyprus	4.3	0.8	97	100	105	106	3.2	-1.0	92	93	96	95	1105
Democratic Rep. of the Congo	1.6	-10.4	50	46	51	51	-1.6	-13.7	44	39	42	41	11
Djibouti	1.0	-1.9	103	95	81	98	-5.0	-4.7	93	84	69	82	31
Dominica	5.8	2.9	105	109	112	116	6.1	2.9	105	109	112	116	180
Dominican Republic	2.9	3.8	117	121	120	125	0.6	1.8	111	112	109	112	199
Ecuador	-0.0	3.2	110	114	117	121	-2.5	1.0	102	105	105	106	214

a/ At constant 1990 prices.
b/ Provisional.

TABLE 1.3
(continued)

ANNUAL GROWTH OF MVA, 1980-1996 AND PER-CAPITA MVA, 1996[a/]

Country group or country/area	Total MVA						Per-capita MVA						
	Growth rate (percentage)		Index (1990 = 100)				Growth rate (percentage)		Index (1990 = 100)				Value (dollars)
	1980-1990	1990-1996	1993	1994	1995	1996 b/	1980-1990	1990-1996	1993	1994	1995	1996 b/	1996 b/
Egypt	6.5	4.3	110	114	123	131	3.8	2.3	103	106	111	117	232
El Salvador	1.0	5.1	115	123	132	135	0.1	2.6	107	112	117	118	270
Equatorial Guinea	2.8	5.0	115	124	129	134	-2.2	2.3	107	113	114	115	7
Ethiopia	2.6	6.3	83	89	99	107	-0.2	3.1	75	79	85	88	11
Fiji	1.1	4.7	114	122	123	127	-0.2	3.1	109	115	114	116	231
French Guiana	1.4	...	...	...	...	...	-4.0	...	...	...	...	...	...
French Polynesia	6.2	4.1	114	118	122	127	3.4	2.0	107	108	109	112	947
Gabon	-3.8	0.2	112	95	107	116	-6.7	-2.5	103	85	93	98	349
Gambia	4.1	1.2	104	108	105	104	0.4	-2.4	92	93	87	84	16
Ghana	3.9	2.6	109	110	112	116	0.5	-0.3	100	98	97	98	37
Grenada	6.2	-0.8	103	99	98	104	5.9	-1.0	102	98	97	102	130
Guadeloupe	2.4	0.8	102	103	100	103	0.5	-0.8	97	96	92	93	394
Guatemala	0.0	2.9	109	112	116	118	-2.8	-0.0	100	100	100	99	124
Guinea	5.3	2.3	103	109	113	117	2.7	-2.3	88	88	89	89	19
Guinea-Bissau	-5.0	0.8	99	100	103	104	-6.7	-1.2	93	92	93	92	16
Guyana	-8.0	5.8	112	119	134	138	-8.4	4.9	110	115	128	131	59
Haiti	-1.7	-14.7	38	35	39	40	-3.5	-16.3	36	33	36	36	22
Honduras	3.7	3.7	115	113	119	124	0.5	0.7	105	100	102	104	95
India	7.4	7.5	109	120	136	147	5.1	5.7	103	112	125	133	79
Indonesia	12.6	11.2	136	152	169	189	10.5	9.5	129	143	156	172	222
Iran (Islamic Republic of)	4.5	5.0	121	125	133	144	0.3	2.1	111	111	115	122	231
Iraq	1.8	...	...	...	...	...	-1.6	...	...	...	...	...	...
Jamaica	2.7	-1.5	91	92	91	88	1.7	-2.4	89	89	87	84	291
Jordan	2.2	10.8	117	150	161	171	-1.5	5.8	102	125	128	130	198
Kenya	4.9	2.5	107	109	113	117	1.3	-0.4	98	97	98	99	36
Kuwait	2.8	27.0	187	197	220	243	-2.0	32.9	215	241	279	309	3082
Lebanon	-7.6	1.3	108	114	115	113	-7.1	-2.0	98	100	97	94	159
Lesotho	13.6	9.5	120	129	153	174	10.6	6.7	111	116	135	149	54
Liberia	1.0	3.0	108	111	113	115	-2.4	6.1	125	135	138	132	46
Libyan Arab Jamahiriya	8.9	9.7	126	142	155	170	4.7	6.0	113	124	131	138	601
Madagascar	0.9	3.5	95	99	117	119	-2.4	0.2	86	87	99	98	27
Malawi	3.6	0.7	95	98	104	108	-0.8	-0.0	93	95	100	103	34
Malaysia	8.9	13.2	142	163	187	209	6.1	10.6	132	148	166	182	1154
Maldives	12.0	8.2	131	142	152	158	8.6	4.7	118	125	129	130	48
Mali	6.8	4.9	116	119	127	135	3.7	1.6	106	105	108	111	24
Malta	1.7	5.0	116	121	129	134	0.8	4.3	114	117	124	129	2269
Martinique	10.1	-3.9	60	62	61	63	9.0	-5.0	58	60	58	59	417
Mauritania	4.0	2.1	125	102	113	123	1.3	-0.5	116	92	99	105	49
Mauritius	11.1	5.7	117	124	131	139	10.1	4.5	113	119	124	130	643
Mexico	1.5	2.0	107	111	106	117	-0.6	0.2	101	103	97	105	633
Mongolia	5.8	-1.8	74	75	86	87	2.7	-3.8	69	69	78	76	187
Montserrat	3.3	...	...	...	...	...	4.0	...	...	...	...	...	...
Morocco	4.1	2.5	105	109	113	117	1.9	0.5	99	101	102	104	206

a/ At constant 1990 prices.
b/ Provisional.

TABLE 1.3
(continued)

ANNUAL GROWTH OF MVA, 1980-1996 AND PER-CAPITA MVA, 1996 a/

Country group or country/area	Total MVA						Per-capita MVA						
	Growth rate (percentage)		Index (1990 = 100)				Growth rate (percentage)		Index (1990 = 100)				Value (dollars)
	1980-1990	1990-1996	1993	1994	1995	1996 b/	1980-1990	1990-1996	1993	1994	1995	1996 b/	1996 b/
Myanmar	-0.1	7.1	116	126	136	143	-2.1	5.3	110	118	124	129	58
Namibia	4.3	3.8	113	119	123	114	1.4	1.2	105	107	108	98	204
Nepal	6.6	12.5	165	185	189	206	3.9	9.5	152	166	165	176	19
Netherlands Antilles	-1.0	-0.4	94	94	95	97	-1.7	-1.0	92	91	92	94	532
New Caledonia	4.4	2.1	110	112	113	115	2.7	0.6	106	106	105	105	701
Nicaragua	-3.1	0.6	101	102	105	107	-5.5	-2.2	93	91	91	90	47
Niger	6.1	1.2	95	96	104	104	2.7	-2.2	86	84	88	85	18
Nigeria	0.7	-1.5	100	95	97	97	-2.2	-4.4	91	84	83	81	15
Oman	21.0	9.2	137	136	159	167	15.6	4.7	120	115	128	129	248
Pakistan	7.7	5.5	121	127	132	138	4.1	2.8	112	114	116	117	60
Panama	0.4	5.1	128	134	134	135	-1.7	3.2	121	124	122	121	253
Papua New Guinea	0.8	5.2	127	136	135	140	-1.3	2.8	119	125	121	122	92
Paraguay	2.1	1.2	104	105	108	106	-1.0	-1.4	95	94	94	90	195
Peru	-0.4	5.6	109	126	132	135	-2.6	3.8	103	117	121	122	550
Philippines	0.2	2.6	99	104	111	117	-2.1	0.4	92	95	99	102	185
Puerto Rico	3.7	4.6	117	125	127	132	2.7	3.6	114	120	121	124	4457
Qatar	8.7	3.2	103	107	113	118	0.7	0.9	95	96	100	102	1997
Republic of Korea	13.0	7.9	120	133	147	158	11.7	6.9	117	128	141	150	2584
Réunion	4.8	2.2	100	102	105	109	2.9	0.6	95	95	97	99	858
Rwanda	2.6	-10.5	72	47	53	61	-0.8	-5.9	88	61	71	78	43
Saint Lucia	4.5	1.0	106	93	106	108	3.0	-0.3	101	88	99	100	168
Sao Tome and Principe	0.9	1.9	108	110	111	113	-1.4	-0.3	101	100	100	100	23
Saudi Arabia	6.9	2.3	117	118	118	121	1.5	-0.3	108	106	103	103	547
Senegal	4.6	3.5	100	107	116	120	1.7	0.9	93	96	102	103	88
Seychelles	7.2	3.5	113	114	116	118	6.1	2.4	110	109	111	111	533
Sierra Leone	4.1	3.6	104	109	98	101	1.8	2.5	102	105	93	94	7
Singapore	6.6	7.9	119	134	147	152	5.4	5.9	112	124	134	136	5363
Solomon Islands	2.3	3.7	116	125	115	122	-1.2	0.4	105	109	98	100	19
Somalia	1.8	-3.1	115	91	93	93	-0.7	-5.2	109	85	84	81	5
Sri Lanka	4.9	8.5	129	140	151	162	3.5	7.5	125	134	144	152	122
St. Kitts and Nevis	0.8	2.9	109	110	114	118	1.4	3.4	109	112	117	120	539
St. Vincent and the Grenadines	4.7	1.5	111	111	108	111	3.9	0.6	108	107	103	105	140
Sudan	1.1	4.6	124	126	129	133	-1.4	2.5	116	116	116	117	103
Suriname	-3.4	-6.7	75	72	71	71	-4.6	-7.9	72	68	66	66	342
Swaziland	15.1	3.1	109	113	118	121	11.9	0.2	101	101	102	102	333
Syrian Arab Republic	3.5	8.2	137	144	153	163	-0.2	5.3	126	129	133	138	140
Thailand	9.5	10.4	138	151	168	180	7.6	9.4	134	145	160	170	711
Togo	1.7	-0.1	67	84	102	110	-1.3	-3.0	61	74	88	92	42
Tonga	5.8	-4.7	98	83	70	80	5.3	-5.0	96	81	68	78	48
Trinidad and Tobago	-1.4	1.1	101	103	108	108	-2.7	0.3	99	100	104	103	366
Tunisia	3.7	5.2	116	120	131	134	1.2	3.2	110	111	119	120	305
Turkey	7.3	4.6	118	109	125	133	4.7	3.0	113	102	115	121	714
Uganda	4.4	13.4	133	153	179	215	2.0	9.7	120	133	152	177	18

a/ At constant 1990 prices.
b/ Provisional.

TABLE 1.3
(continued)

ANNUAL GROWTH OF MVA, 1980-1996 AND PER-CAPITA MVA, 1996[a/]

Country group or country/area	Total MVA: Growth rate (percentage) 1980-1990	Total MVA: Growth rate (percentage) 1990-1996	Total MVA: Index (1990 = 100) 1993	Total MVA: Index (1990 = 100) 1994	Total MVA: Index (1990 = 100) 1995	Total MVA: Index (1990 = 100) 1996 b/	Per-capita MVA: Growth rate (percentage) 1980-1990	Per-capita MVA: Growth rate (percentage) 1990-1996	Per-capita MVA: Index (1990 = 100) 1993	Per-capita MVA: Index (1990 = 100) 1994	Per-capita MVA: Index (1990 = 100) 1995	Per-capita MVA: Index (1990 = 100) 1996 b/	Per-capita MVA: Value (dollars) 1996 b/
United Arab Emirates	2.9	4.6	104	112	121	131	-3.3	1.8	95	99	105	111	1455
United Republic of Tanzania	-0.8	2.0	119	114	115	119	-3.9	-1.2	107	100	98	98	12
Uruguay	0.4	-1.0	92	96	93	97	-0.2	-1.5	90	93	90	94	668
Vanuatu	15.1	0.4	103	103	107	110	12.3	-2.2	95	93	94	94	51
Venezuela	2.5	1.5	111	109	117	112	-0.1	-0.7	104	99	104	98	501
Yemen	7.2	0.2	119	93	108	120	3.5	-4.7	102	76	84	89	64
Yugoslavia (former)	1.7	...	...	...	...	...	0.9	...	...	...	...	...	...
Zambia	4.0	-1.9	103	94	92	94	1.7	-4.1	97	86	82	82	135
Zimbabwe	3.1	-2.7	87	95	85	88	-0.2	-5.1	80	86	74	76	138
Low income	6.7	7.4	117	126	139	150	4.3	5.3	110	117	126	134	105
Middle income	7.1	6.0	115	122	134	142	4.6	3.7	108	112	120	125	481
High income	2.6	2.6	104	109	110	115	0.3	0.9	99	101	101	104	831
Africa	4.2	1.5	100	102	106	110	1.3	-1.1	92	92	93	94	76
North Africa	4.7	2.4	103	106	111	115	2.1	0.2	96	98	100	102	202
UMA	4.2	0.4	94	98	100	101	1.5	-1.8	88	89	90	89	209
Central Africa	4.0	-3.3	78	74	80	84	0.9	-5.9	72	67	70	71	43
CEPGL	2.1	-10.2	59	50	54	54	-1.1	-12.5	55	45	48	46	14
UDEAC	6.9	-1.9	91	84	88	94	4.1	-4.6	84	75	77	80	100
Western Africa (ECOWAS)	2.5	1.2	102	102	106	110	-0.5	-1.8	94	91	91	92	31
Mano River Union	3.3	2.7	105	110	111	114	0.7	0.5	99	101	100	100	20
Eastern and southern Africa	4.1	1.5	100	103	105	109	1.0	-1.3	92	92	91	92	40
Latin America	1.3	2.7	106	111	111	116	-0.6	1.0	101	104	102	105	631
LAIA	1.2	2.7	106	112	111	116	-0.8	1.0	101	104	102	105	665
Andean group	1.4	3.0	109	115	120	119	-0.9	1.0	103	106	108	105	357
CACM	1.2	3.9	114	118	124	125	-1.2	1.1	105	106	108	106	166
CARICOM	0.1	-0.8	93	94	95	95	-0.9	-1.7	91	91	91	90	276
OECS	3.9	1.0	103	101	104	107	3.4	0.4	101	99	101	103	189
South and East Asia	9.1	10.6	131	148	164	180	7.1	8.9	125	139	152	164	252
ASEAN	7.5	9.8	129	144	159	173	5.4	8.0	123	135	147	157	357
West Asia and Europe	3.9	0.8	95	91	98	103	1.1	-1.2	89	84	89	92	550
Least developed countries	2.1	2.8	103	104	112	117	-0.6	0.3	95	95	99	101	31
African LDCs	2.1	1.2	96	97	102	106	-0.8	-1.6	88	87	89	90	30
NICs	4.1	4.1	106	113	118	125	2.0	2.4	101	106	109	113	402
Second-generation NICs	7.1	7.8	125	131	145	157	5.0	6.1	119	123	134	142	381
World	3.1	2.3	99	104	109	114	1.4	0.8	95	98	102	105	994

a/ At constant 1990 prices.
b/ Provisional.

TABLE 1.4

SHARE OF MVA IN GDP, SELECTED YEARS

(Percentage)

Country group or country/area	At constant 1990 prices						At current prices					
	1980	1985	1990	1994	1995	1996a/	1980	1985	1990	1994	1995	1996a/
Industrialized countries	23.5	23.3	22.9	21.8	22.3	22.5	...	...	22.9	...	...	...
Eastern Europe and former USSR	31.4	30.9	31.7	28.3	29.1	29.3	...	...	31.7	...	...	...
EU	26.2	25.2	24.4	23.2	23.2	22.9	27.4	25.6	24.4	22.0	22.0	21.6
Austria	23.1	23.7	23.6	22.6	22.2	22.2	25.8	24.7	23.6	21.2	20.8	20.6
Belgium	20.2	22.1	21.9	20.9	21.0	20.6	22.7	22.4	21.9	19.5	19.9	19.1
Denmark	20.7	20.7	18.3	18.0	18.1	17.7	19.7	19.6	18.3	19.0	19.5	19.2
Finland	23.0	23.2	22.7	25.9	27.2	27.1	27.6	25.1	22.7	24.4	26.0	25.1
France	25.4	23.1	22.3	21.1	21.5	21.3	25.5	23.1	22.3	20.0	20.1	19.7
Germany, western part	34.3	33.3	31.7	28.0	27.9	27.6	33.6	32.6	31.7	26.8	26.3	26.0
Greece	18.8	17.6	16.4	14.8	14.7	14.4	19.5	18.2	16.4	15.0	13.9	13.7
Ireland	26.2	29.3	28.5	...	...	...	24.3	26.0	28.5	...	...	...
Italy	22.4	21.8	22.7	22.3	22.8	22.4	28.3	24.6	22.7	20.5	20.9	20.5
Luxembourg	24.6	25.3	22.0	17.8	17.3	16.5	24.8	26.2	22.0	16.1	15.5	15.0
Netherlands	19.8	20.2	20.1	19.6	19.7	19.3	19.0	18.6	20.1	18.6	18.7	18.5
Portugal	28.2	26.8	25.3	23.3	23.1	22.8	29.4	29.6	25.3	23.5	23.3	23.0
Spain	24.7	23.6	22.4	22.4	20.5	19.8	26.7	25.7	22.4	20.5	18.4	17.9
Sweden	22.2	22.6	21.4	22.7	24.4	24.6	23.0	23.7	21.4	21.4	22.8	22.6
United Kingdom	26.0	24.0	22.1	21.5	21.3	21.1	25.9	23.9	22.1	20.4	20.7	20.5
Other Western Europe	22.9	20.9	20.1	20.2	20.3	20.0	22.9	20.9	20.1	19.5	19.9	19.2
Iceland	22.5	19.5	16.3	16.1	16.2	16.1	19.8	18.2	16.3	16.6	16.1	16.1
Norway	16.4	15.0	12.5	11.6	11.4	11.1	15.8	13.7	12.5	12.8	13.4	12.5
Switzerland	25.8	23.7	23.7	24.8	25.1	25.2	26.7	25.1	23.7	22.3	22.7	22.4
Japan	25.1	26.8	26.8	25.2	26.0	25.8	28.2	28.4	26.8	23.5	23.6	23.3
North America	18.6	18.5	18.2	18.3	19.4	20.3	21.2	19.4	18.2	17.7	17.9	17.6
Canada	18.0	18.3	17.5	17.6	18.1	18.0	18.8	18.4	17.5	18.0	19.3	19.5
United States of America	18.6	18.5	18.2	18.4	19.5	20.5	21.5	19.5	18.2	17.7	17.8	17.5
Others	20.2	18.4	17.5	16.9	16.9	16.6	19.7	18.9	17.5	17.2	17.3	16.8
Australia	17.1	14.9	14.3	13.8	13.4	13.1	19.0	17.0	14.3	14.2	14.0	13.7
Israel	20.6	22.6	21.1	22.1	22.4	22.3	16.3	21.6	21.1	21.2	21.1	21.1
New Zealand	20.7	21.0	18.4	19.1	18.8	18.4	21.8	21.5	18.4	19.3	19.3	19.1
South Africa	28.2	24.8	24.7	23.3	24.3	23.7	21.9	22.4	24.7	22.7	23.5	23.1

a/ Provisional.

TABLE 1.4
(continued)

SHARE OF MVA IN GDP, SELECTED YEARS

(Percentage)

Country group or country/area	At constant 1990 prices						At current prices					
	1980	1985	1990	1994	1995	1996a/	1980	1985	1990	1994	1995	1996a/
Developing countries	20.7	21.5	22.4	23.7	24.2	24.6	20.9	21.5	22.4	21.8	22.8	22.8
excluding China	19.9	20.6	21.1	21.1	21.4	21.6	18.4	19.6	21.1	19.9	20.5	20.3
Algeria	13.2	15.2	12.1	8.2	7.5	6.3	9.5	12.2	12.1	10.0	9.4	8.3
Angola	7.8	9.7	5.0	5.7	6.0	6.0	9.3	9.7	5.0	6.7	7.2	6.8
Anguilla	0.7	0.7	0.7	0.7	0.8	0.8	1.1	1.0	0.7	0.7	0.7	0.7
Antigua and Barbuda	3.3	3.5	3.3	2.5	2.4	2.3	5.3	4.2	3.3	2.2	2.0	1.9
Argentina	28.5	26.8	26.5	25.8	24.9	25.0	29.1	29.3	26.5	19.8	19.8	19.8
Bahrain	7.1	13.2	15.2	18.6	19.1	19.0	14.7	9.2	15.2	16.0	18.8	19.0
Bangladesh	10.8	8.7	8.7	9.6	10.0	10.0	11.0	9.9	8.7	9.8	9.6	9.6
Barbados	9.8	8.9	8.0	7.3	7.5	7.2	12.0	10.6	8.0	7.1	7.0	6.6
Belize	18.7	17.2	15.0	15.0	15.0	15.6	22.8	16.0	15.0	15.4	15.4	16.0
Benin	9.3	6.4	7.8	8.0	8.0	8.1	8.0	7.6	7.8	8.7	8.6	8.3
Bermuda	10.3	10.0	10.0	10.0	9.9	9.9	...	...	10.0	...	...	...
Bhutan	3.8	5.7	8.1	9.6	10.3	11.2	3.3	5.4	8.1	10.6	11.5	12.6
Bolivia	19.6	16.1	18.2	17.7	17.8	17.8	14.5	15.0	18.2	17.8	17.9	18.0
Botswana	5.1	3.6	5.0	4.6	4.7	4.6	4.1	5.4	5.0	4.5	4.7	4.7
Brazil	31.8	29.0	26.3	24.3	23.9	23.9	33.5	33.8	26.3	22.9	23.8	23.4
British Virgin Islands	2.2	2.4	3.0	3.7	3.8	3.8	2.8	2.7	3.0	3.1	3.1	3.1
Brunei Darussalam	10.7	7.4	8.8	6.2	6.2	6.2	11.6	9.9	8.8	8.1	8.1	8.2
Burkina Faso	20.2	16.6	15.8	14.7	14.5	14.1	15.9	15.3	15.8	20.2	19.8	19.0
Burundi	12.0	11.6	12.9	12.4	11.5	9.4	7.4	8.0	12.9	21.7	19.2	16.9
Cambodia	2.5	4.1	5.2	5.5	5.6	6.0	...	...	5.2	5.3	5.1	5.5
Cameroon	8.6	12.2	16.2	15.4	15.2	15.6	10.0	12.5	16.2	11.0	11.4	11.1
Cape Verde	7.2	7.9	7.5	6.0	5.8	5.5	4.5	5.5	7.5	6.1	5.1	4.7
Central African Republic	7.7	13.1	11.5	9.6	8.9	7.2	7.2	10.0	11.5	9.2	8.8	7.4
Chad	13.2	17.7	21.9	13.9	15.3	16.2	15.9	15.9	21.9	14.0	16.3	14.8
Chile	20.8	19.9	20.9	20.4	20.0	20.0	24.8	18.1	20.9	19.6	19.3	19.1
China	32.6	31.6	33.1	39.5	40.4	41.6	39.8	34.6	33.1	37.2	38.0	38.4
China (Hong Kong SAR)	22.5	20.9	16.3	13.1	12.6	11.5	21.9	20.5	16.3	8.5	7.7	6.7
China (Taiwan Province)	34.3	35.7	32.7	30.0	30.0	29.7	35.4	36.9	32.7	28.5	27.7	27.4
Colombia	21.6	20.0	19.9	18.1	17.4	16.5	23.2	21.7	19.9	17.6	18.9	15.8
Comoros	4.2	4.6	4.5	5.2	5.3	5.4	4.3	4.0	4.5	6.6	5.9	5.2
Congo	6.3	7.5	8.3	6.7	7.7	7.6	7.5	5.6	8.3	6.3	6.6	6.0
Costa Rica	19.2	19.3	19.1	19.4	19.6	18.9	18.4	21.8	19.1	18.4	18.9	18.2
Cote d'Ivoire	13.4	15.5	14.4	14.6	13.6	13.8	10.8	10.0	14.4	11.8	12.7	12.9
Cuba	21.8	25.6	23.6	25.8	26.0	26.0	20.9	27.5	23.6	...	...	...
Cyprus	17.2	16.6	14.8	12.8	12.7	12.6	18.2	16.3	14.8	13.1	12.8	12.7
Democratic Rep of the Congo	11.7	12.6	11.0	7.7	8.7	8.6	14.1	9.7	11.0	4.3	4.9	5.5
Djibouti	5.8	5.3	5.3	5.1	4.5	5.7	4.9	4.8	5.3	5.2	4.6	5.8
Dominica	5.5	6.5	6.6	6.5	6.8	7.0	4.8	6.0	6.6	6.8	6.8	6.9
Dominican Republic	18.2	16.9	18.0	18.5	17.6	17.0	15.3	12.3	18.0	18.5	17.6	17.0
Ecuador	23.0	21.9	20.1	19.6	19.6	19.9	18.3	19.7	20.1	22.6	21.9	22.3

a/ Provisional.

TABLE 1.4
(continued)

SHARE OF MVA IN GDP, SELECTED YEARS

(Percentage)

Country group or country/area	At constant 1990 prices						At current prices					
	1980	1985	1990	1994	1995	1996a/	1980	1985	1990	1994	1995	1996a/
Egypt	22.1	21.9	24.4	24.9	25.5	25.9	12.2	13.5	24.4	24.5	25.0	24.3
El Salvador	21.0	20.8	21.8	22.5	22.7	22.8	16.5	17.9	21.8	22.2	21.1	21.0
Equatorial Guinea	1.4	2.5	1.3	1.3	1.2	0.9	0.9	1.9	1.3	1.1	1.0	1.1
Ethiopia	7.0	9.0	7.8	5.9	6.2	6.1	7.8	7.2	7.8	6.7	6.9	6.9
Fiji	10.7	9.9	10.5	11.7	11.5	11.6	12.0	9.5	10.5	9.7	10.1	10.0
French Guiana	15.4	8.4	5.2	5.5	5.4	5.3	...	...	5.2	...	...	...
French Polynesia	7.1	8.5	7.3	7.7	7.7	7.8	6.6	8.5	7.3	6.7	6.7	6.7
Gabon	7.5	7.3	5.6	4.8	5.2	5.5	4.6	6.0	5.6	4.9	5.8	5.7
Gambia	4.7	5.3	5.8	5.4	5.6	5.3	6.7	5.6	5.8	6.7	6.7	6.7
Ghana	11.2	9.0	9.8	9.1	8.8	8.7	7.8	11.5	9.8	9.4	9.6	9.4
Grenada	5.2	5.6	6.6	6.1	5.9	5.9	4.2	5.3	6.6	5.7	5.6	5.7
Guadeloupe	6.8	5.3	5.9	6.0	5.9	5.9	...	...	5.9	...	...	...
Guatemala	16.6	15.8	15.0	14.3	14.1	13.9	16.6	15.8	15.0	14.4	14.3	14.0
Guinea	3.5	3.6	4.5	4.2	4.1	4.1	2.8	4.5	4.5	1.9	2.1	4.5
Guinea-Bissau	13.5	11.9	7.1	6.3	6.2	6.0	12.4	9.1	7.1	6.7	5.8	5.6
Guyana	19.0	16.1	10.3	8.7	9.3	8.8	12.1	13.9	10.3	11.4	11.3	11.2
Haiti	18.8	16.7	15.8	6.8	7.3	7.3	18.4	16.0	15.8	7.4	6.0	5.7
Honduras	15.4	15.7	16.3	16.0	16.1	16.4	15.0	14.5	16.3	17.1	17.7	18.3
India	15.5	17.1	18.7	18.6	19.7	20.0	17.7	17.9	18.7	18.2	19.7	20.1
Indonesia	12.0	17.2	20.7	23.4	23.9	24.7	13.0	16.0	20.7	23.3	24.2	25.2
Iran (Islamic Republic of)	8.6	9.0	12.3	12.2	12.6	12.9	9.4	8.5	12.3	13.6	14.4	15.1
Iraq	10.2	12.1	8.4	...	...	...	4.3	9.1	8.4	...	...	...
Jamaica	18.0	19.2	18.2	15.6	15.3	15.1	15.6	18.4	18.2	17.6	16.3	15.7
Jordan	11.4	11.9	17.0	19.3	19.5	19.7	14.5	13.2	17.0	18.2	18.4	18.6
Kenya	11.2	11.0	11.4	11.7	11.6	11.5	12.4	11.4	11.4	11.2	10.8	9.8
Kuwait	6.7	7.7	11.5	16.3	17.5	18.7	5.5	5.9	11.5	10.4	10.8	11.4
Lebanon	12.7	13.9	13.1	8.9	8.4	7.9	12.3	12.8	13.1	6.1	5.8	5.6
Lesotho	6.4	10.2	11.8	12.7	14.1	14.4	6.0	10.4	11.8	14.5	15.2	15.5
Liberia	6.3	6.6	6.9	7.1	7.0	7.2	8.4	6.1	6.9	6.4	6.4	6.4
Libyan Arab Jamahiriya	3.3	6.8	7.9	10.4	11.2	12.0	1.5	3.7	7.9	...	...	...
Madagascar	15.0	13.0	12.7	12.5	14.6	14.5	12.8	11.5	12.7	12.0	12.5	12.3
Malawi	15.7	16.8	18.8	19.1	18.1	16.8	13.6	14.5	18.8	18.5	18.6	14.0
Malaysia	20.2	19.9	26.5	31.2	32.6	33.7	21.2	19.0	26.5	32.6	33.5	35.3
Maldives	4.1	5.3	5.4	5.8	5.8	5.6	4.9	5.4	5.4	5.4	5.4	5.3
Mali	6.2	7.9	8.6	9.4	9.4	9.6	6.6	7.3	8.6	7.0	7.2	7.1
Malta	33.3	30.2	27.0	27.0	27.1	27.2	33.1	29.5	27.0	23.5	22.7	22.2
Martinique	5.1	5.8	7.2	4.4	4.4	4.4	...	...	7.2	...	...	...
Mauritania	8.3	12.7	10.3	9.1	9.5	10.0	6.5	12.9	10.3	10.9	11.3	12.0
Mauritius	16.7	19.7	23.6	23.8	23.9	23.8	15.3	20.6	23.6	23.3	23.7	23.3
Mexico.	19.9	19.3	20.6	19.8	20.1	21.3	19.3	20.4	20.6	18.2	19.8	21.0
Mongolia	23.8	26.5	29.0	27.2	29.5	29.7	...	...	29.0	...	...	...
Montserrat	6.2	6.3	5.8	6.5	6.6	6.6	5.7	5.7	5.8	...	...	...
Morocco	18.8	19.9	19.4	18.4	20.5	18.9	17.7	19.5	19.4	18.0	19.3	17.9

a/ Provisional.

TABLE 1.4
(continued)

SHARE OF MVA IN GDP, SELECTED YEARS

(Percentage)

Country group or country/area	At constant 1990 prices						At current prices					
	1980	1985	1990	1994	1995	1996a/	1980	1985	1990	1994	1995	1996a/
Myanmar	8.1	8.5	7.8	8.0	8.1	8.1	9.5	9.9	7.8	6.2	6.9	6.8
Namibia	7.9	10.7	13.6	13.8	13.6	12.2	4.6	10.1	13.6	15.0	15.0	12.2
Nepal	5.6	5.9	6.0	8.9	8.9	9.2	4.2	5.6	6.0	9.3	9.3	9.5
Netherlands Antilles	8.5	6.8	6.8	6.3	6.3	6.3	8.5	6.8	6.8	6.4	6.3	6.2
New Caledonia	5.8	4.7	4.4	4.5	4.4	4.3	4.0	3.2	4.4	4.8	4.8	4.8
Nicaragua	19.5	19.8	16.9	16.6	16.4	16.0	26.0	28.0	16.9	16.8	16.6	16.3
Niger	2.7	5.2	6.6	6.3	6.6	6.4	3.7	7.1	6.6	6.3	6.4	6.5
Nigeria	5.1	5.7	5.5	4.7	4.7	4.6	8.4	8.7	5.5	6.6	8.2	8.1
Oman	0.8	2.2	2.9	3.1	3.5	3.6	0.6	2.2	2.9	4.3	4.5	5.1
Pakistan	15.7	16.4	17.4	18.3	18.0	18.0	15.9	15.9	17.4	17.5	17.2	16.9
Panama	11.2	10.4	10.5	10.8	10.7	10.5	11.8	13.1	10.5	9.5	9.7	9.4
Papua New Guinea	10.8	11.5	9.2	8.3	8.5	8.6	9.7	11.2	9.2	7.8	7.9	8.4
Paraguay	18.8	17.8	17.3	16.3	16.0	15.6	16.0	16.2	17.3	15.7	15.7	15.8
Peru	29.3	26.7	26.7	26.7	26.3	26.3	20.0	25.2	26.7	22.9	22.8	22.9
Philippines	27.0	24.6	24.8	24.2	24.7	24.6	25.7	25.2	24.8	23.3	23.0	22.6
Puerto Rico	43.2	41.2	38.9	40.1	40.0	40.1	37.5	39.2	38.9	41.4	41.3	41.8
Qatar	7.1	11.1	12.7	12.2	12.8	13.0	3.2	7.8	12.7	11.4	10.1	8.9
Republic of Korea	22.5	25.4	29.2	29.4	30.0	30.2	28.6	29.7	29.2	26.6	26.7	25.8
Réunion	9.0	9.2	10.0	9.1	9.1	9.1	...	...	10.0	...	...	...
Rwanda	17.1	15.3	16.2	15.8	14.5	14.4	16.5	15.0	16.2	15.2	15.4	14.0
Saint Lucia	6.8	7.4	6.7	5.4	5.8	5.8	7.9	7.0	6.7	5.2	5.7	5.6
Sao Tome and Principe	6.5	6.4	5.6	5.8	5.8	5.8	9.8	9.9	5.6	4.6	7.5	6.9
Saudi Arabia	3.6	7.3	8.2	8.5	8.4	8.5	5.3	8.4	8.2	9.6	9.8	9.5
Senegal	8.8	10.0	11.0	11.5	11.9	11.7	12.9	11.3	11.0	11.4	11.8	11.5
Seychelles	6.4	6.7	9.0	8.9	9.3	9.3	7.3	9.5	9.0	9.7	9.7	9.8
Sierra Leone	2.8	3.4	3.7	4.7	4.7	4.6	5.0	3.7	3.7	5.9	6.3	6.1
Singapore	28.8	22.2	27.2	26.1	26.4	25.4	27.7	22.4	27.2	24.2	24.8	24.1
Solomon Islands	3.9	3.6	3.5	3.5	3.1	3.1	4.6	4.5	3.5	3.1	3.0	2.9
Somalia	5.5	4.1	4.6	5.8	5.8	5.8	4.7	5.0	4.6	5.4	5.4	5.5
Sri Lanka	17.1	16.7	18.3	20.5	21.0	21.6	21.9	18.2	18.3	19.0	19.4	19.7
St. Kitts and Nevis	22.3	16.7	13.9	13.3	13.2	13.0	16.8	13.3	13.9	11.0	11.8	11.7
St. Vincent and the Grenadines	10.4	9.9	8.2	8.4	7.6	7.5	9.3	9.7	8.2	7.9	7.2	7.2
Sudan	9.5	8.7	8.6	8.5	8.3	8.3	6.6	8.3	8.6	9.8	10.3	10.9
Suriname	16.3	13.9	12.3	8.4	7.9	7.7	17.6	12.5	12.3	11.4	10.9	10.9
Swaziland	21.2	16.0	35.9	36.4	36.8	36.9	22.4	16.8	35.9	34.1	34.4	35.1
Syrian Arab Republic	5.5	6.8	5.3	5.4	5.6	5.6	3.6	7.7	5.3	6.0	5.9	5.8
Thailand	22.6	22.0	27.2	29.7	30.3	30.8	21.5	21.9	27.2	28.5	28.5	28.6
Togo	8.1	7.5	9.9	9.4	10.7	10.9	7.8	6.7	9.9	10.3	10.7	10.7
Tonga	2.9	6.0	6.1	4.3	3.5	4.1	6.8	5.1	6.1	5.2	4.2	3.9
Trinidad and Tobago	7.0	7.0	8.7	9.0	9.3	9.0	8.6	6.8	8.7	8.2	9.0	8.6
Tunisia	18.0	19.9	16.9	17.1	18.2	17.5	11.8	15.1	16.9	18.3	18.9	18.3
Turkey	17.6	20.4	22.2	22.2	23.6	23.8	17.0	19.0	22.2	21.9	22.6	20.8
Uganda	5.1	5.4	5.7	7.0	7.5	8.3	4.3	5.8	5.7	6.5	6.8	7.8

a/ Provisional.

TABLE 1.4
(continued)

SHARE OF MVA IN GDP, SELECTED YEARS

(Percentage)

Country group or country/area	At constant 1990 prices						At current prices					
	1980	1985	1990	1994	1995	1996a/	1980	1985	1990	1994	1995	1996a/
United Arab Emirates	3.5	8.6	7.2	7.8	8.0	8.5	3.5	8.6	7.2	7.6	7.3	7.1
United Republic of Tanzania	13.1	9.6	8.7	8.2	8.1	8.0	13.7	9.8	8.7	7.3	7.1	7.1
Uruguay	28.8	26.3	26.3	20.5	20.4	20.4	26.1	29.4	26.3	18.4	17.8	17.8
Vanuatu	2.1	3.2	5.3	4.5	4.5	4.6	3.8	3.5	5.3	5.6	5.5	5.7
Venezuela	18.3	21.5	20.4	19.5	20.5	19.9	16.0	21.9	20.4	17.2	17.2	18.1
Yemen	7.4	10.3	8.2	7.1	7.6	8.1	6.5	11.7	8.2	9.3	10.3	10.8
Yugoslavia (former)	29.5	34.0	31.2	...	...	...	33.1	41.0	31.2	...	...	...
Zambia	23.3	24.7	31.9	31.6	32.3	31.0	18.5	22.9	31.9	26.6	27.0	28.9
Zimbabwe	20.9	20.7	22.5	20.2	18.1	17.6	29.0	20.2	22.5	23.0	21.9	21.0
Low income	15.2	16.3	18.5	19.4	20.1	20.4	15.4	16.2	18.5	19.1	19.7	20.0
Middle income	18.2	20.0	22.1	22.5	23.2	23.3	16.2	18.2	22.1	21.8	22.1	21.2
High income	22.0	22.5	21.9	21.3	21.2	21.3	20.2	22.0	21.9	19.4	20.0	20.0
Africa	11.5	13.2	13.2	12.6	12.7	12.6	9.2	10.6	13.2	12.8	13.1	12.5
North Africa	13.4	15.4	15.4	14.9	15.2	14.9	8.9	11.6	15.4	15.7	16.4	15.7
UMA	11.8	14.6	13.2	12.2	12.5	11.8	8.3	11.0	13.2	12.0	12.4	11.5
Central Africa	9.4	11.1	10.7	9.4	9.6	9.7	11.0	10.0	10.7	8.0	8.6	8.3
CEPGL	12.6	13.0	12.1	9.4	10.0	9.7	13.9	10.3	12.1	8.1	8.1	8.1
UDEAC	8.1	10.6	12.5	10.8	11.0	11.2	8.2	9.9	12.5	8.6	9.2	8.8
Western Africa (ECOWAS)	7.7	8.5	8.3	7.9	7.8	7.8	8.5	8.9	8.3	7.9	8.8	8.7
Mano River Union	4.2	4.5	5.0	5.0	5.0	4.9	4.8	4.7	5.0	4.2	4.2	5.4
Eastern and southern Africa	12.8	13.1	14.2	13.3	13.1	12.8	10.8	11.6	14.2	13.4	13.2	12.9
Latin America	26.5	25.0	24.1	23.0	22.7	22.9	25.3	25.7	24.1	20.8	21.8	21.8
LAIA	26.8	25.0	24.1	22.8	22.5	22.8	25.8	26.1	24.1	20.2	21.3	21.3
Andean group	22.9	22.6	21.8	21.1	21.1	20.7	18.4	21.7	21.8	19.2	19.5	18.8
CACM	18.4	18.1	17.9	17.9	17.9	17.7	17.8	18.2	17.9	17.6	17.5	17.2
CARICOM	11.4	11.4	11.9	10.6	10.6	10.3	11.4	9.7	11.9	11.1	11.2	11.0
OECS	7.3	7.1	6.6	5.9	6.0	5.9	7.2	6.8	6.6	5.6	5.7	5.6
South and East Asia	21.5	22.8	25.2	27.6	28.4	29.0	25.7	24.5	25.2	25.3	26.1	26.3
ASEAN	18.8	19.0	23.2	25.3	25.9	26.4	18.5	19.1	23.2	23.4	23.6	23.9
West Asia and Europe	13.0	16.8	16.3	16.0	16.7	16.9	11.3	14.3	16.3	14.7	15.7	15.1
Least developed countries	9.7	9.8	9.3	8.8	9.0	9.0	9.4	9.6	9.3	8.1	8.2	8.1
African LDCs	9.9	10.3	9.9	9.2	9.2	9.1	9.3	9.3	9.9	9.2	9.4	9.6
NICs	26.1	25.5	25.2	24.0	24.2	24.3	26.6	26.8	25.2	21.8	22.7	22.5
Second-generation NICs	18.9	20.2	22.8	24.3	25.2	25.5	18.3	19.4	22.8	24.2	24.8	24.5
World	23.1	23.0	22.8	22.1	22.7	22.9	...	...	22.8	...	...	...

a/ Provisional.

Section 1.2

THE MANUFACTURING BRANCHES

TABLE 1.5

DISTRIBUTION OF WORLD VALUE ADDED, SELECTED BRANCHES AND YEARS[a/]

(Percentage)

Branch (ISIC)	Year	Industrialized countries							Developing countries			World
		All countries	Eastern Europe and former USSR	Western Europe: EU b/	Western Europe: Other	Japan	North America	Others	All countries	NICs	Others	
Food products (311/2)	1980	85.4	16.3	27.8	1.6	14.7	22.5	2.5	14.6	7.3	7.3	100.0
	1985	84.8	16.5	27.4	1.4	14.0	23.0	2.5	15.2	7.6	7.6	100.0
	1990	84.1	14.7	28.9	1.4	13.8	22.8	2.5	15.9	8.2	7.7	100.0
	1996	81.1	5.2	33.2	1.4	13.8	24.6	2.9	18.9	9.3	9.6	100.0
Beverages (313)	1980	79.2	13.9	32.9	1.4	10.3	18.4	2.3	20.8	11.0	9.8	100.0
	1985	78.1	13.1	33.0	1.3	9.6	18.5	2.6	21.9	11.4	10.5	100.0
	1990	76.7	9.4	35.4	1.3	9.4	18.4	2.8	23.3	11.9	11.4	100.0
	1996	72.8	5.2	36.8	1.3	8.1	18.7	2.7	27.2	12.8	14.4	100.0
Tobacco (314)	1980	73.5	5.6	33.3	1.2	3.2	29.6	0.6	26.5	12.2	14.3	100.0
	1985	69.7	6.2	32.6	1.2	2.9	26.2	0.6	30.3	12.9	17.4	100.0
	1990	69.3	5.0	33.1	1.2	2.7	26.6	0.7	30.7	13.2	17.5	100.0
	1996	63.2	1.8	32.1	1.2	2.5	24.9	0.7	36.8	13.9	22.9	100.0
Textiles (321)	1980	78.5	17.8	29.3	0.9	14.7	14.2	1.6	21.5	13.2	8.3	100.0
	1985	77.0	18.6	27.6	0.9	14.3	14.0	1.6	23.0	13.6	9.4	100.0
	1990	74.9	17.8	27.4	0.8	12.6	14.8	1.5	25.1	14.5	10.6	100.0
	1996	69.3	5.5	31.6	0.9	9.8	19.8	1.7	30.7	16.6	14.1	100.0
Wearing apparel (322)	1980	81.6	11.6	34.4	0.8	11.0	21.8	2.0	18.4	10.9	7.5	100.0
	1985	79.6	13.1	32.1	0.7	11.1	20.5	2.1	20.4	12.4	8.0	100.0
	1990	77.3	13.1	29.3	0.5	10.8	21.3	2.3	22.7	12.9	9.8	100.0
	1996	74.7	5.0	29.2	0.5	12.9	24.6	2.5	25.3	12.0	13.3	100.0
Leather and fur products (323)	1980	76.7	18.8	33.3	0.3	9.9	13.3	1.1	23.3	15.2	8.1	100.0
	1985	75.2	19.1	34.0	0.3	9.2	11.3	1.3	24.8	17.6	7.2	100.0
	1990	74.0	18.2	33.6	0.4	9.9	10.5	1.4	26.0	18.6	7.4	100.0
	1996	70.1	4.8	42.9	0.5	10.0	10.1	1.8	29.9	19.0	10.9	100.0
Footwear (324)	1980	73.0	11.8	42.7	0.7	4.1	11.7	2.0	27.0	17.8	9.2	100.0
	1985	71.4	14.5	40.5	0.7	4.5	9.0	2.2	28.6	20.4	8.2	100.0
	1990	71.7	16.0	38.5	0.5	5.6	8.4	2.7	28.3	20.4	7.9	100.0
	1996	70.4	6.3	47.2	0.4	5.6	8.0	2.9	29.6	19.2	10.4	100.0
Wood and cork products (331)	1980	89.5	7.5	33.6	3.7	22.0	19.5	3.2	10.5	4.9	5.6	100.0
	1985	88.8	8.8	29.9	3.5	17.7	25.5	3.4	11.2	5.6	5.6	100.0
	1990	88.4	7.6	32.3	3.6	16.7	25.2	3.0	11.6	4.6	7.0	100.0
	1996	87.9	4.5	35.2	3.4	13.6	27.7	3.5	12.1	3.8	8.3	100.0

a/ At constant 1990 prices.
b/ In 1996 including estimates for the eastern part of Germany.

TABLE 1.5
(continued)

DISTRIBUTION OF WORLD VALUE ADDED, SELECTED BRANCHES AND YEARS[a/]

(Percentage)

Branch (ISIC)	Year	Industrialized countries							Developing countries			World
		All countries	Eastern Europe and former USSR	Western Europe: EU b/	Western Europe: Other	Japan	North America	Others	All countries	NICs	Others	
Paper (341)	1980	90.6	6.0	32.7	1.3	12.6	35.7	2.3	9.4	6.2	3.2	100.0
	1985	90.3	6.3	31.6	1.4	12.6	36.1	2.3	9.7	6.7	3.0	100.0
	1990	89.5	3.9	32.7	1.3	14.2	35.2	2.2	10.5	7.1	3.4	100.0
	1996	88.2	2.9	32.6	1.3	13.7	35.7	2.0	11.8	7.8	4.0	100.0
Industrial chemicals (351)	1980	88.6	10.8	37.3	0.3	14.7	24.0	1.5	11.4	7.8	3.6	100.0
	1985	86.6	11.0	36.6	0.5	13.6	23.6	1.3	13.4	9.0	4.4	100.0
	1990	85.2	8.4	35.1	0.5	14.7	25.2	1.3	14.8	10.0	4.8	100.0
	1996	82.1	3.6	37.1	0.6	14.5	25.0	1.3	17.9	12.1	5.8	100.0
Other chemicals (352)	1980	85.3	6.1	31.5	2.4	16.0	27.7	1.6	14.7	10.2	4.5	100.0
	1985	85.9	5.9	30.8	2.5	16.8	28.3	1.6	14.1	9.8	4.3	100.0
	1990	85.6	4.0	30.5	2.9	18.2	28.5	1.5	14.4	9.8	4.6	100.0
	1996	83.2	1.6	31.6	3.8	17.3	27.3	1.6	16.8	11.1	5.7	100.0
Petroleum refineries (353)	1980	70.0	12.2	36.8	0.1	4.1	15.0	1.8	30.0	9.9	20.1	100.0
	1985	64.0	13.7	29.5	0.2	3.6	14.7	2.3	36.0	12.1	23.9	100.0
	1990	60.7	10.9	28.6	0.2	3.5	15.2	2.3	39.3	12.8	26.5	100.0
	1996	56.8	6.7	29.3	0.2	3.6	14.4	2.6	43.2	14.9	28.3	100.0
Prods. of petroleum and coal (354)	1980	90.4	15.1	54.7	0.8	5.3	13.5	1.0	9.6	6.1	3.5	100.0
	1985	87.4	17.4	47.8	0.9	5.8	13.9	1.6	12.6	8.3	4.3	100.0
	1990	86.7	16.4	46.7	0.8	6.0	15.1	1.7	13.3	8.3	5.0	100.0
	1996	83.3	10.8	46.8	0.9	6.8	15.8	2.2	16.7	11.0	5.7	100.0
Rubber products (355)	1980	84.6	11.3	36.3	0.6	17.9	16.8	1.7	15.4	10.4	5.0	100.0
	1985	83.9	12.0	32.9	0.6	18.0	18.8	1.6	16.1	11.2	4.9	100.0
	1990	81.5	8.5	32.5	0.6	18.3	19.9	1.7	18.5	12.6	5.9	100.0
	1996	78.5	4.0	32.0	0.5	16.3	24.0	1.7	21.5	13.6	7.9	100.0
Plastic products (356)	1980	87.7	4.0	35.8	1.6	22.8	21.1	2.4	12.3	9.0	3.3	100.0
	1985	87.8	4.0	34.1	1.4	22.1	24.1	2.1	12.2	9.5	2.7	100.0
	1990	87.9	2.3	35.4	1.4	22.4	24.3	2.1	12.1	9.5	2.6	100.0
	1996	86.8	1.2	35.1	1.0	19.0	28.1	2.4	13.2	9.8	3.4	100.0
Pottery, china, earthenware (361)	1980	87.7	7.7	56.4	1.5	14.2	7.1	0.8	12.3	6.9	5.4	100.0
	1985	86.4	9.6	52.0	1.4	14.3	8.2	0.9	13.6	7.8	5.8	100.0
	1990	84.5	7.7	52.6	1.2	14.5	7.7	0.8	15.5	8.1	7.4	100.0
	1996	79.2	7.1	48.5	1.0	13.5	8.2	0.9	20.8	9.5	11.3	100.0

a/ At constant 1990 prices.
b/ In 1996 including estimates for the eastern part of Germany.

TABLE 1.5
(continued)

DISTRIBUTION OF WORLD VALUE ADDED, SELECTED BRANCHES AND YEARS[a/]

(Percentage)

Branch (ISIC)	Year	Industrialized countries							Developing countries			World
		All countries	Eastern Europe and former USSR	Western Europe: EU b/	Western Europe: Other	Japan	North America	Others	All countries	NICs	Others	
Glass (362)	1980	88.6	7.1	37.1	1.6	18.9	22.0	1.9	11.4	8.5	2.9	100.0
	1985	87.2	8.5	35.6	1.5	18.4	21.3	1.9	12.8	9.0	3.8	100.0
	1990	86.0	6.7	37.6	1.3	18.7	19.7	2.0	14.0	9.2	4.8	100.0
	1996	82.2	3.6	37.8	1.1	17.3	20.5	1.9	17.8	10.8	7.0	100.0
Other non-metallic mineral prods.(369)	1980	85.0	9.2	38.7	2.0	18.2	14.5	2.4	15.0	8.7	6.3	100.0
	1985	83.2	10.3	33.9	2.0	18.2	16.5	2.3	16.8	9.2	7.6	100.0
	1990	82.2	9.3	35.0	1.6	18.5	15.5	2.3	17.8	9.5	8.3	100.0
	1996	76.9	6.0	34.6	1.4	16.8	15.8	2.3	23.1	11.8	11.3	100.0
Iron and steel (371)	1980	87.9	12.7	33.1	0.7	22.2	16.8	2.4	12.1	9.1	3.0	100.0
	1985	85.7	13.9	31.7	0.8	22.7	14.3	2.3	14.3	10.6	3.7	100.0
	1990	83.0	11.6	30.9	0.8	23.3	14.0	2.4	17.0	12.7	4.3	100.0
	1996	76.7	6.0	32.0	0.8	20.1	15.5	2.3	23.3	16.8	6.5	100.0
Non-ferrous metals (372)	1980	84.6	18.0	27.9	1.6	12.2	20.5	4.4	15.4	7.6	7.8	100.0
	1985	83.5	18.7	26.7	1.6	11.7	20.5	4.3	16.5	8.1	8.4	100.0
	1990	83.0	16.1	27.2	1.8	13.6	19.6	4.7	17.0	8.9	8.1	100.0
	1996	79.7	10.0	27.2	1.7	14.3	21.2	5.3	20.3	10.6	9.7	100.0
Metal products (381)	1980	91.8	4.2	40.2	1.9	20.6	22.2	2.7	8.2	5.5	2.7	100.0
	1985	91.0	5.1	37.1	1.8	20.4	23.8	2.8	9.0	6.2	2.8	100.0
	1990	90.5	3.8	38.6	1.8	21.7	22.1	2.5	9.5	6.6	2.9	100.0
	1996	89.0	1.8	38.1	1.9	20.0	24.5	2.7	11.0	7.2	3.8	100.0
Non-electrical machinery (382)	1980	92.6	11.7	41.0	2.4	16.6	19.8	1.1	7.4	6.2	1.2	100.0
	1985	93.1	13.2	36.7	2.0	20.0	20.2	1.0	6.9	5.5	1.4	100.0
	1990	93.3	10.6	35.2	1.9	22.3	22.4	0.9	6.7	5.5	1.2	100.0
	1996	93.1	3.5	32.4	1.6	16.6	38.2	0.8	6.9	5.6	1.3	100.0
Electrical machinery (383)	1980	90.2	8.7	42.1	2.8	14.6	20.4	1.6	9.8	7.7	2.1	100.0
	1985	91.0	9.3	36.8	2.0	22.5	19.1	1.3	9.0	7.2	1.8	100.0
	1990	88.9	7.0	33.5	2.0	25.9	19.4	1.1	11.1	9.1	2.0	100.0
	1996	87.1	2.1	31.4	1.6	23.8	27.2	1.0	12.9	10.4	2.5	100.0
Transport equipment (384)	1980	89.1	6.2	37.0	0.7	17.7	25.5	2.0	10.9	8.5	2.4	100.0
	1985	89.3	7.0	33.6	0.5	17.0	29.5	1.7	10.7	8.5	2.2	100.0
	1990	89.5	5.7	34.9	0.5	19.0	27.9	1.5	10.5	8.2	2.3	100.0
	1996	84.5	2.5	32.9	0.5	18.1	28.8	1.7	15.5	12.0	3.5	100.0

a/ At constant 1990 prices.
b/ In 1996 including estimates for the eastern part of Germany.

TABLE 1.6 DISTRIBUTION OF VALUE ADDED OF SELECTED BRANCHES AMONG DEVELOPING REGIONS, 1985 AND 1995[a/]

(Percentage)

Branch (ISIC)	Developing regions										Least developed countries	
	Africa		Latin America		South and East Asia		West Asia and Europe		All countries			
	1985	1995	1985	1995	1985	1995	1985	1995	1985	1995	1985	1995
Alimentation (311/2)	11.0	9.3	45.1	43.9	31.4	37.9	12.5	8.9	100.0	100.0	5.9	5.0
Boissons (313)	15.0	12.7	56.9	53.6	20.5	25.8	7.6	7.9	100.0	100.0	8.6	4.3b/
Tabac (314)	9.9	7.5	47.3	40.7	32.8	41.8	10.0	10.0	100.0	100.0	5.5	3.6
Textiles (321)	9.3	7.6	25.6	22.5	50.8	57.8	14.3	12.1	100.0	100.0	4.0	3.8b/
Habillement (322)	6.1	7.0	33.5	25.2	44.2	54.9	16.2	12.9	100.0	100.0	2.2	...
Cuir et fourrure (323)	6.5	6.8b/	45.8	49.4b/	29.3	32.7b/	18.4	11.1b/	100.0	100.0	2.3	...
Chaussures (324)	9.1	7.9b/	51.7	53.8b/	18.9	26.4b/	20.3	11.9b/	100.0	100.0	4.0	...
Articles en bois et liège (331)	14.1	12.0b/	24.8	24.0b/	42.8	55.8b/	18.3	8.2b/	100.0	100.0	5.7	2.9b/
Papier (341)	5.8	3.7	52.6	44.5	29.5	42.8	12.1	9.0	100.0	100.0	1.9	0.9b/
Chimie industrielle (351)	5.1	3.0b/	47.9	35.5b/	32.1	48.7b/	14.9	12.8b/	100.0	100.0	1.1	0.8b/
Autres produits chimiques (352)	5.6	4.3	57.8	44.5	26.8	43.6	9.8	7.6	100.0	100.0	1.9	1.4
Raffineries de pétrole (353)	10.6	7.3	40.3	31.2	28.4	40.7	20.7	20.8	100.0	100.0	1.4	1.0
Dérivés pétrole et charbon (354)	3.0	2.2	44.9	38.6	27.1	38.0	25.0	21.2	100.0	100.0	...	...
Caoutchouc (355)	4.8	3.9b/	34.7	30.0b/	46.5	57.7b/	14.0	8.4b/	100.0	100.0	0.8	0.5b/
Grès, porcelaines et faïences (361)	9.6	7.7	31.3	22.8	37.2	45.0	21.8	24.5	100.0	100.0	...	...
Verre (362)	3.9	3.9	53.1	41.0	29.1	42.0	13.9	13.1	100.0	100.0	1.0	1.2
Autres minéraux non métal. (369)	12.4	9.5	35.9	29.3	35.4	49.3	16.3	11.9	100.0	100.0	2.3	1.8
Sidérurgie (371)	5.6	3.0	41.0	31.4	42.8	58.9	10.6	6.7	100.0	100.0	0.7	0.4
Métaux non ferreux (372)	4.0	3.9	56.7	51.2	25.8	36.0	13.5	8.9	100.0	100.0	...	...
Ouvrages en métaux (381)	8.5	5.6	39.9	34.0	38.2	51.7	13.4	8.7	100.0	100.0	...	...
Machines non élect. (382)	3.0	1.5	43.4	33.1	38.8	57.1	14.8	8.3	100.0	100.0	...	...
Machines électriques (383)	4.3	1.5	38.4	22.8	43.5	70.3	13.8	5.4	100.0	100.0	0.7	0.3
Matériel de transport (384)	4.8	2.0	47.9	39.3	38.5	52.9	8.8	5.8	100.0	100.0	0.7	0.4

a/ At constant 1990 prices.
b/ Figure refers to 1994.

TABLE 1.7

LEADING PRODUCERS IN SELECTED BRANCHES, 1990 AND 1996

World leading countries				Leading developing countries			
1990		1996		1990		1996	
Country or area	Share a/ (percentage)	Country or area	Share a/ (percentage)	Country or area	Share b/ (percentage)	Country or area	Share b/ (percentage)
Food products (311/2)							
United States of America	24.1	United States of America	24.0	Brazil	13.5	Brazil	13.5
Japan	16.1	Japan	14.9	Argentina	8.9	Argentina	9.6
France	6.6	Germany, western part	6.6	Mexico	6.9	India	6.7
Germany, western part	6.3	France	6.6	India	6.2	Republic of Korea	6.3
United Kingdom	5.1	United Kingdom	4.8	Republic of Korea	6.2	Mexico	6.1
Italy	4.2	Italy	3.9	Yugoslavia (former)	4.8	Indonesia	5.8
Spain	3.5	Spain	3.1	Turkey	4.0	Philippines	4.6
Canada	2.6	Brazil	2.8	China (Taiwan Province)	3.9	Turkey	4.0
Brazil	2.5	Canada	2.7	Thailand	3.9	China (Taiwan Province)	3.8
Netherlands	1.9	Netherlands	2.0	Philippines	3.8	Thailand	3.3
Argentina	1.7	Argentina	2.0	Indonesia	2.9	Chile	2.8
Australia	1.6	Australia	1.6	Chile	2.4	Peru	2.1
Belgium	1.5	Belgium	1.5	Peru	2.0	Egypt	1.9
Mexico	1.3	India	1.4	Colombia	1.9	Colombia	1.7
India	1.2	Republic of Korea	1.3	Venezuela	1.7	Iran (Islamic Republic of)	1.6
Sum of above	80.2	Sum of above	79.2	Sum of above	73.0	Sum of above	73.8
Textiles (321)							
United States of America	16.5	United States of America	20.2	India	13.1	India	17.0
Japan	15.4	Italy	11.4	Brazil	10.1	China (Taiwan Province)	8.9
Italy	10.6	Japan	10.7	Republic of Korea	10.0	Brazil	8.9
Germany, western part	6.1	India	5.7	China (Taiwan Province)	9.1	Turkey	8.5
France	4.6	Germany, western part	4.6	Turkey	7.3	Republic of Korea	7.4
India	4.0	France	4.3	Yugoslavia (former)	5.0	Iran (Islamic Republic of)	4.3
United Kingdom	3.3	United Kingdom	3.0	Pakistan	4.0	Pakistan	4.1
Brazil	3.1	China (Taiwan Province)	3.0	China (Hong Kong SAR)	3.6	Indonesia	4.0
Republic of Korea	3.1	Brazil	3.0	Mexico	3.5	China (Hong Kong SAR)	3.2
China (Taiwan Province)	2.8	Turkey	2.8	Argentina	3.2	Argentina	3.1
Spain	2.5	Republic of Korea	2.5	Iran (Islamic Republic of)	3.1	Mexico	2.9
Turkey	2.2	Spain	2.3	Indonesia	2.8	Peru	2.3
Yugoslavia (former)	1.5	Canada	1.5	Egypt	1.9	Colombia	1.9
Canada	1.5	Iran (Islamic Republic of)	1.4	Peru	1.7	Egypt	1.8
Portugal	1.3	Pakistan	1.4	Colombia	1.6	Malaysia	1.2
Sum of above	78.5	Sum of above	77.8	Sum of above	80.0	Sum of above	79.5

a/ In world total value added (excluding eastern Europe and the former USSR) at constant 1990 prices.
b/ In total value added of developing countries at constant 1990 prices.

TABLE 1.7

LEADING PRODUCERS IN SELECTED BRANCHES, 1990 AND 1996

World leading countries				Leading developing countries			
1990		1996		1990		1996	
Country or area	Share a/ (percentage)	Country or area	Share a/ (percentage)	Country or area	Share b/ (percentage)	Country or area	Share b/ (percentage)
Wearing apparel (322)							
United States of America	22.0	United States of America	24.1	Brazil	15.5	Brazil	12.8
Japan	12.4	Japan	13.8	Republic of Korea	10.6	China (Hong Kong SAR)	10.5
Italy	9.1	Italy	10.5	China (Hong Kong SAR)	10.4	Republic of Korea	8.5
France	6.4	France	4.4	Yugoslavia (former)	5.9	Indonesia	7.0
Germany, western part	5.6	United Kingdom	4.2	Turkey	4.6	Turkey	4.6
Brazil	4.0	Brazil	3.5	China (Taiwan Province)	4.4	Argentina	4.2
United Kingdom	4.0	Germany, western part	3.4	Argentina	3.7	China (Taiwan Province)	2.7
Spain	3.2	China (Hong Kong SAR)	2.9	India	2.7	Tunisia	2.7
Republic of Korea	2.8	Spain	2.7	Philippines	2.7	India	2.5
China (Hong Kong SAR)	2.7	Canada	2.3	Mexico	2.1	Philippines	2.2
Canada	2.5	Republic of Korea	2.3	Indonesia	2.1	Mexico	1.9
Yugoslavia (former)	1.6	Indonesia	1.9	Tunisia	1.6	Morocco	1.7
Portugal	1.4	Portugal	1.3	Algeria	1.5	Iraq	1.6
Turkey	1.2	Turkey	1.3	Iraq	1.5	Sri Lanka	1.4
China (Taiwan Province)	1.2	Argentina	1.1	Singapore	1.2	Malaysia	1.2
Sum of above	80.1	Sum of above	79.7	Sum of above	70.5	Sum of above	65.5
Leather and fur products (323)							
Italy	14.5	Italy	18.4	Republic of Korea	18.4	Argentina	17.0
Japan	12.1	Japan	11.2	Brazil	14.0	Brazil	12.6
United States of America	11.9	United States of America	10.6	Mexico	11.3	Mexico	10.8
France	7.8	France	6.8	Argentina	8.2	Republic of Korea	8.0
Republic of Korea	5.8	Argentina	5.7	Yugoslavia (former)	7.3	India	6.2
Germany, western part	5.6	Spain	4.7	China (Taiwan Province)	5.8	Bangladesh	5.0
Spain	5.4	Brazil	4.2	India	5.4	China (Taiwan Province)	3.5
Brazil	4.4	Germany, western part	3.9	Iran (Islamic Republic of)	1.7	Uruguay	2.6
Mexico	3.6	Mexico	3.6	Algeria	1.5	Indonesia	2.3
United Kingdom	2.9	United Kingdom	3.4	Turkey	1.5	Paraguay	1.7
Argentina	2.6	Republic of Korea	2.7	Uruguay	1.5	Morocco	1.4
Yugoslavia (former)	2.3	India	2.1	Colombia	1.5	Turkey	1.2
China (Taiwan Province)	1.9	Bangladesh	1.7	Bangladesh	1.1	Iran (Islamic Republic of)	1.2
India	1.7	Portugal	1.3	Chile	1.1	Tunisia	1.1
Portugal	1.1	China (Taiwan Province)	1.2	Indonesia	1.0	Chile	1.1
Sum of above	83.6	Sum of above	81.5	Sum of above	81.3	Sum of above	75.7

a/ In world total value added (excluding eastern Europe and the former USSR) at constant 1990 prices.
b/ In total value added of developing countries at constant 1990 prices.

TABLE 1.7

LEADING PRODUCERS IN SELECTED BRANCHES, 1990 AND 1996

World leading countries				Leading developing countries			
1990		1996		1990		1996	
Country or area	Share a/ (percentage)	Country or area	Share a/ (percentage)	Country or area	Share b/ (percentage)	Country or area	Share b/ (percentage)
Footwear (324)							
Italy	18.2	Italy	24.3	Brazil	26.8	Brazil	26.3
Brazil	9.0	Brazil	8.6	Yugoslavia (former)	12.9	Argentina	12.2
United States of America	8.7	United States of America	7.8	China (Taiwan Province)	8.8	Mexico	6.5
France	6.8	Japan	6.2	Argentina	7.5	Indonesia	6.2
Japan	6.7	France	6.0	Republic of Korea	6.3	China (Taiwan Province)	5.8
Spain	4.8	United Kingdom	4.6	Mexico	6.3	India	3.3
United Kingdom	4.8	Spain	4.1	India	3.0	Republic of Korea	3.0
Germany, western part	4.8	Argentina	4.0	Indonesia	2.9	Tunisia	2.4
Yugoslavia (former)	4.3	Portugal	3.2	Chile	1.9	Iraq	2.3
China (Taiwan Province)	3.0	Germany, western part	3.1	Iraq	1.8	Chile	2.1
Portugal	2.9	Mexico	2.1	Algeria	1.8	Turkey	1.6
Argentina	2.5	Indonesia	2.0	Colombia	1.5	Colombia	1.5
Republic of Korea	2.1	China (Taiwan Province)	1.9	Iran (Islamic Republic of)	1.4	Iran (Islamic Republic of)	1.4
Mexico	2.1	South Africa	1.4	Venezuela	1.3	Venezuela	1.4
South Africa	1.6	Austria	1.3	Turkey	1.1	Morocco	1.0
Sum of above	82.3	Sum of above	80.6	Sum of above	85.3	Sum of above	77.0
Paper (341)							
United States of America	31.6	United States of America	32.2	Brazil	19.5	Brazil	18.2
Japan	14.8	Japan	14.3	Mexico	10.6	Republic of Korea	12.2
Germany, western part	8.2	Germany, western part	7.3	Republic of Korea	10.2	India	9.5
Canada	5.0	Canada	5.0	India	7.6	Mexico	8.2
France	4.8	France	4.8	China (Taiwan Province)	7.2	China (Taiwan Province)	6.6
Italy	4.7	Italy	4.6	Argentina	5.6	Argentina	6.4
United Kingdom	4.4	United Kingdom	4.2	Yugoslavia (former)	4.3	Indonesia	6.0
Sweden	2.8	Finland	2.8	Turkey	4.2	Turkey	4.6
Finland	2.6	Sweden	2.7	Chile	3.8	Chile	4.6
Brazil	2.1	Brazil	2.2	Indonesia	3.4	China (Hong Kong SAR)	2.1
Spain	1.9	Spain	2.0	Colombia	2.0	Colombia	1.9
Netherlands	1.4	Republic of Korea	1.5	Venezuela	1.8	Pakistan	1.4
Austria	1.2	Austria	1.4	China (Hong Kong SAR)	1.8	Peru	1.2
Mexico	1.2	Netherlands	1.3	Philippines	1.5	Venezuela	1.0
Republic of Korea	1.1	India	1.2	Singapore	1.2	Singapore	1.0
Sum of above	87.8	Sum of above	87.5	Sum of above	84.7	Sum of above	84.9

a/ In world total value added (excluding eastern Europe and the former USSR) at constant 1990 prices.
b/ In total value added of developing countries at constant 1990 prices.

TABLE 1.7

LEADING PRODUCERS IN SELECTED BRANCHES, 1990 AND 1996

World leading countries				Leading developing countries			
1990		1996		1990		1996	
Country or area	Share a/ (percentage)	Country or area	Share a/ (percentage)	Country or area	Share b/ (percentage)	Country or area	Share b/ (percentage)
Industrial chemicals (351)							
United States of America	25.8	United States of America	24.7	Brazil	15.8	China (Taiwan Province)	14.5
Japan	16.1	Japan	15.3	Mexico	14.6	Brazil	12.4
Germany, western part	13.7	Germany, western part	12.9	China (Taiwan Province)	10.8	Republic of Korea	12.1
United Kingdom	5.0	France	5.0	India	10.3	Mexico	12.0
France	4.9	United Kingdom	4.8	Republic of Korea	8.6	India	10.8
Italy	4.5	Italy	4.1	Saudi Arabia	5.7	Saudi Arabia	7.2
Netherlands	3.0	Netherlands	3.0	Turkey	4.8	Turkey	4.0
Brazil	2.5	China (Taiwan Province)	2.7	Argentina	3.2	Malaysia	3.0
Mexico	2.4	Brazil	2.3	Yugoslavia (former)	2.7	Argentina	3.0
Belgium	2.1	Republic of Korea	2.3	Malaysia	2.1	Indonesia	2.4
Spain	2.0	Mexico	2.3	Indonesia	2.1	Venezuela	1.9
China (Taiwan Province)	1.7	Belgium	2.1	Singapore	1.6	Pakistan	1.7
Canada	1.7	India	2.0	Pakistan	1.6	Singapore	1.6
India	1.7	Spain	1.8	Colombia	1.5	Colombia	1.1
Republic of Korea	1.4	Canada	1.7	Venezuela	1.2	Philippines	0.9
Sum of above	88.5	Sum of above	87.0	Sum of above	86.6	Sum of above	88.6
Other chemicals (352)							
United States of America	27.5	United States of America	26.1	Brazil	16.4	Republic of Korea	14.8
Japan	18.9	Japan	17.8	Mexico	12.1	Brazil	12.9
Germany, western part	10.3	Germany, western part	9.2	Republic of Korea	10.4	Argentina	10.4
France	5.3	France	5.4	Argentina	10.0	India	10.1
United Kingdom	5.0	United Kingdom	5.3	India	9.5	Mexico	10.1
Spain	3.1	Switzerland	3.8	Turkey	4.7	Turkey	5.2
Italy	2.9	Spain	2.9	China (Taiwan Province)	3.8	China (Taiwan Province)	4.2
Switzerland	2.8	Italy	2.6	Yugoslavia (former)	3.6	Philippines	3.3
Brazil	2.5	Republic of Korea	2.6	Philippines	2.7	Thailand	2.6
Canada	2.2	Brazil	2.2	Thailand	2.4	Chile	2.4
Mexico	1.8	Canada	2.1	Venezuela	1.9	Peru	2.0
Republic of Korea	1.6	Argentina	1.8	Chile	1.9	Indonesia	1.9
Argentina	1.5	India	1.7	Colombia	1.7	Singapore	1.7
India	1.4	Mexico	1.7	Singapore	1.7	Colombia	1.5
Sweden	1.0	Ireland	1.3	Indonesia	1.7	Venezuela	1.4
Sum of above	87.8	Sum of above	86.5	Sum of above	84.5	Sum of above	84.5

a/ In world total value added (excluding eastern Europe and the former USSR) at constant 1990 prices.
b/ In total value added of developing countries at constant 1990 prices.

TABLE 1.7

LEADING PRODUCERS IN SELECTED BRANCHES, 1990 AND 1996

World leading countries				Leading developing countries			
1990		1996		1990		1996	
Country or area	Share a/ (percentage)	Country or area	Share a/ (percentage)	Country or area	Share b/ (percentage)	Country or area	Share b/ (percentage)
Rubber products (355)							
Japan	20.0	United States of America	22.9	Republic of Korea	20.9	Republic of Korea	23.0
United States of America	19.6	Japan	17.3	Brazil	12.0	Brazil	10.5
Germany, western part	10.3	Germany, western part	8.3	India	10.6	India	10.3
Italy	7.1	Italy	6.6	Mexico	9.9	Mexico	8.7
France	6.2	France	6.0	China (Taiwan Province)	7.5	Malaysia	8.4
United Kingdom	4.4	Republic of Korea	5.3	Indonesia	4.9	Turkey	6.5
Republic of Korea	4.2	Spain	3.7	Malaysia	4.9	Indonesia	6.1
Spain	3.5	United Kingdom	3.6	Turkey	4.8	China (Taiwan Province)	5.7
Brazil	2.4	Canada	2.6	Yugoslavia (former)	3.9	Argentina	2.9
India	2.1	Brazil	2.4	Argentina	3.1	Thailand	2.0
Canada	2.1	India	2.3	Philippines	1.8	Venezuela	1.5
Mexico	2.0	Mexico	2.0	Thailand	1.7	Iran (Islamic Republic of)	1.3
China (Taiwan Province)	1.5	Malaysia	1.9	Venezuela	1.3	Philippines	1.1
Indonesia	1.0	Turkey	1.5	Iran (Islamic Republic of)	1.2	Chile	0.7
Malaysia	1.0	Indonesia	1.4	Colombia	1.2	Colombia	0.7
Sum of above	87.4	Sum of above	87.8	Sum of above	89.7	Sum of above	89.4
Iron and steel (371)							
Japan	26.4	Japan	22.0	Brazil	15.7	India	18.5
United States of America	14.3	United States of America	15.2	India	15.5	Republic of Korea	16.1
Germany, western part	9.5	Germany, western part	7.8	Republic of Korea	13.7	Brazil	12.3
Italy	8.0	Italy	7.7	Mexico	12.5	China (Taiwan Province)	10.7
France	4.9	India	4.7	China (Taiwan Province)	10.2	Mexico	10.6
United Kingdom	3.6	France	4.3	Turkey	4.8	Indonesia	6.8
Brazil	3.0	Republic of Korea	4.1	Yugoslavia (former)	3.6	Turkey	4.4
India	3.0	United Kingdom	3.3	Indonesia	3.4	Argentina	2.4
Spain	2.8	Brazil	3.1	Argentina	2.9	Venezuela	2.0
Republic of Korea	2.6	Spain	2.8	Venezuela	1.5	Malaysia	1.4
Mexico	2.4	China (Taiwan Province)	2.7	Egypt	1.1	Philippines	1.2
China (Taiwan Province)	2.0	Mexico	2.7	Algeria	1.0	Chile	1.0
Austria	1.6	Canada	1.8	Chile	0.9	Peru	0.9
Canada	1.5	Indonesia	1.7	Philippines	0.9	Egypt	0.8
South Africa	1.4	Austria	1.5	Malaysia	0.9	Colombia	0.8
Sum of above	87.0	Sum of above	85.4	Sum of above	88.6	Sum of above	89.9

a/ In world total value added (excluding eastern Europe and the former USSR) at constant 1990 prices.
b/ In total value added of developing countries at constant 1990 prices.

TABLE 1.7

LEADING PRODUCERS IN SELECTED BRANCHES, 1990 AND 1996

World leading countries				Leading developing countries			
1990		1996		1990		1996	
Country or area	Share a/ (percentage)	Country or area	Share a/ (percentage)	Country or area	Share b/ (percentage)	Country or area	Share b/ (percentage)
Non-ferrous metals (372)							
United States of America	19.7	United States of America	19.8	Chile	13.0	India	12.4
Japan	16.2	Japan	16.1	Brazil	11.8	Peru	11.8
Germany, western part	9.5	Germany, western part	7.6	Mexico	11.6	Mexico	10.9
France	6.5	France	5.5	India	9.4	Chile	10.6
Italy	4.4	Italy	4.7	Peru	8.7	Brazil	10.2
Australia	4.4	Canada	4.2	Republic of Korea	6.3	Republic of Korea	8.1
Canada	3.7	Australia	4.0	Yugoslavia (former)	5.9	China (Taiwan Province)	6.1
United Kingdom	3.1	India	2.8	Venezuela	5.6	Iran (Islamic Republic of)	5.2
Chile	2.6	Peru	2.7	China (Taiwan Province)	5.3	Venezuela	4.8
Brazil	2.4	Mexico	2.5	Turkey	4.7	Turkey	3.2
Mexico	2.3	Chile	2.4	Iran (Islamic Republic of)	3.4	Philippines	2.1
Spain	2.3	United Kingdom	2.4	Argentina	1.6	Argentina	1.4
India	1.9	Brazil	2.3	Egypt	1.4	Egypt	1.2
Peru	1.8	Spain	2.2	Morocco	1.2	Morocco	1.1
Belgium	1.7	Republic of Korea	1.9	Philippines	1.0	Malaysia	0.8
Sum of above	82.5	Sum of above	81.1	Sum of above	90.9	Sum of above	89.9
Metal products (381)							
Japan	22.5	United States of America	23.3	Republic of Korea	14.7	Republic of Korea	16.9
United States of America	21.0	Japan	20.6	Brazil	12.5	China (Taiwan Province)	12.0
Germany, western part	12.8	Germany, western part	13.3	China (Taiwan Province)	11.9	Brazil	11.4
France	7.6	France	6.5	Mexico	8.5	Mexico	7.3
Italy	5.2	Italy	4.5	Argentina	6.9	Argentina	6.7
United Kingdom	4.5	United Kingdom	3.7	India	4.8	India	4.9
Spain	2.6	Spain	2.4	Yugoslavia (former)	4.4	Malaysia	4.3
Canada	2.0	Canada	1.9	Turkey	4.0	Turkey	3.4
Sweden	1.5	Republic of Korea	1.9	Singapore	2.8	Singapore	3.3
Republic of Korea	1.4	Austria	1.5	China (Hong Kong SAR)	2.8	Chile	2.1
Netherlands	1.3	Sweden	1.4	Algeria	1.9	Indonesia	1.9
Australia	1.3	China (Taiwan Province)	1.4	Indonesia	1.7	Iran (Islamic Republic of)	1.9
Austria	1.3	Netherlands	1.3	Chile	1.6	Peru	1.7
Brazil	1.2	Brazil	1.3	Iran (Islamic Republic of)	1.5	China (Hong Kong SAR)	1.7
China (Taiwan Province)	1.2	Australia	1.3	Venezuela	1.3	Syrian Arab Republic	1.2
Sum of above	87.4	Sum of above	86.3	Sum of above	81.3	Sum of above	80.7

a/ In world total value added (excluding eastern Europe and the former USSR) at constant 1990 prices.
b/ In total value added of developing countries at constant 1990 prices.

TABLE 1.7

LEADING PRODUCERS IN SELECTED BRANCHES, 1990 AND 1996

World leading countries				Leading developing countries			
1990		1996		1990		1996	
Country or area	Share a/ (percentage)	Country or area	Share a/ (percentage)	Country or area	Share b/ (percentage)	Country or area	Share b/ (percentage)
Non-electrical machinery (382)							
Japan	24.9	United States of America	38.5	Brazil	22.6	Republic of Korea	19.4
United States of America	23.8	Japan	17.5	Republic of Korea	14.4	Brazil	17.9
Germany, western part	14.8	Germany, western part	10.3	India	11.4	India	12.8
Italy	7.2	Italy	7.7	Singapore	7.6	Singapore	9.4
France	5.2	United Kingdom	4.4	China (Taiwan Province)	7.3	China (Taiwan Province)	7.9
United Kingdom	4.9	France	3.6	Argentina	5.9	Turkey	5.7
Brazil	1.7	Canada	1.8	Yugoslavia (former)	5.8	Argentina	5.1
Spain	1.5	Republic of Korea	1.4	Mexico	4.8	Mexico	4.1
Canada	1.3	Spain	1.3	Turkey	4.5	Iran (Islamic Republic of)	2.7
Sweden	1.1	Brazil	1.3	China (Hong Kong SAR)	3.0	Malaysia	2.5
Republic of Korea	1.1	India	0.9	Iran (Islamic Republic of)	2.3	China (Hong Kong SAR)	1.9
Austria	0.9	Netherlands	0.9	Algeria	1.0	Chile	0.9
Netherlands	0.9	Finland	0.9	Malaysia	1.0	Philippines	0.5
India	0.9	Singapore	0.7	Indonesia	0.5	Venezuela	0.4
Belgium	0.8	Sweden	0.7	Chile	0.5	Egypt	0.4
Sum of above	91.0	Sum of above	91.9	Sum of above	92.6	Sum of above	91.6
Electrical machinery (383)							
Japan	27.9	United States of America	27.0	Republic of Korea	20.6	Republic of Korea	23.2
United States of America	19.5	Japan	24.6	China (Taiwan Province)	17.6	China (Taiwan Province)	22.0
Germany, western part	13.8	Germany, western part	11.8	Brazil	15.0	Brazil	13.4
France	5.7	France	4.7	India	7.5	India	6.9
Italy	5.6	Italy	4.2	Mexico	6.6	Malaysia	6.4
United Kingdom	3.9	United Kingdom	3.1	Singapore	5.0	Mexico	4.6
Republic of Korea	2.5	Republic of Korea	3.1	Yugoslavia (former)	4.3	Singapore	4.4
China (Taiwan Province)	2.1	China (Taiwan Province)	2.9	Malaysia	3.6	Turkey	3.5
Brazil	1.8	Brazil	1.8	Turkey	3.1	Argentina	2.7
Spain	1.7	Spain	1.5	Argentina	2.7	Philippines	1.9
Netherlands	1.4	Netherlands	1.3	China (Hong Kong SAR)	2.1	China (Hong Kong SAR)	1.6
Canada	1.3	Sweden	1.2	Philippines	1.8	Iran (Islamic Republic of)	0.8
Austria	1.1	Austria	1.2	Algeria	1.1	Indonesia	0.8
India	0.9	Canada	1.1	Indonesia	0.8	Algeria	0.4
Mexico	0.8	India	0.9	Iran (Islamic Republic of)	0.7	Peru	0.4
Sum of above	90.0	Sum of above	90.4	Sum of above	92.5	Sum of above	93.0

a/ In world total value added (excluding eastern Europe and the former USSR) at constant 1990 prices.
b/ In total value added of developing countries at constant 1990 prices.

TABLE 1.8

STRUCTURE OF MVA IN SELECTED COUNTRY GROUPS, SELECTED YEARS[a/]

(Percentage)

Branch (ISIC)	Year	Industrialized countries						Developing countries			
		Eastern Europe and former USSR	Western Europe		Japan	North America	All countries	NICs	Second-generation NICs	Others	All countries
			EU b/	Other							
Food products (311/2)	1980	16.5	8.0	9.3	9.5	10.0	9.9	9.2	14.9	14.6	11.2
	1985	15.8	8.6	9.2	8.7	9.9	10.0	9.3	14.6	15.7	11.5
	1990	16.2	8.5	8.5	7.5	9.3	9.4	9.0	12.1	16.1	10.8
	1996c/	13.5	9.2	8.5	7.7	8.2	8.9	8.7	11.5	...	10.6
Beverages (313)	1980	3.3	2.2	2.1	1.6	1.9	2.2	3.3	3.9	5.0	3.7
	1985	2.8	2.3	2.1	1.3	1.8	2.1	3.2	3.7	5.1	3.7
	1990	2.3	2.4	1.9	1.2	1.7	1.9	3.0	4.0	5.3	3.6
	1996c/	3.3	2.5	1.9	1.1	1.5	1.9	2.9	4.2	...	3.7
Tobacco (314)	1980	1.0	1.6	1.3	0.3	2.2	1.4	2.6	5.5	5.0	3.5
	1985	1.0	1.7	1.3	0.3	1.8	1.3	2.6	5.8	6.1	3.8
	1990	0.8	1.5	1.2	0.2	1.6	1.2	2.2	4.8	5.3	3.2
	1996c/	0.7	1.4	1.2	0.2	1.3	1.1	2.0	5.2	...	3.2
Textiles (321)	1980	9.3	4.3	2.9	4.9	3.2	4.7	8.5	8.8	9.0	8.7
	1985	8.4	4.1	2.9	4.2	2.8	4.3	7.9	9.2	9.0	8.3
	1990	8.7	3.6	2.4	3.0	2.6	3.7	7.0	8.7	8.8	7.6
	1996c/	6.0	3.2	2.0	2.0	2.4	2.7	5.8	7.2	...	6.4
Wearing apparel (322)	1980	3.3	2.8	1.3	2.0	2.7	2.6	3.8	6.6	2.8	4.0
	1985	3.2	2.5	1.1	1.7	2.2	2.4	3.8	6.2	2.4	3.9
	1990	3.3	2.0	0.8	1.3	2.0	2.0	3.2	5.7	2.4	3.5
	1996c/	2.2	1.6	0.7	1.4	1.6	1.6	2.2	5.0	...	2.7
Leather and fur products (323)	1980	1.0	0.5	0.1	0.3	0.3	0.4	1.0	0.3	1.0	0.9
	1985	0.8	0.5	0.1	0.3	0.2	0.4	1.0	0.3	0.8	0.8
	1990	0.8	0.4	0.1	0.2	0.2	0.3	0.8	0.3	0.7	0.7
	1996c/	0.4	0.3	0.1	0.2	0.1	0.2	0.5	0.2	...	0.5
Footwear (324)	1980	0.9	0.9	0.4	0.2	0.4	0.6	1.7	0.7	1.6	1.5
	1985	0.9	0.8	0.3	0.2	0.3	0.5	1.6	0.6	1.3	1.4
	1990	1.0	0.6	0.2	0.2	0.2	0.4	1.2	0.5	1.0	1.1
	1996c/	0.7	0.5	0.1	0.1	0.1	0.3	0.7	0.6	...	0.7
Wood and cork products (331)	1980	1.4	1.8	4.4	2.7	1.7	2.0	1.2	2.6	1.9	1.5
	1985	1.4	1.6	4.1	1.8	1.9	1.8	1.1	2.1	1.8	1.4
	1990	1.4	1.6	4.1	1.6	1.8	1.7	0.9	3.1	1.5	1.4
	1996c/	1.9	1.6	3.6	1.3	1.5	1.6	0.6	2.7	...	1.1

a/ Percentage shares of individual branches in total MVA at constant 1990 prices.
b/ In 1996 including estimates for the eastern part of Germany.
c/ 1995 for developing countries.

TABLE 1.8
(continued)

STRUCTURE OF MVA IN SELECTED COUNTRY GROUPS, SELECTED YEARS[a/]

(Percentage)

Branch (ISIC)	Year	Industrialized countries						Developing countries			
		Eastern Europe and former USSR	Western Europe		Japan	North America	All countries	NICs	Second-generation NICs	Others	All countries
			EU b/	Other							
Furniture, fixtures excl. metallic (332)	1980	1.3	1.9	2.1	1.4	1.2	1.6	1.2	0.7	2.2	1.4
	1985	1.4	1.6	2.0	1.0	1.4	1.4	1.2	0.6	1.2	1.1
	1990	1.4	1.7	1.9	1.0	1.3	1.4	1.0	0.8	0.7	0.9
	1996c/	1.5	1.6	1.7	0.7	1.2	1.3	0.8	0.7	...	0.7
Paper (341)	1980	1.8	2.8	2.4	2.4	4.7	3.1	2.3	1.8	2.1	2.2
	1985	1.8	3.0	2.8	2.3	4.7	3.2	2.4	1.8	1.8	2.2
	1990	1.4	3.1	2.8	2.5	4.6	3.2	2.5	1.9	2.1	2.3
	1996c/	2.5	3.2	2.7	2.7	4.2	3.4	2.6	2.0	...	2.4
Printing and publishing (342)	1980	0.4	4.0	6.2	6.4	7.2	4.9	2.2	1.6	2.2	2.1
	1985	0.4	4.0	7.9	6.0	7.9	5.1	2.2	1.5	1.9	2.0
	1990	0.5	4.4	7.9	5.4	7.7	5.2	2.3	1.5	1.9	2.1
	1996c/	1.0	4.2	8.0	6.3	5.8	5.1	2.6	1.1	...	2.3
Industrial chemicals (351)	1980	5.3	5.2	1.0	4.6	5.1	4.9	4.7	3.8	3.3	4.3
	1985	5.3	5.7	1.7	4.2	5.1	5.1	5.5	4.5	4.4	5.1
	1990	5.0	5.5	1.8	4.3	5.5	5.1	5.9	4.4	5.1	5.5
	1996c/	5.5	6.1	2.3	4.8	4.9	5.3	6.4	4.1	...	5.8
Other chemicals (352)	1980	2.8	4.1	6.6	4.7	5.6	4.5	5.8	4.2	4.6	5.3
	1985	2.7	4.6	8.3	5.0	5.8	4.8	5.7	4.1	4.6	5.2
	1990	2.3	4.8	10.0	5.2	6.1	5.1	5.7	4.4	5.1	5.4
	1996c/	2.5	5.3	14.5	5.9	5.5	5.5	6.0	4.5	...	5.7
Petroleum refineries (353)	1980	4.0	3.5	0.2	0.9	2.2	2.7	4.1	12.6	14.4	7.6
	1985	3.7	2.6	0.3	0.6	1.8	2.1	4.1	12.9	13.7	7.5
	1990	3.4	2.4	0.4	0.5	1.8	1.9	4.0	12.4	15.0	7.5
	1996c/	5.5	2.6	0.4	0.6	1.5	1.9	4.1	12.5	...	7.5
Prods. of petroleum and coal (354)	1980	1.0	1.0	0.4	0.2	0.4	0.7	0.5	0.5	0.4	0.5
	1985	0.9	0.8	0.3	0.2	0.3	0.6	0.6	0.6	0.4	0.5
	1990	1.0	0.7	0.3	0.2	0.3	0.5	0.5	0.6	0.4	0.5
	1996c/	1.5	0.7	0.3	0.2	0.3	0.5	0.5	0.4	...	0.5
Rubber products (355)	1980	1.4	1.3	0.4	1.4	0.9	1.2	1.6	2.0	0.9	1.5
	1985	1.4	1.2	0.5	1.4	1.0	1.2	1.7	1.9	0.8	1.5
	1990	1.2	1.2	0.5	1.3	1.0	1.2	1.8	1.9	1.0	1.7
	1996c/	1.4	1.2	0.4	1.2	1.1	1.2	1.7	2.1	...	1.7

a/ Percentage shares of individual branches in total MVA at constant 1990 prices.
b/ In 1996 including estimates for the eastern part of Germany.
c/ 1995 for developing countries.

TABLE 1.8
(continued)

STRUCTURE OF MVA IN SELECTED COUNTRY GROUPS, SELECTED YEARS[a/]

(Percentage)

Branch (ISIC)	Year	Industrialized countries						Developing countries			
		Eastern Europe and former USSR	Western Europe		Japan	North America	All countries	NICs	Second-generation NICs	Others	All countries
			EU b/	Other							
Plastic products (356)	1980	0.9	2.3	2.2	3.4	2.1	2.3	2.6	1.5	1.7	2.2
	1985	0.9	2.7	2.4	3.4	2.6	2.6	2.9	1.3	1.5	2.4
	1990	0.7	3.0	2.5	3.5	2.8	2.8	3.0	1.3	1.5	2.4
	1996c/	1.0	3.1	2.0	3.4	3.0	3.0	2.7	1.5	...	2.3
Pottery, china, earthenware (361)	1980	0.4	0.7	0.4	0.4	0.1	0.5	0.4	0.9	0.3	0.4
	1985	0.4	0.7	0.4	0.3	0.1	0.4	0.4	0.8	0.3	0.4
	1990	0.4	0.6	0.3	0.3	0.1	0.4	0.4	0.9	0.3	0.5
	1996c/	0.8	0.6	0.2	0.3	0.1	0.4	0.4	1.0	...	0.5
Glass (362)	1980	0.7	1.0	0.9	1.2	0.9	1.0	1.0	0.7	0.5	0.9
	1985	0.7	1.0	0.9	1.0	0.8	0.9	1.0	0.9	0.5	0.9
	1990	0.7	1.0	0.8	1.0	0.8	0.9	0.9	1.1	0.6	0.9
	1996c/	0.9	1.0	0.6	0.9	0.6	0.8	0.9	1.2	...	0.9
Other non-metallic mineral prods.(369)	1980	3.0	3.6	4.0	3.7	2.1	3.2	3.5	4.5	4.0	3.8
	1985	2.8	3.0	3.8	3.2	2.0	2.8	3.2	4.3	4.4	3.6
	1990	3.0	3.1	3.2	3.0	1.9	2.7	3.1	4.3	4.8	3.6
	1996c/	4.6	2.9	2.5	2.8	1.6	2.5	3.2	4.9	...	3.9
Iron and steel (371)	1980	6.3	4.6	2.1	7.0	3.6	4.9	5.5	2.6	3.6	4.7
	1985	5.8	4.3	2.3	6.2	2.7	4.4	5.6	2.9	3.9	4.9
	1990	5.5	3.9	2.3	5.4	2.4	4.0	6.0	3.5	3.8	5.1
	1996c/	6.0	3.8	2.0	4.9	2.2	3.7	6.5	4.5	...	5.6
Non-ferrous metals (372)	1980	3.4	1.5	1.9	1.5	1.7	1.8	1.8	2.1	3.8	2.3
	1985	3.2	1.5	2.0	1.3	1.6	1.7	1.8	1.9	4.0	2.3
	1990	3.2	1.5	2.1	1.3	1.4	1.7	1.8	1.3	4.2	2.1
	1996c/	4.3	1.4	2.0	1.5	1.3	1.7	1.8	1.1	...	2.1
Metal products (381)	1980	2.7	7.4	7.5	8.5	6.2	6.8	4.3	2.6	3.9	4.0
	1985	2.8	6.6	7.0	7.2	5.9	6.1	4.3	2.5	3.4	3.9
	1990	2.5	6.8	7.2	7.1	5.4	6.1	4.3	2.9	3.3	3.9
	1996c/	2.9	6.5	7.2	6.8	5.0	5.9	4.1	3.0	...	3.8
Non-electrical machinery (382)	1980	11.8	11.7	14.6	10.6	8.7	10.6	7.7	2.3	2.6	5.8
	1985	13.0	11.8	14.6	12.8	9.0	11.3	6.9	2.5	3.2	5.5
	1990	13.8	12.2	14.8	14.2	10.6	12.2	7.2	2.6	2.6	5.5
	1996c/	12.1	12.2	13.8	12.6	17.3	13.8	7.3	2.8	...	5.5

a/ Percentage shares of individual branches in total MVA at constant 1990 prices.
b/ In 1996 including estimates for the eastern part of Germany.
c/ 1995 for developing countries.

TABLE 1.8
(continued)

STRUCTURE OF MVA IN SELECTED COUNTRY GROUPS, SELECTED YEARS[a/]

(Percentage)

Branch (ISIC)	Year	Industrialized countries						Developing countries			
		Eastern Europe and former USSR	Western Europe		Japan	North America	All countries	NICs	Second-generation NICs	Others	All countries
			EU b/	Other							
Electrical machinery (383)	1980	6.7	9.3	13.4	7.2	6.9	8.0	7.4	3.6	2.6	5.8
	1985	8.1	10.6	12.8	12.8	7.5	9.8	8.0	4.1	2.7	6.3
	1990	8.2	10.5	13.7	15.0	8.4	10.6	10.6	5.7	2.8	8.3
	1996c/	7.2	11.7	13.3	17.9	12.1	12.8	12.4	6.8	...	9.5
Transport equipment (384)	1980	5.7	9.7	4.2	10.4	10.3	9.4	9.7	4.9	4.7	7.9
	1985	6.1	9.8	3.2	9.8	11.8	9.7	9.7	5.0	3.9	7.7
	1990	6.5	10.7	2.9	10.7	11.7	10.4	9.3	6.8	2.7	7.7
	1996c/	6.6	9.3	3.2	10.3	9.7	9.4	10.6	7.2	...	8.6
Prof., scient. equipment (385)	1980	1.3	1.3	5.3	1.1	6.1	2.6	0.9	0.5	0.2	0.7
	1985	1.6	1.4	3.9	1.4	5.7	2.6	0.9	0.5	0.2	0.7
	1990	1.5	1.3	3.7	1.4	5.4	2.5	1.0	0.4	0.2	0.8
	1996c/	1.1	1.4	3.3	1.1	4.6	2.4	0.9	0.4	...	0.7
Other manufactures (390)	1980	2.4	1.0	2.4	1.5	1.6	1.5	1.5	3.3	1.1	1.6
	1985	2.7	1.0	1.8	1.4	1.4	1.4	1.4	2.9	1.0	1.5
	1990	3.3	1.0	1.7	1.5	1.4	1.5	1.4	2.1	0.8	1.4
	1996c/	2.4	0.9	1.5	1.1	1.3	1.1	1.1	1.6	...	1.1
Total manufacturing (3)	1980	100.0	100.0	100.0	100.0	100.0	100.0	100.0	100.0	100.0	100.0
	1985	100.0	100.0	100.0	100.0	100.0	100.0	100.0	100.0	100.0	100.0
	1990	100.0	100.0	100.0	100.0	100.0	100.0	100.0	100.0	100.0	100.0
	1996c/	100.0	100.0	100.0	100.0	100.0	100.0	100.0	100.0	100.0	100.0

a/ Percentage shares of individual branches in total MVA at constant 1990 prices.
b/ In 1996 including estimates for the eastern part of Germany.
c/ 1995 for developing countries.

TABLE 1.9

ANNUAL GROWTH OF VALUE ADDED OF BRANCHES, SELECTED COUNTRY GROUPS, 1980-1990 AND 1990-1996[a/]

(Percentage)

Branch (ISIC)	Industrialized countries excluding eastern Europe and former USSR		Eastern Europe and former USSR		Developing countries							
					All countries		NICs		Second-generation NICs		Others	
	1980-1990	1990-1996	1980-1990	1990-1996	1980-1990	1990-1996	1980-1990	1990-1996	1980-1990	1990-1996	1980-1990	1990-1996
Food products (311/2)	1.8	1.3	1.7	...	2.4	3.3	2.8	2.4	2.9	6.2	1.7	2.7
Beverages (313)	1.7	0.9	-1.4	...	2.4	3.9	2.2	2.4	4.7	7.4	1.6	4.1
Tobacco (314)	0.0	-0.0	0.7	...	1.7	4.1	1.6	1.6	3.0	...	0.9	...
Textiles (321)	0.1	-1.7	1.1	...	2.3	0.4	2.1	-0.8	5.5	3.3	0.8	0.7
Wearing apparel (322)	-0.6	-1.1	1.7	...	2.5	-0.6	2.2	-3.4	4.6	...	...	...
Leather and fur products (323)	-1.5	-3.0	-0.0	...	0.8	-2.3	2.0	-4.2	2.2	2.0	...	...
Footwear (324)	-2.8	-2.3	2.4	...	-0.6	-3.5	0.6	-5.1	2.2	6.1	...	...
Wood and cork products (331)	1.5	0.5	2.2	...	2.0	...	1.0	...	6.8	3.7	...	...
Furniture, fixtures excl. metallic (332)	1.7	-0.7	3.0	...	-0.3	...	2.5	...	5.6	4.4	...	...
Paper (341)	3.2	1.8	1.2	...	4.3	4.0	4.8	3.5	6.5	6.6	1.5	3.8
Printing and publishing (342)	3.2	0.7	2.9	...	3.2	4.6	4.4	4.8	3.0	1.0	...	...
Industrial chemicals (351)	3.3	2.2	2.0	...	6.0	5.5	6.0	5.5	7.6	5.2	5.2	...
Other chemicals (352)	4.0	2.5	1.2	...	3.6	5.2	3.4	4.8	6.8	6.3	...	...
Petroleum refineries (353)	-0.7	1.0	0.9	...	3.6	4.0	3.4	4.6	5.5	6.0	2.7	2.2b/
Prods. of petroleum and coal (354)	-0.8	-0.1	1.3	...	3.1	4.0	3.0	4.9	6.0	0.6	...	...
Rubber products (355)	3.0	1.7	1.6	...	5.1	4.0	5.4	2.8	5.8	7.8	2.2	3.1c/
Plastic products (356)	4.9	2.4	1.4	...	5.3	3.4	6.3	2.2	4.5	9.7	...	...
Pottery, china, earthenware (361)	0.9	-1.1	2.6	...	3.9	5.2	2.7	3.0	7.4	8.8	2.1	2.2c/
Glass (362)	1.4	-0.0	2.8	...	3.5	4.2	2.4	2.7	8.9	8.3	3.5	4.2b/
Other non-metallic mineral prods.(369)	1.1	0.2	2.0	...	3.1	4.9	2.5	4.1	5.6	8.7	2.8	2.4b/
Iron and steel (371)	0.6	0.2	0.8	...	4.8	6.3	4.7	5.8	9.1	11.1	2.6	...
Non-ferrous metals (372)	2.1	1.7	1.5	...	2.8	4.4	4.0	4.7	-0.2	...	2.0	4.0b/
Metal products (381)	1.4	0.8	2.5	...	3.3	3.5	4.2	2.6	6.4	8.2	...	...
Non-electrical machinery (382)	4.2	4.1	4.0	...	3.5	3.9	4.0	3.8	4.5	7.8	...	...
Electrical machinery (383)	5.5	4.8	5.0	...	7.7	6.9	8.4	7.0	10.2	9.8	...	...
Transport equipment (384)	3.5	-0.6	3.8	...	3.2	6.3	3.7	6.4	6.9	7.5	...	...
Prof., scient. equipment (385)	2.5	-0.1	4.8	...	...	...	4.9	1.6	...	...	...	...
Other manufactures (390)	2.0	-1.4	4.8	...	...	...	3.8	...	...	...	...	...

a/ At constant 1990 prices.
b/ Figure refers to the period 1990-1995.
c/ Figure refers to the period 1990-1994.

TABLE 1.10

SHARE OF FEMALES IN TOTAL EMPLOYMENT BY BRANCH, SELECTED YEARS

(Percentage)

Branch (ISIC)	Albania		Argentina		Austria		Bangladesh		Bermuda	
	1990	1996	1990	1994	1990	1994	1990	1992	1990	1996
Food products (311/2)	...	64.4	...	19.0	39.8	39.6	5.9	5.3	36.9	33.7
Beverages (313)	...	70.0	...	11.6	20.5	20.8	-	8.5	13.5	12.9
Tobacco (314)	...	83.8	...	14.6	42.9	35.6	10.3	7.9	...	...
Textiles (321)	...	11.3	...	22.6	55.8	53.5	2.3	1.8	...	...
Wearing apparel (322)	...	80.1	...	65.9	88.8	85.7	71.2	69.4	74.1	68.4
Leather and fur products (323)	...	54.8	...	13.3	60.7	59.0	0.2	0.1	...	...
Footwear (324)	...	64.8	...	28.1	67.9	65.9	-	2.6	30.8	...
Wood and cork products (331)	...	5.1	...	4.8	16.6	15.7	15.8	24.5	12.9	15.0
Furniture, fixtures excl. metallic (332)	...	...	...	7.3	20.1	20.5	6.0	-	26.9	30.3
Paper (341)	...	...	...	13.7	20.0	18.1	0.6	1.4	...	...
Printing and publishing (342)	...	58.0	...	21.1	34.6	34.7	1.3	0.5	47.4	44.0
Industrial chemicals (351)	...	17.6	...	9.1	18.2	16.7	2.8	3.0	23.5	16.7
Other chemicals (352)	...	18.3	...	28.8	40.1	39.0	4.1	4.1	...	...
Petroleum refineries (353)	...	34.7	...	6.7	18.9	20.6	1.5	1.6	10.5	...
Prods. of petroleum and coal (354)	...	...	...	7.9	9.1	14.5	1.7	-	...	...
Rubber products (355)	...	19.3	...	10.1	23.9	20.8	-	0.8	...	...
Plastic products (356)	...	25.2	...	18.1	36.5	32.1	0.9	0.9	...	...
Pottery, china, earthenware (361)	...	...	...	13.7	46.7	43.2	4.1	1.5	50.0	55.6
Glass (362)	...	...	...	5.6	34.4	34.6	4.6	10.5	35.0	...
Other non-metallic mineral prods.(369)	...	19.8	...	4.3	12.0	12.4	0.4	1.5	50.0	...
Iron and steel (371)	...	7.1	...	3.2	9.9	9.8	-	0.1	...	...
Non-ferrous metals (372)	...	19.4	...	6.0	17.7	18.6	-	-	...	...
Metal products (381)	...	46.6	...	8.0	21.1	19.9	0.7	0.6	17.1	12.0
Non-electrical machinery (382)	...	29.1	...	7.7	12.7	12.8	2.0	1.0	9.1	...
Electrical machinery (383)	...	42.0	...	20.1	35.7	31.5	2.9	2.7	33.3	28.6
Transport equipment (384)	...	...	...	5.3	14.8	15.2	0.3	0.4	7.7	13.3
Prof., scient equipment (385)	...	...	...	22.7	47.1	46.3	4.1	3.5	42.9	...
Other manufactures (390)	...	37.9	...	27.1	36.6	36.1	20.6	18.7	35.3	40.5
Total manufacturing (3)	...	44.0	...	17.0	29.4	27.4	14.0	15.3	35.6	33.9

TABLE 1.10

SHARE OF FEMALES IN TOTAL EMPLOYMENT BY BRANCH, SELECTED YEARS

(Percentage)

Branch (ISIC)	Bulgaria		Chile		China (Taiwan Prov.)		Colombia		Croatia	
	1990	1996	1990	1995	1990	1996	1989	1994	1990	1996
Food products (311/2)	...	50.6	25.4	26.9	44.8	45.4	26.2	31.9	43.8	42.9
Beverages (313)	...	44.9	8.3	8.9	34.9	34.1	14.7	15.2	33.5	34.9
Tobacco (314)	...	59.2	8.9	8.9	67.8	90.4	24.3	27.5	56.1	49.1
Textiles (321)	...	68.4	30.4	35.0	57.4	53.6	35.6	39.9	69.9	71.7
Wearing apparel (322)	...	74.0	65.9	62.1	79.1	78.9	81.2	79.5	86.2	88.0
Leather and fur products (323)	...	61.2	11.8	14.6	46.5	33.8	41.5	45.6	64.2	64.0
Footwear (324)	...	78.0	37.8	36.5	65.8	65.8	51.2	50.5	74.5	73.0
Wood and cork products (331)	...	39.6	5.4	6.5	42.4	40.4	15.5	19.5	30.5	32.8
Furniture, fixtures excl. metallic (332)	...	45.5	9.4	11.4	37.9	38.3	21.9	24.9	35.6	34.1
Paper (341)	...	47.4	5.6	7.4	31.8	32.3	19.9	19.8	42.5	39.3
Printing and publishing (342)	...	52.5	15.8	18.6	34.9	36.7	33.8	39.5	49.9	49.0
Industrial chemicals (351)	...	37.7	7.1	19.3	26.4	24.5	13.8	17.1	24.8	25.8
Other chemicals (352)	...	53.9	32.0	31.9	43.8	44.7	42.4	46.0	51.3	51.9
Petroleum refineries (353)	...	...	7.1	6.4	9.0	9.6	10.4	11.1	21.4	22.8
Prods. of petroleum and coal (354)	...	38.8	4.1	9.5	17.9	10.4	12.9	17.2	12.9	16.1
Rubber products (355)	...	45.5	10.5	9.1	45.4	41.5	13.6	23.6	49.1	41.4
Plastic products (356)	...	52.3	16.9	15.7	53.1	45.4	31.2	35.5	41.5	36.8
Pottery, china, earthenware (361)	...	44.7	14.3	16.0	53.3	40.7	22.2	19.6	41.0	43.5
Glass (362)	...	44.2	5.0	5.9	36.3	36.1	14.4	17.2	39.1	35.7
Other non-metallic mineral prods. (369)	...	29.7	5.0	5.3	25.4	22.7	9.5	10.3	17.6	18.9
Iron and steel (371)	...	32.2	2.9	3.2	15.6	15.4	10.7	11.0	11.1	20.2
Non-ferrous metals (372)	...	27.1	2.3	3.8	22.5	23.0	13.2	14.6	17.9	18.4
Metal products (381)	...	36.0	6.0	6.9	31.3	32.9	17.3	18.5	23.3	23.9
Non-electrical machinery (382)	...	...	5.6	4.6	33.2	34.1	14.0	15.0	15.2	15.0
Electrical machinery (383)	...	45.1	12.1	14.4	54.6	52.6	32.8	37.9	39.0	39.4
Transport equipment (384)	...	27.8	6.9	6.8	21.6	24.8	12.8	14.8	17.2	16.7
Prof., scient. equipment (385)	...	...	21.4	17.3	56.8	58.1	45.0	52.1	46.5	32.0
Other manufactures (390)	...	54.7	36.0	28.4	56.5	52.3	46.5	45.9	55.6	59.0
Total manufacturing (3)	...	...	20.2	20.6	45.1	42.3	31.1	35.2	41.5	42.8

TABLE 1.10

SHARE OF FEMALES IN TOTAL EMPLOYMENT BY BRANCH, SELECTED YEARS

(Percentage)

Branch (ISIC)	Cyprus		Czech Republic		Denmark		Egypt		El Salvador	
	1990	1994	1990	1993	1990	1992	1991	1994	1990	1996
Food products (311/2)	44.4	44.1	50.0	53.3	44.6	43.8	9.0	13.0	...	31.8
Beverages (313)	29.1	27.5	41.7	43.5	25.4	24.9	10.9	7.0	...	9.4
Tobacco (314)	45.7	56.5	50.0	50.0	57.0	54.8	16.1	16.3	...	16.5
Textiles (321)	77.6	73.7	68.3	69.0	58.0	59.8	12.6	14.9	...	46.5
Wearing apparel (322)	94.7	96.3	82.9	87.9	91.9	93.9	53.6	58.3	...	78.5
Leather and fur products (323)	71.6	67.1	84.6	75.0	59.6	54.2	9.4	11.0	...	40.5
Footwear (324)	63.9	64.8	52.8	70.4	50.7	48.9	22.0	18.6	...	42.2
Wood and cork products (331)	8.7	10.4	40.0	33.3	20.0	19.3	2.7	3.4	...	10.8
Furniture, fixtures excl metallic (332)	21.3	38.2	55.6	46.2	27.6	27.0	4.9	3.4	...	14.3
Paper (341)	41.8	38.4	44.0	45.5	26.5	27.5	7.6	10.9	...	55.8
Printing and publishing (342)	38.3	42.3	50.0	56.3	37.5	38.0	7.8	8.7	...	26.7
Industrial chemicals (351)	25.5	24.6	36.2	33.3	26.6	30.5	5.9	5.2	...	11.9
Other chemicals (352)	46.1	43.9	53.8	57.1	48.1	48.5	24.4	26.5	...	45.3
Petroleum refineries (353)	7.0	6.5	46.2	35.7	10.3	11.7	7.8	7.8	...	2.9
Prods. of petroleum and coal (354)	...	...	29.4	...	10.8	11.8	5.1	10.7	...	14.7
Rubber products (355)	25.0	34.2	43.8	33.3	26.0	26.3	3.0	9.6	...	25.1
Plastic products (356)	33.4	31.0	57.1	50.0	38.4	40.2	11.8	14.6	...	29.3
Pottery, china, earthenware (361)	75.8	61.9	55.6	63.6	69.7	75.9	14.5	17.7	...	32.7
Glass (362)	24.7	25.3	48.3	45.2	30.7	29.7	8.9	11.7	...	16.1
Other non-metallic mineral prods.(369)	11.4	12.1	26.7	27.0	16.8	16.9	3.2	3.5	...	6.4
Iron and steel (371)	...	...	28.6	25.5	16.0	16.1	2.5	2.6	...	5.1
Non-ferrous metals (372)	...	...	28.6	33.3	23.6	20.1	1.7	2.6	...	...
Metal products (381)	14.1	15.4	44.8	32.9	21.7	21.8	5.6	7.0	...	11.9
Non-electrical machinery (382)	13.4	14.2	31.8	26.3	20.8	21.0	4.5	4.6	...	8.3
Electrical machinery (383)	34.4	34.8	48.0	44.6	39.1	37.9	17.4	14.9	...	43.5
Transport equipment (384)	19.1	17.1	30.9	33.3	12.2	12.3	3.5	4.1	...	14.6
Prof., scient. equipment (385)	50.0	68.1	47.1	43.5	43.2	44.3	14.4	18.9	...	62.3
Other manufactures (390)	33.8	28.7	58.3	47.7	50.3	51.3	24.5	14.0	...	47.8
Total manufacturing (3)	51.1	45.9	42.7	42.1	33.9	33.7	10.7	13.0	...	47.8

TABLE 1.10

SHARE OF FEMALES IN TOTAL EMPLOYMENT BY BRANCH, SELECTED YEARS

(Percentage)

Branch (ISIC)	Ethiopia		Ghana		Hungary		India		Indonesia	
	1991	1996	1990	1993	1990	1993	1990	1994	1990	1996
Food products (311/2)	18.1	18.3	...	8.7	41.4	41.0	...	18.5	...	40.5
Beverages (313)	25.1	25.2	...	10.9	40.0	38.9	...	6.5	...	35.3
Tobacco (314)	33.5	37.6	...	6.7	40.0	66.7	...	32.1	...	80.8
Textiles (321)	44.8	43.7	...	2.1	59.2	65.3	...	7.3	...	53.5
Wearing apparel (322)	70.2	67.9	...	...	71.0	79.7	...	51.2	...	76.1
Leather and fur products (323)	15.9	17.0	...	...	90.0	55.6	...	15.3	...	47.2
Footwear (324)	38.9	41.5	...	...	67.9	68.2	...	36.2	...	76.0
Wood and cork products (331)	11.8	13.4	...	3.4	33.3	27.8	...	9.7	...	35.9
Furniture, fixtures excl. metallic (332)	12.8	12.4	...	3.6	30.8	30.0	...	1.6	...	30.1
Paper (341)	25.9	33.9	...	8.5	38.5	45.5	...	3.8	...	20.6
Printing and publishing (342)	37.7	36.3	...	29.3	47.6	50.0	...	3.6	...	30.9
Industrial chemicals (351)	23.6	12.4	...	6.8	37.8	39.1	...	0.8	...	18.1
Other chemicals (352)	33.0	34.2	...	15.5	50.0	46.2	...	19.2	...	49.5
Petroleum refineries (353)	...	...	...	...	33.3	25.0	...	0.4	...	14.4
Prods. of petroleum and coal (354)	...	...	...	...	...	...	...	5.9	...	20.2
Rubber products (355)	9.4	8.5	...	35.2	37.5	40.0	...	3.7	...	24.2
Plastic products (356)	31.8	37.1	...	5.2	44.4	40.0	...	5.4	...	49.1
Pottery, china, earthenware (361)	...	...	...	...	50.0	50.0	...	8.7	...	32.3
Glass (362)	15.4	18.4	...	...	40.0	40.0	...	2.6	...	16.6
Other non-metallic mineral prods.(369)	10.3	10.4	...	...	28.6	26.3	...	7.5	...	23.9
Iron and steel (371)	6.9	9.0	...	28.2	27.3	28.1	...	1.0	...	5.1
Non-ferrous metals (372)	...	...	...	4.2	30.0	25.0	...	0.8	...	9.3
Metal products (381)	15.3	15.9	...	3.5	34.0	23.8	...	2.0	...	21.1
Non-electrical machinery (382)	22.6	14.1	...	5.1	22.8	18.6	...	1.4	...	11.3
Electrical machinery (383)	18.6	18.0	...	4.5	45.0	45.8	...	7.7	...	54.0
Transport equipment (384)	17.8	14.2	...	...	25.4	27.3	...	1.0	...	12.3
Prof., scient. equipment (385)	...	...	...	...	40.9	43.8	...	13.0	...	62.4
Other manufactures (390)	...	...	...	...	52.8	50.0	...	15.6	...	67.4
Total manufacturing (3)	32.4	30.9	...	8.4	41.3	42.2	...	10.9	...	46.8

TABLE 1.10

SHARE OF FEMALES IN TOTAL EMPLOYMENT BY BRANCH, SELECTED YEARS

(Percentage)

Branch (ISIC)	Italy		Jordan		Kenya		Macau		Malaysia	
	1991	1994	1990	1995	1990	1993	1990	1996	1990	1995
Food products (311/2)	29.0	25.5	9.3	6.6	18.6	19.6	26.0	44.5	34.7	34.7
Beverages (313)	19.2	20.3	11.2	6.7	5.7	5.7	22.4	24.4	33.3	32.7
Tobacco (314)	10.1	6.5	4.4	3.1	13.9	13.7	48.7	...	46.5	67.1
Textiles (321)	57.2	49.6	32.1	32.9	8.6	8.4	60.6	69.7	58.2	45.3
Wearing apparel (322)	78.7	78.6	29.2	41.6	24.4	20.1	74.5	79.6	85.3	83.4
Leather and fur products (323)	45.2	45.1	15.0	18.2	18.8	20.1	48.2	61.5	61.1	58.6
Footwear (324)	53.3	50.0	12.4	9.1	1.4	1.0	52.7	72.7	50.0	48.0
Wood and cork products (331)	22.1	21.1	-	1.4	8.6	8.6	12.6	4.8	26.0	32.2
Furniture, fixtures excl. metallic (332)	23.9	24.9	0.4	1.4	2.7	3.2	5.9	8.7	29.7	23.5
Paper (341)	20.2	19.4	13.8	16.4	4.3	4.9	10.5	16.4	33.3	31.9
Printing and publishing (342)	28.0	24.7	4.5	6.8	14.0	14.3	23.0	27.8	41.2	40.9
Industrial chemicals (351)	10.8	9.7	6.0	3.7	16.5	13.5	...	...	16.3	15.7
Other chemicals (352)	27.6	26.6	27.6	22.6	17.3	18.3	50.5	46.0	41.5	36.4
Petroleum refineries (353)	7.6	...	1.9	1.8	7.2	7.2	...	...	9.1	11.1
Prods. of petroleum and coal (354)	9.8	...	...	...	...	...	...	...	20.0	21.4
Rubber products (355)	18.2	15.6	5.9	1.2	4.5	5.7	12.5	...	50.3	44.1
Plastic products (356)	28.8	27.5	3.2	6.6	8.5	8.9	14.0	35.5	53.4	46.3
Pottery, china, earthenware (361)	30.6	24.4	8.0	6.5	3.8	5.4	29.5	...	59.2	46.1
Glass (362)	13.3	15.0	1.3	0.5	0.3	0.5	3.4	16.7	13.9	12.1
Other non-metallic mineral prods.(369)	7.1	15.7	0.8	0.7	2.7	3.1	13.5	16.6	19.6	17.6
Iron and steel (371)	6.8	5.4	1.4	1.2	...	...	...	...	11.7	10.5
Non-ferrous metals (372)	10.4	11.2	3.0	2.4	...	...	...	...	16.7	17.4
Metal products (381)	17.3	17.0	2.3	1.6	5.6	5.8	4.0	10.8	30.5	23.4
Non-electrical machinery (382)	14.2	14.8	4.3	5.8	2.2	1.9	5.8	12.5	25.2	29.7
Electrical machinery (383)	30.0	24.7	12.0	16.4	7.0	6.8	66.8	74.0	75.4	66.5
Transport equipment (384)	12.4	7.7	4.1	4.3	2.4	2.0	2.1	3.6	20.7	20.2
Prof., scient. equipment (385)	38.0	31.6	34.6	22.7	13.8	15.6	57.1	...	72.6	72.2
Other manufactures (390)	54.1	42.2	13.9	24.1	26.4	24.8	64.5	72.1	62.8	52.1
Total manufacturing (3)	27.3	25.5	8.9	9.6	11.3	11.6	63.9	71.3	50.7	46.3

TABLE 1.10

SHARE OF FEMALES IN TOTAL EMPLOYMENT BY BRANCH, SELECTED YEARS

(Percentage)

Branch (ISIC)	Malta		Mongolia		Morocco		Mozambique		Nepal	
	1990	1994	1990	1994	1992	1996	1990	1996	1990	1994
Food products (311/2)	18.0	17.9	...	56.2	11.6	14.6	...	35.9	12.6	11.1
Beverages (313)	11.5	11.3	...	56.0	3.2	4.2	...	7.2	12.1	9.6
Tobacco (314)	66.4	29.2	...	...	3.3	8.4	...	7.8	5.8	7.6
Textiles (321)	63.1	51.5	...	70.5	36.0	39.7	...	13.7	47.9	38.8
Wearing apparel (322)	81.8	80.3	...	76.5	75.5	76.9	...	46.6	15.4	17.1
Leather and fur products (323)	67.8	70.6	...	68.0	21.5	23.8	...	...	2.8	8.3
Footwear (324)	58.3	61.1	...	69.0	33.3	40.5	...	...	17.5	14.9
Wood and cork products (331)	0.6	2.5	...	20.1	7.9	5.1	...	2.4	5.4	3.7
Furniture, fixtures excl. metallic (332)	5.8	6.7	...	33.4	12.9	12.5	...	0.5	1.2	2.1
Paper (341)	17.8	13.8	...	21.1	13.5	13.4	...	20.4	5.3	12.8
Printing and publishing (342)	26.9	26.8	...	53.0	15.5	16.2	...	21.4	8.2	9.8
Industrial chemicals (351)	25.8	28.3	...	50.0	4.7	6.8	...	6.3	...	...
Other chemicals (352)	...	...	...	62.4	25.3	17.7	...	9.5	17.0	12.5
Petroleum refineries (353)	...	...	...	...	...	...	...	7.0	...	...
Prods. of petroleum and coal (354)	...	...	...	27.7	...	...	...	...	...	...
Rubber products (355)	32.8	36.4	...	...	4.3	3.3	...	10.2	5.0	2.9
Plastic products (356)	22.2	26.3	...	...	25.2	20.5	...	18.8	10.9	3.9
Pottery, china, earthenware (361)	12.1	18.8	...	56.1	24.2	28.2	...	...	...	...
Glass (362)	14.0	13.0	...	41.7	5.4	6.3	...	...	...	5.4
Other non-metallic mineral prods.(369)	3.9	2.5	...	45.5	2.4	2.8	...	4.6	17.5	15.0
Iron and steel (371)	...	...	..	20.4	3.1	4.2	...	12.3	0.7	0.6
Non-ferrous metals (372)	...	...	...	20.3	5.4	3.6	...	...	...	...
Metal products (381)	...	...	...	28.3	6.0	7.0	...	9.6	1.7	2.3
Non-electrical machinery (382)	2.8	5.7	...	15.5	6.8	6.2	...	6.3	...	...
Electrical machinery (383)	36.2	47.1	...	23.5	45.9	38.6	...	14.8	2.7	4.4
Transport equipment (384)	2.1	2.0	...	21.1	13.8	20.5	...	6.0	...	...
Prof., scient. equipment (385)	70.7	69.1	...	37.2	28.1	26.8	...	...	...	...
Other manufactures (390)	38.6	38.5	..	47.1	25.1	18.4	...	...	6.6	27.0
Total manufacturing (3)	38.4	36.3	...	53.7	30.0	32.5	...	19.6	23.1	21.5

TABLE 1.10

SHARE OF FEMALES IN TOTAL EMPLOYMENT BY BRANCH, SELECTED YEARS

(Percentage)

Branch (ISIC)	New Zealand		Nigeria		Philippines		Puerto Rico		Republic of Korea	
	1990	1993	1990	1992	1990	1995	1990	1995	1990	1995
Food products (311/2)	27.1	29.6	...	19.3	...	33.4	...	...	48.8	49.6
Beverages (313)	29.4	...	...	10.3	...	9.1	...	...	25.4	27.9
Tobacco (314)	42.1	...	...	21.8	...	45.0	38.3	43.5	30.6	21.2
Textiles (321)	44.2	45.1	...	26.1	...	52.4	54.4	53.6	57.4	51.4
Wearing apparel (322)	81.4	81.3	...	35.8	...	79.6	88.9	85.6	72.7	70.0
Leather and fur products (323)	33.6	30.9	...	12.4	...	66.6	...	...	37.3	42.0
Footwear (324)	58.8	59.0	...	11.5	...	57.6	...	...	49.3	53.0
Wood and cork products (331)	12.5	11.3	...	8.9	...	16.6	...	...	26.1	24.1
Furniture, fixtures excl. metallic (332)	22.5	21.8	...	7.7	...	28.6	28.9	22.2	28.0	27.2
Paper (341)	16.9	18.9	...	21.5	...	23.0	25.3	20.6	23.6	22.3
Printing and publishing (342)	40.3	39.1	...	17.5	...	31.4	47.6	47.1	28.9	30.4
Industrial chemicals (351)	20.9	21.0	...	8.5	...	19.8	...	...	15.7	17.9
Other chemicals (352)	40.8	38.9	...	29.7	...	33.4	...	...	37.0	34.3
Petroleum refineries (353)	10.5	...	...	12.8	...	12.8	...	...	4.2	3.0
Prods. of petroleum and coal (354)	22.3	...	...	12.6	...	22.7	...	...	11.8	13.3
Rubber products (355)	18.4	18.3	...	27.0	...	40.9	...	...	58.7	20.8
Plastic products (356)	26.7	25.6	...	12.0	...	27.3	...	...	28.2	25.0
Pottery, china, earthenware (361)	43.5	52.2	...	...	...	43.7	...	11.9	50.0	52.7
Glass (362)	15.8	14.9	...	2.4	...	9.0	...	...	22.4	21.1
Other non-metallic mineral prods.(369)	11.0	12.4	...	5.3	...	14.1	...	...	18.7	16.2
Iron and steel (371)	11.1	10.6	...	2.1	...	7.5	...	...	7.5	8.4
Non-ferrous metals (372)	13.7	11.9	...	1.2	...	18.2	...	...	12.3	13.2
Metal products (381)	17.6	16.6	...	7.5	...	18.5	17.7	21.6	19.8	20.6
Non-electrical machinery (382)	12.8	12.4	...	7.1	...	48.3	38.7	28.2	16.0	18.3
Electrical machinery (383)	33.5	34.3	...	13.2	...	70.1	61.0	53.4	49.1	45.5
Transport equipment (384)	17.7	16.5	...	0.5	...	12.3	52.6	43.3	12.7	12.2
Prof., scient. equipment (385)	47.8	45.2	...	...	...	80.3	67.0	61.1	40.7	38.4
Other manufactures (390)	39.2	35.7	...	3.3	...	65.3	58.5	50.8	49.0	43.9
Total manufacturing (3)	28.9	28.8	...	15.6	...	45.5	55.3	53.4	38.7	33.1

TABLE 1.10

SHARE OF FEMALES IN TOTAL EMPLOYMENT BY BRANCH, SELECTED YEARS

(Percentage)

Branch (ISIC)	Republic of Moldova		Sri Lanka		Thailand		United Kingdom		Zambia	
	1990	1995	1990	1993	1990	1994	1990	1995	1990	1994
Food products (311/2)	...	56.8	33.3	34.6	30.9	51.8	40.9	38.5	...	8.0
Beverages (313)	...	48.0	23.6	17.2	4.8	21.6	24.9	38.2	...	5.8
Tobacco (314)	...	73.3	55.2	57.4	49.9	57.6	38.2	25.0	...	5.2
Textiles (321)	...	75.3	62.1	58.0	66.6	67.1	47.9	46.4	...	10.9
Wearing apparel (322)	...	85.1	90.2	89.0	84.1	92.1	78.7	76.1	...	13.6
Leather and fur products (323)	...	70.1	47.7	63.1	55.1	63.4	41.9	46.7	...	42.6
Footwear (324)	...	67.5	47.6	54.0	76.2	67.7	55.2	44.7	...	12.6
Wood and cork products (331)	...	29.2	15.4	23.2	37.1	39.2	14.5	17.6	...	2.9
Furniture, fixtures excl. metallic (332)	...	46.0	5.1	11.5	46.0	43.1	21.8	10.4	...	2.8
Paper (341)	...	42.9	13.2	11.2	35.6	37.4	28.7	29.5	...	4.1
Printing and publishing (342)	...	66.6	13.2	11.2	43.6	42.1	35.4	40.8	...	17.1
Industrial chemicals (351)	...	37.0	8.1	15.0	13.9	24.3	17.4	29.1	...	7.0
Other chemicals (352)	...	66.1	30.3	28.0	55.9	54.3	38.9	30.9	...	11.6
Petroleum refineries (353)	...	...	...	...	...	19.0	14.9	23.1	...	...
Prods. of petroleum and coal (354)	...	...	...	...	...	17.2	5.0	...	...	...
Rubber products (355)	...	...	33.0	25.0	40.6	49.5	24.0	24.0	...	5.9
Plastic products (356)	...	64.8	60.7	43.4	33.4	51.1	32.1	24.3	...	5.0
Pottery, china, earthenware (361)	...	...	54.3	59.8	54.2	61.1	15.7	20.6	...	...
Glass (362)	...	45.6	5.8	7.9	35.7	37.4	8.9	20.9	...	...
Other non-metallic mineral prods.(369)	...	28.2	23.7	20.6	16.8	22.0	15.5	20.7	...	3.6
Iron and steel (371)	...	28.1	6.8	5.1	18.0	18.7	6.8	10.7	...	1.4
Non-ferrous metals (372)	...	...	4.7	16.2	8.2	14.9	9.8	12.0	...	3.0
Metal products (381)	...	27.9	17.7	8.4	33.5	42.5	18.1	18.2	...	3.5
Non-electrical machinery (382)	...	...	3.9	29.5	16.0	24.5	16.9	22.3	...	...
Electrical machinery (383)	...	...	38.0	24.3	40.6	56.4	29.9	33.2	...	...
Transport equipment (384)	...	...	9.4	10.4	19.6	21.7	11.2	13.3	...	4.8
Prof., scient. equipment (385)	...	...	39.8	24.6	...	67.9	31.9	34.3	...	9.1
Other manufactures (390)	...	...	68.0	75.9	69.3	68.2	44.6	29.2	...	17.8
Total manufacturing (3)	...	58.4	55.5	59.2	50.0	62.2	28.2	29.5	...	7.6

TABLE 1.11

SELECTED CHARACTERISTICS OF BRANCHES, SELECTED YEARS AND COUNTRIES

Food products (311/2)

Country or area	Latest year	Value added per employee		Wages per employee		Percentage in output a/								
		Real annual growth rate (percentage)	Value (current 1000 dollars)	Real annual growth rate (percentage)	Value (current 1000 dollars)	Costs of input materials and utilities			Costs of labour			Operating surplus		
	(LY)	1985-LY	LY	1985-LY	LY	1985	1990	LY	1985	1990	LY	1985	1990	LY
Industrialized countries b/														
Austria	1994	...	52.3	1.5	27.9	78.8	77.5	76.2	11.0	11.8	12.7	10.1	10.7	11.1
Canada	1994	...	65.2	-0.0	23.0	72.0	67.8	67.2	11.3	12.3	11.6	16.7	20.0	21.3
Finland	1995	...	60.3	2.6	28.5	76.9	78.0	75.6	9.2	10.6	11.5	13.9	11.4	12.9
France	1995	...	70.7	...	...	74.6	73.3	71.7	14.7	15.3	...	10.7	11.4	...
Germany	1994	...	...	...	27.3	...	...	...	...	...	11.2	...	...	...
Iceland	1995	...	41.9	2.4	28.2	78.9	79.5	72.8	18.6	18.4	18.3	2.5	2.2	8.9
Israel	1994	...	25.8	...	17.6	75.4	71.1	75.5	12.2	15.7	16.6	12.4	13.2	7.8
Italy	1994	...	56.7	...	...	83.8	80.7	80.2	7.1	11.9	12.0	9.1	7.4	7.8
Japan	1995	-0.5	94.5	0.6	32.0	67.4	63.0	59.5	10.8	11.9	13.7	21.7	25.1	26.8
Norway	1994	...	34.5	1.9	26.6	88.2	87.3	85.1	10.9	10.9	11.5	0.9	1.8	3.4
South Africa	1994	1.9	...	2.7	7.9	77.0	76.4	...	10.4	12.5	...	12.6	11.1	...
Spain	1995	...	38.7	2.3	17.5	77.1	75.8	79.6	7.2	8.3	9.2	15.7	16.0	11.2
Sweden	1994	...	46.6	2.0	22.8	71.9	69.0	76.9	8.7	10.1	11.3	19.3	20.9	11.8
United Kingdom	1995	2.0	43.5	1.3	20.3	69.8	65.2	74.9	11.2	12.8	11.7	19.0	22.0	13.4
United States of America	1995	...	110.6	-0.7	25.2	66.5	64.5	60.6	9.0	8.7	9.0	24.4	26.9	30.5
Countries of eastern Europe and the former USSR														
Albania	1996	...	...	...	...	...	...	...	...	...	6.3	...	...	...
Azerbaijan	1994	...	...	...	...	...	...	...	...	4.7	3.1	...	...	...
Bulgaria	1996	...	...	...	1.0	...	...	...	2.8	4.2	5.0	...	...	...
Latvia	1996	...	8.2	...	...	...	...	65.9	...	...	...	...	...	...
Lithuania	1994	...	...	...	1.3	...	...	...	...	...	10.3	...	...	...
Republic of Moldova	1995	...	...	...	0.7	...	...	...	...	5.1	8.5	...	...	...
Russian Federation	1995	...	6.0	...	1.5	...	...	68.1	...	...	7.8	...	...	...
Slovakia	1994	...	7.1	...	2.3	...	...	78.2	...	...	7.0	...	...	24.1
Ukraine	1996	...	...	...	1.0	...	...	...	...	5.8	8.1	...	...	14.8
Developing countries														
Bolivia	1995	...	21.9	...	2.9	...	75.2	72.0	...	3.3	3.7	...	21.4	24.2
Brazil	1994	5.1	38.2	...	5.4	66.7	59.3	55.4	4.8	7.1	6.3	28.6	33.6	38.3
Cameroon	1996	...	6.8	...	2.4	...	38.5	62.1	...	20.0	13.3	...	41.4	24.6
Chile	1995	...	36.8	3.4	7.3	61.7	62.1	59.6	5.9	7.4	8.1	32.4	30.4	32.4
China	1996	...	...	...	...	83.9	84.5	78.3	3.5	...	...	12.5	...	...
China (Hong Kong SAR)	1995	...	35.7	2.9	14.9	74.4	67.8	62.9	13.2	15.3	15.4	12.4	16.9	21.7
China (Taiwan Province)	1996	...	35.7	5.9	14.3	79.5	79.1	79.1	5.6	7.6	8.3	14.8	13.3	12.5
Colombia	1995	-2.0	29.2	0.8	4.2	71.4	73.2	65.0	4.4	3.7	5.0	24.2	23.0	30.0
Costa Rica	1996	...	...	...	...	76.1	76.6	76.6	...	...	...	...	...	...
Croatia	1996	...	...	...	5.0	...	62.4	...	...	10.7	...	...	26.9	...
Cyprus	1996	...	24.7	3.5	13.0	74.3	70.1	67.2	11.1	14.8	17.3	14.7	15.1	15.5
Ecuador	1996	...	12.1	...	2.7	77.6	81.5	81.4	8.7	7.6	4.2	13.7	10.9	14.4

a/ At current prices.

b/ Excluding countries of eastern Europe and the former USSR.

TABLE 1.11
(continued)

SELECTED CHARACTERISTICS OF BRANCHES, SELECTED YEARS AND COUNTRIES

Food products (311/2)

Country or area	Latest year	Value added per employee		Wages per employee		Percentage in output a/								
		Real annual growth rate (percentage)	Value (current 1000 dollars)	Real annual growth rate (percentage)	Value (current 1000 dollars)	Costs of input materials and utilities			Costs of labour			Operating surplus		
	(LY)	1985-LY	LY	1985-LY	LY	1985	1990	LY	1985	1990	LY	1985	1990	LY
Egypt	1994	...	4.5	...	1.4	77.1	79.7	79.8	13.0	6.7	6.3	9.9	13.6	13.9
El Salvador	1996	...	12.9	...	3.1	65.1	...	69.8	7.9	...	7.2	27.0	...	23.1
Ethiopia	1996	...	6.9	...	0.9	...	57.7	47.7	...	7.4	6.6	...	34.9	45.6
Gabon	1995	...	9.6	...	7.0	...	...	68.5	...	...	23.0	...	...	8.5
Honduras	1995	...	5.0	...	1.9	76.7	78.9	79.4	9.2	8.4	7.8	14.1	12.7	12.8
India	1994	...	2.4	3.1	0.7	88.2	89.4	86.6	4.9	4.3	4.0	6.9	6.2	9.4
Indonesia	1996	...	6.0	2.7	1.2	74.3	66.1	75.4	7.2	4.0	5.0	18.5	29.9	19.6
Jamaica	1996	...	10.0	...	...	...	75.6	...	10.8	11.4	...	...	13.0	...
Jordan	1995	...	7.9	...	2.3	77.5	73.5	81.3	8.8	7.2	5.3	13.7	19.3	13.3
Kenya	1995	-0.0	5.4	...	1.1	88.4	92.0	91.5	4.2	1.8	1.8	7.4	6.1	6.7
Kuwait	1995	...	17.9	...	7.3	62.0	60.1	59.6	19.7	18.7	16.5	18.4	21.1	24.0
Macau	1996	...	11.5	...	7.0	78.7	66.2	53.1	13.2	22.1	28.3	8.0	11.8	18.6
Malawi	1994	...	4.5	0.2	1.1	87.4	...	65.1	10.0	...	8.8	2.7	...	26.2
Malaysia	1995	...	21.7	2.3	4.7	85.4	85.4	85.4	3.6	3.6	3.2	11.1	11.0	11.5
Malta	1994	...	23.6	2.5	9.9	72.5	69.5	71.1	10.6	10.7	12.1	16.9	19.8	16.8
Mauritius	1994	...	7.1	3.1	3.9	86.0	84.5	83.9	5.6	6.6	8.8	8.5	8.9	7.3
Mexico	1994	...	34.8	1.8	7.1	73.0	70.0	69.9	5.3	5.4	6.1	21.7	24.6	23.9
Mongolia	1995	...	1.8	...	0.6	...	75.4	79.8	...	5.3	6.5	...	19.3	13.7
Morocco	1996	...	10.0	...	3.8	84.8	90.1	79.9	7.1	6.9	7.8	8.1	3.0	12.4
Namibia	1994	...	19.2	...	6.0	...	...	62.4	...	...	11.9	...	...	25.7
Nepal	1996	...	2.6	...	0.4	...	73.3	74.5	...	4.7	4.3	...	21.9	21.3
Peru	1994	0.2	17.3	...	3.9	74.8	58.0	72.2	4.7	5.5	6.3	20.4	36.5	21.5
Philippines	1995	...	18.1	3.3	2.9	75.1	63.3	64.3	5.8	6.5	5.7	19.2	30.2	30.0
Qatar	1994	...	13.6	...	5.6	...	67.5	63.7	...	16.4	15.0	...	16.1	21.2
Republic of Korea	1995	...	63.0	8.4	13.6	72.2	64.6	60.7	6.4	8.1	8.5	21.4	27.3	30.9
Senegal	1996	...	6.3	...	2.8	...	72.9	78.4	...	10.1	9.6	...	17.0	11.9
Singapore	1996	...	57.9	3.6	20.7	82.9	71.5	67.1	6.8	10.1	11.8	10.4	18.4	21.1
Slovenia	1995	...	...	...	...	...	...	63.5	...	...	...	...	...	...
St. Vincent and the Grenadines	1994	...	...	...	6.7	...	...	...	...	...	...	...	...	...
The f.Yugosl.Rep.of Macedonia	1996	...	7.5	...	5.5	...	55.1	69.6	...	18.6	22.2	...	26.3	8.2
Thailand	1994	...	12.4	...	2.6	...	77.6	73.0	...	3.4	5.8	...	19.0	21.3
Trinidad and Tobago	1995	...	6.3	...	3.3	71.9	77.0	80.2	17.4	11.9	10.3	10.7	11.1	9.4
Tunisia	1996	...	...	...	...	...	83.4	82.5	...	6.5	7.4	...	10.1	10.1
Turkey	1994	3.0	23.9	...	4.9	76.8	71.4	69.7	5.9	8.2	6.3	17.3	20.4	24.1
Uruguay	1995	...	24.6	...	6.2	71.6	69.5	64.0	8.2	8.8	9.0	20.2	21.7	27.0
Venezuela	1996	...	20.2	...	2.6	71.9	69.3	66.9	10.1	7.3	4.3	18.0	23.4	28.8
Yugoslavia	1996	...	9.4	...	1.9	...	63.2	70.7	...	...	6.0	...	...	23.3
Zambia	1994	...	4.7	...	2.1	...	48.8	69.9	...	9.0	13.6	...	42.2	16.5
Zimbabwe	1995	...	10.4	...	3.2	80.2	72.6	72.6	12.9	11.1	8.4	6.9	16.3	19.0

TABLE 1.11 SELECTED CHARACTERISTICS OF BRANCHES, SELECTED YEARS AND COUNTRIES

Country or area	Latest year	Value added per employee		Wages per employee		Percentage in output a/								
Textiles (321)		Real annual growth rate (percentage)	Value (current 1000 dollars)	Real annual growth rate (percentage)	Value (current 1000 dollars)	Costs of input materials and utilities			Costs of labour			Operating surplus		
	(LY)	1985-LY	LY	1985-LY	LY	1985	1990	LY	1985	1990	LY	1985	1990	LY
Industrialized countries b/														
Austria	1994	3.9	44.0	2.8	25.2	64.7	64.1	62.2	20.4	20.8	21.6	14.9	15.1	16.2
Belgium	1994	...	...	...	...	73.1	70.6	71.0	13.0	12.0	12.7	13.8	17.4	16.3
Canada	1994	1.5	46.4	0.4	21.4	58.2	58.6	57.5	21.6	21.5	19.6	20.2	19.9	22.9
Finland	1995	7.7	51.3	2.5	25.0	53.7	57.7	58.2	23.3	25.7	20.3	23.1	16.6	21.5
France	1995	2.8	47.1	...	...	64.7	63.9	66.7	24.7	23.5	...	10.5	12.6	...
Germany	1994	...	...	...	27.1	...	...	...	...	...	21.6	...	...	...
Iceland	1995	...	40.2	1.4	24.5	68.1	65.2	65.8	26.6	30.8	20.8	5.3	4.1	13.4
Israel	1994	...	25.5	...	16.8	70.3	68.7	70.7	19.2	17.9	19.2	10.6	13.4	10.1
Italy	1994	...	45.7	...	...	67.2	68.5	69.1	13.2	19.8	18.1	19.6	11.7	12.8
Japan	1995	-1.9	68.4	1.2	32.7	60.7	57.7	54.6	17.2	18.5	21.7	22.2	23.8	23.7
Norway	1994	3.6	34.3	1.2	22.2	63.8	62.3	61.7	25.1	26.3	24.7	11.1	11.4	13.5
South Africa	1994	2.5	...	1.7	6.5	71.4	65.3	...	18.9	20.8	...	9.8	13.8	...
Spain	1995	2.4	32.0	1.7	16.3	61.4	60.6	68.4	16.9	18.6	16.1	21.7	20.8	15.6
Sweden	1994	4.3	41.3	1.8	21.0	53.0	50.4	60.1	20.1	21.2	20.3	26.8	28.4	19.6
Switzerland	1996	...	61.9	...	...	...	58.7	58.5	...	...	...	...	...	...
United Kingdom	1995	-0.6	31.6	2.0	18.1	59.6	55.2	62.8	20.6	23.1	21.3	19.8	21.8	15.8
United States of America	1995	2.4	52.2	0.0	21.6	60.0	58.6	57.7	19.0	17.9	17.6	21.0	23.5	24.8
Countries of eastern Europe and the former USSR														
Azerbaijan	1994	...	...	...	...	...	...	...	...	7.9	7.4	...	...	...
Bulgaria	1996	...	1.6	...	0.8	...	...	75.3	11.6	12.7	12.4	...	...	12.3
Latvia	1996	...	4.9	...	...	...	...	59.6	...	...	...	...	...	...
Lithuania	1994	...	...	...	1.0	...	...	...	...	...	20.8	...	...	...
Republic of Moldova	1995	...	...	...	0.3	...	...	...	...	10.7	12.2	...	...	...
Romania	1994	...	...	...	0.7	...	58.5	...	...	18.8	...	...	...	...
Russian Federation	1995	...	2.0	...	0.7	...	...	60.1	...	...	14.2	...	22.7	25.7
Slovakia	1994	...	3.5	...	1.7	...	...	65.8	...	...	16.4	...	...	17.8
Ukraine	1996	...	...	...	0.5	...	...	...	...	8.1	15.8	...	...	...
Developing countries														
Bolivia	1995	...	7.0	...	1.7	...	66.4	63.8	...	7.8	8.9	...	25.8	27.3
Brazil	1994	3.4	27.4	...	5.3	56.5	45.3	43.1	8.7	9.5	11.0	34.8	45.3	45.9
Cameroon	1996	...	18.2	...	5.3	...	...	73.2	...	14.5	7.9	...	...	18.9
Chile	1995	...	20.0	5.1	6.9	49.5	51.5	54.0	12.1	13.2	15.9	38.4	35.3	30.1
China	1996	...	...	...	...	75.3	78.5	78.0	4.2	...	...	20.5	...	...
China (Hong Kong SAR)	1995	11.8	26.7	2.5	15.3	74.1	72.6	75.3	15.8	16.3	14.1	10.2	11.1	10.5
China (Taiwan Province)	1996	5.0	23.9	4.9	12.6	73.8	67.4	64.7	15.1	18.6	18.7	11.0	14.0	16.6
Colombia	1995	1.2	16.7	0.9	3.8	52.8	49.8	51.8	9.4	6.9	11.1	37.8	43.2	37.2
Costa Rica	1996	...	...	...	...	64.6	65.5	67.7	...	...	...	...	...	...
Croatia	1996	...	...	...	3.1	...	49.5	...	...	18.4	...	...	32.1	...

a/ At current prices.

b/ Excluding countries of eastern Europe and the former USSR.

TABLE 1.11
(continued)

SELECTED CHARACTERISTICS OF BRANCHES, SELECTED YEARS AND COUNTRIES

Textiles (321)

Country or area	Latest year	Value added per employee		Wages per employee		Percentage in output a/								
		Real annual growth rate (percentage)	Value (current 1000 dollars)	Real annual growth rate (percentage)	Value (current 1000 dollars)	Costs of input materials and utilities			Costs of labour			Operating surplus		
	(LY)	1985-LY	LY	1985-LY	LY	1985	1990	LY	1985	1990	LY	1985	1990	LY
Cyprus	1996	...	17.5	2.6	9.7	57.4	59.2	58.8	22.9	20.3	22.8	19.8	20.5	18.4
Ecuador	1996	...	9.0	...	1.7	57.9	62.1	66.6	17.4	13.7	6.2	24.7	24.2	27.2
Egypt	1994	...	2.1	...	1.3	67.5	72.1	75.4	24.5	15.1	15.3	8.0	12.8	9.3
El Salvador	1996	...	6.2	...	2.6	46.8	...	64.6	17.5	...	15.1	35.7	...	20.3
Ethiopia	1996	...	1.5	...	0.6	...	60.3	61.8	...	24.9	15.0	...	14.8	23.2
Honduras	1995	...	1.3	...	0.8	72.4	66.6	68.7	18.5	19.2	18.8	9.2	14.2	12.5
India	1994	...	2.4	0.9	1.0	81.1	79.7	81.2	13.0	10.4	7.8	5.9	9.8	11.0
Indonesia	1996	4.5	6.5	5.3	1.2	68.0	69.5	66.1	8.7	5.0	6.5	23.3	25.6	27.4
Jordan	1995	...	9.0	...	2.3	62.2	57.4	62.6	10.5	7.2	9.7	27.3	35.5	27.7
Kenya	1995	-3.6	1.5	...	1.0	77.4	71.6	75.7	12.5	15.1	17.2	10.1	13.3	7.1
Kuwait	1995	...	15.9	...	6.4	60.3	50.9	45.6	17.5	14.8	21.9	22.2	34.2	32.5
Macau	1996	...	11.2	...	6.3	74.2	71.9	77.6	12.5	13.5	12.6	13.3	14.6	9.8
Malawi	1994	...	3.9	0.5	0.9	61.8	87.0	41.7	12.0	11.1	13.5	26.2	1.8	44.8
Malaysia	1995	8.2	15.2	3.8	4.6	71.9	71.8	69.3	13.7	9.5	9.3	14.4	18.7	21.4
Malta	1994	13.6	20.0	4.3	9.0	43.3	54.1	62.9	30.6	20.3	16.8	26.2	25.6	20.3
Mauritius	1994	...	7.3	3.4	2.9	75.4	62.8	70.4	7.8	13.9	11.6	16.8	23.3	18.1
Mexico	1994	...	14.7	...	5.8	55.7	53.0	55.6	14.7	15.4	17.4	29.6	31.6	27.0
Mongolia	1995	...	11.1	...	0.8	...	55.6	25.8	...	6.1	5.5	...	38.2	68.7
Morocco	1996	...	6.7	...	3.8	74.1	72.6	66.9	14.8	14.1	19.0	11.1	13.3	14.1
Nepal	1996	...	1.4	...	0.4	...	60.0	54.6	...	15.7	12.9	...	24.3	32.4
Peru	1994	2.1	10.7	...	3.6	60.2	51.6	74.7	6.8	9.9	8.6	33.0	38.4	16.8
Philippines	1995	...	8.7	4.4	2.5	80.3	65.5	61.7	10.6	12.6	11.0	9.1	21.9	27.3
Qatar	1994	...	10.8	...	3.7	...	...	40.0	...	...	20.6	...	...	39.4
Republic of Korea	1995	4.3	42.3	9.6	14.2	62.2	61.4	55.4	12.1	15.4	15.0	25.6	23.2	29.6
Senegal	1996	...	5.2	...	1.2	...	...	74.4	...	...	5.7	...	...	19.8
Singapore	1996	...	32.3	4.5	17.8	67.7	67.1	66.5	17.9	14.0	18.4	14.4	18.9	15.1
Slovenia	1995	...	...	...	...	...	...	68.9	...	...	...	...	...	...
Thailand	1994	...	8.1	...	2.9	...	71.4	64.2	...	3.1	12.9	...	25.4	22.9
Tonga	1994	...	...	...	1.2	...	...	...	...	...	8.7	...	...	...
Trinidad and Tobago	1995	...	10.6	...	4.4	...	55.9	67.1	...	15.0	13.5	...	29.1	19.4
Tunisia	1996	...	...	...	...	...	71.5	67.1	...	14.4	13.1	...	14.0	19.8
Turkey	1994	2.7	20.9	...	3.6	64.2	59.2	61.6	10.3	11.3	6.6	25.6	29.6	31.8
Uruguay	1995	...	27.8	...	7.0	54.4	58.9	55.4	12.5	12.0	11.3	33.1	29.2	33.3
Venezuela	1996	...	13.5	...	2.4	55.2	59.1	57.5	17.8	13.9	7.5	27.0	27.1	35.0
Yugoslavia	1996	...	2.6	...	0.7	...	50.2	53.2	...	...	13.0	...	...	33.7
Zambia	1994	...	4.0	...	1.8	...	46.1	65.2	...	11.6	16.1	...	42.3	18.7
Zimbabwe	1995	...	8.6	...	2.0	66.8	51.7	52.7	14.0	14.2	11.1	19.2	34.0	36.2

current prices.

TABLE 1.11

SELECTED CHARACTERISTICS OF BRANCHES, SELECTED YEARS AND COUNTRIES

Country or area	Latest year	Wearing apparel (322)												
		Value added per employee		Wages per employee		Percentage in output a/								
		Real annual growth rate (percentage)	Value (current 1000 dollars)	Real annual growth rate (percentage)	Value (current 1000 dollars)	Costs of input materials and utilities			Costs of labour			Operating surplus		
	(LY)	1985-LY	LY	1985-LY	LY	1985	1990	LY	1985	1990	LY	1985	1990	LY
Industrialized countries b/														
Austria	1994	3.6	29.5	3.1	19.0	60.1	60.6	62.8	25.3	24.9	24.0	14.6	14.5	13.3
Belgium	1994	...	...	...	...	63.2	66.1	65.8	21.9	16.0	9.4	14.8	17.9	24.8
Canada	1994	5.1	29.6	0.7	15.6	51.4	52.6	53.7	27.3	25.8	24.4	21.3	21.6	21.9
Finland	1995	1.5	37.2	2.4	21.2	46.8	52.3	53.7	30.0	31.1	26.4	23.2	16.5	19.9
France	1995	-1.0	49.1	...	...	57.7	57.4	57.2	31.9	30.2	...	10.4	12.5	...
Germany	1994	...	...	...	22.5	...	...	...	...	...	17.2	...	...	...
Iceland	1995	...	28.7	...	22.6	62.2	66.5	56.0	26.5	27.7	34.7	11.3	5.8	9.3
Israel	1994	...	14.1	...	10.8	62.7	57.8	65.1	25.4	28.9	26.7	11.9	13.4	8.2
Italy	1994	...	33.6	...	...	65.9	71.5	69.3	16.4	22.3	18.8	17.7	6.2	11.9
Japan	1995	1.8	39.9	1.4	22.6	49.2	47.2	45.5	27.1	28.0	30.8	23.8	24.9	23.6
Norway	1994	4.0	38.0	1.8	20.9	61.8	62.0	64.1	27.2	27.4	19.8	11.1	10.7	16.1
South Africa	1994	0.8	...	1.4	4.7	60.0	59.4	...	30.9	28.6	...	9.1	12.0	...
Spain	1995	...	21.3	0.4	12.6	57.8	59.1	66.1	20.2	19.0	20.1	22.0	21.9	13.8
Sweden	1994	6.6	33.1	2.2	18.1	46.2	47.8	61.5	30.8	29.5	21.1	23.0	22.7	17.4
United Kingdom	1995	1.6	20.8	1.0	12.7	51.6	48.3	62.0	25.7	26.3	23.2	22.7	25.4	14.8
United States of America	1995	2.5	40.6	-0.1	15.6	49.3	46.3	47.4	22.6	22.8	20.2	28.1	30.9	32.4
Countries of eastern Europe and the former USSR														
Albania	1996	...	...	...	...	...	...	...	...	...	33.3	...	...	...
Bulgaria	1996	...	2.0	...	0.6	...	...	48.5	10.6	14.3	16.5	...	...	35.0
Latvia	1996	...	3.8	...	...	...	...	35.1	...	...	...	...	...	...
Lithuania	1994	...	...	...	0.9	...	...	...	...	...	24.4	...	...	...
Republic of Moldova	1995	...	...	...	0.2	...	...	...	...	16.6	25.6	...	...	...
Romania	1994	...	...	...	0.8	...	57.4	...	...	23.8	...	...	18.7	...
Russian Federation	1995	...	1.4	...	0.5	...	...	48.8	...	...	20.2	...	...	31.0
Slovakia	1994	...	3.6	...	1.7	...	...	47.3	...	...	25.0	...	...	27.7
Ukraine	1996	...	...	...	0.5	...	...	...	...	13.9	30.1	...	...	...
Developing countries														
Bolivia	1995	...	3.5	...	1.5	...	61.9	65.1	...	10.6	15.3	...	27.4	19.6
Cameroon	1996	...	12.8	...	2.6	...	...	52.8	...	...	9.6	...	...	37.6
Chile	1995	...	20.3	5.7	6.2	46.8	51.9	50.2	11.5	14.7	15.3	41.7	33.4	34.5
China (Hong Kong SAR)	1995	16.5	20.5	2.7	13.4	67.4	70.2	72.4	25.1	20.9	18.1	7.4	8.9	9.5
China (Taiwan Province)	1996	...	21.9	4.6	9.9	72.9	67.8	64.0	8.5	11.0	16.3	18.5	21.2	19.7
Colombia	1995	-1.9	7.3	0.2	2.3	55.4	61.2	51.3	15.3	11.2	15.5	29.3	27.6	33.3
Costa Rica	1996	...	...	...	...	60.7	...	62.5	...	...	...	...	...	...
Croatia	1996	...	...	...	3.3	...	41.6	...	...	22.9	...	...	35.5	...
Cyprus	1996	1.8	15.0	2.9	8.7	61.5	62.2	62.1	20.7	22.5	22.1	17.8	15.3	15.8
Ecuador	1996	...	4.1	...	1.0	62.5	69.0	63.3	21.4	14.8	8.7	16.2	16.2	27.9
Egypt	1994	...	3.6	...	0.7	75.3	79.2	61.7	12.0	11.3	7.5	12.7	9.5	30.7

a/ At current prices.

b/ Excluding countries of eastern Europe and the former USSR.

TABLE 1.11
(continued)

SELECTED CHARACTERISTICS OF BRANCHES, SELECTED YEARS AND COUNTRIES

Wearing apparel (322)														
Country or area	Latest year	Value added per employee		Wages per employee		Percentage in output a/								
		Real annual growth rate (percentage)	Value (current 1000 dollars)	Real annual growth rate (percentage)	Value (current 1000 dollars)	Costs of input materials and utilities			Costs of labour			Operating surplus		
	(LY)	1985-LY	LY	1985-LY	LY	1985	1990	LY	1985	1990	LY	1985	1990	LY
El Salvador	1996	...	3.7	...	2.1	47.1	...	27.0	18.5	...	41.3	34.5	...	31.7
Ethiopia	1996	...	1.3	...	0.5	...	68.9	54.4	...	11.7	17.2	...	19.3	28.5
Gabon	1995	...	8.2	...	3.4	...	...	62.5	...	...	15.7	...	...	21.8
Honduras	1995	...	1.6	...	1.2	57.8	54.2	39.6	31.1	35.1	44.4	11.1	10.7	15.9
India	1994	...	3.1	0.9	0.6	85.4	77.7	71.2	6.7	5.8	5.7	7.9	16.5	23.1
Indonesia	1996	5.8	3.6	3.7	1.1	66.3	64.3	60.8	14.7	9.9	12.3	19.0	25.8	26.8
Jordan	1995	...	4.6	...	1.8	65.3	51.1	56.4	19.4	14.3	17.1	15.4	34.6	26.4
Kenya	1995	...	2.0	...	0.9	77.6	...	...	11.2	...	...	11.2	...	...
Kuwait	1995	...	10.8	...	4.6	27.1	48.5	23.5	34.6	15.2	32.9	38.3	36.3	43.6
Macau	1996	...	10.3	...	5.9	72.2	72.9	74.8	16.2	15.9	14.4	11.6	11.2	10.8
Malaysia	1995	...	6.6	3.6	3.6	66.5	68.2	64.7	19.3	16.1	19.1	14.2	15.8	16.2
Malta	1994	4.9	14.8	2.3	8.9	54.8	57.2	60.5	26.0	27.1	23.9	19.2	15.7	15.6
Mauritius	1994	...	3.9	7.2	2.3	66.1	68.4	65.5	18.5	17.8	20.5	15.4	13.8	14.0
Mexico	1994	...	9.8	0.4	4.6	58.8	47.8	46.0	15.7	21.5	25.5	25.5	30.7	28.4
Mongolia	1995	...	0.4	...	0.4	...	70.0	60.1	...	18.4	35.0	...	11.6	4.9
Morocco	1996	...	3.9	...	2.5	72.6	67.5	59.3	16.6	20.9	26.2	10.8	11.5	14.5
Nepal	1996	...	1.6	...	0.4	...	56.9	63.8	...	16.3	9.9	...	26.8	26.3
Peru	1994	3.3	6.3	...	1.6	70.5	69.3	75.1	8.5	8.0	6.3	21.1	22.7	18.6
Philippines	1995	...	5.1	2.0	2.2	59.6	51.8	48.3	34.4	24.8	22.4	6.0	23.4	29.3
Republic of Korea	1995	2.7	35.7	9.8	12.5	58.8	56.6	50.9	19.2	19.1	17.3	22.0	24.3	31.9
Singapore	1996	3.1	16.7	3.9	12.1	66.6	69.2	69.7	22.0	18.7	22.0	11.4	12.1	8.2
Slovenia	1995	...	...	...	...	...	...	44.5	...	...	...	...	...	...
St. Vincent and the Grenadines	1994	...	...	...	1.9	...	...	...	...	...	...	...	...	...
The f.Yugosl.Rep.of Macedonia	1996	...	2.5	...	2.5	...	45.0	...	...	27.9	...	...	27.1	...
Thailand	1994	...	5.4	...	3.6	...	75.3	71.4	...	14.0	19.2	...	10.7	9.3
Tonga	1994	...	...	...	1.5	...	...	...	18.9	17.2	20.8	...	...	...
Trinidad and Tobago	1995	...	3.3	...	2.0	57.8	64.2	66.7	34.8	26.3	20.0	7.3	9.5	13.3
Tunisia	1996	...	...	...	...	...	68.8	65.8	...	15.1	15.7	...	16.1	18.5
Turkey	1994	...	14.8	...	2.2	72.3	68.5	68.7	7.0	7.5	4.6	20.7	23.9	26.7
Uruguay	1995	...	11.9	...	3.4	62.9	64.3	48.5	14.6	12.4	14.8	22.5	23.3	36.7
Venezuela	1996	...	14.7	...	2.1	59.6	62.8	48.0	19.9	17.6	7.5	20.5	19.6	44.4
Yugoslavia	1996	...	1.8	...	0.6	...	46.9	48.1	...	...	18.5	...	...	33.4
Zambia	1994	...	1.7	...	1.3	...	66.3	72.4	...	13.6	22.0	...	20.1	5.6
Zimbabwe	1995	...	3.1	...	1.5	54.1	54.3	59.6	26.4	21.4	19.1	19.4	24.3	21.3

At current prices.

TABLE 1.11

SELECTED CHARACTERISTICS OF BRANCHES, SELECTED YEARS AND COUNTRIES

Leather and fur products (323)

Country or area	Latest year	Value added per employee		Wages per employee		Percentage in output a/								
		Real annual growth rate (percentage)	Value (current 1000 dollars)	Real annual growth rate (percentage)	Value (current 1000 dollars)	Costs of input materials and utilities			Costs of labour			Operating surplus		
	(LY)	1985-LY	LY	1985-LY	LY	1985	1990	LY	1985	1990	LY	1985	1990	LY
Industrialized countries b/														
Austria	1994	...	26.9	1.3	19.5	74.9	73.7	75.6	15.8	15.7	17.7	9.2	10.7	6.7
Canada	1994	...	34.2	0.8	18.8	58.0	59.6	60.0	21.8	23.2	22.0	20.2	17.2	18.0
Finland	1995	...	35.7	2.7	22.5	65.8	60.6	63.8	19.9	23.5	22.9	14.2	15.9	13.3
France	1995	...	93.8	...	...	60.3	55.2	48.7	28.4	29.7	...	11.3	15.2	...
Germany	1994	...	...	...	23.2	...	...	...	...	...	20.9	...	...	...
Iceland	1995	...	51.1	2.9	30.0	53.8	73.0	55.0	25.9	10.0	26.4	20.2	17.0	18.5
Israel	1994	...	18.4	...	14.1	63.4	64.5	72.2	19.5	19.6	21.2	17.1	15.9	6.6
Italy	1994	...	50.1	...	...	77.3	76.5	78.0	8.9	14.3	11.2	13.8	9.2	10.8
Japan	1995	...	75.3	1.7	34.3	62.5	63.2	59.6	15.8	15.8	18.4	21.7	21.0	22.0
Norway	1994	...	36.5	2.7	24.4	69.3	70.4	71.1	26.1	20.0	19.2	4.7	9.6	9.6
South Africa	1994	0.9	...	1.1	5.3	76.5	76.8	...	11.7	14.6	...	11.7	8.6	...
Spain	1995	...	29.0	0.6	16.1	71.8	69.8	74.3	11.4	14.1	14.3	16.8	16.1	11.5
Sweden	1994	...	44.5	1.1	19.6	62.6	53.0	65.6	14.8	18.6	15.2	22.5	28.3	19.2
United Kingdom	1995	7.9	27.2	2.1	17.8	66.7	66.5	69.1	16.0	17.0	20.2	17.4	16.5	10.8
United States of America	1995	...	57.3	0.6	22.1	56.1	56.6	58.5	21.1	16.9	16.0	22.8	26.5	25.5
Countries of eastern Europe and the former USSR														
Azerbaijan	1994	...	...	...	...	...	...	...	...	11.2	10.8	...	...	...
Bulgaria	1996	...	...	...	0.8	...	...	...	8.7	11.5	9.1	...	...	...
Kyrgyzstan	1994	...	...	...	...	...	...	...	...	3.1	6.1	...	...	...
Latvia	1996	...	2.3	...	...	...	...	67.7	...	...	...	...	...	...
Lithuania	1994	...	...	...	1.0	...	...	...	...	...	17.7	...	...	...
Republic of Moldova	1995	...	...	...	0.3	...	...	...	...	7.3	9.5	...	...	...
Russian Federation	1995	...	2.5	...	1.0	...	...	52.2	...	...	18.5	...	...	29.3
Slovakia	1994	...	3.3	...	1.8	...	...	69.2	...	...	17.2	...	...	13.6
Ukraine	1996	...	...	...	0.6	...	...	...	...	16.1	11.6	...	...	...
Developing countries														
Bolivia	1995	...	4.6	...	1.4	...	73.1	72.5	...	5.5	8.3	...	21.4	19.2
Chile	1995	...	27.1	4.5	7.5	62.8	56.4	59.1	7.8	8.1	11.3	29.4	35.5	29.6
China	1996	...	...	...	...	72.5	77.3	75.0	2.7	...	...	24.7	...	...
China (Hong Kong SAR)	1995	...	33.6	5.9	18.7	79.6	78.3	77.2	16.1	11.9	12.7	4.3	9.8	10.1
China (Taiwan Province)	1996	...	16.0	6.8	13.3	67.3	64.5	63.3	13.6	24.4	30.3	19.1	11.1	6.3
Colombia	1995	1.0	11.5	-0.8	2.9	68.4	70.5	65.4	9.0	6.5	8.8	22.6	23.0	25.7
Costa Rica	1996	...	...	...	...	61.4	62.2	67.8	...	...	...	...	...	...
Croatia	1996	...	...	...	2.9	...	64.1	...	...	16.4	...	...	19.5	...
Cyprus	1996	...	17.9	2.7	9.5	65.7	64.0	61.1	19.9	22.3	20.6	14.4	13.8	18.3
Ecuador	1996	...	5.3	...	1.0	71.7	71.3	71.3	13.8	10.4	5.4	14.6	18.3	23.3
El Salvador	1996	...	8.1	...	2.9	48.6	...	48.2	15.5	...	18.7	35.9	...	33.0
Ethiopia	1996	...	6.3	...	1.3	...	65.2	70.4	...	7.2	6.1	...	27.6	23.5

a/ At current prices.

b/ Excluding countries of eastern Europe and the former USSR.

TABLE 1.11
(continued)

SELECTED CHARACTERISTICS OF BRANCHES, SELECTED YEARS AND COUNTRIES

Leather and fur products (323)															
Country or area	Latest year	Value added per employee		Wages per employee		Percentage in output a/									
		Real annual growth rate (percentage)	Value (current 1000 dollars)	Real annual growth rate (percentage)	Value (current 1000 dollars)	Costs of input materials and utilities			Costs of labour			Operating surplus			
	(LY)	1985-LY	LY	1985-LY	LY	1985	1990	LY	1985	1990	LY	1985	1990	LY
Honduras	1995	...	3.4	...	1.3	74.7	72.9	69.5	13.8	11.0	11.9	11.6	16.1	18.6
India	1994	...	2.0	1.8	0.7	90.4	86.5	88.1	5.2	4.5	4.4	4.4	9.1	7.5
Indonesia	1996	1.3	4.7	2.4	1.0	68.1	67.3	64.0	7.2	5.1	7.8	24.7	27.5	28.1
Jordan	1995	...	8.5	...	3.1	48.6	55.0	83.8	20.2	9.1	5.9	31.2	35.8	10.3
Kenya	1995	...	1.9	...	1.0	85.6	77.3	70.4	8.4	10.7	16.4	6.0	12.0	13.2
Kuwait	1995	...	22.5	...	4.5	...	...	58.0	...	...	8.5	...	...	33.5
Macau	1996	...	29.7	...	8.9	71.4	67.1	47.2	21.5	16.5	15.9	7.1	16.4	36.9
Malaysia	1995	...	8.7	4.1	4.0	70.6	74.6	66.2	14.2	12.5	15.7	15.2	12.8	18.0
Malta	1994	...	18.0	4.2	8.9	37.6	52.5	54.8	32.7	23.0	22.2	29.7	24.5	23.0
Mauritius	1994	...	3.8	2.8	2.7	66.5	62.4	63.7	15.3	15.2	26.0	18.2	22.5	10.3
Mongolia	1995	...	1.2	...	0.8	...	78.1	76.5	...	5.4	16.3	...	16.4	7.2
Morocco	1996	...	4.5	...	2.8	...	...	80.4	...	...	12.0	...	...	7.6
Nepal	1996	...	5.3	...	0.5	...	70.8	65.0	...	2.3	3.3	...	27.0	31.7
Peru	1994	...	8.6	...	2.6	67.4	49.9	72.0	6.9	10.8	8.4	25.7	39.3	19.6
Philippines	1995	...	3.6	4.8	2.0	70.7	45.3	56.5	16.6	26.5	24.6	12.7	28.2	18.9
Republic of Korea	1995	...	50.0	9.7	15.1	74.9	70.7	66.6	8.7	8.8	10.1	16.5	20.5	23.3
Senegal	1996	...	32.6	...	1.3	...	...	70.9	...	...	1.2	...	...	27.9
Singapore	1996	...	29.3	5.8	17.3	68.1	63.8	62.5	19.4	18.9	22.2	12.5	17.3	15.3
Slovenia	1995	...	...	...	...	...	...	64.1	...	...	...	...	...	...
Thailand	1994	...	5.6	...	2.0	...	72.4	55.3	...	20.4	15.7	...	7.2	29.0
Trinidad and Tobago	1995	...	4.6	...	2.7	66.7	70.6	60.7	26.7	17.6	22.6	6.7	11.8	16.7
Turkey	1994	-5.5	14.2	...	3.4	71.1	72.5	70.0	5.6	7.9	7.1	23.2	19.6	22.9
Uruguay	1995	...	24.4	...	7.5	52.6	68.8	73.7	8.2	10.2	8.1	39.2	21.1	18.3
Venezuela	1996	...	7.8	...	2.2	68.4	69.0	67.9	11.2	9.1	8.9	20.5	21.9	23.2
Yugoslavia	1996	...	3.9	...	0.9	...	58.5	57.0	...	...	9.6	...	...	33.4
Zambia	1994	...	2.0	...	0.3	...	...	35.1	...	...	8.5	...	...	56.4
Zimbabwe	1995	...	4.1	...	2.2	73.1	67.8	69.8	13.7	10.0	16.3	13.2	22.2	13.9

a/ At current prices

TABLE 1.11

SELECTED CHARACTERISTICS OF BRANCHES, SELECTED YEARS AND COUNTRIES

Country or area	Latest year	Footwear (324)												
		Value added per employee		Wages per employee		Percentage in output a/								
		Real annual growth rate (percentage)	Value (current 1000 dollars)	Real annual growth rate (percentage)	Value (current 1000 dollars)	Costs of input materials and utilities			Costs of labour			Operating surplus		
	(LY)	1985-LY	LY	1985-LY	LY	1985	1990	LY	1985	1990	LY	1985	1990	LY
Industrialized countries b/														
Austria	1994	...	31.4	1.8	19.6	68.7	69.9	69.4	20.6	18.7	19.1	10.7	11.4	11.5
Canada	1994	...	29.3	-0.1	16.2	53.0	53.6	52.9	27.9	27.9	26.0	19.1	18.6	21.1
Finland	1995	...	35.9	2.0	20.5	57.2	59.1	58.7	25.5	27.9	23.6	17.4	13.1	17.7
France	1995	...	32.8	...	...	48.1	50.9	53.3	37.9	35.9	...	14.0	13.2	...
Germany	1994	...	...	...	26.3	...	...	...	...	...	16.8	...	...	...
Israel	1994	...	17.2	...	13.4	56.3	55.5	70.1	25.9	27.1	23.3	17.9	17.4	6.6
Italy	1994	...	31.5	...	...	68.2	73.5	73.3	15.0	19.3	17.4	16.8	7.2	9.2
Japan	1995	...	64.8	0.6	31.7	61.7	60.4	55.3	18.5	18.0	21.9	19.8	21.7	22.8
Norway	1994	...	30.0	1.6	21.8	60.0	57.6	54.2	28.8	30.9	33.3	11.2	11.5	12.4
South Africa	1994	1.8	...	-0.1	5.2	68.0	52.2	...	21.6	21.4	...	10.4	26.4	...
Spain	1995	...	23.3	0.4	12.2	63.1	67.0	79.5	15.8	13.9	10.8	21.1	19.0	9.7
Sweden	1994	...	32.9	1.2	17.8	52.3	52.9	59.1	24.3	22.6	22.2	23.4	24.4	18.7
United Kingdom	1995	-1.0	21.2	0.3	15.7	45.3	49.6	62.7	29.4	26.8	27.6	25.3	23.6	9.6
United States of America	1995	...	41.0	0.1	16.6	47.4	50.1	50.5	22.8	21.3	20.0	29.8	28.6	29.4
Countries of eastern Europe and the former USSR														
Albania	1996	...	...	...	...	...	...	...	...	...	7.1	...	...	...
Azerbaijan	1994	...	...	...	...	...	...	...	...	14.2	12.6	...	...	...
Bulgaria	1996	...	...	...	0.7	...	...	...	12.9	16.2	12.9	...	...	...
Latvia	1996	...	3.1	...	...	...	...	50.9	...	...	...	...	...	...
Lithuania	1994	...	...	...	0.9	...	...	...	...	...	18.8	...	...	...
Republic of Moldova	1995	...	...	...	0.3	...	...	...	...	18.8	20.3	...	...	...
Russian Federation	1995	...	1.7	...	0.7	...	...	56.3	...	...	17.3	...	...	26.5
Slovakia	1994	...	2.6	...	1.7	...	...	60.8	...	...	25.7	...	...	13.5
Ukraine	1996	...	...	...	0.4	...	...	...	...	19.4	20.2	...	...	...
Developing countries														
Bolivia	1995	...	8.7	...	2.1	...	54.9	67.0	...	10.6	8.0	...	34.4	25.1
Chile	1995	...	21.5	3.0	6.0	51.6	52.3	47.6	14.7	13.1	14.6	33.8	34.6	37.8
China (Hong Kong SAR)	1995	...	13.4	...	9.5	64.1	71.6	55.7	29.3	21.4	31.4	6.6	7.0	12.9
China (Taiwan Province)	1996	...	12.8	4.3	10.8	78.8	78.8	78.9	11.5	12.9	17.7	9.7	8.3	3.3
Colombia	1995	-1.9	10.4	-0.2	2.6	55.7	62.1	54.8	14.1	9.0	11.3	30.1	28.9	33.9
Costa Rica	1996	...	...	...	...	59.9	60.7	61.8	...	...	...	...	...	...
Croatia	1996	...	...	...	2.9	...	54.8	...	...	24.0	...	...	21.1	...
Cyprus	1996	...	18.8	2.4	11.0	60.9	61.8	58.8	24.2	21.2	24.2	14.9	17.0	17.1
Ecuador	1996	...	7.8	...	1.4	64.9	68.0	65.8	19.6	15.8	6.0	15.5	16.2	28.1
El Salvador	1996	...	4.8	...	2.2	42.9	...	54.1	13.7	...	21.3	43.4	...	24.6
Ethiopia	1996	...	2.2	...	0.7	...	64.7	59.5	...	12.9	13.3	...	22.4	27.2
Honduras	1995	...	2.1	...	1.7	64.6	73.1	67.8	24.1	17.5	26.1	11.3	9.5	6.1
India	1994	...	2.0	...	0.7	78.8	82.9	81.6	13.6	8.0	6.1	7.6	9.0	12.3

a/ At current prices.

b/ Excluding countries of eastern Europe and the former USSR.

TABLE 1.11
(continued)

SELECTED CHARACTERISTICS OF BRANCHES, SELECTED YEARS AND COUNTRIES

Footwear (324)														
Country or area	Latest year	Value added per employee		Wages per employee		Percentage in output a/								
		Real annual growth rate (percentage)	Value (current 1000 dollars)	Real annual growth rate (percentage)	Value (current 1000 dollars)	Costs of input materials and utilities			Costs of labour			Operating surplus		
	(LY)	1985-LY	LY	1985-LY	LY	1985	1990	LY	1985	1990	LY	1985	1990	LY
Indonesia	1996	...	3.9	1.2	1.3	54.1	50.3	58.7	13.5	12.4	14.0	32.4	37.3	27.4
Jordan	1995	...	7.4	...	2.2	45.7	58.1	57.7	18.3	18.9	12.7	36.0	23.0	29.7
Kenya	1995	...	3.5	...	1.6	80.0	66.7	78.4	10.0	9.7	10.0	10.0	23.6	11.6
Kuwait	1995	...	4.2	...	3.8	...	...	56.4	...	...	39.2	...	...	4.4
Malaysia	1995	...	8.7	1.5	3.8	57.8	66.4	59.9	19.0	17.1	17.6	23.2	16.5	22.5
Malta	1994	...	13.5	2.1	8.4	56.8	63.9	61.7	29.6	24.3	23.9	13.6	11.7	14.4
Mauritius	1994	...	6.5	...	1.5	51.8	55.1	39.6	18.1	19.3	14.3	30.0	25.6	46.2
Mexico	1994	...	10.0	0.4	5.7	66.4	62.0	56.1	16.6	22.5	25.2	16.9	15.5	18.7
Mongolia	1995	...	0.8	...	0.3	...	56.8	54.8	...	11.9	15.3	...	31.3	30.0
Morocco	1996	...	4.9	...	3.1	...	...	65.5	...	...	22.2	...	...	12.4
Nepal	1996	...	1.3	...	0.4	...	38.6	64.3	...	23.7	10.1	...	37.7	25.6
Peru	1994	4.6	6.2	...	1.5	69.2	56.5	77.2	10.2	14.9	5.4	20.6	28.6	17.4
Philippines	1995	...	2.9	1.7	1.6	68.6	61.4	64.9	23.6	20.9	19.7	7.9	17.6	15.5
Republic of Korea	1995	...	29.0	8.6	12.1	60.4	55.6	53.3	15.2	15.1	19.4	24.4	29.3	27.3
Senegal	1996	...	5.4	...	1.9	...	...	70.1	...	...	10.5	...	...	19.4
Singapore	1996	...	33.5	9.0	18.1	64.5	67.4	59.6	20.6	18.1	21.9	15.0	14.5	18.5
Slovenia	1995	...	...	...	...	...	...	58.4	...	...	...	...	...	...
Swaziland	1994	...	7.1	...	3.7	...	...	68.5	...	...	16.3	...	...	15.2
The f.Yugosl.Rep.of Macedonia	1996	...	3.2	...	2.1	...	51.0	66.5	...	19.7	22.3	...	29.3	11.2
Thailand	1994	...	5.3	...	2.3	...	63.5	55.6	...	18.3	19.2	...	18.2	25.2
Trinidad and Tobago	1995	...	4.0	...	2.3	57.2	70.5	72.5	33.9	20.9	16.0	8.9	8.7	11.5
Turkey	1994	-0.7	12.8	...	3.1	68.5	68.0	62.4	16.7	14.9	9.1	14.7	17.1	28.5
Uruguay	1995	...	3.7	...	3.1	66.2	72.3	83.1	11.9	9.9	13.9	21.9	17.9	3.0
Venezuela	1996	...	8.1	...	2.1	61.5	67.0	57.8	19.7	14.1	11.1	18.8	18.9	31.1
Yugoslavia	1996	...	1.9	...	0.6	...	59.0	52.9	...	...	16.0	...	...	31.1
Zambia	1994	...	2.3	...	1.3	...	...	72.4	...	...	16.2	...	...	11.4
Zimbabwe	1995	...	5.7	...	2.2	38.8	43.9	55.3	18.6	16.5	17.2	42.6	39.7	27.5

a/ At current prices.

TABLE 1.11

SELECTED CHARACTERISTICS OF BRANCHES, SELECTED YEARS AND COUNTRIES

Wood and cork products (331)

Country or area	Latest year	Value added per employee		Wages per employee		Percentage in output [a]								
		Real annual growth rate (percentage)	Value (current 1000 dollars)	Real annual growth rate (percentage)	Value (current 1000 dollars)	Costs of input materials and utilities			Costs of labour			Operating surplus		
	(LY)	1985-LY	LY	1985-LY	LY	1985	1990	LY	1985	1990	LY	1985	1990	LY
Industrialized countries [b]														
Austria	1994	2.8	52.2	1.4	24.2	74.2	72.7	73.2	13.4	12.0	12.4	12.4	15.3	14.4
Belgium	1994	...	...	...	...	74.6	73.1	74.0	...	...	...	...	...	...
Canada	1994	0.3	65.9	0.1	26.2	59.7	64.3	58.1	23.6	22.3	16.6	16.6	13.4	25.2
Finland	1995	5.2	54.8	3.0	27.2	66.8	65.4	69.2	18.1	16.4	15.3	15.0	18.2	15.6
France	1995	2.6	63.5	...	...	61.6	60.1	60.4	25.7	22.7	...	12.7	17.2	...
Germany	1994	...	...	...	29.8	...	...	...	...	...	...	...	...	...
Iceland	1995	...	57.8	...	30.9	56.3	75.7	64.8	9.0	14.1	18.8	34.7	10.2	16.4
Israel	1994	...	20.9	...	16.9	59.6	61.6	67.9	28.1	26.7	26.0	12.3	11.6	6.1
Italy	1994	...	43.1	...	...	68.6	69.4	70.6	13.3	19.3	17.6	18.1	11.3	11.8
Japan	1995	-0.5	77.6	1.4	35.6	63.0	61.2	60.2	17.4	17.0	18.3	19.6	21.8	21.5
Norway	1994	4.5	47.2	1.9	27.8	69.7	69.6	68.9	19.1	19.0	18.3	11.2	11.4	12.8
South Africa	1994	-1.4	...	1.2	4.1	66.0	60.0	...	18.7	19.1	...	15.3	20.9	...
Spain	1995	-0.7	28.6	2.3	14.6	58.6	62.9	69.0	17.0	14.8	15.8	24.4	22.3	15.1
Sweden	1994	5.5	55.8	2.0	22.8	63.9	60.4	68.0	14.6	13.2	13.1	21.5	26.4	18.9
United Kingdom	1995	...	33.3	0.8	19.9	63.2	61.5	68.9	18.1	17.8	18.6	18.7	20.7	12.6
United States of America	1995	-0.4	54.2	-0.7	22.5	60.6	61.7	61.3	19.6	18.6	16.1	19.7	19.8	22.6
Countries of eastern Europe and the former USSR														
Azerbaijan	1994	...	...	...	...	...	...	...	...	13.7	18.3	...	...	...
Bulgaria	1996	...	...	...	0.8	...	...	...	9.4	14.9	10.8	...	...	...
Latvia	1996	...	4.7	...	...	...	...	64.3	...	...	...	...	...	...
Lithuania	1994	...	...	...	0.9	...	...	...	...	...	15.4	...	...	...
Republic of Moldova	1995	...	...	...	0.4	...	...	...	...	27.6	10.1	...	...	...
Romania	1994	...	...	...	0.8	...	56.3	...	...	19.2	...	...	24.6	...
Russian Federation	1995	...	2.1	...	1.1	...	...	62.6	...	...	18.8	...	...	18.7
Slovakia	1994	...	4.2	...	2.0	...	...	63.4	...	...	17.6	...	...	18.9
Ukraine	1996	...	...	...	0.5	...	...	...	...	18.7	13.0	...	...	...
Developing countries														
Bolivia	1995	...	8.0	...	1.3	...	68.5	65.3	...	6.9	5.8	...	24.6	28.8
Brazil	1994	...	17.0	...	3.9	40.0	37.5	38.7	20.0	16.7	14.2	40.0	45.8	47.0
Cameroon	1996	...	9.8	...	3.6	...	64.9	69.5	...	18.5	11.2	...	16.6	19.3
Chile	1995	...	24.2	6.2	6.1	48.6	60.3	60.8	8.3	9.8	9.8	43.2	29.9	29.4
China	1996	...	...	...	...	69.5	76.7	72.1	5.0	...	...	25.5	...	...
China (Hong Kong SAR)	1995	...	31.0	4.7	15.9	72.7	78.3	74.9	16.0	12.7	12.9	11.4	9.0	12.3
China (Taiwan Province)	1996	...	14.3	4.8	10.9	62.2	59.3	66.1	23.3	27.8	25.7	14.5	12.9	8.2
Colombia	1995	2.4	11.7	1.6	3.4	49.0	50.9	63.3	12.1	10.3	10.7	38.9	38.8	26.0
Costa Rica	1996	...	...	...	...	57.4	58.1	59.4	...	...	...	...	...	...
Croatia	1996	...	...	...	3.2	...	62.1	...	...	14.8	...	...	23.1	...
Cyprus	1996	...	23.8	2.5	12.4	56.7	57.5	57.1	19.2	17.9	22.4	24.1	24.5	20.5

a/ At current prices.

b/ Excluding countries of eastern Europe and the former USSR.

TABLE 1.11
(continued)

SELECTED CHARACTERISTICS OF BRANCHES, SELECTED YEARS AND COUNTRIES

Wood and cork products (331)														
Country or area	Latest year	Value added per employee		Wages per employee		Percentage in output a/								
		Real annual growth rate (percentage)	Value (current 1000 dollars)	Real annual growth rate (percentage)	Value (current 1000 dollars)	Costs of input materials and utilities			Costs of labour			Operating surplus		
	(LY)	1985-LY	LY	1985-LY	LY	1985	1990	LY	1985	1990	LY	1985	1990	LY
Ecuador	1996	...	7.8	...	1.8	66.6	65.8	63.1	21.9	15.1	8.3	11.5	19.1	28.6
Egypt	1994	...	5.3	...	1.0	75.0	78.5	45.8	15.1	16.7	10.0	9.8	4.8	44.2
El Salvador	1996	...	4.0	...	2.0	60.0	...	46.5	15.0	...	26.5	25.0	...	27.0
Ethiopia	1996	...	2.8	...	0.7	...	38.2	33.7	...	29.0	17.4	...	32.7	48.9
Gabon	1995	...	7.6	...	6.4	...	...	66.9	...	...	28.2	...	...	4.9
Honduras	1995	...	2.3	...	1.5	67.6	72.7	74.0	24.6	19.3	17.0	7.7	8.0	8.9
India	1994	...	1.4	1.7	0.5	79.1	78.9	79.4	10.1	7.8	7.9	10.8	13.3	12.7
Indonesia	1996	1.5	6.2	2.1	1.3	64.6	65.3	63.8	8.9	5.7	7.5	26.6	29.0	28.7
Jordan	1995	...	5.1	...	1.9	75.9	61.0	68.3	16.1	10.2	11.9	8.0	28.8	19.7
Kenya	1995	0.4	1.6	...	0.8	67.5	78.4	80.4	15.3	10.0	10.1	17.2	11.6	9.5
Kuwait	1995	...	15.8	...	6.1	56.1	43.1	62.3	32.4	28.0	14.4	11.4	28.9	23.3
Macau	1996	...	8.7	...	5.3	55.4	51.6	47.0	25.1	28.9	32.1	19.5	19.5	20.9
Malaysia	1995	0.2	9.3	-0.3	3.3	69.3	70.1	69.9	16.2	12.0	10.7	14.5	17.9	19.4
Malta	1994	3.3	19.7	3.2	7.5	50.4	48.5	48.0	25.0	23.6	19.8	24.6	27.9	32.2
Mexico	1994	...	15.2	...	4.5	56.4	58.9	59.0	10.8	11.9	12.2	32.8	29.2	28.8
Mongolia	1995	...	0.4	...	0.2	...	70.2	65.1	...	17.9	21.3	...	12.0	13.6
Morocco	1996	...	6.8	...	3.4	...	...	76.6	...	...	11.6	...	...	11.8
Namibia	1994	...	19.5	...	5.8	...	...	48.2	...	...	15.5	...	...	36.3
Nepal	1996	...	1.6	...	0.4	...	58.7	61.8	...	14.6	9.4	...	26.7	28.8
Peru	1994	4.7	6.9	...	1.7	74.8	45.9	67.7	7.0	11.2	8.0	18.2	42.9	24.3
Philippines	1995	...	4.8	0.9	1.8	70.6	63.2	65.2	14.8	15.3	13.2	14.6	21.5	21.6
Qatar	1994	...	9.9	...	4.9	...	44.5	61.2	...	22.1	19.2	...	33.4	19.6
Republic of Korea	1995	1.1	44.2	9.3	15.2	72.8	64.4	58.4	12.2	14.0	14.3	15.0	21.6	27.3
Senegal	1996	...	14.5	...	4.5	...	84.7	88.8	...	9.6	3.5	...	5.7	7.7
Singapore	1996	3.6	39.7	4.9	17.2	72.1	71.8	70.0	14.2	12.5	13.0	13.7	15.8	17.0
Slovenia	1996	...	13.7	...	7.8	...	73.6	70.5	...	20.8	16.7	...	5.7	12.8
Thailand	1994	...	10.3	...	2.3	...	70.1	55.6	...	7.4	9.9	...	22.5	34.5
Tonga	1994	...	...	...	1.8	...	...	...	36.8	39.2	58.7	...	...	...
Trinidad and Tobago	1995	...	5.1	...	3.6	56.7	...	46.4	34.4	30.2	37.9	8.9	...	15.7
Turkey	1994	2.4	11.2	...	4.2	72.5	68.7	72.2	9.9	10.4	10.4	17.6	20.9	17.4
Uruguay	1995	...	10.5	...	4.2	54.3	49.1	51.2	18.1	14.9	19.5	27.6	36.0	29.2
Venezuela	1996	...	6.0	...	1.8	57.4	59.9	58.9	18.7	17.4	12.6	23.9	22.7	28.5
Yugoslavia	1996	...	3.9	...	0.9	...	60.9	63.1	...	...	8.8	...	...	28.1
Zambia	1994	...	3.3	...	1.1	...	51.4	44.4	...	16.3	17.8	...	32.3	37.8
Zimbabwe	1995	...	6.3	...	1.9	56.7	47.5	36.8	29.5	19.2	19.4	13.8	33.4	43.8

a/ At current prices.

TABLE 1.11

SELECTED CHARACTERISTICS OF BRANCHES, SELECTED YEARS AND COUNTRIES

Furniture, fixtures excl. metallic (332)

Country or area	Latest year	Value added per employee		Wages per employee		Percentage in output a/								
		Real annual growth rate (percentage)	Value (current 1000 dollars)	Real annual growth rate (percentage)	Value (current 1000 dollars)	Costs of input materials and utilities			Costs of labour			Operating surplus		
	(LY)	1985-LY	LY	1985-LY	LY	1985	1990	LY	1985	1990	LY	1985	1990	LY
Industrialized countries b/														
Austria	1994	...	42.6	2.2	24.7	59.6	60.0	57.8	25.2	23.2	24.5	15.2	16.8	17.7
Belgium	1994	...	...	...	...	67.5	67.4	66.1	...	...	...	...	...	...
Canada	1994	...	36.2	0.2	19.3	48.7	49.1	49.5	27.7	29.9	26.9	23.5	21.0	23.6
Finland	1995	...	47.0	2.7	25.5	48.5	49.7	54.6	27.4	24.7	24.7	24.1	25.6	20.8
France	1995	...	63.9	...	...	56.6	56.7	53.7	29.7	26.0	...	13.6	17.3	...
Germany	1994	...	...	...	31.1	...	...	...	...	...	23.6	...	...	...
Iceland	1995	...	37.9	2.5	30.0	50.4	59.1	59.8	30.8	34.0	31.8	18.8	6.9	8.4
Israel	1994	...	22.1	...	15.5	60.3	56.6	62.7	25.1	25.5	26.1	14.6	17.9	11.2
Italy	1994	...	38.8	...	...	66.2	70.0	72.0	15.9	20.0	18.6	17.9	10.0	9.3
Japan	1995	...	89.7	2.2	40.0	56.0	55.5	55.0	19.8	18.5	20.0	24.2	26.0	24.9
Norway	1994	...	40.9	1.5	26.8	64.7	65.4	64.2	22.4	24.0	23.4	13.0	10.7	12.4
South Africa	1994	...	...	...	6.1	66.7	64.7	...	27.4	22.9	...	5.9	12.4	...
Spain	1995	...	25.6	1.8	15.1	53.0	59.0	64.2	21.1	19.6	21.1	25.9	21.4	14.7
Sweden	1994	...	41.2	1.8	21.2	54.5	54.7	64.0	18.8	19.0	18.6	26.7	26.4	17.4
United Kingdom	1995	...	32.5	0.5	20.5	52.1	53.2	64.0	23.5	24.0	22.7	24.4	22.8	13.3
United States of America	1995	...	47.2	0.0	21.9	48.0	49.0	51.5	25.6	24.6	22.5	26.3	26.4	26.0
Countries of eastern Europe and the former USSR														
Azerbaijan	1994	...	...	...	...	...	...	...	...	12.7	24.4	...	...	...
Bulgaria	1996	...	...	...	0.8	...	...	...	9.5	13.9	13.2	...	...	...
Latvia	1996	...	4.0	...	...	...	...	50.8	...	...	...	...	...	...
Lithuania	1994	...	...	...	1.0	...	...	...	...	...	21.2	...	...	...
Republic of Moldova	1995	...	...	...	0.5	...	...	...	...	15.5	11.8	...	...	...
Romania	1994	...	...	...	0.8	...	63.8	...	...	36.0	...	...	0.2	...
Russian Federation	1995	...	2.2	...	0.9	...	...	63.2	...	...	14.5	...	...	22.4
Ukraine	1996	...	...	...	0.4	...	...	...	...	20.0	19.4	...	...	...
Developing countries														
Bolivia	1995	...	2.6	...	1.0	...	66.9	66.4	...	12.6	12.6	...	20.6	21.1
Brazil	1994	...	21.0	...	4.2	60.0	35.1	38.9	20.0	14.0	12.3	20.0	50.9	48.9
Cameroon	1996	...	3.4	...	2.8	...	65.0	65.1	...	18.4	28.7	...	16.6	6.2
Chile	1995	...	18.0	7.7	6.5	50.0	50.1	54.5	13.5	14.5	16.5	36.5	35.4	29.0
China	1996	...	...	...	...	66.0	73.3	71.7	1.5	...	...	32.5	...	...
China (Hong Kong SAR)	1995	...	21.2	2.4	14.2	67.1	61.1	64.6	23.8	25.6	23.7	9.1	13.3	11.7
China (Taiwan Province)	1996	2.7	25.3	4.9	12.6	41.0	34.9	70.5	36.3	25.6	14.7	22.7	39.5	14.8
Colombia	1995	0.6	7.8	0.9	2.7	50.7	54.8	49.2	18.1	14.6	17.3	31.2	30.7	33.4
Costa Rica	1996	...	...	...	...	68.1	68.7	69.6	...	...	...	...	...	...
Croatia	1996	...	...	...	3.1	...	53.9	...	...	22.3	...	...	23.8	...
Cyprus	1996	...	23.3	3.1	12.1	55.0	54.4	53.5	20.9	24.7	24.1	24.1	20.9	22.4
Ecuador	1996	...	5.7	...	2.1	48.8	67.1	67.1	21.5	22.7	11.8	29.8	10.2	21.1

a/ At current prices.

b/ Excluding countries of eastern Europe and the former USSR.

TABLE 1.11
(continued)

SELECTED CHARACTERISTICS OF BRANCHES, SELECTED YEARS AND COUNTRIES

Furniture, fixtures excl. metallic (332)

Country or area	Latest year	Value added per employee		Wages per employee		Percentage in output a/								
		Real annual growth rate (percentage)	Value (current 1000 dollars)	Real annual growth rate (percentage)	Value (current 1000 dollars)	Costs of input materials and utilities			Costs of labour			Operating surplus		
	(LY)	1985-LY	LY	1985-LY	LY	1985	1990	LY	1985	1990	LY	1985	1990	LY
Egypt	1994	...	2.1	...	1.4	64.2	79.7	78.5	17.9	15.0	13.9	17.9	5.2	7.6
El Salvador	1996	...	6.3	...	2.3	44.4	...	55.8	13.0	...	16.4	42.5	...	27.8
Ethiopia	1996	...	2.3	...	0.7	...	43.8	49.6	...	25.7	15.3	...	30.5	35.2
Gabon	1995	...	12.6	...	10.6	...	...	65.5	...	...	29.2	...	...	5.3
Honduras	1995	...	1.1	...	0.6	60.2	66.7	68.0	29.2	15.7	18.3	10.6	17.6	13.7
India	1994	...	0.9	2.2	0.8	78.8	73.9	83.5	19.4	18.9	15.4	1.8	7.2	1.0
Indonesia	1996	...	2.7	1.8	1.0	60.8	62.7	61.3	19.6	13.0	14.3	19.6	24.3	24.4
Jamaica	1996	...	9.4	...	...	...	66.9	...	16.1	16.3	...	...	16.8	...
Jordan	1995	...	5.0	...	2.2	69.7	63.0	65.3	19.5	11.9	15.3	10.8	25.1	19.4
Kenya	1995	-3.7	1.6	...	1.2	68.3	70.0	55.3	14.4	14.7	32.1	17.3	15.4	12.6
Kuwait	1995	...	14.5	...	6.2	55.1	46.5	49.6	25.1	27.8	21.7	19.8	25.7	28.7
Macau	1996	...	11.3	...	6.6	54.4	52.3	50.1	33.7	30.5	29.1	11.9	17.1	20.8
Malaysia	1995	...	8.4	1.2	3.6	61.2	64.8	67.1	20.7	15.8	14.1	18.0	19.4	18.7
Malta	1994	...	17.0	2.6	9.0	46.8	41.6	50.5	36.7	24.6	26.1	16.5	33.8	23.4
Mauritius	1994	...	5.3	7.7	3.8	69.3	73.6	60.6	19.6	20.0	28.1	11.1	6.5	11.3
Mexico	1994	...	13.5	1.4	5.4	61.2	61.3	60.8	12.2	13.8	15.5	26.6	24.9	23.7
Morocco	1996	...	7.3	...	5.4	...	...	63.4	...	...	27.0	...	...	9.5
Namibia	1994	...	6.6	...	2.9	...	...	36.2	...	...	27.9	...	...	35.9
Nepal	1996	...	1.0	...	0.4	...	58.5	57.0	...	10.5	19.1	...	31.1	23.9
Peru	1994	...	7.4	...	1.9	60.3	61.1	69.4	13.9	14.8	7.9	25.9	24.2	22.6
Philippines	1995	...	3.7	3.0	1.8	64.7	51.9	61.1	23.5	24.8	18.3	11.8	23.2	20.6
Qatar	1994	...	7.7	...	4.3	...	33.3	54.3	...	34.2	25.3	...	32.5	20.3
Republic of Korea	1995	-3.3	45.4	9.1	15.0	59.0	52.2	50.1	17.5	17.2	16.5	23.6	30.7	33.4
Senegal	1996	...	2.5	...	1.4	...	75.6	83.0	...	15.0	9.5	...	9.4	7.5
Singapore	1996	...	29.4	5.6	16.6	63.1	68.6	64.9	20.4	19.2	19.8	16.5	12.1	15.3
Slovenia	1995	...	...	...	...	...	...	73.2	...	...	...	...	...	...
Swaziland	1995	...	4.4	...	2.2	...	...	75.0	...	...	12.5	...	...	12.5
The f.Yugosl.Rep.of Macedonia	1996	...	2.7	...	2.4	...	58.7	70.2	...	21.7	26.3	...	19.5	3.5
Thailand	1994	...	5.7	...	2.1	...	67.6	57.5	...	11.3	15.6	...	21.1	26.9
Trinidad and Tobago	1995	...	5.9	...	3.5	69.2	...	70.0	20.2	18.5	17.8	10.6	...	12.2
Turkey	1994	-6.9	16.2	...	2.7	44.3	58.0	53.8	6.1	8.8	7.6	49.6	33.3	38.5
Uruguay	1995	...	12.1	...	3.5	52.2	51.5	50.5	20.3	15.3	14.5	27.5	33.2	35.0
Venezuela	1996	...	6.5	...	2.0	55.9	60.7	55.2	21.5	17.0	13.7	22.5	22.3	31.0
Yugoslavia	1996	...	4.1	...	1.1	...	55.9	59.2	...	...	11.4	...	...	29.3
Zambia	1994	...	1.9	...	0.8	...	41.2	64.0	...	7.1	15.7	...	51.7	20.3
Zimbabwe	1995	...	5.0	...	1.7	50.5	50.3	49.5	25.1	17.2	17.3	24.4	32.5	33.2

a/ At current prices.

TABLE 1.11

SELECTED CHARACTERISTICS OF BRANCHES, SELECTED YEARS AND COUNTRIES

Paper (341)

Country or area	Latest year	Value added per employee		Wages per employee		Percentage in output a/								
		Real annual growth rate (percentage)	Value (current 1000 dollars)	Real annual growth rate (percentage)	Value (current 1000 dollars)	Costs of input materials and utilities			Costs of labour			Operating surplus		
	(LY)	1985-LY	LY	1985-LY	LY	1985	1990	LY	1985	1990	LY	1985	1990	LY
Industrialized countries b/														
Austria	1994	5.8	73.8	1.7	36.4	72.3	68.1	68.1	14.5	14.8	15.7	13.2	17.2	16.1
Belgium	1994	...	...	...	...	73.2	73.8	73.9	11.8	10.7	12.2	15.1	15.5	13.9
Canada	1994	2.9	79.9	0.7	34.6	60.0	58.3	59.5	20.1	18.9	17.5	20.0	22.7	22.9
Finland	1995	4.9	162.6	3.1	39.6	70.6	69.0	63.7	10.1	13.3	8.8	19.3	17.6	27.4
France	1995	3.8	77.1	...	...	67.9	65.9	68.3	20.9	19.0	...	11.2	15.1	...
Germany	1994	...	...	...	33.4	...	...	...	...	...	19.0	...	...	...
Iceland	1995	...	48.8	1.8	32.2	64.0	61.5	64.2	25.8	27.1	23.7	10.1	11.4	12.1
Israel	1994	...	34.7	...	21.4	71.0	65.1	66.8	18.8	18.8	20.5	10.2	16.2	12.7
Italy	1994	...	61.0	...	...	71.8	70.0	70.5	11.0	17.6	16.4	17.3	12.4	13.1
Japan	1995	2.4	144.0	1.2	46.6	66.4	61.0	57.1	12.0	12.2	13.9	21.6	26.8	29.0
Norway	1994	5.2	63.1	2.3	33.2	74.1	73.5	73.1	13.2	11.9	14.1	12.7	14.7	12.7
South Africa	1994	-1.4	...	1.2	10.9	67.0	63.9	...	13.8	13.5	...	19.2	22.6	...
Spain	1995	1.6	66.2	2.1	24.2	68.4	69.6	70.3	10.8	12.6	10.9	20.8	17.7	18.8
Sweden	1994	4.9	81.0	1.4	26.6	62.5	61.5	67.0	11.8	11.8	10.8	25.7	26.7	22.2
Switzerland	1996	...	78.6	...	...	...	65.2	62.5	...	...	...	...	...	...
United Kingdom	1995	4.7	56.6	1.8	26.3	59.1	56.9	66.7	18.8	18.8	15.5	22.1	24.3	17.8
United States of America	1995	3.1	130.1	-0.0	35.9	56.8	54.6	53.7	16.4	14.4	12.8	26.8	31.1	33.5
Countries of eastern Europe and the former USSR														
Azerbaijan	1994	...	...	...	...	...	...	...	...	9.8	30.4	...	...	...
Bulgaria	1996	...	1.4	...	0.9	...	...	87.4	7.1	8.6	8.6	...	...	4.0
Kyrgyzstan	1994	...	...	...	...	...	...	...	...	1.3	4.9	...	...	...
Latvia	1996	...	5.1	...	...	...	...	64.2	...	...	...	...	...	...
Lithuania	1994	...	...	...	1.2	...	...	...	...	...	17.2	...	...	...
Republic of Moldova	1995	...	...	...	0.6	...	...	...	...	12.7	6.8	...	...	...
Romania	1994	...	...	...	0.9	...	71.9	...	...	12.7	...	...	15.4	...
Russian Federation	1995	...	10.7	...	2.0	...	...	60.0	...	...	7.6	...	...	32.4
Slovakia	1994	...	8.8	...	2.3	...	...	69.2	...	...	8.0	...	...	22.8
Ukraine	1996	...	...	...	1.0	...	...	...	...	9.6	9.6	...	...	...
Developing countries														
Bolivia	1995	...	7.1	...	1.6	...	79.6	68.2	...	5.7	7.1	...	14.7	24.7
Brazil	1994	4.4	45.2	...	9.3	54.5	46.4	43.7	9.1	11.4	11.6	36.4	42.2	44.7
Cameroon	1996	...	11.2	...	5.2	...	73.5	82.0	...	11.3	8.4	...	15.2	9.6
Chile	1995	...	130.5	3.0	12.6	49.1	50.2	44.3	5.3	5.0	5.4	45.6	44.7	50.3
China	1996	...	...	...	...	69.3	76.0	72.9	4.2	...	...	26.4	...	...
China (Hong Kong SAR)	1995	17.0	31.9	4.4	17.2	75.4	74.8	75.3	15.3	13.7	13.3	9.3	11.4	11.4
China (Taiwan Province)	1996	4.2	23.9	4.8	14.8	56.7	70.8	74.2	16.8	13.3	16.0	26.5	15.9	9.8
Colombia	1995	3.8	45.7	1.3	6.3	63.2	64.2	56.9	5.5	4.6	6.0	31.4	31.2	37.1
Costa Rica	1996	...	...	...	...	72.5	75.0	75.8	...	...	...	...	...	...

a/ At current prices.

b/ Excluding countries of eastern Europe and the former USSR.

TABLE 1.11
(continued)

SELECTED CHARACTERISTICS OF BRANCHES, SELECTED YEARS AND COUNTRIES

Paper (341)

Country or area	Latest year	Value added per employee		Wages per employee		Percentage in output a/								
		Real annual growth rate (percentage)	Value (current 1000 dollars)	Real annual growth rate (percentage)	Value (current 1000 dollars)	Costs of input materials and utilities			Costs of labour			Operating surplus		
	(LY)	1985-LY	LY	1985-LY	LY	1985	1990	LY	1985	1990	LY	1985	1990	LY
Croatia	1996	...	...	...	4.3	...	55.3	...	...	11.1	...	...	33.7	...
Cyprus	1996	2.0	31.3	2.8	14.1	71.1	73.5	68.0	12.2	11.8	14.5	16.7	14.7	17.5
Ecuador	1996	...	15.5	...	3.1	78.2	84.9	81.0	8.5	5.4	3.9	13.2	9.7	15.2
Egypt	1994	...	5.5	...	1.7	69.8	77.6	72.5	19.0	9.6	8.6	11.2	12.8	18.9
El Salvador	1996	...	25.8	...	3.6	47.6	...	34.4	11.6	...	9.2	40.8	...	56.4
Ethiopia	1996	...	5.7	...	1.0	...	83.2	62.4	...	12.6	6.3	...	4.1	31.3
Gabon	1995	...	6.5	...	3.5	...	...	75.8	...	...	13.0	...	...	11.2
Honduras	1995	...	5.2	...	2.9	82.7	80.9	82.4	10.2	8.1	9.8	7.0	11.0	7.9
India	1994	...	3.6	1.8	1.2	85.9	80.2	79.5	8.7	6.8	6.7	5.5	13.0	13.8
Indonesia	1996	...	14.2	5.4	2.3	70.5	64.6	66.7	6.5	3.1	5.3	23.0	32.3	28.0
Jordan	1995	...	10.1	...	3.4	77.2	69.6	77.8	13.5	7.3	7.4	9.3	23.1	14.8
Kenya	1995	-4.3	4.3	...	1.6	79.4	73.9	81.3	7.2	8.0	6.8	13.3	18.1	12.0
Kuwait	1995	...	30.7	...	8.7	64.1	50.7	64.6	17.5	6.7	10.0	18.4	42.6	25.4
Macau	1996	...	10.1	...	5.7	73.7	69.5	74.2	15.3	17.9	14.4	11.1	12.6	11.3
Malaysia	1995	...	18.7	3.8	5.2	65.5	67.9	68.0	11.6	9.3	8.8	22.9	22.8	23.1
Malta	1994	14.3	23.2	2.6	10.2	62.0	63.1	55.7	17.3	16.3	19.4	20.7	20.6	24.9
Mauritius	1994	...	9.4	3.0	2.1	65.6	61.5	59.7	14.4	10.1	9.0	19.9	28.4	31.3
Mexico	1994	...	30.0	0.9	7.9	68.1	68.8	71.5	7.3	7.4	7.5	24.6	23.8	21.0
Morocco	1996	...	14.3	...	4.9	...	...	73.7	...	...	9.0	...	...	17.3
Nepal	1996	...	2.0	...	0.4	...	64.8	64.8	...	8.1	7.3	...	27.1	27.9
Peru	1994	0.1	16.3	...	4.6	68.0	55.2	74.8	5.6	8.7	7.2	26.4	36.1	18.0
Philippines	1995	...	16.5	3.6	3.4	66.6	64.4	65.3	4.9	6.7	7.1	28.5	28.9	27.6
Qatar	1994	...	9.0	...	4.2	...	50.0	50.0	...	46.1	23.0	...	3.9	26.9
Republic of Korea	1995	7.4	72.9	9.0	17.4	69.5	66.1	62.0	8.3	9.3	9.1	22.2	24.7	28.9
Senegal	1996	...	2.8	...	1.3	...	73.1	87.0	...	10.0	6.1	...	16.9	6.9
Singapore	1996	0.7	61.1	4.5	22.2	53.5	58.0	53.8	13.8	12.1	16.8	32.7	29.9	29.4
Slovenia	1995	...	...	...	...	...	...	71.2	...	...	...	...	...	...
St. Vincent and the Grenadines	1994	...	...	...	5.5	...	...	...	...	...	...	...	...	...
Swaziland	1995	...	16.8	...	6.3	...	...	49.1	...	...	19.1	...	...	31.8
The f.Yugosl.Rep.of Macedonia	1996	...	4.3	...	3.5	...	68.0	70.1	...	21.1	24.3	...	10.8	5.6
Thailand	1994	...	34.7	...	5.0	...	76.9	66.8	...	3.7	4.8	...	19.4	28.4
Trinidad and Tobago	1995	...	17.7	...	3.8	62.3	68.4	65.6	27.4	16.0	7.4	10.3	15.6	27.0
Turkey	1994	8.5	30.7	...	6.6	64.9	58.6	58.9	8.7	12.5	8.8	26.4	28.9	32.3
Uruguay	1995	...	34.3	...	10.4	50.2	59.7	56.1	10.5	10.4	13.3	39.4	29.8	30.6
Venezuela	1996	...	21.7	...	3.6	59.8	62.5	62.3	12.1	9.7	6.3	28.0	27.8	31.4
Yugoslavia	1996	...	6.4	...	1.4	...	65.9	68.2	...	...	6.9	...	...	24.9
Zambia	1994	...	3.4	...	1.3	...	57.9	47.3	...	13.3	20.8	...	28.8	31.9
Zimbabwe	1995	...	8.2	...	3.5	57.7	58.6	68.9	21.9	15.9	13.0	20.4	25.5	18.0

a/ At current prices.

TABLE 1.11

SELECTED CHARACTERISTICS OF BRANCHES, SELECTED YEARS AND COUNTRIES

Printing and publishing (342)

Country or area	Latest year	Value added per employee		Wages per employee		Percentage in output a/								
		Real annual growth rate (percentage)	Value (current 1000 dollars)	Real annual growth rate (percentage)	Value (current 1000 dollars)	Costs of input materials and utilities			Costs of labour			Operating surplus		
	(LY)	1985-LY	LY	1985-LY	LY	1985	1990	LY	1985	1990	LY	1985	1990	LY
Industrialized countries b/														
Austria	1994	5.9	58.6	3.5	38.8	52.8	58.9	58.9	29.3	26.9	27.3	17.8	14.2	13.9
Belgium	1994	...	...	...	...	58.7	58.4	58.4	24.9	21.0	19.6	16.3	20.6	22.0
Canada	1994	-2.4	53.3	0.4	26.6	38.5	37.8	37.1	30.1	32.6	31.4	31.4	29.7	31.4
Finland	1995	3.6	60.7	1.7	31.8	41.9	55.6	58.5	24.6	24.9	21.7	33.5	19.5	19.8
France	1995	1.6	76.0	...	...	58.9	58.5	56.6	30.8	28.5	...	10.3	13.0	...
Germany	1994	...	...	...	37.8	...	...	...	...	...	31.1	...	...	...
Iceland	1995	...	48.3	4.6	36.4	49.5	46.3	48.6	33.3	36.6	38.7	17.2	17.1	12.7
Israel	1994	...	30.1	...	20.5	49.9	48.8	52.7	29.0	31.3	32.2	21.1	20.0	15.1
Italy	1994	...	59.4	...	...	59.3	54.3	60.6	18.9	29.2	28.8	21.8	16.6	10.6
Japan	1995	2.2	139.8	1.4	55.5	47.2	47.4	45.4	22.3	20.3	21.7	30.5	32.3	32.9
Norway	1994	1.4	43.8	1.2	28.7	55.8	56.7	54.2	27.9	28.2	30.0	16.2	15.1	15.8
South Africa	1994	-2.1	...	0.1	11.9	45.5	50.1	...	38.2	34.1	...	16.3	15.8	...
Spain	1995	...	47.1	2.0	23.3	46.7	54.5	61.9	20.8	18.2	18.8	32.5	27.3	19.2
Sweden	1994	-1.6	46.0	0.2	25.0	34.7	36.8	63.1	25.0	23.7	20.1	40.3	39.6	16.8
Switzerland	1996	...	73.1	...	...	...	51.5	50.6	...	...	...	...	...	...
United Kingdom	1995	3.2	52.3	0.2	26.8	38.2	38.4	54.2	28.3	25.9	23.5	33.5	35.7	22.4
United States of America	1995	-0.2	82.1	-0.0	29.2	34.9	34.3	33.1	25.1	24.7	23.7	40.0	41.0	43.1
Countries of eastern Europe and the former USSR														
Albania	1996	...	...	...	...	...	...	...	...	...	31.1	...	...	...
Azerbaijan	1994	...	...	...	...	...	...	...	...	39.0	28.4	...	...	...
Bulgaria	1996	...	6.3	...	1.6	...	...	69.3	12.2	11.6	7.6	...	...	23.1
Latvia	1996	...	8.1	...	...	...	...	44.8	...	...	...	...	...	...
Lithuania	1994	...	...	...	1.8	...	...	...	...	...	26.0	...	...	...
Republic of Moldova	1995	...	...	...	0.8	...	...	...	...	28.5	17.5	...	...	...
Romania	1994	...	...	...	1.1	...	52.9	...	...	15.2	...	...	31.8	...
Russian Federation	1995	...	3.5	...	1.3	...	...	42.5	...	...	20.6	...	...	36.8
Slovakia	1994	...	8.2	...	3.0	...	...	59.0	...	...	14.9	...	...	26.0
Ukraine	1996	...	...	...	1.2	...	...	...	...	...	26.8	...	...	...
Developing countries														
Bolivia	1995	...	7.5	...	2.1	...	68.3	66.2	...	10.3	9.4	...	21.5	24.4
Brazil	1994	7.8	38.4	...	9.8	40.0	23.5	25.0	20.0	22.5	19.0	40.0	53.9	55.9
Chile	1995	...	52.8	5.5	14.0	43.3	43.7	34.7	15.0	14.3	17.3	41.6	42.0	48.0
China	1996	...	...	...	...	65.4	71.4	68.0	6.3	...	...	28.3	...	...
China (Hong Kong SAR)	1995	9.1	31.4	4.9	21.4	59.4	57.7	62.6	21.6	19.7	25.5	18.9	22.5	11.9
Colombia	1995	-2.3	19.1	2.9	4.7	51.8	54.5	47.5	12.0	10.1	13.0	36.2	35.4	39.5
Costa Rica	1996	...	...	...	...	65.0	65.7	66.7	...	...	...	...	...	...
Croatia	1996	...	...	...	5.1	...	46.0	...	...	13.6	...	...	40.5	...
Cyprus	1996	...	28.7	2.3	15.9	55.8	57.7	53.5	23.7	23.2	25.7	20.5	19.1	20.7

a/ At current prices.

b/ Excluding countries of eastern Europe and the former USSR.

TABLE 1.11
(continued)

SELECTED CHARACTERISTICS OF BRANCHES, SELECTED YEARS AND COUNTRIES

Printing and publishing (342)

Country or area	Latest year	Value added per employee		Wages per employee		Percentage in output a/								
		Real annual growth rate (percentage)	Value (current 1000 dollars)	Real annual growth rate (percentage)	Value (current 1000 dollars)	Costs of input materials and utilities			Costs of labour			Operating surplus		
	(LY)	1985-LY	LY	1985-LY	LY	1985	1990	LY	1985	1990	LY	1985	1990	LY
Ecuador	1996	...	10.6	...	3.1	59.0	69.2	69.1	24.4	13.9	9.1	16.6	16.9	21.8
Egypt	1994	...	7.5	...	4.1	59.1	70.8	75.0	19.8	14.5	13.5	21.1	14.7	11.5
El Salvador	1996	...	13.5	...	3.5	49.2	...	42.2	13.0	...	14.9	37.9	...	42.9
Ethiopia	1996	...	3.6	...	1.0	...	38.3	41.3	...	19.2	16.4	...	42.4	42.3
Gabon	1995	...	24.8	...	14.4	...	...	58.3	...	...	24.3	...	...	17.5
Honduras	1995	...	3.5	...	2.9	52.8	62.0	67.6	29.4	27.5	26.7	17.8	10.5	5.7
India	1994	...	3.2	5.5	1.7	70.4	74.2	69.7	19.5	17.1	16.6	10.1	8.7	13.7
Indonesia	1996	2.0	10.2	3.4	2.1	61.7	69.7	52.7	19.2	8.9	10.0	19.2	21.4	37.4
Jordan	1995	...	11.3	...	4.0	61.5	62.5	55.0	27.6	17.8	16.0	10.9	19.6	29.0
Kenya	1995	0.8	3.1	...	1.7	71.4	64.4	58.9	14.9	17.8	22.8	13.7	17.8	18.3
Malaysia	1995	...	19.0	1.5	6.5	48.0	52.0	52.0	22.6	17.5	16.3	29.4	30.4	31.6
Malta	1994	6.5	30.9	2.6	12.0	46.3	45.8	47.4	25.8	24.3	20.5	27.9	29.9	32.1
Mauritius	1994	...	12.3	7.4	5.7	57.8	53.6	48.5	24.2	20.9	24.0	18.0	25.5	27.4
Mexico	1994	...	19.1	1.5	8.6	55.7	55.9	53.8	15.2	14.2	20.8	29.1	29.9	25.4
Mongolia	1995	...	0.7	...	0.5	...	43.5	71.8	...	12.8	20.5	...	43.7	7.7
Morocco	1996	...	8.7	...	5.0	...	...	65.3	...	...	19.7	...	...	15.0
Namibia	1994	...	12.5	...	7.4	...	...	54.7	...	...	26.6	...	...	18.7
Peru	1994	5.7	20.4	...	5.5	61.9	55.2	56.5	9.8	13.1	11.8	28.3	31.7	31.7
Philippines	1995	...	9.2	4.5	3.1	64.9	58.6	58.7	12.8	16.4	14.0	22.3	25.0	27.2
Qatar	1994	...	20.8	...	8.3	...	37.0	31.9	...	26.1	27.2	...	37.0	40.9
Republic of Korea	1995	4.2	59.4	7.3	18.0	45.8	40.2	39.9	18.2	19.0	18.3	36.0	40.8	41.9
Senegal	1996	...	12.6	...	4.9	...	68.2	66.8	...	15.7	12.9	...	16.1	20.3
Singapore	1996	4.0	60.8	5.3	25.2	45.9	46.5	40.7	23.4	21.7	24.6	30.7	31.8	34.7
Slovenia	1995	...	...	...	...	...	...	58.5	...	...	...	...	...	...
Swaziland	1995	...	7.3	...	6.2	...	...	81.9	...	...	15.5	...	...	2.6
The f.Yugosl.Rep.of Macedonia	1996	...	6.1	...	4.4	...	46.0	60.5	...	25.9	28.8	...	28.1	10.7
Thailand	1994	...	...	...	5.7	...	48.1	21.4	...	17.2	7.5	...	34.7	71.1
Trinidad and Tobago	1995	...	11.3	...	4.7	49.9	55.4	57.5	34.1	29.0	17.7	16.0	15.7	24.9
Turkey	1994	-5.4	43.3	...	4.9	54.7	49.2	54.1	12.0	11.6	5.2	33.3	39.1	40.8
Uruguay	1995	...	26.4	...	7.8	53.1	48.9	37.7	20.3	14.4	18.4	26.6	36.7	43.9
Venezuela	1996	...	15.7	...	3.3	53.5	62.9	49.6	22.9	15.1	10.5	23.5	21.9	39.9
Yugoslavia	1996	...	8.7	...	2.0	...	42.5	54.3	...	...	10.4	...	...	35.3
Zambia	1994	...	3.4	...	1.2	...	37.7	64.9	...	6.0	12.5	...	56.3	22.5
Zimbabwe	1995		10.0	...	4.7	33.6	35.3	46.3	31.8	27.5	25.2	34.6	37.1	28.4

a/ At current prices.

TABLE 1.11

SELECTED CHARACTERISTICS OF BRANCHES, SELECTED YEARS AND COUNTRIES

Industrial chemicals (351)

Country or area	Latest year	Value added per employee		Wages per employee		Percentage in output a/								
		Real annual growth rate (percentage)	Value (current 1000 dollars)	Real annual growth rate (percentage)	Value (current 1000 dollars)	Costs of input materials and utilities			Costs of labour			Operating surplus		
	(LY)	1985-LY	LY	1985-LY	LY	1985	1990	LY	1985	1990	LY	1985	1990	LY
Industrialized countries b/														
Austria	1994	...	72.4	1.8	38.3	76.0	72.4	69.9	13.1	13.9	15.9	10.9	13.7	14.2
Belgium	1994	...	...	...	...	71.1	67.0	68.7	...	...	...	...	...	...
Canada	1994	...	173.4	0.4	38.9	70.9	62.4	60.6	9.8	10.4	8.8	19.3	27.2	30.5
Finland	1994	...	90.8	2.4	28.0	68.5	61.2	62.7	10.8	12.7	11.5	20.8	26.1	25.8
France	1995	...	102.0	...	...	73.1	64.2	68.5	16.1	17.4	...	10.9	18.4	...
Germany	1994	...	...	...	45.2	...	...	...	...	...	...	...	...	...
Iceland	1995	...	47.7	2.1	35.1	73.4	59.0	72.9	19.1	21.5	19.9	7.5	19.5	7.1
Israel	1994	...	77.0	...	41.5	64.2	67.1	66.4	12.5	17.8	18.1	23.3	15.1	15.5
Italy	1994	...	73.6	...	...	75.4	73.0	72.5	10.1	16.8	15.2	14.6	10.2	12.3
Japan	1995	...	366.2	1.6	67.3	66.1	54.5	49.1	7.6	8.3	9.3	26.3	37.2	41.5
Norway	1994	...	99.1	3.2	42.2	71.5	67.9	69.2	10.6	12.0	13.1	17.9	20.1	17.7
Spain	1995	...	97.5	3.1	32.4	73.6	70.5	71.1	6.7	9.5	9.6	19.7	20.0	19.3
Sweden	1994	...	88.5	1.8	28.0	63.2	54.9	65.4	10.1	11.6	11.0	26.7	33.5	23.7
United Kingdom	1995	5.6	111.2	0.2	28.5	67.5	61.0	65.1	9.5	11.9	8.9	23.0	27.1	26.0
United States of America	1995	...	246.0	0.4	45.5	60.5	53.8	52.6	11.2	9.6	8.8	28.2	36.6	38.7
Countries of eastern Europe and the former USSR														
Albania	1996	...	...	...	...	...	...	...	...	...	5.4	...	...	...
Azerbaijan	1994	...	...	...	...	...	...	...	...	8.7	6.2	...	...	...
Bulgaria	1996	...	...	...	2.0	...	...	...	7.0	10.9	7.1	...	...	...
Latvia	1996	...	4.9	...	...	...	...	71.4	...	...	...	...	...	...
Lithuania	1994	...	...	...	1.4	...	...	...	...	...	6.6	...	...	...
Republic of Moldova	1995	...	...	...	0.5	...	...	...	...	10.7	13.7	...	...	...
Russian Federation	1995	...	6.2	...	1.4	...	...	69.1	...	...	7.0	...	...	23.9
Slovakia	1994	...	8.4	...	2.6	...	...	73.0	...	...	8.4	...	...	18.6
Ukraine	1996	...	...	...	1.0	...	...	...	...	10.4	9.7	...	...	...
Developing countries														
Bolivia	1995	...	9.2	...	2.5	...	57.2	62.2	...	11.7	10.4	...	31.1	27.4
Chile	1995	...	100.4	4.0	15.1	51.3	46.7	53.7	7.0	6.6	6.9	41.7	46.7	39.3
China (Taiwan Province)	1996	7.9	93.4	5.9	22.2	72.4	72.8	70.9	5.9	7.4	6.9	21.7	19.8	22.2
Colombia	1995	4.5	61.9	1.2	7.4	63.8	67.2	59.2	6.2	4.3	4.9	30.0	28.5	35.9
Costa Rica	1996	...	...	...	...	75.3	75.8	76.4	...	...	...	...	...	...
Croatia	1996	...	...	...	5.5	...	81.6	...	...	13.1	...	...	5.3	...
Cyprus	1996	...	44.5	1.6	16.3	69.0	64.9	70.7	23.4	11.5	10.8	7.6	23.6	18.6
Ecuador	1996	...	39.2	...	4.6	70.9	73.3	63.9	9.6	11.6	4.2	19.5	15.1	31.9
Egypt	1994	...	7.0	...	2.5	63.7	69.5	59.4	22.6	13.2	14.7	13.7	17.3	25.9
El Salvador	1996	...	27.3	...	8.5	51.8	...	64.8	5.9	...	11.0	42.3	...	24.2
Ethiopia	1995	...	3.6	...	1.0	...	32.8	30.3	...	21.9	20.5	...	45.3	49.2
Gabon	1995	...	21.0	...	11.6	...	...	63.6	...	...	20.1	...	...	16.3

a/ At current prices.

b/ Excluding countries of eastern Europe and the former USSR.

TABLE 1.11
(continued)

SELECTED CHARACTERISTICS OF BRANCHES, SELECTED YEARS AND COUNTRIES

Industrial chemicals (351)

Country or area	Latest year	Value added per employee		Wages per employee		Percentage in output a/								
		Real annual growth rate (percentage)	Value (current 1000 dollars)	Real annual growth rate (percentage)	Value (current 1000 dollars)	Costs of input materials and utilities			Costs of labour			Operating surplus		
	(LY)	1985-LY	LY	1985-LY	LY	1985	1990	LY	1985	1990	LY	1985	1990	LY
Honduras	1995	...	4.5	...	1.4	60.2	62.9	69.9	18.3	10.2	9.7	21.4	26.9	20.4
India	1994	...	11.2	2.2	2.2	82.2	83.2	76.1	6.3	5.2	4.7	11.5	11.6	19.2
Indonesia	1996	...	32.0	1.0	3.9	65.4	69.9	60.1	8.3	3.7	4.9	26.4	26.3	35.1
Jordan	1995	...	28.3	...	5.3	82.4	77.4	85.6	10.1	3.9	2.7	7.5	18.7	11.7
Kenya	1995	0.9	4.3	...	2.0	85.6	89.5	91.1	7.0	4.1	4.1	7.4	6.4	4.8
Kuwait	1995	...	114.0	...	32.7	43.7	53.2	21.3	51.7	36.9	22.6	4.6	9.9	56.1
Malawi	1994	...	8.7	...	1.1	62.5	78.0	61.1	3.7	5.6	5.0	33.8	16.4	33.9
Malaysia	1995	...	...	1.6	11.0	55.5	58.4	68.1	3.2	3.9	3.3	41.3	37.7	28.6
Malta	1994	...	26.2	3.1	10.2	24.2	43.9	52.1	18.4	23.5	18.5	57.4	32.7	29.3
Mauritius	1994	...	20.8	9.1	7.1	78.8	65.9	68.6	5.8	6.3	10.7	15.3	27.7	20.7
Mexico	1994	...	58.7	2.4	11.1	62.1	58.7	57.2	6.2	7.4	8.1	31.6	33.9	34.8
Morocco	1996	...	42.1	...	9.5	...	...	62.8	...	...	8.4	...	...	28.8
Peru	1994	3.0	23.9	...	6.9	58.4	51.6	66.2	6.2	9.7	9.7	35.4	38.7	24.1
Philippines	1995	...	31.8	4.6	4.9	74.4	63.4	65.1	4.1	5.2	5.4	21.5	31.4	29.5
Qatar	1994	...	...	...	...	...	23.0	34.4	...	16.3	13.4	...	60.7	52.2
Republic of Korea	1995	...	139.0	8.7	23.7	73.5	66.9	59.8	4.0	5.7	6.8	22.4	27.4	33.3
Senegal	1996	...	22.9	...	5.6	...	...	71.3	...	8.8	7.0	...	...	21.7
Singapore	1996	...	...	2.7	34.6	79.8	66.4	67.4	6.2	6.2	9.9	14.0	27.4	22.7
Slovenia	1995	...	...	...	...	...	...	66.4	...	...	...	...	...	...
Swaziland	1995	...	3.3	...	2.4	...	...	83.9	...	...	11.9	...	...	4.2
The f.Yugosl.Rep.of Macedonia	1996	...	6.0	...	4.4	...	66.3	71.4	...	18.7	20.8	...	15.0	7.8
Thailand	1994	...	32.4	...	6.0	...	62.0	71.6	...	6.6	5.3	...	31.3	23.2
Tunisia	1996	...	...	...	...	...	...	82.5	...	...	5.8	...	...	11.7
Turkey	1994	7.3	63.5	...	10.0	75.1	61.1	52.4	5.9	9.0	7.5	19.0	29.9	40.1
Uruguay	1995	...	57.9	...	16.0	63.7	63.4	54.3	8.1	5.5	12.6	28.2	31.2	33.1
Venezuela	1996	...	96.9	...	8.3	55.9	57.4	48.4	10.0	7.1	4.4	34.0	35.5	47.1
Yugoslavia	1996	...	4.0	...	2.2	...	76.6	...	...	...	...	...	...	...
Zambia	1994	...	8.5	...	3.8	...	89.3	47.0	...	4.1	23.4	...	6.7	29.6

a/ At current prices.

TABLE 1.11

SELECTED CHARACTERISTICS OF BRANCHES, SELECTED YEARS AND COUNTRIES

Other chemicals (352)														
Country or area	Latest year	Value added per employee		Wages per employee		Percentage in output a/								
		Real annual growth rate (percentage)	Value (current 1000 dollars)	Real annual growth rate (percentage)	Value (current 1000 dollars)	Costs of input materials and utilities			Costs of labour			Operating surplus		
	(LY)	1985-LY	LY	1985-LY	LY	1985	1990	LY	1985	1990	LY	1985	1990	LY
Industrialized countries b/														
Austria	1994	...	73.1	2.6	36.6	72.6	68.4	66.7	15.7	16.2	16.7	11.7	15.4	16.6
Belgium	1994	...	...	...	...	66.2	63.9	65.3	...	...	...	...	...	...
Canada	1994	...	92.8	1.1	30.0	49.9	46.3	49.1	16.5	17.2	16.4	33.6	36.5	34.4
Finland	1994	...	65.2	2.1	24.9	46.1	54.5	53.9	18.9	19.6	17.6	35.0	25.9	28.5
France	1995	...	94.2	...	...	66.4	64.3	64.5	23.4	21.6	...	10.2	14.1	...
Germany	1994	...	...	...	42.0	...	...	...	...	...	18.8	...	...	...
Iceland	1995	...	52.8	0.4	25.7	66.8	68.0	59.1	16.4	17.7	19.9	16.8	14.2	21.0
Italy	1994	...	80.7	...	...	75.0	68.7	63.9	9.6	17.6	20.3	15.4	13.7	15.8
Japan	1995	...	349.6	1.4	60.6	46.0	41.1	39.6	10.3	9.8	10.5	43.7	49.1	49.9
Norway	1994	...	83.2	3.4	39.0	67.2	61.7	64.0	17.1	16.7	16.9	15.7	21.5	19.1
Spain	1995	...	65.5	3.3	31.8	62.0	62.0	67.1	13.8	14.2	16.0	24.2	23.7	16.9
Sweden	1994	...	124.3	2.1	28.3	41.0	36.1	44.9	17.7	16.7	12.5	41.4	47.2	42.6
United Kingdom	1995	3.6	74.2	3.1	31.7	48.8	45.9	63.7	15.1	16.3	15.5	36.2	37.8	20.8
United States of America	1995	...	218.5	0.8	39.3	40.3	39.0	38.3	13.2	11.7	11.1	46.5	49.3	50.6
Countries of eastern Europe and the former USSR														
Albania	1996	...	...	...	...	...	...	...	...	...	7.1	...	...	...
Azerbaijan	1994	...	...	...	...	...	...	...	...	10.8	30.2	...	...	...
Bulgaria	1996	...	...	...	1.3	...	...	...	5.9	8.3	7.3	...	...	...
Kyrgyzstan	1994	...	...	...	...	...	...	...	...	3.2	8.8	...	...	...
Latvia	1996	...	8.7	...	...	...	...	52.6	...	...	...	...	...	...
Lithuania	1994	...	...	...	1.2	...	...	...	...	...	16.1	...	...	...
Republic of Moldova	1995	...	...	...	0.6	...	...	...	...	6.1	14.1	...	...	...
Russian Federation	1995	...	7.0	...	1.3	...	...	54.4	...	...	8.5	...	...	37.1
Slovakia	1994	...	12.8	...	3.0	...	...	64.2	...	...	8.4	...	...	27.5
Ukraine	1996	...	...	...	1.2	...	...	...	...	8.4	10.5	...	...	...
Developing countries														
Bolivia	1995	...	13.6	...	3.2	...	60.2	59.8	...	10.4	9.6	...	29.4	30.6
Cameroon	1996	...	13.8	...	4.9	...	...	70.1	...	...	10.6	...	...	19.3
Chile	1995	...	65.1	1.5	14.2	43.0	46.4	43.1	12.9	11.1	12.4	44.1	42.5	44.5
China (Taiwan Province)	1996	6.3	24.1	6.1	15.9	73.8	71.4	76.2	14.7	15.2	15.7	11.5	13.4	8.1
Colombia	1995	0.4	40.1	1.9	6.3	57.7	56.9	44.1	7.7	5.9	8.8	34.6	37.2	47.1
Costa Rica	1996	...	...	...	...	68.8	70.3	71.3	...	...	...	...	...	...
Croatia	1996	...	...	...	5.5	...	55.4	...	...	9.7	...	...	34.9	...
Cyprus	1996	...	28.4	3.7	13.9	71.5	72.9	70.1	12.9	11.7	14.7	15.6	15.4	15.3
Ecuador	1996	...	15.4	...	4.7	65.6	68.2	75.3	17.9	10.8	7.5	16.5	21.0	17.2
Egypt	1994	...	6.9	...	2.3	73.4	65.7	69.0	12.5	9.4	10.2	14.1	24.9	20.8
El Salvador	1996	...	30.0	...	5.2	42.3	...	44.8	9.0	...	9.5	48.6	...	45.7
Ethiopia	1996	...	7.3	...	0.9	...	64.5	65.4	...	8.9	4.1	...	26.7	30.5

a/ At current prices.

b/ Excluding countries of eastern Europe and the former USSR.

TABLE 1.11
(continued)

SELECTED CHARACTERISTICS OF BRANCHES, SELECTED YEARS AND COUNTRIES

Country or area	Latest year	Other chemicals (352)												
		Value added per employee		Wages per employee		Percentage in output a/								
		Real annual growth rate (percentage)	Value (current 1000 dollars)	Real annual growth rate (percentage)	Value (current 1000 dollars)	Costs of input materials and utilities			Costs of labour			Operating surplus		
	(LY)	1985-LY	LY	1985-LY	LY	1985	1990	LY	1985	1990	LY	1985	1990	LY
Gabon	1995	...	22.0	...	17.1	...	...	78.8	...	...	16.5	...	...	4.7
Honduras	1995	...	6.1	...	3.0	74.5	76.4	80.9	13.0	10.9	9.3	12.5	12.7	9.8
India	1994	...	5.3	1.3	1.4	81.5	79.5	76.4	7.4	6.7	6.1	11.1	13.8	17.5
Indonesia	1996	...	11.7	2.3	2.6	67.1	68.0	67.2	10.5	6.5	7.4	22.4	25.6	25.4
Jordan	1995	...	10.9	...	4.5	81.4	73.8	75.5	10.0	7.4	10.1	8.6	18.8	14.5
Kenya	1995	3.0	5.4	...	2.3	79.5	...	...	12.1	...	...	8.4	...	...
Kuwait	1995	...	34.3	...	10.0	65.0	58.3	61.4	13.9	12.7	11.3	21.2	29.0	27.3
Macau	1996	...	20.8	...	10.5	53.0	50.4	68.4	27.4	13.3	15.9	19.6	36.3	15.6
Malawi	1994	...	8.9	...	1.8	61.0	75.0	41.9	6.1	8.1	11.7	32.9	16.9	46.4
Malaysia	1995	...	28.9	1.8	6.7	59.5	65.1	64.6	11.0	8.6	8.2	29.5	26.3	27.2
Mauritius	1994	...	14.5	5.4	4.2	78.4	74.3	63.3	7.5	7.6	10.5	14.1	18.1	26.2
Mexico	1994	...	52.0	5.1	13.3	52.6	56.8	53.0	8.8	10.2	12.0	38.6	33.0	35.0
Mongolia	1995	...	2.3	...	1.0	...	58.5	59.8	...	7.1	18.0	...	34.4	22.2
Morocco	1996	...	12.1	...	5.9	...	...	68.6	...	...	15.3	...	...	16.1
Nepal	1996	...	4.7	...	0.6	...	66.3	64.5	...	7.1	4.3	...	26.6	31.1
Peru	1994	6.1	31.2	...	7.8	63.9	47.7	63.0	7.3	9.5	9.2	28.8	42.7	27.8
Philippines	1995	...	44.0	5.1	7.8	75.0	55.4	47.0	8.0	9.2	9.4	17.0	35.3	43.6
Qatar	1994	...	12.0	...	6.6	...	...	79.4	...	...	11.4	...	...	9.3
Republic of Korea	1995	...	99.5	6.9	18.1	52.3	47.7	47.2	9.1	8.6	9.6	38.5	43.6	43.2
Senegal	1996	...	14.7	...	3.2	...	69.5	66.4	...	10.2	7.2	...	20.4	26.4
Singapore	1996	...	...	5.2	35.4	45.1	38.6	47.0	10.0	8.8	9.3	44.9	52.6	43.7
Slovenia	1995	...	...	...	...	...	...	64.7	...	...	...	...	...	...
The f.Yugosl.Rep.of Macedonia	1996	...	10.1	...	8.1	...	39.9	62.7	...	27.8	30.0	...	32.3	7.3
Thailand	1994	...	21.5	...	5.1	...	61.2	64.6	...	7.0	8.3	...	31.7	27.1
Tonga	1994	...	...	...	4.5	...	...	...	3.7	4.0	2.0	...	...	...
Trinidad and Tobago	1995	...	9.1	...	4.8	76.3	59.8	78.6	22.8	16.4	11.4	0.9	23.7	10.1
Tunisia	1996	...	...	...	...	...	68.9	66.0	...	9.8	12.3	...	21.2	21.7
Turkey	1994	2.6	71.6	...	9.3	61.5	56.4	50.7	7.4	8.7	6.4	31.1	34.9	43.0
Uruguay	1995	...	63.5	...	14.6	50.4	53.5	44.8	12.6	12.0	12.7	37.0	34.5	42.5
Venezuela	1996	...	29.4	...	4.4	48.3	48.3	51.8	16.4	12.7	7.3	35.2	39.0	40.9
Yugoslavia	1996	...	22.9	...	2.6	...	57.1	47.4	...	...	5.9	...	...	46.8
Zambia	1994	...	12.8	...	1.9	...	58.0	50.7	...	5.0	7.5	...	37.0	41.9
Zimbabwe	1995	...	16.4	...	6.2	50.5	52.6	60.8	15.5	12.4	14.8	34.0	35.0	24.4

a/ At current prices.

TABLE 1.11

SELECTED CHARACTERISTICS OF BRANCHES, SELECTED YEARS AND COUNTRIES

Rubber products (355)

Country or area	Latest year	Value added per employee		Wages per employee		Percentage in output a/								
		Real annual growth rate (percentage)	Value (current 1000 dollars)	Real annual growth rate (percentage)	Value (current 1000 dollars)	Costs of input materials and utilities			Costs of labour			Operating surplus		
	(LY)	1985-LY	LY	1985-LY	LY	1985	1990	LY	1985	1990	LY	1985	1990	LY
Industrialized countries b/														
Austria	1994	...	67.8	2.8	36.9	68.6	67.1	61.2	18.4	23.4	21.1	13.0	9.6	17.7
Belgium	1994	...	...	...	...	64.3	63.8	62.2	18.3	15.7	17.1	17.4	20.5	20.7
Canada	1994	...	72.3	-0.1	27.6	58.2	57.1	65.6	20.0	22.1	13.1	21.8	20.8	21.3
Finland	1995	...	74.1	3.6	31.5	45.3	52.1	51.9	29.0	24.1	20.5	25.7	23.8	27.6
France	1995	...	42.5	...	...	53.3	51.8	54.8	36.7	36.1	...	10.0	12.1	...
Germany	1994	...	...	...	35.9	...	...	...	...	...	25.6	...	...	...
Israel	1994	...	34.7	...	22.3	61.6	55.0	60.5	27.3	24.7	25.4	11.1	20.3	14.1
Italy	1994	...	70.9	...	...	64.0	61.4	48.7	17.1	28.5	24.5	18.9	10.0	26.9
Japan	1995	...	127.1	1.9	50.5	56.4	51.1	49.0	17.6	18.2	20.3	25.9	30.7	30.7
Norway	1994	...	41.1	2.5	31.3	55.8	58.1	60.9	25.4	24.5	29.8	18.8	17.3	9.4
South Africa	1994	4.2	...	0.9	11.6	65.8	61.5	...	21.2	16.5	...	13.0	22.0	...
Spain	1995	...	51.2	2.8	26.4	53.3	49.7	57.9	20.6	24.8	21.7	26.1	25.5	20.3
Sweden	1994	...	51.2	1.9	23.1	50.5	47.4	55.8	21.2	23.0	19.9	28.2	29.7	24.3
United Kingdom	1995	3.9	46.5	2.0	25.7	50.0	47.8	61.0	24.2	24.6	21.5	25.8	27.6	17.4
United States of America	1995	...	78.5	-1.0	29.9	49.4	47.6	47.3	21.7	20.9	20.1	28.8	31.5	32.6
Countries of eastern Europe and the former USSR														
Azerbaijan	1994	...	...	...	...	...	...	...	...	12.9	17.9	...	...	...
Bulgaria	1996	...	...	...	0.9	...	...	...	6.8	10.9	9.2	...	...	...
Kyrgyzstan	1994	...	...	...	...	...	...	...	...	...	5.8	...	...	...
Latvia	1996	...	2.1	...	...	...	...	66.5	...	...	...	...	...	...
Lithuania	1994	...	...	...	0.7	...	...	...	...	...	23.8	...	...	...
Russian Federation	1995	...	5.7	...	1.2	...	...	64.2	...	...	7.2	...	...	28.5
Slovakia	1994	...	9.1	...	3.2	...	...	71.9	...	...	9.8	...	...	18.3
Ukraine	1996	...	...	...	1.2	...	...	...	...	9.4	6.2	...	...	...
Developing countries														
Bolivia	1995	...	4.4	...	1.8	...	70.4	56.8	...	13.1	17.4	...	16.5	25.9
Brazil	1994	5.1	39.1	...	9.1	50.0	46.7	40.8	16.7	12.0	13.8	33.3	41.3	45.4
Cameroon	1996	...	3.2	...	1.5	...	...	57.8	...	...	20.1	...	...	22.2
Chile	1995	...	41.5	4.4	10.9	55.8	50.6	52.9	8.8	12.2	12.4	35.4	37.2	34.7
China	1996	...	...	...	...	64.1	73.1	74.8	3.3	...	...	32.6	...	...
China (Hong Kong SAR)	1995	...	32.3	4.0	16.4	68.2	65.1	60.3	21.4	18.1	20.1	10.5	16.8	19.6
China (Taiwan Province)	1996	4.1	19.4	4.8	12.9	69.9	64.4	66.2	18.2	23.4	22.5	11.9	12.2	11.3
Colombia	1995	-0.9	25.2	1.2	5.7	52.8	57.1	55.5	8.2	7.0	10.1	39.0	35.8	34.3
Costa Rica	1996	...	...	...	...	64.8	66.7	67.7	...	...	...	...	...	...
Croatia	1996	...	...	...	3.5	...	64.1	...	...	15.7	...	...	20.2	...
Cyprus	1996	...	26.5	2.4	13.4	66.7	59.0	56.7	15.3	17.8	22.0	18.0	23.2	21.4
Ecuador	1996	...	19.4	...	5.0	67.4	67.2	72.5	13.1	18.4	7.1	19.5	14.5	20.4
Egypt	1994	...	3.5	...	2.0	63.3	70.3	72.7	16.9	19.9	15.8	19.8	9.8	11.5

a/ At current prices.

b/ Excluding countries of eastern Europe and the former USSR.

TABLE 1.11
(continued)

SELECTED CHARACTERISTICS OF BRANCHES, SELECTED YEARS AND COUNTRIES

Rubber products (355)

Country or area	Latest year	Value added per employee		Wages per employee		Percentage in output a/								
		Real annual growth rate (percentage)	Value (current 1000 dollars)	Real annual growth rate (percentage)	Value (current 1000 dollars)	Costs of input materials and utilities			Costs of labour			Operating surplus		
	(LY)	1985-LY	LY	1985-LY	LY	1985	1990	LY	1985	1990	LY	1985	1990	LY
El Salvador	1996	...	11.0	...	2.9	41.2	...	48.2	10.5	...	13.7	48.3	...	38.1
Ethiopia	1996	...	4.7	...	0.9	...	58.2	63.3	...	11.2	7.1	...	30.6	29.6
Honduras	1995	...	2.5	...	1.5	68.7	77.6	78.5	15.2	11.5	13.0	16.1	10.9	8.5
India	1994	...	3.6	0.3	1:2	79.0	81.4	83.3	6.5	5.7	5.7	14.5	12.9	11.0
Indonesia	1996	...	5.8	2.2	1.3	72.4	71.1	79.5	7.1	5.4	4.5	20.4	23.5	16.0
Jordan	1995	...	11.6	...	2.5	30.0	78.9	49.6	20.0	7.0	11.0	50.0	14.1	39.4
Kenya	1995	7.1	10.8	...	2.5	65.6	71.9	64.2	11.7	5.5	8.1	22.7	22.6	27.7
Kuwait	1995	...	18.5	...	6.4	60.4	63.4	72.2	9.4	12.3	9.6	30.2	24.3	18.1
Malaysia	1995	...	14.8	1.4	4.3	77.3	73.0	71.4	7.1	8.0	8.3	15.5	19.1	20.3
Malta	1994	...	22.5	2.2	13.0	42.2	31.2	33.7	34.4	40.5	38.3	23.5	28.3	28.0
Mauritius	1994	...	6.1	2.2	3.6	70.5	62.9	65.6	15.8	15.0	20.0	13.8	22.1	14.4
Mexico	1994	...	35.4	...	12.9	55.1	53.1	54.7	12.0	12.8	16.5	32.9	34.1	28.8
Morocco	1996	...	22.0	...	11.1	...	...	60.0	...	...	20.1	...	...	19.9
Nepal	1996	...	8.7	...	0.6	...	58.1	53.8	...	6.4	3.3	...	35.5	42.8
Peru	1994	1.1	28.4	...	7.7	57.1	45.8	61.7	7.4	12.7	10.3	35.5	41.5	27.9
Philippines	1995	...	10.0	2.0	2.7	77.7	56.8	50.4	15.0	17.0	13.3	7.3	26.2	36.3
Republic of Korea	1995	...	62.1	...	17.4	63.2	57.9	52.3	15.4	18.4	13.3	21.4	23.7	34.3
Senegal	1994	...	7.5	...	1.5	...	...	...	...	...	...	...	...	...
Singapore	1996	...	42.4	4.1	21.5	81.8	57.1	54.9	10.8	21.9	22.9	7.5	21.0	22.2
Slovenia	1995	...	...	...	...	...	...	66.8	...	...	...	...	...	...
Thailand	1994	...	12.1	...	2.6	...	74.0	78.9	...	5.5	4.6	...	20.5	16.5
Trinidad and Tobago	1995	...	8.2	...	7.8	...	57.3	58.0	...	28.1	39.6	...	14.6	2.4
Tunisia	1996	...	...	...	...	...	65.1	54.5	...	13.5	21.2	...	21.5	24.4
Turkey	1994	-0.5	45.9	...	9.9	62.5	50.3	47.5	6.8	13.7	11.3	30.7	36.0	41.2
Uruguay	1995	...	18.1	...	7.4	37.5	38.5	52.3	14.6	15.0	19.5	47.9	46.5	28.1
Venezuela	1996	...	49.5	...	6.2	49.2	52.1	37.5	18.8	11.3	7.8	32.0	36.6	54.7
Yugoslavia	1996	...	5.6	...	1.3	...	52.5	59.6	...	...	9.0	...	...	31.4
Zambia	1994	...	5.7	...	2.5	...	43.5	63.8	...	32.3	15.9	...	24.2	20.2
Zimbabwe	1995	...	14.9	...	4.2	55.7	61.7	61.2	17.7	13.6	10.8	26.6	24.7	28.0

a/ At current prices.

TABLE 1.11

SELECTED CHARACTERISTICS OF BRANCHES, SELECTED YEARS AND COUNTRIES

Country or area	Latest year	Plastic products (356)												
		Value added per employee		Wages per employee		Percentage in output a/								
		Real annual growth rate (percentage)	Value (current 1000 dollars)	Real annual growth rate (percentage)	Value (current 1000 dollars)	Costs of input materials and utilities			Costs of labour			Operating surplus		
	(LY)	1985-LY	LY	1985-LY	LY	1985	1990	LY	1985	1990	LY	1985	1990	LY
Industrialized countries b/														
Austria	1994	...	48.4	2.3	26.6	63.1	63.6	59.1	20.3	19.5	22.5	16.6	16.9	18.4
Canada	1994	...	48.6	0.4	21.6	58.1	56.2	55.4	18.6	21.2	19.8	23.3	22.6	24.8
Finland	1995	...	62.6	2.9	28.9	50.5	53.2	59.2	21.7	22.5	18.8	27.8	24.3	22.0
France	1995	...	67.4	...	...	64.3	63.3	64.0	24.6	22.0	...	11.0	14.7	...
Germany	1994	...	...	...	31.8	...	...	...	...	...	22.7	...	...	...
Iceland	1995	...	57.0	4.0	35.3	64.1	58.8	61.6	22.1	23.1	23.8	13.8	18.1	14.6
Israel	1994	...	35.2	...	18.7	52.4	56.6	62.3	15.0	16.9	20.1	32.6	26.5	17.6
Italy	1994	...	52.8	...	...	68.4	67.9	68.1	13.0	20.1	18.5	18.6	12.0	13.4
Japan	1995	...	110.3	1.6	42.6	61.0	58.6	55.6	14.1	14.4	17.2	24.9	27.0	27.2
Norway	1994	...	49.7	2.7	30.3	64.8	64.3	63.8	19.9	19.8	22.0	15.3	16.0	14.1
South Africa	1994	3.5	...	-1.7	7.8	65.6	68.2	...	21.0	18.6	...	13.4	13.2	...
Spain	1995	...	43.8	1.8	20.6	65.0	65.4	68.2	14.6	16.6	15.0	20.4	18.1	16.8
Sweden	1994	...	46.1	2.3	23.3	51.4	46.1	59.2	19.2	20.0	20.6	29.3	33.9	20.2
United Kingdom	1995	0.3	40.7	1.2	22.4	54.3	53.1	64.6	20.2	20.3	19.5	25.4	26.6	15.9
United States of America	1995	...	70.3	-0.1	25.8	50.3	52.3	51.1	20.1	19.1	18.0	29.6	28.6	30.9
Countries of eastern Europe and the former USSR														
Albania	1996	...	...	...	...	...	...	...	...	...	34.6	...	...	...
Azerbaijan	1994	...	...	...	...	...	...	...	...	17.1	7.4	...	...	...
Bulgaria	1996	...	...	...	1.4	...	...	...	6.5	7.9	8.5	...	...	...
Kyrgyzstan	1994	...	...	...	...	...	...	...	...	3.2	9.1	...	...	...
Latvia	1996	...	5.7	...	...	...	...	54.1	...	...	...	...	...	...
Lithuania	1994	...	...	...	1.0	...	...	...	...	...	20.5	...	...	...
Republic of Moldova	1995	...	...	...	0.1	...	...	...	...	15.7	18.8	...	...	...
Russian Federation	1995	...	3.7	...	1.0	...	...	58.1	...	...	11.2	...	...	30.7
Slovakia	1994	...	7.1	...	2.4	...	...	68.0	...	...	10.7	...	...	21.3
Ukraine	1996	...	...	...	0.6	...	...	...	...	15.6	17.4	...	...	...
Developing countries														
Bolivia	1995	...	7.6	...	2.1	...	67.3	67.3	...	8.5	9.0	...	24.2	23.7
Brazil	1994	3.0	30.5	...	6.5	50.0	40.1	41.1	12.5	13.4	12.5	37.5	46.5	46.3
Cameroon	1996	...	6.0	...	2.4	...	...	68.1	...	...	12.6	...	...	19.4
Chile	1995	...	30.5	6.0	8.4	51.2	57.5	55.8	9.7	10.2	12.2	39.1	32.4	31.9
China	1996	...	...	...	...	71.2	76.3	75.8	1.4	...	...	27.4	...	...
China (Hong Kong SAR)	1995	13.6	32.0	5.1	16.4	69.6	69.2	71.2	18.0	15.8	14.8	12.3	15.1	14.1
China (Taiwan Province)	1996	5.1	22.6	6.5	13.8	70.9	68.7	65.3	17.4	16.9	21.2	11.7	14.4	13.5
Colombia	1995	1.1	18.7	2.3	3.9	65.6	64.1	59.1	7.7	6.3	8.6	26.7	29.6	32.4
Costa Rica	1996	...	...	...	...	64.2	64.9	65.9	...	...	...	...	...	...
Croatia	1996	...	...	...	5.4	...	62.6	...	...	14.8	...	...	22.6	...
Cyprus	1996	...	28.1	3.6	14.9	65.6	61.5	54.8	17.9	17.8	24.0	16.5	20.7	21.2

a/ At current prices.

b/ Excluding countries of eastern Europe and the former USSR.

TABLE 1.11
(continued)

SELECTED CHARACTERISTICS OF BRANCHES, SELECTED YEARS AND COUNTRIES

Plastic products (356)														
Country or area	Latest year	Value added per employee		Wages per employee		Percentage in output a/								
		Real annual growth rate (percentage)	Value (current 1000 dollars)	Real annual growth rate (percentage)	Value (current 1000 dollars)	Costs of input materials and utilities			Costs of labour			Operating surplus		
	(LY)	1985-LY	LY	1985-LY	LY	1985	1990	LY	1985	1990	LY	1985	1990	LY
Ecuador	1996	...	12.9	...	2.3	64.3	68.4	68.3	13.3	10.0	5.5	22.4	21.7	26.2
Egypt	1994	...	3.1	...	1.4	...	81.8	78.3	13.8	7.3	9.8	...	10.9	12.0
El Salvador	1996	...	7.8	...	2.8	51.3	...	63.1	12.1	...	13.2	36.6	...	23.7
Ethiopia	1996	...	5.3	...	1.0	...	50.5	61.0	...	9.6	7.2	...	39.9	31.8
Honduras	1995	...	6.7	...	3.7	62.1	72.1	75.7	20.6	9.7	13.2	17.3	18.1	11.1
India	1994	...	2.8	0.6	0.9	82.1	84.1	87.0	5.6	4.5	4.1	12.3	11.3	8.9
Indonesia	1996	...	4.7	4.7	1.2	61.0	70.7	72.7	7.2	5.5	7.3	31.7	23.8	20.0
Jordan	1995	...	7.3	...	2.6	71.6	73.6	77.4	13.4	8.0	8.1	15.0	18.4	14.5
Kenya	1995	-1.0	6.5	...	1.5	74.5	71.7	78.3	11.8	5.6	4.9	13.8	22.6	16.9
Kuwait	1995	...	29.6	...	7.4	57.6	54.4	58.3	15.4	12.6	10.4	27.0	33.1	31.3
Macau	1996	...	12.8	...	5.5	80.4	70.0	70.0	11.4	15.6	12.9	8.2	14.4	17.2
Malaysia	1995	...	12.8	3.8	4.3	63.3	65.4	64.1	13.2	10.7	11.9	23.5	24.0	23.9
Malta	1994	...	17.8	2.6	10.1	45.6	56.0	49.0	27.2	25.7	28.8	27.3	18.3	22.2
Mauritius	1994	...	8.8	3.3	3.3	66.7	65.5	51.0	15.7	14.5	18.5	17.6	20.0	30.5
Mexico	1994	...	21.1	1.3	6.4	45.4	48.2	51.1	11.8	12.4	14.8	42.8	39.4	34.0
Morocco	1996	...	7.8	...	3.4	...	...	73.3	...	...	11.7	...	...	15.0
Nepal	1996	...	2.6	...	0.4	...	65.4	71.7	...	5.6	4.4	...	29.0	23.8
Peru	1994	2.6	17.4	...	5.2	61.9	50.1	69.4	6.4	9.0	9.1	31.7	40.9	21.5
Philippines	1995	...	11.4	4.7	2.9	77.2	71.4	64.1	7.9	8.1	9.0	14.9	20.5	26.9
Qatar	1994	...	12.6	...	5.7	...	65.7	58.5	...	14.9	18.8	...	19.4	22.7
Republic of Korea	1995	...	79.5	9.5	16.8	65.6	61.3	57.6	10.0	12.0	9.0	24.4	26.8	33.5
Senegal	1996	...	6.3	...	2.2	...	72.8	81.1	...	13.3	6.7	...	13.9	12.2
Singapore	1996	...	33.7	4.6	17.4	61.8	64.3	60.3	17.5	15.1	20.5	20.7	20.7	19.1
Slovenia	1995	...	...	...	...	...	...	67.4	...	...	...	...	...	...
Swaziland	1995	...	13.4	...	6.5	...	...	78.2	...	...	10.6	...	...	11.2
The f.Yugosl.Rep.of Macedonia	1996	...	5.3	...	4.6	...	50.1	59.3	...	24.7	34.9	...	25.2	5.8
Thailand	1994	...	8.5	...	2.6	...	62.9	68.0	...	4.4	9.8	...	32.8	22.2
Trinidad and Tobago	1995	...	17.1	...	5.3	56.0	42.6	57.4	27.7	22.2	13.1	16.4	35.2	29.6
Tunisia	1996	...	...	...	...	...	75.2	67.6	...	7.1	8.4	...	17.7	24.0
Turkey	1994	-1.2	27.0	...	3.4	74.3	66.3	63.3	7.2	8.2	4.7	18.5	25.5	32.0
Uruguay	1995	...	23.1	...	7.1	50.6	54.9	53.1	12.4	11.0	14.5	37.0	34.2	32.4
Venezuela	1996	...	14.5	...	3.2	55.3	60.7	54.5	16.8	13.1	10.0	27.8	26.2	35.5
Yugoslavia	1996	...	7.4	...	1.7	...	58.5	58.7	...	...	9.4	...	...	31.9
Zambia	1994	...	5.7	...	1.4	...	50.8	50.2	...	6.8	12.3	...	42.4	37.5
Zimbabwe	1995	...	5.8	...	2.9	48.2	44.6	66.6	17.9	16.6	16.6	33.9	38.8	16.8

a/ At current prices.

TABLE 1.11

SELECTED CHARACTERISTICS OF BRANCHES, SELECTED YEARS AND COUNTRIES

Pottery, china, earthenware (361)

Country or area	Latest year	Value added per employee		Wages per employee		Percentage in output a/								
		Real annual growth rate (percentage)	Value (current 1000 dollars)	Real annual growth rate (percentage)	Value (current 1000 dollars)	Costs of input materials and utilities			Costs of labour			Operating surplus		
	(LY)	1985-LY	LY	1985-LY	LY	1985	1990	LY	1985	1990	LY	1985	1990	LY
Industrialized countries b/														
Austria	1994	...	46.6	2.8	29.6	45.6	44.0	46.5	38.0	35.2	33.9	16.5	20.8	19.6
Canada	1994	...	36.6	-2.0	18.3	42.9	38.5	50.0	31.4	26.9	25.0	25.7	34.6	25.0
Finland	1994	...	51.9	2.5	22.7	23.4	35.4	38.4	30.2	29.1	27.0	46.4	35.5	34.6
Germany	1994	...	...	...	25.6	...	...	...	...	...	37.9	...	...	...
Iceland	1995	...	35.0	1.5	13.5	53.9	50.0	50.0	28.6	49.0	19.3	17.5	1.1	30.7
Israel	1994	...	21.5	...	20.9	44.2	43.4	...	38.5	34.9	...	17.3	21.7	...
Italy	1994	...	43.1	...	...	61.6	54.9	44.5	17.4	29.2	37.7	21.0	15.8	17.8
Japan	1995	...	84.2	2.6	40.6	45.3	45.5	43.7	27.1	27.4	27.2	27.6	27.1	29.1
Spain	1995	...	34.9	2.4	19.2	35.6	44.7	50.3	31.9	30.8	27.3	32.6	24.6	22.4
Sweden	1994	...	47.6	2.8	23.1	31.5	29.1	43.0	29.9	28.1	27.7	38.7	42.8	29.4
United Kingdom	1995	2.0	30.8	1.9	19.5	33.0	32.3	46.0	33.4	35.3	34.3	33.6	32.5	19.7
United States of America	1995	...	57.0	-1.0	24.5	35.0	29.5	29.0	32.5	31.8	30.5	32.5	38.7	40.5
Countries of eastern Europe and the former USSR														
Azerbaijan	1994	...	...	...	...	...	...	...	...	36.3	36.0	...	...	...
Bulgaria	1996	...	...	...	1.2	...	...	...	17.2	17.6	14.0	...	...	...
Latvia	1996	...	1.9	...	...	...	...	39.7	...	...	...	...	...	...
Lithuania	1994	...	...	...	0.7	...	...	...	...	...	40.7	...	...	...
Russian Federation	1995	...	7.9	...	0.9	...	...	52.8	...	...	5.2	...	...	42.1
Slovakia	1994	...	4.2	...	2.4	...	...	63.4	...	...	20.7	...	...	16.0
Ukraine	1996	...	...	...	0.7	...	...	...	...	34.7	26.7	...	...	...
Developing countries														
Bolivia	1995	...	1.4	...	0.7	...	...	...	...	...	...	...	...	...
Chile	1995	...	14.2	5.2	6.1	48.9	45.2	51.1	19.9	22.4	20.9	31.2	32.4	28.0
China (Hong Kong SAR)	1994	...	15.5	1.4	10.4	74.7	58.1	55.6	15.4	27.4	29.6	9.9	14.5	14.8
China (Taiwan Province)	1996	...	15.6	6.8	13.3	51.1	51.8	50.9	34.6	35.1	41.8	14.2	13.0	7.3
Colombia	1995	5.1	21.7	2.9	4.7	44.4	44.4	37.9	13.3	10.9	13.4	42.2	44.7	48.8
Costa Rica	1996	...	...	...	...	64.0	64.7	65.8	...	...	...	...	...	...
Croatia	1996	...	...	...	3.8	...	40.5	...	...	18.0	...	...	41.5	...
Cyprus	1996	...	21.0	0.7	7.7	42.4	43.3	34.2	23.1	22.8	24.1	34.5	33.9	41.7
Ecuador	1996	...	8.4	...	2.2	34.5	60.2	69.7	21.7	17.3	8.1	43.8	22.5	22.2
Egypt	1994	...	2.3	...	1.4	53.9	58.4	66.6	23.5	9.7	20.2	22.7	31.9	13.2
El Salvador	1996	...	3.0	...	1.5	...	...	29.9	...	...	35.1	...	...	35.0
Honduras	1995	...	2.0	...	1.3	63.1	57.7	60.8	33.0	16.0	25.1	4.0	26.3	14.1
India	1994	...	2.2	2.0	0.9	78.7	72.7	67.2	19.4	16.2	12.9	1.9	11.0	19.9
Indonesia	1996	...	7.8	6.4	1.8	60.3	57.8	54.9	16.2	8.9	10.3	23.5	33.3	34.8
Jordan	1995	...	11.6	...	3.0	43.8	57.8	45.8	17.8	12.1	13.9	38.4	30.1	40.3
Malaysia	1995	...	9.1	3.1	4.1	47.6	48.3	48.9	21.3	20.9	22.9	31.1	30.8	28.2
Malta	1994	...	19.0	2.1	7.3	33.3	37.0	23.7	54.0	39.0	29.4	12.7	24.0	46.9

a/ At current prices.

b/ Excluding countries of eastern Europe and the former USSR.

TABLE 1.11
(continued)

SELECTED CHARACTERISTICS OF BRANCHES, SELECTED YEARS AND COUNTRIES

Pottery, china, earthenware (361)

Country or area	Latest year	Value added per employee		Wages per employee		Percentage in output a/								
		Real annual growth rate (percentage)	Value (current 1000 dollars)	Real annual growth rate (percentage)	Value (current 1000 dollars)	Costs of input materials and utilities			Costs of labour			Operating surplus		
	(LY)	1985-LY	LY	1985-LY	LY	1985	1990	LY	1985	1990	LY	1985	1990	LY
Mauritius	1994	...	3.2	3.8	2.3	60.0	66.7	58.1	10.5	23.3	30.2	29.5	10.0	11.6
Mexico	1994	...	29.2	0.6	6.9	36.5	35.6	37.0	15.0	14.2	14.8	48.6	50.2	48.2
Mongolia	1995	...	...	...	...	...	53.2	66.9	...	18.5	19.2	...	28.2	13.9
Morocco	1996	...	10.9	...	4.6	...	...	65.5	...	...	14.6	...	...	19.8
Peru	1994	12.4	11.6	...	3.9	53.5	37.0	58.7	9.1	19.9	13.7	37.4	43.0	27.5
Philippines	1995	...	6.5	3.4	2.8	54.3	42.0	40.7	16.2	21.9	25.8	29.5	36.1	33.5
Republic of Korea	1995	...	31.4	9.2	12.9	36.8	33.5	34.7	26.3	28.0	26.8	37.0	38.5	38.4
Thailand	1994	...	5.5	...	2.1	...	46.0	39.8	...	19.7	22.7	...	34.3	37.4
Trinidad and Tobago	1994	...	5.8	...	3.5	53.3	...	61.6	26.7	...	23.3	20.0	...	15.1
Tunisia	1996	...	...	...	...	...	57.8	56.0	...	21.6	19.7	...	20.7	24.3
Turkey	1994	...	46.0	...	5.3	43.1	33.7	31.2	22.0	12.3	8.0	34.9	54.1	60.8
Uruguay	1995	...	17.3	...	7.4	49.6	39.1	41.5	24.3	18.9	25.0	26.1	42.0	33.4
Venezuela	1996	...	11.8	...	2.9	28.4	45.0	45.7	31.3	29.7	13.4	40.3	25.3	40.8
Yugoslavia	1996	...	4.5	...	0.8	...	41.6	42.9	...	...	10.3	...	...	46.9
Zimbabwe	1995	...	3.0	...	1.4	31.4	37.0	31.3	41.2	42.0	32.0	27.5	21.0	36.7

a/ At current prices.

TABLE 1.11

SELECTED CHARACTERISTICS OF BRANCHES, SELECTED YEARS AND COUNTRIES

Glass (362)														
Country or area	Latest year	Value added per employee		Wages per employee		Percentage in output a/								
		Real annual growth rate (percentage)	Value (current 1000 dollars)	Real annual growth rate (percentage)	Value (current 1000 dollars)	Costs of input materials and utilities			Costs of labour			Operating surplus		
	(LY)	1985-LY	LY	1985-LY	LY	1985	1990	LY	1985	1990	LY	1985	1990	LY
Industrialized countries b/														
Austria	1994	...	70.3	1.7	31.0	48.3	47.1	42.8	23.1	23.7	25.2	28.6	29.2	32.0
Canada	1994	...	63.5	-0.0	27.4	46.3	53.4	46.6	24.4	24.0	23.1	29.3	22.5	30.3
Finland	1995	...	58.4	3.2	32.0	45.4	53.1	57.8	26.2	26.4	23.1	28.4	20.5	19.1
France	1995	...	65.0	...	...	48.2	46.1	51.4	36.5	31.6	...	15.3	22.3	...
Germany	1994	...	...	...	33.1	...	...	...	...	...	25.3	...	...	...
Iceland	1995	...	44.5	0.8	26.1	59.7	63.4	57.1	24.3	26.2	25.1	16.0	10.4	17.8
Israel	1994	...	30.4	...	21.7	50.0	52.5	65.9	35.2	24.7	24.4	14.8	22.8	9.7
Italy	1994	...	58.3	...	...	61.6	60.8	56.3	16.6	25.6	25.5	21.8	13.6	18.2
Japan	1995	...	181.7	1.2	52.8	45.6	42.4	41.0	14.0	14.6	17.1	40.4	43.0	41.9
Norway	1994	...	50.3	1.7	30.7	56.1	57.5	58.7	24.5	23.5	25.2	19.5	19.1	16.1
South Africa	1994	-0.5	...	3.0	12.2	56.2	47.5	...	16.3	17.5	...	27.5	35.0	...
Spain	1995	...	53.8	0.8	21.9	48.3	50.9	55.9	19.5	18.0	18.0	32.2	31.0	26.1
Sweden	1994	...	44.7	2.1	23.8	45.7	42.4	60.5	20.1	21.2	21.1	34.3	36.5	18.5
United Kingdom	1995	1.0	40.2	-0.4	21.4	46.8	43.0	61.6	25.0	26.3	20.4	28.2	30.7	18.0
United States of America	1995	...	94.1	-0.7	31.7	44.9	41.9	39.5	23.7	22.0	20.4	31.4	36.1	40.2
Countries of eastern Europe and the former USSR														
Azerbaijan	1994	...	...	...	...	...	...	...	...	16.3	17.9	...	...	...
Bulgaria	1996	...	...	...	1.2	...	...	...	19.4	17.7	14.3	...	...	...
Latvia	1996	...	3.7	...	...	...	...	66.6	...	...	...	...	...	...
Lithuania	1994	...	...	...	1.3	...	...	...	...	...	25.0	...	...	...
Republic of Moldova	1995	...	...	...	0.8	...	...	...	...	7.8	7.7	...	...	...
Russian Federation	1995	...	3.6	...	1.0	...	...	53.2	...	...	13.3	...	...	33.6
Slovakia	1994	...	7.6	...	2.4	...	...	51.6	...	...	15.4	...	...	33.1
Ukraine	1996	...	...	...	0.8	...	...	...	...	16.4	15.8	...	...	...
Developing countries														
Bolivia	1995	...	11.6	...	2.8	...	51.4	58.4	...	10.9	10.0	...	37.6	31.6
Chile	1995	...	53.1	4.2	10.3	33.5	38.2	38.8	10.2	13.1	11.9	56.3	48.6	49.4
China (Taiwan Province)	1996	...	24.0	3.9	13.5	39.2	40.5	51.5	33.0	32.2	27.2	27.8	27.2	21.3
Colombia	1995	1.7	27.0	0.7	4.9	40.8	44.7	40.8	11.7	9.1	10.7	47.5	46.2	48.4
Costa Rica	1996	...	...	...	...	63.1	63.8	64.8	...	...	...	...	...	...
Croatia	1996	...	...	...	3.8	...	45.7	...	...	12.2	...	...	42.1	...
Cyprus	1996	...	22.7	3.9	13.3	20.9	67.3	63.0	27.1	15.7	21.7	51.9	17.0	15.3
Ecuador	1996	...	39.9	...	3.4	45.9	63.7	52.1	13.3	9.5	4.1	40.9	26.8	43.8
Egypt	1994	...	2.8	...	1.5	59.0	71.3	70.0	36.9	19.0	16.3	4.1	9.7	13.7
El Salvador	1996	...	4.8	...	2.3	60.0	...	50.2	8.0	...	24.3	32.0	...	25.4
Ethiopia	1996	...	3.5	...	0.7	...	...	36.2	...	...	12.8	...	...	51.0
India	1994	...	2.2	2.9	1.0	73.7	77.8	78.8	12.6	11.0	9.4	13.8	11.2	11.8
Indonesia	1996	...	14.4	2.0	2.1	50.2	70.2	49.5	8.2	6.5	7.5	41.6	23.2	43.0

a/ At current prices.

b/ Excluding countries of eastern Europe and the former USSR.

TABLE 1.11
(continued)

SELECTED CHARACTERISTICS OF BRANCHES, SELECTED YEARS AND COUNTRIES

Glass (362)

Country or area	Latest year	Value added per employee		Wages per employee		Percentage in output a/								
		Real annual growth rate (percentage)	Value (current 1000 dollars)	Real annual growth rate (percentage)	Value (current 1000 dollars)	Costs of input materials and utilities			Costs of labour			Operating surplus		
	(LY)	1985-LY	LY	1985-LY	LY	1985	1990	LY	1985	1990	LY	1985	1990	LY
Jordan	1995	...	5.1	...	2.2	62.6	71.9	71.2	23.7	13.7	12.5	13.7	14.4	16.3
Kenya	1995	...	2.6	...	1.3	61.3	53.8	...	24.7	19.8	...	14.0	26.4	...
Kuwait	1995	...	27.2	...	9.5	...	58.7	43.5	...	8.0	19.8	...	33.3	36.8
Macau	1996	...	25.6	...	9.7	62.6	57.2	70.3	16.8	20.4	11.3	20.6	22.4	18.4
Malaysia	1995	...	38.1	0.5	6.9	63.0	50.7	61.6	18.1	11.7	6.9	18.9	37.6	31.4
Malta	1994	...	14.8	1.2	9.4	52.7	51.2	45.5	25.8	26.5	34.5	21.5	22.4	20.0
Mauritius	1994	...	4.9	2.4	3.7	58.3	50.0	41.2	29.9	38.3	44.3	11.8	11.7	14.5
Mexico	1994	...	41.2	2.3	10.4	43.8	40.7	40.5	11.7	13.9	14.9	44.4	45.4	44.5
Morocco	1996	...	11.4	...	4.5	...	...	56.3	...	...	17.3	...	...	26.4
Peru	1994	0.7	18.0	...	5.0	74.3	66.0	63.1	9.0	8.8	10.2	16.7	25.2	26.7
Philippines	1995	...	28.8	2.9	4.5	71.8	45.8	39.0	10.1	21.6	9.5	18.1	32.6	51.5
Republic of Korea	1995	...	83.8	9.8	20.7	52.7	41.9	39.8	12.7	18.1	14.9	34.6	40.0	45.3
Swaziland	1995	...	6.3	...	3.5	...	...	57.3	...	...	23.7	...	...	19.1
Thailand	1994	...	21.1	...	5.6	...	58.3	48.4	...	34.2	13.6	...	7.5	38.0
Trinidad and Tobago	1995	...	21.7	...	9.4	44.3	46.4	52.7	34.0	29.9	20.3	21.6	23.7	26.9
Tunisia	1996	...	...	...	...	...	59.3	57.5	...	13.8	15.4	...	27.0	27.0
Turkey	1994	...	43.4	...	8.6	52.2	42.5	40.1	12.5	16.8	11.9	35.2	40.7	48.1
Uruguay	1995	...	24.6	...	9.9	54.4	43.7	43.2	19.1	13.7	22.9	26.5	42.7	33.9
Venezuela	1996	...	43.2	...	3.6	46.7	42.6	34.2	20.6	13.4	5.5	32.7	44.1	60.3
Yugoslavia	1996	...	4.0	...	1.2	...	61.8	55.8	...	...	13.1	...	...	31.2
Zimbabwe	1995	...	5.4	...	3.7	47.5	50.4	72.9	29.8	24.0	18.5	22.7	25.6	8.6

a/ At current prices.

TABLE 1.11

SELECTED CHARACTERISTICS OF BRANCHES, SELECTED YEARS AND COUNTRIES

Other non-metallic mineral prods. (369)

Country or area	Latest year	Value added per employee		Wages per employee		Percentage in output a/								
		Real annual growth rate (percentage)	Value (current 1000 dollars)	Real annual growth rate (percentage)	Value (current 1000 dollars)	Costs of input materials and utilities			Costs of labour			Operating surplus		
	(LY)	1985-LY	LY	1985-LY	LY	1985	1990	LY	1985	1990	LY	1985	1990	LY
Industrialized countries b/														
Austria	1994	...	74.2	1.9	35.8	62.2	61.1	61.2	19.2	20.2	18.7	18.6	18.7	20.1
Canada	1994	...	65.0	-0.5	26.6	53.4	51.8	51.2	20.3	20.4	19.9	26.3	27.7	28.8
Finland	1994	...	55.1	1.7	22.3	49.2	52.8	53.9	21.9	20.3	18.7	28.8	26.9	27.4
France	1995	...	117.7	...	...	56.7	55.7	54.6	27.6	24.0	...	15.7	20.4	...
Germany	1994	...	...	...	34.9	...	...	...	...	...	19.1	...	...	...
Iceland	1995	...	52.0	-0.5	30.2	57.9	55.4	57.0	23.2	28.0	24.9	18.9	16.6	18.1
Israel	1994	...	47.3	...	24.6	65.0	61.8	67.9	19.5	18.1	16.7	15.5	20.0	15.4
Italy	1994	...	57.0	...	...	63.0	60.7	61.6	15.3	20.3	22.2	21.7	19.1	16.3
Japan	1995	...	138.2	1.7	46.7	53.3	50.2	47.7	16.1	15.5	17.6	30.6	34.3	34.6
Norway	1994	...	73.0	2.2	34.6	65.4	63.5	61.5	18.6	19.5	18.3	16.0	17.0	20.2
Spain	1995	...	49.6	2.1	20.5	55.2	55.5	60.8	15.1	14.7	16.2	29.6	29.8	23.0
Sweden	1994	...	58.2	1.9	25.2	44.6	47.3	52.7	18.3	18.4	20.5	37.0	34.3	26.8
United Kingdom	1995	4.5	57.8	1.3	25.3	48.7	46.0	59.1	16.6	17.6	17.9	34.6	36.4	22.9
United States of America	1995	...	83.1	-0.3	29.6	49.1	48.5	46.5	19.2	20.1	19.1	31.6	31.4	34.4
Countries of eastern Europe and the former USSR														
Albania	1996	...	...	...	...	...	...	...	...	...	12.8	...	...	...
Azerbaijan	1994	...	...	...	...	...	...	...	...	18.0	9.6	...	...	...
Bulgaria	1996	...	3.1	...	1.2	...	...	71.3	7.6	10.2	10.7	...	...	18.0
Kyrgyzstan	1994	...	...	...	...	...	...	...	...	4.5	3.6	...	...	...
Latvia	1996	...	5.4	...	...	...	...	54.6	...	...	...	...	...	...
Lithuania	1994	...	...	...	1.2	...	...	...	...	...	21.5	...	...	...
Republic of Moldova	1995	...	...	...	0.3	...	...	...	...	19.8	6.7	...	...	...
Russian Federation	1995	...	4.1	...	1.4	...	...	61.0	...	...	13.1	...	...	26.0
Slovakia	1994	...	5.9	...	2.5	...	...	62.4	...	...	15.8	...	...	21.8
Ukraine	1996	...	...	...	0.8	...	...	...	...	22.4	14.8	...	...	...
Developing countries														
Bolivia	1995	...	16.4	...	2.7	...	52.9	50.3	...	8.7	8.0	...	38.3	41.7
Cameroon	1996	...	28.2	...	14.3	...	...	72.5	...	...	14.0	...	...	13.5
Chile	1995	...	72.0	4.3	13.3	42.6	47.3	44.9	9.1	9.7	10.1	48.3	43.0	44.9
China (Hong Kong SAR)	1995	...	67.5	3.6	22.7	82.2	82.6	76.8	6.8	6.9	7.8	11.0	10.5	15.4
China (Taiwan Province)	1996	...	40.2	5.8	15.3	62.7	56.4	67.0	15.6	14.1	12.6	21.7	29.5	20.4
Colombia	1995	2.2	33.1	1.0	4.3	49.7	48.5	46.2	10.2	7.7	7.0	40.1	43.8	46.8
Costa Rica	1996	...	...	...	...	62.6	61.3	65.1	...	...	...	...	...	...
Croatia	1996	...	...	...	4.3	...	52.2	...	...	16.6	...	...	31.2	...
Cyprus	1996	...	40.9	3.1	17.9	64.5	58.0	57.9	20.4	18.6	18.4	15.1	23.4	23.7
Ecuador	1996	...	25.0	...	4.0	56.4	61.8	63.0	14.2	13.3	5.9	29.4	24.9	31.1
Egypt	1994	...	11.2	...	2.4	64.1	64.6	65.5	16.4	11.5	7.3	19.6	23.9	27.2
El Salvador	1996	...	17.7	...	3.8	52.9	...	55.3	12.4	...	9.6	34.6	...	35.1

a/ At current prices.

b/ Excluding countries of eastern Europe and the former USSR.

TABLE 1.11
(continued)

SELECTED CHARACTERISTICS OF BRANCHES, SELECTED YEARS AND COUNTRIES

Other non-metallic mineral prods. (369)

Country or area	Latest year	Value added per employee		Wages per employee		Percentage in output a/								
		Real annual growth rate (percentage)	Value (current 1000 dollars)	Real annual growth rate (percentage)	Value (current 1000 dollars)	Costs of input materials and utilities			Costs of labour			Operating surplus		
	(LY)	1985-LY	LY	1985-LY	LY	1985	1990	LY	1985	1990	LY	1985	1990	LY
Ethiopia	1996	...	5.6	...	0.8	...	53.0	51.6	...	11.1	7.2	...	35.9	41.2
Gabon	1995	...	15.2	...	12.8	...	...	75.7	...	...	20.5	...	...	3.8
Honduras	1995	...	6.8	...	1.8	60.3	64.0	65.0	17.6	14.3	9.5	22.1	21.8	25.5
India	1994	...	2.8	2.7	0.9	75.3	75.5	77.6	8.5	6.9	6.9	16.2	17.6	15.5
Indonesia	1996	...	7.5	5.4	1.8	66.7	61.8	60.8	7.4	5.1	9.5	25.8	33.2	29.7
Jordan	1995	...	13.8	...	3.2	43.3	46.5	52.7	11.3	9.9	10.8	45.4	43.6	36.4
Kenya	1995	3.5	5.3	...	2.0	85.3	76.0	73.5	8.8	8.1	10.2	6.0	15.9	16.3
Kuwait	1995	...	28.8	...	7.8	60.8	72.1	60.4	15.9	8.9	10.8	23.3	19.0	28.8
Macau	1996	...	29.8	...	10.4	59.2	65.5	79.0	38.3	22.5	7.3	2.5	12.0	13.6
Malawi	1994	...	0.8	...	0.5	86.6	90.2	86.3	9.1	6.0	8.7	4.3	3.8	4.9
Malaysia	1995	...	27.5	3.1	5.9	53.5	53.2	58.9	11.4	9.6	8.9	35.1	37.2	32.3
Malta	1994	...	21.6	1.9	8.6	70.9	66.8	62.2	13.0	13.2	15.1	16.1	20.0	22.7
Mauritius	1994	...	15.7	9.4	5.4	65.7	62.7	61.2	13.5	10.8	13.2	20.9	26.5	25.6
Mexico	1994	...	68.7	3.9	11.8	47.8	47.1	45.6	9.2	10.3	9.3	43.0	42.6	45.0
Mongolia	1995	...	1.3	...	0.8	...	82.2	71.3	...	11.5	17.3	...	6.3	11.3
Morocco	1996	...	16.0	...	5.6	...	...	44.1	...	...	19.5	...	...	36.4
Namibia	1994	...	10.4	...	3.7	...	...	56.5	...	...	15.5	...	...	28.1
Nepal	1996	...	0.6	...	0.2	...	39.4	45.4	...	18.0	18.8	...	42.6	35.7
Peru	1994	8.1	29.6	...	4.4	56.0	50.1	53.5	6.2	7.6	7.0	37.8	42.3	39.5
Philippines	1995	...	26.1	5.7	3.9	72.8	58.1	50.8	7.8	8.6	7.3	19.4	33.4	41.8
Republic of Korea	1995	...	83.4	8.9	18.2	61.6	54.8	52.3	10.1	10.2	10.4	28.3	35.0	37.2
Senegal	1996	...	52.1	...	8.1	...	54.1	66.6	...	6.2	5.2	...	39.7	28.2
Singapore	1996	...	77.3	4.1	23.2	65.6	68.8	71.4	13.1	10.2	8.6	21.3	21.1	20.0
Swaziland	1995	...	4.3	...	3.9	...	...	60.4	...	...	36.1	...	...	3.5
Thailand	1994	...	19.8	...	4.4	...	55.5	53.4	...	6.7	10.4	...	37.8	36.3
Trinidad and Tobago	1995	...	19.9	...	6.1	44.4	49.4	57.8	34.0	18.8	13.0	21.6	31.8	29.2
Tunisia	1996	...	...	...	...	...	63.2	61.0	...	17.7	17.8	...	19.1	21.2
Turkey	1994	4.6	32.6	...	4.7	58.7	44.6	44.5	10.6	13.3	8.0	30.7	42.0	47.4
Uruguay	1995	...	23.8	...	6.6	51.5	58.1	44.8	16.2	13.1	15.3	32.2	28.8	39.9
Venezuela	1996	...	23.9	...	3.0	45.9	47.5	46.7	21.1	15.4	6.6	32.9	37.2	46.7
Yugoslavia	1996	...	6.7	...	1.9	...	51.3	55.2	...	...	12.6	...	...	32.1
Zambia	1994	...	3.9	...	1.8	...	45.7	69.1	...	8.0	14.0	...	46.3	16.9
Zimbabwe	1995	...	12.0	...	2.9	54.9	47.0	37.3	25.8	21.6	15.3	19.3	31.5	47.4

a/ At current prices.

TABLE 1.11

SELECTED CHARACTERISTICS OF BRANCHES, SELECTED YEARS AND COUNTRIES

Country or area	Latest year	Iron and steel (371)												
		Value added per employee		Wages per employee		Percentage in output a/								
		Real annual growth rate (percentage)	Value (current 1000 dollars)	Real annual growth rate (percentage)	Value (current 1000 dollars)	Costs of input materials and utilities			Costs of labour			Operating surplus		
	(LY)	1985-LY	LY	1985-LY	LY	1985	1990	LY	1985	1990	LY	1985	1990	LY
Industrialized countries b/														
Austria	1994	...	56.1	1.6	34.3	64.4	56.9	64.4	20.5	22.2	21.7	15.1	21.0	13.9
Belgium	1994	...	...	...	...	73.5	68.9	65.0	...	...	...	...	...	...
Canada	1994	...	78.3	0.5	36.2	60.2	62.3	62.1	21.3	22.6	17.5	18.5	15.1	20.4
Finland	1994	...	87.8	1.7	26.7	73.3	73.7	69.8	11.0	12.7	9.2	15.7	13.5	21.0
France	1995	...	53.1	...	...	76.0	68.8	69.2	20.3	18.2	...	3.7	13.0	...
Germany	1994	...	...	...	35.4	...	...	...	...	...	20.6	...	...	...
Iceland	1995	...	...	1.9	44.5	65.2	77.4	60.9	12.9	18.5	13.6	21.9	4.1	25.5
Israel	1994	...	43.5	...	25.9	64.0	73.2	75.9	19.4	15.9	14.4	16.6	10.9	9.8
Italy	1994	...	60.1	...	...	76.5	72.4	75.3	11.8	18.2	14.7	11.7	9.4	10.0
Japan	1995	3.6	215.8	1.6	66.7	66.2	61.6	58.4	10.1	10.3	12.8	23.6	28.1	28.7
Norway	1994	...	58.4	2.3	36.2	73.8	76.0	73.0	15.3	16.6	16.7	10.9	7.4	10.3
South Africa	1994	3.0	...	2.5	14.9	65.7	53.6	...	19.3	18.7	...	15.0	27.7	...
Spain	1995	...	76.2	2.0	27.3	74.4	69.0	70.5	13.3	15.1	10.6	12.4	15.9	18.9
Sweden	1994	...	70.5	2.1	27.0	64.7	66.6	71.6	13.5	13.2	10.9	21.7	20.3	17.6
United Kingdom	1995	8.0	68.8	2.7	29.9	64.3	60.9	68.4	16.9	17.6	13.7	18.8	21.5	17.9
United States of America	1995	...	106.1	0.0	40.2	60.5	58.0	56.8	20.9	18.4	16.4	18.6	23.6	26.9
Countries of eastern Europe and the former USSR														
Albania	1996	...	...	...	...	...	...	...	...	...	10.8	...	...	...
Azerbaijan	1994	...	...	...	...	...	...	...	...	15.4	14.5	...	...	...
Bulgaria	1996	...	3.0	...	1.8	...	...	87.0	8.1	8.9	7.7	...	...	5.3
Latvia	1996	...	5.9	...	...	...	...	76.4	...	...	...	...	...	...
Lithuania	1994	...	...	...	1.2	...	...	...	...	...	19.3	...	...	...
Republic of Moldova	1995	...	...	...	0.4	...	...	...	...	10.6	19.9	...	...	...
Russian Federation	1995	...	8.0	...	1.6	...	...	70.6	...	...	5.8	...	...	23.6
Slovakia	1994	...	11.7	...	3.5	...	...	80.1	...	...	6.0	...	...	13.9
Ukraine	1996	...	...	...	1.5	...	...	...	...	8.7	6.6	...	...	...
Developing countries														
Bolivia	1995	...	18.5	...	1.2	...	70.3	66.4	...	10.7	2.2	...	18.9	31.4
Chile	1995	...	61.1	5.3	15.7	55.6	55.5	62.4	7.4	9.2	9.7	37.0	35.3	27.9
China	1996	...	...	...	...	68.5	75.8	73.3	5.5	...	...	26.0	...	...
China (Hong Kong SAR)	1995	...	73.2	6.0	23.9	82.8	78.1	71.2	11.6	8.8	9.4	5.7	13.1	19.4
China (Taiwan Province)	1996	...	53.5	6.0	18.4	66.3	65.4	68.0	8.7	11.3	11.0	25.0	23.3	21.0
Colombia	1995	7.2	38.2	-0.1	5.2	56.8	55.9	57.9	8.0	4.2	5.7	35.2	39.9	36.4
Croatia	1996	...	...	...	3.4	...	67.8	...	...	7.7	...	...	24.5	...
Ecuador	1996	...	18.8	...	3.6	60.8	82.6	84.9	6.5	6.2	2.9	32.7	11.2	12.3
El Salvador	1996	...	15.7	...	4.2	45.7	...	74.3	13.7	...	6.8	40.7	...	18.9
Ethiopia	1996	...	11.5	...	1.2	...	83.8	70.9	...	7.5	3.0	...	8.7	26.1
Honduras	1995	...	3.4	...	1.1	69.9	72.3	78.6	11.7	4.7	6.6	18.4	23.0	14.8

a/ At current prices.

b/ Excluding countries of eastern Europe and the former USSR.

TABLE 1.11
(continued)

SELECTED CHARACTERISTICS OF BRANCHES, SELECTED YEARS AND COUNTRIES

Iron and steel (371)														
Country or area	Latest year	Value added per employee		Wages per employee		Percentage in output a/								
		Real annual growth rate (percentage)	Value (current 1000 dollars)	Real annual growth rate (percentage)	Value (current 1000 dollars)	Costs of input materials and utilities			Costs of labour			Operating surplus		
	(LY)	1985-LY	LY	1985-LY	LY	1985	1990	LY	1985	1990	LY	1985	1990	LY
India	1994	...	5.8	3.2	1.8	82.5	83.7	81.7	8.1	5.7	5.6	9.4	10.6	12.7
Jordan	1995	...	23.7	...	4.2	88.8	72.3	73.8	4.7	3.4	4.6	6.5	24.4	21.5
Kuwait	1995	...	29.2	...	7.4	50.6	63.5	54.3	20.5	10.7	11.6	28.9	25.8	34.1
Malaysia	1995	...	15.8	2.2	6.8	75.4	80.4	89.6	7.0	4.1	4.5	17.6	15.5	5.9
Mexico	1994	...	62.6	2.3	9.8	68.0	67.5	66.1	5.5	5.4	5.3	26.4	27.1	28.6
Morocco	1996	...	63.6	...	7.8	...	...	74.7	...	...	3.1	...	...	22.2
Nepal	1996	...	6.4	...	0.5	...	78.8	80.0	...	2.3	1.5	...	18.9	18.5
Peru	1994	6.4	21.4	...	7.9	60.4	45.9	67.4	7.9	14.4	12.0	31.7	39.6	20.5
Philippines	1995	...	23.9	3.9	3.6	68.0	80.5	71.0	4.2	4.5	4.3	27.8	15.0	24.6
Qatar	1994	...	...	...	...	...	45.7	57.8	...	10.1	12.1	...	44.2	30.1
Republic of Korea	1995	...	129.3	8.2	21.7	69.2	64.4	63.0	5.5	6.8	6.2	25.3	28.8	30.8
Singapore	1996	...	61.7	3.1	31.4	68.5	69.8	74.6	11.5	8.4	13.0	20.0	21.8	12.5
Slovenia	1995	...	...	...	...	...	...	69.9	...	...	...	...	...	...
The f. Yugosl. Rep. of Macedonia	1996	...	4.7	...	4.0	...	74.7	79.9	...	15.1	16.8	...	10.2	3.2
Thailand	1994	...	41.0	...	3.3	...	79.6	58.5	...	6.6	3.4	...	13.8	38.1
Trinidad and Tobago	1995	...	47.2	...	9.9	...	78.0	75.4	...	10.7	5.2	...	11.3	19.4
Tunisia	1996	...	...	...	...	...	80.5	79.5	...	9.2	11.3	...	10.3	9.1
Turkey	1994	9.0	49.6	...	9.7	75.5	76.0	63.9	6.6	10.1	7.1	17.9	13.9	29.0
Uruguay	1995	...	53.0	...	9.3	49.8	46.1	52.7	9.5	8.4	8.3	40.7	45.5	39.0
Venezuela	1996	...	47.1	...	9.9	52.4	66.0	51.1	16.8	14.1	10.3	30.9	19.9	38.6
Yugoslavia	1996	...	4.1	...	1.3	...	85.5	81.4	...	...	6.1	...	...	12.5
Zambia	1994	...	3.8	...	2.7	...	61.1	65.8	...	11.7	23.9	...	27.2	10.3
Zimbabwe	1995	...	11.7	...	3.5	57.7	54.6	55.5	24.6	22.8	13.2	17.8	22.6	31.3

a/ At current prices.

TABLE 1.11

SELECTED CHARACTERISTICS OF BRANCHES, SELECTED YEARS AND COUNTRIES

Non-ferrous metals (372)

Country or area	Latest year	Value added per employee		Wages per employee		Percentage in output a/								
		Real annual growth rate (percentage)	Value (current 1000 dollars)	Real annual growth rate (percentage)	Value (current 1000 dollars)	Costs of input materials and utilities			Costs of labour			Operating surplus		
	(LY)	1985-LY	LY	1985-LY	LY	1985	1990	LY	1985	1990	LY	1985	1990	LY
Industrialized countries b/														
Austria	1994	...	55.3	2.2	34.9	75.2	83.1	80.5	12.4	10.4	12.3	12.4	6.6	7.2
Belgium	1994	...	...	...	...	80.6	76.3	75.9	...	...	...	...	...	...
Canada	1994	...	86.9	0.1	34.9	59.4	61.2	58.9	20.9	19.6	16.5	19.7	19.2	24.6
Finland	1994	...	89.4	2.6	28.6	88.0	81.4	79.4	7.7	7.2	6.6	4.2	11.4	14.0
France	1995	...	135.6	...	...	70.2	70.1	66.4	15.3	15.5	...	14.5	14.4	...
Germany	1994	...	...	...	37.2	...	...	...	...	...	19.0	...	...	...
Iceland	1995	...	84.7	0.6	37.0	...	78.3	76.0	...	15.2	10.5	...	6.4	13.5
Israel	1994	...	33.7	...	17.9	56.1	65.2	66.1	20.4	19.7	18.0	23.5	15.1	15.9
Italy	1994	...	54.1	...	...	79.0	78.2	76.7	9.5	16.5	14.8	11.5	5.3	8.4
Japan	1995	3.5	152.4	1.2	54.1	73.4	69.1	65.3	9.9	10.2	12.3	16.8	20.7	22.4
Norway	1994	...	82.5	3.4	41.5	70.1	77.1	77.4	11.7	10.4	11.4	18.2	12.5	11.3
South Africa	1994	5.1	...	1.9	13.4	53.6	66.8	...	11.4	10.4	...	35.1	22.9	...
Spain	1995	...	67.5	2.7	27.6	73.7	73.7	74.5	8.5	10.4	10.4	17.7	15.9	15.1
Sweden	1994	...	57.7	2.1	24.9	74.7	71.4	76.7	10.4	9.8	10.1	14.9	18.8	13.3
United Kingdom	1995	2.2	58.2	1.4	25.7	74.7	73.7	74.7	12.4	13.5	11.2	13.0	12.8	14.2
United States of America	1995	...	95.3	-0.8	33.2	71.5	70.1	66.5	15.5	12.6	11.7	13.0	17.3	21.8
Countries of eastern Europe and the former USSR														
Albania	1996	...	...	...	...	...	...	...	...	...	5.6	...	...	...
Azerbaijan	1994	...	...	...	...	...	...	...	...	11.6	9.6	...	...	...
Bulgaria	1996	...	14.2	...	1.9	...	...	56.6	3.6	7.7	5.7	...	...	37.8
Kyrgyzstan	1994	...	...	...	...	...	...	...	...	3.2	5.6	...	...	...
Latvia	1996	...	5.3	...	...	...	...	69.1	...	...	...	...	...	...
Lithuania	1994	...	...	...	0.5	...	...	...	...	...	23.1	...	...	...
Russian Federation	1995	...	24.5	...	3.7	...	...	48.9	...	...	7.8	...	...	43.3
Slovakia	1994	...	6.3	...	2.9	...	...	80.4	...	...	9.1	...	...	10.5
Ukraine	1996	...	...	...	1.5	...	...	...	...	...	13.5	...	...	...
Developing countries														
Bolivia	1995	...	23.0	...	2.7	...	87.2	73.8	...	3.1	3.1	...	9.7	23.1
Cameroon	1996	...	36.3	...	12.0	...	...	78.3	...	...	7.2	...	...	14.5
Chile	1995	...	203.5	4.5	19.3	45.9	65.6	67.0	2.5	1.7	3.1	51.7	32.7	29.8
China	1996	...	...	...	...	74.0	80.8	78.5	3.6	...	...	22.4	...	...
China (Hong Kong SAR)	1995	...	55.9	6.9	22.3	79.5	88.1	88.4	10.4	5.7	4.6	10.1	6.2	7.0
China (Taiwan Province)	1996	...	40.9	4.1	14.9	83.2	78.2	78.6	5.0	7.1	7.8	11.8	14.6	13.6
Colombia	1995	3.1	24.8	0.8	5.1	56.5	56.9	68.1	6.9	4.6	6.5	36.6	38.5	25.4
Costa Rica	1996	...	...	...	...	...	...	76.9	...	...	...	...	...	...
Croatia	1996	...	...	...	3.2	...	62.1	...	...	10.5	...	...	27.3	...
Ecuador	1996	...	13.6	...	3.9	70.1	89.8	80.2	7.9	5.7	5.7	22.0	4.5	14.1
Egypt	1994	...	6.2	...	2.1	32.5	74.2	75.9	13.6	8.3	8.2	53.9	17.5	15.9

a/ At current prices.

b/ Excluding countries of eastern Europe and the former USSR.

TABLE 1.11
(continued)

SELECTED CHARACTERISTICS OF BRANCHES, SELECTED YEARS AND COUNTRIES

Non-ferrous metals (372)

Country or area	Latest year	Value added per employee		Wages per employee		Percentage in output a/								
		Real annual growth rate (percentage)	Value (current 1000 dollars)	Real annual growth rate (percentage)	Value (current 1000 dollars)	Costs of input materials and utilities			Costs of labour			Operating surplus		
	(LY)	1985-LY	LY	1985-LY	LY	1985	1990	LY	1985	1990	LY	1985	1990	LY
Honduras	1995	...	2.8	...	1.4	44.8	58.2	55.2	29.1	20.5	22.8	26.0	21.3	22.0
India	1994	...	4.4	...	1.3	91.5	82.3	80.5	6.8	6.4	5.6	1.7	11.4	13.9
Indonesia	1996	...	27.9	...	2.4	...	71.6	61.5	...	1.3	3.3	...	27.1	35.2
Jordan	1995	...	15.5	...	3.6	77.5	55.8	75.3	7.4	5.7	5.8	15.1	38.5	18.9
Malaysia	1995	...	26.6	0.7	6.5	93.6	86.3	79.7	2.6	4.0	4.9	3.8	9.7	15.4
Mexico	1994	...	55.7	2.9	9.5	72.6	68.2	61.7	4.0	4.3	6.6	23.3	27.5	31.7
Morocco	1996	...	15.2	...	6.9	...	...	82.4	...	...	8.0	...	...	9.7
Peru	1994	...	70.2	...	10.1	67.2	46.8	59.1	1.8	3.1	5.9	31.0	50.1	35.0
Republic of Korea	1995	...	83.4	8.4	18.9	75.5	74.1	70.8	7.8	7.4	6.6	16.7	18.5	22.6
Singapore	1996	...	54.0	3.0	21.4	83.9	65.9	51.0	5.2	9.8	19.4	10.9	24.3	29.6
Slovenia	1995	...	...	...	...	...	...	78.2	...	...	...	...	...	...
Thailand	1994	...	4.7	...	3.6	...	82.1	76.7	...	6.2	17.8	...	11.7	5.6
Turkey	1994	5.0	29.0	...	6.9	74.2	62.7	67.2	8.5	9.6	7.8	17.2	27.7	25.0
Uruguay	1995	...	37.7	...	10.3	44.8	52.0	57.2	9.9	12.6	11.7	45.3	35.4	31.1
Venezuela	1996	...	68.5	...	6.7	61.2	51.3	47.2	7.8	5.5	5.2	31.0	43.2	47.6
Yugoslavia	1996	...	6.6	...	2.2	...	73.5	77.1	...	...	7.7	...	...	15.2
Zambia	1994	...	2.8	...	1.3	...	43.2	69.8	...	4.3	13.6	...	52.5	16.6
Zimbabwe	1995	...	10 9	...	2.8	53.6	64.9	54.9	14.4	14.2	11.6	32.0	20.9	33.5

a/ At current prices.

TABLE 1.11

SELECTED CHARACTERISTICS OF BRANCHES, SELECTED YEARS AND COUNTRIES

Metal products (381)															
Country or area	Latest year	Value added per employee		Wages per employee		Percentage in output a/									
		Real annual growth rate (percentage)	Value (current 1000 dollars)	Real annual growth rate (percentage)	Value (current 1000 dollars)	Costs of input materials and utilities			Costs of labour			Operating surplus			
	(LY)	1985-LY	LY	1985-LY	LY	1985	1990	LY	1985	1990	LY	1985	1990	LY	
Industrialized countries b/															
Austria	1994	1.6	51.2	1.9	29.3	60.4	57.2	56.8	24.6	24.1	24.7	15.0	18.7	18.5	
Canada	1994	1.2	48.2	-0.1	24.1	56.7	55.8	55.8	21.3	23.6	22.1	22.0	20.6	22.1	
Finland	1995	6.4	53.4	2.9	30.3	47.9	54.1	66.0	25.2	23.4	19.3	26.8	22.5	14.7	
France	1995	1.4	78.6	...	...	53.3	51.8	50.4	33.7	32.2	...	12.9	16.0	...	
Germany	1994	...	...	...	32.7	...	...	...	...	...	26.1	...	...	...	
Iceland	1995	...	39.9	...	28.9	41.3	51.4	62.7	42.1	34.3	27.0	16.7	14.3	10.4	
Israel	1994	...	28.8	...	21.2	51.1	51.0	58.5	29.2	33.4	30.6	19.7	15.6	10.9	
Italy	1994	...	44.7	...	...	61.3	64.0	63.7	18.4	24.7	24.1	20.3	11.3	12.3	
Japan	1995	0.4	116.7	1.8	47.7	55.5	54.5	51.4	18.6	17.1	19.9	25.9	28.4	28.7	
Norway	1994	8.0	44.6	1.9	30.2	59.9	62.7	59.6	28.1	27.8	27.4	12.0	9.5	13.0	
South Africa	1994	...	...	...	8.5	67.2	60.1	...	22.9	25.3	...	9.9	14.6	...	
Spain	1995	...	36.0	1.1	19.4	55.7	59.7	63.1	20.5	19.0	19.9	23.7	21.3	17.1	
Sweden	1994	2.6	50.1	1.7	23.4	47.7	47.1	58.9	20.1	20.1	19.2	32.2	32.8	21.9	
United Kingdom	1995	-2.9	36.4	0.6	22.1	52.8	51.9	57.5	24.0	23.5	25.7	23.2	24.7	16.7	
United States of America	1995	2.0	67.5	-0.5	28.4	50.7	51.5	50.2	23.0	22.0	21.0	26.4	26.5	28.8	
Countries of eastern Europe and the former USSR															
Azerbaijan	1994	...	...	...	...	...	...	...	...	9.8	6.2	...	...	...	
Bulgaria	1996	...	...	...	0.8	...	...	...	8.6	15.1	11.2	...	...	...	
Kyrgyzstan	1994	...	...	...	...	...	...	...	...	...	7.5	...	...	...	
Latvia	1996	...	5.5	...	...	...	...	52.3	...	...	...	...	...	...	
Lithuania	1994	...	...	...	0.8	...	...	...	...	...	26.2	...	...	...	
Republic of Moldova	1995	...	...	...	0.5	...	...	...	...	29.4	10.8	...	...	...	
Romania	1994	...	...	...	0.9	...	62.3	...	...	14.3	...	...	23.4	...	
Russian Federation	1995	...	3.2	...	1.1	...	...	53.1	...	...	15.4	...	...	31.5	
Slovakia	1994	...	4.7	...	2.3	...	...	59.7	...	...	19.6	...	...	20.7	
Ukraine	1996	...	...	...	0.9	...	...	...	...	...	17.1	...	...	...	
Developing countries															
Bolivia	1995	...	6.8	...	1.7	...	71.1	63.0	...	6.0	9.5	...	22.9	27.5	
Cameroon	1996	...	9.2	...	6.1	...	...	75.7	...	...	16.0	...	...	8.3	
Chile	1995	...	25.4	3.9	8.0	55.2	57.6	57.8	11.6	11.1	13.3	33.2	31.2	28.9	
China	1996	...	...	...	...	65.8	73.0	74.7	...	...	...	...	...	...	
China (Hong Kong SAR)	1995	13.2	30.0	5.3	17.0	66.5	68.7	76.4	21.2	16.8	13.4	12.2	14.4	10.2	
China (Taiwan Province)	1996	2.8	21.0	5.1	13.4	66.5	63.8	62.1	26.0	26.2	24.2	7.5	10.0	13.6	
Colombia	1995	3.4	15.5	0.9	3.5	56.8	59.9	53.4	10.6	8.6	10.6	32.6	31.5	36.0	
Costa Rica	1996	...	...	...	...	75.9	76.9	76.8	...	...	...	...	...	...	
Croatia	1996	...	...	...	3.7	...	54.5	...	...	19.8	...	...	25.7	...	
Cyprus	1996	...	23.5	2.3	12.2	65.3	65.4	64.4	16.4	15.5	18.4	18.3	19.2	17.2	
Ecuador	1996	...	10.2	...	3.3	64.0	70.5	72.8	14.8	12.4	8.7	21.1	17.1	18.5	

a/ At current prices.

b/ Excluding countries of eastern Europe and the former USSR.

TABLE 1.11
(continued)

SELECTED CHARACTERISTICS OF BRANCHES, SELECTED YEARS AND COUNTRIES

Country or area	Latest year	Metal products (381)												
		Value added per employee		Wages per employee		Percentage in output a/								
		Real annual growth rate (percentage)	Value (current 1000 dollars)	Real annual growth rate (percentage)	Value (current 1000 dollars)	Costs of input materials and utilities			Costs of labour			Operating surplus		
	(LY)	1985-LY	LY	1985-LY	LY	1985	1990	LY	1985	1990	LY	1985	1990	LY
Egypt	1994	...	3.6	...	1.3	70.1	77.3	66.8	19.6	15.0	12.0	10.3	7.7	21.3
El Salvador	1996	...	6.1	...	2.7	47.1	...	63.1	12.8	...	16.4	40.1	...	20.5
Ethiopia	1996	...	4.1	...	0.9	...	54.3	53.0	...	23.7	10.7	...	22.1	36.3
Gabon	1995	...	26.3	...	16.1	...	...	66.5	...	...	20.4	...	...	13.1
Honduras	1995	...	5.1	...	2.2	67.4	69.5	77.0	14.7	10.7	9.9	17.9	19.8	13.2
India	1994	...	2.9	1.8	1.2	77.6	81.6	79.5	11.1	8.6	8.3	11.2	9.7	12.2
Indonesia	1996	...	10.3	2.9	1.9	70.5	70.6	60.8	7.7	4.8	7.2	21.8	24.6	32.0
Jordan	1995	...	6.4	...	2.3	68.1	60.8	67.3	15.1	13.3	11.6	16.8	25.9	21.1
Kenya	1995	5.1	3.9	...	1.5	86.9	82.6	83.0	6.0	6.0	6.5	7.1	11.3	10.5
Kuwait	1995	...	18.2	...	7.4	60.0	45.0	54.0	19.5	27.2	18.6	20.5	27.8	27.4
Macau	1996	...	15.8	...	7.4	56.9	56.8	57.6	26.6	21.7	19.9	16.5	21.4	22.5
Malawi	1994	...	2.4	...	0.9	60.8	57.8	85.5	9.8	5.2	5.4	29.4	37.1	9.1
Malaysia	1995	2.8	14.0	1.8	4.9	68.7	73.5	70.7	13.2	9.0	10.3	18.1	17.6	18.9
Mauritius	1994	...	12.5	6.9	4.4	62.8	50.9	50.5	13.5	11.2	17.5	23.7	37.9	32.0
Mexico	1994	...	24.5	1.9	7.9	56.0	55.8	57.4	11.6	11.2	13.8	32.4	33.0	28.8
Mongolia	1995	...	1.4	...	0.7	...	43.7	59.9	...	14.2	19.9	...	42.1	20.2
Morocco	1996	...	8.7	...	4.8	68.9	74.3	75.6	15.9	13.4	13.4	15.2	12.3	10.9
Namibia	1994	...	17.1	...	8.2	...	...	57.6	...	...	20.4	...	...	22.0
Nepal	1996	...	4.1	...	0.5	...	66.1	70.8	...	6.2	3.7	...	27.7	25.5
Peru	1994	0.9	13.4	...	3.4	66.1	57.4	66.5	6.7	7.9	8.4	27.2	34.7	25.1
Philippines	1995	...	6.9	0.6	2.3	76.3	65.7	66.7	9.2	11.6	11.1	14.5	22.7	22.1
Republic of Korea	1995	1.6	51.1	9.0	17.0	59.9	57.7	56.8	14.6	13.6	14.3	25.4	28.7	28.9
Senegal	1996	...	16.5	...	4.4	...	70.3	70.8	...	11.1	7.8	...	18.6	21.4
Singapore	1996	1.6	44.5	3.7	20.5	62.6	65.2	65.4	17.5	14.8	16.0	19.9	20.0	18.7
Slovenia	1995	...	...	...	...	...	...	63.0	...	...	...	...	...	...
Swaziland	1995	...	11.9	1.3	6.9	67.1	70.8	64.6	15.3	14.6	20.6	17.6	14.6	14.8
The f.Yugosl.Rep.of Macedonia	1996	...	4.0	...	3.6	...	48.1	63.7	...	28.4	33.0	...	23.5	3.2
Thailand	1994	...	9.3	...	2.8	...	81.3	62.9	...	3.7	11.3	...	15.0	25.8
Tonga	1994	...	...	...	2.4	...	...	...	17.5	23.2	18.6	...	...	...
Trinidad and Tobago	1995	...	7.9	...	3.7	...	61.7	70.9	...	23.5	13.8	...	14.8	15.3
Turkey	1994	0.8	22.5	...	4.4	58.2	55.6	56.0	11.9	11.1	8.6	29.9	33.3	35.5
Uruguay	1995	...	18.1	...	6.9	46.0	52.8	48.9	17.4	14.6	19.4	36.6	32.7	31.7
Venezuela	1996	...	14.2	...	3.1	58.4	64.5	58.1	15.5	11.6	9.0	26.1	23.9	32.8
Yugoslavia	1996	...	4.1	...	1.0	...	53.3	56.3	...	...	10.7	...	...	33.0
Zambia	1994	...	3.9	...	1.7	...	42.1	54.9	...	17.1	19.4	...	40.9	25.7
Zimbabwe	1995	...	7.9	...	3.3	57.2	53.5	55.4	23.3	19.2	19.0	19.5	27.3	25.6

a/ At current prices.

TABLE 1.11

SELECTED CHARACTERISTICS OF BRANCHES, SELECTED YEARS AND COUNTRIES

Non-electrical machinery (382)

Country or area	Latest year	Value added per employee		Wages per employee		Percentage in output a/								
		Real annual growth rate (percentage)	Value (current 1000 dollars)	Real annual growth rate (percentage)	Value (current 1000 dollars)	Costs of input materials and utilities			Costs of labour			Operating surplus		
	(LY)	1985-LY	LY	1985-LY	LY	1985	1990	LY	1985	1990	LY	1985	1990	LY
Industrialized countries b/														
Austria	1994	2.4	57.2	2.0	34.4	63.8	63.9	62.9	22.0	22.6	22.3	14.2	13.4	14.8
Canada	1994	6.6	56.0	0.4	26.7	52.8	55.0	57.7	23.4	23.5	20.2	23.8	21.5	22.2
Finland	1995	6.3	63.0	2.4	33.8	46.8	53.7	67.4	25.6	22.4	17.5	27.6	23.8	15.1
France	1995	1.8	60.8	...	...	58.1	60.0	65.2	30.7	26.9	...	11.2	13.1	...
Germany	1994	...	...	...	38.5	...	...	...	...	...	27.3	...	...	...
Israel	1994	...	32.2	...	23.9	47.8	58.3	62.4	35.4	30.6	27.8	16.8	11.1	9.7
Italy	1994	...	51.7	...	...	42.3	65.6	67.9	18.0	24.3	21.4	39.7	10.1	10.6
Japan	1995	0.9	133.6	1.2	52.3	56.8	57.9	60.2	16.6	14.6	15.6	26.6	27.6	24.2
Norway	1994	4.5	49.8	1.4	36.3	74.4	77.1	66.4	16.7	16.4	24.5	8.9	6.6	9.1
South Africa	1994	2.6	...	-0.1	11.8	56.7	61.7	...	29.2	21.7	...	14.0	16.6	...
Spain	1995	0.8	46.1	3.1	25.0	55.4	59.5	63.9	19.5	20.3	19.6	25.1	20.2	16.5
Sweden	1994	0.1	55.5	2.0	26.3	50.0	50.1	57.5	20.1	20.3	20.1	29.9	29.5	22.4
United Kingdom	1995	4.3	48.8	1.7	26.6	52.1	54.0	68.2	22.1	20.9	17.4	25.7	25.1	14.5
United States of America	1995	9.1	89.6	-0.3	34.8	48.6	48.3	50.5	23.7	22.1	19.2	27.8	29.6	30.2
Countries of eastern Europe and the former USSR														
Azerbaijan	1994	...	...	...	...	...	...	...	...	14.6	24.9	...	...	...
Latvia	1996	...	4.5	...	...	...	...	50.6	...	...	...	...	...	...
Lithuania	1994	...	...	...	0.9	...	...	...	...	...	22.7	...	...	...
Romania	1994	...	...	...	1.0	...	...	...	...	...	...	...	...	...
Russian Federation	1995	...	3.3	...	1.0	...	...	43.7	...	...	17.2	...	...	39.1
Slovakia	1994	...	3.4	...	2.2	...	...	58.3	...	...	27.2	...	...	14.5
Ukraine	1996	...	...	...	0.7	...	...	...	...	...	20.1	...	...	...
Developing countries														
Bolivia	1995	...	4.5	...	0.2	...	58.6	50.6	...	4.0	2.3	...	37.4	47.1
Brazil	1994	10.3	37.8	...	10.3	40.7	34.1	39.1	18.5	16.7	16.6	40.7	49.2	44.3
Chile	1995	...	29.9	-0.0	11.5	59.6	62.5	57.1	29.9	20.0	16.5	10.4	17.5	26.4
China	1996	...	...	...	...	63.9	71.1	73.3	9.0	...	...	27.1	...	...
China (Hong Kong SAR)	1995	1.0	39.7	5.0	18.4	70.1	71.8	76.1	18.2	12.6	11.1	11.7	15.7	12.8
China (Taiwan Province)	1996	3.1	24.2	5.2	14.9	67.8	65.6	70.1	17.5	20.1	18.4	14.7	14.2	11.5
Colombia	1995	7.0	13.7	1.1	3.6	56.8	65.2	53.8	11.3	8.2	12.2	32.0	26.7	33.9
Costa Rica	1996	...	...	...	...	65.2	66.0	67.6	...	...	...	...	...	...
Croatia	1996	...	...	...	3.9	...	53.4	...	...	17.7	...	...	28.8	...
Cyprus	1996	...	26.5	1.9	13.4	56.8	58.5	55.6	24.6	22.5	22.4	18.7	19.1	22.0
Ecuador	1996	...	9.7	...	2.3	59.5	70.6	71.4	18.2	14.9	6.9	22.2	14.6	21.7
Egypt	1994	...	10.0	...	1.8	73.0	75.6	45.3	16.7	14.9	9.7	10.3	9.5	45.0
El Salvador	1996	...	13.1	...	3.6	43.2	...	52.9	10.3	...	12.8	46.5	...	34.3
Ethiopia	1996	...	2.1	...	0.8	...	...	43.5	...	...	21.1	...	...	35.3
Honduras	1995	...	3.5	...	1.6	60.5	58.3	70.2	22.9	14.1	13.6	16.6	27.6	16.2

a/ At current prices.

b/ Excluding countries of eastern Europe and the former USSR.

TABLE 1.11
(continued)

SELECTED CHARACTERISTICS OF BRANCHES, SELECTED YEARS AND COUNTRIES

Non-electrical machinery (382)

Country or area	Latest year	Value added per employee: Real annual growth rate (percentage)	Value added per employee: Value (current 1000 dollars)	Wages per employee: Real annual growth rate (percentage)	Wages per employee: Value (current 1000 dollars)	Percentage in output a/ — Costs of input materials and utilities			Costs of labour			Operating surplus		
	(LY)	1985-LY	LY	1985-LY	LY	1985	1990	LY	1985	1990	LY	1985	1990	LY
India	1994	...	4.3	1.6	1.6	73.0	77.8	76.6	12.2	9.6	8.5	14.8	12.6	14.9
Indonesia	1996	...	13.0	4.7	2.1	64.3	66.1	65.1	8.9	6.2	5.8	26.8	27.7	29.1
Jordan	1995	...	8.7	...	3.0	64.8	57.2	70.3	19.9	8.4	10.1	15.3	34.4	19.5
Kenya	1995	...	3.1	...	1.5	81.6	75.0	...	10.3	10.4	...	8.0	14.6	...
Kuwait	1995	...	9.1	...	5.2	36.6	40.5	37.8	47.2	47.5	35.5	16.2	12.0	26.7
Macau	1996	...	10.5	...	6.5	48.8	39.5	43.1	38.3	29.2	35.4	12.9	31.3	21.5
Malaysia	1995	1.2	19.1	1.2	5.3	65.7	68.0	74.2	16.0	8.7	7.1	18.3	23.3	18.7
Malta	1994	8.3	20.6	2.8	11.0	42.4	46.8	59.7	27.1	39.3	21.6	30.5	13.9	18.7
Mexico	1994	...	37.6	1.8	9.6	53.2	53.0	63.0	11.9	11.9	9.5	34.9	35.1	27.5
Peru	1994	4.5	17.8	...	4.3	65.4	51.4	61.5	10.3	12.6	9.4	24.4	36.0	29.1
Philippines	1995	...	10.9	4.4	3.0	66.3	58.3	62.5	16.7	19.0	10.3	17.0	22.7	27.2
Republic of Korea	1995	3.6	59.0	8.2	17.8	58.7	56.8	59.5	14.2	13.3	12.2	27.1	29.9	28.2
Senegal	1996	...	6.8	...	3.0	...	58.5	80.3	...	32.1	8.8	...	9.5	10.9
Singapore	1996	...	...	0.6	18.9	54.9	68.4	72.7	22.1	8.2	5.7	23.0	23.4	21.7
Slovenia	1995	...	...	...	...	...	...	72.4	...	...	...	...	...	...
Thailand	1994	...	...	...	3.3	...	46.1	20.0	...	6.7	1.3	...	47.2	78.7
Trinidad and Tobago	1995	...	4.4	...	3.4	...	74.7	55.8	...	10.8	34.6	...	14.5	9.6
Tunisia	1996	...	...	...	...	...	85.2	83.1	...	12.6	11.4	...	2.2	5.5
Turkey	1994	4.7	30.9	...	5.4	68.1	57.2	53.9	10.7	10.5	8.1	21.2	32.3	38.0
Uruguay	1995	...	16.3	...	6.4	26.0	45.1	40.5	20.8	17.4	23.3	53.3	37.5	36.2
Venezuela	1996	...	15.7	...	2.8	55.3	57.9	51.6	16.5	11.8	8.8	28.1	30.3	39.6
Yugoslavia	1996	...	3.8	...	1.0	...	49.7	48.6	...	...	13.6	...	...	37.8
Zimbabwe	1995	...	8.1	...	3.1	45.2	45.2	50.1	24.2	17.9	19.1	30.6	36.9	30.8

a/ At current prices.

TABLE 1.11

SELECTED CHARACTERISTICS OF BRANCHES, SELECTED YEARS AND COUNTRIES

Country or area	Latest year	Value added per employee: Real annual growth rate (percentage)	Value added per employee: Value (current 1000 dollars)	Wages per employee: Real annual growth rate (percentage)	Wages per employee: Value (current 1000 dollars)	Percentage in output a/: Costs of input materials and utilities			Costs of labour			Operating surplus		
	(LY)	1985-LY	LY	1985-LY	LY	1985	1990	LY	1985	1990	LY	1985	1990	LY
Electrical machinery (383)														
Industrialized countries b/														
Austria	1994	5.6	59.2	3.2	35.8	62.8	62.8	63.0	22.8	22.0	22.4	14.4	15.2	14.6
Canada	1994	3.0	69.8	1.1	28.5	50.8	49.2	54.6	23.4	23.5	18.5	25.8	27.3	26.9
Finland	1995	11.4	81.5	3.1	32.7	48.5	52.3	67.5	25.7	21.1	13.0	25.8	26.6	19.4
France	1995	3.2	73.9	...	...	52.3	53.3	54.2	35.3	31.3	...	12.5	15.4	...
Germany	1994	...	...	...	38.1	...	...	...	...	...	26.1	...	...	...
Israel	1994	...	48.6	...	34.8	45.6	45.2	58.2	33.7	34.2	29.9	20.7	20.6	11.9
Italy	1994	...	51.0	...	...	59.0	61.8	62.5	19.9	25.2	24.8	21.2	12.9	12.7
Japan	1995	6.5	125.7	2.4	46.6	60.5	60.3	59.4	13.6	13.8	15.1	25.9	25.9	25.6
Norway	1994	8.4	54.3	1.5	35.3	58.3	65.6	63.8	28.8	23.8	23.5	12.9	10.6	12.7
South Africa	1994	...	...	0.2	11.1	63.9	71.2	...	21.7	22.7	...	14.4	6.1	...
Spain	1995	8.1	50.1	2.6	25.3	56.2	60.0	65.7	19.6	16.3	17.3	24.2	23.7	16.9
Sweden	1994	11.0	55.6	2.8	26.6	46.1	45.7	66.6	20.8	18.3	16.0	33.2	35.9	17.5
Switzerland	1996	...	87.3	...	...	...	59.8	61.2	...	...	...	...	...	...
United Kingdom	1995	2.7	47.8	1.5	24.3	52.3	53.5	64.2	22.9	23.5	18.2	24.8	23.0	17.6
United States of America	1995	10.8	113.8	-0.2	33.8	43.3	45.0	42.2	25.2	21.4	17.1	31.6	33.6	40.6
Countries of eastern Europe and the former USSR														
Azerbaijan	1994	...	...	...	...	...	...	...	...	12.3	12.6	...	...	...
Bulgaria	1996	...	2.1	...	1.0	...	...	74.7	10.8	13.7	11.5	...	...	13.8
Kyrgyzstan	1994	...	...	...	...	...	...	...	...	4.1	5.7	...	...	...
Latvia	1996	...	3.2	...	...	...	...	55.0	...	...	...	...	...	...
Lithuania	1994	...	...	...	0.9	...	...	...	...	...	20.8	...	...	...
Romania	1994	...	...	...	0.9	...	59.7	...	...	10.1	...	...	30.2	...
Russian Federation	1995	...	3.9	...	0.8	...	...	48.3	...	...	10.5	...	...	41.1
Slovakia	1994	...	4.9	...	2.2	...	...	69.5	...	...	13.9	...	...	16.6
Ukraine	1996	...	...	...	0.6	...	...	...	...	17.8	17.4	...	...	...
Developing countries														
Bolivia	1995	...	6.8	...	1.4	...	60.1	63.4	...	6.2	7.3	...	33.7	29.3
Brazil	1994	7.3	56.6	...	11.8	43.5	34.1	38.1	13.0	14.1	12.9	43.5	51.8	49.0
Cameroon	1996	...	13.6	...	5.3	...	76.7	70.6	...	15.8	11.4	...	7.5	18.0
Chile	1995	...	42.2	1.5	11.7	37.8	48.4	45.9	16.6	10.8	15.1	45.6	40.8	39.0
China	1996	...	...	...	...	65.6	74.2	77.0	3.5	...	...	30.9	...	...
China (Hong Kong SAR)	1995	...	47.6	6.0	17.4	77.1	76.1	65.4	14.5	12.7	12.7	8.5	11.2	22.0
China (Taiwan Province)	1996	9.0	32.1	6.9	15.2	70.6	70.3	72.6	14.2	15.3	13.0	15.2	14.4	14.4
Colombia	1995	-1.3	19.1	0.5	4.4	55.6	58.0	52.1	9.1	7.2	10.9	35.2	34.8	36.9
Costa Rica	1996	...	...	...	...	73.3	74.8	76.9	...	...	...	...	...	...
Croatia	1996	...	...	...	4.8	...	46.8	...	...	18.4	...	...	34.8	...
Cyprus	1996	4.4	23.7	4.2	13.9	72.3	64.1	63.2	12.1	19.4	21.6	15.5	16.5	15.2
Ecuador	1996	...	21.2	...	2.5	65.2	71.1	67.2	13.0	10.5	3.8	21.8	18.4	29.0

a/ At current prices.

b/ Excluding countries of eastern Europe and the former USSR.

TABLE 1.11
(continued)

SELECTED CHARACTERISTICS OF BRANCHES, SELECTED YEARS AND COUNTRIES

Electrical machinery (383)

Country or area	Latest year	Value added per employee: Real annual growth rate (percentage)	Value added per employee: Value (current 1000 dollars)	Wages per employee: Real annual growth rate (percentage)	Wages per employee: Value (current 1000 dollars)	Percentage in output a/: Costs of input materials and utilities			Costs of labour			Operating surplus		
	(LY)	1985-LY	LY	1985-LY	LY	1985	1990	LY	1985	1990	LY	1985	1990	LY
Egypt	1994	...	6.9	...	2.1	61.8	77.0	70.0	11.0	11.4	9.2	27.2	11.7	20.8
El Salvador	1996	...	10.1	...	3.3	44.2	...	70.1	9.5	...	9.7	46.4	...	20.2
Ethiopia	1996	...	1.0	...	1.0	...	45.1	...	...	17.1	...	...	37.8	...
Gabon	1995	...	49.1	...	16.9	...	...	75.5	...	...	8.4	...	...	16.1
Honduras	1995	...	6.9	...	2.5	65.0	69.3	77.3	14.2	6.4	8.4	20.8	24.3	14.4
India	1994	...	6.1	1.3	1.7	76.5	77.4	73.7	11.4	8.4	7.1	12.1	14.2	19.2
Indonesia	1996	...	17.4	4.2	2.3	70.5	71.3	62.7	6.7	3.9	4.9	22.8	24.7	32.4
Jordan	1995	...	14.7	...	3.6	51.5	64.0	75.6	27.3	5.8	6.0	21.2	30.3	18.4
Kenya	1995	12.2	16.1	...	2.7	75.4	83.1	...	11.7	2.5	...	12.9	14.4	...
Kuwait	1995	...	30.1	...	8.7	71.2	26.6	65.5	10.9	9.6	9.9	17.9	63.8	24.6
Macau	1996	...	12.1	...	6.8	70.5	80.6	69.7	18.4	11.1	17.1	11.0	8.3	13.3
Malaysia	1995	5.7	17.3	1.3	5.0	68.9	78.4	79.8	11.3	6.7	5.8	19.8	14.9	14.4
Malta	1994	16.4	29.4	5.2	12.2	66.3	88.6	90.7	12.4	4.9	3.8	21.3	6.5	5.4
Mauritius	1994	...	11.1	8.4	5.2	77.7	74.2	71.7	10.5	11.3	13.2	11.8	14.5	15.1
Mexico	1994	...	21.7	...	5.9	53.4	45.9	47.7	13.2	13.8	14.1	33.4	40.3	38.2
Mongolia	1995	...	0.3	...	0.1	...	35.5	78.8	...	5.5	8.9	...	59.0	12.2
Morocco	1996	...	13.5	...	6.0	69.0	74.3	59.4	15.5	11.6	18.0	15.5	14.1	22.6
Nepal	1996	...	5.4	...	0.5	...	67.8	71.0	...	4.2	2.8	...	28.0	26.1
Peru	1994	...	14.3	...	4.4	60.1	55.5	68.6	6.3	6.9	9.6	33.6	37.6	21.8
Philippines	1995	...	13.3	1.4	3.3	73.2	61.2	65.5	10.8	9.2	8.6	16.0	29.5	26.0
Republic of Korea	1995	11.8	94.2	9.0	16.4	62.5	58.7	49.2	10.5	11.2	8.8	27.0	30.0	41.9
Senegal	1995	...	8.9	...	6.0	...	83.9	85.1	...	10.8	10.1	...	5.3	4.8
Singapore	1996	7.7	66.3	5.2	22.3	67.7	72.8	69.8	11.6	10.1	10.1	20.7	17.2	20.0
Slovenia	1996	...	19.0	...	9.7	...	62.7	64.7	...	26.2	18.2	...	11.0	17.2
The f.Yugosl.Rep.of Macedonia	1996	...	4.9	...	3.8	...	55.1	72.1	...	21.6	21.5	...	23.4	6.4
Thailand	1994	...	17.4	...	3.7	...	60.7	70.2	...	4.3	6.3	...	35.0	23.4
Trinidad and Tobago	1995	...	13.0	...	4.8	61.8	72.7	64.5	24.9	14.9	13.1	13.3	12.4	22.4
Tunisia	1996	...	...	...	...	...	74.4	73.9	...	12.1	9.4	...	13.5	16.7
Turkey	1994	4.3	38.9	...	6.5	63.8	58.3	53.0	8.3	9.8	7.9	28.0	31.9	39.1
Uruguay	1995	...	21.5	...	6.9	43.9	55.1	49.2	14.0	11.0	16.4	42.1	33.9	34.4
Venezuela	1996	...	22.3	...	3.8	58.5	58.6	49.3	15.8	12.1	8.7	25.6	29.4	42.0
Yugoslavia	1996	...	5.6	...	1.3	...	61.5	65.4	...	...	7.9	...	...	26.7
Zimbabwe	1995	...	10.3	...	3.2	52.6	41.8	53.5	23.5	20.3	14.5	23.9	37.9	32.0

a/ At current prices.

TABLE 1.11

SELECTED CHARACTERISTICS OF BRANCHES, SELECTED YEARS AND COUNTRIES

Transport equipment (384)

Country or area	Latest year	Value added per employee		Wages per employee		Percentage in output a/								
		Real annual growth rate (percentage)	Value (current 1000 dollars)	Real annual growth rate (percentage)	Value (current 1000 dollars)	Costs of input materials and utilities			Costs of labour			Operating surplus		
	(LY)	1985-LY	LY	1985-LY	LY	1985	1990	LY	1985	1990	LY	1985	1990	LY
Industrialized countries b/														
Austria	1994	2.6	64.6	1.8	33.0	61.6	65.2	68.1	20.5	17.1	16.3	17.9	17.7	15.6
Canada	1994	2.0	87.9	0.7	33.1	76.0	75.1	77.2	10.4	11.4	8.6	13.6	13.4	14.2
Finland	1995	3.8	52.8	2.9	33.4	53.8	63.6	65.5	25.3	22.1	21.9	20.9	14.3	12.6
France	1995	2.2	68.0	...	...	68.3	68.8	69.7	29.1	20.6	...	2.7	10.6	...
Germany	1994	...	...	...	41.2	...	...	...	...	...	21.2	...	...	...
Iceland	1995	...	47.2	...	39.6	...	42.8	47.2	...	48.6	44.3	...	8.6	8.5
Israel	1994	...	36.3	...	33.6	46.2	47.1	55.8	49.7	43.1	40.9	4.0	9.8	3.3
Italy	1994	...	38.7	...	...	65.7	68.3	70.4	15.8	25.7	24.4	18.4	6.0	5.2
Japan	1995	2.7	163.6	1.4	57.3	69.9	70.3	68.6	10.8	9.7	11.0	19.3	20.0	20.4
Norway	1994	-1.5	44.6	2.5	34.2	66.8	69.2	66.7	26.7	21.6	25.5	6.5	9.3	7.8
South Africa	1994	3.2	...	0.2	11.1	...	74.8	...	...	15.5	...	...	9.7	...
Spain	1995	7.2	53.2	2.5	26.1	71.5	70.8	75.2	17.5	13.3	12.2	11.0	15.9	12.7
Sweden	1994	5.5	53.7	2.2	25.8	63.1	57.9	66.8	15.6	17.5	15.9	21.2	24.6	17.3
United Kingdom	1995	5.4	51.8	2.0	28.6	59.0	58.7	71.5	22.0	19.7	15.7	19.0	21.6	12.8
United States of America	1995	2.6	109.1	-0.5	41.6	59.7	60.0	62.4	18.4	17.4	14.4	21.9	22.6	23.3
Countries of eastern Europe and the former USSR														
Azerbaijan	1994	...	...	...	...	...	...	...	...	22.0	43.8	...	...	...
Bulgaria	1996	...	...	...	1.1	...	...	...	11.4	12.4	13.7	...	...	...
Kyrgyzstan	1994	...	...	...	...	...	...	...	...	...	7.0	...	...	...
Latvia	1996	...	4.3	...	...	...	...	51.1	...	...	...	...	...	...
Lithuania	1994	...	...	...	1.0	...	...	...	...	...	17.5	...	...	...
Romania	1994	...	...	...	1.1	...	72.1	...	...	25.9	...	...	2.0	...
Russian Federation	1995	...	1.8	...	1.4	...	...	82.3	...	...	13.6	...	...	4.1
Slovakia	1994	...	5.5	...	2.4	...	...	70.3	...	...	12.7	...	...	17.0
Ukraine	1996	...	...	...	0.8	...	...	...	...	...	22.2	...	...	...
Developing countries														
Bolivia	1995	...	4.8	...	1.5	...	54.6	76.7	...	13.4	7.1	...	31.9	16.2
Brazil	1994	3.5	61.5	...	13.5	62.1	47.6	42.9	10.3	13.9	12.5	27.6	38.4	44.6
Chile	1995	...	23.9	2.8	8.5	62.6	64.5	73.1	8.6	8.3	9.6	28.8	27.2	17.2
China	1996	...	...	...	...	64.9	73.8	75.5	4.3	...	...	30.8	...	...
China (Hong Kong SAR)	1995	1.7	39.6	4.5	25.7	48.5	38.1	37.8	36.2	39.5	40.4	15.3	22.4	21.8
China (Taiwan Province)	1996	4.8	41.4	5.3	17.0	65.6	67.4	63.4	14.7	13.5	15.0	19.6	19.1	21.6
Colombia	1995	6.7	24.7	1.1	4.9	68.9	71.5	70.9	7.6	4.4	5.8	23.5	24.1	23.3
Costa Rica	1996	...	...	...	...	51.0	50.2	44.2	...	...	...	...	...	...
Croatia	1996	...	...	...	4.1	...	64.5	...	...	21.5	...	...	14.0	...
Cyprus	1996	...	25.9	2.3	13.9	54.6	54.3	50.8	25.0	23.0	26.4	20.4	22.7	22.8
Ecuador	1996	...	9.7	...	2.6	78.5	84.9	87.6	6.9	4.5	3.3	14.6	10.6	9.1
Egypt	1994	...	4.1	...	2.0	77.1	62.5	77.3	17.5	19.7	11.1	5.4	17.8	11.5

a/ At current prices.

b/ Excluding countries of eastern Europe and the former USSR.

TABLE 1.11
(continued)

SELECTED CHARACTERISTICS OF BRANCHES, SELECTED YEARS AND COUNTRIES

Transport equipment (384)

Country or area	Latest year	Value added per employee		Wages per employee		Percentage in output a/								
		Real annual growth rate (percentage)	Value (current 1000 dollars)	Real annual growth rate (percentage)	Value (current 1000 dollars)	Costs of input materials and utilities			Costs of labour			Operating surplus		
	(LY)	1985-LY	LY	1985-LY	LY	1985	1990	LY	1985	1990	LY	1985	1990	LY
El Salvador	1996	...	6.4	...	2.6	...	...	57.7	...	...	17.1	...	...	25.2
Ethiopia	1996	...	11.0	...	1.3	...	61.4	77.5	...	10.5	2.6	...	28.1	19.9
Honduras	1995	...	2.4	...	1.3	52.0	61.3	57.2	27.4	21.3	23.5	20.6	17.4	19.3
India	1994	...	3.1	1.0	1.6	76.1	75.6	78.4	15.3	12.5	11.1	8.6	11.9	10.5
Indonesia	1996	0.2	30.1	3.1	2.6	66.6	60.4	56.0	9.5	3.6	3.8	23.9	36.0	40.2
Jordan	1995	...	10.9	...	2.8	30.4	70.2	71.8	27.0	10.7	7.3	42.6	19.1	20.8
Kenya	1995	-2.2	2.1	...	1.8	82.9	88.9	...	9.9	9.3	...	7.2	1.9	...
Kuwait	1995	...	14.9	...	8.3	...	...	64.6	...	...	19.7	...	...	15.7
Malaysia	1995	5.7	24.0	0.6	6.0	63.5	71.0	77.2	14.0	5.5	5.7	22.5	23.6	17.1
Mauritius	1994	...	8.4	4.7	4.1	42.6	52.1	57.2	17.5	13.1	21.0	39.9	34.8	21.8
Mexico	1994	...	51.1	4.0	10.9	66.2	70.2	71.3	6.8	5.6	6.1	27.1	24.2	22.6
Morocco	1996	...	15.3	...	6.8	77.6	72.8	68.7	9.9	10.9	13.9	12.4	16.3	17.4
Peru	1994	3.6	24.0	...	5.0	62.9	48.5	62.8	6.4	6.7	7.8	30.7	44.7	29.4
Philippines	1995	...	24.4	5.4	3.8	74.7	74.3	74.0	11.5	4.9	4.1	13.8	20.8	22.0
Republic of Korea	1995	2.3	75.7	9.2	23.2	64.6	63.4	60.6	10.7	11.8	12.1	24.7	24.8	27.3
Senegal	1996	...	19.0	...	4.1	...	41.4	57.0	...	24.6	9.4	...	34.1	33.7
Singapore	1996	2.3	44.9	2.7	23.7	42.2	57.4	54.2	24.8	16.6	24.1	33.0	25.9	21.7
Slovenia	1996	...	15.6	...	9.4	...	75.4	87.3	...	18.2	7.6	...	6.4	5.0
The f.Yugosl.Rep.of Macedonia	1996	...	3.5	...	3.2	...	47.9	56.8	...	17.2	39.1	...	34.9	4.1
Thailand	1994	...	28.7	...	4.5	...	77.1	63.5	...	4.1	5.7	...	18.8	30.8
Tonga	1994	...	...	...	1.6	...	...	...	17.2	22.2	16.8	...	...	...
Trinidad and Tobago	1995	...	7.3	...	3.1	44.9	67.6	74.2	18.2	14.3	11.0	36.8	18.1	14.8
Tunisia	1996	...	...	...	...	...	72.4	70.1	...	13.0	12.5	...	14.5	17.4
Turkey	1994	2.7	28.9	...	6.9	67.1	63.5	58.9	10.3	11.1	9.8	22.5	25.5	31.3
Uruguay	1995	...	33.7	...	7.8	54.4	52.6	38.4	10.4	8.4	14.3	35.2	39.0	47.2
Venezuela	1996	...	47.8	...	3.6	73.3	74.4	57.1	11.0	9.6	3.2	15.7	16.1	39.6
Yugoslavia	1996	...	3.4	...	0.9	...	59.9	45.6	...	...	13.8	...	...	40.6
Zambia	1994	...	3.2	...	1.7	...	36.7	67.7	...	21.1	17.5	...	42.2	14.8
Zimbabwe	1995	...	9.2	...	3.8	46.5	64.1	76.6	26.5	14.3	9.6	27.0	21.6	13.7

a/ At current prices.

Part II

COUNTRY TABLES

ALBANIA

Supplier of information:
Directorate of Statistics, Ministry of Economy, Tirana.

Basic source of data:
Not reported.

Major deviations from ISIC (Revision 2):
None reported.

Reference period (if not calendar year):

Scope:
The data relate to the state sector only. However, in 1996, food products and beverages include establishments from the private sector.

Method of enumeration:
Not reported.

Adjusted for non-response:
Not reported.

Concepts and definitions of variables:
No deviations from the standard UN concepts and definitions are reported.

Related national publications:

Albania

ISIC Revision 2	Number of establishments					Number of employees					Wages and salaries paid to employees				
		(numbers)					(numbers)					(thousand LEKS)			
ISIC Industry	Note	1993	1994	1995	1996	Note	1993	1994	1995	1996	Note	1993	1994	1995	1996
311/2 Food products		182	136	91	1790		14392	6766	4094	4461		645449	755850	326713	638691
3111 Slaughtering, preparing & preserving meat		13	-	-	79		291	-	-	354		14832	-	-	32501
3112 Dairy products		15	30	14	230		1052	806	141	466		46089	41671	11296	53921
3113 Canning, preserving of fruits & vegetables		-	-	-	26		-	-	-	160		-	-	-	14236
3114 Canning, preserving and processing of fish		1	18	20	6		10	430	162	270		248	60001	10951	15453
3115 Vegetable and animal oils and fats		13	12	10	23		1100	506	223	348		36372	70640	18024	54092
3116 Grain mill products		46	29	20	655		6085	2943	2103	878		293309	370694	143614	117516
3117 Bakery products		31	20	13	738		2559	1073	846	1366		134472	118872	84740	301545
3118 Sugar factories and refineries		-	1	1	-		-	392	432	-		-	34512	46285	-
3119 Cocoa, chocolate and sugar confectionery		7	8	1	20		553	254	29	260		19387	21644	176	17024
3121 Other food products		56	18	12	11		2742	362	158	88		100740	37816	11627	9966
3122 Prepared animal feeds		-	-	-	2		-	-	-	271		-	-	-	22437
313 Beverages		17	27	10	178		708	454	421	1375		25456	54322	42522	159898
3131 Distilling, rectifying and blending spirits		11	10	1	94		464	...	...	349		18057	...	...	31613
3132 Wine industries		2	3	2	17		56	...	...	437		1565	...	...	46297
3133 Malt liquors and malt		3	3	1	11		168	...	...	171		4970	...	...	32733
3134 Soft drinks and carbonated waters		1	1	2	56		20	...	...	418		864	...	...	49255
314 Tobacco		3	6	6	9		2253	1311	976	2148		71968	123125	69564	172972
321 Textiles		16	14	6	6		7946	3338	172	106		296632	53248	5362	4450
3211 Spinning, weaving and finishing textiles		7	10	5	5		6233	2900	154	88		218878	46077	4368	3456
3212 Made-up textile goods excl. wearing apparel		-	-	-	-		-	-	-	-		-	-	-	-
3213 Knitting mills		8	3	1	1		1691	352	18	18		76052	6139	994	994
3214 Carpets and rugs		-	-	-	-		-	-	-	-		-	-	-	-
3215 Cordage, rope and twine		-	-	-	-		-	-	-	-		-	-	-	-
3219 Other textiles		1	1	-	-		22	86	-	-		1702	1032	-	-
322 Wearing apparel, except footwear		30	17	9	8		6376	3565	1522	1265		230368	34886	115358	87977
323 Leather and fur products		9	1	1	1		648	146	10	520		29268	2252	2746	31632
3231 Tanneries and leather finishing		5	1	1	1		317	146	10	520		12512	2252	2746	31632
3232 Fur dressing and dyeing industries		1	-	-	-		118	-	-	-		8502	-	-	-
3233 Leather prods. excl. wearing apparel		3	-	-	-		213	-	-	-		8254	-	-	-
324 Footwear, except rubber or plastic		4	5	4	3		2248	836	...	458		106954	16457	...	22080
331 Wood products, except furniture		31	16	13	9		1624	1784	756	567		57962	51968	87974	49741
3311 Sawmills, planing and other wood mills		22	7	6	4		1410	1042	400	137		49879	22584	46312	13677
3312 Wooden and cane containers		3	1	1	-		156	63	75	-		5036	1026	8126	-
3319 Other wood and cork products		6	8	6	5		58	679	281	430		3047	28358	33536	36064
332 Furniture and fixtures, excl. metal		13	-	-	-		1398	-	-	-		71934	-	-	-
341 Paper and products		6	2	1	-		463	46	10	-		17850	595	1296	-
3411 Pulp, paper and paperboard articles		4	2	1	-		279	46	10	-		11594	595	1296	-
3412 Containers of paper and paperboard		1	-	-	-		144	-	-	-		4910	-	-	-
3419 Other pulp, paper and paperboard articles		1	-	-	-		40	-	-	-		1346	-	-	-
342 Printing and publishing		20	17	2	1		1067	803	187	224		41590	10675	26752	18805
351 Industrial chemicals		8	3	1	2		2102	175	17	17		77915	2226	1870	1870
3511 Basic chemicals excl. fertilizers		5	-	-	1		530	-	-	-		17504	-	-	-
3512 Fertilizers and pesticides		3	3	1	1		1572	175	17	17		60411	2226	1870	1870
3513 Synthetic resins and plastic materials		-	-	-	-		-	-	-	-		-	-	-	-
352 Other chemicals		4	3	3	2		675	228	118	120		35383	6353	13424	8264
3521 Paints, varnishes and lacquers		1	1	1	1		77	156	71	70		3115	1700	9634	5288
3522 Drugs and medicines		-	-	-	-		-	-	-	-		-	-	-	-
3523 Soap, cleaning preps., perfumes, cosmetics		-	-	-	-		-	-	-	-		-	-	-	-
3529 Other chemical products		3	2	2	1		598	72	47	50		32268	4653	3790	2976
353 Petroleum refineries		5	4	4	4		2586	1917	1675	1827		106972	122082	128247	156771

Code	Industry												
354	Misc. petroleum and coal products	-	-	-	-	-	-	-	-	-	-	-	-
355	Rubber products	-	2	2	1	-	344	353	109	-	5664	28876	8274
3551	Tyres and tubes	-	2	2	1	-	344	353	109	-	5664	28876	8274
3559	Other rubber products	-	-	-	-	-	-	-	-	-	-	-	-
356	Plastic products	4	4	1	2	1405	686	438	735	53232	9555	41015	33604
361	Pottery, china, earthenware	-	5	1	2	-	...	...	101	-	...	...	4012
362	Glass and products	3	-	-	-	248	-	-	-	8507	-	-	-
369	Other non-metallic mineral products	40	26	14	13	6638	4640	3801	3217	321948	1033464	828997	254620
3691	Structural clay products	18	5	1	1	2702	132	9	-	136669	3015	1564	-
3692	Cement, lime and plaster	6	3	3	3	2209	1716	1683	1980	104656	393881	367259	251608
3699	Other non-metallic mineral products	16	18	10	9	1727	2792	2109	1237	80623	636568	460174	3012
371	Iron and steel	1	2	1	1	1985	1720	1700	1700	82091	51636	82032	82032
372	Non-ferrous metals	-	4	4	4	-	2158	2185	2160	-	99886	217723	217723
381	Fabricated metal products	23	21	20	24	1685	2297	1109	861	59030	181013	89042	66695
3811	Cutlery, hand tools and general hardware	5	-	-	8	378	-	-	430	11646	-	-	38572
3812	Furniture and fixtures primarily of metal	-	-	-	-	-	-	-	-	-	-	-	-
3813	Structural metal products	-	-	-	-	-	-	-	-	-	-	-	-
3819	Other fabricated metal products	18	21	20	16	1307	2297	1109	431	47384	181013	89042	28123
382	Non-electrical machinery	13	19	19	6	1517	1691	1328	1032	51045	113678	115804	117928
3821	Engines and turbines	1	-	-	-	35	-	-	-	750	-	-	-
3822	Agricultural machinery and equipment	7	14	14	3	1040	534	359	62	36552	45920	33340	5700
3823	Metal and wood working machinery	-	-	-	-	-	-	-	-	-	-	-	-
3824	Other special industrial machinery	3	5	5	2	336	1157	969	936	10008	67758	82464	110272
3825	Office, computing and accounting machinery	-	-	-	-	-	-	-	-	-	-	-	-
3829	Other non-electrical machinery & equipment	2	-	-	1	106	-	-	34	3735	-	-	1956
383	Electrical machinery	7	13	8	6	894	1294	571	455	30636	29268	64923	35712
3831	Electrical industrial machinery	3	4	3	4	434	554	266	331	14058	12604	31092	25912
3832	Radio, television and communication equipm.	1	1	1	-	180	135	88	-	12767	3385	9458	-
3833	Electrical appliances and housewares	1	6	2	-	74	391	93	-	764	7436	10348	-
3839	Other electrical apparatus and supplies	2	2	2	2	206	214	124	124	3047	5843	14025	9800
384	Transport equipment	2	-	-	-	101	-	-	-	3076	-	-	-
3841	Shipbuilding and repairing	-	-	-	-	-	-	-	-	-	-	-	-
3842	Railroad equipment	-	-	-	-	-	-	-	-	-	-	-	-
3843	Motor vehicles	1	-	-	-	69	-	-	-	1977	-	-	-
3844	Motorcycles and bicycles	-	-	-	-	-	-	-	-	-	-	-	-
3845	Aircraft	-	-	-	-	-	-	-	-	-	-	-	-
3849	Other transport equipment	1	-	-	-	32	-	-	-	1099	-	-	-
385	Professional and scientific equipment	1	2	2	-	72	206	116	-	2443	12571	14634	-
3851	Prof. and scientific equipment n.e.c.	1	2	2	-	72	206	116	-	2443	12571	14634	-
3852	Photographic and optical goods	-	-	-	-	-	-	-	-	-	-	-	-
3853	Watches and clocks	-	-	-	-	-	-	-	-	-	-	-	-
390	Other manufacturing industries	-	4	3	8	-	239	50	446	-	15108	17478	33521
3901	Jewellery and related articles	-	-	-	-	-	-	-	-	-	-	-	-
3902	Musical instruments	-	-	-	-	-	-	-	-	-	-	-	-
3903	Sporting and athletic goods	-	-	-	-	-	-	-	-	-	-	-	-
3909	Manufacturing industries, n.e.c.	-	4	3	8	-	239	50	446	-	15108	17478	33521
3	Total manufacturing	442	364	238	2080	59031	38398	21609	23904	2427709	2785882	2322352	2207272

Albania

ISIC Revision 2 ISIC Industry	Output in factor values Note	(million LEKS) 1993	1994	1995	1996	Value added Note	(million LEKS) 1993	1994	1995	1996	Gross fixed capital formation Note	(million LEKS) 1995	1996
311/2 Food products		9565	2877	...	10208		...	...	...	...		...	...
3111 Slaughtering, preparing & preserving meat		38	-	-	536		...	...	...	...		...	...
3112 Dairy products		98	3	...	912		...	...	...	...		...	...
3113 Canning, preserving of fruits & vegetables		-	-	-	52		...	...	...	...		...	...
3114 Canning, preserving and processing of fish		...a/	151	...	37		...	...	...	...		...	...
3115 Vegetable and animal oils and fats		685	602	...	396		...	...	...	...		...	...
3116 Grain mill products		6224	1000	...	2117		...	...	...	...		...	...
3117 Bakery products		2085	708	...	5974		...	...	...	...		...	...
3118 Sugar factories and refineries		-	176	...	27		...	...	...	...		...	...
3119 Cocoa, chocolate and sugar confectionery		58	137	...	77		...	...	...	...		...	...
3121 Other food products		378a/	99	...	72		...	...	...	...		...	...
3122 Prepared animal feeds		-	-	-	8		...	...	...	...		...	...
313 Beverages		197	601	...	2218		...	...	...	...		...	...
3131 Distilling, rectifying and blending spirits		167	...	...	415		...	...	...	...		...	...
3132 Wine industries		14	...	...	160		...	...	...	...		...	...
3133 Malt liquors and malt		14	...	...	610		...	...	...	...		...	...
3134 Soft drinks and carbonated waters		2	...	...	1034		...	...	...	...		...	...
314 Tobacco		840	711	...	3149		...	...	...	...		...	...
321 Textiles		1047	131	25	12		...	...	...	...		...	...
3211 Spinning, weaving and finishing textiles		762	86	20	8		...	...	...	...		...	...
3212 Made-up textile goods excl. wearing apparel		-	-	-	-		...	...	...	...		...	...
3213 Knitting mills		238	31	5	5		...	...	...	...		...	...
3214 Carpets and rugs		-	-	-	-		...	...	...	...		...	...
3215 Cordage, rope and twine		-	-	-	-		...	...	...	...		...	...
3219 Other textiles		47	14	-	-		...	...	...	...		...	...
322 Wearing apparel, except footwear		451	315	236	264		...	...	...	...		...	...
323 Leather and fur products		83	3	21	100		...	...	...	...		...	...
3231 Tanneries and leather finishing		73b/	3	21	100		...	...	...	...		...	...
3232 Fur dressing and dyeing industries		10	-	-	-		...	...	...	...		...	...
3233 Leather prods. excl. wearing apparel		...b/	-	-	-		...	...	...	...		...	...
324 Footwear, except rubber or plastic		431	154	66	313		...	...	...	...		...	...
331 Wood products, except furniture		471	251	231	152		...	...	...	...		...	...
3311 Sawmills, planing and other wood mills		450	73	137	72		...	...	...	...		...	...
3312 Wooden and cane containers		17	1	1	-		...	...	...	...		...	...
3319 Other wood and cork products		4	176	94	80		...	...	...	...		...	...
332 Furniture and fixtures, excl. metal		285	-	-	-		...	...	...	...		...	...
341 Paper and products		45	15	3	-		...	...	...	...		...	...
3411 Pulp, paper and paperboard articles		22	15	3	-		...	...	...	...		...	...
3412 Containers of paper and paperboard		21	-	-	-		...	...	...	...		...	...
3419 Other pulp, paper and paperboard articles		2	-	-	-		...	...	...	...		...	...
342 Printing and publishing		297	292	298	60		...	...	...	...		...	...
351 Industrial chemicals		381	93	35	35		...	...	...	...		...	...
3511 Basic chemicals excl. fertilizers		68	-	-	-		...	...	...	...		...	...
3512 Fertilizers and pesticides		313	93	35	35		...	...	...	...		...	...
3513 Synthetic resins and plastic materials		-	-	-	-		...	...	...	...		...	...
352 Other chemicals		200	38	460	116		...	...	...	...		...	...
3521 Paints, varnishes and lacquers		47	20	325	32		...	...	...	...		...	...
3522 Drugs and medicines		-	-	-	-		...	...	...	...		...	...
3523 Soap, cleaning preps., perfumes, cosmetics		-	-	-	-		...	...	...	...		...	...
3529 Other chemical products		153	18	135	84		...	...	...	...		...	...
353 Petroleum refineries		4856	4039	6262	5502		...	...	...	...		...	...

ISIC	Industry										
354	Misc. petroleum and coal products	-	-	-	-	...	...	...	...	...	...
355	Rubber products	-	60	109	16	...	...	...	...	...	...
3551	Tyres and tubes	-	60	109	16	...	...	...	...	...	...
3559	Other rubber products	-	-	-	-	...	...	...	...	...	...
356	Plastic products	282	73	50	97	...	...	...	...	...	...
361	Pottery, china, earthenware	-	...	...	2	...	...	...	...	...	...
362	Glass and products	23	-	-	-	...	...	...	...	...	...
369	Other non-metallic mineral products	1771	2487	1933	1997	...	...	...	...	...	...
3691	Structural clay products	634	17	2	1	...	...	...	...	...	...
3692	Cement, lime and plaster	892	1367	1144	1262	...	...	...	...	...	...
3699	Other non-metallic mineral products	245	1104	787	733	...	...	...	...	...	...
371	Iron and steel	559	709	762	762	...	...	...	...	...	...
372	Non-ferrous metals	-	2323	3865	3865	...	...	...	...	...	...
381	Fabricated metal products	280	382	579	167	...	...	...	...	...	...
3811	Cutlery, hand tools and general hardware	85	-	-	60	...	...	...	...	...	...
3812	Furniture and fixtures primarily of metal	-	-	-	-	...	...	...	...	...	...
3813	Structural metal products	-	-	-	-	...	...	...	...	...	...
3819	Other fabricated metal products	195	382	579	107	...	...	...	...	...	...
382	Non-electrical machinery	170	435	332	309	...	...	...	...	...	...
3821	Engines and turbines	2	-	-	-	...	...	...	...	...	...
3822	Agricultural machinery and equipment	113	150	...	14	...	...	...	...	...	...
3823	Metal and wood working machinery	-	-	-	-	...	...	...	...	...	...
3824	Other special industrial machinery	28	285	332	294	...	...	...	...	...	...
3825	Office, computing and accounting machinery	-	-	-	-	...	...	...	...	...	...
3829	Other non-electrical machinery & equipment	27	-	-	1	...	...	...	...	...	...
383	Electrical machinery	270	268	290	85	...	...	...	...	...	...
3831	Electrical industrial machinery	98	75	43	9	...	...	...	...	...	...
3832	Radio, television and communication equipm.	161	-	142	-	...	...	...	...	...	...
3833	Electrical appliances and housewares	1	134	19	-	...	...	...	...	...	...
3839	Other electrical apparatus and supplies	10	58	87	76	...	...	...	...	...	...
384	Transport equipment	5	-	-	-	...	...	...	...	...	...
3841	Shipbuilding and repairing	-	-	-	-	...	...	...	...	...	...
3842	Railroad equipment	-	-	-	-	...	...	...	...	...	...
3843	Motor vehicles	2	-	-	-	...	...	...	...	...	...
3844	Motorcycles and bicycles	-	-	-	-	...	...	...	...	...	...
3845	Aircraft	-	-	-	-	...	...	...	...	...	...
3849	Other transport equipment	3	-	-	-	...	...	...	...	...	...
385	Professional and scientific equipment	20	135	162	-	...	...	...	...	...	...
3851	Prof. and scientific equipment n.e.c.	20	135	162	-	...	...	...	...	...	...
3852	Photographic and optical goods	-	-	-	-	...	...	...	...	...	...
3853	Watches and clocks	-	-	-	-	...	...	...	...	...	...
390	Other manufacturing industries	-	13	118	93	...	...	...	...	...	...
3901	Jewellery and related articles	-	-	-	-	...	...	...	...	...	...
3902	Musical instruments	-	-	-	-	...	...	...	...	...	...
3903	Sporting and athletic goods	-	-	-	-	...	...	...	...	...	...
3909	Manufacturing industries, n.e.c.	-	13	118	93	...	...	...	...	...	...
3	Total manufacturing	22529	16404	16042	29523	...	...	...	...	...	...

a/ 3121 includes 3114.
b/ 3231 includes 3233.

Albania

ISIC Revision 2		Index numbers of industrial production											
		(1990=100)											
ISIC Industry	Note	1985	1986	1987	1988	1989	1990	1991	1992	1993	1994	1995	1996
311/2 Food products		...	...	...	...	...	...	...	...	...	...	...	...
313 Beverages		...	...	...	...	...	...	...	...	...	...	...	...
314 Tobacco		...	...	...	...	...	...	...	...	...	...	...	...
321 Textiles		...	...	...	...	...	...	...	...	...	...	...	...
322 Wearing apparel, except footwear		...	...	...	...	...	...	...	...	...	...	...	...
323 Leather and fur products		...	...	...	...	...	...	...	...	...	...	...	...
324 Footwear, except rubber or plastic		...	...	...	...	...	...	...	...	...	...	...	...
331 Wood products, except furniture		...	...	...	...	...	...	...	...	...	...	...	...
332 Furniture and fixtures, excl. metal		...	...	...	...	...	...	...	...	...	...	...	...
341 Paper and products		...	...	...	...	...	...	...	...	...	...	...	...
342 Printing and publishing		...	...	...	...	...	...	...	...	...	...	...	...
351 Industrial chemicals		...	...	...	...	...	...	...	...	...	...	...	...
352 Other chemicals		...	...	...	...	...	...	...	...	...	...	...	...
353 Petroleum refineries		...	...	...	...	...	...	...	...	...	...	...	...
354 Misc. petroleum and coal products		...	...	...	...	...	...	...	...	...	...	...	...
355 Rubber products		...	...	...	...	...	...	...	...	...	...	...	...
356 Plastic products		...	...	...	...	...	...	...	...	...	...	...	...
361 Pottery, china, earthenware		...	...	...	...	...	...	...	...	...	...	...	...
362 Glass and products		...	...	...	...	...	...	...	...	...	...	...	...
369 Other non-metallic mineral products		...	...	...	...	...	...	...	...	...	...	...	...
371 Iron and steel		...	...	...	...	...	...	...	...	...	...	...	...
372 Non-ferrous metals		...	...	...	...	...	...	...	...	...	...	...	...
381 Fabricated metal products		...	...	...	...	...	...	...	...	...	...	...	...
382 Non-electrical machinery		...	...	...	...	...	...	...	...	...	...	...	...
383 Electrical machinery		...	...	...	...	...	...	...	...	...	...	...	...
384 Transport equipment		...	...	...	...	...	...	...	...	...	...	...	...
385 Professional and scientific equipment		...	...	...	...	...	...	...	...	...	...	...	...
390 Other manufacturing industries		...	...	...	...	...	...	...	...	...	...	...	...
3 Total manufacturing		...	...	...	...	...	...	...	...	...	...	...	...

ARGENTINA

Supplier of information:
Instituto Nacional de Estatísdica y Censos (INDEC), Buenos Aires.

Basic source of data:
Census of manufacturing industry.

Major deviations from ISIC (Revision 3):
None reported.

Reference period (if not calendar year):

Scope:
All establishments, except that for gross fixed capital formation the scope of the survey is limited to establishments with more than five persons engaged.

Method of enumeration:
Not reported.

Adjusted for non-response:
Not reported.

Concepts and definitions of variables:
Data on the number of establishments and the number of employees for 1994 are as of July of that year.

Related national publications:
Censo Nacional Económico, 1994, Resultados definitivos, Versiòn revisada, Serie A no. 1; published by the Instituto Nacional de Estadística y Censos, INDEC, Buenos Aires.

Argentina

ISIC Revision 3	Number of establishments (numbers)					Number of employees (numbers)					Wages and salaries paid to employees (million PESOS)				
ISIC Industry	Note	1991	1992	1993	1994	Note	1991	1992	1993	1994	Note	1991	1992	1993	1994
151 Processed meat,fish,fruit,vegetables,fats		...	...	1840	2048		...	...	73912	69801		...	...	871.8	...
1511 Processing/preserving of meat		...	...	1079	1208		...	...	45728	46890		...	...	553.7	...
1512 Processing/preserving of fish		...	...	122	140		...	...	7233	6011		...	...	90.0	...
1513 Processing/preserving of fruit & vegetables		...	...	552	606		...	...	15381	12022		...	...	126.2	...
1514 Vegetable and animal oils and fats		...	...	87	94		...	...	5570	4878		...	...	101.9	...
1520 Dairy products		...	...	738	766		...	...	20682	20458		...	...	355.5	...
153 Grain mill products; starches; animal feeds		...	...	389	419		...	...	12331	12129		...	...	196.1	...
1531 Grain mill products		...	...	218	233		...	...	8755	8789		...	...	140.3	...
1532 Starches and starch products		...	...	14	17		...	...	1087	950		...	...	21.8	...
1533 Prepared animal feeds		...	...	157	169		...	...	2489	2390		...	...	34.1	...
154 Other food products		...	...	15162	17320		...	...	83290	96282		...	...	870.4	...
1541 Bakery products		...	...	12640	14504		...	...	48672	54952		...	...	412.8	...
1542 Sugar		...	...	24	33		...	...	8342	14091		...	...	104.0	...
1543 Cocoa, chocolate and sugar confectionery		...	...	169	194		...	...	8603	8572		...	...	138.7	...
1544 Macaroni, noodles & similar products		...	...	1809	2025		...	...	6155	6809		...	...	68.6	...
1549 Other food products n.e.c.		...	...	520	564		...	...	11518	11858		...	...	146.4	...
155 Beverages		...	...	3326	3612		...	...	40851	40638		...	...	682.3	...
1551 Distilling, rectifying & blending of spirits		...	...	20	23		...	...	1196	1190		...	...	23.5	...
1552 Wines		...	...	700	744		...	...	13707	13543		...	...	155.2	...
1553 Malt liquors and malt		...	...	18	20		...	...	3917	3520		...	...	121.7	...
1554 Soft drinks; mineral waters		...	...	2588	2825		...	...	22031	22385		...	...	381.9	...
1600 Tobacco products		...	...	25	27		...	...	5846	4962		...	...	148.2	...
171 Spinning, weaving and finishing of textiles		...	...	1179	1291		...	...	34767	34476		...	...	381.5	...
1711 Textile fibre preparation; textile weaving		...	...	794	870		...	...	27466	26881		...	...	303.2	...
1712 Finishing of textiles		...	...	385	421		...	...	7301	7595		...	...	78.3	...
172 Other textiles		...	...	907	986		...	...	9567	9286		...	...	106.0	...
1721 Made-up textile articles, except apparel		...	...	609	669		...	...	4501	4235		...	...	39.3	...
1722 Carpets and rugs		...	...	47	56		...	...	896	927		...	...	11.7	...
1723 Cordage, rope, twine and netting		...	...	25	26		...	...	502	436		...	...	5.3	...
1729 Other textiles n.e.c.		...	...	226	235		...	...	3668	3688		...	...	49.6	...
1730 Knitted and crocheted fabrics and articles		...	...	769	862		...	...	9791	9646		...	...	87.6	...
1810 Wearing apparel, except fur apparel		...	...	5125	5956		...	...	34285	36030		...	...	267.4	...
1820 Dressing & dyeing of fur; processing of fur		...	...	100	106		...	...	393	365		...	...	3.7	...
191 Tanning, dressing and processing of leather		...	...	835	924		...	...	13461	13797		...	...	139.6	...
1911 Tanning and dressing of leather		...	...	339	366		...	...	11366	11518		...	...	123.8	...
1912 Luggage, handbags, etc.; saddlery & harness		...	...	496	558		...	...	2095	2279		...	...	15.8	...
1920 Footwear		...	...	1388	1547		...	...	24270	24356		...	...	238.9	...
2010 Sawmilling and planing of wood		...	...	1321	1535		...	...	7538	9078		...	...	48.9	...
202 Products of wood, cork, straw, etc.		...	...	3984	4585		...	...	10842	11993		...	...	89.3	...
2021 Veneer sheets, plywood, particle board, etc.		...	...	78	88		...	...	1955	2189		...	...	23.0	...
2022 Builders' carpentry and joinery		...	...	1612	1869		...	...	3866	4325		...	...	30.5	...
2023 Wooden containers		...	...	359	406		...	...	2447	2684		...	...	16.1	...
2029 Other wood products; articles of cork/straw		...	...	1935	2222		...	...	2574	2795		...	...	19.7	...
210 Paper and paper products		...	...	882	961		...	...	23550	23781		...	...	342.2	...
2101 Pulp, paper and paperboard		...	...	86	91		...	...	6422	6573		...	...	103.0	...
2102 Corrugated paper and paperboard		...	...	482	536		...	...	9626	9705		...	...	134.6	...
2109 Other articles of paper and paperboard		...	...	314	334		...	...	7502	7503		...	...	104.5	...
221 Publishing		...	...	929	1070		...	...	15346	15010		...	...	448.6	...
2211 Publishing of books and other publications		...	...	287	323		...	...	1936	1971		...	...	33.5	...
2212 Publishing of newspapers, journals, etc.		...	...	456	545		...	...	12185	11825		...	...	393.8	...
2213 Publishing of recorded media		...	...	18	15		...	...	172	170		...	...	5.2	...
2219 Other publishing		...	...	168	187		...	...	1053	1044		...	...	16.2	...

222 Printing and related service activities	...	...	5354	6323	...	...	18959	20926	...	...	267.9	...
2221 Printing	...	...	4869	5759	...	...	16458	18235	...	...	235.1	...
2222 Service activities related to printing	...	...	485	564	...	...	2501	2691	...	...	32.8	...
2230 Reproduction of recorded media	...	...	24	27	...	...	224	245	...	...	5.8	...
2310 Coke oven products	...	...	24	26	...	...	267	303	...	...	5.4	...
2320 Refined petroleum products	...	...	70	85	...	...	7071	6002	...	...	240.5	...
2330 Processing of nuclear fuel	...	...	3	3	...	...	874	952	...	...	19.1	...
241 Basic chemicals	...	...	499	503	...	...	13773	13811	...	...	270.5	...
2411 Basic chemicals, except fertilizers	...	...	291	285	...	...	7744	7956	...	...	155.4	...
2412 Fertilizers and nitrogen compounds	...	...	16	18	...	...	1359	1134	...	...	21.6	...
2413 Plastics in primary forms; synthetic rubber	...	...	192	200	...	...	4670	4721	...	...	93.5	...
242 Other chemicals	...	...	1809	1898	...	...	44845	45772	...	...	1065.3	...
2421 Pesticides and other agro-chemical products	...	...	67	68	...	...	1254	1149	...	...	27.2	...
2422 Paints, varnishes, printing ink and mastics	...	...	290	313	...	...	5193	5347	...	...	119.5	...
2423 Pharmaceuticals, medicinal chemicals, etc.	...	...	458	485	...	...	18675	19571	...	...	550.6	...
2424 Soap, cleaning & cosmetic preparations	...	...	567	601	...	...	12819	12353	...	...	242.6	...
2429 Other chemical products n.e.c.	...	...	427	431	...	...	6904	7352	...	...	125.3	...
2430 Man-made fibres	...	...	44	50	...	...	2299	1819	...	...	46.9	...
251 Rubber products	...	...	551	585	...	...	10206	10119	...	...	172.0	...
2511 Rubber tyres and tubes	...	...	123	135	...	...	4790	4770	...	...	108.3	...
2519 Other rubber products	...	...	428	450	...	...	5416	5349	...	...	63.7	...
2520 Plastic products	...	...	2679	2899	...	...	27827	29754	...	...	356.4	...
2610 Glass and glass products	...	...	252	277	...	...	7921	7797	...	...	140.8	...
269 Non-metallic mineral products n.e.c.	...	...	3844	4286	...	...	31103	31996	...	...	405.8	...
2691 Pottery, china and earthenware	...	...	223	249	...	...	3163	3005	...	...	56.8	...
2692 Refractory ceramic products	...	...	63	85	...	...	870	865	...	...	11.2	...
2693 Struct.non-refractory clay; ceramic products	...	...	1092	1328	...	...	8466	8347	...	...	112.5	...
2694 Cement, lime and plaster	...	...	139	142	...	...	6285	6198	...	...	108.3	...
2695 Articles of concrete, cement and plaster	...	...	1490	1642	...	...	7445	8467	...	...	67.6	...
2696 Cutting, shaping & finishing of stone	...	...	654	681	...	...	3136	3323	...	...	26.3	...
2699 Other non-metallic mineral products n.e.c.	...	...	183	159	...	...	1738	1791	...	...	23.1	...
2710 Basic iron and steel	...	...	119	116	...	...	19487	18886	...	...	390.3	...
2720 Basic precious and non-ferrous metals	...	...	45	46	...	...	4227	3899	...	...	107.2	...
273 Casting of metals	...	...	832	889	...	...	10536	10953	...	...	126.7	...
2731 Casting of iron and steel	...	...	409	434	...	...	6723	6908	...	...	82.6	...
2732 Casting of non-ferrous metals	...	...	423	455	...	...	3813	4045	...	...	44.1	...
281 Struct.metal products;tanks;steam generators	...	...	4944	5745	...	...	14284	16530	...	...	124.0	...
2811 Structural metal products	...	...	4674	5455	...	...	11227	13444	...	...	93.2	...
2812 Tanks, reservoirs and containers of metal	...	...	250	271	...	...	2840	2858	...	...	28.1	...
2813 Steam generators	...	...	20	19	...	...	217	228	...	...	2.7	...
289 Other metal products; metal working services	...	...	8623	9442	...	...	36299	38504	...	...	428.3	...
2891 Metal forging/pressing/stamping/roll-forming	...	...	365	383	...	...	3810	3907	...	...	43.7	...
2892 Treatment & coating of metals	...	...	1672	1876	...	...	3438	3871	...	...	30.6	...
2893 Cutlery, hand tools and general hardware	...	...	979	1060	...	...	6422	6693	...	...	86.1	...
2899 Other fabricated metal products n.e.c.	...	...	5607	6123	...	...	22629	24033	...	...	267.9	...
291 General purpose machinery	...	...	2601	2799	...	...	20905	21695	...	...	272.2	...
2911 Engines & turbines(not for transport equip.)	...	...	99	101	...	...	1608	1548	...	...	29.1	...
2912 Pumps, compressors, taps and valves	...	...	487	504	...	...	6254	6368	...	...	92.2	...
2913 Bearings, gears, gearing & driving elements	...	...	114	106	...	...	1423	1381	...	...	19.1	...
2914 Ovens, furnaces and furnace burners	...	...	68	72	...	...	583	563	...	...	7.1	...
2915 Lifting and handling equipment	...	...	562	600	...	...	2621	2850	...	...	30.5	...
2919 Other general purpose machinery	...	...	1271	1416	...	...	8416	8985	...	...	94.2	...
292 Special purpose machinery	...	...	3958	4266	...	...	20665	22076	...	...	240.4	...
2921 Agricultural and forestry machinery	...	...	2382	2571	...	...	7952	8953	...	...	91.2	...
2922 Machine tools	...	...	454	477	...	...	2489	2504	...	...	30.6	...
2923 Machinery for metallurgy	...	...	72	72	...	...	651	834	...	...	7.6	...
2924 Machinery for mining & construction	...	...	254	278	...	...	1593	1814	...	...	19.2	...
2925 Food/beverage/tobacco processing machinery	...	...	310	339	...	...	3889	3761	...	...	48.0	...
2926 Machinery for textile, apparel and leather	...	...	136	146	...	...	982	928	...	...	9.2	...
2927 Weapons and ammunition	...	...	26	26	...	...	1158	1118	...	...	14.5	...
2929 Other special purpose machinery	...	...	324	357	...	...	1951	2164	...	...	20.2	...
2930 Domestic appliances n.e.c.	...	...	391	403	...	...	11677	11159	...	...	176.2	...

continued

Argentina

ISIC Revision 3	Number of establishments (numbers)					Number of employees (numbers)					Wages and salaries paid to employees (million PESOS)				
ISIC Industry	Note	1991	1992	1993	1994	Note	1991	1992	1993	1994	Note	1991	1992	1993	1994
3000 Office, accounting and computing machinery		...	...	120	133		...	...	873	1106		...	...	27.2	...
3110 Electric motors, generators and transformers		...	...	1058	1164		...	...	4652	4658		...	...	55.1	...
3120 Electricity distribution & control apparatus		...	...	201	216		...	...	3557	3325		...	...	50.3	...
3130 Insulated wire and cable		...	...	156	168		...	...	4305	4158		...	...	78.8	...
3140 Accumulators, primary cells and batteries		...	...	752	786		...	...	2407	2330		...	...	34.3	...
3150 Lighting equipment and electric lamps		...	...	380	394		...	...	2552	2824		...	...	38.6	...
3190 Other electrical equipment n.e.c.		...	...	541	571		...	...	5484	6046		...	...	73.4	...
3210 Electronic valves, tubes, etc.		...	...	200	216		...	...	1134	1259		...	...	15.7	...
3220 TV/radio transmitters; line comm. apparatus		...	...	194	227		...	...	3936	3760		...	...	90.5	...
3230 TV and radio receivers and associated goods		...	...	124	134		...	...	4698	4274		...	...	102.9	...
331 Medical, measuring, testing appliances, etc.		...	...	1058	1231		...	...	5142	5442		...	...	61.1	...
3311 Medical, surgical and orthopaedic equipment		...	...	788	934		...	...	2568	2887		...	...	27.5	...
3312 Measuring/testing/navigating appliances,etc.		...	...	213	227		...	...	2163	2124		...	...	27.5	...
3313 Industrial process control equipment		...	...	57	70		...	...	411	431		...	...	6.1	...
3320 Optical instruments & photographic equipment		...	...	119	129		...	...	1158	1218		...	...	13.6	...
3330 Watches and clocks		...	...	19	22		...	...	209	299		...	...	3.1	...
3410 Motor vehicles		...	...	18	33		...	...	22884	24087		...	...	701.2	...
3420 Automobile bodies, trailers & semi-trailers		...	...	439	474		...	...	6109	6495		...	...	74.5	...
3430 Parts/accessories for automobiles		...	...	2076	2547		...	...	35154	36217		...	...	548.9	...
351 Building and repairing of ships and boats		...	...	301	347		...	...	1609	2721		...	...	21.9	...
3511 Building and repairing of ships		...	...	164	180		...	...	1351	2383		...	...	19.9	...
3512 Building/repairing of pleasure/sport. boats		...	...	137	167		...	...	258	338		...	...	2.0	...
3520 Railway/tramway locomotives & rolling stock		...	...	19	23		...	...	723	694		...	...	9.7	...
3530 Aircraft and spacecraft		...	...	44	54		...	...	226	334		...	...	3.7	...
359 Transport equipment n.e.c.		...	...	344	350		...	...	3922	3676		...	...	48.2	...
3591 Motorcycles		...	...	64	64		...	...	1981	1872		...	...	34.3	...
3592 Bicycles and invalid carriages		...	...	219	222		...	...	1656	1499		...	...	11.5	...
3599 Other transport equipment n.e.c.		...	...	61	64		...	...	285	305		...	...	2.4	...
3610 Furniture		...	...	4872	5582		...	...	16436	19194		...	...	125.5	...
369 Manufacturing n.e.c.		...	...	1488	2121		...	...	7653	8087		...	...	83.7	...
3691 Jewellery and related articles		...	...	212	233		...	...	665	681		...	...	6.2	...
3692 Musical instruments		...	...	35	34		...	...	103	104		...	...	0.9	...
3693 Sports goods		...	...	123	126		...	...	608	545		...	...	5.1	...
3694 Games and toys		...	...	195	202		...	...	1280	1474		...	...	11.9	...
3699 Other manufacturing n.e.c.		...	...	923	1526		...	...	4997	5283		...	...	59.6	...
3710 Recycling of metal waste and scrap		...	...	...	...		...	...	...	...		...	...	...	...
3720 Recycling of non-metal waste and scrap		...	...	...	...		...	...	...	...		...	...	...	...
D Total manufacturing		...	...	90088	101605		...	...	858994	887490		...	...	12401.7	...

Argentina

ISIC Revision 3	Output in producers' prices					Value added in producers' prices					Gross fixed capital formation		
		(million PESOS)					(million PESOS)					(million PESOS)	
ISIC Industry	Note	1991	1992	1993	1994	Note	1991	1992	1993	1994	Note	1993	1994
151 Processed meat, fish, fruit, vegetables, fats		...	...	9144.8	...		...	...	1594.0	...		301.5	...
1511 Processing/preserving of meat		...	...	4607.3	...		...	...	913.4	...		153.0	...
1512 Processing/preserving of fish		...	...	463.5	...		...	...	72.5	...		29.7	...
1513 Processing/preserving of fruit & vegetables		...	...	1164.8	...		...	...	397.2	...		46.4	...
1514 Vegetable and animal oils and fats		...	...	2909.2	...		...	...	210.9	...		72.4	...
1520 Dairy products		...	...	2767.8	...		...	...	623.5	...		133.5	...
153 Grain mill products; starches; animal feeds		...	...	1882.5	...		...	...	406.0	...		52.9	...
1531 Grain mill products		...	...	1288.8	...		...	...	304.5	...		32.9	...
1532 Starches and starch products		...	...	181.9	...		...	...	35.6	...		9.4	...
1533 Prepared animal feeds		...	...	411.8	...		...	...	65.9	...		10.7	...
154 Other food products		...	...	5281.6	...		...	...	1841.7	...		232.6	...
1541 Bakery products		...	...	2268.9	...		...	...	915.0	...		103.7	...
1542 Sugar		...	...	442.7	...		...	...	145.9	...		9.3	...
1543 Cocoa, chocolate and sugar confectionery		...	...	781.5	...		...	...	218.5	...		49.7	...
1544 Macaroni, noodles & similar products		...	...	428.0	...		...	...	168.4	...		16.9	...
1549 Other food products n.e.c.		...	...	1360.5	...		...	...	393.9	...		53.0	...
155 Beverages		...	...	4819.5	...		...	...	1745.5	...		383.0	...
1551 Distilling, rectifying & blending of spirits		...	...	330.8	...		...	...	119.1	...		6.6	...
1552 Wines		...	...	1623.8	...		...	...	440.4	...		49.5	...
1553 Malt liquors and malt		...	...	564.3	...		...	...	277.8	...		86.9	...
1554 Soft drinks; mineral waters		...	...	2300.5	...		...	...	908.2	...		239.9	...
1600 Tobacco products		...	...	2341.6	...		...	...	1764.8	...		47.3	...
171 Spinning, weaving and finishing of textiles		...	...	2331.4	...		...	...	796.0	...		93.9	...
1711 Textile fibre preparation; textile weaving		...	...	1869.2	...		...	...	628.5	...		70.5	...
1712 Finishing of textiles		...	...	462.2	...		...	...	167.5	...		23.4	...
172 Other textiles		...	...	672.2	...		...	...	253.4	...		31.3	...
1721 Made-up textile articles, except apparel		...	...	308.8	...		...	...	105.4	...		7.5	...
1722 Carpets and rugs		...	...	65.7	...		...	...	17.6	...		3.9	...
1723 Cordage, rope, twine and netting		...	...	22.2	...		...	...	9.1	...		1.0	...
1729 Other textiles n.e.c.		...	...	275.5	...		...	...	121.4	...		19.0	...
1730 Knitted and crocheted fabrics and articles		...	...	639.4	...		...	...	241.6	...		20.3	...
1810 Wearing apparel, except fur apparel		...	...	1983.8	...		...	...	719.5	...		32.6	...
1820 Dressing & dyeing of fur; processing of fur		...	...	36.4	...		...	...	12.2	...		0.3	...
191 Tanning, dressing and processing of leather		...	...	1121.9	...		...	...	287.4	...		22.8	...
1911 Tanning and dressing of leather		...	...	992.6	...		...	...	244.2	...		21.3	...
1912 Luggage, handbags, etc.; saddlery & harness		...	...	129.3	...		...	...	43.2	...		1.5	...
1920 Footwear		...	...	1046.0	...		...	...	405.3	...		59.8	...
2010 Sawmilling and planing of wood		...	...	328.6	...		...	...	136.4	...		11.3	...
202 Products of wood, cork, straw, etc.		...	...	576.7	...		...	...	222.2	...		26.5	...
2021 Veneer sheets, plywood, particle board, etc.		...	...	122.4	...		...	...	38.1	...		15.8	...
2022 Builders' carpentry and joinery		...	...	206.0	...		...	...	82.0	...		5.4	...
2023 Wooden containers		...	...	80.6	...		...	...	31.6	...		2.2	...
2029 Other wood products; articles of cork/straw		...	...	167.7	...		...	...	70.4	...		3.1	...
210 Paper and paper products		...	...	2321.7	...		...	...	575.6	...		172.3	...
2101 Pulp, paper and paperboard		...	...	628.4	...		...	...	102.6	...		31.8	...
2102 Corrugated paper and paperboard		...	...	854.4	...		...	...	244.5	...		40.8	...
2109 Other articles of paper and paperboard		...	...	838.9	...		...	...	228.5	...		99.8	...
221 Publishing		...	...	2047.8	...		...	...	886.4	...		106.7	...
2211 Publishing of books and other publications		...	...	246.1	...		...	...	105.0	...		4.1	...
2212 Publishing of newspapers, journals, etc.		...	...	1616.9	...		...	...	697.3	...		95.7	...
2213 Publishing of recorded media		...	...	91.3	...		...	...	43.2	...		-	...
2219 Other publishing		...	...	93.5	...		...	...	40.9	...		6.9	...

continued

Argentina

ISIC Revision 3	Output in producers' prices					Value added in producers' prices					Gross fixed capital formation		
		(million PESOS)					(million PESOS)					(million PESOS)	
ISIC Industry	Note	1991	1992	1993	1994	Note	1991	1992	1993	1994	Note	1993	1994
222 Printing and related service activities		...	...	1439.6	...		...	...	635.4	...		98.2	...
2221 Printing		...	...	1256.2	...		...	...	556.0	...		86.4	...
2222 Service activities related to printing		...	...	183.4	...		...	...	79.4	...		11.8	...
2230 Reproduction of recorded media		...	...	43.6	...		...	...	20.5	...		4.0	...
2310 Coke oven products		...	...	52.8	...		...	...	16.9	...		1.1	...
2320 Refined petroleum products		...	...	7831.9	...		...	...	3230.8	...		279.5	...
2330 Processing of nuclear fuel		...	...	41.7	...		...	...	12.9	...		8.5	...
241 Basic chemicals		...	...	2220.6	...		...	...	477.9	...		81.4	...
2411 Basic chemicals, except fertilizers		...	...	1332.3	...		...	...	339.7	...		59.1	...
2412 Fertilizers and nitrogen compounds		...	...	56.4	...		...	...	15.4	...		-0.2	...
2413 Plastics in primary forms; synthetic rubber		...	...	831.9	...		...	...	122.8	...		22.4	...
242 Other chemicals		...	...	7228.4	...		...	...	2288.1	...		216.7	...
2421 Pesticides and other agro-chemical products		...	...	391.2	...		...	...	55.1	...		7.5	...
2422 Paints, varnishes, printing ink and mastics		...	...	697.0	...		...	...	229.2	...		21.4	...
2423 Pharmaceuticals, medicinal chemicals, etc.		...	...	3243.4	...		...	...	1155.0	...		94.7	...
2424 Soap, cleaning & cosmetic preparations		...	...	1942.3	...		...	...	566.7	...		51.0	...
2429 Other chemical products n.e.c.		...	...	954.4	...		...	...	282.1	...		42.1	...
2430 Man-made fibres		...	...	264.2	...		...	...	78.6	...		13.7	...
251 Rubber products		...	...	663.5	...		...	...	267.9	...		23.2	...
2511 Rubber tyres and tubes		...	...	386.9	...		...	...	143.6	...		14.5	...
2519 Other rubber products		...	...	276.6	...		...	...	124.3	...		8.7	...
2520 Plastic products		...	...	2340.3	...		...	...	876.9	...		269.9	...
2610 Glass and glass products		...	...	581.3	...		...	...	257.6	...		35.8	...
269 Non-metallic mineral products n.e.c.		...	...	2106.8	...		...	...	827.6	...		142.0	...
2691 Pottery, china and earthenware		...	...	148.5	...		...	...	90.0	...		3.4	...
2692 Refractory ceramic products		...	...	51.5	...		...	...	15.1	...		1.8	...
2693 Struct.non-refractory clay; ceramic products		...	...	430.7	...		...	...	209.7	...		47.9	...
2694 Cement, lime and plaster		...	...	642.1	...		...	...	193.5	...		57.3	...
2695 Articles of concrete, cement and plaster		...	...	435.4	...		...	...	157.7	...		16.9	...
2696 Cutting, shaping & finishing of stone		...	...	194.5	...		...	...	88.9	...		10.3	...
2699 Other non-metallic mineral products n.e.c.		...	...	204.0	...		...	...	72.7	...		4.3	...
2710 Basic iron and steel		...	...	2581.9	...		...	...	553.8	...		130.0	...
2720 Basic precious and non-ferrous metals		...	...	571.5	...		...	...	124.5	...		10.0	...
273 Casting of metals		...	...	769.3	...		...	...	273.3	...		50.0	...
2731 Casting of iron and steel		...	...	416.7	...		...	...	162.8	...		30.6	...
2732 Casting of non-ferrous metals		...	...	352.6	...		...	...	110.5	...		19.4	...
281 Struct.metal products;tanks;steam generators		...	...	903.1	...		...	...	328.7	...		20.4	...
2811 Structural metal products		...	...	693.6	...		...	...	249.5	...		14.2	...
2812 Tanks, reservoirs and containers of metal		...	...	191.2	...		...	...	68.8	...		6.0	...
2813 Steam generators		...	...	18.3	...		...	...	10.4	...		0.2	...
289 Other metal products; metal working services		...	...	2601.2	...		...	...	1045.8	...		100.9	...
2891 Metal forging/pressing/stamping/roll-forming		...	...	273.0	...		...	...	107.2	...		12.4	...
2892 Treatment & coating of metals		...	...	252.7	...		...	...	92.6	...		21.1	...
2893 Cutlery, hand tools and general hardware		...	...	402.2	...		...	...	208.9	...		13.5	...
2899 Other fabricated metal products n.e.c.		...	...	1673.3	...		...	...	637.1	...		53.9	...
291 General purpose machinery		...	...	1623.3	...		...	...	666.5	...		39.5	...
2911 Engines & turbines(not for transport equip.)		...	...	155.4	...		...	...	64.8	...		11.2	...
2912 Pumps, compressors, taps and valves		...	...	476.2	...		...	...	214.6	...		9.7	...
2913 Bearings, gears, gearing & driving elements		...	...	97.5	...		...	...	43.0	...		1.4	...
2914 Ovens, furnaces and furnace burners		...	...	40.5	...		...	...	19.4	...		0.3	...
2915 Lifting and handling equipment		...	...	207.9	...		...	...	91.2	...		3.9	...
2919 Other general purpose machinery		...	...	645.9	...		...	...	233.5	...		13.0	...

292 Special purpose machinery		...	...	1367.7	...		...	...	536.4	...		33.3	...
2921 Agricultural and forestry machinery		...	...	602.7	...		...	...	220.0	...		8.5	...
2922 Machine tools		...	...	164.9	...		...	...	73.5	...		4.7	...
2923 Machinery for metallurgy		...	...	29.3	...		...	...	11.4	...		0.6	...
2924 Machinery for mining & construction		...	...	112.9	...		...	...	48.2	...		6.8	...
2925 Food/beverage/tobacco processing machinery		...	...	251.4	...		...	...	97.8	...		4.0	...
2926 Machinery for textile, apparel and leather		...	...	47.3	...		...	...	19.9	...		1.3	...
2927 Weapons and ammunition		...	...	30.8	...		...	...	5.8	...		1.4	...
2929 Other special purpose machinery		...	...	128.5	...		...	...	59.8	...		5.9	...
2930 Domestic appliances n.e.c.		...	...	1293.2	...		...	...	461.4	...		57.2	...
3000 Office, accounting and computing machinery		...	...	216.0	...		...	...	64.8	...		16.4	...
3110 Electric motors, generators and transformers		...	...	313.9	...		...	...	132.7	...		7.0	...
3120 Electricity distribution & control apparatus		...	...	212.8	...		...	...	70.9	...		8.0	...
3130 Insulated wire and cable		...	...	465.8	...		...	...	141.7	...		24.9	...
3140 Accumulators, primary cells and batteries		...	...	204.2	...		...	...	72.6	...		2.4	...
3150 Lighting equipment and electric lamps		...	...	225.6	...		...	...	77.9	...		4.8	...
3190 Other electrical equipment n.e.c.		...	...	467.4	...		...	...	178.5	...		16.1	...
3210 Electronic valves, tubes, etc.		...	...	83.5	...		...	...	37.6	...		1.3	...
3220 TV/radio transmitters; line comm. apparatus		...	...	706.5	...		...	...	184.8	...		29.1	...
3230 TV and radio receivers and associated goods		...	...	947.2	...		...	...	214.7	...		26.9	...
331 Medical, measuring, testing appliances, etc.		...	...	381.8	...		...	...	160.0	...		6.9	...
3311 Medical, surgical and orthopaedic equipment		...	...	181.7	...		...	...	79.0	...		4.6	...
3312 Measuring/testing/navigating appliances,etc.		...	...	160.4	...		...	...	59.9	...		1.7	...
3313 Industrial process control equipment		...	...	39.7	...		...	...	21.1	...		0.7	...
3320 Optical instruments & photographic equipment		...	...	59.5	...		...	...	28.1	...		2.7	...
3330 Watches and clocks		...	...	31.5	...		...	...	13.9	...		0.4	...
3410 Motor vehicles		...	...	5374.8	...		...	...	1127.2	...		80.1	...
3420 Automobile bodies, trailers & semi-trailers		...	...	471.6	...		...	...	161.2	...		14.0	...
3430 Parts/accessories for automobiles		...	...	2475.1	...		...	...	906.6	...		80.4	...
351 Building and repairing of ships and boats		...	...	133.3	...		...	...	54.7	...		2.0	...
3511 Building and repairing of ships		...	...	115.8	...		...	...	47.5	...		1.7	...
3512 Building/repairing of pleasure/sport. boats		...	...	17.5	...		...	...	7.2	...		0.3	...
3520 Railway/tramway locomotives & rolling stock		...	...	27.7	...		...	...	8.8	...		2.8	...
3530 Aircraft and spacecraft		...	...	13.9	...		...	...	7.2	...		-	...
359 Transport equipment n.e.c.		...	...	418.4	...		...	...	109.3	...		14.7	...
3591 Motorcycles		...	...	291.6	...		...	...	66.3	...		10.7	...
3592 Bicycles and invalid carriages		...	...	107.8	...		...	...	36.6	...		3.7	...
3599 Other transport equipment n.e.c.		...	...	19.0	...		...	...	6.4	...		0.2	...
3610 Furniture		...	...	924.3	...		...	...	348.7	...		25.4	...
369 Manufacturing n.e.c.		...	...	437.6	...		...	...	191.1	...		20.2	...
3691 Jewellery and related articles		...	...	71.3	...		...	...	20.5	...		2.6	...
3692 Musical instruments		...	...	4.7	...		...	...	1.9	...		-0.1	...
3693 Sports goods		...	...	33.4	...		...	...	16.3	...		1.8	...
3694 Games and toys		...	...	81.5	...		...	...	42.6	...		2.9	...
3699 Other manufacturing n.e.c.		...	...	246.8	...		...	...	109.8	...		13.0	...
3710 Recycling of metal waste and scrap		...	...	...	...		...	...	...	...		...	...
3720 Recycling of non-metal waste and scrap		...	...	...	...		...	...	...	...		...	...
D Total manufacturing		...	...	90461.8	...		...	...	29787.4	...		3730.4	...

Argentina

ISIC Revision 3			Index numbers of industrial production (1990=100)											
ISIC Industry		Note	1985	1986	1987	1988	1989	1990	1991	1992	1993	1994	1995	1996
15	Food and beverages		...	...	...	...	...	100	111	117	116	124	134	131
16	Tobacco products		115	118	112	101	101	100	104	111	116	119	119	119
17	Textiles	a/	...	...	...	...	...	100	112	117	107	111	100	111
18	Wearing apparel, fur	a/	...	...	...	...	...	...	...	...	...	...	...	...
19	Leather, leather products and footwear	a/	...	...	...	...	...	...	...	...	...	...	...	...
20	Wood products (excl. furniture)		106	113	117	118	110	100	111	109	125	137	99	103
21	Paper and paper products		93	108	116	108	101	100	108	118	118	130	140	143
22	Printing and publishing		102	115	116	103	106	100	122	184	195	196	156	171
23	Coke,refined petroleum products,nuclear fuel	b/	...	...	...	...	...	100	107	114	118	121	114	121
24	Chemicals and chemical products	b/	...	...	...	...	...	...	...	...	...	...	...	...
25	Rubber and plastics products	b/	...	...	...	...	...	...	...	...	...	...	...	...
26	Non-metallic mineral products		100	127	141	121	108	100	114	131	141	146	128	132
27	Basic metals		71	91	101	104	94	100	91	88	93	101	104	116
28	Fabricated metal products		117	115	115	114	103	100	113	126	137	136	118	118
29	Machinery and equipment n.e.c.	c/	114	104	110	112	92	100	95	101	102	100	104	106
30	Office, accounting and computing machinery	c/	...	...	...	...	...	...	...	...	...	...	...	...
31	Electrical machinery and apparatus	d/	158	166	178	152	119	100	123	158	159	146	117	150
32	Radio,television and communication equipment	d/	...	...	...	...	...	...	...	...	...	...	...	...
33	Medical, precision and optical instruments		124	123	139	134	109	100	...	...	...	...	...	...
34	Motor vehicles, trailers, semi-trailers	e/	129	155	175	142	120	100	118	190	222	252	189	212
35	Other transport equipment	e/	...	...	...	...	...	...	...	...	...	...	...	...
36	Furniture; manufacturing n.e.c.		...	...	...	...	...	...	...	...	...	...	...	...
37	Recycling		...	...	...	...	...	...	...	...	...	...	...	...
D	Total manufacturing		98	109	111	106	98	100	110	123	127	133	123	130

a/ 17 includes 18 and 19.
b/ 23 includes 24 and 25.
c/ 29 includes 30.
d/ 31 includes 32.
e/ 34 includes 35.

ARMENIA

Supplier of information:
State Committee on Statistics of the Republic of Armenia, Yerevan.

Basic source of data:
Not reported.

Major deviations from ISIC (Revision 2):
None reported.

Reference period (if not calendar year):

Scope:
Not reported.

Method of enumeration:
Not reported.

Adjusted for non-response:
Not reported.

Concepts and definitions of variables:
No deviations from the standard UN concepts and definitions are reported.

Related national publications:

Armenia

ISIC Revision 2	Number of establishments					Number of persons engaged					Wages and salaries paid to employees				
		(numbers)					(numbers)					(million DRAMS)			
ISIC Industry	Note	1993	1994	1995	1996	Note	1993	1994	1995	1996	Note	1993a/	1994	1995	1996
311/2 Food products		114	120	119	...		22262	22303	20978	18835		4212.6	631.1	2136.2	2454.9
313 Beverages		46	44	46	...		...	...	...	...		...	...	...	...
314 Tobacco		4	4	4	...		...	...	...	...		...	...	...	...
321 Textiles		53	54	54	...		28664	29412	25443	20925		3691.5	426.4	110.3	514.4
322 Wearing apparel, except footwear		61	62	63	...		25078	...	20036	15971		2214.0	336.4	580.2	376.8
323 Leather and fur products		6	6	4	...		...	...	...	...		...	...	...	...
324 Footwear, except rubber or plastic		23	28	29	...		...	...	...	...		...	...	...	...
331 Wood products, except furniture		12	10	10	...		...	...	...	...		...	...	...	...
332 Furniture and fixtures, excl. metal		22	20	22	...		...	...	...	...		...	...	...	...
341 Paper and products		1	2	2	...		...	...	...	...		...	...	...	...
342 Printing and publishing		54	52	45	...		...	...	...	...		...	...	...	...
351 Industrial chemicals		7	8	8	...		...	...	...	...		...	...	...	...
352 Other chemicals		7	7	7	...		...	...	...	...		...	...	...	...
353 Petroleum refineries		-	-	-	...		-	-	-	-		-	-	-	-
354 Misc. petroleum and coal products		2	1	1	...		...	...	...	...		...	...	...	...
355 Rubber products		5	5	5	...		...	...	...	...		...	...	...	...
356 Plastic products		4	6	4	...		...	...	...	...		...	...	...	...
361 Pottery, china, earthenware		2	2	2	...		...	...	...	...		...	...	...	...
362 Glass and products		5	5	5	...		...	...	...	...		...	...	...	...
369 Other non-metallic mineral products		49	44	41	...		...	...	...	...		...	...	...	...
371 Iron and steel		4	4	4	...		...	...	...	...		...	...	...	...
372 Non-ferrous metals		3	3	3	...		...	...	...	...		...	...	...	...
381 Fabricated metal products		53	52	55	...		...	...	...	...		...	...	...	...
382 Non-electrical machinery		73	85	78	...		...	...	...	...		...	...	...	...
383 Electrical machinery		38	37	37	...		...	...	...	...		...	...	...	...
384 Transport equipment		5	7	8	...		...	...	...	...		...	...	...	...
385 Professional and scientific equipment		32	28	28	...		...	...	...	...		...	...	...	...
390 Other manufacturing industries		34	36	34	...		...	...	...	...		...	...	...	...
3 Total manufacturing		719	732	718	...		281309	273252	239859	...		43982.0	7886.1	22755.9	22175.8

a/ Data reported in Roubles.

Armenia

ISIC Revision 2		Output in producers' prices					Value added					Gross fixed capital formation		
			(million DRAMS)					(million DRAMS)					(thousand DRAMS)	
ISIC	Industry	Note	1993a/	1994	1995	1996	Note	1993	1994	1995	1996	Note	1995	1996
311/2	Food products		67658.7	10115.9	48185.8	...		...	...	...	...		...	...
313	Beverages		18121.0	4061.3	4772.8	...		...	...	...	...		...	...
314	Tobacco		6788.5	2015.1	1753.9	...		...	...	...	...		...	...
321	Textiles		24331.9	2469.2	2472.5	...		...	...	...	...		...	...
322	Wearing apparel, except footwear		8833.3	2064.9	8014.4	...		...	...	...	...		...	...
323	Leather and fur products		3820.6	806.8	179.5	...		...	...	...	...		...	...
324	Footwear, except rubber or plastic		17823.9	1436.1	1313.9	...		...	...	...	...		...	...
331	Wood products, except furniture		629.2	128.6	457.2	...		...	...	...	...		...	...
332	Furniture and fixtures, excl. metal		2932.8	321.5	417.1	...		...	...	...	...		...	...
341	Paper and products		686.2	121.3	139.5	...		...	...	...	...		...	...
342	Printing and publishing		736.2	291.9	989.8	...		...	...	...	...		...	...
351	Industrial chemicals		7884.0	3876.5	5049.4	...		...	...	...	...		...	...
352	Other chemicals		8581.7	820.7	1730.7	...		...	...	...	...		...	...
353	Petroleum refineries		-	-	-	...		...	...	...	...		...	...
354	Misc. petroleum and coal products		606.4	235.8	411.6	...		...	...	...	...		...	...
355	Rubber products		2991.7	633.9	976.0	...		...	...	...	...		...	...
356	Plastic products		527.2	110.7	186.0	...		...	...	...	...		...	...
361	Pottery, china, earthenware		486.1	69.6	87.4	...		...	...	...	...		...	...
362	Glass and products		2739.7	426.3	507.3	...		...	...	...	...		...	...
369	Other non-metallic mineral products		14935.3	3652.1	6561.3	...		...	...	...	...		...	...
371	Iron and steel		970.4	154.7	251.2	...		...	...	...	...		...	...
372	Non-ferrous metals		2431.4	1164.9	2785.9	...		...	...	...	...		...	...
381	Fabricated metal products		4456.5	1289.8	2905.7	...		...	...	...	...		...	...
382	Non-electrical machinery		26150.7	4408.3	5455.0	...		...	...	...	...		...	...
383	Electrical machinery		41818.8	6874.0	8657.5	...		...	...	...	...		...	...
384	Transport equipment		5597.8	1167.9	812.7	...		...	...	...	...		...	...
385	Professional and scientific equipment		24138.9	4592.3	4729.0	...		...	...	...	...		...	...
390	Other manufacturing industries		146812.3	22111.7	21063.7	...		...	...	...	...		...	...
3	Total manufacturing		443491.3	75421.7	130866.6	...		...	...	...	...		...	...

a/ Data reported in Roubles.

Armenia

ISIC Revision 2			Index numbers of industrial production											
			(1990=100)											
ISIC	Industry	Note	1985	1986	1987	1988	1989	1990	1991	1992	1993	1994	1995	1996
311/2	Food products		...	...	...	...	...	...	...	...	...	...	...	...
313	Beverages		...	...	...	...	...	...	...	...	...	...	...	...
314	Tobacco		...	...	...	...	...	...	...	...	...	...	...	...
321	Textiles		...	...	...	...	...	...	...	...	...	...	...	...
322	Wearing apparel, except footwear		...	...	...	...	...	...	...	...	...	...	...	...
323	Leather and fur products		...	...	...	...	...	...	...	...	...	...	...	...
324	Footwear, except rubber or plastic		...	...	...	...	...	...	...	...	...	...	...	...
331	Wood products, except furniture		...	...	...	...	...	...	...	...	...	...	...	...
332	Furniture and fixtures, excl. metal		...	...	...	...	...	...	...	...	...	...	...	...
341	Paper and products		...	...	...	...	...	...	...	...	...	...	...	...
342	Printing and publishing		...	...	...	...	...	...	...	...	...	...	...	...
351	Industrial chemicals		...	...	...	...	...	...	...	...	...	...	...	...
352	Other chemicals		...	...	...	...	...	...	...	...	...	...	...	...
353	Petroleum refineries		...	...	...	...	...	...	...	...	...	...	...	...
354	Misc. petroleum and coal products		...	...	...	...	...	...	...	...	...	...	...	...
355	Rubber products		...	...	...	...	...	...	...	...	...	...	...	...
356	Plastic products		...	...	...	...	...	...	...	...	...	...	...	...
361	Pottery, china, earthenware		...	...	...	...	...	...	...	...	...	...	...	...
362	Glass and products		...	...	...	...	...	...	...	...	...	...	...	...
369	Other non-metallic mineral products		...	...	...	...	...	...	...	...	...	...	...	...
371	Iron and steel		...	...	...	...	...	...	...	...	...	...	...	...
372	Non-ferrous metals		...	...	...	...	...	...	...	...	...	...	...	...
381	Fabricated metal products		...	...	...	...	...	...	...	...	...	...	...	...
382	Non-electrical machinery		...	...	...	...	...	...	...	...	...	...	...	...
383	Electrical machinery		...	...	...	...	...	...	...	...	...	...	...	...
384	Transport equipment		...	...	...	...	...	...	...	...	...	...	...	...
385	Professional and scientific equipment		...	...	...	...	...	...	...	...	...	...	...	...
390	Other manufacturing industries		...	...	...	...	...	...	...	...	...	...	...	...
3	Total manufacturing		...	...	...	...	...	...	...	...	...	...	...	...

AUSTRIA

Supplier of information:
Austrian Central Statistical Office, Vienna.
Industrial statistics for the OECD countries are compiled by the OECD secretariat, which supplies them to UNIDO.

Basic source of data:
Up to 1994, Annual Industrial Statistical Survey; for 1995, Non-agricultural Census.

Major deviations from ISIC (Revision 3):
Up to 1994, data collected under the national classification system have been reclassified to correspond with ISIC (Revision 3). The exact correspondance with the current ISIC could not be achieved.

Reference period (if not calendar year):

Scope:
Up to 1994, all establishments affiliated to the Industrial Section of the Federal Economic Chamber, and established with 20 or more employees which affiliate to the Section "Gewerbe". For 1995, all enterprises in the non-agricultural sector.

Method of enumeration:
Not reported.

Adjusted for non-response:
Not reported.

Concepts and definitions of variables:
Establishment refers to the local kind of activity unit.
Enterprise refers to the smallest legal unit which may consist of one or more establishments. The definitions correspond to those referred to by the EU-Council regulation on statistical units.
Number of employees refers to persons employed on 31 December.
Wages and salaries is compensation of employees covering both wages and salaries, plus employers' contributions to social security schemes and pension funds. It includes regular and overtime payments, bonuses, cost-of-living allowances, vacation and sick leave pay, taxes and social insurance contributions payable by employees and deducted by employers, payments in kind and allowances.
Output is gross output valued in producers' prices, including all indirect taxes but excluding value added tax and all subsidies. It includes all products, net change in work in progress, work done on own account, services rendered, goods shipped in the same condition as received, electricity sold, fixed assets produced for own use, net changes in stock levels of finished goods and goods made by homeworkers and handicraft workers.
Value added is based on the census concept. It is calculated as the value of gross output less the cost of materials, fuels and other supplies, contract and commission work done by others, repair and maintenance work done by others, goods shipped in the same condition as received and electricity purchased. Input estimates are on a consumed basis. The cost of, and receipts for, non-industrial services are included.
Gross fixed capital formation is investment expenditure defined as the value of purchases of fixed assets, including own-account construction of assets. The value of sales of fixed assets is not deducted. "Fixed assets" are those with a productive life of at least one year, including assets made by a unit's labour force; additions, alterations, and repairs to existing assets; new assets, whether yet in use or not; and used assets. The valuation is at full cost including delivered price, cost of installation, fees and taxes (except value added tax). The value of sales of used assets is the actual amount realized.

Related national publications:
Industriestatistik, Vol. 2, published by the Austrian Central Statistical Office, Vienna.

Austria

ISIC Revision 3	Number of establishments					Number of employees					Wages and salaries paid to employees				
		(numbers)					(numbers)					(million SCHILLINGS)			
ISIC Industry	Note	1992	1993	1994	1995a/b/	Note	1992	1993	1994	1995b/	Note	1992	1993	1994	1995b/
151 Processed meat,fish,fruit,vegetables,fats		225	218	202	1561		15792	15887	15345	22878		4175	4309	4443	6606
1511 Processing/preserving of meat		197	192	177	1402		14296	14408	13907	18301		3769	3870	3976	4612
1512 Processing/preserving of fish		...	...	...	4		...	...	...	240		...	...	...	43
1513 Processing/preserving of fruit & vegetables		28	26	25	128		1496	1479	1438	3134		406	438	467	1052
1514 Vegetable and animal oils and fats		...	...	...	27		...	...	...	1203		...	...	...	899
1520 Dairy products		116	119	103	106		6753	5838	5401	6765		2386	2204	2039	2861
153 Grain mill products; starches; animal feeds		46	41	40	227		1042	990	912	3623		422	410	403	1364
1531 Grain mill products		...	...	...	171		...	...	...	...		...	...	...	...
1532 Starches and starch products		...	...	...	3		...	...	...	...		...	...	...	...
1533 Prepared animal feeds		...	...	...	53		...	...	...	1664		...	...	...	598
154 Other food products		421	418	416	2580		27535	27240	27360	36936		8201	8595	8710	9896
1541 Bakery products		239	237	237	2439		13089	12975	13450	29002		3259	3437	3575	6784
1542 Sugar		7	4	5	1		1205	1116	1067	...		465	464	442	...
1543 Cocoa, chocolate and sugar confectionery		24	25	25	26		2952	3078	2950	2793		858	937	930	971
1544 Macaroni, noodles & similar products		151	152	149	23		10289	10071	9893	342		3618	3757	3762	102
1549 Other food products n.e.c.		...	...	...	91		...	...	...	...		...	...	...	...
155 Beverages		226	222	225	262		12472	12345	11947	11189		4643	4866	4928	4670
1551 Distilling, rectifying & blending of spirits		96	91	91	82		2154	2206	2009	1094		727	787	738	372
1552 Wines		...	...	...	53		...	...	...	...		...	...	...	...
1553 Malt liquors and malt		81	81	83	52		6647	6481	6199	...		2717	2849	2796	...
1554 Soft drinks; mineral waters		49	50	51	75		3671	3658	3739	3584		1199	1230	1394	1341
1600 Tobacco products		14	14	13	1		1296	1248	1195	...		584	626	627	...
171 Spinning, weaving and finishing of textiles		104	101	99	176		13467	10771	11092	12236		4020	3556	3449	4538
1711 Textile fibre preparation; textile weaving		78	73	75	103		10901	8764	9027	9849		3173	2750	2692	3691
1712 Finishing of textiles		26	28	24	73		2566	2007	2065	2387		846	806	758	847
172 Other textiles		210	200	200	662		9900	9316	9226	8853		2642	2598	2626	2510
1721 Made-up textile articles, except apparel		142	134	135	121		4730	4420	4497	2791		1184	1142	1154	837
1722 Carpets and rugs		27	25	24	59		2005	1898	1904	1101		548	530	573	336
1723 Cordage, rope, twine and netting		41	41	41	20		3165	2998	2825	364		910	926	899	121
1729 Other textiles n.e.c.		...	...	...	462		...	...	...	4597		...	...	...	1216
1730 Knitted and crocheted fabrics and articles		96	99	88	124		9492	8506	7809	5519		2236	2149	2014	1462
1810 Wearing apparel, except fur apparel		336	303	275	1232		18766	15738	13319	15552		3553	3271	2892	3482
1820 Dressing & dyeing of fur; processing of fur		6	5	5	122		150	116	125	352		37	31	29	67
191 Tanning, dressing and processing of leather		41	41	35	140		2566	2242	2383	2382		558	529	531	514
1911 Tanning and dressing of leather		...	...	...	47		...	...	...	1232		...	...	...	246
1912 Luggage, handbags, etc.; saddlery & harness		...	...	...	93		...	...	...	1150		...	...	...	269
1920 Footwear		51	49	47	103		5953	5595	5152	5259		1354	1269	1151	1305
2010 Sawmilling and planing of wood		1737	1672	1638	1311		10387	9828	9423	8894		2494	2448	2451	2422
202 Products of wood, cork, straw, etc.		728	695	668	2176		39048	38182	38270	27142		10302	10577	10934	7401
2021 Veneer sheets, plywood, particle board, etc.		32	30	29	24		3046	2944	3142	3582		1028	1037	1068	1233
2022 Builders' carpentry and joinery		582	559	535	1458		32867	32312	32167	20523		8447	8777	9089	5460
2023 Wooden containers		37	36	33	112		773	668	659	762		196	178	170	181
2029 Other wood products; articles of cork/straw		77	70	71	582		2362	2258	2302	2275		631	584	606	527
210 Paper and paper products		141	141	136	143		19718	18860	18306	17861		7887	7562	7621	7490
2101 Pulp, paper and paperboard		39	38	35	34		12066	11328	10966	9498		5343	5012	4992	4294
2102 Corrugated paper and paperboard		102	103	101	73		7652	7532	7340	5941		2544	2550	2629	2172
2109 Other articles of paper and paperboard		...	...	...	36		...	...	...	2422		...	...	...	1024
221 Publishing		55	55	58	364		5272	4797	4862	7198		2233	2178	2276	3128
2211 Publishing of books and other publications		...	...	...	139		...	...	...	2056		...	...	...	706
2212 Publishing of newspapers, journals, etc.		...	...	...	161		...	...	...	4768		...	...	...	2321
2213 Publishing of recorded media		...	...	...	24		...	...	...	222		...	...	...	57
2219 Other publishing		...	...	...	40		...	...	...	152		...	...	...	44

222 Printing and related service activities	257	253	239	1065	17233	16253	15356	18451	7189	7062	6791	7698
2221 Printing	228	220	209	840	15744	14772	14074	15722	6747	6571	6343	6467
2222 Service activities related to printing	29	33	30	225	1489	1481	1282	2729	442	490	448	1231
2230 Reproduction of recorded media	17	16	16	7	864	715	762	794	374	250	241	294
2310 Coke oven products	27	29	34	...	840	885	941	...	352	394	467	...
2320 Refined petroleum products	27	27	25	8	3521	3308	3552	...	2576	2536	2525	...
2330 Processing of nuclear fuel	...	...	...	...	...	...	...	...	...	...	...	...
241 Basic chemicals	143	143	136	66	19383	17920	17112	7532	7817	7606	7494	3832
2411 Basic chemicals, except fertilizers	54	53	50	43	6657	6226	5851	...	3016	2920	2888	...
2412 Fertilizers and nitrogen compounds	...	...	...	7	...	...	...	1394	...	...	...	794
2413 Plastics in primary forms; synthetic rubber	89	90	86	16	12726	11694	11261	...	4801	4687	4606	...
242 Other chemicals	257	253	242	308	18082	17584	17206	...	6842	7092	7201	...
2421 Pesticides and other agro-chemical products	...	...	...	2	...	...	...	...	...	...	...	...
2422 Paints, varnishes, printing ink and mastics	71	68	66	51	3066	2972	3045	3222	1068	1075	1115	1199
2423 Pharmaceuticals, medicinal chemicals, etc.	59	61	58	76	8123	8162	7977	8061	3136	3328	3460	3697
2424 Soap, cleaning & cosmetic preparations	34	30	28	116	2987	2648	2363	2325	1225	1248	1157	903
2429 Other chemical products n.e.c.	93	94	90	63	3906	3802	3821	1977	1412	1442	1469	876
2430 Man-made fibres	...	...	...	4	...	...	...	...	...	...	...	...
251 Rubber products	35	33	33	45	5914	5339	5142	5090	2346	2136	2168	2094
2511 Rubber tyres and tubes	13	13	14	12	3283	2977	2791	2801	1416	1285	1296	1267
2519 Other rubber products	22	20	19	33	2631	2362	2351	2289	930	851	872	827
2520 Plastic products	256	257	252	560	14487	14627	14891	21674	4091	4353	4531	7307
2610 Glass and glass products	73	72	75	181	8933	8375	8641	7966	3030	2955	3056	2922
269 Non-metallic mineral products n.e.c.	464	454	448	1017	27315	25859	25830	27635	10363	10173	10375	11702
2691 Pottery, china and earthenware	29	29	26	168	2710	2440	2448	2685	860	826	827	909
2692 Refractory ceramic products	75	76	71	15	2627	2535	2465	2612	934	947	938	1498
2693 Struct.non-refractory clay; ceramic products	...	...	...	37	...	...	...	1664	...	...	...	657
2694 Cement, lime and plaster	34	32	30	17	3542	3088	3017	2337	1419	1400	1360	1229
2695 Articles of concrete, cement and plaster	253	244	248	337	11573	11501	11790	11744	4386	4342	4675	4992
2696 Cutting, shaping & finishing of stone	51	52	51	391	2189	2170	2060	3560	647	681	646	1212
2699 Other non-metallic mineral products n.e.c.	22	21	22	52	4674	4125	4050	3033	2117	1977	1928	1205
2710 Basic iron and steel	39	37	37	41	23190	20813	20459	21817	8681	8217	8389	9834
2720 Basic precious and non-ferrous metals	54	51	49	41	7582	6984	6746	6081	2907	2719	2690	2394
273 Casting of metals	70	66	68	70	7879	7118	7257	5225	2608	2426	2461	1828
2731 Casting of iron and steel	...	...	...	27	...	...	...	1507	...	...	...	570
2732 Casting of non-ferrous metals	...	...	...	43	...	...	...	3718	...	...	...	1258
281 Struct.metal products;tanks;steam generators	323	322	328	832	21268	20606	21151	29535	7115	7116	7363	10807
2811 Structural metal products	...	...	...	775	...	...	...	23906	...	...	...	8686
2812 Tanks, reservoirs and containers of metal	...	...	...	39	...	...	...	4039	...	...	...	1557
2813 Steam generators	...	...	...	18	...	...	...	1590	...	...	...	564
289 Other metal products; metal working services	565	556	555	2136	34531	33011	34063	34384	10993	10742	11128	11509
2891 Metal forging/pressing/stamping/roll-forming	124	129	130	489	6673	6723	7151	3704	2141	2135	2213	1144
2892 Treatment & coating of metals	...	...	...	396	...	...	...	6480	...	...	...	2127
2893 Cutlery, hand tools and general hardware	210	206	209	829	16760	15611	16194	13439	5355	5237	5432	4587
2899 Other fabricated metal products n.e.c.	231	221	216	422	11098	10677	10718	10761	3497	3370	3484	3651
291 General purpose machinery	144	143	146	589	13791	14163	14522	27759	4756	5117	5348	10814
2911 Engines & turbines(not for transport equip.)	58	59	64	19	7207	7195	7550	295	2626	2774	2969	102
2912 Pumps, compressors, taps and valves	...	...	...	88	...	...	...	5547	...	...	...	2092
2913 Bearings, gears, gearing & driving elements	44	44	46	32	4208	4137	4193	2892	1355	1398	1441	1117
2914 Ovens, furnaces and furnace burners	42	40	36	46	2376	2831	2779	2786	776	945	938	1150
2915 Lifting and handling equipment	...	...	...	138	...	...	...	7779	...	...	...	3305
2919 Other general purpose machinery	...	...	...	266	...	...	...	8460	...	...	...	3047
292 Special purpose machinery	521	525	503	1058	48070	44001	42939	37668	17914	17248	17198	14781
2921 Agricultural and forestry machinery	87	87	83	498	6280	5932	5668	6269	1854	1872	1815	1975
2922 Machine tools	434	438	420	125	41790	38069	37271	6264	16060	15376	15383	2420
2923 Machinery for metallurgy	...	...	...	8	...	...	...	640	...	...	...	269
2924 Machinery for mining & construction	...	...	...	53	...	...	...	4938	...	...	...	2045
2925 Food/beverage/tobacco processing machinery	...	...	...	66	...	...	...	1969	...	...	...	778
2926 Machinery for textile, apparel and leather	...	...	...	34	...	...	...	1466	...	...	...	550
2927 Weapons and ammunition	...	...	...	33	...	...	...	1347	...	...	...	522
2929 Other special purpose machinery	...	...	...	241	...	...	...	14775	...	...	...	6222
2930 Domestic appliances n.e.c.	29	29	28	80	4838	4350	4526	5432	1396	1358	1389	1778

continued

Austria

ISIC Revision 3		Number of establishments					Number of employees					Wages and salaries paid to employees			
		(numbers)					(numbers)					(million SCHILLINGS)			
ISIC Industry	Note	1992	1993	1994	1995a/b/	Note	1992	1993	1994	1995b/	Note	1992	1993	1994	1995b/
3000 Office, accounting and computing machinery		...	...	...	49		...	...	...	322		...	...	...	123
3110 Electric motors, generators and transformers		85	87	85	87		11669	11310	10922	8399		3774	3907	3864	3420
3120 Electricity distribution & control apparatus		...	...	...	114		...	...	...	8427		...	...	...	3334
3130 Insulated wire and cable		23	22	21	23		3428	3348	3423	4544		1304	1380	1400	1895
3140 Accumulators, primary cells and batteries		183	184	184	9		29435	27155	26502	1203		12031	12462	12315	513
3150 Lighting equipment and electric lamps		...	...	...	74		...	...	...	3143		...	...	...	1135
3190 Other electrical equipment n.e.c.		...	...	...	78		...	...	...	6331		...	...	...	2043
3210 Electronic valves, tubes, etc.		58	59	53	58		16906	15878	15994	6713		5529	5566	5718	2600
3220 TV/radio transmitters; line comm. apparatus		60	55	61	24		7795	7024	7331	20274		3157	3108	3448	11443
3230 TV and radio receivers and associated goods		...	...	...	47		...	...	...	5798		...	...	...	2422
331 Medical, measuring, testing appliances, etc.		96	98	100	855		7177	6913	7214	10871		2413	2490	2700	3550
3311 Medical, surgical and orthopaedic equipment		26	26	28	650		1449	1507	1643	6301		405	428	495	1686
3312 Measuring/testing/navigating appliances, etc.		70	72	72	197		5728	5406	5571	3760		2008	2062	2205	1489
3313 Industrial process control equipment		...	...	...	8		...	...	...	810		...	...	...	375
3320 Optical instruments & photographic equipment		21	21	20	89		4108	3492	3099	2338		1355	1223	1066	821
3330 Watches and clocks		17	15	12	10		623	507	511	42		178	151	150	21
3410 Motor vehicles		...	...	...	22		...	...	...	11370		...	...	...	4524
3420 Automobile bodies, trailers & semi-trailers		...	...	...	134		...	...	...	3436		...	...	...	1007
3430 Parts/accessories for automobiles		...	...	...	45		...	...	...	9058		...	...	...	3399
351 Building and repairing of ships and boats		5	5	5	34		577	376	385	322		269	289	144	110
3511 Building and repairing of ships		...	...	...	3		...	...	...	...		...	...	...	...
3512 Building/repairing of pleasure/sport. boats		...	...	...	31		...	...	...	...		...	...	...	...
3520 Railway/tramway locomotives & rolling stock		8	8	8	11		3254	3023	2855	3871		1203	1189	1066	2048
3530 Aircraft and spacecraft		4	4	5	23		...	...	...	191		...	...	...	67
359 Transport equipment n.e.c.		4	4	3	11		...	...	...	637		...	...	...	189
3591 Motorcycles		...	...	...	2		...	...	...	...		...	...	...	...
3592 Bicycles and invalid carriages		...	...	...	6		...	...	...	...		...	...	...	...
3599 Other transport equipment n.e.c.		...	...	...	3		...	...	...	...		...	...	...	...
3610 Furniture		9	9	9	3191		404	333	381	38254		95	100	101	9563
369 Manufacturing n.e.c.		52	46	44	1032		6993	6314	6395	11646		1987	1962	1939	3607
3691 Jewellery and related articles		...	...	...	400		...	...	...	1211		...	...	...	356
3692 Musical instruments		5	5	5	158		419	387	358	621		137	143	115	179
3693 Sports goods		47	41	39	56		6574	5927	6037	4680		1850	1819	1823	1687
3694 Games and toys		...	...	...	108		...	...	...	1638		...	...	...	440
3699 Other manufacturing n.e.c.		...	...	...	310		...	...	...	3496		...	...	...	945
3710 Recycling of metal waste and scrap		...	...	...	59		...	...	...	494		...	...	...	179
3720 Recycling of non-metal waste and scrap		...	...	...	32		...	...	...	473		...	...	...	155
D Total manufacturing		8598	8385	8185	25509		596088	559957	553754	629747		201581	199411	201470	228712

a/ Number of enterprises.
b/ Data for 1995 are not strictly comparable with those provided for earlier years.

Austria

ISIC Revision 3		Output in producers' prices (million SCHILLINGS)					Value added in producers' prices (million SCHILLINGS)					Gross fixed capital formation (million SCHILLINGS)	
ISIC Industry	Note	1992	1993	1994	1995a/	Note	1992	1993	1994	1995a/b/	Note	1994	1995a/
151 Processed meat,fish,fruit,vegetables,fats		39081	38354	37789	46741		7358	7538	6757	12605		1740	2452
1511 Processing/preserving of meat		35369	34423	33572	32359		6466	6521	5803	8532		1487	1524
1512 Processing/preserving of fish		...	...	...	353		...	...	...	105		...	17
1513 Processing/preserving of fruit & vegetables		3712	3931	4217	9119		892	1017	954	2519		253	835
1514 Vegetable and animal oils and fats		...	...	...	4910		...	...	...	1450		...	76
1520 Dairy products		27363	28935	25604	30880		4323	4457	3646	3140		1255	1179
153 Grain mill products; starches; animal feeds		4675	4512	4477	9051		970	988	936	2173		153	547
1531 Grain mill products		...	...	...	...		...	...	...	...		...	...
1532 Starches and starch products		...	...	...	...		...	...	...	...		...	...
1533 Prepared animal feeds		...	...	...	4262		...	...	...	959		...	133
154 Other food products		52896	54550	55212	42145		17169	18065	17959	18616		3066	2446
1541 Bakery products		13192	13761	13936	21440		6283	6625	6581	12018		1195	1483
1542 Sugar		4186	4103	4369	...		1104	1070	1133	...		461	...
1543 Cocoa, chocolate and sugar confectionery		5804	6538	6721	6172		1739	1861	2122	1559		306	351
1544 Macaroni, noodles & similar products		29714	30148	30186	592		8044	8509	8122	275		1104	63
1549 Other food products n.e.c.		...	...	...	...		...	...	...	...		...	...
155 Beverages		31795	31972	33696	26141		12505	12761	13588	9699		3302	2689
1551 Distilling, rectifying & blending of spirits		5869	5655	5587	2587		1428	1481	1387	655		214	75
1552 Wines		...	...	...	...		...	...	...	...		...	...
1553 Malt liquors and malt		14825	14933	15823	...		7604	7764	8428	...		1948	...
1554 Soft drinks; mineral waters		11101	11384	12286	8914		3473	3516	3773	3033		1141	651
1600 Tobacco products		20086	19921	20849	...		17204	16853	17948	...		290	...
171 Spinning, weaving and finishing of textiles		17819	16147	15818	21479		6452	5840	5893	8895		714	1145
1711 Textile fibre preparation; textile weaving		14613	13159	12985	18068		5175	4778	4886	7605		616	1036
1712 Finishing of textiles		3207	2988	2833	3411		1277	1062	1008	1289		98	108
172 Other textiles		14309	13779	13579	11804		5141	5130	4875	4790		649	597
1721 Made-up textile articles, except apparel		5816	5688	5617	3397		2063	2014	1880	1537		308	173
1722 Carpets and rugs		3328	2985	2985	1597		1117	1045	1090	512		180	172
1723 Cordage, rope, twine and netting		5165	5106	4977	589		1961	2071	1905	223		161	15
1729 Other textiles n.e.c.		...	...	...	6221		...	...	...	2518		...	237
1730 Knitted and crocheted fabrics and articles		8924	8290	7998	6095		3700	3592	3368	2463		380	286
1810 Wearing apparel, except fur apparel		14450	13298	12014	13992		5607	5037	4480	5658		282	362
1820 Dressing & dyeing of fur; processing of fur		232	161	173	307		61	59	57	139		6	8
191 Tanning, dressing and processing of leather		3346	3112	3001	3360		947	907	733	799		75	55
1911 Tanning and dressing of leather		...	...	...	2469		...	...	...	391		...	37
1912 Luggage, handbags, etc.; saddlery & harness		...	...	...	892		...	...	...	408		...	18
1920 Footwear		6820	6294	6023	6048		2317	2166	1846	2221		175	206
2010 Sawmilling and planing of wood		22495	19653	21789	20993		5786	5221	5702	5677		1344	1691
202 Products of wood, cork, straw, etc.		46468	46232	49814	33696		18777	18358	19248	13820		2810	2695
2021 Veneer sheets, plywood, particle board, etc.		8015	7174	8480	8259		2412	1963	2069	2612		500	629
2022 Builders' carpentry and joinery		34301	35232	37092	22545		14911	15013	15698	9811		2110	1865
2023 Wooden containers		925	812	790	821		363	336	315	356		38	65
2029 Other wood products; articles of cork/straw		3227	3014	3452	2070		1091	1047	1166	1040		162	136
210 Paper and paper products		47126	43232	48478	56697		14319	13100	15441	19690		3042	3205
2101 Pulp, paper and paperboard		34179	30632	34779	38762		9571	8448	10389	13259		2019	1705
2102 Corrugated paper and paperboard		12947	12599	13699	11512		4747	4653	5051	4388		1023	586
2109 Other articles of paper and paperboard		...	...	...	6423		...	...	...	2043		...	914
221 Publishing		10483	9945	11216	16143		2260	2765	3267	5110		543	652
2211 Publishing of books and other publications		...	...	...	3746		...	...	...	1216		...	128
2212 Publishing of newspapers, journals, etc.		...	...	...	11721		...	...	...	3605		...	397
2213 Publishing of recorded media		...	...	...	421		...	...	...	198		...	103
2219 Other publishing		...	...	...	255		...	...	...	91		...	23

continued

Austria

ISIC Revision 3		Output in producers' prices					Value added in producers' prices					Gross fixed capital formation	
		(million SCHILLINGS)					(million SCHILLINGS)					(million SCHILLINGS)	
ISIC Industry	Note	1992	1993	1994	1995a/	Note	1992	1993	1994	1995a/b/	Note	1994	1995a/
222 Printing and related service activities		23478	22333	22034	25098		11155	10415	10326	12770		1354	1912
2221 Printing		21939	20817	20632	22066		10413	9694	9621	10898		1269	1736
2222 Service activities related to printing		1538	1517	1402	3032		743	721	705	1872		85	176
2230 Reproduction of recorded media		993	947	894	2101		428	495	452	1306		38	183
2310 Coke oven products		1758	1999	2279	...		625	704	635	...		213	...
2320 Refined petroleum products		31152	30797	30768	...		4829	5051	6265	...		616	...
2330 Processing of nuclear fuel		...	...	...	...		...	...	...	...		...	...
241 Basic chemicals		48076	42555	47051	26972		13389	12456	14156	7170		2333	1237
2411 Basic chemicals, except fertilizers		19612	15585	17915	...		5375	4797	5478	...		867	...
2412 Fertilizers and nitrogen compounds		...	...	...	4439		...	...	...	1731		...	88
2413 Plastics in primary forms; synthetic rubber		28464	26971	29136	...		8014	7659	8678	...		1466	...
242 Other chemicals		41392	42885	43187	...		13681	14801	14367	...		3058	...
2421 Pesticides and other agro-chemical products		...	...	...	...		...	...	...	...		...	...
2422 Paints, varnishes, printing ink and mastics		5714	5872	6276	5489		1659	1818	1890	2211		341	340
2423 Pharmaceuticals, medicinal chemicals, etc.		19018	20589	20990	19346		7053	7913	7725	8648		2060	1971
2424 Soap, cleaning & cosmetic preparations		9059	8550	7808	4455		2328	2291	1951	1524		237	204
2429 Other chemical products n.e.c.		7601	7874	8113	4498		2642	2779	2800	1767		420	180
2430 Man-made fibres		...	...	...	...		...	...	...	...		...	...
251 Rubber products		10936	9679	10258	7853		3926	3543	3980	3357		354	388
2511 Rubber tyres and tubes		7175	6415	6599	4503		2289	2009	2239	1872		222	234
2519 Other rubber products		3760	3265	3659	3350		1637	1533	1741	1485		132	153
2520 Plastic products		19032	19617	20117	34360		7676	8207	8234	14063		1741	2379
2610 Glass and glass products		12126	11732	12139	11170		6702	6630	6941	6324		1197	1490
269 Non-metallic mineral products n.e.c.		48977	49549	53596	50593		19618	18983	21131	22470		4324	3989
2691 Pottery, china and earthenware		2387	2339	2436	2293		1257	1277	1304	1304		149	179
2692 Refractory ceramic products		4744	5222	5458	6219		1993	2030	2303	2666		694	262
2693 Struct.non-refractory clay; ceramic products		...	...	...	2921		...	...	...	1410		...	441
2694 Cement, lime and plaster		7588	7441	8034	4798		3288	3277	3402	2212		1004	307
2695 Articles of concrete, cement and plaster		22688	23142	26087	24660		8427	8768	9940	10550		1926	2191
2696 Cutting, shaping & finishing of stone		2185	2248	2183	3816		1056	1115	1116	2035		125	280
2699 Other non-metallic mineral products n.e.c.		9385	9157	9397	5886		3597	2516	3066	2293		426	329
2710 Basic iron and steel		40116	36851	40652	50301		12989	11888	13381	20113		2048	3444
2720 Basic precious and non-ferrous metals		25575	21372	21880	21628		4662	3858	4259	4464		993	493
273 Casting of metals		9548	8559	9307	6936		4762	4236	4390	3190		800	537
2731 Casting of iron and steel		...	...	...	1736		...	...	...	899		...	146
2732 Casting of non-ferrous metals		...	...	...	5200		...	...	...	2291		...	392
281 Struct.metal products;tanks;steam generators		28923	29354	31203	43822		11476	10881	12475	17347		1595	2219
2811 Structural metal products		...	...	...	36364		...	...	...	14053		...	1841
2812 Tanks, reservoirs and containers of metal		...	...	...	5780		...	...	...	2503		...	331
2813 Steam generators		...	...	...	1678		...	...	...	791		...	47
289 Other metal products; metal working services		43128	40871	43664	43146		19001	18511	19834	21503		2884	3322
2891 Metal forging/pressing/stamping/roll-forming		7020	7118	7700	4851		3359	3342	3705	2109		464	333
2892 Treatment & coating of metals		...	...	...	7063		...	...	...	3897		...	536
2893 Cutlery, hand tools and general hardware		21705	20143	21343	16462		9769	9386	10067	9103		1537	1264
2899 Other fabricated metal products n.e.c.		14404	13609	14621	14769		5873	5784	6062	6394		882	1190
291 General purpose machinery		18974	19911	22268	42108		6585	8146	9167	17809		1710	1708
2911 Engines & turbines(not for transport equip.)		9655	10411	12409	355		2579	3953	5211	159		763	32
2912 Pumps, compressors, taps and valves		...	...	...	7270		...	...	...	3302		...	372
2913 Bearings, gears, gearing & driving elements		5670	5462	5731	4168		2565	2510	2356	1831		567	279
2914 Ovens, furnaces and furnace burners		3649	4038	4127	3962		1442	1682	1600	1704		379	120
2915 Lifting and handling equipment		...	...	...	14618		...	...	...	5879		...	380
2919 Other general purpose machinery		...	...	...	11736		...	...	...	4934		...	524

292 Special purpose machinery	78262	71724	78872	59253	27479	24657	28385	23293	2472	2351
2921 Agricultural and forestry machinery	9032	8894	9019	8940	2549	2913	2910	4273	307	402
2922 Machine tools	69231	62830	69853	8438	24929	21744	25475	3566	2165	362
2923 Machinery for metallurgy	...	...	...	980	...	...	...	379	...	60
2924 Machinery for mining & construction	...	...	...	9079	...	...	...	3085	...	290
2925 Food/beverage/tobacco processing machinery	...	...	...	3148	...	...	...	1319	...	123
2926 Machinery for textile, apparel and leather	...	...	...	1751	...	...	...	705	...	73
2927 Weapons and ammunition	...	...	...	1877	...	...	...	850	...	149
2929 Other special purpose machinery	...	...	...	25040	...	...	...	9114	...	890
2930 Domestic appliances n.e.c.	7057	6615	6900	7528	2868	2644	2659	3199	360	401
3000 Office, accounting and computing machinery	...	...	...	565	...	...	...	212	...	30
3110 Electric motors, generators and transformers	12832	16700	14751	13240	5870	7161	6349	6201	511	465
3120 Electricity distribution & control apparatus	...	...	...	10965	...	...	...	5048	...	590
3130 Insulated wire and cable	5730	6021	6041	7083	2373	2594	2640	2831	340	219
3140 Accumulators, primary cells and batteries	52430	49141	50778	1907	19057	18459	18745	733	1313	70
3150 Lighting equipment and electric lamps	...	...	...	4230	...	...	...	2015	...	167
3190 Other electrical equipment n.e.c.	...	...	...	8013	...	...	...	3879	...	555
3210 Electronic valves, tubes, etc.	27926	28380	35061	11468	8721	9107	10398	5747	2484	1364
3220 TV/radio transmitters; line comm. apparatus	13572	11457	14943	34943	5529	4993	6012	16629	612	1895
3230 TV and radio receivers and associated goods	...	...	...	15553	...	...	...	3593	...	526
331 Medical, measuring, testing appliances, etc.	8116	8396	8912	11604	3688	3907	4138	6114	642	673
3311 Medical, surgical and orthopaedic equipment	1731	1637	1779	4974	709	707	792	2970	256	425
3312 Measuring/testing/navigating appliances,etc.	6386	6759	7133	5033	2979	3200	3346	2486	385	210
3313 Industrial process control equipment	...	...	...	1597	...	...	...	658	...	38
3320 Optical instruments & photographic equipment	4174	3550	2995	2452	2053	1814	1454	1226	170	95
3330 Watches and clocks	611	647	654	54	249	252	275	32	21	1
3410 Motor vehicles	...	...	...	46829	...	...	...	12356	...	2611
3420 Automobile bodies, trailers & semi-trailers	...	...	...	4491	...	...	...	1737	...	232
3430 Parts/accessories for automobiles	...	...	...	13431	...	...	...	5241	...	744
351 Building and repairing of ships and boats	714	931	405	365	266	472	210	185	14	34
3511 Building and repairing of ships	...	...	...	...	...	...	...	...	...	...
3512 Building/repairing of pleasure/sport. boats	...	...	...	...	...	...	...	...	...	...
3520 Railway/tramway locomotives & rolling stock	4303	4580	3885	10368	2053	2103	1883	3317	171	294
3530 Aircraft and spacecraft	...	...	...	214	...	...	...	90	...	39
359 Transport equipment n.e.c.	...	...	...	1305	...	...	...	372	...	24
3591 Motorcycles	...	...	...	...	...	...	...	...	...	...
3592 Bicycles and invalid carriages	...	...	...	...	...	...	...	...	...	...
3599 Other transport equipment n.e.c.	...	...	...	...	...	...	...	...	...	...
3610 Furniture	445	410	419	33762	156	140	150	16191	10	2276
369 Manufacturing n.e.c.	7930	7603	7920	18940	3134	3047	3005	6195	331	758
3691 Jewellery and related articles	...	...	...	7085	...	...	...	1176	...	58
3692 Musical instruments	426	430	300	496	193	205	181	305	11	28
3693 Sports goods	7504	7174	7620	6594	2941	2843	2824	2371	319	411
3694 Games and toys	...	...	...	1417	...	...	...	700	...	43
3699 Other manufacturing n.e.c.	...	...	...	3348	...	...	...	1643	...	219
3710 Recycling of metal waste and scrap	...	...	...	897	...	...	...	342	...	77
3720 Recycling of non-metal waste and scrap	...	...	...	564	...	...	...	289	...	85
D Total manufacturing	1058828	1020148	1073536	1100497	369703	359832	381165	420731	57422	64346

a/ Data for 1995 are not strictly comparable with those provided for earlier years.
b/ Value added in factor values.

Austria

ISIC Revision 3		Note	Index numbers of industrial production (1990=100)											
ISIC	Industry		1985	1986	1987	1988	1989	1990	1991	1992	1993	1994	1995	1996
15	Food and beverages		...	...	...	...	...	100	97	97	100	94	98	97
16	Tobacco products		...	...	...	...	...	...	...	...	...	...	...	...
17	Textiles		...	...	...	...	...	100	101	103	95	86	88	91
18	Wearing apparel, fur		...	...	...	...	...	100	99	95	75	65	52	45
19	Leather, leather products and footwear		...	...	...	...	...	100	92	87	84	85	81	79
20	Wood products (excl. furniture)		...	...	...	...	...	100	79	89	82	86	132	136
21	Paper and paper products		...	...	...	...	...	100	103	107	111	118	120	124
22	Printing and publishing		...	...	...	...	...	100	94	104	89	87	91	130
23	Coke,refined petroleum products,nuclear fuel		...	...	...	...	...	100	105	110	110	103	100	126
24	Chemicals and chemical products		...	...	...	...	...	100	96	101	104	100	113	120
25	Rubber and plastics products		...	...	...	...	...	100	95	94	89	89	116	116
26	Non-metallic mineral products		...	...	...	...	...	100	59	64	63	68	110	110
27	Basic metals		...	...	...	...	...	100	95	89	83	90	105	101
28	Fabricated metal products		...	...	...	...	...	100	91	92	89	93	116	124
29	Machinery and equipment n.e.c.		...	...	...	...	...	100	87	80	76	73	137	141
30	Office, accounting and computing machinery		...	...	...	...	...	100	76	96	70	80	83	40
31	Electrical machinery and apparatus		...	...	...	...	...	100	90	98	97	129	154	158
32	Radio,television and communication equipment		...	...	...	...	...	100	87	79	87	106	121	123
33	Medical, precision and optical instruments		...	...	...	...	...	100	91	90	94	97	107	108
34	Motor vehicles, trailers, semi-trailers		...	...	...	...	...	100	99	101	99	102	129	139
35	Other transport equipment		...	...	...	...	...	100	72	58	55	68	80	71
36	Furniture; manufacturing n.e.c.		...	...	...	...	...	100	90	95	89	80	109	104
37	Recycling		...	...	...	...	...	...	...	...	...	...	...	...
D	Total manufacturing		...	...	...	...	...	100	92	92	91	92	113	116

AZERBAIJAN

Supplier of information:
State Committee of the Republic of Azerbaijan on Statistics, Baku.

Basic source of data:
Not reported.

Major deviations from ISIC (Revision 3):
None reported.

Reference period (if not calendar year):

Scope:
Not reported.

Method of enumeration:
Not reported.

Adjusted for non-response:
Not reported.

Concepts and definitions of variables:
No deviations from the standard UN concepts and definitions are reported.

Related national publications:

ISIC Revision 3	Number of establishments					Number of persons engaged					Wages and salaries paid to employees				
		(numbers)					(numbers)					(thousand MANAT)			
ISIC Industry	Note	1993	1994	1995	1996	Note	1993	1994	1995	1996	Note	1993	1994	1995	1996
151 Processed meat,fish,fruit,vegetables,fats		...	...	...	40		...	...	3500	2989		...	...	...	...
1511 Processing/preserving of meat		...	...	...	36		...	...	2918	2553		...	...	...	...
1512 Processing/preserving of fish		...	...	...	2		...	...	228	175		...	...	...	...
1513 Processing/preserving of fruit & vegetables		...	...	...	2		...	...	354	261		...	...	...	...
1514 Vegetable and animal oils and fats		...	...	...	-		...	...	-	-		...	...	...	...
1520 Dairy products		...	...	...	13		...	...	1147	1163		...	...	...	...
153 Grain mill products; starches; animal feeds		...	...	...	40		...	...	3969	3276		...	...	...	...
1531 Grain mill products		...	...	...	-		...	...	-	-		...	...	...	...
1532 Starches and starch products		...	...	...	13		...	...	981	767		...	...	...	...
1533 Prepared animal feeds		...	...	...	27		...	...	2988	2509		...	...	...	...
154 Other food products		...	...	...	4		...	...	968	860		...	...	...	...
1541 Bakery products		...	...	...	2		...	...	773	729		...	...	...	...
1542 Sugar		...	...	...	-		...	...	-	-		...	...	...	...
1543 Cocoa, chocolate and sugar confectionery		...	...	...	2		...	...	195	131		...	...	...	...
1544 Macaroni, noodles & similar products		...	...	...	-		...	...	-	-		...	...	...	...
1549 Other food products n.e.c.		...	...	...	-		...	...	-	-		...	...	...	...
155 Beverages		...	...	...	22		...	...	927	749		...	...	...	...
1551 Distilling, rectifying & blending of spirits		...	...	...	22		...	...	927	749		...	...	...	...
1552 Wines		...	...	...	-		...	...	-	-		...	...	...	...
1553 Malt liquors and malt		...	...	...	-		...	...	-	-		...	...	...	...
1554 Soft drinks; mineral waters		...	...	...	-		...	...	-	-		...	...	...	...
1600 Tobacco products		...	...	...	8		...	...	1686	1331		...	...	...	...
171 Spinning, weaving and finishing of textiles		...	...	...	39		...	...	16281	13457		...	...	...	...
1711 Textile fibre preparation; textile weaving		...	...	...	34		...	...	12480	10695		...	...	...	...
1712 Finishing of textiles		...	...	...	3		...	...	3317	2379		...	...	...	...
172 Other textiles		...	...	...	17		...	...	24216	24791		...	...	...	...
1721 Made-up textile articles, except apparel		...	...	...	7		...	...	5072	4387		...	...	...	...
1722 Carpets and rugs		...	...	...	4		...	...	1883	1272		...	...	...	...
1723 Cordage, rope, twine and netting		...	...	...	...		...	...	...	...		...	...	...	...
1729 Other textiles n.e.c.		...	...	...	...		...	...	...	...		...	...	...	...
1730 Knitted and crocheted fabrics and articles		...	...	...	-		...	...	-	-		...	...	...	...
1810 Wearing apparel, except fur apparel		...	...	...	1		...	...	20	15		...	...	...	...
1820 Dressing & dyeing of fur; processing of fur		...	...	...	-		...	...	-	-		...	...	...	...
191 Tanning, dressing and processing of leather		...	...	...	2		...	...	309	162		...	...	...	...
1911 Tanning and dressing of leather		...	...	...	...		...	...	...	...		...	...	...	...
1912 Luggage, handbags, etc.; saddlery & harness		...	...	...	...		...	...	...	...		...	...	...	...
1920 Footwear		...	...	...	4		...	...	1042	841		...	...	...	...
2010 Sawmilling and planing of wood		...	...	...	26		...	...	6412	5031		...	...	...	...
202 Products of wood, cork, straw, etc.		...	...	...	1		...	...	222	231		...	...	...	...
2021 Veneer sheets, plywood, particle board, etc.		...	...	...	...		...	...	...	...		...	...	...	...
2022 Builders' carpentry and joinery		...	...	...	...		...	...	...	...		...	...	...	...
2023 Wooden containers		...	...	...	...		...	...	...	...		...	...	...	...
2029 Other wood products; articles of cork/straw		...	...	...	...		...	...	...	...		...	...	...	...
210 Paper and paper products		...	...	...	...		...	...	...	...		...	...	...	...
2101 Pulp, paper and paperboard		...	...	...	...		...	...	...	...		...	...	...	...
2102 Corrugated paper and paperboard		...	...	...	...		...	...	...	...		...	...	...	...
2109 Other articles of paper and paperboard		...	...	...	...		...	...	...	...		...	...	...	...
221 Publishing		...	...	...	25		...	...	1024	1092		...	...	...	...
2211 Publishing of books and other publications		...	...	...	13		...	...	676	729		...	...	...	...
2212 Publishing of newspapers, journals, etc.		...	...	...	10		...	...	241	243		...	...	...	...
2213 Publishing of recorded media		...	...	...	...		...	...	...	...		...	...	...	...
2219 Other publishing		...	...	...	...		...	...	...	...		...	...	...	...

222 Printing and related service activities	...	...	...	14	...	...	981	889	...	...	...	...
2221 Printing	...	...	...	6	...	...	272	257	...	...	...	...
2222 Service activities related to printing	...	...	...	8	...	...	709	632	...	...	...	...
2230 Reproduction of recorded media	...	...	...	...	...	...	...	...	...	...	...	...
2310 Coke oven products	...	...	...	...	...	...	...	...	...	...	...	...
2320 Refined petroleum products	...	...	...	3	...	...	6138	6037	...	...	...	...
2330 Processing of nuclear fuel	...	...	...	-	...	...	-	-	...	...	...	...
241 Basic chemicals	...	...	...	8	...	...	11434	10720	...	...	...	...
2411 Basic chemicals, except fertilizers	...	...	...	...	...	...	...	...	...	...	...	...
2412 Fertilizers and nitrogen compounds	...	...	...	...	...	...	...	...	...	...	...	...
2413 Plastics in primary forms; synthetic rubber	...	...	...	5	...	...	6639	6179	...	...	...	...
242 Other chemicals	...	...	...	...	...	...	...	...	...	...	...	...
2421 Pesticides and other agro-chemical products	...	...	...	...	...	...	...	...	...	...	...	...
2422 Paints, varnishes, printing ink and mastics	...	...	...	...	...	...	...	...	...	...	...	...
2423 Pharmaceuticals, medicinal chemicals, etc.	...	...	...	...	...	...	...	...	...	...	...	...
2424 Soap, cleaning & cosmetic preparations	...	...	...	...	...	...	...	...	...	...	...	...
2429 Other chemical products n.e.c.	...	...	...	...	...	...	...	...	...	...	...	...
2430 Man-made fibres	...	...	...	1	...	...	26	25	...	...	...	...
251 Rubber products	...	...	...	3	...	...	2968	2687	...	...	...	...
2511 Rubber tyres and tubes	...	...	...	...	...	...	...	...	...	...	...	...
2519 Other rubber products	...	...	...	...	...	...	...	...	...	...	...	...
2520 Plastic products	...	...	...	...	...	...	...	...	...	...	...	...
2610 Glass and glass products	...	...	...	...	...	...	...	...	...	...	...	...
269 Non-metallic mineral products n.e.c.	...	...	...	...	...	...	...	...	...	...	...	...
2691 Pottery, china and earthenware	...	...	...	...	...	...	...	...	...	...	...	...
2692 Refractory ceramic products	...	...	...	...	...	...	...	...	...	...	...	...
2693 Struct.non-refractory clay; ceramic products	...	...	...	...	...	...	...	...	...	...	...	...
2694 Cement, lime and plaster	...	...	...	...	...	...	...	...	...	...	...	...
2695 Articles of concrete, cement and plaster	...	...	...	...	...	...	...	...	...	...	...	...
2696 Cutting, shaping & finishing of stone	...	...	...	...	...	...	...	...	...	...	...	...
2699 Other non-metallic mineral products n.e.c.	...	...	...	...	...	...	...	...	...	...	...	...
2710 Basic iron and steel	...	...	...	1	...	...	809	752	...	...	...	...
2720 Basic precious and non-ferrous metals	...	...	...	-	...	...	-	-	...	...	...	...
273 Casting of metals	...	...	...	1	...	...	97	96	...	...	...	...
2731 Casting of iron and steel	...	...	...	...	...	...	...	...	...	...	...	...
2732 Casting of non-ferrous metals	...	...	...	...	...	...	...	...	...	...	...	...
281 Struct.metal products;tanks;steam generators	...	...	...	17	...	...	2280	1898	...	...	...	...
2811 Structural metal products	...	...	...	13	...	...	1223	1015	...	...	...	...
2812 Tanks, reservoirs and containers of metal	...	...	...	4	...	...	1057	883	...	...	...	...
2813 Steam generators	...	...	...	-	...	...	-	-	...	...	...	...
289 Other metal products; metal working services	...	...	...	...	...	...	...	...	...	...	...	...
2891 Metal forging/pressing/stamping/roll-forming	...	...	...	...	...	...	...	...	...	...	...	...
2892 Treatment & coating of metals	...	...	...	...	...	...	...	...	...	...	...	...
2893 Cutlery, hand tools and general hardware	...	...	...	...	...	...	...	...	...	...	...	...
2899 Other fabricated metal products n.e.c.	...	...	...	...	...	...	...	...	...	...	...	...
291 General purpose machinery	...	...	...	6	...	...	3531	3134	...	...	...	...
2911 Engines & turbines(not for transport equip.)	...	...	...	-	...	...	-	-	...	...	...	...
2912 Pumps, compressors, taps and valves	...	...	...	5	...	...	3339	2961	...	...	...	...
2913 Bearings, gears, gearing & driving elements	...	...	...	-	...	...	-	-	...	...	...	...
2914 Ovens, furnaces and furnace burners	...	...	...	1	...	...	192	173	...	...	...	...
2915 Lifting and handling equipment	...	...	...	-	...	...	-	-	...	...	...	...
2919 Other general purpose machinery	...	...	...	-	...	...	-	-	...	...	...	...
292 Special purpose machinery	...	...	...	19	...	...	6028	5411	...	...	...	...
2921 Agricultural and forestry machinery	...	...	...	1	...	...	...	...	...	...	...	...
2922 Machine tools	...	...	...	10	...	...	4057	3773	...	...	...	...
2923 Machinery for metallurgy	...	...	...	1	...	...	201	165	...	...	...	...
2924 Machinery for mining & construction	...	...	...	7	...	...	1493	1220	...	...	...	...
2925 Food/beverage/tobacco processing machinery	...	...	...	-	...	...	-	-	...	...	...	...
2926 Machinery for textile, apparel and leather	...	...	...	-	...	...	-	-	...	...	...	...
2927 Weapons and ammunition	...	...	...	-	...	...	-	-	...	...	...	...
2929 Other special purpose machinery	...	...	...	-	...	...	-	-	...	...	...	...
2930 Domestic appliances n.e.c.	...	...	...	-	...	...	-	-	...	...	...	...

continued

Azerbaijan

ISIC Revision 3	Number of establishments					Number of persons engaged					Wages and salaries paid to employees				
		(numbers)					(numbers)					(thousand MANAT)			
ISIC Industry	Note	1993	1994	1995	1996	Note	1993	1994	1995	1996	Note	1993	1994	1995	1996
3000 Office, accounting and computing machinery		...	...	...	-		...	...	-	-		...	...	...	...
3110 Electric motors, generators and transformers		...	...	...	9		...	...	2947	2611		...	...	...	...
3120 Electricity distribution & control apparatus		...	...	...	6		...	...	2001	2411		...	...	...	...
3130 Insulated wire and cable		...	...	...	1		...	...	609	549		...	...	...	...
3140 Accumulators, primary cells and batteries		...	...	...	8		...	...	481	371		...	...	...	...
3150 Lighting equipment and electric lamps		...	...	...	1		...	...	1040	721		...	...	...	...
3190 Other electrical equipment n.e.c.		...	...	...	-		...	...	-	-		...	...	...	...
3210 Electronic valves, tubes, etc.		...	...	...	1		...	...	145	52		...	...	...	...
3220 TV/radio transmitters; line comm. apparatus		...	...	...	15		...	...	5227	4050		...	...	...	...
3230 TV and radio receivers and associated goods		...	...	...	-		...	...	-	-		...	...	...	...
331 Medical, measuring, testing appliances, etc.		...	...	...	5		...	...	602	338		...	...	...	...
3311 Medical, surgical and orthopaedic equipment		...	...	...	...		...	...	...	...		...	...	...	...
3312 Measuring/testing/navigating appliances,etc.		...	...	...	...		...	...	...	...		...	...	...	...
3313 Industrial process control equipment		...	...	...	...		...	...	...	...		...	...	...	...
3320 Optical instruments & photographic equipment		...	...	...	4		...	...	1849	1685		...	...	...	...
3330 Watches and clocks		...	...	...	2		...	...	108	95		...	...	...	...
3410 Motor vehicles		...	...	...	1		...	...	883	838		...	...	...	...
3420 Automobile bodies, trailers & semi-trailers		...	...	...	-		...	...	-	-		...	...	...	...
3430 Parts/accessories for automobiles		...	...	...	-		...	...	-	-		...	...	...	...
351 Building and repairing of ships and boats		...	...	...	5		...	...	3022	3171		...	...	...	...
3511 Building and repairing of ships		...	...	...	5		...	...	3022	3171		...	...	...	...
3512 Building/repairing of pleasure/sport. boats		...	...	...	-		...	...	-	-		...	...	...	...
3520 Railway/tramway locomotives & rolling stock		...	...	...	...		...	...	...	...		...	...	...	...
3530 Aircraft and spacecraft		...	...	...	...		...	...	...	...		...	...	...	...
359 Transport equipment n.e.c.		...	...	...	...		...	...	...	...		...	...	...	...
3591 Motorcycles		...	...	...	...		...	...	...	...		...	...	...	...
3592 Bicycles and invalid carriages		...	...	...	...		...	...	...	...		...	...	...	...
3599 Other transport equipment n.e.c.		...	...	...	...		...	...	...	...		...	...	...	...
3610 Furniture		...	...	...	...		...	...	...	...		...	...	...	...
369 Manufacturing n.e.c.		...	...	...	...		...	...	...	...		...	...	...	...
3691 Jewellery and related articles		...	...	...	...		...	...	...	...		...	...	...	...
3692 Musical instruments		...	...	...	...		...	...	...	...		...	...	...	...
3693 Sports goods		...	...	...	...		...	...	...	...		...	...	...	...
3694 Games and toys		...	...	...	...		...	...	...	...		...	...	...	...
3699 Other manufacturing n.e.c.		...	...	...	...		...	...	...	...		...	...	...	...
3710 Recycling of metal waste and scrap		...	...	...	2		...	...	257	222		...	...	...	...
3720 Recycling of non-metal waste and scrap		...	...	...	...		...	...	...	...		...	...	...	...
D Total manufacturing		...	...	...	1020		...	...	251107	224534		...	...	...	...

Azerbaijan

ISIC Revision 3	Output					Value added					Gross fixed capital formation		
		(billion MANAT)					(billion MANAT)					(million MANAT)	
ISIC Industry	Note	1993	1994	1995	1996	Note	1993	1994	1995	1996	Note	1995	1996
151 Processed meat,fish,fruit,vegetables,fats		...	...	52.3	40.7		...	...	...	...		...	34055.8
1511 Processing/preserving of meat		...	...	45.7	32.4		...	...	...	...		...	30125.4
1512 Processing/preserving of fish		...	...	3.3	7.0		...	...	...	...		...	24.1
1513 Processing/preserving of fruit & vegetables		...	...	3.3	1.3		...	...	...	...		...	-
1514 Vegetable and animal oils and fats		...	...	-	-		...	...	...	...		...	-
1520 Dairy products		...	...	3.7	3.5		...	...	...	...		...	2486.0
153 Grain mill products; starches; animal feeds		...	...	19.0	12.2		...	...	...	...		...	6023.4
1531 Grain mill products		...	...	-	-		...	...	...	...		...	...
1532 Starches and starch products		...	...	2.2	2.4		...	...	...	...		...	...
1533 Prepared animal feeds		...	...	16.8	9.8		...	...	...	...		...	6261.4
154 Other food products		...	...	37.2	15.8		...	...	...	...		...	3047.6
1541 Bakery products		...	...	33.3	14.0		...	...	...	...		...	3047.6
1542 Sugar		...	...	-	-		...	...	...	...		...	-
1543 Cocoa, chocolate and sugar confectionery		...	...	3.9	1.8		...	...	...	...		...	-
1544 Macaroni, noodles & similar products		...	...	-	-		...	...	...	...		...	-
1549 Other food products n.e.c.		...	...	-	-		...	...	...	...		...	-
155 Beverages		...	...	21.1	13.2		...	...	...	...		...	62737.2
1551 Distilling, rectifying & blending of spirits		...	...	21.1	13.2		...	...	...	...		...	62737.2
1552 Wines		...	...	-	-		...	...	...	...		...	-
1553 Malt liquors and malt		...	...	-	-		...	...	...	...		...	-
1554 Soft drinks; mineral waters		...	...	-	-		...	...	...	...		...	-
1600 Tobacco products		...	...	34.9	27.1		...	...	...	...		...	-
171 Spinning, weaving and finishing of textiles		...	...	581.8	556.3		...	...	...	...		...	24442.5
1711 Textile fibre preparation; textile weaving		...	...	545.9	549.1		...	...	...	...		...	23812.6
1712 Finishing of textiles		...	...	35.6	7.2		...	...	...	...		...	...
172 Other textiles		...	...	172.7	274.0		...	...	...	...		...	...
1721 Made-up textile articles, except apparel		...	...	94.5	58.2		...	...	...	...		...	-
1722 Carpets and rugs		...	...	9.2	3.8		...	...	...	...		...	-
1723 Cordage, rope, twine and netting		...	...	...	...		...	...	...	...		...	...
1729 Other textiles n.e.c.		...	...	...	...		...	...	...	...		...	...
1730 Knitted and crocheted fabrics and articles		...	...	-	-		...	...	...	...		...	-
1810 Wearing apparel, except fur apparel		...	...	0.1	0.1		...	...	...	...		...	14.3
1820 Dressing & dyeing of fur; processing of fur		...	...	-	-		...	...	...	...		...	-
191 Tanning, dressing and processing of leather		...	...	0.5	0.3		...	...	...	...		...	...
1911 Tanning and dressing of leather		...	...	...	...		...	...	...	...		...	...
1912 Luggage, handbags, etc.; saddlery & harness		...	...	...	...		...	...	...	...		...	...
1920 Footwear		...	...	2.7	1.4		...	...	...	...		...	112.5
2010 Sawmilling and planing of wood		...	...	59.6	63.1		...	...	...	...		...	1107.7
202 Products of wood, cork, straw, etc.		...	...	0.2	0.2		...	...	...	...		...	...
2021 Veneer sheets, plywood, particle board, etc.		...	...	...	...		...	...	...	...		...	...
2022 Builders' carpentry and joinery		...	...	...	...		...	...	...	...		...	...
2023 Wooden containers		...	...	...	...		...	...	...	...		...	...
2029 Other wood products; articles of cork/straw		...	...	...	...		...	...	...	...		...	...
210 Paper and paper products		...	...	...	...		...	...	...	...		...	...
2101 Pulp, paper and paperboard		...	...	...	...		...	...	...	...		...	...
2102 Corrugated paper and paperboard		...	...	...	...		...	...	...	...		...	...
2109 Other articles of paper and paperboard		...	...	...	...		...	...	...	...		...	...
221 Publishing		...	...	10.1	12.4		...	...	...	...		...	6241.2
2211 Publishing of books and other publications		...	...	6.2	5.8		...	...	...	...		...	4911.6
2212 Publishing of newspapers, journals, etc.		...	...	3.1	5.2		...	...	...	...		...	...
2213 Publishing of recorded media		...	...	...	...		...	...	...	...		...	...
2219 Other publishing		...	...	...	...		...	...	...	...		...	...

continued

ISIC Revision 3	Output					Value added					Gross fixed capital formation		
		(billion MANAT)					(billion MANAT)					(million MANAT)	
ISIC Industry	Note	1993	1994	1995	1996	Note	1993	1994	1995	1996	Note	1995	1996
222 Printing and related service activities		...	...	1.7	2.4		...	...	...	...		...	2951.1
2221 Printing		...	...	0.7	0.9		...	...	...	...		...	44.0
2222 Service activities related to printing		...	...	0.9	1.4		...	...	...	...		...	2729.7
2230 Reproduction of recorded media		...	...	...	...		...	...	...	...		...	...
2310 Coke oven products		...	...	...	...		...	...	...	...		...	...
2320 Refined petroleum products		...	...	2314.7	3038.5		...	...	...	...		...	445362.0
2330 Processing of nuclear fuel		...	...	-	-		...	...	...	...		...	-
241 Basic chemicals		...	...	220.0	206.0		...	...	...	...		...	31997.5
2411 Basic chemicals, except fertilizers		...	...	...	...		...	...	...	...		...	...
2412 Fertilizers and nitrogen compounds		...	...	...	...		...	...	...	...		...	...
2413 Plastics in primary forms; synthetic rubber		...	...	124.1	96.2		...	...	...	...		...	16610.9
242 Other chemicals		...	...	...	...		...	...	...	...		...	...
2421 Pesticides and other agro-chemical products		...	...	...	...		...	...	...	...		...	...
2422 Paints, varnishes, printing ink and mastics		...	...	...	...		...	...	...	...		...	...
2423 Pharmaceuticals, medicinal chemicals, etc.		...	...	...	...		...	...	...	...		...	...
2424 Soap, cleaning & cosmetic preparations		...	...	...	...		...	...	...	...		...	...
2429 Other chemical products n.e.c.		...	...	...	...		...	...	...	...		...	...
2430 Man-made fibres		...	...	-	-		...	...	...	...		...	-
251 Rubber products		...	...	36.2	37.9		...	...	...	...		...	...
2511 Rubber tyres and tubes		...	...	...	...		...	...	...	...		...	...
2519 Other rubber products		...	...	...	...		...	...	...	...		...	...
2520 Plastic products		...	...	...	...		...	...	...	...		...	...
2610 Glass and glass products		...	...	...	...		...	...	...	...		...	...
269 Non-metallic mineral products n.e.c.		...	...	...	...		...	...	...	...		...	...
2691 Pottery, china and earthenware		...	...	...	...		...	...	...	...		...	...
2692 Refractory ceramic products		...	...	...	...		...	...	...	...		...	...
2693 Struct.non-refractory clay; ceramic products		...	...	...	...		...	...	...	...		...	...
2694 Cement, lime and plaster		...	...	...	...		...	...	...	...		...	...
2695 Articles of concrete, cement and plaster		...	...	...	...		...	...	...	...		...	...
2696 Cutting, shaping & finishing of stone		...	...	...	...		...	...	...	...		...	...
2699 Other non-metallic mineral products n.e.c.		...	...	...	...		...	...	...	...		...	...
2710 Basic iron and steel		...	...	5.6	7.1		...	...	...	...		...	-
2720 Basic precious and non-ferrous metals		...	...	-	-		...	...	...	...		...	-
273 Casting of metals		...	...	0.8	1.6		...	...	...	...		...	105.3
2731 Casting of iron and steel		...	...	...	...		...	...	...	...		...	...
2732 Casting of non-ferrous metals		...	...	...	...		...	...	...	...		...	...
281 Struct.metal products;tanks;steam generators		...	...	10.8	13.9		...	...	...	...		...	8372.4
2811 Structural metal products		...	...	6.9	6.1		...	...	...	...		...	...
2812 Tanks, reservoirs and containers of metal		...	...	3.9	7.8		...	...	...	...		...	8702.6
2813 Steam generators		...	...	-	-		...	...	...	...		...	...
289 Other metal products; metal working services		...	...	...	...		...	...	...	...		...	...
2891 Metal forging/pressing/stamping/roll-forming		...	...	...	...		...	...	...	...		...	...
2892 Treatment & coating of metals		...	...	...	...		...	...	...	...		...	...
2893 Cutlery, hand tools and general hardware		...	...	...	...		...	...	...	...		...	...
2899 Other fabricated metal products n.e.c.		...	...	...	...		...	...	...	...		...	...
291 General purpose machinery		...	...	14.9	13.1		...	...	...	...		...	-
2911 Engines & turbines(not for transport equip.)		...	...	-	-		...	...	...	...		...	-
2912 Pumps, compressors, taps and valves		...	...	14.4	12.4		...	...	...	...		...	-
2913 Bearings, gears, gearing & driving elements		...	...	-	-		...	...	...	...		...	-
2914 Ovens, furnaces and furnace burners		...	...	0.5	0.7		...	...	...	...		...	-
2915 Lifting and handling equipment		...	...	-	-		...	...	...	...		...	-
2919 Other general purpose machinery		...	...	-	-		...	...	...	...		...	-

292 Special purpose machinery	...	...	56.0	59.4	...	...	...	...	...	74644.1
2921 Agricultural and forestry machinery	...	...	2.4	1.4	...	...	...	...	...	3069.6
2922 Machine tools	...	...	45.9	48.2	...	...	...	...	...	47839.0
2923 Machinery for metallurgy	...	...	...	...	...	...	...	...	...	...
2924 Machinery for mining & construction	...	...	7.7	9.8	...	...	...	...	...	22661.9
2925 Food/beverage/tobacco processing machinery	...	...	-	-	...	...	...	...	...	-
2926 Machinery for textile, apparel and leather	...	...	-	-	...	...	...	...	...	-
2927 Weapons and ammunition	...	...	-	-	...	...	...	...	...	-
2929 Other special purpose machinery	...	...	-	-	...	...	...	...	...	-
2930 Domestic appliances n.e.c.	...	...	-	-	...	...	...	...	...	-
3000 Office, accounting and computing machinery	...	...	-	-	...	...	...	...	...	-
3110 Electric motors, generators and transformers	...	...	22.0	28.3	...	...	...	...	...	428.8
3120 Electricity distribution & control apparatus	...	...	7.3	15.1	...	...	...	...	...	2242.2
3130 Insulated wire and cable	...	...	2.6	7.0	...	...	...	...	...	-
3140 Accumulators, primary cells and batteries	...	...	0.7	0.5	...	...	...	...	...	-
3150 Lighting equipment and electric lamps	...	...	2.1	1.8	...	...	...	...	...	-
3190 Other electrical equipment n.e.c.	...	...	-	-	...	...	...	...	...	-
3210 Electronic valves, tubes, etc.	...	...	-	-	...	...	...	...	...	-
3220 TV/radio transmitters; line comm. apparatus	...	...	9.3	9.2	...	...	...	...	...	185006.1
3230 TV and radio receivers and associated goods	...	...	-	-	...	...	...	...	...	-
331 Medical, measuring, testing appliances, etc.	...	...	1.9	1.8	...	...	...	...	...	18.8
3311 Medical, surgical and orthopaedic equipment	...	...	...	...	...	...	...	...	...	...
3312 Measuring/testing/navigating appliances,etc.	...	...	...	...	...	...	...	...	...	...
3313 Industrial process control equipment	...	...	...	...	...	...	...	...	...	...
3320 Optical instruments & photographic equipment	...	...	20.2	16.9	...	...	...	...	...	1747.9
3330 Watches and clocks	...	...	-	-	...	...	...	...	...	-
3410 Motor vehicles	...	...	0.5	1.9	...	...	...	...	...	-
3420 Automobile bodies, trailers & semi-trailers	...	...	-	-	...	...	...	...	...	-
3430 Parts/accessories for automobiles	...	...	-	-	...	...	...	...	...	-
351 Building and repairing of ships and boats	...	...	21.8	31.8	...	...	...	...	...	942.0
3511 Building and repairing of ships	...	...	21.8	31.8	...	...	...	...	...	942.0
3512 Building/repairing of pleasure/sport. boats	...	...	-	-	...	...	...	...	...	-
3520 Railway/tramway locomotives & rolling stock	...	...	...	...	...	...	...	...	...	...
3530 Aircraft and spacecraft	...	...	...	...	...	...	...	...	...	...
359 Transport equipment n.e.c.	...	...	...	...	...	...	...	...	...	...
3591 Motorcycles	...	...	...	...	...	...	...	...	...	...
3592 Bicycles and invalid carriages	...	...	...	...	...	...	...	...	...	...
3599 Other transport equipment n.e.c.	...	...	...	...	...	...	...	...	...	...
3610 Furniture	...	...	...	...	...	...	...	...	...	...
369 Manufacturing n.e.c.	...	...	...	...	...	...	...	...	...	...
3691 Jewellery and related articles	...	...	...	...	...	...	...	...	...	...
3692 Musical instruments	...	...	...	...	...	...	...	...	...	...
3693 Sports goods	...	...	...	...	...	...	...	...	...	...
3694 Games and toys	...	...	...	...	...	...	...	...	...	...
3699 Other manufacturing n.e.c.	...	...	...	...	...	...	...	...	...	...
3710 Recycling of metal waste and scrap	...	...	0.6	0.4	...	...	...	...	...	...
3720 Recycling of non-metal waste and scrap	...	...	...	...	...	...	...	...	...	...
D Total manufacturing	...	...	5409.7	6379.5	...	...	...	...	...	977000.0

Azerbaijan

ISIC Revision 3			Index numbers of industrial production											
			(1990=100)											
ISIC	Industry	Note	1985	1986	1987	1988	1989	1990	1991	1992	1993	1994	1995	1996
15	Food and beverages		...	...	...	...	...	...	...	...	...	...	...	...
16	Tobacco products		...	...	...	...	...	...	...	...	...	...	...	...
17	Textiles		...	...	...	...	...	...	...	...	...	...	...	...
18	Wearing apparel, fur		...	...	...	...	...	...	...	...	...	...	...	...
19	Leather, leather products and footwear		...	...	...	...	...	...	...	...	...	...	...	...
20	Wood products (excl. furniture)		...	...	...	...	...	...	...	...	...	...	...	...
21	Paper and paper products		...	...	...	...	...	...	...	...	...	...	...	...
22	Printing and publishing		...	...	...	...	...	...	...	...	...	...	...	...
23	Coke,refined petroleum products,nuclear fuel		...	...	...	...	...	...	...	...	...	...	...	...
24	Chemicals and chemical products		...	...	...	...	...	...	...	...	...	...	...	...
25	Rubber and plastics products		...	...	...	...	...	...	...	...	...	...	...	...
26	Non-metallic mineral products		...	...	...	...	...	...	...	...	...	...	...	...
27	Basic metals		...	...	...	...	...	...	...	...	...	...	...	...
28	Fabricated metal products		...	...	...	...	...	...	...	...	...	...	...	...
29	Machinery and equipment n.e.c.		...	...	...	...	...	...	...	...	...	...	...	...
30	Office, accounting and computing machinery		...	...	...	...	...	...	...	...	...	...	...	...
31	Electrical machinery and apparatus		...	...	...	...	...	...	...	...	...	...	...	...
32	Radio,television and communication equipment		...	...	...	...	...	...	...	...	...	...	...	...
33	Medical, precision and optical instruments		...	...	...	...	...	...	...	...	...	...	...	...
34	Motor vehicles, trailers, semi-trailers		...	...	...	...	...	...	...	...	...	...	...	...
35	Other transport equipment		...	...	...	...	...	...	...	...	...	...	...	...
36	Furniture; manufacturing n.e.c.		...	...	...	...	...	...	...	...	...	...	...	...
37	Recycling		...	...	...	...	...	...	...	...	...	...	...	...
D	Total manufacturing		...	...	...	...	...	...	...	...	...	...	...	...

BELGIUM

Supplier of information:
Office national de sécurité sociale (ONSS), Ministère de l'emploi et du travail, Brussels. Industrial statistics for the OECD countries are compiled by the OECD secretariat, which supplies them to UNIDO. The notes appearing here are based on information in the OECD publication *Industrial Structure Statistics* (annual), OECD, Paris.

Basic source of data:
Not reported.

Major deviations from ISIC (Revision 2):
Data have been converted from NACE (Revision 1) to ISIC (Rev. 2).

Reference period (if not calendar year):

Scope:
Not reported.

Method of enumeration:
Not reported.

Adjusted for non-response:
Not reported.

Concepts and definitions of variables:
Wages and salaries does not include employers' social security contributions.

Related national publications:

Belgium

ISIC Revision 2	Number of establishments					Number of employees					Wages and salaries paid to employees				
		(numbers)					(thousands)					(million FRANCS)			
ISIC Industry	Note	1993	1994	1995	1996	Note	1993	1994	1995	1996	Note	1993	1994	1995	1996
311/2 Food products		6813	6790	...	...		...	...	...	...		55432	56576	...	...
313 Beverages		198	200	...	...		...	...	...	...		11206	11500	...	...
314 Tobacco		43	39	...	...		...	...	...	...		4033	4253	...	...
321 Textiles		1537	1476	...	...		...	...	...	...		30082	31233	...	...
322 Wearing apparel, except footwear		1314	1172	...	...		...	...	...	...		10881	9853	...	...
323 Leather and fur products		108	95	...	...		...	...	...	...		1464	1400	...	...
324 Footwear, except rubber or plastic		80	81	...	...		...	...	...	...		576	499	...	...
331 Wood products, except furniture		3139a/	3087a/	...	...		...	...	...	...		25860a/	26055a/	...	...
332 Furniture and fixtures, excl. metal		...a/	...a/	...	...		...	...	...	...		...a/	...a/	...	...
341 Paper and products		289	291	...	...		...	...	...	...		14250	14557	...	...
342 Printing and publishing		2561	2520	...	...		...	...	...	...		30655	30968	...	...
351 Industrial chemicals		778b/	772b/	...	...		...	...	...	...		91894b/	91557b/	...	...
352 Other chemicals		...b/	...b/	...	...		...	...	...	...		...b/	...b/	...	...
353 Petroleum refineries		40c/	35c/	...	...		...	...	...	...		6801c/	6809c/	...	...
354 Misc. petroleum and coal products		...c/	...c/	...	...		...	...	...	...		...c/	...c/	...	...
355 Rubber products		98	97	...	...		...	...	...	...		4087	4316	...	...
356 Plastic products		585	571	...	...		...	...	...	...		18453	17772	...	...
361 Pottery, china, earthenware		...d/	...d/	...	...		...	...	...	...		...d/	...d/	...	...
362 Glass and products		157	165	...	...		...	...	...	...		11102	11229	...	...
369 Other non-metallic mineral products		1216d/	1208d/	...	...		...	...	...	...		18246d/	18792d/	...	...
371 Iron and steel		290e/	284e/	...	...		...	...	...	...		50244e/	50132e/	...	...
372 Non-ferrous metals		...e/	...e/	...	...		...	...	...	...		...e/	...e/	...	...
381 Fabricated metal products		3439	3438	...	...		...	...	...	...		43274	43657	...	...
382 Non-electrical machinery		1045	1086	...	...		...	...	...	...		38324	39756	...	...
383 Electrical machinery		791	675	...	...		...	...	...	...		46710	46927	...	...
384 Transport equipment		528	528	...	...		...	...	...	...		63181	62840	...	...
385 Professional and scientific equipment		606	635	...	...		...	...	...	...		5955	5865	...	...
390 Other manufacturing industries		556	564	...	...		...	...	...	...		3314	3411	...	...
3 Total manufacturing		26211	25809	...	...		...	...	...	...		586024	589957	...	...

a/ 331 includes 332.
b/ 351 includes 352.
c/ 353 includes 354.
d/ 369 includes 361.
e/ 371 includes 372.

Belgium

ISIC Revision 2	Output in producers' prices					Value added in factor values					Gross fixed capital formation		
		(million FRANCS)					(million FRANCS)					(million FRANCS)	
ISIC Industry	Note	1993	1994	1995	1996	Note	1993	1994	1995	1996	Note	1995	1996
311/2 Food products		...	...	...	...		218571	230414	243648	263382		29169	33073
313 Beverages		102091	103769	108820	103247		31118	30916	31773	30879		9010	7961
314 Tobacco		58626	63778	63976	58966		9761	11371	11406	10496		645	882
321 Textiles		227797	246108	234505	228433		66871	71441	68316	66524		14577	13254
322 Wearing apparel, except footwear		100356	104853	105991	89646		34456	35907	36297	30655		2218	1955
323 Leather and fur products	a/	3940	3377	3082	2968	a/	1559	1333	1214	1165		9	5
324 Footwear, except rubber or plastic	a/	...	...	...	...	a/	...	...	...	...		54	44
331 Wood products, except furniture		35662	36784	37736	35460		9485	9551	9872	9165		1032	955
332 Furniture and fixtures, excl. metal		158994	160931	170254	171492		54198	54598	57782	58115		6577	8209
341 Paper and products		111347	119128	130796	127686		29130	31068	34063	33181		13663	13276
342 Printing and publishing		151677	158382	174249	168143		63145	65852	72448	69911		15479	14776
351 Industrial chemicals		449754	510463	583545	593510		140670	159603	182453	185453		79275	99577
352 Other chemicals		134842	143671	168356	166063		46765	49880	59734	58334		...	...
353 Petroleum refineries	b/	167256	163204	179207	258050	b/	15164	14574	15775	22184	b/	6620	7133
354 Misc. petroleum and coal products	b/	...	...	...	...	b/	...	...	...	...	b/	...	...
355 Rubber products		21492	25254	26649	24275		8136	9541	10061	9168		1750	1651
356 Plastic products		...	...	...	...	c/	...	...	...	...	c/	...	...
361 Pottery, china, earthenware	d/	154174	163930	170965	165034	d/	65029	68837	72031	69185	d/	18619	13749
362 Glass and products	d/	...	...	...	...	d/	...	...	...	...	d/	...	...
369 Other non-metallic mineral products	d/	...	...	...	...	d/	...	...	...	...	d/	...	...
371 Iron and steel		163706	187154	212506	173160		57132	65413	74274	60456		18627	17055
372 Non-ferrous metals		94965	109483	119149	133106		22746	26341	28668	32005		3685	5502
381 Fabricated metal products	e/	1362845	1451769	1477289	1484505	e/	430919	459036	467080	468894	e/	58712	64344
382 Non-electrical machinery	e/	...	...	...	...	e/	...	...	...	...	e/	...	...
383 Electrical machinery	e/	...	...	...	...	e/	...	...	...	...	e/	...	...
384 Transport equipment	e/	...	...	...	...	e/	...	...	...	...	e/	...	...
385 Professional and scientific equipment	e/	...	...	...	...	e/	...	...	...	...	e/	...	...
390 Other manufacturing industries		...	...	...	...	c/	89594	91766	104291	100602	c/	1804	2190
3 Total manufacturing		...	...	...	...		1394449	1487442	1581186	1579754		302034	329704

a/ 323 includes 324.
b/ 353 includes 354.
c/ 390 includes 356.
d/ 361 includes 362 and 369.
e/ 381 includes 382, 383, 384 and 385.

Belgium

ISIC Revision 2 ISIC Industry	Note	Index numbers of industrial production (1990=100) 1985	1986	1987	1988	1989	1990	1991	1992	1993	1994	1995	1996
311/2 Food products	a/	...	...	...	...	...	100	102	103	102	100	104	106
313 Beverages	a/	...	...	...	...	...	...	...	...	...	...	...	...
314 Tobacco		116	109	106	104	104	100	106	98	93	97	98	60
321 Textiles		99	100	100	101	102	100	88	94	85	85	85	84
322 Wearing apparel, except footwear		83	87	80	77	99	100	107	108	117	114	113	84
323 Leather and fur products	b/	146	135	118	112	110	100	77	59	46	42	45	45
324 Footwear, except rubber or plastic	b/	...	...	...	...	...	...	...	...	...	...	...	...
331 Wood products, except furniture		74	77	85	89	100	100	98	92	89	91	96	95
332 Furniture and fixtures, excl. metal		...	...	...	...	...	100	105	100	95	94	98	97
341 Paper and products		77	78	86	94	95	100	98	102	93	97	95	96
342 Printing and publishing		...	...	...	...	...	...	...	...	...	...	...	...
351 Industrial chemicals	c/	86	88	89	94	94	100	100	112	108	107	112	116
352 Other chemicals	c/	...	...	...	...	...	...	...	...	...	...	...	...
353 Petroleum refineries		...	...	...	...	...	100	112	116	108	109	100	121
354 Misc. petroleum and coal products		...	...	...	...	...	100	84	77	63	62	62	59
355 Rubber products	d/	...	...	...	...	...	100	102	112	101	102	109	109
356 Plastic products	d/	...	...	...	...	...	...	...	...	...	...	...	...
361 Pottery, china, earthenware	e/	85	88	87	101	123	100	94	97	97	103	103	99
362 Glass and products	e/	...	...	...	...	...	...	...	...	...	...	...	...
369 Other non-metallic mineral products	e/	...	...	...	...	...	...	...	...	...	...	...	...
371 Iron and steel	f/	96	88	89	102	108	100	98	89	95	103	106	104
372 Non-ferrous metals	f/	...	...	...	...	...	...	...	...	...	...	...	...
381 Fabricated metal products		79	75	77	83	92	100	101	97	90	92	99	105
382 Non-electrical machinery	g/	97	93	94	96	97	100	95	87	81	86	91	89
383 Electrical machinery	g/	...	...	...	...	...	...	...	...	...	...	...	...
384 Transport equipment		78	84	83	99	86	100	98	97	89	88	88	87
385 Professional and scientific equipment		134	121	101	100	84	100	105	105	95	107	127	115
390 Other manufacturing industries		...	...	...	...	...	...	...	...	...	...	...	...
3 Total manufacturing		...	...	...	...	...	...	...	...	...	...	...	...

a/ 311/2 includes 313.
b/ 323 includes 324.
c/ 351 includes 352.
d/ 355 includes 356.
e/ 361 includes 362 and 369.
f/ 371 includes 372.
g/ 382 includes 383.

BERMUDA

Supplier of information:
Statistics Department, Bermuda.

Basic source of data:
Employment survey.

Major deviations from ISIC (Revision 2):
None reported.

Reference period (if not calendar year):

Scope:
Not reported.

Method of enumeration:
Not reported.

Adjusted for non-response:
Not reported.

Concepts and definitions of variables:
No deviations from the standard UN concepts and definitions are reported.

Related national publications:

Bermuda

ISIC Revision 2	Number of establishments					Number of employees					Wages and salaries paid to employees				
		(numbers)					(numbers)					(thousand DOLLARS)			
ISIC Industry	Note	1993	1994	1995	1996	Note	1993	1994	1995	1996	Note	1993	1994	1995	1996
311/2 Food products		...	...	...	...		169	176	189	175		...	...	...	...
313 Beverages		...	...	...	...		105	129	131	116		...	...	...	...
314 Tobacco		...	...	...	...		...	...	...	...		...	...	...	...
321 Textiles		...	...	...	...		...	...	...	...		...	...	...	...
322 Wearing apparel, except footwear		...	...	...	...		22	23	20	19		...	...	...	...
323 Leather and fur products		...	...	...	...		...	...	...	...		...	...	...	...
324 Footwear, except rubber or plastic		...	...	...	...		14	14	-	-		...	...	...	...
331 Wood products, except furniture		...	...	...	...		67	67	56	60		...	...	...	...
332 Furniture and fixtures, excl. metal		...	...	...	...		37	39	36	33		...	...	...	...
341 Paper and products		...	...	...	...		...	...	...	...		...	...	...	...
342 Printing and publishing		...	...	...	...		380	369	375	361		...	...	...	...
351 Industrial chemicals		...	...	...	...		16	17	14	12		...	...	...	...
352 Other chemicals		...	...	...	...		...	...	...	...		...	...	...	...
353 Petroleum refineries		...	...	...	...		65	70	-	-		...	...	...	...
354 Misc. petroleum and coal products		...	...	...	...		...	...	...	...		...	...	...	...
355 Rubber products		...	...	...	...		...	...	...	...		...	...	...	...
356 Plastic products		...	...	...	...		...	...	...	...		...	...	...	...
361 Pottery, china, earthenware		...	...	...	...		12	10	7	9		...	...	...	...
362 Glass and products		...	...	...	...		65	63	17	1		...	...	...	...
369 Other non-metallic mineral products		...	...	...	...		-	-	-	-		...	...	...	...
371 Iron and steel		...	...	...	...		...	...	...	...		...	...	...	...
372 Non-ferrous metals		...	...	...	...		...	...	...	...		...	...	...	...
381 Fabricated metal products		...	...	...	...		34	33	24	25		...	...	...	...
382 Non-electrical machinery		...	...	...	...		8	6	-	-		...	...	...	...
383 Electrical machinery		...	...	...	...		8	17	7	7		...	...	...	...
384 Transport equipment		...	...	...	...		14	17	21	15		...	...	...	...
385 Professional and scientific equipment		...	...	...	...		4	3	3	1		...	...	...	...
390 Other manufacturing industries		...	...	...	...		20	45	25	42		...	...	...	...
3 Total manufacturing		...	...	...	...		1040	1098	925	876		...	...	...	...

BOLIVIA

Supplier of information:
Instituto Nacional de Estadística, La Paz.

Basic source of data:
Annual industrial survey.

Major deviations from ISIC (Revision 3):
None reported.

Reference period (if not calendar year):
The data refer to the business year or accounting period.

Scope:
Establishments with 5 or more persons engaged.

Method of enumeration:
Not reported.

Adjusted for non-response:
Not reported.

Concepts and definitions of variables:
No deviations from the standard UN concepts and definitions are reported.

Related national publications:
Encuesta Económica Anual, Industria Manufacturera, published by the Instituto Nacional de Estadística, La Paz.

Bolivia

ISIC Revision 3	Number of establishments					Number of employees					Wages and salaries paid to employees				
		(numbers)					(numbers)					(thousand BOLIVIANOS)			
ISIC Industry	Note	1992	1993	1994	1995	Note	1992	1993	1994	1995	Note	1992	1993	1994	1995
151 Processed meat,fish,fruit,vegetables,fats		...	...	...	60		...	...	...	2910		...	...	...	35269
1511 Processing/preserving of meat		...	...	...	45		...	...	...	1693		...	...	...	14373
1512 Processing/preserving of fish		...	...	...	2		...	...	...	38		...	...	...	404
1513 Processing/preserving of fruit & vegetables		...	...	...	9		...	...	...	339		...	...	...	3246
1514 Vegetable and animal oils and fats		...	...	...	4		...	...	...	840		...	...	...	17246
1520 Dairy products		...	...	...	42		...	...	...	1329		...	...	...	14026
153 Grain mill products; starches; animal feeds		...	...	...	56		...	...	...	1088		...	...	...	14253
1531 Grain mill products		...	...	...	40		...	...	...	937		...	...	...	13127
1532 Starches and starch products		...	...	...	1		...	...	...	-		...	...	...	-
1533 Prepared animal feeds		...	...	...	15		...	...	...	151		...	...	...	1126
154 Other food products		...	...	...	236		...	...	...	4210		...	...	...	44440
1541 Bakery products		...	...	...	110		...	...	...	1232		...	...	...	6455
1542 Sugar		...	...	...	5		...	...	...	1412		...	...	...	27108
1543 Cocoa, chocolate and sugar confectionery		...	...	...	17		...	...	...	253		...	...	...	1589
1544 Macaroni, noodles & similar products		...	...	...	41		...	...	...	548		...	...	...	3738
1549 Other food products n.e.c.		...	...	...	63		...	...	...	765		...	...	...	5550
155 Beverages		...	...	...	66		...	...	...	4896		...	...	...	96226
1551 Distilling, rectifying & blending of spirits		...	...	...	9		...	...	...	488		...	...	...	4437
1552 Wines		...	...	...	6		...	...	...	62		...	...	...	603
1553 Malt liquors and malt		...	...	...	9		...	...	...	2059		...	...	...	63028
1554 Soft drinks; mineral waters		...	...	...	42		...	...	...	2287		...	...	...	28158
1600 Tobacco products		...	...	...	1		...	...	...	203		...	...	...	3762
171 Spinning, weaving and finishing of textiles		...	...	...	38		...	...	...	1870		...	...	...	18067
1711 Textile fibre preparation; textile weaving		...	...	...	35		...	...	...	1817		...	...	...	17556
1712 Finishing of textiles		...	...	...	3		...	...	...	53		...	...	...	511
172 Other textiles		...	...	...	26		...	...	...	1128		...	...	...	5487
1721 Made-up textile articles, except apparel		...	...	...	13		...	...	...	896		...	...	...	3980
1722 Carpets and rugs		...	...	...	4		...	...	...	30		...	...	...	195
1723 Cordage, rope, twine and netting		...	...	...	3		...	...	...	39		...	...	...	282
1729 Other textiles n.e.c.		...	...	...	6		...	...	...	163		...	...	...	1030
1730 Knitted and crocheted fabrics and articles		...	...	...	44		...	...	...	815		...	...	...	6407
1810 Wearing apparel, except fur apparel		...	...	...	88		...	...	...	2081		...	...	...	12605
1820 Dressing & dyeing of fur; processing of fur		...	...	...	...		...	...	...	...		...	...	...	...
191 Tanning, dressing and processing of leather		...	...	...	35		...	...	...	1139		...	...	...	6647
1911 Tanning and dressing of leather		...	...	...	29		...	...	...	912		...	...	...	5516
1912 Luggage, handbags, etc.; saddlery & harness		...	...	...	6		...	...	...	227		...	...	...	1131
1920 Footwear		...	...	...	29		...	...	...	1002		...	...	...	11023
2010 Sawmilling and planing of wood		...	...	...	107		...	...	...	2219		...	...	...	14870
202 Products of wood, cork, straw, etc.		...	...	...	64		...	...	...	883		...	...	...	5625
2021 Veneer sheets, plywood, particle board, etc.		...	...	...	12		...	...	...	359		...	...	...	2168
2022 Builders' carpentry and joinery		...	...	...	50		...	...	...	514		...	...	...	3415
2023 Wooden containers		...	...	...	2		...	...	...	10		...	...	...	42
2029 Other wood products; articles of cork/straw		...	...	...	...		...	...	...	...		...	...	...	...
210 Paper and paper products		...	...	...	27		...	...	...	1762		...	...	...	24523
2101 Pulp, paper and paperboard		...	...	...	1		...	...	...	18		...	...	...	442
2102 Corrugated paper and paperboard		...	...	...	7		...	...	...	92		...	...	...	1170
2109 Other articles of paper and paperboard		...	...	...	19		...	...	...	1652		...	...	...	22911
221 Publishing		...	...	...	29		...	...	...	1114		...	...	...	17013
2211 Publishing of books and other publications		...	...	...	12		...	...	...	135		...	...	...	1301
2212 Publishing of newspapers, journals, etc.		...	...	...	16		...	...	...	968		...	...	...	15666
2213 Publishing of recorded media		...	...	...	...		...	...	...	...		...	...	...	...
2219 Other publishing		...	...	...	1		...	...	...	11		...	...	...	46

ISIC	Industry												
222	Printing and related service activities	...	...	...	126	...	...	...	1059	...	...	...	6055
2221	Printing	...	...	...	126	...	...	...	1059	...	...	...	6055
2222	Service activities related to printing	...	...	...	...	...	...	...	...	...	...	...	...
2230	Reproduction of recorded media	...	...	...	3	...	...	...	234	...	...	...	1305
2310	Coke oven products	...	...	...	...	...	...	...	...	...	...	...	...
2320	Refined petroleum products	...	...	...	3	...	...	...	816	...	...	...	32105
2330	Processing of nuclear fuel	...	...	...	...	...	...	...	...	...	...	...	...
241	Basic chemicals	...	...	...	27	...	...	...	411	...	...	...	4990
2411	Basic chemicals, except fertilizers	...	...	...	19	...	...	...	355	...	...	...	4701
2412	Fertilizers and nitrogen compounds	...	...	...	...	...	...	...	...	...	...	...	...
2413	Plastics in primary forms; synthetic rubber	...	...	...	8	...	...	...	56	...	...	...	289
242	Other chemicals	...	...	...	66	...	...	...	2333	...	...	...	35837
2421	Pesticides and other agro-chemical products	...	...	...	2	...	...	...	21	...	...	...	170
2422	Paints, varnishes, printing ink and mastics	...	...	...	9	...	...	...	238	...	...	...	5046
2423	Pharmaceuticals, medicinal chemicals, etc.	...	...	...	27	...	...	...	1540	...	...	...	24849
2424	Soap, cleaning & cosmetic preparations	...	...	...	24	...	...	...	469	...	...	...	4775
2429	Other chemical products n.e.c.	...	...	...	4	...	...	...	65	...	...	...	997
2430	Man-made fibres	...	...	...	...	...	...	...	...	...	...	...	...
251	Rubber products	...	...	...	9	...	...	...	48	...	...	...	482
2511	Rubber tyres and tubes	...	...	...	4	...	...	...	1	...	...	...	4
2519	Other rubber products	...	...	...	5	...	...	...	47	...	...	...	478
2520	Plastic products	...	...	...	89	...	...	...	1939	...	...	...	15966
2610	Glass and glass products	...	...	...	12	...	...	...	346	...	...	...	4261
269	Non-metallic mineral products n.e.c.	...	...	...	137	...	...	...	3367	...	...	...	47282
2691	Pottery, china and earthenware	...	...	...	2	...	...	...	9	...	...	...	29
2692	Refractory ceramic products	...	...	...	3	...	...	...	52	...	...	...	371
2693	Struct.non-refractory clay; ceramic products	...	...	...	68	...	...	...	1333	...	...	...	8613
2694	Cement, lime and plaster	...	...	...	12	...	...	...	1034	...	...	...	29284
2695	Articles of concrete, cement and plaster	...	...	...	49	...	...	...	895	...	...	...	8685
2696	Cutting, shaping & finishing of stone	...	...	...	3	...	...	...	44	...	...	...	300
2699	Other non-metallic mineral products n.e.c.	...	...	...	...	...	...	...	...	...	...	...	...
2710	Basic iron and steel	...	...	...	10	...	...	...	229	...	...	...	1760
2720	Basic precious and non-ferrous metals	...	...	...	6	...	...	...	1101	...	...	...	18368
273	Casting of metals	...	...	...	...	...	...	...	...	...	...	...	...
2731	Casting of iron and steel	...	...	...	...	...	...	...	...	...	...	...	...
2732	Casting of non-ferrous metals	...	...	...	...	...	...	...	...	...	...	...	...
281	Struct.metal products;tanks;steam generators	...	...	...	37	...	...	...	431	...	...	...	2380
2811	Structural metal products	...	...	...	33	...	...	...	334	...	...	...	1761
2812	Tanks, reservoirs and containers of metal	...	...	...	4	...	...	...	97	...	...	...	619
2813	Steam generators	...	...	...	...	...	...	...	...	...	...	...	...
289	Other metal products; metal working services	...	...	...	62	...	...	...	754	...	...	...	7792
2891	Metal forging/pressing/stamping/roll-forming	...	...	...	...	...	...	...	...	...	...	...	...
2892	Treatment & coating of metals	...	...	...	...	...	...	...	...	...	...	...	...
2893	Cutlery, hand tools and general hardware	...	...	...	3	...	...	...	21	...	...	...	68
2899	Other fabricated metal products n.e.c.	...	...	...	59	...	...	...	733	...	...	...	7724
291	General purpose machinery	...	...	...	1	...	...	...	9	...	...	...	97
2911	Engines & turbines(not for transport equip.)	...	...	...	...	...	...	...	...	...	...	...	...
2912	Pumps, compressors, taps and valves	...	...	...	...	...	...	...	...	...	...	...	...
2913	Bearings, gears, gearing & driving elements	...	...	...	1	...	...	...	9	...	...	...	97
2914	Ovens, furnaces and furnace burners	...	...	...	...	...	...	...	...	...	...	...	...
2915	Lifting and handling equipment	...	...	...	...	...	...	...	...	...	...	...	...
2919	Other general purpose machinery	...	...	...	...	...	...	...	...	...	...	...	...
292	Special purpose machinery	...	...	...	21	...	...	...	521	...	...	...	3623
2921	Agricultural and forestry machinery	...	...	...	4	...	...	...	24	...	...	...	105
2922	Machine tools	...	...	...	2	...	...	...	-	...	...	...	-
2923	Machinery for metallurgy	...	...	...	2	...	...	...	-	...	...	...	-
2924	Machinery for mining & construction	...	...	...	5	...	...	...	100	...	...	...	744
2925	Food/beverage/tobacco processing machinery	...	...	...	4	...	...	...	190	...	...	...	2045
2926	Machinery for textile, apparel and leather	...	...	...	1	...	...	...	89	...	...	...	314
2927	Weapons and ammunition	...	...	...	1	...	...	...	89	...	...	...	314
2929	Other special purpose machinery	...	...	...	2	...	...	...	29	...	...	...	101
2930	Domestic appliances n.e.c.	...	...	...	3	...	...	...	6	...	...	...	21

continued

Bolivia

ISIC Revision 3	Number of establishments					Number of employees					Wages and salaries paid to employees				
		(numbers)					(numbers)					(thousand BOLIVIANOS)			
ISIC Industry	Note	1992	1993	1994	1995	Note	1992	1993	1994	1995	Note	1992	1993	1994	1995
3000 Office, accounting and computing machinery		...	...	...	...		...	...	...	...		...	...	...	...
3110 Electric motors, generators and transformers		...	...	...	3		...	...	...	36		...	...	...	115
3120 Electricity distribution & control apparatus		...	...	...	1		...	...	...	3		...	...	...	11
3130 Insulated wire and cable		...	...	...	1		...	...	...	67		...	...	...	527
3140 Accumulators, primary cells and batteries		...	...	...	2		...	...	...	65		...	...	...	441
3150 Lighting equipment and electric lamps		...	...	...	6		...	...	...	262		...	...	...	1775
3190 Other electrical equipment n.e.c.		...	...	...	6		...	...	...	48		...	...	...	211
3210 Electronic valves, tubes, etc.		...	...	...	...		...	...	...	...		...	...	...	...
3220 TV/radio transmitters; line comm. apparatus		...	...	...	...		...	...	...	...		...	...	...	...
3230 TV and radio receivers and associated goods		...	...	...	...		...	...	...	...		...	...	...	...
331 Medical, measuring, testing appliances, etc.		...	...	...	4		...	...	...	45		...	...	...	422
3311 Medical, surgical and orthopaedic equipment		...	...	...	4		...	...	...	45		...	...	...	422
3312 Measuring/testing/navigating appliances,etc.		...	...	...	...		...	...	...	...		...	...	...	...
3313 Industrial process control equipment		...	...	...	...		...	...	...	...		...	...	...	...
3320 Optical instruments & photographic equipment		...	...	...	13		...	...	...	75		...	...	...	628
3330 Watches and clocks		...	...	...	...		...	...	...	...		...	...	...	...
3410 Motor vehicles		...	...	...	...		...	...	...	...		...	...	...	...
3420 Automobile bodies, trailers & semi-trailers		...	...	...	20		...	...	...	278		...	...	...	1921
3430 Parts/accessories for automobiles		...	...	...	17		...	...	...	267		...	...	...	1685
351 Building and repairing of ships and boats		...	...	...	...		...	...	...	...		...	...	...	...
3511 Building and repairing of ships		...	...	...	...		...	...	...	...		...	...	...	...
3512 Building/repairing of pleasure/sport. boats		...	...	...	...		...	...	...	...		...	...	...	...
3520 Railway/tramway locomotives & rolling stock		...	...	...	...		...	...	...	...		...	...	...	...
3530 Aircraft and spacecraft		...	...	...	...		...	...	...	...		...	...	...	...
359 Transport equipment n.e.c.		...	...	...	4		...	...	...	124		...	...	...	1224
3591 Motorcycles		...	...	...	...		...	...	...	...		...	...	...	...
3592 Bicycles and invalid carriages		...	...	...	...		...	...	...	...		...	...	...	...
3599 Other transport equipment n.e.c.		...	...	...	4		...	...	...	124		...	...	...	1224
3610 Furniture		...	...	...	160		...	...	...	1672		...	...	...	7858
369 Manufacturing n.e.c.		...	...	...	29		...	...	...	1126		...	...	...	4205
3691 Jewellery and related articles		...	...	...	12		...	...	...	969		...	...	...	3494
3692 Musical instruments		...	...	...	2		...	...	...	13		...	...	...	63
3693 Sports goods		...	...	...	...		...	...	...	...		...	...	...	...
3694 Games and toys		...	...	...	1		...	...	...	14		...	...	...	70
3699 Other manufacturing n.e.c.		...	...	...	14		...	...	...	130		...	...	...	578
3710 Recycling of metal waste and scrap		...	...	...	...		...	...	...	...		...	...	...	...
3720 Recycling of non-metal waste and scrap		...	...	...	...		...	...	...	...		...	...	...	...
D Total manufacturing		...	...	...	1826		...	...	...	46321		...	...	...	533590

ISIC Revision 3 ISIC Industry	Note	Output in producers' prices (thousand BOLIVIANOS) 1992	1993	1994	1995	Note	Value added in producers' prices (thousand BOLIVIANOS) 1992	1993	1994	1995	Note	Gross fixed capital formation (million BOLIVIANOS) 1994	1995
151 Processed meat, fish, fruit, vegetables, fats		...	...	...	1762534		...	...	...	399401		...	...
1511 Processing/preserving of meat		...	...	...	1290500		...	...	...	284380		...	...
1512 Processing/preserving of fish		...	...	...	2215		...	...	...	399		...	...
1513 Processing/preserving of fruit & vegetables		...	...	...	42212		...	...	...	12951		...	...
1514 Vegetable and animal oils and fats		...	...	...	427607		...	...	...	101671		...	...
1520 Dairy products		...	...	...	248940		...	...	...	69750		...	...
153 Grain mill products; starches; animal feeds		...	...	...	815035		...	...	...	142435		...	...
1531 Grain mill products		...	...	...	741945		...	...	...	93727		...	...
1532 Starches and starch products		...	...	...	44		...	...	...	24		...	...
1533 Prepared animal feeds		...	...	...	73046		...	...	...	48684		...	...
154 Other food products		...	...	...	855907		...	...	...	301441		...	...
1541 Bakery products		...	...	...	95273		...	...	...	25339		...	...
1542 Sugar		...	...	...	492875		...	...	...	219398		...	...
1543 Cocoa, chocolate and sugar confectionery		...	...	...	15976		...	...	...	3953		...	...
1544 Macaroni, noodles & similar products		...	...	...	75151		...	...	...	13734		...	...
1549 Other food products n.e.c.		...	...	...	176632		...	...	...	39017		...	...
155 Beverages		...	...	...	1154050		...	...	...	589209		...	...
1551 Distilling, rectifying & blending of spirits		...	...	...	61403		...	...	...	25002		...	...
1552 Wines		...	...	...	7654		...	...	...	2220		...	...
1553 Malt liquors and malt		...	...	...	813893		...	...	...	450326		...	...
1554 Soft drinks; mineral waters		...	...	...	271100		...	...	...	111661		...	...
1600 Tobacco products		...	...	...	81869		...	...	...	26601		...	...
171 Spinning, weaving and finishing of textiles		...	...	...	193467		...	...	...	61138		...	...
1711 Textile fibre preparation; textile weaving		...	...	...	191286		...	...	...	60206		...	...
1712 Finishing of textiles		...	...	...	2181		...	...	...	932		...	...
172 Other textiles		...	...	...	87983		...	...	...	34116		...	...
1721 Made-up textile articles, except apparel		...	...	...	76480		...	...	...	30261		...	...
1722 Carpets and rugs		...	...	...	1638		...	...	...	451		...	...
1723 Cordage, rope, twine and netting		...	...	...	2065		...	...	...	781		...	...
1729 Other textiles n.e.c.		...	...	...	7800		...	...	...	2623		...	...
1730 Knitted and crocheted fabrics and articles		...	...	...	43356		...	...	...	18566		...	...
1810 Wearing apparel, except fur apparel		...	...	...	117173		...	...	...	36826		...	...
1820 Dressing & dyeing of fur; processing of fur		...	...	...	...		...	...	...	...		...	...
191 Tanning, dressing and processing of leather		...	...	...	113956		...	...	...	26393		...	...
1911 Tanning and dressing of leather		...	...	...	105262		...	...	...	21914		...	...
1912 Luggage, handbags, etc.; saddlery & harness		...	...	...	8694		...	...	...	4479		...	...
1920 Footwear		...	...	...	122974		...	...	...	39537		...	...
2010 Sawmilling and planing of wood		...	...	...	303205		...	...	...	91705		...	...
202 Products of wood, cork, straw, etc.		...	...	...	69568		...	...	...	19888		...	...
2021 Veneer sheets, plywood, particle board, etc.		...	...	...	39279		...	...	...	10324		...	...
2022 Builders' carpentry and joinery		...	...	...	30055		...	...	...	9455		...	...
2023 Wooden containers		...	...	...	234		...	...	...	109		...	...
2029 Other wood products; articles of cork/straw		...	...	...	...		...	...	...	...		...	...
210 Paper and paper products		...	...	...	259000		...	...	...	71493		...	...
2101 Pulp, paper and paperboard		...	...	...	4042		...	...	...	566		...	...
2102 Corrugated paper and paperboard		...	...	...	10508		...	...	...	3276		...	...
2109 Other articles of paper and paperboard		...	...	...	244450		...	...	...	67651		...	...
221 Publishing		...	...	...	132831		...	...	...	45547		...	...
2211 Publishing of books and other publications		...	...	...	10589		...	...	...	4735		...	...
2212 Publishing of newspapers, journals, etc.		...	...	...	118424		...	...	...	39878		...	...
2213 Publishing of recorded media		...	...	...	...		...	...	...	...		...	...
2219 Other publishing		...	...	...	3818		...	...	...	934		...	...

continued

Bolivia

ISIC Revision 3 ISIC Industry	Note	Output in producers' prices (thousand BOLIVIANOS) 1992	1993	1994	1995	Note	Value added in producers' prices (thousand BOLIVIANOS) 1992	1993	1994	1995	Note	Gross fixed capital formation (million BOLIVIANOS) 1994	1995
222 Printing and related service activities		...	...	...	85207		...	...	...	33563		...	...
2221 Printing		...	...	...	85207		...	...	...	33563		...	...
2222 Service activities related to printing		...	...	...	...		...	...	...	...		...	...
2230 Reproduction of recorded media		...	...	...	14664		...	...	...	4221		...	...
2310 Coke oven products		...	...	...	...		...	...	...	...		...	...
2320 Refined petroleum products		...	...	...	2324386		...	...	...	1590054		...	...
2330 Processing of nuclear fuel		...	...	...	...		...	...	...	...		...	...
241 Basic chemicals		...	...	...	47935		...	...	...	19659		...	...
2411 Basic chemicals, except fertilizers		...	...	...	38067		...	...	...	18578		...	...
2412 Fertilizers and nitrogen compounds		...	...	...	...		...	...	...	...		...	...
2413 Plastics in primary forms; synthetic rubber		...	...	...	9868		...	...	...	1081		...	...
242 Other chemicals		...	...	...	339568		...	...	...	124877		...	...
2421 Pesticides and other agro-chemical products		...	...	...	2913		...	...	...	982		...	...
2422 Paints, varnishes, printing ink and mastics		...	...	...	60556		...	...	...	15243		...	...
2423 Pharmaceuticals, medicinal chemicals, etc.		...	...	...	176301		...	...	...	76902		...	...
2424 Soap, cleaning & cosmetic preparations		...	...	...	92210		...	...	...	28418		...	...
2429 Other chemical products n.e.c.		...	...	...	7588		...	...	...	3332		...	...
2430 Man-made fibres		...	...	...	...		...	...	...	...		...	...
251 Rubber products		...	...	...	5216		...	...	...	1544		...	...
2511 Rubber tyres and tubes		...	...	...	58		...	...	...	14		...	...
2519 Other rubber products		...	...	...	5158		...	...	...	1530		...	...
2520 Plastic products		...	...	...	192657		...	...	...	66607		...	...
2610 Glass and glass products		...	...	...	76397		...	...	...	27915		...	...
269 Non-metallic mineral products n.e.c.		...	...	...	633512		...	...	...	263026		...	...
2691 Pottery, china and earthenware		...	...	...	754		...	...	...	168		...	...
2692 Refractory ceramic products		...	...	...	1977		...	...	...	773		...	...
2693 Struct.non-refractory clay; ceramic products		...	...	...	76110		...	...	...	30070		...	...
2694 Cement, lime and plaster		...	...	...	464825		...	...	...	189685		...	...
2695 Articles of concrete, cement and plaster		...	...	...	85841		...	...	...	40377		...	...
2696 Cutting, shaping & finishing of stone		...	...	...	4005		...	...	...	1953		...	...
2699 Other non-metallic mineral products n.e.c.		...	...	...	...		...	...	...	...		...	...
2710 Basic iron and steel		...	...	...	30451		...	...	...	9695		...	...
2720 Basic precious and non-ferrous metals		...	...	...	466187		...	...	...	102607		...	...
273 Casting of metals		...	...	...	...		...	...	...	...		...	...
2731 Casting of iron and steel		...	...	...	...		...	...	...	...		...	...
2732 Casting of non-ferrous metals		...	...	...	...		...	...	...	...		...	...
281 Struct.metal products;tanks;steam generators		...	...	...	41196		...	...	...	10806		...	...
2811 Structural metal products		...	...	...	25756		...	...	...	6898		...	...
2812 Tanks, reservoirs and containers of metal		...	...	...	15440		...	...	...	3908		...	...
2813 Steam generators		...	...	...	...		...	...	...	...		...	...
289 Other metal products; metal working services		...	...	...	112471		...	...	...	36653		...	...
2891 Metal forging/pressing/stamping/roll-forming		...	...	...	...		...	...	...	...		...	...
2892 Treatment & coating of metals		...	...	...	...		...	...	...	...		...	...
2893 Cutlery, hand tools and general hardware		...	...	...	407		...	...	...	184		...	...
2899 Other fabricated metal products n.e.c.		...	...	...	112064		...	...	...	36469		...	...
291 General purpose machinery		...	...	...	417		...	...	...	300		...	...
2911 Engines & turbines(not for transport equip.)		...	...	...	...		...	...	...	...		...	...
2912 Pumps, compressors, taps and valves		...	...	...	...		...	...	...	...		...	...
2913 Bearings, gears, gearing & driving elements		...	...	...	417		...	...	...	300		...	...
2914 Ovens, furnaces and furnace burners		...	...	...	...		...	...	...	...		...	...
2915 Lifting and handling equipment		...	...	...	...		...	...	...	...		...	...
2919 Other general purpose machinery		...	...	...	...		...	...	...	...		...	...

292 Special purpose machinery		...	...	...	33881		...	...	...	11250		...	...
2921 Agricultural and forestry machinery		...	...	...	2830		...	...	...	341		...	...
2922 Machine tools		...	...	...	189		...	...	...	34		...	...
2923 Machinery for metallurgy		...	...	...	189		...	...	...	34		...	...
2924 Machinery for mining & construction		...	...	...	5656		...	...	...	1483		...	...
2925 Food/beverage/tobacco processing machinery		...	...	...	11599		...	...	...	7348		...	...
2926 Machinery for textile, apparel and leather		...	...	...	6508		...	...	...	939		...	...
2927 Weapons and ammunition		...	...	...	6508		...	...	...	939		...	...
2929 Other special purpose machinery		...	...	...	402		...	...	...	132		...	...
2930 Domestic appliances n.e.c.		...	...	...	502		...	...	...	81		...	...
3000 Office, accounting and computing machinery		...	...	...	...		...	...	...	...		...	...
3110 Electric motors, generators and transformers		...	...	...	1890		...	...	...	448		...	...
3120 Electricity distribution & control apparatus		...	...	...	119		...	...	...	23		...	...
3130 Insulated wire and cable		...	...	...	23813		...	...	...	10003		...	...
3140 Accumulators, primary cells and batteries		...	...	...	4459		...	...	...	1136		...	...
3150 Lighting equipment and electric lamps		...	...	...	18655		...	...	...	6335		...	...
3190 Other electrical equipment n.e.c.		...	...	...	2380		...	...	...	758		...	...
3210 Electronic valves, tubes, etc.		...	...	...	...		...	...	...	...		...	...
3220 TV/radio transmitters; line comm. apparatus		...	...	...	...		...	...	...	...		...	...
3230 TV and radio receivers and associated goods		...	...	...	...		...	...	...	...		...	...
331 Medical, measuring, testing appliances, etc.		...	...	...	2391		...	...	...	913		...	...
3311 Medical, surgical and orthopaedic equipment		...	...	...	2391		...	...	...	913		...	...
3312 Measuring/testing/navigating appliances,etc.		...	...	...	...		...	...	...	...		...	...
3313 Industrial process control equipment		...	...	...	...		...	...	...	...		...	...
3320 Optical instruments & photographic equipment		...	...	...	9783		...	...	...	1902		...	...
3330 Watches and clocks		...	...	...	...		...	...	...	...		...	...
3410 Motor vehicles		...	...	...	...		...	...	...	...		...	...
3420 Automobile bodies, trailers & semi-trailers		...	...	...	32910		...	...	...	6180		...	...
3430 Parts/accessories for automobiles		...	...	...	19268		...	...	...	4662		...	...
351 Building and repairing of ships and boats		...	...	...	...		...	...	...	...		...	...
3511 Building and repairing of ships		...	...	...	...		...	...	...	...		...	...
3512 Building/repairing of pleasure/sport. boats		...	...	...	...		...	...	...	...		...	...
3520 Railway/tramway locomotives & rolling stock		...	...	...	...		...	...	...	...		...	...
3530 Aircraft and spacecraft		...	...	...	...		...	...	...	...		...	...
359 Transport equipment n.e.c.		...	...	...	10194		...	...	...	3491		...	...
3591 Motorcycles		...	...	...	...		...	...	...	...		...	...
3592 Bicycles and invalid carriages		...	...	...	...		...	...	...	...		...	...
3599 Other transport equipment n.e.c.		...	...	...	10194		...	...	...	3491		...	...
3610 Furniture		...	...	...	67064		...	...	...	19760		...	...
369 Manufacturing n.e.c.		...	...	...	356044		...	...	...	35489		...	...
3691 Jewellery and related articles		...	...	...	348225		...	...	...	33063		...	...
3692 Musical instruments		...	...	...	107		...	...	...	20		...	...
3693 Sports goods		...	...	...	...		...	...	...	...		...	...
3694 Games and toys		...	...	...	855		...	...	...	265		...	...
3699 Other manufacturing n.e.c.		...	...	...	6857		...	...	...	2141		...	...
3710 Recycling of metal waste and scrap		...	...	...	...		...	...	...	...		...	...
3720 Recycling of non-metal waste and scrap		...	...	...	...		...	...	...	...		...	...
D Total manufacturing		...	...	...	11315465		...	...	...	4368004		...	...

Bolivia

ISIC Revision 3		Index numbers of industrial production (1990=100)												
ISIC	Industry	Note	1985	1986	1987	1988	1989	1990	1991	1992	1993	1994	1995	1996
15	Food and beverages		92	97	95	99	93	100	111	110	117	120	127	135
16	Tobacco products		54	87	90	96	104	100	105	121	118	131	168	141
17	Textiles		148	152	152	144	109	100	109	119	117	139	143	133
18	Wearing apparel, fur		81	92	78	80	93	100	110	113	166	187	214	219
19	Leather, leather products and footwear		95	105	65	70	71	100	105	121	134	132	147	160
20	Wood products (excl. furniture)		90	106	145	118	145	100	104	104	112	114	114	111
21	Paper and paper products		...	...	...	...	...	...	...	...	...	...	...	...
22	Printing and publishing		74	60	77	79	98	100	103	118	121	111	106	89
23	Coke,refined petroleum products,nuclear fuel		92	83	85	82	85	100	102	99	96	101	102	112
24	Chemicals and chemical products		57	55	54	63	77	100	92	96	92	128	156	196
25	Rubber and plastics products		90	113	127	91	98	100	118	138	159	172	191	221
26	Non-metallic mineral products		61	54	66	86	93	100	105	111	118	131	146	147
27	Basic metals		97	59	21	40	72	100	118	119	130	134	103	96
28	Fabricated metal products		62	79	88	122	141	100	104	111	116	136	132	121
29	Machinery and equipment n.e.c.		...	...	...	...	...	...	...	...	...	...	...	...
30	Office, accounting and computing machinery		...	...	...	...	...	...	...	...	...	...	...	...
31	Electrical machinery and apparatus		...	...	...	...	...	...	...	...	...	...	...	...
32	Radio,television and communication equipment		...	...	...	...	...	...	...	...	...	...	...	...
33	Medical, precision and optical instruments		...	...	...	...	...	...	...	...	...	...	...	...
34	Motor vehicles, trailers, semi-trailers		...	...	...	...	...	...	...	...	...	...	...	...
35	Other transport equipment		...	...	...	...	...	...	...	...	...	...	...	...
36	Furniture; manufacturing n.e.c.		...	...	...	...	...	100	107	115	162	189	179	150
37	Recycling		...	...	...	...	...	...	...	...	...	...	...	...
D	Total manufacturing		80	84	86	90	92	100	107	109	116	122	128	133

BOSNIA AND HERZEGOVINA

Supplier of information:
Statistical Office, Sarajevo.

Basic source of data:
Not reported.

Major deviations from ISIC (Revision 2):
None reported.

Reference period (if not calendar year):

Scope:
Data refer to the Federation of Bosnia and Herzegovina only.

Method of enumeration:
Not reported.

Adjusted for non-response:
Not reported.

Concepts and definitions of variables:
Number of employees refers to the numbers actively employed as of 31 December of the year indicated.

Related national publications:

ISIC Revision 2	Number of establishments					Number of employees					Wages and salaries paid to employees				
		(numbers)					(numbers)					(million DINARS)			
ISIC Industry	Note	1993	1994a/	1995a/	1996a/	Note	1993	1994a/	1995a/	1996a/	Note	1993	1994	1995	1996
311/2 Food products		...	29	39	48		...	2013	2798	4421		...	...	...	...
3111 Slaughtering, preparing & preserving meat		...	5	5	3		...	126	375	232		...	...	...	...
3112 Dairy products		...	1	1	1		...	28	25	50		...	...	...	...
3113 Canning, preserving of fruits & vegetables		...	3	3	4		...	65	90	295		...	...	...	...
3114 Canning, preserving and processing of fish		...	-	-	-		...	-	-	-		...	...	...	...
3115 Vegetable and animal oils and fats		...	-	-	-		...	-	-	-		...	...	...	...
3116 Grain mill products		...	2	4	6		...	225	288	376		...	...	...	...
3117 Bakery products		...	11	15	20		...	857	1153	1648		...	...	...	...
3118 Sugar factories and refineries		...	-	-	-		...	-	-	-		...	...	...	...
3119 Cocoa, chocolate and sugar confectionery		...	1	2	3		...	53	180	768		...	...	...	...
3121 Other food products		...	5	8	10		...	565	593	943		...	...	...	...
3122 Prepared animal feeds		...	1	1	1		...	94	94	109		...	...	...	...
313 Beverages		...	4	8	9		...	727	842	1268		...	...	...	...
3131 Distilling, rectifying and blending spirits		...	-	-	1		...	-	-	202		...	...	...	...
3132 Wine industries		...	-	4	3		...	-	390	234		...	...	...	...
3133 Malt liquors and malt		...	3	3	4		...	527	396	736		...	...	...	...
3134 Soft drinks and carbonated waters		...	1	1	1		...	200	56	96		...	...	...	...
314 Tobacco		...	2	6	7		...	440	676	849		...	...	...	...
321 Textiles		...	4	9	17		...	469	1509	2817		...	...	...	...
3211 Spinning, weaving and finishing textiles		...	3	4	4		...	451	455	675		...	...	...	...
3212 Made-up textile goods excl. wearing apparel		...	-	-	1		...	-	-	163		...	...	...	...
3213 Knitting mills		...	-	5	10		...	-	1054	1626		...	...	...	...
3214 Carpets and rugs		...	-	-	-		...	-	-	-		...	...	...	...
3215 Cordage, rope and twine		...	1	-	1		...	18	-	24		...	...	...	...
3219 Other textiles		...	-	-	1		...	-	-	329		...	...	...	...
322 Wearing apparel, except footwear		...	8	14	18		...	1443	3670	4380		...	...	...	...
323 Leather and fur products		...	-	1	2		...	-	30	69		...	...	...	...
3231 Tanneries and leather finishing		...	-	-	-		...	-	-	-		...	...	...	...
3232 Fur dressing and dyeing industries		...	-	-	1		...	-	-	22		...	...	...	...
3233 Leather prods. excl. wearing apparel		...	-	1	1		...	-	30	47		...	...	...	...
324 Footwear, except rubber or plastic		...	7	11	11		...	2507	3028	6155		...	...	...	...
331 Wood products, except furniture		...	8	16	25		...	623	1397	4749		...	...	...	...
3311 Sawmills, planing and other wood mills		...	2	7	14		...	112	787	3572		...	...	...	...
3312 Wooden and cane containers		...	6	8	10		...	511	575	1132		...	...	...	...
3319 Other wood and cork products		...	-	1	1		...	-	35	45		...	...	...	...
332 Furniture and fixtures, excl. metal		...	9	14	18		...	1281	996	2807		...	...	...	...
341 Paper and products		...	8	6	6		...	345	468	2209		...	...	...	...
3411 Pulp, paper and paperboard articles		...	5	1	3		...	252	319	1931		...	...	...	...
3412 Containers of paper and paperboard		...	3	5	3		...	93	149	278		...	...	...	...
3419 Other pulp, paper and paperboard articles		...	-	-	-		...	-	-	-		...	...	...	...
342 Printing and publishing		...	5	11	13		...	1168	702	750		...	...	...	...
351 Industrial chemicals		...	3	6	6		...	924	767	2038		...	...	...	...
3511 Basic chemicals excl. fertilizers		...	3	5	5		...	924	742	2016		...	...	...	...
3512 Fertilizers and pesticides		...	-	-	-		...	-	-	-		...	...	...	...
3513 Synthetic resins and plastic materials		...	-	1	1		...	-	25	22		...	...	...	...
352 Other chemicals		...	3	6	5		...	1213	1510	1854		...	...	...	...
3521 Paints, varnishes and lacquers		...	-	-	-		...	-	-	-		...	...	...	...
3522 Drugs and medicines		...	1	1	1		...	751	247	299		...	...	...	...
3523 Soap, cleaning preps., perfumes, cosmetics		...	2	2	2		...	462	518	660		...	...	...	...
3529 Other chemical products		...	-	3	2		...	-	745	895		...	...	...	...
353 Petroleum refineries		...	-	-	-		...	-	-	-		...	...	...	...

ISIC	Industry														
354	Misc. petroleum and coal products		...	-	-	-		...	-	-	-		...	...	...	...
355	Rubber products		...	1	1	1		...	180	140	144		...	...	...	...
3551	Tyres and tubes		...	-	-	-		...	-	-	-		...	...	...	...
3559	Other rubber products		...	1	1	1		...	180	140	144		...	...	...	...
356	Plastic products		...	3	5	6		...	105	163	536		...	...	...	...
361	Pottery, china, earthenware		...	-	-	-		...	-	-	-		...	...	...	...
362	Glass and products		...	-	-	-		...	-	-	-		...	...	...	...
369	Other non-metallic mineral products		...	2	12	17		...	596	707	2849		...	...	...	...
3691	Structural clay products		...	1	3	4		...	283	153	595		...	...	...	...
3692	Cement, lime and plaster		...	1	3	5		...	313	371	567		...	...	...	...
3699	Other non-metallic mineral products		...	-	6	8		...	-	183	1687		...	...	...	...
371	Iron and steel		...	1	2	6		...	404	197	5105		...	...	...	...
372	Non-ferrous metals		...	-	1	1		...	-	117	146		...	...	...	...
381	Fabricated metal products		...	4	11	18		...	1035	1040	2726		...	...	...	...
3811	Cutlery, hand tools and general hardware		...	2	5	11		...	408	402	1278		...	...	...	...
3812	Furniture and fixtures primarily of metal		...	-	2	1		...	-	85	43		...	...	...	...
3813	Structural metal products		...	2	4	6		...	627	553	1405		...	...	...	...
3819	Other fabricated metal products		...	-	-	-		...	-	-	-		...	...	...	...
382	Non-electrical machinery		...	1	3	7		...	838	330	1421		...	...	...	...
3821	Engines and turbines		...	-	-	-		...	-	-	-		...	...	...	...
3822	Agricultural machinery and equipment		...	-	-	-		...	-	-	-		...	...	...	...
3823	Metal and wood working machinery		...	-	-	-		...	-	-	-		...	...	...	...
3824	Other special industrial machinery		...	-	-	3		...	-	-	881		...	...	...	...
3825	Office, computing and accounting machinery		...	-	-	1		...	-	-	6		...	...	...	...
3829	Other non-electrical machinery & equipment		...	1	3	3		...	838	330	534		...	...	...	...
383	Electrical machinery		...	1	5	7		...	13	865	934		...	...	...	...
3831	Electrical industrial machinery		...	1	2	3		...	13	338	346		...	...	...	...
3832	Radio, television and communication equipm.		...	-	-	1		...	-	-	24		...	...	...	...
3833	Electrical appliances and housewares		...	-	1	1		...	-	21	43		...	...	...	...
3839	Other electrical apparatus and supplies		...	-	2	2		...	-	506	521		...	...	...	...
384	Transport equipment		...	-	3	6		...	-	579	1456		...	...	...	...
3841	Shipbuilding and repairing		...	-	-	-		...	-	-	-		...	...	...	...
3842	Railroad equipment		...	-	-	1		...	-	-	142		...	...	...	...
3843	Motor vehicles		...	-	3	5		...	-	579	1314		...	...	...	...
3844	Motorcycles and bicycles		...	-	-	-		...	-	-	-		...	...	...	...
3845	Aircraft		...	-	-	-		...	-	-	-		...	...	...	...
3849	Other transport equipment		...	-	-	-		...	-	-	-		...	...	...	...
385	Professional and scientific equipment		...	-	-	1		...	-	-	6		...	...	...	...
3851	Prof. and scientific equipment n.e.c.		...	-	-	1		...	-	-	6		...	...	...	...
3852	Photographic and optical goods		...	-	-	-		...	-	-	-		...	...	...	...
3853	Watches and clocks		...	-	-	-		...	-	-	-		...	...	...	...
390	Other manufacturing industries		...	1	2	4		...	298	109	382		...	...	...	...
3901	Jewellery and related articles		...	-	-	1		...	-	-	63		...	...	...	...
3902	Musical instruments		...	-	-	-		...	-	-	-		...	...	...	...
3903	Sporting and athletic goods		...	-	-	-		...	-	-	-		...	...	...	...
3909	Manufacturing industries, n.e.c.		...	1	2	3		...	298	109	319		...	...	...	...
3	Total manufacturing		...	104	192	259		...	16622	22640	50071		...	...	...	...

a/ Data refer to the Federation of Bosnia and Herzegovina only.

Bosnia and Herzegovina

ISIC Revision 2		Output					Value added					Gross fixed capital formation		
			(million DINARS)					(million DINARS)					(thousand DINARS)	
ISIC	Industry	Note	1993	1994	1995	1996	Note	1993	1994	1995	1996	Note	1995	1996
311/2	Food products		...	...	...	...		...	...	...	...		...	...
313	Beverages		...	...	...	...		...	...	...	...		...	...
314	Tobacco		...	...	...	...		...	...	...	...		...	...
321	Textiles		...	...	...	...		...	...	...	...		...	...
322	Wearing apparel, except footwear		...	...	...	...		...	...	...	...		...	...
323	Leather and fur products		...	...	...	...		...	...	...	...		...	...
324	Footwear, except rubber or plastic		...	...	...	...		...	...	...	...		...	...
331	Wood products, except furniture		...	...	...	...		...	...	...	...		...	...
332	Furniture and fixtures, excl. metal		...	...	...	...		...	...	...	...		...	...
341	Paper and products		...	...	...	...		...	...	...	...		...	...
342	Printing and publishing		...	...	...	...		...	...	...	...		...	...
351	Industrial chemicals		...	...	...	...		...	...	...	...		...	...
352	Other chemicals		...	...	...	...		...	...	...	...		...	...
353	Petroleum refineries		...	...	...	...		...	...	...	...		...	...
354	Misc. petroleum and coal products		...	...	...	...		...	...	...	...		...	...
355	Rubber products		...	...	...	...		...	...	...	...		...	...
356	Plastic products		...	...	...	...		...	...	...	...		...	...
361	Pottery, china, earthenware		...	...	...	...		...	...	...	...		...	...
362	Glass and products		...	...	...	...		...	...	...	...		...	...
369	Other non-metallic mineral products		...	...	...	...		...	...	...	...		...	...
371	Iron and steel		...	...	...	...		...	...	...	...		...	...
372	Non-ferrous metals		...	...	...	...		...	...	...	...		...	...
381	Fabricated metal products		...	...	...	...		...	...	...	...		...	...
382	Non-electrical machinery		...	...	...	...		...	...	...	...		...	...
383	Electrical machinery		...	...	...	...		...	...	...	...		...	...
384	Transport equipment		...	...	...	...		...	...	...	...		...	...
385	Professional and scientific equipment		...	...	...	...		...	...	...	...		...	...
390	Other manufacturing industries		...	...	...	...		...	...	...	...		...	...
3	Total manufacturing		...	...	...	...		...	...	...	...		...	...

BOTSWANA

Supplier of information:
Central Statistics Office, Gaborone.

Basic source of data:
Survey of Employment and Earnings (biannually), Survey of Industrial Production (quarterly) and Census of Production and Distribution (annual).

Major deviations from ISIC (Revision 2):
None reported.

Reference period (if not calendar year):
Fiscal year ending 30 June of the year indicated.

Scope:
Licensed establishments with one or more paid employees.

Method of enumeration:
Questionnaires are distributed by mail.

Adjusted for non-response:
Yes.

Concepts and definitions of variables:
Number of employees is the average for September of the reference year.
Output and value added are gross output and total value added, respectively, and are derived from national accounts estimates.
For the years 1995 and 1996, wages and salaries is the compensation of employees and computed from monthly wages and salaries for all employees.

Related national publications:
Statistical Bulletin (quarterly); Employment Survey Report (annual); National Accounts of Botswana (annual), all published by the Central Statistics Office, Gaborone.

Botswana

ISIC Revision 2		Number of establishments (numbers)					Number of employees (numbers)					Wages and salaries paid to employees (million PULA)			
ISIC Industry	Note	1993	1994	1995	1996	Note	1993	1994	1995	1996	Note	1993	1994	1995	1996
311/2 Food products		88	90	134	106		5100	5200	5473	5330		66.9	...	57.4	47.8
313 Beverages		5	5	7	7		900	800	1315	1192		20.5	...	22.4	18.5
314 Tobacco		-	-	-	-		-	-	-	-		-	...	-	-
321 Textiles	a/	105	112	176	116	a/	3600	4800	4547	4329		28.6a/	...	24.9a/	22.0a/
322 Wearing apparel, except footwear	a/	...	...	...	...	a/	...	...	...	...		...a/	...	...a/	...a/
323 Leather and fur products	b/	19	15	19	20	b/	600	500	423	359		5.6b/	...	2.2b/	2.1b/
324 Footwear, except rubber or plastic	b/	...	...	...	...	b/	...	...	...	...		...b/	...	...b/	...b/
331 Wood products, except furniture	c/	36	42	60	36	c/	1100	1000	1313	1338		7.9c/	...	9.6c/	14.7c/
332 Furniture and fixtures, excl. metal	c/	...	...	...	...	c/	...	...	...	...		...c/	...	...c/	...c/
341 Paper and products	d/	43	46	58	44	d/	1100	1200	1301	1275		19.1d/	...	11.0d/	10.7d/
342 Printing and publishing	d/	...	...	...	...	d/	...	...	...	...		...d/	...	...d/	...d/
351 Industrial chemicals	e/	32	37	50	34	e/	900	1100	969	938		13.6e/	...	13.7e/	12.8e/
352 Other chemicals	e/	...	...	...	...	e/	...	...	...	...		...e/	...	...e/	...e/
353 Petroleum refineries		-	-	-	-		-	-	-	-		-	...	-	-
354 Misc. petroleum and coal products		-	-	-	-		-	-	-	-		-	...	-	-
355 Rubber products	e/	...	...	...	...	e/	...	...	...	...		...e/	...	...e/	...e/
356 Plastic products	e/	...	...	...	...	e/	...	...	...	...		...e/	...	...e/	...e/
361 Pottery, china, earthenware		-	-	-	-		-	-	-	-		-	...	-	-
362 Glass and products		-	-	-	-		-	-	-	-		-	...	-	-
369 Other non-metallic mineral products		-	-	-	-		-	-	-	-		-	...	-	-
371 Iron and steel		-	-	-	-		-	-	-	-		-	...	-	-
372 Non-ferrous metals		-	-	-	-		-	-	-	-		-	...	-	-
381 Fabricated metal products	f/	83	85	125	105	f/	3100	3000	3763	3982		31.4f/	...	49.0f/	60.1f/
382 Non-electrical machinery	f/	...	...	...	...	f/	...	...	...	...		...f/	...	...f/	...f/
383 Electrical machinery	f/	...	...	...	...	f/	...	...	...	...		...f/	...	...f/	...f/
384 Transport equipment	f/	...	...	...	...	f/	...	...	...	...		...f/	...	...f/	...f/
385 Professional and scientific equipment		-	-	-	-		-	-	-	-		-	...	-	-
390 Other manufacturing industries		96	102	168	120		4400	4500	5046	5022		34.4	...	29.8	33.1
3 Total manufacturing		507	534	797	588		20800	22100	24150	23765		228.0	191.9	220.0	221.7

a/ 321 includes 322.
b/ 323 includes 324.
c/ 331 includes 332.
d/ 341 includes 342.
e/ 351 includes 352, 355 and 356.
f/ 381 includes 382, 383 and 384.

Botswana

ISIC Revision 2	Output a/					Value added					Gross fixed capital formation		
		(million PULA)					(million PULA)					(million PULA)	
ISIC Industry	Note	1993	1994	1995	1996	Note	1993	1994	1995	1996	Note	1995	1996
311/2 Food products		720.1	...	...	...		146.6	164.3	...	...		...	...
313 Beverages		246.0	...	...	...		57.8	64.4	...	...		...	...
314 Tobacco		-	...	...	...		-	-	...	...		...	...
321 Textiles		202.1b/	...	...	...		59.5b/	66.3b/	...	...		...	...
322 Wearing apparel, except footwear		...b/	...	...	...		...b/	...b/	...	...		...	...
323 Leather and fur products		27.3c/	...	...	...		10.7c/	12.6c/	...	...		...	...
324 Footwear, except rubber or plastic		...c/	...	...	...		...c/	...c/	...	...		...	...
331 Wood products, except furniture		34.9d/	...	...	...		14.4d/	17.5d/	...	...		...	...
332 Furniture and fixtures, excl. metal		...d/	...	...	...		...d/	...d/	...	...		...	...
341 Paper and products		139.3e/	...	...	...		31.0e/	28.0e/	...	...		...	...
342 Printing and publishing		...e/	...	...	...		...e/	...e/	...	...		...	...
351 Industrial chemicals		80.7f/	...	...	...		16.8f/	18.7f/	...	...		...	...
352 Other chemicals		...f/	...	...	...		...f/	...f/	...	...		...	...
353 Petroleum refineries		-	...	...	...		-	-	...	...		...	...
354 Misc. petroleum and coal products		-	...	...	...		-	-	...	...		...	...
355 Rubber products		...f/	...	...	...		...f/	...f/	...	...		...	...
356 Plastic products		...f/	...	...	...		...f/	...f/	...	...		...	...
361 Pottery, china, earthenware		-	...	...	...		-	-	...	...		...	...
362 Glass and products		-	...	...	...		-	-	...	...		...	...
369 Other non-metallic mineral products		-	...	...	...		-	-	...	...		...	...
371 Iron and steel		-	...	...	...		-	-	...	...		...	...
372 Non-ferrous metals		-	...	...	...		-	-	...	...		...	...
381 Fabricated metal products		170.9g/	...	...	...		25.6g/	28.5g/	...	...		...	...
382 Non-electrical machinery		...g/	...	...	...		...g/	...g/	...	...		...	...
383 Electrical machinery		...g/	...	...	...		...g/	...g/	...	...		...	...
384 Transport equipment		...g/	...	...	...		...g/	...g/	...	...		...	...
385 Professional and scientific equipment		-	...	...	...		-	-	...	...		...	...
390 Other manufacturing industries		239.1	...	...	...		86.2	99.2	...	...		...	...
3 Total manufacturing		1860.4	...	...	...		448.6	499.5	...	...		...	...

a/ Output (in purchasers' prices).
b/ 321 includes 322.
c/ 323 includes 324.
d/ 331 includes 332.
e/ 341 includes 342.
f/ 351 includes 352, 355 and 356.
g/ 381 includes 382, 383 and 384.

Botswana

ISIC Revision 2		Index numbers of industrial production											
		(1990=100)											
ISIC Industry	Note	1985	1986	1987	1988	1989	1990	1991	1992	1993	1994	1995	1996
311/2 Food products		...	...	...	...	...	...	...	...	...	...	...	...
313 Beverages		...	...	...	...	...	...	...	...	...	...	...	...
314 Tobacco		...	...	...	...	...	...	...	...	...	...	...	...
321 Textiles		...	...	...	...	...	...	...	...	...	...	...	...
322 Wearing apparel, except footwear		...	...	...	...	...	...	...	...	...	...	...	...
323 Leather and fur products		...	...	...	...	...	...	...	...	...	...	...	...
324 Footwear, except rubber or plastic		...	...	...	...	...	...	...	...	...	...	...	...
331 Wood products, except furniture		...	...	...	...	...	...	...	...	...	...	...	...
332 Furniture and fixtures, excl. metal		...	...	...	...	...	...	...	...	...	...	...	...
341 Paper and products		...	...	...	...	...	...	...	...	...	...	...	...
342 Printing and publishing		...	...	...	...	...	...	...	...	...	...	...	...
351 Industrial chemicals		...	...	...	...	...	...	...	...	...	...	...	...
352 Other chemicals		...	...	...	...	...	...	...	...	...	...	...	...
353 Petroleum refineries		...	...	...	...	...	...	...	...	...	...	...	...
354 Misc. petroleum and coal products		...	...	...	...	...	...	...	...	...	...	...	...
355 Rubber products		...	...	...	...	...	...	...	...	...	...	...	...
356 Plastic products		...	...	...	...	...	...	...	...	...	...	...	...
361 Pottery, china, earthenware		...	...	...	...	...	...	...	...	...	...	...	...
362 Glass and products		...	...	...	...	...	...	...	...	...	...	...	...
369 Other non-metallic mineral products		...	...	...	...	...	...	...	...	...	...	...	...
371 Iron and steel		...	...	...	...	...	...	...	...	...	...	...	...
372 Non-ferrous metals		...	...	...	...	...	...	...	...	...	...	...	...
381 Fabricated metal products		...	...	...	...	...	...	...	...	...	...	...	...
382 Non-electrical machinery		...	...	...	...	...	...	...	...	...	...	...	...
383 Electrical machinery		...	...	...	...	...	...	...	...	...	...	...	...
384 Transport equipment		...	...	...	...	...	...	...	...	...	...	...	...
385 Professional and scientific equipment		...	...	...	...	...	...	...	...	...	...	...	...
390 Other manufacturing industries		...	...	...	...	...	...	...	...	...	...	...	...
3 Total manufacturing		...	...	...	...	...	...	...	...	...	...	...	...

BRAZIL

Supplier of information:
Fundaçao Instituto Brasileiro de Geografía e Estatística (IBGE), Rio de Janeiro.

Basic source of data:
Pesquisa Industrial Anual.

Major deviations from ISIC (Revision 2):
The data are based on the national classification scheme, which is not strictly comparable with the ISIC, but are arranged to represent ISIC (Rev. 2) as far as details permit.

Reference period (if not calendar year):

Scope:
The survey covers all registered establishments.

Method of enumeration:
Not reported.

Adjusted for non-response:
Not reported.

Concepts and definitions of variables:
Number of employees refers to persons actively engaged as of 31 December of the year indicated.
Output and value added exclude discount and cancelled sales. The valuation of output and value added is approximate to factor values.
In July 1994, the national currency was changed from cruzeiros reais to reais (1 real = 2750 cruzeiros reais). All data reported in terms of national currency are in reais.

Related national publications:

Brazil

ISIC Revision 2	Number of establishments					Number of employees					Wages and salaries paid to employees				
		(numbers)					(thousands)					(thousand REAIS)			
ISIC Industry	Note	1991	1992	1993	1994	Note	1991	1992	1993	1994	Note	1991	1992	1993	1994
311/2 Food products		...	5274	5088	4805		...	548.8	520.8	539.2		...	3822	84320	1854020
313 Beverages		...	509	530	481		...	85.0	82.7	74.0		...	867	18916	338263
314 Tobacco		...	194	158	120		...	23.4	20.3	19.9		...	356	8396	144616
321 Textiles		...	1446	1386	1367		...	243.4	258.8	250.4		...	1722	43675	847820
322 Wearing apparel, except footwear		...	2430a/	2303a/	2231a/		...	461.2a/	421.4a/	397.7a/		...	2481a/	56466a/	1016204a/
323 Leather and fur products		...	...a/	...a/	...a/		...	...a/	...a/	...a/		...	...a/	...a/	...a/
324 Footwear, except rubber or plastic		...	...a/	...a/	...a/		...	...a/	...a/	...a/		...	...a/	...a/	...a/
331 Wood products, except furniture		...	885	877	832		...	81.8	87.8	81.2		...	405	10408	204624
332 Furniture and fixtures, excl. metal		...	896	838	776		...	78.7	76.7	78.9		...	411	9498	212543
341 Paper and products		...	850	822	740		...	120.1	120.9	113.1		...	1353	35449	672738
342 Printing and publishing		...	947	883	851		...	112.1	106.2	107.3		...	1413	32551	669026
351 Industrial chemicals		...	2825b/	2775b/	2538b/		...	363.7b/	360.1b/	327.6b/		...	6825b/	154222b/	2980498b/
352 Other chemicals		...	...b/	...b/	...b/		...	...b/	...b/	...b/		...	...b/	...b/	...b/
353 Petroleum refineries		...	...b/	...b/	...b/		...	...b/	...b/	...b/		...	...b/	...b/	...b/
354 Misc. petroleum and coal products		...	...b/	...b/	...b/		...	...b/	...b/	...b/		...	...b/	...b/	...b/
355 Rubber products		...	443	433	430		...	56.2	52.3	57.4		...	593	15575	335170
356 Plastic products		...	836	844	792		...	107.4	111.2	113.6		...	982	22258	471381
361 Pottery, china, earthenware		...	1695c/	1704c/	1656c/		...	152.5c/	150.6c/	145.4c/		...	1539c/	33876c/	689441c/
362 Glass and products		...	...c/	...c/	...c/		...	...c/	...c/	...c/		...	...c/	...c/	...c/
369 Other non-metallic mineral products		...	...c/	...c/	...c/		...	...c/	...c/	...c/		...	...c/	...c/	...c/
371 Iron and steel		...	2404d/	2326d/	2273d/		...	384.8d/	390.5d/	378.5d/		...	5202d/	113568d/	2498997d/
372 Non-ferrous metals		...	...d/	...d/	...d/		...	...d/	...d/	...d/		...	...d/	...d/	...d/
381 Fabricated metal products		...	...d/	...d/	...d/		...	...d/	...d/	...d/		...	...d/	...d/	...d/
382 Non-electrical machinery		...	2156	1951	1937		...	305.2	279.2	264.7		...	4079	87496	1743158
383 Electrical machinery		...	1397	1268	1248		...	224.9	208.4	211.0		...	3356	74464	1596867
384 Transport equipment		...	844	834	777		...	286.6	298.3	303.4		...	5091	129639	2617613
385 Professional and scientific equipment		...	800e/	690e/	699e/		...	87.3e/	76.6e/	85.3e/		...	930e/	18521e/	445914e/
390 Other manufacturing industries		...	...e/	...e/	...e/		...	...e/	...e/	...e/		...	...e/	...e/	...e/
3 Total manufacturing		...	26831	25710	24553		...	3723.0	3622.8	3548.6		...	41427	949298	19338890

a/ 322 includes 323 and 324.
b/ 351 includes 352, 353 and 354.
c/ 361 includes 362 and 369.
d/ 371 includes 372 and 381.
e/ 385 includes 390.

Brazil

ISIC Revision 2	Output in factor values					Value added in factor values					Gross fixed capital formation		
		(million REAIS)					(million REAIS)					(million REAIS)	
ISIC Industry	Note	1991	1992	1993	1994	Note	1991	1992	1993	1994	Note	1993	1994
311/2 Food products		...	60.3	1305.8	29521.0		...	28.1	628.2	13174.0		56.7	...
313 Beverages		...	6.2	145.9	3420.0		...	4.1	98.6	2341.0		8.7	...
314 Tobacco		...	3.7	77.6	1685.0		...	2.6	55.5	947.0		9.6	...
321 Textiles		...	17.0	362.3	7722.0		...	10.3	224.5	4391.0		30.8	...
322 Wearing apparel, except footwear		...	18.3a/	461.2a/	9572.0a/		...	10.8a/	278.5a/	5059.0a/		9.6a/	...
323 Leather and fur products		...	...a/	...a/	...a/		...	...a/	...a/	...a/		...a/	...
324 Footwear, except rubber or plastic		...	...a/	...a/	...a/		...	...a/	...a/	...a/		...a/	...
331 Wood products, except furniture		...	2.7	83.6	1438.0		...	1.8	58.4	881.0		3.4	...
332 Furniture and fixtures, excl. metal		...	2.6	72.5	1732.0		...	1.5	47.5	1059.0		3.9	...
341 Paper and products		...	12.0	275.8	5809.0		...	7.0	166.0	3271.0		21.2	...
342 Printing and publishing		...	6.0	141.8	3517.0		...	4.7	105.6	2636.0		4.5	...
351 Industrial chemicals		...	79.9b/	1841.8b/	38801.0b/		...	40.1b/	1101.0b/	22854.0b/		171.3b/	...
352 Other chemicals		...	...b/	...b/	...b/		...	...b/	...b/	...b/		...b/	...
353 Petroleum refineries		...	...b/	...b/	...b/		...	...b/	...b/	...b/		...b/	...
354 Misc. petroleum and coal products		...	...b/	...b/	...b/		...	...b/	...b/	...b/		...b/	...
355 Rubber products		...	5.0	111.6	2423.0		...	3.2	74.0	1435.0		4.6	...
356 Plastic products		...	8.5	166.6	3758.0		...	5.8	105.1	2213.0		7.8	...
361 Pottery, china, earthenware		...	13.5c/	282.4c/	6097.0c/		...	9.5c/	199.7c/	4175.0c/		12.2c/	...
362 Glass and products		...	...c/	...c/	...c/		...	...c/	...c/	...c/		...c/	...
369 Other non-metallic mineral products		...	...c/	...c/	...c/		...	...c/	...c/	...c/		...c/	...
371 Iron and steel		...	42.2d/	954.6d/	19212.0d/		...	24.0d/	567.2d/	10712.0d/		62.9d/	...
372 Non-ferrous metals		...	...d/	...d/	...d/		...	...d/	...d/	...d/		...d/	...
381 Fabricated metal products		...	...d/	...d/	...d/		...	...d/	...d/	...d/		...d/	...
382 Non-electrical machinery		...	22.1	477.5	10516.0		...	15.7	325.7	6401.0		11.3	...
383 Electrical machinery		...	24.6	643.5	12344.0		...	17.5	461.5	7642.0		12.7	...
384 Transport equipment		...	36.1	965.2	20878.0		...	23.1	565.2	11921.0		17.1	...
385 Professional and scientific equipment		...	6.1e/	130.6e/	2971.0e/		...	4.6e/	100.1e/	2196.0e/		5.7e/	...
390 Other manufacturing industries		...	...e/	...e/	...e/		...	...e/	...e/	...e/		...e/	...
3 Total manufacturing		...	367.0	8500.3	181416.0		...	214.4	5162.2	103308.0		453.9	...

a/ 322 includes 323 and 324.
b/ 351 includes 352, 353 and 354.
c/ 361 includes 362 and 369.
d/ 371 includes 372 and 381.
e/ 385 includes 390.

Brazil

ISIC Revision 2		Index numbers of industrial production (1990=100)											
ISIC Industry	Note	1985	1986	1987	1988	1989	1990	1991	1992	1993	1994	1995	1996
311/2 Food products		92	93	99	97	98	100	104	104	104	106	115	121
313 Beverages		70	87	84	85	98	100	118	99	107	118	138	134
314 Tobacco		87	94	95	96	101	100	107	126	132	112	107	120
321 Textiles		105	119	118	111	111	100	103	98	98	101	96	90
322 Wearing apparel, except footwear	a/	126	135	122	114	116	100	87	80	89	87	81	79
323 Leather and fur products		...	...	...	...	...	...	...	...	...	...	...	...
324 Footwear, except rubber or plastic	a/	...	...	...	...	...	...	...	...	...	...	...	...
331 Wood products, except furniture		...	...	...	...	...	...	...	...	...	...	...	...
332 Furniture and fixtures, excl. metal		...	...	...	...	...	...	...	...	...	...	...	...
341 Paper and products		90	99	102	101	107	100	107	105	110	113	113	117
342 Printing and publishing		84	86	92	100	93	100	104	98	108	108	115	112
351 Industrial chemicals	b/	105	107	113	110	109	100	92	92	96	102	102	107
352 Other chemicals	b/	...	...	...	...	...	...	...	...	...	...	...	...
353 Petroleum refineries	b/	...	...	...	...	...	...	...	...	...	...	...	...
354 Misc. petroleum and coal products	b/	...	...	...	...	...	...	...	...	...	...	...	...
355 Rubber products		89	101	105	107	105	100	99	99	108	112	112	111
356 Plastic products		98	118	113	105	118	100	100	89	95	99	109	121
361 Pottery, china, earthenware	c/	94	111	114	109	113	100	101	93	98	100	105	111
362 Glass and products	c/	...	...	...	...	...	...	...	...	...	...	...	...
369 Other non-metallic mineral products	c/	...	...	...	...	...	...	...	...	...	...	...	...
371 Iron and steel	d/	100	113	113	108	115	100	94	94	101	111	109	111
372 Non-ferrous metals	d/	...	...	...	...	...	...	...	...	...	...	...	...
381 Fabricated metal products	d/	...	...	...	...	...	...	...	...	...	...	...	...
382 Non-electrical machinery		99	119	125	114	119	100	90	81	95	115	110	96
383 Electrical machinery		88	107	106	101	107	100	94	82	93	111	127	133
384 Transport equipment		111	125	112	122	119	100	100	98	118	134	139	139
385 Professional and scientific equipment		...	...	...	...	...	...	...	...	...	...	...	...
390 Other manufacturing industries		...	...	...	...	...	...	...	...	...	...	...	...
3 Total manufacturing		100	110	111	108	110	100	97	93	101	108	111	112

a/ 322 includes 324.
b/ 351 includes 352, 353 and 354.
c/ 361 includes 362 and 369.
d/ 371 includes 372 and 381.

BULGARIA

Supplier of information:
Central Statistical Office of the Council of Ministers, Sofia.

Basic source of data:
Statistical reports collected regularly by the above office.

Major deviations from ISIC (Revision 2):
The classification of all of the enterprise's primary and subsidiary units is determined by its basic activity. Where the enterprise engages in more than one kind of activity, the nature of the main product determines the classification; if no product accounts for more than 80 per cent of total output, the enterprise is classified under miscellaneous manufacturing (ISIC 390). Repair services for the general public are included in total manufacturing (ISIC major division 3). Publishing (part of ISIC 342) is not included in manufacturing. Up to 1993 data for co-operative enterprises are included in ISIC 390. All other ISICs include only state-owned enterprises. As of 1994 all ISICs include all enterprises.

Reference period (if not calendar year):

Scope:
The index numbers of industrial production cover, in principle, all industrial establishments.

Method of enumeration:
Not reported.

Adjusted for non-response:
Not reported.

Concepts and definitions of variables:
Figures for wages and salaries are computed by UNIDO from reported wages and salaries per employee.
Output refers to gross output.
Value added is gross value added in basic prices.
Gross fixed capital formation refers to the net increase in fixed assets other than land during the reference year. Valuation is at full original cost.

Related national publications:
Statisticheski Godishnik Na Narodna Republika Bulgaria (Statistical Yearbook of the People's Republic of Bulgaria), published by the Central Statistical Office of the Council of Ministers, Sofia.

Bulgaria

ISIC Revision 2		Number of enterprises					Number of employees					Wages and salaries paid to employees			
		(numbers)					(thousands)					(million LEVA)			
ISIC Industry	Note	1993	1994	1995	1996	Note	1993	1994	1995	1996	Note	1993	1994	1995	1996
311/2 Food products		3280	4703	5107	4915		55.6	59.7	51.7	49.8		2153.7	3365.6	4651.2	8512.4
313 Beverages		1855	2258	2023	1698		12.1	15.0	14.5	13.6		645.0	1158.3	1785.7	3267.1
314 Tobacco		27	27	27	32		14.5	14.6	13.1	12.5		751.4	1350.4	2222.4	4523.5
321 Textiles		643	729	818	762		64.5	63.5	61.0	55.7		1711.4	2821.9	4194.1	8088.0
322 Wearing apparel, except footwear		2175	2950	3097	2278		38.7	48.5	47.0	39.3		920.6	1912.1	2899.1	4491.7
323 Leather and fur products		250	306	280	265		6.8	6.5	6.0	4.9		174.9	295.7	417.1	672.8
324 Footwear, except rubber or plastic		246	389	459	257		14.5	16.3	15.5	15.9		370.1	700.7	1060.3	2099.7
331 Wood products, except furniture		1344	1961	2324	1637		13.9	14.6	13.6	13.4		428.2	709.2	1044.7	1974.6
332 Furniture and fixtures, excl. metal		616	1052	1130	923		12.2	15.6	15.3	13.4		327.5	709.9	1001.8	1810.6
341 Paper and products		101	167	176	216		10.7	13.7	14.3	13.5		366.9	674.2	1234.4	2233.0
342 Printing and publishing	a/	341	515	547	558	a/	7.3	6.9	6.3	5.9	a/	373.9	587.5	883.0	1647.5
351 Industrial chemicals		79	146	90	59		22.9	22.3	24.4	24.4		1133.1	1750.0	3384.3	8779.8
352 Other chemicals		256	386	385	397		22.9	22.2	20.7	19.3		1155.8	1772.3	2526.0	4611.9
353 Petroleum refineries	b/	...	...	...	...	b/	...	...	...	...	b/	...	...	...	...
354 Misc. petroleum and coal products		15	12	14	12		13.5	13.6	13.9	12.1		1277.2	2051.9	3290.9	5879.2
355 Rubber products		227	329	429	423		13.0	11.7	11.3	11.0		425.1	598.2	938.8	1727.9
356 Plastic products		740	939	980	951		7.6	9.8	9.5	8.6		336.5	654.9	1068.4	2111.8
361 Pottery, china, earthenware		59	97	111	118		3.8	4.0	3.6	3.8		122.4	227.0	346.4	829.6
362 Glass and products		174	162	115	70		12.5	12.5	13.1	13.8		421.5	693.0	1278.1	2885.9
369 Other non-metallic mineral products		289	360	392	398		21.5	21.6	20.0	19.2		839.9	1370.4	2056.6	3963.1
371 Iron and steel		18	18	18	15		25.6	25.4	26.5	26.7		1556.6	2581.6	3940.3	8312.1
372 Non-ferrous metals		38	44	34	31		10.6	10.6	11.0	10.7		651.0	1046.3	1672.1	3528.7
381 Fabricated metal products		1265	2048	2546	2207		44.9	55.7	40.1	23.9		1459.5	2896.3	3402.1	3601.3
382 Non-electrical machinery	c/	1940	2536	2799	2507	c/	106.7	83.5	91.1	110.2	c/	3639.3	2529.4	7556.1	19095.0
383 Electrical machinery		2943	4425	5138	3442		66.2	54.1	50.8	44.8		2120.8	2919.6	4148.9	7652.3
384 Transport equipment		2142	3919	4539	2752		51.6	52.4	49.3	37.4		2344.2	3541.8	4940.9	7611.4
385 Professional and scientific equipment	c/	...	...	...	...	c/	...	...	...	...	c/	...	...	...	...
390 Other manufacturing industries		3996	2904	1599	1319		92.9	21.4	10.2	7.5		2192.0	873.9	821.6	1065.6
3 Total manufacturing	b/	25059	33382	35177	28242	b/	767.0	695.7	653.8	611.3	b/	27898.9	42067.6	63053.1	120976.2

a/ Excluding publishing.
b/ Total manufacturing excludes 353.
c/ 382 includes 385.

Bulgaria

ISIC Revision 2	Output					Value added					Gross fixed capital formation		
		(million LEVA)					(million LEVA)					(million LEVA)	
ISIC Industry	Note	1993	1994	1995	1996	Note	1993	1994	1995	1996	Note	1995	1996
311/2 Food products		31659	52605	78052	169211	a/	13554	20871	37084	73745		4642.1	1525.3
313 Beverages		8479	18542	32081	76474	a/	...	...	...	...		2890.0	1373.5
314 Tobacco		8142	18121	28385	65104	a/	...	...	...	...		483.1	4288.5
321 Textiles		9757	19143	27998	65015		3372	5414	8662	16072		807.3	1303.6
322 Wearing apparel, except footwear		4085	8138	12489	27183		2368	3957	6237	14003		584.0	383.0
323 Leather and fur products		1379	2718	3744	7381	b/	1362	2267	3169	6204		152.9	64.6
324 Footwear, except rubber or plastic		2272	4872	6832	16227	b/	...	...	...	...		238.0	150.2
331 Wood products, except furniture	c/	3058	5704	9369	18222	d/c/	2683	4477	6918	11456		202.5	...
332 Furniture and fixtures, excl. metal		2462	4687	7255	13736	d/	...	...	...	...		117.1	227.0
341 Paper and products		3233	6978	15501	25953		907	1756	3706	3267		371.4	275.4
342 Printing and publishing	e/	2891	6659	10712	21657	e/	1062	1885	3017	6657	e/	325.5	399.5
351 Industrial chemicals		9412	23968	45362	123603	f/	12834	23773	39928	79728		1698.0	3423.2
352 Other chemicals		8730	16921	26996	63138	f/	...	...	...	...		726.0	936.0
353 Petroleum refineries	g/	...	...	...	...	f/	...	...	...	...	g/	...	...
354 Misc. petroleum and coal products		21721	61458	93782	275371	f/	...	...	...	...		7461.4	2390.0
355 Rubber products		2454	4233	7942	18722	f/	...	...	...	...		148.1	154.0
356 Plastic products		2970	7019	12220	24706	f/	...	...	...	...		254.4	352.1
361 Pottery, china, earthenware		978	2068	2524	5924	h/	1032	1962	5976	8773		280.0	291.0
362 Glass and products		2196	4947	8817	20151	h/	...	...	...	...		218.1	421.2
369 Other non-metallic mineral products		4803	9496	15629	37007		2299	3938	6359	10625		564.0	623.5
371 Iron and steel		13212	29261	51076	108580	i/	2833	4661	10758	14118		4385.7	1195.2
372 Non-ferrous metals		5917	15697	27000	62382	i/	3126	6595	13533	27079		781.7	1401.5
381 Fabricated metal products		7111	18224	21704	32224	j/	12725	18033	35097	69845		925.1	664.1
382 Non-electrical machinery	k/	13539	20377	37939	101595	j/	...	...	...	...	k/	824.4	972.2
383 Electrical machinery		11521	20218	31560	66529		5232	6916	12157	16806		881.6	676.6
384 Transport equipment		10119	17621	26883	55429	j/	...	...	...	...		1141.2	695.3
385 Professional and scientific equipment	k/	...	...	...	...	j/	...	...	...	...	k/	...	...
390 Other manufacturing industries		9770	10542	13441	22907		2848	2951	3926	8257		55.0	7.0
3 Total manufacturing	g/	201870	410217	655293	1524431	i/	68237	109456	196527	366635	g/	31158.6	24193.0

a/ 311/2 includes 313 and 314.
b/ 323 includes 324.
c/ Including logging.
d/ 331 includes 332.
e/ Excluding publishing.
f/ 351 includes 352, 353, 354, 355 and 356.
g/ Total manufacturing excludes 353.
h/ 361 includes 362.
i/ Including ore extraction.
j/ 381 includes 382, 384 and 385.
k/ 382 includes 385.

Bulgaria

ISIC Revision 2		Index numbers of industrial production											
		(1990=100)											
ISIC Industry	Note	1985	1986	1987	1988	1989	1990	1991	1992	1993	1994	1995	1996
311/2 Food products	a/	104	100	99	108	107	100	79	68	52	51	52	...
313 Beverages	a/	...	...	...	...	...	...	...	...	...	...	...	...
314 Tobacco	a/	...	...	...	...	...	...	...	...	...	...	...	...
321 Textiles		85	83	88	95	98	100	69	60	50	52	48	...
322 Wearing apparel, except footwear		78	97	95	88	88	100	87	74	62	75	63	...
323 Leather and fur products	b/	82	81	85	98	111	100	88	78	65	67	58	...
324 Footwear, except rubber or plastic	b/	...	...	...	...	...	...	...	...	...	...	...	...
331 Wood products, except furniture		102	91	92	108	109	100	83	74	65	75	74	...
332 Furniture and fixtures, excl. metal		...	...	...	...	...	...	...	...	...	...	...	...
341 Paper and products		105	103	104	109	104	100	71	65	63	74	87	...
342 Printing and publishing		81	77	80	84	95	100	109	115	154	181	152	...
351 Industrial chemicals	c/	121	135	128	158	133	100	82	68	60	82	96	...
352 Other chemicals	c/	...	...	...	...	...	...	...	...	...	...	...	...
353 Petroleum refineries	c/	...	...	...	...	...	...	...	...	...	...	...	...
354 Misc. petroleum and coal products	c/	...	...	...	...	...	...	...	...	...	...	...	...
355 Rubber products	c/	...	...	...	...	...	...	...	...	...	...	...	...
356 Plastic products	c/	...	...	...	...	...	...	...	...	...	...	...	...
361 Pottery, china, earthenware	d/	97	89	98	102	101	100	81	67	66	80	84	...
362 Glass and products	d/	...	...	...	...	...	...	...	...	...	...	...	...
369 Other non-metallic mineral products		109	116	113	112	105	100	60	52	48	52	57	...
371 Iron and steel		114	119	120	122	119	100	55	50	63	81	91	...
372 Non-ferrous metals		123	124	124	127	122	100	73	70	82	92	88	...
381 Fabricated metal products	e/	110	102	108	122	118	100	81	64	48	48	50	...
382 Non-electrical machinery	e/	...	...	...	...	...	...	...	...	...	...	...	...
383 Electrical machinery		100	91	108	149	142	100	64	41	39	39	39	...
384 Transport equipment		...	...	...	...	...	...	...	...	...	...	...	...
385 Professional and scientific equipment		...	...	...	...	...	...	...	...	...	...	...	...
390 Other manufacturing industries		91	92	94	103	109	100	96	85	88	63	49	...
3 Total manufacturing		...	...	...	...	...	...	...	...	...	...	...	...

a/ 311/2 includes 313 and 314.
b/ 323 includes 324.
c/ 351 includes 352, 353, 354, 355 and 356.
d/ 361 includes 362.
e/ 381 includes 382.

CAMBODIA

Supplier of information:
National Institute of Statistics, Ministry of Planning, Phnom Penh.

Basic source of data:
Survey of industrial establishments.

Major deviations from ISIC (Revision 3):

Reference period (if not calendar year):

Scope:
For 1993, all establishments are covered. For 1995, establishments with 10 or more workers engaged are covered.

Method of enumeration:
For 1993, establishments with 10 or more workers engaged are completely enumerated, and those with less than 10 workers engaged are sampled. The survey is carried out through personal visits.

Adjusted for non-response:
No.

Concepts and definitions of variables:
Output refers to census output.
Value added refers to census value added.

Related national publications:
Survey of Industrial Establishments,1993; Survey of Establishments, 1995, both published by National Institute of Statistics, Ministry of Planning, Phnom Penh.

Cambodia

ISIC Revision 3	Number of establishments					Number of employees					Wages and salaries paid to employees				
		(numbers)					(numbers)					(million RIELS)			
ISIC Industry	Note	1993	1994	1995	1996	Note	1993	1994	1995	1996	Note	1993	1994	1995	1996
151 Processed meat,fish,fruit,vegetables,fats		5a/	...	101b/	...		172a/	...	1673b/	...		389a/	...	3013b/	...
1511 Processing/preserving of meat		...	...	...	...		...	...	...	...		...	...	...	...
1512 Processing/preserving of fish		...	...	...	...		...	...	...	...		...	...	...	...
1513 Processing/preserving of fruit & vegetables		...	...	...	...		...	...	...	...		...	...	...	...
1514 Vegetable and animal oils and fats		...	...	...	...		...	...	...	...		...	...	...	...
1520 Dairy products		...	...	...	...		...	...	...	...		...	...	...	...
153 Grain mill products; starches; animal feeds		...a/	...	...b/	...		...a/	...	...b/	...		...a/	...	...b/	...
1531 Grain mill products		11	...	...b/	...		185	...	...b/	...		70	...	...b/	...
1532 Starches and starch products		...	...	...	...		...	...	...	...		...	...	...	...
1533 Prepared animal feeds		...	...	...	...		...	...	...	...		...	...	...	...
154 Other food products		47	...	...b/	...		800	...	...b/	...		522	...	...b/	...
1541 Bakery products		...	...	...	...		...	...	...	...		...	...	...	...
1542 Sugar		...	...	...	...		...	...	...	...		...	...	...	...
1543 Cocoa, chocolate and sugar confectionery		...	...	...	...		...	...	...	...		...	...	...	...
1544 Macaroni, noodles & similar products		...	...	...	...		...	...	...	...		...	...	...	...
1549 Other food products n.e.c.		...	...	...	...		...	...	...	...		...	...	...	...
155 Beverages		16	...	...b/	...		775	...	...b/	...		1108	...	...b/	...
1551 Distilling, rectifying & blending of spirits		...	...	...	...		...	...	...	...		...	...	...	...
1552 Wines		...	...	...	...		...	...	...	...		...	...	...	...
1553 Malt liquors and malt		...	...	...	...		...	...	...	...		...	...	...	...
1554 Soft drinks; mineral waters		...	...	...	...		...	...	...	...		...	...	...	...
1600 Tobacco products		126	...	157	...		2804	...	1239	...		1935	...	1663	...
171 Spinning, weaving and finishing of textiles		-	...	5c/	...		-	...	208c/	...		-	...	299c/	...
1711 Textile fibre preparation; textile weaving		...	...	...	...		...	...	...	...		...	...	...	...
1712 Finishing of textiles		...	...	...	...		...	...	...	...		...	...	...	...
172 Other textiles		4	...	...c/	...		669	...	...c/	...		500	...	...c/	...
1721 Made-up textile articles, except apparel		...	...	...	...		...	...	...	...		...	...	...	...
1722 Carpets and rugs		...	...	...	...		...	...	...	...		...	...	...	...
1723 Cordage, rope, twine and netting		...	...	...	...		...	...	...	...		...	...	...	...
1729 Other textiles n.e.c.		...	...	...	...		...	...	...	...		...	...	...	...
1730 Knitted and crocheted fabrics and articles		-	...	...c/	...		-	...	...c/	...		-	...	...c/	...
1810 Wearing apparel, except fur apparel		4	...	15d/	...		507	...	5192d/	...		499	...	6770d/	...
1820 Dressing & dyeing of fur; processing of fur		-	...	...d/	...		-	...	...d/	...		-	...	...d/	...
191 Tanning, dressing and processing of leather		-	...	...d/	...		-	...	...d/	...		-	...	...d/	...
1911 Tanning and dressing of leather		...	...	...	...		...	...	...	...		...	...	...	...
1912 Luggage, handbags, etc.; saddlery & harness		...	...	...	...		...	...	...	...		...	...	...	...
1920 Footwear		-	...	...d/	...		-	...	...d/	...		-	...	...d/	...
2010 Sawmilling and planing of wood		25	...	52e/	...		616	...	1315e/	...		1374	...	9795e/	...
202 Products of wood, cork, straw, etc.		10	...	...e/	...		693	...	...e/	...		1596	...	...e/	...
2021 Veneer sheets, plywood, particle board, etc.		...	...	...	...		...	...	...	...		...	...	...	...
2022 Builders' carpentry and joinery		...	...	...	...		...	...	...	...		...	...	...	...
2023 Wooden containers		...	...	...	...		...	...	...	...		...	...	...	...
2029 Other wood products; articles of cork/straw		...	...	...	...		...	...	...	...		...	...	...	...
210 Paper and paper products		2	...	...e/	...		37	...	...e/	...		23	...	...e/	...
2101 Pulp, paper and paperboard		...	...	...	...		...	...	...	...		...	...	...	...
2102 Corrugated paper and paperboard		...	...	...	...		...	...	...	...		...	...	...	...
2109 Other articles of paper and paperboard		...	...	...	...		...	...	...	...		...	...	...	...
221 Publishing		-	...	6f/	...		-	...	142f/	...		-	...	176f/	...
2211 Publishing of books and other publications		...	...	...	...		...	...	...	...		...	...	...	...
2212 Publishing of newspapers, journals, etc.		...	...	...	...		...	...	...	...		...	...	...	...
2213 Publishing of recorded media		...	...	...	...		...	...	...	...		...	...	...	...
2219 Other publishing		...	...	...	...		...	...	...	...		...	...	...	...

222 Printing and related service activities	3	...	...f/	...	102	...	...f/	...	115	...	...f/	...
2221 Printing	...	...	...	...	...	...	...	...	...	...	...	...
2222 Service activities related to printing	...	...	...	...	...	...	...	...	...	...	...	...
2230 Reproduction of recorded media	-	...	...f/	...	-	...	...f/	...	-	...	...f/	...
2310 Coke oven products	...	...	...	...	...	...	...	...	...	...	...	...
2320 Refined petroleum products	...	...	...	...	...	...	...	...	...	...	...	...
2330 Processing of nuclear fuel	...	...	...	...	...	...	...	...	...	...	...	...
241 Basic chemicals	3g/	...	6h/	...	94g/	...	90h/	...	244g/	...	170h/	...
2411 Basic chemicals, except fertilizers	...	...	...	...	...	...	...	...	...	...	...	...
2412 Fertilizers and nitrogen compounds	...	...	...	...	...	...	...	...	...	...	...	...
2413 Plastics in primary forms; synthetic rubber	...	...	...	...	...	...	...	...	...	...	...	...
242 Other chemicals	...g/	...	...h/	...	...g/	...	...h/	...	...g/	...	...h/	...
2421 Pesticides and other agro-chemical products	...	...	...	...	...	...	...	...	...	...	...	...
2422 Paints, varnishes, printing ink and mastics	...	...	...	...	...	...	...	...	...	...	...	...
2423 Pharmaceuticals, medicinal chemicals, etc.	...	...	...	...	...	...	...	...	...	...	...	...
2424 Soap, cleaning & cosmetic preparations	...	...	...	...	...	...	...	...	...	...	...	...
2429 Other chemical products n.e.c.	...	...	...	...	...	...	...	...	...	...	...	...
2430 Man-made fibres	-	...	...h/	...	-	...	...h/	...	-	...	...h/	...
251 Rubber products	10	...	8i/	...	9882	...	874i/	...	8083	...	1302i/	...
2511 Rubber tyres and tubes	...	...	...	...	...	...	...	...	...	...	...	...
2519 Other rubber products	...	...	...	...	...	...	...	...	...	...	...	...
2520 Plastic products	-	...	...i/	...	-	...	...i/	...	-	...	...i/	...
2610 Glass and glass products	250j/	...	398j/	...	4188j/	...	4981j/	...	2001j/	...	4331j/	...
269 Non-metallic mineral products n.e.c.	...j/	...	...j/	...	...j/	...	...j/	...	...j/	...	...j/	...
2691 Pottery, china and earthenware	...	...	...	...	...	...	...	...	...	...	...	...
2692 Refractory ceramic products	...	...	...	...	...	...	...	...	...	...	...	...
2693 Struct.non-refractory clay; ceramic products	...	...	...	...	...	...	...	...	...	...	...	...
2694 Cement, lime and plaster	...	...	...	...	...	...	...	...	...	...	...	...
2695 Articles of concrete, cement and plaster	...	...	...	...	...	...	...	...	...	...	...	...
2696 Cutting, shaping & finishing of stone	...	...	...	...	...	...	...	...	...	...	...	...
2699 Other non-metallic mineral products n.e.c.	...	...	...	...	...	...	...	...	...	...	...	...
2710 Basic iron and steel	4k/	...	6k/	...	81k/	...	170k/	...	74k/	...	285k/	...
2720 Basic precious and non-ferrous metals	...k/	...	...k/	...	...k/	...	...k/	...	...k/	...	...k/	...
273 Casting of metals	...k/	...	...k/	...	...k/	...	...k/	...	...k/	...	...k/	...
2731 Casting of iron and steel	...	...	...	...	...	...	...	...	...	...	...	...
2732 Casting of non-ferrous metals	...	...	...	...	...	...	...	...	...	...	...	...
281 Struct.metal products;tanks;steam generators	12m/	...	15m/	...	261n/	...	216m/	...	290n/	...	305m/	...
2811 Structural metal products	...	...	...	...	...	...	...	...	...	...	...	...
2812 Tanks, reservoirs and containers of metal	...	...	...	...	...	...	...	...	...	...	...	...
2813 Steam generators	...	...	...	...	...	...	...	...	...	...	...	...
289 Other metal products; metal working services	...m/	...	...m/	...	...n/	...	...m/	...	...n/	...	...m/	...
2891 Metal forging/pressing/stamping/roll-forming	...	...	...	...	...	...	...	...	...	...	...	...
2892 Treatment & coating of metals	...	...	...	...	...	...	...	...	...	...	...	...
2893 Cutlery, hand tools and general hardware	...	...	...	...	...	...	...	...	...	...	...	...
2899 Other fabricated metal products n.e.c.	...	...	...	...	...	...	...	...	...	...	...	...
291 General purpose machinery	1	...	-	...	...n/	...	-	...	...n/	...	-	...
2911 Engines & turbines(not for transport equip.)	...	...	...	...	...	...	...	...	...	...	...	...
2912 Pumps, compressors, taps and valves	...	...	...	...	...	...	...	...	...	...	...	...
2913 Bearings, gears, gearing & driving elements	...	...	...	...	...	...	...	...	...	...	...	...
2914 Ovens, furnaces and furnace burners	...	...	...	...	...	...	...	...	...	...	...	...
2915 Lifting and handling equipment	...	...	...	...	...	...	...	...	...	...	...	...
2919 Other general purpose machinery	...	...	...	...	...	...	...	...	...	...	...	...
292 Special purpose machinery	-	...	-	...	-	...	-	...	-	...	-	...
2921 Agricultural and forestry machinery	...	...	...	...	...	...	...	...	...	...	...	...
2922 Machine tools	...	...	...	...	...	...	...	...	...	...	...	...
2923 Machinery for metallurgy	...	...	...	...	...	...	...	...	...	...	...	...
2924 Machinery for mining & construction	...	...	...	...	...	...	...	...	...	...	...	...
2925 Food/beverage/tobacco processing machinery	...	...	...	...	...	...	...	...	...	...	...	...
2926 Machinery for textile, apparel and leather	...	...	...	...	...	...	...	...	...	...	...	...
2927 Weapons and ammunition	...	...	...	...	...	...	...	...	...	...	...	...
2929 Other special purpose machinery	...	...	...	...	...	...	...	...	...	...	...	...
2930 Domestic appliances n.e.c.	-	...	-	...	-	...	-	...	-	...	-	...

continued

Cambodia

ISIC Revision 3	Number of establishments					Number of employees					Wages and salaries paid to employees				
		(numbers)					(numbers)					(million RIELS)			
ISIC Industry	Note	1993	1994	1995	1996	Note	1993	1994	1995	1996	Note	1993	1994	1995	1996
3000 Office, accounting and computing machinery		-	...	-	...		-	...	-	...		-	...	-	...
3110 Electric motors, generators and transformers		-	...	-	...		-	...	-	...		-	...	-	...
3120 Electricity distribution & control apparatus		-	...	-	...		-	...	-	...		-	...	-	...
3130 Insulated wire and cable		-	...	-	...		-	...	-	...		-	...	-	...
3140 Accumulators, primary cells and batteries		-	...	-	...		-	...	-	...		-	...	-	...
3150 Lighting equipment and electric lamps		-	...	-	...		-	...	-	...		-	...	-	...
3190 Other electrical equipment n.e.c.		-	...	-	...		-	...	-	...		-	...	-	...
3210 Electronic valves, tubes, etc.		-	...	-	...		-	...	-	...		-	...	-	...
3220 TV/radio transmitters; line comm. apparatus		-	...	-	...		-	...	-	...		-	...	-	...
3230 TV and radio receivers and associated goods		-	...	-	...		-	...	-	...		-	...	-	...
331 Medical, measuring, testing appliances, etc.		-	...	-	...		-	...	-	...		-	...	-	...
3311 Medical, surgical and orthopaedic equipment		...	...	...	...		...	...	...	...		...	...	...	...
3312 Measuring/testing/navigating appliances,etc.		...	...	...	...		...	...	...	...		...	...	...	...
3313 Industrial process control equipment		...	...	...	...		...	...	...	...		...	...	...	...
3320 Optical instruments & photographic equipment		-	...	-	...		-	...	-	...		-	...	-	...
3330 Watches and clocks		-	...	-	...		-	...	-	...		-	...	-	...
3410 Motor vehicles		-	...	-	...		-	...	-	...		-	...	-	...
3420 Automobile bodies, trailers & semi-trailers		-	...	-	...		-	...	-	...		-	...	-	...
3430 Parts/accessories for automobiles		-	...	-	...		-	...	-	...		-	...	-	...
351 Building and repairing of ships and boats		-	...	-	...		-	...	-	...		-	...	-	...
3511 Building and repairing of ships		...	...	...	...		...	...	...	...		...	...	...	...
3512 Building/repairing of pleasure/sport. boats		...	...	...	...		...	...	...	...		...	...	...	...
3520 Railway/tramway locomotives & rolling stock		-	...	-	...		-	...	-	...		-	...	-	...
3530 Aircraft and spacecraft		-	...	-	...		-	...	-	...		-	...	-	...
359 Transport equipment n.e.c.		-	...	-	...		-	...	-	...		-	...	-	...
3591 Motorcycles		...	...	...	...		...	...	...	...		...	...	...	...
3592 Bicycles and invalid carriages		...	...	...	...		...	...	...	...		...	...	...	...
3599 Other transport equipment n.e.c.		...	...	...	...		...	...	...	...		...	...	...	...
3610 Furniture		5	...	13p/	...		98	...	128p/	...		378	...	97p/	...
369 Manufacturing n.e.c.		4	...	...p/	...		42	...	...p/	...		33	...	...p/	...
3691 Jewellery and related articles		...	...	...	...		...	...	...	...		...	...	...	...
3692 Musical instruments		...	...	...	...		...	...	...	...		...	...	...	...
3693 Sports goods		...	...	...	...		...	...	...	...		...	...	...	...
3694 Games and toys		...	...	...	...		...	...	...	...		...	...	...	...
3699 Other manufacturing n.e.c.		...	...	...	...		...	...	...	...		...	...	...	...
3710 Recycling of metal waste and scrap		1	...	...	...		...	...	...	...		...	...	...	...
3720 Recycling of non-metal waste and scrap		-	...	...	...		-	...	...	...		-	...	...	...
D Total manufacturing		543	...	782	...		22006	...	16225	...		19235	...	26206	...

a/ 151 includes 1520.
b/ 151 includes 1520, 153, 154 and 155.
c/ 171 includes 172 and 1730.
d/ 1810 includes 1820, 191 and 1920.
e/ 2010 includes 202 and 210.
f/ 221 includes 222 and 2230.
g/ 241 includes 242.
h/ 241 includes 242 and 2430.
i/ 251 includes 2520.
j/ 2610 includes 269.
k/ 2710 includes 2720 and 273.
m/ 281 includes 289.
n/ 281 includes 289 and 291.
p/ 3610 includes 369.

Cambodia

ISIC Revision 3 ISIC Industry	Output in producers' prices Note	(million RIELS) 1993	1994	1995	1996	Value added in producers' prices Note	(million RIELS) 1993	1994	1995	1996	Gross fixed capital formation Note	(million RIELS) 1995	1996
151 Processed meat,fish,fruit,vegetables,fats		12156a/	...	57534b/	...		1637a/	...	24521b/	...		...	...
1511 Processing/preserving of meat		...	...	...	...		...	...	...	...		...	...
1512 Processing/preserving of fish		...	...	...	...		...	...	...	...		...	...
1513 Processing/preserving of fruit & vegetables		...	...	...	...		...	...	...	...		...	...
1514 Vegetable and animal oils and fats		...	...	...	...		...	...	...	...		...	...
1520 Dairy products		...a/	...	...b/	...		...a/	...	...b/	...		...	...
153 Grain mill products; starches; animal feeds		1878	...	...b/	...		956	...	...b/	...		...	...
1531 Grain mill products		...	...	...	...		...	...	...	...		...	...
1532 Starches and starch products		...	...	...	...		...	...	...	...		...	...
1533 Prepared animal feeds		...	...	...	...		...	...	...	...		...	...
154 Other food products		4060	...	...b/	...		1460	...	...b/	...		...	...
1541 Bakery products		...	...	...	...		...	...	...	...		...	...
1542 Sugar		...	...	...	...		...	...	...	...		...	...
1543 Cocoa, chocolate and sugar confectionery		...	...	...	...		...	...	...	...		...	...
1544 Macaroni, noodles & similar products		...	...	...	...		...	...	...	...		...	...
1549 Other food products n.e.c.		...	...	...	...		...	...	...	...		...	...
155 Beverages		51440	...	...b/	...		34593	...	...b/	...		...	...
1551 Distilling, rectifying & blending of spirits		...	...	...	...		...	...	...	...		...	...
1552 Wines		...	...	...	...		...	...	...	...		...	...
1553 Malt liquors and malt		...	...	...	...		...	...	...	...		...	...
1554 Soft drinks; mineral waters		...	...	...	...		...	...	...	...		...	...
1600 Tobacco products		36117	...	23115	...		8810	...	10163	...		...	...
171 Spinning, weaving and finishing of textiles		-	...	2800c/	...		-	...	1153c/	...		...	...
1711 Textile fibre preparation; textile weaving		...	...	...	...		...	...	...	...		...	...
1712 Finishing of textiles		...	...	...	...		...	...	...	...		...	...
172 Other textiles		1886	...	...c/	...		655	...	...c/	...		...	...
1721 Made-up textile articles, except apparel		...	...	...	...		...	...	...	...		...	...
1722 Carpets and rugs		...	...	...	...		...	...	...	...		...	...
1723 Cordage, rope, twine and netting		...	...	...	...		...	...	...	...		...	...
1729 Other textiles n.e.c.		...	...	...	...		...	...	...	...		...	...
1730 Knitted and crocheted fabrics and articles		-	...	...c/	...		-	...	...c/	...		...	...
1810 Wearing apparel, except fur apparel		2724	...	114502d/	...		1707	...	37567d/	...		...	...
1820 Dressing & dyeing of fur; processing of fur		-	...	...d/	...		-	...	...d/	...		...	...
191 Tanning, dressing and processing of leather		-	...	...d/	...		-	...	...d/	...		...	...
1911 Tanning and dressing of leather		...	...	...	...		...	...	...	...		...	...
1912 Luggage, handbags, etc.; saddlery & harness		...	...	...	...		...	...	...	...		...	...
1920 Footwear		-	...	...d/	...		-	...	...d/	...		...	...
2010 Sawmilling and planing of wood		11027	...	40865e/	...		4089	...	18099e/	...		...	...
202 Products of wood, cork, straw, etc.		22119	...	...e/	...		15856	...	...e/	...		...	...
2021 Veneer sheets, plywood, particle board, etc.		...	...	...	...		...	...	...	...		...	...
2022 Builders' carpentry and joinery		...	...	...	...		...	...	...	...		...	...
2023 Wooden containers		...	...	...	...		...	...	...	...		...	...
2029 Other wood products; articles of cork/straw		...	...	...	...		...	...	...	...		...	...
210 Paper and paper products		342	...	...e/	...		123	...	...e/	...		...	...
2101 Pulp, paper and paperboard		...	...	...	...		...	...	...	...		...	...
2102 Corrugated paper and paperboard		...	...	...	...		...	...	...	...		...	...
2109 Other articles of paper and paperboard		...	...	...	...		...	...	...	...		...	...
221 Publishing		-	...	1549f/	...		-	...	784f/	...		...	...
2211 Publishing of books and other publications		...	...	...	...		...	...	...	...		...	...
2212 Publishing of newspapers, journals, etc.		...	...	...	...		...	...	...	...		...	...
2213 Publishing of recorded media		...	...	...	...		...	...	...	...		...	...
2219 Other publishing		...	...	...	...		...	...	...	...		...	...

continued

Cambodia

ISIC	Industry (ISIC Revision 3)	Note	Output in producers' prices (million RIELS) 1993	1994	1995	1996	Note	Value added in producers' prices (million RIELS) 1993	1994	1995	1996	Note	Gross fixed capital formation (million RIELS) 1995	1996
222	Printing and related service activities		369	...	...f/	...		150	...	...f/	...		...	...
2221	Printing		...	...	...	...		...	...	...	...		...	...
2222	Service activities related to printing		...	...	...	...		...	...	...	...		...	...
2230	Reproduction of recorded media		-	...	...f/	...		-	...	...f/	...		...	...
2310	Coke oven products		...	...	...	...		...	...	...	...		...	...
2320	Refined petroleum products		...	...	...	...		...	...	...	...		...	...
2330	Processing of nuclear fuel		...	...	...	...		...	...	...	...		...	...
241	Basic chemicals		3169g/	...	1793h/	...		970g/	...	551h/	...		...	...
2411	Basic chemicals, except fertilizers		...	...	...	...		...	...	...	...		...	...
2412	Fertilizers and nitrogen compounds		...	...	...	...		...	...	...	...		...	...
2413	Plastics in primary forms; synthetic rubber		...	...	...	...		...	...	...	...		...	...
242	Other chemicals		...g/	...	...h/	...		...g/	...	...h/	...		...	...
2421	Pesticides and other agro-chemical products		...	...	...	...		...	...	...	...		...	...
2422	Paints, varnishes, printing ink and mastics		...	...	...	...		...	...	...	...		...	...
2423	Pharmaceuticals, medicinal chemicals, etc.		...	...	...	...		...	...	...	...		...	...
2424	Soap, cleaning & cosmetic preparations		...	...	...	...		...	...	...	...		...	...
2429	Other chemical products n.e.c.		...	...	...	...		...	...	...	...		...	...
2430	Man-made fibres		-	...	...h/	...		-	...	...h/	...		...	...
251	Rubber products		23407	...	80388i/	...		12389	...	30114i/	...		...	...
2511	Rubber tyres and tubes		...	...	...	...		...	...	...	...		...	...
2519	Other rubber products		...	...	...	...		...	...	...	...		...	...
2520	Plastic products		-	...	...i/	...		-	...	...i/	...		...	...
2610	Glass and glass products		7571j/	...	90689j/	...		3457j/	...	42659j/	...		...	...
269	Non-metallic mineral products n.e.c.		...j/	...	...j/	...		...j/	...	...j/	...		...	...
2691	Pottery, china and earthenware		...	...	...	...		...	...	...	...		...	...
2692	Refractory ceramic products		...	...	...	...		...	...	...	...		...	...
2693	Struct.non-refractory clay; ceramic products		...	...	...	...		...	...	...	...		...	...
2694	Cement, lime and plaster		...	...	...	...		...	...	...	...		...	...
2695	Articles of concrete, cement and plaster		...	...	...	...		...	...	...	...		...	...
2696	Cutting, shaping & finishing of stone		...	...	...	...		...	...	...	...		...	...
2699	Other non-metallic mineral products n.e.c.		...	...	...	...		...	...	...	...		...	...
2710	Basic iron and steel		1487k/	...	19633k/	...		221k/	...	6574k/	...		...	...
2720	Basic precious and non-ferrous metals		...k/	...	...k/	...		...k/	...	...k/	...		...	...
273	Casting of metals		...k/	...	...k/	...		...k/	...	...k/	...		...	...
2731	Casting of iron and steel		...	...	...	...		...	...	...	...		...	...
2732	Casting of non-ferrous metals		...	...	...	...		...	...	...	...		...	...
281	Struct.metal products;tanks;steam generators		1697m/	...	1717n/	...		559m/	...	934n/	...		...	...
2811	Structural metal products		...	...	...	...		...	...	...	...		...	...
2812	Tanks, reservoirs and containers of metal		...	...	...	...		...	...	...	...		...	...
2813	Steam generators		...	...	...	...		...	...	...	...		...	...
289	Other metal products; metal working services		...m/	...	...n/	...		...m/	...	...n/	...		...	...
2891	Metal forging/pressing/stamping/roll-forming		...	...	...	...		...	...	...	...		...	...
2892	Treatment & coating of metals		...	...	...	...		...	...	...	...		...	...
2893	Cutlery, hand tools and general hardware		...	...	...	...		...	...	...	...		...	...
2899	Other fabricated metal products n.e.c.		...	...	...	...		...	...	...	...		...	...
291	General purpose machinery		...m/	...	-	...		...m/	...	-	...		...	...
2911	Engines & turbines(not for transport equip.)		...	...	...	...		...	...	...	...		...	...
2912	Pumps, compressors, taps and valves		...	...	...	...		...	...	...	...		...	...
2913	Bearings, gears, gearing & driving elements		...	...	...	...		...	...	...	...		...	...
2914	Ovens, furnaces and furnace burners		...	...	...	...		...	...	...	...		...	...
2915	Lifting and handling equipment		...	...	...	...		...	...	...	...		...	...
2919	Other general purpose machinery		...	...	...	...		...	...	...	...		...	...

292 Special purpose machinery		-	...	-	...		-	...	-	...		...	...
2921 Agricultural and forestry machinery		...	...	...	...		...	...	...	...		...	...
2922 Machine tools		...	...	...	...		...	...	...	...		...	...
2923 Machinery for metallurgy		...	...	...	...		...	...	...	...		...	...
2924 Machinery for mining & construction		...	...	...	...		...	...	...	...		...	...
2925 Food/beverage/tobacco processing machinery		...	...	...	...		...	...	...	...		...	...
2926 Machinery for textile, apparel and leather		...	...	...	...		...	...	...	...		...	...
2927 Weapons and ammunition		...	...	...	...		...	...	...	...		...	...
2929 Other special purpose machinery		...	...	...	...		...	...	...	...		...	...
2930 Domestic appliances n.e.c.		-	...	-	...		-	...	-	...		...	...
3000 Office, accounting and computing machinery		-	...	-	...		-	...	-	...		...	...
3110 Electric motors, generators and transformers		-	...	-	...		-	...	-	...		...	...
3120 Electricity distribution & control apparatus		-	...	-	...		-	...	-	...		...	...
3130 Insulated wire and cable		-	...	-	...		-	...	-	...		...	...
3140 Accumulators, primary cells and batteries		-	...	-	...		-	...	-	...		...	...
3150 Lighting equipment and electric lamps		-	...	-	...		-	...	-	...		...	...
3190 Other electrical equipment n.e.c.		-	...	-	...		-	...	-	...		...	...
3210 Electronic valves, tubes, etc.		-	...	-	...		-	...	-	...		...	...
3220 TV/radio transmitters; line comm. apparatus		-	...	-	...		-	...	-	...		...	...
3230 TV and radio receivers and associated goods		-	...	-	...		-	...	-	...		...	...
331 Medical, measuring, testing appliances, etc.		-	...	-	...		-	...	-	...		...	...
3311 Medical, surgical and orthopaedic equipment		...	...	...	...		...	...	...	...		...	...
3312 Measuring/testing/navigating appliances,etc.		...	...	...	...		...	...	...	...		...	...
3313 Industrial process control equipment		...	...	...	...		...	...	...	...		...	...
3320 Optical instruments & photographic equipment		-	...	-	...		-	...	-	...		...	...
3330 Watches and clocks		-	...	-	...		-	...	-	...		...	...
3410 Motor vehicles		-	...	-	...		-	...	-	...		...	...
3420 Automobile bodies, trailers & semi-trailers		-	...	-	...		-	...	-	...		...	...
3430 Parts/accessories for automobiles		-	...	-	...		-	...	-	...		...	...
351 Building and repairing of ships and boats		-	...	-	...		-	...	-	...		...	...
3511 Building and repairing of ships		...	...	...	...		...	...	...	...		...	...
3512 Building/repairing of pleasure/sport. boats		...	...	...	...		...	...	...	...		...	...
3520 Railway/tramway locomotives & rolling stock		-	...	-	...		-	...	-	...		...	...
3530 Aircraft and spacecraft		-	...	-	...		-	...	-	...		...	...
359 Transport equipment n.e.c.		-	...	-	...		-	...	-	...		...	...
3591 Motorcycles		...	...	...	...		...	...	...	...		...	...
3592 Bicycles and invalid carriages		...	...	...	...		...	...	...	...		...	...
3599 Other transport equipment n.e.c.		...	...	...	...		...	...	...	...		...	...
3610 Furniture		3231	...	293p/	...		1565	...	139p/	...		...	...
369 Manufacturing n.e.c.		86	...	...p/	...		60	...	...p/	...		...	...
3691 Jewellery and related articles		...	...	...	...		...	...	...	...		...	...
3692 Musical instruments		...	...	...	...		...	...	...	...		...	...
3693 Sports goods		...	...	...	...		...	...	...	...		...	...
3694 Games and toys		...	...	...	...		...	...	...	...		...	...
3699 Other manufacturing n.e.c.		...	...	...	...		...	...	...	...		...	...
3710 Recycling of metal waste and scrap		...	...	...	...		...	...	...	...		...	...
3720 Recycling of non-metal waste and scrap		-	...	...	...		-	...	...	...		...	...
D Total manufacturing		184763	...	434878	...		89255	...	173259	...		...	...

a/ 151 includes 1520.
b/ 151 includes 1520, 153, 154 and 155.
c/ 171 includes 172 and 1730.
d/ 1810 includes 1820, 191 and 1920.
e/ 2010 includes 202 and 210.
f/ 221 includes 222 and 2230.
g/ 241 includes 242.
h/ 241 includes 242 and 2430.
i/ 251 includes 2520.
j/ 2610 includes 269.
k/ 2710 includes 2720 and 273.
m/ 281 includes 289 and 291.
n/ 281 includes 289.
p/ 3610 includes 369.

Cambodia

ISIC Revision 3			Index numbers of industrial production											
			(1990=100)											
ISIC	Industry	Note	1985	1986	1987	1988	1989	1990	1991	1992	1993	1994	1995	1996
15	Food and beverages		...	...	...	...	...	...	...	...	...	...	...	...
16	Tobacco products		...	...	...	...	...	...	...	...	...	...	...	...
17	Textiles		...	...	...	...	...	...	...	...	...	...	...	...
18	Wearing apparel, fur		...	...	...	...	...	...	...	...	...	...	...	...
19	Leather, leather products and footwear		...	...	...	...	...	...	...	...	...	...	...	...
20	Wood products (excl. furniture)		...	...	...	...	...	...	...	...	...	...	...	...
21	Paper and paper products		...	...	...	...	...	...	...	...	...	...	...	...
22	Printing and publishing		...	...	...	...	...	...	...	...	...	...	...	...
23	Coke,refined petroleum products,nuclear fuel		...	...	...	...	...	...	...	...	...	...	...	...
24	Chemicals and chemical products		...	...	...	...	...	...	...	...	...	...	...	...
25	Rubber and plastics products		...	...	...	...	...	...	...	...	...	...	...	...
26	Non-metallic mineral products		...	...	...	...	...	...	...	...	...	...	...	...
27	Basic metals		...	...	...	...	...	...	...	...	...	...	...	...
28	Fabricated metal products		...	...	...	...	...	...	...	...	...	...	...	...
29	Machinery and equipment n.e.c.		...	...	...	...	...	...	...	...	...	...	...	...
30	Office, accounting and computing machinery		...	...	...	...	...	...	...	...	...	...	...	...
31	Electrical machinery and apparatus		...	...	...	...	...	...	...	...	...	...	...	...
32	Radio,television and communication equipment		...	...	...	...	...	...	...	...	...	...	...	...
33	Medical, precision and optical instruments		...	...	...	...	...	...	...	...	...	...	...	...
34	Motor vehicles, trailers, semi-trailers		...	...	...	...	...	...	...	...	...	...	...	...
35	Other transport equipment		...	...	...	...	...	...	...	...	...	...	...	...
36	Furniture; manufacturing n.e.c.		...	...	...	...	...	...	...	...	...	...	...	...
37	Recycling		...	...	...	...	...	...	...	...	...	...	...	...
D	Total manufacturing		...	...	...	...	...	...	...	...	...	...	...	...

CAMEROON

Supplier of information:
Direction de la statistique et de la comptabilité nationale, Ministère de l'économie et des finances, Yaoundé.

Basic source of data:
Annual industrial survey.

Major deviations from ISIC (Revision 2):
Data collected under the national classification system have been reclassified by the national authorities to correspond with ISIC (Rev. 2). Lack of detail in national data, however, results in several cases where exact correspondence with the ISIC cannot be achieved. Manufacture of rubber footwear (part of ISIC 355) and plastic footwear (part of ISIC 356) are included in ISIC 324. Repair of bicycles and motorcycles (part of ISIC major division 9) is included in ISIC 384.

Reference period (if not calendar year):
Fiscal year ending 30 June of the year indicated.

Scope:
All industrial enterprises in the modern sector which keep accounting records.

Method of enumeration:
Questionnaires are distributed by mail with follow-up site visits as required.

Adjusted for non-response:
No.

Concepts and definitions of variables:
Output includes revenues from goods shipped in the same condition as received. It excludes the value of goods and capital assets produced by the enterprise for its own use.
Value added is the value of all products and services rendered by the enterprise, including the value of fixed capital assets produced on own account and the net change in the value of work in progress less the costs of intermediate goods and services.

Related national publications:
Résultats des recensements industriels et commerciaux (occasional), published by the Direction de la statistique et de la comptabilité nationale, Ministère de l'économie et des finances, Yaoundé.

Cameroon

ISIC Revision 2	Number of enterprises					Number of employees					Wages and salaries paid to employees				
		(numbers)					(numbers)					(million CFA FRANCS)			
ISIC Industry	Note	1993	1994	1995	1996a/	Note	1993	1994	1995	1996a/	Note	1993	1994	1995	1996a/
311/2 Food products		65	69	57	55		16504	15372	14903	15365		17269	17966	17136	18643
3111 Slaughtering, preparing & preserving meat		...	...	...	...		...	...	...	...		...	...	...	...
3112 Dairy products		3	2	1	2		219	94	112	145		337	107	131	215
3113 Canning, preserving of fruits & vegetables		1	1	1	-		36	28	28	-		37	13	26	-
3114 Canning, preserving and processing of fish		...	...	...	...		...	...	...	...		...	...	...	...
3115 Vegetable and animal oils and fats		5	5	6	6		8590	8643	7667	8109		6090	7033	6478	7527
3116 Grain mill products		13	18	9	13		1013	797	821	948		1521	1147	1247	1127
3117 Bakery products		31	31	27	21		828	779	728	587		876	902	833	716
3118 Sugar factories and refineries		3	2	3	3		4950	4219	4670	4655		5632	5162	5310	5449
3119 Cocoa, chocolate and sugar confectionery		3	3	3	3		466	385	385	401		1576	1999	1802	1847
3121 Other food products		3	4	5	5		247	302	367	371		980	1382	1054	1517
3122 Prepared animal feeds		3	3	2	2		155	125	125	149		220	222	255	245
313 Beverages		11	11	9	8		4476	3224	1548	1957		20429	16293	8356	7972
3131 Distilling, rectifying and blending spirits		1	1	1	1		...	...	...	...		161	147	131	168
3132 Wine industries		2	2	2	2		...	...	...	...		207	136	36	26
3133 Malt liquors and malt		5	4	3	3		...	...	...	...		19807	15601	7865	7529
3134 Soft drinks and carbonated waters		3	4	3	2		...	...	...	...		254	409	324	249
314 Tobacco		3	3	2	2		854	770	567	557		3027	2215	2408	2331
321 Textiles		4	7	7	4		2819	3047	3064	3046		5763	7460	8291	8325
3211 Spinning, weaving and finishing textiles		...	...	...	...		...	...	...	...		...	...	...	...
3212 Made-up textile goods excl. wearing apparel		...	...	...	...		...	...	...	...		...	...	...	...
3213 Knitting mills		...	...	...	...		...	...	...	...		...	...	...	...
3214 Carpets and rugs		...	...	...	...		...	...	...	...		...	...	...	...
3215 Cordage, rope and twine		...	...	...	...		...	...	...	...		...	...	...	...
3219 Other textiles		...	...	...	...		...	...	...	...		...	...	...	...
322 Wearing apparel, except footwear		12	6	6	6		838	266	85	141		1275	416	54	187
323 Leather and fur products	b/	2	1	2	2	b/	58	36	68	24	b/	48	23	46	11
3231 Tanneries and leather finishing		...	...	...	...		...	...	...	...		...	...	...	...
3232 Fur dressing and dyeing industries		...	...	...	...		...	...	...	...		...	...	...	...
3233 Leather prods. excl. wearing apparel		...	...	...	...		...	...	...	...		...	...	...	...
324 Footwear, except rubber or plastic	b/	...	...	...	...	b/	...	...	...	...	b/	...	...	...	..
331 Wood products, except furniture		19	21	21	25		5249	5912	6306	7095		9013	9802	11187	13044
3311 Sawmills, planing and other wood mills		16	19	18	...		...	...	...	...		7585	8368	9251	10863
3312 Wooden and cane containers		-	-	-	...		...	...	...	...		-	-	-	-
3319 Other wood and cork products		3	2	3	...		...	...	...	...		1428	1434	1936	2181
332 Furniture and fixtures, excl. metal		5	5	7	4		81	53	98	80		93	56	131	116
341 Paper and products		12	12	14	11		898	845	1014	916		2274	1890	2449	2441
3411 Pulp, paper and paperboard articles		...	...	...	...		...	...	...	...		...	...	...	...
3412 Containers of paper and paperboard		...	...	...	...		...	...	...	...		...	...	...	...
3419 Other pulp, paper and paperboard articles		...	...	...	...		...	...	...	...		...	...	...	...
342 Printing and publishing		11	12	13	15		1131	820	809	921		2352	1160	1156	1861
351 Industrial chemicals		-	-	-	-		-	-	-	-		-	-	-	-
3511 Basic chemicals excl. fertilizers		...	...	...	...		...	...	...	...		...	...	...	...
3512 Fertilizers and pesticides		...	...	...	...		...	...	...	...		...	...	...	...
3513 Synthetic resins and plastic materials		...	...	...	...		...	...	...	...		...	...	...	...
352 Other chemicals		21	21	23	21		1825	1881	1786	1618		4403	4656	4653	4046
3521 Paints, varnishes and lacquers		...	...	1	...		...	...	...	...		...	...	...	...
3522 Drugs and medicines		...	...	-	...		...	...	...	...		...	...	...	...
3523 Soap, cleaning preps., perfumes, cosmetics		...	...	22	...		...	...	...	...		...	...	...	...
3529 Other chemical products		...	...	-	...		...	...	...	...		...	...	...	...
353 Petroleum refineries	c/	2	3	3	2	c/	542	567	560	563	c/	3853	4450	4855	5136

354	Misc. petroleum and coal products	c/	...	...	...	...	c/	...	...	...	...	c/	...	...	...	...
355	Rubber products		4	4	4	4		17383	15519	16625	17848		10508	11574	12223	13951
3551	Tyres and tubes		...	...	...	...		...	...	...	...		...	...	...	...
3559	Other rubber products		...	...	...	...		...	...	...	...		...	...	...	...
356	Plastic products		10	13	14	11		465	455	578	548		673	699	713	660
361	Pottery, china, earthenware		-	-	-	-		-	-	-	-		-	-	-	-
362	Glass and products		-	-	-	-		-	-	-	-		-	-	-	-
369	Other non-metallic mineral products		2	3	3	2		644	629	604	557		3437	3771	4113	4079
3691	Structural clay products		...	...	...	...		...	...	...	...		...	...	...	...
3692	Cement, lime and plaster		...	...	...	...		...	...	...	...		...	...	...	...
3699	Other non-metallic mineral products		...	...	...	...		...	...	...	...		...	...	...	...
371	Iron and steel		-	-	-	-		-	-	-	-		-	-	-	-
372	Non-ferrous metals		5	5	6	5		1311	1032	1011	1112		5821	6001	6590	6846
381	Fabricated metal products		9	11	14	7		376	491	523	368		798	1211	1619	1140
3811	Cutlery, hand tools and general hardware		...	...	...	...		...	...	...	...		...	...	...	...
3812	Furniture and fixtures primarily of metal		...	...	...	...		...	...	...	...		...	...	...	...
3813	Structural metal products		...	...	...	...		...	...	...	...		...	...	...	...
3819	Other fabricated metal products		...	...	...	...		...	...	...	...		...	...	...	...
382	Non-electrical machinery		-	-	-	-		-	-	-	-		-	-	-	-
3821	Engines and turbines		...	...	...	...		...	...	...	...		...	...	...	...
3822	Agricultural machinery and equipment		...	...	...	...		...	...	...	...		...	...	...	...
3823	Metal and wood working machinery		...	...	...	...		...	...	...	...		...	...	...	...
3824	Other special industrial machinery		...	...	...	...		...	...	...	...		...	...	...	...
3825	Office, computing and accounting machinery		...	...	...	...		...	...	...	...		...	...	...	...
3829	Other non-electrical machinery & equipment		...	...	...	...		...	...	...	...		...	...	...	...
383	Electrical machinery		5	3	2	2		670	588	442	444		1513	1551	1295	1197
3831	Electrical industrial machinery		...	...	...	...		...	...	...	...		...	...	...	...
3832	Radio, television and communication equipm.		...	...	...	...		...	...	...	...		...	...	...	...
3833	Electrical appliances and housewares		...	...	...	...		...	...	...	...		...	...	...	...
3839	Other electrical apparatus and supplies		1	...	1	...		...	...	...	...		...	...	...	...
384	Transport equipment		4	4	2	5		209	168	69	218		588	612	249	412
3841	Shipbuilding and repairing		...	...	...	...		...	...	...	...		...	...	...	...
3842	Railroad equipment		...	...	...	...		...	...	...	...		...	...	...	...
3843	Motor vehicles		...	...	...	...		...	...	...	...		...	...	...	...
3844	Motorcycles and bicycles		...	...	...	...		...	...	...	...		...	...	...	...
3845	Aircraft		...	...	...	...		...	...	...	...		...	...	...	...
3849	Other transport equipment		...	...	...	...		...	...	...	...		...	...	...	...
385	Professional and scientific equipment		-	-	-	-		-	-	-	-		-	-	-	-
3851	Prof. and scientific equipment n.e.c.		...	...	...	...		...	...	...	...		...	...	...	...
3852	Photographic and optical goods		...	...	...	...		...	...	...	...		...	...	...	...
3853	Watches and clocks		...	...	...	...		...	...	...	...		...	...	...	...
390	Other manufacturing industries		8	6	3	3		379	292	203	228		890	980	552	801
3901	Jewellery and related articles		...	...	...	...		...	...	...	...		...	...	...	...
3902	Musical instruments		...	...	...	...		...	...	...	...		...	...	...	...
3903	Sporting and athletic goods		...	...	...	...		...	...	...	...		...	...	...	...
3909	Manufacturing industries, n.e.c.		...	...	...	...		...	...	...	...		...	...	...	...
3	Total manufacturing		214	220	212	194		56712	51967	50863	53606		94027	92786	88077	93199

a/ Data are provisional.
b/ 323 includes 324.
c/ 353 includes 354.

ISIC Revision 2		Output in producers' prices					Value added in producers' prices					Gross fixed capital formation	
		(million CFA FRANCS)					(million CFA FRANCS)					(million CFA FRANCS)	
ISIC Industry	Note	1993	1994	1995	1996a/	Note	1993	1994	1995	1996a/	Note	1995	1996a/
311/2 Food products		81072	109709	139047	140409		17719	27747	54660	53181		10344	11730
3111 Slaughtering, preparing & preserving meat		...	...	...	...		...	...	...	...		...	...
3112 Dairy products		1803	836	848	1704		-95	-138	43	374		92	235
3113 Canning, preserving of fruits & vegetables		189	80	63	-		33	46	-4	-		112	-
3114 Canning, preserving and processing of fish		...	...	...	...		...	...	...	...		...	...
3115 Vegetable and animal oils and fats		21206	27451	33300	43785		5871	-1171	16754	19710		2885	6062
3116 Grain mill products		18315	29755	26538	17346		1047	4097	3672	2279		1766	1069
3117 Bakery products		4548	4714	4561	4177		1076	1303	874	894		489	578
3118 Sugar factories and refineries		15185	20812	40454	30552		1472	14800	25573	17332		3623	2587
3119 Cocoa, chocolate and sugar confectionery		8931	12057	20238	30085		3784	3262	4792	11306		703	818
3121 Other food products		7590	10555	10621	9864		4257	5000	2373	1185		599	275
3122 Prepared animal feeds		3305	3449	2424	2896		274	547	582	101		75	106
313 Beverages		103781	102651	96530	121821		39161	49314	33227	57509		3907	1472
3131 Distilling, rectifying and blending spirits		...	...	...	...		...	...	...	...		...	...
3132 Wine industries		...	...	...	...		...	...	...	...		...	...
3133 Malt liquors and malt		...	...	...	...		...	...	...	...		...	...
3134 Soft drinks and carbonated waters		...	...	...	...		...	...	...	...		...	...
314 Tobacco		23846	26610	29099	18650		7031	2645	6270	6308		7325	5923
321 Textiles		38323	61202	101009	106022		16259	20113	43373	28367		10258	10401
3211 Spinning, weaving and finishing textiles		...	...	...	...		...	...	...	...		...	...
3212 Made-up textile goods excl. wearing apparel		...	...	...	...		...	...	...	...		...	...
3213 Knitting mills		...	...	...	...		...	...	...	...		...	...
3214 Carpets and rugs		...	...	...	...		...	...	...	...		...	...
3215 Cordage, rope and twine		...	...	...	...		...	...	...	...		...	...
3219 Other textiles		...	...	...	...		...	...	...	...		...	...
322 Wearing apparel, except footwear		6204	2031	398	1952		1520	695	124	921		43	56
323 Leather and fur products	b/	669	1034	2186	111	b/	285	504	755	-7	b/	4	2
3231 Tanneries and leather finishing		...	...	...	...		...	...	...	...		...	...
3232 Fur dressing and dyeing industries		...	...	...	...		...	...	...	...		...	...
3233 Leather prods. excl. wearing apparel		...	...	...	...		...	...	...	...		...	...
324 Footwear, except rubber or plastic	b/	...	...	...	...	b/	...	...	...	...	b/	...	...
331 Wood products, except furniture		52755	103032	125381	116706		14050	44107	43773	35562		14083	15324
3311 Sawmills, planing and other wood mills		...	...	...	...		...	...	...	...		...	...
3312 Wooden and cane containers		...	...	...	...		...	...	...	...		...	...
3319 Other wood and cork products		...	...	...	...		...	...	...	...		...	...
332 Furniture and fixtures, excl. metal		314	251	413	404		52	53	178	141		21	35
341 Paper and products		14497	18698	27294	29020		3718	3652	4905	5231		1677	372
3411 Pulp, paper and paperboard articles		...	...	...	...		...	...	...	...		...	...
3412 Containers of paper and paperboard		...	...	...	...		...	...	...	...		...	...
3419 Other pulp, paper and paperboard articles		...	...	...	...		...	...	...	...		...	...
342 Printing and publishing		3410	3560	5441	6125		2088	1413	2775	1498		903	620
351 Industrial chemicals		-	-	-	-		-	-	-	-		-	-
3511 Basic chemicals excl. fertilizers		...	...	...	...		...	...	...	...		...	...
3512 Fertilizers and pesticides		...	...	...	...		...	...	...	...		...	...
3513 Synthetic resins and plastic materials		...	...	...	...		...	...	...	...		...	...
352 Other chemicals		29897	30254	39874	38202		10063	8559	12701	11432		2084	4171
3521 Paints, varnishes and lacquers		...	...	...	...		...	...	...	...		...	...
3522 Drugs and medicines		...	...	...	...		...	...	...	...		...	...
3523 Soap, cleaning preps., perfumes, cosmetics		...	...	...	...		...	...	...	...		...	...
3529 Other chemical products		...	...	...	...		...	...	...	...		...	...
353 Petroleum refineries	c/	71043	89386	136165	120976	c/	15615	17888	19954	6711	c/	1651	10534

354	Misc. petroleum and coal products	c/	...	...	...	...	c/	...	...	...	...	c/	...	...
355	Rubber products		28928	43064	63262	69573		13021	20796	29550	29382		21219	22519
3551	Tyres and tubes		...	...	...	...		...	...	...	...		...	...
3559	Other rubber products		...	...	...	...		...	...	...	...		...	...
356	Plastic products		3487	21667	5455	5254		1240	18843	1869	1678		388	1510
361	Pottery, china, earthenware		-	-	-	-		-	-	-	-		-	-
362	Glass and products		-	-	-	-		-	-	-	-		-	-
369	Other non-metallic mineral products		21167	21010	36149	29198		9727	6773	15403	8030		772	666
3691	Structural clay products		...	...	...	...		...	...	...	...		...	...
3692	Cement, lime and plaster		...	...	...	...		...	...	...	...		...	...
3699	Other non-metallic mineral products		...	...	...	...		...	...	...	...		...	...
371	Iron and steel		-	-	-	-		-	-	-	-		-	-
372	Non-ferrous metals		52157	66296	84672	95367		7049	29424	14733	20657		2264	2902
381	Fabricated metal products		3454	5288	7888	7131		844	1982	2819	1735		316	302
3811	Cutlery, hand tools and general hardware		...	...	...	...		...	...	...	...		...	...
3812	Furniture and fixtures primarily of metal		...	...	...	...		...	...	...	...		...	...
3813	Structural metal products		...	...	...	...		...	...	...	...		...	...
3819	Other fabricated metal products		...	...	...	...		...	...	...	...		...	...
382	Non-electrical machinery		-	-	-	-		-	-	-	-		-	-
3821	Engines and turbines		...	...	...	...		...	...	...	...		...	...
3822	Agricultural machinery and equipment		...	...	...	...		...	...	...	...		...	...
3823	Metal and wood working machinery		...	...	...	...		...	...	...	...		...	...
3824	Other special industrial machinery		...	...	...	...		...	...	...	...		...	...
3825	Office, computing and accounting machinery		...	...	...	...		...	...	...	...		...	...
3829	Other non-electrical machinery & equipment		...	...	...	...		...	...	...	...		...	...
383	Electrical machinery		7136	9490	7790	10500		1488	1804	1857	3092		266	112
3831	Electrical industrial machinery		...	...	...	...		...	...	...	...		...	...
3832	Radio, television and communication equipm.		...	...	...	...		...	...	...	...		...	...
3833	Electrical appliances and housewares		...	...	...	...		...	...	...	...		...	...
3839	Other electrical apparatus and supplies		...	...	...	...		...	...	...	...		...	...
384	Transport equipment		2763	3793	1852	2775		737	-137	55	126		30	682
3841	Shipbuilding and repairing		...	...	...	...		...	...	...	...		...	...
3842	Railroad equipment		...	...	...	...		...	...	...	...		...	...
3843	Motor vehicles		...	...	...	...		...	...	...	...		...	...
3844	Motorcycles and bicycles		...	...	...	...		...	...	...	...		...	...
3845	Aircraft		...	...	...	...		...	...	...	...		...	...
3849	Other transport equipment		...	...	...	...		...	...	...	...		...	...
385	Professional and scientific equipment		-	-	-	-		-	-	-	-		-	-
3851	Prof. and scientific equipment n.e.c.		...	...	...	...		...	...	...	...		...	...
3852	Photographic and optical goods		...	...	...	...		...	...	...	...		...	...
3853	Watches and clocks		...	...	...	...		...	...	...	...		...	...
390	Other manufacturing industries		5406	5816	5017	9563		2570	2702	2021	2866		178	316
3901	Jewellery and related articles		...	...	...	...		...	...	...	...		...	...
3902	Musical instruments		...	...	...	...		...	...	...	...		...	...
3903	Sporting and athletic goods		...	...	...	...		...	...	...	...		...	...
3909	Manufacturing industries, n.e.c.		...	...	...	...		...	...	...	...		...	...
3	Total manufacturing		550309	724842	914922	929759		164237	258876	291004	274420		77733	89649

a/ Data are provisional.
b/ 323 includes 324.
c/ 353 includes 354.

Cameroon

ISIC Revision 2		Index numbers of industrial production											
		(1990=100)											
ISIC Industry	Note	1985	1986	1987	1988	1989	1990	1991	1992	1993	1994	1995	1996
311/2 Food products		...	...	...	...	...	...	...	...	...	...	...	...
313 Beverages		...	...	...	...	...	...	...	...	...	...	...	...
314 Tobacco		...	...	...	...	...	...	...	...	...	...	...	...
321 Textiles		...	...	...	...	...	...	...	...	...	...	...	...
322 Wearing apparel, except footwear		...	...	...	...	...	...	...	...	...	...	...	...
323 Leather and fur products		...	...	...	...	...	...	...	...	...	...	...	...
324 Footwear, except rubber or plastic		...	...	...	...	...	...	...	...	...	...	...	...
331 Wood products, except furniture		...	...	...	...	...	...	...	...	...	...	...	...
332 Furniture and fixtures, excl. metal		...	...	...	...	...	...	...	...	...	...	...	...
341 Paper and products		...	...	...	...	...	...	...	...	...	...	...	...
342 Printing and publishing		...	...	...	...	...	...	...	...	...	...	...	...
351 Industrial chemicals		...	...	...	...	...	...	...	...	...	...	...	...
352 Other chemicals		...	...	...	...	...	...	...	...	...	...	...	...
353 Petroleum refineries		...	...	...	...	...	...	...	...	...	...	...	...
354 Misc. petroleum and coal products		...	...	...	...	...	...	...	...	...	...	...	...
355 Rubber products		...	...	...	...	...	...	...	...	...	...	...	...
356 Plastic products		...	...	...	...	...	...	...	...	...	...	...	...
361 Pottery, china, earthenware		...	...	...	...	...	...	...	...	...	...	...	...
362 Glass and products		...	...	...	...	...	...	...	...	...	...	...	...
369 Other non-metallic mineral products		...	...	...	...	...	...	...	...	...	...	...	...
371 Iron and steel		...	...	...	...	...	...	...	...	...	...	...	...
372 Non-ferrous metals		97	90	78	91	98	100	97	...	...	...	...	...
381 Fabricated metal products		...	...	...	...	...	...	...	...	...	...	...	...
382 Non-electrical machinery		...	...	...	...	...	...	...	...	...	...	...	...
383 Electrical machinery		...	...	...	...	...	...	...	...	...	...	...	...
384 Transport equipment		...	...	...	...	...	...	...	...	...	...	...	...
385 Professional and scientific equipment		...	...	...	...	...	...	...	...	...	...	...	...
390 Other manufacturing industries		...	...	...	...	...	...	...	...	...	...	...	...
3 Total manufacturing		...	...	...	...	...	...	...	...	...	...	...	...

CANADA

Supplier of information:
Statistics Canada, Ottawa.
Industrial statistics for the OECD countries are compiled by the OECD secretariat, which supplies them to UNIDO.

Basic source of data:
Census of manufactures.

Major deviations from ISIC (Revision 3):
None reported.

Reference period (if not calendar year):

Scope:
All establishments.

Method of enumeration:
Not reported.

Adjusted for non-response:
Not reported

Concepts and definitions of variables:
Number of employees refers to the average number of employees throughout the year, whether full-or part-time.
Wages and salaries includes: regular and overtime cash payments; bonuses and cost-of-living allowances; vacation and sick leave pay; taxes and social insurance contributions, etc. payable by employees and deduced by employers; payments in kind, and allowances.
Output is gross output including all products, work done on own account, manufacturing services rendered, goods shipped in the same condition as received, electricity sold, fixed assets produced for own use, goods made by homeworkers and handicraft workers if the establishment has a pay deduction number, and revenue from rental of own products, allowing for net changes of work in progress and in stocks of finished goods.
Value added is based on the census concept. It is calculated as gross output less the cost of materials, fuels and other supplies, goods shipped in the same condition as received and electricity purchased. It includes receipts for various non-industrial services, but does not include interest or rental other than on machinery produced and rented. The cost of non-industrial services is not deducted.

Related national publications:

Canada

ISIC Revision 3	Number of establishments					Number of employees					Wages and salaries paid to employees				
		(numbers)					(thousands)					(million DOLLARS)			
ISIC Industry	Note	1992	1993	1994	1995	Note	1992	1993	1994	1995a/	Note	1992	1993	1994	1995
151 Processed meat,fish,fruit,vegetables,fats		...	...	1189	1195		...	...	92	95		...	...	2567	2692
1511 Processing/preserving of meat		...	...	552	557		...	...	46	48		...	...	1383	1477
1512 Processing/preserving of fish		...	...	409	400		...	...	22	22		...	...	459	463
1513 Processing/preserving of fruit & vegetables		...	...	218	227		...	...	23	24		...	...	685	704
1514 Vegetable and animal oils and fats		...	...	10	11		...	...	1	1		...	...	40	48
1520 Dairy products		...	...	278	270		...	...	23	22		...	...	828	831
153 Grain mill products; starches; animal feeds		...	...	539	531		...	...	14	14		...	...	536	532
1531 Grain mill products		...	...	60	65		...	...	5	5		...	...	231	231
1532 Starches and starch products		...	...	...b/	...b/		...	...	...b/	...b/		...	...	...b/	...b/
1533 Prepared animal feeds		...	...	479	466		...	...	9	9		...	...	305	301
154 Other food products		...	...	943	961		...	...	60	59		...	...	1973	1948
1541 Bakery products		...	...	492	485		...	...	28	27		...	...	887	838
1542 Sugar		...	...	94	108		...	...	11	11		...	...	397	411
1543 Cocoa, chocolate and sugar confectionery		...	...	...	...		...	...	...	...		...	...	...	...
1544 Macaroni, noodles & similar products		...	...	29	38		...	...	2	2		...	...	49	46
1549 Other food products n.e.c.		...	...	328b/	330b/		...	...	19b/	19b/		...	...	640b/	653b/
155 Beverages		...	...	197	233		...	...	26	24		...	...	1182	1163
1551 Distilling, rectifying & blending of spirits		...	...	19	19		...	...	3	2		...	...	138	126
1552 Wines		...	...	30	35		...	...	1	1		...	...	42	42
1553 Malt liquors and malt		...	...	55	76		...	...	11	11		...	...	576	567
1554 Soft drinks; mineral waters		...	...	93	103		...	...	11	10		...	...	426	428
1600 Tobacco products		...	...	17	16		...	...	5	4		...	...	271	261
171 Spinning, weaving and finishing of textiles		...	...	227	251		...	...	15	16		...	...	437	472
1711 Textile fibre preparation; textile weaving		...	...	90	91		...	...	11	12		...	...	346	367
1712 Finishing of textiles		...	...	137	160		...	...	4	4		...	...	91	105
172 Other textiles		...	...	545	606		...	...	24	24		...	...	629	638
1721 Made-up textile articles, except apparel		...	...	447c/	504c/		...	...	15c/	15c/		...	...	340c/	350c/
1722 Carpets and rugs		...	...	27	28		...	...	4	4		...	...	125	123
1723 Cordage, rope, twine and netting		...	...	...c/	...c/		...	...	...c/	...c/		...	...	...c/	...c/
1729 Other textiles n.e.c.		...	...	71	74		...	...	5	5		...	...	164	165
1730 Knitted and crocheted fabrics and articles		...	...	146	148		...	...	11	11		...	...	264	270
1810 Wearing apparel, except fur apparel		...	...	1549	1524		...	...	72	71		...	...	1538	1553
1820 Dressing & dyeing of fur; processing of fur		...	...	125	117		...	...	1	1		...	...	16	18
191 Tanning, dressing and processing of leather		...	...	70	73		...	...	2	2		...	...	55	56
1911 Tanning and dressing of leather		...	...	18	21		...	...	1	1		...	...	28	29
1912 Luggage, handbags, etc.; saddlery & harness		...	...	52	52		...	...	1	1		...	...	27	27
1920 Footwear		...	...	146	156		...	...	11	10		...	...	243	224
2010 Sawmilling and planing of wood		...	...	837	883		...	...	62	63		...	...	2405	2541
202 Products of wood, cork, straw, etc.		...	...	1352	1330		...	...	44	46		...	...	1439	1495
2021 Veneer sheets, plywood, particle board, etc.		...	...	117	121		...	...	13	14		...	...	540	589
2022 Builders' carpentry and joinery		...	...	828	792		...	...	25	24		...	...	716	697
2023 Wooden containers		...	...	159	160		...	...	2	3		...	...	63	69
2029 Other wood products; articles of cork/straw		...	...	248	257		...	...	4	5		...	...	120	140
210 Paper and paper products		...	...	649	668		...	...	100	103		...	...	4691	4987
2101 Pulp, paper and paperboard		...	...	209	219		...	...	71	72		...	...	3619	3856
2102 Corrugated paper and paperboard		...	...	244	245		...	...	18	20		...	...	688	749
2109 Other articles of paper and paperboard		...	...	196	204		...	...	11	11		...	...	384	382
221 Publishing		...	...	1300	1269		...	...	50	50		...	...	1975	2000
2211 Publishing of books and other publications		...	...	177	173		...	...	6	6		...	...	247	255
2212 Publishing of newspapers, journals, etc.		...	...	1073	1051		...	...	42	43		...	...	1676	1699
2213 Publishing of recorded media		...	...	...d/	...d/		...	...	...d/	...d/		...	...	...d/	...d/
2219 Other publishing		...	...	50	45		...	...	2	1		...	...	52	46

222 Printing and related service activities	...	...	3172	3153	...	...	72	74	...	...	2501	2600
2221 Printing	...	...	2469	2464	...	...	58	60	...	...	2035	2133
2222 Service activities related to printing	...	...	703	689	...	...	14	14	...	...	466	467
2230 Reproduction of recorded media	...	...	42d/	46d/	...	...	3d/	4d/	...	...	92d/	126d/
2310 Coke oven products	...	...	...e/	...e/	...	...	...e/	...e/	...	...	...e/	...e/
2320 Refined petroleum products	...	...	61	64	...	...	12	11	...	...	690	653
2330 Processing of nuclear fuel	...	...	...f/	...	...	...	...f/	...	...	...	...f/	...
241 Basic chemicals	...	...	434	450	...	...	27	27	...	...	1464	1447
2411 Basic chemicals, except fertilizers	...	...	211f/	216	...	...	15f/	15	...	...	852f/	863
2412 Fertilizers and nitrogen compounds	...	...	134	138	...	...	3	4	...	...	157	168
2413 Plastics in primary forms; synthetic rubber	...	...	89	96	...	...	9	8	...	...	455	416
242 Other chemicals	...	...	971	982	...	...	65	66	...	...	2647	2661
2421 Pesticides and other agro-chemical products	...	...	10	11	...	...	1	1	...	...	25	29
2422 Paints, varnishes, printing ink and mastics	...	...	188	180	...	...	9	9	...	...	343	338
2423 Pharmaceuticals, medicinal chemicals, etc.	...	...	112	119	...	...	20	20	...	...	938	950
2424 Soap, cleaning & cosmetic preparations	...	...	189	187	...	...	15	14	...	...	553	534
2429 Other chemical products n.e.c.	...	...	472g/	485g/	...	...	20g/	22g/	...	...	788g/	810g/
2430 Man-made fibres	...	...	24	27	...	...	5	5	...	...	194	211
251 Rubber products	...	...	175	200	...	...	24	24	...	...	903	974
2511 Rubber tyres and tubes	...	...	14	13	...	...	10	9	...	...	420	422
2519 Other rubber products	...	...	161	187	...	...	14	15	...	...	483	552
2520 Plastic products	...	...	1132	1274	...	...	53	56	...	...	1547	1707
2610 Glass and glass products	...	...	182	191	...	...	12	12	...	...	426	440
269 Non-metallic mineral products n.e.c.	...	...	1459	1472	...	...	34	35	...	...	1190	1259
2691 Pottery, china and earthenware	...	...	31	33	...	...	1	1	...	...	25	27
2692 Refractory ceramic products	...	...	29	30	...	...	2	2	...	...	55	74
2693 Struct.non-refractory clay; ceramic products	...	...	17	18	...	...	1	1	...	...	31	36
2694 Cement, lime and plaster	...	...	33	31	...	...	4	4	...	...	179	186
2695 Articles of concrete, cement and plaster	...	...	1050	1059	...	...	20	20	...	...	678	706
2696 Cutting, shaping & finishing of stone	...	...	145	145	...	...	2	3	...	...	78	79
2699 Other non-metallic mineral products n.e.c.	...	...	154e/	156e/	...	...	4e/	4e/	...	...	144e/	151e/
2710 Basic iron and steel	...	...	121	123	...	...	39	39	...	...	1971	2062
2720 Basic precious and non-ferrous metals	...	...	140h/	144h/	...	...	32h/	34h/	...	...	1605h/	1727h/
273 Casting of metals	...	...	186	189	...	...	15	17	...	...	633	673
2731 Casting of iron and steel	...	...	98	96	...	...	10	11	...	...	424	427
2732 Casting of non-ferrous metals	...	...	88	93	...	...	5	6	...	...	209	246
281 Struct.metal products;tanks;steam generators	...	...	1672	1656	...	...	49	52	...	...	1631	1790
2811 Structural metal products	...	...	1549	1533	...	...	40	43	...	...	1292	1439
2812 Tanks, reservoirs and containers of metal	...	...	85	86	...	...	4	4	...	...	134	150
2813 Steam generators	...	...	38	37	...	...	5	5	...	...	205	201
289 Other metal products; metal working services	...	...	3134	3157	...	...	81	88	...	...	2713	3030
2891 Metal forging/pressing/stamping/roll-forming	...	...	...h/	...h/	...	...	...h/	...h/	...	...	...h/	...h/
2892 Treatment & coating of metals	...	...	1651	1665	...	...	31	35	...	...	983	1141
2893 Cutlery, hand tools and general hardware	...	...	728	731	...	...	22	23	...	...	785	874
2899 Other fabricated metal products n.e.c.	...	...	755	761	...	...	28	30	...	...	945	1015
291 General purpose machinery	...	...	900	937	...	...	41	44	...	...	1517	1704
2911 Engines & turbines(not for transport equip.)	...	...	123	122	...	...	8	8	...	...	330	326
2912 Pumps, compressors, taps and valves	...	...	173	184	...	...	8	8	...	...	292	312
2913 Bearings, gears, gearing & driving elements	...	...	...i/	...i/	...	...	...i/	...i/	...	...	...i/	...i/
2914 Ovens, furnaces and furnace burners	...	...	...j/	...j/	...	...	...j/	...j/	...	...	...j/	...j/
2915 Lifting and handling equipment	...	...	505k/	530k/	...	...	21k/	24k/	...	...	765k/	917k/
2919 Other general purpose machinery	...	...	99	101	...	...	4	4	...	...	130	149
292 Special purpose machinery	...	...	971	1018	...	...	43	49	...	...	1554	1839
2921 Agricultural and forestry machinery	...	...	196	201	...	...	10	10	...	...	307	331
2922 Machine tools	...	...	49	56	...	...	3	3	...	...	97	126
2923 Machinery for metallurgy	...	...	...i/	...i/	...	...	...i/	...i/	...	...	...i/	...i/
2924 Machinery for mining & construction	...	...	...k/	...k/	...	...	...k/	...k/	...	...	...k/	...k/
2925 Food/beverage/tobacco processing machinery	...	...	...i/	...i/	...	...	...i/	...i/	...	...	...i/	...i/
2926 Machinery for textile, apparel and leather	...	...	...i/	...i/	...	...	...i/	...i/	...	...	...i/	...i/
2927 Weapons and ammunition	...	...	...	...	...	...	...	...	...	...	...	...
2929 Other special purpose machinery	...	...	726i/	761i/	...	...	30i/	36i/	...	...	1150i/	1382i/
2930 Domestic appliances n.e.c.	...	...	186j/	193j/	...	...	15j/	14j/	...	...	482j/	441j/

continued

Canada

ISIC Revision 3 ISIC Industry	Number of establishments Note	(numbers) 1992	1993	1994	1995	Number of employees Note	(thousands) 1992	1993	1994	1995a/	Wages and salaries paid to employees Note	(million DOLLARS) 1992	1993	1994	1995
3000 Office, accounting and computing machinery		...	...	147	157		...	...	15	15		...	...	599	631
3110 Electric motors, generators and transformers		...	...	168	186		...	...	11	11		...	...	418	428
3120 Electricity distribution & control apparatus		...	...	136	132		...	...	8	8		...	...	292	300
3130 Insulated wire and cable		...	...	58	59		...	...	7	7		...	...	288	296
3140 Accumulators, primary cells and batteries		...	...	16	20		...	...	1	1		...	...	47	43
3150 Lighting equipment and electric lamps		...	...	150	151		...	...	5	6		...	...	162	174
3190 Other electrical equipment n.e.c.		...	...	95	109		...	...	10	10		...	...	309	344
3210 Electronic valves, tubes, etc.		...	...	209	239		...	...	14	18		...	...	456	560
3220 TV/radio transmitters; line comm. apparatus		...	...	249m/	272		...	...	38m/	39m/		...	...	1727m/	1747m/
3230 TV and radio receivers and associated goods		...	...	16	17		...	...	2	1		...	...	46	33
331 Medical, measuring, testing appliances, etc.		...	...	216	212		...	...	9	10		...	...	343	381
3311 Medical, surgical and orthopaedic equipment		...	...	...g/	...g/		...	...	...g/	...g/		...	...	...g/	...g/
3312 Measuring/testing/navigating appliances,etc.		...	...	216	212		...	...	9	10		...	...	343	381
3313 Industrial process control equipment		...	...	...m/	...		...	...	...m/	...m/		...	...	...m/	...m/
3320 Optical instruments & photographic equipment		...	...	139	127		...	...	3	2		...	...	73	49
3330 Watches and clocks		...	...	15	13		...	...	...	...		...	...	9	7
3410 Motor vehicles		...	...	86n/	93n/		...	...	64n/	65n/		...	...	3503n/	3605n/
3420 Automobile bodies, trailers & semi-trailers		...	...	279	292		...	...	12	14		...	...	382	449
3430 Parts/accessories for automobiles		...	...	473	488		...	...	73	79		...	...	2767	3086
351 Building and repairing of ships and boats		...	...	240	276		...	...	10	11		...	...	419	397
3511 Building and repairing of ships		...	...	44	49		...	...	7	7		...	...	327	285
3512 Building/repairing of pleasure/sport. boats		...	...	196	227		...	...	3	4		...	...	92	112
3520 Railway/tramway locomotives & rolling stock		...	...	21	18		...	...	8	8		...	...	370	386
3530 Aircraft and spacecraft		...	...	177	193		...	...	36	39		...	...	1649	1873
359 Transport equipment n.e.c.		...	...	...	...		...	...	...	-		...	...	...	...
3591 Motorcycles		...	...	...n/	...n/		...	...	...n/	...n/		...	...	...n/	...n/
3592 Bicycles and invalid carriages		...	...	...p/	...p/		...	...	...p/	...p/		...	...	...p/	...p/
3599 Other transport equipment n.e.c.		...	...	...	...		...	...	...	...		...	...	...	...
3610 Furniture		...	...	1927	2016		...	...	65	67		...	...	1831	1940
369 Manufacturing n.e.c.		...	...	2086	2141		...	...	43	43		...	...	1147	1178
3691 Jewellery and related articles		...	...	288	291		...	...	5	5		...	...	125	120
3692 Musical instruments		...	...	...d/	...d/		...	...	...d/	...d/		...	...	...d/	...d/
3693 Sports goods		...	...	180p/	186p/		...	...	9p/	9p/		...	...	224p/	224p/
3694 Games and toys		...	...	43	51		...	...	2	3		...	...	43	62
3699 Other manufacturing n.e.c.		...	...	1575	1613		...	...	27	26		...	...	755	772
3710 Recycling of metal waste and scrap		...	...	...	...		...	...	...	...		...	...	...	...
3720 Recycling of non-metal waste and scrap		...	...	...	...		...	...	...	...		...	...	...	...
D Total manufacturing		...	...	31974	32718		...	...	1670	1715		...	...	61638	64936

a/ Number of persons engaged.
b/ 1549 includes 1532.
c/ 1721 includes 1723.
d/ 2230 includes 2213 and 3692.
e/ 2699 includes 2310.
f/ 2411 includes 2330.
g/ 2429 includes 3311.
h/ 2720 includes 2891.
i/ 2929 includes 2913, 2923, 2925 and 2926.
j/ 2930 includes 2914.
k/ 2915 includes 2924.
m/ 3220 includes 3313.
n/ 3410 includes 3591.
p/ 3693 includes 3592.

Canada

ISIC Revision 3		Output in producers' prices					Value added in producers' prices					Gross fixed capital formation		
			(million DOLLARS)					(million DOLLARS)					(thousand DOLLARS)	
ISIC	Industry	Note	1992	1993	1994	1995	Note	1992	1993	1994	1995	Note	1994	1995
151	Processed meat,fish,fruit,vegetables,fats		...	...	23580	24390		...	...	6930	6930		...	...
1511	Processing/preserving of meat		...	...	12910	13050		...	...	2850	2920		...	...
1512	Processing/preserving of fish		...	...	3970	4020		...	...	1210	1080		...	...
1513	Processing/preserving of fruit & vegetables		...	...	5060	5290		...	...	2540	2580		...	...
1514	Vegetable and animal oils and fats		...	...	1640	2030		...	...	330	350		...	...
1520	Dairy products		...	...	8960	9420		...	...	2300	2200		...	...
153	Grain mill products; starches; animal feeds		...	...	5630	6070		...	...	1670	1770		...	...
1531	Grain mill products		...	...	2010	2160		...	...	820	920		...	...
1532	Starches and starch products		...	...	...a/	...a/		...	...	...a/	...a/		...	...
1533	Prepared animal feeds		...	...	3620	3910		...	...	850	850		...	...
154	Other food products		...	...	12890	13420		...	...	5840	5820		...	...
1541	Bakery products		...	...	4100	3960		...	...	2190	2060		...	...
1542	Sugar		...	...	2580	2770		...	...	1100	1110		...	...
1543	Cocoa, chocolate and sugar confectionery		...	...	...	...		...	...	...	...		...	...
1544	Macaroni, noodles & similar products		...	...	400	410		...	...	200	180		...	...
1549	Other food products n.e.c.		...	...	5810a/	6280a/		...	...	2350a/	2470a/		...	...
155	Beverages		...	...	7290	8200		...	...	4290	4280		...	...
1551	Distilling, rectifying & blending of spirits		...	...	890	880		...	...	600	580		...	...
1552	Wines		...	...	310	320		...	...	170	150		...	...
1553	Malt liquors and malt		...	...	3640	4510		...	...	2640	2800		...	...
1554	Soft drinks; mineral waters		...	...	2450	2490		...	...	880	750		...	...
1600	Tobacco products		...	...	3870	3880		...	...	1630	1660		...	...
171	Spinning, weaving and finishing of textiles		...	...	1800	1990		...	...	850	930		...	...
1711	Textile fibre preparation; textile weaving		...	...	1520	1690		...	...	700	770		...	...
1712	Finishing of textiles		...	...	280	300		...	...	150	160		...	...
172	Other textiles		...	...	3140	3280		...	...	1370	1380		...	...
1721	Made-up textile articles, except apparel		...	...	1420b/	1540b/		...	...	680b/	720b/		...	...
1722	Carpets and rugs		...	...	890	880		...	...	260	260		...	...
1723	Cordage, rope, twine and netting		...	...	...b/	...b/		...	...	...b/	...b/		...	...
1729	Other textiles n.e.c.		...	...	830	860		...	...	430	400		...	...
1730	Knitted and crocheted fabrics and articles		...	...	1130	1170		...	...	520	520		...	...
1810	Wearing apparel, except fur apparel		...	...	6280	6500		...	...	2910	3080		...	...
1820	Dressing & dyeing of fur; processing of fur		...	...	90	90		...	...	40	40		...	...
191	Tanning, dressing and processing of leather		...	...	270	280		...	...	110	110		...	...
1911	Tanning and dressing of leather		...	...	180	190		...	...	60	60		...	...
1912	Luggage, handbags, etc.; saddlery & harness		...	...	90	90		...	...	50	50		...	...
1920	Footwear		...	...	930	880		...	...	440	400		...	...
2010	Sawmilling and planing of wood		...	...	15500	15350		...	...	6360	5220		...	...
202	Products of wood, cork, straw, etc.		...	...	7650	7800		...	...	3360	3270		...	...
2021	Veneer sheets, plywood, particle board, etc.		...	...	3330	3540		...	...	1730	1670		...	...
2022	Builders' carpentry and joinery		...	...	3300	3110		...	...	1280	1190		...	...
2023	Wooden containers		...	...	290	320		...	...	110	120		...	...
2029	Other wood products; articles of cork/straw		...	...	730	830		...	...	240	290		...	...
210	Paper and paper products		...	...	26740	39070		...	...	10790	18160		...	...
2101	Pulp, paper and paperboard		...	...	21320	32130		...	...	8700	15660		...	...
2102	Corrugated paper and paperboard		...	...	3350	4130		...	...	1270	1460		...	...
2109	Other articles of paper and paperboard		...	...	2070	2810		...	...	820	1040		...	...
221	Publishing		...	...	6240	6550		...	...	4440	4560		...	...
2211	Publishing of books and other publications		...	...	1390	1400		...	...	890	900		...	...
2212	Publishing of newspapers, journals, etc.		...	...	4680	4980		...	...	3450	3560		...	...
2213	Publishing of recorded media		...	...	...c/	...c/		...	...	...c/	...c/		...	...
2219	Other publishing		...	...	170	170		...	...	100	100		...	...

continued

Canada

ISIC Revision 3		Output in producers' prices					Value added in producers' prices					Gross fixed capital formation		
			(million DOLLARS)					(million DOLLARS)					(thousand DOLLARS)	
ISIC	Industry	Note	1992	1993	1994	1995	Note	1992	1993	1994	1995	Note	1994	1995
222	Printing and related service activities		...	...	8000	8900		...	...	4520	4770		...	...
2221	Printing		...	...	6850	7730		...	...	3730	3990		...	...
2222	Service activities related to printing		...	...	1150	1170		...	...	790	780		...	...
2230	Reproduction of recorded media		...	...	460c/	610c/		...	...	310c/	410c/		...	...
2310	Coke oven products		...	...	...d/	...d/		...	...	...d/	...d/		...	...
2320	Refined petroleum products		...	...	17900	18170		...	...	2620	2740		...	...
2330	Processing of nuclear fuel		...	...	...e/	...		...	...	...e/	...		...	...
241	Basic chemicals		...	...	16480	18250		...	...	6450	8310		...	...
2411	Basic chemicals, except fertilizers		...	...	9120e/	10210		...	...	4140e/	5140		...	...
2412	Fertilizers and nitrogen compounds		...	...	1730	2230		...	...	620	1080		...	...
2413	Plastics in primary forms; synthetic rubber		...	...	5630	5810		...	...	1690	2090		...	...
242	Other chemicals		...	...	16300	17640		...	...	8290	8870		...	...
2421	Pesticides and other agro-chemical products		...	...	360	380		...	...	180	140		...	...
2422	Paints, varnishes, printing ink and mastics		...	...	2450	2440		...	...	1040	990		...	...
2423	Pharmaceuticals, medicinal chemicals, etc.		...	...	5630	5820		...	...	3250	3350		...	...
2424	Soap, cleaning & cosmetic preparations		...	...	3370	3820		...	...	1790	2080		...	...
2429	Other chemical products n.e.c.		...	...	4490f/	5180f/		...	...	2030f/	2310f/		...	...
2430	Man-made fibres		...	...	1310	1840		...	...	570	640		...	...
251	Rubber products		...	...	6880	7570		...	...	2370	2350		...	...
2511	Rubber tyres and tubes		...	...	4570	4890		...	...	1190	1010		...	...
2519	Other rubber products		...	...	2310	2680		...	...	1180	1340		...	...
2520	Plastic products		...	...	7930	8880		...	...	3520	3820		...	...
2610	Glass and glass products		...	...	2110	2260		...	...	1110	1210		...	...
269	Non-metallic mineral products n.e.c.		...	...	6120	6510		...	...	2890	3140		...	...
2691	Pottery, china and earthenware		...	...	100	90		...	...	50	50		...	...
2692	Refractory ceramic products		...	...	260	360		...	...	120	180		...	...
2693	Struct.non-refractory clay; ceramic products		...	...	110	100		...	...	70	60		...	...
2694	Cement, lime and plaster		...	...	1110	1180		...	...	640	700		...	...
2695	Articles of concrete, cement and plaster		...	...	3090	3180		...	...	1350	1400		...	...
2696	Cutting, shaping & finishing of stone		...	...	290	300		...	...	170	180		...	...
2699	Other non-metallic mineral products n.e.c.		...	...	1160d/	1300d/		...	...	490d/	570d/		...	...
2710	Basic iron and steel		...	...	12280	13560		...	...	4400	5160		...	...
2720	Basic precious and non-ferrous metals		...	...	9950g/	12240g/		...	...	4050g/	5130g/		...	...
273	Casting of metals		...	...	2400	2770		...	...	1230	1410		...	...
2731	Casting of iron and steel		...	...	1390	1520		...	...	780	860		...	...
2732	Casting of non-ferrous metals		...	...	1010	1250		...	...	450	550		...	...
281	Struct.metal products;tanks;steam generators		...	...	7360	8330		...	...	3120	3790		...	...
2811	Structural metal products		...	...	5820	6750		...	...	2450	2890		...	...
2812	Tanks, reservoirs and containers of metal		...	...	470	520		...	...	220	270		...	...
2813	Steam generators		...	...	1070	1060		...	...	450	630		...	...
289	Other metal products; metal working services		...	...	10100	11470		...	...	5260	5840		...	...
2891	Metal forging/pressing/stamping/roll-forming		...	...	...g/	...g/		...	...	...g/	...g/		...	...
2892	Treatment & coating of metals		...	...	3110	3640		...	...	1850	2130		...	...
2893	Cutlery, hand tools and general hardware		...	...	2410	2670		...	...	1490	1650		...	...
2899	Other fabricated metal products n.e.c.		...	...	4580	5160		...	...	1920	2060		...	...
291	General purpose machinery		...	...	7270	8340		...	...	3300	3870		...	...
2911	Engines & turbines(not for transport equip.)		...	...	1370	1410		...	...	710	770		...	...
2912	Pumps, compressors, taps and valves		...	...	1610	1670		...	...	660	750		...	...
2913	Bearings, gears, gearing & driving elements		...	...	...h/	...h/		...	...	...h/	...h/		...	...
2914	Ovens, furnaces and furnace burners		...	...	...i/	...i/		...	...	...i/	...i/		...	...
2915	Lifting and handling equipment		...	...	3710j/	4600j/		...	...	1660j/	2020j/		...	...
2919	Other general purpose machinery		...	...	580	660		...	...	270	330		...	...

292 Special purpose machinery	...	...	7230	8950	...	...	3430	4290	...	...
2921 Agricultural and forestry machinery	...	...	1760	2020	...	...	770	890	...	...
2922 Machine tools	...	...	420	470	...	...	230	260	...	...
2923 Machinery for metallurgy	...	...	...h/	...h/	...	...	...h/	...h/	...	...
2924 Machinery for mining & construction	...	...	...j/	...j/	...	...	...j/	...j/	...	...
2925 Food/beverage/tobacco processing machinery	...	...	...h/	...h/	...	...	...h/	...h/	...	...
2926 Machinery for textile, apparel and leather	...	...	...h/	...h/	...	...	...h/	...h/	...	...
2927 Weapons and ammunition	...	...	...	...	...	...	...	...	...	...
2929 Other special purpose machinery	...	...	5050h/	6460h/	...	...	2430h/	3140h/	...	...
2930 Domestic appliances n.e.c.	...	...	2500i/	2480i/	...	...	1020i/	1000i/	...	...
3000 Office, accounting and computing machinery	...	...	5990	7930	...	...	1280	1170	...	...
3110 Electric motors, generators and transformers	...	...	1580	1810	...	...	760	790	...	...
3120 Electricity distribution & control apparatus	...	...	1340	1390	...	...	700	670	...	...
3130 Insulated wire and cable	...	...	1890	2030	...	...	740	710	...	...
3140 Accumulators, primary cells and batteries	...	...	340	350	...	...	180	170	...	...
3150 Lighting equipment and electric lamps	...	...	910	990	...	...	390	390	...	...
3190 Other electrical equipment n.e.c.	...	...	1850	1960	...	...	880	830	...	...
3210 Electronic valves, tubes, etc.	...	...	3930	5000	...	...	1120	1540	...	...
3220 TV/radio transmitters; line comm. apparatus	...	...	7710k/	9140k/	...	...	4220k/	5140k/	...	...
3230 TV and radio receivers and associated goods	...	...	840	820	...	...	160	140	...	...
331 Medical, measuring, testing appliances, etc.	...	...	1400	1510	...	...	810	840	...	...
3311 Medical, surgical and orthopaedic equipment	...	...	...f/	...f/	...	...	...f/	...f/	...	...
3312 Measuring/testing/navigating appliances,etc.	...	...	1400	1510	...	...	810	840	...	...
3313 Industrial process control equipment	...	...	...k/	...k/	...	...	...k/	...k/	...	...
3320 Optical instruments & photographic equipment	...	...	290	200	...	...	150	90	...	...
3330 Watches and clocks	...	...	40	30	...	...	20	10	...	...
3410 Motor vehicles	...	...	77580m/	81740m/	...	...	11810m/	13710m/	...	...
3420 Automobile bodies, trailers & semi-trailers	...	...	1700	2070	...	...	690	800	...	...
3430 Parts/accessories for automobiles	...	...	14700	16240	...	...	6230	6720	...	...
351 Building and repairing of ships and boats	...	...	1300	1460	...	...	780	910	...	...
3511 Building and repairing of ships	...	...	960	970	...	...	610	690	...	...
3512 Building/repairing of pleasure/sport. boats	...	...	340	490	...	...	170	220	...	...
3520 Railway/tramway locomotives & rolling stock	...	...	2310	2520	...	...	930	940	...	...
3530 Aircraft and spacecraft	...	...	5930	7610	...	...	3530	4340	...	...
359 Transport equipment n.e.c.	...	...	...	...	...	...	...	...	...	...
3591 Motorcycles	...	...	...m/	...m/	...	...	...m/	...m/	...	...
3592 Bicycles and invalid carriages	...	...	...n/	...n/	...	...	...n/	...n/	...	...
3599 Other transport equipment n.e.c.	...	...	...	...	...	...	...	...	...	...
3610 Furniture	...	...	7830	8430	...	...	3660	4000	...	...
369 Manufacturing n.e.c.	...	...	4570	4800	...	...	2420	2560	...	...
3691 Jewellery and related articles	...	...	540	480	...	...	260	220	...	...
3692 Musical instruments	...	...	...c/	...c/	...	...	...c/	...c/	...	...
3693 Sports goods	...	...	1220n/	1280n/	...	...	570n/	630n/	...	...
3694 Games and toys	...	...	360	520	...	...	170	270	...	...
3699 Other manufacturing n.e.c.	...	...	2450	2520	...	...	1420	1440	...	...
3710 Recycling of metal waste and scrap	...	...	...	...	...	...	...	...	...	...
3720 Recycling of non-metal waste and scrap	...	...	...	...	...	...	...	...	...	...
D Total manufacturing	...	...	418630	465170	...	...	153790	173560	...	...

a/ 1549 includes 1532.
b/ 1721 includes 1723.
c/ 2230 includes 2213 and 3692.
d/ 2699 includes 2310.
e/ 2411 includes 2330.
f/ 2429 includes 3311.
g/ 2720 includes 2891.
h/ 2929 includes 2913, 2923, 2925 and 2926.
i/ 2930 includes 2914.
j/ 2915 includes 2924.
k/ 3220 includes 3313.
m/ 3410 includes 3591.
n/ 3693 includes 3592.

Canada

ISIC Revision 3		Index numbers of industrial production											
		(1990=100)											
ISIC Industry	Note	1985	1986	1987	1988	1989	1990	1991	1992	1993	1994	1995	1996
15 Food and beverages		...	...	...	...	...	100	101	103	104	108	109	112
16 Tobacco products		...	...	...	...	...	100	96	88	84	96	89	88
17 Textiles		...	...	...	...	...	100	91	84	88	93	96	96
18 Wearing apparel, fur		...	...	...	...	...	100	89	87	87	88	92	85
19 Leather, leather products and footwear		...	...	...	...	...	100	79	79	80	82	72	66
20 Wood products (excl. furniture)		...	...	...	...	...	100	88	92	99	103	102	107
21 Paper and paper products		...	...	...	...	...	100	94	97	104	110	112	111
22 Printing and publishing		...	...	...	...	...	100	86	81	79	78	78	76
23 Coke,refined petroleum products,nuclear fuel		...	...	...	...	...	100	97	97	102	104	105	111
24 Chemicals and chemical products		...	...	...	...	...	100	92	95	102	107	111	112
25 Rubber and plastics products		...	...	...	...	...	100	94	103	116	126	134	140
26 Non-metallic mineral products		...	...	...	...	...	100	83	80	81	85	87	89
27 Basic metals		...	...	...	...	...	100	99	103	117	120	123	127
28 Fabricated metal products		...	...	...	...	...	100	88	82	85	95	101	102
29 Machinery and equipment n.e.c.		...	...	...	...	...	100	82	77	90	104	118	115
30 Office, accounting and computing machinery		...	...	...	...	...	100	117	131	157	227	320	278
31 Electrical machinery and apparatus		...	...	...	...	...	100	85	79	80	81	83	84
32 Radio,television and communication equipment		...	...	...	...	...	100	98	106	100	109	131	135
33 Medical, precision and optical instruments		...	...	...	...	...	100	107	105	104	107	114	118
34 Motor vehicles, trailers, semi-trailers		...	...	...	...	...	100	91	95	118	131	141	142
35 Other transport equipment		...	...	...	...	...	100	88	89	85	87	91	95
36 Furniture; manufacturing n.e.c.		...	...	...	...	...	100	89	88	93	103	108	112
37 Recycling		...	...	...	...	...	...	...	...	...	...	...	...
D Total manufacturing		...	...	...	...	...	100	93	94	99	106	111	112

CHILE

Supplier of information:
Instituto Nacional de Estadísticas, Santiago.

Basic source of data:
Annual industrial survey.

Major deviations from ISIC (Revision 2):
None reported.

Reference period (if not calendar year):

Scope:
Establishments with 50 or more persons engaged. The index numbers of industrial production cover, in principle, all establishments employing 10 or more persons.

Method of enumeration:
Not reported.

Adjusted for non-response:
No.

Concepts and definitions of variables:
Number of employees is the average of the numbers for the months of February, May, August and November.
Output includes gross revenues from goods shipped in the same condition as received.

Related national publications:
Industrias Manufactureras (annual), published by the Instituto Nacional de Estadísticas, Santiago.

Chile

ISIC Revision 2	Number of establishments					Number of employees					Wages and salaries paid to employees				
		(numbers)					(numbers)					(million PESOS)			
ISIC Industry	Note	1992	1993	1994	1995	Note	1992	1993	1994	1995	Note	1992	1993	1994	1995
311/2 Food products		424	426	419	457		84603	83365	86253	91404		157924	183624	224559	265975
3111 Slaughtering, preparing & preserving meat		51	50	50	52		9894	10604	11248	11348		18984	23213	29631	33896
3112 Dairy products		33	34	35	36		8301	8441	8513	9273		18660	22133	28232	35007
3113 Canning, preserving of fruits & vegetables		52	55	59	63		16044	13999	15472	14501		19115	23085	26502	30755
3114 Canning, preserving and processing of fish		110	107	96	118		18689	19069	19068	23377		27968	32334	37088	49224
3115 Vegetable and animal oils and fats		50	46	49	44		10185	8031	8004	7604		27551	24354	31066	32765
3116 Grain mill products		23	23	21	27		1887	1779	1635	2192		4630	5361	5801	8018
3117 Bakery products		58	61	54	58		7479	7669	7554	8427		11069	13995	15696	20830
3118 Sugar factories and refineries		5	5	4	4		2073	1941	1607	1571		5091	5716	5550	6800
3119 Cocoa, chocolate and sugar confectionery		10	11	11	12		4564	4889	4530	4332		9854	11670	13507	15213
3121 Other food products		23	26	32	33		4394	5873	7109	7101		12742	18788	26848	27594
3122 Prepared animal feeds		9	8	8	10		1093	1070	1513	1678		2260	2975	4638	5873
313 Beverages		51	50	48	46		11635	11750	11308	11225		30720	36029	38205	45823
3131 Distilling, rectifying and blending spirits		4	5	4	4		1081	1234	1180	1326		2803	3751	4148	5634
3132 Wine industries		19	21	20	21		3877	4262	4092	4073		6666	8786	10143	12955
3133 Malt liquors and malt		8	8	8	7		2014	1817	1657	1403		6086	5733	5987	5677
3134 Soft drinks and carbonated waters		20	16	16	14		4663	4437	4379	4423		15165	17759	17927	21557
314 Tobacco		3	3	2	2		679	719	722	583		3022	4309	4614	4175
321 Textiles		135	137	131	131		25976	24544	22382	21560		44205	50311	55402	59311
3211 Spinning, weaving and finishing textiles		64	59	61	65		17879	15592	14265	13806		32276	34330	37649	39511
3212 Made-up textile goods excl. wearing apparel		8	14	13	10		768	1251	1187	900		1154	2089	2285	2066
3213 Knitting mills		55	58	51	51		6714	7235	6465	6481		9744	12793	14141	16476
3214 Carpets and rugs		3	1	1	1		253	92	81	90		464	271	317	373
3215 Cordage, rope and twine		2	2	2	1		134	156	167	82		240	370	490	307
3219 Other textiles		3	3	3	3		228	218	217	201		327	458	520	578
322 Wearing apparel, except footwear		120	121	118	106		19349	18887	19155	18053		27998	32692	43979	44616
323 Leather and fur products		18	21	20	18		2017	2568	2554	2178		3801	5919	6493	6488
3231 Tanneries and leather finishing		14	14	14	12		1550	1658	1678	1414		3034	3915	4329	4248
3232 Fur dressing and dyeing industries		-	-	-	-		-	-	-	-		-	-	-	-
3233 Leather prods. excl. wearing apparel		4	7	6	6		467	910	876	764		767	2004	2164	2240
324 Footwear, except rubber or plastic		67	57	59	55		12557	11676	12156	11007		18289	21473	26406	26112
331 Wood products, except furniture		126	149	154	149		20691	24529	22539	22890		31030	42995	48408	55004
3311 Sawmills, planing and other wood mills		103	131	139	132		17467	21608	19955	20050		27407	38996	44514	49830
3312 Wooden and cane containers		18	12	11	10		2320	2013	2033	1841		2505	2615	2930	3082
3319 Other wood and cork products		5	6	4	7		904	908	551	999		1118	1384	964	2092
332 Furniture and fixtures, excl. metal		38	48	47	47		5934	6242	7155	7084		8920	11816	15163	18394
341 Paper and products		41	41	46	45		11583	11107	11543	12232		34334	39630	53738	61049
3411 Pulp, paper and paperboard articles		13	12	14	16		5877	4744	5299	5860		21895	22751	33087	36955
3412 Containers of paper and paperboard		14	12	16	16		3011	3449	3286	3496		6111	8560	10482	13059
3419 Other pulp, paper and paperboard articles		14	17	16	13		2695	2914	2958	2876		6328	8319	10169	11035
342 Printing and publishing		60	63	58	59		9874	11300	11074	10896		35167	45975	53946	60552
351 Industrial chemicals		30	31	31	29		4898	5106	5621	4750		17875	22503	28384	28392
3511 Basic chemicals excl. fertilizers		23	21	23	21		2754	3066	4136	3293		12653	15056	22037	20320
3512 Fertilizers and pesticides		3	5	4	3		1419	1477	1070	897		3127	4558	3336	4198
3513 Synthetic resins and plastic materials		4	5	4	5		725	563	415	560		2095	2889	3011	3874
352 Other chemicals		102	105	105	98		17337	19266	18528	18102		61924	79131	92198	101759
3521 Paints, varnishes and lacquers		15	15	15	14		2052	2146	2311	2308		6767	8360	10356	11306
3522 Drugs and medicines		37	39	39	35		6001	6485	6443	6286		23738	29742	33958	37366
3523 Soap, cleaning preps., perfumes, cosmetics		23	25	24	24		4222	5814	6107	5852		12593	24091	29522	34144
3529 Other chemical products		27	26	27	25		5062	4821	3667	3656		18826	16938	18362	18943
353 Petroleum refineries		2	2	2	2		1315	1319	1324	1306		8980	10694	12289	17063

Code	Industry														
354	Misc. petroleum and coal products		8	7	8	11		1074	661	845	1024		2855	2736	3702	5211
355	Rubber products		19	24	23	24		3686	4715	4279	4193		9563	14926	17496	18186
3551	Tyres and tubes		5	4	4	5		1621	1355	1345	1559		5941	7259	8686	10145
3559	Other rubber products		14	20	19	19		2065	3360	2934	2634		3622	7667	8810	8041
356	Plastic products		98	101	109	109		12957	14111	14600	15327		25779	34476	42004	51340
361	Pottery, china, earthenware		8	8	7	12		2794	2859	2046	2836		3815	5158	5108	6844
362	Glass and products		11	12	13	14		2216	2527	2446	2353		6078	7172	3602	9598
369	Other non-metallic mineral products		46	52	54	56		7525	8566	8865	8030		23554	31734	38976	42287
3691	Structural clay products		13	15	13	16		1773	1881	1487	1822		3706	5009	4193	6294
3692	Cement, lime and plaster		5	6	7	8		1665	1915	1981	1923		9290	12544	16113	18024
3699	Other non-metallic mineral products	a/	28	31	34	32	a/	4087	4770	5397	4285	a/	10558	14181	18670	17969
371	Iron and steel		20	18	23	18		7500	7171	7324	6583		26054	32706	40560	41075
372	Non-ferrous metals		22	25	21	28		7884	8225	7710	9318		40850	47556	53072	71232
381	Fabricated metal products		150	160	179	183		21427	22673	24754	24226		45880	58057	72019	76904
3811	Cutlery, hand tools and general hardware		12	13	15	11		1236	1616	1759	1758		2499	3705	5055	4131
3812	Furniture and fixtures primarily of metal		10	12	15	19		1066	1197	1365	1734		1602	2393	3079	4440
3813	Structural metal products		62	66	70	79		8468	9007	9979	10284		17690	23140	27535	32626
3819	Other fabricated metal products		66	69	79	74		10657	10853	11651	10450		24089	28819	36350	35707
382	Non-electrical machinery		71	79	73	80		12458	11843	12643	12313		41491	46887	53323	56144
3821	Engines and turbines		2	-	-	-		130	-	-	-		250	-	-	-
3822	Agricultural machinery and equipment		3	5	5	4		229	395	376	316		466	776	1062	962
3823	Metal and wood working machinery		7	4	5	4		493	344	405	261		1227	620	1216	1088
3824	Other special industrial machinery		11	16	16	23		2720	2996	2720	2964		13982	17527	17677	19360
3825	Office, computing and accounting machinery		-	-	-	-		-	-	-	-		-	-	-	-
3829	Other non-electrical machinery & equipment		48	54	47	49		8886	8108	9142	8772		25566	27964	33368	34734
383	Electrical machinery		29	29	29	34		4386	4310	4292	4928		13517	15188	18445	22941
3831	Electrical industrial machinery		8	9	8	8		1330	1433	1299	1274		4330	5830	5787	5863
3832	Radio, television and communication equipm.		3	2	3	6		257	207	315	656		575	646	1470	3674
3833	Electrical appliances and housewares		3	3	2	2		491	542	158	178		1067	1336	544	575
3839	Other electrical apparatus and supplies		15	15	16	18		2308	2128	2520	2820		7545	7376	10644	12829
384	Transport equipment		50	44	45	44		12061	11645	11452	10943		26251	26326	34151	37103
3841	Shipbuilding and repairing		14	10	9	11		5027	4684	4075	4558		12549	10908	14048	16525
3842	Railroad equipment		4	4	3	2		643	569	444	265		1053	1124	1071	608
3843	Motor vehicles		27	26	28	24		4236	4227	4843	4011		9615	11092	15226	14808
3844	Motorcycles and bicycles		3	3	3	4		407	644	682	730		735	845	1045	1723
3845	Aircraft		1	1	1	1		1565	1521	1344	1240		2168	2357	2627	3005
3849	Other transport equipment		1	-	1	2		183	-	64	139		131	-	134	434
385	Professional and scientific equipment		6	6	8	8		645	651	835	762		1567	1983	2879	2868
3851	Prof. and scientific equipment n.e.c.		4	4	6	6		349	332	481	517		932	1175	1936	2048
3852	Photographic and optical goods		2	2	2	2		296	319	354	245		635	808	943	820
3853	Watches and clocks		-	-	-	-		-	-	-	-		-	-	-	-
390	Other manufacturing industries		15	11	12	14		1554	1120	1232	1516		2369	2736	2846	4146
3901	Jewellery and related articles		1	1	2	1		249	256	324	249		407	691	877	808
3902	Musical instruments		1	-	-	-		47	-	-	-		26	-	-	-
3903	Sporting and athletic goods		-	-	-	-		-	-	-	-		-	-	-	-
3909	Manufacturing industries, n.e.c.		13	10	10	13		1258	864	908	1267		1936	2045	1969	3338
3	Total manufacturing		1770	1830	1844	1879		326615	333455	335637	337622		753812	914742	1091967	1240592

a/ Including cement for construction as well as fibre cement.

Chile

ISIC Revision 2	Output in producers' prices					Value added in producers' prices					Gross fixed capital formation		
		(billion PESOS)					(billion PESOS)					(billion PESOS)	
ISIC Industry	Note	1992	1993	1994	1995	Note	1992	1993	1994	1995	Note	1994	1995
311/2 Food products		2078.8	2380.0	2802.1	3303.5		787.9	938.0	1092.8	1336.1		129.9	193.5
3111 Slaughtering, preparing & preserving meat		349.6	373.0	363.6	404.3		133.8	134.9	128.3	138.3		...	...
3112 Dairy products		313.0	356.9	386.2	452.6		104.8	143.5	141.5	163.4		...	...
3113 Canning, preserving of fruits & vegetables		186.7	220.9	298.0	304.0		74.2	90.6	111.2	111.7		...	...
3114 Canning, preserving and processing of fish		222.4	241.1	257.2	403.1		105.8	96.6	115.3	197.3		...	...
3115 Vegetable and animal oils and fats		368.1	357.8	452.4	508.5		142.7	149.0	193.4	224.9		...	...
3116 Grain mill products		83.6	95.8	114.8	159.8		21.7	22.0	36.8	53.7		...	...
3117 Bakery products		108.9	139.7	156.6	186.1		53.7	68.3	66.9	91.5		...	...
3118 Sugar factories and refineries		113.6	153.8	160.5	170.5		19.4	39.8	58.4	61.3		...	...
3119 Cocoa, chocolate and sugar confectionery		81.6	105.5	138.0	134.2		35.4	45.9	49.6	57.1		...	...
3121 Other food products		164.6	223.7	307.2	382.7		82.6	126.6	152.1	191.6		...	...
3122 Prepared animal feeds		86.8	111.8	167.5	197.7		13.8	20.7	39.3	45.3		...	...
313 Beverages		422.8	474.7	530.1	614.3		236.3	244.2	287.1	326.7		43.4	42.8
3131 Distilling, rectifying and blending spirits		42.9	61.0	59.6	71.1		19.1	27.9	32.6	46.5		...	...
3132 Wine industries		115.2	111.2	124.1	149.1		59.3	52.6	57.5	61.6		...	...
3133 Malt liquors and malt		79.7	87.9	69.1	79.7		53.8	51.1	35.4	35.5		...	...
3134 Soft drinks and carbonated waters		185.0	214.6	277.3	314.4		104.1	112.6	161.6	183.1		...	...
314 Tobacco		164.9	206.6	228.9	258.9		141.2	177.9	205.9	225.2		3.2	1.3
321 Textiles		314.3	334.8	336.8	372.6		149.4	152.2	151.5	171.3		12.3	5.3
3211 Spinning, weaving and finishing textiles		208.1	210.9	216.8	240.6		102.0	99.8	95.4	110.8		...	...
3212 Made-up textile goods excl. wearing apparel		10.4	16.3	12.8	12.3		5.5	7.8	7.6	7.3		...	...
3213 Knitting mills		85.0	97.5	96.6	108.3		37.4	40.6	44.6	48.7		...	...
3214 Carpets and rugs		2.9	1.7	1.8	1.9		1.1	0.7	0.7	0.8		...	...
3215 Cordage, rope and twine		2.2	2.7	2.9	1.6		1.0	1.2	1.4	0.7		...	...
3219 Other textiles		5.8	5.8	6.0	8.0		2.5	2.0	1.8	2.9		...	...
322 Wearing apparel, except footwear		198.9	240.0	270.4	291.8		86.7	116.7	131.3	145.2		11.2	8.7
323 Leather and fur products		36.3	50.1	53.7	57.2		12.2	17.1	22.5	23.4		0.9	0.9
3231 Tanneries and leather finishing		32.2	39.5	44.1	46.4		9.7	11.2	16.8	16.8		...	...
3232 Fur dressing and dyeing industries		-	-	-	-		-	-	-	-		...	...
3233 Leather prods. excl. wearing apparel		4.0	10.6	9.6	10.8		2.4	5.9	5.7	6.6		...	...
324 Footwear, except rubber or plastic		142.5	146.5	168.8	179.1		62.6	68.7	81.4	93.8		5.7	1.1
331 Wood products, except furniture		273.3	402.9	498.3	561.2		117.7	170.0	196.1	219.9		24.6	28.0
3311 Sawmills, planing and other wood mills		246.2	376.5	472.8	531.2		104.6	157.3	185.5	205.3		...	...
3312 Wooden and cane containers		18.2	17.4	19.5	18.2		9.3	9.0	8.6	9.0		...	...
3319 Other wood and cork products		8.9	9.0	6.0	11.8		3.8	3.8	2.0	5.6		...	...
332 Furniture and fixtures, excl. metal		61.8	76.9	92.7	111.2		32.4	36.0	48.2	50.6		3.1	4.8
341 Paper and products		576.6	605.6	817.3	1137.6		274.3	272.2	426.2	633.5		34.6	82.5
3411 Pulp, paper and paperboard articles		387.9	386.0	573.5	845.2		187.0	160.4	298.5	503.6		...	...
3412 Containers of paper and paperboard		81.5	95.3	102.1	145.4		32.0	39.9	43.7	57.3		...	...
3419 Other pulp, paper and paperboard articles		107.2	124.3	141.7	147.0		55.4	71.9	84.0	72.6		...	...
342 Printing and publishing		215.3	252.3	294.6	349.4		123.1	154.2	179.3	228.2		18.1	18.5
351 Industrial chemicals		282.1	440.4	474.6	409.0		140.9	165.9	198.2	189.1		29.1	39.9
3511 Basic chemicals excl. fertilizers		168.7	287.2	337.2	243.9		91.1	95.4	155.6	132.5		...	...
3512 Fertilizers and pesticides		95.8	115.5	92.4	98.5		42.0	55.2	25.5	34.5		...	...
3513 Synthetic resins and plastic materials		17.6	37.7	45.1	66.5		7.9	15.3	17.1	22.2		...	...
352 Other chemicals		554.0	682.8	745.5	821.8		309.7	377.1	416.2	467.6		22.7	19.8
3521 Paints, varnishes and lacquers		62.8	74.0	84.1	87.6		20.5	26.3	33.6	28.6		...	...
3522 Drugs and medicines		182.5	237.0	255.3	259.8		109.0	142.8	153.6	162.9		...	...
3523 Soap, cleaning preps., perfumes, cosmetics		104.1	218.1	256.2	306.7		57.8	124.4	145.6	188.1		...	...
3529 Other chemical products		204.5	153.7	149.9	167.7		122.4	83.6	83.4	88.0		...	...
353 Petroleum refineries		706.4	864.0	913.7	897.3		230.2	355.0	362.7	335.1		21.6	12.0

ISIC	Industry												
354	Misc. petroleum and coal products		74.3	80.5	104.8	129.3		31.9	37.8	54.5	55.7	1.1	3.2
355	Rubber products		73.7	113.7	118.6	146.6		33.1	53.1	57.2	69.0	2.3	4.7
3551	Tyres and tubes		53.0	66.7	67.8	91.2		22.6	28.3	29.4	39.4	...	...
3559	Other rubber products		20.7	46.9	50.8	55.4		10.6	24.9	27.9	29.7	...	...
356	Plastic products		209.5	278.9	339.1	419.2		81.1	130.1	156.5	185.2	21.0	28.9
361	Pottery, china, earthenware		16.9	20.1	14.7	32.8		10.1	11.3	9.0	16.0	0.6	2.2
362	Glass and products		46.6	58.6	69.6	81.0		23.2	32.1	41.4	49.6	2.9	9.2
369	Other non-metallic mineral products		259.4	343.4	370.1	416.8		144.8	195.6	193.7	229.5	22.4	37.0
3691	Structural clay products		29.1	37.8	22.5	43.6		16.8	21.8	12.0	23.5	...	...
3692	Cement, lime and plaster		125.6	165.8	187.0	212.3		80.9	115.0	117.2	133.7	...	...
3699	Other non-metallic mineral products	a/	104.7	139.8	160.7	160.9	a/	47.1	58.9	64.5	72.3	...	...
371	Iron and steel		240.5	292.3	330.5	424.7		93.2	114.9	135.8	159.7	12.4	6.6
372	Non-ferrous metals		1826.0	1673.3	1905.1	2281.6		629.3	491.9	547.8	752.2	50.0	133.7
381	Fabricated metal products		385.3	453.5	520.2	578.6		158.6	197.0	219.7	244.0	25.5	23.9
3811	Cutlery, hand tools and general hardware		14.0	18.0	22.9	15.5		8.9	11.5	11.8	8.4	...	...
3812	Furniture and fixtures primarily of metal		10.9	15.4	19.9	29.1		5.5	8.4	10.1	13.4	...	...
3813	Structural metal products		151.3	205.4	222.0	255.6		59.6	86.2	91.1	105.1	...	...
3819	Other fabricated metal products		209.1	214.7	255.4	278.4		84.5	91.0	106.7	117.1	...	...
382	Non-electrical machinery		216.0	259.1	285.3	341.2		79.7	86.4	114.1	146.3	5.8	14.4
3821	Engines and turbines		0.8	-	-	-		0.6	-	-	-	...	...
3822	Agricultural machinery and equipment		3.4	5.1	5.2	4.6		1.2	2.4	2.8	2.8	...	...
3823	Metal and wood working machinery		7.6	2.8	5.8	8.0		3.8	1.7	3.2	3.6	...	...
3824	Other special industrial machinery		75.9	98.5	75.2	90.6		13.6	22.5	23.1	37.5	...	...
3825	Office, computing and accounting machinery		-	-	-	-		-	-	-	-	...	...
3829	Other non-electrical machinery & equipment		128.4	152.8	199.1	238.0		60.4	59.8	85.0	102.4	...	...
383	Electrical machinery		102.3	127.9	112.8	152.3		54.9	73.9	64.9	82.4	4.5	4.7
3831	Electrical industrial machinery		29.4	38.4	34.0	50.1		19.1	24.8	20.9	20.9	...	...
3832	Radio, television and communication equipm.		9.9	10.4	11.1	19.0		5.6	7.8	8.9	12.9	...	...
3833	Electrical appliances and housewares		11.9	18.1	2.9	2.9		5.9	6.4	1.0	1.3	...	...
3839	Other electrical apparatus and supplies		51.2	60.9	64.9	80.3		24.3	34.9	34.1	47.3	...	...
384	Transport equipment		290.3	342.9	354.9	386.0		89.9	100.6	90.0	103.6	5.2	5.2
3841	Shipbuilding and repairing		48.2	59.6	59.1	58.6		29.5	30.4	34.2	38.7	...	...
3842	Railroad equipment		3.5	3.1	2.4	2.8		2.3	1.8	1.4	2.0	...	...
3843	Motor vehicles		213.4	254.6	268.7	289.3		48.3	51.1	46.0	49.7	...	...
3844	Motorcycles and bicycles		9.3	9.4	10.9	16.2		3.5	5.9	4.3	7.6	...	...
3845	Aircraft		15.0	16.1	13.0	16.1		5.9	11.4	3.7	4.0	...	...
3849	Other transport equipment		0.7	-	0.8	2.9		0.5	-	0.4	1.6	...	...
385	Professional and scientific equipment		9.6	12.6	18.0	20.4		5.4	7.8	10.5	11.3	0.2	0.7
3851	Prof. and scientific equipment n.e.c.		7.0	9.0	13.8	15.4		4.0	6.1	8.4	9.1	...	...
3852	Photographic and optical goods		2.6	3.5	4.2	5.1		1.4	1.7	2.2	2.3	...	...
3853	Watches and clocks		-	-	-	-		-	-	-	-	...	...
390	Other manufacturing industries		12.4	13.3	14.6	21.4		7.5	7.9	8.1	11.3	0.3	2.0
3901	Jewellery and related articles		2.4	3.6	3.5	2.9		1.9	2.8	2.4	2.2	...	...
3902	Musical instruments		0.2	-	-	-		0.1	-	-	-	...	...
3903	Sporting and athletic goods		-	-	-	-		-	-	-	-	...	...
3909	Manufacturing industries, n.e.c.		9.8	9.7	11.1	18.5		5.5	5.1	5.7	9.0	...	...
3	Total manufacturing		9790.7	11227.7	12785.9	14796.8		4147.3	4785.6	5502.5	6561.6	514.3	735.5

a/ Including cement for construction as well as fibre cement.

Chile

ISIC Revision 2		Index numbers of industrial production (1990=100)											
ISIC Industry	Note	1985	1986	1987	1988	1989	1990	1991	1992	1993	1994	1995	1996
311/2 Food products	a/	89	97	93	97	104	100	101	119	123	137	143	142
313 Beverages		70	71	69	83	100	100	98	108	115	110	122	129
314 Tobacco		81	83	82	91	97	100	100	108	105	105	106	113
321 Textiles		89	105	110	105	107	100	110	105	101	93	97	98
322 Wearing apparel, except footwear		83	92	100	97	107	100	113	108	97	88	84	80
323 Leather and fur products		92	86	78	74	91	100	115	111	107	97	101	89
324 Footwear, except rubber or plastic		88	89	88	94	106	100	119	123	118	105	93	90
331 Wood products, except furniture	b/	98	100	120	114	97	100	94	82	70	72	70	73
332 Furniture and fixtures, excl. metal		27	41	68	85	97	100	100	98	98	103	105	100
341 Paper and products		82	87	87	96	97	100	109	131	132	141	149	152
342 Printing and publishing		55	65	69	74	88	100	130	181	184	198	230	226
351 Industrial chemicals		76	76	87	99	101	100	108	116	112	119	124	130
352 Other chemicals		72	82	85	93	102	100	106	121	130	139	157	176
353 Petroleum refineries		64	67	71	81	98	100	102	106	112	119	130	135
354 Misc. petroleum and coal products		...	...	111	104	110	100	143	155	150	216	215	213
355 Rubber products		96	88	95	92	102	100	142	163	150	141	139	127
356 Plastic products		...	...	122	114	109	100	122	128	132	143	152	162
361 Pottery, china, earthenware		89	94	99	103	113	100	95	93	99	103	108	106
362 Glass and products		51	60	56	71	101	100	109	125	134	146	158	181
369 Other non-metallic mineral products		71	84	75	101	114	100	108	130	152	152	167	192
371 Iron and steel		85	87	91	113	113	100	101	120	129	124	147	149
372 Non-ferrous metals	c/	81	85	86	90	96	100	97	104	100	96	101	104
381 Fabricated metal products		71	76	86	93	102	100	100	124	139	141	151	161
382 Non-electrical machinery		47	62	71	72	90	100	96	143	186	200	222	204
383 Electrical machinery		54	68	78	88	96	100	107	123	127	128	134	140
384 Transport equipment		86	77	88	91	114	100	107	125	120	115	105	106
385 Professional and scientific equipment		...	...	84	94	107	100	110	133	133	139	149	162
390 Other manufacturing industries		89	94	98	91	98	100	92	90	85	78	79	78
3 Total manufacturing	d/	79	85	88	94	101	100	104	117	120	124	131	135

a/ Excluding slaughtering.
b/ Excluding sawmills.
c/ Excluding smelting and refining of copper.
d/ Excluding slaughtering, sawmills, and smelting and refining of copper.

CHINA

Supplier of information:
State Statistical Bureau, Beijing.

Basic source of data:
Not reported.

Major deviations from ISIC (Revision 2):
None reported.

Reference period (if not calendar year):

Scope:
Industrial enterprises with independent accounting systems.

Method of enumeration:
Not reported.

Adjusted for non-response:
Not reported.

Concepts and definitions of variables:
No deviations from the standard UN concepts and definitions are reported.

Related national publications:
Statistical Yearbook of China (annual), published by the State Statistical Bureau, Beijing.

China

ISIC Revision 2	Number of enterprises					Number of employees					Wages and salaries paid to employees				
		(numbers)					(thousands)					(billion YUAN)			
ISIC Industry	Note	1993	1994	1995	1996	Note	1993	1994	1995	1996	Note	1993	1994	1995	1996
311/2 Food products		42457	43130	46841	45860		3130	3180	3220	3170		...	...	...	...
313 Beverages		12705	13161	14719	14130		1130	1170	1210	1210		...	...	...	...
314 Tobacco		391	382	423	416		290	340	330	330		...	...	...	...
321 Textiles		24613	24774	25686	24297		6840	6910	6730	6340		...	...	...	...
322 Wearing apparel, except footwear	a/	17921	18439	20007	19502	a/	1640	1810	1750	1680		...	...	...	...
323 Leather and fur products		9370	9773	10468	9728		850	920	990	910		...	...	...	...
324 Footwear, except rubber or plastic	a/	...	...	...	...	a/	...	...	...	...		...	...	...	...
331 Wood products, except furniture		12410	13486	15480	15259		730	770	730	720		...	...	...	...
332 Furniture and fixtures, excl. metal		8014	8171	8760	8716		340	350	350	310		...	...	...	...
341 Paper and products		11940	12282	13890	13893		1250	1280	1330	1280		...	...	...	...
342 Printing and publishing		13174	13576	15436	15378		930	990	970	960		...	...	...	...
351 Industrial chemicals	b/	28839	30473	35092	35405	b/	5230	5470	5610	5580		...	...	...	...
352 Other chemicals	b/	...	...	...	...	b/	...	...	...	...		...	...	...	...
353 Petroleum refineries	c/	1901	2176	2734	2612	c/	680	710	720	760		...	...	...	...
354 Misc. petroleum and coal products	c/	...	...	...	...	c/	...	...	...	...		...	...	...	...
355 Rubber products		4155	4242	4663	4656		760	770	770	750		...	...	...	...
356 Plastic products		16274	16826	19255	19432		1010	1010	1090	1050		...	...	...	...
361 Pottery, china, earthenware	d/	54528	56762	61278	61887	d/	3960	4010	4250	4070		...	...	...	...
362 Glass and products	d/	...	...	...	...	d/	...	...	...	...		...	...	...	...
369 Other non-metallic mineral products	d/	...	...	...	...	d/	...	...	...	...		...	...	...	...
371 Iron and steel		5839	6400	7299	6730		3410	3460	3460	3370		...	...	...	...
372 Non-ferrous metals		3460	3609	4621	4611		920	1010	1010	1010		...	...	...	...
381 Fabricated metal products		28427	29311	30728	30388		1920	1960	1930	1810		...	...	...	...
382 Non-electrical machinery		44310	45188	48332	49059		7240	7360	7090	7020		...	...	...	...
383 Electrical machinery		23446	24632	27668	27184		3770	3960	4160	3990		...	...	...	...
384 Transport equipment		15439	16411	19445	20339		3380	3450	3700	3540		...	...	...	...
385 Professional and scientific equipment		4975	5165	5637	5774		860	900	860	820		...	...	...	...
390 Other manufacturing industries		21865	22309	22429	21277		2030	2530	2160	1660		...	...	...	...
3 Total manufacturing		406453	420678	460891	456533		52300	54320	54390	52340		...	...	...	...

a/ 322 includes 324.
b/ 351 includes 352.
c/ 353 includes 354.
d/ 361 includes 362 and 369.

China

ISIC Revision 2	Output					Value added					Gross fixed capital formation		
		(billion YUAN)					(billion YUAN)					(billion YUAN)	
ISIC Industry	Note	1993	1994	1995	1996	Note	1993	1994	1995	1996	Note	1995	1996
311/2 Food products		235.7	333.5	404.0	462.6		68.3	83.4	70.8	100.2		...	...
313 Beverages		76.7	101.0	115.6	142.3		27.8	33.0	35.4	45.7		...	...
314 Tobacco		77.6	96.9	100.4	120.2		42.2	55.3	61.3	75.7		...	...
321 Textiles		352.1	495.0	460.4	472.2		95.1	111.7	89.8	104.0		...	...
322 Wearing apparel, except footwear	a/	99.4	144.1	147.0	177.7	a/	32.5	35.5	34.7	44.7		...	...
323 Leather and fur products		57.1	84.3	97.4	111.2		15.2	20.2	20.1	27.8		...	...
324 Footwear, except rubber or plastic	a/	...	...	...	...	a/	...	...	...	...		...	...
331 Wood products, except furniture		27.9	36.6	40.6	51.3		9.5	10.0	9.5	14.3		...	...
332 Furniture and fixtures, excl. metal		15.4	21.9	22.6	28.2		4.8	5.9	5.6	8.0		...	...
341 Paper and products		61.1	75.9	101.4	121.5		15.1	19.2	23.2	32.9		...	...
342 Printing and publishing		33.9	40.5	41.2	53.1		12.4	12.4	12.3	17.0		...	...
351 Industrial chemicals	b/	352.1	467.7	559.1	642.5	b/	105.8	121.6	141.0	174.1		...	...
352 Other chemicals	b/	...	...	...	...	b/	...	...	...	...		...	...
353 Petroleum refineries	c/	144.6	188.0	202.8	221.2	c/	34.6	43.4	56.1	55.9		...	...
354 Misc. petroleum and coal products	c/	...	...	...	...	c/	...	...	...	...		...	...
355 Rubber products		44.8	55.0	62.0	74.9		12.6	13.8	13.8	18.8		...	...
356 Plastic products		71.2	92.7	112.8	133.8		20.9	22.2	22.5	32.4		...	...
361 Pottery, china, earthenware	d/	233.3	299.7	301.8	356.0	d/	89.8	94.2	90.0	105.5		...	...
362 Glass and products	d/	...	...	...	...	d/	...	...	...	...		...	...
369 Other non-metallic mineral products	d/	...	...	...	...	d/	...	...	...	...		...	...
371 Iron and steel		393.1	416.5	366.0	374.6		128.5	129.0	105.3	99.9		...	...
372 Non-ferrous metals		97.4	120.2	137.2	142.5		26.1	26.3	30.2	30.7		...	...
381 Fabricated metal products		130.2	170.8	165.1	194.4		39.8	44.0	38.4	49.1		...	...
382 Non-electrical machinery		346.5	418.4	412.2	466.9		104.9	117.4	111.9	124.7		...	...
383 Electrical machinery		315.0	432.7	512.5	611.1		88.6	106.6	123.9	140.4		...	...
384 Transport equipment		259.9	318.6	330.3	378.5		69.8	75.5	80.5	92.9		...	...
385 Professional and scientific equipment		36.6	42.4	42.6	52.9		12.2	12.9	12.3	14.4		...	...
390 Other manufacturing industries		78.9	105.3	107.1	125.4		26.0	28.3	26.8	36.4		...	...
3 Total manufacturing		3540.4	4557.9	4842.1	5514.9		1082.4	1222.0	1215.6	1445.8		...	...

a/ 322 includes 324.
b/ 351 includes 352.
c/ 353 includes 354.
d/ 361 includes 362 and 369.

China

ISIC Revision 2			Index numbers of industrial production											
			(1990=100)											
ISIC	Industry	Note	1985	1986	1987	1988	1989	1990	1991	1992	1993	1994	1995	1996
311/2	Food products		...	...	...	...	...	...	...	...	...	...	...	...
313	Beverages		...	...	...	...	...	...	...	...	...	...	...	...
314	Tobacco		...	...	...	...	...	...	...	...	...	...	...	...
321	Textiles		...	...	...	...	...	...	...	...	...	...	...	...
322	Wearing apparel, except footwear		...	...	...	...	...	...	...	...	...	...	...	...
323	Leather and fur products		...	...	...	...	...	...	...	...	...	...	...	...
324	Footwear, except rubber or plastic		...	...	...	...	...	...	...	...	...	...	...	...
331	Wood products, except furniture		...	...	...	...	...	...	...	...	...	...	...	...
332	Furniture and fixtures, excl. metal		...	...	...	...	...	...	...	...	...	...	...	...
341	Paper and products		...	...	...	...	...	...	...	...	...	...	...	...
342	Printing and publishing		...	...	...	...	...	...	...	...	...	...	...	...
351	Industrial chemicals		...	...	...	...	...	...	...	...	...	...	...	...
352	Other chemicals		...	...	...	...	...	...	...	...	...	...	...	...
353	Petroleum refineries		...	...	...	...	...	...	...	...	...	...	...	...
354	Misc. petroleum and coal products		...	...	...	...	...	...	...	...	...	...	...	...
355	Rubber products		...	...	...	...	...	...	...	...	...	...	...	...
356	Plastic products		...	...	...	...	...	...	...	...	...	...	...	...
361	Pottery, china, earthenware		...	...	...	...	...	...	...	...	...	...	...	...
362	Glass and products		...	...	...	...	...	...	...	...	...	...	...	...
369	Other non-metallic mineral products		...	...	...	...	...	...	...	...	...	...	...	...
371	Iron and steel		...	...	...	...	...	...	...	...	...	...	...	...
372	Non-ferrous metals		...	...	...	...	...	...	...	...	...	...	...	...
381	Fabricated metal products		...	...	...	...	...	...	...	...	...	...	...	...
382	Non-electrical machinery		...	...	...	...	...	...	...	...	...	...	...	...
383	Electrical machinery		...	...	...	...	...	...	...	...	...	...	...	...
384	Transport equipment		...	...	...	...	...	...	...	...	...	...	...	...
385	Professional and scientific equipment		...	...	...	...	...	...	...	...	...	...	...	...
390	Other manufacturing industries		...	...	...	...	...	...	...	...	...	...	...	...
3	Total manufacturing		...	...	...	...	...	...	...	...	...	...	...	...

CHINA (HONG KONG SAR)

Supplier of information:
Census and Statistics Department, Hong Kong.

Basic source of data:
Annual survey.

Major deviations from ISIC (Revision 2):
None reported.

Reference period (if not calendar year):
For establishments that do not have data available for the calendar year, data may be supplied for any 12 month period between 1 January of the reference year and 31 March of the following year.

Scope:
All establishments listed in a comprehensive and up-to-date register maintained by the Census and Statistics Department of Hong Kong.

Method of enumeration:
Establishments are sampled. Questionnaires are mailed to establishments in the sample for completion. Staff of the Census and Statistics Department visit these establishments to collect completed questionnaires or to assist with their completion.

Adjusted for non-response:
Yes.

Concepts and definitions of variables:
Wages and salaries excludes payments in kind and includes severance and termination pay.
Value added is total value added.
... denotes data suppressed because of confidentiality rules, except for the index numbers of industrial production.

Related national publications:
Report on the Survey of Industrial Production (annual); Hong Kong Monthly Digest of Statistics; Hong Kong Annual Digest of Statistics, all published by the Census and Statistics Department, Hong Kong.

China (Hong Kong SAR)

ISIC Revision 2	Number of establishments					Number of employees					Wages and salaries paid to employees				
		(numbers)					(thousands)					(million DOLLARS)			
ISIC Industry	Note	1992	1993	1994	1995	Note	1992	1993	1994	1995	Note	1992	1993	1994	1995
311/2 Food products		790	734	692	703		19.9	19.5	18.2	17.8		1843	2069	2016	2047
3111 Slaughtering, preparing & preserving meat		138	101	99	108		2.7	3.2	1.7	2.0		259	401	193	225
3112 Dairy products		11	11	10	11		1.5	1.4	1.5	1.5		173	178	192	227
3113 Canning, preserving of fruits & vegetables		9	14	9	13		0.2	0.3	0.2	0.3		20	30	...	...
3114 Canning, preserving and processing of fish		181	173	124	123		1.7	1.3	1.2	1.2		162	157	171	182
3115 Vegetable and animal oils and fats		3	3	4	3		0.6	0.6	0.2	0.4		48	59	28	44
3116 Grain mill products		39	41	29	41		0.8	0.5	0.4	0.4		62	45	44	39
3117 Bakery products		255	285	273	241		6.2	6.2	6.1	5.4		549	616	653	614
3118 Sugar factories and refineries		2	2	1	1		0.1	0.2	0.2	0.2		...	...	...	...
3119 Cocoa, chocolate and sugar confectionery		23	12	12	10		0.5	0.3	0.7	0.6		39	23	65	62
3121 Other food products		117	84	127	141		5.4	5.4	5.9	5.8		495	532	612	635
3122 Prepared animal feeds		12	8	5	11		0.2	0.1	0.1	0.1		...	...	...	19
313 Beverages		11	16	18	21		4.1	4.1	4.3	4.3		546	597	684	739
3131 Distilling, rectifying and blending spirits		3	4	3	3		-	0.1	-	-		...	...	...	2
3132 Wine industries		-	-	-	-		-	-	-	-		-	-	-	-
3133 Malt liquors and malt		2	2	2	3		1.1	1.0	1.0	0.9		...	...	...	166
3134 Soft drinks and carbonated waters		6	11	13	15		3.0	3.1	3.2	3.4		399	438	518	571
314 Tobacco		4	4	4	5		1.3	1.3	1.2	1.2		219	231	225	237
321 Textiles		4606	3619	3466	2926		84.7	78.6	65.2	49.2		8068	8082	7275	5838
3211 Spinning, weaving and finishing textiles		1838	1519	1573	1398		43.6	34.3	28.2	21.8		4413a/	3968	3575	2779
3212 Made-up textile goods excl. wearing apparel		824	680	539	400		3.7	3.5	2.1	1.8		317	338	278	180
3213 Knitting mills		1736	1289	1259	1032		35.9	39.7	34.1	24.8a/		...	3632a/	3325	2776a/
3214 Carpets and rugs		9	9	7	7		0.1	0.1	0.1	0.1		8	...	6	9
3215 Cordage, rope and twine		93	44	40	56		0.2	0.1	0.1	0.1		17	8	11	15
3219 Other textiles		105	80	48	33		1.0	0.9	0.6	0.5		99	121	80	72
322 Wearing apparel, except footwear		6711	4803	3842	3200		164.3	126.1	102.3	78.0		12769	10296	9310	8079
323 Leather and fur products		87	114	78	99		1.0	1.3	0.8	0.8		104	135	104	116
3231 Tanneries and leather finishing		15	25	25	17		0.3	0.4	0.4	0.3		34	44	46	39
3232 Fur dressing and dyeing industries		-	-	-	-		-	-	-	-		-	-	-	-
3233 Leather prods. excl. wearing apparel		72	89	53	82		0.7	0.9	0.4	0.5		71	91	59	77
324 Footwear, except rubber or plastic		172	121	99	76		1.5	0.7	0.5	0.3		104	40	34	22
331 Wood products, except furniture		646	478	483	381		1.9	1.6	1.2	1.0		158	157	134	123
3311 Sawmills, planing and other wood mills		97	81	57	43		0.9	0.8	0.5	0.4		83	89	64	54
3312 Wooden and cane containers		239	193	217	154		0.5	0.4	0.4	0.2a/		...	30a/	39a/	21a/
3319 Other wood and cork products		309	204	210	184		0.5	0.4	0.3	0.4		...	37	31a/	45
332 Furniture and fixtures, excl. metal		713	475	453	358		2.6	1.5	1.3	0.7		251	140	126	77
341 Paper and products		1456	1235	1117	957		12.2	11.6	8.6	7.4		1295	1401	1076	983
3411 Pulp, paper and paperboard articles		25	59	25	104		1.2	1.2	1.1	1.5		150	146	146	205
3412 Containers of paper and paperboard		1146	808	731	650		8.5	8.0	5.6	3.9		902	1014	727	512
3419 Other pulp, paper and paperboard articles		286	368	361	203		2.5	2.4	1.9	1.9		244	240	204	266
342 Printing and publishing		4925	4688	4651	4546		33.2	35.5	37.1	41.3		3712	4395	5467	6850
351 Industrial chemicals		248	268	188	174		2.0	2.1	1.9	1.6		262	842b/	938b/	938b/
3511 Basic chemicals excl. fertilizers		101	73	92	63		1.1	1.0	0.9	0.7		163	164	150	152
3512 Fertilizers and pesticides		2	1	1	1		-	-	-	-		...	...	...	...
3513 Synthetic resins and plastic materials		145	194	95	110		0.9	1.1	1.0	0.9		99	152	171	152
352 Other chemicals		374	416	400	355		4.9	4.5	4.7	4.1		395	...b/	...b/	...b/
3521 Paints, varnishes and lacquers		17	14	19	14		0.9	0.7	0.7	0.6		112	106	131	111
3522 Drugs and medicines		228	249	229	194		2.3	2.1	2.1	2.1		203	191	206	256
3523 Soap, cleaning preps., perfumes, cosmetics		59	53	84	89		0.7	0.6	0.8	0.7		80	75	105	95
3529 Other chemical products		70	100	68	58		1.0	1.2	1.1	0.7a/		...	105a/	130a/	123a/
353 Petroleum refineries		3c/	1	2	1	c/	0.1	0.1	0.1	0.1	c/	22	23	25	25

354 Misc. petroleum and coal products	...c/	3	3	4	c/	...	...	...	...	c/	...	...	...	...
355 Rubber products	106	96	80	70		0.6	0.4	0.4	0.3		52	46	45	38
3551 Tyres and tubes	9	12	10	10		0.2	0.2	0.2	0.1		18	21	24	23
3559 Other rubber products	97	85	71	59		0.5	0.3	0.2	0.2		34	25	18a/	15
356 Plastic products	3511	2374	2041	1653		28.5	20.0	13.1	9.6		2639	1978	1386	1220
361 Pottery, china, earthenware	37	23	23	16		0.1	0.1	0.1	...		...	...	8	...
362 Glass and products	68	88	46	21		0.8	0.7	0.6	0.4		78	89	...	77
369 Other non-metallic mineral products	167	112	165	183		2.6	2.5	3.2	3.3a/		...	371a/	477a/	579a/
3691 Structural clay products	2	2	2	2		0.1	0.1	0.1	0.1		...	...	...	...
3692 Cement, lime and plaster	15	14	16	13		1.3	1.3	1.7	1.9		188	213	296	370
3699 Other non-metallic mineral products	150	96	147	168		1.2	1.1	1.3	1.4		144	159	181	209
371 Iron and steel	74	75	32	36		1.0	1.1	0.9	0.8		129	174	150	148
372 Non-ferrous metals	90	101	89	77		1.3	1.6	1.2	1.3		166	220	200	224
381 Fabricated metal products	5618	4612	4262	3319		35.8	27.1	22.0	19.0		3209	2830	2511	2501
3811 Cutlery, hand tools and general hardware	128	150	81	93		1.6	1.4	1.2	0.8a/		121	90a/	104a/	8a/
3812 Furniture and fixtures primarily of metal	209	77	121	84		1.3	0.8	0.9	0.6		115	73	86	74
3813 Structural metal products	1166	1014	846	806		4.3	4.2	2.6	2.6		456	499	341	393
3819 Other fabricated metal products	4115	3371	3214	2336		28.5	20.7	17.2	14.7a/		...	2131a/	1955a/	1909a/
382 Non-electrical machinery	5486	4582	4538	3849		36.5	31.2	28.8	26.6		3845	3602a/	3525	3784
3821 Engines and turbines	74	45	23	19		0.7	0.4	0.3	0.3		88	52	51	51
3822 Agricultural machinery and equipment	4	2	4	3		0.2	0.2	0.2	0.2		17	...	19	21
3823 Metal and wood working machinery	156	98	156	114		0.5	0.4	0.2	0.2		47	46	30	31
3824 Other special industrial machinery	1522	1229	1150	914		9.2	7.3	5.9	5.6		1017	903	767	821
3825 Office, computing and accounting machinery	177	158	171	186		14.2	13.3	12.8	12.8		1465	1410	1475	1777
3829 Other non-electrical machinery & equipment	3554	3050	3034	2613		11.7	9.7	9.3	7.5		1212	1192	1184	1083
383 Electrical machinery	1091	940	842	828		48.9	43.1	37.6	31.9		4668	4590a/	4643	4289
3831 Electrical industrial machinery	194	208	238	264		4.1	3.3	3.5	2.8		402	432a/	474	498
3832 Radio, television and communication equipm.	484	367	300	266		30.8	29.2	24.7	21.4		3061	3293	3195	2875
3833 Electrical appliances and housewares	135	152	121	126		5.5	3.1	2.2	1.5		486	295	206	185
3839 Other electrical apparatus and supplies	279	213	183	172		8.5	7.5	7.2	6.1		719	571a/	768	731
384 Transport equipment	706	570	606	534		14.2	14.1	13.4	11.4		2052	2322	2359	2269
3841 Shipbuilding and repairing	421	408	486	370		7.7	7.4	6.6	4.7		951	1088	1015	844
3842 Railroad equipment	2	2	2	-		0.1	-	-	-		...	...	...	-
3843 Motor vehicles	230	127	85	135		1.3	1.2	1.0	1.1		132	138	135	157
3844 Motorcycles and bicycles	-	-	1	2		-	-	...	0.2		-	-	...	...
3845 Aircraft	2	3	2	2		5.2	5.3	5.4	5.2		...	1075	...	...
3849 Other transport equipment	53	31	30	24		...	0.1	0.4	0.3		3	...	58	44
385 Professional and scientific equipment	1424	1124	932	804		22.8	18.5	15.8	12.9		2035	1791	1668	1590
3851 Prof. and scientific equipment n.e.c.	39	68	23	17		0.3	0.3	0.1	0.2		...	32	10	20
3852 Photographic and optical goods	136	89	80	85		6.5	5.4	5.2	4.3		491	446	484	494
3853 Watches and clocks	1250	967	829	702		16.1	12.7	10.5	8.4		...	1313	1174	1076
390 Other manufacturing industries	2582	2708	2835	2406		19.6	19.1	16.3	13.7		1981	2027	1923	1886
3901 Jewellery and related articles	875	1074	1061	1092		9.9	11.5	9.1	7.7		1141	1305	1136	1197
3902 Musical instruments	-	-	1	1		-	-	...	...		-	-	...	...
3903 Sporting and athletic goods	33	18	20	12		0.4	0.3	0.4	0.2		45	41	57	25
3909 Manufacturing industries, n.e.c.	1673	1616	1751	1301		9.4	7.4	6.7	5.7a/		795	681	725a/	652a/
3 Total manufacturing	41706	34382	31988	27599		546.4	468.1	400.6	339.5		51081	48631	46406	44679

a/ Data are incomplete due to confidentiality rules.
b/ 351 includes 352.
c/ 353 includes 354.

China (Hong Kong SAR)

ISIC Revision 2 ISIC Industry	Note	Output in producers' prices (million DOLLARS) 1992	1993	1994	1995	Note	Value added in producers' prices (million DOLLARS) 1992	1993	1994	1995	Note	Gross fixed capital formation (million DOLLARS) 1994	1995
311/2 Food products		11273	11256	11860	13255		3801	3999	4027	4917		345	854
3111 Slaughtering, preparing & preserving meat		1377	1510	1068	1327		346	565	324	359		6	34
3112 Dairy products		1010	1013	1170	1195		431	434	476	516		-61	517
3113 Canning, preserving of fruits & vegetables		145	180	...	...		58	42	...	...		...	...
3114 Canning, preserving and processing of fish		1506	1384	2001	2565		471	372	385	999		26	99
3115 Vegetable and animal oils and fats		794	738	340	672		146	87	27	120		-4	16
3116 Grain mill products		499	343	354	369		137	76	53	80		89	15
3117 Bakery products		2504	2864	2970	2900		936	1108	1170	1131		96	110
3118 Sugar factories and refineries		...	...	...	...		...	...	...	...		...	...
3119 Cocoa, chocolate and sugar confectionery		198	115	350	345		68	50	132	132		7	3
3121 Other food products		2932	2953	3335	3499		1150	1223	1373	1466		168	49
3122 Prepared animal feeds		...	...	...	...		...	...	...	29		...	1
313 Beverages		3771	4058	4729	4776		1628	1826	2053	1989		-2679	221
3131 Distilling, rectifying and blending spirits		...	...	...	17		...	...	...	3		...	-
3132 Wine industries		-	-	-	-		-	-	-	-		-	-
3133 Malt liquors and malt		...	...	...	1199		...	...	...	453		...	42
3134 Soft drinks and carbonated waters		2405	2710	3184	3333		879	1064	1283	1306		162	179
314 Tobacco		7903	6256	7986	4599		4714	3832	5441	2072		35	-282
321 Textiles		52209	49245	45854	41273		14800	13180	11595	10179		872	-150
3211 Spinning, weaving and finishing textiles		26363a/	22211	19916	18483		7494a/	6548	5506	4704		372	-297
3212 Made-up textile goods excl. wearing apparel		1516	1363	1349	1073		701	513	450	325		51	26
3213 Knitting mills		22834a/	24822a/	23971	21066a/		6062a/	5832a/	5435	4982a/		433	120a/
3214 Carpets and rugs		25	...	22	29		9	...	9	8		-	-
3215 Cordage, rope and twine		155	64	65	132		33	19	20	30		1	1
3219 Other textiles		846	749	530	472		336	256	176	118		15	-
322 Wearing apparel, except footwear		65760	57420	48412	44749		19705	16092	13622	12342		253	477
323 Leather and fur products		773	1015	1017	913		198	250	232	208		14	13
3231 Tanneries and leather finishing		307	477	550	441		68	94	109	71		18	1
3232 Fur dressing and dyeing industries		-	-	-	-		-	-	-	-		-	-
3233 Leather prods. excl. wearing apparel		467	539	467	472		130	156	122	137		-4	11
324 Footwear, except rubber or plastic		726	130	101	70		153	48	44	31		-	1
331 Wood products, except furniture		1118	1043	1037	955		282	256	254	240		19	4
3311 Sawmills, planing and other wood mills		686	726	692	550		128	132	129	120		2	12
3312 Wooden and cane containers	a/	169	120	176	101	a/	67	47	63	40	a/	3	-
3319 Other wood and cork products		259a/	194	164a/	296		85a/	76	60a/	77		4a/	-8
332 Furniture and fixtures, excl. metal		1171	623	477	325		402	223	172	115		6	6
341 Paper and products		9109	9633	6984	7399		2584	2735	1972	1825		343	267
3411 Pulp, paper and paperboard articles		1237	1216	983	1746		390	325	311	382		200	135
3412 Containers of paper and paperboard		6359	6819	4477	3691		1703	1872	1191	965		101	66
3419 Other pulp, paper and paperboard articles		1514	1598	1524	1962		491	537	470	478		41	66
342 Printing and publishing		18389	20998	24431	26882		7815	9065	9949	10041		1798	1280
351 Industrial chemicals		3139a/	7096b/	8396b/	8966b/		742a/	1966b/	2101b/	1902b/	b/	214	407
3511 Basic chemicals excl. fertilizers		1083	970	874	820		443	401	457	439		82	172
3512 Fertilizers and pesticides		...	...	...	...		...	...	...	...		...	-
3513 Synthetic resins and plastic materials		2057	2675	3824	4107		299	332	380	137		63	86
352 Other chemicals		3006a/	...b/	...b/	...b/		1115a/	...b/	...b/	...b/	b/	...	...
3521 Paints, varnishes and lacquers		658	536	562	531		281	197	206	205		7	6
3522 Drugs and medicines		954	1201	1329	1573		393	521	484	536		13	24
3523 Soap, cleaning preps., perfumes, cosmetics		748	631	707	707		253	222	286	269		11	9
3529 Other chemical products	a/	646	847	897	991	a/	188	226	208	230	a/	17	3
353 Petroleum refineries	c/	191	306	286	275	c/	62	106	107	123	c/	30	38

354 Misc. petroleum and coal products	c/	...	...	...	...	c/	...	...	...	...	c/	...	...
355 Rubber products		265	212	221	189		95	81	76	75		3	8
3551 Tyres and tubes		101	109	121	110		39	42	44	49		2	7
3559 Other rubber products		164	103	89a/	79		56	39	26a/	26		1a/	1
356 Plastic products		15865	11026	8460	8253		4824	3804	2495	2380		259	300
361 Pottery, china, earthenware		...	...	27	...		...	...	12	...		1	...
362 Glass and products		519	467	...	476		194	231	...	222		...	10
369 Other non-metallic mineral products	a/	3923	4187	5905	7422	a/	636	811	1142	1724	a/	210	169
3691 Structural clay products		...	...	...	...		...	...	...	...		...	-
3692 Cement, lime and plaster		3063	3270	4776	6312		347	460	835	1321		140	158
3699 Other non-metallic mineral products		860	917	1129	1110		290	351	307	403		69	11
371 Iron and steel		1288	1608	1749	1575		300	340	250	453		216	268
372 Non-ferrous metals		4737	5054	3844	4836		395	527	414	562		78	84
381 Fabricated metal products		19470	17887	15858	18728		6137	5463	4883	4411		527	610
3811 Cutlery, hand tools and general hardware		1039	918a/	985a/	1154a/		407	441a/	445a/	484a/	a/	32	23
3812 Furniture and fixtures primarily of metal		458	347	370	343		187	115	134	100		9	11
3813 Structural metal products		2299	2570	1648	1745		754	804	561	614		11	20
3819 Other fabricated metal products		15674	13814a/	12714a/	15372a/		4789	4035a/	3701a/	3183a/	a/	442	553
382 Non-electrical machinery		32522	29333a/	27154	34216		8681	7278a/	7233	8171		871	1375
3821 Engines and turbines		531	295	384	349		228	109	171	117		20	12
3822 Agricultural machinery and equipment		111	...	162	167		43	...	66	64		7	11
3823 Metal and wood working machinery		213	282	239	201		79	90	68	59		9	14
3824 Other special industrial machinery		5109	4823	4279	4025		1733	1557	1247	1195		239	62
3825 Office, computing and accounting machinery		21464	19352	17002	24453		4453	3417	3547	4622		751	1111
3829 Other non-electrical machinery & equipment		5093	4580	5088	5022		2144	2104	2133	2112		-156	164
383 Electrical machinery		35213	33238a/	35351	33896		10453	10362a/	11988	11739		2496	2246
3831 Electrical industrial machinery		3280	2745a/	4079	3112		1051	997a/	1521	904		297	319
3832 Radio, television and communication equipm.		22979	24239	24113	23581		7060	7725	8694	9064		1987	1764
3833 Electrical appliances and housewares		3666	2315	1660	1832		883	574	380	373		38	45
3839 Other electrical apparatus and supplies		5288	3939a/	5499	5371		1459	1066a/	1394	1397		147	118
384 Transport equipment		5452	5894	5923	5615		3366	3647	3579	3491		371	864
3841 Shipbuilding and repairing		2726	3072	3048	2539		1375	1561	1428	1284		289	789
3842 Railroad equipment		...	...	...	-		...	...	...	-		...	-
3843 Motor vehicles	a/	497	480	399	554	a/	217	195	214	252		-7	10
3844 Motorcycles and bicycles		-	-	...	...		-	-	...	...		...	...
3845 Aircraft		...	2292	...	...		...	1861	...	...		...	...
3849 Other transport equipment		21	...	101	69		7	...	73	56		-	-
385 Professional and scientific equipment		23039	20223	21364	19161		3956	3592	3523	3246		532	299
3851 Prof. and scientific equipment n.e.c.		...	82	158	278		...	26	49	68		2	4
3852 Photographic and optical goods		3852	3545	4543	4605		949	921	1013	940		118	145
3853 Watches and clocks		18615a/	16596	16664	14278		2873a/	2644	2462	2238		413	149
390 Other manufacturing industries		13202	14840	12510	12306		3361	3614	3417	3029		251	288
3901 Jewellery and related articles		7408	9594	7684	8210		1690	2089	1764	1727		106	123
3902 Musical instruments		-	-	...	...		-	-	...	...		...	...
3903 Sporting and athletic goods		417	404	367	211		101	90	87	44		34	7
3909 Manufacturing industries, n.e.c.		5377	4842	4441a/	3885a/		1569	1435	1560a/	1229a/	a/	109	142
3 Total manufacturing		334293	314511	300520	301250		100495	93846	90866	85512		7051	9657

a/ Data are incomplete due to confidentiality rules.
b/ 351 includes 352.
c/ 353 includes 354.

China (Hong Kong SAR)

ISIC Revision 2		Index numbers of industrial production (1990=100)											
ISIC Industry	Note	1985	1986	1987	1988	1989	1990	1991	1992	1993	1994	1995	1996
311/2 Food products	a/	65	70	76	86	89	100	104	109	112	114	113	112
313 Beverages	a/	...	...	...	...	...	...	...	...	...	...	...	...
314 Tobacco	a/	...	...	...	...	...	...	...	...	...	...	...	...
321 Textiles		70	87	99	97	102	100	105	109	101	101	97	91
322 Wearing apparel, except footwear		74	89	101	101	102	100	97	98	100	100	101	97
323 Leather and fur products	b/	86	96	105	109	101	100	95	93	85	81	78	79
324 Footwear, except rubber or plastic	b/	...	...	...	...	...	...	...	...	...	...	...	...
331 Wood products, except furniture	c/	86	96	104	109	101	100	95	93	85	81	78	79
332 Furniture and fixtures, excl. metal	c/	...	...	...	...	...	...	...	...	...	...	...	...
341 Paper and products		47	55	69	84	92	100	111	130	146	150	150	146
342 Printing and publishing		47	55	69	84	92	100	110	129	146	150	150	145
351 Industrial chemicals	d/	98	111	119	116	106	100	94	90	81	74	70	70
352 Other chemicals	d/	...	...	...	...	...	...	...	...	...	...	...	...
353 Petroleum refineries		...	...	...	...	...	...	...	...	...	...	...	...
354 Misc. petroleum and coal products		...	...	...	...	...	...	...	...	...	...	...	...
355 Rubber products		98	111	118	115	106	100	94	90	81	74	70	70
356 Plastic products		114	131	139	133	115	100	92	85	71	58	49	47
361 Pottery, china, earthenware	e/	97	111	119	115	106	100	94	90	81	74	70	70
362 Glass and products	e/	...	...	...	...	...	...	...	...	...	...	...	...
369 Other non-metallic mineral products	e/	...	...	...	...	...	...	...	...	...	...	...	...
371 Iron and steel	f/	78	88	102	122	111	100	98	93	85	84	83	75
372 Non-ferrous metals	f/	...	...	...	...	...	...	...	...	...	...	...	...
381 Fabricated metal products		79	91	105	126	113	100	99	94	86	85	82	73
382 Non-electrical machinery		79	89	103	122	112	100	98	94	85	84	83	75
383 Electrical machinery		60	67	84	97	99	100	103	105	107	111	121	114
384 Transport equipment		85	96	105	109	101	100	95	93	85	81	78	79
385 Professional and scientific equipment		60	67	85	97	99	100	103	105	107	111	121	114
390 Other manufacturing industries		85	96	105	110	101	100	95	93	85	81	77	79
3 Total manufacturing		73	85	97	104	102	100	101	102	101	100	100	95

a/ 311/2 includes 313 and 314.
b/ 323 includes 324.
c/ 331 includes 332.
d/ 351 includes 352.
e/ 361 includes 362 and 369.
f/ 371 includes 372.

COLOMBIA

Supplier of information:
Departamento Administrativo Nacional de Estadística, Bogotá. The index numbers of industrial production are compiled by the Banco de la República.

Basic source of data:
Annual manufacturing survey.

Major deviations from ISIC (Revision 2):
None reported.

Reference period (if not calendar year):

Scope:
Establishments with 10 or more persons engaged.

Method of enumeration:
Not reported.

Adjusted for non-response:
Not reported.

Concepts and definitions of variables:
Number of employees is as of the pay period that includes 15 November of the reference year. Persons on strike are excluded.
Wages and salaries excludes employers' contributions to social insurance, welfare funds and other similar schemes unless otherwise indicated.
Output includes revenues from goods shipped in the same condition as received.
Gross fixed capital formation is net of depreciation. The revaluation of fixed assets over the year is taken into account.

Related national publications:
Encuesta anual manufacturera; Boletín Mensual de Estadística (la Industria Manufacturera); Anuario General de Estadística, Tomo IV; Informe al Congreso Nacional (annual), all published by the Departamento Administrativo Nacional de Estadística, Bogotá.

Colombia

ISIC Revision 2	Number of establishments					Number of employees					Wages and salaries paid to employees				
		(numbers)					(numbers)					(million PESOS)			
ISIC Industry	Note	1992	1993	1994	1995	Note	1992	1993	1994	1995	Note	1992	1993	1994	1995
311/2 Food products		1415	1345	1347	1435		102999	101596	105301	100818		197518	253059	323211	382949
3111 Slaughtering, preparing & preserving meat		118	115	112	115		11583	10379	11553	10837		18156	20190	28002	32740
3112 Dairy products		112	115	112	121		11939	12803	13953	12844		24657	33248	45409	63155
3113 Canning, preserving of fruits & vegetables		44	46	46	51		2076	2552	2224	3342		3144	6830	5575	12217
3114 Canning, preserving and processing of fish		12	13	15	15		1410	1318	1500	1543		2169	3137	4358	4155
3115 Vegetable and animal oils and fats		63	61	61	62		9461	8816	9404	9500		23926	23667	32375	38463
3116 Grain mill products		345	316	297	283		15478	14178	13117	12662		22839	28103	33573	39762
3117 Bakery products		381	364	370	422		18429	19071	19145	18947		30144	38874	48834	59544
3118 Sugar factories and refineries		34	30	30	31		12459	11872	12291	8962		27085	38027	45246	42789
3119 Cocoa, chocolate and sugar confectionery		64	64	67	72		5376	5664	5618	5588		12052	16527	16979	23578
3121 Other food products		173	159	168	189		10721	10900	12137	12290		24982	33387	47946	47804
3122 Prepared animal feeds		69	62	69	74		4067	4043	4359	4303		8364	11069	14912	18741
313 Beverages		144	142	141	142		23547	24043	23544	21583		63271	74949	95957	116199
3131 Distilling, rectifying and blending spirits		34	32	33	32		4532	4864	4511	4014		11172	13295	14477	18855
3132 Wine industries		21	21	22	22		681	705	748	674		1102	1708	1875	2076
3133 Malt liquors and malt		23	22	22	22		7354	7373	7378	7039		24538	27401	38169	46588
3134 Soft drinks and carbonated waters		66	67	64	66		10980	11101	10907	9856		26459	32545	41436	48679
314 Tobacco		12	10	10	9		1937	1591	1496	1240		3892	4762	5029	5037
321 Textiles		502	479	468	465		61057	59993	59450	56816		105564	140134	167176	198708
3211 Spinning, weaving and finishing textiles		235	208	198	200		39801	36944	35831	33663		75206	96202	112671	131284
3212 Made-up textile goods excl. wearing apparel		40	38	41	49		2609	2641	2856	2990		3724	4592	5969	7022
3213 Knitting mills		182	189	181	172		16179	17763	17811	17183		22294	32608	37775	47543
3214 Carpets and rugs		17	16	16	15		807	894	1126	1091		1142	1838	3721	4207
3215 Cordage, rope and twine		9	8	8	10		459	462	402	651		582	827	902	2122
3219 Other textiles		19	20	24	19		1202	1289	1424	1238		2616	4067	6137	6530
322 Wearing apparel, except footwear		983	940	901	944		66229	65058	66424	66649		77757	100923	127585	141532
323 Leather and fur products		133	125	111	118		8960	9040	7735	7030		13043	17616	18803	18812
3231 Tanneries and leather finishing		42	37	31	38		3499	3618	3187	2901		6416	9062	9568	9168
3232 Fur dressing and dyeing industries		8	8	8	10		458	460	504	539		569	679	1212	1367
3233 Leather prods. excl. wearing apparel		83	80	72	70		5003	4962	4044	3590		6058	7875	8023	8278
324 Footwear, except rubber or plastic		297	262	250	254		16986	14999	14071	11985		22041	25482	29535	28359
331 Wood products, except furniture		195	181	186	196		8019	7732	7545	7435		12544	15784	19482	23055
3311 Sawmills, planing and other wood mills		154	141	146	155		6490	6073	6388	6387		10580	12989	17154	20615
3312 Wooden and cane containers		5	...a/	...a/	5		135	...a/	...a/	107		160	...a/	...a/	248
3319 Other wood and cork products		36	40a/	40a/	36		1394	1659a/	1157a/	941		1804	2795a/	2328a/	2192
332 Furniture and fixtures, excl. metal		262	239	262	270		8926	9385	11125	9585		10038	14567	21788	23280
341 Paper and products		164	158	163	170		13756	14276	14873	14931		40749	56011	71053	86398
3411 Pulp, paper and paperboard articles		33	29	32	33		6108	6253	6361	5705		23220	31526	37238	43707
3412 Containers of paper and paperboard		83	86	85	93		4820	4932	5198	5862		11058	14474	19524	25623
3419 Other pulp, paper and paperboard articles		48	43	46	44		2828	3091	3314	3364		6471	10011	14290	17068
342 Printing and publishing		426	423	413	434		26774	27211	28464	29244		49796	64946	84674	126284
351 Industrial chemicals		150	159	163	177		15008	14766	14822	14021		52723	64712	84745	94427
3511 Basic chemicals excl. fertilizers		98	104	103	114		5819	5244	5020	5805		15916	15533	19819	28627
3512 Fertilizers and pesticides		25	28	30	31		3541	3736	4247	3558		16882	21815	30107	31409
3513 Synthetic resins and plastic materials		27	27	30	32		5648	5786	5555	4658		19925	27364	34819	34392
352 Other chemicals		351	356	358	356		34539	38342	38117	38948		100207	151486	193419	224587
3521 Paints, varnishes and lacquers		32	32	34	32		2803	2863	3006	2955		6682	8930	11844	13680
3522 Drugs and medicines		132	130	130	132		15748	15947	16740	17132		54303	74713	101593	120499
3523 Soap, cleaning preps., perfumes, cosmetics		80	87	81	81		9453	12706	11243	11512		22870	43382	49934	57873
3529 Other chemical products		107	107	113	111		6535	6826	7128	7349		16352	24461	30048	32534
353 Petroleum refineries		6	6	6	6		6303	6623	6301	6090		31568	42499	48725	51189

ISIC	Industry														
354	Misc. petroleum and coal products		32	30	34	40		1517	1265	1487	1589		4077	7426	6873	10234
355	Rubber products		105	100	91	93		7585	7513	7012	6770		22417	26921	31787	35454
3551	Tyres and tubes		28	27	25	26		4230	3891	3626	3515		17166	19626	23241	26055
3559	Other rubber products		77	73	66	67		3355	3622	3386	3255		5251	7295	8546	9399
356	Plastic products		428	416	404	428		24700	25384	24035	25641		46920	63345	70959	91646
361	Pottery, china, earthenware		19	17	15	13		5878	6337	6366	6073		11594	17914	22545	25884
362	Glass and products		80	80	75	82		7554	7555	7169	7445		16938	22801	28012	33350
369	Other non-metallic mineral products		327	326	330	365		21146	22701	23257	23833		45922	61421	79356	93576
3691	Structural clay products		102	103	103	113		6294	7000	7264	7683		9167	12735	16679	21405
3692	Cement, lime and plaster		26	27	29	30		5493	6361	6431	6328		17082	22896	29724	34117
3699	Other non-metallic mineral products		199	196	198	222		9359	9340	9562	9822		19673	25790	32953	38054
371	Iron and steel		86	90	81	86		9870	9153	9041	9176		36125	32050	34730	43478
372	Non-ferrous metals		36	38	41	42		2497	2456	2447	2263		6305	8069	9394	10434
381	Fabricated metal products		628	622	600	664		30415	32698	32621	32561		50255	69231	89787	105101
3811	Cutlery, hand tools and general hardware		39	43	37	37		4962	5086	4912	4955		9589	12128	16342	19611
3812	Furniture and fixtures primarily of metal		145	147	143	160		4608	5335	5287	5244		5737	8365	10445	12526
3813	Structural metal products		172	159	171	199		6619	6490	7604	7979		11216	13675	20273	25965
3819	Other fabricated metal products		272	273	249	268		14226	15787	14818	14383		23713	35064	42727	46999
382	Non-electrical machinery		369	365	349	374		19138	19804	20086	20863		31144	42016	55779	68923
3821	Engines and turbines	b/	...	...	...	...	b/	...	...	...	...	b/	...	...	...	...
3822	Agricultural machinery and equipment		40	37	34	39		966	1075	1039	905		1297	2005	2941	2277
3823	Metal and wood working machinery		29	25	25	27		621	619	636	700		993	1493	1735	2436
3824	Other special industrial machinery		71	75	69	73		2756	2764	2596	2602		4641	6239	6711	8627
3825	Office, computing and accounting machinery		12	13	12	10		347	399	415	369		671	987	1237	1183
3829	Other non-electrical machinery & equipment	b/	217	215	209	225	b/	14448	14947	15400	16287	b/	23542	31292	43155	54400
383	Electrical machinery		226	214	205	209		19414	19519	19801	19998		40285	52567	68249	79712
3831	Electrical industrial machinery		92	77	79	82		5452	5330	5206	5943		11835	15829	22059	26391
3832	Radio, television and communication equipm.		35	32	31	33		4605	4599	4682	4844		7047	9442	11622	16013
3833	Electrical appliances and housewares		11	12	9	9		1017	960	921	862		2114	2480	2911	3264
3839	Other electrical apparatus and supplies		88	93	86	85		8340	8630	8992	8349		19289	24816	31658	34044
384	Transport equipment		305	283	253	274		22133	23501	21595	20562		47048	68918	82543	91638
3841	Shipbuilding and repairing		15	8	9	9		1327	730	603	701		2411	1730	1655	2370
3842	Railroad equipment	c/	...	...	...	...	c/	...	...	...	...	c/	...	...	...	...
3843	Motor vehicles		239	227	202	217		16748	18314	16589	15108		34115	51876	62705	67133
3844	Motorcycles and bicycles		33	29	28	30		2372	2740	2891	2991		3897	6079	7722	9365
3845	Aircraft		8	8	5	9		1470	1542	1362	1550		6364	8927	10202	11931
3849	Other transport equipment	c/	10	11	9	9	c/	216	175	150	212	c/	261	306	259	840
385	Professional and scientific equipment		79	75	63	67		4282	4711	3655	3847		9748	13445	11029	13582
3851	Prof. and scientific equipment n.e.c.		60	59	51	56		3571	3991	3209	3324		8786	12104	9883	11948
3852	Photographic and optical goods		16	16d/	12d/	11d/		665	720d/	446d/	523d/		908	1341d/	1145d/	1634d/
3853	Watches and clocks		3	...d/	...d/	...d/		46	...d/	...d/	...d/		54	...d/	...d/	...d/
390	Other manufacturing industries		195	182	168	196		9596	9892	8965	9293		15104	21062	26834	33529
3901	Jewellery and related articles		18	19	18	21		1094	1346	1240	1252		1702	2954	3338	4328
3902	Musical instruments		5	3	5	4		128	106	117	65		151	156	194	132
3903	Sporting and athletic goods		9	8	6	8		277	293	268	342		286	408	463	786
3909	Manufacturing industries, n.e.c.		163	152	139	163		8097	8147	7340	7634		12965	17543	22839	28282
3	Total manufacturing		7955	7663	7488	7909		580765	587144	586805	576289		1164593	1534114	1909059	2257356

a/ 3319 includes 3312.
b/ 3829 includes 3821.
c/ 3849 includes 3842.
d/ 3852 includes 3853.

Colombia

ISIC Revision 2	Output in producers' prices					Value added in producers' prices					Gross fixed capital formation		
		(billion PESOS)					(billion PESOS)					(million PESOS)	
ISIC Industry	Note	1992	1993	1994	1995	Note	1992	1993	1994	1995	Note	1994	1995
311/2 Food products		4002.6	4653.6	6300.9	7682.3		1262.5	1383.0	2147.6	2690.6		115149	120683
3111 Slaughtering, preparing & preserving meat		309.1	299.3	404.8	537.4		90.3	85.9	126.5	168.4		4270	612
3112 Dairy products		452.3	558.3	761.4	1109.8		147.9	142.2	232.2	372.0		10797	2271
3113 Canning, preserving of fruits & vegetables		58.5	81.9	60.9	155.7		23.1	27.9	26.8	98.6		970	7473
3114 Canning, preserving and processing of fish		64.0	63.3	81.4	138.0		23.0	13.3	20.3	59.6		281	-12565
3115 Vegetable and animal oils and fats		456.4	512.4	580.2	766.4		135.5	132.7	163.6	252.6		12021	7431
3116 Grain mill products		938.4	958.5	1554.3	1642.1		171.6	167.2	443.4	395.6		8398	20630
3117 Bakery products		260.9	375.6	463.0	571.5		110.7	163.2	203.5	257.6		12825	6719
3118 Sugar factories and refineries		438.3	536.5	696.9	846.1		202.2	240.5	316.9	399.2		11652	25420
3119 Cocoa, chocolate and sugar confectionery		169.7	218.9	290.5	350.0		76.8	100.9	148.8	162.9		9431	12349
3121 Other food products		472.5	558.9	788.3	846.1		225.3	243.6	368.7	378.9		43877	28494
3122 Prepared animal feeds		382.5	490.2	619.2	719.3		56.1	65.5	96.8	145.2		626	21848
313 Beverages		1119.8	1244.6	1636.6	2023.0		704.8	675.7	992.2	1301.7		78811	270001
3131 Distilling, rectifying and blending spirits		169.5	163.1	227.3	318.7		105.1	73.9	135.5	213.1		4230	1219
3132 Wine industries		14.2	22.6	22.7	25.9		5.4	8.4	8.2	12.0		64	544
3133 Malt liquors and malt		554.8	585.2	763.0	946.6		379.5	322.8	463.9	631.1		34770	118376
3134 Soft drinks and carbonated waters		381.3	473.8	623.7	731.8		214.8	270.6	384.5	445.4		39747	149862
314 Tobacco		91.7	100.7	101.7	102.5		47.3	45.2	60.6	63.3		-602	-2642
321 Textiles		1197.0	1382.7	1537.5	1796.2		518.9	598.5	712.5	866.0		-26250	-85484
3211 Spinning, weaving and finishing textiles		883.8	995.2	1084.3	1231.5		406.0	451.7	525.3	624.8		-25858	-81144
3212 Made-up textile goods excl. wearing apparel		31.4	33.4	41.5	56.3		13.3	13.5	18.8	28.9		2174	-617
3213 Knitting mills		217.3	271.0	293.4	388.5		79.0	105.8	120.9	160.7		3152	111
3214 Carpets and rugs		14.4	18.7	38.8	38.2		5.7	5.8	16.6	15.3		-465	-1552
3215 Cordage, rope and twine		5.0	5.9	6.7	17.6		2.0	1.9	2.7	8.7		352	508
3219 Other textiles		45.2	58.7	72.7	64.1		13.0	19.8	28.1	27.7		-5605	-2790
322 Wearing apparel, except footwear		527.6	646.7	802.0	915.7		241.7	284.2	372.7	446.1		8696	21641
323 Leather and fur products		181.2	222.6	194.0	212.9		58.0	62.6	57.6	73.6		1280	6161
3231 Tanneries and leather finishing		127.9	150.3	130.0	139.7		34.3	38.6	31.4	40.5		169	7362
3232 Fur dressing and dyeing industries		6.1	6.8	13.8	15.5		1.9	1.5	4.7	5.4		628	15
3233 Leather prods. excl. wearing apparel		47.2	65.4	50.2	57.7		21.7	22.5	21.5	27.7		483	-1216
324 Footwear, except rubber or plastic		204.8	206.2	252.3	251.4		79.9	84.3	98.8	113.5		-2028	-3800
331 Wood products, except furniture		118.9	165.1	200.3	215.6		51.7	75.0	84.1	79.1		5871	32430
3311 Sawmills, planing and other wood mills		106.3	147.2	186.1	201.2		45.4	66.3	77.0	72.9		6224	32576
3312 Wooden and cane containers		1.2	...a/	...a/	2.1		0.5	...a/	...a/	0.7		...a/	67
3319 Other wood and cork products		11.4	17.9a/	14.3a/	12.3		5.8	8.7a/	7.0a/	5.6		-353a/	-213
332 Furniture and fixtures, excl. metal		61.4	78.5	132.4	134.3		29.0	35.7	64.0	68.2		2865	5886
341 Paper and products		704.2	844.9	1064.4	1447.5		245.5	276.3	429.6	623.4		-337	-8714
3411 Pulp, paper and paperboard articles		398.3	445.0	538.5	781.6		132.1	135.0	209.4	357.5		-12199	-27319
3412 Containers of paper and paperboard		193.5	229.6	303.3	389.0		65.5	72.6	113.7	147.2		6503	2762
3419 Other pulp, paper and paperboard articles		112.5	170.3	222.5	276.8		47.9	68.7	106.5	118.8		5359	15843
342 Printing and publishing		411.2	513.6	680.0	968.3		208.0	266.3	368.5	508.7		34552	-15426
351 Industrial chemicals		981.2	1222.4	1470.4	1942.0		407.1	498.6	593.0	792.6		-15222	-37551
3511 Basic chemicals excl. fertilizers		210.0	290.2	316.6	431.8		116.0	176.8	183.4	257.4		2891	-32243
3512 Fertilizers and pesticides		361.4	409.1	512.9	626.0		136.1	136.5	165.9	228.4		-15891	-3397
3513 Synthetic resins and plastic materials		409.8	523.1	641.0	884.2		154.9	185.2	243.7	306.8		-2222	-1911
352 Other chemicals		1202.8	1680.2	1972.0	2553.0		621.0	861.6	1077.9	1426.2		43092	54574
3521 Paints, varnishes and lacquers		115.6	170.5	190.9	238.1		40.8	62.9	68.3	91.4		3601	9053
3522 Drugs and medicines		511.4	599.2	763.7	1023.2		298.0	336.2	459.0	622.9		23840	35030
3523 Soap, cleaning preps., perfumes, cosmetics		374.2	646.1	718.0	956.2		187.7	336.2	399.7	527.2		12945	7037
3529 Other chemical products		201.5	264.4	299.3	335.5		94.6	126.4	150.8	184.7		2706	3454
353 Petroleum refineries		532.1	639.3	782.2	1496.1		167.4	116.8	259.7	608.1		60024	65638

354 Misc. petroleum and coal products		85.7	121.6	165.7	222.9		32.3	40.8	64.3	97.2		1592	7
355 Rubber products		225.6	276.2	342.8	349.5		111.7	111.5	182.7	155.5		-1440	54171
3551 Tyres and tubes		178.7	217.4	276.1	273.1		90.0	85.6	150.6	119.0		-1625	51556
3559 Other rubber products		46.9	58.8	66.7	76.4		21.6	25.9	32.1	36.5		185	2615
356 Plastic products		541.0	683.1	814.6	1069.4		231.3	291.6	353.9	437.7		20812	66805
361 Pottery, china, earthenware		101.5	149.6	182.3	193.7		60.7	92.7	117.0	120.3		5299	-2404
362 Glass and products		153.8	198.1	250.1	310.7		83.0	104.6	147.0	183.8		269	32846
369 Other non-metallic mineral products		577.5	819.6	1155.4	1340.9		314.6	414.8	609.4	721.2		53308	107049
3691 Structural clay products		58.3	80.0	110.5	147.2		37.7	48.4	70.1	92.1		9593	17089
3692 Cement, lime and plaster		297.9	393.8	553.2	654.5		176.5	217.5	316.6	397.5		33421	78823
3699 Other non-metallic mineral products		221.3	345.9	491.7	539.2		100.4	148.9	222.7	231.6		10294	11136
371 Iron and steel		495.8	493.4	588.5	758.8		265.6	182.4	235.4	319.7		9072	-10438
372 Non-ferrous metals		83.0	104.9	132.9	160.6		31.6	38.2	46.4	51.2		-3048	1907
381 Fabricated metal products		506.3	631.8	803.9	988.3		219.8	260.2	362.2	460.5		13218	17073
3811 Cutlery, hand tools and general hardware		92.6	108.1	125.8	165.8		50.9	66.9	73.1	112.1		918	-1888
3812 Furniture and fixtures primarily of metal		38.6	55.4	75.5	77.5		17.0	21.1	32.1	38.3		1183	1582
3813 Structural metal products		106.9	96.1	170.8	244.4		43.5	33.5	73.5	113.0		2690	7038
3819 Other fabricated metal products		268.3	372.3	431.8	500.6		108.5	138.8	183.4	197.1		8426	10341
382 Non-electrical machinery		273.5	386.7	464.6	563.1		116.8	159.9	206.4	260.0		8969	6826
3821 Engines and turbines	b/	...	...	...	...	b/	...	...	...	...	b/	...	...
3822 Agricultural machinery and equipment		7.1	12.5	17.4	11.6		3.2	5.3	8.7	5.7		99	4
3823 Metal and wood working machinery		6.5	8.7	10.2	12.5		3.4	4.8	4.2	6.1		263	1725
3824 Other special industrial machinery		29.5	37.4	41.4	53.2		14.2	17.4	19.8	25.8		1368	-757
3825 Office, computing and accounting machinery		4.4	5.6	6.5	7.6		2.3	2.6	3.3	3.8		594	317
3829 Other non-electrical machinery & equipment	b/	226.0	322.4	389.1	478.2	b/	93.6	129.9	170.4	218.6	b/	6646	5537
383 Electrical machinery		454.7	525.7	627.5	728.1		211.6	221.7	260.4	348.5		17290	27380
3831 Electrical industrial machinery		103.4	121.7	147.9	189.3		43.8	51.1	64.6	80.3		1446	565
3832 Radio, television and communication equipm.		79.8	103.5	114.7	144.6		36.5	45.6	48.2	81.4		3272	15550
3833 Electrical appliances and housewares		32.9	40.9	39.0	35.3		12.0	18.3	15.0	13.7		-88	-108
3839 Other electrical apparatus and supplies		238.6	259.7	325.9	358.8		119.3	106.7	132.7	173.0		12659	11373
384 Transport equipment		740.3	1209.7	1421.1	1590.4		222.9	294.5	367.8	462.8		7553	9861
3841 Shipbuilding and repairing		13.6	6.0	7.9	13.6		6.4	2.7	3.8	10.0		54	-218
3842 Railroad equipment	c/	...	...	...	...	c/	...	...	...	...	c/	...	...
3843 Motor vehicles		621.9	1056.1	1221.1	1260.2		181.2	247.8	325.1	349.9		856	9667
3844 Motorcycles and bicycles		67.3	119.0	160.8	217.9		12.2	30.4	26.2	44.6		1146	2365
3845 Aircraft		34.8	26.6	29.2	94.0		22.2	12.9	11.8	56.1		5490	-1908
3849 Other transport equipment	c/	2.7	1.8	2.1	4.7	c/	0.8	0.7	0.8	2.1	c/	8	-44
385 Professional and scientific equipment		84.9	103.3	96.9	128.6		51.0	53.7	53.9	72.2		308	-1542
3851 Prof. and scientific equipment n.e.c.		79.7	97.9	91.5	121.2		48.0	50.7	50.7	67.5		263	-1752
3852 Photographic and optical goods		4.8	5.3d/	5.4d/	7.4d/		2.8	2.9d/	3.2d/	4.7d/	d/	46	210
3853 Watches and clocks		0.4	...d/	...d/	...d/		0.2	...d/	...d/	...d/	d/	...	...
390 Other manufacturing industries		114.1	149.0	200.7	240.7		62.1	81.2	118.4	141.0		4496	5421
3901 Jewellery and related articles		10.9	21.3	24.1	29.4		5.1	12.5	13.4	15.4		-455	-1084
3902 Musical instruments		1.0	0.8	0.9	0.5		0.5	0.4	0.5	0.3		3	15
3903 Sporting and athletic goods		1.2	1.9	2.6	8.8		0.7	0.9	1.1	4.2		126	9
3909 Manufacturing industries, n.e.c.		101.0	125.1	173.1	201.9		55.9	67.3	103.4	121.2		4823	6481
3 Total manufacturing		15774.2	19453.9	24373.4	30386.2		6657.8	7611.3	10443.8	13492.6		443595	738358

a/ 3319 includes 3312.
b/ 3829 includes 3821.
c/ 3849 includes 3842.
d/ 3852 includes 3853.

Colombia

ISIC Revision 2		Note	Index numbers of industrial production (1990=100)											
ISIC	Industry		1985	1986	1987	1988	1989	1990	1991	1992	1993	1994	1995	1996
311/2	Food products		87	88	90	90	90	100	98	111	105	103	106	110
313	Beverages		90	93	100	97	98	100	100	95	101	109	118	109
314	Tobacco		125	126	115	107	101	100	116	97	85	70	59	67
321	Textiles		90	100	109	103	97	100	100	107	106	108	113	116
322	Wearing apparel, except footwear		63	65	71	84	94	100	97	101	95	78	77	81
323	Leather and fur products		60	72	76	81	85	100	109	105	97	91	77	58
324	Footwear, except rubber or plastic		99	105	98	100	107	100	122	124	119	115	104	84
331	Wood products, except furniture		59	62	75	82	94	100	96	95	107	117	102	74
332	Furniture and fixtures, excl. metal		97	90	90	113	107	100	94	104	121	149	154	77
341	Paper and products		65	68	76	78	89	100	112	122	113	122	133	120
342	Printing and publishing		95	101	105	118	105	100	104	105	114	132	121	116
351	Industrial chemicals		79	88	95	99	98	100	104	101	102	104	113	103
352	Other chemicals		69	78	83	87	93	100	101	109	114	119	121	113
353	Petroleum refineries		80	91	99	95	98	100	102	90	91	97	98	118
354	Misc. petroleum and coal products		98	96	101	111	109	100	92	96	95	110	116	108
355	Rubber products		93	91	86	99	95	100	104	112	111	100	85	73
356	Plastic products		87	103	103	96	91	100	99	115	128	148	143	144
361	Pottery, china, earthenware		71	82	95	104	102	100	111	124	141	157	156	155
362	Glass and products		72	72	85	93	93	100	99	97	101	106	110	100
369	Other non-metallic mineral products		92	98	102	102	104	100	111	116	128	136	138	122
371	Iron and steel		75	81	91	99	100	100	98	111	113	130	132	127
372	Non-ferrous metals		66	79	102	99	82	100	99	108	106	110	115	102
381	Fabricated metal products		78	88	89	101	88	100	91	100	114	125	134	131
382	Non-electrical machinery		46	53	60	65	69	100	101	116	130	142	143	116
383	Electrical machinery		96	101	104	112	107	100	91	106	114	120	111	106
384	Transport equipment		72	81	98	117	109	100	84	100	142	158	159	145
385	Professional and scientific equipment		83	88	100	113	102	100	106	88	85	89	118	139
390	Other manufacturing industries		94	100	108	109	112	100	103	106	120	121	117	112
3	Total manufacturing		83	89	94	97	96	100	100	106	110	114	117	112

COOK ISLANDS

Supplier of information:
Statistics Office, Ministry of Finance and Economic Management, Rarotonga.

Basic source of data:
Survey of Employment and Earnings, 1993; Cook Islands National Accounts, 1982 - 1996; Census of Population and Dwellings, 1996.

Major deviations from ISIC (Revision 2):
None reported.

Reference period (if not calendar year):

Scope:
All establishments.

Method of enumeration:
The inquiry is conducted by mail and personal visits.

Adjusted for non-response:
No.

Concepts and definitions of variables:
No deviations from the standard UN concepts and definitions are reported.

Related national publications:

Cooks Islands

ISIC Revision 2	Number of establishments					Number of employees					Wages and salaries paid to employees				
		(numbers)					(numbers)					(thousand DOLLARS)			
ISIC Industry	Note	1993	1994	1995	1996	Note	1993	1994	1995	1996	Note	1993	1994	1995	1996
3 Total manufacturing		59	...	...	...		290	...	...	303		2084	2364	1908	1947

ISIC Revision 2	Output					Value added					Gross fixed capital formation		
		(thousand DOLLARS)					(thousand DOLLARS)					(thousand DOLLARS)	
ISIC Industry	Note	1993	1994	1995	1996	Note	1993	1994	1995	1996	Note	1995	1996
3 Total manufacturing		8884	9299	8061	8225		3820	3995	3698	3773		...	...

ISIC Revision 2	Index numbers of industrial production												
		(1990=100)											
ISIC Industry	Note	1985	1986	1987	1988	1989	1990	1991	1992	1993	1994	1995	1996
3 Total manufacturing		...	...	...	...	...	...	...	...	...	...	...	...

COSTA RICA

Supplier of information:
Departamento de Contabilidad Social, Banco Central de Costa Rica, San José.

Basic source of data:
Data collection of the Banco Central de Costa Rica.

Major deviations from ISIC (Revision 2):
None reported.

Reference period (if not calendar year):

Scope:
Number of establishments, employees and wages and salaries relate to enterprises registered under the social security scheme while other variables refer to all enterprises.

Method of enumeration:
Not reported.

Adjusted for non-response:
Not reported.

Concepts and definitions of variables:
Figures for wages and salaries were computed by UNIDO from the reported monthly averages.
Output is gross output and is derived from national accounts estimates.
Value added is total value added.
Output and value added are net of indirect taxes.

Related national publications:

ISIC Revision 2	Number of establishments (numbers)					Number of employees (numbers)					Wages and salaries paid to employees (million COLONES)				
ISIC Industry	Note	1993	1994	1995	1996	Note	1993	1994	1995	1996	Note	1993	1994	1995	1996
311/2 Food products		1219	1193	1232	1273		34882	36636	38132	39084		15476.3	...	...	...
3111 Slaughtering, preparing & preserving meat		55	68	86	87		5117	6205	6479	6159		2571.5	...	...	...
3112 Dairy products		37	35	42	48		3586	3816	3951	3896		2212.0	...	...	...
3113 Canning, preserving of fruits & vegetables		95	103	105	107		3721	4251	4248	5149		1602.7	...	...	...
3114 Canning, preserving and processing of fish		18	19	18	27		2008	1896	1734	1988		779.9	...	...	...
3115 Vegetable and animal oils and fats		12	8	6	8		1183	1176	1004	1126		901.8	...	...	...
3116 Grain mill products		197	173	167	159		6157	5788	6125	6298		2684.6	...	...	...
3117 Bakery products		562	554	555	565		6288	6457	6875	6934		2345.3	...	...	...
3118 Sugar factories and refineries		25	22	20	20		2309	2585	2775	3037		1196.3	...	...	...
3119 Cocoa, chocolate and sugar confectionery		27	23	27	29		1639	1592	1423	1242		912.9	...	...	...
3121 Other food products		150	146	164	185		2280	2175	2989	2735		13.2	...	...	...
3122 Prepared animal feeds		41	42	42	38		594	695	529	520		256.1	...	...	...
313 Beverages		56	46	49	49		4183	3447	3397	4739		2558.0	...	...	...
3131 Distilling, rectifying and blending spirits		6	5	6	5		393	410	406	472		298.6	...	...	...
3132 Wine industries		4	2	2	1		44	19	16	14		23.6	...	...	...
3133 Malt liquors and malt		5	2	3	4		746	214	270	1593		469.7	...	...	...
3134 Soft drinks and carbonated waters		41	37	38	39		3000	2804	2705	2660		1766.2	...	...	...
314 Tobacco		8	4	5	6		624	565	544	522		738.5	...	...	...
321 Textiles		207	192	187	149		10754	6681	10362	4972		4273.8	...	...	...
3211 Spinning, weaving and finishing textiles		47	39	35	31		3118	1758	2283	1763		1238.0	...	...	...
3212 Made-up textile goods excl. wearing apparel		56	60	55	48		1036	1095	723	507		476.4	...	...	...
3213 Knitting mills		72	65	70	54		4851	3217	6494	2454		1806.1	...	...	...
3214 Carpets and rugs		10	11	10	6		218	126	90	49		100.6	...	...	...
3215 Cordage, rope and twine		4	4	3	4		24	161	99	157		5.5	...	...	...
3219 Other textiles		18	13	14	6		1507	324	673	42		647.1	...	...	...
322 Wearing apparel, except footwear		588	569	529	513		34855	39783	36796	35088		13265.7	...	...	...
323 Leather and fur products		73	68	66	70		1454	1405	1548	1782		537.7	...	...	...
3231 Tanneries and leather finishing		13	13	13	10		757	680	727	712		345.2	...	...	...
3232 Fur dressing and dyeing industries		4	4	4	4		17	24	12	9		4.6	...	...	...
3233 Leather prods. excl. wearing apparel		56	51	49	56		680	701	809	1061		187.9	...	...	...
324 Footwear, except rubber or plastic		104	98	99	88		1750	1620	1709	1851		637.3	...	...	...
331 Wood products, except furniture		270	297	322	333		4639	4863	4531	4526		1694.3	...	...	...
3311 Sawmills, planing and other wood mills		205	227	238	242		4023	4209	3916	3680		1494.9	...	...	...
3312 Wooden and cane containers		2	2	5	6		35	24	24	32		10.3	...	...	...
3319 Other wood and cork products		63	68	79	85		581	630	591	814		189.1	...	...	...
332 Furniture and fixtures, excl. metal		486	493	501	481		2536	2654	2645	2512		785.6	...	...	...
341 Paper and products		50	52	51	59		2932	3249	2893	3410		2127.7	...	...	...
3411 Pulp, paper and paperboard articles		6	5	8	8		37	42	84	77		11.8	...	...	...
3412 Containers of paper and paperboard		26	25	22	25		1807	1997	1860	2282		1321.8	...	...	...
3419 Other pulp, paper and paperboard articles		18	22	21	26		1088	1210	949	1051		794.1	...	...	...
342 Printing and publishing		348	371	377	398		4846	5098	5029	4927		2948.1	...	...	...
351 Industrial chemicals		58	54	49	50		2574	2452	1869	1541		1625.9	...	...	...
3511 Basic chemicals excl. fertilizers		17	19	14	14		159	288	187	260		92.9	...	...	...
3512 Fertilizers and pesticides		19	17	17	17		1814	1604	1461	1053		1107.8	...	...	...
3513 Synthetic resins and plastic materials		22	18	18	19		601	560	221	228		425.2	...	...	...
352 Other chemicals		183	169	171	177		5347	5443	5223	4710		2686.4	...	...	...
3521 Paints, varnishes and lacquers		33	31	35	34		980	953	941	669		689.5	...	...	...
3522 Drugs and medicines		46	43	42	47		1240	1273	1153	1550		1.1	...	...	...
3523 Soap, cleaning preps., perfumes, cosmetics		48	42	44	47		1958	2046	1943	1450		1266.5	...	...	...
3529 Other chemical products		56	53	50	49		1169	1171	1186	1041		729.4	...	...	...
353 Petroleum refineries		11	2	3	1		2389	2516	2340	1379		2672.5	...	...	...

354 Misc. petroleum and coal products	2	1	1	3	25	7	7	11	9.0	...	...	...
355 Rubber products	54	55	60	61	3419	3185	4306	2784	1912.0	...	...	...
3551 Tyres and tubes	26	29	30	30	1297	1271	1257	1257	913.6	...	...	...
3559 Other rubber products	28	26	30	31	2122	1914	3049	1527	998.4	...	...	...
356 Plastic products	118	104	111	104	6480	6732	6193	6046	3349.7	...	...	...
361 Pottery, china, earthenware	56	46	38	41	903	742	779	729	422.8	...	...	...
362 Glass and products	49	45	41	41	914	843	779	884	417.1	...	...	...
369 Other non-metallic mineral products	201	190	192	193	4046	3859	3542	3391	2042.5	...	...	...
3691 Structural clay products	18	24	31	33	229	244	269	295	78.3	...	...	...
3692 Cement, lime and plaster	44	42	49	47	865	831	987	755	584.3	...	...	...
3699 Other non-metallic mineral products	139	124	112	113	2952	2784	2286	2341	1379.9	...	...	...
371 Iron and steel	28	31	35	35	558	785	670	730	310.2	...	...	...
372 Non-ferrous metals	7	7	6	9	340	317	315	345	187.2	...	...	...
381 Fabricated metal products	374	381	388	392	5211	4926	5366	4793	2232.7	...	...	...
3811 Cutlery, hand tools and general hardware	21	21	18	17	297	379	381	374	114.9	...	...	...
3812 Furniture and fixtures primarily of metal	66	60	61	62	993	838	946	854	348.1	...	...	...
3813 Structural metal products	190	205	211	209	1571	1452	1496	1374	590.2	...	...	...
3819 Other fabricated metal products	97	95	98	104	2350	2257	2543	2191	1179.5	...	...	...
382 Non-electrical machinery	170	162	167	192	3459	3469	2789	2765	1625.8	...	...	...
3821 Engines and turbines	27	21	20	16	215	158	153	115	74.2	...	...	...
3822 Agricultural machinery and equipment	29	29	25	26	461	474	518	522	229.2	...	...	...
3823 Metal and wood working machinery	17	10	15	15	95	63	75	85	32.5	...	...	...
3824 Other special industrial machinery	36	32	46	55	335	347	372	487	144.4	...	...	...
3825 Office, computing and accounting machinery	13	24	17	21	922	1044	181	196	400.2	...	...	...
3829 Other non-electrical machinery & equipment	48	46	44	59	1431	1383	1490	1360	745.4	...	...	...
383 Electrical machinery	121	110	108	116	6972	7670	9896	9288	3918.5	...	...	...
3831 Electrical industrial machinery	38	33	32	34	1150	1411	2404	2724	742.7	...	...	...
3832 Radio, television and communication equipm.	28	25	24	29	2210	1696	2570	1855	1352.1	...	...	...
3833 Electrical appliances and housewares	15	13	10	9	1988	2120	2440	2180	791.3	...	...	...
3839 Other electrical apparatus and supplies	40	39	42	44	1624	2443	2482	2529	1032.4	...	...	...
384 Transport equipment	105	168	213	240	1720	2138	1952	2291	1037.0	...	...	...
3841 Shipbuilding and repairing	15	19	16	18	218	233	198	224	91.3	...	...	...
3842 Railroad equipment	-	-	-	-	-	-	-	-	-	...	...	...
3843 Motor vehicles	66	124	171	194	589	884	819	1086	232.1	...	...	...
3844 Motorcycles and bicycles	13	13	13	16	116	173	61	134	38.7	...	...	...
3845 Aircraft	7	5	5	5	758	773	735	724	658.7	...	...	...
3849 Other transport equipment	4	7	8	7	39	75	139	123	16.1	...	...	...
385 Professional and scientific equipment	24	34	47	48	284	332	366	569	105.5	...	...	...
3851 Prof. and scientific equipment n.e.c.	5	11	17	15	37	63	104	81	9.0	...	...	...
3852 Photographic and optical goods	19	23	30	32	247	269	262	317	96.5	...	...	...
3853 Watches and clocks	-	-	-	1	-	-	-	171	-	...	...	...
390 Other manufacturing industries	116	119	129	120	3827	3121	2064	3156	1414.3	...	...	...
3901 Jewellery and related articles	27	37	39	40	531	426	473	548	189.9	...	...	...
3902 Musical instruments	6	3	3	3	17	12	11	11	4.0	...	...	...
3903 Sporting and athletic goods	14	17	16	16	1660	1600	327	1419	381.3	...	...	...
3909 Manufacturing industries, n.e.c.	69	62	71	61	1619	1083	1253	1178	839.2	...	...	...
3 Total manufacturing	5086	5061	5177	5242	151923	154538	156042	148825	71012.1	...	...	...

Costa Rica

ISIC Revision 2	Output in producers' prices					Value added in producers' prices					Gross fixed capital formation		
		(million COLONES)					(million COLONES)					(million COLONES)	
ISIC Industry	Note	1993	1994	1995a/	1996a/	Note	1993	1994	1995a/	1996a/	Note	1995	1996
311/2 Food products		220544	257216	366672	387189		51902	59542	83707	90498		...	...
3111 Slaughtering, preparing & preserving meat		27337	28272	30154	33005		5057	5137	5446	5960		...	...
3112 Dairy products		44546	50066	63023	72671		8913	9839	12310	14195		...	...
3113 Canning, preserving of fruits & vegetables		7846	9174	11886	15060		2304	2646	3408	4318		...	...
3114 Canning, preserving and processing of fish		3959	5830	7133	8376		707	1022	1243	1459		...	...
3115 Vegetable and animal oils and fats		19955	19111	24269	30934		4643	4367	5512	7026		...	...
3116 Grain mill products		45355	56823	114559	82961		8731	10741	21481	15601		...	...
3117 Bakery products		35643	43764	58366	72621		11651	14052	18627	23176		...	...
3118 Sugar factories and refineries		14242	16139	22134	26278		5709	6355	8663	10285		...	...
3119 Cocoa, chocolate and sugar confectionery		6394	7428	9768	11158		1850	2111	2759	3152		...	...
3121 Other food products		3168	5308	8075	8446		912	1501	2270	2374		...	...
3122 Prepared animal feeds		12099	15302	17305	25679		1425	1771	1990	2953		...	...
313 Beverages		45344	57197	68586	84895		23859	29083	34784	43101		...	...
3131 Distilling, rectifying and blending spirits		3347	3240	3209	4059		2238	2129	2096	2651		...	...
3132 Wine industries		33	38	45	56		15	18	21	26		...	...
3133 Malt liquors and malt		17839	20421	26479	32985		10561	11875	15304	19065		...	...
3134 Soft drinks and carbonated waters		24126	33498	38852	47795		11044	15062	17363	21360		...	...
314 Tobacco		5464	6764	10532	12512		3384	4115	6368	7566		...	...
321 Textiles		13785	13985	14288	15607		4581	4551	4631	5039		...	...
3211 Spinning, weaving and finishing textiles		7896	8220	8143	9154		2529	2586	2546	2862		...	...
3212 Made-up textile goods excl. wearing apparel		106	90	102	127		30	25	28	35		...	...
3213 Knitting mills		1612	1458	1590	1512		652	579	628	597		...	...
3214 Carpets and rugs		-	-	-	-		-	-	-	-		...	...
3215 Cordage, rope and twine		4171	4217	4454	4814		1370	1361	1429	1544		...	...
3219 Other textiles		...	...	...	...		...	...	...	...		...	...
322 Wearing apparel, except footwear		18087	19815	23920	25402		6943	7471	8964	9519		...	...
323 Leather and fur products		1897	1949	2311	2734		712	721	849	881		...	...
3231 Tanneries and leather finishing		1393	1387	1654	1966		502	491	582	692		...	...
3232 Fur dressing and dyeing industries		...	...	...	...		...	...	...	...		...	...
3233 Leather prods. excl. wearing apparel		503	563	657	768		210	230	267	190		...	...
324 Footwear, except rubber or plastic		3900	3978	4721	3623		1524	1527	1801	1382		...	...
331 Wood products, except furniture		7973	9633	9711	9311		3317	3935	3943	3782		...	...
3311 Sawmills, planing and other wood mills		7277	8741	8864	8403		3045	3593	3621	3433		...	...
3312 Wooden and cane containers		456	587	573	548		168	212	206	197		...	...
3319 Other wood and cork products		240	305	274	360		104	130	116	152		...	...
332 Furniture and fixtures, excl. metal		8010	8601	10340	11338		2496	2633	3146	3449		...	...
341 Paper and products		26340	26713	40868	43695		6566	6539	9856	10589		...	...
3411 Pulp, paper and paperboard articles		...	...	...	...		...	...	...	...		...	...
3412 Containers of paper and paperboard		22265	22595	35396	37355		5180	5163	8040	8484		...	...
3419 Other pulp, paper and paperboard articles		4074	4118	5472	6341		1386	1376	1817	2105		...	...
342 Printing and publishing		20573	22935	26665	29580		7026	7694	8891	9862		...	...
351 Industrial chemicals		21434	29918	53606	79622		5143	7059	12668	18826		...	...
3511 Basic chemicals excl. fertilizers		138	157	188	225		84	94	112	133		...	...
3512 Fertilizers and pesticides		19778	27908	51769	77315		4811	6668	12293	18360		...	...
3513 Synthetic resins and plastic materials		1518	1853	1649	2082		248	298	263	333		...	...
352 Other chemicals		42913	59312	62258	58690		12962	17658	18226	16848		...	...
3521 Paints, varnishes and lacquers		5917	8241	9712	11622		1327	1815	2127	2545		...	...
3522 Drugs and medicines		17745	27487	23819	14627		5781	8796	7576	4652		...	...
3523 Soap, cleaning preps., perfumes, cosmetics		14407	17623	21555	24060		4055	4872	5922	6610		...	...
3529 Other chemical products		4844	5961	7172	8382		1800	2176	2601	3040		...	...
353 Petroleum refineries		19506	20263	32039	33676		5147	5252	8253	8675		...	...

Code	Industry													
354	Misc. petroleum and coal products		28	38	50	55		9	12	16	18		...	...
355	Rubber products		6841	9029	11765	15391		2298	2972	3795	4970		...	...
3551	Tyres and tubes		4968	6608	8955	11676		1453	1899	2557	3334		...	...
3559	Other rubber products		1874	2421	2810	3715		845	1073	1238	1636		...	...
356	Plastic products		19495	23415	31065	35816		6800	8022	10578	12196		...	...
361	Pottery, china, earthenware		1771	2012	2244	2573		621	693	768	881		...	...
362	Glass and products		4219	5058	6409	7469		1520	1790	2254	2627		...	...
369	Other non-metallic mineral products		15634	18672	21665	22158		5897	6755	7763	7743		...	...
3691	Structural clay products		2377	2071	2276	1372		1326	1135	1239	747		...	...
3692	Cement, lime and plaster		4434	5272	6151	6819		1559	1820	2111	2341		...	...
3699	Other non-metallic mineral products		8823	11329	13239	13967		3013	3799	4413	4656		...	...
371	Iron and steel		...	...	...	...		...	...	...	...		...	...
372	Non-ferrous metals		831	969	1292	1682		197	225	299	389		...	...
381	Fabricated metal products		17607	20742	25434	27385		4122	4753	5769	6352		...	...
3811	Cutlery, hand tools and general hardware		...	...	...	...		...	...	...	...		...	...
3812	Furniture and fixtures primarily of metal		2229	2569	2984	3711		985	1115	1287	1601		...	...
3813	Structural metal products		1770	2053	2710	3157		496	565	741	864		...	...
3819	Other fabricated metal products		13608	16120	19740	20517		2641	3073	3740	3888		...	...
382	Non-electrical machinery		9199	10515	11768	12744		3033	3420	3805	4124		...	...
3821	Engines and turbines		...	...	...	...		...	...	...	...		...	...
3822	Agricultural machinery and equipment		...	...	...	...		...	...	...	...		...	...
3823	Metal and wood working machinery		175	206	230	245		56	65	72	77		...	...
3824	Other special industrial machinery		985	1252	1411	1563		424	529	593	657		...	...
3825	Office, computing and accounting machinery		...	...	...	...		...	...	...	...		...	...
3829	Other non-electrical machinery & equipment		8039	9058	10127	10936		2553	2826	3140	3391		...	...
383	Electrical machinery		40897	47639	52032	59724		9774	11152	12186	13767		...	...
3831	Electrical industrial machinery		886	976	1304	1227		308	333	443	417		...	...
3832	Radio, television and communication equipm.		34431	40346	43452	51556		7494	8626	9233	10955		...	...
3833	Electrical appliances and housewares		...	...	...	...		...	...	...	...		...	...
3839	Other electrical apparatus and supplies		5581	6317	7277	6941		1972	2193	2511	2395		...	...
384	Transport equipment		5493	6451	5990	5700		2787	3408	3162	3182		...	...
3841	Shipbuilding and repairing		405	362	464	519		182	160	204	228		...	...
3842	Railroad equipment		-	-	-	-		-	-	-	-		...	...
3843	Motor vehicles		2955	2541	2153	1045		1278	1079	909	441		...	...
3844	Motorcycles and bicycles		...	...	...	...		...	...	...	...		...	...
3845	Aircraft		2134	3548	3373	4136		1328	2169	2049	2513		...	...
3849	Other transport equipment		...	...	...	...		...	...	...	...		...	...
385	Professional and scientific equipment		...	...	...	...		...	...	...	...		...	...
3851	Prof. and scientific equipment n.e.c.		...	...	...	...		...	...	...	...		...	...
3852	Photographic and optical goods		...	...	...	...		...	...	...	...		...	...
3853	Watches and clocks		...	...	...	...		...	...	...	...		...	...
390	Other manufacturing industries		1508	2180	1632	1540		572	814	614	573		...	...
3901	Jewellery and related articles		168	274	322	219		74	119	138	94		...	...
3902	Musical instruments		...	...	...	...		...	...	...	...		...	...
3903	Sporting and athletic goods		...	...	...	...		...	...	...	...		...	...
3909	Manufacturing industries, n.e.c.		1340	1906	1310	1321		498	696	475	479		...	...
3	Total manufacturing		579289	684998	897860	990112		173192	201795	257093	286838		...	...

a/ Data are provisional.

Costa Rica

ISIC Revision 2		Index numbers of industrial production											
		(1990=100)											
ISIC Industry	Note	1985	1986	1987	1988	1989	1990	1991	1992	1993	1994	1995	1996
311/2 Food products		82	86	92	96	97	100	102	113	123	127	133	138
313 Beverages		77	84	89	87	92	100	109	112	115	119	119	121
314 Tobacco		126	120	107	109	99	100	105	104	119	122	131	135
321 Textiles		96	99	102	103	103	100	83	75	66	58	50	44
322 Wearing apparel, except footwear		156	129	106	110	100	100	105	133	135	128	132	118
323 Leather and fur products		114	107	99	80	88	100	84	93	104	98	99	106
324 Footwear, except rubber or plastic		...	...	...	...	...	...	...	...	...	...	...	...
331 Wood products, except furniture		113	99	116	119	96	100	92	93	88	97	84	73
332 Furniture and fixtures, excl. metal		73	85	90	95	104	100	84	80	64	61	63	55
341 Paper and products		75	74	75	86	94	100	104	89	92	85	92	96
342 Printing and publishing		84	95	104	105	102	100	97	108	128	130	118	115
351 Industrial chemicals		73	73	59	69	94	100	99	133	102	129	163	192
352 Other chemicals		90	88	96	93	98	100	112	126	157	195	171	135
353 Petroleum refineries		111	167	167	153	158	100	90	128	131	140	183	151
354 Misc. petroleum and coal products		...	...	...	...	...	...	...	...	...	...	...	...
355 Rubber products		87	86	91	93	97	100	90	95	96	112	114	117
356 Plastic products		76	80	85	84	88	100	104	113	131	142	145	150
361 Pottery, china, earthenware		...	...	...	...	...	...	...	...	...	...	...	...
362 Glass and products		...	...	...	...	...	...	...	...	...	...	...	...
369 Other non-metallic mineral products		74	77	87	102	102	100	104	114	123	126	119	108
371 Iron and steel		...	...	...	...	...	...	...	...	...	...	...	...
372 Non-ferrous metals		...	...	...	...	...	...	...	...	...	...	...	...
381 Fabricated metal products		69	68	82	81	96	100	95	108	123	127	116	107
382 Non-electrical machinery		96	103	120	115	99	100	86	111	116	127	130	123
383 Electrical machinery		74	89	91	94	100	100	97	138	168	186	180	168
384 Transport equipment		71	93	88	106	98	100	84	112	101	88	84	82
385 Professional and scientific equipment		...	...	...	...	...	...	...	...	...	...	...	...
390 Other manufacturing industries		73	69	77	68	82	100	96	101	105	136	112	110
3 Total manufacturing		86	91	94	97	99	100	101	112	119	125	128	125

CROATIA

Supplier of information:
Central Bureau of Statistics (CBS) of the Republic of Croatia, Zagreb.

Basic source of data:
The Complex Annual Report of Economic Establishments and the Annual Report on Investment in Fixed Assets. Data on number of establishments are provided by the Register Division.

Major deviations from ISIC (Revision 2) and ISIC (Revision 3):
None reported.

Reference period (if not calendar year):

Scope:
Data refer to industrial activities of the legal entities.

Method of enumeration:
Questionnaires are distributed by mail.

Adjusted for non-response:
Not reported.

Concepts and definitions of variables:
Number of establishments is the number as of 31 December of the reference year (whether active or not).
Number of employees is the number as of 31 March of the reference year.
Figures for wages and salaries were derived from reported monthly wages and salaries per employee. They refer to net wages after subtraction of social insurance contributions, contributions to pension and welfare funds and taxes. In all other respects they conform to the UN concepts and definitions.
Gross fixed capital formation refers to investment in industry for new fixed assets during the reference year, regardless of the time of payment.

Related national publications:

Croatia

ISIC Revision 2	Number of establishments a/					Number of employees					Wages and salaries paid to employees				
		(numbers)					(numbers)					(thousand KUNAS)			
ISIC Industry	Note	1993	1994	1995	1996	Note	1993	1994	1995	1996	Note	1993	1994	1995	1996
311/2 Food products		1102	1367	1515	1603		45420	45470	45390	40567		322119	787359	1154722	1107479
313 Beverages		240	307	332	347		7630	7490	7990	7664		59239	150549	225126	236542
314 Tobacco		17	16	16	15		3170	2860	2680	2197		24003	57314	87218	82862
321 Textiles		422	530	570	584		32990	31410	29790	24248		171020	370512	475091	402420
322 Wearing apparel, except footwear		683	879	986	996		31350	31190	30180	27639		196376	410585	522235	493854
323 Leather and fur products		159	192	203	209		4530	4620	3930	3268		23157	50173	58101	50942
324 Footwear, except rubber or plastic		144	184	195	208		19840	20760	19850	14433		112136	233924	300847	230524
331 Wood products, except furniture		881	1078	1196	1273		16200	15800	14850	13307		93506	195667	248767	230105
332 Furniture and fixtures, excl. metal		271	396	465	486		15350	14430	13250	13135		83995	171775	217989	217988
341 Paper and products		196	239	253	255		6740	6340	6620	5918		42705	94187	146090	136990
342 Printing and publishing		1744	2289	2613	2732		12110	11150	11270	12070		80071	190397	285762	333711
351 Industrial chemicals		113	128	135	143		11470	11400	10910	9717		72261	200138	239715	291044
352 Other chemicals		273	334	369	381		12290	11830	11360	11257		96157	207687	222883	334873
353 Petroleum refineries		6	6	6	6		5150	5010	4970	6014		40046	103527	136695	182874
354 Misc. petroleum and coal products		11	11	10	10		680	650	280	217		4806	12316	6250	5023
355 Rubber products		80	89	101	107		3230	2470	2380	954		15039	30500	43040	18053
356 Plastic products		575	695	766	782		7090	6470	6420	6353		55302	113354	168795	188074
361 Pottery, china, earthenware		28	39	47	52		2360	2170	2000	1575		15123	30857	38760	32357
362 Glass and products		42	49	53	57		3400	3350	3150	3023		21787	47637	61047	62105
369 Other non-metallic mineral products		354	416	457	463		14100	13120	12840	11994		82570	179796	253153	278501
371 Iron and steel		22	20	20	23		7300	6450	5620	4382		39420	71208	84030	80979
372 Non-ferrous metals		53	63	67	66		2650	2520	2520	2322		13801	28516	39766	39790
381 Fabricated metal products		1776	2221	2491	2555		28900	27030	25080	21991		178949	351931	468294	440964
382 Non-electrical machinery		642	760	843	887		23710	21100	18260	16874		134862	275228	300414	359619
383 Electrical machinery		1529	1848	1991	2004		24000	21590	20610	20852		166752	338358	469661	543737
384 Transport equipment		323	381	431	450		26050	24550	23640	22126		139420	296073	443959	488542
385 Professional and scientific equipment		102	123	133	133		1340	1140	1260	1549		7445	14405	22287	32101
390 Other manufacturing industries		130	179	208	219		1550	1420	1290	1282		10639	21436	25310	24507
3 Total manufacturing		11918	14839	16472	17046		370600	353790	338390	306928		2302706	5035409	6746007	6926560

a/ See country note for definition.

Croatia

ISIC Revision 3	Output					Value added					Gross fixed capital formation		
		(thousand KUNAS)					(thousand KUNAS)					(thousand KUNAS)	
ISIC Industry	Note	1993	1994	1995	1996	Note	1993	1994	1995	1996	Note	1995	1996
151 Processed meat,fish,fruit,vegetables,fats		...	...	...	...		...	...	...	...		...	229683
1511 Processing/preserving of meat		...	...	...	...		...	...	...	...		...	...
1512 Processing/preserving of fish		...	...	...	...		...	...	...	...		...	...
1513 Processing/preserving of fruit & vegetables		...	...	...	...		...	...	...	...		...	...
1514 Vegetable and animal oils and fats		...	...	...	...		...	...	...	...		...	...
1520 Dairy products		...	...	...	...		...	...	...	...		...	...
153 Grain mill products; starches; animal feeds		...	...	...	...		...	...	...	...		...	174011
1531 Grain mill products		...	...	...	...		...	...	...	...		...	106194
1532 Starches and starch products		...	...	...	...		...	...	...	...		...	...
1533 Prepared animal feeds		...	...	...	...		...	...	...	...		...	...
154 Other food products		...	...	...	...		...	...	...	...		...	...
1541 Bakery products		...	...	...	...		...	...	...	...		...	157099
1542 Sugar		...	...	...	...		...	...	...	...		...	...
1543 Cocoa, chocolate and sugar confectionery		...	...	...	...		...	...	...	...		...	...
1544 Macaroni, noodles & similar products		...	...	...	...		...	...	...	...		...	...
1549 Other food products n.e.c.		...	...	...	...		...	...	...	...		...	...
155 Beverages		...	...	...	...		...	...	...	...		...	...
1551 Distilling, rectifying & blending of spirits		...	...	...	...		...	...	...	...		...	712877
1552 Wines		...	...	...	...		...	...	...	...		...	...
1553 Malt liquors and malt		...	...	...	...		...	...	...	...		...	...
1554 Soft drinks; mineral waters		...	...	...	...		...	...	...	...		...	...
1600 Tobacco products		...	...	...	...		...	...	...	...		...	145050
171 Spinning, weaving and finishing of textiles		...	...	...	...		...	...	...	...		...	14383
1711 Textile fibre preparation; textile weaving		...	...	...	...		...	...	...	...		...	...
1712 Finishing of textiles		...	...	...	...		...	...	...	...		...	...
172 Other textiles		...	...	...	...		...	...	...	...		...	4163
1721 Made-up textile articles, except apparel		...	...	...	...		...	...	...	...		...	...
1722 Carpets and rugs		...	...	...	...		...	...	...	...		...	...
1723 Cordage, rope, twine and netting		...	...	...	...		...	...	...	...		...	...
1729 Other textiles n.e.c.		...	...	...	...		...	...	...	...		...	...
1730 Knitted and crocheted fabrics and articles		...	...	...	...		...	...	...	...		...	3126
1810 Wearing apparel, except fur apparel		...	...	...	...		...	...	...	...		...	99620
1820 Dressing & dyeing of fur; processing of fur		...	...	...	...		...	...	...	...		...	32
191 Tanning, dressing and processing of leather		...	...	...	...		...	...	...	...		...	5048
1911 Tanning and dressing of leather		...	...	...	...		...	...	...	...		...	...
1912 Luggage, handbags, etc.; saddlery & harness		...	...	...	...		...	...	...	...		...	...
1920 Footwear		...	...	...	...		...	...	...	...		...	12328
2010 Sawmilling and planing of wood		...	...	...	...		...	...	...	...		...	18427
202 Products of wood, cork, straw, etc.		...	...	...	...		...	...	...	...		...	40883
2021 Veneer sheets, plywood, particle board, etc.		...	...	...	...		...	...	...	...		...	...
2022 Builders' carpentry and joinery		...	...	...	...		...	...	...	...		...	...
2023 Wooden containers		...	...	...	...		...	...	...	...		...	...
2029 Other wood products; articles of cork/straw		...	...	...	...		...	...	...	...		...	...
210 Paper and paper products		...	...	...	...		...	...	...	...		...	135476
2101 Pulp, paper and paperboard		...	...	...	...		...	...	...	...		...	...
2102 Corrugated paper and paperboard		...	...	...	...		...	...	...	...		...	...
2109 Other articles of paper and paperboard		...	...	...	...		...	...	...	...		...	...
221 Publishing		...	...	...	...		...	...	...	...		...	100764
2211 Publishing of books and other publications		...	...	...	...		...	...	...	...		...	6164
2212 Publishing of newspapers, journals, etc.		...	...	...	...		...	...	...	...		...	...
2213 Publishing of recorded media		...	...	...	...		...	...	...	...		...	4262
2219 Other publishing		...	...	...	...		...	...	...	...		...	18401

continued

Croatia

ISIC Revision 3		Output					Value added					Gross fixed capital formation		
			(thousand KUNAS)					(thousand KUNAS)					(thousand KUNAS)	
ISIC	Industry	Note	1993	1994	1995	1996	Note	1993	1994	1995	1996	Note	1995	1996
222	Printing and related service activities		...	...	...	...		...	...	...	...		...	61368
2221	Printing		...	...	...	...		...	...	...	...		...	...
2222	Service activities related to printing		...	...	...	...		...	...	...	...		...	...
2230	Reproduction of recorded media		...	...	...	...		...	...	...	...		...	-
2310	Coke oven products		...	...	...	...		...	...	...	...		...	-
2320	Refined petroleum products		...	...	...	...		...	...	...	...		...	562651
2330	Processing of nuclear fuel		...	...	...	...		...	...	...	...		...	-
241	Basic chemicals		...	...	...	...		...	...	...	...		...	51240
2411	Basic chemicals, except fertilizers		...	...	...	...		...	...	...	...		...	...
2412	Fertilizers and nitrogen compounds		...	...	...	...		...	...	...	...		...	...
2413	Plastics in primary forms; synthetic rubber		...	...	...	...		...	...	...	...		...	...
242	Other chemicals		...	...	...	...		...	...	...	...		...	297481
2421	Pesticides and other agro-chemical products		...	...	...	...		...	...	...	...		...	...
2422	Paints, varnishes, printing ink and mastics		...	...	...	...		...	...	...	...		...	...
2423	Pharmaceuticals, medicinal chemicals, etc.		...	...	...	...		...	...	...	...		...	...
2424	Soap, cleaning & cosmetic preparations		...	...	...	...		...	...	...	...		...	...
2429	Other chemical products n.e.c.		...	...	...	...		...	...	...	...		...	...
2430	Man-made fibres		...	...	...	...		...	...	...	...		...	-
251	Rubber products		...	...	...	...		...	...	...	...		...	9077
2511	Rubber tyres and tubes		...	...	...	...		...	...	...	...		...	-
2519	Other rubber products		...	...	...	...		...	...	...	...		...	9077
2520	Plastic products		...	...	...	...		...	...	...	...		...	82610
2610	Glass and glass products		...	...	...	...		...	...	...	...		...	12750
269	Non-metallic mineral products n.e.c.		...	...	...	...		...	...	...	...		...	256493
2691	Pottery, china and earthenware		...	...	...	...		...	...	...	...		...	...
2692	Refractory ceramic products		...	...	...	...		...	...	...	...		...	...
2693	Struct.non-refractory clay; ceramic products		...	...	...	...		...	...	...	...		...	...
2694	Cement, lime and plaster		...	...	...	...		...	...	...	...		...	...
2695	Articles of concrete, cement and plaster		...	...	...	...		...	...	...	...		...	...
2696	Cutting, shaping & finishing of stone		...	...	...	...		...	...	...	...		...	...
2699	Other non-metallic mineral products n.e.c.		...	...	...	...		...	...	...	...		...	...
2710	Basic iron and steel		...	...	...	...		...	...	...	...		...	3320
2720	Basic precious and non-ferrous metals		...	...	...	...		...	...	...	...		...	1532
273	Casting of metals		...	...	...	...		...	...	...	...		...	20883
2731	Casting of iron and steel		...	...	...	...		...	...	...	...		...	...
2732	Casting of non-ferrous metals		...	...	...	...		...	...	...	...		...	...
281	Struct.metal products;tanks;steam generators		...	...	...	...		...	...	...	...		...	26560
2811	Structural metal products		...	...	...	...		...	...	...	...		...	...
2812	Tanks, reservoirs and containers of metal		...	...	...	...		...	...	...	...		...	...
2813	Steam generators		...	...	...	...		...	...	...	...		...	...
289	Other metal products; metal working services		...	...	...	...		...	...	...	...		...	85815
2891	Metal forging/pressing/stamping/roll-forming		...	...	...	...		...	...	...	...		...	7306
2892	Treatment & coating of metals		...	...	...	...		...	...	...	...		...	...
2893	Cutlery, hand tools and general hardware		...	...	...	...		...	...	...	...		...	...
2899	Other fabricated metal products n.e.c.		...	...	...	...		...	...	...	...		...	...
291	General purpose machinery		...	...	...	...		...	...	...	...		...	79609
2911	Engines & turbines(not for transport equip.)		...	...	...	...		...	...	...	...		...	43916
2912	Pumps, compressors, taps and valves		...	...	...	...		...	...	...	...		...	...
2913	Bearings, gears, gearing & driving elements		...	...	...	...		...	...	...	...		...	2536
2914	Ovens, furnaces and furnace burners		...	...	...	...		...	...	...	...		...	-
2915	Lifting and handling equipment		...	...	...	...		...	...	...	...		...	19116
2919	Other general purpose machinery		...	...	...	...		...	...	...	...		...	...

292 Special purpose machinery		...	...	...	...		...	...	...	...	...	21006
2921 Agricultural and forestry machinery		...	...	...	...		...	...	...	...	...	...
2922 Machine tools		...	...	...	...		...	...	...	...	...	...
2923 Machinery for metallurgy		...	...	...	...		...	...	...	...	...	...
2924 Machinery for mining & construction		...	...	...	...		...	...	...	...	...	...
2925 Food/beverage/tobacco processing machinery		...	...	...	...		...	...	...	...	...	...
2926 Machinery for textile, apparel and leather		...	...	...	...		...	...	...	...	...	...
2927 Weapons and ammunition		...	...	...	...		...	...	...	...	...	...
2929 Other special purpose machinery		...	...	...	...		...	...	...	...	...	...
2930 Domestic appliances n.e.c.		...	...	...	...		...	...	...	...	...	16570
3000 Office, accounting and computing machinery		...	...	...	...		...	...	...	...	...	6708
3110 Electric motors, generators and transformers		...	...	...	...		...	...	...	...	...	10279
3120 Electricity distribution & control apparatus		...	...	...	...		...	...	...	...	...	32698
3130 Insulated wire and cable		...	...	...	...		...	...	...	...	...	14623
3140 Accumulators, primary cells and batteries		...	...	...	...		...	...	...	...	...	2099
3150 Lighting equipment and electric lamps		...	...	...	...		...	...	...	...	...	1805
3190 Other electrical equipment n.e.c.		...	...	...	...		...	...	...	...	...	13840
3210 Electronic valves, tubes, etc.		...	...	...	...		...	...	...	...	...	-
3220 TV/radio transmitters; line comm. apparatus		...	...	...	...		...	...	...	...	...	52172
3230 TV and radio receivers and associated goods		...	...	...	...		...	...	...	...	...	520
331 Medical, measuring, testing appliances, etc.		...	...	...	...		...	...	...	...	...	4507
3311 Medical, surgical and orthopaedic equipment		...	...	...	...		...	...	...	...	...	...
3312 Measuring/testing/navigating appliances,etc.		...	...	...	...		...	...	...	...	...	...
3313 Industrial process control equipment		...	...	...	...		...	...	...	...	...	...
3320 Optical instruments & photographic equipment		...	...	...	...		...	...	...	...	...	5915
3330 Watches and clocks		...	...	...	...		...	...	...	...	...	-
3410 Motor vehicles		...	...	...	...		...	...	...	...	...	10285
3420 Automobile bodies, trailers & semi-trailers		...	...	...	...		...	...	...	...	...	-
3430 Parts/accessories for automobiles		...	...	...	...		...	...	...	...	...	20819
351 Building and repairing of ships and boats		...	...	...	...		...	...	...	...	...	49035
3511 Building and repairing of ships		...	...	...	...		...	...	...	...	...	49035
3512 Building/repairing of pleasure/sport. boats		...	...	...	...		...	...	...	...	...	-
3520 Railway/tramway locomotives & rolling stock		...	...	...	...		...	...	...	...	...	12663
3530 Aircraft and spacecraft		...	...	...	...		...	...	...	...	...	930
359 Transport equipment n.e.c.		...	...	...	...		...	...	...	...	...	-
3591 Motorcycles		...	...	...	...		...	...	...	...	...	-
3592 Bicycles and invalid carriages		...	...	...	...		...	...	...	...	...	-
3599 Other transport equipment n.e.c.		...	...	...	...		...	...	...	...	...	-
3610 Furniture		...	...	...	...		...	...	...	...	...	109667
369 Manufacturing n.e.c.		...	...	...	...		...	...	...	...	...	5386
3691 Jewellery and related articles		...	...	...	...		...	...	...	...	...	...
3692 Musical instruments		...	...	...	...		...	...	...	...	...	...
3693 Sports goods		...	...	...	...		...	...	...	...	...	...
3694 Games and toys		...	...	...	...		...	...	...	...	...	...
3699 Other manufacturing n.e.c.		...	...	...	...		...	...	...	...	...	...
3710 Recycling of metal waste and scrap		...	...	...	...		...	...	...	...	...	24065
3720 Recycling of non-metal waste and scrap		...	...	...	...		...	...	...	...	...	4966
D Total manufacturing		...	...	...	...		...	...	...	...	...	3931111

Croatia

ISIC Revision 3		Index numbers of industrial production											
		(1990=100)											
ISIC Industry	Note	1985	1986	1987	1988	1989	1990	1991	1992	1993	1994	1995	1996
15 Food and beverages		...	...	...	...	104	100	79	70	62	65	67	69
16 Tobacco products		...	...	...	...	117	100	91	99	84	84	78	88
17 Textiles		...	...	...	...	125	100	66	59	56	52	48	39
18 Wearing apparel, fur		...	...	...	...	103	100	80	69	73	69	64	58
19 Leather, leather products and footwear		...	...	...	...	117	100	49	41	44	42	33	29
20 Wood products (excl. furniture)		...	...	...	...	120	100	65	67	69	62	58	62
21 Paper and paper products		...	...	...	...	115	100	66	57	59	59	58	53
22 Printing and publishing		...	...	...	...	104	100	76	62	57	61	61	62
23 Coke,refined petroleum products,nuclear fuel		...	...	...	...	102	100	70	59	66	65	75	72
24 Chemicals and chemical products		...	...	...	...	111	100	75	69	63	65	66	64
25 Rubber and plastics products		...	...	...	...	116	100	62	46	44	46	45	42
26 Non-metallic mineral products		...	...	...	...	112	100	77	60	58	62	62	74
27 Basic metals		...	...	...	...	114	100	66	41	42	42	35	32
28 Fabricated metal products		...	...	...	...	123	100	69	46	40	37	35	35
29 Machinery and equipment n.e.c.		...	...	...	...	117	100	58	36	31	26	30	29
30 Office, accounting and computing machinery		...	...	...	...	124	100	72	34	17	12	13	12
31 Electrical machinery and apparatus		...	...	...	...	140	100	71	59	52	53	55	56
32 Radio,television and communication equipment		...	...	...	...	93	100	73	73	76	62	67	76
33 Medical, precision and optical instruments		...	...	...	...	135	100	59	51	44	42	34	24
34 Motor vehicles, trailers, semi-trailers		...	...	...	...	244	100	49	28	45	60	30	23
35 Other transport equipment		...	...	...	...	114	100	70	59	47	41	41	50
36 Furniture; manufacturing n.e.c.		...	...	...	...	119	100	70	57	58	54	51	49
37 Recycling		...	...	...	...	110	100	64	62	45	41	41	43
D Total manufacturing		108	113	116	114	114	100	70	59	55	53	53	54

CYPRUS

Supplier of information:
Department of Statistics and Research, Ministry of Finance, Nicosia.

Basic source of data:
Annual survey of industrial production.

Major deviations from ISIC (Revision 2):
Data exclude cottage industry (embroidery, weaving and cane products).

Reference period (if not calendar year):

Scope:
All establishments in the Government controlled areas, with adjustments on the basis of the results of the 1992 census.

Method of enumeration:
For the annual survey establishments are sampled. Data are collected for establishments in the sample through interviews. Every five years, the Department conducts a census of industrial production covering establishments with 5 or more persons engaged on a complete enumeration basis and establishments with 4 or fewer persons engaged on a sample basis. The census provides the basis for reviewing the intercensal estimates of output, value added and employment that are compiled from the annual survey. The frame for the census as well as for the annual survey is provided by a registry of establishments, which is updated prior to each census.

Adjusted for non-response:
Yes.

Concepts and definitions of variables:
Output is gross output. It does not include VAT.
Value added is total value added.

Related national publications:
Industrial Statistics (annual); Statistical Abstract (annual); Economic Report (annual); all published by the Department of Statistics and Research, Ministry of Finance, Nicosia.

ISIC Revision 2	Number of establishments					Number of employees					Wages and salaries paid to employees				
		(numbers)					(numbers)					(thousand POUNDS)			
ISIC Industry	Note	1993	1994	1995	1996	Note	1993	1994	1995	1996	Note	1993	1994	1995	1996
311/2 Food products		922	993	1054	1063		5945	6392	7095	7346		31050	34801	46721	44629
3111 Slaughtering, preparing & preserving meat		86	80	75	77		592	623	673	701		4163	4629	5570	5461
3112 Dairy products		110	110	112	114		1025	1074	1153	1192		5814	6509	8608	7973
3113 Canning, preserving of fruits & vegetables		16	30	41	41		420	417	627	691		2099	2135	4981	4468
3114 Canning, preserving and processing of fish		-	-	-	-		-	-	-	-		-	-	-	-
3115 Vegetable and animal oils and fats		37	33	29	30		135	142	149	142		889	950	1182	1107
3116 Grain mill products		28	23	20	20		152	152	182	179		1223	1270	1620	1564
3117 Bakery products		474	553	617	622		2281	2470	3001	3130		9911	11528	16021	15732
3118 Sugar factories and refineries		-	-	-	-		-	-	-	-		-	-	-	-
3119 Cocoa, chocolate and sugar confectionery		51	48	45	45		272	317	234	218		1216	1376	1246	1195
3121 Other food products		62	56	54	50		742	838	762	711		3853	4309	5223	4617
3122 Prepared animal feeds		58	60	61	64		326	359	314	382		1882	2095	2270	2512
313 Beverages		57	62	64	65		2039	2027	1866	1854		14780	15378	17560	15894
3131 Distilling, rectifying and blending spirits	a/	39	46	49	48	a/	1347	1276	1343	1322	a/	9865	9558	12846	11271
3132 Wine industries	a/	...	...	...	...	a/	...	...	...	...	a/	...	...	...	...
3133 Malt liquors and malt	a/	...	...	...	...	a/	...	...	...	...	a/	...	...	...	...
3134 Soft drinks and carbonated waters		18	16	15	17		692	751	523	532		4915	5820	4714	4623
314 Tobacco		7	4	4	4		355	294	255	285		2728	2581	2812	2915
321 Textiles		227	251	260	255		2307	1976	2186	2098		9542	8827	11653	9493
3211 Spinning, weaving and finishing textiles		17	15	14	10		331	337	306	142		1626	1610	1823	772
3212 Made-up textile goods excl. wearing apparel		103	138	150	148		531	484	700	685		2136	2193	3560	3212
3213 Knitting mills		107	98	96	97		1445	1155	1180	1271		5780	5024	6270	5509
3214 Carpets and rugs		-	-	-	-		-	-	-	-		-	-	-	-
3215 Cordage, rope and twine		-	-	-	-		-	-	-	-		-	-	-	-
3219 Other textiles		-	-	-	-		-	-	-	-		-	-	-	-
322 Wearing apparel, except footwear		1350	1266	1206	1061		8681	6901	6670	5444		30228	25969	29935	22158
323 Leather and fur products		86	88	90	79		747	465	346	301		2915	2160	1900	1334
3231 Tanneries and leather finishing		6	6	6	6		45	44	41	40		252	279	306	245
3232 Fur dressing and dyeing industries		-	-	-	-		-	-	-	-		-	-	-	-
3233 Leather prods. excl. wearing apparel		80	82	84	73		702	421	305	261		2663	1881	1594	1089
324 Footwear, except rubber or plastic		145	151	156	135		1723	1580	1270	984		7716	7483	7004	5056
331 Wood products, except furniture		962	1089	1179	1181		2249	2316	2530	2554		10743	12279	16235	14767
3311 Sawmills, planing and other wood mills	b/	862	972	1057	1055	b/	2116	2171	2388	2427	b/	10188	11437	15495	13950
3312 Wooden and cane containers	b/	...	...	...	...	b/	...	...	...	...	b/	...	...	...	...
3319 Other wood and cork products		100	117	122	126		133	145	142	127		555	842	740	817
332 Furniture and fixtures, excl. metal		702	730	742	720		2539	2712	2202	1875		11610	12986	13493	10575
341 Paper and products		60	56	54	56		748	756	738	773		4078	4711	5047	5099
3411 Pulp, paper and paperboard articles		-	-	-	-		-	-	-	-		-	-	-	-
3412 Containers of paper and paperboard		14	15	15	15		264	269	227	253		1564	2055	1796	1922
3419 Other pulp, paper and paperboard articles		46	41	39	41		484	487	511	520		2514	2656	3251	3177
342 Printing and publishing		320	340	350	348		1818	2046	1951	1868		11708	13081	15143	13824
351 Industrial chemicals		7	10	12	12		153	179	123	118		871	1133	1008	898
3511 Basic chemicals excl. fertilizers		1	1	1	1		27	32	35	28		241	304	308	218
3512 Fertilizers and pesticides		6	9	11	11		126	147	88	90		630	829	700	680
3513 Synthetic resins and plastic materials		-	-	-	-		-	-	-	-		-	-	-	-
352 Other chemicals		107	113	115	115		1477	1537	1552	1581		8417	10030	11492	10237
3521 Paints, varnishes and lacquers		14	13	13	13		221	229	234	231		1429	1504	1975	1775
3522 Drugs and medicines		4	9	11	13		287	351	439	512		1462	2399	3062	2909
3523 Soap, cleaning preps., perfumes, cosmetics		31	38	42	42		638	649	674	652		3774	4313	5085	4464
3529 Other chemical products		58	53	49	47		331	308	205	186		1752	1814	1370	1089
353 Petroleum refineries		1	1	1	1		152	153	143	144		2614	2560	3622	3246

ISIC	Industry														
354	Misc. petroleum and coal products		-	-	-	-		-	-	-	-		-	-	-	-
355	Rubber products		15	19	23	23		148	155	158	153		891	937	1148	959
3551	Tyres and tubes		5	7	10	10		66	64	73	70		440	451	572	427
3559	Other rubber products		10	12	13	13		82	91	85	83		451	486	576	532
356	Plastic products		43	55	62	60		1194	1152	1334	1267		7035	7310	9378	8812
361	Pottery, china, earthenware		66	62	57	61		180	155	94	107		571	523	406	384
362	Glass and products		33	25	23	21		97	99	115	103		531	542	666	639
369	Other non-metallic mineral products		236	275	307	304		2486	2519	2660	2526		17654	18458	24472	21102
3691	Structural clay products		92	97	99	99		1150	1083	1029	983		6900	6884	8055	6574
3692	Cement, lime and plaster		5	6	8	10		525	499	464	451		6473	6640	7716	6971
3699	Other non-metallic mineral products		139	172	200	195		811	937	1167	1092		4281	4934	8701	7557
371	Iron and steel		-	-	-	-		-	-	-	-		-	-	-	-
372	Non-ferrous metals		-	-	-	-		-	-	-	-		-	-	-	-
381	Fabricated metal products		906	1038	1119	1132		2790	3033	3058	3179		14412	15893	19621	18036
3811	Cutlery, hand tools and general hardware		102	102	102	105		148	151	160	181		770	799	978	1040
3812	Furniture and fixtures primarily of metal		53	56	59	57		538	524	575	506		2633	2682	3640	2920
3813	Structural metal products		650	753	817	820		1405	1636	1700	1722		7248	8472	10667	9475
3819	Other fabricated metal products		101	127	141	150		699	722	623	770		3761	3940	4336	4601
382	Non-electrical machinery		280	324	348	350		1337	1187	1121	1045		7365	6980	7916	6513
3821	Engines and turbines		-	-	-	-		-	-	-	-		-	-	-	-
3822	Agricultural machinery and equipment	c/	280	324	348	350	c/	1337	1187	1121	1045	c/	7365	6980	7916	6513
3823	Metal and wood working machinery		-	-	-	-		-	-	-	-		-	-	-	-
3824	Other special industrial machinery		-	-	-	-		-	-	-	-		-	-	-	-
3825	Office, computing and accounting machinery	c/	...	...	...	...	c/	...	...	...	...	c/	...	...	...	...
3829	Other non-electrical machinery & equipment	c/	...	...	...	...	c/	...	...	...	...	c/	...	...	...	...
383	Electrical machinery		91	107	115	113		614	555	517	500		3408	3364	3502	3247
3831	Electrical industrial machinery		33	32	32	33		77	75	22	21		434	388	144	105
3832	Radio, television and communication equipm.		6	6	6	5		14	12	4	4		47	56	24	23
3833	Electrical appliances and housewares		-	-	-	-		-	-	-	-		-	-	-	-
3839	Other electrical apparatus and supplies		52	69	77	75		523	468	491	475		2927	2920	3334	3119
384	Transport equipment		75	93	101	96		341	433	455	416		1895	2542	3130	2700
3841	Shipbuilding and repairing		23	38	43	40		105	127	106	96		668	866	818	761
3842	Railroad equipment		-	-	-	-		-	-	-	-		-	-	-	-
3843	Motor vehicles		52	55	58	56		236	306	349	320		1227	1676	2312	1939
3844	Motorcycles and bicycles		-	-	-	-		-	-	-	-		-	-	-	-
3845	Aircraft		-	-	-	-		-	-	-	-		-	-	-	-
3849	Other transport equipment		-	-	-	-		-	-	-	-		-	-	-	-
385	Professional and scientific equipment		3	10	13	13		10	47	58	61		43	246	366	313
3851	Prof. and scientific equipment n.e.c.		2	7	9	9	d/	10	47	58	61	d/	43	246	366	313
3852	Photographic and optical goods		1	3	4	4	d/	...	...	...	...	d/	...	...	...	...
3853	Watches and clocks		-	-	-	-		-	-	-	-		-	-	-	-
390	Other manufacturing industries		381	393	399	406		899	908	869	920		4079	4252	4796	4482
3901	Jewellery and related articles		280	278	275	280		674	679	652	677		3071	3145	3679	3285
3902	Musical instruments		-	-	-	-		-	-	-	-		-	-	-	-
3903	Sporting and athletic goods		-	-	-	-		-	-	-	-		-	-	-	-
3909	Manufacturing industries, n.e.c.		101	115	124	126		225	229	217	243		1008	1107	1117	1197
3	Total manufacturing		7082	7555	7854	7674		41029	39577	39366	37502		206884	215026	259026	227312

a/ 3131 includes 3132 and 3133.
b/ 3311 includes 3312.
c/ 3822 includes 3825 and 3829.
d/ 3851 includes 3852.

Cyprus

ISIC Revision 2		Output in producers' prices					Value added in producers' prices					Gross fixed capital formation	
		(thousand POUNDS)					(thousand POUNDS)					(thousand POUNDS)	
ISIC Industry	Note	1993	1994	1995	1996	Note	1993	1994	1995	1996	Note	1995	1996
311/2 Food products		188110	209348	243247	258338		62508	66808	80144	84668		15688	15917
3111 Slaughtering, preparing & preserving meat		15119	15450	18808	21175		6445	6832	8177	9290		2224	2242
3112 Dairy products		43901	47094	50973	52939		12065	12221	13890	14013		3508	4343
3113 Canning, preserving of fruits & vegetables		10876	11818	23301	22892		3805	3920	7775	7528		1386	2248
3114 Canning, preserving and processing of fish		-	-	-	-		-	-	-	-		-	-
3115 Vegetable and animal oils and fats		14847	18449	18675	19346		2922	2480	2426	3762		829	730
3116 Grain mill products		8615	9303	11573	13542		2312	1925	2754	3317		404	195
3117 Bakery products		43281	49259	58045	61436		20128	22519	26529	28596		4012	3853
3118 Sugar factories and refineries		-	-	-	-		-	-	-	-		-	-
3119 Cocoa, chocolate and sugar confectionery		8374	11035	9539	9587		2483	2688	2418	2532		240	429
3121 Other food products		22001	24789	27686	23182		9050	10385	11873	8859		2208	1646
3122 Prepared animal feeds		21096	22151	24647	34239		3298	3838	4302	6771		877	231
313 Beverages		78542	90190	88968	92782		35054	41271	36966	37448		6968	5752
3131 Distilling, rectifying and blending spirits	a/	43097	48361	55114	55943	a/	22596	27971	27753	27293	a/	3934	3315
3132 Wine industries	a/	...	...	...	...	a/	...	...	...	...	a/	...	...
3133 Malt liquors and malt	a/	...	...	...	...	a/	...	...	...	...	a/	...	...
3134 Soft drinks and carbonated waters		35445	41829	33854	36839		12458	13300	9213	10155		3034	2437
314 Tobacco		42811	42929	43190	46396		28661	30837	32450	34333		123	315
321 Textiles		38522	34632	43013	41612		16546	15369	17678	17142		-402	1511
3211 Spinning, weaving and finishing textiles		8906	8607	7084	4183		3560	3629	3045	1616		343	59
3212 Made-up textile goods excl. wearing apparel		9265	9212	16050	17191		3843	3930	5589	6147		280	589
3213 Knitting mills		20351	16813	19879	20238		9143	7810	9044	9379		-1025	863
3214 Carpets and rugs		-	-	-	-		-	-	-	-		-	-
3215 Cordage, rope and twine		-	-	-	-		-	-	-	-		-	-
3219 Other textiles		-	-	-	-		-	-	-	-		-	-
322 Wearing apparel, except footwear		126193	104418	110006	100285		46895	44378	42093	38040		1574	1056
323 Leather and fur products		9630	8887	7489	6465		4154	3501	2904	2515		127	204
3231 Tanneries and leather finishing		2019	2217	2325	2377		806	607	462	513		20	30
3232 Fur dressing and dyeing industries		-	-	-	-		-	-	-	-		-	-
3233 Leather prods. excl. wearing apparel		7611	6670	5164	4088		3348	2894	2442	2002		107	174
324 Footwear, except rubber or plastic		27434	29325	22697	20914		11928	12289	9276	8622		532	437
331 Wood products, except furniture		51020	55066	62925	66009		22561	23798	26886	28304		1546	1924
3311 Sawmills, planing and other wood mills	b/	48226	52060	60054	62520	b/	21193	22310	25337	26489	b/	1432	1715
3312 Wooden and cane containers	b/	...	...	...	...	b/	...	...	...	...	b/	...	...
3319 Other wood and cork products		2794	3006	2871	3489		1368	1488	1549	1815		114	209
332 Furniture and fixtures, excl. metal		42361	45754	46706	43889		18750	20756	20924	20409		1519	1065
341 Paper and products		24308	27159	30694	35284		8226	10084	9979	11279		1014	2293
3411 Pulp, paper and paperboard articles		-	-	-	-		-	-	-	-		-	-
3412 Containers of paper and paperboard		7531	8911	10839	11897		2708	3928	4456	4777		272	1248
3419 Other pulp, paper and paperboard articles		16777	18248	19855	23387		5518	6156	5523	6502		742	1045
342 Printing and publishing		44757	48939	53847	53732		20567	21797	23579	24959		3228	3154
351 Industrial chemicals		5574	9384	8204	8352		1563	2599	2793	2450		185	334
3511 Basic chemicals excl. fertilizers		1139	1176	1192	1259		634	623	628	647		85	38
3512 Fertilizers and pesticides		4435	8208	7012	7093		929	1976	2165	1803		100	296
3513 Synthetic resins and plastic materials		-	-	-	-		-	-	-	-		-	-
352 Other chemicals		58982	67648	69604	69820		20097	22538	21399	20905		2749	3127
3521 Paints, varnishes and lacquers		9506	10045	10895	11513		2953	3169	3426	4141		404	155
3522 Drugs and medicines		15122	19384	22002	23805		5046	6067	6182	6271		1185	968
3523 Soap, cleaning preps., perfumes, cosmetics		24102	26224	28789	27595		8515	9196	9001	8373		1096	1085
3529 Other chemical products		10252	11995	7918	6907		3583	4106	2790	2120		64	919
353 Petroleum refineries		53972	60539	56322	65784		5053	4695	6301	5921		529	5340

ISIC	Industry													
354	Misc. petroleum and coal products		-	-	-	-		-	-	-	-		-	-
355	Rubber products		3788	4321	4580	4367		1604	1867	1905	1892		123	35
3551	Tyres and tubes		1689	1852	1803	1800		729	833	834	758		70	-1
3559	Other rubber products		2099	2469	2777	2567		875	1034	1071	1134		53	36
356	Plastic products		32563	33263	39266	36691		14024	14272	16560	16585		2153	2408
361	Pottery, china, earthenware		2220	1888	1314	1593		1244	1098	860	1048		68	42
362	Glass and products		2567	2730	3452	2941		959	1008	1176	1088		173	63
369	Other non-metallic mineral products		86474	90351	113641	114537		38839	41685	46695	48221		7862	9737
3691	Structural clay products		28566	28864	28298	26590		12719	12980	12739	12306		1560	1029
3692	Cement, lime and plaster		31900	34965	33234	35941		17434	19160	17249	18935		3435	4074
3699	Other non-metallic mineral products		26008	26522	52109	52006		8686	9545	16707	16980		2867	4634
371	Iron and steel		-	-	-	-		-	-	-	-		-	-
372	Non-ferrous metals		-	-	-	-		-	-	-	-		-	-
381	Fabricated metal products		75216	78176	94562	98102		27694	28524	32251	34876		4044	7570
3811	Cutlery, hand tools and general hardware		3916	3995	3680	4214		1735	1758	1569	1978		221	192
3812	Furniture and fixtures primarily of metal		11101	10872	12627	12056		4366	4729	5270	5377		881	635
3813	Structural metal products		42147	43862	54942	55895		15021	15155	18135	18511		2176	1988
3819	Other fabricated metal products		18052	19447	23313	25937		6572	6882	7277	9010		766	4755
382	Non-electrical machinery		28030	28065	28589	29136		12685	12704	12957	12933		1125	1022
3821	Engines and turbines		-	-	-	-		-	-	-	-		-	-
3822	Agricultural machinery and equipment	c/	28030	28065	28589	29136	c/	12685	12704	12957	12933	c/	1125	1022
3823	Metal and wood working machinery		-	-	-	-		-	-	-	-		-	-
3824	Other special industrial machinery		-	-	-	-		-	-	-	-		-	-
3825	Office, computing and accounting machinery	c/	...	...	...	...	c/	...	...	...	...	c/	...	...
3829	Other non-electrical machinery & equipment	c/	...	...	...	...	c/	...	...	...	...	c/	...	...
383	Electrical machinery		17281	16022	15074	15019		5995	5842	5482	5529		803	259
3831	Electrical industrial machinery		1789	1254	693	909		766	685	422	509		2	9
3832	Radio, television and communication equipm.		130	176	62	99		80	95	30	33		-	16
3833	Electrical appliances and housewares		-	-	-	-		-	-	-	-		-	-
3839	Other electrical apparatus and supplies		15362	14592	14319	14011		5149	5062	5030	4987		801	234
384	Transport equipment		8323	10407	11553	10214		3820	5002	5443	5027		391	325
3841	Shipbuilding and repairing		2611	3115	2431	2016		1318	1830	1255	1221		30	13
3842	Railroad equipment		-	-	-	-		-	-	-	-		-	-
3843	Motor vehicles		5712	7292	9122	8198		2502	3172	4188	3806		361	312
3844	Motorcycles and bicycles		-	-	-	-		-	-	-	-		-	-
3845	Aircraft		-	-	-	-		-	-	-	-		-	-
3849	Other transport equipment		-	-	-	-		-	-	-	-		-	-
385	Professional and scientific equipment		425	2042	1875	1658		109	454	546	582		146	28
3851	Prof. and scientific equipment n.e.c.	d/	425	2042	1875	1658	d/	109	454	546	582	d/	146	28
3852	Photographic and optical goods	d/	...	...	...	...	d/	...	...	...	...	d/	...	...
3853	Watches and clocks		-	-	-	-		-	-	-	-		-	-
390	Other manufacturing industries		27827	30016	31149	32736		7997	8618	8237	9924		1036	912
3901	Jewellery and related articles		23179	24778	25527	26990		6187	6635	5971	7255		804	529
3902	Musical instruments		-	-	-	-		-	-	-	-		-	-
3903	Sporting and athletic goods		-	-	-	-		-	-	-	-		-	-
3909	Manufacturing industries, n.e.c.		4648	5238	5622	5746		1810	1983	2266	2669		232	383
3	Total manufacturing		1076930	1131499	1233047	1256656		417533	441794	466294	474700		53304	64830

a/ 3131 includes 3132 and 3133.
b/ 3311 includes 3312.
c/ 3822 includes 3825 and 3829.
d/ 3851 includes 3852.

Cyprus

ISIC Revision 2		Index numbers of industrial production											
		(1990=100)											
ISIC Industry	Note	1985	1986	1987	1988	1989	1990	1991	1992	1993	1994	1995	1996
311/2 Food products	a/	78	79	82	86	94	100	97	102	101	113	113	106
313 Beverages	a/	...	...	...	...	...	...	...	...	...	...	...	...
314 Tobacco		49	40	78	92	91	100	119	134	76	54	54	59
321 Textiles		76	75	82	99	90	100	94	108	99	95	82	66
322 Wearing apparel, except footwear		85	91	112	106	93	100	96	84	71	71	72	63
323 Leather and fur products	b/	98	100	106	109	111	100	94	89	69	68	62	47
324 Footwear, except rubber or plastic	b/	...	...	...	...	...	...	...	...	...	...	...	...
331 Wood products, except furniture		117	111	100	113	108	100	117	120	103	105	115	119
332 Furniture and fixtures, excl. metal	c/	...	...	...	...	...	...	...	...	...	...	...	...
341 Paper and products		75	66	72	91	91	100	91	85	89	102	117	116
342 Printing and publishing		91	71	75	80	92	100	87	105	96	100	97	94
351 Industrial chemicals	d/	69	77	80	93	102	100	95	103	101	111	111	112
352 Other chemicals	d/	...	...	...	...	...	...	...	...	...	...	...	...
353 Petroleum refineries		...	...	...	...	...	...	...	...	...	...	...	...
354 Misc. petroleum and coal products		...	...	...	...	...	...	...	...	...	...	...	...
355 Rubber products	e/	90	80	79	86	101	100	94	116	81	79	89	86
356 Plastic products	e/	...	...	...	...	...	...	...	...	...	...	...	...
361 Pottery, china, earthenware	f/	70	82	78	81	92	100	98	100	101	101	99	96
362 Glass and products	f/	...	...	...	...	...	...	...	...	...	...	...	...
369 Other non-metallic mineral products	f/	...	...	...	...	...	...	...	...	...	...	...	...
371 Iron and steel		...	...	...	...	...	...	...	...	...	...	...	...
372 Non-ferrous metals		...	...	...	...	...	...	...	...	...	...	...	...
381 Fabricated metal products	g/	84	79	92	103	99	100	102	104	108	115	121	122
382 Non-electrical machinery	g/	...	...	...	...	...	...	...	...	...	...	...	...
383 Electrical machinery		110	90	73	87	108	100	105	133	147	134	146	144
384 Transport equipment		142	124	168	169	114	100	123	122	141	110	98	76
385 Professional and scientific equipment		...	...	...	...	...	100	101	102	103	154	138	125
390 Other manufacturing industries	c/	71	73	80	76	91	100	94	99	95	102	96	90
3 Total manufacturing		82	81	89	94	96	100	99	102	94	97	97	92

a/ 311/2 includes 313.
b/ 323 includes 324.
c/ 390 includes 332.
d/ 351 includes 352.
e/ 355 includes 356.
f/ 361 includes 362 and 369.
g/ 381 includes 382.

CZECH REPUBLIC

Supplier of information:
Czech Statistical Office, Prague.
Industrial statistics for the OECD countries are compiled by the OECD secretariat, which supplies them to UNIDO.

Basic source of data:
Not reported.

Major deviations from ISIC (Revision 3):
None reported.

Reference period (if not calendar year):

Scope:
Not reported.

Method of enumeration:
Not reported.

Adjusted for non-response:
Not reported.

Concepts and definitions of variables:
No deviations from the standard UN concepts and definitions are reported.

Related national publications:

ISIC Revision 3		Number of establishments					Number of employees					Wages and salaries paid to employees				
			(numbers)					(thousands)					(million KORUNAS)			
ISIC	Industry	Note	1993	1994	1995	1996	Note	1993	1994	1995	1996	Note	1993	1994	1995	1996
151	Processed meat,fish,fruit,vegetables,fats		...	...	5595a/	5623a/		...	...	139a/	152a/		...	...	12661a/	15381a/
1511	Processing/preserving of meat		...	...	...	...		...	...	...	...		...	...	...	...
1512	Processing/preserving of fish		...	...	...	...		...	...	...	...		...	...	...	...
1513	Processing/preserving of fruit & vegetables		...	...	...	...		...	...	...	...		...	...	...	...
1514	Vegetable and animal oils and fats		...	...	...	...		...	...	...	...		...	...	...	...
1520	Dairy products		...	...	...a/	...a/		...	...	...a/	...a/		...	...	...a/	...a/
153	Grain mill products; starches; animal feeds		...	...	...a/	...a/		...	...	...a/	...a/		...	...	...a/	...a/
1531	Grain mill products		...	...	...	...		...	...	...	...		...	...	...	...
1532	Starches and starch products		...	...	...	...		...	...	...	...		...	...	...	...
1533	Prepared animal feeds		...	...	...	...		...	...	...	...		...	...	...	...
154	Other food products		...	...	...a/	...a/		...	...	...a/	...a/		...	...	...a/	...a/
1541	Bakery products		...	...	...	...		...	...	...	...		...	...	...	...
1542	Sugar		...	...	...	...		...	...	...	...		...	...	...	...
1543	Cocoa, chocolate and sugar confectionery		...	...	...	...		...	...	...	...		...	...	...	...
1544	Macaroni, noodles & similar products		...	...	...	...		...	...	...	...		...	...	...	...
1549	Other food products n.e.c.		...	...	...	...		...	...	...	...		...	...	...	...
155	Beverages		...	...	...a/	...a/		...	...	...a/	...a/		...	...	...a/	...a/
1551	Distilling, rectifying & blending of spirits		...	...	...	...		...	...	...	...		...	...	...	...
1552	Wines		...	...	...	...		...	...	...	...		...	...	...	...
1553	Malt liquors and malt		...	...	...	...		...	...	...	...		...	...	...	...
1554	Soft drinks; mineral waters		...	...	...	...		...	...	...	...		...	...	...	...
1600	Tobacco products		...	...	...	...		...	...	...	...		...	...	...	...
171	Spinning, weaving and finishing of textiles		...	...	3525b/	3195b/		...	...	92b/	88b/		...	...	6452b/	7102b/
1711	Textile fibre preparation; textile weaving		...	...	...	...		...	...	...	...		...	...	...	...
1712	Finishing of textiles		...	...	...	...		...	...	...	...		...	...	...	...
172	Other textiles		...	...	...b/	...b/		...	...	...b/	...b/		...	...	...b/	...b/
1721	Made-up textile articles, except apparel		...	...	...	...		...	...	...	...		...	...	...	...
1722	Carpets and rugs		...	...	...	...		...	...	...	...		...	...	...	...
1723	Cordage, rope, twine and netting		...	...	...	...		...	...	...	...		...	...	...	...
1729	Other textiles n.e.c.		...	...	...	...		...	...	...	...		...	...	...	...
1730	Knitted and crocheted fabrics and articles		...	...	...b/	...b/		...	...	...b/	...b/		...	...	...b/	...b/
1810	Wearing apparel, except fur apparel		...	...	11383c/	8768c/		...	...	56c/	53c/		...	...	3685c/	3523c/
1820	Dressing & dyeing of fur; processing of fur		...	...	...c/	...c/		...	...	...c/	...c/		...	...	...c/	...c/
191	Tanning, dressing and processing of leather		...	...	1064d/	1107d/		...	...	43d/	31d/		...	...	2562d/	2582d/
1911	Tanning and dressing of leather		...	...	...	...		...	...	...	...		...	...	...	...
1912	Luggage, handbags, etc.; saddlery & harness		...	...	...	...		...	...	...	...		...	...	...	...
1920	Footwear		...	...	...d/	...d/		...	...	...d/	...d/		...	...	...d/	...d/
2010	Sawmilling and planing of wood		...	...	15093e/	17370e/		...	...	53e/	49e/		...	...	4919e/	4668e/
202	Products of wood, cork, straw, etc.		...	...	...e/	...e/		...	...	...e/	...e/		...	...	...e/	...e/
2021	Veneer sheets, plywood, particle board, etc.		...	...	...	...		...	...	...	...		...	...	...	...
2022	Builders' carpentry and joinery		...	...	...	...		...	...	...	...		...	...	...	...
2023	Wooden containers		...	...	...	...		...	...	...	...		...	...	...	...
2029	Other wood products; articles of cork/straw		...	...	...	...		...	...	...	...		...	...	...	...
210	Paper and paper products		...	...	366	391		...	...	31	25		...	...	2244	2674
2101	Pulp, paper and paperboard		...	...	...	...		...	...	...	...		...	...	...	...
2102	Corrugated paper and paperboard		...	...	...	...		...	...	...	...		...	...	...	...
2109	Other articles of paper and paperboard		...	...	...	...		...	...	...	...		...	...	...	...
221	Publishing		...	...	4166f/	4202f/		...	...	26f/	34f/		...	...	3701f/	4376f/
2211	Publishing of books and other publications		...	...	...	...		...	...	...	...		...	...	...	...
2212	Publishing of newspapers, journals, etc.		...	...	...	...		...	...	...	...		...	...	...	...
2213	Publishing of recorded media		...	...	...	...		...	...	...	...		...	...	...	...
2219	Other publishing		...	...	...	...		...	...	...	...		...	...	...	...

222 Printing and related service activities	...	...	...f/	...f/	...	...	...f/	...f/	...	...	...f/	...f/
2221 Printing	...	...	...	...	...	...	...	...	...	...	...	...
2222 Service activities related to printing	...	...	...	...	...	...	...	...	...	...	...	...
2230 Reproduction of recorded media	...	...	...f/	...f/	...	...	...f/	...f/	...	...	...f/	...f/
2310 Coke oven products	...	...	...	...	...	...	...	...	...	...	...	...
2320 Refined petroleum products	...	...	...	...	...	...	...	...	...	...	...	...
2330 Processing of nuclear fuel	...	...	...	...	...	...	...	...	...	...	...	...
241 Basic chemicals	...	...	1024g/	893g/	...	...	49g/	54g/	...	...	5064g/	6945g/
2411 Basic chemicals, except fertilizers	...	...	...	...	...	...	...	...	...	...	...	...
2412 Fertilizers and nitrogen compounds	...	...	...	...	...	...	...	...	...	...	...	...
2413 Plastics in primary forms; synthetic rubber	...	...	...	...	...	...	...	...	...	...	...	...
242 Other chemicals	...	...	...g/	...g/	...	...	...g/	...g/	...	...	...g/	...g/
2421 Pesticides and other agro-chemical products	...	...	...	...	...	...	...	...	...	...	...	...
2422 Paints, varnishes, printing ink and mastics	...	...	...	...	...	...	...	...	...	...	...	...
2423 Pharmaceuticals, medicinal chemicals, etc.	...	...	...	...	...	...	...	...	...	...	...	...
2424 Soap, cleaning & cosmetic preparations	...	...	...	...	...	...	...	...	...	...	...	...
2429 Other chemical products n.e.c.	...	...	...	...	...	...	...	...	...	...	...	...
2430 Man-made fibres	...	...	...g/	...g/	...	...	...g/	...g/	...	...	...g/	...g/
251 Rubber products	...	...	1637h/	1988h/	...	...	40h/	44h/	...	...	3878h/	5061h/
2511 Rubber tyres and tubes	...	...	...	...	...	...	...	...	...	...	...	...
2519 Other rubber products	...	...	...	...	...	...	...	...	...	...	...	...
2520 Plastic products	...	...	...h/	...h/	...	...	...h/	...h/	...	...	...h/	...h/
2610 Glass and glass products	...	...	4573i/	5587i/	...	...	76i/	80i/	...	...	7769i/	9029i/
269 Non-metallic mineral products n.e.c.	...	...	...i/	...i/	...	...	...i/	...i/	...	...	...i/	...i/
2691 Pottery, china and earthenware	...	...	...	...	...	...	...	...	...	...	...	...
2692 Refractory ceramic products	...	...	...	...	...	...	...	...	...	...	...	...
2693 Struct.non-refractory clay; ceramic products	...	...	...	...	...	...	...	...	...	...	...	...
2694 Cement, lime and plaster	...	...	...	...	...	...	...	...	...	...	...	...
2695 Articles of concrete, cement and plaster	...	...	...	...	...	...	...	...	...	...	...	...
2696 Cutting, shaping & finishing of stone	...	...	...	...	...	...	...	...	...	...	...	...
2699 Other non-metallic mineral products n.e.c.	...	...	...	...	...	...	...	...	...	...	...	...
2710 Basic iron and steel	...	...	364j/	310j/	...	...	122j/	107j/	...	...	12089j/	13773j/
2720 Basic precious and non-ferrous metals	...	...	...j/	...j/	...	...	...j/	...j/	...	...	...j/	...j/
273 Casting of metals	...	...	...j/	...j/	...	...	...j/	...j/	...	...	...j/	...j/
2731 Casting of iron and steel	...	...	...	...	...	...	...	...	...	...	...	...
2732 Casting of non-ferrous metals	...	...	...	...	...	...	...	...	...	...	...	...
281 Struct.metal products;tanks;steam generators	...	...	21562k/	28181k/	...	...	121k/	132k/	...	...	12259k/	14675k/
2811 Structural metal products	...	...	...	...	...	...	...	...	...	...	...	...
2812 Tanks, reservoirs and containers of metal	...	...	...	...	...	...	...	...	...	...	...	...
2813 Steam generators	...	...	...	...	...	...	...	...	...	...	...	...
289 Other metal products; metal working services	...	...	...k/	...k/	...	...	...k/	...k/	...	...	...k/	...k/
2891 Metal forging/pressing/stamping/roll-forming	...	...	...	...	...	...	...	...	...	...	...	...
2892 Treatment & coating of metals	...	...	...	...	...	...	...	...	...	...	...	...
2893 Cutlery, hand tools and general hardware	...	...	...	...	...	...	...	...	...	...	...	...
2899 Other fabricated metal products n.e.c.	...	...	...	...	...	...	...	...	...	...	...	...
291 General purpose machinery	...	...	5858m/	6351m/	...	...	184m/	182m/	...	...	18259m/	20447m/
2911 Engines & turbines(not for transport equip.)	...	...	...	...	...	...	...	...	...	...	...	...
2912 Pumps, compressors, taps and valves	...	...	...	...	...	...	...	...	...	...	...	...
2913 Bearings, gears, gearing & driving elements	...	...	...	...	...	...	...	...	...	...	...	...
2914 Ovens, furnaces and furnace burners	...	...	...	...	...	...	...	...	...	...	...	...
2915 Lifting and handling equipment	...	...	...	...	...	...	...	...	...	...	...	...
2919 Other general purpose machinery	...	...	...	...	...	...	...	...	...	...	...	...
292 Special purpose machinery	...	...	...m/	...m/	...	...	...m/	...m/	...	...	...m/	...m/
2921 Agricultural and forestry machinery	...	...	...	...	...	...	...	...	...	...	...	...
2922 Machine tools	...	...	...	...	...	...	...	...	...	...	...	...
2923 Machinery for metallurgy	...	...	...	...	...	...	...	...	...	...	...	...
2924 Machinery for mining & construction	...	...	...	...	...	...	...	...	...	...	...	...
2925 Food/beverage/tobacco processing machinery	...	...	...	...	...	...	...	...	...	...	...	...
2926 Machinery for textile, apparel and leather	...	...	...	...	...	...	...	...	...	...	...	...
2927 Weapons and ammunition	...	...	...	...	...	...	...	...	...	...	...	...
2929 Other special purpose machinery	...	...	...	...	...	...	...	...	...	...	...	...
2930 Domestic appliances n.e.c.	...	...	...m/	...m/	...	...	...m/	...m/	...	...	...m/	...m/

continued

Czech Republic

ISIC Revision 3	Number of establishments					Number of employees					Wages and salaries paid to employees				
		(numbers)					(thousands)					(million KORUNAS)			
ISIC Industry	Note	1993	1994	1995	1996	Note	1993	1994	1995	1996	Note	1993	1994	1995	1996
3000 Office, accounting and computing machinery		...	...	160	152		...	...	8	4		...	...	306	361
3110 Electric motors, generators and transformers		...	...	9936n/	9641n/		...	...	67n/	73n/		...	...	6710n/	8339n/
3120 Electricity distribution & control apparatus		...	...	...n/	...n/		...	...	...n/	...n/		...	...	...n/	...n/
3130 Insulated wire and cable		...	...	...n/	...n/		...	...	...n/	...n/		...	...	...n/	...n/
3140 Accumulators, primary cells and batteries		...	...	...n/	...n/		...	...	...n/	...n/		...	...	...n/	...n/
3150 Lighting equipment and electric lamps		...	...	...n/	...n/		...	...	...n/	...n/		...	...	...n/	...n/
3190 Other electrical equipment n.e.c.		...	...	...n/	...n/		...	...	...n/	...n/		...	...	...n/	...n/
3210 Electronic valves, tubes, etc.		...	...	2548p/	1796p/		...	...	24p/	23p/		...	...	2179p/	2451p/
3220 TV/radio transmitters; line comm. apparatus		...	...	...p/	...p/		...	...	...p/	...p/		...	...	...p/	...p/
3230 TV and radio receivers and associated goods		...	...	...p/	...p/		...	...	...p/	...p/		...	...	...p/	...p/
331 Medical, measuring, testing appliances, etc.		...	...	2740q/	3422q/		...	...	25q/	29q/		...	...	2686q/	3261q/
3311 Medical, surgical and orthopaedic equipment		...	...	...	...		...	...	...	...		...	...	...	...
3312 Measuring/testing/navigating appliances,etc.		...	...	...	...		...	...	...	...		...	...	...	...
3313 Industrial process control equipment		...	...	...	...		...	...	...	...		...	...	...	...
3320 Optical instruments & photographic equipment		...	...	...q/	...q/		...	...	...q/	...q/		...	...	...q/	...q/
3330 Watches and clocks		...	...	...q/	...q/		...	...	...q/	...q/		...	...	...q/	...q/
3410 Motor vehicles		...	...	548r/	311r/		...	...	56r/	57r/		...	...	5839r/	7412r/
3420 Automobile bodies, trailers & semi-trailers		...	...	...r/	...r/		...	...	...r/	...r/		...	...	...r/	...r/
3430 Parts/accessories for automobiles		...	...	...r/	...r/		...	...	...r/	...r/		...	...	...r/	...r/
351 Building and repairing of ships and boats		...	...	305s/	422s/		...	...	42s/	36s/		...	...	3478s/	4114s/
3511 Building and repairing of ships		...	...	...	...		...	...	...	...		...	...	...	...
3512 Building/repairing of pleasure/sport. boats		...	...	...	...		...	...	...	...		...	...	...	...
3520 Railway/tramway locomotives & rolling stock		...	...	...s/	...s/		...	...	...s/	...s/		...	...	...s/	...s/
3530 Aircraft and spacecraft		...	...	...s/	...s/		...	...	...s/	...s/		...	...	...s/	...s/
359 Transport equipment n.e.c.		...	...	...s/	...s/		...	...	...s/	...s/		...	...	...s/	...s/
3591 Motorcycles		...	...	...	...		...	...	...	...		...	...	...	...
3592 Bicycles and invalid carriages		...	...	...	...		...	...	...	...		...	...	...	...
3599 Other transport equipment n.e.c.		...	...	...	...		...	...	...	...		...	...	...	...
3610 Furniture		...	...	7992t/	10058t/		...	...	67t/	74t/		...	...	5650t/	6617t/
369 Manufacturing n.e.c.		...	...	...t/	...t/		...	...	...t/	...t/		...	...	...t/	...t/
3691 Jewellery and related articles		...	...	...	...		...	...	...	...		...	...	...	...
3692 Musical instruments		...	...	...	...		...	...	...	...		...	...	...	...
3693 Sports goods		...	...	...	...		...	...	...	...		...	...	...	...
3694 Games and toys		...	...	...	...		...	...	...	...		...	...	...	...
3699 Other manufacturing n.e.c.		...	...	...	...		...	...	...	...		...	...	...	...
3710 Recycling of metal waste and scrap		...	...	437u/	386u/		...	...	7u/	7u/		...	...	697u/	704u/
3720 Recycling of non-metal waste and scrap		...	...	...u/	...u/		...	...	...u/	...u/		...	...	...u/	...u/
D Total manufacturing		...	...	100889	110163		...	...	1347	1341		...	...	125039	144650

a/ 151 includes 1520, 153, 154 and 155.
b/ 171 includes 172 and 1730.
c/ 1810 includes 1820.
d/ 191 includes 1920.
e/ 2010 includes 202.
f/ 221 includes 222 and 2230.
g/ 241 includes 242 and 2430.
h/ 251 includes 2520.
i/ 2610 includes 269.
j/ 2710 includes 2720 and 273.
k/ 281 includes 289.
m/ 291 includes 292 and 2930.
n/ 3110 includes 3120, 3130, 3140, 3150 and 3190.
p/ 3210 includes 3220 and 3230.
q/ 331 includes 3320 and 3330.
r/ 3410 includes 3420 and 3430.
s/ 351 includes 3520, 3530 and 359.
t/ 3610 includes 369.
u/ 3710 includes 3720.

Czech Republic

ISIC Revision 3		Output					Value added					Gross fixed capital formation		
			(million KORUNAS)					(million KORUNAS)					(million KORUNAS)	
ISIC	Industry	Note	1993	1994	1995	1996	Note	1993	1994	1995	1996	Note	1995	1996
151	Processed meat,fish,fruit,vegetables,fats		...	...	194309a/	232056a/		...	...	41918a/	44588a/	a/	12246	16390
1511	Processing/preserving of meat		...	...	...	...		...	...	...	...		...	...
1512	Processing/preserving of fish		...	...	...	...		...	...	...	...		...	...
1513	Processing/preserving of fruit & vegetables		...	...	...	...		...	...	...	...		...	...
1514	Vegetable and animal oils and fats		...	...	...	...		...	...	...	...		...	...
1520	Dairy products		...	...	...	...		...	...	...	...		...	...
153	Grain mill products; starches; animal feeds		...	...	...a/	...a/		...	...	...a/	...a/	a/	...	...
1531	Grain mill products		...	...	...a/	...a/		...	...	...a/	...a/	a/	...	...
1532	Starches and starch products		...	...	...	...		...	...	...	...		...	...
1533	Prepared animal feeds		...	...	...	...		...	...	...	...		...	...
154	Other food products		...	...	...	...		...	...	...	...		...	...
1541	Bakery products		...	...	...a/	...a/		...	...	...a/	...a/	a/	...	...
1542	Sugar		...	...	...	...		...	...	...	...		...	...
1543	Cocoa, chocolate and sugar confectionery		...	...	...	...		...	...	...	...		...	...
1544	Macaroni, noodles & similar products		...	...	...	...		...	...	...	...		...	...
1549	Other food products n.e.c.		...	...	...	...		...	...	...	...		...	...
155	Beverages		...	...	...	...		...	...	...	...		...	...
1551	Distilling, rectifying & blending of spirits		...	...	...a/	...a/		...	...	...a/	...a/	a/	...	...
1552	Wines		...	...	...	...		...	...	...	...		...	...
1553	Malt liquors and malt		...	...	...	...		...	...	...	...		...	...
1554	Soft drinks; mineral waters		...	...	...	...		...	...	...	...		...	...
1600	Tobacco products		...	...	...	...		...	...	...	...		...	...
171	Spinning, weaving and finishing of textiles		...	...	55374b/	55590b/		...	...	14149b/	15136b/	b/	3696	4366
1711	Textile fibre preparation; textile weaving		...	...	...	...		...	...	...	...		...	...
1712	Finishing of textiles		...	...	...	...		...	...	...	...		...	...
172	Other textiles		...	...	...b/	...b/		...	...	...b/	...b/	b/	...	...
1721	Made-up textile articles, except apparel		...	...	...	...		...	...	...	...		...	...
1722	Carpets and rugs		...	...	...	...		...	...	...	...		...	...
1723	Cordage, rope, twine and netting		...	...	...	...		...	...	...	...		...	...
1729	Other textiles n.e.c.		...	...	...	...		...	...	...	...		...	...
1730	Knitted and crocheted fabrics and articles		...	...	...b/	...b/		...	...	...b/	...b/	b/	...	...
1810	Wearing apparel, except fur apparel		...	...	16878c/	16528c/		...	...	7485c/	6035c/	c/	758	963
1820	Dressing & dyeing of fur; processing of fur		...	...	...c/	...c/		...	...	...c/	...c/	c/	...	...
191	Tanning, dressing and processing of leather		...	...	17203d/	16380d/		...	...	5225d/	5118d/	d/	626	533
1911	Tanning and dressing of leather		...	...	...	...		...	...	...	...		...	...
1912	Luggage, handbags, etc.; saddlery & harness		...	...	...	...		...	...	...	...		...	...
1920	Footwear		...	...	...d/	...d/		...	...	...d/	...d/	d/	...	...
2010	Sawmilling and planing of wood		...	...	36331e/	40349e/		...	...	11133e/	12183e/	e/	2268	4466
202	Products of wood, cork, straw, etc.		...	...	...e/	...e/		...	...	...e/	...e/	e/	...	...
2021	Veneer sheets, plywood, particle board, etc.		...	...	...	...		...	...	...	...		...	...
2022	Builders' carpentry and joinery		...	...	...	...		...	...	...	...		...	...
2023	Wooden containers		...	...	...	...		...	...	...	...		...	...
2029	Other wood products; articles of cork/straw		...	...	...	...		...	...	...	...		...	...
210	Paper and paper products		...	...	36797	33693		...	...	9745	7676		3515	5196
2101	Pulp, paper and paperboard		...	...	...	...		...	...	...	...		...	...
2102	Corrugated paper and paperboard		...	...	...	...		...	...	...	...		...	...
2109	Other articles of paper and paperboard		...	...	...	...		...	...	...	...		...	...
221	Publishing		...	...	32198f/	37599f/		...	...	9078f/	11804f/	f/	3446	2880
2211	Publishing of books and other publications		...	...	...	...		...	...	...	...		...	...
2212	Publishing of newspapers, journals, etc.		...	...	...	...		...	...	...	...		...	...
2213	Publishing of recorded media		...	...	...	...		...	...	...	...		...	...
2219	Other publishing		...	...	...	...		...	...	...	...		...	...

continued

Czech Republic

ISIC Revision 3		Output					Value added					Gross fixed capital formation		
			(million KORUNAS)					(million KORUNAS)					(million KORUNAS)	
ISIC	Industry	Note	1993	1994	1995	1996	Note	1993	1994	1995	1996	Note	1995	1996
222	Printing and related service activities		...	...	...f/	...f/		...	...	...f/	...f/	f/	...	...
2221	Printing		...	...	...	...		...	...	...	...		...	...
2222	Service activities related to printing		...	...	...	...		...	...	...	...		...	...
2230	Reproduction of recorded media		...	...	...f/	...f/		...	...	...f/	...f/	f/	...	...
2310	Coke oven products		...	...	...	...		...	...	...	...		...	...
2320	Refined petroleum products		...	...	...	...		...	...	...	...		...	...
2330	Processing of nuclear fuel		...	...	...	...		...	...	...	...		...	...
241	Basic chemicals		...	...	72696g/	100559g/		...	...	20303g/	25156g/	g/	7516	10905
2411	Basic chemicals, except fertilizers		...	...	...	...		...	...	...	...		...	...
2412	Fertilizers and nitrogen compounds		...	...	...	...		...	...	...	...		...	...
2413	Plastics in primary forms; synthetic rubber		...	...	...	...		...	...	...	...		...	...
242	Other chemicals		...	...	...g/	...g/		...	...	...g/	...g/	g/	...	...
2421	Pesticides and other agro-chemical products		...	...	...	...		...	...	...	...		...	...
2422	Paints, varnishes, printing ink and mastics		...	...	...	...		...	...	...	...		...	...
2423	Pharmaceuticals, medicinal chemicals, etc.		...	...	...	...		...	...	...	...		...	...
2424	Soap, cleaning & cosmetic preparations		...	...	...	...		...	...	...	...		...	...
2429	Other chemical products n.e.c.		...	...	...	...		...	...	...	...		...	...
2430	Man-made fibres		...	...	...g/	...g/		...	...	...g/	...g/	g/	...	...
251	Rubber products		...	...	37966h/	48027h/		...	...	10689h/	14188h/	h/	3542	3603
2511	Rubber tyres and tubes		...	...	...	...		...	...	...	...		...	...
2519	Other rubber products		...	...	...	...		...	...	...	...		...	...
2520	Plastic products		...	...	...h/	...h/		...	...	...h/	...h/	h/	...	...
2610	Glass and glass products		...	...	64207i/	75712i/		...	...	23374i/	27605i/	i/	11885	12219
269	Non-metallic mineral products n.e.c.		...	...	...i/	...i/		...	...	...i/	...i/	i/	...	...
2691	Pottery, china and earthenware		...	...	...	...		...	...	...	...		...	...
2692	Refractory ceramic products		...	...	...	...		...	...	...	...		...	...
2693	Struct.non-refractory clay; ceramic products		...	...	...	...		...	...	...	...		...	...
2694	Cement, lime and plaster		...	...	...	...		...	...	...	...		...	...
2695	Articles of concrete, cement and plaster		...	...	...	...		...	...	...	...		...	...
2696	Cutting, shaping & finishing of stone		...	...	...	...		...	...	...	...		...	...
2699	Other non-metallic mineral products n.e.c.		...	...	...	...		...	...	...	...		...	...
2710	Basic iron and steel		...	...	219590j/	179985j/		...	...	30445j/	29369j/	j/	6727	10387
2720	Basic precious and non-ferrous metals		...	...	...j/	...j/		...	...	...j/	...j/	j/	...	...
273	Casting of metals		...	...	...j/	...j/		...	...	...j/	...j/	j/	...	...
2731	Casting of iron and steel		...	...	...	...		...	...	...	...		...	...
2732	Casting of non-ferrous metals		...	...	...	...		...	...	...	...		...	...
281	Struct.metal products;tanks;steam generators		...	...	93512k/	108352k/		...	...	32832k/	35918k/	k/	6193	7162
2811	Structural metal products		...	...	...	...		...	...	...	...		...	...
2812	Tanks, reservoirs and containers of metal		...	...	...	...		...	...	...	...		...	...
2813	Steam generators		...	...	...	...		...	...	...	...		...	...
289	Other metal products; metal working services		...	...	...k/	...k/		...	...	...k/	...k/	k/	...	...
2891	Metal forging/pressing/stamping/roll-forming		...	...	...	...		...	...	...	...		...	...
2892	Treatment & coating of metals		...	...	...	...		...	...	...	...		...	...
2893	Cutlery, hand tools and general hardware		...	...	...	...		...	...	...	...		...	...
2899	Other fabricated metal products n.e.c.		...	...	...	...		...	...	...	...		...	...
291	General purpose machinery		...	...	112000m/	127827m/		...	...	37868m/	40862m/	m/	6636	7386
2911	Engines & turbines(not for transport equip.)		...	...	...	...		...	...	...	...		...	...
2912	Pumps, compressors, taps and valves		...	...	...	...		...	...	...	...		...	...
2913	Bearings, gears, gearing & driving elements		...	...	...	...		...	...	...	...		...	...
2914	Ovens, furnaces and furnace burners		...	...	...	...		...	...	...	...		...	...
2915	Lifting and handling equipment		...	...	...	...		...	...	...	...		...	...
2919	Other general purpose machinery		...	...	...	...		...	...	...	...		...	...

ISIC													
292 Special purpose machinery		...	...	...m/	...m/		...	...	...m/	...m/	m/	...	...
2921 Agricultural and forestry machinery		...	...	...	...		...	...	...	...		...	...
2922 Machine tools		...	...	...	...		...	...	...	...		...	...
2923 Machinery for metallurgy		...	...	...	...		...	...	...	...		...	...
2924 Machinery for mining & construction		...	...	...	...		...	...	...	...		...	...
2925 Food/beverage/tobacco processing machinery		...	...	...	...		...	...	...	...		...	...
2926 Machinery for textile, apparel and leather		...	...	...	...		...	...	...	...		...	...
2927 Weapons and ammunition		...	...	...	...		...	...	...	...		...	...
2929 Other special purpose machinery		...	...	...	...		...	...	...	...		...	...
2930 Domestic appliances n.e.c.		...	...	...m/	...m/		...	...	...m/	...m/	m/	...	...
3000 Office, accounting and computing machinery		...	...	2270	2280		...	...	618	743		69	83
3110 Electric motors, generators and transformers		...	...	53688n/	61849n/		...	...	16254n/	19284n/	n/	3660	4370
3120 Electricity distribution & control apparatus		...	...	...n/	...n/		...	...	...n/	...n/	n/	...	...
3130 Insulated wire and cable		...	...	...n/	...n/		...	...	...n/	...n/	n/	...	...
3140 Accumulators, primary cells and batteries		...	...	...n/	...n/		...	...	...n/	...n/	n/	...	...
3150 Lighting equipment and electric lamps		...	...	...n/	...n/		...	...	...n/	...n/	n/	...	...
3190 Other electrical equipment n.e.c.		...	...	...n/	...n/		...	...	...n/	...n/	n/	...	...
3210 Electronic valves, tubes, etc.		...	...	14037p/	18849p/		...	...	5315p/	6100p/	p/	892	1185
3220 TV/radio transmitters; line comm. apparatus		...	...	...p/	...p/		...	...	...p/	...p/	p/	...	...
3230 TV and radio receivers and associated goods		...	...	...p/	...p/		...	...	...p/	...p/	p/	...	...
331 Medical, measuring, testing appliances, etc.		...	...	15263q/	18655q/		...	...	6256q/	7354q/	q/	1419	1402
3311 Medical, surgical and orthopaedic equipment		...	...	...	...		...	...	...	...		...	...
3312 Measuring/testing/navigating appliances,etc.		...	...	...	...		...	...	...	...		...	...
3313 Industrial process control equipment		...	...	...	...		...	...	...	...		...	...
3320 Optical instruments & photographic equipment		...	...	...q/	...q/		...	...	...q/	...q/	q/	...	...
3330 Watches and clocks		...	...	...q/	...q/		...	...	...q/	...q/	q/	...	...
3410 Motor vehicles		...	...	76444r/	98407r/		...	...	15928r/	21018r/	r/	8330	14598
3420 Automobile bodies, trailers & semi-trailers		...	...	...r/	...r/		...	...	...r/	...r/	r/	...	...
3430 Parts/accessories for automobiles		...	...	...r/	...r/		...	...	...r/	...r/	r/	...	...
351 Building and repairing of ships and boats		...	...	22487s/	27000s/		...	...	6766s/	7308s/	s/	1795	1937
3511 Building and repairing of ships		...	...	...	...		...	...	...	...		...	...
3512 Building/repairing of pleasure/sport. boats		...	...	...	...		...	...	...	...		...	...
3520 Railway/tramway locomotives & rolling stock		...	...	...s/	...s/		...	...	...s/	...s/	s/	...	...
3530 Aircraft and spacecraft		...	...	...s/	...s/		...	...	...s/	...s/	s/	...	...
359 Transport equipment n.e.c.		...	...	...s/	...s/		...	...	...s/	...s/	s/	...	...
3591 Motorcycles		...	...	...	...		...	...	...	...		...	...
3592 Bicycles and invalid carriages		...	...	...	...		...	...	...	...		...	...
3599 Other transport equipment n.e.c.		...	...	...	...		...	...	...	...		...	...
3610 Furniture		...	...	39948t/	48177t/		...	...	14166t/	16326t/	t/	2516	2437
369 Manufacturing n.e.c.		...	...	...t/	...t/		...	...	...t/	...t/	t/	...	...
3691 Jewellery and related articles		...	...	...	...		...	...	...	...		...	...
3692 Musical instruments		...	...	...	...		...	...	...	...		...	...
3693 Sports goods		...	...	...	...		...	...	...	...		...	...
3694 Games and toys		...	...	...	...		...	...	...	...		...	...
3699 Other manufacturing n.e.c.		...	...	...	...		...	...	...	...		...	...
3710 Recycling of metal waste and scrap		...	...	11116u/	9450u/		...	...	2119u/	1788u/	u/	959	371
3720 Recycling of non-metal waste and scrap		...	...	...u/	...u/		...	...	...u/	...u/	u/	...	...
D Total manufacturing		...	...	1296686	1419906		...	...	337157	362696		94691	115260

a/ 151 includes 1520, 153, 154 and 155.
b/ 171 includes 172 and 1730.
c/ 1810 includes 1820.
d/ 191 includes 1920.
e/ 2010 includes 202.
f/ 221 includes 222 and 2230.
g/ 241 includes 242 and 2430.
h/ 251 includes 2520.
i/ 2610 includes 269.
j/ 2710 includes 2720 and 273.
k/ 281 includes 289.
m/ 291 includes 292 and 2930.
n/ 3110 includes 3120, 3130, 3140, 3150 and 3190.
p/ 3210 includes 3220 and 3230.
q/ 331 includes 3320 and 3330.
r/ 3410 includes 3420 and 3430.
s/ 351 includes 3520, 3530 and 359.
t/ 3610 includes 369.
u/ 3710 includes 3720.

Czech Republic

ISIC Revision 3			Index numbers of industrial production											
			(1990=100)											
ISIC	Industry	Note	1985	1986	1987	1988	1989	1990	1991	1992	1993	1994	1995	1996
15	Food and beverages		...	...	...	...	...	...	...	...	...	...	...	...
16	Tobacco products		...	...	...	...	...	...	...	...	...	...	...	...
17	Textiles		...	...	...	...	...	...	...	...	...	...	...	...
18	Wearing apparel, fur		...	...	...	...	...	...	...	...	...	...	...	...
19	Leather, leather products and footwear		...	...	...	...	...	...	...	...	...	...	...	...
20	Wood products (excl. furniture)		...	...	...	...	...	...	...	...	...	...	...	...
21	Paper and paper products		...	...	...	...	...	...	...	...	...	...	...	...
22	Printing and publishing		...	...	...	...	...	...	...	...	...	...	...	...
23	Coke,refined petroleum products,nuclear fuel		...	...	...	...	...	...	...	...	...	...	...	...
24	Chemicals and chemical products		...	...	...	...	...	...	...	...	...	...	...	...
25	Rubber and plastics products		...	...	...	...	...	...	...	...	...	...	...	...
26	Non-metallic mineral products		...	...	...	...	...	...	...	...	...	...	...	...
27	Basic metals		...	...	...	...	...	...	...	...	...	...	...	...
28	Fabricated metal products		...	...	...	...	...	...	...	...	...	...	...	...
29	Machinery and equipment n.e.c.		...	...	...	...	...	...	...	...	...	...	...	...
30	Office, accounting and computing machinery		...	...	...	...	...	...	...	...	...	...	...	...
31	Electrical machinery and apparatus		...	...	...	...	...	...	...	...	...	...	...	...
32	Radio,television and communication equipment		...	...	...	...	...	...	...	...	...	...	...	...
33	Medical, precision and optical instruments		...	...	...	...	...	...	...	...	...	...	...	...
34	Motor vehicles, trailers, semi-trailers		...	...	...	...	...	...	...	...	...	...	...	...
35	Other transport equipment		...	...	...	...	...	...	...	...	...	...	...	...
36	Furniture; manufacturing n.e.c.		...	...	...	...	...	...	...	...	...	...	...	...
37	Recycling		...	...	...	...	...	...	...	...	...	...	...	...
D	Total manufacturing		...	...	...	...	...	...	...	...	...	...	...	...

DENMARK

Supplier of information:
Danmarks Statistik, Copenhagen.
Industrial statistics for the OECD countries are compiled by the OECD secretariat, which supplies them to UNIDO.

Basic source of data:
Surveys based partly on the establishment as a local unit (employment, wages and salaries, gross fixed capital formation) and partly on kind-of-activity units (output, value added).

Major deviations from ISIC (Revision 3):
The data presented in ISIC Revision 3 were originally classified according to NACE (Revision 1).

Reference period (if not calendar year):

Scope:
The figures for number of establishments, employment and wages and salaries were derived from the register-based statistics of establishments and employment. All establishments with any employment in manufacturing are covered. Data for production, value added and investment refer to enterprises employing 20 or more persons engaged.

Method of enumeration:
Not reported.

Adjusted for non-response:
Not reported.

Concepts and definitions of variables:
Number of employees refers to all full-time and part-time employees and all self-employed at end November.
Wages and salaries include all outlays of these kinds reported to the tax authorities by establishments operating during the year. This means that outlays even in establishments which are not in activity at end November are included in the figures.
Output is given as gross output in factor values. It includes the value of all products, net change of work in progress, work done on own account, services rendered, goods shipped in the same condition as received, electricity sold, fixed assets produced for own use, net changes in stocks of finished goods, goods made by homeworkers and handicraft workers and other elements of turnover.
Value added is calculated as the value of gross output less the cost of materials, fuels and other supplies, contract and commission work done by others, goods shipped in the same condition as received and electricity purchased. Input estimates are on a consumed basis.
Gross fixed capital formation is given as the value of purchases of fixed assets, including own-account construction of assets, less the value of sales of fixed assets. Fixed assets are those with a productive life of more than three years, including assets made by a unit's labour force for its own use, additions, alterations and improvements to existing assets, new and used assets.
Valuation is a full cost incurred, including the delivered price and the installation cost. For assets produced by the unit, the cost of work put in progress is used. The actual amount realized is taken when deducting sales and used assets.

Related national publications:

Denmark

ISIC	ISIC Revision 3 Industry	Note	Number of establishments (numbers) 1992	1993	1994	1995	Note	Number of employees (numbers) 1992	1993	1994	1995	Note	Wages and salaries paid to employees (million KRONER) 1992	1993	1994	1995
151	Processed meat,fish,fruit,vegetables,fats		...	655	634	631		...	38406	37900	36379		...	7667	7735	7829
1511	Processing/preserving of meat		...	342	325	313		...	25709	25208	23152		...	5444	5409	5404
1512	Processing/preserving of fish		...	228	222	230		...	8890	8653	8938		...	1446	1511	1519
1513	Processing/preserving of fruit & vegetables		...	67	67	68		...	2782	2998	3263		...	523	552	644
1514	Vegetable and animal oils and fats		...	18	20	20		...	1025	1041	1026		...	254	263	262
1520	Dairy products		...	184	181	180		...	11988	12119	12356		...	2642	2643	2791
153	Grain mill products; starches; animal feeds		...	102	105	103		...	2770	2963	3175		...	582	626	706
1531	Grain mill products		...	25	26	24		...	900	895	935		...	210	216	232
1532	Starches and starch products		...	4	7	7		...	184	241	280		...	42	53	60
1533	Prepared animal feeds		...	73	72	72		...	1686	1827	1960		...	329	357	414
154	Other food products		...	1737	1678	1616		...	30311	31036	30790		...	4095	4409	4419
1541	Bakery products		...	1569	1516	1471		...	20486	20714	20964		...	2155	2253	2278
1542	Sugar		...	11	13	10		...	1789	1698	1596		...	352	363	343
1543	Cocoa, chocolate and sugar confectionery		...	48	43	42		...	4413	4493	3278		...	805	841	623
1544	Macaroni, noodles & similar products		...	12	11	9		...	103	61	74		...	13	8	10
1549	Other food products n.e.c.		...	97	95	84		...	3520	4070	4878		...	770	944	1165
155	Beverages		...	69	65	65		...	6796	6818	6925		...	1676	1685	1751
1551	Distilling, rectifying & blending of spirits		...	5	7	10a/		...	312	440	571a/		...	79	109	127a/
1552	Wines		...	4	4	...a/		...	176	198	...a/		...	31	29	...a/
1553	Malt liquors and malt		...	25	26	27		...	4957	4940	4921		...	1308	1295	1320
1554	Soft drinks; mineral waters		...	35	28	28		...	1351	1240	1433		...	258	252	304
1600	Tobacco products		...	17	15	13		...	1461	1460	1472		...	316	312	324
171	Spinning, weaving and finishing of textiles		...	178	173	156		...	3084	3013	2233		...	561	554	447
1711	Textile fibre preparation; textile weaving		...	122	113	103		...	1707	1702	1276		...	314	318	265
1712	Finishing of textiles		...	56	60	53		...	1377	1311	957		...	247	236	182
172	Other textiles		...	579	558	535		...	5615	6010	5891		...	974	1042	1065
1721	Made-up textile articles, except apparel		...	372	366	349		...	3123	3554	3397		...	485	552	550
1722	Carpets and rugs		...	31	32	30		...	939	929	924		...	213	203	212
1723	Cordage, rope, twine and netting		...	84	76	74		...	567	550	528		...	94	94	94
1729	Other textiles n.e.c.		...	92	84	82		...	986	977	1042		...	182	193	209
1730	Knitted and crocheted fabrics and articles		...	204	193	185		...	3523	3192	3039		...	526	527	535
1810	Wearing apparel, except fur apparel		...	1311	1131	1069		...	9640	8867	7520		...	1370	1301	1188
1820	Dressing & dyeing of fur; processing of fur		...	89	86	80		...	225	240	201		...	22	23	18
191	Tanning, dressing and processing of leather		...	97	92	83		...	611	601	527		...	104	101	91
1911	Tanning and dressing of leather		...	7	8	6		...	288	280	195		...	55	55	43
1912	Luggage, handbags, etc.; saddlery & harness		...	90	84	77		...	323	321	332		...	49	46	48
1920	Footwear		...	108	104	106		...	1367	1441	1348		...	237	272	259
2010	Sawmilling and planing of wood		...	218	217	196		...	1931	2171	1998		...	295	354	343
202	Products of wood, cork, straw, etc.		...	779	747	742		...	11837	13682	13713		...	2068	2449	2654
2021	Veneer sheets, plywood, particle board, etc.		...	68	66	57		...	1616	1671	1434		...	262	287	263
2022	Builders' carpentry and joinery		...	273	271	280		...	7532	9334	9609		...	1384	1734	1946
2023	Wooden containers		...	87	79	83		...	816	744	952		...	127	119	155
2029	Other wood products; articles of cork/straw		...	351	331	322		...	1873	1933	1718		...	295	309	290
210	Paper and paper products		...	269	260	252		...	9578	10039	10304		...	2162	2286	2457
2101	Pulp, paper and paperboard		...	28	25	24		...	1209	1140	1255		...	317	277	321
2102	Corrugated paper and paperboard		...	120	118	113		...	5348	5734	5613		...	1219	1306	1333
2109	Other articles of paper and paperboard		...	121	117	115		...	3021	3165	3436		...	626	702	803
221	Publishing		...	1418	1393	1391		...	31202	30940	33522		...	4805	4979	5245
2211	Publishing of books and other publications		...	537	525	537		...	2848	2642	3348		...	525	517	699
2212	Publishing of newspapers, journals, etc.		...	488	484	467		...	25739	25728	28160		...	3786	3947	4128
2213	Publishing of recorded media		...	35	50	72		...	97	111	136		...	10	17	21
2219	Other publishing		...	358	334	315		...	2518	2459	1878		...	483	498	398

222 Printing and related service activities	...	2168	2071	1991	...	18017	17852	16963	...	3912	3888	3822
2221 Printing	...	1488	1414	1360	...	12755	12953	12376	...	2753	2777	2757
2222 Service activities related to printing	...	680	657	631	...	5262	4899	4587	...	1160	1110	1065
2230 Reproduction of recorded media	...	19	20	27	...	61	82	224	...	14	18	43
2310 Coke oven products	...	...	...	...	...	...	...	...	...	...	...	...
2320 Refined petroleum products	...	17	17	18	...	901	977	989	...	257	283	302
2330 Processing of nuclear fuel	...	...	...	...	...	...	...	...	...	...	...	...
241 Basic chemicals	...	95	92	94	...	6418	5783	5955	...	1653	1512	1622
2411 Basic chemicals, except fertilizers	...	47	41	42	...	5129	4263	4467	...	1373	1171	1276
2412 Fertilizers and nitrogen compounds	...	13	13	12	...	734	778	744	...	177	191	189
2413 Plastics in primary forms; synthetic rubber	...	35	38	40	...	555	742	744	...	103	149	157
242 Other chemicals	...	383	383	366	...	18815	21256	22020	...	4634	5319	5769
2421 Pesticides and other agro-chemical products	...	8	7	12	...	192	108	108	...	42	23	23
2422 Paints, varnishes, printing ink and mastics	...	88	88	87	...	2811	2810	2920	...	683	692	725
2423 Pharmaceuticals, medicinal chemicals, etc.	...	95	99	90	...	10256	11676	12349	...	2714	3212	3542
2424 Soap, cleaning & cosmetic preparations	...	129	121	108	...	3605	3653	3548	...	753	764	762
2429 Other chemical products n.e.c.	...	63b/	68b/	69b/	...	1951b/	3009b/	3095b/	...	442b/	628b/	717b/
2430 Man-made fibres	...	...b/	...b/	...b/	...	...b/	...b/	...b/	...	...b/	...b/	...b/
251 Rubber products	...	134	124	118	...	2809	2708	2540	...	569	552	543
2511 Rubber tyres and tubes	...	73	72	70	...	309	363	292	...	53	70	53
2519 Other rubber products	...	61	52	48	...	2500	2345	2248	...	515	482	490
2520 Plastic products	...	644	631	612	...	17786	18316	18560	...	3540	3686	3807
2610 Glass and glass products	...	176	192	191	...	3386	4148	4615	...	648	772	918
269 Non-metallic mineral products n.e.c.	...	1253	1190	1127	...	14874	15571	15513	...	3144	3333	3567
2691 Pottery, china and earthenware	...	464c/	430	386c/	...	1379c/	1189	1352c/	...	279c/	242	268c/
2692 Refractory ceramic products	...	...c/	3	...c/	...	...c/	46	...c/	...	...c/	8	...c/
2693 Struct.non-refractory clay; ceramic products	...	43	41	39	...	746	850	928	...	143	162	189
2694 Cement, lime and plaster	...	18	16	14	...	993	938	841	...	246	238	220
2695 Articles of concrete, cement and plaster	...	437	435	429	...	7541	8389	8111	...	1571	1800	1906
2696 Cutting, shaping & finishing of stone	...	157	138	135	...	541	533	496	...	89	92	95
2699 Other non-metallic mineral products n.e.c.	...	134	127	124	...	3674	3626	3785	...	816	790	889
2710 Basic iron and steel	...	85	93	101	...	4439	4895	5466	...	958	1058	1210
2720 Basic precious and non-ferrous metals	...	39	45	46	...	2129	1879	2183	...	501	430	516
273 Casting of metals	...	67	52	42	...	1090	429	104	...	184	69	18
2731 Casting of iron and steel	...	17	9	7	...	241	109	15	...	41	17	1
2732 Casting of non-ferrous metals	...	50	43	35	...	849	320	89	...	144	51	17
281 Struct.metal products;tanks;steam generators	...	524	528	502	...	14001	15050	15525	...	2939	3147	3414
2811 Structural metal products	...	428	429	416	...	10054	10851	11477	...	2080	2192	2462
2812 Tanks, reservoirs and containers of metal	...	89	91	77	...	2866	2949	2342	...	587	637	493
2813 Steam generators	...	7	8	9	...	1081	1250	1706	...	272	318	459
289 Other metal products; metal working services	...	3726	3587	3515	...	28750	31379	31813	...	5212	5719	6143
2891 Metal forging/pressing/stamping/roll-forming	...	9	11	12	...	94	67	30	...	17	13	5
2892 Treatment & coating of metals	...	2545	2418	2347	...	13562	13627	11979	...	2375	2380	2223
2893 Cutlery, hand tools and general hardware	...	309	299	297	...	3732	3918	4339	...	695	727	873
2899 Other fabricated metal products n.e.c.	...	863	859	859	...	11362	13767	15465	...	2125	2599	3042
291 General purpose machinery	...	1014	1003	1029	...	37493	41705	44602	...	8115	8849	9969
2911 Engines & turbines(not for transport equip.)	...	72	69	70	...	3095	3217	3085	...	740	789	781
2912 Pumps, compressors, taps and valves	...	163	155	167	...	17406	19283	20819	...	3520	3763	4362
2913 Bearings, gears, gearing & driving elements	...	32	34	37	...	750	720	839	...	152	147	178
2914 Ovens, furnaces and furnace burners	...	42	38	37	...	565	389	362	...	126	77	76
2915 Lifting and handling equipment	...	228	240	251	...	6447	8010	8812	...	1473	1815	2079
2919 Other general purpose machinery	...	477	467	467	...	9230	10086	10685	...	2105	2257	2492
292 Special purpose machinery	...	1182	1202	1210	...	22195	23248	23807	...	4724	4884	5260
2921 Agricultural and forestry machinery	...	356	356	366	...	5315	5618	5917	...	1018	1042	1137
2922 Machine tools	...	149	159	161	...	2341	2858	2854	...	494	564	594
2923 Machinery for metallurgy	...	23	26	25	...	186	184	175	...	40	42	37
2924 Machinery for mining & construction	...	45	53	57	...	1989	2184	2566	...	449	491	597
2925 Food/beverage/tobacco processing machinery	...	175	169	167	...	5369	5357	4970	...	1212	1244	1221
2926 Machinery for textile, apparel and leather	...	36	40	32	...	673	826	875	...	145	176	185
2927 Weapons and ammunition	...	14	11	8	...	305	61	13	...	68	17	4
2929 Other special purpose machinery	...	384	388	394	...	6017	6160	6437	...	1297	1308	1485
2930 Domestic appliances n.e.c.	...	103	91	89	...	7378	7324	6892	...	1488	1479	1495

continued

Denmark

ISIC Revision 3 ISIC Industry	Note	Number of establishments (numbers) 1992	1993	1994	1995	Note	Number of employees (numbers) 1992	1993	1994	1995	Note	Wages and salaries paid to employees (million KRONER) 1992	1993	1994	1995
3000 Office, accounting and computing machinery		...	138	145	140		...	2017	2145	2009		...	536	586	551
3110 Electric motors, generators and transformers		...	75	77	79		...	3087	3434	4410		...	617	706	936
3120 Electricity distribution & control apparatus		...	172	167	150		...	4174	4183	3861		...	893	882	835
3130 Insulated wire and cable		...	30	30	31		...	1487	1445	1411		...	319	296	320
3140 Accumulators, primary cells and batteries		...	19	18	20		...	322	276	273		...	61	56	58
3150 Lighting equipment and electric lamps		...	221	205	201		...	2254	2689	2719		...	385	473	524
3190 Other electrical equipment n.e.c.		...	580	586	582		...	3289	3233	3455		...	645	603	659
3210 Electronic valves, tubes, etc.		...	123	104	104		...	3057	2661	2801		...	647	560	592
3220 TV/radio transmitters; line comm. apparatus		...	57	55	51		...	2749	3126	2979		...	744	736	717
3230 TV and radio receivers and associated goods		...	117	113	107		...	5088	5352	5671		...	914	967	1098
331 Medical, measuring, testing appliances, etc.		...	624	628	621		...	13212	13068	14152		...	2898	2924	3237
3311 Medical, surgical and orthopaedic equipment		...	389	387	386		...	7397	7601	7741		...	1496	1582	1654
3312 Measuring/testing/navigating appliances,etc.		...	142	148	153		...	5259	4819	6038		...	1286	1217	1508
3313 Industrial process control equipment		...	93	93	82		...	556	648	373		...	116	125	75
3320 Optical instruments & photographic equipment		...	51	49	49		...	1047	1376	1415		...	255	297	330
3330 Watches and clocks		...	3	5	3		...	14	13	10		...	2	2	2
3410 Motor vehicles		...	11	9	...		...	83	55	...		...	17	10	...
3420 Automobile bodies, trailers & semi-trailers		...	137	131	134		...	3339	3890	4320		...	649	737	854
3430 Parts/accessories for automobiles		...	68	81	80		...	2066	3106	3524		...	379	555	689
351 Building and repairing of ships and boats		...	437	415	396		...	11605	13092	12108		...	2781	2940	2983
3511 Building and repairing of ships		...	261	233	205		...	10821	12083	10866		...	2641	2748	2738
3512 Building/repairing of pleasure/sport. boats		...	176	182	191		...	784	1009	1242		...	140	192	246
3520 Railway/tramway locomotives & rolling stock		...	4	5	7		...	895	774	717		...	217	180	165
3530 Aircraft and spacecraft		...	45	42	44		...	560	687	734		...	116	138	166
359 Transport equipment n.e.c.		...	63	62	64		...	1064	1145	1255		...	186	208	243
3591 Motorcycles		...	-	...d/	...d/		...	-	...d/	...d/		...	-	...d/	...d/
3592 Bicycles and invalid carriages		...	45	46d/	50d/		...	484	676d/	860d/		...	85	115d/	157d/
3599 Other transport equipment n.e.c.		...	18	16	14		...	580	469	395		...	101	93	86
3610 Furniture		...	1670	1603	1583		...	23991	25720	25038		...	3919	4420	4584
369 Manufacturing n.e.c.		...	1162	1093	1067		...	7914	7955	8219		...	1394	1427	1514
3691 Jewellery and related articles		...	334	325	309		...	897	923	950		...	161	160	168
3692 Musical instruments		...	89	85	82		...	230	243	248		...	44	48	51
3693 Sports goods		...	37	39	42		...	184	378	415		...	35	75	87
3694 Games and toys		...	91	81	89		...	4220	4143	4013		...	817	812	827
3699 Other manufacturing n.e.c.		...	611	563	545		...	2383	2268	2593		...	337	332	381
3710 Recycling of metal waste and scrap		...	14	15	17		...	348	187	224		...	58	39	46
3720 Recycling of non-metal waste and scrap		...	13	12	13		...	146	176	165		...	32	38	40
D Total manufacturing		...	25477	24603	24024		...	464695	484882	490634		...	91258	96073	101688

a/ 1551 includes 1552.
b/ 2429 includes 2430.
c/ 2691 includes 2692.
d/ 3592 includes 3591.

Denmark

ISIC Revision 3	Output in factor values					Value added in factor values					Gross fixed capital formation		
		(million KRONER)					(million KRONER)					(million KRONER)	
ISIC Industry	Note	1992	1993	1994	1995	Note	1992	1993	1994	1995	Note	1994	1995
151 Processed meat,fish,fruit,vegetables,fats		59137	52995	55318	...		15170	15378	16047	...		1067	...
1511 Processing/preserving of meat		41807	37173	39892	...		10104	10682	11281	...		707	...
1512 Processing/preserving of fish		11012	10227	9838	...		2894	2777	2923	...		247	...
1513 Processing/preserving of fruit & vegetables		3970	3329	3133	...		1437	1296	1229	...		62	...
1514 Vegetable and animal oils and fats		2349	2265	2454	...		734	623	614	...		51	...
1520 Dairy products		25954	26033	27381	...		5455	5762	5763	...		605	...
153 Grain mill products; starches; animal feeds		4234	3904	4289	...		1536	1421	1601	...		160	...
1531 Grain mill products		2299a/	1876	1986	...		898a/	674	763	...		33	...
1532 Starches and starch products		...a/	529	511	...		...a/	172	139	...		25	...
1533 Prepared animal feeds		1935	1499	1793	...		638	575	698	...		102	...
154 Other food products		10531	14378	16260	...		5260	6777	7673	...		871	...
1541 Bakery products		3976	4136	4528	...		1950	2026	2215	...		187	...
1542 Sugar		...	...	...	...		...	...	...	...		...	...
1543 Cocoa, chocolate and sugar confectionery		2172	2301	2405	...		1146	1170	1206	...		90	...
1544 Macaroni, noodles & similar products		...	...	...	...		...	...	...	...		...	...
1549 Other food products n.e.c.		...	...	...	...		...	...	...	...		...	...
155 Beverages		9722	9718	9973	...		5811	5616	5833	...		442	...
1551 Distilling, rectifying & blending of spirits		...	...	...	...		...	...	...	...		...	...
1552 Wines		...	...	...	...		...	...	...	...		...	...
1553 Malt liquors and malt		...	...	...	...		...	...	...	...		...	...
1554 Soft drinks; mineral waters		969	1115	1294	...		563	598	659	...		108	...
1600 Tobacco products		2852	2762	2916	...		1801	1781	1894	...		99	...
171 Spinning, weaving and finishing of textiles		1554	1304	1333	...		839	684	742	...		97	...
1711 Textile fibre preparation; textile weaving		1125	892	909	...		559	413	468	...		24	...
1712 Finishing of textiles		429	412	424	...		280	271	275	...		73	...
172 Other textiles		3560	3176	3297	...		1602	1518	1616	...		89	...
1721 Made-up textile articles, except apparel		1143	1257	1276	...		589	667	676	...		41	...
1722 Carpets and rugs		1605	1231	1259	...		579	456	495	...		8	...
1723 Cordage, rope, twine and netting		235	110	137	...		107	54	66	...		2	...
1729 Other textiles n.e.c.		578	578	625	...		328	341	380	...		39	...
1730 Knitted and crocheted fabrics and articles		2071	2022	2003	...		934	927	860	...		55	...
1810 Wearing apparel, except fur apparel		...	...	...	...		...	...	...	...		...	...
1820 Dressing & dyeing of fur; processing of fur		...	...	...	...		...	...	...	...		...	...
191 Tanning, dressing and processing of leather		278	368	397	...		127	143	129	...		-	...
1911 Tanning and dressing of leather		...	...	...	...		...	...	...	...		...	...
1912 Luggage, handbags, etc.; saddlery & harness		...	...	...	...		...	...	...	...		...	...
1920 Footwear		1374	1463	1579	...		455	470	513	...		38	...
2010 Sawmilling and planing of wood		786	809	893	...		363	383	404	...		21	...
202 Products of wood, cork, straw, etc.		5909	6187	7231	...		2825	3046	3563	...		337	...
2021 Veneer sheets, plywood, particle board, etc.		791	680	680	...		375	331	340	...		51	...
2022 Builders' carpentry and joinery		4394	4758	5640	...		2098	2327	2739	...		248	...
2023 Wooden containers		244	218	281	...		112	106	127	...		7	...
2029 Other wood products; articles of cork/straw		480	531	631	...		240	281	356	...		30	...
210 Paper and paper products		9053	7473	8024	...		4543	3877	4168	...		493	...
2101 Pulp, paper and paperboard		1715	1173	1313	...		867	597	651	...		140	...
2102 Corrugated paper and paperboard		5283	4164	4328	...		2548	2136	2255	...		251	...
2109 Other articles of paper and paperboard		2055	2135	2383	...		1128	1145	1262	...		101	...
221 Publishing		7854	7950	7706	...		5712	5904	5773	...		231	...
2211 Publishing of books and other publications		390	384	330	...		187	185	171	...		6	...
2212 Publishing of newspapers, journals, etc.		7111	7222	7294	...		5302	5498	5552	...		223	...
2213 Publishing of recorded media		...	...	...	...		...	...	...	...		...	...
2219 Other publishing		...	...	...	...		...	...	...	...		...	...

continued

Denmark

ISIC Revision 3		Output in factor values (million KRONER)					Value added in factor values (million KRONER)					Gross fixed capital formation (million KRONER)	
ISIC Industry	Note	1992	1993	1994	1995	Note	1992	1993	1994	1995	Note	1994	1995
222 Printing and related service activities		6622	6433	6669	...		3853	3740	3871	...		444	...
2221 Printing		5336	5263	5475	...		2851	2799	2922	...		355	...
2222 Service activities related to printing		1286b/	1170b/	1194b/	...		1002b/	940b/	950b/	...		89b/	...
2230 Reproduction of recorded media		...b/	...b/	...b/	...		...b/	...b/	...b/	...		...b/	...
2310 Coke oven products		...	...	...	...		...	...	...	...		...	...
2320 Refined petroleum products		10648	10149	9790	...		1005	1277	1124	...		1713	...
2330 Processing of nuclear fuel		...	...	...	...		...	...	...	...		...	...
241 Basic chemicals		10227	7362	8260	...		5498	4165	4566	...		624	...
2411 Basic chemicals, except fertilizers		...	...	...	...		...	...	...	...		...	...
2412 Fertilizers and nitrogen compounds		...	...	...	...		...	...	...	...		...	...
2413 Plastics in primary forms; synthetic rubber		...	...	...	...		...	...	...	...		...	...
242 Other chemicals		21237	21179	23103	...		12526	12790	13796	...		1828	...
2421 Pesticides and other agro-chemical products		...c/	...c/	...c/	...		...c/	...c/	...c/	...		...c/	...
2422 Paints, varnishes, printing ink and mastics		4306c/	4127c/	4549c/	...		1937c/	1923c/	2097c/	...		276c/	...
2423 Pharmaceuticals, medicinal chemicals, etc.		11281	11706	13168	...		7756	8164	8985	...		1280	...
2424 Soap, cleaning & cosmetic preparations		4257	3657	3906	...		2096	1735	1918	...		120	...
2429 Other chemical products n.e.c.		1393	1690	1480	...		736	968	796	...		152	...
2430 Man-made fibres		...c/	...c/	...c/	...		...c/	...c/	...c/	...		...c/	...
251 Rubber products		1156	1099	1270	...		708	678	764	...		36	...
2511 Rubber tyres and tubes		...	...	...	...		...	...	...	...		...	...
2519 Other rubber products		...	...	...	...		...	...	...	...		...	...
2520 Plastic products		11371	10691	11520	...		6322	6021	6490	...		520	...
2610 Glass and glass products		1940	2300	2299	...		1160	1561	1422	...		79	...
269 Non-metallic mineral products n.e.c.		10183	9273	10649	...		6012	5604	6409	...		381	...
2691 Pottery, china and earthenware		...	...	...	...		...	...	...	...		...	...
2692 Refractory ceramic products		...	...	...	...		...	...	...	...		...	...
2693 Struct.non-refractory clay; ceramic products		...	...	...	...		...	...	...	...		...	...
2694 Cement, lime and plaster		...	...	...	...		...	...	...	...		...	...
2695 Articles of concrete, cement and plaster		5679	5112	5898	...		3148	2948	3348	...		150	...
2696 Cutting, shaping & finishing of stone		...	...	102	...		...	...	61	...		10	...
2699 Other non-metallic mineral products n.e.c.		2282	2390	2616	...		1304	1465	1596	...		144	...
2710 Basic iron and steel		4854	4605	5385	...		2370	2136	2307	...		149	...
2720 Basic precious and non-ferrous metals		2513	2941	3252	...		1050	1462	1510	...		51	...
273 Casting of metals		...	...	...	...		...	...	...	...		...	...
2731 Casting of iron and steel		...	...	...	...		...	...	...	...		...	...
2732 Casting of non-ferrous metals		...	...	...	...		...	...	...	...		...	...
281 Struct.metal products;tanks;steam generators		...	...	...	...		...	...	...	...		...	...
2811 Structural metal products		5792	5144	4772	...		2981	2748	2462	...		158	...
2812 Tanks, reservoirs and containers of metal		1190	1067	1097	...		687	643	646	...		32	...
2813 Steam generators		...	...	...	...		...	...	...	...		...	...
289 Other metal products; metal working services		...	...	...	...		...	...	...	...		...	...
2891 Metal forging/pressing/stamping/roll-forming		...	...	...	...		...	...	...	...		...	...
2892 Treatment & coating of metals		666	621	806	...		472	435	560	...		37	...
2893 Cutlery, hand tools and general hardware		1728	1676	2014	...		1022	1030	1208	...		115	...
2899 Other fabricated metal products n.e.c.		7511	7093	7492	...		4003	3828	4036	...		389	...
291 General purpose machinery		23185	24159	26139	...		12913	13328	14329	...		1128	...
2911 Engines & turbines(not for transport equip.)		...d/	...d/	3080	...		...d/	...d/	1514	...		69	...
2912 Pumps, compressors, taps and valves		12587d/	12025d/	10206	...		7546d/	7100d/	6382	...		791	...
2913 Bearings, gears, gearing & driving elements		387	354	362	...		230	215	220	...		20	...
2914 Ovens, furnaces and furnace burners		...e/	...e/	120	...		...e/	...e/	63	...		1	...
2915 Lifting and handling equipment		4087e/	5211e/	5757	...		2143e/	2737e/	3130	...		46	...
2919 Other general purpose machinery		6124	6569	6614	...		2993	3275	3021	...		201	...

292 Special purpose machinery	12014	10138	11390	...	6514	5725	6296	...	339	...
2921 Agricultural and forestry machinery	2648	2412	2577	...	1408	1347	1414	...	72	...
2922 Machine tools	1302	995	1037	...	746	557	605	...	30	...
2923 Machinery for metallurgy	...	...	...	...	...	...	...	...	...	...
2924 Machinery for mining & construction	1666	1582	1634	...	910	880	867	...	40	...
2925 Food/beverage/tobacco processing machinery	3074	2221	2902	...	1598	1222	1561	...	87	...
2926 Machinery for textile, apparel and leather	530	456	482	...	273	232	239	...	10	...
2927 Weapons and ammunition	...	...	...	...	...	...	...	...	...	...
2929 Other special purpose machinery	...	...	...	...	...	...	...	...	...	...
2930 Domestic appliances n.e.c.	5094	4695	5676	...	2372	2228	2673	...	144	...
3000 Office, accounting and computing machinery	1512	1228	1603	...	914	691	827	...	26	...
3110 Electric motors, generators and transformers	2392	1827	3139	...	1021	777	1188	...	146	...
3120 Electricity distribution & control apparatus	2136	2059	2293	...	1164	991	1191	...	75	...
3130 Insulated wire and cable	907	1114	1560	...	449	510	707	...	91	...
3140 Accumulators, primary cells and batteries	...f/	...f/	...f/	...	...f/	...f/	...f/	...	...f/	...
3150 Lighting equipment and electric lamps	1213f/	1467f/	1638f/	...	706f/	942f/	1027f/	...	64f/	...
3190 Other electrical equipment n.e.c.	532	837	844	...	304	388	395	...	12	...
3210 Electronic valves, tubes, etc.	2128	2149	2351	...	1174	1149	1210	...	58	...
3220 TV/radio transmitters; line comm. apparatus	1564	1237	1518	...	740	604	763	...	60	...
3230 TV and radio receivers and associated goods	3782	3700	3973	...	1769	1685	1854	...	181	...
331 Medical, measuring, testing appliances, etc.	6162	6506	7637	...	3905	4080	4780	...	289	...
3311 Medical, surgical and orthopaedic equipment	3013	3342	3932	...	1858	2071	2455	...	182	...
3312 Measuring/testing/navigating appliances,etc.	2942	2965	3475	...	1928	1896	2193	...	105	...
3313 Industrial process control equipment	206	200	230	...	119	113	131	...	3	...
3320 Optical instruments & photographic equipment	838	956	1189	...	402	473	598	...	34	...
3330 Watches and clocks	...	...	...	...	...	...	...	...	...	...
3410 Motor vehicles	...	...	...	...	...	...	...	...	...	...
3420 Automobile bodies, trailers & semi-trailers	2571	2424	2588	...	1026	989	1044	...	32	...
3430 Parts/accessories for automobiles	1785	1788	1974	...	944	957	1054	...	69	...
351 Building and repairing of ships and boats	10132	9256	8489	...	4251	4172	3466	...	300	...
3511 Building and repairing of ships	9673	8976	8164	...	3981	4008	3289	...	289	...
3512 Building/repairing of pleasure/sport. boats	459	280	325	...	270	165	177	...	11	...
3520 Railway/tramway locomotives & rolling stock	...	...	...	...	...	...	...	...	...	...
3530 Aircraft and spacecraft	...	...	...	...	...	...	...	...	...	...
359 Transport equipment n.e.c.	801	706	...	...	335	316	...	...	...	...
3591 Motorcycles	...	...	...	...	...	...	...	...	...	...
3592 Bicycles and invalid carriages	...	...	...	...	...	...	...	...	...	...
3599 Other transport equipment n.e.c.	291	238	...	...	133	117	...	...	...	...
3610 Furniture	11642	11218	13435	...	5978	5947	6998	...	564	...
369 Manufacturing n.e.c.	5659	6140	6296	...	3208	3571	3602	...	485	...
3691 Jewellery and related articles	301	284	238	...	181	182	143	...	1	...
3692 Musical instruments	...	...	...	...	...	...	...	...	...	...
3693 Sports goods	...	...	...	...	...	...	...	...	...	...
3694 Games and toys	4071	4656	4821	...	2328	2760	2824	...	479	...
3699 Other manufacturing n.e.c.	950	853	891	...	511	452	461	...	2	...
3710 Recycling of metal waste and scrap	...	...	...	...	...	...	...	...	...	...
3720 Recycling of non-metal waste and scrap	...	...	...	...	...	...	...	...	...	...
D Total manufacturing	345756	331814	357546	...	155315	154141	164923	...	15387	...

a/ 1531 includes 1532.
b/ 2222 includes 2230.
c/ 2422 includes 2421 and 2430.
d/ 2912 includes 2911.
e/ 2915 includes 2914.
f/ 3150 includes 3140.

Denmark

ISIC Revision 3		Note	Index numbers of industrial production											
			(1990=100)											
ISIC	Industry		1985	1986	1987	1988	1989	1990	1991	1992	1993	1994	1995	1996
15	Food and beverages		92	94	94	97	96	100	102	105	107	114	110	109
16	Tobacco products		101	104	103	99	101	100	125	111	106	99	98	93
17	Textiles		109	110	107	103	104	100	98	92	87	89	86	92
18	Wearing apparel, fur		141	138	123	106	100	100	108	105	98	104	107	108
19	Leather, leather products and footwear		114	110	115	93	94	100	111	118	122	142	130	119
20	Wood products (excl. furniture)		94	105	114	109	104	100	95	105	108	128	140	135
21	Paper and paper products		90	93	92	97	99	100	104	104	89	101	103	97
22	Printing and publishing		87	99	99	105	99	100	100	103	105	110	117	123
23	Coke,refined petroleum products,nuclear fuel		105	104	109	109	106	100	104	108	108	114	121	133
24	Chemicals and chemical products		90	92	90	93	98	100	101	110	109	122	134	139
25	Rubber and plastics products		81	91	93	100	101	100	98	104	101	112	111	109
26	Non-metallic mineral products		100	112	105	104	101	100	96	93	88	101	107	107
27	Basic metals		90	98	95	96	103	100	105	118	122	130	133	129
28	Fabricated metal products		86	98	94	92	100	100	100	105	93	106	111	112
29	Machinery and equipment n.e.c.		96	98	91	98	102	100	98	100	94	102	111	109
30	Office, accounting and computing machinery		66	76	72	82	97	100	84	111	114	124	143	177
31	Electrical machinery and apparatus		86	97	97	98	100	100	91	87	85	101	125	133
32	Radio,television and communication equipment		88	100	102	99	101	100	96	112	114	120	123	153
33	Medical, precision and optical instruments		87	94	94	101	102	100	103	109	112	129	134	141
34	Motor vehicles, trailers, semi-trailers		90	90	86	83	94	100	99	97	77	122	136	135
35	Other transport equipment		110	105	85	84	86	100	106	108	98	112	117	107
36	Furniture; manufacturing n.e.c.		94	99	94	94	100	100	101	102	99	111	114	113
37	Recycling		...	...	...	...	...	...	...	...	...	...	...	...
D	Total manufacturing		92	98	95	97	100	100	100	104	101	111	116	117

ECUADOR

Supplier of information:
Instituto Nacional de Estadística y Censos (INEC), Quito. The index numbers of industrial production are compiled by the Banco del Ecuador.

Basic source of data:
Annual survey of manufacturing and mining.

Major deviations from ISIC (Revision 3):
None reported.

Reference period (if not calendar year):

Scope:
Establishments with 10 or more persons engaged.

Method of enumeration:
Questionnaires were distributed by mail with follow-up site visits as required.

Adjusted for non-response:
No.

Concepts and definitions of variables:
Number of employees is as of the last pay period in November of the reference year.
Output is gross output.
Value added is total value added.

Related national publications:
Encuesta Anual de Manufacturera y Minería (annual), published by the Instituto Nacional de Estadística y Censos, (INEC), Quito.

Ecuador

ISIC Revision 3	Number of establishments					Number of employees					Wages and salaries paid to employees				
		(numbers)					(numbers)					(million SUCRES)			
ISIC Industry	Note	1993	1994	1995	1996	Note	1993	1994	1995	1996	Note	1993	1994	1995	1996
151 Processed meat,fish,fruit,vegetables,fats		...	...	164	167		...	...	19673	21251		...	...	120401	171791
1511 Processing/preserving of meat		...	...	29	31		...	...	2668	2745		...	...	15658	17088
1512 Processing/preserving of fish		...	...	92	96		...	...	12527	14263		...	...	72938	115091
1513 Processing/preserving of fruit & vegetables		...	...	17	16		...	...	1283	1221		...	...	7160	8620
1514 Vegetable and animal oils and fats		...	...	26	24		...	...	3195	3022		...	...	24645	30992
1520 Dairy products		...	...	34	32		...	...	2076	1874		...	...	15543	20173
153 Grain mill products; starches; animal feeds		...	...	79	78		...	...	3040	3007		...	...	18074	23742
1531 Grain mill products		...	...	54	53		...	...	2204	2169		...	...	12633	16510
1532 Starches and starch products		...	...	3	3		...	...	42	39		...	...	128	125
1533 Prepared animal feeds		...	...	22	22		...	...	794	799		...	...	5313	7107
154 Other food products		...	...	115	116		...	...	9520	9196		...	...	84378	89764
1541 Bakery products		...	...	45	46		...	...	2678	2729		...	...	17446	20713
1542 Sugar		...	...	6	6		...	...	3212	3093		...	...	40039	35873
1543 Cocoa, chocolate and sugar confectionery		...	...	14	13		...	...	1492	1226		...	...	10931	12823
1544 Macaroni, noodles & similar products		...	...	19	19		...	...	675	705		...	...	3353	3863
1549 Other food products n.e.c.		...	...	31	32		...	...	1463	1443		...	...	12609	16492
155 Beverages		...	...	70	65		...	...	6809	6455		...	...	61375	65562
1551 Distilling, rectifying & blending of spirits		...	...	30	28		...	...	1004	887		...	...	5609	7378
1552 Wines		...	...	2	1		...	...	108	97		...	...	103	108
1553 Malt liquors and malt		...	...	5	5		...	...	406	402		...	...	32052	28135
1554 Soft drinks; mineral waters		...	...	33	31		...	...	5291	5069		...	...	23611	29941
1600 Tobacco products		...	...	2	1		...	...	376	385		...	...	3584	4814
171 Spinning, weaving and finishing of textiles		...	...	66	66		...	...	6780	6811		...	...	36600	42458
1711 Textile fibre preparation; textile weaving		...	...	66	66		...	...	6780	6811		...	...	36600	42458
1712 Finishing of textiles		...	...	-	-		...	...	-	-		...	...	-	-
172 Other textiles		...	...	30	27		...	...	1511	1341		...	...	4242	4481
1721 Made-up textile articles, except apparel		...	...	13	13		...	...	916	859		...	...	2892	3110
1722 Carpets and rugs		...	...	9	9		...	...	276	219		...	...	840	895
1723 Cordage, rope, twine and netting		...	...	2	1		...	...	36	27		...	...	85	83
1729 Other textiles n.e.c.		...	...	6	4		...	...	283	236		...	...	425	393
1730 Knitted and crocheted fabrics and articles		...	...	42	37		...	...	2595	2461		...	...	8262	9740
1810 Wearing apparel, except fur apparel		...	...	115	103		...	...	4151	3999		...	...	10980	12482
1820 Dressing & dyeing of fur; processing of fur		...	...	2	-		...	...	7	-		...	...	16	-
191 Tanning, dressing and processing of leather		...	...	22	20		...	...	800	720		...	...	2095	2293
1911 Tanning and dressing of leather		...	...	20	18		...	...	713	644		...	...	1966	2094
1912 Luggage, handbags, etc.; saddlery & harness		...	...	2	2		...	...	87	76		...	...	129	199
1920 Footwear		...	...	40	42		...	...	2693	2664		...	...	11398	11658
2010 Sawmilling and planing of wood		...	...	24	21		...	...	869	810		...	...	5266	5741
202 Products of wood, cork, straw, etc.		...	...	45	45		...	...	2885	2859		...	...	12667	14744
2021 Veneer sheets, plywood, particle board, etc.		...	...	9	13		...	...	1847	1955		...	...	9167	10699
2022 Builders' carpentry and joinery		...	...	25	23		...	...	871	758		...	...	3025	3597
2023 Wooden containers		...	...	5	2		...	...	51	17		...	...	174	45
2029 Other wood products; articles of cork/straw		...	...	6	7		...	...	116	129		...	...	301	403
210 Paper and paper products		...	...	50	46		...	...	5442	5175		...	...	40347	51712
2101 Pulp, paper and paperboard		...	...	5	5		...	...	781	733		...	...	6453	8333
2102 Corrugated paper and paperboard		...	...	24	22		...	...	2703	2564		...	...	21977	31891
2109 Other articles of paper and paperboard		...	...	21	19		...	...	1958	1878		...	...	11917	11488
221 Publishing		...	...	19	22		...	...	2288	3052		...	...	23289	33987
2211 Publishing of books and other publications		...	...	1	2		...	...	97	752		...	...	459	2579
2212 Publishing of newspapers, journals, etc.		...	...	17	20		...	...	2171	2300		...	...	22800	31408
2213 Publishing of recorded media		...	...	-	-		...	...	-	-		...	...	-	-
2219 Other publishing		...	...	1	-		...	...	20	-		...	...	30	-

222 Printing and related service activities	...	...	55	57	...	...	1301	1471	...	...	5273	10936
2221 Printing	...	...	52	55	...	...	1175	1361	...	...	4954	10653
2222 Service activities related to printing	...	...	3	2	...	...	126	110	...	...	319	283
2230 Reproduction of recorded media	...	...	2	1	...	...	199	65	...	...	530	393
2310 Coke oven products	...	...	-	-	...	...	-	-	...	...	-	-
2320 Refined petroleum products	...	...	7	6	...	...	2618	2570	...	...	40827	77953
2330 Processing of nuclear fuel	...	...	-	-	...	...	-	-	...	...	-	-
241 Basic chemicals	...	...	31	31	...	...	1159	1089	...	...	12230	16136
2411 Basic chemicals, except fertilizers	...	...	15	15	...	...	629	624	...	...	7193	10218
2412 Fertilizers and nitrogen compounds	...	...	1	1	...	...	62	38	...	...	558	859
2413 Plastics in primary forms; synthetic rubber	...	...	15	15	...	...	468	427	...	...	4479	5059
242 Other chemicals	...	...	84	86	...	...	6162	6280	...	...	65357	93489
2421 Pesticides and other agro-chemical products	...	...	1	1	...	...	24	21	...	...	156	128
2422 Paints, varnishes, printing ink and mastics	...	...	16	16	...	...	955	881	...	...	7899	11374
2423 Pharmaceuticals, medicinal chemicals, etc.	...	...	31	33	...	...	2733	2933	...	...	33340	49465
2424 Soap, cleaning & cosmetic preparations	...	...	26	26	...	...	2048	2081	...	...	20832	28166
2429 Other chemical products n.e.c.	...	...	10	10	...	...	402	364	...	...	3130	4356
2430 Man-made fibres	...	...	-	-	...	...	-	-	...	...	-	-
251 Rubber products	...	...	15	15	...	...	1114	1178	...	...	17428	18890
2511 Rubber tyres and tubes	...	...	6	6	...	...	853	877	...	...	16661	18151
2519 Other rubber products	...	...	9	9	...	...	261	301	...	...	767	739
2520 Plastic products	...	...	96	89	...	...	6262	5811	...	...	40709	41804
2610 Glass and glass products	...	...	13	11	...	...	578	500	...	...	5224	5501
269 Non-metallic mineral products n.e.c.	...	...	100	104	...	...	5064	5404	...	...	50013	64797
2691 Pottery, china and earthenware	...	...	11	13	...	...	824	784	...	...	6791	5613
2692 Refractory ceramic products	...	...	1	1	...	...	13	20	...	...	47	37
2693 Struct.non-refractory clay; ceramic products	...	...	14	14	...	...	840	845	...	...	3923	4252
2694 Cement, lime and plaster	...	...	5	6	...	...	1083	1316	...	...	23391	34931
2695 Articles of concrete, cement and plaster	...	...	61	61	...	...	2163	2232	...	...	15213	19124
2696 Cutting, shaping & finishing of stone	...	...	7	8	...	...	110	174	...	...	385	507
2699 Other non-metallic mineral products n.e.c.	...	...	1	1	...	...	31	33	...	...	263	333
2710 Basic iron and steel	...	...	14	13	...	...	1722	1371	...	...	12106	16138
2720 Basic precious and non-ferrous metals	...	...	7	7	...	...	554	605	...	...	7140	7533
273 Casting of metals	...	...	2	2	...	...	32	66	...	...	61	173
2731 Casting of iron and steel	...	...	2	2	...	...	32	66	...	...	61	173
2732 Casting of non-ferrous metals	...	...	-	-	...	...	-	-	...	...	-	-
281 Struct.metal products;tanks;steam generators	...	...	61	55	...	...	2066	1865	...	...	12982	12824
2811 Structural metal products	...	...	49	45	...	...	1378	1522	...	...	10133	10928
2812 Tanks, reservoirs and containers of metal	...	...	12	10	...	...	688	343	...	...	2849	1896
2813 Steam generators	...	...	-	-	...	...	-	-	...	...	-	-
289 Other metal products; metal working services	...	...	50	47	...	...	2628	2458	...	...	30181	32300
2891 Metal forging/pressing/stamping/roll-forming	...	...	1	1	...	...	12	13	...	...	50	44
2892 Treatment & coating of metals	...	...	2	1	...	...	24	11	...	...	68	40
2893 Cutlery, hand tools and general hardware	...	...	9	9	...	...	361	308	...	...	1241	1397
2899 Other fabricated metal products n.e.c.	...	...	38	36	...	...	2231	2126	...	...	28822	30819
291 General purpose machinery	...	...	24	24	...	...	1846	1813	...	...	9426	11524
2911 Engines & turbines(not for transport equip.)	...	...	1	2	...	...	33	34	...	...	87	105
2912 Pumps, compressors, taps and valves	...	...	8	7	...	...	359	346	...	...	2331	2338
2913 Bearings, gears, gearing & driving elements	...	...	-	-	...	...	-	-	...	...	-	-
2914 Ovens, furnaces and furnace burners	...	...	5	5	...	...	246	240	...	...	811	837
2915 Lifting and handling equipment	...	...	2	1	...	...	128	132	...	...	1533	2170
2919 Other general purpose machinery	...	...	8	9	...	...	1080	1061	...	...	4664	6074
292 Special purpose machinery	...	...	12	12	...	...	345	318	...	...	1416	1399
2921 Agricultural and forestry machinery	...	...	1	1	...	...	11	11	...	...	18	18
2922 Machine tools	...	...	3	4	...	...	192	179	...	...	1073	1043
2923 Machinery for metallurgy	...	...	-	-	...	...	-	-	...	...	-	-
2924 Machinery for mining & construction	...	...	3	2	...	...	41	27	...	...	130	40
2925 Food/beverage/tobacco processing machinery	...	...	3	3	...	...	42	44	...	...	110	208
2926 Machinery for textile, apparel and leather	...	...	-	-	...	...	-	-	...	...	-	-
2927 Weapons and ammunition	...	...	1	1	...	...	24	23	...	...	33	33
2929 Other special purpose machinery	...	...	1	1	...	...	35	34	...	...	52	57
2930 Domestic appliances n.e.c.	...	...	7	7	...	...	1341	995	...	...	7401	10339

continued

Ecuador

ISIC Revision 3 — ISIC Industry	Number of establishments: Note	1993 (numbers)	1994	1995	1996	Number of employees: Note	1993 (numbers)	1994	1995	1996	Wages and salaries paid to employees: Note	1993 (million SUCRES)	1994	1995	1996
3000 Office, accounting and computing machinery		...	...	-	-		...	...	-	-		...	...	-	-
3110 Electric motors, generators and transformers		...	...	5	5		...	...	179	196		...	...	733	890
3120 Electricity distribution & control apparatus		...	...	8	6		...	...	296	214		...	...	1726	1671
3130 Insulated wire and cable		...	...	6	6		...	...	532	531		...	...	3767	5026
3140 Accumulators, primary cells and batteries		...	...	6	5		...	...	200	155		...	...	1244	1255
3150 Lighting equipment and electric lamps		...	...	3	3		...	...	67	58		...	...	839	1110
3190 Other electrical equipment n.e.c.		...	...	3	2		...	...	62	34		...	...	360	214
3210 Electronic valves, tubes, etc.		...	...	-	-		...	...	-	-		...	...	-	-
3220 TV/radio transmitters; line comm. apparatus		...	...	2	1		...	...	89	90		...	...	81	93
3230 TV and radio receivers and associated goods		...	...	7	4		...	...	593	69		...	...	3048	487
331 Medical, measuring, testing appliances, etc.		...	...	3	3		...	...	69	54		...	...	449	350
3311 Medical, surgical and orthopaedic equipment		...	...	3	3		...	...	69	54		...	...	449	350
3312 Measuring/testing/navigating appliances,etc.		...	...	-	-		...	...	-	-		...	...	-	-
3313 Industrial process control equipment		...	...	-	-		...	...	-	-		...	...	-	-
3320 Optical instruments & photographic equipment		...	...	2	1		...	...	67	31		...	...	135	62
3330 Watches and clocks		...	...	-	-		...	...	-	-		...	...	-	-
3410 Motor vehicles		...	...	4	4		...	...	1360	1268		...	...	14780	17096
3420 Automobile bodies, trailers & semi-trailers		...	...	28	27		...	...	734	676		...	...	2603	3055
3430 Parts/accessories for automobiles		...	...	20	18		...	...	648	653		...	...	2264	2658
351 Building and repairing of ships and boats		...	...	4	5		...	...	59	537		...	...	154	3145
3511 Building and repairing of ships		...	...	4	5		...	...	59	537		...	...	154	3145
3512 Building/repairing of pleasure/sport. boats		...	...	-	-		...	...	-	-		...	...	-	-
3520 Railway/tramway locomotives & rolling stock		...	...	-	-		...	...	-	-		...	...	-	-
3530 Aircraft and spacecraft		...	...	-	-		...	...	-	-		...	...	-	-
359 Transport equipment n.e.c.		...	...	1	2		...	...	15	32		...	...	68	86
3591 Motorcycles		...	...	-	1		...	...	-	20		...	...	-	47
3592 Bicycles and invalid carriages		...	...	-	-		...	...	-	-		...	...	-	-
3599 Other transport equipment n.e.c.		...	...	1	1		...	...	15	12		...	...	68	39
3610 Furniture		...	...	113	107		...	...	4015	3514		...	...	18155	23092
369 Manufacturing n.e.c.		...	...	41	41		...	...	1536	1573		...	...	5375	5495
3691 Jewellery and related articles		...	...	10	10		...	...	302	426		...	...	1232	1605
3692 Musical instruments		...	...	-	-		...	...	-	-		...	...	-	-
3693 Sports goods		...	...	1	1		...	...	12	11		...	...	63	39
3694 Games and toys		...	...	6	8		...	...	377	362		...	...	1010	1054
3699 Other manufacturing n.e.c.		...	...	24	22		...	...	845	774		...	...	3070	2797
3710 Recycling of metal waste and scrap		...	...	-	-		...	...	-	-		...	...	-	-
3720 Recycling of non-metal waste and scrap		...	...	-	-		...	...	-	-		...	...	-	-
D Total manufacturing		...	...	1755	1695		...	...	117027	115604		...	...	832602	1053056

Ecuador

ISIC Revision 3	Output in producers' prices					Value added in producers' prices					Gross fixed capital formation		
		(million SUCRES)					(million SUCRES)					(million SUCRES)	
ISIC Industry	Note	1993	1994	1995	1996	Note	1993	1994	1995	1996	Note	1995	1996
151 Processed meat,fish,fruit,vegetables,fats		...	...	3687670	4417093		...	...	722285	780447		165979	152757
1511 Processing/preserving of meat		...	...	457435	552794		...	...	96816	95062		19662	26228
1512 Processing/preserving of fish		...	...	2232366	2669389		...	...	406701	423645		115258	82676
1513 Processing/preserving of fruit & vegetables		...	...	118779	165981		...	...	31372	49827		-497	-4967
1514 Vegetable and animal oils and fats		...	...	879090	1028929		...	...	187396	211913		31556	48820
1520 Dairy products		...	...	391947	499870		...	...	97399	121610		29342	23586
153 Grain mill products; starches; animal feeds		...	...	795808	1064670		...	...	114278	149381		27097	65178
1531 Grain mill products		...	...	601777	797069		...	...	95396	109170		19729	59160
1532 Starches and starch products		...	...	1376	1820		...	...	281	561		-167	25
1533 Prepared animal feeds		...	...	192655	265781		...	...	18601	39650		7535	5993
154 Other food products		...	...	1111419	1374946		...	...	301500	314727		158799-	69218
1541 Bakery products		...	...	215841	341511		...	...	73484	94675		3405	-30680
1542 Sugar		...	...	355852	433236		...	...	115297	117355		99679	26427
1543 Cocoa, chocolate and sugar confectionery		...	...	266272	235749		...	...	48226	15299		29502	27644
1544 Macaroni, noodles & similar products		...	...	60698	86198		...	...	12601	15671		-187	4063
1549 Other food products n.e.c.		...	...	212756	278252		...	...	51892	71727		26400	41764
155 Beverages		...	...	883448	965349		...	...	385860	413729		111739	137728
1551 Distilling, rectifying & blending of spirits		...	...	111483	147087		...	...	35495	50698		10548	16996
1552 Wines		...	...	580	598		...	...	242	237		-18	-12
1553 Malt liquors and malt		...	...	384053	389956		...	...	251199	236571		74889	47494
1554 Soft drinks; mineral waters		...	...	387332	427708		...	...	98924	126223		26320	73250
1600 Tobacco products		...	...	48007	65799		...	...	11887	18873		8888	6422
171 Spinning, weaving and finishing of textiles		...	...	647728	679784		...	...	273626	215697		62175	-654
1711 Textile fibre preparation; textile weaving		...	...	647728	679784		...	...	273626	215697		62175	-654
1712 Finishing of textiles		...	...	-	-		...	...	-	-		-	-
172 Other textiles		...	...	55274	79630		...	...	16465	31373		12723	11442
1721 Made-up textile articles, except apparel		...	...	38033	62520		...	...	10576	26033		13207	8388
1722 Carpets and rugs		...	...	10768	13668		...	...	3394	4346		319	2114
1723 Cordage, rope, twine and netting		...	...	1788	1436		...	...	566	459		217	807
1729 Other textiles n.e.c.		...	...	4685	2006		...	...	1929	535		-1020	133
1730 Knitted and crocheted fabrics and articles		...	...	126229	154830		...	...	52698	58299		14485	24785
1810 Wearing apparel, except fur apparel		...	...	122552	142935		...	...	49587	52390		4830	10691
1820 Dressing & dyeing of fur; processing of fur		...	...	79	-		...	...	22	-		-	-
191 Tanning, dressing and processing of leather		...	...	35358	42270		...	...	11299	12127		2182	4556
1911 Tanning and dressing of leather		...	...	34591	41159		...	...	10878	11502		2147	4264
1912 Luggage, handbags, etc.; saddlery & harness		...	...	767	1111		...	...	421	625		35	292
1920 Footwear		...	...	144522	193624		...	...	43079	66151		6575	10843
2010 Sawmilling and planing of wood		...	...	49140	57510		...	...	20210	24838		6930	3134
202 Products of wood, cork, straw, etc.		...	...	196075	188659		...	...	88713	66042		34400	58255
2021 Veneer sheets, plywood, particle board, etc.		...	...	126183	149486		...	...	44262	53838		29601	56461
2022 Builders' carpentry and joinery		...	...	66013	36170		...	...	43283	10957		4771	1798
2023 Wooden containers		...	...	1738	414		...	...	278	67		-15	-
2029 Other wood products; articles of cork/straw		...	...	2141	2589		...	...	890	1180		43	-4
210 Paper and paper products		...	...	1152980	1340680		...	...	178896	255375		163450	74719
2101 Pulp, paper and paperboard		...	...	178783	204077		...	...	42914	74724		26613	22789
2102 Corrugated paper and paperboard		...	...	778366	932544		...	...	90514	140074		99202	30491
2109 Other articles of paper and paperboard		...	...	195831	204059		...	...	45468	40577		37635	21439
221 Publishing		...	...	308159	395595		...	...	90887	120271		59441	9884
2211 Publishing of books and other publications		...	...	3529	10054		...	...	1228	4277		355	456
2212 Publishing of newspapers, journals, etc.		...	...	304551	385541		...	...	89618	115994		59083	9428
2213 Publishing of recorded media		...	...	-	-		...	...	-	-		-	-
2219 Other publishing		...	...	79	-		...	...	41	-		3	-

continued

Ecuador

ISIC Revision 3		Output in producers' prices					Value added in producers' prices					Gross fixed capital formation		
			(million SUCRES)					(million SUCRES)					(million SUCRES)	
ISIC	Industry	Note	1993	1994	1995	1996	Note	1993	1994	1995	1996	Note	1995	1996
222	Printing and related service activities		...	...	62654	99900		...	...	21962	32671		22312	7803
2221	Printing		...	...	56385	91667		...	...	20437	30356		19850	5886
2222	Service activities related to printing		...	...	6269	8233		...	...	1525	2315		2462	1917
2230	Reproduction of recorded media		...	...	4068	1327		...	...	2562	809		1606	-516
2310	Coke oven products		...	...	-	-		...	...	-	-		-	-
2320	Refined petroleum products		...	...	3407272	3668759		...	...	2437890	2226740		579706	507961
2330	Processing of nuclear fuel		...	...	-	-		...	...	-	-		-	-
241	Basic chemicals		...	...	239747	381258		...	...	68098	137351		47796	7842
2411	Basic chemicals, except fertilizers		...	...	111438	143106		...	...	42021	52711		11799	19658
2412	Fertilizers and nitrogen compounds		...	...	52710	145036		...	...	9108	58018		29144	-16238
2413	Plastics in primary forms; synthetic rubber		...	...	75599	93116		...	...	16969	26622		6853	4422
242	Other chemicals		...	...	867136	1243110		...	...	190842	308014		106934	76955
2421	Pesticides and other agro-chemical products		...	...	2416	2817		...	...	1197	1392		272	-66
2422	Paints, varnishes, printing ink and mastics		...	...	182097	249144		...	...	31052	68320		18486	5501
2423	Pharmaceuticals, medicinal chemicals, etc.		...	...	273795	414180		...	...	68763	116122		25320	28118
2424	Soap, cleaning & cosmetic preparations		...	...	361701	503365		...	...	75461	101843		58391	33675
2429	Other chemical products n.e.c.		...	...	47127	73604		...	...	14369	20337		4465	9727
2430	Man-made fibres		...	...	-	-		...	...	-	-		-	-
251	Rubber products		...	...	194624	265722		...	...	55819	73021		19867	-1527
2511	Rubber tyres and tubes		...	...	186557	257424		...	...	51878	70055		20751	-28
2519	Other rubber products		...	...	8067	8298		...	...	3941	2966		-884	-1499
2520	Plastic products		...	...	620150	754831		...	...	192458	239365		88206	96724
2610	Glass and glass products		...	...	109664	132971		...	...	46328	63689		24666	13892
269	Non-metallic mineral products n.e.c.		...	...	853594	1064174		...	...	285570	389459		-234411	182019
2691	Pottery, china and earthenware		...	...	65179	69142		...	...	24834	20963		4636	2607
2692	Refractory ceramic products		...	...	257	424		...	...	-	184		-171	140
2693	Struct.non-refractory clay; ceramic products		...	...	77500	103164		...	...	24817	39384		6068	38110
2694	Cement, lime and plaster		...	...	498479	631694		...	...	176351	255128		-257528	113146
2695	Articles of concrete, cement and plaster		...	...	203701	250120		...	...	55620	70108		11541	27981
2696	Cutting, shaping & finishing of stone		...	...	3345	3842		...	...	1484	1773		437	191
2699	Other non-metallic mineral products n.e.c.		...	...	5133	5788		...	...	2464	1919		606	-156
2710	Basic iron and steel		...	...	416105	568820		...	...	43519	85805		67499	14632
2720	Basic precious and non-ferrous metals		...	...	130530	132253		...	...	27999	26179		37712	-5244
273	Casting of metals		...	...	613	948		...	...	379	431		162	-113
2731	Casting of iron and steel		...	...	613	948		...	...	379	431		162	-113
2732	Casting of non-ferrous metals		...	...	-	-		...	...	-	-		-	-
281	Struct.metal products;tanks;steam generators		...	...	152134	144276		...	...	40675	44747		19242	8851
2811	Structural metal products		...	...	92753	114146		...	...	28166	37826		11415	9616
2812	Tanks, reservoirs and containers of metal		...	...	59381	30130		...	...	12509	6921		7827	-765
2813	Steam generators		...	...	-	-		...	...	-	-		-	-
289	Other metal products; metal working services		...	...	333654	375472		...	...	79293	96555		59916	22
2891	Metal forging/pressing/stamping/roll-forming		...	...	568	472		...	...	219	320		-60	-7
2892	Treatment & coating of metals		...	...	539	468		...	...	264	208		-5	16
2893	Cutlery, hand tools and general hardware		...	...	13289	13715		...	...	4555	5881		2982	1816
2899	Other fabricated metal products n.e.c.		...	...	319258	360817		...	...	74255	90146		56999	-1803
291	General purpose machinery		...	...	129255	156475		...	...	36764	42333		15387	1358
2911	Engines & turbines(not for transport equip.)		...	...	769	962		...	...	390	475		-83	31
2912	Pumps, compressors, taps and valves		...	...	27935	34486		...	...	11041	11366		726	1618
2913	Bearings, gears, gearing & driving elements		...	...	-	-		...	...	-	-		-	-
2914	Ovens, furnaces and furnace burners		...	...	6381	6637		...	...	2929	3356		1056	1084
2915	Lifting and handling equipment		...	...	5863	7477		...	...	2526	3666		1552	2528
2919	Other general purpose machinery		...	...	88307	106913		...	...	19878	23470		12136	-3903

292 Special purpose machinery	...	...	16653	11126	...	...	4427	3193	3164	-3559
2921 Agricultural and forestry machinery	...	...	105	139	...	...	17	79	-1	50
2922 Machine tools	...	...	14069	8171	...	...	3311	1788	2906	-3799
2923 Machinery for metallurgy	...	...	-	-	...	...	-	-	-	-
2924 Machinery for mining & construction	...	...	958	234	...	...	411	173	117	10
2925 Food/beverage/tobacco processing machinery	...	...	807	1751	...	...	308	710	22	67
2926 Machinery for textile, apparel and leather	...	...	-	-	...	...	-	-	-	-
2927 Weapons and ammunition	...	...	167	211	...	...	132	154	98	49
2929 Other special purpose machinery	...	...	547	620	...	...	248	289	22	64
2930 Domestic appliances n.e.c.	...	...	162388	171267	...	...	43431	51307	31642	6446
3000 Office, accounting and computing machinery	...	...	-	-	...	...	-	-	-	-
3110 Electric motors, generators and transformers	...	...	16225	22700	...	...	4482	5426	1541	2441
3120 Electricity distribution & control apparatus	...	...	19657	14507	...	...	5671	5239	-121	2390
3130 Insulated wire and cable	...	...	107417	187741	...	...	21519	71731	8980	31102
3140 Accumulators, primary cells and batteries	...	...	25082	33179	...	...	4602	6068	-145	33
3150 Lighting equipment and electric lamps	...	...	19846	22295	...	...	6205	4011	3033	1474
3190 Other electrical equipment n.e.c.	...	...	8652	6264	...	...	1553	1105	1863	651
3210 Electronic valves, tubes, etc.	...	...	-	-	...	...	-	-	-	-
3220 TV/radio transmitters; line comm. apparatus	...	...	457	560	...	...	282	334	55	-35
3230 TV and radio receivers and associated goods	...	...	56083	3208	...	...	12919	975	13922	-215
331 Medical, measuring, testing appliances, etc.	...	...	3167	3419	...	...	1310	1152	-352	10
3311 Medical, surgical and orthopaedic equipment	...	...	3167	3419	...	...	1310	1152	-352	10
3312 Measuring/testing/navigating appliances,etc.	...	...	-	-	...	...	-	-	-	-
3313 Industrial process control equipment	...	...	-	-	...	...	-	-	-	-
3320 Optical instruments & photographic equipment	...	...	1167	878	...	...	592	618	-77	-269
3330 Watches and clocks	...	...	-	-	...	...	-	-	-	-
3410 Motor vehicles	...	...	814565	715447	...	...	90224	77001	37220	10019
3420 Automobile bodies, trailers & semi-trailers	...	...	20638	23340	...	...	7127	7270	173	261
3430 Parts/accessories for automobiles	...	...	27264	26917	...	...	8538	3971	3289	1849
351 Building and repairing of ships and boats	...	...	1331	22312	...	...	576	8320	88	-2137
3511 Building and repairing of ships	...	...	1331	22312	...	...	576	8320	88	-2137
3512 Building/repairing of pleasure/sport. boats	...	...	-	-	...	...	-	-	-	-
3520 Railway/tramway locomotives & rolling stock	...	...	-	-	...	...	-	-	-	-
3530 Aircraft and spacecraft	...	...	-	-	...	...	-	-	-	-
359 Transport equipment n.e.c.	...	...	592	3435	...	...	225	1504	-1	-256
3591 Motorcycles	...	...	-	2859	...	...	-	1258	-	-733
3592 Bicycles and invalid carriages	...	...	-	-	...	...	-	-	-	-
3599 Other transport equipment n.e.c.	...	...	592	576	...	...	225	246	-1	477
3610 Furniture	...	...	177153	195062	...	...	53748	64240	12689	15982
369 Manufacturing n.e.c.	...	...	54759	76535	...	...	18099	25846	9694	7490
3691 Jewellery and related articles	...	...	7728	12493	...	...	3338	5726	945	1298
3692 Musical instruments	...	...	-	-	...	...	-	-	-	-
3693 Sports goods	...	...	410	377	...	...	164	141	-10	20
3694 Games and toys	...	...	10985	13836	...	...	3593	3840	290	698
3699 Other manufacturing n.e.c.	...	...	35636	49829	...	...	11004	16139	8469	5474
3710 Recycling of metal waste and scrap	...	...	-	-	...	...	-	-	-	-
3720 Recycling of non-metal waste and scrap	...	...	-	-	...	...	-	-	-	-
D Total manufacturing	...	...	18810691	22193732	...	...	6274379	6807810	1852292	1646880

Ecuador

ISIC Revision 3			Index numbers of industrial production (1990=100)											
ISIC	Industry	Note	1985	1986	1987	1988	1989	1990	1991	1992	1993	1994	1995	1996
15	Food and beverages		...	...	...	...	...	...	...	...	...	...	...	...
16	Tobacco products		137	131	121	107	107	100	97	101	106	104	...	...
17	Textiles		98	95	90	93	96	100	99	88	77	81	...	...
18	Wearing apparel, fur		...	...	...	...	...	...	...	...	...	...	...	...
19	Leather, leather products and footwear		...	...	...	...	...	...	...	...	...	...	...	...
20	Wood products (excl. furniture)		73	81	86	86	89	100	113	132	156	173	...	...
21	Paper and paper products		68	79	81	83	92	100	115	105	118	124	...	...
22	Printing and publishing		55	63	70	79	91	100	123	137	146	165	...	...
23	Coke,refined petroleum products,nuclear fuel		...	...	...	...	...	...	...	...	...	...	...	...
24	Chemicals and chemical products		...	...	...	...	...	...	...	...	...	...	...	...
25	Rubber and plastics products		...	...	...	...	...	...	...	...	...	...	...	...
26	Non-metallic mineral products		...	...	...	...	...	...	...	...	...	...	...	...
27	Basic metals		...	...	...	...	...	...	...	...	...	...	...	...
28	Fabricated metal products		81	90	91	95	96	100	114	133	148	170	...	...
29	Machinery and equipment n.e.c.		...	...	...	...	...	...	...	...	...	...	...	...
30	Office, accounting and computing machinery		...	...	...	...	...	...	...	...	...	...	...	...
31	Electrical machinery and apparatus	a/	76	84	96	101	92	100	117	137	146	187	...	...
32	Radio,television and communication equipment	a/	...	...	...	...	...	...	...	...	...	...	...	...
33	Medical, precision and optical instruments		...	...	...	...	...	...	...	...	...	...	...	...
34	Motor vehicles, trailers, semi-trailers	b/	49	57	42	55	93	100	123	134	138	156	...	...
35	Other transport equipment	b/	...	...	...	...	...	...	...	...	...	...	...	...
36	Furniture; manufacturing n.e.c.		...	...	...	...	...	...	...	...	...	...	...	...
37	Recycling		...	...	...	...	...	...	...	...	...	...	...	...
D	Total manufacturing		80	83	86	89	93	100	113	118	121	...	...	...

a/ 31 includes 32.
b/ 34 includes 35.

EGYPT

Supplier of information:
Central Agency for Public Mobilisation and Statistics (CAPMAS), Cairo.

Basic source of data:
Survey of industrial production.

Major deviations from ISIC (Revision 2):
The Egyptian industrial classification system is based on the preceding version of the ISIC, but the data have been adjusted by the national authorities to correspond with ISIC (Rev. 2) as far as details permit.

Reference period (if not calendar year):
Fiscal year beginning 1 July of the year indicated.

Scope:
All establishments in the public sector and establishments with 10 or more persons engaged in the private sector. The indices of industrial production cover all industrial establishments.

Method of enumeration:
Individual sites were visited by enumerators.

Adjusted for non-response:
Not reported.

Concepts and definitions of variables:
Output is gross output.
Value added is net of depreciation.

Related national publications:
Statistics of Industrial Production (irregular); Basic Statistics (irregular); Statistical Handbook (annual), all published by the Central Agency for Public Mobilisation and Statistics (CAPMAS), Cairo.

Egypt

ISIC Revision 2	Number of establishments					Number of persons engaged					Wages and salaries paid to employees				
		(numbers)					(thousands)					(million POUNDS)			
ISIC Industry	Note	1991	1992	1993	1994	Note	1991	1992	1993	1994	Note	1991	1992	1993	1994
311/2 Food products		3864	4165	4057	4083		243.0	193.0	191.0	184.7		828.6	677.1	748.9	874.2
3111 Slaughtering, preparing & preserving meat		39	24	27	36		4.4	5.2	5.3	5.6		14.2	17.8	20.3	22.3
3112 Dairy products		29	37	35	49		8.8	9.3	8.2	8.9		29.5	40.3	31.5	40.6
3113 Canning, preserving of fruits & vegetables		52	50	57	56		11.7	9.4	9.0	9.8		29.2	33.1	33.9	45.0
3114 Canning, preserving and processing of fish		10	8	9	8		1.1	1.1	1.6	1.7		10.3	6.3	10.4	10.7
3115 Vegetable and animal oils and fats		35	30	29	26		18.9	16.2	14.0	14.7		210.5	63.6	56.1	59.3
3116 Grain mill products		240	222	220	210		68.4	33.8	31.1	32.0		138.2	135.2	148.7	179.9
3117 Bakery products		3080	3450	3318	3290		76.3	72.4	68.0	55.4		212.2	203.1	210.8	211.3
3118 Sugar factories and refineries		10	10	11	11		15.2	13.4	16.5	18.0		71.7	63.0	98.0	126.9
3119 Cocoa, chocolate and sugar confectionery		90	68	69	86		10.9	9.8	12.0	12.5		29.2	33.5	39.2	73.5
3121 Other food products		227	216	227	252		15.0	10.4	11.3	14.0		46.7	37.8	42.5	60.1
3122 Prepared animal feeds		52	50	55	59		12.3	12.0	14.0	12.1		36.9	43.4	57.5	44.6
313 Beverages		27	53	38	36		12.1	21.3	15.2	13.0		80.9	90.0	84.4	73.9
3131 Distilling, rectifying and blending spirits		7	8	8	6		1.1	1.0	1.0	1.5		5.9	5.3	5.8	7.6
3132 Wine industries		2	1	1	1		0.6	0.5	0.5	0.5		2.8	2.8	3.3	3.1
3133 Malt liquors and malt		3	3	3	4		2.7	1.8	2.3	1.9		11.4	11.3	15.8	17.0
3134 Soft drinks and carbonated waters		15	41	26	25		7.7	18.0	11.4	9.1		60.8	70.6	59.5	46.3
314 Tobacco		27	32	30	32		16.6	17.0	16.7	17.1		83.7	96.5	108.1	122.2
321 Textiles		839	938	940	1028		247.3	267.5	279.2	287.0		899.8	1018.2	1134.3	1280.8
3211 Spinning, weaving and finishing textiles		605	593	612	639		215.0	231.9	241.4	243.2		787.2	880.0	975.1	1106.1
3212 Made-up textile goods excl. wearing apparel		57	65	52	73		13.3	2.9	2.1	7.2		46.7	6.6	5.3	16.3
3213 Knitting mills		127	152	144	172		12.8	14.9	16.5	16.6		39.2	45.8	51.0	55.5
3214 Carpets and rugs		28	30	26	34		4.8	7.0	7.3	5.8		11.6	33.9	36.7	35.4
3215 Cordage, rope and twine		1	3	3	7		1.0	1.1	1.2	2.4		14.8	5.9	9.8	6.3
3219 Other textiles		21	95	103	103		0.4	9.7	10.7	11.8		0.3	46.0	56.4	61.3
322 Wearing apparel, except footwear		371	349	344	538		30.4	28.9	29.7	38.0		60.9	74.2	79.4	91.3
323 Leather and fur products		69	60	50	71		3.7	3.1	3.1	3.7		13.8	11.6	13.6	15.7
3231 Tanneries and leather finishing		40	36	22	48		2.9	2.3	2.4	3.0		12.3	9.6	12.0	14.0
3232 Fur dressing and dyeing industries		8	3	11	-		0.2	0.2	0.2	-		0.2	0.4	0.8	-
3233 Leather prods. excl. wearing apparel		21	21	17	23		0.6	0.6	0.5	0.8		1.3	1.6	0.8	1.7
324 Footwear, except rubber or plastic		94	97	91	120		9.8	9.1	6.9	6.2		27.9	30.2	25.9	17.1
331 Wood products, except furniture		98	109	108	112		6.3	6.7	6.0	9.2		23.7	26.5	25.5	30.2
3311 Sawmills, planing and other wood mills		88	102	98	101		6.1	6.6	5.9	8.9		23.4	26.4	25.2	29.8
3312 Wooden and cane containers		-	-	4	3		-	-	...	0.1		-	-	0.2	0.2
3319 Other wood and cork products		10	7	6	8		0.2	0.1	0.1	0.1		0.3	0.1	0.1	0.2
332 Furniture and fixtures, excl. metal		128	113	116	138		8.2	6.7	8.0	8.5		28.9	25.3	30.7	39.9
341 Paper and products		99	98	96	109		33.4	19.2	18.6	19.6		120.6	86.2	96.7	113.9
3411 Pulp, paper and paperboard articles		34	33	27	33		14.9	10.6	10.2	9.0		74.7	44.9	53.2	54.0
3412 Containers of paper and paperboard		46	43	52	41		15.3	5.0	5.1	5.9		27.1	20.7	25.4	33.8
3419 Other pulp, paper and paperboard articles		19	22	17	35		3.2	3.6	3.3	4.7		18.8	20.6	18.1	26.1
342 Printing and publishing		164	163	154	160		15.5	20.4	18.8	11.0		71.0	163.5	188.2	152.1
351 Industrial chemicals		60	46	52	61		57.0	46.1	38.6	44.0		318.2	292.6	298.5	379.5
3511 Basic chemicals excl. fertilizers		22	17	24	33		15.7	10.6	11.1	16.8		77.4	66.9	76.8	157.3
3512 Fertilizers and pesticides		24	22	20	23		30.5	25.1	27.1	26.8		190.1	173.5	220.3	219.3
3513 Synthetic resins and plastic materials		14	7	8	5		10.8	10.4	0.4	0.4		50.7	52.2	1.4	2.9
352 Other chemicals		187	178	178	194		51.8	54.0	53.4	63.4		343.1	331.6	366.0	484.8
3521 Paints, varnishes and lacquers		37	33	33	38		3.9	3.3	4.9	4.1		15.8	17.4	31.6	23.5
3522 Drugs and medicines		25	26	26	28		26.0	27.8	25.8	31.8		213.6	211.6	230.7	319.2
3523 Soap, cleaning preps., perfumes, cosmetics		79	77	76	88		16.7	15.1	15.3	19.2		92.8	65.8	67.1	99.6
3529 Other chemical products		46	42	43	40		5.2	7.8	7.4	8.3		20.9	36.8	36.6	42.5
353 Petroleum refineries		8	8	8	8		18.4	17.5	17.7	18.3		185.1	220.0	253.8	301.3

354	Misc. petroleum and coal products	17	16	15	20	1.4	0.9	1.1	7.8	8.2	8.7	10.9	81.8
355	Rubber products	32	36	24	30	9.7	8.3	7.3	6.9	11.4	43.3	46.7	47.4
3551	Tyres and tubes	4	4	2	5	7.1	6.0	4.1	4.1	0.5	33.7	27.3	32.8
3559	Other rubber products	28	32	22	25	2.6	2.3	3.2	2.9	10.9	9.6	19.4	14.6
356	Plastic products	217	214	225	276	27.6	18.6	18.0	21.7	99.6	69.5	75.6	103.6
361	Pottery, china, earthenware	21	16	15	18	11.6	6.2	5.6	6.0	59.2	28.0	29.3	28.5
362	Glass and products	67	70	60	65	13.3	14.9	14.7	15.3	48.0	67.0	68.8	78.3
369	Other non-metallic mineral products	611	571	584	617	57.8	59.8	60.2	57.2	267.2	297.3	342.5	461.9
3691	Structural clay products	339	339	325	402	16.5	18.7	18.0	14.1	51.7	70.7	76.3	71.2
3692	Cement, lime and plaster	16	12	16	13	21.4	22.2	22.1	24.2	149.7	152.9	187.1	228.8
3699	Other non-metallic mineral products	256	220	243	202	19.9	18.9	20.1	18.9	65.8	73.7	79.1	161.9
371	Iron and steel	105	102	103	102	47.6	47.8	48.6	50.9	324.5	341.0	393.5	406.8
372	Non-ferrous metals	25	30	22	29	19.7	20.5	18.9	24.4	118.9	117.3	129.6	174.3
381	Fabricated metal products	419	409	392	505	48.6	52.6	46.5	60.0	325.7	272.0	237.0	266.2
3811	Cutlery, hand tools and general hardware	34	33	39	50	5.0	6.0	4.9	6.1	16.8	26.4	20.9	23.8
3812	Furniture and fixtures primarily of metal	47	38	31	47	4.7	4.3	4.5	6.5	22.1	26.7	29.8	60.6
3813	Structural metal products	67	49	56	64	10.0	9.5	10.0	10.3	45.1	48.7	59.9	54.7
3819	Other fabricated metal products	271	289	266	344	28.9	32.8	27.1	37.0	241.7	170.2	126.4	127.2
382	Non-electrical machinery	168	160	153	145	41.6	37.8	38.9	45.3	186.9	198.0	227.3	274.3
3821	Engines and turbines	2	2	5	2	3.8	3.2	3.4	3.3	20.4	20.6	22.0	22.3
3822	Agricultural machinery and equipment	22	23	21	17	2.7	2.8	2.9	0.5	11.4	11.5	9.9	1.3
3823	Metal and wood working machinery	8	7	5	6	2.1	3.1	3.2	3.2	8.8	14.4	14.7	16.6
3824	Other special industrial machinery	32	36	32	34	6.9	6.6	5.8	11.0	37.1	37.8	40.6	69.1
3825	Office, computing and accounting machinery	3	1	2	2	0.5	0.1	0.6	0.3	7.6	0.1	5.3	11.3
3829	Other non-electrical machinery & equipment	101	91	88	84	25.6	22.0	23.0	27.0	101.6	113.6	134.8	153.8
383	Electrical machinery	107	105	109	124	33.0	32.8	31.9	33.2	250.1	226.7	232.6	237.5
3831	Electrical industrial machinery	22	19	20	28	8.1	4.6	4.4	5.7	53.2	29.0	35.5	45.2
3832	Radio, television and communication equipm.	9	9	11	13	9.8	9.5	9.7	8.4	62.6	72.7	84.4	71.0
3833	Electrical appliances and housewares	16	16	15	20	1.8	4.4	3.5	4.8	68.2	21.2	19.8	22.8
3839	Other electrical apparatus and supplies	60	61	63	63	13.3	14.3	14.3	14.2	66.1	103.8	92.9	98.5
384	Transport equipment	141	140	128	137	54.3	60.4	47.8	51.8	247.0	313.5	289.6	351.4
3841	Shipbuilding and repairing	21	21	22	25	12.5	13.0	13.0	12.6	58.4	74.5	82.8	85.5
3842	Railroad equipment	5	2	2	4	3.8	2.7	2.8	2.8	19.8	19.3	20.7	26.3
3843	Motor vehicles	113	115	101	105	35.1	41.6	29.2	33.0	155.4	204.4	169.4	220.1
3844	Motorcycles and bicycles	2	2	2	2	2.9	2.9	2.8	2.8	13.4	14.8	16.5	16.5
3845	Aircraft	-	-	-	-	-	-	-	-	-	-	-	-
3849	Other transport equipment	-	...	1	1	-	0.2	-	0.5	-	0.5	0.2	3.0
385	Professional and scientific equipment	19	18	18	21	10.9	7.3	6.8	9.8	44.2	53.5	38.0	65.9
3851	Prof. and scientific equipment n.e.c.	15	10	10	13	10.6	6.1	6.0	8.7	31.8	28.6	29.9	55.6
3852	Photographic and optical goods	3	6	6	6	0.2	1.1	0.6	1.0	12.4	24.8	7.9	10.2
3853	Watches and clocks	1	2	2	2	0.1	0.1	0.2	0.1	-	0.1	0.2	0.1
390	Other manufacturing industries	34	38	44	57	1.7	1.7	2.3	4.0	5.6	7.2	10.3	13.9
3901	Jewellery and related articles	14	9	12	23	0.1	0.1	0.5	0.6	0.5	0.5	2.5	2.7
3902	Musical instruments	-	-	-	-	-	-	-	-	-	-	-	-
3903	Sporting and athletic goods	-	-	-	-	-	-	-	-	-	-	-	-
3909	Manufacturing industries, n.e.c.	20	29	32	34	1.6	1.6	1.8	3.5	5.1	6.7	7.8	11.1
3	Total manufacturing	8018	8334	8154	8836	1132.3	1080.1	1051.5	1118.1	5082.7	5186.5	5585.7	6568.4

ISIC Revision 2		Output in factor values					Value added in factor values					Gross fixed capital formation	
		(million POUNDS)					(million POUNDS)					(million POUNDS)	
ISIC Industry	Note	1991	1992	1993	1994	Note	1991	1992	1993	1994	Note	1993	1994
311/2 Food products		9045.3	10606.3	12260.9	13864.6		1563.8	1964.4	3062.5	2798.1		203.2	133.7
3111 Slaughtering, preparing & preserving meat		560.5	325.1	436.4	423.9		28.5	45.0	145.8	89.6		...	...
3112 Dairy products		334.2	629.6	370.2	517.4		43.4	145.6	92.1	159.7		...	...
3113 Canning, preserving of fruits & vegetables		305.5	271.2	300.8	508.7		66.9	67.3	112.7	121.1		...	...
3114 Canning, preserving and processing of fish		86.4	26.1	53.2	54.1		22.0	3.8	17.3	27.4		...	...
3115 Vegetable and animal oils and fats		1061.5	1590.4	1483.5	1830.8		159.6	146.6	253.1	171.9		...	...
3116 Grain mill products		2198.9	3082.6	2929.5	3683.4		334.6	412.8	410.2	620.6		...	...
3117 Bakery products		1695.4	1792.1	2422.3	1844.1		437.2	449.7	1013.9	426.5		...	...
3118 Sugar factories and refineries		931.8	1043.5	1567.7	2298.6		100.8	272.4	401.0	638.6		...	...
3119 Cocoa, chocolate and sugar confectionery		250.3	317.3	424.7	474.7		168.9	78.9	130.9	125.2		...	...
3121 Other food products		642.9	572.2	792.5	1220.1		106.9	104.4	145.0	262.4		...	...
3122 Prepared animal feeds		977.9	956.2	1480.1	1008.8		95.0	237.9	340.5	155.1		...	...
313 Beverages		707.1	850.6	955.6	649.6		193.6	279.9	423.0	351.9		34.8	-349.5
3131 Distilling, rectifying and blending spirits		81.5	77.1	35.1	38.9		54.6	58.3	8.8	14.4		...	...
3132 Wine industries		21.6	17.9	12.9	12.1		14.8	6.5	4.8	-0.1		...	...
3133 Malt liquors and malt		79.9	42.0	91.2	179.4		32.4	12.5	52.4	134.1		...	...
3134 Soft drinks and carbonated waters		524.1	713.6	816.4	419.2		91.8	202.6	357.0	203.5		...	...
314 Tobacco		1179.1	1642.1	1622.4	1757.0		278.5	372.2	331.4	409.7		371.7	204.8
321 Textiles		6407.5	6967.7	7551.7	8373.5		1937.3	1774.2	1913.0	2058.2		-27.0	-1071.5
3211 Spinning, weaving and finishing textiles		5647.3	5907.8	6393.6	6961.1		1690.8	1478.9	1520.5	1640.0		...	...
3212 Made-up textile goods excl. wearing apparel		96.9	108.5	59.9	171.7		58.1	25.9	10.1	77.5		...	...
3213 Knitting mills		327.7	366.5	398.9	500.3		107.9	90.7	86.1	132.0		...	...
3214 Carpets and rugs		263.4	408.0	367.1	444.3		66.3	84.9	135.6	61.7		...	...
3215 Cordage, rope and twine		27.5	36.0	37.9	41.2		9.1	11.9	13.6	15.4		...	...
3219 Other textiles		44.7	140.9	294.3	254.9		5.1	81.9	147.1	131.5		...	...
322 Wearing apparel, except footwear		687.0	677.5	719.9	1210.6		110.6	188.4	228.7	463.2		25.9	141.7
323 Leather and fur products		111.1	92.6	70.7	96.9		21.3	31.2	0.4	15.3		-11.4	0.1
3231 Tanneries and leather finishing		79.3	67.7	46.8	79.4		10.7	22.2	-5.1	10.4		...	...
3232 Fur dressing and dyeing industries		10.9	2.6	12.4	-		2.7	0.6	3.7	-		...	...
3233 Leather prods. excl. wearing apparel		20.9	22.3	11.5	17.5		7.9	8.4	1.8	4.9		...	...
324 Footwear, except rubber or plastic		164.9	350.1	121.6	102.0		55.3	250.2	20.8	13.5		-24.8	-79.4
331 Wood products, except furniture		137.4	222.2	125.7	302.3		36.9	80.1	18.5	163.8		-4.7	7.2
3311 Sawmills, planing and other wood mills		135.6	221.7	123.0	297.9		36.3	79.9	18.0	162.9		...	...
3312 Wooden and cane containers		-	-	2.2	2.9		-	-	0.3	0.4		...	...
3319 Other wood and cork products		1.8	0.5	0.5	1.5		0.6	0.2	0.2	0.5		...	...
332 Furniture and fixtures, excl. metal		200.6	140.1	242.2	286.9		58.9	44.2	58.8	61.8		15.6	18.2
341 Paper and products		1227.5	1274.9	1160.7	1317.2		264.4	432.6	296.0	362.6		-53.2	196.3
3411 Pulp, paper and paperboard articles		676.5	462.8	412.2	535.2		148.6	95.5	88.5	173.0		...	...
3412 Containers of paper and paperboard		393.9	366.8	627.8	550.8		56.8	64.7	181.1	135.7		...	...
3419 Other pulp, paper and paperboard articles		157.1	445.3	120.7	231.2		59.0	272.4	26.4	54.0		...	...
342 Printing and publishing		598.6	1042.6	889.3	1130.3		197.8	265.9	361.5	282.2		906.2	6.7
351 Industrial chemicals		2767.6	2460.3	2482.8	2576.0		734.1	809.9	782.6	1046.9		89.4	370.3
3511 Basic chemicals excl. fertilizers		697.7	537.9	535.5	1063.7		223.6	190.3	156.1	469.8		...	...
3512 Fertilizers and pesticides		1695.5	1531.4	1902.3	1446.5		493.3	520.8	619.2	556.0		...	...
3513 Synthetic resins and plastic materials		374.4	391.0	45.0	65.8		17.2	98.8	7.3	21.1		...	...
352 Other chemicals		3375.9	3392.4	4252.4	4752.9		845.9	725.5	1255.5	1474.5		229.2	645.9
3521 Paints, varnishes and lacquers		347.9	321.1	431.6	503.9		75.6	82.9	132.3	215.8		...	...
3522 Drugs and medicines		1546.5	1668.1	1846.3	2360.5		414.7	445.4	676.6	774.0		...	...
3523 Soap, cleaning preps., perfumes, cosmetics		1213.3	972.9	1597.7	1514.4		304.9	84.8	371.5	380.8		...	...
3529 Other chemical products		268.2	430.3	376.8	374.1		50.7	112.4	75.1	103.8		...	...
353 Petroleum refineries		6967.9	10109.0	10980.5	12120.2		4113.4	5809.1	5399.2	3449.5		800.7	907.4

354	Misc. petroleum and coal products	225.9	226.0	285.6	943.7	81.9	74.0	55.1	121.2	1.1	13.3
355	Rubber products	138.9	278.5	267.5	300.1	63.3	53.8	64.1	82.0	-5.9	35.5
3551	Tyres and tubes	1.4	220.7	196.6	224.9	0.7	39.6	33.2	54.4	...	...
3559	Other rubber products	137.5	57.8	70.9	75.2	62.6	14.2	30.9	27.6	...	...
356	Plastic products	984.5	897.9	799.4	1062.6	206.7	272.5	143.5	230.9	-71.3	-521.3
361	Pottery, china, earthenware	419.9	163.9	148.6	141.3	89.8	30.0	43.4	47.2	9.7	16.0
362	Glass and products	248.3	371.9	394.2	479.6	87.6	105.9	140.7	143.9	70.0	83.9
369	Other non-metallic mineral products	2428.5	3453.3	3665.2	6321.2	466.8	1250.5	1350.9	2181.7	127.7	456.7
3691	Structural clay products	321.5	614.7	670.4	536.2	58.6	143.9	251.8	224.7	...	...
3692	Cement, lime and plaster	1651.9	2053.9	2484.9	2772.7	274.3	686.3	942.7	1053.9	...	...
3699	Other non-metallic mineral products	455.1	784.7	509.9	3012.3	133.9	420.3	156.4	903.1	...	...
371	Iron and steel	2805.6	3146.7	3600.8	2539.9	818.3	636.1	689.4	376.6	258.4	163.7
372	Non-ferrous metals	1385.5	1510.5	1400.4	2119.9	241.1	257.7	277.3	511.0	158.7	846.8
381	Fabricated metal products	1379.4	2705.9	1940.9	2221.7	437.7	1022.9	795.8	738.7	43.0	247.8
3811	Cutlery, hand tools and general hardware	100.2	219.7	471.7	141.8	29.4	20.4	382.2	40.2	...	...
3812	Furniture and fixtures primarily of metal	121.0	132.1	126.8	216.2	27.1	35.6	31.7	64.9	...	...
3813	Structural metal products	268.1	733.7	460.0	432.2	98.6	504.8	120.0	140.9	...	...
3819	Other fabricated metal products	890.1	1620.4	882.4	1431.5	282.6	462.1	261.9	492.6	...	...
382	Non-electrical machinery	1505.6	1351.0	1567.9	2820.2	354.9	309.6	379.9	1542.7	53.0	65.1
3821	Engines and turbines	114.9	120.4	115.1	93.5	31.4	41.8	37.8	19.5	...	...
3822	Agricultural machinery and equipment	94.9	81.9	85.3	11.2	17.9	15.8	20.4	6.6	...	...
3823	Metal and wood working machinery	32.1	63.5	16.9	24.8	17.5	10.7	6.4	19.9	...	...
3824	Other special industrial machinery	84.8	82.5	121.4	278.7	30.7	19.3	39.5	107.1	...	...
3825	Office, computing and accounting machinery	40.6	0.3	41.3	54.8	13.2	0.1	25.5	46.1	...	...
3829	Other non-electrical machinery & equipment	1138.3	1002.4	1187.9	2357.2	244.2	221.9	250.3	1343.6	...	...
383	Electrical machinery	1780.1	1979.1	2290.5	2577.8	494.6	662.9	644.6	773.2	130.2	256.2
3831	Electrical industrial machinery	387.2	373.8	393.4	887.2	52.1	174.1	-54.4	295.7	...	...
3832	Radio, television and communication equipm.	365.3	476.3	492.8	499.3	141.2	150.5	119.3	129.7	...	...
3833	Electrical appliances and housewares	184.1	241.4	213.7	294.1	44.2	27.1	67.8	81.1	...	...
3839	Other electrical apparatus and supplies	843.5	887.6	1190.6	897.2	257.1	311.2	511.9	266.7	...	...
384	Transport equipment	1825.1	2080.1	1761.7	3156.1	755.2	545.7	519.5	714.9	193.7	-12.1
3841	Shipbuilding and repairing	206.5	466.3	297.9	340.9	46.1	173.8	114.9	143.6	...	...
3842	Railroad equipment	160.9	169.9	206.9	358.3	33.8	73.6	28.6	84.7	...	...
3843	Motor vehicles	1389.8	1374.5	1125.7	2333.4	653.5	282.2	375.4	493.4	...	...
3844	Motorcycles and bicycles	67.9	68.8	126.6	122.9	21.8	15.9	0.2	-6.7	...	...
3845	Aircraft	-	-	-	-	-	-	-	-	...	...
3849	Other transport equipment	-	0.6	4.6	0.6	-	0.2	0.4	-0.1	...	...
385	Professional and scientific equipment	198.7	184.5	118.9	132.9	73.1	31.5	38.0	80.3	-15.2	19.6
3851	Prof. and scientific equipment n.e.c.	104.1	59.7	60.7	98.4	43.1	18.1	24.7	73.2	...	...
3852	Photographic and optical goods	92.9	122.1	55.4	33.3	29.4	12.6	12.7	6.9	...	...
3853	Watches and clocks	1.7	2.7	2.8	1.2	0.6	0.8	0.6	0.3	...	...
390	Other manufacturing industries	97.8	87.6	70.9	141.9	29.9	36.2	13.6	17.6	-3.5	16.6
3901	Jewellery and related articles	24.6	6.7	20.2	21.0	2.1	3.8	0.1	-1.6	...	...
3902	Musical instruments	-	-	-	-	-	-	-	-	...	...
3903	Sporting and athletic goods	-	-	-	-	-	-	-	-	...	...
3909	Manufacturing industries, n.e.c.	73.2	80.9	50.7	120.9	27.8	32.4	13.5	19.2	...	...
3	Total manufacturing	49001.3	58265.3	61748.9	73498.9	14612.7	18317.1	19307.7	20512.8	3505.2	2819.5

Egypt

ISIC Revision 2		Index numbers of industrial production											
		(1990=100)											
ISIC Industry	Note	1985	1986	1987	1988	1989	1990	1991	1992	1993	1994	1995	1996
311/2 Food products	a/	113	126	112	109	123	100	97	98	113	119	148	...
313 Beverages	a/	...	...	...	...	...	...	...	...	...	...	...	...
314 Tobacco		117	106	117	112	106	100	105	106	111	121	129	...
321 Textiles		127	131	114	95	98	100	108	98	92	92	96	...
322 Wearing apparel, except footwear		45	42	39	98	122	100	85	81	79	81	87	...
323 Leather and fur products	b/	228	174	157	165	164	100	108	103	101	103	104	...
324 Footwear, except rubber or plastic	b/	...	...	...	...	...	...	...	...	...	...	...	...
331 Wood products, except furniture		138	132	133	112	102	100	92	89	92	98	95	...
332 Furniture and fixtures, excl. metal		112	107	97	113	111	100	90	101	104	103	101	...
341 Paper and products		51	65	55	66	69	100	101	105	75	77	72	...
342 Printing and publishing		138	92	138	114	111	100	98	94	77	70	59	...
351 Industrial chemicals	c/	87	76	107	110	99	100	101	84	91	95	91	...
352 Other chemicals	c/	...	...	...	...	...	...	...	...	...	...	...	...
353 Petroleum refineries	d/	142	113	108	100	95	100	122	121	117	114	103	...
354 Misc. petroleum and coal products	d/	...	...	...	...	...	...	...	...	...	...	...	...
355 Rubber products	e/	82	106	107	113	124	100	98	90	80	76	75	...
356 Plastic products	e/	...	...	...	...	...	...	...	...	...	...	...	...
361 Pottery, china, earthenware	f/	45	59	66	80	83	100	93	93	95	89	98	...
362 Glass and products	f/	...	...	...	...	...	...	...	...	...	...	...	...
369 Other non-metallic mineral products	f/	...	...	...	...	...	...	...	...	...	...	...	...
371 Iron and steel	g/	75	83	94	94	101	100	112	91	90	97	103	...
372 Non-ferrous metals	g/	...	...	...	...	...	...	...	...	...	...	...	...
381 Fabricated metal products		99	98	106	114	108	100	98	98	98	99	99	...
382 Non-electrical machinery		113	99	122	110	111	100	90	80	83	89	102	...
383 Electrical machinery		140	125	119	128	114	100	106	97	91	95	97	...
384 Transport equipment		201	145	134	146	150	100	121	85	99	101	92	...
385 Professional and scientific equipment		59	77	94	164	141	100	101	67	46	42	63	...
390 Other manufacturing industries		105	110	148	131	121	100	283	271	255	251	194	...
3 Total manufacturing		112	105	106	104	105	100	107	99	100	102	106	...

a/ 311/2 includes 313.
b/ 323 includes 324.
c/ 351 includes 352.
d/ 353 includes 354.
e/ 355 includes 356.
f/ 361 includes 362 and 369.
g/ 371 includes 372.

EL SALVADOR

Supplier of information:
Departamento de Estadísticas Industriales, Dirección General de Estadística y Censos (DIGESTYC), Ministerio de Economía, San Salvador.

Basic source of data:
Annual survey of the manufacturing industry.

Major deviations from ISIC (Revision 2):
None reported.

Reference period (if not calendar year):

Scope:
Establishments with 5 or more persons engaged and with fixed capital of 20,000 colones or more. Establishments processing coffee or cotton are excluded.

Method of enumeration:
Not reported.

Adjusted for non-response:
Not reported.

Concepts and definitions of variables:
Number of persons engaged is as of 31 August of the reference year.
Output includes receipts for the right to use patents, copyrights and the like, and purchases of goods for resale without transformation.

Related national publications:
Anuario Estadístico, Tomo III, published by the Dirección General de Estadística y Censos (DIGESTYC), Ministerio de Economía, San Salvador.

El Salvador

ISIC Revision 2	Number of establishments					Number of persons engaged					Wages and salaries paid to employees				
		(numbers)					(numbers)					(million COLONES)			
ISIC Industry	Note	1993	1994	1995	1996	Note	1993	1994	1995	1996	Note	1993	1994	1995	1996
311/2 Food products		100	107	122	248		7400	9347	5778	12651		249.3	443.1	202.1	338.2
3111 Slaughtering, preparing & preserving meat		11	10	3	12		1918	1878	116	564		36.8	66.5	1.8	18.8
3112 Dairy products		9	9	11	21		597	656	466	1028		7.9	41.9	24.4	20.8
3113 Canning, preserving of fruits & vegetables		7	2	7	9		388	35	129	580		4.1	0.6	2.2	27.1
3114 Canning, preserving and processing of fish		-	2	2	5		-	280	346	1036		-	3.4	5.3	18.3
3115 Vegetable and animal oils and fats		5	5	6	8		841	900	1047	1100		100.1	61.8	57.2	50.8
3116 Grain mill products		5	6	1	9		180	189	7	78		2.8	4.3	0.1	1.2
3117 Bakery products		34	51	63	124		952	3227	1409	2801		12.7	166.8	24.2	47.8
3118 Sugar factories and refineries		3	2	4	6		1043	891	1249	3282		39.3	57.3	60.7	75.2
3119 Cocoa, chocolate and sugar confectionery		7	6	5	9		407	752	402	673		7.2	20.7	8.0	18.8
3121 Other food products		12	8	12	31		909	379	449	1310		35.4	14.3	13.1	53.4
3122 Prepared animal feeds		7	6	8	14		165	160	158	199		3.0	5.6	5.1	6.0
313 Beverages		10	16	14	17		971	2407	3405	3893		31.4	137.7	177.6	172.1
3131 Distilling, rectifying and blending spirits		8	10	9	9		264	249	185	262		4.2	4.5	3.8	6.9
3132 Wine industries		-	-	-	-		-	-	-	-		-	-	-	-
3133 Malt liquors and malt		-	1	1	1		-	842	882	855		-	76.9	68.1	48.9
3134 Soft drinks and carbonated waters		2	5	4	7		707	1316	2338	2776		27.2	56.4	105.7	116.3
314 Tobacco		1	1	1	1		228	237	250	231		17.2	21.7	20.3	18.2
321 Textiles		51	40	52	77		7423	7838	8549	10853		134.6	223.9	172.3	251.1
3211 Spinning, weaving and finishing textiles		14	14	17	23		5164	4222	4650	5873		101.6	117.4	87.6	136.7
3212 Made-up textile goods excl. wearing apparel		4	8	13	16		152	1345	1428	901		2.7	55.7	42.0	21.2
3213 Knitting mills		33	18	22	37		2107	2271	2471	4072		30.3	50.8	42.6	93.1
3214 Carpets and rugs		-	-	-	1		-	-	-	7		-	-	-	0.1
3215 Cordage, rope and twine		-	-	-	-		-	-	-	-		-	-	-	-
3219 Other textiles		-	-	-	-		-	-	-	-		-	-	-	-
322 Wearing apparel, except footwear		61	102	78	166		10420	11568	12060	31079		139.7	232.7	201.2	570.3
323 Leather and fur products		10	6	1	8		698	366	140	538		12.8	10.9	4.8	13.8
3231 Tanneries and leather finishing		3	2	1	2		335	74	140	130		5.9	2.1	4.8	3.3
3232 Fur dressing and dyeing industries		-	-	-	-		-	-	-	-		-	-	-	-
3233 Leather prods. excl. wearing apparel		7	4	...	6		363	292	...	408		7.0	8.8	...	10.5
324 Footwear, except rubber or plastic		8	4	5	29		1003	409	1294	857		18.6	8.8	22.9	16.7
331 Wood products, except furniture		3	7	6	21		99	311	171	204		1.6	8.6	4.2	3.5
3311 Sawmills, planing and other wood mills		1	-	1	7		8	-	17	56		0.2	-	0.2	1.3
3312 Wooden and cane containers		-	-	-	-		-	-	-	-		-	-	-	-
3319 Other wood and cork products		2	7	5	14		91	311	154	148		1.5	8.6	4.0	2.3
332 Furniture and fixtures, excl. metal		10	19	34	45		823	994	1279	1078		15.9	28.0	28.4	22.1
341 Paper and products		9	6	8	9		1837	1636	1614	1132		137.3	85.3	30.8	36.0
3411 Pulp, paper and paperboard articles		2	2	...	3		189	266	...	373		3.5	3.5	...	11.3
3412 Containers of paper and paperboard		3	2	7	3		963	680	1596	720		30.6	29.3	29.9	23.9
3419 Other pulp, paper and paperboard articles		4	2	1	3		685	690	18	39		103.2	52.5	0.9	0.8
342 Printing and publishing		36	41	79	112		1962	2139	3008	3284		46.8	90.3	81.9	100.2
351 Industrial chemicals		4	6	4	7		564	508	923	955		31.0	16.0	52.6	71.1
3511 Basic chemicals excl. fertilizers		2	1	1	3		67	24	35	77		1.7	1.1	2.4	3.0
3512 Fertilizers and pesticides		2	3	2	2		497	247	801	807		29.3	8.8	48.0	66.7
3513 Synthetic resins and plastic materials		-	2	1	2		-	237	87	71		-	6.1	2.1	1.5
352 Other chemicals		51	50	56	65		4628	4243	4339	5433		155.6	211.4	48.4	245.3
3521 Paints, varnishes and lacquers		2	3	2	2		94	315	46	229		2.1	13.8	9.5	9.7
3522 Drugs and medicines		20	27	35	31		2182	2188	3364	2454		69.6	104.5	0.1	81.3
3523 Soap, cleaning preps., perfumes, cosmetics		15	11	9	18		1893	1322	616	2170		73.1	82.5	20.2	144.0
3529 Other chemical products		14	9	10	14		459	418	313	580		10.8	10.6	18.6	10.3
353 Petroleum refineries		1	1	1	1		64	72	69	69		10.6	14.8	15.3	15.3

Code	Industry														
354	Misc. petroleum and coal products		2	1	3	2		38	14	36	34		2.0	0.2	1.0	2.3
355	Rubber products		11	9	11	13		425	373	1743	398		10.9	12.9	41.7	10.2
3551	Tyres and tubes		6	4	5	4		286	227	292	157		8.7	9.7	11.3	4.6
3559	Other rubber products		5	5	6	9		139	146	1451	241		2.1	3.2	30.3	5.5
356	Plastic products		21	17	16	37		2239	1640	1884	3988		44.6	53.9	47.1	97.6
361	Pottery, china, earthenware		1	3	5	5		12	43	65	55		0.2	0.7	1.0	0.7
362	Glass and products		1	1	4	7		24	25	74	124		0.3	0.5	16.3	2.5
369	Other non-metallic mineral products		19	30	38	68		1355	2112	2284	2922		37.7	92.1	76.8	97.5
3691	Structural clay products		-	-	2	7		-	-	62	81		-	-	1.2	1.5
3692	Cement, lime and plaster		1	1	1	2		382	777	794	794		13.8	42.7	39.7	39.7
3699	Other non-metallic mineral products		18	29	35	59		973	1335	1428	2047		23.9	49.4	36.0	56.3
371	Iron and steel		5	7	7	3		462	679	895	490		8.0	22.8	24.5	17.8
372	Non-ferrous metals		-	2	-	-		-	20	-	-		-	0.6	-	-
381	Fabricated metal products		39	34	52	92		1352	1353	2032	3582		24.8	35.4	49.7	85.6
3811	Cutlery, hand tools and general hardware		2	3	2	3		375	435	381	490		7.0	14.2	9.3	12.9
3812	Furniture and fixtures primarily of metal		10	13	24	21		211	315	487	381		3.1	6.2	9.2	7.1
3813	Structural metal products		9	9	11	38		326	247	684	1183		7.2	6.1	15.4	23.8
3819	Other fabricated metal products		18	9	15	30		440	356	480	1528		7.4	9.0	15.8	41.7
382	Non-electrical machinery		4	11	24	30		88	699	966	971		2.2	29.2	26.5	30.2
3821	Engines and turbines		-	-	-	-		-	-	-	-		-	-	-	-
3822	Agricultural machinery and equipment		-	1	-	1		-	10	-	27		-	0.8	...	0.6
3823	Metal and wood working machinery		-	-	-	2		-	-	-	87		-	-	-	2.2
3824	Other special industrial machinery		2	1	18	14		16	22	432	195		0.4	0.4	10.1	4.6
3825	Office, computing and accounting machinery		-	-	-	1		-	-	-	7		-	-	-	0.1
3829	Other non-electrical machinery & equipment		2	9	6	12		72	667	534	655		1.8	28.0	16.4	22.8
383	Electrical machinery		8	14	7	18		603	726	180	2425		26.2	58.3	6.3	69.4
3831	Electrical industrial machinery		-	2	3	3		-	11	51	60		-	0.1	1.3	1.4
3832	Radio, television and communication equipm.		2	3	1	5		74	83	75	1333		1.4	5.0	3.8	24.4
3833	Electrical appliances and housewares		-	1	-	-		-	41	-	-		-	1.6	-	-
3839	Other electrical apparatus and supplies		6	8	3	10		529	591	54	1032		24.8	51.7	1.2	43.6
384	Transport equipment		5	2	16	10		135	118	170	281		2.7	4.5	2.7	6.4
3841	Shipbuilding and repairing		1	-	1	1		7	-	11	36		0.1	-	0.2	0.9
3842	Railroad equipment		-	-	-	-		-	-	-	-		-	-	-	-
3843	Motor vehicles		3	-	14	8		21	-	153	175		0.4	-	2.4	3.8
3844	Motorcycles and bicycles		-	-	1	1		-	-	6	70		-	-	0.1	1.7
3845	Aircraft		-	-	-	-		-	-	-	-		-	-	-	-
3849	Other transport equipment		1	2	-	-		107	118	-	-		2.1	4.5	-	-
385	Professional and scientific equipment		7	3	1	8		382	107	8	138		8.1	5.2	0.1	4.4
3851	Prof. and scientific equipment n.e.c.		4	-	1	6		328	-	8	104		6.4	-	0.1	2.8
3852	Photographic and optical goods		3	3	-	2		54	107	-	34		1.6	5.2	-	1.5
3853	Watches and clocks		-	-	-	-		-	-	-	-		-	-	...	-
390	Other manufacturing industries		...	19	25	13		...	1193	1309	919		...	32.3	27.3	24.9
3901	Jewellery and related articles		...	2	3	-		...	25	39	-		...	0.6	0.9	-
3902	Musical instruments		...	-	-	-		...	-	-	-		...	-	...	...
3903	Sporting and athletic goods		...	-	2	1		...	-	466	204		...	-	5.4	2.8
3909	Manufacturing industries, n.e.c.		...	17	20	12		...	1168	804	715		...	31.7	21.0	22.1
3	Total manufacturing	a/	478	559	670	1112	a/	45235	51177	54525	88584	a/	1170.1	1881.8	1383.9	2323.5

a/ Sum of available data.

El Salvador

ISIC Revision 2	Output					Value added in producers' prices					Gross fixed capital formation		
		(million COLONES)					(million COLONES)					(million COLONES)	
ISIC Industry	Note	1993	1994	1995	1996	Note	1993	1994	1995	1996	Note	1995	1996
311/2 Food products		1993.9	3513.7	2929.9	4718.9		705.9	276.9	948.2	1426.0		209.4	297.7
3111 Slaughtering, preparing & preserving meat		100.9	833.0	19.5	156.7		53.4	330.0	9.0	55.6		1.2	3.9
3112 Dairy products		71.7	254.5	213.3	255.9		16.5	109.3	90.9	86.3		8.2	8.6
3113 Canning, preserving of fruits & vegetables		58.6	2.3	10.3	184.9		18.8	1.1	4.2	72.2		1.0	0.5
3114 Canning, preserving and processing of fish		-	17.8	41.8	125.2		-	8.4	24.9	47.7		3.2	8.2
3115 Vegetable and animal oils and fats		871.4	815.4	1208.8	1499.4		270.1	269.6	252.4	368.1		19.0	36.8
3116 Grain mill products		36.8	30.2	...	17.2		15.5	21.4	0.4	4.0		...	0.7
3117 Bakery products		97.5	597.8	125.2	356.9		41.1	-907.9	7.7	132.8		11.2	59.3
3118 Sugar factories and refineries		266.2	400.0	679.9	762.7		67.9	278.3	418.0	275.5		145.5	147.0
3119 Cocoa, chocolate and sugar confectionery		57.5	100.0	84.1	124.0		26.0	67.8	29.5	47.1		9.9	5.4
3121 Other food products		338.4	87.0	102.5	648.5		178.3	32.5	40.7	244.7		4.1	11.0
3122 Prepared animal feeds		94.9	375.6	444.4	587.5		18.3	66.3	70.7	92.1		6.2	16.2
313 Beverages		305.1	1061.5	1521.6	1308.9		179.0	906.8	1015.3	756.3		252.4	119.8
3131 Distilling, rectifying and blending spirits		104.6	57.2	45.6	100.6		46.7	17.2	19.6	28.3		2.1	7.0
3132 Wine industries		-	-	-	-		-	-	-	-		-	-
3133 Malt liquors and malt		-	762.3	461.5	401.9		-	648.4	333.1	301.8		89.2	-
3134 Soft drinks and carbonated waters		200.6	242.0	1014.5	806.5		132.3	241.2	662.6	426.3		161.1	112.8
314 Tobacco		264.5	307.0	341.5	358.5		217.8	261.1	281.3	264.6		13.0	18.3
321 Textiles		905.5	1112.1	1375.4	1666.1		381.9	507.9	635.8	589.1		136.9	88.6
3211 Spinning, weaving and finishing textiles		723.2	644.7	775.6	1157.8		307.0	295.2	319.6	318.7		47.5	54.6
3212 Made-up textile goods excl. wearing apparel		15.0	281.9	328.5	110.7		7.4	111.8	120.5	60.9		52.9	15.2
3213 Knitting mills		167.2	185.5	271.3	397.2		67.5	100.9	195.6	209.1		36.5	18.7
3214 Carpets and rugs		-	-	-	0.4		-	-	-	0.3		-	-
3215 Cordage, rope and twine		-	-	-	-		-	-	-	-		-	-
3219 Other textiles		-	-	-	-		-	-	-	-		-	-
322 Wearing apparel, except footwear		418.7	...	566.5	1381.3		243.0	370.1	466.2	1008.8		74.6	42.9
323 Leather and fur products		88.5	30.6	23.1	73.8		40.5	17.0	4.2	38.2		13.0	2.3
3231 Tanneries and leather finishing		50.9	8.5	23.1	20.5		19.7	3.7	4.2	1.0		13.0	1.7
3232 Fur dressing and dyeing industries		-	-	-	-		-	-	-	-		-	-
3233 Leather prods. excl. wearing apparel		37.6	22.1	...	53.2		20.8	13.3	...	37.2		...	0.6
324 Footwear, except rubber or plastic		86.0	27.9	133.0	78.2		...	14.2	64.1	35.9		11.0	0.5
331 Wood products, except furniture		5.8	31.0	10.9	13.3		3.5	25.6	19.8	7.1		1.0	0.2
3311 Sawmills, planing and other wood mills		0.4	-	0.6	6.1		0.2	-	0.5	2.9		0.1	0.2
3312 Wooden and cane containers		-	-	-	-		-	-	-	-		-	-
3319 Other wood and cork products		5.4	31.0	10.3	7.2		3.3	25.6	19.3	4.3		1.0	0.1
332 Furniture and fixtures, excl. metal		107.0	100.4	167.2	135.0		48.5	36.4	42.4	59.7		19.7	3.6
341 Paper and products		488.8	512.4	697.7	389.4		183.8	216.3	309.6	255.5		19.5	30.6
3411 Pulp, paper and paperboard articles		14.1	22.0	...	286.5		5.6	8.9	...	194.3		...	30.0
3412 Containers of paper and paperboard		225.0	243.0	693.4	96.2		57.8	67.5	307.6	57.9		19.5	0.6
3419 Other pulp, paper and paperboard articles		249.7	247.4	4.4	6.6		120.3	140.0	2.0	3.3		...	-
342 Printing and publishing		415.2	...	312.0	673.1		233.7	342.1	419.5	388.8		42.9	42.8
351 Industrial chemicals		391.7	181.5	272.9	648.1		114.0	45.5	160.4	228.1		18.8	6.6
3511 Basic chemicals excl. fertilizers		30.0	15.4	18.2	24.6		14.9	9.4	8.7	14.9		0.7	0.9
3512 Fertilizers and pesticides		361.7	127.0	239.8	594.3		99.2	16.6	144.8	208.5		18.1	5.6
3513 Synthetic resins and plastic materials		-	39.0	15.0	29.2		-	19.6	6.9	4.7		...	0.1
352 Other chemicals		1673.6	1375.9	644.3	2585.8		776.4	745.3	223.1	1426.6		51.1	114.5
3521 Paints, varnishes and lacquers		25.1	170.5	178.6	190.8		10.3	66.4	65.2	68.4		0.2	2.2
3522 Drugs and medicines		626.0	466.7	1.8	638.2		349.9	307.8	0.4	398.9		...	35.3
3523 Soap, cleaning preps., perfumes, cosmetics		936.9	687.3	208.8	1687.1		376.9	347.3	62.5	932.1		5.6	77.0
3529 Other chemical products		85.6	51.4	255.1	69.8		39.3	23.8	94.9	27.2		45.4	-
353 Petroleum refineries		1867.0	1256.8	1243.5	2075.1		520.1	59.9	735.4	865.2		18.8	18.8

ISIC	Industry													
354	Misc. petroleum and coal products		99.6	...	9.2	167.6		21.7	0.4	2.4	37.5		5.1	8.0
355	Rubber products		93.5	...	108.0	74.1		40.6	31.3	104.6	38.4		31.2	2.8
3551	Tyres and tubes		77.4	...	35.4	26.5		31.9	23.3	60.5	15.4		11.7	0.3
3559	Other rubber products		16.1	15.0	72.6	47.6		8.7	7.9	44.1	23.1		19.5	2.5
356	Plastic products		354.7	314.7	234.1	741.2		166.1	145.5	91.0	273.3		51.1	28.3
361	Pottery, china, earthenware		1.0	2.1	2.1	2.1		0.8	1.6	2.3	1.4		0.7	1.3
362	Glass and products		4.3	3.5	4.2	10.4		0.9	0.7	-1.0	5.2		0.1	-
369	Other non-metallic mineral products		268.7	830.1	861.9	1013.8		138.9	487.5	458.5	453.3		-286.9	50.9
3691	Structural clay products		-	-	6.5	5.9		-	-	2.7	2.1		-335.1	0.1
3692	Cement, lime and plaster		82.2	532.9	582.0	597.5		46.1	349.6	326.5	264.9		32.4	32.4
3699	Other non-metallic mineral products		186.6	297.1	273.3	410.4		92.8	137.8	129.2	186.3		15.8	18.5
371	Iron and steel		95.8	213.9	475.9	262.3		21.8	82.9	120.1	67.3		64.6	6.2
372	Non-ferrous metals		-	7.3	-	-		-	1.1	-	-		-	-
381	Fabricated metal products		173.4	140.3	262.1	521.0		82.9	107.4	249.1	192.4		15.5	41.5
3811	Cutlery, hand tools and general hardware		59.1	63.8	43.6	75.3		31.8	34.0	155.4	30.5		1.9	3.1
3812	Furniture and fixtures primarily of metal		17.9	26.6	41.0	30.6		9.1	19.2	27.4	16.6		3.4	1.4
3813	Structural metal products		50.2	15.6	74.8	96.1		20.5	14.0	25.4	54.0		5.3	2.9
3819	Other fabricated metal products		46.3	34.4	102.8	319.1		21.4	40.2	40.9	91.3		4.8	34.1
382	Non-electrical machinery		21.0	206.7	175.2	236.6		16.4	104.5	40.8	111.5		5.6	8.4
3821	Engines and turbines		-	-	-	-		-	-	-	-		-	-
3822	Agricultural machinery and equipment		-	3.1	...	2.0		-	1.9	...	1.3		...	0.3
3823	Metal and wood working machinery		-	-	-	8.6		-	-	-	3.8		-	-
3824	Other special industrial machinery		1.6	1.6	46.7	14.3		0.8	1.4	20.8	8.6		2.9	1.4
3825	Office, computing and accounting machinery		-	-	-	1.5		-	-	-	0.7		-	-0.3
3829	Other non-electrical machinery & equipment		19.5	201.9	128.5	210.1		15.6	101.1	20.1	97.2		2.8	7.0
383	Electrical machinery		411.2	329.2	26.9	717.9		160.1	164.1	36.8	214.5		1.4	96.0
3831	Electrical industrial machinery		-	0.4	3.4	5.7		-	0.1	6.2	2.3		...	0.5
3832	Radio, television and communication equipm.		69.9	14.4	13.7	328.2		21.5	22.8	26.4	71.3		0.6	0.5
3833	Electrical appliances and housewares		-	4.6	-	-		-	3.2	-	-		-	-
3839	Other electrical apparatus and supplies		341.3	309.8	9.8	384.0		138.7	138.0	4.1	140.9		0.8	95.0
384	Transport equipment		27.8	29.7	2.3	37.5		13.1	18.8	5.3	15.9		3.0	2.0
3841	Shipbuilding and repairing		0.7	-	0.8	11.8		0.2	-	-	3.7		0.1	0.9
3842	Railroad equipment		-	-	-	-		-	-	-	-		-	-
3843	Motor vehicles		2.6	-	1.2	24.9		1.4	-	4.8	12.0		2.9	1.1
3844	Motorcycles and bicycles		-	-	0.3	0.8		-	-	0.5	0.1		-	-
3845	Aircraft		-	-	-	-		-	-	-	-		-	-
3849	Other transport equipment		24.5	29.7	-	-		11.5	18.8	-	-		-	-
385	Professional and scientific equipment		47.1	26.3	0.3	18.6		27.4	17.2	-	12.5		-0.1	1.8
3851	Prof. and scientific equipment n.e.c.		36.1	-	0.3	13.6		19.0	-	-	9.5		-0.1	1.8
3852	Photographic and optical goods		11.0	26.3	-	5.0		8.4	17.2	-	3.1		-	-
3853	Watches and clocks		-	-	-	-		-	-	-	-		-	-
390	Other manufacturing industries		...	108.6	108.1	143.9		...	60.2	72.7	83.1		29.7	7.4
3901	Jewellery and related articles		...	1.3	3.2	-		...	1.1	2.1	-		0.1	-
3902	Musical instruments		...	-	...	-		...	-	...	-		...	-
3903	Sporting and athletic goods		...	-	14.0	4.9		...	-	13.3	4.2		0.3	0.2
3909	Manufacturing industries, n.e.c.		...	107.3	90.9	139.0		...	59.1	57.2	78.9		29.3	7.3
3	Total manufacturing	a/	10609.4	11723.3	12509.7	20052.4	a/	4338.9	5048.3	6507.9	8856.1	a/	803.0	1041.8

a/ Sum of available data.

El Salvador

ISIC Revision 2		Index numbers of industrial production (1990=100)											
ISIC Industry	Note	1985	1986	1987	1988	1989	1990	1991	1992	1993	1994	1995	1996
311/2 Food products	a/	...	...	...	...	...	100	103	112	115	121	127	129
313 Beverages	a/	...	...	...	...	...	...	...	...	...	...	...	...
314 Tobacco		85	88	89	95	96	100	104	104	89	92	94	88
321 Textiles		80	95	100	90	97	100	104	113	101	102	111	108
322 Wearing apparel, except footwear		...	...	...	...	...	100	106	113	83	87	90	89
323 Leather and fur products		98	83	81	89	97	100	106	111	111	120	128	124
324 Footwear, except rubber or plastic		...	...	...	...	...	...	...	...	...	...	...	...
331 Wood products, except furniture	b/	...	...	...	...	...	100	104	107	122	142	156	144
332 Furniture and fixtures, excl. metal	b/	...	...	...	...	...	...	...	...	...	...	...	...
341 Paper and products		104	84	82	84	91	100	104	111	111	119	121	119
342 Printing and publishing		93	80	83	85	93	100	104	112	118	128	136	148
351 Industrial chemicals	c/	84	88	89	90	97	100	107	117	109	130	143	138
352 Other chemicals	c/	...	...	...	...	...	...	...	...	...	...	...	...
353 Petroleum refineries		89	90	93	91	98	100	128	167	141	136	119	119
354 Misc. petroleum and coal products		...	...	...	...	...	...	...	...	...	...	...	...
355 Rubber products	d/	...	...	...	...	...	100	105	112	75	77	82	77
356 Plastic products	d/	...	...	...	...	...	...	...	...	...	...	...	...
361 Pottery, china, earthenware	e/	78	82	94	94	100	100	106	115	128	135	138	137
362 Glass and products	e/	...	...	...	...	...	...	...	...	...	...	...	...
369 Other non-metallic mineral products	e/	...	...	...	...	...	...	...	...	...	...	...	...
371 Iron and steel	f/	...	...	...	...	...	100	103	109	106	111	118	126
372 Non-ferrous metals	f/	...	...	...	...	...	...	...	...	...	...	...	...
381 Fabricated metal products	f/	...	...	...	...	...	...	...	...	...	...	...	...
382 Non-electrical machinery		...	...	...	...	...	...	...	...	...	...	...	...
383 Electrical machinery		...	...	...	...	...	...	...	...	...	...	...	...
384 Transport equipment	g/	...	...	...	...	...	100	105	129	138	159	184	184
385 Professional and scientific equipment		...	...	...	...	...	...	...	...	...	...	...	...
390 Other manufacturing industries	g/	...	...	...	...	...	...	...	...	...	...	...	...
3 Total manufacturing		...	...	...	...	...	...	...	...	...	...	...	...

a/ 311/2 includes 313.
b/ 331 includes 332.
c/ 351 includes 352.
d/ 355 includes 356.
e/ 361 includes 362 and 369.
f/ 371 includes 372 and 381.
g/ 384 includes 390.

ERITREA

Supplier of information:
Ministry of Trade and Industry, Department of Industry, Asmara.

Basic source of data:
Survey of the manufacturing industry.

Major deviations from ISIC (Revision 3):
None reported.

Reference period (if not calendar year):

Scope:
Establishments with 10 or more persons engaged.

Method of enumeration:
Complete enumeration.

Adjusted for non-response:
Not reported.

Concepts and definitions of variables:
Wages and salaries is compensation of employees.

Related national publications:

Eritrea

ISIC Revision 3		Number of establishments					Number of employees					Wages and salaries paid to employees			
		(numbers)					(numbers)					(thousand NAKFA)			
ISIC Industry	Note	1993	1994	1995	1996	Note	1993	1994	1995	1996	Note	1993	1994	1995	1996
15 Food and beverages	a/	36	38	43	53	a/	3974	4218	4357	4292	a/	12837	14682	14172	17789
16 Tobacco products	a/	...	...	...	...	a/	...	...	...	...	a/	...	...	...	...
17 Textiles	b/	12	13	12	12	b/	5331	4518	4310	3967	b/	13746	17194	15998	18828
18 Wearing apparel, fur	b/	...	...	...	...	b/	...	...	...	...	b/	...	...	...	
19 Leather, leather products and footwear		12	16	18	18		1065	1100	963	958		5489	6054	6009	5291
20 Wood products (excl. furniture)		...	...	...	...		...	...	...	...		...	...	...	...
21 Paper and paper products	c/	5	5	6	7	c/	414	412	436	466	c/	2248	2310	2461	2550
22 Printing and publishing	c/	...	...	...	...	c/	...	...	...	...	c/	...	...	...	...
23 Coke,refined petroleum products,nuclear fuel		...	...	...	...		...	...	...	...		...	...	...	...
24 Chemicals and chemical products		10	9	10	10		1286	1230	1052	777		6579	6700	7545	6486
25 Rubber and plastic products		2	2	2	4		664	728	670	697		3365	3836	4247	4149
26 Non-metallic mineral products		15	19	21	26		1088	1113	922	1075		5045	5837	5139	5961
27 Basic metals	d/	6	6	6	6	d/	708	648	559	516	d/	2449	2740	2549	2621
28 Fabricated metal products	d/	...	...	...	...	d/	...	...	...	...	d/	...	...	...	...
29 Machinery and equipment n.e.c.	e/	2	3	4	4	e/	105	113	112	95	e/	811	916	928	845
30 Office, accounting and computing machinery		...	...	...	...		...	...	...	...		...	...	...	...
31 Electrical machinery and apparatus	e/	...	...	...	...	e/	...	...	...	...	e/	...	...	...	...
32 Radio,television and communication equipment		...	...	...	...		...	...	...	...		...	...	...	...
33 Medical, precision and optical instruments		2	3	4	4		37	62	79	86		111	478	551	648
34 Motor vehicles, trailers, semi-trailers	e/	...	...	...	...	e/	...	...	...	...	e/	...	...	...	...
35 Other transport equipment		...	...	...	...		...	...	...	...		...	...	...	...
36 Furniture; manufacturing n.e.c.		7	9	10	13		269	293	276	292		1600	1577	1933	1936
37 Recycling		...	...	...	...		...	...	...	...		...	...	...	...
D Total manufacturing		109	123	136	157		14941	14435	13736	13221		54279	62323	61532	67105

a/ 15 includes 16.
b/ 17 includes 18.
c/ 21 includes 22.
d/ 27 includes 28.
e/ 29 includes 31 and 34.

Eritrea

ISIC Revision 3		Note	Output in producers' prices (thousand NAKFA) 1993	1994	1995	1996	Note	Value added in producers' prices (thousand NAKFA) 1993	1994	1995	1996	Note	Gross fixed capital formation (thousand NAKFA) 1995	1996
15	Food and beverages	a/	212842	248935	342183	451410	a/	123786	135267	188894	222570		...	...
16	Tobacco products	a/	...	...	...	...	a/	...	...	...	...		...	...
17	Textiles	b/	57703	52735	79178	80761	b/	7885	5265	11220	8761		...	...
18	Wearing apparel, fur	b/	...	...	...	...	b/	...	...	...	...		...	...
19	Leather, leather products and footwear		24445	33636	52476	63809		1675	2322	12263	18785		...	...
20	Wood products (excl. furniture)		...	...	...	...		...	...	...	...		...	...
21	Paper and paper products	c/	18093	18248	20558	21154	c/	9364	5743	6600	7554		...	...
22	Printing and publishing	c/	...	...	...	...	c/	...	...	...	...		...	...
23	Coke,refined petroleum products,nuclear fuel		...	...	...	...		...	...	...	...		...	...
24	Chemicals and chemical products		70083	82230	98620	73841		48437	52342	68683	42595		...	...
25	Rubber and plastic products		20893	25220	41991	52141		8004	5332	12414	6912		...	...
26	Non-metallic mineral products		43714	45477	44501	47183		19577	19786	22409	23955		...	...
27	Basic metals	d/	30777	31598	43381	47701	d/	11143	17334	16097	744		...	...
28	Fabricated metal products	d/	...	...	...	...	d/	...	...	...	...		...	...
29	Machinery and equipment n.e.c.	e/	6979	8024	8541	4741	e/	3492	2131	2170	1570		...	...
30	Office, accounting and computing machinery		...	...	...	...		...	...	...	...		...	...
31	Electrical machinery and apparatus	e/	...	...	...	...	e/	...	...	...	...		...	...
32	Radio,television and communication equipment		...	...	...	...		...	...	...	...		...	...
33	Medical, precision and optical instruments		752	962	1713	2490		441	725	550	574		...	...
34	Motor vehicles, trailers, semi-trailers	e/	...	...	...	...	e/	...	...	...	...		...	...
35	Other transport equipment		...	...	...	...		...	...	...	...		...	...
36	Furniture; manufacturing n.e.c.		8554	8177	10373	11377		4282	2536	3249	4784		...	...
37	Recycling		...	...	...	...		...	...	...	...		...	...
D	Total manufacturing		494835	555240	743514	856607		238086	248782	344549	338804		...	...

a/ 15 includes 16.
b/ 17 includes 18.
c/ 21 includes 22.
d/ 27 includes 28.
e/ 29 includes 31and 34.

ESTONIA

Supplier of information:
State Statistical Office of Estonia, Tallin.

Basic source of data:
Not reported.

Major deviations from ISIC (Revision 3):
None reported.

Reference period (if not calendar year):

Scope:
Not reported.

Method of enumeration:
Not reported.

Adjusted for non-response:
Not reported.

Concepts and definitions of variables:
No deviations from the standard UN concepts and definitions are reported.

Related national publications:
National Accounts in Estonia, published by the State Statistical Office of Estonia. Tallin.

Estonia

ISIC Revision 3	Number of establishments					Number of employees a/					Wages and salaries paid a/ to employees				
		(numbers)					(numbers)					(thousand KROON)			
ISIC Industry	Note	1993	1994	1995	1996	Note	1993	1994	1995	1996	Note	1993	1994	1995	1996
151 Processed meat,fish,fruit,vegetables,fats		110	165	154	147		...	...	...	...		...	...	...	...
1511 Processing/preserving of meat		56	88	81	71		...	...	...	...		...	...	...	...
1512 Processing/preserving of fish		38	56	57	57		...	...	...	...		...	...	...	...
1513 Processing/preserving of fruit & vegetables		13	18	13	15		...	...	...	...		...	...	...	...
1514 Vegetable and animal oils and fats		3	3	3	4		...	...	...	...		...	...	...	...
1520 Dairy products		32	39	39	38		...	...	...	...		...	...	...	...
153 Grain mill products; starches; animal feeds		29	41	46	44		...	...	...	...		...	...	...	...
1531 Grain mill products		10	16	19	20		...	...	...	...		...	...	...	...
1532 Starches and starch products		5	5	5	5		...	...	...	...		...	...	...	...
1533 Prepared animal feeds		14	20	22	19		...	...	...	...		...	...	...	...
154 Other food products		84	143	156	154		...	...	...	...		...	...	...	...
1541 Bakery products		67	116	129	124		...	...	...	...		...	...	...	...
1542 Sugar		-	-	-	-		...	...	...	...		...	...	...	...
1543 Cocoa, chocolate and sugar confectionery		5	5	4	10		...	...	...	...		...	...	...	...
1544 Macaroni, noodles & similar products		-	-	-	-		...	...	...	...		...	...	...	...
1549 Other food products n.e.c.		12	22	23	20		...	...	...	...		...	...	...	...
155 Beverages		28	35	36	33		...	...	...	...		...	...	...	...
1551 Distilling, rectifying & blending of spirits		3	7	7	7		...	...	...	...		...	...	...	...
1552 Wines		5	6	6	6		...	...	...	...		...	...	...	...
1553 Malt liquors and malt		13	13	14	12		...	...	...	...		...	...	...	...
1554 Soft drinks; mineral waters		7	9	9	8		...	...	...	...		...	...	...	...
1600 Tobacco products		1	1	1	1		...	...	...	...		...	...	...	...
171 Spinning, weaving and finishing of textiles		26	33	40	32		...	...	...	...		...	...	...	...
1711 Textile fibre preparation; textile weaving		26	30	35	27		...	...	...	...		...	...	...	...
1712 Finishing of textiles		-	3	5	5		...	...	...	...		...	...	...	...
172 Other textiles		50	75	84	88		...	...	...	...		...	...	...	...
1721 Made-up textile articles, except apparel		16	37	45	51		...	...	...	...		...	...	...	...
1722 Carpets and rugs		15	21	24	22		...	...	...	...		...	...	...	...
1723 Cordage, rope, twine and netting		4	7	7	9		...	...	...	...		...	...	...	...
1729 Other textiles n.e.c.		15	10	8	6		...	...	...	...		...	...	...	...
1730 Knitted and crocheted fabrics and articles		72	120	102	84		...	...	...	...		...	...	...	...
1810 Wearing apparel, except fur apparel		290	408	430	412		...	...	...	...		...	...	...	...
1820 Dressing & dyeing of fur; processing of fur		21	25	21	21		...	...	...	...		...	...	...	...
191 Tanning, dressing and processing of leather		42	70	64	57		...	...	...	...		...	...	...	...
1911 Tanning and dressing of leather		5	11	5	5		...	...	...	...		...	...	...	...
1912 Luggage, handbags, etc.; saddlery & harness		37	59	59	52		...	...	...	...		...	...	...	...
1920 Footwear		45	53	43	37		...	...	...	...		...	...	...	...
2010 Sawmilling and planing of wood		230	432	473	481		...	...	...	...		...	...	...	...
202 Products of wood, cork, straw, etc.		284	386	401	371		...	...	...	...		...	...	...	...
2021 Veneer sheets, plywood, particle board, etc.		11	16	13	12		...	...	...	...		...	...	...	...
2022 Builders' carpentry and joinery		170	234	246	241		...	...	...	...		...	...	...	...
2023 Wooden containers		14	16	14	11		...	...	...	...		...	...	...	...
2029 Other wood products; articles of cork/straw		89	120	128	107		...	...	...	...		...	...	...	...
210 Paper and paper products		26	39	41	44		...	...	...	...		...	...	...	...
2101 Pulp, paper and paperboard		8	8	6	7		...	...	...	...		...	...	...	...
2102 Corrugated paper and paperboard		11	17	19	15		...	...	...	...		...	...	...	...
2109 Other articles of paper and paperboard		7	14	16	22		...	...	...	...		...	...	...	...
221 Publishing		203	280	330	307		...	...	...	...		...	...	...	...
2211 Publishing of books and other publications		72	123	133	141		...	...	...	...		...	...	...	...
2212 Publishing of newspapers, journals, etc.		111	141	169	140		...	...	...	...		...	...	...	...
2213 Publishing of recorded media		1	2	3	4		...	...	...	...		...	...	...	...
2219 Other publishing		19	14	25	22		...	...	...	...		...	...	...	...

222	Printing and related service activities	81	116	125	118	...	...	...	...	...	...	...	...
2221	Printing	69	95	106	108	...	...	...	...	...	...	...	...
2222	Service activities related to printing	12	21	19	10	...	...	...	...	...	...	...	...
2230	Reproduction of recorded media	10	9	8	9	...	...	...	...	...	...	...	...
2310	Coke oven products	-	-	-	-	...	...	...	...	...	...	...	...
2320	Refined petroleum products	7	7	7	11	...	...	...	...	...	...	...	...
2330	Processing of nuclear fuel	-	1	-	-	...	...	...	...	...	...	...	...
241	Basic chemicals	11	14	18	16	...	...	...	...	...	...	...	...
2411	Basic chemicals, except fertilizers	7	11	13	11	...	...	...	...	...	...	...	...
2412	Fertilizers and nitrogen compounds	4	3	4	4	...	...	...	...	...	...	...	...
2413	Plastics in primary forms; synthetic rubber	-	-	1	1	...	...	...	...	...	...	...	...
242	Other chemicals	64	82	81	79	...	...	...	...	...	...	...	...
2421	Pesticides and other agro-chemical products	2	2	4	4	...	...	...	...	...	...	...	...
2422	Paints, varnishes, printing ink and mastics	12	17	14	16	...	...	...	...	...	...	...	...
2423	Pharmaceuticals, medicinal chemicals, etc.	15	22	21	17	...	...	...	...	...	...	...	...
2424	Soap, cleaning & cosmetic preparations	21	23	31	31	...	...	...	...	...	...	...	...
2429	Other chemical products n.e.c.	14	18	11	11	...	...	...	...	...	...	...	...
2430	Man-made fibres	1	-	-	-	...	...	...	...	...	...	...	...
251	Rubber products	17	22	16	15	...	...	...	...	...	...	...	...
2511	Rubber tyres and tubes	7	10	7	8	...	...	...	...	...	...	...	...
2519	Other rubber products	10	12	9	7	...	...	...	...	...	...	...	...
2520	Plastic products	67	95	100	105	...	...	...	...	...	...	...	...
2610	Glass and glass products	11	18	22	16	...	...	...	...	...	...	...	...
269	Non-metallic mineral products n.e.c.	172	191	176	164	...	...	...	...	...	...	...	...
2691	Pottery, china and earthenware	15	20	16	16	...	...	...	...	...	...	...	...
2692	Refractory ceramic products	7	7	5	5	...	...	...	...	...	...	...	...
2693	Struct.non-refractory clay; ceramic products	13	11	11	13	...	...	...	...	...	...	...	...
2694	Cement, lime and plaster	3	5	4	5	...	...	...	...	...	...	...	...
2695	Articles of concrete, cement and plaster	91	89	84	72	...	...	...	...	...	...	...	...
2696	Cutting, shaping & finishing of stone	31	46	45	45	...	...	...	...	...	...	...	...
2699	Other non-metallic mineral products n.e.c.	12	13	11	8	...	...	...	...	...	...	...	...
2710	Basic iron and steel	-	-	1	1	...	...	...	...	...	...	...	...
2720	Basic precious and non-ferrous metals	2	3	5	3	...	...	...	...	...	...	...	...
273	Casting of metals	7	6	7	10	...	...	...	...	...	...	...	...
2731	Casting of iron and steel	2	3	2	4	...	...	...	...	...	...	...	...
2732	Casting of non-ferrous metals	5	3	4	6	...	...	...	...	...	...	...	...
281	Struct.metal products;tanks;steam generators	72	90	104	102	...	...	...	...	...	...	...	...
2811	Structural metal products	60	72	86	86	...	...	...	...	...	...	...	...
2812	Tanks, reservoirs and containers of metal	8	12	10	11	...	...	...	...	...	...	...	...
2813	Steam generators	4	6	8	5	...	...	...	...	...	...	...	...
289	Other metal products; metal working services	185	251	277	277	...	...	...	...	...	...	...	...
2891	Metal forging/pressing/stamping/roll-forming	19	21	24	21	...	...	...	...	...	...	...	...
2892	Treatment & coating of metals	28	43	56	65	...	...	...	...	...	...	...	...
2893	Cutlery, hand tools and general hardware	32	35	35	28	...	...	...	...	...	...	...	...
2899	Other fabricated metal products n.e.c.	106	152	162	163	...	...	...	...	...	...	...	...
291	General purpose machinery	71	97	89	97	...	...	...	...	...	...	...	...
2911	Engines & turbines(not for transport equip.)	12	9	6	3	...	...	...	...	...	...	...	...
2912	Pumps, compressors, taps and valves	7	6	6	5	...	...	...	...	...	...	...	...
2913	Bearings, gears, gearing & driving elements	-	-	-	-	...	...	...	...	...	...	...	...
2914	Ovens, furnaces and furnace burners	5	9	4	3	...	...	...	...	...	...	...	...
2915	Lifting and handling equipment	8	18	14	14	...	...	...	...	...	...	...	...
2919	Other general purpose machinery	39	55	59	72	...	...	...	...	...	...	...	...
292	Special purpose machinery	167	202	176	158	...	...	...	...	...	...	...	...
2921	Agricultural and forestry machinery	123	146	118	109	...	...	...	...	...	...	...	...
2922	Machine tools	5	9	14	12	...	...	...	...	...	...	...	...
2923	Machinery for metallurgy	-	-	-	-	...	...	...	...	...	...	...	...
2924	Machinery for mining & construction	5	6	5	5	...	...	...	...	...	...	...	...
2925	Food/beverage/tobacco processing machinery	5	8	9	9	...	...	...	...	...	...	...	...
2926	Machinery for textile, apparel and leather	2	4	2	2	...	...	...	...	...	...	...	...
2927	Weapons and ammunition	-	1	2	1	...	...	...	...	...	...	...	...
2929	Other special purpose machinery	27	28	26	20	...	...	...	...	...	...	...	...
2930	Domestic appliances n.e.c.	3	6	8	6	...	...	...	...	...	...	...	...

continued

Estonia

ISIC Revision 3 ISIC Industry	Number of establishments Note	(numbers) 1993	1994	1995	1996	Number of employees a/ Note	(numbers) 1993	1994	1995	1996	Wages and salaries paid a/ to employees Note	(thousand KROON) 1993	1994	1995	1996
3000 Office, accounting and computing machinery		75	76	78	8		...	...	...	...		...	...	...	...
3110 Electric motors, generators and transformers		20	30	30	30		...	...	...	...		...	...	...	...
3120 Electricity distribution & control apparatus		26	29	27	25		...	...	...	...		...	...	...	...
3130 Insulated wire and cable		9	7	6	5		...	...	...	...		...	...	...	...
3140 Accumulators, primary cells and batteries		-	1	2	1		...	...	...	...		...	...	...	...
3150 Lighting equipment and electric lamps		3	8	8	7		...	...	...	...		...	...	...	...
3190 Other electrical equipment n.e.c.		57	64	58	54		...	...	...	...		...	...	...	...
3210 Electronic valves, tubes, etc.		16	24	32	41		...	...	...	...		...	...	...	...
3220 TV/radio transmitters; line comm. apparatus		5	5	3	3		...	...	...	...		...	...	...	...
3230 TV and radio receivers and associated goods		25	26	29	81		...	...	...	...		...	...	...	...
331 Medical, measuring, testing appliances, etc.		51	65	79	78		...	...	...	...		...	...	...	...
3311 Medical, surgical and orthopaedic equipment		15	17	25	27		...	...	...	...		...	...	...	...
3312 Measuring/testing/navigating appliances,etc.		27	43	46	39		...	...	...	...		...	...	...	...
3313 Industrial process control equipment		9	5	8	12		...	...	...	...		...	...	...	...
3320 Optical instruments & photographic equipment		13	16	18	19		...	...	...	...		...	...	...	...
3330 Watches and clocks		-	1	1	1		...	...	...	...		...	...	...	...
3410 Motor vehicles		13	16	17	17		...	...	...	...		...	...	...	...
3420 Automobile bodies, trailers & semi-trailers		4	10	5	4		...	...	...	...		...	...	...	...
3430 Parts/accessories for automobiles		20	12	14	11		...	...	...	...		...	...	...	...
351 Building and repairing of ships and boats		37	59	53	52		...	...	...	...		...	...	...	...
3511 Building and repairing of ships		23	35	31	34		...	...	...	...		...	...	...	...
3512 Building/repairing of pleasure/sport. boats		14	24	22	18		...	...	...	...		...	...	...	...
3520 Railway/tramway locomotives & rolling stock		1	2	2	2		...	...	...	...		...	...	...	...
3530 Aircraft and spacecraft		-	-	1	1		...	...	...	...		...	...	...	...
359 Transport equipment n.e.c.		1	-	-	-		...	...	...	...		...	...	...	...
3591 Motorcycles		-	-	-	-		...	...	...	...		...	...	...	...
3592 Bicycles and invalid carriages		-	-	-	-		...	...	...	...		...	...	...	...
3599 Other transport equipment n.e.c.		1	-	-	-		...	...	...	...		...	...	...	...
3610 Furniture		130	167	199	210		...	...	...	...		...	...	...	...
369 Manufacturing n.e.c.		154	204	226	207		...	...	...	...		...	...	...	...
3691 Jewellery and related articles		13	19	28	25		...	...	...	...		...	...	...	...
3692 Musical instruments		4	5	5	3		...	...	...	...		...	...	...	...
3693 Sports goods		11	13	13	16		...	...	...	...		...	...	...	...
3694 Games and toys		5	14	15	14		...	...	...	...		...	...	...	...
3699 Other manufacturing n.e.c.		121	153	165	149		...	...	...	...		...	...	...	...
3710 Recycling of metal waste and scrap		12	10	10	4		...	...	...	...		...	...	...	...
3720 Recycling of non-metal waste and scrap		11	11	14	14		...	...	...	...		...	...	...	...
D Total manufacturing		3204	4398	4593	4413		...	...	134111	123285		...	2899368	2874060	4336488

a/ Data are based on "Economic indicators of enterprises in Estonia".

Estonia

ISIC Revision 3		Output				Value added a/					Gross fixed capital formation a/		
		(million KROON)					(million KROON)					(million KROON)	
ISIC Industry	Note	1993	1994	1995	1996	Note	1993	1994	1995	1996	Note	1995	1996
151 Processed meat,fish,fruit,vegetables,fats		2065.3	2490.8	2407.8	2888.1		...	...	...	...		...	...
1511 Processing/preserving of meat		1381.9	1228.4	1241.5	1236.9		...	...	...	...		...	...
1512 Processing/preserving of fish		626.6	1155.9	1038.9	1492.2		...	...	...	...		...	...
1513 Processing/preserving of fruit & vegetables		43.2	92.8	105.6	127.0		...	...	...	...		...	...
1514 Vegetable and animal oils and fats		13.6	13.7	21.8	32.0		...	...	...	...		...	...
1520 Dairy products		1195.0	1368.2	1883.3	2259.7		...	...	...	...		...	...
153 Grain mill products; starches; animal feeds		420.6	428.3	373.9	340.9		...	...	...	...		...	...
1531 Grain mill products		51.4	62.5	78.8	90.7		...	...	...	...		...	...
1532 Starches and starch products		6.2	4.8	2.7	4.2		...	...	...	...		...	...
1533 Prepared animal feeds		363.0	361.1	292.4	246.0		...	...	...	...		...	...
154 Other food products		752.4	961.0	1146.0	1384.3		...	...	...	...		...	...
1541 Bakery products		506.6	606.0	755.8	928.8		...	...	...	...		...	...
1542 Sugar		-	-	-	-		...	...	...	...		...	...
1543 Cocoa, chocolate and sugar confectionery		207.0	272.4	235.7	323.0		...	...	...	...		...	...
1544 Macaroni, noodles & similar products		-	-	-	-		...	...	...	...		...	...
1549 Other food products n.e.c.		38.7	82.6	154.5	132.5		...	...	...	...		...	...
155 Beverages		890.3	1090.5	1545.9	1566.2		...	...	...	...		...	...
1551 Distilling, rectifying & blending of spirits		610.8	607.6	842.3	686.5		...	...	...	...		...	...
1552 Wines		20.5	20.7	20.2	34.0		...	...	...	...		...	...
1553 Malt liquors and malt		157.5	276.3	357.9	410.9		...	...	...	...		...	...
1554 Soft drinks; mineral waters		101.5	185.9	325.5	434.8		...	...	...	...		...	...
1600 Tobacco products		149.0	179.9	197.1	...		...	...	...	...		...	...
171 Spinning, weaving and finishing of textiles		462.8	...	1002.8	1471.5		...	...	...	...		...	...
1711 Textile fibre preparation; textile weaving		462.8	583.4	941.0	1363.2		...	...	...	...		...	...
1712 Finishing of textiles		-	...	61.8	108.3		...	...	...	...		...	...
172 Other textiles		111.8	181.0	365.5	520.7		...	...	...	...		...	...
1721 Made-up textile articles, except apparel		1.8	62.0	214.7	366.9		...	...	...	...		...	...
1722 Carpets and rugs		93.6	93.3	128.6	132.4		...	...	...	...		...	...
1723 Cordage, rope, twine and netting		3.4	12.0	10.9	11.4		...	...	...	...		...	...
1729 Other textiles n.e.c.		13.0	13.7	11.3	10.0		...	...	...	...		...	...
1730 Knitted and crocheted fabrics and articles		89.6	143.8	177.6	159.6		...	...	...	...		...	...
1810 Wearing apparel, except fur apparel		541.3	631.4	886.2	1082.2		...	...	...	...		...	...
1820 Dressing & dyeing of fur; processing of fur		7.9	11.6	15.2	10.3		...	...	...	...		...	...
191 Tanning, dressing and processing of leather		62.8	97.2	94.7	86.9		...	...	...	...		...	...
1911 Tanning and dressing of leather		43.2	68.2	61.0	49.7		...	...	...	...		...	...
1912 Luggage, handbags, etc.; saddlery & harness		19.5	29.0	33.7	37.2		...	...	...	...		...	...
1920 Footwear		148.3	174.6	220.5	262.8		...	...	...	...		...	...
2010 Sawmilling and planing of wood		168.1	374.0	737.5	900.4		...	...	...	...		...	...
202 Products of wood, cork, straw, etc.		341.0	548.1	1005.5	1153.4		...	...	...	...		...	...
2021 Veneer sheets, plywood, particle board, etc.		109.0	161.1	300.2	361.6		...	...	...	...		...	...
2022 Builders' carpentry and joinery		194.7	338.1	495.9	652.8		...	...	...	...		...	...
2023 Wooden containers		8.5	11.6	16.9	13.2		...	...	...	...		...	...
2029 Other wood products; articles of cork/straw		28.7	37.2	192.5	125.8		...	...	...	...		...	...
210 Paper and paper products		47.9	123.0	264.8	418.8		...	...	...	...		...	...
2101 Pulp, paper and paperboard		12.8	26.4	79.5	161.2		...	...	...	...		...	...
2102 Corrugated paper and paperboard		20.1	54.4	137.3	136.7		...	...	...	...		...	...
2109 Other articles of paper and paperboard		15.0	42.2	48.0	120.9		...	...	...	...		...	...
221 Publishing		...	...	512.2	741.8		...	...	...	...		...	...
2211 Publishing of books and other publications		111.0	29.1	223.3	210.2		...	...	...	...		...	...
2212 Publishing of newspapers, journals, etc.		126.9	228.1	282.6	509.0		...	...	...	...		...	...
2213 Publishing of recorded media		...	...	0.5	...		...	...	...	...		...	...
2219 Other publishing		33.1	...	5.8	22.6		...	...	...	...		...	...

continued

Estonia

ISIC Revision 3	Output					Value added a/					Gross fixed capital formation a/		
		(million KROON)					(million KROON)					(million KROON)	
ISIC Industry	Note	1993	1994	1995	1996	Note	1993	1994	1995	1996	Note	1995	1996
222 Printing and related service activities		...	230.1	421.0	406.7		...	...	...	...		...	...
2221 Printing		159.5	217.2	391.9	386.9		...	...	...	...		...	...
2222 Service activities related to printing		...	12.9	29.1	19.8		...	...	...	...		...	...
2230 Reproduction of recorded media		2.2	4.7	2.5	1.3		...	...	...	...		...	...
2310 Coke oven products		-	-	-	-		...	...	...	...		...	...
2320 Refined petroleum products		32.9	40.8	66.9	88.9		...	...	...	...		...	...
2330 Processing of nuclear fuel		-	...	-	-		...	...	...	...		...	...
241 Basic chemicals		563.7	354.9	619.2	635.5		...	...	...	...		...	...
2411 Basic chemicals, except fertilizers		11.7	2.5	127.9	161.2		...	...	...	...		...	...
2412 Fertilizers and nitrogen compounds		552.0	352.5	491.3	474.3		...	...	...	...		...	...
2413 Plastics in primary forms; synthetic rubber		-	-	...	...		...	...	...	...		...	...
242 Other chemicals		...	...	1483.3	1615.5		...	...	...	...		...	...
2421 Pesticides and other agro-chemical products		...	...	...	...		...	...	...	...		...	...
2422 Paints, varnishes, printing ink and mastics		79.3	179.9	255.0	387.9		...	...	...	...		...	...
2423 Pharmaceuticals, medicinal chemicals, etc.		61.8	133.3	169.8	200.9		...	...	...	...		...	...
2424 Soap, cleaning & cosmetic preparations		50.0	110.6	100.9	110.5		...	...	...	...		...	...
2429 Other chemical products n.e.c.		219.7	723.3	957.6	916.2		...	...	...	...		...	...
2430 Man-made fibres		1.3	-	-	-		...	...	...	...		...	...
251 Rubber products		27.4	22.8	27.1	34.7		...	...	...	...		...	...
2511 Rubber tyres and tubes		16.0	17.1	19.4	25.4		...	...	...	...		...	...
2519 Other rubber products		11.4	5.7	7.7	9.3		...	...	...	...		...	...
2520 Plastic products		106.3	185.4	279.7	380.9		...	...	...	...		...	...
2610 Glass and glass products		112.1	189.4	270.7	325.6		...	...	...	...		...	...
269 Non-metallic mineral products n.e.c.		...	733.2	712.5	859.1		...	...	...	...		...	...
2691 Pottery, china and earthenware		4.1	13.4	7.6	8.3		...	...	...	...		...	...
2692 Refractory ceramic products		...	0.7	3.1	14.7		...	...	...	...		...	...
2693 Struct.non-refractory clay; ceramic products		20.9	31.6	33.0	39.5		...	...	...	...		...	...
2694 Cement, lime and plaster		127.9	231.4	277.2	270.0		...	...	...	...		...	...
2695 Articles of concrete, cement and plaster		240.4	399.6	303.3	454.9		...	...	...	...		...	...
2696 Cutting, shaping & finishing of stone		31.1	43.6	42.9	67.7		...	...	...	...		...	...
2699 Other non-metallic mineral products n.e.c.		2.7	12.8	45.4	4.0		...	...	...	...		...	...
2710 Basic iron and steel		-	-	...	...		...	...	...	...		...	...
2720 Basic precious and non-ferrous metals		...	...	...	...		...	...	...	...		...	...
273 Casting of metals		...	...	22.0	18.3		...	...	...	...		...	...
2731 Casting of iron and steel		10.5	18.0	19.0	12.1		...	...	...	...		...	...
2732 Casting of non-ferrous metals		...	...	3.0	6.2		...	...	...	...		...	...
281 Struct.metal products;tanks;steam generators		209.7	215.0	328.4	477.0		...	...	...	...		...	...
2811 Structural metal products		181.6	167.4	241.3	375.4		...	...	...	...		...	...
2812 Tanks, reservoirs and containers of metal		7.5	24.0	62.8	55.0		...	...	...	...		...	...
2813 Steam generators		20.5	23.6	24.3	46.6		...	...	...	...		...	...
289 Other metal products; metal working services		169.5	382.2	639.8	914.8		...	...	...	...		...	...
2891 Metal forging/pressing/stamping/roll-forming		5.2	69.4	166.7	252.8		...	...	...	...		...	...
2892 Treatment & coating of metals		21.4	21.9	62.4	109.3		...	...	...	...		...	...
2893 Cutlery, hand tools and general hardware		37.3	71.1	63.6	96.9		...	...	...	...		...	...
2899 Other fabricated metal products n.e.c.		105.7	219.8	347.1	455.8		...	...	...	...		...	...
291 General purpose machinery		...	305.8	304.4	406.8		...	...	...	...		...	...
2911 Engines & turbines(not for transport equip.)		1.8	1.3	2.2	7.3		...	...	...	...		...	...
2912 Pumps, compressors, taps and valves		11.1	21.4	26.1	41.6		...	...	...	...		...	...
2913 Bearings, gears, gearing & driving elements		-	-	-	-		...	...	...	...		...	...
2914 Ovens, furnaces and furnace burners		...	9.0	22.6	17.9		...	...	...	...		...	...
2915 Lifting and handling equipment		106.5	118.5	67.8	65.1		...	...	...	...		...	...
2919 Other general purpose machinery		92.5	155.6	185.7	274.9		...	...	...	...		...	...

292 Special purpose machinery	...	...	223.3	290.2	...	...	...	...	...	...
2921 Agricultural and forestry machinery	63.3	111.7	121.9	171.8	...	...	...	...	...	...
2922 Machine tools	...	1.1	22.8	39.4	...	...	...	...	...	...
2923 Machinery for metallurgy	-	-	-	-	...	...	...	...	...	...
2924 Machinery for mining & construction	19.1	...	...	...	...	...	...	...	...	...
2925 Food/beverage/tobacco processing machinery	25.8	42.3	53.2	47.0	...	...	...	...	...	...
2926 Machinery for textile, apparel and leather	2.6	2.7	3.7	4.2	...	...	...	...	...	...
2927 Weapons and ammunition	-	2.8	1.3	...	...	...	...	...	...	...
2929 Other special purpose machinery	6.8	22.1	20.4	26.9	...	...	...	...	...	...
2930 Domestic appliances n.e.c.	7.4	10.1	6.1	0.2	...	...	...	...	...	...
3000 Office, accounting and computing machinery	10.9	45.4	131.0	132.7	...	...	...	...	...	...
3110 Electric motors, generators and transformers	53.1	42.8	60.2	47.1	...	...	...	...	...	...
3120 Electricity distribution & control apparatus	110.7	181.6	240.2	314.6	...	...	...	...	...	...
3130 Insulated wire and cable	23.2	46.5	38.8	61.0	...	...	...	...	...	...
3140 Accumulators, primary cells and batteries	-	0.1	8.6	...	...	...	...	...	...	...
3150 Lighting equipment and electric lamps	9.4	33.1	56.1	17.4	...	...	...	...	...	...
3190 Other electrical equipment n.e.c.	3.8	1.5	17.0	40.5	...	...	...	...	...	...
3210 Electronic valves, tubes, etc.	63.5	46.3	82.3	70.5	...	...	...	...	...	...
3220 TV/radio transmitters; line comm. apparatus	6.5	...	...	2.7	...	...	...	...	...	...
3230 TV and radio receivers and associated goods	7.8	11.3	12.5	228.4	...	...	...	...	...	...
331 Medical, measuring, testing appliances, etc.	118.3	140.6	159.2	202.7	...	...	...	...	...	...
3311 Medical, surgical and orthopaedic equipment	20.0	34.3	28.3	44.6	...	...	...	...	...	...
3312 Measuring/testing/navigating appliances,etc.	62.3	69.5	85.0	114.6	...	...	...	...	...	...
3313 Industrial process control equipment	36.0	36.8	45.9	43.5	...	...	...	...	...	...
3320 Optical instruments & photographic equipment	...	...	1.6	...	...	...	...	...	...	...
3330 Watches and clocks	-	...	...	...	...	...	...	...	...	...
3410 Motor vehicles	27.8	24.0	33.5	48.6	...	...	...	...	...	...
3420 Automobile bodies, trailers & semi-trailers	6.5	7.0	13.9	12.3	...	...	...	...	...	...
3430 Parts/accessories for automobiles	309.6	376.6	421.5	448.0	...	...	...	...	...	...
351 Building and repairing of ships and boats	219.4	385.9	470.7	511.3	...	...	...	...	...	...
3511 Building and repairing of ships	217.2	378.1	458.9	507.5	...	...	...	...	...	...
3512 Building/repairing of pleasure/sport. boats	2.2	7.8	11.8	3.8	...	...	...	...	...	...
3520 Railway/tramway locomotives & rolling stock	15.6	14.2	13.6	15.6	...	...	...	...	...	...
3530 Aircraft and spacecraft	-	-	...	...	...	...	...	...	...	...
359 Transport equipment n.e.c.	...	-	-	-	...	...	...	...	...	...
3591 Motorcycles	-	-	-	-	...	...	...	...	...	...
3592 Bicycles and invalid carriages	-	-	-	-	...	...	...	...	...	...
3599 Other transport equipment n.e.c.	...	-	-	-	...	...	...	...	...	...
3610 Furniture	651.6	887.9	1234.8	1483.4	...	...	...	...	...	...
369 Manufacturing n.e.c.	68.6	97.8	144.6	212.7	...	...	...	...	...	...
3691 Jewellery and related articles	41.6	57.1	54.1	48.1	...	...	...	...	...	...
3692 Musical instruments	6.9	9.6	8.5	13.9	...	...	...	...	...	...
3693 Sports goods	2.6	4.5	20.4	23.7	...	...	...	...	...	...
3694 Games and toys	0.9	1.9	1.3	2.7	...	...	...	...	...	...
3699 Other manufacturing n.e.c.	16.6	24.7	60.3	124.3	...	...	...	...	...	...
3710 Recycling of metal waste and scrap	1.1	3.8	12.7	8.9	...	...	...	...	...	...
3720 Recycling of non-metal waste and scrap	6.4	5.4	3.8	7.0	...	...	...	...	...	...
D Total manufacturing	12008.3	16014.0	21400.0	25677.2	4038.3	6465.6	9100.3	8826.4	2948.3	3361.8

a/ Data are based on "Economic indicators of enterprises in Estonia".

Estonia

ISIC Revision 3		Note	Index numbers of industrial production											
			(1990=100)											
ISIC	Industry		1985	1986	1987	1988	1989	1990	1991	1992	1993	1994	1995	1996
15	Food and beverages		...	...	...	...	...	...	...	...	...	...	...	...
16	Tobacco products		...	...	...	...	...	...	...	...	...	...	...	...
17	Textiles		...	...	...	...	...	...	...	...	...	...	...	...
18	Wearing apparel, fur		...	...	...	...	...	...	...	...	...	...	...	...
19	Leather, leather products and footwear		...	...	...	...	...	...	...	...	...	...	...	...
20	Wood products (excl. furniture)		...	...	...	...	...	...	...	...	...	...	...	...
21	Paper and paper products		...	...	...	...	...	...	...	...	...	...	...	...
22	Printing and publishing		...	...	...	...	...	...	...	...	...	...	...	...
23	Coke,refined petroleum products,nuclear fuel		...	...	...	...	...	...	...	...	...	...	...	...
24	Chemicals and chemical products		...	...	...	...	...	...	...	...	...	...	...	...
25	Rubber and plastics products		...	...	...	...	...	...	...	...	...	...	...	...
26	Non-metallic mineral products		...	...	...	...	...	...	...	...	...	...	...	...
27	Basic metals		...	...	...	...	...	...	...	...	...	...	...	...
28	Fabricated metal products		...	...	...	...	...	...	...	...	...	...	...	...
29	Machinery and equipment n.e.c.		...	...	...	...	...	...	...	...	...	...	...	...
30	Office, accounting and computing machinery		...	...	...	...	...	...	...	...	...	...	...	...
31	Electrical machinery and apparatus		...	...	...	...	...	...	...	...	...	...	...	...
32	Radio,television and communication equipment		...	...	...	...	...	...	...	...	...	...	...	...
33	Medical, precision and optical instruments		...	...	...	...	...	...	...	...	...	...	...	...
34	Motor vehicles, trailers, semi-trailers		...	...	...	...	...	...	...	...	...	...	...	...
35	Other transport equipment		...	...	...	...	...	...	...	...	...	...	...	...
36	Furniture; manufacturing n.e.c.		...	...	...	...	...	...	...	...	...	...	...	...
37	Recycling		...	...	...	...	...	...	...	...	...	...	...	...
D	Total manufacturing		89	93	95	99	100	100	92	57	47	45	46	47

ETHIOPIA

Supplier of information:
Central Statistical Authority, Ministry of Economic Development and Cooperation, Addis Ababa.

Basic source of data:
Annual survey of the manufacturing industry.

Major deviations from ISIC (Revision 3):
None reported.

Reference period (if not calendar year):
Fiscal year ending 7 July of the year indicated.

Scope:
Establishments with 10 or more persons engaged and using power driven machines.

Method of enumeration:
Individual sites are visited by enumerators.

Adjusted for non-response:
Yes.

Concepts and definitions of variables:
An establishment is defined as an entity comprising the whole of the premises under the same ownership or management at a particular address.
Number of employees is expressed in terms of full-time equivalents. The number of part-time workers is converted to its full-time equivalent on the basis of the number of months worked.
Gross fixed capital formation is not adjusted for the value of sales and disposals of used fixed assets.

Related national publications:
Statistical Abstract (annual); Results of Annual Survey of Manufacturing Industries, both published by the Central Statistical Authority, Ministry of Economic Development and Cooperation, Addis Ababa.

Ethiopia

ISIC Revision 3	Note	Number of establishments (numbers)				Note	Number of employees (numbers)				Note	Wages and salaries paid to employees (thousand BIRR)			
ISIC Industry		1993	1994	1995	1996		1993	1994	1995	1996		1993	1994	1995	1996
151 Processed meat,fish,fruit,vegetables,fats		22	29	29	35		4958	5416	4903	4668		18508	20352	18142	18975
1511 Processing/preserving of meat	a/	7	8	7	7	a/	3152	3695	3040	3003	a/	10608	13256	10444	11552
1512 Processing/preserving of fish	a/	...	...	...	...	a/	...	...	...	...	a/	...	...	...	...
1513 Processing/preserving of fruit & vegetables	a/	...	...	...	...	a/	...	...	...	...	a/	...	...	...	...
1514 Vegetable and animal oils and fats		15	21	22	28		1806	1721	1863	1665		7900	7096	7698	7423
1520 Dairy products		1	1	1	1		49	97	43	265		155	303	148	869
153 Grain mill products; starches; animal feeds		20	20	17	20		3859	3873	3769	2671		15091	17446	20263	14742
1531 Grain mill products		18	18	15	18		3643	3670	3546	2469		14704	16969	19470	13918
1532 Starches and starch products		-	-	-	-		-	-	-	-		-	-	-	-
1533 Prepared animal feeds		2	2	2	2		216	203	223	202		387	477	793	824
154 Other food products		60	96	83	92		6169	7131	6787	8144		28416	35756	37918	52628
1541 Bakery products		47	80	71	79		1317	1610	1621	2676		2875	5568	4242	9837
1542 Sugar	b/	9	9	5	5	b/	4305	3970	4061	4376	b/	24023	25469	29806	38745
1543 Cocoa, chocolate and sugar confectionery	b/	...	...	...	...	b/	...	...	...	...	b/	...	...	...	...
1544 Macaroni, noodles & similar products		3	3	3	3		419	462	459	337		778	1501	2046	1521
1549 Other food products n.e.c.		1	4	4	5		128	1089	646	755		740	3218	1824	2525
155 Beverages		21	22	23	26		7413	7381	8051	7450		35938	39786	45771	48454
1551 Distilling, rectifying & blending of spirits		6	7	7	10		846	794	1070	802		4348	4470	4692	4911
1552 Wines		3	3	3	3		772	727	724	407		2955	3252	3826	4534
1553 Malt liquors and malt		4	5	5	5		2531	2718	2854	2865		12943	15332	18103	20050
1554 Soft drinks; mineral waters		8	7	8	8		3264	3142	3403	3376		15692	16732	19150	18959
1600 Tobacco products		1	1	1	1		984	993	987	982		4638	6340	8591	8914
171 Spinning, weaving and finishing of textiles		16	21	20	20		26138	26924	27446	24982		92534	106445	105692	94747
1711 Textile fibre preparation; textile weaving		16	21	20	20		26138	26924	27446	24982		92534	106445	105692	94747
1712 Finishing of textiles		-	-	-	-		-	-	-	-		-	-	-	-
172 Other textiles		2	2	4	3		3370	3304	3352	3274		7839	9849	9133	9871
1721 Made-up textile articles, except apparel		-	-	-	-		-	-	-	-		-	-	-	-
1722 Carpets and rugs		-	-	-	-		-	-	-	-		-	-	-	-
1723 Cordage, rope, twine and netting		2	2	4	3		3370	3304	3352	3274		7839	9849	9133	9871
1729 Other textiles n.e.c.		-	-	-	-		-	-	-	-		-	-	-	-
1730 Knitted and crocheted fabrics and articles		5	6	5	9		150	178	143	131		374	404	364	318
1810 Wearing apparel, except fur apparel		8	17	13	23		3839	4043	3962	4054		11520	12163	11443	12331
1820 Dressing & dyeing of fur; processing of fur		-	-	-	-		-	-	-	-		-	-	-	-
191 Tanning, dressing and processing of leather		7	7	7	8		3181	3349	3369	3610		17846	22609	26389	30056
1911 Tanning and dressing of leather		7	7	7	8		3181	3349	3369	3610		17846	22609	26389	30056
1912 Luggage, handbags, etc.; saddlery & harness		-	-	-	-		-	-	-	-		-	-	-	-
1920 Footwear		14	45	43	55		3086	3840	3666	4138		13291	15370	15307	19119
2010 Sawmilling and planing of wood	c/d/	...	...	...	...	c/d/	...	...	...	...	c/d/	...	...	...	...
202 Products of wood, cork, straw, etc.	c/	10	24	22	26	c/	2838	2717	2554	2495	c/	7808	11282	11046	11582
2021 Veneer sheets, plywood, particle board, etc.	d/	...	...	...	...	d/	...	...	...	...	d/	...	...	...	...
2022 Builders' carpentry and joinery	d/	...	...	...	...	d/	...	...	...	...	d/	...	...	...	...
2023 Wooden containers		-	-	-	-		-	-	-	-		-	-	-	-
2029 Other wood products; articles of cork/straw	d/	10	24	22	26	d/	2838	2717	2554	2495	d/	7808	11282	11046	11582
210 Paper and paper products		4	3	4	5		1290	1357	1362	1270		6565	7143	8360	7758
2101 Pulp, paper and paperboard		4	3	4	5		1290	1357	1362	1270		6565	7143	8360	7758
2102 Corrugated paper and paperboard		-	-	-	-		-	-	-	-		-	-	-	-
2109 Other articles of paper and paperboard		-	-	-	-		-	-	-	-		-	-	-	-
221 Publishing		-	-	-	-		-	-	-	-		-	-	-	-
2211 Publishing of books and other publications		-	-	-	-		-	-	-	-		-	-	-	-
2212 Publishing of newspapers, journals, etc.		-	-	-	-		-	-	-	-		-	-	-	-
2213 Publishing of recorded media		-	-	-	-		-	-	-	-		-	-	-	-
2219 Other publishing		-	-	-	-		-	-	-	-		-	-	-	-

ISIC	Industry														
222	Printing and related service activities		19	25	28	38		3139	3243	3636	4280		17251	19250	22664	27701
2221	Printing	e/	...	...	...	...	e/	...	...	...	...	e/	...	...	...	...
2222	Service activities related to printing	e/	19	25	28	38	e/	3139	3243	3636	4280	e/	17251	19250	22664	27701
2230	Reproduction of recorded media		-	-	-	-		-	-	-	-		-	-	-	-
2310	Coke oven products		-	-	-	-		-	-	-	-		-	-	-	-
2320	Refined petroleum products		-	-	-	-		-	-	-	-		-	-	-	-
2330	Processing of nuclear fuel		-	-	-	-		-	-	-	-		-	-	-	-
241	Basic chemicals		1	2	1	2		178	190	170	499		944	1148	1091	3012
2411	Basic chemicals, except fertilizers		1	2	1	2		178	190	170	499		944	1148	1091	3012
2412	Fertilizers and nitrogen compounds		-	-	-	-		-	-	-	-		-	-	-	-
2413	Plastics in primary forms; synthetic rubber		-	-	-	-		-	-	-	-		-	-	-	-
242	Other chemicals		10	22	26	33		1630	1900	2511	2326		8136	9900	11976	12736
2421	Pesticides and other agro-chemical products		-	-	-	-		-	-	-	-		-	-	-	-
2422	Paints, varnishes, printing ink and mastics		2	2	3	5		285	272	465	429		1607	1774	2661	2816
2423	Pharmaceuticals, medicinal chemicals, etc.		1	1	2	2		525	501	510	500		2657	2734	3096	3288
2424	Soap, cleaning & cosmetic preparations		5	16	17	23		751	1045	1407	1290		3260	4542	5152	5784
2429	Other chemical products n.e.c.		2	3	4	3		69	82	129	107		612	850	1067	848
2430	Man-made fibres		-	-	-	-		-	-	-	-		-	-	-	-
251	Rubber products		4	5	4	4		856	875	940	1121		5612	6241	7188	6445
2511	Rubber tyres and tubes		4	5	4	4		856	875	940	1121		5612	6241	7188	6445
2519	Other rubber products		-	-	-	-		-	-	-	-		-	-	-	-
2520	Plastic products		5	11	9	11		933	1128	1064	1098		5027	6093	6772	6885
2610	Glass and glass products		1	1	1	2		371	434	468	663		1094	2028	2457	2919
269	Non-metallic mineral products n.e.c.		17	41	48	83		2865	4172	4864	5375		11419	16720	20156	28613
2691	Pottery, china and earthenware		-	-	-	-		-	-	-	-		-	-	-	-
2692	Refractory ceramic products		-	-	-	-		-	-	-	-		-	-	-	-
2693	Struct.non-refractory clay; ceramic products		4	5	5	7		450	781	631	640		1291	2375	2207	2213
2694	Cement, lime and plaster		4	4	5	7		1588	1648	1810	1730		6935	8240	9624	15394
2695	Articles of concrete, cement and plaster		8	30	35	64		513	1399	1814	2545		1726	4497	5977	7956
2696	Cutting, shaping & finishing of stone		-	-	-	-		-	-	-	-		-	-	-	-
2699	Other non-metallic mineral products n.e.c.		1	2	3	5		314	344	609	460		1467	1608	2348	3050
2710	Basic iron and steel		3	3	3	3		1137	1120	1183	1121		6858	7173	7424	8346
2720	Basic precious and non-ferrous metals		-	-	-	-		-	-	-	-		-	-	-	-
273	Casting of metals		-	-	-	-		-	-	-	-		-	-	-	-
2731	Casting of iron and steel		-	-	-	-		-	-	-	-		-	-	-	-
2732	Casting of non-ferrous metals		-	-	-	-		-	-	-	-		-	-	-	-
281	Struct.metal products;tanks;steam generators		5	23	27	29		167	452	572	562		1061	1907	2314	2285
2811	Structural metal products	f/	5	23	27	29	f/	167	452	572	562	f/	1061	1907	2314	2285
2812	Tanks, reservoirs and containers of metal	f/	...	...	...	...	f/	...	...	...	...	f/	...	...	...	...
2813	Steam generators		-	-	-	-		-	-	-	-		-	-	-	-
289	Other metal products; metal working services		9	12	13	10		1399	1346	1479	1444		8206	8395	9230	9642
2891	Metal forging/pressing/stamping/roll-forming		-	-	-	-		-	-	-	-		-	-	-	-
2892	Treatment & coating of metals		-	-	-	-		-	-	-	-		-	-	-	-
2893	Cutlery, hand tools and general hardware		5	8	9	4		529	534	640	571		2773	2892	3715	3519
2899	Other fabricated metal products n.e.c.		4	4	4	6		870	812	839	873		5433	5503	5515	6123
291	General purpose machinery		1	1	1	8		185	178	175	226		973	1094	1114	1282
2911	Engines & turbines(not for transport equip.)		-	-	-	-		-	-	-	-		-	-	-	-
2912	Pumps, compressors, taps and valves		1	1	1	1		185	178	175	143		973	1094	1114	1007
2913	Bearings, gears, gearing & driving elements		-	-	-	-		-	-	-	-		-	-	-	-
2914	Ovens, furnaces and furnace burners		-	-	-	5		-	-	-	56		-	-	-	217
2915	Lifting and handling equipment		-	-	-	-		-	-	-	-		-	-	-	-
2919	Other general purpose machinery		-	-	-	2		-	-	-	27		-	-	-	58
292	Special purpose machinery		-	-	-	6		-	-	-	121		-	-	-	475
2921	Agricultural and forestry machinery		-	-	-	-		-	-	-	-		-	-	-	-
2922	Machine tools		-	-	-	-		-	-	-	-		-	-	-	-
2923	Machinery for metallurgy		-	-	-	-		-	-	-	-		-	-	-	-
2924	Machinery for mining & construction		-	-	-	-		-	-	-	-		-	-	-	-
2925	Food/beverage/tobacco processing machinery		-	-	-	6		-	-	-	121		-	-	-	475
2926	Machinery for textile, apparel and leather		-	-	-	-		-	-	-	-		-	-	-	-
2927	Weapons and ammunition		-	-	-	-		-	-	-	-		-	-	-	-
2929	Other special purpose machinery		-	-	-	-		-	-	-	-		-	-	-	-
2930	Domestic appliances n.e.c.		-	-	-	-		-	-	-	-		-	-	-	-

continued

Ethiopia

ISIC Revision 3	Number of establishments					Number of employees					Wages and salaries paid to employees				
		(numbers)					(numbers)					(thousand BIRR)			
ISIC Industry	Note	1993	1994	1995	1996	Note	1993	1994	1995	1996	Note	1993	1994	1995	1996
3000 Office, accounting and computing machinery		-	-	-	-		-	-	-	-		-	-	-	-
3110 Electric motors, generators and transformers		-	-	-	-		-	-	-	-		-	-	-	-
3120 Electricity distribution & control apparatus		-	-	-	-		-	-	-	-		-	-	-	-
3130 Insulated wire and cable		-	-	-	-		-	-	-	-		-	-	-	-
3140 Accumulators, primary cells and batteries		1	2	2	1		100	109	112	89		628	585	677	543
3150 Lighting equipment and electric lamps		-	-	-	-		-	-	-	-		-	-	-	-
3190 Other electrical equipment n.e.c.		-	-	-	-		-	-	-	-		-	-	-	-
3210 Electronic valves, tubes, etc.		-	-	-	-		-	-	-	-		-	-	-	-
3220 TV/radio transmitters; line comm. apparatus		-	-	-	-		-	-	-	-		-	-	-	-
3230 TV and radio receivers and associated goods		-	-	-	-		-	-	-	-		-	-	-	-
331 Medical, measuring, testing appliances, etc.		-	-	-	-		-	-	-	-		-	-	-	-
3311 Medical, surgical and orthopaedic equipment		-	-	-	-		-	-	-	-		-	-	-	-
3312 Measuring/testing/navigating appliances,etc.		-	-	-	-		-	-	-	-		-	-	-	-
3313 Industrial process control equipment		-	-	-	-		-	-	-	-		-	-	-	-
3320 Optical instruments & photographic equipment		-	-	-	-		-	-	-	-		-	-	-	-
3330 Watches and clocks		-	-	-	-		-	-	-	-		-	-	-	-
3410 Motor vehicles		-	-	-	-		-	-	-	-		-	-	-	-
3420 Automobile bodies, trailers & semi-trailers		2	3	3	11		365	386	404	681		3502	3875	4719	5616
3430 Parts/accessories for automobiles		-	-	-	2		-	-	-	24		-	-	-	63
351 Building and repairing of ships and boats		-	-	-	-		-	-	-	-		-	-	-	-
3511 Building and repairing of ships		-	-	-	-		-	-	-	-		-	-	-	-
3512 Building/repairing of pleasure/sport. boats		-	-	-	-		-	-	-	-		-	-	-	-
3520 Railway/tramway locomotives & rolling stock		-	-	-	-		-	-	-	-		-	-	-	-
3530 Aircraft and spacecraft		-	-	-	-		-	-	-	-		-	-	-	-
359 Transport equipment n.e.c.		-	-	-	-		-	-	-	-		-	-	-	-
3591 Motorcycles		-	-	-	-		-	-	-	-		-	-	-	-
3592 Bicycles and invalid carriages		-	-	-	-		-	-	-	-		-	-	-	-
3599 Other transport equipment n.e.c.		-	-	-	-		-	-	-	-		-	-	-	-
3610 Furniture		20	54	63	75		1433	2106	2241	2275		6369	8851	9981	10076
369 Manufacturing n.e.c.		-	-	-	-		-	-	-	-		-	-	-	-
3691 Jewellery and related articles		-	-	-	-		-	-	-	-		-	-	-	-
3692 Musical instruments		-	-	-	-		-	-	-	-		-	-	-	-
3693 Sports goods		-	-	-	-		-	-	-	-		-	-	-	-
3694 Games and toys		-	-	-	-		-	-	-	-		-	-	-	-
3699 Other manufacturing n.e.c.		-	-	-	-		-	-	-	-		-	-	-	-
3710 Recycling of metal waste and scrap		-	-	-	-		-	-	-	-		-	-	-	-
3720 Recycling of non-metal waste and scrap		-	-	-	-		-	-	-	-		-	-	-	-
D Total manufacturing		289	499	501	642		82082	88242	90213	90039		337603	398508	426330	457003

a/ 1511 includes 1512 and 1513.
b/ 1542 includes 1543.
c/ 202 includes 2010.
d/ 2029 includes 2010, 2021 and 2022.
e/ 2222 includes 2221.
f/ 2811 includes 2812.

Ethiopia

ISIC	Industry	Note	Output in producers' prices (thousand BIRR) 1993	1994	1995	1996	Note	Value added in producers' prices (thousand BIRR) 1993	1994	1995	1996	Note	Gross fixed capital formation (thousand BIRR) 1995	1996
151	Processed meat,fish,fruit,vegetables,fats		82311	109383	116067	126083		33301	56141	43638	47588		2726	8384
1511	Processing/preserving of meat	a/	36891	64399	46445	64345	a/	15911	41593	19559	25395	a/	2305	2507
1512	Processing/preserving of fish	a/	...	...	...	...	a/	...	...	...	...	a/	...	...
1513	Processing/preserving of fruit & vegetables	a/	...	...	...	...	a/	...	...	...	...	a/	...	...
1514	Vegetable and animal oils and fats		45420	44984	69622	61738		17390	14548	24079	22193		421	5877
1520	Dairy products		4653	8602	12949	10384		2118	5358	4592	1801		808	-
153	Grain mill products; starches; animal feeds		152933	239779	376942	335476		42864	77840	116416	82891		4186	9273
1531	Grain mill products		150428	234900	369145	331465		43750	76243	112973	81155		4091	9241
1532	Starches and starch products		-	-	-	-		-	-	-	-		-	-
1533	Prepared animal feeds		2505	4879	7797	4011		-886	1597	3443	1736		95	32
154	Other food products		281698	360156	442170	844802		174893	227734	275543	555787		14188	45317
1541	Bakery products		28360	52282	69925	160321		4810	17158	16915	47541		2766	3204
1542	Sugar	b/	222355	231864	283795	577466	b/	158687	171280	225784	459320	b/	9016	41726
1543	Cocoa, chocolate and sugar confectionery	b/	...	...	...	...	b/	...	...	...	...	b/	...	...
1544	Macaroni, noodles & similar products		15130	32757	52579	52620		9479	13573	16520	25987		479	287
1549	Other food products n.e.c.		15853	43253	35871	54395		1917	25723	16324	22939		1927	100
155	Beverages		474909	601473	792465	863945		363041	448798	589465	619210		21862	31713
1551	Distilling, rectifying & blending of spirits		48167	48887	54687	60849		41705	38399	46879	43038		1343	816
1552	Wines		22712	22816	33613	30173		16878	16875	22262	20049		100	53
1553	Malt liquors and malt		278383	345927	459424	508285		220736	271278	362182	379732		15589	27113
1554	Soft drinks; mineral waters		125648	183843	244741	264638		83722	122246	158142	176391		4830	3731
1600	Tobacco products		188537	191227	199936	244188		147836	154039	155768	120085		409	1414
171	Spinning, weaving and finishing of textiles		359535	565491	524763	627684		181488	256138	229251	234944		3807	6939
1711	Textile fibre preparation; textile weaving		359535	565491	524763	627684		181488	256138	229251	234944		3807	6939
1712	Finishing of textiles		-	-	-	-		-	-	-	-		-	-
172	Other textiles		26360	77456	59430	68260		14282	24647	27982	31435		2951	4299
1721	Made-up textile articles, except apparel		-	-	-	-		-	-	-	-		-	-
1722	Carpets and rugs		-	-	-	-		-	-	-	-		-	-
1723	Cordage, rope, twine and netting		26360	77456	59430	68260		14282	24647	27982	31435		2951	4299
1729	Other textiles n.e.c.		-	-	-	-		-	-	-	-		-	-
1730	Knitted and crocheted fabrics and articles		2318	2925	2536	3296		398	778	929	1055		10	90
1810	Wearing apparel, except fur apparel		65881	76259	64452	71729		27663	30757	24916	32738		794	2752
1820	Dressing & dyeing of fur; processing of fur		-	-	-	-		-	-	-	-		-	-
191	Tanning, dressing and processing of leather		216872	288401	482044	490895		118772	137760	136156	145211		16797	8632
1911	Tanning and dressing of leather		216872	288401	482044	490895		118772	137760	136156	145211		16797	8632
1912	Luggage, handbags, etc.; saddlery & harness		-	-	-	-		-	-	-	-		-	-
1920	Footwear		71160	88569	119315	143605		28787	38623	47039	58124		5881	13543
2010	Sawmilling and planing of wood	c/d/	...	...	...	...	c/d/	...	...	...	...	c/d/	...	...
202	Products of wood, cork, straw, etc.	c/	28746	59969	65993	66595	c/	19169	39683	45971	44133	c/	599	1214
2021	Veneer sheets, plywood, particle board, etc.	d/	...	...	...	...	d/	...	...	...	...	d/	...	...
2022	Builders' carpentry and joinery	d/	...	...	...	...	d/	...	...	...	...	d/	...	...
2023	Wooden containers		-	-	-	-		-	-	-	-		-	-
2029	Other wood products; articles of cork/straw	d/	28746	59969	65993	66595	d/	19169	39683	45971	44133	d/	599	1214
210	Paper and paper products		65462	107816	86424	122973		29111	58797	31904	46229		2218	1529
2101	Pulp, paper and paperboard		65462	107816	86424	122973		29111	58797	31904	46229		2218	1529
2102	Corrugated paper and paperboard		-	-	-	-		-	-	-	-		-	-
2109	Other articles of paper and paperboard		-	-	-	-		-	-	-	-		-	-
221	Publishing		-	-	-	-		-	-	-	-		-	-
2211	Publishing of books and other publications		-	-	-	-		-	-	-	-		-	-
2212	Publishing of newspapers, journals, etc.		-	-	-	-		-	-	-	-		-	-
2213	Publishing of recorded media		-	-	-	-		-	-	-	-		-	-
2219	Other publishing		-	-	-	-		-	-	-	-		-	-

continued

Ethiopia

ISIC Revision 3 ISIC Industry	Note	Output in producers' prices (thousand BIRR) 1993	1994	1995	1996	Note	Value added in producers' prices (thousand BIRR) 1993	1994	1995	1996	Note	Gross fixed capital formation (thousand BIRR) 1995	1996
222 Printing and related service activities		76373	100681	114383	168591		47871	58519	66845	98995		15046	7041
2221 Printing	e/	...	...	...	...	e/	...	...	...	...	e/	...	...
2222 Service activities related to printing	e/	76373	100681	114383	168591	e/	47871	58519	66845	98995	e/	15046	7041
2230 Reproduction of recorded media		-	-	-	-		-	-	-	-		-	-
2310 Coke oven products		-	-	-	-		-	-	-	-		-	-
2320 Refined petroleum products		-	-	-	-		-	-	-	-		-	-
2330 Processing of nuclear fuel		-	-	-	-		-	-	-	-		-	-
241 Basic chemicals		4312	6047	5333	5829		2901	3701	3717	-4572		378	1380
2411 Basic chemicals, except fertilizers		4312	6047	5333	5829		2901	3701	3717	-4572		378	1380
2412 Fertilizers and nitrogen compounds		-	-	-	-		-	-	-	-		-	-
2413 Plastics in primary forms; synthetic rubber		-	-	-	-		-	-	-	-		-	-
242 Other chemicals		144291	237706	277055	311697		57567	81135	85364	107917		12810	9235
2421 Pesticides and other agro-chemical products		-	-	-	-		-	-	-	-		-	-
2422 Paints, varnishes, printing ink and mastics		32414	44793	55213	80373		14430	15745	19087	28814		805	1297
2423 Pharmaceuticals, medicinal chemicals, etc.		47057	69793	59078	59345		16607	29922	23240	20567		3424	6107
2424 Soap, cleaning & cosmetic preparations		53832	86385	107474	161754		23435	31194	34940	52553		6602	1826
2429 Other chemical products n.e.c.		10988	36734	55290	10225		3095	4274	8097	5983		1979	5
2430 Man-made fibres		-	-	-	-		-	-	-	-		-	-
251 Rubber products		56485	94683	76337	90938		28323	48250	36339	33368		42362	16041
2511 Rubber tyres and tubes		56485	94683	76337	90938		28323	48250	36339	33368		42362	16041
2519 Other rubber products		-	-	-	-		-	-	-	-		-	-
2520 Plastic products		43467	84442	84908	95323		21327	32947	38082	37217		2608	10787
2610 Glass and glass products		4991	18481	20899	22841		2798	12452	13940	14565		2052	41
269 Non-metallic mineral products n.e.c.		122847	204937	315754	396831		55654	102358	149482	192029		23032	27498
2691 Pottery, china and earthenware		-	-	-	-		-	-	-	-		-	-
2692 Refractory ceramic products		-	-	-	-		-	-	-	-		-	-
2693 Struct.non-refractory clay; ceramic products		7974	10455	8592	8662		4998	4543	5185	5668		77	2316
2694 Cement, lime and plaster		102091	160101	222710	276798		43672	76418	103044	131926		20685	17914
2695 Articles of concrete, cement and plaster		7256	22785	70685	78157		4040	13679	34026	36891		1473	3403
2696 Cutting, shaping & finishing of stone		-	-	-	-		-	-	-	-		-	-
2699 Other non-metallic mineral products n.e.c.		5526	11596	13766	33214		2944	7718	7227	17544		797	3865
2710 Basic iron and steel		58208	218911	222574	282160		26901	67820	95340	82096		2707	2226
2720 Basic precious and non-ferrous metals		-	-	-	-		-	-	-	-		-	-
273 Casting of metals		-	-	-	-		-	-	-	-		-	-
2731 Casting of iron and steel		-	-	-	-		-	-	-	-		-	-
2732 Casting of non-ferrous metals		-	-	-	-		-	-	-	-		-	-
281 Struct.metal products;tanks;steam generators		4180	11133	15728	19067		2307	4240	5871	8341		4249	5256
2811 Structural metal products	f/	4180	11133	15728	19067	f/	2307	4240	5871	8341	f/	4249	5256
2812 Tanks, reservoirs and containers of metal	f/	...	...	...	...	f/	...	...	...	...	f/	...	...
2813 Steam generators		-	-	-	-		-	-	-	-		-	-
289 Other metal products; metal working services		37515	70946	70873	92081		17716	30478	33066	43930		3772	2207
2891 Metal forging/pressing/stamping/roll-forming		-	-	-	-		-	-	-	-		-	-
2892 Treatment & coating of metals		-	-	-	-		-	-	-	-		-	-
2893 Cutlery, hand tools and general hardware		15597	28478	24360	26126		8510	11716	12809	13481		1998	1211
2899 Other fabricated metal products n.e.c.		21918	42468	46513	65955		9206	18762	20257	30449		1774	996
291 General purpose machinery		1080	2757	4034	6636		260	1707	1916	3371		33	119
2911 Engines & turbines(not for transport equip.)		-	-	-	-		-	-	-	-		-	-
2912 Pumps, compressors, taps and valves		1080	2757	4034	3756		260	1707	1916	2026		33	40
2913 Bearings, gears, gearing & driving elements		-	-	-	-		-	-	-	-		-	-
2914 Ovens, furnaces and furnace burners		-	-	-	2383		-	-	-	1068		-	3
2915 Lifting and handling equipment		-	-	-	-		-	-	-	-		-	-
2919 Other general purpose machinery		-	-	-	497		-	-	-	277		-	76

292 Special purpose machinery	-	-	-	1675	-	-	-	1321	-	37
2921 Agricultural and forestry machinery	-	-	-	-	-	-	-	-	-	-
2922 Machine tools	-	-	-	-	-	-	-	-	-	-
2923 Machinery for metallurgy	-	-	-	-	-	-	-	-	-	-
2924 Machinery for mining & construction	-	-	-	-	-	-	-	-	-	-
2925 Food/beverage/tobacco processing machinery	-	-	-	1675	-	-	-	1321	-	37
2926 Machinery for textile, apparel and leather	-	-	-	-	-	-	-	-	-	-
2927 Weapons and ammunition	-	-	-	-	-	-	-	-	-	-
2929 Other special purpose machinery	-	-	-	-	-	-	-	-	-	-
2930 Domestic appliances n.e.c.	-	-	-	-	-	-	-	-	-	-
3000 Office, accounting and computing machinery	-	-	-	-	-	-	-	-	-	-
3110 Electric motors, generators and transformers	-	-	-	-	-	-	-	-	-	-
3120 Electricity distribution & control apparatus	-	-	-	-	-	-	-	-	-	-
3130 Insulated wire and cable	-	-	-	-	-	-	-	-	-	-
3140 Accumulators, primary cells and batteries	3546	4424	2752	1624	2087	2337	1497	586	19	8
3150 Lighting equipment and electric lamps	-	-	-	-	-	-	-	-	-	-
3190 Other electrical equipment n.e.c.	-	-	-	-	-	-	-	-	-	-
3210 Electronic valves, tubes, etc.	-	-	-	-	-	-	-	-	-	-
3220 TV/radio transmitters; line comm. apparatus	-	-	-	-	-	-	-	-	-	-
3230 TV and radio receivers and associated goods	-	-	-	-	-	-	-	-	-	-
331 Medical, measuring, testing appliances, etc.	-	-	-	-	-	-	-	-	-	-
3311 Medical, surgical and orthopaedic equipment	-	-	-	-	-	-	-	-	-	-
3312 Measuring/testing/navigating appliances,etc.	-	-	-	-	-	-	-	-	-	-
3313 Industrial process control equipment	-	-	-	-	-	-	-	-	-	-
3320 Optical instruments & photographic equipment	-	-	-	-	-	-	-	-	-	-
3330 Watches and clocks	-	-	-	-	-	-	-	-	-	-
3410 Motor vehicles	-	-	-	-	-	-	-	-	-	-
3420 Automobile bodies, trailers & semi-trailers	71240	133330	320340	217747	30645	43271	50696	49018	4095	2420
3430 Parts/accessories for automobiles	-	-	-	125	-	-	-	107	-	-
351 Building and repairing of ships and boats	-	-	-	-	-	-	-	-	-	-
3511 Building and repairing of ships	-	-	-	-	-	-	-	-	-	-
3512 Building/repairing of pleasure/sport. boats	-	-	-	-	-	-	-	-	-	-
3520 Railway/tramway locomotives & rolling stock	-	-	-	-	-	-	-	-	-	-
3530 Aircraft and spacecraft	-	-	-	-	-	-	-	-	-	-
359 Transport equipment n.e.c.	-	-	-	-	-	-	-	-	-	-
3591 Motorcycles	-	-	-	-	-	-	-	-	-	-
3592 Bicycles and invalid carriages	-	-	-	-	-	-	-	-	-	-
3599 Other transport equipment n.e.c.	-	-	-	-	-	-	-	-	-	-
3610 Furniture	24255	44720	54035	66026	13283	23841	28207	33293	5638	9871
369 Manufacturing n.e.c.	-	-	-	-	-	-	-	-	-	-
3691 Jewellery and related articles	-	-	-	-	-	-	-	-	-	-
3692 Musical instruments	-	-	-	-	-	-	-	-	-	-
3693 Sports goods	-	-	-	-	-	-	-	-	-	-
3694 Games and toys	-	-	-	-	-	-	-	-	-	-
3699 Other manufacturing n.e.c.	-	-	-	-	-	-	-	-	-	-
3710 Recycling of metal waste and scrap	-	-	-	-	-	-	-	-	-	-
3720 Recycling of non-metal waste and scrap	-	-	-	-	-	-	-	-	-	-
D Total manufacturing	2674167	4010703	4930487	5799106	1493363	2070149	2339932	2722813	196037	229266

a/ 1511 includes 1512 and 1513.
b/ 1542 includes 1543.
c/ 202 includes 2010.
d/ 2029 includes 2010, 2021 and 2022.
e/ 2222 includes 2221.
f/ 2811 includes 2812.

Ethiopia

ISIC Revision 3		Note	Index numbers of industrial production (1990=100)											
ISIC	Industry		1985	1986	1987	1988	1989	1990	1991	1992	1993	1994	1995	1996
15	Food and beverages		...	...	...	...	...	...	...	...	...	...	...	...
16	Tobacco products		...	...	...	...	...	...	...	...	...	...	...	...
17	Textiles		...	...	...	...	...	...	...	...	...	...	...	...
18	Wearing apparel, fur		...	...	...	...	...	...	...	...	...	...	...	...
19	Leather, leather products and footwear		...	...	...	...	...	...	...	...	...	...	...	...
20	Wood products (excl. furniture)		...	...	...	...	...	...	...	...	...	...	...	...
21	Paper and paper products		...	...	...	...	...	...	...	...	...	...	...	...
22	Printing and publishing		...	...	...	...	...	...	...	...	...	...	...	...
23	Coke,refined petroleum products,nuclear fuel		...	...	...	...	...	...	...	...	...	...	...	...
24	Chemicals and chemical products		...	...	...	...	...	...	...	...	...	...	...	...
25	Rubber and plastics products		...	...	...	...	...	...	...	...	...	...	...	...
26	Non-metallic mineral products		...	...	...	...	...	...	...	...	...	...	...	...
27	Basic metals		...	...	...	...	...	...	...	...	...	...	...	...
28	Fabricated metal products		...	...	...	...	...	...	...	...	...	...	...	...
29	Machinery and equipment n.e.c.		...	...	...	...	...	...	...	...	...	...	...	...
30	Office, accounting and computing machinery		...	...	...	...	...	...	...	...	...	...	...	...
31	Electrical machinery and apparatus		...	...	...	...	...	...	...	...	...	...	...	...
32	Radio,television and communication equipment		...	...	...	...	...	...	...	...	...	...	...	...
33	Medical, precision and optical instruments		...	...	...	...	...	...	...	...	...	...	...	...
34	Motor vehicles, trailers, semi-trailers		...	...	...	...	...	...	...	...	...	...	...	...
35	Other transport equipment		...	...	...	...	...	...	...	...	...	...	...	...
36	Furniture; manufacturing n.e.c.		...	...	...	...	...	...	...	...	...	...	...	...
37	Recycling		...	...	...	...	...	...	...	...	...	...	...	...
D	Total manufacturing		...	...	...	...	...	...	...	...	...	...	...	...

FINLAND

Supplier of information:
Statistics Finland, Helsinki.
Industrial statistics for the OECD countries are compiled by the OECD secretariat, which supplies them to UNIDO.

Basic source of data:
Data for the years 1993, 1994 are national accounts estimates. Data for 1995 and 1996 are industrial survey results.

Major deviations from ISIC (Revision 3):
Data have been converted from NACE (Revision 1) to ISIC (Rev. 3).

Reference period (if not calendar year):
The survey covers chiefly the calendar year, however, in some cases establishments are allowed to report using their own financial year.

Scope:
Not reported.

Method of enumeration:
Not reported.

Adjusted for non-response:
Not reported.

Concepts and definitions of variables:
Number of employees, defined as "wage earners and salaried personnel", covers salaried employees, wage earners and all full- and part-time employees. It is based on the average number of employees throughout the year.
Output is the gross value of production including the value of all products, allowing for net change of work in progress, goods shipped in the same condition as received, net changes in stocks of finished goods, services rendered and electricity sold.
Value added uses the national accounting concept up to 1994. It is gross output less the value of materials, fuels and other supplies, contract and commission work done by others, repair and maintenance work done by others, and electricity purchases. Input estimates are on a received basis. Valuation is in basic value. Data for 1995 refer to census value added.
Gross fixed capital formation is expenditure on the purchase of fixed assets plus own-account construction of assets, less sales of fixed assets. Fixed assets are those with a productive life of at least one year, and include assets made by a unit's labour force for its own use; additions, alterations, improvements and repairs to existing assets; new assets (whether or not in use) and used assets. Valuation is at full cost incurred, including delivered price, cost of installation and fees and taxes.

Related national publications:

Finland

ISIC Revision 3	Number of establishments					Number of employees					Wages and salaries paid to employees				
		(numbers)					(numbers)					(thousand MARKS)			
ISIC Industry	Note	1993	1994	1995a/	1996a/	Note	1993	1994	1995a/b/	1996	Note	1993c/	1994c/	1995a/b/	1996
151 Processed meat,fish,fruit,vegetables,fats		...	...	488	489		44400d/	42200d/	14382	...		5193000d/	5107000d/	1775658	...
1511 Processing/preserving of meat		...	...	204	204		...	...	10820	...		...	...	1304181	...
1512 Processing/preserving of fish		...	...	123	124		...	...	378	...		...	...	43470	...
1513 Processing/preserving of fruit & vegetables		...	...	145	145		...	...	2280	...		...	...	270522	...
1514 Vegetable and animal oils and fats		...	...	16	16		...	...	904	...		...	...	157485	...
1520 Dairy products		...	...	110	110		...d/	...d/	6470	...		...d/	...d/	855381	...
153 Grain mill products; starches; animal feeds		...	...	172	172		...d/	...d/	2301	...		...d/	...d/	349018	...
1531 Grain mill products		...	...	85	85		...	...	577	...		...	...	83184	...
1532 Starches and starch products		...	...	6	6		...	...	352	...		...	...	47069	...
1533 Prepared animal feeds		...	...	81	81		...	...	1372	...		...	...	218765	...
154 Other food products		...	...	1011	1019		...d/	...d/	15405	...		...d/	...d/	1824561	...
1541 Bakery products		...	...	880	887		...	...	10030	...		...	...	1102673	...
1542 Sugar		...	...	9	9		...	...	687	...		...	...	101992	...
1543 Cocoa, chocolate and sugar confectionery		...	...	42	42		...	...	2558	...		...	...	334274	...
1544 Macaroni, noodles & similar products		...	...	2	-		...	...	...e/	...		...	...	...e/	...
1549 Other food products n.e.c.		...	...	78	81		...	...	2130e/	...		...	...	285622e/	...
155 Beverages		...	...	58	58		...d/	...d/	4079	...		...d/	...d/	643920	...
1551 Distilling, rectifying & blending of spirits		...	...	4	10f/		...	...	1017f/	...		...	...	178985f/	...
1552 Wines		...	...	6	...f/		...	...	...f/	...		...	...	...f/	...
1553 Malt liquors and malt		...	...	31	31		...	...	3062g/	...		...	...	464935g/	...
1554 Soft drinks; mineral waters		...	...	17	17		...	...	...g/	...		...	...	...g/	...
1600 Tobacco products		...	...	5	5		900	900	919	...		128000	126000	135681	...
171 Spinning, weaving and finishing of textiles		...	...	159	160		8200h/	7800h/	1201	...		797000h/	798000h/	121836	...
1711 Textile fibre preparation; textile weaving		...	...	55	55		...	...	890	...		...	...	87827	...
1712 Finishing of textiles		...	...	104	105		...	...	311	...		...	...	34009	...
172 Other textiles		...	...	597	608		...h/	...h/	2923	...		...h/	...h/	344302	...
1721 Made-up textile articles, except apparel		...	...	255	259		...	...	729	...		...	...	70785	...
1722 Carpets and rugs		...	...	179	181		...	...	117	...		...	...	9106	...
1723 Cordage, rope, twine and netting		...	...	18	18		...	...	159	...		...	...	13754	...
1729 Other textiles n.e.c.		...	...	145	150		...	...	1918	...		...	...	250657	...
1730 Knitted and crocheted fabrics and articles		...	...	161	164		...h/	...h/	1776	...		...h/	...h/	176878	...
1810 Wearing apparel, except fur apparel		...	...	1073	1093		7700i/	7100i/	7703	...		619000i/	616000i/	711862	...
1820 Dressing & dyeing of fur; processing of fur		...	...	141	141		...i/	...i/	315	...		...i/	...i/	32073	...
191 Tanning, dressing and processing of leather		...	...	260	264		3200j/	3300j/	788	...		273000j/	284000j/	76471	...
1911 Tanning and dressing of leather		...	...	18	18		...	...	461	...		...	...	49104	...
1912 Luggage, handbags, etc.; saddlery & harness		...	...	242	246		...	...	327	...		...	...	27367	...
1920 Footwear		...	...	91	91		...j/	...j/	2482	...		...j/	...j/	221976	...
2010 Sawmilling and planing of wood		...	...	1044	1053		24700k/	26100k/	9740	...		2522000k/	2864000k/	1197812	...
202 Products of wood, cork, straw, etc.		...	...	1520	1527		...k/	...k/	15162	...		...k/	...k/	1755941	...
2021 Veneer sheets, plywood, particle board, etc.		...	...	65	65		...	...	6968	...		...	...	861381	...
2022 Builders' carpentry and joinery		...	...	993	994		...	...	7205	...		...	...	782353	...
2023 Wooden containers		...	...	163	164		...	...	518	...		...	...	59882	...
2029 Other wood products; articles of cork/straw		...	...	299	304		...	...	471	...		...	...	52325	...
210 Paper and paper products		...	...	315	317		38600	38500	38604	...		5792000	6068000	6670060	...
2101 Pulp, paper and paperboard		...	...	155	157		...	...	32850	...		...	...	5848070	...
2102 Corrugated paper and paperboard		...	...	66	66		...	...	3278	...		...	...	463574	...
2109 Other articles of paper and paperboard		...	...	94	94		...	...	2476	...		...	...	358416	...
221 Publishing		...	...	1034	1042		33300m/	31500m/	14699	...		4230000m/	4111000m/	2045077	...
2211 Publishing of books and other publications		...	...	245	248		...	...	1508	...		...	...	225888	...
2212 Publishing of newspapers, journals, etc.		...	...	527	532		...	...	12822	...		...	...	1761317	...
2213 Publishing of recorded media		...	...	191	191		...	...	369n/	...		...	...	57872n/	...
2219 Other publishing		...	...	71	71		...	...	...n/	...		...	...	...n/	...

222	Printing and related service activities	...	...	1293	1299	...m/	...m/	13092	...	...m/	...m/	1815351	...
2221	Printing	...	...	944	948	...	...	11851	...	...	...	1629894	...
2222	Service activities related to printing	...	...	349	351	...	...	1241p/	...	...	...	185457p/	...
2230	Reproduction of recorded media	...	...	43	43	...m/	...m/	...p/	...	...m/	...m/	...p/	...
2310	Coke oven products	...	...	1	1	3700q/	3600q/	198	...	611000q/	590000q/	34199	...
2320	Refined petroleum products	...	...	13	18	...q/	...q/	3014	...	...q/	...q/	548724	...
2330	Processing of nuclear fuel	...	...	-	-	...q/	...q/	-	...	...q/	...q/	-	...
241	Basic chemicals	...	...	150	151	18100r/	17800r/	8337	...	2458000r/	2535000r/	1424510	...
2411	Basic chemicals, except fertilizers	...	...	91	92	...	...	5262	...	...	...	867347	...
2412	Fertilizers and nitrogen compounds	...	...	18	18	...	...	1281	...	...	...	224371	...
2413	Plastics in primary forms; synthetic rubber	...	...	41	41	...	...	1794	...	...	...	332792	...
242	Other chemicals	...	...	179	188	...r/	...r/	9184	...	...r/	...r/	1261641	...
2421	Pesticides and other agro-chemical products	...	...	1	-	...	...	...s/	...	...	...	...s/	...
2422	Paints, varnishes, printing ink and mastics	...	...	30	30	...	...	1803s/	...	...	...	277426s/	...
2423	Pharmaceuticals, medicinal chemicals, etc.	...	...	32	33	...	...	4144	...	...	...	547721	...
2424	Soap, cleaning & cosmetic preparations	...	...	68	72	...	...	1524	...	...	...	199582	...
2429	Other chemical products n.e.c.	...	...	48	53	...	...	1713	...	...	...	236912	...
2430	Man-made fibres	...	...	2	...	...r/	...r/	676	...	...r/	...r/	83180	...
251	Rubber products	...	...	69	69	12000t/	12700t/	2497	...	1399000t/	1525000t/	343995	...
2511	Rubber tyres and tubes	...	...	17	17	...	...	...	...	...	...	...	...
2519	Other rubber products	...	...	52	52	...	...	...	...	...	...	...	...
2520	Plastic products	...	...	544	546	...t/	...t/	10308	...	...t/	...t/	1299500	...
2610	Glass and glass products	...	...	115	115	12900u/	12500u/	3232	...	1473000u/	1496000u/	451343	...
269	Non-metallic mineral products n.e.c.	...	...	779	786	...u/	...u/	8876	...	...u/	...u/	1104850	...
2691	Pottery, china and earthenware	...	...	110	...	...	...	...	...	...	...	...	...
2692	Refractory ceramic products	...	...	3	...	...	...	...	...	...	...	...	...
2693	Struct.non-refractory clay; ceramic products	...	...	13	13	...	...	...	...	...	...	73070	...
2694	Cement, lime and plaster	...	...	10	11	...	...	497	...	...	...	71645	...
2695	Articles of concrete, cement and plaster	...	...	353	354	...	...	4337	...	...	...	500733	...
2696	Cutting, shaping & finishing of stone	...	...	242	244	...	...	839	...	...	...	100751	...
2699	Other non-metallic mineral products n.e.c.	...	...	48	49	...	...	1612	...	...	...	225453	...
2710	Basic iron and steel	...	...	82	83	15200v/	15400v/	9963	...	2074000v/	2178000v/	1585091	...
2720	Basic precious and non-ferrous metals	...	...	24	25	...v/	...v/	3776	...	...v/	...v/	601797	...
273	Casting of metals	...	...	55	55	...v/	...v/	2629	...	...v/	...v/	370397	...
2731	Casting of iron and steel	...	...	27	27	...	...	...	...	...	...	...	...
2732	Casting of non-ferrous metals	...	...	28	28	...	...	...	...	...	...	...	...
281	Struct.metal products;tanks;steam generators	...	...	1256	1261	22700w/	23200w/	11382	...	2549000w/	2752000w/	1543742	...
2811	Structural metal products	...	...	1137	1142	...	...	7427	...	...	...	921815	...
2812	Tanks, reservoirs and containers of metal	...	...	96	96	...	...	1899	...	...	...	246907	...
2813	Steam generators	...	...	23	23	...	...	2056	...	...	...	375020	...
289	Other metal products; metal working services	...	...	2296	2305	...w/	...w/	9591	...	...w/	...w/	1234839	...
2891	Metal forging/pressing/stamping/roll-forming	...	...	61	61	...	...	...x/	...	...	...	...x/	...
2892	Treatment & coating of metals	...	...	978	978	...	...	1817x/	...	...	...	242263x/	...
2893	Cutlery, hand tools and general hardware	...	...	362	364	...	...	2812	...	...	...	355462	...
2899	Other fabricated metal products n.e.c.	...	...	895	902	...	...	4962	...	...	...	637114	...
291	General purpose machinery	...	...	1551	1561	45400y/	46800y/	21095	...	5769000y/	6305000y/	3145620	...
2911	Engines & turbines(not for transport equip.)	...	...	117	119	...	...	2371	...	...	...	435733	...
2912	Pumps, compressors, taps and valves	...	...	127	129	...	...	3987	...	...	...	593171	...
2913	Bearings, gears, gearing & driving elements	...	...	40	40	...	...	1228	...	...	...	190032	...
2914	Ovens, furnaces and furnace burners	...	...	13	13	...	...	130	...	...	...	18112	...
2915	Lifting and handling equipment	...	...	343	344	...	...	7821	...	...	...	1124044	...
2919	Other general purpose machinery	...	...	911	916	...	...	5558	...	...	...	784528	...
292	Special purpose machinery	...	...	1615	1620	...y/	...y/	25484	...	...y/	...y/	3823234	...
2921	Agricultural and forestry machinery	...	...	613	616	...	...	2395	...	...	...	323280	...
2922	Machine tools	...	...	167	167	...	...	3259	...	...	...	453753	...
2923	Machinery for metallurgy	...	...	12	12	...	...	166	...	...	...	33304	...
2924	Machinery for mining & construction	...	...	174	174	...	...	3633	...	...	...	545237	...
2925	Food/beverage/tobacco processing machinery	...	...	103	103	...	...	758	...	...	...	98481	...
2926	Machinery for textile, apparel and leather	...	...	27	27	...	...	43	...	...	...	4980	...
2927	Weapons and ammunition	...	...	37	37	...	...	1073	...	...	...	143046	...
2929	Other special purpose machinery	...	...	482	484	...	...	14157	...	...	...	2221153	...
2930	Domestic appliances n.e.c.	...	...	45	45	...y/	...y/	2032	...	...y/	...y/	237889	...

continued

ISIC Revision 3	Number of establishments					Number of employees					Wages and salaries paid to employees				
		(numbers)					(numbers)					(thousand MARKS)			
ISIC Industry	Note	1993	1994	1995a/	1996a/	Note	1993	1994	1995a/b/	1996	Note	1993c/	1994c/	1995a/b/	1996
3000 Office, accounting and computing machinery		...	...	57	58		2900	3200	3449	...		352000	400000	479436	...
3110 Electric motors, generators and transformers		...	...	97	100		12700z/	14000z/	6168	...		1580000z/	1822000z/	912380	...
3120 Electricity distribution & control apparatus		...	...	103	104		...z/	...z/	3938	...		...z/	...z/	508627	...
3130 Insulated wire and cable		...	...	29	30		...z/	...z/	1762A/	...		...z/	...z/	265685A/	...
3140 Accumulators, primary cells and batteries		...	...	4	4		...z/	...z/	...A/	...		...z/	...z/	...A/	...
3150 Lighting equipment and electric lamps		...	...	79	79		...z/	...z/	1353	...		...z/	...z/	171843	...
3190 Other electrical equipment n.e.c.		...	...	134	134		...z/	...z/	2099	...		...z/	...z/	274155	...
3210 Electronic valves, tubes, etc.		...	...	151	152		12500B/	15500B/	2964	...		1598000B/	2098000B/	342356	...
3220 TV/radio transmitters; line comm. apparatus		...	...	85	87		...B/	...B/	17087	...		...B/	...B/	2595392	...
3230 TV and radio receivers and associated goods		...	...	43	43		...B/	...B/	1501	...		...B/	...B/	191861	...
331 Medical, measuring, testing appliances, etc.		...	...	675	677		6100C/	6400C/	6811	...		812000C/	887000C/	1029005	...
3311 Medical, surgical and orthopaedic equipment		...	...	451	451		...	...	3569	...		...	...	499672	...
3312 Measuring/testing/navigating appliances,etc.		...	...	166	167		...	...	1999	...		...	...	306777	...
3313 Industrial process control equipment		...	...	58	59		...	...	1243	...		...	...	222556	...
3320 Optical instruments & photographic equipment		...	...	31	32		...C/	...C/	249	...		...C/	...C/	33906	...
3330 Watches and clocks		...	...	6	6		...C/	...C/	-	...		...C/	...C/	-	...
3410 Motor vehicles		...	...	30	30		6600D/	6600D/	2623	...		634000D/	707000D/	371671	...
3420 Automobile bodies, trailers & semi-trailers		...	...	152	154		...D/	...D/	2311	...		...D/	...D/	296317	...
3430 Parts/accessories for automobiles		...	...	71	72		...D/	...D/	1256	...		...D/	...D/	161625	...
351 Building and repairing of ships and boats		...	...	419	422		15600E/	15800E/	10314	...		1885000E/	2082000E/	1516892	...
3511 Building and repairing of ships		...	...	103	105		...	...	9534	...		...	...	1416864	...
3512 Building/repairing of pleasure/sport. boats		...	...	316	317		...	...	780	...		...	...	100028	...
3520 Railway/tramway locomotives & rolling stock		...	...	6	17		...E/	...E/	2421	...		...E/	...E/	362271	...
3530 Aircraft and spacecraft		...	...	13	15		...E/	...E/	3024	...		...E/	...E/	505782	...
359 Transport equipment n.e.c.		...	...	25	25		...E/	...E/	436	...		...E/	...E/	53304	...
3591 Motorcycles		...	...	4	...		...	...	...	...		...	...	...	...
3592 Bicycles and invalid carriages		...	...	7	...		...	...	...	...		...	...	...	...
3599 Other transport equipment n.e.c.		...	...	14	14		...	...	68	...		...	...	7659	...
3610 Furniture		...	...	1347	1360		13700F/	13300F/	8913	...		1293000F/	1376000F/	993262	...
369 Manufacturing n.e.c.		...	...	806	811		...F/	...F/	3495	...		...F/	...F/	401064	...
3691 Jewellery and related articles		...	...	259	259		...	...	687	...		...	...	85160	...
3692 Musical instruments		...	...	35	36		...	...	-	...		...	...	-	...
3693 Sports goods		...	...	127	128		...	...	1338	...		...	...	142102	...
3694 Games and toys		...	...	59	60		...	...	246	...		...	...	28097	...
3699 Other manufacturing n.e.c.		...	...	326	328		...	...	1224	...		...	...	145705	...
3710 Recycling of metal waste and scrap		...	...	69	69		-	-	149	...		-	-	20750	...
3720 Recycling of non-metal waste and scrap		...	...	13	13		-	-	24	...		-	-	2309	...
D Total manufacturing		...	...	22796	22978		361100	364200	366662	...		44041000	46727000	51338302	...

a/ Industrial survey results.
b/ Data are provisional.
c/ National Accounts estimates.
d/ 151 includes 1520, 153, 154 and 155.
e/ 1549 includes 1544.
f/ 1551 includes 1552.
g/ 1553 includes 1554.
h/ 171 includes 172 and 1730.
i/ 1810 includes 1820.
j/ 191 includes 1920.
k/ 2010 includes 202.
m/ 221 includes 222 and 2230.
n/ 2213 includes 2219.
p/ 2222 includes 2230.
q/ 2310 includes 2320 and 2330.
r/ 241 includes 242 and 2430.
s/ 2422 includes 2421.
t/ 251 includes 2520.
u/ 2610 includes 269.
v/ 2710 includes 2720 and 273.
w/ 281 includes 289.
x/ 2892 includes 2891.
y/ 291 includes 292 and 2930.
z/ 3110 includes 3120, 3130, 3140, 3150 and 3190.
A/ 3130 includes 3140.
B/ 3210 includes 3220 and 3230.
C/ 331 includes 3320 and 3330.
D/ 3410 includes 3420 and 3430.
E/ 351 includes 3520, 3530 and 359.
F/ 3610 includes 369.

Finland

ISIC Revision 3		Output					Value added					Gross fixed capital formation	
		(million MARKS)					(million MARKS)					(thousand MARKS)	
ISIC Industry	Note	1993a/	1994a/	1995b/c/	1996b/c/	Note	1993a/	1994a/	1995c/d/	1996	Note	1995c/d/	1996
151 Processed meat,fish,fruit,vegetables,fats		49691.0e/	48948.0e/	15682.2	17627.2		13095.0e/	12371.0e/	3994.5	...		461371	...
1511 Processing/preserving of meat		...	...	11634.2	13087.7		...	...	2942.1	...		294751	...
1512 Processing/preserving of fish		...	...	303.9	317.9		...	...	79.5	...		16352	...
1513 Processing/preserving of fruit & vegetables		...	...	2094.9	2479.4		...	...	667.9	...		116984	...
1514 Vegetable and animal oils and fats		...	...	1649.2	1742.2		...	...	305.0	...		33284	...
1520 Dairy products		...e/	...e/	10629.4	11469.3		...e/	...e/	1085.2	...		255190	...
153 Grain mill products; starches; animal feeds		...e/	...e/	4567.5	5071.9		...e/	...e/	976.4	...		244542	...
1531 Grain mill products		...	...	909.0	1009.3		...	...	229.6	...		95794	...
1532 Starches and starch products		...	...	702.7	673.0		...	...	113.4	...		32975	...
1533 Prepared animal feeds		...	...	2955.9	3389.6		...	...	633.4	...		115773	...
154 Other food products		...e/	...e/	10725.7	10819.2		...e/	...e/	4102.7	...		422169	...
1541 Bakery products		...	...	4152.8	4557.9		...	...	2263.4	...		113582	...
1542 Sugar		...	...	1762.4	1763.9		...	...	421.4	...		94852	...
1543 Cocoa, chocolate and sugar confectionery		...	...	1753.8	1629.9		...	...	661.8	...		93378	...
1544 Macaroni, noodles & similar products		...	...	...f/	-		...	...	...f/	...		...f/	...
1549 Other food products n.e.c.		...	...	3056.8f/	2867.5		...	...	756.1f/	...		120357f/	...
155 Beverages		...e/	...e/	4650.7	4261.2		...e/	...e/	1713.3	...		484653	...
1551 Distilling, rectifying & blending of spirits		...	...	1403.5g/	1109.0g/		...	...	396.5g/	...		12175g/	...
1552 Wines		...	...	...g/	...g/		...	...	...g/	...		...g/	...
1553 Malt liquors and malt		...	...	3247.2h/	2726.2		...	...	1316.8h/	...		472478h/	...
1554 Soft drinks; mineral waters		...	...	...h/	426.0		...	...	...h/	...		...h/	...
1600 Tobacco products		986.0	974.0	896.7	651.4		490.0	512.0	274.2	...		-74977	...
171 Spinning, weaving and finishing of textiles		3675.0i/	3996.0i/	783.8	700.9		1541.0i/	1787.0i/	235.3	...		21533	...
1711 Textile fibre preparation; textile weaving		...	...	533.9	331.1		...	...	196.1	...		20270	...
1712 Finishing of textiles		...	...	249.8	369.8		...	...	39.2	...		1263	...
172 Other textiles		...i/	...i/	1788.7	2329.7		...i/	...i/	802.5	...		197252	...
1721 Made-up textile articles, except apparel		...	...	362.4	553.2		...	...	151.8	...		9442	...
1722 Carpets and rugs		...	...	44.0	100.0		...	...	25.1	...		647	...
1723 Cordage, rope, twine and netting		...	...	49.7	51.5		...	...	29.1	...		2602	...
1729 Other textiles n.e.c.		...	...	1332.5	1625.0		...	...	596.5	...		184561	...
1730 Knitted and crocheted fabrics and articles		...i/	...i/	593.4	622.4		...i/	...i/	285.0	...		19383	...
1810 Wearing apparel, except fur apparel		2282.0j/	2673.0j/	2698.4	2976.4		1154.0j/	1226.0j/	1249.9	...		42487	...
1820 Dressing & dyeing of fur; processing of fur		...j/	...j/	97.0	152.8		...j/	...j/	34.4	...		966	...
191 Tanning, dressing and processing of leather		1141.0k/	1251.0k/	377.4	445.8		507.0k/	551.0k/	137.3	...		12166	...
1911 Tanning and dressing of leather		...	...	274.7	203.2		...	...	80.3	...		11246	...
1912 Luggage, handbags, etc.; saddlery & harness		...	...	102.8	242.7		...	...	57.1	...		920	...
1920 Footwear		...k/	...k/	940.5	901.3		...k/	...k/	388.7	...		21159	...
2010 Sawmilling and planing of wood		16606.0m/	20624.0m/	11602.7	11237.7		6111.0m/	7587.0m/	3054.9	...		682597	...
202 Products of wood, cork, straw, etc.		...m/	...m/	7730.5	8948.6		...m/	...m/	2906.1	...		326580	...
2021 Veneer sheets, plywood, particle board, etc.		...	...	3833.6	3973.2		...	...	1485.1	...		191717	...
2022 Builders' carpentry and joinery		...	...	3407.3	4251.4		...	...	1194.5	...		125784	...
2023 Wooden containers		...	...	317.6	483.0		...	...	127.2	...		6041	...
2029 Other wood products; articles of cork/straw		...	...	172.1	241.1		...	...	99.3	...		3038	...
210 Paper and paper products		48558.0	55552.0	75591.6	70480.5		15475.0	18275.0	27414.2	...		3734487	...
2101 Pulp, paper and paperboard		...	...	70283.7	64670.2		...	...	25552.4	...		3516246	...
2102 Corrugated paper and paperboard		...	...	2743.5	2858.2		...	...	1009.5	...		124622	...
2109 Other articles of paper and paperboard		...	...	2564.4	2952.1		...	...	852.3	...		93619	...
221 Publishing		16403.0n/	17461.0n/	9702.5	10973.5		7192.0n/	7653.0n/	3774.0	...		196574	...
2211 Publishing of books and other publications		...	...	1616.9	1798.1		...	...	457.2	...		26188	...
2212 Publishing of newspapers, journals, etc.		...	...	7872.9	8748.7		...	...	3195.1	...		163609	...
2213 Publishing of recorded media		...	...	212.8p/	116.3		...	...	121.6p/	...		6777p/	...
2219 Other publishing		...	...	...p/	310.4		...	...	...p/	...		...p/	...

continued

Finland

ISIC Revision 3	Output					Value added					Gross fixed capital formation		
		(million MARKS)					(million MARKS)					(thousand MARKS)	
ISIC Industry	Note	1993a/	1994a/	1995b/c/	1996b/c/	Note	1993a/	1994a/	1995c/d/	1996	Note	1995c/d/	1996
222 Printing and related service activities		...n/	...n/	8020.4	9000.3		...n/	...n/	3616.9	...		410966	...
2221 Printing		...	...	7549.8	8250.3		...	...	3271.3	...		368897	...
2222 Service activities related to printing		...	...	470.5q/	749.9		...	...	345.6q/	...		42069q/	...
2230 Reproduction of recorded media		...n/	...n/	...q/	76.9		...n/	...n/	...q/	...		...q/	...
2310 Coke oven products		12616.0r/	12767.0r/	626.7	684.8		1331.0r/	1979.0r/	177.2	...		21523	...
2320 Refined petroleum products		...r/	...r/	9984.9	13279.4		...r/	...r/	822.1	...		209514	...
2330 Processing of nuclear fuel		...r/	...r/	-	-		...r/	...r/	-	...		-	...
241 Basic chemicals		17981.0s/	20133.0s/	14486.0	15236.9		7169.0s/	7956.0s/	4552.0	...		1525113	...
2411 Basic chemicals, except fertilizers		...	...	8873.3	9416.9		...	...	3133.8	...		1244976	...
2412 Fertilizers and nitrogen compounds		...	...	1850.5	2125.2		...	...	485.3	...		23217	...
2413 Plastics in primary forms; synthetic rubber		...	...	3762.2	3694.8		...	...	933.0	...		256920	...
242 Other chemicals		...s/	...s/	6729.3	7399.5		...s/	...s/	3135.2	...		323779	...
2421 Pesticides and other agro-chemical products		...	...	...t/	-		...	...	...t/	...		...t/	...
2422 Paints, varnishes, printing ink and mastics		...	...	1812.0t/	1976.4		...	...	643.4t/	...		52996t/	...
2423 Pharmaceuticals, medicinal chemicals, etc.		...	..	2570.6	2619.5		...	...	1457.5	...		185727	...
2424 Soap, cleaning & cosmetic preparations		...	...	965.5	1102.5		...	...	370.7	...		27240	...
2429 Other chemical products n.e.c.		...	...	1381.1	1701.0		...	...	663.5	...		57816	...
2430 Man-made fibres		...s/	...s/	604.5	...		...s/	...s/	146.9	...		31204	...
251 Rubber products		7114.0u/	8001.0u/	1681.5	1724.6		3170.0u/	3434.0u/	808.5	...		155927	...
2511 Rubber tyres and tubes		...	...	...	1047.6		...	...	...	...		...	...
2519 Other rubber products		...	...	...	677.1		...	...	...	...		...	...
2520 Plastic products		...u/	...u/	6901.7	7994.1		...u/	...u/	2815.6	...		465029	...
2610 Glass and glass products		6948.0v/	7499.0v/	1951.6	2041.1		3165.0v/	3464.0v/	824.2	...		158450	...
269 Non-metallic mineral products n.e.c.		...v/	...v/	5425.4	6482.2		...v/	...v/	2355.0	...		268926	...
2691 Pottery, china and earthenware		...	...	...	...		...	...	...	...		...	...
2692 Refractory ceramic products		...	...	...	...		...	...	...	...		...	...
2693 Struct.non-refractory clay; ceramic products		...	...	195.1	173.7		...	...	81.9	...		3066	...
2694 Cement, lime and plaster		...	...	612.7	593.7		...	...	291.1	...		13259	...
2695 Articles of concrete, cement and plaster		...	...	2511.5	3207.8		...	...	1085.8	...		142177	...
2696 Cutting, shaping & finishing of stone		...	...	386.7	549.0		...	...	184.9	...		29560	...
2699 Other non-metallic mineral products n.e.c.		...	...	1245.0	1469.7		...	...	445.4	...		57369	...
2710 Basic iron and steel		23769.0w/	25857.0w/	20039.8	18471.7		6519.0w/	7006.0w/	6213.6	...		1017304	...
2720 Basic precious and non-ferrous metals		...w/	...w/	9505.5	10484.8		...w/	...w/	1081.7	...		957889	...
273 Casting of metals		...w/	...w/	1409.5	1399.4		...w/	...w/	687.0	...		78061	...
2731 Casting of iron and steel		...	...	...	1091.3		...	...	...	...		...	...
2732 Casting of non-ferrous metals		...	...	...	...		...	...	...	...		...	...
281 Struct.metal products;tanks;steam generators		13023.0x/	14089.0x/	8914.1	10127.9		5391.0x/	5718.0x/	2747.1	...		152207	...
2811 Structural metal products		...	...	4457.3	5805.7		...	...	1573.5	...		146413	...
2812 Tanks, reservoirs and containers of metal		...	...	1213.7	1143.4		...	...	500.1	...		16809	...
2813 Steam generators		...	...	3243.1	3178.7		...	...	673.4	...		-11015	...
289 Other metal products; metal working services		...x/	...x/	5449.6	7230.7		...x/	...x/	2141.0	...		257031	...
2891 Metal forging/pressing/stamping/roll-forming		...	...	...y/	-		...	...	...y/	...		...y/	...
2892 Treatment & coating of metals		...	...	1589.6y/	2534.6		...	...	455.8y/	...		51396y/	...
2893 Cutlery, hand tools and general hardware		...	...	1281.0	1490.4		...	...	701.6	...		107209	...
2899 Other fabricated metal products n.e.c.		...	...	2579.0	3205.8		...	...	983.5	...		98426	...
291 General purpose machinery		27456.0z/	31936.0z/	16403.3	19620.8		11790.0z/	13081.0z/	6027.2	...		738971	...
2911 Engines & turbines(not for transport equip.)		...	...	3029.9	4007.1		...	...	1036.0	...		128208	...
2912 Pumps, compressors, taps and valves		...	...	2910.7	3361.2		...	...	1192.6	...		108672	...
2913 Bearings, gears, gearing & driving elements		...	...	840.7	955.2		...	...	366.2	...		61024	...
2914 Ovens, furnaces and furnace burners		...	...	97.7	125.6		...	...	26.1	...		8297	...
2915 Lifting and handling equipment		...	...	6237.3	6928.1		...	...	2106.2	...		312427	...
2919 Other general purpose machinery		...	...	3287.0	4243.7		...	...	1300.2	...		120343	...

292 Special purpose machinery	...z/	...z/	20872.6	26696.4	...z/	...z/	7229.5	...	520093	...
2921 Agricultural and forestry machinery	...	...	2683.0	3048.7	...	...	759.6	...	75915	...
2922 Machine tools	...	...	2361.3	2544.6	...	...	884.3	...	120841	...
2923 Machinery for metallurgy	...	...	293.9	305.3	...	...	49.1	...	2757	...
2924 Machinery for mining & construction	...	...	3277.7	3349.1	...	...	1123.9	...	107719	...
2925 Food/beverage/tobacco processing machinery	...	...	277.6	438.4	...	...	153.3	...	4286	...
2926 Machinery for textile, apparel and leather	...	...	17.0	...	...	...	6.9	...	-627	...
2927 Weapons and ammunition	...	...	465.4	624.8	...	...	251.1	...	22679	...
2929 Other special purpose machinery	...	...	11496.8	16027.5	...	...	4001.3	...	186523	...
2930 Domestic appliances n.e.c.	...z/	...z/	1179.2	1278.9	...z/	...z/	398.1	...	38973	...
3000 Office, accounting and computing machinery	4440.0	4765.0	5514.3	4574.3	768.0	589.0	670.4	...	108638	...
3110 Electric motors, generators and transformers	8369.0A/	10066.0A/	5654.0	5660.4	3885.0A/	4409.0A/	1899.9	...	-225640	...
3120 Electricity distribution & control apparatus	...A/	...A/	2530.2	3212.3	...A/	...A/	1102.1	...	65539	...
3130 Insulated wire and cable	...A/	...A/	1686.2B/	1884.3B/	...A/	...A/	811.7B/	...	45104B/	...
3140 Accumulators, primary cells and batteries	...A/	...A/	...B/	...B/	...A/	...A/	...B/	...	...B/	...
3150 Lighting equipment and electric lamps	...A/	...A/	833.7	880.9	...A/	...A/	332.1	...	18771	...
3190 Other electrical equipment n.e.c.	...A/	...A/	1151.1	1335.3	...A/	...A/	519.1	...	66936	...
3210 Electronic valves, tubes, etc.	11568.0C/	17304.0C/	1802.7	2234.7	4489.0C/	5828.0C/	651.6	...	185842	...
3220 TV/radio transmitters; line comm. apparatus	...C/	...C/	25656.7	28434.6	...C/	...C/	7548.0	...	1532546	...
3230 TV and radio receivers and associated goods	...C/	...C/	1285.9	1077.6	...C/	...C/	264.9	...	73358	...
331 Medical, measuring, testing appliances, etc.	3625.0D/	3990.0D/	4758.3	6106.5	1837.0D/	1865.0D/	2019.5	...	112959	...
3311 Medical, surgical and orthopaedic equipment	...	...	2309.0	2867.8	...	...	982.7	...	43005	...
3312 Measuring/testing/navigating appliances,etc.	...	...	1247.8	1816.7	...	...	601.4	...	49734	...
3313 Industrial process control equipment	...	...	1201.5	1422.0	...	...	435.5	...	20220	...
3320 Optical instruments & photographic equipment	...D/	...D/	131.0	171.9	...D/	...D/	60.5	...	4453	...
3330 Watches and clocks	...D/	...D/	-	-	...D/	...D/	-	...	-	...
3410 Motor vehicles	3072.0E/	3395.0E/	1896.6	1653.9	1008.0E/	1482.0E/	660.2	...	89432	...
3420 Automobile bodies, trailers & semi-trailers	...E/	...E/	1402.4	1845.6	...E/	...E/	517.0	...	30499	...
3430 Parts/accessories for automobiles	...E/	...E/	721.5	682.7	...E/	...E/	284.1	...	64366	...
351 Building and repairing of ships and boats	7359.0F/	8772.0F/	8625.7	7478.4	3246.0F/	3301.0F/	2649.2	...	175689	...
3511 Building and repairing of ships	...	...	8281.8	6861.1	...	...	2518.6	...	165276	...
3512 Building/repairing of pleasure/sport. boats	...	...	344.0	617.3	...	...	130.7	...	10413	...
3520 Railway/tramway locomotives & rolling stock	...F/	...F/	886.3	940.4	...F/	...F/	360.3	...	1268	...
3530 Aircraft and spacecraft	...F/	...F/	1155.1	1205.1	...F/	...F/	582.6	...	143205	...
359 Transport equipment n.e.c.	...F/	...F/	259.0	266.6	...F/	...F/	104.2	...	7999	...
3591 Motorcycles	...	...	...	...	...	...	...	...	...	...
3592 Bicycles and invalid carriages	...	...	...	...	...	...	...	...	...	...
3599 Other transport equipment n.e.c.	...	...	32.9	37.6	...	...	20.3	...	794	...
3610 Furniture	5519.0G/	6096.0G/	4023.9	4817.1	2483.0G/	2663.0G/	1828.6	...	116000	...
369 Manufacturing n.e.c.	...G/	...G/	1684.8	2029.1	...G/	...G/	792.1	...	58382	...
3691 Jewellery and related articles	...	...	378.9	404.4	...	...	164.1	...	6035	...
3692 Musical instruments	...	...	-	24.7	...	...	-	...	-	...
3693 Sports goods	...	...	599.5	679.3	...	...	269.3	...	15196	...
3694 Games and toys	...	...	153.2	148.0	...	...	69.1	...	14340	...
3699 Other manufacturing n.e.c.	...	...	553.2	772.7	...	...	289.7	...	22811	...
3710 Recycling of metal waste and scrap	-	-	443.3	497.5	-	-	80.9	...	10903	...
3720 Recycling of non-metal waste and scrap	-	-	8.2	15.7	-	-	5.1	...	1176	...
D Total manufacturing	292201.0	326149.0	371355.4	395904.9	101816.0	112737.0	121951.5	...	17066517	...

a/ National Accounts estimates.
b/ Output in factor values.
c/ Industrial survey results.
d/ Data are provisional.
e/ 151 includes 1520, 153, 154 and 155.
f/ 1549 includes 1544.
g/ 1551 includes 1552.
h/ 1553 includes 1554.
i/ 171 includes 172 and 1730.
j/ 1810 includes 1820.
k/ 191 includes 1920.
m/ 2010 includes 202.
n/ 221 includes 222 and 2230.
p/ 2213 includes 2219.
q/ 2222 includes 2230.
r/ 2310 includes 2320 and 2330.
s/ 241 includes 242 and 2430.
t/ 2422 includes 2421.
u/ 251 includes 2520.
v/ 2610 includes 269.
w/ 2710 includes 2720 and 273.
x/ 281 includes 289.
y/ 2892 includes 2891.
z/ 291 includes 292 and 2930.
A/ 3110 includes 3120, 3130, 3140, 3150 and 3190.
B/ 3130 includes 3140.
C/ 3210 includes 3220 and 3230.
D/ 331 includes 3320 and 3330.
E/ 3410 includes 3420 and 3430.
F/ 351 includes 3520, 3530 and 359.
G/ 3610 includes 369.

Finland

ISIC Revision 3		Note	Index numbers of industrial production											
			(1990=100)											
ISIC Industry			1985	1986	1987	1988	1989	1990	1991	1992	1993	1994	1995	1996
15	Food and beverages		...	...	...	...	...	100	99	100	104	103	105	110
16	Tobacco products		...	...	...	...	...	100	90	90	84	82	78	79
17	Textiles		...	...	...	...	...	100	85	87	88	97	95	98
18	Wearing apparel, fur		...	...	...	...	...	100	77	62	59	65	58	53
19	Leather, leather products and footwear		...	...	...	...	...	100	84	75	70	76	75	72
20	Wood products (excl. furniture)		...	...	...	...	...	100	78	80	92	107	106	109
21	Paper and paper products		...	...	...	...	...	100	97	101	110	121	123	118
22	Printing and publishing		...	...	...	...	...	100	90	84	82	85	89	89
23	Coke,refined petroleum products,nuclear fuel		...	...	...	...	...	100	103	106	103	121	116	126
24	Chemicals and chemical products		...	...	...	...	...	100	95	97	100	112	114	113
25	Rubber and plastics products		...	...	...	...	...	100	87	88	95	103	108	109
26	Non-metallic mineral products		...	...	...	...	...	100	85	72	66	72	74	77
27	Basic metals		...	...	...	...	...	100	98	108	115	123	127	140
28	Fabricated metal products		...	...	...	...	...	100	75	69	73	80	93	100
29	Machinery and equipment n.e.c.		...	...	...	...	...	100	76	74	76	89	109	115
30	Office, accounting and computing machinery		...	...	...	...	...	100	106	171	194	195	191	209
31	Electrical machinery and apparatus		...	...	...	...	...	100	92	98	97	112	120	128
32	Radio,television and communication equipment		...	...	...	...	...	100	87	117	178	264	371	404
33	Medical, precision and optical instruments		...	...	...	...	...	100	88	87	96	102	114	128
34	Motor vehicles, trailers, semi-trailers		...	...	...	...	...	100	80	81	58	67	72	75
35	Other transport equipment		...	...	...	...	...	100	96	102	95	109	124	113
36	Furniture; manufacturing n.e.c.		...	...	...	...	...	100	87	83	79	87	89	94
37	Recycling		...	...	...	...	...	...	...	...	...	...	...	...
D	Total manufacturing		88	89	94	97	101	100	89	91	95	106	118	121

FRANCE

Supplier of information:
Institut National de la Statistique et des Etudes Economiques (INSEE), Paris.
Industrial statistics for the OECD countries are compiled by the OECD secretariat, which supplies them to UNIDO. The notes appearing here are based on information in the OECD publication *Industriall Structure Statistics* (annual),OECD, Paris.

Basic source of data:
National accounts compilations.

Major deviations from ISIC (Revision 2):
None reported.

Reference period (if not calendar year):

Scope:
All establishments.

Method of enumeration:
Not reported.

Adjusted for non-response:
Yes.

Concepts and definitions of variables:
Number of employees refers to the average number of employees throughout the year. Both full- and part-time employees are included.
Output is gross output in basic values.
Value added, also in basic values, is calculated as gross output, less the cost of materials, fuels and other supplies; contract, commission, repair and maintenance work done by others; goods shipped in the same condition as received; and electricity purchased. Inputs are calculated on the basis of the amount consumed.
Gross fixed capital formation is the value of acquisitions of fixed capital (plus own-account construction) less the value of sales of own account construction. Fixed assets covered are those with a productive life of more than one year and include assets made by a unit's labour force for its own use; additions, alterations, improvements, and repairs; new assets not yet in use and used assets. Valuation for new assets is the full cost incurred, including delivered price and installation charges, but excluding fees and taxes. Assets produced by the unit are valued at the cost of work put in progress, while for sales of used assets, the actual amount realized is taken.

Related national publications:
Système élargi de comptabilité nationale; Sources et méthodes d'élaboration des comptes nationaux, both published by Institut National de la Statistique et des Etudes Economiques (INSEE), Paris.

France

ISIC Revision 2		Number of establishments					Number of employees					Wages and salaries paid to employees			
		(numbers)					(thousands)					(million FRANCS)			
ISIC Industry	Note	1993	1994	1995	1996	Note	1993	1994	1995	1996	Note	1993	1994	1995	1996
311/2 Food products		...	...	...	...		449.9	446.0	443.5	441.1		...	...	...	...
313 Beverages		...	...	...	...		40.6	40.4	40.4	40.1		...	...	...	...
314 Tobacco		...	...	...	...		4.8	4.5	4.5	4.4		...	...	...	...
321 Textiles		...	...	...	...		168.5	159.7	154.3	146.6		...	...	...	...
322 Wearing apparel, except footwear		...	...	...	...		122.3	115.9	111.9	106.2		...	...	...	...
323 Leather and fur products		...	...	...	...		15.5	14.5	14.3	13.8		...	...	...	...
324 Footwear, except rubber or plastic		...	...	...	...		41.5	38.9	38.4	36.9		...	...	...	...
331 Wood products, except furniture		...	...	...	...		82.2	80.1	79.6	78.2		...	...	...	...
332 Furniture and fixtures, excl. metal		...	...	...	...		76.6	74.7	74.2	72.9		...	...	...	...
341 Paper and products		...	...	...	...		101.9	100.8	100.3	98.0		...	...	...	...
342 Printing and publishing		...	...	...	...		222.3	219.1	219.0	215.9		...	...	...	...
351 Industrial chemicals		...	...	...	...		104.3	101.3	100.5	98.1		...	...	...	...
352 Other chemicals		...	...	...	...		179.5	177.1	177.6	175.0		...	...	...	...
353 Petroleum refineries		...	...	...	...		18.0	18.0	17.2	16.8		...	...	...	...
354 Misc. petroleum and coal products		...	...	...	...		...	...	...	...		...	...	...	...
355 Rubber products		...	...	...	...		82.9	81.7	82.9	82.7		...	...	...	...
356 Plastic products		...	...	...	...		119.5	117.6	119.3	118.9		...	...	...	...
361 Pottery, china, earthenware		...	...	...	...		...	...	...	...		...	...	...	...
362 Glass and products		...	...	...	...		53.1	51.5	51.3	50.2		...	...	...	...
369 Other non-metallic mineral products		...	...	...	...		77.8	74.9	74.5	72.8		...	...	...	...
371 Iron and steel		...	...	...	...		161.6	156.2	157.6	155.8		...	...	...	...
372 Non-ferrous metals		...	...	...	...		43.1	42.0	41.2	39.8		...	...	...	...
381 Fabricated metal products		...	...	...	...		310.4	299.0	303.3	304.4		...	...	...	...
382 Non-electrical machinery		...	...	...	...		394.0	378.5	382.4	380.7		...	...	...	...
383 Electrical machinery		...	...	...	...		430.7	420.7	425.1	420.5		...	...	...	...
384 Transport equipment		...	...	...	...		506.1	489.2	486.7	482.2		...	...	...	...
385 Professional and scientific equipment		...	...	...	...		60.4	57.9	58.5	58.3		...	...	...	...
390 Other manufacturing industries		...	...	...	...		83.1	81.0	80.3	78.9		...	...	...	...
3 Total manufacturing		...	...	...	...		3950.6	3841.2	3838.8	3789.2		...	...	...	...

France

ISIC Revision 2 ISIC Industry	Output Note	(million FRANCS) 1993	1994	1995	1996	Value added Note	(million FRANCS) 1993	1994	1995	1996	Gross fixed capital formation Note	(million FRANCS) 1995	1996
311/2 Food products		532230	540681	553029	...		156657	153756	156589	...	a/	24379	22901
313 Beverages		76334	75327	76153	...		34097	34461	33499	...	a/	...	...
314 Tobacco		17381	20024	20651	...		14682	17383	17977	...	a/	...	...
321 Textiles		100729	107803	108871	...		33942	35901	36255	...	b/	6344	6173
322 Wearing apparel, except footwear		67860	67908	64080	...		31208	29656	27408	...	b/	...	...
323 Leather and fur products		10798	11957	13045	...		5345	5882	6692	...	c/	414	331
324 Footwear, except rubber or plastic		14859	14099	13447	...		7684	6850	6278	...	c/	...	...
331 Wood products, except furniture		54277	60370	63752	...		22898	23252	25242	...	d/	5722	5445
332 Furniture and fixtures, excl. metal		48843	49035	51109	...		22950	22767	23655	...	d/	...	...
341 Paper and products		96791	105018	121852	...		32843	33193	38585	...		6006	6005
342 Printing and publishing		178909	185379	191306	...		81377	83000	83083	...		8040	7806
351 Industrial chemicals		139570	151555	162247	...		40037	43707	51146	...		10511	11162
352 Other chemicals		216095	228401	234943	...		82829	86109	83487	...		10926	12141
353 Petroleum refineries		192862	192628	195873	...		90686	90969	94221	...	e/	10838	10647
354 Misc. petroleum and coal products		...	...	...	...		...	...	...	...		...	...
355 Rubber products		36219	37769	38985	...		18417	18184	17602	...	f/	9310	8818
356 Plastic products		102400	106143	111680	...		38484	38051	40156	...	f/	...	...
361 Pottery, china, earthenware		...	...	...	...		...	...	...	...		...	...
362 Glass and products		29615	31495	34241	...		14970	15523	16638	...		2770	3365
369 Other non-metallic mineral products		88446	93760	96342	...		39454	41233	43752	...		10078	9825
371 Iron and steel		113247	128624	135886	...		33595	37214	41792	...		226	538
372 Non-ferrous metals		68034	74340	82899	...		22595	25258	27882	...		9159	8649
381 Fabricated metal products		204480	223239	239795	...		104738	111576	118930	...		13457	12759
382 Non-electrical machinery		303730	312384	333933	...		112861	111819	116132	...		13989	14148
383 Electrical machinery		309917	324171	342641	...		145711	149112	156850	...		14427	14148
384 Transport equipment		475657	521940	545331	...		146351	160281	165098	...		27271	28700
385 Professional and scientific equipment		41169	43104	44932	...		21803	22722	23342	...		...	...
390 Other manufacturing industries		48451	50683	53180	...		24083	25208	25720	...		...	...
3 Total manufacturing		3568903	3757837	3930203	...		1380297	1423067	1478011	...		183867	183561

a/ 311/2 includes 313 and 314.
b/ 321 includes 322.
c/ 323 includes 324.
d/ 331 includes 332.
e/ 353 includes production of crude petroleum and natural gas.
f/ 355 includes 356.

France

ISIC Revision 2		Index numbers of industrial production (1990=100)											
ISIC Industry	Note	1985	1986	1987	1988	1989	1990	1991	1992	1993	1994	1995	1996
311/2 Food products	a/	89	90	92	95	97	100	101	102	104	105	108	111
313 Beverages	a/	...	...	...	...	...	...	...	...	...	...	...	...
314 Tobacco		122	108	99	96	97	100	92	97	89	88	85	87
321 Textiles		114	110	105	104	104	100	95	93	87	92	91	86
322 Wearing apparel, except footwear		134	133	124	112	105	100	94	88	81	81	75	63
323 Leather and fur products	b/	121	118	109	98	98	100	94	90	85	83	80	73
324 Footwear, except rubber or plastic	b/	...	...	...	...	...	...	...	...	...	...	...	...
331 Wood products, except furniture		86	86	90	96	101	100	99	95	88	97	97	95
332 Furniture and fixtures, excl. metal	c/	...	...	...	...	...	...	...	...	...	...	...	...
341 Paper and products		83	85	89	94	98	100	103	109	106	113	111	111
342 Printing and publishing		77	77	83	92	97	100	96	93	91	92	94	93
351 Industrial chemicals	d/	86	86	89	94	99	100	101	107	108	115	116	120
352 Other chemicals	d/	...	...	...	...	...	...	...	...	...	...	...	...
353 Petroleum refineries	e/	104	99	93	100	99	100	104	101	105	102	104	106
354 Misc. petroleum and coal products	e/	...	...	...	...	...	...	...	...	...	...	...	...
355 Rubber products	f/	78	81	85	91	97	100	99	102	97	105	109	109
356 Plastic products	f/	...	...	...	...	...	...	...	...	...	...	...	...
361 Pottery, china, earthenware	g/	90	89	91	96	97	100	96	90	83	90	93	87
362 Glass and products	g/	...	...	...	...	...	...	...	...	...	...	...	...
369 Other non-metallic mineral products	g/	...	...	...	...	...	...	...	...	...	...	...	...
371 Iron and steel	h/	94	91	91	98	101	100	97	95	87	96	97	95
372 Non-ferrous metals	h/	...	...	...	...	...	...	...	...	...	...	...	...
381 Fabricated metal products		88	88	89	94	100	100	95	90	83	88	93	90
382 Non-electrical machinery		87	85	85	92	96	100	93	89	82	83	87	87
383 Electrical machinery		91	91	90	92	96	100	99	100	98	103	109	110
384 Transport equipment		89	91	89	96	102	100	99	96	88	93	88	90
385 Professional and scientific equipment		91	92	95	98	97	100	95	89	84	82	81	83
390 Other manufacturing industries	c/	84	85	88	93	96	100	95	91	84	80	79	76
3 Total manufacturing		91	90	91	95	99	100	98	97	93	97	98	98

a/ 311/2 includes 313.
b/ 323 includes 324.
c/ 390 includes 332.
d/ 351 includes 352.
e/ 353 includes 354.
f/ 355 includes 356.
g/ 361 includes 362 and 369.
h/ 371 includes 372.

GAMBIA

Supplier of information:
Department of State for Trade, Industry and Employment, in close cooperation with the Central Statistics Department, Banjul.

Basic source of data:
Census of Industrial Production, 1995/6.

Major deviations from ISIC (Revision 3):
None reported.

Reference period (if not calendar year):
Fiscal year.

Scope:
All establishments with 5 or more persons engaged.

Method of enumeration:
Individual sites are visited by enumerators.

Adjusted for non-response:
Not reported.

Concepts and definitions of variables:
Wages and salaries is the compensation of employees.

Related national publications:
National Accounts of The Gambia, Banjul.

Gambia

ISIC Revision 3		Number of establishments					Number of employees					Wages and salaries paid to employees			
			(numbers)					(numbers)					(thousand DALASIS)		
ISIC	Industry	Note	1992	1993	1994	1995	Note	1992	1993	1994	1995	Note	1992	1993	1994	1995
15	Food and beverages		...	...	...	21		...	...	...	1392		...	...	...	18928
17	Textiles		...	...	...	75a/		...	...	...	380a/		...	...	...	2106a/
18	Wearing apparel, fur		...	...	...	...a/		...	...	...	...a/		...	...	...	...a/
20	Wood products (excl. furniture)		...	...	...	74b/		...	...	...	534b/		...	...	...	2111b/
22	Printing and publishing		...	...	...	4		...	...	...	36		...	...	...	665
24	Chemicals and chemical products		...	...	...	2c/		...	...	...	127c/		...	...	...	1483c/
25	Rubber and plastic products		...	...	...	...c/		...	...	...	...c/		...	...	...	...c/
27	Basic metals		...	...	...	3		...	...	...	25		...	...	...	353
28	Fabricated metal products		...	...	...	51		...	...	...	357		...	...	...	1669
29	Machinery and equipment n.e.c.		...	...	...	2d/		...	...	...	11d/		...	...	...	191d/
35	Other transport equipment		...	...	...	...d/		...	...	...	...d/		...	...	...	...d/
36	Furniture; manufacturing n.e.c.		...	...	...	...b/		...	...	...	...b/		...	...	...	...b/
D	Total manufacturing		...	...	...	232		...	...	...	2862		...	...	...	27506

a/ 17 includes 18.
b/ 20 includes 36.
c/ 24 includes 25.
d/ 29 includes 35.

ISIC Revision 3		Output in producers' prices					Value added in producers' prices					Gross fixed capital formation		
			(thousand DALASIS)					(thousand DALASIS)					(thousand DALASIS)	
ISIC	Industry	Note	1992	1993	1994	1995	Note	1992	1993	1994	1995	Note	1994	1995
15	Food and beverages		...	...	...	208887		...	...	...	57381		...	...
17	Textiles		...	...	...	18309a/		...	...	...	7320a/		...	...
18	Wearing apparel, fur		...	...	...	...a/		...	...	...	...a/		...	...
20	Wood products (excl. furniture)		...	...	...	10830b/		...	...	...	5473b/		...	...
22	Printing and publishing		...	...	...	5468		...	...	...	3711		...	...
24	Chemicals and chemical products		...	...	...	36432c/		...	...	...	7805c/		...	...
25	Rubber and plastic products		...	...	...	...c/		...	...	...	...c/		...	...
27	Basic metals		...	...	...	6007		...	...	...	1608		...	...
28	Fabricated metal products			...	...	9633		...	...	...	4278		...	...
29	Machinery and equipment n.e.c.		...	...	...	2132d/		...	...	...	695d/		...	...
35	Other transport equipment		...	...	...	...d/		...	...	...	...d/		...	...
36	Furniture; manufacturing n.e.c.		...	...	...	...b/		...	...	...	...b/		...	...
D	Total manufacturing		...	...	...	297697		...	...	...	88272		...	...

a/ 17 includes 18.
b/ 20 includes 36.
c/ 24 includes 25.
d/ 29 includes 35.

GREECE

Supplier of information:
National Statistical Service of Greece, Athens.
Industrial statistics for the OECD countries are compiled by the OECD secretariat, which supplies them to UNIDO.

Basic source of data:
Annual industrial survey.

Major deviations from ISIC (Revision 3):
None reported.

Reference period (if not calendar year):

Scope:
Manufacturing establishments with 10 or more persons engaged, excluding government establishments.

Method of enumeration:
Complete enumeration of establishments with 20 or more persons engaged and a stratified random sample of establishments with 10 to 19 persons.

Adjusted for non-response:
Not reported.

Concepts and definitions of variables:
Number of employees covers salaried employees, defined as persons receiving a monthly salary on a contractual basis irrespective of the amount of the remuneration, and wage earners, defined as persons receiving a daily pay or paid on a piece-work basis either in cash or in kind.
Wages and salaries covers wages, salaries, payments for overtime work and regular leave, bonuses, allowances, dismissal compensation and the value of receipts in kind.
Output comprises the value of finished goods produced, receipts from contract work done for others, receipts from repair work, receipts from the sale of goods sold in the same condition as purchased, sales of self-produced steam, electric energy, processing waste, and subsidies and reimbursements for re-export of products. Value is at ex-factory selling price, excluding indirect taxes.
Value added is the value of the output less the cost of materials and supplies, purchased fuels and electricity consumed, the purchase value of goods sold in the same condition as purchased, and payments for contract and repair work.
Gross fixed capital formation represents current expenditure on new and used fixed assets less sales and write-offs due to obsolescence. Own-account construction of fixed assets is included.

Related national publications:

Greece

ISIC Revision 3	Number of establishments					Number of employees					Wages and salaries paid to employees				
		(numbers)					(numbers)					(million DRACHMAS)			
ISIC Industry	Note	1992	1993	1994	1995	Note	1992	1993	1994	1995	Note	1992	1993	1994	1995
151 Processed meat,fish,fruit,vegetables,fats		...	400	387	380		...	16428	16474	16137		...	41636	46999	49924
1511 Processing/preserving of meat		...	...	...	...		...	...	...	...		...	...	...	...
1512 Processing/preserving of fish		...	...	...	...		...	...	...	...		...	...	...	...
1513 Processing/preserving of fruit & vegetables		...	...	...	...		...	...	...	...		...	...	...	...
1514 Vegetable and animal oils and fats		...	...	...	...		...	...	...	...		...	...	...	...
1520 Dairy products		...	88	89	89		...	6794	6938	7059		...	20396	25715	28565
153 Grain mill products; starches; animal feeds		...	134	130	129		...	4037	3509	3499		...	11969	12079	13370
1531 Grain mill products		...	...	...	...		...	...	...	...		...	...	...	...
1532 Starches and starch products		...	...	...	...		...	...	...	...		...	...	...	...
1533 Prepared animal feeds		...	...	...	...		...	...	...	...		...	...	...	...
154 Other food products		...	346	342	339		...	14964	15415	15283		...	40283	49264	53858
1541 Bakery products		...	...	...	...		...	...	...	...		...	...	...	...
1542 Sugar		...	...	...	...		...	...	...	...		...	...	...	...
1543 Cocoa, chocolate and sugar confectionery		...	...	...	...		...	...	...	...		...	...	...	...
1544 Macaroni, noodles & similar products		...	...	...	...		...	...	...	...		...	...	...	...
1549 Other food products n.e.c.		...	...	...	...		...	...	...	...		...	...	...	...
155 Beverages		...	158	158	154		...	9105	8917	8608		...	34431	39308	42443
1551 Distilling, rectifying & blending of spirits		...	...	...	...		...	...	...	...		...	...	...	...
1552 Wines		...	...	...	...		...	...	...	...		...	...	...	...
1553 Malt liquors and malt		...	...	...	...		...	...	...	...		...	...	...	...
1554 Soft drinks; mineral waters		...	...	...	...		...	...	...	...		...	...	...	...
1600 Tobacco products		...	14	14	14		...	3315	2996	2925		...	10289	13475	14663
171 Spinning, weaving and finishing of textiles		...	220	201	194		...	15929	14176	13981		...	42749	43851	47871
1711 Textile fibre preparation; textile weaving		...	...	...	...		...	...	...	...		...	...	...	...
1712 Finishing of textiles		...	...	...	...		...	...	...	...		...	...	...	...
172 Other textiles		...	133	126	124		...	4479	3988	4076		...	9499	9943	10813
1721 Made-up textile articles, except apparel		...	...	...	...		...	...	...	...		...	...	...	...
1722 Carpets and rugs		...	...	...	...		...	...	...	...		...	...	...	...
1723 Cordage, rope, twine and netting		...	...	...	...		...	...	...	...		...	...	...	...
1729 Other textiles n.e.c.		...	...	...	...		...	...	...	...		...	...	...	...
1730 Knitted and crocheted fabrics and articles		...	172	172	162		...	7279	6422	5613		...	14757	14580	14121
1810 Wearing apparel, except fur apparel		...	863	805	759		...	34487	30063	28084		...	64840	63876	67077
1820 Dressing & dyeing of fur; processing of fur		...	40	38	38		...	805	771	689		...	1361	1395	1400
191 Tanning, dressing and processing of leather		...	57	50	47		...	1144	964	865		...	2816	2791	2776
1911 Tanning and dressing of leather		...	...	...	...		...	...	...	...		...	...	...	...
1912 Luggage, handbags, etc.; saddlery & harness		...	...	...	...		...	...	...	...		...	...	...	...
1920 Footwear		...	188	185	181		...	5065	4716	4486		...	9932	11023	11966
2010 Sawmilling and planing of wood		...	36	32	32		...	838	761	754		...	1972	1975	2029
202 Products of wood, cork, straw, etc.		...	141	134	128		...	4787	4267	3988		...	13472	12730	13852
2021 Veneer sheets, plywood, particle board, etc.		...	...	...	...		...	...	...	...		...	...	...	...
2022 Builders' carpentry and joinery		...	...	...	...		...	...	...	...		...	...	...	...
2023 Wooden containers		...	...	...	...		...	...	...	...		...	...	...	...
2029 Other wood products; articles of cork/straw		...	...	...	...		...	...	...	...		...	...	...	...
210 Paper and paper products		...	138	138	139		...	7851	8022	8293		...	24874	27001	31116
2101 Pulp, paper and paperboard		...	...	...	...		...	...	...	...		...	...	...	...
2102 Corrugated paper and paperboard		...	...	...	...		...	...	...	...		...	...	...	...
2109 Other articles of paper and paperboard		...	...	...	...		...	...	...	...		...	...	...	...
221 Publishing		...	112	112	111		...	6685	6787	6872		...	22518	26301	28683
2211 Publishing of books and other publications		...	...	...	...		...	...	...	...		...	...	...	...
2212 Publishing of newspapers, journals, etc.		...	...	...	...		...	...	...	...		...	...	...	...
2213 Publishing of recorded media		...	...	...	...		...	...	...	...		...	...	...	...
2219 Other publishing		...	...	...	...		...	...	...	...		...	...	...	...

ISIC	Description												
222	Printing and related service activities	...	126	122	125	...	3357	3379	3216	...	9422	11299	11434
2221	Printing	...	...	...	...	...	...	...	...	...	...	...	...
2222	Service activities related to printing	...	...	...	...	...	...	...	...	...	...	...	...
2230	Reproduction of recorded media	...	-	-	-	...	-	-	-	...	-	-	-
2310	Coke oven products	...	-	-	-	...	-	-	-	...	-	-	-
2320	Refined petroleum products	...	18	17	17	...	4182	4261	4117	...	18783	23716	28334
2330	Processing of nuclear fuel	...	-	-	-	...	-	-	-	...	-	-	-
241	Basic chemicals	...	66	65	65	...	4593	4430	4342	...	21990	23997	26932
2411	Basic chemicals, except fertilizers	...	...	...	...	...	...	...	...	...	...	...	...
2412	Fertilizers and nitrogen compounds	...	...	...	...	...	...	...	...	...	...	...	...
2413	Plastics in primary forms; synthetic rubber	...	...	...	...	...	...	...	...	...	...	...	...
242	Other chemicals	...	266	257	253	...	14949	14761	13929	...	54009	60058	64344
2421	Pesticides and other agro-chemical products	...	...	...	...	...	...	...	...	...	...	...	...
2422	Paints, varnishes, printing ink and mastics	...	...	...	...	...	...	...	...	...	...	...	...
2423	Pharmaceuticals, medicinal chemicals, etc.	...	...	...	...	...	...	...	...	...	...	...	...
2424	Soap, cleaning & cosmetic preparations	...	...	...	...	...	...	...	...	...	...	...	...
2429	Other chemical products n.e.c.	...	...	...	...	...	...	...	...	...	...	...	...
2430	Man-made fibres	...	5	5	5	...	1056	955	937	...	2687	3313	3465
251	Rubber products	...	25	25	25	...	1005	998	1012	...	4185	4805	5492
2511	Rubber tyres and tubes	...	...	...	...	...	...	...	...	...	...	...	...
2519	Other rubber products	...	...	...	...	...	...	...	...	...	...	...	...
2520	Plastic products	...	232	238	243	...	7963	8062	8380	...	21118	24015	27314
2610	Glass and glass products	...	25	22	20	...	1089	1018	906	...	2859	2973	3089
269	Non-metallic mineral products n.e.c.	...	489	483	476	...	17624	16562	16087	...	59551	63712	69460
2691	Pottery, china and earthenware	...	...	...	...	...	...	...	...	...	...	...	...
2692	Refractory ceramic products	...	...	...	...	...	...	...	...	...	...	...	...
2693	Struct.non-refractory clay; ceramic products	...	...	...	...	...	...	...	...	...	...	...	...
2694	Cement, lime and plaster	...	...	...	...	...	...	...	...	...	...	...	...
2695	Articles of concrete, cement and plaster	...	...	...	...	...	...	...	...	...	...	...	...
2696	Cutting, shaping & finishing of stone	...	...	...	...	...	...	...	...	...	...	...	...
2699	Other non-metallic mineral products n.e.c.	...	...	...	...	...	...	...	...	...	...	...	...
2710	Basic iron and steel	...	75	70	69	...	6077	5639	5421	...	24035	24618	27433
2720	Basic precious and non-ferrous metals	...	48	51	50	...	4787	4836	4895	...	23068	23287	28005
273	Casting of metals	...	6	5	6	...	100	164	255	...	281	508	817
2731	Casting of iron and steel	...	...	...	...	...	...	...	...	...	...	...	...
2732	Casting of non-ferrous metals	...	...	...	...	...	...	...	...	...	...	...	...
281	Struct.metal products;tanks;steam generators	...	156	140	139	...	4315	3744	3713	...	11190	10516	12078
2811	Structural metal products	...	...	...	...	...	...	...	...	...	...	...	...
2812	Tanks, reservoirs and containers of metal	...	...	...	...	...	...	...	...	...	...	...	...
2813	Steam generators	...	...	...	...	...	...	...	...	...	...	...	...
289	Other metal products; metal working services	...	223	222	222	...	6764	6892	6697	...	18760	21559	23361
2891	Metal forging/pressing/stamping/roll-forming	...	...	...	...	...	...	...	...	...	...	...	...
2892	Treatment & coating of metals	...	...	...	...	...	...	...	...	...	...	...	...
2893	Cutlery, hand tools and general hardware	...	...	...	...	...	...	...	...	...	...	...	...
2899	Other fabricated metal products n.e.c.	...	...	...	...	...	...	...	...	...	...	...	...
291	General purpose machinery	...	150	149	140	...	4316	4260	4132	...	11244	12406	13733
2911	Engines & turbines(not for transport equip.)	...	...	...	...	...	...	...	...	...	...	...	...
2912	Pumps, compressors, taps and valves	...	...	...	...	...	...	...	...	...	...	...	...
2913	Bearings, gears, gearing & driving elements	...	...	...	...	...	...	...	...	...	...	...	...
2914	Ovens, furnaces and furnace burners	...	...	...	...	...	...	...	...	...	...	...	...
2915	Lifting and handling equipment	...	...	...	...	...	...	...	...	...	...	...	...
2919	Other general purpose machinery	...	...	...	...	...	...	...	...	...	...	...	...
292	Special purpose machinery	...	127	127	129	...	4702	4638	4873	...	14084	16243	19545
2921	Agricultural and forestry machinery	...	...	...	...	...	...	...	...	...	...	...	...
2922	Machine tools	...	...	...	...	...	...	...	...	...	...	...	...
2923	Machinery for metallurgy	...	...	...	...	...	...	...	...	...	...	...	...
2924	Machinery for mining & construction	...	...	...	...	...	...	...	...	...	...	...	...
2925	Food/beverage/tobacco processing machinery	...	...	...	...	...	...	...	...	...	...	...	...
2926	Machinery for textile, apparel and leather	...	...	...	...	...	...	...	...	...	...	...	...
2927	Weapons and ammunition	...	...	...	...	...	...	...	...	...	...	...	...
2929	Other special purpose machinery	...	...	...	...	...	...	...	...	...	...	...	...
2930	Domestic appliances n.e.c.	...	65	63	63	...	2266	2210	2162	...	7014	7865	8434

continued

Greece

ISIC Revision 3	Number of establishments					Number of employees					Wages and salaries paid to employees				
		(numbers)					(numbers)					(million DRACHMAS)			
ISIC Industry	Note	1992	1993	1994	1995	Note	1992	1993	1994	1995	Note	1992	1993	1994	1995
3000 Office, accounting and computing machinery		...	5	4	4		...	72	58	102		...	239	186	498
3110 Electric motors, generators and transformers		...	17	16	15		...	1161	1116	1108		...	4208	4355	4949
3120 Electricity distribution & control apparatus		...	35	37	35		...	1525	1535	1518		...	4276	4763	4926
3130 Insulated wire and cable		...	21	21	22		...	1563	1524	1537		...	6135	5977	6996
3140 Accumulators, primary cells and batteries		...	10	8	8		...	571	430	400		...	3133	1530	1728
3150 Lighting equipment and electric lamps		...	29	28	28		...	556	533	541		...	1113	1265	1474
3190 Other electrical equipment n.e.c.		...	6	7	6		...	108	154	140		...	286	417	429
3210 Electronic valves, tubes, etc.		...	11	13	11		...	308	365	338		...	787	957	969
3220 TV/radio transmitters; line comm. apparatus		...	6	6	6		...	2051	2032	2032		...	8073	8943	10207
3230 TV and radio receivers and associated goods		...	14	12	12		...	215	169	149		...	450	457	434
331 Medical, measuring, testing appliances, etc.		...	27	23	23		...	898	893	923		...	2171	2324	2767
3311 Medical, surgical and orthopaedic equipment		...	...	...	...		...	...	...	...		...	...	...	...
3312 Measuring/testing/navigating appliances,etc.		...	...	...	...		...	...	...	...		...	...	...	...
3313 Industrial process control equipment		...	...	...	...		...	...	...	...		...	...	...	...
3320 Optical instruments & photographic equipment		...	8	7	7		...	166	223	322		...	346	519	902
3330 Watches and clocks		...	1	1	1		...	6	6	5		...	11	12	11
3410 Motor vehicles		...	12	11	11		...	1711	1599	1481		...	5749	5976	6306
3420 Automobile bodies, trailers & semi-trailers		...	19	16	16		...	345	249	282		...	919	718	871
3430 Parts/accessories for automobiles		...	16	20	20		...	286	376	364		...	656	1009	1075
351 Building and repairing of ships and boats		...	92	101	101		...	8803	8560	8509		...	34344	36414	40175
3511 Building and repairing of ships		...	...	...	...		...	...	...	...		...	...	...	...
3512 Building/repairing of pleasure/sport. boats		...	...	...	...		...	...	...	...		...	...	...	...
3520 Railway/tramway locomotives & rolling stock		...	12	13	13		...	2373	2398	2214		...	7554	8634	8815
3530 Aircraft and spacecraft		...	5	6	6		...	4892	4778	4595		...	21016	25385	26200
359 Transport equipment n.e.c.		...	5	6	7		...	107	119	151		...	242	278	443
3591 Motorcycles		...	...	...	...		...	...	...	...		...	...	...	...
3592 Bicycles and invalid carriages		...	...	...	...		...	...	...	...		...	...	...	...
3599 Other transport equipment n.e.c.		...	...	...	...		...	...	...	...		...	...	...	...
3610 Furniture		...	319	313	295		...	6414	6011	5569		...	13402	14027	14513
369 Manufacturing n.e.c.		...	94	92	89		...	1904	1835	1771		...	3963	4287	4699
3691 Jewellery and related articles		...	...	...	...		...	...	...	...		...	...	...	...
3692 Musical instruments		...	...	...	...		...	...	...	...		...	...	...	...
3693 Sports goods		...	...	...	...		...	...	...	...		...	...	...	...
3694 Games and toys		...	...	...	...		...	...	...	...		...	...	...	...
3699 Other manufacturing n.e.c.		...	...	...	...		...	...	...	...		...	...	...	...
3710 Recycling of metal waste and scrap		...	13	10	10		...	185	99	123		...	496	222	348
3720 Recycling of non-metal waste and scrap		...	-	-	-		...	-	-	-		...	-	-	-
D Total manufacturing		...	6119	5945	5813		...	269357	257057	250460		...	791644	865853	947536

Greece

ISIC Revision 3	Output in factor values					Value added in factor values					Gross fixed capital formation		
		(million DRACHMAS)					(million DRACHMAS)					(million DRACHMAS)	
ISIC Industry	Note	1992	1993	1994	1995	Note	1992	1993	1994	1995	Note	1994	1995
151 Processed meat,fish,fruit,vegetables,fats		...	423353	469704	531154		...	118542	128941	150053		22704	23298
1511 Processing/preserving of meat		...	...	...	...		...	...	...	...		...	...
1512 Processing/preserving of fish		...	...	...	...		...	...	...	...		...	...
1513 Processing/preserving of fruit & vegetables		...	...	...	...		...	...	...	...		...	...
1514 Vegetable and animal oils and fats		...	...	...	...		...	...	...	...		...	...
1520 Dairy products		...	249894	300757	317593		...	77494	94330	105360		18856	36849
153 Grain mill products; starches; animal feeds		...	208915	199249	206371		...	41215	43982	45790		6101	5076
1531 Grain mill products		...	...	...	...		...	...	...	...		...	...
1532 Starches and starch products		...	...	...	...		...	...	...	...		...	...
1533 Prepared animal feeds		...	...	...	...		...	...	...	...		...	...
154 Other food products		...	303015	331583	354795		...	132573	146289	153957		22956	22538
1541 Bakery products		...	...	...	...		...	...	...	...		...	...
1542 Sugar		...	...	...	...		...	...	...	...		...	...
1543 Cocoa, chocolate and sugar confectionery		...	...	...	...		...	...	...	...		...	...
1544 Macaroni, noodles & similar products		...	...	...	...		...	...	...	...		...	...
1549 Other food products n.e.c.		...	...	...	...		...	...	...	...		...	...
155 Beverages		...	314586	352009	375664		...	137992	156414	156552		19403	23544
1551 Distilling, rectifying & blending of spirits		...	...	...	...		...	...	...	...		...	...
1552 Wines		...	...	...	...		...	...	...	...		...	...
1553 Malt liquors and malt		...	...	...	...		...	...	...	...		...	...
1554 Soft drinks; mineral waters		...	...	...	...		...	...	...	...		...	...
1600 Tobacco products		...	93769	113629	129878		...	38381	44908	48358		5567	4859
171 Spinning, weaving and finishing of textiles		...	221813	243266	270362		...	97602	105206	109641		17066	16623
1711 Textile fibre preparation; textile weaving		...	...	...	...		...	...	...	...		...	...
1712 Finishing of textiles		...	...	...	...		...	...	...	...		...	...
172 Other textiles		...	59394	64677	68762		...	24779	26509	26283		7206	5050
1721 Made-up textile articles, except apparel		...	...	...	...		...	...	...	...		...	...
1722 Carpets and rugs		...	...	...	...		...	...	...	...		...	...
1723 Cordage, rope, twine and netting		...	...	...	...		...	...	...	...		...	...
1729 Other textiles n.e.c.		...	...	...	...		...	...	...	...		...	...
1730 Knitted and crocheted fabrics and articles		...	103697	105367	100850		...	40325	40234	39035		4647	5387
1810 Wearing apparel, except fur apparel		...	310040	306320	333047		...	138128	132799	140595		10999	12231
1820 Dressing & dyeing of fur; processing of fur		...	11664	13219	12621		...	3719	3784	3204		219	175
191 Tanning, dressing and processing of leather		...	26530	23860	23507		...	12127	8056	7595		328	581
1911 Tanning and dressing of leather		...	...	...	...		...	...	...	...		...	...
1912 Luggage, handbags, etc.; saddlery & harness		...	...	...	...		...	...	...	...		...	...
1920 Footwear		...	56017	60887	64753		...	23319	25362	26964		1187	2140
2010 Sawmilling and planing of wood		...	14692	14970	14328		...	3878	4611	4576		306	470
202 Products of wood, cork, straw, etc.		...	92767	82228	97504		...	35427	28650	34278		4484	3167
2021 Veneer sheets, plywood, particle board, etc.		...	...	...	...		...	...	...	...		...	...
2022 Builders' carpentry and joinery		...	...	...	...		...	...	...	...		...	...
2023 Wooden containers		...	...	...	...		...	...	...	...		...	...
2029 Other wood products; articles of cork/straw		...	...	...	...		...	...	...	...		...	...
210 Paper and paper products		...	155032	177871	228518		...	60873	66986	79246		9734	16448
2101 Pulp, paper and paperboard		...	...	...	...		...	...	...	...		...	...
2102 Corrugated paper and paperboard		...	...	...	...		...	...	...	...		...	...
2109 Other articles of paper and paperboard		...	...	...	...		...	...	...	...		...	...
221 Publishing		...	88071	98939	120290		...	51604	55966	64733		8749	5557
2211 Publishing of books and other publications		...	...	...	...		...	...	...	...		...	...
2212 Publishing of newspapers, journals, etc.		...	...	...	...		...	...	...	...		...	...
2213 Publishing of recorded media		...	...	...	...		...	...	...	...		...	...
2219 Other publishing		...	...	...	...		...	...	...	...		...	...

continued

Greece

ISIC Revision 3	Output in factor values					Value added in factor values					Gross fixed capital formation		
		(million DRACHMAS)					(million DRACHMAS)					(million DRACHMAS)	
ISIC Industry	Note	1992	1993	1994	1995	Note	1992	1993	1994	1995	Note	1994	1995
222 Printing and related service activities		...	43990	51730	55578		...	23030	26327	27566		2387	2984
2221 Printing		...	...	...	...		...	...	...	...		...	...
2222 Service activities related to printing		...	...	...	...		...	...	...	...		...	...
2230 Reproduction of recorded media		...	-	-	-		...	-	-	-		-	-
2310 Coke oven products		...	-	-	-		...	-	-	-		-	-
2320 Refined petroleum products		...	567731	658902	735162		...	105191	105745	129570		8968	16973
2330 Processing of nuclear fuel		...	-	-	-		...	-	-	-		-	-
241 Basic chemicals		...	124741	143781	174527		...	47252	50897	61018		5446	8843
2411 Basic chemicals, except fertilizers		...	...	...	...		...	...	...	...		...	...
2412 Fertilizers and nitrogen compounds		...	...	...	...		...	...	...	...		...	...
2413 Plastics in primary forms; synthetic rubber		...	...	...	...		...	...	...	...		...	...
242 Other chemicals		...	411013	476010	496377		...	168937	200739	211370		13186	17445
2421 Pesticides and other agro-chemical products		...	...	...	...		...	...	...	...		...	...
2422 Paints, varnishes, printing ink and mastics		...	...	...	...		...	...	...	...		...	...
2423 Pharmaceuticals, medicinal chemicals, etc.		...	...	...	...		...	...	...	...		...	...
2424 Soap, cleaning & cosmetic preparations		...	...	...	...		...	...	...	...		...	...
2429 Other chemical products n.e.c.		...	...	...	...		...	...	...	...		...	...
2430 Man-made fibres		...	12790	15995	18604		...	5703	6778	7766		1725	1654
251 Rubber products		...	32744	35784	40473		...	12314	13527	14042		819	1480
2511 Rubber tyres and tubes		...	...	...	...		...	...	...	...		...	...
2519 Other rubber products		...	...	...	...		...	...	...	...		...	...
2520 Plastic products		...	146191	173069	220391		...	59317	67347	79037		11570	17176
2610 Glass and glass products		...	17111	17665	18908		...	7937	8706	9203		721	896
269 Non-metallic mineral products n.e.c.		...	322187	335344	361125		...	134607	140990	146606		17127	15510
2691 Pottery, china and earthenware		...	...	...	...		...	...	...	...		...	...
2692 Refractory ceramic products		...	...	...	...		...	...	...	...		...	...
2693 Struct.non-refractory clay; ceramic products		...	...	...	...		...	...	...	...		...	...
2694 Cement, lime and plaster		...	...	...	...		...	...	...	...		...	...
2695 Articles of concrete, cement and plaster		...	...	...	...		...	...	...	...		...	...
2696 Cutting, shaping & finishing of stone		...	...	...	...		...	...	...	...		...	...
2699 Other non-metallic mineral products n.e.c.		...	...	...	...		...	...	...	...		...	...
2710 Basic iron and steel		...	207461	235380	309038		...	45256	46251	69525		5099	10813
2720 Basic precious and non-ferrous metals		...	188707	240795	321765		...	52697	70945	94171		10548	10059
273 Casting of metals		...	1590	1937	3263		...	722	941	1667		100	90
2731 Casting of iron and steel		...	...	...	...		...	...	...	...		...	...
2732 Casting of non-ferrous metals		...	...	...	...		...	...	...	...		...	...
281 Struct.metal products;tanks;steam generators		...	67710	64245	75163		...	26488	25222	28631		4306	3707
2811 Structural metal products		...	...	...	...		...	...	...	...		...	...
2812 Tanks, reservoirs and containers of metal		...	...	...	...		...	...	...	...		...	...
2813 Steam generators		...	...	...	...		...	...	...	...		...	...
289 Other metal products; metal working services		...	121990	142769	157618		...	47540	56535	60986		4381	7125
2891 Metal forging/pressing/stamping/roll-forming		...	...	...	...		...	...	...	...		...	...
2892 Treatment & coating of metals		...	...	...	...		...	...	...	...		...	...
2893 Cutlery, hand tools and general hardware		...	...	...	...		...	...	...	...		...	...
2899 Other fabricated metal products n.e.c.		...	...	...	...		...	...	...	...		...	...
291 General purpose machinery		...	51518	59115	65547		...	23532	27287	29232		3605	3841
2911 Engines & turbines(not for transport equip.)		...	...	...	...		...	...	...	...		...	...
2912 Pumps, compressors, taps and valves		...	...	...	...		...	...	...	...		...	...
2913 Bearings, gears, gearing & driving elements		...	...	...	...		...	...	...	...		...	...
2914 Ovens, furnaces and furnace burners		...	...	...	...		...	...	...	...		...	...
2915 Lifting and handling equipment		...	...	...	...		...	...	...	...		...	...
2919 Other general purpose machinery		...	...	...	...		...	...	...	...		...	...

292 Special purpose machinery		...	58071	59813	71535		...	21069	23843	27825		2712	2863
2921 Agricultural and forestry machinery		...	...	...	...		...	...	...	...		...	...
2922 Machine tools		...	...	...	...		...	...	...	...		...	...
2923 Machinery for metallurgy		...	...	...	...		...	...	...	...		...	...
2924 Machinery for mining & construction		...	...	...	...		...	...	...	...		...	...
2925 Food/beverage/tobacco processing machinery		...	...	...	...		...	...	...	...		...	...
2926 Machinery for textile, apparel and leather		...	...	...	...		...	...	...	...		...	...
2927 Weapons and ammunition		...	...	...	...		...	...	...	...		...	...
2929 Other special purpose machinery		...	...	...	...		...	...	...	...		...	...
2930 Domestic appliances n.e.c.		...	48197	56408	59870		...	19007	22246	23158		3410	2904
3000 Office, accounting and computing machinery		...	1106	909	1473		...	484	473	932		27	59
3110 Electric motors, generators and transformers		...	19293	20118	23389		...	8785	9126	9763		697	714
3120 Electricity distribution & control apparatus		...	24285	26504	25258		...	10495	12332	11262		2592	2746
3130 Insulated wire and cable		...	82114	77236	108287		...	21405	19205	23892		3718	2680
3140 Accumulators, primary cells and batteries		...	10714	11298	7980		...	5061	4409	4034		2768	1447
3150 Lighting equipment and electric lamps		...	7804	8826	10294		...	3429	3989	4468		227	520
3190 Other electrical equipment n.e.c.		...	2130	2464	2430		...	878	1125	1033		141	361
3210 Electronic valves, tubes, etc.		...	3242	5000	4365		...	1514	2010	1895		742	395
3220 TV/radio transmitters; line comm. apparatus		...	126218	101823	85267		...	50125	48392	39205		4276	4044
3230 TV and radio receivers and associated goods		...	1640	1572	1553		...	881	879	935		13	73
331 Medical, measuring, testing appliances, etc.		...	10395	11788	15124		...	4972	5287	6299		460	661
3311 Medical, surgical and orthopaedic equipment		...	...	...	...		...	...	...	...		...	...
3312 Measuring/testing/navigating appliances,etc.		...	...	...	...		...	...	...	...		...	...
3313 Industrial process control equipment		...	...	...	...		...	...	...	...		...	...
3320 Optical instruments & photographic equipment		...	2007	2400	3596		...	935	1256	1673		1549	533
3330 Watches and clocks		...	43	38	36		...	24	16	22		-	...
3410 Motor vehicles		...	52319	42792	38357		...	12839	10011	10985		935	289
3420 Automobile bodies, trailers & semi-trailers		...	6750	4970	5429		...	2258	1547	2088		125	103
3430 Parts/accessories for automobiles		...	3133	4520	4417		...	1627	2313	2194		170	110
351 Building and repairing of ships and boats		...	66907	71978	69301		...	47425	51805	47786		353	1165
3511 Building and repairing of ships		...	...	...	...		...	...	...	...		...	...
3512 Building/repairing of pleasure/sport. boats		...	...	...	...		...	...	...	...		...	...
3520 Railway/tramway locomotives & rolling stock		...	14828	16982	17198		...	11247	12888	13097		2	12
3530 Aircraft and spacecraft		...	42735	47906	49246		...	31810	37191	38530		7049	13803
359 Transport equipment n.e.c.		...	2613	2821	3183		...	841	966	1044		35	1189
3591 Motorcycles		...	...	...	...		...	...	...	...		...	...
3592 Bicycles and invalid carriages		...	...	...	...		...	...	...	...		...	...
3599 Other transport equipment n.e.c.		...	...	...	...		...	...	...	...		...	...
3610 Furniture		...	70762	75030	79599		...	32692	34638	36044		2830	3548
369 Manufacturing n.e.c.		...	22133	22962	28062		...	10891	10316	12252		1534	1124
3691 Jewellery and related articles		...	...	...	...		...	...	...	...		...	...
3692 Musical instruments		...	...	...	...		...	...	...	...		...	...
3693 Sports goods		...	...	...	...		...	...	...	...		...	...
3694 Games and toys		...	...	...	...		...	...	...	...		...	...
3699 Other manufacturing n.e.c.		...	...	...	...		...	...	...	...		...	...
3710 Recycling of metal waste and scrap		...	4819	5624	7641		...	1414	1051	1157		69	484
3720 Recycling of non-metal waste and scrap		...	-	-	-		...	-	-	-		-	-
D Total manufacturing		...	5734980	6292839	7026424		...	2100613	2278580	2488186		286936	344414

Greece

ISIC Revision 3		Index numbers of industrial production											
		(1990=100)											
ISIC Industry	Note	1985	1986	1987	1988	1989	1990	1991	1992	1993	1994	1995	1996
15 Food and beverages		...	...	...	...	...	...	...	...	...	...	...	...
16 Tobacco products		106	98	84	89	82	100	101	96	95	110	122	121
17 Textiles		100	107	109	106	104	100	91	83	78	78	73	70
18 Wearing apparel, fur		110	110	101	107	100	100	105	101	99	88	78	66
19 Leather, leather products and footwear		...	...	...	...	...	...	...	...	...	...	...	...
20 Wood products (excl. furniture)		84	82	86	87	99	100	102	99	91	83	97	95
21 Paper and paper products		90	104	120	108	108	100	108	110	102	109	113	107
22 Printing and publishing		121	106	105	109	108	100	92	89	84	82	82	88
23 Coke,refined petroleum products,nuclear fuel		...	...	...	...	...	...	...	...	...	...	...	...
24 Chemicals and chemical products		...	...	...	...	...	...	...	...	...	...	...	...
25 Rubber and plastics products		...	...	...	...	...	...	...	...	...	...	...	...
26 Non-metallic mineral products		...	...	...	...	...	...	...	...	...	...	...	...
27 Basic metals		...	...	...	...	...	...	...	...	...	...	...	...
28 Fabricated metal products		122	130	109	123	110	100	95	105	98	97	98	95
29 Machinery and equipment n.e.c.	a/	97	87	78	79	98	100	89	89	79	80	96	99
30 Office, accounting and computing machinery	a/	...	...	...	...	...	...	...	...	...	...	...	...
31 Electrical machinery and apparatus	b/	124	125	106	97	105	100	112	114	125	123	127	135
32 Radio,television and communication equipment	b/	...	...	...	...	...	...	...	...	...	...	...	...
33 Medical, precision and optical instruments		137	112	244	142	90	100	116	109	82	67	65	69
34 Motor vehicles, trailers, semi-trailers	c/	71	79	82	91	87	100	104	106	83	73	77	75
35 Other transport equipment	c/	...	...	...	...	...	...	...	...	...	...	...	...
36 Furniture; manufacturing n.e.c.		...	...	...	...	...	...	...	...	...	...	...	...
37 Recycling		...	...	...	...	...	...	...	...	...	...	...	...
D Total manufacturing		98	98	96	101	103	100	99	98	95	96	98	98

a/ 29 includes 30.
b/ 31 includes 32.
c/ 34 includes 35.

GRENADA

Supplier of information:
Central Statistical Office, St. George's.

Basic source of data:
Administrative records, Grenada Industrial Development Corporation, Inland Revenue Department.

Major deviations from ISIC (Revision 2):
None reported.

Reference period (if not calendar year):

Scope:
Not reported.

Method of enumeration:
Not reported.

Adjusted for non-response:
Yes. Adjustments are made on the basis of wages and salaries data from social security records.

Concepts and definitions of variables:
Data follow System of National Accounts (SNA) conventions.

Related national publications:

ISIC Revision 2	Number of establishments					Number of persons engaged					Wages and salaries paid to employees				
		(numbers)					(numbers)					(thousand DOLLARS)			
ISIC Industry	Note	1993	1994	1995	1996	Note	1993	1994a/	1995a/	1996	Note	1993	1994	1995	1996
311/2 Food products		24	20	20	...		237	264	261	...		...	...	...	...
3111 Slaughtering, preparing & preserving meat		1	2	2	1		...	11	11	10		...	...	...	...
3112 Dairy products		...	4	4	5		...	19	17	5		...	...	...	...
3113 Canning, preserving of fruits & vegetables		1	2	2	...		...	50	49	16		...	...	...	...
3114 Canning, preserving and processing of fish		...	...	...	...		...	...	...	...		...	...	...	...
3115 Vegetable and animal oils and fats		...	...	...	...		...	...	...	...		...	...	...	...
3116 Grain mill products		2	1	1	2		42	7	7	42		...	...	...	...
3117 Bakery products		9	8	8	9		147	159	160	149		...	...	...	...
3118 Sugar factories and refineries		...	...	...	...		...	...	...	...		...	...	...	...
3119 Cocoa, chocolate and sugar confectionery		5	...	...	...		41	...	...	...		...	...	...	...
3121 Other food products		6	2	2	8		7	18	17	8		...	...	...	...
3122 Prepared animal feeds		...	1	1	1		...	-	-	...		...	...	...	...
313 Beverages		5	6	6	7		454	532	563	448		...	...	...	...
3131 Distilling, rectifying and blending spirits		3	3	3	5		219	290	315	215		...	...	...	...
3132 Wine industries		-	-	-	-		-	-	-	-		...	...	...	...
3133 Malt liquors and malt		1	1	1	1		166	19	19	166		...	...	...	...
3134 Soft drinks and carbonated waters		1	2	2	1		69	223	229	67		...	...	...	...
314 Tobacco		1	1	1	1		19	17	17	19		...	...	...	...
321 Textiles		1	1	...	5		2	16	16	...		...	...	...	...
3211 Spinning, weaving and finishing textiles		...	...	...	4		...	...	...	4		...	...	...	...
3212 Made-up textile goods excl. wearing apparel		...	...	...	-		...	...	...	-		...	...	...	...
3213 Knitting mills		...	...	...	-		...	...	...	-		...	...	...	...
3214 Carpets and rugs		...	...	...	-		...	...	...	-		...	...	...	...
3215 Cordage, rope and twine		...	...	...	-		...	...	...	-		...	...	...	...
3219 Other textiles		1	1	...	1		2	16	16	...		...	...	...	...
322 Wearing apparel, except footwear		16	17	17	8		187	139	248	188		...	...	...	...
323 Leather and fur products		2	...	...	3		39	...	...	39		...	...	...	...
3231 Tanneries and leather finishing		...	...	...	-		...	...	...	-		...	...	...	...
3232 Fur dressing and dyeing industries		...	...	...	-		...	...	...	-		...	...	...	...
3233 Leather prods. excl. wearing apparel		2	...	...	3		39	...	...	39		...	...	...	...
324 Footwear, except rubber or plastic		...	...	...	...		...	...	...	...		...	...	...	...
331 Wood products, except furniture		4	...	...	4		25	...	...	25		...	...	...	...
3311 Sawmills, planing and other wood mills		...	...	...	1		...	...	...	25		...	...	...	...
3312 Wooden and cane containers		...	...	...	...		...	...	...	...		...	...	...	...
3319 Other wood and cork products		4	...	...	...		25	...	...	...		...	...	...	...
332 Furniture and fixtures, excl. metal		...	4	6	3		...	55	47	3		...	...	...	...
341 Paper and products		1	1	...	1		30	37	...	31		...	...	...	...
3411 Pulp, paper and paperboard articles		1	1	...	1		30	37	...	31		...	...	...	...
3412 Containers of paper and paperboard		...	...	...	-		...	...	...	-		...	...	...	...
3419 Other pulp, paper and paperboard articles		...	...	...	-		...	...	...	-		...	...	...	...
342 Printing and publishing		1	3	...	2		100	37	...	172		...	...	...	...
351 Industrial chemicals		1	...	...	...		5	...	...	...		...	...	...	...
3511 Basic chemicals excl. fertilizers		...	...	...	...		...	...	...	...		...	...	...	...
3512 Fertilizers and pesticides		...	...	...	...		...	...	...	...		...	...	...	...
3513 Synthetic resins and plastic materials		1	...	...	...		5	...	...	...		...	...	...	...
352 Other chemicals		4	3	...	2		120	75	...	122		...	...	...	...
3521 Paints, varnishes and lacquers		1	1	...	1		29	30	...	29		...	...	...	...
3522 Drugs and medicines		1	1	...	...		81	...	...	...		...	...	...	...
3523 Soap, cleaning preps., perfumes, cosmetics		2	1	...	1		10	45	...	1		...	...	...	...
3529 Other chemical products		-	-	...	...		-	-	...	...		...	...	...	...
353 Petroleum refineries		...	...	...	...		...	...	...	...		...	...	...	...

354 Misc. petroleum and coal products		...	...	...	...		...	...	...	...		...	...	...	...
355 Rubber products		1	1	...	2		5	7	...	52		...	...	...	...
3551 Tyres and tubes		1	1	...	2		5	7	...	52		...	...	...	...
3559 Other rubber products		...	...	...	-		...	...	...	-		...	...	...	...
356 Plastic products		...	...	...	...		...	...	...	...		...	...	...	...
361 Pottery, china, earthenware		...	...	...	...		...	...	...	...		...	...	...	...
362 Glass and products		...	1	1	1		...	-	4	2		...	...	...	...
369 Other non-metallic mineral products		7	4	4	12		58	33	31	82		...	...	...	...
3691 Structural clay products		1	...	...	1		...	...	...	1		...	...	...	...
3692 Cement, lime and plaster		...	4	4	1		...	33	31	1		...	...	...	...
3699 Other non-metallic mineral products		6	...	...	10		58	...	...	80		...	...	...	...
371 Iron and steel		...	1	1	1		...	20	22	...		...	...	...	...
372 Non-ferrous metals		...	...	...	...		...	...	...	...		...	...	...	...
381 Fabricated metal products		9	...	...	...		93	...	...	93		...	...	...	...
3811 Cutlery, hand tools and general hardware		...	...	...	...		45	...	...	45		...	...	...	...
3812 Furniture and fixtures primarily of metal		6	...	...	6		38	...	...	38		...	...	...	...
3813 Structural metal products		3	...	...	3		10	...	...	10		...	...	...	...
3819 Other fabricated metal products		-	...	...	-		...	...	...	-		...	...	...	...
382 Non-electrical machinery		1	...	...	1		4	...	...	4		...	...	...	...
3821 Engines and turbines		...	...	...	-		...	...	...	-		...	...	...	...
3822 Agricultural machinery and equipment		...	...	...	-		...	...	...	-		...	...	...	...
3823 Metal and wood working machinery		...	...	...	-		...	...	...	-		...	...	...	...
3824 Other special industrial machinery		...	...	...	-		...	...	...	-		...	...	...	...
3825 Office, computing and accounting machinery		...	...	...	-		...	...	...	-		...	...	...	...
3829 Other non-electrical machinery & equipment		1	...	...	1		4	...	...	4		...	...	...	...
383 Electrical machinery		2	2	...	3		27	33	...	...		...	...	...	...
3831 Electrical industrial machinery		...	...	...	-		...	...	...	-		...	...	...	...
3832 Radio, television and communication equipm.		...	...	...	-		...	...	...	-		...	...	...	...
3833 Electrical appliances and housewares		...	2	...	1		...	33	...	...		...	...	...	...
3839 Other electrical apparatus and supplies		2	...	...	2		27	...	...	27		...	...	...	...
384 Transport equipment		1	2	...	1		13	10	...	13		...	...	...	...
3841 Shipbuilding and repairing		...	1	...	1		...	-	...	13		...	...	...	...
3842 Railroad equipment		...	-	...	-		...	-	...	-		...	...	...	...
3843 Motor vehicles		...	1	...	-		...	10	...	-		...	...	...	...
3844 Motorcycles and bicycles		...	-	...	-		...	-	...	-		...	...	...	...
3845 Aircraft		...	-	...	-		...	-	...	-		...	...	...	...
3849 Other transport equipment		...	-	...	-		...	-	...	-		...	...	...	...
385 Professional and scientific equipment		...	...	...	1		...	...	...	1		...	...	...	...
3851 Prof. and scientific equipment n.e.c.		...	...	...	1		...	...	...	1		...	...	...	...
3852 Photographic and optical goods		...	...	...	-		...	...	...	-		...	...	...	...
3853 Watches and clocks		...	...	...	-		...	...	...	-		...	...	...	...
390 Other manufacturing industries		1	2	...	6		...	9	...	316		...	...	...	...
3901 Jewellery and related articles		1	1	...	1		...	9	...	61		...	...	...	...
3902 Musical instruments		...	...	...	-		...	...	...	-		...	...	...	...
3903 Sporting and athletic goods		...	1	...	-		...	-	...	-		...	...	...	...
3909 Manufacturing industries, n.e.c.		...	...	...	5		...	...	...	255		...	...	...	...
3 Total manufacturing	b/	82	69	56	...	b/	1418	1284	1209	...		...	...	...	...

a/ Number of employees.
b/ Sum of available data.

Grenada

ISIC Revision 2	Output in factor values					Value added in factor values					Gross fixed capital formation		
		(thousand DOLLARS)					(thousand DOLLARS)					(thousand DOLLARS)	
ISIC Industry	Note	1993	1994	1995	1996	Note	1993	1994	1995	1996	Note	1995	1996
311/2 Food products		...	...	...	...		...	...	...	...		...	...
313 Beverages		...	...	...	...		...	...	...	...		...	...
314 Tobacco		...	...	...	...		...	...	...	...		...	...
321 Textiles		...	...	...	...		...	...	...	...		...	...
322 Wearing apparel, except footwear		...	...	...	...		...	...	...	...		...	...
323 Leather and fur products		...	...	...	...		...	...	...	...		...	...
324 Footwear, except rubber or plastic		...	...	...	...		...	...	...	...		...	...
331 Wood products, except furniture		...	...	...	...		...	...	...	...		...	...
332 Furniture and fixtures, excl. metal		...	...	...	...		...	...	...	...		...	...
341 Paper and products		...	...	...	...		...	...	...	...		...	...
342 Printing and publishing		...	...	...	...		...	...	...	...		...	...
351 Industrial chemicals		...	...	...	...		...	...	...	...		...	...
352 Other chemicals		...	...	...	...		...	...	...	...		...	...
353 Petroleum refineries		...	...	...	...		...	...	...	...		...	...
354 Misc. petroleum and coal products		...	...	...	...		...	...	...	...		...	...
355 Rubber products		...	...	...	...		...	...	...	...		...	...
356 Plastic products		...	...	...	...		...	...	...	...		...	...
361 Pottery, china, earthenware		...	...	...	...		...	...	...	...		...	...
362 Glass and products		...	...	...	...		...	...	...	...		...	...
369 Other non-metallic mineral products		...	...	...	...		...	...	...	...		...	...
371 Iron and steel		...	...	...	...		...	...	...	...		...	...
372 Non-ferrous metals		...	...	...	...		...	...	...	...		...	...
381 Fabricated metal products		...	...	...	...		...	...	...	...		...	...
382 Non-electrical machinery		...	...	...	...		...	...	...	...		...	...
383 Electrical machinery		...	...	...	...		...	...	...	...		...	...
384 Transport equipment		...	...	...	...		...	...	...	...		...	...
385 Professional and scientific equipment		...	...	...	...		...	...	...	...		...	...
390 Other manufacturing industries		...	...	...	...		...	...	...	...		...	...
3 Total manufacturing		50000	...	...	...		34120	...	...	...		...	...

HAITI

Supplier of information:
Institut haïtien de statistique et d'informatique, Port-au-Prince.

Basic source of data:
Not reported.

Major deviations from ISIC (Revision 2):
None reported.

Reference period (if not calendar year):
Fiscal year from 1 October to 30 September.

Scope:
Not reported.

Method of enumeration:
Not reported.

Adjusted for non-response:
Not reported.

Concepts and definitions of variables:
No deviations from the standard UN concepts and definitions are reported.

Related national publications:

Haiti

ISIC Revision 2		Number of establishments (numbers)					Number of employees (thousands)					Wages and salaries paid to employees (million GOURDES)				
ISIC	Industry	Note	1993	1994	1995	1996	Note	1993	1994	1995	1996	Note	1993	1994	1995	1996
311/2	Food products		...	...	...	...		...	...	...	...		...	...	...	...
313	Beverages		...	...	...	...		...	...	...	...		...	...	...	...
314	Tobacco		...	...	...	...		...	...	...	...		...	...	...	...
321	Textiles		...	...	...	...		...	...	...	...		...	...	...	...
322	Wearing apparel, except footwear		...	...	...	...		...	...	...	...		...	...	...	...
323	Leather and fur products		...	...	...	...		...	...	...	...		...	...	...	...
324	Footwear, except rubber or plastic		...	...	...	...		...	...	...	...		...	...	...	...
331	Wood products, except furniture		...	...	...	...		...	...	...	...		...	...	...	...
332	Furniture and fixtures, excl. metal		...	...	...	...		...	...	...	...		...	...	...	...
341	Paper and products		...	...	...	...		...	...	...	...		...	...	...	...
342	Printing and publishing		...	...	...	...		...	...	...	...		...	...	...	...
351	Industrial chemicals		...	...	...	...		...	...	...	...		...	...	...	...
352	Other chemicals		...	...	...	...		...	...	...	...		...	...	...	...
353	Petroleum refineries		...	...	...	...		...	...	...	...		...	...	...	...
354	Misc. petroleum and coal products		...	...	...	...		...	...	...	...		...	...	...	...
355	Rubber products		...	...	...	...		...	...	...	...		...	...	...	...
356	Plastic products		...	...	...	...		...	...	...	...		...	...	...	...
361	Pottery, china, earthenware		...	...	...	...		...	...	...	...		...	...	...	...
362	Glass and products		...	...	...	...		...	...	...	...		...	...	...	...
369	Other non-metallic mineral products		...	...	...	...		...	...	...	...		...	...	...	...
371	Iron and steel		...	...	...	...		...	...	...	...		...	...	...	...
372	Non-ferrous metals		...	...	...	...		...	...	...	...		...	...	...	...
381	Fabricated metal products		...	...	...	...		...	...	...	...		...	...	...	...
382	Non-electrical machinery		...	...	...	...		...	...	...	...		...	...	...	...
383	Electrical machinery		...	...	...	...		...	...	...	...		...	...	...	...
384	Transport equipment		...	...	...	...		...	...	...	...		...	...	...	...
385	Professional and scientific equipment		...	...	...	...		...	...	...	...		...	...	...	...
390	Other manufacturing industries		...	...	...	...		...	...	...	...		...	...	...	...
3	Total manufacturing		...	...	...	...		...	...	...	...		...	...	...	...

Haiti

ISIC Revision 2	Output					Value added					Gross fixed capital formation		
		(million GOURDES)					(thousand GOURDES)					(million GOURDES)	
ISIC Industry	Note	1993	1994	1995	1996	Note	1993	1994	1995	1996	Note	1995	1996
311/2 Food products		...	...	...	...		114527	99512	110772	112694		...	...
313 Beverages		...	...	...	...		14342	7556	8245	9349		...	...
314 Tobacco		...	...	...	...		39331	25593	26763	27264		...	...
321 Textiles		...	...	...	...	a/	40632	55368	58026	61521		...	...
322 Wearing apparel, except footwear		...	...	...	...	a/	...	...	...	...		...	...
323 Leather and fur products		...	...	...	...	a/	...	...	...	...		...	...
324 Footwear, except rubber or plastic		...	...	...	...	a/	...	...	...	...		...	...
331 Wood products, except furniture		...	...	...	...		...	...	...	...		...	...
332 Furniture and fixtures, excl. metal		...	...	...	...		...	...	...	...		...	...
341 Paper and products		...	...	...	...		...	...	...	...		...	...
342 Printing and publishing		...	...	...	...		...	...	...	...		...	...
351 Industrial chemicals		...	...	...	...	b/	40185	33603	39466	36707		...	...
352 Other chemicals		...	...	...	...	b/	...	...	...	...		...	...
353 Petroleum refineries		...	...	...	...		-	-	-	-		...	...
354 Misc. petroleum and coal products		...	...	...	...		-	-	-	-		...	...
355 Rubber products		...	...	...	...	b/	...	...	...	...		...	...
356 Plastic products		...	...	...	...	b/	...	...	...	...		...	...
361 Pottery, china, earthenware		...	...	...	...		...	...	...	...		...	...
362 Glass and products		...	...	...	...		...	...	...	...		...	...
369 Other non-metallic mineral products		...	...	...	...		6645	6105	9192	11396		...	...
371 Iron and steel		...	...	...	...		31844	36721	37452	...		...	...
372 Non-ferrous metals		...	...	...	...		...	...	...	...		...	...
381 Fabricated metal products		...	...	...	...		...	...	...	...		...	...
382 Non-electrical machinery		...	...	...	...		...	...	...	...		...	...
383 Electrical machinery		...	...	...	...		-	-	-	-		...	...
384 Transport equipment		...	...	...	...		...	...	...	...		...	...
385 Professional and scientific equipment		...	...	...	...		-	-	-	-		...	...
390 Other manufacturing industries		...	...	...	...	c/	22357	20535	22542	23860		...	...
3 Total manufacturing		...	...	...	...		309862	285015	312458	321827		...	...

a/ 321 includes 322, 323 and 324.
b/ 351 includes 352, 355 and 356.
c/ 390 includes part of metal processing.

Haiti

ISIC Revision 2		Note	Index numbers of industrial production (1990=100)											
ISIC	Industry		1985	1986	1987	1988	1989	1990	1991	1992	1993	1994	1995	1996
311/2	Food products		143	110	128	133	103	100	65	46	39	39	39	...
313	Beverages		68	103	98	129	85	100	67	73	60	52	52	...
314	Tobacco		86	90	95	103	104	100	99	113	73	77	...	...
321	Textiles		65	67	49	96	155	100	78	...	...	...	...	...
322	Wearing apparel, except footwear		...	...	...	...	...	...	...	...	...	...	...	...
323	Leather and fur products		...	...	...	...	...	...	...	...	...	...	...	...
324	Footwear, except rubber or plastic		...	...	...	...	...	...	...	...	...	...	...	...
331	Wood products, except furniture		...	...	...	...	...	...	...	...	...	...	...	...
332	Furniture and fixtures, excl. metal		...	...	...	...	...	...	...	...	...	...	...	...
341	Paper and products		...	...	...	...	...	...	...	...	...	...	...	...
342	Printing and publishing		...	...	...	...	...	...	...	...	...	...	...	...
351	Industrial chemicals	a/	113	114	153	112	101	100	121	113	110	129	...	...
352	Other chemicals	a/	...	...	...	...	...	...	...	...	...	...	...	...
353	Petroleum refineries		...	...	...	...	...	...	...	...	...	...	...	...
354	Misc. petroleum and coal products		...	...	...	...	...	...	...	...	...	...	...	...
355	Rubber products		...	...	...	...	...	...	...	...	...	...	...	...
356	Plastic products		...	...	...	...	...	...	...	...	...	...	...	...
361	Pottery, china, earthenware		...	...	...	...	...	...	...	...	...	...	...	...
362	Glass and products		...	...	...	...	...	...	...	...	...	...	...	...
369	Other non-metallic mineral products		147	137	140	151	120	100	117	111	55	42	28	28
371	Iron and steel		...	...	...	...	...	...	...	...	...	...	...	...
372	Non-ferrous metals		...	...	...	...	...	...	...	...	...	...	...	...
381	Fabricated metal products		...	...	...	...	...	...	...	...	...	...	...	...
382	Non-electrical machinery		...	...	...	...	...	...	...	...	...	...	...	...
383	Electrical machinery		...	...	...	...	...	...	...	...	...	...	...	...
384	Transport equipment		...	...	...	...	...	...	...	...	...	...	...	...
385	Professional and scientific equipment		...	...	...	...	...	...	...	...	...	...	...	...
390	Other manufacturing industries		...	...	...	...	...	...	...	...	...	...	...	...
3	Total manufacturing		...	...	...	...	...	...	...	...	...	...	...	...

a/ 351 includes 352.

HONDURAS

Supplier of information:
Banco Central de Honduras, Tegucigalpa.

Basic source of data:
Annual industrial survey.

Major deviations from ISIC (Revision 2):
Data collected under the national classification system have been reclassified by the national authorities to correspond approximately with ISIC (Rev. 2).

Reference period (if not calendar year):

Scope:
Registered establishments with 5 or more persons engaged.

Method of enumeration:
Individual sites are visited by enumerators.

Adjusted for non-response:
Not reported.

Concepts and definitions of variables:
Number of persons engaged includes homeworkers.
Output is gross output and includes gross revenues from goods shipped in the same condition as received.
Value added is total value added.

Related national publications:

Honduras

ISIC Revision 2	Number of establishments					Number of persons engaged					Wages and salaries paid to employees				
		(numbers)					(numbers)					(thousand LEMPIRAS)			
ISIC Industry	Note	1993	1994	1995	1996	Note	1993	1994	1995	1996	Note	1993	1994	1995	1996
311/2 Food products		166	166	166	...		27071	29661	32672	...		384272	460109	586012	738126
3111 Slaughtering, preparing & preserving meat		15	15	15	...		3715	4071	4582	...		45970	54241	68121	85119
3112 Dairy products		14	14	14	...		2115	2317	2890	...		32918	43451	54314	66831
3113 Canning, preserving of fruits & vegetables		7	7	7	...		2380	2608	2715	...		23632	26385	41806	52257
3114 Canning, preserving and processing of fish		20	20	20	...		3007	3295	4264	...		45069	49008	53259	66574
3115 Vegetable and animal oils and fats		9	9	9	...		3546	3885	3914	...		73502	95711	110837	138547
3116 Grain mill products		23	23	23	...		1881	2061	2267	...		31453	32090	40621	48507
3117 Bakery products		27	27	27	...		3115	3413	3705	...		49797	54381	60140	84148
3118 Sugar factories and refineries		7	7	7	...		3132	3432	3030	...		33103	41095	66042	82552
3119 Cocoa, chocolate and sugar confectionery		4	4	4	...		442	484	489	...		4032	7104	7529	9412
3121 Other food products		30	30	30	...		3302	3618	3898	...		35581	43740	57446	71808
3122 Prepared animal feeds		10	10	10	...		436	477	918	...		9215	12903	25897	32371
313 Beverages		23	23	23	...		4750	5205	5502	...		136510	156170	204496	262973
3131 Distilling, rectifying and blending spirits		16	16	16	...		585	641	611	...	a/	59592	63196	85257	110572
3132 Wine industries		-	-	-	...		-	-	-	...		-	-	-	-
3133 Malt liquors and malt		7	7	7	...		2819	3089	3250	...	a/	...	...	...	...
3134 Soft drinks and carbonated waters		...	...	...	...		1346	1475	1641	...		76918	92974	119239	152401
314 Tobacco		13	13	13	...		3289	3329	3409	...		21499	26879	38580	46064
321 Textiles		25	25	25	...		10359	11348	11182	...		63119	61891	80117	101748
3211 Spinning, weaving and finishing textiles		12	12	12	...		6747	7392	7413	...		43743	47109	63894	81145
3212 Made-up textile goods excl. wearing apparel		...	...	...	...		87	95	109	...		279	849	500	635
3213 Knitting mills		10	10	10	...		3457	3787	3566	...		19031	13756	15483	19663
3214 Carpets and rugs		-	-	-	...		-	-	-	...		-	-	-	-
3215 Cordage, rope and twine		3	3	3	...		68	74	94	...		66	177	240	305
3219 Other textiles		-	-	-	...		-	-	-	...		-	-	-	-
322 Wearing apparel, except footwear		123	153	166	...		41068	51024	64897	...		308924	385335	734346	932620
323 Leather and fur products		13	13	13	...		540	591	908	...		7798	9227	11281	14328
3231 Tanneries and leather finishing		-	-	-	...		-	-	-	...		-	-	-	-
3232 Fur dressing and dyeing industries		4	4	4	...		540b/	591b/	908b/	...		4838	5607	6840	8688
3233 Leather prods. excl. wearing apparel		9	9	9	...		...b/	...b/	...b/	...		2960	3620	4441	5640
324 Footwear, except rubber or plastic		17	17	17	...		1343	1471	1177	...		14614	17029	18581	23598
331 Wood products, except furniture		41	41	41	...		9929	10878	12191	...		123669	143119	174960	213450
3311 Sawmills, planing and other wood mills		24	24	24	...		8117	8893	9920	...		105295	121089	150175	183213
3312 Wooden and cane containers		8	8	8	...		364	399	418	...		6136	7362	8273	10093
3319 Other wood and cork products		9	9	9	...		1448	1586	1853	...		12238	14668	16512	20144
332 Furniture and fixtures, excl. metal		16	16	16	...		6470	7089	7939	...		31336	39170	48501	59171
341 Paper and products		18	18	18	...		1900	2082	3114	...		46231	59487	85553	106941
3411 Pulp, paper and paperboard articles		-	-	-	...		-	-	-	...		-	-	-	-
3412 Containers of paper and paperboard		11	11	11	...		1471	1612	2413	...		34060	44882	60908	76135
3419 Other pulp, paper and paperboard articles		7	7	7	...		429	470	701	...		12171	14605	24645	30806
342 Printing and publishing		28	28	28	...		2968	3252	3642	...		68348	78600	99530	124414
351 Industrial chemicals		8	8	8	...		472	517	528	...		4658	5649	7203	9004
3511 Basic chemicals excl. fertilizers		4	4	4	...		345	378	386	...		2552	2456	2792	3490
3512 Fertilizers and pesticides		4	4	4	...		127	139	142	...		2106	3193	4411	5514
3513 Synthetic resins and plastic materials		-	-	-	...		-	-	-	...		-	-	-	-
352 Other chemicals		46	46	47	...		2932	3082	4425	...		52879	78590	124101	155125
3521 Paints, varnishes and lacquers		1	1	1	...		171	51	61	...		1588	2134	1729	2161
3522 Drugs and medicines		14	14	14	...		905	992	1144	...		14171	18673	22942	28677
3523 Soap, cleaning preps., perfumes, cosmetics		16	16	16	...		1232	1350	2003	...		25025	38661	79832	99790
3529 Other chemical products		15	15	16	...		624	689	1217	...		12095	19122	19598	24497
353 Petroleum refineries		2	2	1	...		160	175	...	...		623	872	1177	1471

Industry												
354 Misc. petroleum and coal products	-	-	-	...	-	-	-	...	-	-	-	-
355 Rubber products	20	20	20	...	1356	1486	2451	...	21961	27094	34812	43515
3551 Tyres and tubes	9	9	9	...	186	204	379	...	4952	5937	8464	10580
3559 Other rubber products	11	11	11	...	1170	1282	2072	...	17009	21157	26348	32935
356 Plastic products	27	27	27	...	1719	1884	2760	...	56391	69239	95690	119612
361 Pottery, china, earthenware	5	5	4	...	153	167	213	...	1930	2410	2530	3163
362 Glass and products	-	-	-	...	-	-	-	...	-	-	-	-
369 Other non-metallic mineral products	32	32	30	...	5332	5791	6283	...	59462	76519	109135	136417
3691 Structural clay products	8	8	6	...	1028	1126	1269	...	2514	3141	3533	4416
3692 Cement, lime and plaster	5	5	5	...	1361	1441	1468	...	25488	33134	50093	62616
3699 Other non-metallic mineral products	19	19	19	...	2943	3224	3546	...	31460	40244	55509	69385
371 Iron and steel	5	5	5	...	495	543	742	...	5938	5691	7396	9632
372 Non-ferrous metals	5	5	5	...	280	307	332	...	4551	3975	4538	6536
381 Fabricated metal products	57	57	57	...	3066	3360	4089	...	53999	74928	84355	102774
3811 Cutlery, hand tools and general hardware	5	5	5	...	288	316	286	...	3290	3438	4028	4995
3812 Furniture and fixtures primarily of metal	19	19	19	...	855	937	883	...	6279	11805	16531	18672
3813 Structural metal products	17	17	17	...	972	1065	1262	...	17418	21673	24663	30582
3819 Other fabricated metal products	16	16	16	...	951	1042	1658	...	27012	38012	39133	48525
382 Non-electrical machinery	41	41	26	...	674	737	1203	...	11632	14271	18037	22365
3821 Engines and turbines	-	-	-	...	-	-	-	...	-	-	-	-
3822 Agricultural machinery and equipment	10	10	10	...	155	169	250	...	3665	4825	6082	7541
3823 Metal and wood working machinery	-	-	-	...	-	-	-	...	-	-	-	-
3824 Other special industrial machinery	-	-	-	...	-	-	-	...	-	-	-	-
3825 Office, computing and accounting machinery	-	-	-	...	-	-	-	...	-	-	-	-
3829 Other non-electrical machinery & equipment	31	31	16	...	519	568	953	...	7967	9446	11955	14824
383 Electrical machinery	20	20	20	...	662	726	832	...	8764	12684	19943	24729
3831 Electrical industrial machinery	5	5	5	...	6	7	7	...	115	173	231	286
3832 Radio, television and communication equipm.	1	1	1	...	180	197	224	...	1444	1733	2280	2827
3833 Electrical appliances and housewares	-	-	-	...	-	-	-	...	-	-	-	-
3839 Other electrical apparatus and supplies	14	14	14	...	476	522	601	...	7205	10778	17432	21616
384 Transport equipment	11	11	11	...	304	334	424	...	4970	4745	5373	6664
3841 Shipbuilding and repairing	4	4	4	...	81	89	129	...	422	548	744	923
3842 Railroad equipment	-	-	-	...	-	-	-	...	-	-	-	-
3843 Motor vehicles	3	3	3	...	154	169	194	...	4548	4197	4629	5741
3844 Motorcycles and bicycles	4	4	4	...	69	76	101	...	...	...	...	...
3845 Aircraft	-	-	-	...	-	-	-	...	-	-	-	-
3849 Other transport equipment	-	-	-	...	-	-	-	...	-	-	-	-
385 Professional and scientific equipment	10	10	10	...	87	96	161	...	1669	2208	2465	3057
3851 Prof. and scientific equipment n.e.c.	1	1	1	...	68	75	25	...	140	167	360	446
3852 Photographic and optical goods	9	9	9	...	19	21	136	...	1529	2041	2105	2611
3853 Watches and clocks	-	-	-	...	-	-	-	...	-	-	-	-
390 Other manufacturing industries	64	64	30	...	1712	1933	2160	...	15307	17472	22964	28603
3901 Jewellery and related articles	12	12	12	...	64	127	145	...	2097	2454	2958	3727
3902 Musical instruments	-	-	-	...	-	-	-	...	-	-	-	-
3903 Sporting and athletic goods	4	4	4	...	322	353	346	...	2117	2405	3167	3658
3909 Manufacturing industries, n.e.c.	48	48	14	...	1326	1453	1669	...	11093	12613	16839	21218
3 Total manufacturing	836	866	827	...	129091	147068	173236	...	1511054	1833363	2621676	3296100

a/ 3131 includes 3133.
b/ 3232 includes 3233.

Honduras

ISIC Revision 2		Output in producers' prices					Value added in factor values					Gross fixed capital formation	
		(thousand LEMPIRAS)					(thousand LEMPIRAS)					(thousand LEMPIRAS)	
ISIC Industry	Note	1993	1994	1995	1996	Note	1993	1994	1995	1996	Note	1995	1996
311/2 Food products		4645118	6185398	7533141	10123330		965194	1199081	1549992	1937288		...	...
3111 Slaughtering, preparing & preserving meat		778268	1052411	1031328	1616119		123069	155198	190571	238123		...	...
3112 Dairy products		421364	688062	858287	1040657		68824	98533	128719	158383		...	...
3113 Canning, preserving of fruits & vegetables		222931	258607	400362	514453		39595	45528	78109	97636		...	...
3114 Canning, preserving and processing of fish		421006	611666	622870	920534		88928	127853	165056	206320		...	...
3115 Vegetable and animal oils and fats		600796	836336	987017	1332473		131357	163631	188106	235133		...	...
3116 Grain mill products		727044	972009	1413650	1913314		145531	174655	212149	253331		...	...
3117 Bakery products		352920	405416	460569	598906		79066	83491	95553	133700		...	...
3118 Sugar factories and refineries		392818	522451	758639	886231		154353	192855	293952	367440		...	...
3119 Cocoa, chocolate and sugar confectionery		47593	62081	74951	98935		9678	11572	14767	18459		...	...
3121 Other food products		359602	379226	498058	627690		71507	80428	99634	124543		...	...
3122 Prepared animal feeds		320776	397133	427410	574013		53286	65337	83376	104220		...	...
313 Beverages		1245099	1692746	2303175	3038027		359911	446157	552226	699588		...	...
3131 Distilling, rectifying and blending spirits		66508	71680	96419	162745		21483	23303	33192	41490		...	...
3132 Wine industries		-	-	-	-		-	-	-	-		...	...
3133 Malt liquors and malt		494843	600175	782252	893868		142886	154733	188052	235065		...	...
3134 Soft drinks and carbonated waters		683748	1020891	1424504	1981414		195542	268121	330982	423033		...	...
314 Tobacco		328407	433017	633204	802349		91662	114206	162517	194044		...	...
321 Textiles		265813	315431	425346	547001		76883	91158	133112	169053		...	...
3211 Spinning, weaving and finishing textiles		207690	246270	334017	418349		58981	69947	105633	134154		...	...
3212 Made-up textile goods excl. wearing apparel		1708	2515	1550	2032		430	519	630	800		...	...
3213 Knitting mills		55749	65964	88373	124123		17276	20354	26274	33368		...	...
3214 Carpets and rugs		-	-	-	-		-	-	-	-		...	...
3215 Cordage, rope and twine		666	682	1406	2497		196	338	575	731		...	...
3219 Other textiles		-	-	-	-		-	-	-	-		...	...
322 Wearing apparel, except footwear		804470	1098912	1652240	2221433		450224	572907	997188	1266429		...	...
323 Leather and fur products		67200	77500	94805	117919		18935	23883	28898	36700		...	...
3231 Tanneries and leather finishing		-	-	-	-		-	-	-	-		...	...
3232 Fur dressing and dyeing industries		51124	58544	71385	88864		14287	15583	18942	24056		...	...
3233 Leather prods. excl. wearing apparel		16076	18956	23420	29055		4648	8300	9956	12644		...	...
324 Footwear, except rubber or plastic		56661	66651	71276	102214		17419	19950	22930	29121		...	...
331 Wood products, except furniture		676973	889835	1028477	1391576		170517	207247	266966	325698		...	...
3311 Sawmills, planing and other wood mills		580745	739024	856808	1183340		142046	172960	225310	274878		...	...
3312 Wooden and cane containers		24874	28689	34190	40554		8167	9800	11704	14279		...	...
3319 Other wood and cork products		71354	122122	137479	167682		20304	24487	29952	36541		...	...
332 Furniture and fixtures, excl. metal		145705	252211	264627	376857		44929	65743	84687	103318		...	...
341 Paper and products		438618	681300	876658	1110765		91218	118484	154509	193136		...	...
3411 Pulp, paper and paperboard articles		-	-	-	-		-	-	-	-		...	...
3412 Containers of paper and paperboard		341030	564286	741848	939343		63645	85825	108949	136186		...	...
3419 Other pulp, paper and paperboard articles		97588	117014	134810	171422		27573	32659	45560	56950		...	...
342 Printing and publishing		239230	285367	372406	494065		90219	96936	120708	150885		...	...
351 Industrial chemicals		47031	65384	74368	98035		16074	17538	22378	27973		...	...
3511 Basic chemicals excl. fertilizers		23943	35295	37302	51702		11824	12622	15587	19484		...	...
3512 Fertilizers and pesticides		23088	30089	37066	46333		4250	4916	6791	8489		...	...
3513 Synthetic resins and plastic materials		-	-	-	-		-	-	-	-		...	...
352 Other chemicals		741380	986984	1339979	1709112		126652	160345	255760	319701		...	...
3521 Paints, varnishes and lacquers		64935	77995	51228	68908		10205	12514	11110	13888		...	...
3522 Drugs and medicines		128439	150392	202444	280356		35095	38690	55805	69756		...	...
3523 Soap, cleaning preps., perfumes, cosmetics		436598	607800	916435	1130249		52867	70168	144423	180529		...	...
3529 Other chemical products		111408	150797	169872	229599		28485	38973	44422	55528		...	...
353 Petroleum refineries		26887	30884	24833	34041		7474	8925	12047	15059		...	...

354	Misc. petroleum and coal products	-	-	-	-	-	-	-	-	...	...
355	Rubber products	177835	224716	267844	349302	38654	42847	57468	71835	...	...
3551	Tyres and tubes	37199	49242	65547	86547	8334	10070	12975	16219	...	...
3559	Other rubber products	140636	175474	202297	262755	30320	32777	44493	55616	...	...
356	Plastic products	356217	498777	724051	823633	91602	119800	176077	220096	...	...
361	Pottery, china, earthenware	9436	6748	10080	18695	3103	3260	3950	4938	...	...
362	Glass and products	-	-	-	-	-	-	-	-	...	...
369	Other non-metallic mineral products	615101	870864	1151175	1554663	226523	286264	402884	503605	...	...
3691	Structural clay products	9766	10601	20575	30075	3266	3356	5725	7156	...	...
3692	Cement, lime and plaster	309001	500686	642436	851396	124486	167033	228258	285323	...	...
3699	Other non-metallic mineral products	296334	359577	488164	673192	98771	115875	168901	211126	...	...
371	Iron and steel	73197	82545	112291	167555	17947	20107	24046	31316	...	...
372	Non-ferrous metals	12585	17410	19879	19880	6291	8005	8902	12821	...	...
381	Fabricated metal products	571486	745515	854152	1163982	118913	152501	196779	241077	...	...
3811	Cutlery, hand tools and general hardware	26655	28014	26468	40615	8128	9447	12056	14950	...	...
3812	Furniture and fixtures primarily of metal	68909	99666	111599	138291	13498	19226	26507	29940	...	...
3813	Structural metal products	133157	179006	234767	338243	30151	41644	52299	64850	...	...
3819	Other fabricated metal products	342765	438829	481318	646833	67136	82184	105917	131337	...	...
382	Non-electrical machinery	88160	96529	132307	202508	21581	30762	39460	48930	...	...
3821	Engines and turbines	-	-	-	-	-	-	-	-	...	...
3822	Agricultural machinery and equipment	15211	17440	23882	26544	6227	7026	9418	11678	...	...
3823	Metal and wood working machinery	-	-	-	-	-	-	-	-	...	...
3824	Other special industrial machinery	-	-	-	-	-	-	-	-	...	...
3825	Office, computing and accounting machinery	-	-	-	-	-	-	-	-	...	...
3829	Other non-electrical machinery & equipment	72949	79089	108425	175964	15354	23736	30042	37252	...	...
383	Electrical machinery	157501	183781	238721	296247	32641	42201	54233	67248	...	...
3831	Electrical industrial machinery	892	1070	1673	2499	195	225	301	373	...	...
3832	Radio, television and communication equipm.	11724	14724	20664	25779	3715	4458	5864	7271	...	...
3833	Electrical appliances and housewares	-	-	-	-	-	-	-	-	...	...
3839	Other electrical apparatus and supplies	144885	167987	216384	267969	28731	37518	48068	59604	...	...
384	Transport equipment	16715	20421	22832	32352	7709	7681	9776	12123	...	...
3841	Shipbuilding and repairing	1154	1405	1686	5110	528	597	811	1006	...	...
3842	Railroad equipment	-	-	-	-	-	-	-	-	...	...
3843	Motor vehicles	15561	19016	21146	27242	7181	7084	8965	11117	...	...
3844	Motorcycles and bicycles	...	...	...	...	...	...	...	...	...	...
3845	Aircraft	-	-	-	-	-	-	-	-	...	...
3849	Other transport equipment	-	-	-	-	-	-	-	-	...	...
385	Professional and scientific equipment	9432	12692	13014	17995	2977	4175	5297	6569	...	...
3851	Prof. and scientific equipment n.e.c.	728	772	1124	1340	82	398	505	626	...	...
3852	Photographic and optical goods	8704	11920	11890	16655	2895	3777	4792	5943	...	...
3853	Watches and clocks	-	-	-	-	-	-	-	-	...	...
390	Other manufacturing industries	78827	91302	118294	171176	27118	31372	37807	47637	...	...
3901	Jewellery and related articles	10582	11609	12764	18798	3612	3977	4793	6039	...	...
3902	Musical instruments	-	-	-	-	-	-	-	-	...	...
3903	Sporting and athletic goods	4200	5011	6002	6628	2117	2510	3384	4264	...	...
3909	Manufacturing industries, n.e.c.	64045	74682	99528	145750	21389	24885	29630	37334	...	...
3	Total manufacturing	11895080	15912920	20359180	26984710	3122370	3891535	5380597	6736188	...	...

Honduras

ISIC Revision 2		Index numbers of industrial production											
		(1990=100)											
ISIC Industry	Note	1985	1986	1987	1988	1989	1990	1991	1992	1993	1994	1995	1996
311/2 Food products		61	59	60	74	77	100	125	134	153	203	258	310
313 Beverages		88	99	94	95	86	100	137	197	212	258	293	356
314 Tobacco		59	60	61	58	71	100	123	136	139	158	226	260
321 Textiles	a/	63	62	63	65	75	100	140	167	194	237	321	355
322 Wearing apparel, except footwear	a/	...	...	...	...	...	...	...	...	...	...	...	...
323 Leather and fur products	b/	71	74	72	74	81	100	133	149	183	188	258	285
324 Footwear, except rubber or plastic	b/	...	...	...	...	...	...	...	...	...	...	...	...
331 Wood products, except furniture	c/	57	59	61	59	73	100	143	185	235	277	370	459
332 Furniture and fixtures, excl. metal	c/	...	...	...	...	...	...	...	...	...	...	...	...
341 Paper and products		59	58	57	66	87	100	128	129	160	203	213	231
342 Printing and publishing		53	54	57	63	72	100	123	147	156	181	236	256
351 Industrial chemicals	d/	58	58	58	61	69	100	146	173	180	219	310	373
352 Other chemicals	d/	...	...	...	...	...	...	...	...	...	...	...	...
353 Petroleum refineries		75	130	87	70	61	100	109	140	64	70	77	92
354 Misc. petroleum and coal products		...	...	...	...	...	...	...	...	...	...	...	...
355 Rubber products		...	...	...	...	...	...	...	...	...	...	...	...
356 Plastic products		52	51	53	78	95	100	138	140	157	200	263	316
361 Pottery, china, earthenware	e/	84	81	80	88	86	100	121	161	180	215	293	385
362 Glass and products		...	...	...	...	...	...	...	...	...	...	...	...
369 Other non-metallic mineral products	e/	...	...	...	...	...	...	...	...	...	...	...	...
371 Iron and steel		...	...	...	...	...	...	...	...	...	...	...	...
372 Non-ferrous metals		54	49	51	55	70	100	118	113	122	148	216	310
381 Fabricated metal products	f/	37	40	40	48	67	100	106	113	127	166	193	230
382 Non-electrical machinery	f/	...	...	...	...	...	...	...	...	...	...	...	...
383 Electrical machinery	g/	57	57	63	72	79	100	116	119	121	145	167	201
384 Transport equipment		...	...	...	...	...	...	...	...	...	...	...	...
385 Professional and scientific equipment	g/	...	...	...	...	...	...	...	...	...	...	...	...
390 Other manufacturing industries		48	47	52	67	70	100	121	122	102	143	167	202
3 Total manufacturing		65	70	67	72	76	100	127	151	161	199	253	303

a/ 321 includes 322.
b/ 323 includes 324.
c/ 331 includes 332.
d/ 351 includes 352.
e/ 361 includes 369.
f/ 381 includes 382.
g/ 383 includes 385.

ICELAND

Supplier of information:
National Economic Institute of Iceland, Reykjavik.
Industrial statistics for the OECD countries are compiled by the OECD secretariat, which supplies them to UNIDO. The notes appearing here are based on information in the OECD publication *Industrial Structure Statistics* (annual), OECD, Paris.

Basic source of data:
Sample drawn from financial statements out of tax records.

Major deviations from ISIC (Revision 2):
None reported.

Reference period (if not calendar year):

Scope:
All establishments.

Method of enumeration:
The sample covers around 50% of the total wage bill in various industries. For production and value added the stratified samples drawn are "grossed" to the total size according to the proportion between the total wage bill and the sample wage bill. Employment figures are based on administrative registers of total coverage.

Adjusted for non-response:
Not reported.

Concepts and definitions of variables:
Number of employees is calculated as the number of work years, based on the number of insured weeks of work provided by a register-based tax-source.
Wages and salaries uses the national accounting concept. Self-employed are excluded. Social contributions incurred by employers are included.
Output is valued in basic values, including all subsidies but excluding VAT.
Value added uses the national accounting concept. It is calculated as the value of output excluding the cost of materials, fuels and other supplies; contract and commission work done by others; repair and maintenance work done by others; and electricity purchased. It includes receipts for non-industrial services but excludes costs of non-industrial services. Input estimates are on a consumed basis. Valuation is in basic values.

Related national publications:
Atvinnuvegaskyrslur (Industrial Statistics) (annual), Historical Statistics, Compiling Icelandic National Accounts documentation of methods applied, output and expenditure approaches, all published by the National Economic Institute of Iceland, Reykjavik.

Iceland

ISIC Revision 2	Number of establishments					Number of employees					Wages and salaries paid to employees				
		(numbers)					(numbers)					(million KRONUR)			
ISIC Industry	Note	1992	1993	1994	1995	Note	1992	1993	1994	1995	Note	1992	1993	1994	1995
311/2 Food products		676	715	756	740		9982	9982	10399	10532		16353.6	17095.0	18354.8	19232.9
3111 Slaughtering, preparing & preserving meat		41	49	60	49		872	891	956	984		1937.1	1885.9	2058.9	2117.3
3112 Dairy products		15	14	12	14		618	530	558	587		1101.9	1145.6	1171.3	1349.0
3113 Canning, preserving of fruits & vegetables		15	14	12	9		251	236	223	73		298.5	286.3	329.4	363.2
3114 Canning, preserving and processing of fish		419	444	474	468		6540	6710	7056	7207		10412.8	11076.2	11765.0	11907.7
3115 Vegetable and animal oils and fats		-	-	-	-		-	-	-	-		-	-	-	-
3116 Grain mill products		-	-	-	-		-	-	-	-		-	-	-	-
3117 Bakery products		95	107	100	111		830	821	835	888		1304.8	1308.8	1408.0	1623.9
3118 Sugar factories and refineries		-	-	-	-		-	-	-	-		-	-	-	-
3119 Cocoa, chocolate and sugar confectionery		14	11	15	14		261	275	255	254		359.2	374.7	371.6	415.4
3121 Other food products		-	-	-	-		-	-	-	-		-	-	-	-
3122 Prepared animal feeds		77	76	83	75		610	520	516	539		939.3	1017.5	1250.6	1456.4
313 Beverages		9	7	7	6		334	294	306	273		738.5	709.5	687.3	755.5
3131 Distilling, rectifying and blending spirits		2	2	2	2		4	9	8	9		...	...	...	...
3132 Wine industries		-	-	-	-		-	-	-	-		-	-	-	-
3133 Malt liquors and malt		-	-	-	-		-	-	-	-		-	-	-	-
3134 Soft drinks and carbonated waters		7	5	5	4		330	285	298	264		738.5	709.5	687.3	755.5
314 Tobacco		1	-	-	1		10	-	-	6		-	-	-	-
321 Textiles		65	64	72	72		440	436	468	506		704.6	683.3	685.4	801.9
3211 Spinning, weaving and finishing textiles		3	3	3	3		65	64	70	69		106.6	103.3	109.4	108.6
3212 Made-up textile goods excl. wearing apparel		10	9	12	12		34	33	43	49		68.6	65.2	74.2	64.0
3213 Knitting mills		21	19	21	20		70	65	70	83		76.2	76.0	78.2	99.5
3214 Carpets and rugs		-	-	-	-		-	-	-	-		-	-	-	-
3215 Cordage, rope and twine		31	33	36	37		271	275	286	306		453.2	438.8	423.6	529.8
3219 Other textiles		-	-	-	-		-	-	-	-		-	-	-	-
322 Wearing apparel, except footwear		98	85	96	95		502	464	495	501		770.1	639.7	704.6	732.8
323 Leather and fur products		19	20	19	20		275	227	184	201		415.2	322.7	386.7	390.3
3231 Tanneries and leather finishing		4	8	7	5		254	205	166	180		385.5	288.6	347.2	344.3
3232 Fur dressing and dyeing industries		-	-	-	-		-	-	-	-		-	-	-	-
3233 Leather prods. excl. wearing apparel		15	12	12	15		21	22	18	21		29.7	34.1	39.5	46.0
324 Footwear, except rubber or plastic		2	2	3	3		16	12	11	9		13.4	11.3	11.8	11.3
331 Wood products, except furniture		37	38	41	39		17	28	21	27		40.5	46.3	43.3	53.9
3311 Sawmills, planing and other wood mills		-	-	-	-		-	-	-	-		-	-	-	-
3312 Wooden and cane containers		2	3	5	5		7	8	8	8		...	...	...	...
3319 Other wood and cork products		35	35	36	34		10	20	13	20		40.5	46.3	43.3	53.9
332 Furniture and fixtures, excl. metal		335	344	347	344		1049	915	904	897		2156.0	1627.1	1480.5	1740.5
341 Paper and products		9	10	11	14		233	231	224	234		433.6	405.9	461.9	487.9
3411 Pulp, paper and paperboard articles		9	10	11	14		233	231	224	234		433.6	405.9	461.9	487.9
3412 Containers of paper and paperboard		-	-	-	-		-	-	-	-		-	-	-	-
3419 Other pulp, paper and paperboard articles		-	-	-	-		-	-	-	-		-	-	-	-
342 Printing and publishing		344	359	379	400		1926	1812	1745	1867		3645.7	3760.3	4193.6	4398.8
351 Industrial chemicals		6	7	7	7		246	234	217	197		641.4	566.4	448.7	447.4
3511 Basic chemicals excl. fertilizers	a/	6	7	7	7	a/	246	234	217	197	a/	641.4	566.4	448.7	447.4
3512 Fertilizers and pesticides	a/	...	...	...	...	a/	...	...	...	...	a/	...	...	...	...
3513 Synthetic resins and plastic materials		-	-	-	-		-	-	-	-		-	-	-	-
352 Other chemicals		25	22	25	25		366	377	353	389		522.0	627.6	634.5	646.9
3521 Paints, varnishes and lacquers		7	5	5	5		161	169	172	169		281.7	327.3	333.6	327.1
3522 Drugs and medicines		-	-	-	-		-	-	-	-		-	-	-	-
3523 Soap, cleaning preps., perfumes, cosmetics		18	17	20	20		205	208	181	219		240.3	300.3	300.9	319.8
3529 Other chemical products		-	-	-	-		-	-	-	-		-	-	-	-
353 Petroleum refineries		-	-	-	-		-	-	-	-		-	-	-	-

ISIC	Industry												
354	Misc. petroleum and coal products	2	2	-	2	10	9	-	1	16.5	11.2	...	...
355	Rubber products	-	-	-	-	-	-	-	-	-	-	-	-
3551	Tyres and tubes	-	-	-	-	-	-	-	-	-	-	-	-
3559	Other rubber products	-	-	-	-	-	-	-	-	-	-	-	-
356	Plastic products	58	52	53	63	485	429	474	482	1079.4	1066.1	1059.2	1101.4
361	Pottery, china, earthenware	24	21	24	24	23	22	8	21	70.5	31.9	27.5	18.4
362	Glass and products	22	24	24	26	102	98	91	82	185.8	159.7	140.0	138.2
369	Other non-metallic mineral products	66	71	78	77	767	700	650	674	1515.5	1219.1	1306.4	1315.5
3691	Structural clay products	1	-	-	-	...	-	-	-	...	-	-	-
3692	Cement, lime and plaster	1	1	1	1	132	114	90	90	257.9	204.7	207.5	219.8
3699	Other non-metallic mineral products	64	70	77	76	635	586	560	584	1257.6	1014.4	1098.9	1095.7
371	Iron and steel	1	1	1	1	190	161	157	162	459.4	376.3	408.2	466.4
372	Non-ferrous metals	1	1	1	1	623	592	534	511	1376.9	1279.8	1262.5	1224.4
381	Fabricated metal products	504	511	538	566	1857	1740	1730	1834	3214.1	2801.5	2803.3	3423.9
3811	Cutlery, hand tools and general hardware	...	...	...	...	...	...	...	...	...	...	...	...
3812	Furniture and fixtures primarily of metal	...	...	...	...	...	...	...	...	...	...	...	...
3813	Structural metal products	...	...	...	...	...	...	...	...	...	...	...	...
3819	Other fabricated metal products	...	...	...	...	...	...	...	...	...	...	...	...
382	Non-electrical machinery	-	-	-	-	-	-	-	-	-	-	-	-
3821	Engines and turbines	-	-	-	-	-	-	-	-	-	-	-	-
3822	Agricultural machinery and equipment	-	-	-	-	-	-	-	-	-	-	-	-
3823	Metal and wood working machinery	-	-	-	-	-	-	-	-	-	-	-	-
3824	Other special industrial machinery	-	-	-	-	-	-	-	-	-	-	-	-
3825	Office, computing and accounting machinery	-	-	-	-	-	-	-	-	-	-	-	-
3829	Other non-electrical machinery & equipment	-	-	-	-	-	-	-	-	-	-	-	-
383	Electrical machinery	-	-	-	-	-	-	-	-	-	-	-	-
3831	Electrical industrial machinery	-	-	-	-	-	-	-	-	-	-	-	-
3832	Radio, television and communication equipm.	-	-	-	-	-	-	-	-	-	-	-	-
3833	Electrical appliances and housewares	-	-	-	-	-	-	-	-	-	-	-	-
3839	Other electrical apparatus and supplies	-	-	-	-	-	-	-	-	-	-	-	-
384	Transport equipment	70	65	64	57	546	538	360	394	1277.2	1176.6	867.8	1008.1
3841	Shipbuilding and repairing	70	65	64	57	546	538	360	394	1277.2	1176.6	867.8	1008.1
3842	Railroad equipment	-	-	-	-	-	-	-	-	-	-	-	-
3843	Motor vehicles	-	-	-	-	-	-	-	-	-	-	-	-
3844	Motorcycles and bicycles	-	-	-	-	-	-	-	-	-	-	-	-
3845	Aircraft	-	-	-	-	-	-	-	-	-	-	-	-
3849	Other transport equipment	-	-	-	-	-	-	-	-	-	-	-	-
385	Professional and scientific equipment	-	-	-	-	-	-	-	-	-	-	-	-
3851	Prof. and scientific equipment n.e.c.	-	-	-	-	-	-	-	-	-	-	-	-
3852	Photographic and optical goods	-	-	-	-	-	-	-	-	-	-	-	-
3853	Watches and clocks	-	-	-	-	-	-	-	-	-	-	-	-
390	Other manufacturing industries	158	157	174	153	495	486	551	629	1158.4	1247.3	1381.7	1627.7
3901	Jewellery and related articles	34	33	39	35	41	38	39	42	66.6	55.0	43.6	55.4
3902	Musical instruments	12	13	12	13	...	1	2	3	0.5	3.7	3.0	7.4
3903	Sporting and athletic goods	-	-	-	-	-	-	-	-	-	-	-	-
3909	Manufacturing industries, n.e.c.	112	111	123	105	454	447	510	585	1091.3	1188.6	1335.1	1564.9
3	Total manufacturing	2532	2578	2720	2736	20493	19784	19880	20430	36788.3	35864.6	37349.7	40024.1

a/ 3511 includes 3512.

Iceland

ISIC Revision 2	Output					Value added					Gross fixed capital formation		
		(million KRONUR)					(million KRONUR)					(million KRONUR)	
ISIC Industry	Note	1992	1993	1994	1995	Note	1992	1993	1994	1995	Note	1994	1995
311/2 Food products		93924.1	93400.6	102929.8	105119.7		25942.3	26824.8	30395.7	28570.5		...	...
3111 Slaughtering, preparing & preserving meat		13693.0	12919.9	12891.6	13403.6		2768.7	2568.5	2817.6	2937.5		...	...
3112 Dairy products		12903.3	10305.1	10260.0	10853.7		2069.5	2135.8	2196.1	2250.1		...	...
3113 Canning, preserving of fruits & vegetables		1886.3	2081.3	2399.6	2449.9		506.5	563.1	553.5	582.7		...	...
3114 Canning, preserving and processing of fish		54659.7	57662.4	65681.6	66005.8		16261.3	17534.1	20257.8	18004.0		...	...
3115 Vegetable and animal oils and fats		-	-	-	-		-	-	-	-		...	...
3116 Grain mill products		-	-	-	-		-	-	-	-		...	...
3117 Bakery products		4032.0	4112.6	4272.5	4568.1		1991.1	1970.8	2030.1	2261.4		...	...
3118 Sugar factories and refineries		-	-	-	-		-	-	-	-		...	...
3119 Cocoa, chocolate and sugar confectionery		1613.6	1237.7	1419.7	1440.5		732.1	538.7	593.6	575.4		...	...
3121 Other food products		-	-	-	-		-	-	-	-		...	...
3122 Prepared animal feeds		5136.2	5081.6	6004.8	6398.1		1613.1	1513.8	1947.0	1959.4		...	...
313 Beverages		3816.2	3624.3	4014.7	3969.9		1315.9	1092.3	1126.8	1280.5		...	...
3131 Distilling, rectifying and blending spirits		...	...	...	...		...	...	...	...		...	...
3132 Wine industries		-	-	-	-		-	-	-	-		...	...
3133 Malt liquors and malt		-	-	-	-		-	-	-	-		...	...
3134 Soft drinks and carbonated waters		3816.2	3624.3	4014.7	3969.9		1315.9	1092.3	1126.8	1280.5		...	...
314 Tobacco		-	-	-	-		-	-	-	-		...	...
321 Textiles		3155.8	3013.3	3145.1	3851.7		1125.5	1014.6	1112.3	1316.3		...	...
3211 Spinning, weaving and finishing textiles		570.3	298.7	334.2	612.0		140.0	68.6	135.1	143.4		...	...
3212 Made-up textile goods excl. wearing apparel		376.5	352.2	385.1	401.9		102.1	77.8	91.5	85.1		...	...
3213 Knitting mills		405.1	477.7	459.0	501.3		190.3	209.8	158.2	213.6		...	...
3214 Carpets and rugs		-	-	-	-		-	-	-	-		...	...
3215 Cordage, rope and twine		1803.9	1884.7	1966.8	2336.5		693.1	658.4	727.5	874.2		...	...
3219 Other textiles		-	-	-	-		-	-	-	-		...	...
322 Wearing apparel, except footwear		1962.6	1940.4	2087.3	2113.9		833.5	839.3	921.6	930.4		...	...
323 Leather and fur products		1128.7	925.7	1297.8	1476.6		481.6	402.3	562.1	664.1		...	...
3231 Tanneries and leather finishing		1021.4	815.4	1177.5	1354.6		429.3	349.7	499.3	596.8		...	...
3232 Fur dressing and dyeing industries		-	-	-	-		-	-	-	-		...	...
3233 Leather prods. excl. wearing apparel		107.3	110.3	120.3	122.0		52.3	52.6	62.8	67.3		...	...
324 Footwear, except rubber or plastic		43.3	12.2	18.9	22.3		1.6	2.9	2.1	5.2		...	...
331 Wood products, except furniture		217.5	226.7	249.8	286.4		88.8	100.3	90.4	100.9		...	...
3311 Sawmills, planing and other wood mills		-	-	-	-		-	-	-	-		...	...
3312 Wooden and cane containers		...	...	...	...		...	...	...	...		...	...
3319 Other wood and cork products		217.5	226.7	249.8	286.4		88.8	100.3	90.4	100.9		...	...
332 Furniture and fixtures, excl. metal		6169.3	5353.9	5459.7	5477.6		2810.0	2275.1	2129.0	2200.3		...	...
341 Paper and products		1531.8	1616.3	1947.9	2061.7		565.6	647.3	745.3	738.0		...	...
3411 Pulp, paper and paperboard articles		1531.8	1616.3	1947.9	2061.7		565.6	647.3	745.3	738.0		...	...
3412 Containers of paper and paperboard		-	-	-	-		-	-	-	-		...	...
3419 Other pulp, paper and paperboard articles		-	-	-	-		-	-	-	-		...	...
342 Printing and publishing		10671.7	10613.7	10711.4	11357.1		5336.8	5019.7	5634.3	5837.1		...	...
351 Industrial chemicals		2436.0	2078.2	2201.6	2244.6		1000.1	779.7	673.1	607.4		...	...
3511 Basic chemicals excl. fertilizers	a/	2436.0	2078.2	2201.6	2244.6	a/	1000.1	779.7	673.1	607.4		...	...
3512 Fertilizers and pesticides	a/	...	...	...	...	a/	...	...	...	...		...	...
3513 Synthetic resins and plastic materials		-	-	-	-		-	-	-	-		...	...
352 Other chemicals		2713.3	2853.7	3013.0	3247.8		1207.4	1288.9	1181.6	1328.8		...	...
3521 Paints, varnishes and lacquers		1322.6	1394.3	1460.4	1524.7		547.8	576.7	580.0	522.5		...	...
3522 Drugs and medicines		-	-	-	-		-	-	-	-		...	...
3523 Soap, cleaning preps., perfumes, cosmetics		1390.7	1459.4	1552.6	1723.1		659.6	712.2	601.6	806.3		...	...
3529 Other chemical products		-	-	-	-		-	-	-	-		...	...
353 Petroleum refineries		-	-	-	-		-	-	-	-		...	...

354 Misc. petroleum and coal products	66.5	48.3	...	...	30.7	21.2	...	...	...	...
355 Rubber products	-	-	-	-	-	-	-	-	...	...
3551 Tyres and tubes	-	-	-	-	-	-	-	-	...	...
3559 Other rubber products	-	-	-	-	-	-	-	-	...	...
356 Plastic products	3975.7	4030.0	4335.6	4630.5	1716.7	1737.5	1779.0	1776.0	...	...
361 Pottery, china, earthenware	106.9	87.6	87.4	95.2	-2.0	54.8	39.5	47.6	...	...
362 Glass and products	604.7	549.2	545.4	550.0	276.8	238.4	234.7	236.0	...	...
369 Other non-metallic mineral products	5017.7	4726.5	5233.3	5276.4	2292.8	2018.4	2409.4	2268.2	...	...
3691 Structural clay products	...	-	-	-	...	-	-	-	...	...
3692 Cement, lime and plaster	657.2	633.8	775.9	771.0	340.1	290.0	379.3	357.0	...	...
3699 Other non-metallic mineral products	4360.5	4092.7	4457.4	4505.4	1952.7	1728.4	2030.1	1911.2	...	...
371 Iron and steel	1923.0	2732.7	2959.0	3431.2	365.3	922.2	995.1	1342.8	...	...
372 Non-ferrous metals	7998.4	8421.2	10837.0	11674.4	1407.5	1164.6	3160.6	2800.0	...	...
381 Fabricated metal products	10044.7	9716.8	11086.2	12698.1	4118.1	3995.8	4110.2	4738.3	...	...
3811 Cutlery, hand tools and general hardware	...	...	...	...	...	...	...	...	...	...
3812 Furniture and fixtures primarily of metal	...	...	...	...	...	...	...	...	...	...
3813 Structural metal products	...	...	...	...	...	...	...	...	...	...
3819 Other fabricated metal products	...	...	...	...	...	...	...	...	...	...
382 Non-electrical machinery	-	-	-	-	-	-	-	-	...	...
3821 Engines and turbines	-	-	-	-	-	-	-	-	...	...
3822 Agricultural machinery and equipment	-	-	-	-	-	-	-	-	...	...
3823 Metal and wood working machinery	-	-	-	-	-	-	-	-	...	...
3824 Other special industrial machinery	-	-	-	-	-	-	-	-	...	...
3825 Office, computing and accounting machinery	-	-	-	-	-	-	-	-	...	...
3829 Other non-electrical machinery & equipment	-	-	-	-	-	-	-	-	...	...
383 Electrical machinery	-	-	-	-	-	-	-	-	...	...
3831 Electrical industrial machinery	-	-	-	-	-	-	-	-	...	...
3832 Radio, television and communication equipm.	-	-	-	-	-	-	-	-	...	...
3833 Electrical appliances and housewares	-	-	-	-	-	-	-	-	...	...
3839 Other electrical apparatus and supplies	-	-	-	-	-	-	-	-	...	...
384 Transport equipment	2527.7	2549.9	2024.5	2275.1	1441.5	1323.1	1068.0	1201.9	...	...
3841 Shipbuilding and repairing	2527.7	2549.9	2024.5	2275.1	1441.5	1323.1	1068.0	1201.9	...	...
3842 Railroad equipment	-	-	-	-	-	-	-	-	...	...
3843 Motor vehicles	-	-	-	-	-	-	-	-	...	...
3844 Motorcycles and bicycles	-	-	-	-	-	-	-	-	...	...
3845 Aircraft	-	-	-	-	-	-	-	-	...	...
3849 Other transport equipment	-	-	-	-	-	-	-	-	...	...
385 Professional and scientific equipment	-	-	-	-	-	-	-	-	...	...
3851 Prof. and scientific equipment n.e.c.	-	-	-	-	-	-	-	-	...	...
3852 Photographic and optical goods	-	-	-	-	-	-	-	-	...	...
3853 Watches and clocks	-	-	-	-	-	-	-	-	...	...
390 Other manufacturing industries	5353.0	5562.6	6062.2	7424.9	1741.6	1977.7	1932.6	2359.8	...	...
3901 Jewellery and related articles	244.5	229.4	238.9	254.5	123.5	108.8	108.1	112.6	...	...
3902 Musical instruments	19.9	25.4	43.1	42.1	9.9	12.7	17.2	18.1	...	...
3903 Sporting and athletic goods	-	-	-	-	-	-	-	-	...	...
3909 Manufacturing industries, n.e.c.	5088.6	5307.8	5780.2	7128.3	1608.2	1856.2	1807.3	2229.1	...	...
3 Total manufacturing	165388.6	164083.8	180247.6	189285.1	54098.1	53740.9	60303.4	60350.1	...	...

a/ 3511 includes 3512.

Iceland

ISIC Revision 2		Index numbers of industrial production											
		(1990=100)											
ISIC Industry	Note	1985	1986	1987	1988	1989	1990	1991	1992	1993	1994	1995	1996
311/2 Food products		...	...	...	...	...	...	...	...	...	...	...	...
313 Beverages		...	...	...	...	...	...	...	...	...	...	...	...
314 Tobacco		...	...	...	...	...	...	...	...	...	...	...	...
321 Textiles		...	...	...	...	...	...	...	...	...	...	...	...
322 Wearing apparel, except footwear		...	...	...	...	...	...	...	...	...	...	...	...
323 Leather and fur products		...	...	...	...	...	...	...	...	...	...	...	...
324 Footwear, except rubber or plastic		...	...	...	...	...	...	...	...	...	...	...	...
331 Wood products, except furniture		...	...	...	...	...	...	...	...	...	...	...	...
332 Furniture and fixtures, excl. metal		...	...	...	...	...	...	...	...	...	...	...	...
341 Paper and products		...	...	...	...	...	...	...	...	...	...	...	...
342 Printing and publishing		...	...	...	...	...	...	...	...	...	...	...	...
351 Industrial chemicals		...	...	...	...	...	...	...	...	...	...	...	...
352 Other chemicals		...	...	...	...	...	...	...	...	...	...	...	...
353 Petroleum refineries		...	...	...	...	...	...	...	...	...	...	...	...
354 Misc. petroleum and coal products		...	...	...	...	...	...	...	...	...	...	...	...
355 Rubber products		...	...	...	...	...	...	...	...	...	...	...	...
356 Plastic products		...	...	...	...	...	...	...	...	...	...	...	...
361 Pottery, china, earthenware		...	...	...	...	...	...	...	...	...	...	...	...
362 Glass and products		...	...	...	...	...	...	...	...	...	...	...	...
369 Other non-metallic mineral products		...	...	...	...	...	...	...	...	...	...	...	...
371 Iron and steel		...	...	...	...	...	...	...	...	...	...	...	...
372 Non-ferrous metals		...	...	...	...	...	...	...	...	...	...	...	...
381 Fabricated metal products		...	...	...	...	...	...	...	...	...	...	...	...
382 Non-electrical machinery		...	...	...	...	...	...	...	...	...	...	...	...
383 Electrical machinery		...	...	...	...	...	...	...	...	...	...	...	...
384 Transport equipment		...	...	...	...	...	...	...	...	...	...	...	...
385 Professional and scientific equipment		...	...	...	...	...	...	...	...	...	...	...	...
390 Other manufacturing industries		...	...	...	...	...	...	...	...	...	...	...	...
3 Total manufacturing		...	...	...	...	...	...	...	...	...	...	...	...

INDIA

Supplier of information:
Central Statistical Organisation, Department of Statistics, Ministry of Planning and Programme Implementation, New Delhi.

Basic source of data:
Annual Survey of Industries.

Major deviations from ISIC (Revision 2):
The Indian industrial classification system is based on the preceding version of the ISIC, but the data have been adjusted by the national authorities to correspond with ISIC (Rev. 2), with three exceptions: the manufacture of inedible oils (part of ISIC 3115) is included in ISIC 352; the manufacture of prime movers, boilers, etc. (part of ISIC 3813) is included in ISIC 382 and the manufacture of electronic computers (part of ISIC 3825) is included in ISIC 383.

Reference period (if not calendar year):
From 1 April of the year indicated to 31 March of the following year. However, individual factory returns for an accounting year ending on any day during the reference period are accepted.

Scope:
Factories using power and employing 10 or more workers on any day of the reference period and all factories employing 20 or more workers. The indices of industrial production for some industries cover only establishments employing plant and machinery worth two million rupees or more.

Method of enumeration:
Factories employing 100 or more workers are completely enumerated. For factories with less than 100 workers, stratified unistage sampling is used.

Adjusted for non-response:
No.

Concepts and definitions of variables:
Number of persons engaged is derived by dividing the person days (paid or unpaid) by the number of days during which the factory was either in operation or repair, maintenance and construction activity was carried out. The number of person days for each category is obtained by summing up the number of persons attending each shift over every shift worked on all days (working and non-working).
Wages and salaries is compensation of employees. It includes payments to contract labourers and excludes payments in kind.
Output is gross output and includes gross revenues from goods shipped in the same condition as received.
Value added is total value added and is net of depreciation.

Related national publications:
Annual Survey of Industries – Summary Results for Factory Sector; Supplement to Annual Survey of Industries – Summary Results for Factory Sector by State Industry, all published by Central Statistical Organisation, Department of Statistics, Ministry of Planning and Programme Implementation, New Delhi.

ISIC Revision 2	Number of establishments					Number of employees					Wages and salaries paid to employees				
		(numbers)					(thousands)					(million RUPEES)			
ISIC Industry	Note	1991	1992	1993	1994	Note	1991	1992	1993	1994	Note	1991	1992	1993	1994
311/2 Food products		19721	21397	21491	21127		1095.9	1189.6	1189.0	1205.8		18278	21887	23581	27108
3111 Slaughtering, preparing & preserving meat		30	33	32	29		3.0	3.8	3.0	3.9		97	126	130	162
3112 Dairy products		465	511	513	563		59.3	68.0	73.6	75.9		1964	2532	3000	3487
3113 Canning, preserving of fruits & vegetables		217	232	294	260		13.0	15.3	15.7	17.0		187	243	253	329
3114 Canning, preserving and processing of fish		183	229	269	275		17.0	18.5	20.0	24.1		224	277	333	468
3115 Vegetable and animal oils and fats		3194	3396	3549	3397		110.4	109.5	112.1	108.9		1768	2057	2315	2356
3116 Grain mill products		9195	10259	9871	9798		195.8	221.8	234.6	218.5		1811	2228	2688	2866
3117 Bakery products		725	758	763	785		32.6	33.3	32.0	35.4		776	878	985	1178
3118 Sugar factories and refineries		1326	1306	1283	1261		340.7	350.0	330.2	327.1		8186	9608	9588	11329
3119 Cocoa, chocolate and sugar confectionery		135	147	209	402		9.0	9.4	9.6	27.7		173	200	216	336
3121 Other food products		3950	4231	4362	3996		302.8	346.5	347.2	352.0		2842	3415	3748	4150
3122 Prepared animal feeds		301	295	346	361		12.1	13.6	11.1	15.3		251	323	327	447
313 Beverages		532	564	606	572		56.5	58.8	57.1	62.6		1394	1648	1725	2157
3131 Distilling, rectifying and blending spirits		210	227	226	220		28.1	29.1	29.2	30.2		700	843	859	1038
3132 Wine industries		45	37	40	42		4.2	2.2	2.7	3.5		95	47	64	94
3133 Malt liquors and malt		78	76	88	81		11.8	14.0	11.8	14.7		340	447	466	602
3134 Soft drinks and carbonated waters		199	224	252	229		12.4	13.5	13.3	14.2		259	311	336	423
314 Tobacco		8299	7786	5158	7708		458.3	490.7	454.7	518.2		3499	4108	4578	5528
321 Textiles		12860	14789	15168	15220		1328.7	1379.5	1395.2	1394.8		30882	35473	39021	43251
3211 Spinning, weaving and finishing textiles		10840	12716	12681	12447		1264.1	1310.8	1305.6	1299.4		29666	34001	37089	40844
3212 Made-up textile goods excl. wearing apparel		96	114	132	128		2.8	3.5	4.6	4.7		49	71	92	112
3213 Knitting mills		1058	1172	1417	1669		30.4	35.8	47.1	49.6		494	667	894	1177
3214 Carpets and rugs		185	167	216	233		5.7	5.1	10.6	9.0		102	108	244	211
3215 Cordage, rope and twine		366	328	369	366		12.7	11.6	13.7	17.4		261	281	302	408
3219 Other textiles		315	292	353	377		13.0	12.6	13.6	14.7		310	345	400	499
322 Wearing apparel, except footwear		1931	2279	3119	3292		126.2	148.0	204.8	244.3		1898	2559	3628	4809
323 Leather and fur products		994	969	1182	1136		49.1	44.4	45.9	52.6		881	922	1020	1232
3231 Tanneries and leather finishing		825	838	941	916		41.9	39.0	37.2	41.3		787	822	855	1022
3232 Fur dressing and dyeing industries		-	-	3	6		-	-	-	0.1		-	-	...	...
3233 Leather prods. excl. wearing apparel		169	131	238	214		7.2	5.5	8.6	11.2		94	100	164	209
324 Footwear, except rubber or plastic		372	364	495	460		47.3	51.8	52.9	60.7		891	1146	1179	1295
331 Wood products, except furniture		3103	3277	3237	3346		56.0	62.5	63.3	64.2		647	847	1001	1102
3311 Sawmills, planing and other wood mills		2681	2806	2772	2849		50.3	55.0	55.2	56.8		574	732	852	950
3312 Wooden and cane containers		184	179	190	200		2.3	2.9	2.8	3.2		31	51	58	73
3319 Other wood and cork products		238	292	275	297		3.4	4.6	5.3	4.1		42	64	91	79
332 Furniture and fixtures, excl. metal		318	331	311	285		7.7	6.6	6.5	5.9		138	134	133	149
341 Paper and products		2111	2278	2602	2504		144.6	153.9	155.2	161.4		3935	4628	5090	5971
3411 Pulp, paper and paperboard articles		839	927	1005	953		115.9	120.7	119.0	123.2		3428	3947	4333	5101
3412 Containers of paper and paperboard		1046	1060	1289	1269		23.5	26.1	27.8	29.0		420	554	596	666
3419 Other pulp, paper and paperboard articles		226	291	308	282		5.2	7.1	8.4	9.2		87	127	161	204
342 Printing and publishing		3111	3287	3261	3131		144.1	147.7	146.0	157.9		4433	5046	5601	8597
351 Industrial chemicals		2175	2345	2496	2528		219.3	251.0	239.6	266.9		10732	15377	14398	18508
3511 Basic chemicals excl. fertilizers		1405	1444	1522	1574		92.6	96.7	96.1	99.8		3708	5659	4665	5599
3512 Fertilizers and pesticides		509	633	652	646		82.9	100.1	92.7	101.4		4600	6008	5858	7891
3513 Synthetic resins and plastic materials		261	268	322	308		43.8	54.3	50.8	65.8		2425	3710	3876	5018
352 Other chemicals		5079	5541	6041	5724		356.6	384.4	399.4	405.2		10913	13792	15312	17522
3521 Paints, varnishes and lacquers		939	1021	1105	1036		46.4	47.1	51.0	46.9		1933	2106	2499	2585
3522 Drugs and medicines		1886	2112	2352	2173		147.0	166.0	174.4	181.5		5751	7371	8249	9941
3523 Soap, cleaning preps., perfumes, cosmetics		808	857	876	757		49.7	51.1	49.4	48.9		1261	1650	1691	1816
3529 Other chemical products		1446	1551	1708	1758		113.5	120.2	124.6	127.9		1968	2665	2873	3180
353 Petroleum refineries		82	79	120	143		21.5	24.4	27.4	30.5		1466	1765	1997	2729

ISIC	Industry												
354	Misc. petroleum and coal products	511	567	566	604	36.1	43.0	42.2	41.4	1223	1553	1646	1822
355	Rubber products	2078	2172	2259	2398	110.5	120.4	125.0	131.3	3103	3753	4512	5028
3551	Tyres and tubes	375	452	461	498	49.9	61.6	62.4	67.3	1777	2437	2968	3320
3559	Other rubber products	1703	1720	1798	1900	60.6	58.8	62.6	64.0	1326	1316	1545	1708
356	Plastic products	2953	3153	3217	3330	85.8	91.6	97.9	101.5	1792	2472	2660	2831
361	Pottery, china, earthenware	557	579	624	624	29.9	25.7	25.1	25.7	659	658	664	697
362	Glass and products	628	590	667	616	65.6	57.7	57.3	53.5	1378	1363	1396	1643
369	Other non-metallic mineral products	8734	9196	9535	9377	358.6	372.6	358.4	365.3	6378	7786	8584	10068
3691	Structural clay products	3976	4072	4261	3981	165.0	165.6	151.0	156.5	1885	2115	2298	2640
3692	Cement, lime and plaster	616	687	745	763	82.6	93.9	93.1	92.2	2583	3466	3800	4225
3699	Other non-metallic mineral products	4142	4437	4529	4633	111.1	113.0	114.2	116.5	1910	2205	2486	3203
371	Iron and steel	3108	3388	3362	3379	412.9	487.6	464.5	452.2	11510	21092	22449	25458
372	Non-ferrous metals	2989	2859	3085	2994	182.9	174.3	160.9	179.1	5423	5640	5514	7099
381	Fabricated metal products	6890	7038	7496	7287	223.0	234.0	231.2	244.1	5428	6753	7315	8982
3811	Cutlery, hand tools and general hardware	2674	2652	2842	2673	68.9	67.5	69.8	70.4	1622	1729	2017	2254
3812	Furniture and fixtures primarily of metal	330	392	413	349	5.8	14.2	13.8	11.7	103	770	802	952
3813	Structural metal products	960	1056	1013	1064	50.0	54.2	44.4	53.6	1367	1622	1456	2063
3819	Other fabricated metal products	2926	2938	3228	3201	98.4	98.1	103.2	108.4	2338	2632	3040	3713
382	Non-electrical machinery	8168	8554	8977	8521	471.4	498.8	478.6	477.1	17000	19996	21187	23506
3821	Engines and turbines	807	747	890	759	62.3	59.2	62.8	56.5	2316	2556	3194	3229
3822	Agricultural machinery and equipment	774	836	825	803	37.5	44.1	41.3	43.0	1325	1970	1978	2549
3823	Metal and wood working machinery	944	1022	1099	1148	46.5	52.2	41.2	47.4	1744	2143	1692	2243
3824	Other special industrial machinery	2687	2976	3069	2843	139.2	156.6	159.9	154.8	4651	5776	6270	6801
3825	Office, computing and accounting machinery	260	262	284	247	30.2	34.8	19.4	24.1	1182	1817	849	1359
3829	Other non-electrical machinery & equipment	2696	2711	2810	2721	155.8	151.9	154.0	151.4	5782	5734	7204	7325
383	Electrical machinery	4835	5120	5110	5385	387.8	399.6	396.1	417.7	14846	17157	18546	21714
3831	Electrical industrial machinery	1783	1924	1896	2031	159.0	161.4	158.4	167.7	7405	8268	8542	10176
3832	Radio, television and communication equipm.	1193	1194	1207	1336	117.2	123.6	118.7	133.3	3932	4770	5245	6368
3833	Electrical appliances and housewares	631	616	581	604	23.4	24.0	25.2	25.4	579	663	804	826
3839	Other electrical apparatus and supplies	1228	1386	1426	1414	88.2	90.6	93.9	91.3	2930	3456	3955	4344
384	Transport equipment	5213	5552	5966	5922	665.9	715.0	707.6	747.4	24908	28998	31866	37767
3841	Shipbuilding and repairing	185	204	241	195	21.1	27.3	30.4	27.8	655	809	1127	1033
3842	Railroad equipment	310	314	325	355	213.8	226.0	210.9	236.5	7228	8564	8568	10808
3843	Motor vehicles	3051	3379	3471	3614	309.3	339.2	334.1	351.4	12817	14902	16626	19651
3844	Motorcycles and bicycles	1242	1241	1362	1237	96.5	98.2	104.2	104.3	2945	3194	3811	4244
3845	Aircraft	19	22	42	42	9.6	8.4	10.5	9.5	867	1070	1263	1447
3849	Other transport equipment	406	392	525	479	15.6	15.9	17.4	17.9	396	459	470	584
385	Professional and scientific equipment	861	796	940	861	49.3	55.2	58.0	58.5	1432	1931	2455	2581
3851	Prof. and scientific equipment n.e.c.	501	476	632	540	25.0	30.7	35.1	34.9	716	1114	1600	1561
3852	Photographic and optical goods	118	109	116	124	3.2	3.4	3.8	3.7	103	104	126	134
3853	Watches and clocks	242	211	192	197	21.1	21.1	19.1	19.8	612	713	729	886
390	Other manufacturing industries	982	1074	1155	1198	45.4	47.8	58.4	61.7	997	1196	1574	1863
3901	Jewellery and related articles	259	273	289	348	20.9	23.2	29.6	32.4	465	634	863	1076
3902	Musical instruments	10	10	10	11	1.2	1.3	1.2	1.3	47	54	59	65
3903	Sporting and athletic goods	63	87	84	89	2.3	2.5	4.3	4.3	40	48	88	100
3909	Manufacturing industries, n.e.c.	650	704	772	750	21.1	20.8	23.3	23.7	445	460	565	622
3	Total manufacturing	109195	115924	118246	119672	7236.9	7716.6	7698.1	7987.5	186062	229680	248630	291017

ISIC Revision 2		Output in factor values					Value added in factor values					Gross fixed capital formation	
		(million RUPEES)					(million RUPEES)					(million RUPEES)	
ISIC Industry	Note	1991	1992	1993	1994	Note	1991	1992	1993	1994	Note	1993	1994
311/2 Food products		434060	498712	563720	679490		44677	48462	68324	90757		17342	33222
3111 Slaughtering, preparing & preserving meat		1459	2242	2352	2945		224	518	274	960		692	216
3112 Dairy products		41198	57694	67943	69337		2940	3847	3657	5628		1676	2585
3113 Canning, preserving of fruits & vegetables		1857	2714	3247	3960		279	694	911	603		413	1070
3114 Canning, preserving and processing of fish		10223	13201	14820	22835		1341	1397	1886	2166		498	1387
3115 Vegetable and animal oils and fats		129109	136134	146767	172665		6652	6652	10587	13170		4192	7147
3116 Grain mill products		80915	94426	113805	132795		5636	4839	6922	10758		2345	1712
3117 Bakery products		10379	11555	13505	16670		1663	1973	2254	2918		308	489
3118 Sugar factories and refineries		90628	103170	117290	157541		12603	15398	24780	36881		6334	13153
3119 Cocoa, chocolate and sugar confectionery		2939	3185	3724	1869		814	605	1055	650		169	104
3121 Other food products		55957	63170	71973	82709		11630	11621	15172	14988		571	5010
3122 Prepared animal feeds		9397	11221	8296	16164		895	918	826	2035		145	349
313 Beverages		22388	25760	29635	42884		5399	5750	6651	9107		4300	5199
3131 Distilling, rectifying and blending spirits		10129	12413	15094	21887		2210	2698	3353	5034		1811	2054
3132 Wine industries		1754	782	1344	2370		312	201	446	436		85	306
3133 Malt liquors and malt		6992	8271	8075	11447		2149	1777	1674	2160		1421	1161
3134 Soft drinks and carbonated waters		3513	4294	5123	7180		728	1074	1179	1477		983	1678
314 Tobacco		39870	47220	53503	55952		10822	12513	14374	17597		1122	1311
321 Textiles		311505	365189	441106	553228		53181	59140	85633	104124		39967	59265
3211 Spinning, weaving and finishing textiles		288577	339090	406572	509169		49228	54500	79267	96424		37125	55187
3212 Made-up textile goods excl. wearing apparel		994	1333	1068	2483		149	251	204	409		184	103
3213 Knitting mills		11305	13990	19119	24277		1875	2252	3437	3776		1072	1285
3214 Carpets and rugs		2647	2768	3418	4858		497	601	694	855		884	113
3215 Cordage, rope and twine		3042	3351	4569	4831		638	785	928	946		427	899
3219 Other textiles		4939	4657	6360	7610		794	751	1104	1714		275	1678
322 Wearing apparel, except footwear		34751	43563	68732	83713		8276	9488	21454	24110		3313	5973
323 Leather and fur products		16716	16433	21670	28129		2599	2456	3332	3334		636	993
3231 Tanneries and leather finishing		14875	14705	18551	23764		2215	2074	2738	2689		494	800
3232 Fur dressing and dyeing industries		-	-	...	...		-	-	...	...		...	...
3233 Leather prods. excl. wearing apparel		1841	1728	3097	4360		385	382	594	644		142	176
324 Footwear, except rubber or plastic		10826	12901	18868	21202		2191	2549	4774	3902		1037	1771
331 Wood products, except furniture		8306	9981	12562	14011		1750	1952	2688	2888		722	769
3311 Sawmills, planing and other wood mills		7461	8826	11277	12281		1592	1760	2429	2524		649	642
3312 Wooden and cane containers		359	581	492	919		58	81	86	232		7	27
3319 Other wood and cork products		486	574	793	811		100	111	174	132		66	100
332 Furniture and fixtures, excl. metal		702	678	852	966		170	159	212	159		36	7
341 Paper and products		56305	62546	70682	89748		10434	11092	13196	18390		11888	49710
3411 Pulp, paper and paperboard articles		47313	51344	57135	72886		9034	9613	11434	16172		8392	48377
3412 Containers of paper and paperboard		7614	9040	10490	12852		1206	1216	1360	1575		3195	819
3419 Other pulp, paper and paperboard articles		1378	2162	3057	4010		193	263	402	643		301	514
342 Printing and publishing		29320	35316	44480	51841		8117	9928	15323	15709		2566	4270
351 Industrial chemicals		220302	289501	306411	393010		31116	60868	77625	94030		34201	49609
3511 Basic chemicals excl. fertilizers		66680	73032	82403	108059		15933	16086	22687	24982		7274	17663
3512 Fertilizers and pesticides		120427	143104	142895	187284		15139	25712	27197	39159		18712	22889
3513 Synthetic resins and plastic materials		33195	73365	81113	97667		44	19070	27742	29889		8215	9057
352 Other chemicals		174672	212447	255877	287710		39567	46651	58738	67846		20426	17823
3521 Paints, varnishes and lacquers		35519	37464	45000	47935		8825	8113	9357	9652		4116	2763
3522 Drugs and medicines		75338	96243	121363	141813		18150	22066	30767	34518		8334	10927
3523 Soap, cleaning preps., perfumes, cosmetics		31073	41093	42123	47560		5868	8001	8551	10706		2082	376
3529 Other chemical products		32742	37647	47391	50402		6724	8471	10063	12970		5894	3757
353 Petroleum refineries		119847	175725	217164	258942		13477	27972	33965	41328		12336	10856

354	Misc. petroleum and coal products	27445	31768	39472	40311	3899	4881	7739	6787	1528	788
355	Rubber products	51490	65867	78066	88956	9485	12541	14009	14843	6736	1708
3551	Tyres and tubes	32505	44970	52852	59615	7019	9455	9928	11371	5228	-19
3559	Other rubber products	18985	20897	25214	29341	2467	3086	4081	3472	1508	1727
356	Plastic products	40914	48334	58254	68922	6164	7677	9684	8977	9719	9527
361	Pottery, china, earthenware	4337	4228	4683	5403	970	956	1268	1774	563	1294
362	Glass and products	14450	12569	14663	17524	3292	2664	3085	3717	2062	3444
369	Other non-metallic mineral products	102542	113951	120906	145177	28523	22687	26173	32564	17338	23672
3691	Structural clay products	14751	18015	20443	21780	3786	4222	5861	6404	2422	2104
3692	Cement, lime and plaster	64477	68454	68177	83097	19456	12568	11901	16112	12088	17075
3699	Other non-metallic mineral products	23313	27482	32286	40300	5281	5897	8411	10048	2829	4493
371	Iron and steel	275935	368186	380226	453765	25140	48123	66426	82988	62006	112043
372	Non-ferrous metals	84602	96328	93670	126644	15706	16219	15246	24742	12537	4679
381	Fabricated metal products	66098	72144	95304	107858	13336	13468	18733	22159	7060	11587
3811	Cutlery, hand tools and general hardware	16256	18060	25294	24227	3636	4129	4592	5681	1126	1453
3812	Furniture and fixtures primarily of metal	1002	3937	4441	5361	181	746	1431	1600	315	373
3813	Structural metal products	14350	13448	16996	23123	2837	2464	3842	4344	1202	2480
3819	Other fabricated metal products	34490	36699	48573	55147	6682	6129	8868	10534	4417	7281
382	Non-electrical machinery	182971	215189	219497	276069	42322	50040	51422	64585	12369	14952
3821	Engines and turbines	29191	31913	32199	40042	5857	7164	7061	9714	1411	2206
3822	Agricultural machinery and equipment	21505	28371	24535	35053	4138	4720	4974	5026	707	925
3823	Metal and wood working machinery	9918	12928	10121	14341	3009	3711	2900	4579	450	1669
3824	Other special industrial machinery	48234	59871	61930	72088	10567	13386	14808	15727	3991	5094
3825	Office, computing and accounting machinery	19495	23650	15615	33266	4918	6707	3418	8286	983	1032
3829	Other non-electrical machinery & equipment	54629	58456	75097	81279	13834	14352	18261	21253	4827	4026
383	Electrical machinery	172590	210052	220482	304000	41003	49161	50680	79981	14526	27716
3831	Electrical industrial machinery	67620	78086	81441	117601	17965	21066	20201	30766	4403	8669
3832	Radio, television and communication equipm.	53211	72265	69642	102329	12998	16050	15726	28898	6219	11735
3833	Electrical appliances and housewares	7915	8433	9900	12886	1169	1203	1577	2870	214	1071
3839	Other electrical apparatus and supplies	43845	51268	59499	71184	8871	10842	13176	17447	3690	6241
384	Transport equipment	173405	222619	253607	339380	43316	50284	57645	73278	20854	18960
3841	Shipbuilding and repairing	4447	10302	12522	13576	947	1490	2353	2113	199	652
3842	Railroad equipment	27824	31739	30520	37779	7781	10086	10344	9237	790	699
3843	Motor vehicles	93491	123470	140808	198246	25736	29028	32754	43522	15660	11926
3844	Motorcycles and bicycles	41333	46166	57342	74615	7105	7061	9512	14935	3477	3881
3845	Aircraft	3068	6361	7572	8144	1028	1613	1687	1986	403	1168
3849	Other transport equipment	3243	4581	4844	7020	720	1006	994	1485	325	634
385	Professional and scientific equipment	13556	16335	21941	26426	3754	3988	5544	6429	3036	2825
3851	Prof. and scientific equipment n.e.c.	6139	9475	13753	16496	1728	2693	3784	4053	1635	1428
3852	Photographic and optical goods	714	739	2107	3619	150	106	468	725	121	376
3853	Watches and clocks	6703	6121	6080	6311	1875	1189	1292	1651	1280	1021
390	Other manufacturing industries	13898	23065	33029	39473	2977	4041	10494	7663	1069	1378
3901	Jewellery and related articles	7162	14151	21827	22836	1527	2293	7993	3339	350	321
3902	Musical instruments	478	524	644	887	174	140	234	336	9	10
3903	Sporting and athletic goods	626	610	1118	2198	141	128	250	745	27	52
3909	Manufacturing industries, n.e.c.	5632	7780	9439	13552	1135	1480	2018	3243	683	995
3	Total manufacturing	2703803	3296607	3739061	4600734	471663	585710	744436	923768	321294	475351

India

ISIC Revision 2		Index numbers of industrial production (1990=100)											
ISIC Industry	Note	1985	1986	1987	1988	1989	1990	1991	1992	1993	1994	1995	1996
311/2 Food products	a/	...	...	...	...	...	100	104	102	98	102	120	132
313 Beverages	a/	...	...	...	...	...	...	...	...	...	...	...	...
314 Tobacco		...	...	...	...	...	100	107	101	110	120	114	121
321 Textiles		89	88	94	88	89	100	108	113	126	122	124	133
322 Wearing apparel, except footwear	b/	92	90	78	106	120	100	92	80	76	76	83	88
323 Leather and fur products		91	88	82	100	111	100	92	81	84	87	96	100
324 Footwear, except rubber or plastic	b/	...	...	...	...	...	...	...	...	...	...	...	...
331 Wood products, except furniture		120	123	95	88	90	100	101	95	104	105	121	126
332 Furniture and fixtures, excl. metal		...	...	...	...	...	...	...	...	...	...	...	...
341 Paper and products		75	84	87	88	93	100	106	111	116	131	148	158
342 Printing and publishing		...	...	...	...	...	...	...	...	...	...	...	...
351 Industrial chemicals	c/	56	65	77	89	94	100	99	105	112	122	131	143
352 Other chemicals	c/	...	...	...	...	...	...	...	...	...	...	...	...
353 Petroleum refineries		79	85	92	93	100	100	99	93	93	96	100	106
354 Misc. petroleum and coal products		...	...	...	...	...	...	...	...	...	...	...	...
355 Rubber products		80	78	66	84	92	100	99	100	98	108	113	123
356 Plastic products		...	...	...	...	...	...	...	...	...	...	...	...
361 Pottery, china, earthenware	d/	87	86	83	94	98	100	101	124	128	138	155	166
362 Glass and products	d/	...	...	...	...	...	...	...	...	...	...	...	...
369 Other non-metallic mineral products	d/	...	...	...	...	...	...	...	...	...	...	...	...
371 Iron and steel	e/	74	78	87	94	93	100	109	107	131	140	144	168
372 Non-ferrous metals	e/	...	...	...	...	...	...	...	...	...	...	...	...
381 Fabricated metal products		77	82	89	91	95	100	93	87	85	96	115	124
382 Non-electrical machinery		71	73	76	83	88	100	98	99	101	106	131	136
383 Electrical machinery		36	41	60	65	72	100	92	94	93	104	119	135
384 Transport equipment		69	73	78	85	91	100	96	101	105	116	136	165
385 Professional and scientific equipment		30	38	91	91	99	100	86	82	80	70	85	84
390 Other manufacturing industries		124	173	84	130	132	100	104	105	136	143	136	108
3 Total manufacturing		...	...	...	...	...	...	...	...	...	...	...	...

a/ 311/2 includes 313.
b/ 322 includes 324.
c/ 351 includes 352.
d/ 361 includes 362 and 369.
e/ 371 includes 372.

INDONESIA

Supplier of information:
Central Bureau of Statistics, Jakarta.

Basic source of data:
Annual industrial survey.

Major deviations from ISIC (Revision 2):
None reported.

Reference period (if not calendar year):

Scope:
Large establishments (with 100 or more persons engaged) and medium scale establishments (with 20-99 persons engaged). Until 1993, ISIC 353 and manufacturing activities on agricultural estates producing tea, tobacco and rubber are excluded.

Method of enumeration:
Establishments are completely enumerated. For provinces where establishments are concentrated, the enquiry is carried out by field enumerators through direct interviews, elsewhere it is carried out by mail.

Adjusted for non-response:
Not reported.

Concepts and definitions of variables:
Wages and salaries is compensation of employees.
Output is gross output and includes: (a) value of all products of the establishment; (b) net change in the value of semi-finished goods and work in progress during the year; (c) receipts from industrial and non-industrial services rendered to others; (d) the value of goods shipped in the same condition as received ; and (e) the value of electricity sold.
Value added is total value added.
Gross fixed capital formation represents the value of acquisitions of new and used fixed assets; sales are not taken into account.

Related national publications:
Industrial Statistics (Survey of Manufacturing Industries) Volumes I and II (annual), published by the Central Bureau of Statistics, Jakarta.

Indonesia

ISIC Revision 2	Number of establishments					Number of employees					Wages and salaries paid to employees				
		(numbers)					(thousands)					(billion RUPIAHS)			
ISIC Industry	Note	1993	1994	1995	1996	Note	1993	1994	1995	1996	Note	1993	1994	1995	1996
311/2 Food products		3739	3863	4272	4501		512.7	496.5	520.3	556.7		849.3	806.8	1759.9	1600.4
3111 Slaughtering, preparing & preserving meat		33	35	37	41		3.0	3.5	3.2	3.7		6.9	6.6	10.2	11.3
3112 Dairy products		31	32	33	36		5.2	6.2	6.7	7.6		17.7	27.6	40.7	51.8
3113 Canning, preserving of fruits & vegetables		50	54	57	59		10.6	14.5	14.2	13.4		19.1	21.2	36.2	51.4
3114 Canning, preserving and processing of fish		374	422	475	485		53.6	61.9	66.6	71.4		62.2	81.7	125.5	167.4
3115 Vegetable and animal oils and fats		244	256	272	293		58.4	52.4	53.2	57.5		95.7	94.6	186.3	222.4
3116 Grain mill products		517	509	520	537		94.3	61.9	60.5	74.6		129.4	73.3	207.3	142.5
3117 Bakery products		698	741	831	895		57.0	63.8	70.7	77.9		72.3	97.4	238.6	250.9
3118 Sugar factories and refineries		116	123	135	128		74.5	70.4	73.9	72.4		134.9	126.8	271.1	250.5
3119 Cocoa, chocolate and sugar confectionery		96	104	110	122		11.5	12.5	15.2	17.0		26.1	30.5	47.4	60.1
3121 Other food products		1369	1375	1575	1685		83.8	82.6	94.9	103.7		225.7	168.8	490.3	292.3
3122 Prepared animal feeds		211	212	227	220		60.7	66.7	61.2	57.6		59.5	78.4	106.3	99.8
313 Beverages		204	215	249	268		21.1	22.2	24.6	25.3		51.5	61.1	104.3	91.7
3131 Distilling, rectifying and blending spirits		4	7	9	7		0.2	0.2	0.5	0.4		0.1	0.2	1.2	1.3
3132 Wine industries		17	16	14	15		1.8	1.7	1.6	2.0		4.9	4.3	4.7	10.8
3133 Malt liquors and malt		14	12	11	10		2.0	2.0	2.5	1.2		11.0	13.1	27.2	13.5
3134 Soft drinks and carbonated waters		169	180	215	236		17.1	18.2	20.0	21.7		35.5	43.5	71.2	66.1
314 Tobacco		880	748	815	839		184.3	215.0	344.7	222.0		252.2	292.4	484.2	499.6
321 Textiles		1953	2017	2242	2255		580.5	609.7	623.8	629.8		961.2	1088.2	1604.1	1840.6
3211 Spinning, weaving and finishing textiles		1319	1318	1502	1473		430.5	455.5	477.1	485.4		710.4	809.6	1270.0	1463.6
3212 Made-up textile goods excl. wearing apparel		216	209	235	243		37.0	35.4	33.4	32.5		51.6	56.2	66.7	72.1
3213 Knitting mills		246	312	316	334		89.2	91.7	87.5	85.9		154.1	167.8	214.3	241.7
3214 Carpets and rugs		11	12	11	15		2.2	2.2	2.0	2.2		3.6	4.1	6.0	7.6
3215 Cordage, rope and twine		49	44	48	51		11.0	11.0	11.1	12.0		16.1	19.8	23.6	30.2
3219 Other textiles		112	122	130	139		10.6	13.7	12.5	11.8		25.4	30.6	23.5	25.3
322 Wearing apparel, except footwear		1798	1862	2110	2329		350.0	356.4	371.4	392.8		611.0	637.0	880.0	1030.1
323 Leather and fur products		180	199	217	226		23.3	20.4	21.9	26.1		31.9	34.3	54.9	62.7
3231 Tanneries and leather finishing		67	72	75	74		9.8	7.9	7.9	7.7		13.4	15.1	24.6	21.3
3232 Fur dressing and dyeing industries		-	-	-	-		-	-	-	-		-	-	-	-
3233 Leather prods. excl. wearing apparel		113	127	142	152		13.5	12.5	14.1	18.3		18.5	19.1	30.3	41.4
324 Footwear, except rubber or plastic		327	345	389	420		230.9	265.3	291.5	301.5		305.0	447.6	746.9	924.6
331 Wood products, except furniture		1474	1589	1754	1782		378.1	393.3	393.0	403.7		655.9	689.0	1108.0	1213.6
3311 Sawmills, planing and other wood mills		1158	1239	1343	1346		340.5	357.5	358.2	367.4		613.4	643.6	1050.9	1151.2
3312 Wooden and cane containers		40	42	51	62		2.3	2.2	2.2	2.8		3.5	2.9	3.6	5.1
3319 Other wood and cork products		276	308	360	374		35.3	33.7	32.6	33.6		39.0	42.6	53.5	57.3
332 Furniture and fixtures, excl. metal		782	898	1159	1363		123.4	132.2	144.0	156.4		166.4	192.0	294.9	367.1
341 Paper and products		268	305	311	359		74.1	78.6	88.7	94.3		173.2	241.2	476.8	498.6
3411 Pulp, paper and paperboard articles		123	135	134	142		46.8	51.1	63.2	66.0		121.6	177.4	378.9	389.4
3412 Containers of paper and paperboard		104	145	150	172		19.1	24.1	23.7	24.1		38.7	57.2	93.3	96.5
3419 Other pulp, paper and paperboard articles		41	25	27	45		8.1	3.4	1.8	4.2		12.9	6.6	4.5	12.7
342 Printing and publishing		511	528	594	676		48.8	53.5	59.9	70.6		136.6	140.7	256.2	353.6
351 Industrial chemicals		325	343	403	414		60.1	63.0	70.4	70.0		260.6	309.2	579.6	643.9
3511 Basic chemicals excl. fertilizers		204	212	240	258		21.9	23.1	26.3	28.3		67.4	86.5	171.2	199.4
3512 Fertilizers and pesticides		29	42	58	49		18.6	18.8	20.1	18.7		132.7	150.3	302.9	309.3
3513 Synthetic resins and plastic materials		92	89	105	107		19.7	21.1	24.0	22.9		60.4	72.4	105.5	135.2
352 Other chemicals		567	579	605	621		100.2	106.1	113.8	115.9		342.7	408.5	659.3	718.6
3521 Paints, varnishes and lacquers		85	94	108	118		9.4	10.4	10.7	11.8		35.2	44.9	53.3	61.4
3522 Drugs and medicines		223	221	226	228		40.9	44.7	48.8	47.8		186.5	223.6	370.2	394.9
3523 Soap, cleaning preps., perfumes, cosmetics		146	145	148	146		27.6	28.0	29.7	30.9		70.4	75.9	126.6	146.7
3529 Other chemical products		113	119	123	129		22.2	23.0	24.6	25.4		50.6	64.1	109.2	115.6
353 Petroleum refineries		...	1	4	8		...	0.3	0.6	0.7		...	2.4	5.6	6.2

ISIC	Industry											
354	Misc. petroleum and coal products	13	11	21	29	0.8	1.2	1.6	1.9	1.5	2.8	7.2	5.0
355	Rubber products	448	448	441	447	121.5	131.0	127.5	126.7	211.9	209.5	343.6	383.5
3551	Tyres and tubes	54	56	56	57	18.7	24.3	26.8	26.8	71.2	71.3	118.8	141.9
3559	Other rubber products	394	392	385	390	102.8	106.7	100.6	99.9	140.7	138.2	224.7	241.7
356	Plastic products	801	854	938	1062	119.6	141.3	157.5	169.4	312.8	251.2	411.3	491.1
361	Pottery, china, earthenware	86	95	95	86	38.7	41.4	45.9	41.6	71.9	90.4	168.1	173.9
362	Glass and products	57	56	71	77	20.1	19.8	21.3	25.5	52.1	64.7	109.9	128.1
369	Other non-metallic mineral products	1355	1452	1861	1995	89.6	94.1	110.7	121.0	212.5	214.7	448.3	514.4
3691	Structural clay products	639	684	...	1058	28.9	30.4	...	45.4	26.7	30.6	...	69.0
3692	Cement, lime and plaster	100	108	...	146	17.7	18.8	...	20.5	98.5	101.3	...	275.8
3699	Other non-metallic mineral products	616	660	...	791	42.9	44.9	...	55.2	87.4	82.8	...	169.6
371	Iron and steel	87	93	103	103	31.5	33.9	32.5	32.8	115.2	138.4	288.6	248.2
372	Non-ferrous metals	52	58	66	79	12.0	12.8	15.1	17.5	37.2	53.9	88.4	98.6
381	Fabricated metal products	723	797	958	1052	117.7	130.3	147.3	162.8	287.3	349.1	612.4	723.9
3811	Cutlery, hand tools and general hardware	161	175	210	234	27.0	28.3	33.3	37.6	48.4	65.4	92.0	121.6
3812	Furniture and fixtures primarily of metal	88	104	127	137	10.2	13.2	15.1	17.1	19.7	27.7	53.7	64.0
3813	Structural metal products	145	172	201	231	25.5	26.4	28.1	37.2	88.6	94.0	146.1	181.8
3819	Other fabricated metal products	329	346	420	450	55.0	62.3	70.8	70.8	130.5	162.1	320.6	356.5
382	Non-electrical machinery	266	269	322	353	36.2	37.1	43.7	45.1	114.9	126.8	219.2	226.8
3821	Engines and turbines	31	26	27	29	3.9	3.2	3.4	3.9	12.7	10.3	19.5	22.7
3822	Agricultural machinery and equipment	16	11	16	26	2.2	1.5	1.9	3.3	5.7	2.6	8.6	11.8
3823	Metal and wood working machinery	10	13	22	29	1.1	1.2	1.3	3.7	3.8	3.3	8.4	19.3
3824	Other special industrial machinery	102	108	120	127	9.1	11.9	14.6	11.8	20.9	35.0	53.8	46.9
3825	Office, computing and accounting machinery	6	4	4	4	1.3	0.9	1.0	0.9	2.8	2.1	3.5	3.5
3829	Other non-electrical machinery & equipment	101	107	133	138	18.5	18.4	21.6	21.6	69.0	73.6	125.4	122.4
383	Electrical machinery	349	407	459	498	107.2	144.1	164.4	166.3	274.5	415.2	887.4	881.6
3831	Electrical industrial machinery	67	75	81	90	7.7	10.9	15.1	14.4	20.3	32.3	75.7	83.6
3832	Radio, television and communication equipm.	118	159	183	202	57.2	81.2	90.6	98.7	139.2	228.9	508.2	541.3
3833	Electrical appliances and housewares	19	19	19	26	6.0	5.5	5.5	5.5	14.7	10.7	17.7	19.4
3839	Other electrical apparatus and supplies	145	154	176	180	36.2	46.5	53.2	47.8	100.3	143.3	285.9	237.3
384	Transport equipment	513	535	577	619	100.2	115.1	128.5	132.4	302.2	338.1	790.5	806.0
3841	Shipbuilding and repairing	156	155	157	163	19.9	17.0	18.1	19.1	75.4	50.5	120.3	130.1
3842	Railroad equipment	-	3	4	4	-	0.9	1.0	1.5	-	4.7	7.2	8.5
3843	Motor vehicles	235	241	259	279	43.8	53.6	61.1	61.4	124.5	162.2	381.2	417.0
3844	Motorcycles and bicycles	115	133	152	168	20.2	26.2	32.4	34.4	43.9	64.3	195.7	165.6
3845	Aircraft	1	1	1	1	...	17.3	15.7	15.7	...	56.2	85.4	84.2
3849	Other transport equipment	-	2	4	4	-	0.1	0.3	0.3	-	0.1	0.6	0.6
385	Professional and scientific equipment	61	66	73	74	6.3	9.6	14.7	15.5	14.7	28.0	48.8	72.8
3851	Prof. and scientific equipment n.e.c.	35	38	38	41	1.9	2.4	2.3	2.5	4.3	6.0	8.4	12.2
3852	Photographic and optical goods	8	11	14	13	1.9	4.0	6.4	7.8	5.8	16.3	19.8	29.1
3853	Watches and clocks	18	17	21	20	2.5	3.2	5.9	5.2	4.6	5.8	20.5	31.5
390	Other manufacturing industries	344	384	442	462	70.5	74.2	77.8	72.1	95.8	120.6	189.1	172.6
3901	Jewellery and related articles	73	82	105	120	4.6	6.1	7.8	8.7	6.5	9.2	15.8	19.4
3902	Musical instruments	8	9	12	13	3.6	3.0	3.4	3.6	5.0	7.8	14.2	4.8
3903	Sporting and athletic goods	37	41	46	40	5.1	5.1	5.6	4.3	7.6	9.6	14.8	11.7
3909	Manufacturing industries, n.e.c.	226	252	279	289	57.2	60.0	60.9	55.5	76.7	94.1	144.3	136.8
3	Total manufacturing	18163a/	19017	21551	22997	3559.4a/	3798.6	4156.9	4196.5	6901.9a/	7753.8	13627.8	14777.6

a/ Excluding ISIC 353.

Indonesia

ISIC Revision 2	Output in producers' prices					Value added in factor values					Gross fixed capital formation		
		(billion RUPIAHS)					(billion RUPIAHS)					(billion RUPIAHS)	
ISIC Industry	Note	1993	1994	1995	1996	Note	1993	1994	1995	1996	Note	1994	1995
311/2 Food products		26251.5	20436.6	26202.6	31952.4		6520.7	5293.3	6328.7	7862.5		1113.0	1115.1
3111 Slaughtering, preparing & preserving meat		89.2	97.6	171.4	188.7		20.4	22.3	56.7	68.9		2.0	2.6
3112 Dairy products		1011.6	1293.6	1558.6	1916.2		253.6	328.2	355.0	536.4		64.0	39.9
3113 Canning, preserving of fruits & vegetables		492.9	249.8	304.6	416.6		88.6	63.9	123.2	134.0		3.0	1.8
3114 Canning, preserving and processing of fish		1889.5	2240.1	2850.7	3196.8		369.4	390.8	572.6	655.4		55.0	46.9
3115 Vegetable and animal oils and fats		3525.1	4831.5	8166.9	9886.3		677.8	922.1	1622.2	2015.0		114.0	215.1
3116 Grain mill products		1996.7	2468.0	2570.9	3207.2		491.0	569.8	466.0	610.2		110.0	159.2
3117 Bakery products		10763.0	1733.8	2252.9	2877.9		2553.8	559.6	740.4	1063.3		61.0	36.5
3118 Sugar factories and refineries		2106.9	2095.8	2105.7	2244.9		782.8	864.2	814.2	940.1		251.0	164.0
3119 Cocoa, chocolate and sugar confectionery		385.0	527.5	544.6	754.9		94.8	171.4	148.1	179.1		22.0	15.3
3121 Other food products		3485.9	4276.8	4928.2	6523.5		995.9	1178.3	1215.1	1442.6		311.0	412.3
3122 Prepared animal feeds		505.7	622.0	748.2	739.3		192.4	222.7	215.2	217.6		120.0	21.4
313 Beverages		921.3	1307.8	1599.6	1865.7		351.2	622.4	587.5	892.0		106.0	194.0
3131 Distilling, rectifying and blending spirits		0.9	1.7	5.6	5.8		0.3	0.7	1.9	3.3		-	-
3132 Wine industries		62.0	50.5	41.7	109.8		10.9	23.5	8.3	23.6		2.0	2.0
3133 Malt liquors and malt		238.2	270.2	474.3	369.4		138.4	195.3	237.3	270.5		1.0	15.7
3134 Soft drinks and carbonated waters		620.2	985.5	1078.1	1380.7		201.7	403.0	340.1	594.6		103.0	176.3
314 Tobacco		8876.5	10358.1	12378.5	14380.7		4245.4	6194.6	5828.5	8839.9		214.0	226.0
321 Textiles		14814.7	20883.7	23528.7	28346.8		4243.1	8055.4	7811.6	9611.8		1693.0	1678.5
3211 Spinning, weaving and finishing textiles		11640.2	17851.3	20658.2	25035.6		3317.5	7087.1	6939.1	8470.2		1540.0	1585.6
3212 Made-up textile goods excl. wearing apparel		489.3	518.4	522.6	558.7		178.3	190.2	186.9	180.9		20.0	20.4
3213 Knitting mills		1768.1	1623.3	1746.8	2003.5		510.7	520.3	513.3	691.4		53.0	39.7
3214 Carpets and rugs		130.4	133.0	118.8	150.0		54.4	50.1	39.8	48.5		21.0	3.4
3215 Cordage, rope and twine		131.4	151.2	167.2	221.7		46.2	59.4	42.1	81.2		15.0	21.0
3219 Other textiles		655.4	606.6	315.1	377.3		136.1	148.3	90.5	139.6		44.0	8.5
322 Wearing apparel, except footwear		6892.0	5548.9	6474.3	8353.4		3430.6	2279.8	2492.3	3271.6		115.0	210.1
323 Leather and fur products		526.4	534.7	661.6	799.7		182.2	175.6	214.8	287.6		17.0	24.9
3231 Tanneries and leather finishing		355.7	352.8	400.3	429.9		115.1	113.6	118.3	141.4		13.0	12.5
3232 Fur dressing and dyeing industries		-	-	-	-		-	-	-	-		-	-
3233 Leather prods. excl. wearing apparel		170.7	181.9	261.2	369.8		67.1	62.0	96.5	146.2		4.0	12.4
324 Footwear, except rubber or plastic		4620.0	5041.2	5503.3	6625.5		1770.5	2262.0	2115.6	2738.0		203.0	370.1
331 Wood products, except furniture		12111.6	13725.8	14639.9	16217.0		4050.7	4663.3	5222.6	5871.3		672.0	416.7
3311 Sawmills, planing and other wood mills		11734.6	13365.5	14287.7	15762.7		3902.5	4522.3	5095.3	5677.7		657.0	401.1
3312 Wooden and cane containers		79.5	20.3	21.0	33.8		20.3	8.2	6.9	12.2		-	0.5
3319 Other wood and cork products		297.5	339.9	331.2	420.5		128.0	132.8	120.4	181.4		15.0	15.1
332 Furniture and fixtures, excl. metal		1482.3	1711.5	2123.4	2564.1		520.1	584.7	746.1	992.7		79.0	77.2
341 Paper and products		4014.0	5423.5	7232.7	9427.0		1381.1	1920.1	2315.9	3135.1		795.0	528.2
3411 Pulp, paper and paperboard articles		2822.1	3867.7	5627.8	7369.9		980.9	1415.0	1936.0	2625.8		667.0	471.2
3412 Containers of paper and paperboard		891.3	1275.8	1535.9	1887.3		335.0	447.0	364.7	469.1		61.0	55.9
3419 Other pulp, paper and paperboard articles		300.5	280.0	69.1	169.7		65.2	58.1	15.2	40.1		67.0	1.1
342 Printing and publishing		1546.2	1885.1	2573.6	3549.9		657.3	854.9	1058.8	1680.7		136.0	341.8
351 Industrial chemicals		6119.3	7564.8	8606.3	13155.7		2324.9	2828.1	3216.5	5255.5		1514.0	814.5
3511 Basic chemicals excl. fertilizers		2119.1	3181.8	3476.8	6828.9		744.6	1213.0	1089.2	2603.8		591.0	420.5
3512 Fertilizers and pesticides		2317.0	2541.0	2897.9	2978.7		1020.6	980.9	1429.9	1414.8		885.0	131.9
3513 Synthetic resins and plastic materials		1683.2	1841.9	2231.6	3348.0		559.7	634.2	697.4	1236.9		38.0	262.1
352 Other chemicals		5719.3	7137.5	8245.1	9674.4		1883.0	2594.7	2472.3	3175.9		360.0	438.9
3521 Paints, varnishes and lacquers		593.5	909.2	823.4	944.0		135.5	293.0	177.8	245.4		54.0	35.5
3522 Drugs and medicines		2142.3	3036.1	3039.2	3591.4		799.0	1314.2	982.5	1361.8		177.0	241.9
3523 Soap, cleaning preps., perfumes, cosmetics		1786.4	1649.8	2601.3	3302.2		562.3	492.0	802.5	966.8		43.0	95.1
3529 Other chemical products		1197.2	1542.5	1781.2	1836.9		386.2	495.5	509.6	601.9		86.0	66.4
353 Petroleum refineries		...	62.4	76.8	176.7		...	61.6	62.9	144.0		-	0.4

ISIC	Industry										
354	Misc. petroleum and coal products	51.7	63.1	80.9	104.3	21.6	22.1	33.7	33.5	-	0.9
355	Rubber products	3653.2	4652.4	6520.8	8457.3	890.7	1174.6	1271.1	1735.4	290.0	259.8
3551	Tyres and tubes	1219.7	1161.7	1789.8	3004.4	322.3	382.1	439.5	799.1	171.0	115.8
3559	Other rubber products	2433.5	3490.7	4731.0	5452.8	568.3	792.5	831.6	936.3	119.0	143.9
356	Plastic products	3111.4	3673.2	5531.2	6756.1	1088.4	1121.9	1807.8	1845.6	255.0	430.2
361	Pottery, china, earthenware	883.6	1119.7	1083.7	1692.2	426.5	591.2	442.4	763.4	290.0	372.1
362	Glass and products	950.7	819.3	1071.2	1703.4	435.0	276.0	461.6	860.9	122.0	118.1
369	Other non-metallic mineral products	3101.8	3447.6	4348.1	5415.0	1224.0	1462.9	1603.1	2124.4	943.0	425.5
3691	Structural clay products	121.0	139.3	...	350.1	57.4	67.9	...	160.1	7.0	...
3692	Cement, lime and plaster	1919.8	2191.8	...	2876.7	754.1	989.1	...	1163.0	847.0	...
3699	Other non-metallic mineral products	1061.0	1116.6	...	2188.2	412.4	405.8	...	801.4	89.0	...
371	Iron and steel	6462.0	7903.0	10044.6	14065.4	2810.6	3462.6	4200.8	8703.1	271.0	377.6
372	Non-ferrous metals	1273.5	2043.3	2558.5	2978.8	391.2	733.5	873.2	1148.2	101.0	59.4
381	Fabricated metal products	4463.6	5333.2	7035.3	10048.3	1738.6	2080.1	2585.0	3938.6	316.0	430.1
3811	Cutlery, hand tools and general hardware	465.8	557.1	677.2	859.6	168.4	193.7	278.6	390.0	28.0	48.7
3812	Furniture and fixtures primarily of metal	216.2	268.8	335.2	519.4	88.5	113.4	115.4	221.3	33.0	52.2
3813	Structural metal products	1336.0	1483.6	1514.2	2716.5	764.9	812.0	635.2	1267.2	51.0	46.4
3819	Other fabricated metal products	2445.6	3023.7	4508.6	5952.7	716.8	961.1	1555.8	2060.2	204.0	282.8
382	Non-electrical machinery	1707.3	2202.8	3023.6	3935.4	510.1	791.8	930.2	1372.3	99.0	216.5
3821	Engines and turbines	366.5	394.8	504.2	927.2	74.3	103.4	121.9	248.9	7.0	10.9
3822	Agricultural machinery and equipment	78.3	28.6	82.5	104.1	29.3	10.2	24.8	47.0	1.0	3.3
3823	Metal and wood working machinery	44.8	55.6	38.8	102.8	12.0	28.8	19.4	45.4	-	6.7
3824	Other special industrial machinery	224.6	350.3	472.5	651.9	101.7	129.4	152.9	249.1	50.0	40.5
3825	Office, computing and accounting machinery	91.8	22.1	91.3	138.0	10.1	9.4	12.5	21.9	-	0.6
3829	Other non-electrical machinery & equipment	901.4	1351.3	1834.3	2011.3	282.7	510.7	598.7	759.9	41.0	154.5
383	Electrical machinery	5988.9	8186.4	13414.2	18134.7	1609.5	2393.7	3944.2	6766.2	455.0	708.4
3831	Electrical industrial machinery	405.8	561.9	847.0	1172.0	143.2	200.4	290.3	406.5	41.0	25.6
3832	Radio, television and communication equipm.	2945.6	4486.5	7072.1	9713.6	736.7	1345.2	1727.9	3122.9	252.0	325.0
3833	Electrical appliances and housewares	296.7	365.9	427.7	481.1	87.1	158.0	166.5	100.7	12.0	28.4
3839	Other electrical apparatus and supplies	2340.8	2772.1	5067.3	6768.0	642.6	690.1	1759.5	3136.1	150.0	329.4
384	Transport equipment	9012.9	13280.1	18184.7	21185.2	4475.8	6796.7	7761.0	9330.6	353.0	1333.1
3841	Shipbuilding and repairing	718.4	404.3	824.3	1207.6	523.0	257.1	614.5	883.7	25.0	694.1
3842	Railroad equipment	-	62.5	60.9	83.3	-	38.9	50.0	66.1	6.0	0.6
3843	Motor vehicles	4028.0	6519.2	8535.2	9129.1	2022.1	3442.2	3293.7	4006.2	217.0	451.1
3844	Motorcycles and bicycles	3646.0	6121.0	8280.8	9838.3	1656.2	2997.5	3506.8	3699.6	96.0	187.0
3845	Aircraft	...	171.6	477.9	921.0	...	60.1	292.8	671.0	9.0	-
3849	Other transport equipment	-	1.6	5.6	5.9	-	0.9	3.2	3.9	-	0.3
385	Professional and scientific equipment	211.6	299.2	495.0	821.4	39.2	115.4	164.0	269.4	132.0	137.5
3851	Prof. and scientific equipment n.e.c.	40.5	60.9	64.6	118.2	9.2	30.3	22.2	56.6	2.0	2.5
3852	Photographic and optical goods	132.4	176.2	291.3	534.4	14.3	50.3	86.2	150.9	130.0	100.1
3853	Watches and clocks	38.7	62.2	139.1	168.7	15.7	34.8	55.6	61.9	-	34.9
390	Other manufacturing industries	1097.4	1179.6	1441.9	1625.4	437.5	443.4	521.7	682.3	60.0	670.4
3901	Jewellery and related articles	184.2	96.3	224.4	303.4	119.9	30.9	44.4	79.5	7.0	535.7
3902	Musical instruments	228.2	184.2	267.3	254.7	76.2	43.7	139.3	157.2	1.0	47.2
3903	Sporting and athletic goods	93.2	135.8	129.6	177.1	33.0	53.4	44.6	64.1	2.0	2.6
3909	Manufacturing industries, n.e.c.	591.8	763.4	820.5	890.1	208.3	315.4	293.4	381.5	50.0	85.0
3	Total manufacturing	135864.4a/	155797.3	194680.0	244011.4	47659.1a/	59856.3	67073.6	93332.5	10704.0	11976.1

a/ Excluding ISIC 353.

Indonesia

ISIC Revision 2		Index numbers of industrial production (1990=100)											
ISIC Industry	Note	1985	1986	1987	1988	1989	1990	1991	1992	1993	1994	1995	1996
311/2 Food products	a/	...	71	78	84	90	100	95	109	136	180	207	245
313 Beverages	a/	...	...	...	...	...	...	...	...	...	...	...	...
314 Tobacco	a/	...	...	...	...	...	...	...	...	...	...	...	...
321 Textiles		42	55	59	71	81	100	107	116	115	126	142	145
322 Wearing apparel, except footwear		...	39	62	88	94	100	183	212	236	251	294	318
323 Leather and fur products		...	29	45	67	81	100	116	199	243	218	223	202
324 Footwear, except rubber or plastic		54	54	44	53	89	100	111	156	171	200	205	171
331 Wood products, except furniture		34	54	75	95	99	100	101	109	105	107	103	96
332 Furniture and fixtures, excl. metal		...	...	...	...	...	100	96	92	83	94	109	73
341 Paper and products		56	54	58	76	83	100	104	150	153	175	210	223
342 Printing and publishing		...	53	60	78	86	100	131	137	159	175	156	139
351 Industrial chemicals	b/	...	65	70	82	91	100	116	129	145	156	159	158
352 Other chemicals	b/	...	...	...	...	...	...	...	...	...	...	...	...
353 Petroleum refineries	b/	...	...	...	...	...	...	...	...	...	...	...	...
354 Misc. petroleum and coal products	b/	...	...	...	...	...	...	...	...	...	...	...	...
355 Rubber products	b/	...	...	...	...	...	...	...	...	...	...	...	...
356 Plastic products	b/	...	...	...	...	...	...	...	...	...	...	...	...
361 Pottery, china, earthenware	c/	...	65	72	76	94	100	114	122	138	174	201	189
362 Glass and products	c/	...	...	...	...	...	...	...	...	...	...	...	...
369 Other non-metallic mineral products	c/	...	...	...	...	...	...	...	...	...	...	...	...
371 Iron and steel		39	60	57	65	77	100	158	165	213	230	291	283
372 Non-ferrous metals		...	...	...	...	...	...	...	...	...	...	...	...
381 Fabricated metal products		50	52	57	62	82	100	91	98	91	102	115	137
382 Non-electrical machinery		...	80	86	88	110	100	103	99	70	38	40	29
383 Electrical machinery		45	57	59	71	85	100	105	129	130	145	153	138
384 Transport equipment		52	68	69	62	75	100	133	103	98	126	127	122
385 Professional and scientific equipment		...	...	...	...	...	100	96	92	83	77	71	62
390 Other manufacturing industries		...	48	53	74	93	100	175	211	180	184	197	219
3 Total manufacturing		...	...	...	...	...	...	...	...	...	...	...	...

a/ 311/2 includes 313 and 314.
b/ 351 includes 352, 353, 354, 355 and 356.
c/ 361 includes 362 and 369.

IRELAND

Supplier of information:
Irish Central Statistics Office, Dublin.
Industrial statistics for the OECD countries are compiled by the OECD secretariat, which supplies them to UNIDO.

Basic source of data:
Annual census of industrial establishments.

Major deviations from ISIC (Revision 3):
All data have been converted from NACE (Revision 1) to ISIC (Rev. 3).
Not covered are: Part of textile fibre preparation and textile weaving (ISIC 1711); part of other textiles n.e.c. (ISIC 1729); part of knitted and crocheted fabrics and articles (ISIC 1730); part of other wood products and articles of cork/straw (ISIC 2029); part of pulp, paper and paperboard (ISIC 2101); and part of other articles of paper and paper board (ISIC 2109).

Reference period (if not calendar year):

Scope:
All establishments engaged in industrial activity which have on average three or more persons engaged during the year. The majority of the industrial establishments covered are individual factories. However, where two or more distinct activities are conducted at the same location each is distinguished, in principle, as a separate establishment. The extent to which separate returns are obtained for each individual establishment, however, depends on the scale of the different activities involved and the availability of separate records in the business for the different establishments. Any sizeable non-industrial activity is excluded.

Method of enumeration:
Not reported.

Adjusted for non-response:
Not reported.

Concepts and definitions of variables:
An establishment is defined as a single economic activity conducted at a particular location. Number of establishments includes all the separate production locations of multi-location enterprises even if separate details are not provided by the respondent.
Number of employees refers to number of persons who are paid a fixed wage or salary. Persons at work or temporarily absent because of illness, holidays, strikes, etc. are included, as are part-time workers. Homeworkers are excluded. The numbers given for each year refer to a week in September.
Wages and salaries represents the gross amount paid to employees before deduction of income tax, employees' contributions to social security etc.
Overtime pay, bonuses, commissions, holiday pay and sick pay are included.
Payments to working proprietors and home workers are excluded.
Output represents the net selling value of all goods manufactured in the year, whether sold or not, and the value of work done. In general, for establishments working on commission on materials supplied to them by other firms, only the payments received by them for the work done are included. The definition of output is amended to include the value of capital work done on own account.
Operating subsidies related to the production or sales of the output are included in the value of output; excise duty and VAT are excluded.
Value added is the difference between the value of output and industrial input.
Industrial input consists of the industrial materials, industrial services, fuel and power used in the production of the output. Industrial materials and services comprise materials for processing and ancillary goods and services, i.e. packing materials, repairs and the cost of contract work done by other firms on materials supplied by the establishment. Valuation is exclusive of deductible VAT.
Gross fixed capital formation is the difference between acquisitions and sales of capital assets. Capital assets (land, buildings, plant and equipment) are defined as goods with an expected useful life of more than one year intended for use by the establishment itself. Acquisitions include purchases from other establishments and production by the establishment itself of capital goods for its own use. Major alterations, improvements and repairs that extend the useful life of an asset or increase its productivity are included. The value of work put in place during the year is included whether or not completed. Acquisitions are valued at total cost including installation charges and fees or duties but excluding deductible VAT and financial costs. Sales are valued at the actual price received excluding VAT.

Related national publications:
Census of Industrial Production (annual), published by the Central Statistics Office, Dublin.

Ireland

ISIC Revision 3	Number of establishments					Number of employees					Wages and salaries paid to employees				
		(numbers)					(numbers)					(million POUNDS)			
ISIC Industry	Note	1992	1993	1994	1995	Note	1992	1993	1994	1995	Note	1992	1993	1994	1995
151 Processed meat,fish,fruit,vegetables,fats		267	273	276	288		16759	16979	16613	17601		184	193	191	205
1511 Processing/preserving of meat		152	153	153	154		12912	13041	12552	13002		139	144	141	150
1512 Processing/preserving of fish		84	87	88	93		2000	2098	2278	2678		18	21	23	27
1513 Processing/preserving of fruit & vegetables		26	28	31	37		1590	1596	1627	1767		22	23	25	25
1514 Vegetable and animal oils and fats		5	5	4	4		257	244	156	154		4	4	3	3
1520 Dairy products		99	98	104	116		7728	7704	7567	7702		135	135	137	145
153 Grain mill products; starches; animal feeds		100	94	94	103		2362	2293	2411	2874		36	36	39	46
1531 Grain mill products		...	...	...	...		...	...	...	...		...	...	...	...
1532 Starches and starch products		...	...	...	...		...	...	...	...		...	...	...	...
1533 Prepared animal feeds		78	77	78	81		1874	1903	1981	2375		28	29	31	37
154 Other food products		265	249	262	258		11118	11116	11222	11238		150	159	170	176
1541 Bakery products		204	192	197	192		5432	5535	5686	5682		53	57	60	62
1542 Sugar	a/	28	24	28	28	a/	3445	3298	3193	3122	a/	57	54	58	58
1543 Cocoa, chocolate and sugar confectionery	a/	...	...	...	...	a/	...	...	...	...	a/	...	...	...	...
1544 Macaroni, noodles & similar products	b/	...	...	...	...	b/	...	...	...	...	b/	...	...	...	...
1549 Other food products n.e.c.	b/	33	33	37	38	b/	2241	2283	2343	2434	b/	40	47	51	56
155 Beverages		65	61	63	65		5193	5068	5188	4870		111	116	119	123
1551 Distilling, rectifying & blending of spirits	c/	44	40	42	46	c/	2756	2726	2931	2708	c/	50	52	54	56
1552 Wines	c/	...	...	...	...	c/	...	...	...	...	c/	...	...	...	...
1553 Malt liquors and malt		21	21	21	19		2437	2342	2257	2162		61	64	65	67
1554 Soft drinks; mineral waters	c/	...	...	...	...	c/	...	...	...	...	c/	...	...	...	...
1600 Tobacco products		6	6	6	6		1276	1178	1027	1018		26	24	23	24
171 Spinning, weaving and finishing of textiles		90	88	94	92		3732	3559	3646	3471		41	42	43	43
1711 Textile fibre preparation; textile weaving		29	29	32	30		2158	2083	2163	1958		27	27	28	27
1712 Finishing of textiles	d/	61	59	62	62	d/	1574	1476	1483	1513	d/	15	14	15	15
172 Other textiles	e/	49	45	44	41	e/	2634	2442	2276	2345	e/	34	31	33	34
1721 Made-up textile articles, except apparel	d/	...	...	...	...	d/	...	...	...	...	d/	...	...	...	...
1722 Carpets and rugs		12	11	10	10		1266	1240	1137	1162		16	16	16	17
1723 Cordage, rope, twine and netting		7	7	7	7		220	194	200	227		4	2	3	4
1729 Other textiles n.e.c.		30	27	27	24		1148	1008	939	956		14	13	13	13
1730 Knitted and crocheted fabrics and articles		56	62	60	57		2389	2428	2305	2136		21	22	22	22
1810 Wearing apparel, except fur apparel		226	215	202	192		11689	10958	11275	11125		94	93	98	103
1820 Dressing & dyeing of fur; processing of fur		6	7	7	7		45	56	64	72		-	-	1	1
191 Tanning, dressing and processing of leather		25	26	24	19		532	547	651	688		5	6	8	6
1911 Tanning and dressing of leather	f/	25	26	24	19	f/	532	547	651	688	f/	5	6	8	6
1912 Luggage, handbags, etc.; saddlery & harness	f/	...	...	...	...	f/	...	...	...	...	f/	...	...	...	...
1920 Footwear		15	15	15	14		639	604	542	511		5	5	6	5
2010 Sawmilling and planing of wood	g/	48	48	45	43	g/	1485	1495	1611	1700	g/	19	20	21	23
202 Products of wood, cork, straw, etc.	h/	181	172	169	165	h/	2680	2539	2382	2701	h/	24	24	23	27
2021 Veneer sheets, plywood, particle board, etc.	g/	...	...	...	...	g/	...	...	...	...	g/	...	...	...	...
2022 Builders' carpentry and joinery		131	123	118	112		2093	1959	1728	1961		19	19	17	20
2023 Wooden containers		19	20	20	21		233	225	248	299		2	2	2	3
2029 Other wood products; articles of cork/straw		31	29	31	32		354	355	406	441		3	3	4	4
210 Paper and paper products		106	110	104	102		4122	4081	4126	4351		65	68	70	78
2101 Pulp, paper and paperboard		8	7	7	7		238	212	230	217		4	3	4	4
2102 Corrugated paper and paperboard	i/	...	...	...	...	i/	...	...	...	...	i/	...	...	...	...
2109 Other articles of paper and paperboard	i/	98	103	97	95	i/	3884	3869	3896	4134	i/	61	65	66	74
221 Publishing	j/	371	392	401	400	j/	11055	11411	11679	11567	j/	189	201	208	210
2211 Publishing of books and other publications		...	...	...	...		...	...	...	...		...	...	...	...
2212 Publishing of newspapers, journals, etc.		...	...	...	...		...	...	...	...		...	...	...	...
2213 Publishing of recorded media		...	...	...	...		...	...	...	...		...	...	...	...
2219 Other publishing		...	...	...	...		...	...	...	...		...	...	...	...

222 Printing and related service activities	j/	...	...	...	...	j/	...	...	...	...	j/	...	...	...	...
2221 Printing		...	...	...	...		...	...	...	...		...	...	...	...
2222 Service activities related to printing		...	...	...	...		...	...	...	...		...	...	...	...
2230 Reproduction of recorded media		25	35	39	43		2035	2590	3049	4020		35	49	58	74
2310 Coke oven products		...	...	...	...		...	...	...	...		...	...	...	...
2320 Refined petroleum products	k/m/	...	...	...	...	k/m/	...	...	...	...	k/m/	...	...	...	...
2330 Processing of nuclear fuel		...	...	...	...		...	...	...	...		...	...	...	...
241 Basic chemicals		70	72	73	73		4351	4465	4702	4846		105	108	115	128
2411 Basic chemicals, except fertilizers		35	37	36	37		2980	3102	3246	3416		79	77	81	93
2412 Fertilizers and nitrogen compounds		27	26	28	27		958	942	1013	971		21	23	26	26
2413 Plastics in primary forms; synthetic rubber		8	9	9	9		413	421	443	459		6	7	8	9
242 Other chemicals		157	162	167	165		9544	10435	11358	11843		151	177	198	215
2421 Pesticides and other agro-chemical products		8	8	7	7		104	117	120	129		1	2	2	2
2422 Paints, varnishes, printing ink and mastics		26	24	24	24		762	610	732	719		12	10	13	13
2423 Pharmaceuticals, medicinal chemicals, etc.		53	61	64	63		4154	4870	5466	5826		69	86	99	111
2424 Soap, cleaning & cosmetic preparations		33	32	35	32		1832	2069	2395	2404		25	30	35	38
2429 Other chemical products n.e.c.		37	37	37	39		2692	2769	2645	2765		44	49	49	52
2430 Man-made fibres		5	5	5	5		1393	1342	1362	1427		23	23	25	26
251 Rubber products		41	41	43	42		2235	2221	2286	2434		36	34	37	42
2511 Rubber tyres and tubes		...	...	...	...		...	...	...	...		...	...	...	...
2519 Other rubber products		...	...	...	...		...	...	...	...		...	...	...	...
2520 Plastic products		197	197	195	189		6164	6263	6516	7062		77	82	88	97
2610 Glass and glass products		49	50	50	52		3804	3284	3348	3607		57	61	65	63
269 Non-metallic mineral products n.e.c.		226	230	242	231		5703	5851	5845	5740		82	86	86	90
2691 Pottery, china and earthenware	n/	...	...	...	...	n/	...	...	...	...	n/	...	...	...	...
2692 Refractory ceramic products	n/	...	...	...	...	n/	...	...	...	...	n/	...	...	...	...
2693 Struct.non-refractory clay; ceramic products	n/	25	30	38	33	n/	927	1011	1081	1024	n/	11	13	12	13
2694 Cement, lime and plaster	p/	12	13	14	15	p/	998	982	1083	1052	p/	21	21	24	24
2695 Articles of concrete, cement and plaster	p/	138	135	134	130	p/	2736	2786	2685	2653	p/	36	38	37	39
2696 Cutting, shaping & finishing of stone		41	40	43	40		556	591	595	551		6	6	6	7
2699 Other non-metallic mineral products n.e.c.		10	12	13	13		486	481	401	460		8	9	7	8
2710 Basic iron and steel		18	20	22	20		996	1079	1086	939		16	20	20	16
2720 Basic precious and non-ferrous metals	q/	22	26	30	31	q/	1342	1287	1208	1248	q/	22	23	21	22
273 Casting of metals	q/	...	...	...	...	q/	...	...	...	...	q/	...	...	...	...
2731 Casting of iron and steel		...	...	...	...		...	...	...	...		...	...	...	...
2732 Casting of non-ferrous metals		...	...	...	...		...	...	...	...		...	...	...	...
281 Struct.metal products;tanks;steam generators		251	240	245	237		4419	4259	4395	4576		51	49	54	57
2811 Structural metal products		204	195	196	194		3220	3058	3098	3364		35	33	36	40
2812 Tanks, reservoirs and containers of metal	r/	47	45	49	43	r/	1199	1201	1297	1212	r/	16	16	18	17
2813 Steam generators	r/	...	...	...	...	r/	...	...	...	...	r/	...	...	...	...
289 Other metal products; metal working services		251	256	258	248		5591	5437	5550	5796		69	68	74	82
2891 Metal forging/pressing/stamping/roll-forming	s/	13	18	18	18	s/	310	331	341	427	s/	4	4	4	5
2892 Treatment & coating of metals	s/	24	26	30	27	s/	378	339	343	335	s/	4	3	4	4
2893 Cutlery, hand tools and general hardware		62	68	66	65		1659	1579	1576	1685		21	20	21	23
2899 Other fabricated metal products n.e.c.		152	144	144	138		3244	3188	3290	3349		41	41	44	49
291 General purpose machinery		161	161	164	163		5803	5672	6117	6722		81	81	93	108
2911 Engines & turbines(not for transport equip.)		...	...	...	...		...	...	...	...		...	...	...	...
2912 Pumps, compressors, taps and valves		...	...	...	...		...	...	...	...		...	...	...	...
2913 Bearings, gears, gearing & driving elements		...	...	...	...		...	...	...	...		...	...	...	...
2914 Ovens, furnaces and furnace burners	t/	21	22	25	29	t/	411	498	576	777	t/	5	6	7	10
2915 Lifting and handling equipment		45	44	43	42		1458	1442	1579	1725		19	21	25	27
2919 Other general purpose machinery	t/	35	42	41	41	t/	1758	1676	1704	1884	t/	25	24	27	33
292 Special purpose machinery		148	148	155	157		3481	3436	3862	3716		44	44	53	53
2921 Agricultural and forestry machinery		30	31	35	37		494	521	607	677		5	5	7	8
2922 Machine tools		21	23	21	20		676	883	1117	756		8	10	14	10
2923 Machinery for metallurgy	u/	...	...	...	...	u/	...	...	...	...	u/	...	...	...	...
2924 Machinery for mining & construction	u/	11	9	11	12	u/	451	379	424	475	u/	8	7	9	10
2925 Food/beverage/tobacco processing machinery		32	31	30	29		705	729	706	720		8	9	10	11
2926 Machinery for textile, apparel and leather	v/	54	54	58	59	v/	1155	924	1008	1088	v/	15	12	13	15
2927 Weapons and ammunition		...	...	...	...		...	...	...	...		...	...	...	...
2929 Other special purpose machinery	v/	...	...	...	...	v/	...	...	...	...	v/	...	...	...	...
2930 Domestic appliances n.e.c.		16	15	16	17		3242	3320	3494	3666		39	40	44	46

continued

Ireland

ISIC Revision 3 — ISIC Industry	Note	Number of establishments (numbers) 1992	1993	1994	1995	Note	Number of employees (numbers) 1992	1993	1994	1995	Note	Wages and salaries paid to employees (million POUNDS) 1992	1993	1994	1995
3000 Office, accounting and computing machinery		66	69	71	71		7939	8886	10235	14413		136	153	175	211
3110 Electric motors, generators and transformers		27	25	26	28		2090	2116	2251	2700		30	32	36	43
3120 Electricity distribution & control apparatus		48	50	48	49		2356	2350	2428	3283		27	30	32	44
3130 Insulated wire and cable		23	22	21	22		1519	1476	1438	2059		20	19	22	31
3140 Accumulators, primary cells and batteries	w/	22	23	24	25	w/	1397	1231	1374	2098	w/	21	17	18	29
3150 Lighting equipment and electric lamps		19	20	19	20		358	328	336	354		3	4	3	4
3190 Other electrical equipment n.e.c.	w/	11	10	10	11	w/	2877	2703	2237	1864	w/	35	32	28	26
3210 Electronic valves, tubes, etc.		24	24	23	24		2717	3297	3706	4072		35	40	50	57
3220 TV/radio transmitters; line comm. apparatus		17	17	18	17		1836	2083	2547	2139		31	35	43	44
3230 TV and radio receivers and associated goods		13	12	12	12		644	713	931	1017		7	9	11	11
331 Medical, measuring, testing appliances, etc.		115	108	109	112		7508	7872	8403	9281		104	113	121	135
3311 Medical, surgical and orthopaedic equipment		47	44	49	51		5814	6248	6745	7505		81	89	95	108
3312 Measuring/testing/navigating appliances,etc.	x/	68	64	60	61	x/	1694	1624	1658	1776	x/	23	23	26	27
3313 Industrial process control equipment	x/	...	...	...	...	x/	...	...	...	...	x/	...	...	...	...
3320 Optical instruments & photographic equipment	y/	22	21	22	23	y/	2135	2297	2203	2515	y/	28	31	34	37
3330 Watches and clocks	y/	...	...	...	...	y/	...	...	...	...	y/	...	...	...	...
3410 Motor vehicles		22	14	15	23		1481	826	849	1444		21	12	14	22
3420 Automobile bodies, trailers & semi-trailers		44	47	46	44		758	660	690	687		8	7	7	8
3430 Parts/accessories for automobiles		37	33	31	32		1616	1786	2109	2272		17	20	26	30
351 Building and repairing of ships and boats		26	27	27	26		561	460	468	496		6	7	6	7
3511 Building and repairing of ships		26	27	27	26		561	460	468	496		6	7	6	7
3512 Building/repairing of pleasure/sport. boats		...	...	...	...		...	...	...	...		...	...	...	...
3520 Railway/tramway locomotives & rolling stock		16	17	16	16		5142	4967	3492	4504		92	84	64	84
3530 Aircraft and spacecraft		...	...	...	...		...	...	...	...		...	...	...	...
359 Transport equipment n.e.c.		4	4	4	6		33	30	28	140		-	-	-	1
3591 Motorcycles		...	...	...	...		...	...	...	...		...	...	...	...
3592 Bicycles and invalid carriages		4	4	4	6		33	30	28	140		-	-	-	1
3599 Other transport equipment n.e.c.		...	...	...	...		...	...	...	...		...	...	...	...
3610 Furniture		255	259	269	282		3703	3835	3906	4064		33	37	38	39
369 Manufacturing n.e.c.	k/	119	123	118	120	k/	5447	5442	5527	5958	k/	78	81	80	86
3691 Jewellery and related articles	z/	38	42	41	43	z/	2007	2013	1935	2053	z/	35	37	33	34
3692 Musical instruments		7	7	6	6		52	41	42	37		-	-	-	-
3693 Sports goods	A/	29	28	27	28	A/	1477	1568	1677	1851	A/	17	17	19	21
3694 Games and toys	A/	...	...	...	...	A/	...	...	...	...	A/	...	...	...	...
3699 Other manufacturing n.e.c.	m/z/	45	46	44	43	m/z/	1911	1820	1873	2017	m/z/	27	27	28	31
3710 Recycling of metal waste and scrap	k/m/	...	...	...	...	k/m/	...	...	...	...	k/m/	...	...	...	...
3720 Recycling of non-metal waste and scrap	k/m/	...	...	...	...	k/m/	...	...	...	...	k/m/	...	...	...	...
D Total manufacturing		4542	4544	4603	4604		197658	198757	203921	218972		2760	2883	3051	3335

a/ 1542 includes 1543.
b/ 1549 includes 1544.
c/ 1551 includes 1552 and 1554.
d/ 1712 includes 1721.
e/ 172 excludes1721.
f/ 1911 includes 1912.
g/ 2010 includes 2021.
h/ 202 excludes 2021.
i/ 2109 includes 2102.
j/ 221 includes 222.
k/ 369 includes 2320, 3710 and 3720.
m/ 3699 includes 2320, 3710 and 3720.
n/ 2693 includes 2691 and 2692.
p/ 2694 includes part of 2695.
q/ 2720 includes 273.
r/ 2812 includes 2813.
s/ 2891 includes part of 2892.
t/ 2914 includes part of 2919.
u/ 2924 includes 2923.
v/ 2926 includes 2929.
w/ 3140 includes part of 3190.
x/ 3312 includes 3313.
y/ 3320 includes 3330.
z/ 3691 includes part of 3699.
A/ 3693 includes 3694.

Ireland

ISIC Revision 3 ISIC Industry	Note	Output in factor values (million POUNDS) 1992	1993	1994	1995	Note	Value added in factor values (million POUNDS) 1992	1993	1994	1995	Note	Gross fixed capital formation (million POUNDS) 1994	1995
151 Processed meat,fish,fruit,vegetables,fats		2570	2696	2651	2918		459	500	502	548		63	64
1511 Processing/preserving of meat		2288	2393	2321	2554		352	380	379	406		46	49
1512 Processing/preserving of fish		150	159	177	208		49	54	58	74		10	12
1513 Processing/preserving of fruit & vegetables		103	117	125	127		46	55	56	56		5	2
1514 Vegetable and animal oils and fats		29	27	29	30		12	11	10	13		2	1
1520 Dairy products		2108	2200	2116	2258		415	449	399	405		94	49
153 Grain mill products; starches; animal feeds		610	581	680	758		127	127	155	161		32	14
1531 Grain mill products		...	...	...	...		...	...	...	...		...	...
1532 Starches and starch products		...	...	...	...		...	...	...	...		...	...
1533 Prepared animal feeds		506	508	586	639		108	110	137	126		31	13
154 Other food products		1779	2144	2365	2569		1225	1501	1676	1814		36	65
1541 Bakery products		239	272	312	321		115	136	150	143		13	18
1542 Sugar	a/	366	419	413	422	a/	141	151	152	149	a/	15	23
1543 Cocoa, chocolate and sugar confectionery	a/	...	...	...	...	a/	...	...	...	...	a/	...	...
1544 Macaroni, noodles & similar products	b/	...	...	...	...	b/	...	...	...	...	b/	...	...
1549 Other food products n.e.c.	b/	1174	1454	1641	1827	b/	969	1214	1374	1522	b/	8	25
155 Beverages		950	937	955	1128		626	578	646	735		57	37
1551 Distilling, rectifying & blending of spirits	c/	448	436	428	545	c/	246	236	241	300	c/	19	15
1552 Wines	c/	...	...	...	...	c/	...	...	...	...	c/	...	...
1553 Malt liquors and malt		501	501	527	583		380	343	406	436		38	23
1554 Soft drinks; mineral waters	c/	...	...	...	...	c/	...	...	...	...	c/	...	...
1600 Tobacco products		155	148	165	173		104	102	113	126		-1	5
171 Spinning, weaving and finishing of textiles		211	223	233	229		76	91	95	84		5	12
1711 Textile fibre preparation; textile weaving		144	152	163	153		49	62	66	55		3	9
1712 Finishing of textiles	d/	67	70	70	76	d/	27	30	29	29	d/	2	3
172 Other textiles	e/	133	120	131	138	e/	68	64	65	63	e/	3	8
1721 Made-up textile articles, except apparel	d/	...	...	...	...	d/	...	...	...	...	d/	...	...
1722 Carpets and rugs		62	59	61	64		29	29	28	29		1	2
1723 Cordage, rope, twine and netting		13	10	12	15		7	5	4	5		-	1
1729 Other textiles n.e.c.		57	52	59	58		32	30	33	29		2	5
1730 Knitted and crocheted fabrics and articles		77	80	81	76		40	43	43	42		4	5
1810 Wearing apparel, except fur apparel		293	299	317	333		134	147	150	158		11	14
1820 Dressing & dyeing of fur; processing of fur		1	2	3	3		1	1	1	2		-	-
191 Tanning, dressing and processing of leather		50	50	70	67		12	14	17	16		4	2
1911 Tanning and dressing of leather	f/	50	50	70	67	f/	12	14	17	16	f/	4	2
1912 Luggage, handbags, etc.; saddlery & harness	f/	...	...	...	...	f/	...	...	...	...	f/	...	...
1920 Footwear		16	15	18	16		7	7	9	9		-	-
2010 Sawmilling and planing of wood	g/	125	131	158	180	g/	46	49	63	62	g/	23	6
202 Products of wood, cork, straw, etc.	h/	112	109	124	142	h/	50	45	45	53	h/	3	6
2021 Veneer sheets, plywood, particle board, etc.	g/	...	...	...	...	g/	...	...	...	...	g/	...	...
2022 Builders' carpentry and joinery		86	84	90	102		39	35	32	40		3	6
2023 Wooden containers		12	12	15	19		4	5	6	6		-	-
2029 Other wood products; articles of cork/straw		14	13	19	20		6	6	7	7		-	1
210 Paper and paper products		343	347	369	467		158	170	174	222		17	18
2101 Pulp, paper and paperboard		26	24	27	33		9	9	10	13		1	1
2102 Corrugated paper and paperboard	i/	...	...	...	...	i/	...	...	...	...	i/	...	...
2109 Other articles of paper and paperboard	i/	317	323	342	434	i/	149	161	163	210	i/	16	17
221 Publishing	j/	598	644	678	702	j/	371	399	419	430	j/	20	26
2211 Publishing of books and other publications		...	...	...	...		...	...	...	...		...	...
2212 Publishing of newspapers, journals, etc.		...	...	...	...		...	...	...	...		...	...
2213 Publishing of recorded media		...	...	...	...		...	...	...	...		...	...
2219 Other publishing		...	...	...	...		...	...	...	...		...	...

continued

Ireland

ISIC Revision 3	Output in factor values					Value added in factor values					Gross fixed capital formation		
		(million POUNDS)					(million POUNDS)					(million POUNDS)	
ISIC Industry	Note	1992	1993	1994	1995	Note	1992	1993	1994	1995	Note	1994	1995
222 Printing and related service activities	j/	...	...	...	...	j/	...	...	...	...	j/	...	...
2221 Printing		...	...	...	...		...	...	...	...		...	...
2222 Service activities related to printing		...	...	...	...		...	...	...	...		...	...
2230 Reproduction of recorded media		899	1071	1557	1871		672	799	1198	1531		22	48
2310 Coke oven products		...	...	...	...		...	...	...	...		...	...
2320 Refined petroleum products	k/m/	...	...	...	...	k/m/	...	...	...	...	k/m/	...	...
2330 Processing of nuclear fuel		...	...	...	...		...	...	...	...		...	...
241 Basic chemicals		1627	1969	2282	2792		1152	1453	1733	2112		118	100
2411 Basic chemicals, except fertilizers		1301	1664	1935	2398		1053	1357	1601	1979		104	87
2412 Fertilizers and nitrogen compounds		261	235	267	305		65	56	84	88		11	7
2413 Plastics in primary forms; synthetic rubber		65	70	80	89		34	40	48	46		3	5
242 Other chemicals		1471	1704	2181	2467		987	1142	1456	1664		137	150
2421 Pesticides and other agro-chemical products		10	11	13	11		3	2	4	5		1	-
2422 Paints, varnishes, printing ink and mastics		62	51	69	66		28	24	33	30		2	2
2423 Pharmaceuticals, medicinal chemicals, etc.		505	651	1086	1306		322	426	718	884		108	108
2424 Soap, cleaning & cosmetic preparations		238	264	318	315		141	156	205	195		9	19
2429 Other chemical products n.e.c.		656	727	695	768		493	533	496	550		17	21
2430 Man-made fibres		131	136	150	187		51	57	64	81		4	22
251 Rubber products		141	134	165	186		80	75	93	107		7	16
2511 Rubber tyres and tubes		...	...	...	...		...	...	...	...		...	...
2519 Other rubber products		...	...	...	...		...	...	...	...		...	...
2520 Plastic products		405	425	463	548		197	206	231	242		30	33
2610 Glass and glass products		141	150	171	194		88	97	115	120		10	17
269 Non-metallic mineral products n.e.c.		415	434	482	523		229	253	266	282		16	25
2691 Pottery, china and earthenware	n/	...	...	...	...	n/	...	...	...	...	n/	...	...
2692 Refractory ceramic products	n/	...	...	...	...	n/	...	...	...	...	n/	...	...
2693 Struct.non-refractory clay; ceramic products	n/	34	42	44	44	n/	21	30	30	29	n/	1	2
2694 Cement, lime and plaster	p/	129	121	144	154	p/	83	80	95	95	p/	3	5
2695 Articles of concrete, cement and plaster	p/	183	195	216	231	p/	94	111	100	109	p/	12	14
2696 Cutting, shaping & finishing of stone		22	22	27	25		11	11	13	14		1	1
2699 Other non-metallic mineral products n.e.c.		48	54	52	69		19	21	27	35		-1	2
2710 Basic iron and steel		74	81	92	97		26	36	18	21		1	2
2720 Basic precious and non-ferrous metals	q/	148	172	180	206	q/	26	52	46	61	q/	8	10
273 Casting of metals	q/	...	...	...	...	q/	...	...	...	...	q/	...	...
2731 Casting of iron and steel		...	...	...	...		...	...	...	...		...	...
2732 Casting of non-ferrous metals		...	...	...	...		...	...	...	...		...	...
281 Struct.metal products;tanks;steam generators		243	242	274	304		102	103	116	119		9	9
2811 Structural metal products		171	171	192	227		68	68	75	87		4	5
2812 Tanks, reservoirs and containers of metal	r/	72	71	82	77	r/	35	35	41	32	r/	5	4
2813 Steam generators	r/	...	...	...	...	r/	...	...	...	...	r/	...	...
289 Other metal products; metal working services		341	343	359	387		162	166	168	188		15	18
2891 Metal forging/pressing/stamping/roll-forming	s/	18	19	16	23	s/	8	10	8	13	s/	1	2
2892 Treatment & coating of metals	s/	11	11	12	11	s/	7	8	7	6	s/	1	1
2893 Cutlery, hand tools and general hardware		86	80	83	96		51	46	50	58		4	5
2899 Other fabricated metal products n.e.c.		226	233	248	257		96	103	103	111		10	11
291 General purpose machinery		393	396	481	588		204	201	225	283		12	16
2911 Engines & turbines(not for transport equip.)		...	...	...	...		...	...	...	...		...	...
2912 Pumps, compressors, taps and valves		...	...	...	...		...	...	...	...		...	...
2913 Bearings, gears, gearing & driving elements		...	...	...	...		...	...	...	...		...	...
2914 Ovens, furnaces and furnace burners	t/	26	31	37	58	t/	13	15	17	19	t/	1	1
2915 Lifting and handling equipment		79	77	102	114		43	40	55	58		4	3
2919 Other general purpose machinery	t/	151	156	180	248	t/	76	74	68	111	t/	3	3

ISIC Revision 3	Note					Note					Note		
292 Special purpose machinery		173	173	207	246		94	100	114	124		10	11
2921 Agricultural and forestry machinery		25	29	37	48		12	15	16	20		1	2
2922 Machine tools		24	31	44	49		15	19	25	21		4	4
2923 Machinery for metallurgy	u/	...	...	...	...	u/	...	...	...	...	u/	...	...
2924 Machinery for mining & construction	u/	35	36	45	46	u/	22	23	30	29	u/	1	1
2925 Food/beverage/tobacco processing machinery		33	35	38	44		15	18	18	18		2	1
2926 Machinery for textile, apparel and leather	v/	56	42	43	59	v/	30	25	25	36	v/	3	3
2927 Weapons and ammunition		...	...	...	...		...	...	...	...		...	...
2929 Other special purpose machinery	v/	...	...	...	...	v/	...	...	...	...	v/	...	...
2930 Domestic appliances n.e.c.		190	200	235	239		89	100	118	112		9	14
3000 Office, accounting and computing machinery		2471	3136	3559	5994		933	923	1001	2163		117	144
3110 Electric motors, generators and transformers		124	151	186	230		77	97	121	147		27	62
3120 Electricity distribution & control apparatus		132	139	153	209		67	74	83	116		9	14
3130 Insulated wire and cable		122	117	134	230		42	37	44	103		2	30
3140 Accumulators, primary cells and batteries	w/	76	82	94	234	w/	44	34	49	104	w/	4	15
3150 Lighting equipment and electric lamps		14	13	12	13		7	6	5	6		-	-
3190 Other electrical equipment n.e.c.	w/	118	109	101	95	w/	66	55	54	48	w/	1	4
3210 Electronic valves, tubes, etc.		204	337	475	681		86	106	113	152		35	46
3220 TV/radio transmitters; line comm. apparatus		240	337	436	405		91	136	168	167		21	18
3230 TV and radio receivers and associated goods		45	63	68	66		14	25	30	22		1	3
331 Medical, measuring, testing appliances, etc.		561	639	682	765		366	412	430	480		30	55
3311 Medical, surgical and orthopaedic equipment		417	487	521	593		293	339	356	395		27	50
3312 Measuring/testing/navigating appliances,etc.	x/	145	153	161	171	x/	74	73	73	86	x/	3	5
3313 Industrial process control equipment	x/	...	...	...	...	x/	...	...	...	...	x/	...	...
3320 Optical instruments & photographic equipment	y/	138	198	222	240	y/	94	147	142	138	y/	12	6
3330 Watches and clocks	y/	...	...	...	...	y/	...	...	...	...	y/	...	...
3410 Motor vehicles		54	44	44	61		27	22	12	25		2	1
3420 Automobile bodies, trailers & semi-trailers		35	36	45	50		14	13	18	18		1	1
3430 Parts/accessories for automobiles		89	106	143	169		42	48	66	73		6	13
351 Building and repairing of ships and boats		25	23	23	29		11	10	10	16		1	1
3511 Building and repairing of ships		25	23	23	29		11	10	10	16		1	1
3512 Building/repairing of pleasure/sport. boats		...	...	...	...		...	...	...	...		...	...
3520 Railway/tramway locomotives & rolling stock		207	205	197	213		118	114	104	116		-1	6
3530 Aircraft and spacecraft		...	...	...	...		...	...	...	...		...	...
359 Transport equipment n.e.c.		1	1	1	3		-	-	1	2		-	4
3591 Motorcycles		...	...	...	...		...	...	...	...		...	...
3592 Bicycles and invalid carriages		1	1	1	3		-	-	1	2		-	4
3599 Other transport equipment n.e.c.		...	...	...	...		...	...	...	...		...	...
3610 Furniture		159	166	173	191		74	78	81	86		9	8
369 Manufacturing n.e.c.	k/	622	643	645	717	k/	233	255	262	278	k/	24	31
3691 Jewellery and related articles	z/	236	259	222	233	z/	120	139	138	131	z/	8	7
3692 Musical instruments		1	1	1	1		1	1	1	1		-	-
3693 Sports goods	A/	95	90	103	130	A/	45	44	50	57	A/	5	7
3694 Games and toys	A/	...	...	...	...	A/	...	...	...	...	A/	...	...
3699 Other manufacturing n.e.c.	m/z/	289	293	319	353	m/z/	67	71	73	89	m/z/	11	17
3710 Recycling of metal waste and scrap	k/m/	...	...	...	...	k/m/	...	...	...	...	k/m/	...	...
3720 Recycling of non-metal waste and scrap	k/m/	...	...	...	...	k/m/	...	...	...	...	k/m/	...	...
D Total manufacturing		22361	24904	27787	33583		10485	11722	13325	16237		1084	1283

a/ 1542 includes 1543.
b/ 1549 includes 1544.
c/ 1551 includes 1552 and 1554.
d/ 1712 includes 1721.
e/ 172 excludes1721.
f/ 1911 includes 1912.
g/ 2010 includes 2021.
h/ 202 excludes 2021.
i/ 2109 includes 2102.
j/ 221 includes 222.
k/ 369 includes 2320, 3710 and 3720.
m/ 3699 includes 2320, 3710 and 3720.
n/ 2693 includes 2691 and 2692.
p/ 2694 includes part of 2695.
q/ 2720 includes 273.
r/ 2812 includes 2813.
s/ 2891 includes part of 2892.
t/ 2914 includes part of 2919.
u/ 2924 includes 2923.
v/ 2926 includes 2929.
w/ 3140 includes part of 3190.
x/ 3312 includes 3313.
y/ 3320 includes 3330.
z/ 3691 includes part of 3699.
A/ 3693 includes 3694.

Ireland

ISIC Revision 3			Index numbers of industrial production											
			(1990=100)											
ISIC	Industry	Note	1985	1986	1987	1988	1989	1990	1991	1992	1993	1994	1995	1996
15	Food and beverages		...	...	...	...	...	...	...	...	...	...	...	...
16	Tobacco products		115	115	108	104	104	100	108	114	104	105	110	113
17	Textiles		84	83	86	89	93	100	100	105	108	111	112	106
18	Wearing apparel, fur		110	110	113	105	98	100	87	85	79	75	72	73
19	Leather, leather products and footwear		134	114	105	101	103	100	91	77	72	77	75	72
20	Wood products (excl. furniture)		...	...	...	...	...	...	...	...	...	...	...	...
21	Paper and paper products		93	97	97	94	101	100	102	104	103	107	107	103
22	Printing and publishing		66	71	80	91	98	100	110	122	133	135	153	155
23	Coke,refined petroleum products,nuclear fuel		...	...	...	...	...	...	...	...	...	...	...	...
24	Chemicals and chemical products		67	67	70	81	97	100	122	143	157	188	217	258
25	Rubber and plastics products		...	...	...	...	...	...	...	...	...	...	...	...
26	Non-metallic mineral products		86	84	80	81	95	100	94	98	94	104	114	125
27	Basic metals		82	76	76	86	95	100	89	81	85	81	87	93
28	Fabricated metal products		93	86	86	89	94	100	95	92	92	97	101	100
29	Machinery and equipment n.e.c.		78	79	89	93	101	100	92	88	85	98	113	116
30	Office, accounting and computing machinery		40	47	64	85	95	100	90	107	113	125	178	192
31	Electrical machinery and apparatus	a/	43	45	54	71	91	100	107	121	133	169	234	250
32	Radio,television and communication equipment	a/	...	...	...	...	...	...	...	...	...	...	...	...
33	Medical, precision and optical instruments		68	68	79	82	91	100	100	112	118	124	145	179
34	Motor vehicles, trailers, semi-trailers	b/	87	80	81	88	102	100	90	85	80	82	84	96
35	Other transport equipment	b/	...	...	...	...	...	...	...	...	...	...	...	...
36	Furniture; manufacturing n.e.c.		...	...	...	...	...	...	...	...	...	...	...	...
37	Recycling		...	...	...	...	...	...	...	...	...	...	...	...
D	Total manufacturing		67	69	76	86	96	100	103	114	120	135	162	176

a/ 31 includes 32.
b/ 34 includes 35.

ISRAEL

Supplier of information:
Central Bureau of Statistics, Jerusalem.

Basic source of data:
Annual industry and crafts survey.

Major deviations from ISIC (Revision 3):
None reported.

Reference period (if not calendar year):

Scope:
All establishments with 5 or more persons engaged and operating during any part of the survey year, except (a) non-profit establishments (such as workshops for training or rehabilitation purposes) and (b) auxiliary industrial units in kibbutz establishments where the bulk of their production is consumed by the kibbutz itself. The survey covers about 95 per cent of employees in the industrial sector. The indices of industrial production cover all industrial establishments and workshops with at least one employee.

Method of enumeration:
Establishments are sampled.

Adjusted for non-response:
Not reported.

Concepts and definitions of variables:
Number of employees is the average of the numbers for four selected months of the reference year.
Wages and salaries covers all payments appearing on the pay-roll on which income tax is due, including basic salary, cost-of-living and other allowances (except child allowance), premiums, bonuses, payments for overtime, leave, sickness etc., bus fare, professional literature, thirteenth month salary, maintenance of vehicles, telephone, clothing, lodging and other payments in kind, such as meals, presents, and housing. It includes certain labour expenses that do not appear on payrolls, such as payments for national insurance and pension fund.
Output does not include net revenues from goods shipped in the same condition as received.
Gross fixed capital formation excludes outlays for land progress payments made for fixed assets on order but not yet completed. Fixed capital formation in new establishments not yet in operation is also excluded. Sales of used fixed assets are not deducted.

Related national publications:
Industry and Crafts Survey (annual); Statistical Abstract of Israel (annual); Monthly Bulletin of Statistics, all published by the Central Bureau of Statistics, Jerusalem.

Israel

ISIC Revision 3	Number of establishments					Number of employees					Wages and salaries paid to employees				
		(numbers)					(thousands)					(million SHEKALIM)			
ISIC Industry	Note	1992	1993	1994	1995	Note	1992	1993	1994	1995	Note	1992	1993	1994	1995
151 Processed meat,fish,fruit,vegetables,fats		...	...	...	178		...	...	...	14.9		...	...	...	917
1511 Processing/preserving of meat		...	...	...	...		...	...	...	...		...	...	...	...
1512 Processing/preserving of fish		...	...	...	...		...	...	...	...		...	...	...	...
1513 Processing/preserving of fruit & vegetables		...	...	...	...		...	...	...	...		...	...	...	...
1514 Vegetable and animal oils and fats		...	...	...	...		...	...	...	...		...	...	...	...
1520 Dairy products		...	...	...	68		...	...	...	5.9		...	...	...	528
153 Grain mill products; starches; animal feeds		...	...	...	50		...	...	...	1.8		...	...	...	154
1531 Grain mill products		...	...	...	...		...	...	...	...		...	...	...	...
1532 Starches and starch products		...	...	...	...		...	...	...	...		...	...	...	...
1533 Prepared animal feeds		...	...	...	...		...	...	...	...		...	...	...	...
154 Other food products		...	...	...	721		...	...	...	24.9		...	...	...	1253
1541 Bakery products		...	...	...	...		...	...	...	...		...	...	...	...
1542 Sugar		...	...	...	...		...	...	...	...		...	...	...	...
1543 Cocoa, chocolate and sugar confectionery		...	...	...	...		...	...	...	...		...	...	...	...
1544 Macaroni, noodles & similar products		...	...	...	...		...	...	...	...		...	...	...	...
1549 Other food products n.e.c.		...	...	...	...		...	...	...	...		...	...	...	...
155 Beverages		...	...	...	45a/		...	...	...	6.3a/		...	...	...	444a/
1551 Distilling, rectifying & blending of spirits		...	...	...	...		...	...	...	...		...	...	...	...
1552 Wines		...	...	...	...		...	...	...	...		...	...	...	...
1553 Malt liquors and malt		...	...	...	...		...	...	...	...		...	...	...	...
1554 Soft drinks; mineral waters		...	...	...	...		...	...	...	...		...	...	...	...
1600 Tobacco products		...	...	...	...a/		...	...	...	...a/		...	...	...	...a/
171 Spinning, weaving and finishing of textiles		...	...	...	156b/		...	...	...	6.3b/		...	...	...	385b/
1711 Textile fibre preparation; textile weaving		...	...	...	...		...	...	...	...		...	...	...	...
1712 Finishing of textiles		...	...	...	...		...	...	...	...		...	...	...	...
172 Other textiles		...	...	...	188c/		...	...	...	5.3c/		...	...	...	256c/
1721 Made-up textile articles, except apparel		...	...	...	...		...	...	...	...		...	...	...	...
1722 Carpets and rugs		...	...	...	...b/		...	...	...	...b/		...	...	...	...b/
1723 Cordage, rope, twine and netting		...	...	...	...		...	...	...	...		...	...	...	...
1729 Other textiles n.e.c.		...	...	...	...		...	...	...	...		...	...	...	...
1730 Knitted and crocheted fabrics and articles		...	...	...	256		...	...	...	15.7		...	...	...	624
1810 Wearing apparel, except fur apparel		...	...	...	731		...	...	...	16.0		...	...	...	613
1820 Dressing & dyeing of fur; processing of fur		...	...	...	...d/e/		...	...	...	...d/e/		...	...	...	...d/e/
191 Tanning, dressing and processing of leather		...	...	...	74d/		...	...	...	1.1d/		...	...	...	46d/
1911 Tanning and dressing of leather		...	...	...	4e/		...	...	...	0.1e/		...	...	...	9e/
1912 Luggage, handbags, etc.; saddlery & harness		...	...	...	70		...	...	...	1.0		...	...	...	37
1920 Footwear		...	...	...	159		...	...	...	3.3		...	...	...	145
2010 Sawmilling and planing of wood		...	...	...	48f/		...	...	...	2.1f/		...	...	...	145f/
202 Products of wood, cork, straw, etc.		...	...	...	199g/		...	...	...	2.6g/		...	...	...	149g/
2021 Veneer sheets, plywood, particle board, etc.		...	...	...	...f/		...	...	...	...f/		...	...	...	...f/
2022 Builders' carpentry and joinery		...	...	...	...		...	...	...	...		...	...	...	...
2023 Wooden containers		...	...	...	...		...	...	...	...		...	...	...	...
2029 Other wood products; articles of cork/straw		...	...	...	...		...	...	...	...		...	...	...	...
210 Paper and paper products		...	...	...	215		...	...	...	8.3		...	...	...	612
2101 Pulp, paper and paperboard		...	...	...	...		...	...	...	...		...	...	...	...
2102 Corrugated paper and paperboard		...	...	...	...		...	...	...	...		...	...	...	...
2109 Other articles of paper and paperboard		...	...	...	...		...	...	...	...		...	...	...	...
221 Publishing		...	...	...	284		...	...	...	9.8		...	...	...	709
2211 Publishing of books and other publications		...	...	...	...		...	...	...	...		...	...	...	...
2212 Publishing of newspapers, journals, etc.		...	...	...	...		...	...	...	...		...	...	...	...
2213 Publishing of recorded media		...	...	...	...		...	...	...	...		...	...	...	...
2219 Other publishing		...	...	...	...		...	...	...	...		...	...	...	...

222 Printing and related service activities	...	...	...	768h/	...	...	...	9.8h/	...	...	...	580h/
2221 Printing	...	...	...	...	...	...	...	...	...	...	...	...
2222 Service activities related to printing	...	...	...	...	...	...	...	...	...	...	...	...
2230 Reproduction of recorded media	...	...	...	...h/	...	...	...	...h/	...	...	...	...h/
2310 Coke oven products	...	...	...	...i/j/	...	...	...	...i/j/	...	...	...	...i/j/
2320 Refined petroleum products	...	...	...	...i/j/	...	...	...	...i/j/	...	...	...	...i/j/
2330 Processing of nuclear fuel	...	...	...	...i/j/	...	...	...	...i/j/	...	...	...	...i/j/
241 Basic chemicals	...	...	...	54i/	...	...	...	8.4i/	...	...	...	1211i/
2411 Basic chemicals, except fertilizers	...	...	...	38k/	...	...	...	4.3k/	...	...	...	613k/
2412 Fertilizers and nitrogen compounds	...	...	...	...k/	...	...	...	...k/	...	...	...	...k/
2413 Plastics in primary forms; synthetic rubber	...	...	...	16j/	...	...	...	4.1j/	...	...	...	598j/
242 Other chemicals	...	...	...	227	...	...	...	14.4	...	...	...	1378
2421 Pesticides and other agro-chemical products	...	...	...	...	...	...	...	...	...	...	...	...
2422 Paints, varnishes, printing ink and mastics	...	...	...	...	...	...	...	...	...	...	...	...
2423 Pharmaceuticals, medicinal chemicals, etc.	...	...	...	...	...	...	...	...	...	...	...	...
2424 Soap, cleaning & cosmetic preparations	...	...	...	...	...	...	...	...	...	...	...	...
2429 Other chemical products n.e.c.	...	...	...	...	...	...	...	...	...	...	...	...
2430 Man-made fibres	...	...	...	...i/j/	...	...	...	...i/j/	...	...	...	...i/j/
251 Rubber products	...	...	...	43	...	...	...	2.1	...	...	...	168
2511 Rubber tyres and tubes	...	...	...	...	...	...	...	...	...	...	...	...
2519 Other rubber products	...	...	...	...	...	...	...	...	...	...	...	...
2520 Plastic products	...	...	...	511	...	...	...	17.6	...	...	...	1042
2610 Glass and glass products	...	...	...	...m/n/	...	...	...	...m/n/	...	...	...	...m/n/
269 Non-metallic mineral products n.e.c.	...	...	...	418m/	...	...	...	12.0m/	...	...	...	978m/
2691 Pottery, china and earthenware	...	...	...	71n/	...	...	...	2.7n/	...	...	...	188n/
2692 Refractory ceramic products	...	...	...	...	...	...	...	...	...	...	...	...
2693 Struct.non-refractory clay; ceramic products	...	...	...	...n/	...	...	...	...n/	...	...	...	...n/
2694 Cement, lime and plaster	...	...	...	200p/	...	...	...	7.2p/	...	...	...	658p/
2695 Articles of concrete, cement and plaster	...	...	...	...p/	...	...	...	...p/	...	...	...	...p/
2696 Cutting, shaping & finishing of stone	...	...	...	147q/	...	...	...	2.1q/	...	...	...	132q/
2699 Other non-metallic mineral products n.e.c.	...	...	...	...q/	...	...	...	...q/	...	...	...	...q/
2710 Basic iron and steel	...	...	...	35	...	...	...	1.9	...	...	...	175
2720 Basic precious and non-ferrous metals	...	...	...	56	...	...	...	2.1	...	...	...	158
273 Casting of metals	...	...	...	51	...	...	...	2.4	...	...	...	216
2731 Casting of iron and steel	...	...	...	...	...	...	...	...	...	...	...	...
2732 Casting of non-ferrous metals	...	...	...	...	...	...	...	...	...	...	...	...
281 Struct.metal products;tanks;steam generators	...	...	...	729	...	...	...	16.6	...	...	...	922
2811 Structural metal products	...	...	...	...	...	...	...	...	...	...	...	...
2812 Tanks, reservoirs and containers of metal	...	...	...	...	...	...	...	...	...	...	...	...
2813 Steam generators	...	...	...	...	...	...	...	...	...	...	...	...
289 Other metal products; metal working services	...	...	...	1138	...	...	...	24.3	...	...	...	1736
2891 Metal forging/pressing/stamping/roll-forming	...	...	...	...	...	...	...	...	...	...	...	...
2892 Treatment & coating of metals	...	...	...	...	...	...	...	...	...	...	...	...
2893 Cutlery, hand tools and general hardware	...	...	...	...	...	...	...	...	...	...	...	...
2899 Other fabricated metal products n.e.c.	...	...	...	...	...	...	...	...	...	...	...	...
291 General purpose machinery	...	...	...	222	...	...	...	10.2	...	...	...	1020
2911 Engines & turbines(not for transport equip.)	...	...	...	...	...	...	...	...	...	...	...	...
2912 Pumps, compressors, taps and valves	...	...	...	...	...	...	...	...	...	...	...	...
2913 Bearings, gears, gearing & driving elements	...	...	...	...	...	...	...	...	...	...	...	...
2914 Ovens, furnaces and furnace burners	...	...	...	...	...	...	...	...	...	...	...	...
2915 Lifting and handling equipment	...	...	...	...	...	...	...	...	...	...	...	...
2919 Other general purpose machinery	...	...	...	...	...	...	...	...	...	...	...	...
292 Special purpose machinery	...	...	...	81	...	...	...	2.6	...	...	...	241
2921 Agricultural and forestry machinery	...	...	...	...	...	...	...	...	...	...	...	...
2922 Machine tools	...	...	...	...	...	...	...	...	...	...	...	...
2923 Machinery for metallurgy	...	...	...	...	...	...	...	...	...	...	...	...
2924 Machinery for mining & construction	...	...	...	...	...	...	...	...	...	...	...	...
2925 Food/beverage/tobacco processing machinery	...	...	...	...	...	...	...	...	...	...	...	...
2926 Machinery for textile, apparel and leather	...	...	...	...	...	...	...	...	...	...	...	...
2927 Weapons and ammunition	...	...	...	...	...	...	...	...	...	...	...	...
2929 Other special purpose machinery	...	...	...	...	...	...	...	...	...	...	...	...
2930 Domestic appliances n.e.c.	...	...	...	94r/	...	...	...	4.4r/	...	...	...	346r/

continued

ISIC Revision 3

ISIC Industry	Number of establishments					Number of employees					Wages and salaries paid to employees				
		(numbers)					(thousands)					(million SHEKALIM)			
	Note	1992	1993	1994	1995	Note	1992	1993	1994	1995	Note	1992	1993	1994	1995
3000 Office, accounting and computing machinery		...	...	...	...r/		...	...	...	...r/		...	...	...	...r/
3110 Electric motors, generators and transformers		...	...	...	69		...	...	...	3.0		...	...	...	243
3120 Electricity distribution & control apparatus		...	...	...	191s/		...	...	...	4.3s/		...	...	...	274s/
3130 Insulated wire and cable		...	...	...	31t/		...	...	...	2.6t/		...	...	...	262t/
3140 Accumulators, primary cells and batteries		...	...	...	...t/		...	...	...	...t/		...	...	...	...t/
3150 Lighting equipment and electric lamps		...	...	...	...s/		...	...	...	...s/		...	...	...	...s/
3190 Other electrical equipment n.e.c.		...	...	...	...s/		...	...	...	...s/		...	...	...	...s/
3210 Electronic valves, tubes, etc.		...	...	...	177		...	...	...	9.7		...	...	...	701
3220 TV/radio transmitters; line comm. apparatus		...	...	...	35		...	...	...	9.5		...	...	...	1351
3230 TV and radio receivers and associated goods		...	...	...	24		...	...	...	2.4		...	...	...	315
331 Medical, measuring, testing appliances, etc.		...	...	...	252u/		...	...	...	23.8u/		...	...	...	3268u/
3311 Medical, surgical and orthopaedic equipment		...	...	...	...		...	...	...	...		...	...	...	...
3312 Measuring/testing/navigating appliances,etc.		...	...	...	...		...	...	...	...		...	...	...	...
3313 Industrial process control equipment		...	...	...	...		...	...	...	...		...	...	...	...
3320 Optical instruments & photographic equipment		...	...	...	43		...	...	...	2.6		...	...	...	328
3330 Watches and clocks		...	...	...	...u/		...	...	...	...u/		...	...	...	...u/
3410 Motor vehicles		...	...	...	...v/		...	...	...	...v/		...	...	...	...v/
3420 Automobile bodies, trailers & semi-trailers		...	...	...	140v/		...	...	...	4.5v/		...	...	...	369v/
3430 Parts/accessories for automobiles		...	...	...	...v/		...	...	...	...v/		...	...	...	...v/
351 Building and repairing of ships and boats		...	...	...	...w/		...	...	...	...w/		...	...	...	...w/
3511 Building and repairing of ships		...	...	...	...		...	...	...	...		...	...	...	...
3512 Building/repairing of pleasure/sport. boats		...	...	...	...		...	...	...	...		...	...	...	...
3520 Railway/tramway locomotives & rolling stock		...	...	...	80w/		...	...	...	10.8w/		...	...	...	1400w/
3530 Aircraft and spacecraft		...	...	...	...w/		...	...	...	...w/		...	...	...	...w/
359 Transport equipment n.e.c.		...	...	...	...w/		...	...	...	...w/		...	...	...	...w/
3591 Motorcycles		...	...	...	...		...	...	...	...		...	...	...	...
3592 Bicycles and invalid carriages		...	...	...	...		...	...	...	...		...	...	...	...
3599 Other transport equipment n.e.c.		...	...	...	...		...	...	...	...		...	...	...	...
3610 Furniture		...	...	...	721		...	...	...	11.5		...	...	...	641
369 Manufacturing n.e.c.		...	...	...	304		...	...	...	6.7		...	...	...	337
3691 Jewellery and related articles		...	...	...	...		...	...	...	...		...	...	...	...
3692 Musical instruments		...	...	...	...		...	...	...	...		...	...	...	...
3693 Sports goods		...	...	...	...		...	...	...	...		...	...	...	...
3694 Games and toys		...	...	...	...		...	...	...	...		...	...	...	...
3699 Other manufacturing n.e.c.		...	...	...	...		...	...	...	...		...	...	...	...
3710 Recycling of metal waste and scrap		...	...	...	...		...	...	...	...		...	...	...	...
3720 Recycling of non-metal waste and scrap		...	...	...	...		...	...	...	...		...	...	...	...
D Total manufacturing		...	...	...	9866		...	...	...	344.5		...	...	...	26640

a/ 155 includes 1600.
b/ 171 includes 1722.
c/ 172 excludes 1722.
d/ 191 includes 1820.
e/ 1911 includes 1820.
f/ 2010 includes 2021.
g/ 202 excludes 2021.
h/ 222 includes 2230.
i/ 241 includes 2310, 2320, 2330 and 2430.
j/ 2413 includes 2310, 2320, 2330 and 2430.
k/ 2411 includes 2412.
m/ 269 includes 2610.
n/ 2691 includes 2610 and 2693.
p/ 2694 includes 2695.
q/ 2696 includes 2699.
r/ 2930 includes 3000.
s/ 3120 includes 3150 and 3190.
t/ 3130 includes 3140.
u/ 331 includes 3330.
v/ 3420 includes 3410 and 3430.
w/ 3520 includes 351, 3530 and 359.

Israel

ISIC Revision 3 ISIC Industry	Note	Output in producers' prices (million SHEKALIM) 1992	1993	1994	1995	Note	Value added in producers' prices (million SHEKALIM) 1992	1993	1994	1995	Note	Gross fixed capital formation (million SHEKALIM) 1994	1995
151 Processed meat,fish,fruit,vegetables,fats		...	...	...	6434		...	...	...	1265		...	325
1511 Processing/preserving of meat		...	...	...	...		...	...	...	...		...	...
1512 Processing/preserving of fish		...	...	...	...		...	...	...	...		...	...
1513 Processing/preserving of fruit & vegetables		...	...	...	...		...	...	...	...		...	...
1514 Vegetable and animal oils and fats		...	...	...	...		...	...	...	...		...	...
1520 Dairy products		...	...	...	3635		...	...	...	996		...	248
153 Grain mill products; starches; animal feeds		...	...	...	2366		...	...	...	307		...	85
1531 Grain mill products		...	...	...	...		...	...	...	...		...	...
1532 Starches and starch products		...	...	...	...		...	...	...	...		...	...
1533 Prepared animal feeds		...	...	...	...		...	...	...	...		...	...
154 Other food products		...	...	...	5098		...	...	...	1830		...	378
1541 Bakery products		...	...	...	...		...	...	...	...		...	...
1542 Sugar		...	...	...	...		...	...	...	...		...	...
1543 Cocoa, chocolate and sugar confectionery		...	...	...	...		...	...	...	...		...	...
1544 Macaroni, noodles & similar products		...	...	...	...		...	...	...	...		...	...
1549 Other food products n.e.c.		...	...	...	...		...	...	...	...		...	...
155 Beverages		...	...	...	2411a/		...	...	...	705a/		...	223a/
1551 Distilling, rectifying & blending of spirits		...	...	...	...		...	...	...	...		...	...
1552 Wines		...	...	...	...		...	...	...	...		...	...
1553 Malt liquors and malt		...	...	...	...		...	...	...	...		...	...
1554 Soft drinks; mineral waters		...	...	...	...		...	...	...	...		...	...
1600 Tobacco products		...	...	...	...a/		...	...	...	...a/		...	...a/
171 Spinning, weaving and finishing of textiles		...	...	...	1619b/		...	...	...	582b/		...	136b/
1711 Textile fibre preparation; textile weaving		...	...	...	...		...	...	...	...		...	...
1712 Finishing of textiles		...	...	...	...		...	...	...	...		...	...
172 Other textiles		...	...	...	1003c/		...	...	...	316c/		...	276c/
1721 Made-up textile articles, except apparel		...	...	...	...		...	...	...	...		...	...
1722 Carpets and rugs		...	...	...	...b/		...	...	...	...b/		...	...b/
1723 Cordage, rope, twine and netting		...	...	...	...		...	...	...	...		...	...
1729 Other textiles n.e.c.		...	...	...	...		...	...	...	...		...	...
1730 Knitted and crocheted fabrics and articles		...	...	...	2193		...	...	...	772		...	173
1810 Wearing apparel, except fur apparel		...	...	...	2767		...	...	...	875		...	67
1820 Dressing & dyeing of fur; processing of fur		...	...	...	...d/e/		...	...	...	...d/e/		...	...d/e/
191 Tanning, dressing and processing of leather		...	...	...	177d/		...	...	...	53d/		...	3d/
1911 Tanning and dressing of leather		...	...	...	34e/		...	...	...	9e/		...	- e/
1912 Luggage, handbags, etc.; saddlery & harness		...	...	...	143		...	...	...	44		...	3
1920 Footwear		...	...	...	634		...	...	...	201		...	25
2010 Sawmilling and planing of wood		...	...	...	607f/		...	...	...	191f/		...	13f/
202 Products of wood, cork, straw, etc.		...	...	...	610g/		...	...	...	197g/		...	27g/
2021 Veneer sheets, plywood, particle board, etc.		...	...	...	...f/		...	...	...	...f/		...	...f/
2022 Builders' carpentry and joinery		...	...	...	...		...	...	...	...		...	...
2023 Wooden containers		...	...	...	...		...	...	...	...		...	...
2029 Other wood products; articles of cork/straw		...	...	...	...		...	...	...	...		...	...
210 Paper and paper products		...	...	...	3357		...	...	...	1022		...	203
2101 Pulp, paper and paperboard		...	...	...	...		...	...	...	...		...	...
2102 Corrugated paper and paperboard		...	...	...	...		...	...	...	...		...	...
2109 Other articles of paper and paperboard		...	...	...	...		...	...	...	...		...	...
221 Publishing		...	...	...	2448		...	...	...	926		...	81
2211 Publishing of books and other publications		...	...	...	...		...	...	...	...		...	...
2212 Publishing of newspapers, journals, etc.		...	...	...	...		...	...	...	...		...	...
2213 Publishing of recorded media		...	...	...	...		...	...	...	...		...	...
2219 Other publishing		...	...	...	...		...	...	...	...		...	...

continued

Israel

ISIC Revision 3		Output in producers' prices					Value added in producers' prices					Gross fixed capital formation		
		(million SHEKALIM)					(million SHEKALIM)					(million SHEKALIM)		
ISIC	Industry	Note	1992	1993	1994	1995	Note	1992	1993	1994	1995	Note	1994	1995
222	Printing and related service activities		...	...	...	2022h/		...	...	...	1016h/		...	205h/
2221	Printing		...	...	...	...		...	...	...	...		...	...
2222	Service activities related to printing		...	...	...	...		...	...	...	...		...	...
2230	Reproduction of recorded media		...	...	...	...h/		...	...	...	...h/		...	...h/
2310	Coke oven products		...	...	...	...i/j/		...	...	...	...i/j/		...	...i/j/
2320	Refined petroleum products		...	...	...	...i/j/		...	...	...	...i/j/		...	...i/j/
2330	Processing of nuclear fuel		...	...	...	...i/j/		...	...	...	...i/j/		...	...i/j/
241	Basic chemicals		...	...	...	10243i/		...	...	...	2411i/		...	1021i/
2411	Basic chemicals, except fertilizers		...	...	...	3180k/		...	...	...	1061k/		...	759k/
2412	Fertilizers and nitrogen compounds		...	...	...	...k/		...	...	...	...k/		...	...k/
2413	Plastics in primary forms; synthetic rubber		...	...	...	7063j/		...	...	...	1350j/		...	262j/
242	Other chemicals		...	...	...	7144		...	...	...	2344		...	562
2421	Pesticides and other agro-chemical products		...	...	...	...		...	...	...	...		...	...
2422	Paints, varnishes, printing ink and mastics		...	...	...	...		...	...	...	...		...	...
2423	Pharmaceuticals, medicinal chemicals, etc.		...	...	...	...		...	...	...	...		...	...
2424	Soap, cleaning & cosmetic preparations		...	...	...	...		...	...	...	...		...	...
2429	Other chemical products n.e.c.		...	...	...	...		...	...	...	...		...	...
2430	Man-made fibres		...	...	...	...i/j/		...	...	...	...i/j/		...	...i/j/
251	Rubber products		...	...	...	636		...	...	...	243		...	78
2511	Rubber tyres and tubes		...	...	...	...		...	...	...	...		...	...
2519	Other rubber products		...	...	...	...		...	...	...	...		...	...
2520	Plastic products		...	...	...	5491		...	...	...	2024		...	779
2610	Glass and glass products		...	...	...	...m/n/		...	...	...	...m/n/		...	...m/n/
269	Non-metallic mineral products n.e.c.		...	...	...	6477m/		...	...	...	1938m/		...	503m/
2691	Pottery, china and earthenware		...	...	...	748n/		...	...	...	302n/		...	83n/
2692	Refractory ceramic products		...	...	...	...		...	...	...	...		...	...
2693	Struct.non-refractory clay; ceramic products		...	...	...	...n/		...	...	...	...n/		...	...n/
2694	Cement, lime and plaster		...	...	...	5286p/		...	...	...	1450p/		...	387p/
2695	Articles of concrete, cement and plaster		...	...	...	...p/		...	...	...	...p/		...	...p/
2696	Cutting, shaping & finishing of stone		...	...	...	443q/		...	...	...	186q/		...	33q/
2699	Other non-metallic mineral products n.e.c.		...	...	...	...q/		...	...	...	...q/		...	...q/
2710	Basic iron and steel		...	...	...	1661		...	...	...	288		...	53
2720	Basic precious and non-ferrous metals		...	...	...	1157		...	...	...	290		...	68
273	Casting of metals		...	...	...	949		...	...	...	374		...	110
2731	Casting of iron and steel		...	...	...	...		...	...	...	...		...	...
2732	Casting of non-ferrous metals		...	...	...	...		...	...	...	...		...	...
281	Struct.metal products;tanks;steam generators		...	...	...	3450		...	...	...	1199		...	144
2811	Structural metal products		...	...	...	...		...	...	...	...		...	...
2812	Tanks, reservoirs and containers of metal		...	...	...	...		...	...	...	...		...	...
2813	Steam generators		...	...	...	...		...	...	...	...		...	...
289	Other metal products; metal working services		...	...	...	6096		...	...	...	2921		...	593
2891	Metal forging/pressing/stamping/roll-forming		...	...	...	...		...	...	...	...		...	...
2892	Treatment & coating of metals		...	...	...	...		...	...	...	...		...	...
2893	Cutlery, hand tools and general hardware		...	...	...	...		...	...	...	...		...	...
2899	Other fabricated metal products n.e.c.		...	...	...	...		...	...	...	...		...	...
291	General purpose machinery		...	...	...	2857		...	...	...	1076		...	62
2911	Engines & turbines(not for transport equip.)		...	...	...	...		...	...	...	...		...	...
2912	Pumps, compressors, taps and valves		...	...	...	...		...	...	...	...		...	...
2913	Bearings, gears, gearing & driving elements		...	...	...	...		...	...	...	...		...	...
2914	Ovens, furnaces and furnace burners		...	...	...	...		...	...	...	...		...	...
2915	Lifting and handling equipment		...	...	...	...		...	...	...	...		...	...
2919	Other general purpose machinery		...	...	...	...		...	...	...	...		...	...

ISIC Industry												
292 Special purpose machinery		...	...	...	1136		...	...	...	524	...	63
2921 Agricultural and forestry machinery		...	...	...	...		...	...	...	...	...	...
2922 Machine tools		...	...	...	...		...	...	...	...	...	...
2923 Machinery for metallurgy		...	...	...	...		...	...	...	...	...	...
2924 Machinery for mining & construction		...	...	...	...		...	...	...	...	...	...
2925 Food/beverage/tobacco processing machinery		...	...	...	...		...	...	...	...	...	...
2926 Machinery for textile, apparel and leather		...	...	...	...		...	...	...	...	...	...
2927 Weapons and ammunition		...	...	...	...		...	...	...	...	...	...
2929 Other special purpose machinery		...	...	...	...		...	...	...	...	...	...
2930 Domestic appliances n.e.c.		...	...	...	1801r/		...	...	...	510r/	...	71r/
3000 Office, accounting and computing machinery		...	...	...	...r/		...	...	...	...r/	...	...r/
3110 Electric motors, generators and transformers		...	...	...	785		...	...	...	336	...	31
3120 Electricity distribution & control apparatus		...	...	...	1124s/		...	...	...	378s/	...	33s/
3130 Insulated wire and cable		...	...	...	1518t/		...	...	...	429t/	...	75t/
3140 Accumulators, primary cells and batteries		...	...	...	...t/		...	...	...	...t/	...	...t/
3150 Lighting equipment and electric lamps		...	...	...	...s/		...	...	...	...s/	...	...s/
3190 Other electrical equipment n.e.c.		...	...	...	...s/		...	...	...	...s/	...	...s/
3210 Electronic valves, tubes, etc.		...	...	...	2789		...	...	...	1511	...	741
3220 TV/radio transmitters; line comm. apparatus		...	...	...	5049		...	...	...	2077	...	213
3230 TV and radio receivers and associated goods		...	...	...	1151		...	...	...	458	...	40
331 Medical, measuring, testing appliances, etc.		...	...	...	8220u/		...	...	...	3459u/	...	356u/
3311 Medical, surgical and orthopaedic equipment		...	...	...	...		...	...	...	...	...	...
3312 Measuring/testing/navigating appliances,etc.		...	...	...	...		...	...	...	...	...	...
3313 Industrial process control equipment		...	...	...	...		...	...	...	...	...	...
3320 Optical instruments & photographic equipment		...	...	...	976		...	...	...	480	...	48
3330 Watches and clocks		...	...	...	...u/		...	...	...	...u/	...	...u/
3410 Motor vehicles		...	...	...	...v/		...	...	...	...v/	...	...v/
3420 Automobile bodies, trailers & semi-trailers		...	...	...	1098v/		...	...	...	410v/	...	38v/
3430 Parts/accessories for automobiles		...	...	...	...v/		...	...	...	...v/	...	...v/
351 Building and repairing of ships and boats		...	...	...	...w/		...	...	...	...w/	...	...w/
3511 Building and repairing of ships		...	...	...	...		...	...	...	...	...	...
3512 Building/repairing of pleasure/sport. boats		...	...	...	...		...	...	...	...	...	...
3520 Railway/tramway locomotives & rolling stock		...	...	...	2917w/		...	...	...	1495w/	...	205w/
3530 Aircraft and spacecraft		...	...	...	...w/		...	...	...	...w/	...	...w/
359 Transport equipment n.e.c.		...	...	...	...w/		...	...	...	...w/	...	...w/
3591 Motorcycles		...	...	...	...		...	...	...	...	...	...
3592 Bicycles and invalid carriages		...	...	...	...		...	...	...	...	...	...
3599 Other transport equipment n.e.c.		...	...	...	...		...	...	...	...	...	...
3610 Furniture		...	...	...	2536		...	...	...	889	...	141
369 Manufacturing n.e.c.		...	...	...	1750		...	...	...	417	...	195
3691 Jewellery and related articles		...	...	...	...		...	...	...	...	...	...
3692 Musical instruments		...	...	...	...		...	...	...	...	...	...
3693 Sports goods		...	...	...	...		...	...	...	...	...	...
3694 Games and toys		...	...	...	...		...	...	...	...	...	...
3699 Other manufacturing n.e.c.		...	...	...	...		...	...	...	...	...	...
3710 Recycling of metal waste and scrap		...	...	...	...		...	...	...	...	...	...
3720 Recycling of non-metal waste and scrap		...	...	...	...		...	...	...	...	...	...
D Total manufacturing		...	...	...	116392		...	...	...	39735	...	8691

a/ 155 includes 1600.
b/ 171 includes 1722.
c/ 172 excludes 1722.
d/ 191 includes 1820.
e/ 1911 includes 1820.
f/ 2010 includes 2021.
g/ 202 excludes 2021.
h/ 222 includes 2230.
i/ 241 includes 2310, 2320, 2330 and 2430.
j/ 2413 includes 2310, 2320, 2330 and 2430.
k/ 2411 includes 2412.
m/ 269 includes 2610.
n/ 2691 includes 2610 and 2693.
p/ 2694 includes 2695.
q/ 2696 includes 2699.
r/ 2930 includes 3000.
s/ 3120 includes 3150 and 3190.
t/ 3130 includes 3140.
u/ 331 includes 3330.
v/ 3420 includes 3410 and 3430.
w/ 3520 includes 351, 3530 and 359.

Israel

ISIC Revision 3		Index numbers of industrial production (1990=100)											
ISIC Industry	Note	1985	1986	1987	1988	1989	1990	1991	1992	1993	1994	1995	1996
15 Food and beverages	a/	79	90	101	102	99	100	102	105	113	120	130	130
16 Tobacco products	a/	...	...	...	...	...	...	...	...	...	...	...	...
17 Textiles		102	101	102	95	95	100	108	111	111	120	128	121
18 Wearing apparel, fur		...	...	...	...	...	...	...	...	...	...	...	...
19 Leather, leather products and footwear		...	...	...	...	...	...	...	...	...	...	...	...
20 Wood products (excl. furniture)		...	...	...	...	...	...	...	...	...	...	...	...
21 Paper and paper products		79	91	97	95	95	100	102	109	113	118	121	122
22 Printing and publishing		77	87	99	98	96	100	98	107	126	130	135	139
23 Coke,refined petroleum products,nuclear fuel	b/	79	80	90	91	95	100	104	115	127	140	145	158
24 Chemicals and chemical products	b/	...	...	...	...	...	...	...	...	...	...	...	...
25 Rubber and plastics products		83	87	96	87	89	100	111	125	141	158	184	195
26 Non-metallic mineral products		77	79	88	86	84	100	130	151	145	155	192	212
27 Basic metals		80	78	81	85	80	100	111	116	121	139	166	176
28 Fabricated metal products		96	97	99	98	95	100	111	117	122	134	150	158
29 Machinery and equipment n.e.c.		88	99	109	108	100	100	100	114	129	141	143	149
30 Office, accounting and computing machinery		...	...	...	...	...	...	...	...	...	...	...	...
31 Electrical machinery and apparatus		...	...	...	...	93	100	106	114	124	132	142	139
32 Radio,television and communication equipment		...	...	...	...	...	...	...	...	...	...	...	...
33 Medical, precision and optical instruments		...	...	...	...	94	100	106	112	124	130	138	...
34 Motor vehicles, trailers, semi-trailers		...	...	...	...	...	...	...	...	...	...	...	...
35 Other transport equipment		...	...	...	...	...	...	...	...	...	...	...	...
36 Furniture; manufacturing n.e.c.		...	...	...	...	...	...	...	...	...	...	...	...
37 Recycling		...	...	...	...	...	...	...	...	...	...	...	...
D Total manufacturing		91	94	98	96	94	100	107	116	124	132	143	151

a/ 15 includes 16.
b/ 23 includes 24.

JAMAICA

Supplier of information:
Statistical Institute of Jamaica, Kingston.

Basic source of data:
Quarterly surveys carried out by the Factories Inspectorate, Ministry of Labour and Employment.

Major deviations from ISIC (Revision 2):
Repair services for the general public (part of ISIC major division 9) are included in manufacturing according to the type of products repaired.

Reference period (if not calendar year):

Scope:
Establishments with 10 or more persons engaged.

Method of enumeration:
Establishments with 50 or more persons engaged are completely enumerated. A 20 percent sample is used for establishments with 10-49 persons engaged.

Adjusted for non-response:
Not reported.

Concepts and definitions of variables:
Wages and salaries is compensation of employees.
Output is gross output and is derived from national accounts estimates.
Value added is total value added.

Related national publications:
Statistical Abstract; Statistical Yearbook; National Income and Product; Employment, Earnings and Hours worked in Large Establishments, all published by the Statistical Institute of Jamaica, Kingston.

Jamaica

ISIC Revision 2	Number of establishments					Number of employees					Wages and salaries paid to employees				
		(numbers)					(numbers)					(thousand DOLLARS)			
ISIC Industry	Note	1993	1994	1995	1996	Note	1993	1994	1995	1996	Note	1993	1994	1995	1996
311/2 Food products		...	...	...	193		25236	23356	23292	23170		...	...	...	...
3111 Slaughtering, preparing & preserving meat		...	...	...	...		...	...	...	...		...	...	...	...
3112 Dairy products		...	...	...	...		...	...	...	...		...	...	...	...
3113 Canning, preserving of fruits & vegetables		...	...	...	...		...	...	...	...		...	...	...	...
3114 Canning, preserving and processing of fish		...	...	...	...		...	...	...	...		...	...	...	...
3115 Vegetable and animal oils and fats		...	...	...	...		...	...	...	...		...	...	...	...
3116 Grain mill products		...	...	...	...		...	...	...	...		...	...	...	...
3117 Bakery products		...	...	...	...		...	...	...	...		...	...	...	...
3118 Sugar factories and refineries		...	...	...	...		12706	10729	...	...		...	...	...	...
3119 Cocoa, chocolate and sugar confectionery		...	...	...	...		...	...	...	...		...	...	...	...
3121 Other food products		...	...	...	...		...	...	...	...		...	...	...	...
3122 Prepared animal feeds		...	...	...	...		...	...	...	...		...	...	...	...
313 Beverages		...	...	...	19		3738	3757	3720	3393		...	...	...	...
3131 Distilling, rectifying and blending spirits		...	...	...	...		...	...	...	...		...	...	...	...
3132 Wine industries		...	...	...	...		...	...	...	...		...	...	...	...
3133 Malt liquors and malt		...	...	...	...		...	...	...	...		...	...	...	...
3134 Soft drinks and carbonated waters		...	...	...	...		...	...	...	...		...	...	...	...
314 Tobacco		...	...	...	6		795	765	803	750		...	...	...	...
321 Textiles		...	...	...	25		764	620	654	531		...	...	...	...
3211 Spinning, weaving and finishing textiles		...	...	...	...		...	...	...	...		...	...	...	...
3212 Made-up textile goods excl. wearing apparel		...	...	...	...		...	...	...	...		...	...	...	...
3213 Knitting mills		...	...	...	...		...	...	...	...		...	...	...	...
3214 Carpets and rugs		...	...	...	...		...	...	...	...		...	...	...	...
3215 Cordage, rope and twine		...	...	...	...		...	...	...	...		...	...	...	...
3219 Other textiles		...	...	...	...		...	...	...	...		...	...	...	...
322 Wearing apparel, except footwear		...	...	...	125		14160	13966	13872	13679		...	...	...	...
323 Leather and fur products		...	...	...	15a/	a/	394	385	432	427		...	...	...	...
3231 Tanneries and leather finishing		...	...	...	...		...	...	...	...		...	...	...	...
3232 Fur dressing and dyeing industries		...	...	...	...		...	...	...	...		...	...	...	...
3233 Leather prods. excl. wearing apparel		...	...	...	...		...	...	...	...		...	...	...	...
324 Footwear, except rubber or plastic		...	...	...	...a/	a/	...	...	...	...		...	...	...	...
331 Wood products, except furniture		...	...	...	22		716	868	1039	1084		...	...	...	...
3311 Sawmills, planing and other wood mills		...	...	...	...		...	...	...	...		...	...	...	...
3312 Wooden and cane containers		...	...	...	...		...	...	...	...		...	...	...	...
3319 Other wood and cork products		...	...	...	...		...	...	...	...		...	...	...	...
332 Furniture and fixtures, excl. metal		...	...	...	63		2333	2416	2288	2344		...	...	...	...
341 Paper and products		...	...	...	25		1301	1262	1257	1183		...	...	...	...
3411 Pulp, paper and paperboard articles		...	...	...	...		...	...	...	...		...	...	...	...
3412 Containers of paper and paperboard		...	...	...	...		...	...	...	...		...	...	...	...
3419 Other pulp, paper and paperboard articles		...	...	...	...		...	...	...	...		...	...	...	...
342 Printing and publishing		...	...	...	48		2020	1908	1952	2028		...	...	...	...
351 Industrial chemicals		...	...	...	14		643	660	661	639		...	...	...	...
3511 Basic chemicals excl. fertilizers		...	...	...	...		...	...	...	...		...	...	...	...
3512 Fertilizers and pesticides		...	...	...	...		...	...	...	...		...	...	...	...
3513 Synthetic resins and plastic materials		...	...	...	...		...	...	...	...		...	...	...	...
352 Other chemicals		...	...	...	47		2688	2709	2468	2060		...	...	...	...
3521 Paints, varnishes and lacquers		...	...	...	...		...	...	...	...		...	...	...	...
3522 Drugs and medicines		...	...	...	...		...	...	...	...		...	...	...	...
3523 Soap, cleaning preps., perfumes, cosmetics		...	...	...	...		...	...	...	...		...	...	...	...
3529 Other chemical products		...	...	...	...		...	...	...	...		...	...	...	...
353 Petroleum refineries		...	...	...	2b/	b/	216	213	212	218		...	...	...	...

354	Misc. petroleum and coal products		...	...	...	...b/	b/	...	...	...	...		...	...	...	...
355	Rubber products		...	...	...	11		683	659	586	599		...	...	...	...
3551	Tyres and tubes		...	...	...	...		...	...	...	...		...	...	...	...
3559	Other rubber products		...	...	...	...		...	...	...	...		...	...	...	...
356	Plastic products		...	...	...	17		1819	1801	1741	1615		...	...	...	...
361	Pottery, china, earthenware		...	...	...	6c/	c/	630	708	770	694		...	...	...	...
362	Glass and products		...	...	...	...c/	c/	...	...	...	...		...	...	...	...
369	Other non-metallic mineral products		...	...	...	42		2264	2203	1952	1965		...	...	...	...
3691	Structural clay products		...	...	...	...		...	...	...	...		...	...	...	...
3692	Cement, lime and plaster		...	...	...	...		594	583	...	...		...	...	...	...
3699	Other non-metallic mineral products		...	...	...	...		...	...	...	...		...	...	...	...
371	Iron and steel		...	...	...	109d/	d/	3965	3712	3606	3493		...	...	...	...
372	Non-ferrous metals		...	...	...	...d/	d/	...	...	...	...		...	...	...	...
381	Fabricated metal products		...	...	...	...d/	d/	...	...	...	...		...	...	...	...
3811	Cutlery, hand tools and general hardware		...	...	...	...		...	...	...	...		...	...	...	...
3812	Furniture and fixtures primarily of metal		...	...	...	...		...	...	...	...		...	...	...	...
3813	Structural metal products		...	...	...	...		...	...	...	...		...	...	...	...
3819	Other fabricated metal products		...	...	...	...		...	...	...	...		...	...	...	...
382	Non-electrical machinery		...	...	...	...d/	d/	...	...	...	...		...	...	...	...
3821	Engines and turbines		...	...	...	...		...	...	...	...		...	...	...	...
3822	Agricultural machinery and equipment		...	...	...	...		...	...	...	...		...	...	...	...
3823	Metal and wood working machinery		...	...	...	...		...	...	...	...		...	...	...	...
3824	Other special industrial machinery		...	...	...	...		...	...	...	...		...	...	...	...
3825	Office, computing and accounting machinery		...	...	...	...		...	...	...	...		...	...	...	...
3829	Other non-electrical machinery & equipment		...	...	...	...		...	...	...	...		...	...	...	...
383	Electrical machinery		...	...	...	...d/	d/	...	...	...	...		...	...	...	...
3831	Electrical industrial machinery		...	...	...	...		...	...	...	...		...	...	...	...
3832	Radio, television and communication equipm.		...	...	...	...		...	...	...	...		...	...	...	...
3833	Electrical appliances and housewares		...	...	...	...		...	...	...	...		...	...	...	...
3839	Other electrical apparatus and supplies		...	...	...	...		...	...	...	...		...	...	...	...
384	Transport equipment		...	...	...	...d/	d/	...	...	...	...		...	...	...	...
3841	Shipbuilding and repairing		...	...	...	...		...	...	...	...		...	...	...	...
3842	Railroad equipment		...	...	...	...		...	...	...	...		...	...	...	...
3843	Motor vehicles		...	...	...	...		...	...	...	...		...	...	...	...
3844	Motorcycles and bicycles		...	...	...	...		...	...	...	...		...	...	...	...
3845	Aircraft		...	...	...	...		...	...	...	...		...	...	...	...
3849	Other transport equipment		...	...	...	...		...	...	...	...		...	...	...	...
385	Professional and scientific equipment		...	...	...	...d/	d/	...	...	...	...		...	...	...	...
3851	Prof. and scientific equipment n.e.c.		...	...	...	...		...	...	...	...		...	...	...	...
3852	Photographic and optical goods		...	...	...	...		...	...	...	...		...	...	...	...
3853	Watches and clocks		...	...	...	...		...	...	...	...		...	...	...	...
390	Other manufacturing industries		...	...	...	24		551	605	611	608		...	...	...	...
3901	Jewellery and related articles		...	...	...	...		...	...	...	...		...	...	...	...
3902	Musical instruments		...	...	...	...		...	...	...	...		...	...	...	...
3903	Sporting and athletic goods		...	...	...	...		...	...	...	...		...	...	...	...
3909	Manufacturing industries, n.e.c.		...	...	...	...		...	...	...	...		...	...	...	...
3	Total manufacturing		...	...	...	813		64916	62573	61915	60478		6270799	8285711	9945923	11628810

a/ 323 includes 324.
b/ 353 includes 354.
c/ 361 includes 362.
d/ 371 includes 372, 381, 382, 383, 384 and 385.

Jamaica

ISIC Revision 2	Output					Value added in producers' prices					Gross fixed capital formation		
		(thousand DOLLARS)					(thousand DOLLARS)					(thousand DOLLARS)	
ISIC Industry	Note	1993	1994	1995	1996	Note	1993	1994	1995	1996	Note	1995	1996
311/2 Food products		...	...	...	...		4671639	6078567	7048956	8632538		...	...
313 Beverages		...	...	...	...		1970421	2626065	3194262	3908869		...	...
314 Tobacco		...	...	...	...		1573870	2510832	2964308	3610971		...	...
321 Textiles		...	...	...	...	a/	967778	1563045	1894351	2120605		...	...
322 Wearing apparel, except footwear		...	...	...	...	a/	...	...	...	...		...	...
323 Leather and fur products		...	...	...	...		41494	41886	54627	63376		...	...
324 Footwear, except rubber or plastic		...	...	...	...		91259	121944	141173	148573		...	...
331 Wood products, except furniture		...	...	...	...		37023	53241	54016	58124		...	...
332 Furniture and fixtures, excl. metal		...	...	...	...		385601	641648	739397	819331		...	...
341 Paper and products		...	...	...	...	b/	749724	917716	1090332	1337171		...	...
342 Printing and publishing		...	...	...	...	b/	...	...	...	...		...	...
351 Industrial chemicals		...	...	...	...	c/	2127256	2698667	2861110	3224963		...	...
352 Other chemicals		...	...	...	...	c/	...	...	...	...		...	...
353 Petroleum refineries		...	...	...	...		1979858	2405326	2739825	3156134		...	...
354 Misc. petroleum and coal products		...	...	...	...	c/	...	...	...	...		...	...
355 Rubber products		...	...	...	...	c/	...	...	...	...		...	...
356 Plastic products		...	...	...	...	c/	...	...	...	...		...	...
361 Pottery, china, earthenware		...	...	...	...	d/	956276	1360900	1703036	1997700		...	...
362 Glass and products		...	...	...	...	d/	...	...	...	...		...	...
369 Other non-metallic mineral products		...	...	...	...	d/	...	...	...	...		...	...
371 Iron and steel		...	...	...	...	e/	2509610	3241680	4322589	4843468		...	...
372 Non-ferrous metals		...	...	...	...	e/	...	...	...	...		...	...
381 Fabricated metal products		...	...	...	...	e/	...	...	...	...		...	...
382 Non-electrical machinery		...	...	...	...	e/	...	...	...	...		...	...
383 Electrical machinery		...	...	...	...	e/	...	...	...	...		...	...
384 Transport equipment		...	...	...	...	e/	...	...	...	...		...	...
385 Professional and scientific equipment		...	...	...	...	e/	...	...	...	...		...	...
390 Other manufacturing industries		...	...	...	...		41672	51155	62629	79319		...	...
3 Total manufacturing		...	...	...	...		18103480	24312670	28870610	34001140		...	...

a/ 321 includes 322.
b/ 341 includes 342.
c/ 351 includes 352, 354, 355 and 356.
d/ 361 includes 362 and 369.
e/ 371 includes 372, 381, 382, 383, 384 and 385.

JAPAN

Supplier of information:
Ministry of International Trade and Industry (MITI), Tokyo.
Industrial statistics for the OECD countries are compiled by the OECD secretariat, which supplies them to UNIDO.

Basic source of data:
Annual census of manufactures.

Major deviations from ISIC (Revision 3):
All data have been converted from the Japanese Standard Industrial Classification to ISIC (Rev. 3).

Reference period (if not calendar year):

Scope:
All establishments classified under manufacturing except those belonging to the government and public service corporations. Surveys cover all such establishments only in years where the last digit is 0, 3, 5 or 8. In all other years, the survey is limited to those establishments with four or more employees. Investment figures cover establishments with 30 or more persons engaged.

Method of enumeration:
Not reported.

Adjusted for non-response:
Not reported.

Concepts and definitions of variables:
Persons engaged refers to the number at the end of the year, full- or part-time. Persons engaged comprises employees (including apprentices and temporary workers, meeting minimum time requirements), working proprietors and unpaid family workers. Temporary and daily workers are excluded, though their remuneration is included in wages and salaries.
Wages and salaries relates to total cash payments, including basic wages, bonuses and other premiums, allowances and employees' retirement and termination allowances.
Output represents the value of shipments of finished goods, adjusted for changes in stocks of finished goods and work in progress. Receipts for contract and repair and maintenance work are included. The value of goods shipped in the same condition as received is excluded.
Value added is output less the cost of materials and fuels consumed, electricity purchases, contract work and indirect taxes, depreciation, and purchases of non-industrial services. Receipts for non-industrial services performed for others are excluded. Input estimates are made on a received basis, not allowing for changes in stock levels.
Gross fixed capital formation is defined as the value of purchases of fixed assets, including own account construction, less the value of sales. Fixed assets covered are those with a productive life of more than one year and include repairs to existing assets, new assets whether not yet in use, unused, or previously used abroad, and used assets. Valuation is at full cost incurred, including delivered price, cost of installation and fees and taxes. For own-produced assets, the cost of work put in progress covers labour costs, materials and supplies and includes an allocation for overheads. The amount realized is taken for sales of used assets.

Related national publications:

Japan

ISIC Revision 3	Number of establishments					Number of persons engaged					Wages and salaries paid to employees				
		(numbers)					(thousands)					(billion YEN)			
ISIC Industry	Note	1992	1993	1994	1995	Note	1992	1993	1994	1995	Note	1992	1993	1994	1995
151 Processed meat,fish,fruit,vegetables,fats		...	...	13908	13949		...	...	340	342		...	...	928	941
1511 Processing/preserving of meat		...	...	1150	1142		...	...	61	62		...	...	205	205
1512 Processing/preserving of fish		...	...	9990	10002		...	...	212	212		...	...	533	542
1513 Processing/preserving of fruit & vegetables		...	...	2574	2603		...	...	62	63		...	...	160	163
1514 Vegetable and animal oils and fats		...	...	194	202		...	...	6	6		...	...	30	30
1520 Dairy products		...	...	797	800		...	...	45	45		...	...	195	201
153 Grain mill products; starches; animal feeds		...	...	1407	1399		...	...	31	30		...	...	150	150
1531 Grain mill products		...	...	942	952		...	...	18	18		...	...	82	83
1532 Starches and starch products		...	...	140	134		...	...	4	4		...	...	22	22
1533 Prepared animal feeds		...	...	325	313		...	...	9	9		...	...	47	45
154 Other food products		...	...	26726	27687		...	...	721	743		...	...	2128	2204
1541 Bakery products		...	...	7053	7231		...	...	233	237		...	...	711	736
1542 Sugar		...	...	117	116		...	...	7	7		...	...	38	38
1543 Cocoa, chocolate and sugar confectionery		...	...	1194	1222		...	...	42	42		...	...	149	147
1544 Macaroni, noodles & similar products		...	...	4196	4325		...	...	63	65		...	...	176	183
1549 Other food products n.e.c.		...	...	14166	14793		...	...	375	392		...	...	1055	1100
155 Beverages		...	...	3387	3410		...	...	89	89		...	...	397	405
1551 Distilling, rectifying & blending of spirits		...	...	345	355		...	...	11	11		...	...	51	52
1552 Wines		...	...	1850	1851		...	...	37	36		...	...	137	139
1553 Malt liquors and malt		...	...	417	413		...	...	15	15		...	...	85	83
1554 Soft drinks; mineral waters		...	...	775	791		...	...	26	27		...	...	123	132
1600 Tobacco products		...	...	26	26		...	...	8	8		...	...	55	58
171 Spinning, weaving and finishing of textiles		...	...	12326	11735		...	...	218	200		...	...	760	712
1711 Textile fibre preparation; textile weaving		...	...	8552	8105		...	...	134	122		...	...	415	386
1712 Finishing of textiles		...	...	3774	3630		...	...	84	78		...	...	345	326
172 Other textiles		...	...	10055	10031		...	...	139	137		...	...	426	428
1721 Made-up textile articles, except apparel		...	...	6143	6207		...	...	78	77		...	...	215	216
1722 Carpets and rugs		...	...	483	456		...	...	9	9		...	...	33	32
1723 Cordage, rope, twine and netting		...	...	716	714		...	...	10	10		...	...	31	32
1729 Other textiles n.e.c.		...	...	2713	2654		...	...	41	41		...	...	146	148
1730 Knitted and crocheted fabrics and articles		...	...	8898	8684		...	...	161	154		...	...	381	370
1810 Wearing apparel, except fur apparel		...	...	20166	19205		...	...	406	373		...	...	854	792
1820 Dressing & dyeing of fur; processing of fur		...	...	76	78		...	...	1	1		...	...	3	3
191 Tanning, dressing and processing of leather		...	...	2985	2851		...	...	36	34		...	...	116	110
1911 Tanning and dressing of leather		...	...	609	587		...	...	11	11		...	...	49	48
1912 Luggage, handbags, etc.; saddlery & harness		...	...	2376	2264		...	...	25	23		...	...	67	62
1920 Footwear		...	...	2427	2949		...	...	47	52		...	...	142	155
2010 Sawmilling and planing of wood		...	...	9887	9628		...	...	108	104		...	...	347	340
202 Products of wood, cork, straw, etc.		...	...	14083	14216		...	...	167	167		...	...	565	568
2021 Veneer sheets, plywood, particle board, etc.		...	...	1362	1379		...	...	40	39		...	...	162	155
2022 Builders' carpentry and joinery		...	...	7341	7299		...	...	73	75		...	...	251	262
2023 Wooden containers		...	...	1330	1323		...	...	17	16		...	...	55	53
2029 Other wood products; articles of cork/straw		...	...	4050	4215		...	...	37	37		...	...	97	98
210 Paper and paper products		...	...	10392	10538		...	...	269	268		...	...	1166	1175
2101 Pulp, paper and paperboard		...	...	1099	1095		...	...	80	79		...	...	438	439
2102 Corrugated paper and paperboard		...	...	6336	6413		...	...	125	125		...	...	480	485
2109 Other articles of paper and paperboard		...	...	2957	3030		...	...	65	64		...	...	249	251
221 Publishing		...	...	2307	2308		...	...	115	114		...	...	948	964
2211 Publishing of books and other publications	a/b/	...	...	1456	1446	a/b/	...	...	46	46	a/b/	...	...	336	352
2212 Publishing of newspapers, journals, etc.	a/	...	...	851	862	a/	...	...	68	69	a/	...	...	612	611
2213 Publishing of recorded media	a/	...	...	...	...	a/	...	...	...	...	a/	...	...	...	...
2219 Other publishing	b/	...	...	...	...	b/	...	...	...	...	b/	...	...	...	...

ISIC															
222 Printing and related service activities		...	...	24154	24837		...	...	421	427		...	...	1833	1869
2221 Printing		...	...	17584	18200		...	...	329	335		...	...	1434	1473
2222 Service activities related to printing		...	...	6570	6637		...	...	92	92		...	...	399	395
2230 Reproduction of recorded media	a/b/	...	...	75	90	a/b/	...	...	6	6	a/b/	...	...	29	29
2310 Coke oven products		...	...	801	813		...	...	10	10		...	...	54	54
2320 Refined petroleum products		...	...	268	274		...	...	24	23		...	...	183	181
2330 Processing of nuclear fuel		...	...	7	7		...	...	4	4		...	...	23	25
241 Basic chemicals		...	...	1217	1231		...	...	124	120		...	...	783	768
2411 Basic chemicals, except fertilizers		...	...	849	856		...	...	71	68		...	...	448	429
2412 Fertilizers and nitrogen compounds		...	...	180	180		...	...	6	6		...	...	33	33
2413 Plastics in primary forms; synthetic rubber		...	...	188	195		...	...	47	46		...	...	301	306
242 Other chemicals		...	...	3928	3979		...	...	249	248		...	...	1398	1412
2421 Pesticides and other agro-chemical products		...	...	94	96		...	...	7	6		...	...	41	39
2422 Paints, varnishes, printing ink and mastics		...	...	579	595		...	...	28	28		...	...	166	168
2423 Pharmaceuticals, medicinal chemicals, etc.		...	...	1083	1069		...	...	98	98		...	...	570	582
2424 Soap, cleaning & cosmetic preparations		...	...	817	826		...	...	47	46		...	...	219	219
2429 Other chemical products n.e.c.		...	...	1355	1393		...	...	69	69		...	...	402	404
2430 Man-made fibres		...	...	87	92		...	...	25	23		...	...	139	136
251 Rubber products		...	...	3339	3505		...	...	128	128		...	...	598	608
2511 Rubber tyres and tubes		...	...	148	145		...	...	29	27		...	...	178	179
2519 Other rubber products		...	...	3191	3360		...	...	99	101		...	...	420	429
2520 Plastic products		...	...	18832	19404		...	...	439	445		...	...	1739	1785
2610 Glass and glass products		...	...	1094	1104		...	...	56	55		...	...	282	273
269 Non-metallic mineral products n.e.c.		...	...	18105	18193		...	...	374	371		...	...	1571	1589
2691 Pottery, china and earthenware		...	...	3342	3270		...	...	61	62		...	...	216	237
2692 Refractory ceramic products		...	...	768	749		...	...	27	26		...	...	120	113
2693 Struct.non-refractory clay; ceramic products		...	...	934	902		...	...	14	13		...	...	47	48
2694 Cement, lime and plaster		...	...	223	222		...	...	13	11		...	...	79	67
2695 Articles of concrete, cement and plaster		...	...	7891	7892		...	...	175	173		...	...	744	752
2696 Cutting, shaping & finishing of stone		...	...	3038	3163		...	...	38	38		...	...	157	159
2699 Other non-metallic mineral products n.e.c.		...	...	1909	1995		...	...	47	47		...	...	208	213
2710 Basic iron and steel		...	...	3143	3156		...	...	231	218		...	...	1501	1436
2720 Basic precious and non-ferrous metals		...	...	1131	1155		...	...	67	69		...	...	380	383
273 Casting of metals		...	...	3384	3382		...	...	92	92		...	...	412	428
2731 Casting of iron and steel		...	...	1485	1460		...	...	50	51		...	...	236	251
2732 Casting of non-ferrous metals		...	...	1899	1922		...	...	42	41		...	...	176	177
281 Struct.metal products;tanks;steam generators		...	...	21681	22505		...	...	382	383		...	...	1798	1810
2811 Structural metal products		...	...	13741	14211		...	...	256	255		...	...	1150	1152
2812 Tanks, reservoirs and containers of metal		...	...	7773	8128		...	...	96	97		...	...	419	423
2813 Steam generators		...	...	167	166		...	...	31	31		...	...	229	235
289 Other metal products; metal working services		...	...	26769	27325		...	...	500	498		...	...	2142	2146
2891 Metal forging/pressing/stamping/roll-forming		...	...	5794	5988		...	...	115	117		...	...	490	502
2892 Treatment & coating of metals		...	...	7719	7866		...	...	122	122		...	...	517	520
2893 Cutlery, hand tools and general hardware		...	...	3583	3523		...	...	71	69		...	...	315	307
2899 Other fabricated metal products n.e.c.		...	...	9673	9948		...	...	191	191		...	...	820	818
291 General purpose machinery		...	...	15060	15801		...	...	456	455		...	...	2304	2322
2911 Engines & turbines(not for transport equip.)		...	...	807	893		...	...	40	36		...	...	237	205
2912 Pumps, compressors, taps and valves		...	...	1554	1622		...	...	56	57		...	...	286	290
2913 Bearings, gears, gearing & driving elements		...	...	1559	1624		...	...	72	76		...	...	357	392
2914 Ovens, furnaces and furnace burners		...	...	168	161		...	...	4	4		...	...	23	27
2915 Lifting and handling equipment		...	...	2453	2452		...	...	69	65		...	...	349	328
2919 Other general purpose machinery		...	...	8519	9049		...	...	215	217		...	...	1052	1080
292 Special purpose machinery		...	...	22705	23841		...	...	515	525		...	...	2559	2624
2921 Agricultural and forestry machinery		...	...	940	956		...	...	29	29		...	...	128	137
2922 Machine tools		...	...	6799	7268		...	...	134	139		...	...	651	681
2923 Machinery for metallurgy		...	...	151	167		...	...	5	3		...	...	27	17
2924 Machinery for mining & construction		...	...	1712	1760		...	...	59	57		...	...	329	306
2925 Food/beverage/tobacco processing machinery		...	...	1039	1083		...	...	18	18		...	...	87	92
2926 Machinery for textile, apparel and leather		...	...	1350	1325		...	...	38	34		...	...	175	162
2927 Weapons and ammunition		...	...	34	29		...	...	8	7		...	...	47	46
2929 Other special purpose machinery		...	...	10680	11253		...	...	225	235		...	...	1116	1182
2930 Domestic appliances n.e.c.		...	...	3336	3348		...	...	156	156		...	...	665	685

continued

Japan

ISIC Revision 3	Number of establishments					Number of persons engaged					Wages and salaries paid to employees				
		(numbers)					(thousands)					(billion YEN)			
ISIC Industry	Note	1992	1993	1994	1995	Note	1992	1993	1994	1995	Note	1992	1993	1994	1995
3000 Office, accounting and computing machinery		...	...	3124	3075		...	...	225	220		...	...	1005	1022
3110 Electric motors, generators and transformers		...	...	2665	2708		...	...	108	108		...	...	475	493
3120 Electricity distribution & control apparatus		...	...	5162	5189		...	...	182	177		...	...	836	819
3130 Insulated wire and cable		...	...	598	625		...	...	46	46		...	...	239	248
3140 Accumulators, primary cells and batteries		...	...	197	212		...	...	23	22		...	...	114	113
3150 Lighting equipment and electric lamps		...	...	1374	1386		...	...	51	50		...	...	214	212
3190 Other electrical equipment n.e.c.		...	...	4477	4488		...	...	202	195		...	...	786	772
3210 Electronic valves, tubes, etc.		...	...	2592	2697		...	...	350	351		...	...	1586	1628
3220 TV/radio transmitters; line comm. apparatus		...	...	482	507		...	...	87	90		...	...	428	466
3230 TV and radio receivers and associated goods		...	...	8887	8628		...	...	434	429		...	...	1614	1682
331 Medical, measuring, testing appliances, etc.		...	...	4525	4608		...	...	156	157		...	...	745	759
3311 Medical, surgical and orthopaedic equipment		...	...	1550	1547		...	...	49	48		...	...	216	216
3312 Measuring/testing/navigating appliances,etc.		...	...	2662	2738		...	...	93	95		...	...	443	464
3313 Industrial process control equipment		...	...	313	323		...	...	15	13		...	...	85	78
3320 Optical instruments & photographic equipment		...	...	2018	1984		...	...	69	63		...	...	273	254
3330 Watches and clocks		...	...	508	472		...	...	30	27		...	...	126	109
3410 Motor vehicles	c/	...	...	49	51	c/	...	...	184	183	c/	...	...	1191	1223
3420 Automobile bodies, trailers & semi-trailers		...	...	262	272		...	...	58	56		...	...	327	329
3430 Parts/accessories for automobiles	c/	...	...	10156	10325	c/	...	...	546	531	c/	...	...	2595	2585
351 Building and repairing of ships and boats		...	...	1334	1365		...	...	57	57		...	...	322	311
3511 Building and repairing of ships		...	...	867	860		...	...	51	51		...	...	302	290
3512 Building/repairing of pleasure/sport. boats		...	...	467	505		...	...	6	6		...	...	21	21
3520 Railway/tramway locomotives & rolling stock		...	...	406	436		...	...	15	17		...	...	84	98
3530 Aircraft and spacecraft		...	...	217	221		...	...	27	26		...	...	157	159
359 Transport equipment n.e.c.		...	...	799	783		...	...	17	16		...	...	69	67
3591 Motorcycles	c/	...	...	...	...	c/	...	...	...	...	c/	...	...	...	...
3592 Bicycles and invalid carriages		...	...	559	521		...	...	13	12		...	...	52	51
3599 Other transport equipment n.e.c.		...	...	240	262		...	...	4	4		...	...	17	16
3610 Furniture		...	...	9537	9433		...	...	160	155		...	...	591	583
369 Manufacturing n.e.c.		...	...	13795	14011		...	...	219	215		...	...	825	806
3691 Jewellery and related articles		...	...	841	913		...	...	14	15		...	...	57	61
3692 Musical instruments		...	...	452	441		...	...	18	14		...	...	99	79
3693 Sports goods		...	...	992	998		...	...	22	23		...	...	81	86
3694 Games and toys		...	...	1764	1710		...	...	25	24		...	...	74	70
3699 Other manufacturing n.e.c.		...	...	9746	9949		...	...	140	138		...	...	514	510
3710 Recycling of metal waste and scrap		...	...	692d/	714d/		...	...	10d/	11d/		...	...	48d/	54d/
3720 Recycling of non-metal waste and scrap		...	...	...d/	...d/		...	...	...d/	...d/		...	...	...d/	...d/
D Total manufacturing		...	...	382825	387726		...	...	10416	10321		...	...	44603	44931

a/ 2213 is included in 2211, 2212 and 2230.
b/ 2219 is included in 2211 and 2230.
c/ 3591 is included in 3410 and 3430.
d/ 3710 includes 3720.

Japan

ISIC Revision 3		Output					Value added					Gross fixed capital formation	
		(billion YEN)					(billion YEN)					(billion YEN)	
ISIC Industry	Note	1992	1993	1994	1995	Note	1992	1993	1994	1995	Note	1994	1995
151 Processed meat,fish,fruit,vegetables,fats		...	...	7830	7883		...	...	2600	2671		167	...
1511 Processing/preserving of meat		...	...	2146	2191		...	...	588	610		50	...
1512 Processing/preserving of fish		...	...	4216	4207		...	...	1436	1471		70	...
1513 Processing/preserving of fruit & vegetables		...	...	942	962		...	...	398	411		30	...
1514 Vegetable and animal oils and fats		...	...	526	524		...	...	179	180		18	...
1520 Dairy products		...	...	2261	2299		...	...	780	807		95	...
153 Grain mill products; starches; animal feeds		...	...	2823	2610		...	...	633	647		74	...
1531 Grain mill products		...	...	1710	1573		...	...	319	345		35	...
1532 Starches and starch products		...	...	273	262		...	...	111	101		22	...
1533 Prepared animal feeds		...	...	840	775		...	...	203	201		17	...
154 Other food products		...	...	12472	12705		...	...	6006	6205		473	...
1541 Bakery products		...	...	3182	3201		...	...	1785	1829		126	...
1542 Sugar		...	...	420	403		...	...	143	136		13	...
1543 Cocoa, chocolate and sugar confectionery		...	...	1084	1066		...	...	578	581		46	...
1544 Macaroni, noodles & similar products		...	...	1003	1042		...	...	447	471		27	...
1549 Other food products n.e.c.		...	...	6783	6993		...	...	3054	3187		261	...
155 Beverages		...	...	6722	6702		...	...	2480	2529		229	...
1551 Distilling, rectifying & blending of spirits		...	...	1006	1013		...	...	482	508		20	...
1552 Wines		...	...	1017	1019		...	...	488	497		33	...
1553 Malt liquors and malt		...	...	2565	2500		...	...	533	543		129	...
1554 Soft drinks; mineral waters		...	...	2135	2169		...	...	976	980		47	...
1600 Tobacco products		...	...	2290	2252		...	...	377	404		30	...
171 Spinning, weaving and finishing of textiles		...	...	3298	3047		...	...	1550	1442		105	...
1711 Textile fibre preparation; textile weaving		...	...	2095	1955		...	...	879	831		58	...
1712 Finishing of textiles		...	...	1203	1091		...	...	671	611		47	...
172 Other textiles		...	...	2223	2199		...	...	972	981		42	...
1721 Made-up textile articles, except apparel		...	...	1120	1087		...	...	482	475		15	...
1722 Carpets and rugs		...	...	248	240		...	...	78	78		3	...
1723 Cordage, rope, twine and netting		...	...	134	129		...	...	63	62		2	...
1729 Other textiles n.e.c.		...	...	722	743		...	...	350	367		22	...
1730 Knitted and crocheted fabrics and articles		...	...	1789	1707		...	...	765	735		29	...
1810 Wearing apparel, except fur apparel		...	...	2704	2568		...	...	1471	1399		33	...
1820 Dressing & dyeing of fur; processing of fur		...	...	14	13		...	...	6	6		...	...
191 Tanning, dressing and processing of leather		...	...	615	601		...	...	242	242		14	...
1911 Tanning and dressing of leather		...	...	263	274		...	...	95	101		13	...
1912 Luggage, handbags, etc.; saddlery & harness		...	...	352	327		...	...	146	141		1	...
1920 Footwear		...	...	638	709		...	...	287	317		7	...
2010 Sawmilling and planing of wood		...	...	2094	1973		...	...	774	731		18	...
202 Products of wood, cork, straw, etc.		...	...	3005	3003		...	...	1225	1246		58	...
2021 Veneer sheets, plywood, particle board, etc.		...	...	1092	1024		...	...	377	379		30	...
2022 Builders' carpentry and joinery		...	...	1282	1361		...	...	550	576		21	...
2023 Wooden containers		...	...	228	213		...	...	99	96		2	...
2029 Other wood products; articles of cork/straw		...	...	403	404		...	...	199	196		4	...
210 Paper and paper products		...	...	8068	8468		...	...	3465	3629		381	...
2101 Pulp, paper and paperboard		...	...	3803	4106		...	...	1647	1790		239	...
2102 Corrugated paper and paperboard		...	...	2825	2902		...	...	1171	1183		77	...
2109 Other articles of paper and paperboard		...	...	1441	1459		...	...	647	657		64	...
221 Publishing		...	...	4620	4825		...	...	2913	3032		151	...
2211 Publishing of books and other publications	a/b/	...	...	2165	2272	a/b/	...	...	1195	1280		42	...
2212 Publishing of newspapers, journals, etc.	a/	...	...	2455	2553	a/	...	...	1718	1752		108	...
2213 Publishing of recorded media	a/	...	...	...	...	a/	...	...	...	...		...	...
2219 Other publishing	b/	...	...	...	...	b/	...	...	...	...		...	...

continued

Japan

ISIC Revision 3	Output					Value added					Gross fixed capital formation		
		(billion YEN)					(billion YEN)					(billion YEN)	
ISIC Industry	Note	1992	1993	1994	1995	Note	1992	1993	1994	1995	Note	1994	1995
222 Printing and related service activities		...	...	7869	8232		...	...	3935	4094		244	...
2221 Printing		...	...	6815	7159		...	...	3219	3363		221	...
2222 Service activities related to printing		...	...	1054	1073		...	...	716	731		23	...
2230 Reproduction of recorded media	a/b/	...	...	225	266	a/b/	...	...	163	168		8	...
2310 Coke oven products		...	...	633	632		...	...	209	208		14	...
2320 Refined petroleum products		...	...	7153	6961		...	...	1767	1413		296	...
2330 Processing of nuclear fuel		...	...	82	95		...	...	54	70		64	...
241 Basic chemicals		...	...	8390	8995		...	...	4268	4597		605	...
2411 Basic chemicals, except fertilizers		...	...	4301	4993		...	...	2099	2581		306	...
2412 Fertilizers and nitrogen compounds		...	...	322	320		...	...	119	124		16	...
2413 Plastics in primary forms; synthetic rubber		...	...	3768	3682		...	...	2050	1892		283	...
242 Other chemicals		...	...	13143	13511		...	...	7838	8089		524	...
2421 Pesticides and other agro-chemical products		...	...	384	385		...	...	162	163		23	...
2422 Paints, varnishes, printing ink and mastics		...	...	1315	1324		...	...	530	535		40	...
2423 Pharmaceuticals, medicinal chemicals, etc.		...	...	5690	6005		...	...	3974	4202		213	...
2424 Soap, cleaning & cosmetic preparations		...	...	2585	2516		...	...	1600	1549		102	...
2429 Other chemical products n.e.c.		...	...	3168	3283		...	...	1573	1639		146	...
2430 Man-made fibres		...	...	880	884		...	...	448	440		83	...
251 Rubber products		...	...	2841	3002		...	...	1499	1530		137	...
2511 Rubber tyres and tubes		...	...	953	1003		...	...	549	542		58	...
2519 Other rubber products		...	...	1888	1999		...	...	950	988		79	...
2520 Plastic products		...	...	10263	10400		...	...	4553	4617		414	...
2610 Glass and glass products		...	...	1687	1593		...	...	1033	940		101	...
269 Non-metallic mineral products n.e.c.		...	...	8544	8533		...	...	4496	4495		341	...
2691 Pottery, china and earthenware		...	...	809	872		...	...	461	491		51	...
2692 Refractory ceramic products		...	...	537	539		...	...	290	300		20	...
2693 Struct.non-refractory clay; ceramic products		...	...	215	211		...	...	139	137		9	...
2694 Cement, lime and plaster		...	...	931	822		...	...	533	456		62	...
2695 Articles of concrete, cement and plaster		...	...	4266	4270		...	...	2044	2046		136	...
2696 Cutting, shaping & finishing of stone		...	...	753	723		...	...	466	455		14	...
2699 Other non-metallic mineral products n.e.c.		...	...	1033	1096		...	...	562	610		49	...
2710 Basic iron and steel		...	...	11693	12057		...	...	4684	4899		858	...
2720 Basic precious and non-ferrous metals		...	...	3176	3624		...	...	1030	1118		162	...
273 Casting of metals		...	...	1889	1996		...	...	980	1019		100	...
2731 Casting of iron and steel		...	...	1004	1080		...	...	525	561		70	...
2732 Casting of non-ferrous metals		...	...	885	916		...	...	455	459		30	...
281 Struct.metal products;tanks;steam generators		...	...	10052	10149		...	...	4680	4737		262	...
2811 Structural metal products		...	...	6790	6769		...	...	3049	3044		191	...
2812 Tanks, reservoirs and containers of metal		...	...	1576	1599		...	...	791	824		25	...
2813 Steam generators		...	...	1686	1780		...	...	839	868		46	...
289 Other metal products; metal working services		...	...	9591	9782		...	...	4817	4944		318	...
2891 Metal forging/pressing/stamping/roll-forming		...	...	2497	2563		...	...	1144	1162		111	...
2892 Treatment & coating of metals		...	...	1607	1660		...	...	992	1039		48	...
2893 Cutlery, hand tools and general hardware		...	...	1182	1197		...	...	667	700		32	...
2899 Other fabricated metal products n.e.c.		...	...	4305	4362		...	...	2013	2044		126	...
291 General purpose machinery		...	...	12056	12515		...	...	5387	5545		356	...
2911 Engines & turbines(not for transport equip.)		...	...	1406	1257		...	...	570	505		49	...
2912 Pumps, compressors, taps and valves		...	...	1658	1731		...	...	764	777		60	...
2913 Bearings, gears, gearing & driving elements		...	...	1600	1795		...	...	781	865		68	...
2914 Ovens, furnaces and furnace burners		...	...	154	188		...	...	85	97		3	...
2915 Lifting and handling equipment		...	...	2077	2000		...	...	790	768		51	...
2919 Other general purpose machinery		...	...	5161	5543		...	...	2397	2534		125	...

292 Special purpose machinery		...	...	12193	13828		...	...	5300	6005		308	...
2921 Agricultural and forestry machinery		...	...	704	746		...	...	325	335		18	...
2922 Machine tools		...	...	2348	2937		...	...	1103	1335		55	...
2923 Machinery for metallurgy		...	...	156	81		...	...	65	33		3	...
2924 Machinery for mining & construction		...	...	2361	2468		...	...	776	837		58	...
2925 Food/beverage/tobacco processing machinery		...	...	394	400		...	...	204	203		8	...
2926 Machinery for textile, apparel and leather		...	...	834	755		...	...	347	323		17	...
2927 Weapons and ammunition		...	...	405	419		...	...	158	198		16	...
2929 Other special purpose machinery		...	...	4990	6023		...	...	2323	2742		132	...
2930 Domestic appliances n.e.c.		...	...	4984	5354		...	...	2273	2394		186	...
3000 Office, accounting and computing machinery		...	...	10565	11010		...	...	3315	3059		404	...
3110 Electric motors, generators and transformers		...	...	2207	2369		...	...	887	966		48	...
3120 Electricity distribution & control apparatus		...	...	4316	4325		...	...	1893	1887		105	...
3130 Insulated wire and cable		...	...	1719	1848		...	...	498	593		72	...
3140 Accumulators, primary cells and batteries		...	...	750	730		...	...	370	349		55	...
3150 Lighting equipment and electric lamps		...	...	1327	1276		...	...	562	536		36	...
3190 Other electrical equipment n.e.c.		...	...	4708	4858		...	...	1953	2060		208	...
3210 Electronic valves, tubes, etc.		...	...	10533	11841		...	...	4531	5242		780	...
3220 TV/radio transmitters; line comm. apparatus		...	...	3576	4160		...	...	1312	1547		83	...
3230 TV and radio receivers and associated goods		...	...	10669	11209		...	...	3729	4079		379	...
331 Medical, measuring, testing appliances, etc.		...	...	3417	3710		...	...	1647	1808		92	...
3311 Medical, surgical and orthopaedic equipment		...	...	1070	1136		...	...	523	563		33	...
3312 Measuring/testing/navigating appliances,etc.		...	...	2078	2293		...	...	998	1100		46	...
3313 Industrial process control equipment		...	...	270	281		...	...	126	146		14	...
3320 Optical instruments & photographic equipment		...	...	1188	1091		...	...	500	453		37	...
3330 Watches and clocks		...	...	727	669		...	...	181	191		30	...
3410 Motor vehicles	c/	...	...	19283	19548	c/	...	...	4078	4869		458	...
3420 Automobile bodies, trailers & semi-trailers		...	...	2868	2824		...	...	682	693		90	...
3430 Parts/accessories for automobiles	c/	...	...	17355	17184	c/	...	...	6499	6487		808	...
351 Building and repairing of ships and boats		...	...	2162	2110		...	...	842	811		95	...
3511 Building and repairing of ships		...	...	2080	2030		...	...	812	778		94	...
3512 Building/repairing of pleasure/sport. boats		...	...	82	81		...	...	31	33		1	...
3520 Railway/tramway locomotives & rolling stock		...	...	366	428		...	...	164	195		10	...
3530 Aircraft and spacecraft		...	...	837	839		...	...	342	366		30	...
359 Transport equipment n.e.c.		...	...	463	441		...	...	229	215		13	...
3591 Motorcycles	c/	...	...	...	...	c/	...	...	...	...		...	...
3592 Bicycles and invalid carriages		...	...	368	361		...	...	191	178		12	...
3599 Other transport equipment n.e.c.		...	...	95	81		...	...	38	37		1	...
3610 Furniture		...	...	2919	2909		...	...	1312	1308		60	...
369 Manufacturing n.e.c.		...	...	4960	4931		...	...	2110	2048		133	...
3691 Jewellery and related articles		...	...	379	407		...	...	132	142		4	...
3692 Musical instruments		...	...	464	328		...	...	217	142		26	...
3693 Sports goods		...	...	395	431		...	...	213	235		14	...
3694 Games and toys		...	...	835	816		...	...	349	312		18	...
3699 Other manufacturing n.e.c.		...	...	2888	2949		...	...	1201	1217		71	...
3710 Recycling of metal waste and scrap		...	...	385d/	451d/		...	...	149d/	188d/		...	...
3720 Recycling of non-metal waste and scrap		...	...	...d/	...d/		...	...	...d/	...d/		...	...
D Total manufacturing		...	...	298112	306731		...	...	123750	128296		11316	...

a/ 2213 is included in 2211, 2212 and 2230.
b/ 2219 is included in 2211 and 2230.
c/ 3591 is included in 3410 and 3430.
d/ 3710 includes 3720.

Japan

ISIC Revision 3		Index numbers of industrial production											
		(1990=100)											
ISIC Industry	Note	1985	1986	1987	1988	1989	1990	1991	1992	1993	1994	1995	1996
15 Food and beverages		...	...	...	99	100	100	100	101	100	102	101	102
16 Tobacco products		...	...	...	97	98	100	101	105	104	103	102	99
17 Textiles		...	...	...	106	105	100	97	93	80	75	68	65
18 Wearing apparel, fur		...	...	...	103	103	100	99	95	87	84	79	75
19 Leather, leather products and footwear		...	...	...	97	100	100	99	96	89	85	79	77
20 Wood products (excl. furniture)		...	...	...	101	101	100	97	93	89	86	81	80
21 Paper and paper products		...	...	...	90	96	100	103	101	99	101	105	107
22 Printing and publishing		...	...	...	96	97	100	104	106	111	113	115	117
23 Coke,refined petroleum products,nuclear fuel		...	...	...	90	94	100	105	108	110	114	116	116
24 Chemicals and chemical products		...	...	...	91	96	100	102	102	100	104	110	111
25 Rubber and plastics products		...	...	...	92	96	100	101	97	93	93	95	97
26 Non-metallic mineral products		...	...	...	93	97	100	100	94	91	92	92	93
27 Basic metals		...	...	...	94	97	100	102	93	91	91	94	93
28 Fabricated metal products		...	...	...	93	97	100	101	97	93	95	95	96
29 Machinery and equipment n.e.c.		...	...	...	87	96	100	100	84	75	77	84	88
30 Office, accounting and computing machinery		...	...	...	...	...	...	...	...	...	...	...	...
31 Electrical machinery and apparatus		...	...	...	88	96	100	106	95	90	94	103	113
32 Radio,television and communication equipment		...	...	...	87	94	100	107	96	100	107	119	123
33 Medical, precision and optical instruments		...	...	...	90	92	100	104	95	83	77	76	80
34 Motor vehicles, trailers, semi-trailers		...	...	...	87	94	100	101	98	91	87	86	88
35 Other transport equipment		...	...	...	69	84	100	95	109	103	100	96	103
36 Furniture; manufacturing n.e.c.		...	...	...	86	91	100	94	90	85	75	70	70
37 Recycling		...	...	...	...	...	...	...	...	...	...	...	...
D Total manufacturing		80	80	83	91	96	100	102	96	91	92	95	97

JORDAN

Supplier of information:
Department of Statistics, Amman.

Basic source of data:
Annual survey of manufacturing establishments.

Major deviations from ISIC (Revision 3):
None reported.

Reference period (if not calendar year):

Scope:
All establishments.

Method of enumeration:
Sample survey of establishments.

Adjusted for non-response:
Yes.

Concepts and definitions of variables:
Number of persons engaged is as of 30 June of the reference year.
Output is gross output and includes gross revenues from goods shipped in the same condition as received.
Value added is total value added.

Related national publications:
Industry Survey (annual); Statistical Yearbook, both published by the Department of Statistics, Amman.

Jordan

ISIC Revision 3 ISIC Industry	Note	Number of establishments (numbers) 1992	1993	1994	1995	Note	Number of persons engaged (numbers) 1992	1993	1994	1995	Note	Wages and salaries paid to employees (thousand DINARS) 1992	1993	1994	1995
151 Processed meat,fish,fruit,vegetables,fats		...	...	129	132		...	...	3150	2819		...	...	4913	5228
1511 Processing/preserving of meat		...	...	21	23		...	...	978	822		...	...	1352	1370
1512 Processing/preserving of fish		...	...	-	-		...	...	-	-		...	...	-	-
1513 Processing/preserving of fruit & vegetables		...	...	11	11		...	...	662	537		...	...	1241	1090
1514 Vegetable and animal oils and fats		...	...	97	98		...	...	1510	1460		...	...	2320	2768
1520 Dairy products		...	...	236	274		...	...	1459	2349		...	...	2242	2862
153 Grain mill products; starches; animal feeds		...	...	118	124		...	...	899	933		...	...	1627	1949
1531 Grain mill products		...	...	93	95		...	...	710	740		...	...	1231	1474
1532 Starches and starch products		...	...	-	-		...	...	-	-		...	...	-	-
1533 Prepared animal feeds		...	...	25	29		...	...	189	193		...	...	396	475
154 Other food products		...	...	1267	1372		...	...	9755	10361		...	...	11273	12492
1541 Bakery products		...	...	1099	1188		...	...	7582	8482		...	...	8360	9648
1542 Sugar		...	...	-	-		...	...	-	-		...	...	-	-
1543 Cocoa, chocolate and sugar confectionery		...	...	44	50		...	...	600	561		...	...	666	590
1544 Macaroni, noodles & similar products		...	...	-	-		...	...	-	-		...	...	-	-
1549 Other food products n.e.c.		...	...	124	134		...	...	1573	1318		...	...	2247	2254
155 Beverages		...	...	28	37		...	...	2044	2045		...	...	3330	4380
1551 Distilling, rectifying & blending of spirits		...	...	3	3		...	...	165	166		...	...	346	349
1552 Wines		...	...	-	-		...	...	-	-		...	...	-	-
1553 Malt liquors and malt		...	...	3	3		...	...	121	111		...	...	339	371
1554 Soft drinks; mineral waters		...	...	22	31		...	...	1758	1768		...	...	2645	3660
1600 Tobacco products		...	...	6	6		...	...	1224	1264		...	...	3890	4125
171 Spinning, weaving and finishing of textiles		...	...	20	21		...	...	1038	1369		...	...	2274	2787
1711 Textile fibre preparation; textile weaving		...	...	20	21		...	...	1038	1369		...	...	2274	2787
1712 Finishing of textiles		...	...	-	-		...	...	-	-		...	...	-	-
172 Other textiles		...	...	206	233		...	...	1272	1310		...	...	1579	1576
1721 Made-up textile articles, except apparel		...	...	170	189		...	...	593	712		...	...	367	471
1722 Carpets and rugs		...	...	27	35		...	...	642	561		...	...	1180	1058
1723 Cordage, rope, twine and netting		...	...	-	-		...	...	-	-		...	...	-	-
1729 Other textiles n.e.c.		...	...	9	9		...	...	37	37		...	...	32	47
1730 Knitted and crocheted fabrics and articles		...	...	83	94		...	...	981	1033		...	...	978	982
1810 Wearing apparel, except fur apparel		...	...	1306	1485		...	...	7122	7209		...	...	6151	6903
1820 Dressing & dyeing of fur; processing of fur		...	...	-	-		...	...	-	-		...	...	-	-
191 Tanning, dressing and processing of leather		...	...	33	34		...	...	493	508		...	...	926	1028
1911 Tanning and dressing of leather		...	...	3	4		...	...	300	348		...	...	756	878
1912 Luggage, handbags, etc.; saddlery & harness		...	...	30	30		...	...	193	160		...	...	170	150
1920 Footwear		...	...	206	215		...	...	1558	1168		...	...	1976	1409
2010 Sawmilling and planing of wood		...	...	12	13		...	...	58	113		...	...	95	216
202 Products of wood, cork, straw, etc.		...	...	1033	1227		...	...	2784	3310		...	...	1863	2391
2021 Veneer sheets, plywood, particle board, etc.		...	...	4	3		...	...	24	18		...	...	22	18
2022 Builders' carpentry and joinery		...	...	874	1059		...	...	2261	2686		...	...	1487	1838
2023 Wooden containers		...	...	25	21		...	...	179	167		...	...	152	166
2029 Other wood products; articles of cork/straw		...	...	130	144		...	...	320	439		...	...	202	369
210 Paper and paper products		...	...	64	66		...	...	3194	2998		...	...	6494	6787
2101 Pulp, paper and paperboard		...	...	13	11		...	...	662	446		...	...	1602	1041
2102 Corrugated paper and paperboard		...	...	29	35		...	...	862	945		...	...	2013	2530
2109 Other articles of paper and paperboard		...	...	22	20		...	...	1670	1607		...	...	2879	3216
221 Publishing		...	...	4	4		...	...	1017	867		...	...	3230	4020
2211 Publishing of books and other publications		...	...	-	-		...	...	-	-		...	...	-	-
2212 Publishing of newspapers, journals, etc.		...	...	4	4		...	...	1017	867		...	...	3230	4020
2213 Publishing of recorded media		...	...	-	-		...	...	-	-		...	...	-	-
2219 Other publishing		...	...	-	-		...	...	-	-		...	...	-	-

222 Printing and related service activities	...	...	198	199	...	...	2038	2133	...	...	3040	3775
2221 Printing	...	...	193	195	...	...	2024	2118	...	...	3034	3760
2222 Service activities related to printing	...	...	5	4	...	...	14	15	...	...	6	15
2230 Reproduction of recorded media	...	...	-	-	...	...	-	-	...	...	-	-
2310 Coke oven products	...	...	-	-	...	...	-	-	...	...	-	-
2320 Refined petroleum products	...	...	1	1	...	...	3947	3863	...	...	13818	15053
2330 Processing of nuclear fuel	...	...	-	-	...	...	-	-	...	...	-	-
241 Basic chemicals	...	...	46	51	...	...	2599	2617	...	...	9048	9536
2411 Basic chemicals, except fertilizers	...	...	13	14	...	...	478	544	...	...	1097	1423
2412 Fertilizers and nitrogen compounds	...	...	5	5	...	...	1115	994	...	...	5752	6214
2413 Plastics in primary forms; synthetic rubber	...	...	28	32	...	...	1006	1079	...	...	2199	1899
242 Other chemicals	...	...	138	147	...	...	5951	5889	...	...	15701	18212
2421 Pesticides and other agro-chemical products	...	...	5	5	...	...	84	78	...	...	132	321
2422 Paints, varnishes, printing ink and mastics	...	...	46	48	...	...	867	848	...	...	1527	1622
2423 Pharmaceuticals, medicinal chemicals, etc.	...	...	16	16	...	...	3066	2809	...	...	10221	10136
2424 Soap, cleaning & cosmetic preparations	...	...	57	63	...	...	1814	1925	...	...	3621	3927
2429 Other chemical products n.e.c.	...	...	14	15	...	...	120	229	...	...	200	2206
2430 Man-made fibres	...	...	-	-	...	...	-	-	...	...	-	-
251 Rubber products	...	...	27	27	...	...	218	218	...	...	270	291
2511 Rubber tyres and tubes	...	...	6	8	...	...	69	117	...	...	104	218
2519 Other rubber products	...	...	21	19	...	...	149	101	...	...	166	73
2520 Plastic products	...	...	152	161	...	...	3860	4268	...	...	6275	7563
2610 Glass and glass products	...	...	42	24	...	...	291	221	...	...	372	304
269 Non-metallic mineral products n.e.c.	...	...	1906	2021	...	...	13135	13471	...	...	20087	25482
2691 Pottery, china and earthenware	...	...	4	4	...	...	70	71	...	...	84	119
2692 Refractory ceramic products	...	...	-	-	...	...	-	-	...	...	-	-
2693 Struct.non-refractory clay; ceramic products	...	...	7	9	...	...	860	839	...	...	849	1760
2694 Cement, lime and plaster	...	...	4	4	...	...	2921	3083	...	...	9640	12570
2695 Articles of concrete, cement and plaster	...	...	1364	1441	...	...	6113	6182	...	...	6120	6845
2696 Cutting, shaping & finishing of stone	...	...	505	526	...	...	2910	2891	...	...	2965	3382
2699 Other non-metallic mineral products n.e.c.	...	...	22	37	...	...	261	405	...	...	429	806
2710 Basic iron and steel	...	...	10	11	...	...	1249	1159	...	...	3293	3525
2720 Basic precious and non-ferrous metals	...	...	6	12	...	...	394	577	...	...	1248	1452
273 Casting of metals	...	...	25	10	...	...	401	126	...	...	648	201
2731 Casting of iron and steel	...	...	22	7	...	...	222	126a/	...	...	223	201a/
2732 Casting of non-ferrous metals	...	...	3	3	...	...	179	...a/	...	...	425	...a/
281 Struct.metal products;tanks;steam generators	...	...	2002	2278	...	...	6316	7664	...	...	5206	7168
2811 Structural metal products	...	...	1909	2174	...	...	5973	6657	...	...	4848	5681
2812 Tanks, reservoirs and containers of metal	...	...	93	104	...	...	343	1007	...	...	358	1487
2813 Steam generators	...	...	-	-	...	...	-	-	...	...	-	-
289 Other metal products; metal working services	...	...	676	691	...	...	3363	3140	...	...	3564	3846
2891 Metal forging/pressing/stamping/roll-forming	...	...	-	-	...	...	-	-	...	...	-	-
2892 Treatment & coating of metals	...	...	9	10	...	...	47	73	...	...	41	156
2893 Cutlery, hand tools and general hardware	...	...	40	38	...	...	193	197	...	...	183	249
2899 Other fabricated metal products n.e.c.	...	...	627	643	...	...	3123	2870	...	...	3340	3441
291 General purpose machinery	...	...	12	16	...	...	701	855	...	...	1584	1955
2911 Engines & turbines(not for transport equip.)	...	...	-	-	...	...	-	-	...	...	-	-
2912 Pumps, compressors, taps and valves	...	...	-	-	...	...	-	-	...	...	-	-
2913 Bearings, gears, gearing & driving elements	...	...	-	-	...	...	-	-	...	...	-	-
2914 Ovens, furnaces and furnace burners	...	...	-	-	...	...	-	-	...	...	-	-
2915 Lifting and handling equipment	...	...	3	5	...	...	237	305	...	...	630	723
2919 Other general purpose machinery	...	...	9	11	...	...	464	550	...	...	954	1232
292 Special purpose machinery	...	...	69	75	...	...	406	399	...	...	414	580
2921 Agricultural and forestry machinery	...	...	26	27	...	...	70	62	...	...	46	42
2922 Machine tools	...	...	9	12	...	...	53	54	...	...	56	72
2923 Machinery for metallurgy	...	...	-	-	...	...	-	-	...	...	-	-
2924 Machinery for mining & construction	...	...	26	26	...	...	182	191	...	...	148	292
2925 Food/beverage/tobacco processing machinery	...	...	5	7	...	...	54	50	...	...	84	66
2926 Machinery for textile, apparel and leather	...	...	-	-	...	...	-	-	...	...	-	-
2927 Weapons and ammunition	...	...	-	-	...	...	-	-	...	...	-	-
2929 Other special purpose machinery	...	...	3	3	...	...	47	42	...	...	80	108
2930 Domestic appliances n.e.c.	...	...	75	79	...	...	1537	1346	...	...	2453	2527

continued

Jordan

ISIC Revision 3	Number of establishments					Number of persons engaged					Wages and salaries paid to employees				
		(numbers)					(numbers)					(thousand DINARS)			
ISIC Industry	Note	1992	1993	1994	1995	Note	1992	1993	1994	1995	Note	1992	1993	1994	1995
3000 Office, accounting and computing machinery		...	...	-	-		...	...	-	-		...	...	-	-
3110 Electric motors, generators and transformers		...	...	2	2		...	...	174b/	111b/		...	...	344b/	174b/
3120 Electricity distribution & control apparatus		...	...	8	6		...	...	...b/	...b/		...	...	...b/	...b/
3130 Insulated wire and cable		...	...	4	4		...	...	397	489		...	...	878	1240
3140 Accumulators, primary cells and batteries		...	...	2	2		...	...	391c/	318c/		...	...	692c/	551c/
3150 Lighting equipment and electric lamps		...	...	11	13		...	...	...c/	...c/		...	...	...c/	...c/
3190 Other electrical equipment n.e.c.		...	...	-	-		...	...	-	-		...	...	-	-
3210 Electronic valves, tubes, etc.		...	...	-	-		...	...	-	-		...	...	-	-
3220 TV/radio transmitters; line comm. apparatus		...	...	-	-		...	...	-	-		...	...	-	-
3230 TV and radio receivers and associated goods		...	...	3	3		...	...	435	411		...	...	838	1319
331 Medical, measuring, testing appliances, etc.		...	...	50	64		...	...	328d/	493d/		...	...	261d/	599d/
3311 Medical, surgical and orthopaedic equipment		...	...	50	64		...	...	328e/	493e/		...	...	261e/	599e/
3312 Measuring/testing/navigating appliances,etc.		...	...	-	-		...	...	-	-		...	...	-	-
3313 Industrial process control equipment		...	...	-	-		...	...	-	-		...	...	-	-
3320 Optical instruments & photographic equipment		...	...	2	2		...	...	...d/e/	...d/e/		...	...	...d/e/	...d/e/
3330 Watches and clocks		...	...	-	-		...	...	-	-		...	...	-	-
3410 Motor vehicles		...	...	-	-		...	...	-	-		...	...	-	-
3420 Automobile bodies, trailers & semi-trailers		...	...	22	22		...	...	792	834		...	...	1742	1794
3430 Parts/accessories for automobiles		...	...	10	9		...	...	311	273		...	...	435	329
351 Building and repairing of ships and boats		...	...	3	4		...	...	22	20		...	...	27	22
3511 Building and repairing of ships		...	...	-	-		...	...	-	-		...	...	-	-
3512 Building/repairing of pleasure/sport. boats		...	...	3	4		...	...	22	20		...	...	27	22
3520 Railway/tramway locomotives & rolling stock		...	...	-	-		...	...	-	-		...	...	-	-
3530 Aircraft and spacecraft		...	...	-	-		...	...	-	-		...	...	-	-
359 Transport equipment n.e.c.		...	...	-	-		...	...	-	-		...	...	-	-
3591 Motorcycles		...	...	-	-		...	...	-	-		...	...	-	-
3592 Bicycles and invalid carriages		...	...	-	-		...	...	-	-		...	...	-	-
3599 Other transport equipment n.e.c.		...	...	-	-		...	...	-	-		...	...	-	-
3610 Furniture		...	...	2017	2283		...	...	7701	8585		...	...	7663	9159
369 Manufacturing n.e.c.		...	...	88	95		...	...	838	649		...	...	1020	908
3691 Jewellery and related articles		...	...	55	62		...	...	300	294		...	...	228	320
3692 Musical instruments		...	...	2	2		...	...	538f/	355f/		...	...	792f/	588f/
3693 Sports goods		...	...	-	-		...	...	-	-		...	...	-	-
3694 Games and toys		...	...	-	-		...	...	-	-		...	...	-	-
3699 Other manufacturing n.e.c.		...	...	31	31		...	...	...f/	...f/		...	...	...f/	...f/
3710 Recycling of metal waste and scrap		...	...	-	-		...	...	-	-		...	...	-	-
3720 Recycling of non-metal waste and scrap		...	...	-	-		...	...	-	-		...	...	-	-
D Total manufacturing		...	...	12358	13649		...	...	95843	99785		...	...	153762	176700

a/ 2731 includes 2732.
b/ 3110 includes 3120.
c/ 3140 includes 3150.
d/ 331 includes 3320.
e/ 3311 includes 3320.
f/ 3692 includes 3699.

Jordan

ISIC Revision 3	Output in producers' prices					Value added in producers' prices					Gross fixed capital formation		
		(thousand DINARS)					(thousand DINARS)					(thousand DINARS)	
ISIC Industry	Note	1992	1993	1994	1995	Note	1992	1993	1994	1995	Note	1994	1995
151 Processed meat,fish,fruit,vegetables,fats		...	...	133366	213158		...	...	25476	27615		1953	4580
1511 Processing/preserving of meat		...	...	20532	15313		...	...	5026	4645		775	412
1512 Processing/preserving of fish		...	...	-	-		...	...	-	-		-	-
1513 Processing/preserving of fruit & vegetables		...	...	10933	14260		...	...	3706	3644		-	-
1514 Vegetable and animal oils and fats		...	...	101901	183585		...	...	16744	19326		1178	4168
1520 Dairy products		...	...	35624	38465		...	...	9109	8830		147	210
153 Grain mill products; starches; animal feeds		...	...	53970	56759		...	...	8362	6006		138	344
1531 Grain mill products		...	...	40861	39593		...	...	6781	5076		90	221
1532 Starches and starch products		...	...	-	-		...	...	-	-		-	-
1533 Prepared animal feeds		...	...	13109	17166		...	...	1581	930		48	123
154 Other food products		...	...	105076	114051		...	...	35128	36365		1222	776
1541 Bakery products		...	...	64098	74108		...	...	21879	26657		670	292
1542 Sugar		...	...	-	-		...	...	-	-		-	-
1543 Cocoa, chocolate and sugar confectionery		...	...	8856	7316		...	...	3555	1690		-	-
1544 Macaroni, noodles & similar products		...	...	-	-		...	...	-	-		-	-
1549 Other food products n.e.c.		...	...	32122	32627		...	...	9694	8018		552	484
155 Beverages		...	...	77695	81760		...	...	36757	36211		26490	3823
1551 Distilling, rectifying & blending of spirits		...	...	3487	4205		...	...	1431	1922		-	-
1552 Wines		...	...	-	-		...	...	-	-		-	-
1553 Malt liquors and malt		...	...	7276	7130		...	...	5335	5117		10	1838
1554 Soft drinks; mineral waters		...	...	66932	70425		...	...	29991	29172		26480	1985
1600 Tobacco products		...	...	107400	117468		...	...	86025	94335		9409	3396
171 Spinning, weaving and finishing of textiles		...	...	22629	27216		...	...	10352	10843		117	1406
1711 Textile fibre preparation; textile weaving		...	...	22629	27216		...	...	10352	10843		117	1406
1712 Finishing of textiles		...	...	-	-		...	...	-	-		-	-
172 Other textiles		...	...	19884	20705		...	...	6027	7474		2238	56
1721 Made-up textile articles, except apparel		...	...	4547	3626		...	...	1588	1426		27	2
1722 Carpets and rugs		...	...	14984	16806		...	...	4312	5925		2211	54
1723 Cordage, rope, twine and netting		...	...	-	-		...	...	-	-		-	-
1729 Other textiles n.e.c.		...	...	353	273		...	...	127	123		-	-
1730 Knitted and crocheted fabrics and articles		...	...	8522	7141		...	...	2755	2303		76	45
1810 Wearing apparel, except fur apparel		...	...	42038	40314		...	...	17069	17565		104	354
1820 Dressing & dyeing of fur; processing of fur		...	...	-	-		...	...	-	-		-	-
191 Tanning, dressing and processing of leather		...	...	11452	17476		...	...	2761	2834		92	316
1911 Tanning and dressing of leather		...	...	10325	16668		...	...	2265	2491		108	316
1912 Luggage, handbags, etc.; saddlery & harness		...	...	1127	808		...	...	496	343		-16	-
1920 Footwear		...	...	17656	11115		...	...	6816	4705		170	42
2010 Sawmilling and planing of wood		...	...	1748	5534		...	...	1336	349		-	-
202 Products of wood, cork, straw, etc.		...	...	16412	16361		...	...	6729	6582		37	20
2021 Veneer sheets, plywood, particle board, etc.		...	...	130	74		...	...	59	35		-	-
2022 Builders' carpentry and joinery		...	...	12409	12575		...	...	5006	5108		37	20
2023 Wooden containers		...	...	2035	908		...	...	938	263		-	-
2029 Other wood products; articles of cork/straw		...	...	1838	2804		...	...	726	1176		-	-
210 Paper and paper products		...	...	81040	91143		...	...	23798	20256		1795	2002
2101 Pulp, paper and paperboard		...	...	27763	20865		...	...	8426	4150		495	1093
2102 Corrugated paper and paperboard		...	...	21104	32885		...	...	7951	8904		1112	514
2109 Other articles of paper and paperboard		...	...	32173	37393		...	...	7421	7202		188	395
221 Publishing		...	...	15064	19181		...	...	7040	12515		6278	558
2211 Publishing of books and other publications		...	...	-	-		...	...	-	-		-	-
2212 Publishing of newspapers, journals, etc.		...	...	15064	19181		...	...	7040	12515		6278	558
2213 Publishing of recorded media		...	...	-	-		...	...	-	-		-	-
2219 Other publishing		...	...	-	-		...	...	-	-		-	-

continued

Jordan

ISIC Revision 3		Output in producers' prices					Value added in producers' prices					Gross fixed capital formation		
		Note	(thousand DINARS)				Note	(thousand DINARS)				Note	(thousand DINARS)	
ISIC	Industry		1992	1993	1994	1995		1992	1993	1994	1995		1994	1995
222	Printing and related service activities		...	...	22097	29596		...	...	7282	9430		351	280
2221	Printing		...	...	22040	29523		...	...	7254	9394		351	280
2222	Service activities related to printing		...	...	57	73		...	...	28	36		-	-
2230	Reproduction of recorded media		...	...	-	-		...	...	-	-		-	-
2310	Coke oven products		...	...	-	-		...	...	-	-		-	-
2320	Refined petroleum products		...	...	380864	398554		...	...	30458	37988		2912	4941
2330	Processing of nuclear fuel		...	...	-	-		...	...	-	-		-	-
241	Basic chemicals		...	...	313426	365674		...	...	38246	52132		31804	13889
2411	Basic chemicals, except fertilizers		...	...	19072	22198		...	...	3856	4622		111	56
2412	Fertilizers and nitrogen compounds		...	...	264132	298712		...	...	23911	29079		30638	13763
2413	Plastics in primary forms; synthetic rubber		...	...	30222	44764		...	...	10479	18431		1055	70
242	Other chemicals		...	...	202669	200497		...	...	56044	53088		10170	4886
2421	Pesticides and other agro-chemical products		...	...	10996	2052		...	...	779	771		-	3
2422	Paints, varnishes, printing ink and mastics		...	...	28967	33798		...	...	6989	2885		438	350
2423	Pharmaceuticals, medicinal chemicals, etc.		...	...	102682	97052		...	...	36750	33676		7284	2625
2424	Soap, cleaning & cosmetic preparations		...	...	56969	58814		...	...	10824	14099		2447	766
2429	Other chemical products n.e.c.		...	...	3055	8781		...	...	702	1657		1	1142
2430	Man-made fibres		...	...	-	-		...	...	-	-		-	-
251	Rubber products		...	...	1842	2604		...	...	773	1315		-15	5
2511	Rubber tyres and tubes		...	...	999	2156		...	...	414	1092		-	5
2519	Other rubber products		...	...	843	448		...	...	359	223		-15	-
2520	Plastic products		...	...	68340	93526		...	...	25342	21677		2717	2229
2610	Glass and glass products		...	...	3465	2428		...	...	1067	699		10	10
269	Non-metallic mineral products n.e.c.		...	...	233571	231073		...	...	116969	110174		5107	3757
2691	Pottery, china and earthenware		...	...	456	525		...	...	174	235		-	-
2692	Refractory ceramic products		...	...	-	-		...	...	-	-		-	-
2693	Struct.non-refractory clay; ceramic products		...	...	14904	12997		...	...	7867	7089		-	-
2694	Cement, lime and plaster		...	...	134529	141797		...	...	75260	77488		3972	2537
2695	Articles of concrete, cement and plaster		...	...	49197	44243		...	...	17785	15395		462	108
2696	Cutting, shaping & finishing of stone		...	...	32363	23097		...	...	15028	8197		654	516
2699	Other non-metallic mineral products n.e.c.		...	...	2122	8414		...	...	855	1770		19	596
2710	Basic iron and steel		...	...	77165	79110		...	...	16317	20481		373	1766
2720	Basic precious and non-ferrous metals		...	...	18784	25198		...	...	9431	6213		63	-
273	Casting of metals		...	...	8278	950		...	...	3086	481		2727	58
2731	Casting of iron and steel		...	...	1365	950a/		...	...	660	481a/		7	58a/
2732	Casting of non-ferrous metals		...	...	6913	...a/		...	...	2426	...a/		2720	...a/
281	Struct.metal products;tanks;steam generators		...	...	48363	61685		...	...	18047	19874		341	615
2811	Structural metal products		...	...	45575	47180		...	...	17076	16588		217	141
2812	Tanks, reservoirs and containers of metal		...	...	2788	14505		...	...	971	3286		124	474
2813	Steam generators		...	...	-	-		...	...	-	-		-	-
289	Other metal products; metal working services		...	...	33203	35620		...	...	12013	11676		2387	19443
2891	Metal forging/pressing/stamping/roll-forming		...	...	-	-		...	...	-	-		-	-
2892	Treatment & coating of metals		...	...	280	583		...	...	129	314		-	7
2893	Cutlery, hand tools and general hardware		...	...	1661	1398		...	...	486	451		3	-
2899	Other fabricated metal products n.e.c.		...	...	31262	33639		...	...	11398	10911		2384	19436
291	General purpose machinery		...	...	12996	14388		...	...	4406	4257		6	269
2911	Engines & turbines(not for transport equip.)		...	...	-	-		...	...	-	-		-	-
2912	Pumps, compressors, taps and valves		...	...	-	-		...	...	-	-		-	-
2913	Bearings, gears, gearing & driving elements		...	...	-	-		...	...	-	-		-	-
2914	Ovens, furnaces and furnace burners		...	...	-	-		...	...	-	-		-	-
2915	Lifting and handling equipment		...	...	3005	4113		...	...	1139	1380		-	269
2919	Other general purpose machinery		...	...	9991	10275		...	...	3267	2877		6	-

292	Special purpose machinery	...	...	3240	4199	...	...	1340	1716		-	-
2921	Agricultural and forestry machinery	...	...	178	156	...	...	104	108		-	-
2922	Machine tools	...	...	500	568	...	...	178	252		-	-
2923	Machinery for metallurgy	...	...	-	-	...	...	-	-		-	-
2924	Machinery for mining & construction	...	...	1476	2576	...	...	518	950		-	-
2925	Food/beverage/tobacco processing machinery	...	...	561	389	...	...	224	144		-	-
2926	Machinery for textile, apparel and leather	...	...	-	-	...	...	-	-		-	-
2927	Weapons and ammunition	...	...	-	-	...	...	-	-		-	-
2929	Other special purpose machinery	...	...	525	510	...	...	316	262		-	-
2930	Domestic appliances n.e.c.	...	...	27684	30910	...	...	8408	7239		918	1098
3000	Office, accounting and computing machinery	...	...	-	-	...	...	-	-		-	-
3110	Electric motors, generators and transformers	...	...	2788b/	1160b/	...	...	1111b/	493b/		-	14b/
3120	Electricity distribution & control apparatus	...	...	...b/	...b/	...	...	...b/	...b/		-	...b/
3130	Insulated wire and cable	...	...	18440	25187	...	...	2747	5024		3599	2868
3140	Accumulators, primary cells and batteries	...	...	8443c/	5073c/	...	...	5148c/	1721c/	c/	7	11
3150	Lighting equipment and electric lamps	...	...	...c/	...c/	...	...	...c/	...c/	c/	...	...
3190	Other electrical equipment n.e.c.	...	...	-	-	...	...	-	-		-	-
3210	Electronic valves, tubes, etc.	...	...	-	-	...	...	-	-		-	-
3220	TV/radio transmitters; line comm. apparatus	...	...	-	-	...	...	-	-		-	-
3230	TV and radio receivers and associated goods	...	...	12465	25299	...	...	5217	6681		-	-
331	Medical, measuring, testing appliances, etc.	...	...	2009d/	3413d/	...	...	852d/	1489d/	d/	6	292
3311	Medical, surgical and orthopaedic equipment	...	...	2009e/	3413e/	...	...	852e/	1489e/	e/	6	292
3312	Measuring/testing/navigating appliances,etc.	...	...	-	-	...	...	-	-		-	-
3313	Industrial process control equipment	...	...	-	-	...	...	-	-		-	-
3320	Optical instruments & photographic equipment	...	...	...d/e/	...d/e/	...	...	...d/e/	...d/e/	d/e/	...	...
3330	Watches and clocks	...	...	-	-	...	...	-	-		-	-
3410	Motor vehicles	...	...	-	-	...	...	-	-		-	-
3420	Automobile bodies, trailers & semi-trailers	...	...	39215	27034	...	...	13852	7590		764	706
3430	Parts/accessories for automobiles	...	...	3803	2181	...	...	1899	604		-	15
351	Building and repairing of ships and boats	...	...	134	73	...	...	67	53		-	-
3511	Building and repairing of ships	...	...	-	-	...	...	-	-		-	-
3512	Building/repairing of pleasure/sport. boats	...	...	134	73	...	...	67	53		-	-
3520	Railway/tramway locomotives & rolling stock	...	...	-	-	...	...	-	-		-	-
3530	Aircraft and spacecraft	...	...	-	-	...	...	-	-		-	-
359	Transport equipment n.e.c.	...	...	-	-	...	...	-	-		-	-
3591	Motorcycles	...	...	-	-	...	...	-	-		-	-
3592	Bicycles and invalid carriages	...	...	-	-	...	...	-	-		-	-
3599	Other transport equipment n.e.c.	...	...	-	-	...	...	-	-		-	-
3610	Furniture	...	...	54486	59680	...	...	20358	20824		894	233
369	Manufacturing n.e.c.	...	...	11088	9973	...	...	3352	2819		23	206
3691	Jewellery and related articles	...	...	3249	1090	...	...	832	703		20	172
3692	Musical instruments	...	...	7839f/	8883f/	...	...	2520f/	2116f/	f/	3	34
3693	Sports goods	...	...	-	-	...	...	-	-		-	-
3694	Games and toys	...	...	-	-	...	...	-	-		-	-
3699	Other manufacturing n.e.c.	...	...	...f/	...f/	...	...	...f/	...f/	f/	...	...
3710	Recycling of metal waste and scrap	...	...	-	-	...	...	-	-		-	-
3720	Recycling of non-metal waste and scrap	...	...	-	-	...	...	-	-		-	-
D	Total manufacturing	...	...	2358434	2612932	...	...	689372	700526		115430	75519

a/ 2731 includes 2732.
b/ 3110 includes 3120.
c/ 3140 includes 3150.
d/ 331 includes 3320.
e/ 3311 includes 3320.
f/ 3692 includes 3699.

Jordan

ISIC Revision 3		Note	Index numbers of industrial production (1990=100)											
ISIC	Industry		1985	1986	1987	1988	1989	1990	1991	1992	1993	1994	1995	1996
15	Food and beverages		111	81	86	97	95	100	93	136	137	134	158	130
16	Tobacco products		...	...	...	...	92	100	112	98	109	132	116	149
17	Textiles		105	93	105	110	94	100	87	74	82	81	92	122
18	Wearing apparel, fur		105	93	105	110	94	100	87	74	82	81	61	54
19	Leather, leather products and footwear		105	93	105	110	94	100	111	131	127	113	101	88
20	Wood products (excl. furniture)		...	...	...	...	...	...	...	...	...	...	...	...
21	Paper and paper products		73	62	89	76	96	100	93	91	110	117	117	115
22	Printing and publishing		...	...	...	...	...	...	...	...	...	...	...	...
23	Coke,refined petroleum products,nuclear fuel		...	...	...	...	...	...	...	...	...	...	...	...
24	Chemicals and chemical products		68	80	83	71	98	100	90	81	71	66	102	81
25	Rubber and plastics products		87	111	105	119	90	100	110	129	138	149	221	96
26	Non-metallic mineral products		66	58	77	58	63	100	99	99	111	110	108	109
27	Basic metals		113	119	125	111	101	100	112	133	105	89	85	92
28	Fabricated metal products		...	...	...	...	...	...	...	...	...	...	...	...
29	Machinery and equipment n.e.c.		...	...	...	...	...	...	...	...	...	...	...	...
30	Office, accounting and computing machinery		...	...	...	...	...	...	...	...	...	...	...	...
31	Electrical machinery and apparatus		...	...	...	...	...	...	...	...	...	...	...	...
32	Radio,television and communication equipment		...	...	...	...	...	...	...	...	...	...	...	...
33	Medical, precision and optical instruments		...	...	...	...	...	...	...	...	...	...	...	...
34	Motor vehicles, trailers, semi-trailers		...	...	...	...	...	...	...	...	...	...	...	...
35	Other transport equipment		...	...	...	...	...	...	...	...	...	...	...	...
36	Furniture; manufacturing n.e.c.		...	...	...	...	...	...	...	...	...	...	...	...
37	Recycling		...	...	...	...	...	...	...	...	...	...	...	...
D	Total manufacturing		89	92	103	93	95	100	95	111	121	127	137	130

KAZAKHSTAN

Supplier of information:
State Committee of the Republic of Kazakhstan on Statistics and Analysis, Almaty.

Basic source of data:
Not reported

Major deviations from ISIC (Revision 3):
None reported.

Reference period (if not calendar year):

Scope:
Not reported.

Method of enumeration:
Not reported.

Adjusted for non-response:
Not reported.

Concepts and definitions of variables:
No deviations from the standard UN concepts and definitions are reported.

Related national publications:

Kazakhstan

ISIC Revision 3	Number of establishments					Number of employees					Wages and salaries paid to employees				
		(numbers)					(numbers)					(thousand TENGE)			
ISIC Industry	Note	1993	1994	1995	1996	Note	1993	1994	1995	1996	Note	1993	1994	1995	1996
151 Processed meat,fish,fruit,vegetables,fats		1738	2015	2348	2879		...	...	...	...		...	...	...	...
1511 Processing/preserving of meat		1304	1414	1603	2148		...	...	...	...		...	...	...	...
1512 Processing/preserving of fish		156	157	154	160		...	...	...	...		...	...	...	...
1513 Processing/preserving of fruit & vegetables		100	90	122	99		...	...	...	...		...	...	...	...
1514 Vegetable and animal oils and fats		178	354	469	472		...	...	...	...		...	...	...	...
1520 Dairy products		535	603	674	1080		...	...	...	...		...	...	...	...
153 Grain mill products; starches; animal feeds		...	...	...	...		...	...	...	...		...	...	...	...
1531 Grain mill products		375	526	793	1039		...	...	...	...		...	...	...	...
1532 Starches and starch products		...	...	...	...		...	...	...	...		...	...	...	...
1533 Prepared animal feeds		464	370	351	103		...	...	...	...		...	...	...	...
154 Other food products		...	...	...	...		...	...	...	...		...	...	...	...
1541 Bakery products		672	782	1092	1675		...	...	...	...		...	...	...	...
1542 Sugar		8	8	9	8		...	...	...	...		...	...	...	...
1543 Cocoa, chocolate and sugar confectionery		27	67	94	71		...	...	...	...		...	...	...	...
1544 Macaroni, noodles & similar products		...	...	...	...		...	...	...	...		...	...	...	...
1549 Other food products n.e.c.		10	45	84	30		...	...	...	...		...	...	...	...
155 Beverages		...	...	...	...		...	...	...	...		...	...	...	...
1551 Distilling, rectifying & blending of spirits		...	...	...	...		...	...	...	...		...	...	...	...
1552 Wines		55	60	58	45		...	...	...	...		...	...	...	...
1553 Malt liquors and malt		40	43	39	52		...	...	...	...		...	...	...	...
1554 Soft drinks; mineral waters		115	121	116	99		...	...	...	...		...	...	...	...
1600 Tobacco products		1	...	2	3		...	...	...	...		...	...	...	...
171 Spinning, weaving and finishing of textiles		...	...	...	...		...	...	...	...		...	...	...	...
1711 Textile fibre preparation; textile weaving		20	29	31	24		...	...	...	...		...	...	...	...
1712 Finishing of textiles		...	...	...	...		...	...	...	...		...	...	...	...
172 Other textiles		...	...	...	...		...	...	...	...		...	...	...	...
1721 Made-up textile articles, except apparel		...	...	...	...		...	...	...	...		...	...	...	...
1722 Carpets and rugs		...	...	...	...		...	...	...	...		...	...	...	...
1723 Cordage, rope, twine and netting		...	...	...	...		...	...	...	...		...	...	...	...
1729 Other textiles n.e.c.		54	173	123	96		...	...	...	...		...	...	...	...
1730 Knitted and crocheted fabrics and articles		28	140	86	53		...	...	...	...		...	...	...	...
1810 Wearing apparel, except fur apparel		331	822	706	433		...	...	...	...		...	...	...	...
1820 Dressing & dyeing of fur; processing of fur		46	111	114	107		...	...	...	...		...	...	...	...
191 Tanning, dressing and processing of leather		...	...	...	...		...	...	...	...		...	...	...	...
1911 Tanning and dressing of leather		4	5	6	11		...	...	...	...		...	...	...	...
1912 Luggage, handbags, etc.; saddlery & harness		...	...	...	...		...	...	...	...		...	...	...	...
1920 Footwear		23	128	111	35		...	...	...	...		...	...	...	...
2010 Sawmilling and planing of wood		1299	1111	894	615		...	...	...	...		...	...	...	...
202 Products of wood, cork, straw, etc.		...	...	...	...		...	...	...	...		...	...	...	...
2021 Veneer sheets, plywood, particle board, etc.		...	...	...	...		...	...	...	...		...	...	...	...
2022 Builders' carpentry and joinery		1304	1	1	1		...	...	...	...		...	...	...	...
2023 Wooden containers		55	51	39	27		...	...	...	...		...	...	...	...
2029 Other wood products; articles of cork/straw		...	...	...	...		...	...	...	...		...	...	...	...
210 Paper and paper products		...	...	...	...		...	...	...	...		...	...	...	...
2101 Pulp, paper and paperboard		1	1	1	1		...	...	...	...		...	...	...	...
2102 Corrugated paper and paperboard		...	...	...	...		...	...	...	...		...	...	...	...
2109 Other articles of paper and paperboard		1	1	2	1		...	...	...	...		...	...	...	...
221 Publishing		...	...	...	...		...	...	...	...		...	...	...	...
2211 Publishing of books and other publications		...	...	...	...		...	...	...	...		...	...	...	...
2212 Publishing of newspapers, journals, etc.		...	...	...	...		...	...	...	...		...	...	...	...
2213 Publishing of recorded media		...	...	...	...		...	...	...	...		...	...	...	...
2219 Other publishing		...	...	...	...		...	...	...	...		...	...	...	...

222 Printing and related service activities	...	...	...	...	...	...	...	...	...	...	...	...
2221 Printing	39	134	183	208	...	...	...	...	...	...	...	...
2222 Service activities related to printing	...	...	...	...	...	...	...	...	...	...	...	...
2230 Reproduction of recorded media	...	...	...	...	...	...	...	...	...	...	...	...
2310 Coke oven products	...	...	...	...	...	...	...	...	...	...	...	...
2320 Refined petroleum products	5	4	4	5	...	...	...	...	...	...	...	...
2330 Processing of nuclear fuel	...	...	...	...	...	...	...	...	...	...	...	...
241 Basic chemicals	15	22	33	25	...	...	...	...	...	...	...	...
2411 Basic chemicals, except fertilizers	3	8	17	11	...	...	...	...	...	...	...	...
2412 Fertilizers and nitrogen compounds	8	9	12	10	...	...	...	...	...	...	...	...
2413 Plastics in primary forms; synthetic rubber	4	5	4	4	...	...	...	...	...	...	...	...
242 Other chemicals	...	...	...	...	...	...	...	...	...	...	...	...
2421 Pesticides and other agro-chemical products	...	...	...	...	...	...	...	...	...	...	...	...
2422 Paints, varnishes, printing ink and mastics	4	32	22	34	...	...	...	...	...	...	...	...
2423 Pharmaceuticals, medicinal chemicals, etc.	16	23	29	22	...	...	...	...	...	...	...	...
2424 Soap, cleaning & cosmetic preparations	...	...	...	...	...	...	...	...	...	...	...	...
2429 Other chemical products n.e.c.	25	79	94	40	...	...	...	...	...	...	...	...
2430 Man-made fibres	...	...	...	...	...	...	...	...	...	...	...	...
251 Rubber products	4	8	8	10	...	...	...	...	...	...	...	...
2511 Rubber tyres and tubes	1	1	1	1	...	...	...	...	...	...	...	...
2519 Other rubber products	3	7	7	9	...	...	...	...	...	...	...	...
2520 Plastic products	9	38	57	43	...	...	...	...	...	...	...	...
2610 Glass and glass products	5	13	12	24	...	...	...	...	...	...	...	...
269 Non-metallic mineral products n.e.c.	...	...	...	...	...	...	...	...	...	...	...	...
2691 Pottery, china and earthenware	6	11	11	12	...	...	...	...	...	...	...	...
2692 Refractory ceramic products	704	742	425	252	...	...	...	...	...	...	...	...
2693 Struct.non-refractory clay; ceramic products	4	8	8	5	...	...	...	...	...	...	...	...
2694 Cement, lime and plaster	119	32	37	26	...	...	...	...	...	...	...	...
2695 Articles of concrete, cement and plaster	396	489	340	259	...	...	...	...	...	...	...	...
2696 Cutting, shaping & finishing of stone	...	...	...	...	...	...	...	...	...	...	...	...
2699 Other non-metallic mineral products n.e.c.	...	...	...	...	...	...	...	...	...	...	...	...
2710 Basic iron and steel	2	4	6	3	...	...	...	...	...	...	...	...
2720 Basic precious and non-ferrous metals	28	48	61	66	...	...	...	...	...	...	...	...
273 Casting of metals	...	...	...	...	...	...	...	...	...	...	...	...
2731 Casting of iron and steel	...	...	...	...	...	...	...	...	...	...	...	...
2732 Casting of non-ferrous metals	...	...	...	...	...	...	...	...	...	...	...	...
281 Struct.metal products;tanks;steam generators	282	413	391	316	...	...	...	...	...	...	...	...
2811 Structural metal products	280	409	386	310	...	...	...	...	...	...	...	...
2812 Tanks, reservoirs and containers of metal	1	2	4	4	...	...	...	...	...	...	...	...
2813 Steam generators	1	2	1	2	...	...	...	...	...	...	...	...
289 Other metal products; metal working services	...	...	...	...	...	...	...	...	...	...	...	...
2891 Metal forging/pressing/stamping/roll-forming	...	...	...	...	...	...	...	...	...	...	...	...
2892 Treatment & coating of metals	...	...	...	...	...	...	...	...	...	...	...	...
2893 Cutlery, hand tools and general hardware	13	18	21	21	...	...	...	...	...	...	...	...
2899 Other fabricated metal products n.e.c.	122	185	182	144	...	...	...	...	...	...	...	...
291 General purpose machinery	...	...	...	...	...	...	...	...	...	...	...	...
2911 Engines & turbines(not for transport equip.)	1	1	1	-	...	...	...	...	...	...	...	...
2912 Pumps, compressors, taps and valves	2	3	3	3	...	...	...	...	...	...	...	...
2913 Bearings, gears, gearing & driving elements	1	2	3	3	...	...	...	...	...	...	...	...
2914 Ovens, furnaces and furnace burners	2	2	1	2	...	...	...	...	...	...	...	...
2915 Lifting and handling equipment	1	2	2	1	...	...	...	...	...	...	...	...
2919 Other general purpose machinery	...	...	...	...	...	...	...	...	...	...	...	...
292 Special purpose machinery	...	...	...	...	...	...	...	...	...	...	...	...
2921 Agricultural and forestry machinery	35	46	42	24	...	...	...	...	...	...	...	...
2922 Machine tools	6	7	6	6	...	...	...	...	...	...	...	...
2923 Machinery for metallurgy	1	2	4	4	...	...	...	...	...	...	...	...
2924 Machinery for mining & construction	17	24	28	30	...	...	...	...	...	...	...	...
2925 Food/beverage/tobacco processing machinery	3	6	10	10	...	...	...	...	...	...	...	...
2926 Machinery for textile, apparel and leather	1	1	...	...	...	...	...	...	...	...	...	...
2927 Weapons and ammunition	...	...	...	...	...	...	...	...	...	...	...	...
2929 Other special purpose machinery	44	55	83	60	...	...	...	...	...	...	...	...
2930 Domestic appliances n.e.c.	1	3	4	4	...	...	...	...	...	...	...	...

continued

Kazakhstan

ISIC Revision 3 ISIC Industry	Note	Number of establishments (numbers) 1993	1994	1995	1996	Note	Number of employees (numbers) 1993	1994	1995	1996	Note	Wages and salaries paid to employees (thousand TENGE) 1993	1994	1995	1996
3000 Office, accounting and computing machinery		...	...	...	...		...	...	...	...		...	...	...	...
3110 Electric motors, generators and transformers		...	...	...	...		...	...	...	...		...	...	...	...
3120 Electricity distribution & control apparatus		...	...	...	...		...	...	...	...		...	...	...	...
3130 Insulated wire and cable		3	18	17	21		...	...	...	...		...	...	...	...
3140 Accumulators, primary cells and batteries		3	15	8	6		...	...	...	...		...	...	...	...
3150 Lighting equipment and electric lamps		...	...	...	...		...	...	...	...		...	...	...	...
3190 Other electrical equipment n.e.c.		15	20	21	20		...	...	...	...		...	...	...	...
3210 Electronic valves, tubes, etc.		...	...	...	...		...	...	...	...		...	...	...	...
3220 TV/radio transmitters; line comm. apparatus		...	...	...	...		...	...	...	...		...	...	...	...
3230 TV and radio receivers and associated goods		...	...	...	...		...	...	...	...		...	...	...	...
331 Medical, measuring, testing appliances, etc.		11	13	11	11		...	...	...	...		...	...	...	...
3311 Medical, surgical and orthopaedic equipment		1	1	1	-		...	...	...	...		...	...	...	...
3312 Measuring/testing/navigating appliances,etc.		6	7	6	8		...	...	...	...		...	...	...	...
3313 Industrial process control equipment		4	5	4	3		...	...	...	...		...	...	...	...
3320 Optical instruments & photographic equipment		...	...	...	...		...	...	...	...		...	...	...	...
3330 Watches and clocks		...	...	...	...		...	...	...	...		...	...	...	...
3410 Motor vehicles		4	11	12	12		...	...	...	...		...	...	...	...
3420 Automobile bodies, trailers & semi-trailers		...	...	...	...		...	...	...	...		...	...	...	...
3430 Parts/accessories for automobiles		...	...	...	...		...	...	...	...		...	...	...	...
351 Building and repairing of ships and boats		...	...	...	...		...	...	...	...		...	...	...	...
3511 Building and repairing of ships		5	5	5	5		...	...	...	...		...	...	...	...
3512 Building/repairing of pleasure/sport. boats		...	...	...	...		...	...	...	...		...	...	...	...
3520 Railway/tramway locomotives & rolling stock		...	...	...	...		...	...	...	...		...	...	...	...
3530 Aircraft and spacecraft		...	...	...	...		...	...	...	...		...	...	...	...
359 Transport equipment n.e.c.		...	...	...	...		...	...	...	...		...	...	...	...
3591 Motorcycles		...	...	...	...		...	...	...	...		...	...	...	...
3592 Bicycles and invalid carriages		...	...	...	...		...	...	...	...		...	...	...	...
3599 Other transport equipment n.e.c.		...	...	...	...		...	...	...	...		...	...	...	...
3610 Furniture		44	329	224	158		...	...	...	...		...	...	...	...
369 Manufacturing n.e.c.		...	...	...	...		...	...	...	...		...	...	...	...
3691 Jewellery and related articles		2	2	3	3		...	...	...	...		...	...	...	...
3692 Musical instruments		1	1	1	1		...	...	...	...		...	...	...	...
3693 Sports goods		...	...	...	...		...	...	...	...		...	...	...	...
3694 Games and toys		2	14	4	3		...	...	...	...		...	...	...	...
3699 Other manufacturing n.e.c.		12	25	26	37		...	...	...	...		...	...	...	...
3710 Recycling of metal waste and scrap		...	...	...	...		...	...	...	...		...	...	...	...
3720 Recycling of non-metal waste and scrap		...	...	...	...		...	...	...	...		...	...	...	...
D Total manufacturing		18380	17801	17104	16516		...	...	...	...		...	...	...	...

Kazakhstan

ISIC Revision 3		Output					Value added					Gross fixed capital formation	
		(million TENGE)					(million TENGE)					(million TENGE)	
ISIC Industry	Note	1993	1994	1995	1996	Note	1993	1994	1995	1996	Note	1995	1996
151 Processed meat,fish,fruit,vegetables,fats		1185	13971	21058	19371		...	...	...	...		...	...
1511 Processing/preserving of meat		1024	10856	16371	14166		...	...	...	...		...	...
1512 Processing/preserving of fish		68	1054	1824	1930		...	...	...	...		...	...
1513 Processing/preserving of fruit & vegetables		55	608	514	733		...	...	...	...		...	...
1514 Vegetable and animal oils and fats		38	1453	2349	2542		...	...	...	...		...	...
1520 Dairy products		399	6560	12804	10705		...	...	...	...		...	...
153 Grain mill products; starches; animal feeds		...	...	...	...		...	...	...	...		...	...
1531 Grain mill products		382	5671	10340	10254		...	...	...	...		...	...
1532 Starches and starch products		...	...	...	...		...	...	...	...		...	...
1533 Prepared animal feeds		292	3621	4813	3210		...	...	...	...		...	...
154 Other food products		...	...	...	...		...	...	...	...		...	...
1541 Bakery products		400	7910	15580	16656		...	...	...	...		...	...
1542 Sugar		153	788	1178	1395		...	...	...	...		...	...
1543 Cocoa, chocolate and sugar confectionery		156	1532	1842	3187		...	...	...	...		...	...
1544 Macaroni, noodles & similar products		...	...	...	...		...	...	...	...		...	...
1549 Other food products n.e.c.		2	152	1101	425		...	...	...	...		...	...
155 Beverages		...	...	...	...		...	...	...	...		...	...
1551 Distilling, rectifying & blending of spirits		...	...	...	...		...	...	...	...		...	...
1552 Wines		51	451	1018	1420		...	...	...	...		...	...
1553 Malt liquors and malt		35	578	1193	1875		...	...	...	...		...	...
1554 Soft drinks; mineral waters		6	190	446	2025		...	...	...	...		...	...
1600 Tobacco products		78	...	3899	9846		...	...	...	...		...	...
171 Spinning, weaving and finishing of textiles		...	...	...	...		...	...	...	...		...	...
1711 Textile fibre preparation; textile weaving		500	4391	4435	3752		...	...	...	...		...	...
1712 Finishing of textiles		...	...	...	...		...	...	...	...		...	...
172 Other textiles		...	...	...	...		...	...	...	...		...	...
1721 Made-up textile articles, except apparel		...	...	...	...		...	...	...	...		...	...
1722 Carpets and rugs		...	...	...	...		...	...	...	...		...	...
1723 Cordage, rope, twine and netting		...	...	...	...		...	...	...	...		...	...
1729 Other textiles n.e.c.		339	4048	6374	8057		...	...	...	...		...	...
1730 Knitted and crocheted fabrics and articles		152	1451	1041	705		...	...	...	...		...	...
1810 Wearing apparel, except fur apparel		273	2685	2617	2048		...	...	...	...		...	...
1820 Dressing & dyeing of fur; processing of fur		49	635	678	534		...	...	...	...		...	...
191 Tanning, dressing and processing of leather		...	...	...	...		...	...	...	...		...	...
1911 Tanning and dressing of leather		16	81	82	137		...	...	...	...		...	...
1912 Luggage, handbags, etc.; saddlery & harness		...	...	...	...		...	...	...	...		...	...
1920 Footwear		129	922	482	365		...	...	...	...		...	...
2010 Sawmilling and planing of wood		91	393	737	582		...	...	...	...		...	...
202 Products of wood, cork, straw, etc.		...	...	...	...		...	...	...	...		...	...
2021 Veneer sheets, plywood, particle board, etc.		...	...	...	...		...	...	...	...		...	...
2022 Builders' carpentry and joinery		223	3	5	4		...	...	...	...		...	...
2023 Wooden containers		3	46	64	40		...	...	...	...		...	...
2029 Other wood products; articles of cork/straw		...	...	...	...		...	...	...	...		...	...
210 Paper and paper products		...	...	...	...		...	...	...	...		...	...
2101 Pulp, paper and paperboard		9	121	161	222		...	...	...	...		...	...
2102 Corrugated paper and paperboard		...	...	...	...		...	...	...	...		...	...
2109 Other articles of paper and paperboard		8	156	160	223		...	...	...	...		...	...
221 Publishing		...	...	...	...		...	...	...	...		...	...
2211 Publishing of books and other publications		...	...	...	...		...	...	...	...		...	...
2212 Publishing of newspapers, journals, etc.		...	...	...	...		...	...	...	...		...	...
2213 Publishing of recorded media		...	...	...	...		...	...	...	...		...	...
2219 Other publishing		...	...	...	...		...	...	...	...		...	...

continued

Kazakhstan

ISIC	Industry	Note	Output (million TENGE) 1993	1994	1995	1996	Note	Value added (million TENGE) 1993	1994	1995	1996	Note	Gross fixed capital formation (million TENGE) 1995	1996
222	Printing and related service activities		...	...	...	...		...	...	...	...		...	...
2221	Printing		34	843	1927	2400		...	...	...	...		...	...
2222	Service activities related to printing		...	...	...	...		...	...	...	...		...	...
2230	Reproduction of recorded media		...	...	...	...		...	...	...	...		...	...
2310	Coke oven products		...	...	...	...		...	...	...	...		...	...
2320	Refined petroleum products		1221	21802	21251	38984		...	...	...	...		...	...
2330	Processing of nuclear fuel		...	...	...	...		...	...	...	...		...	...
241	Basic chemicals		598	8446	15126	16473		...	...	...	...		...	...
2411	Basic chemicals, except fertilizers		49	730	2058	2025		...	...	...	...		...	...
2412	Fertilizers and nitrogen compounds		418	5889	10841	12561		...	...	...	...		...	...
2413	Plastics in primary forms; synthetic rubber		131	1827	2227	1887		...	...	...	...		...	...
242	Other chemicals		...	...	...	...		...	...	...	...		...	...
2421	Pesticides and other agro-chemical products		...	...	...	...		...	...	...	...		...	...
2422	Paints, varnishes, printing ink and mastics		4	113	381	712		...	...	...	...		...	...
2423	Pharmaceuticals, medicinal chemicals, etc.		6	152	382	334		...	...	...	...		...	...
2424	Soap, cleaning & cosmetic preparations		...	...	...	...		...	...	...	...		...	...
2429	Other chemical products n.e.c.		630	9304	17118	18836		...	...	...	...		...	...
2430	Man-made fibres		...	...	...	...		...	...	...	...		...	...
251	Rubber products		107	732	1084	1193		...	...	...	...		...	...
2511	Rubber tyres and tubes		62	229	233	616		...	...	...	...		...	...
2519	Other rubber products		45	503	851	577		...	...	...	...		...	...
2520	Plastic products		33	399	401	349		...	...	...	...		...	...
2610	Glass and glass products		4	65	93	92		...	...	...	...		...	...
269	Non-metallic mineral products n.e.c.		...	...	...	...		...	...	...	...		...	...
2691	Pottery, china and earthenware		22	167	228	164		...	...	...	...		...	...
2692	Refractory ceramic products		165	1187	1830	1506		...	...	...	...		...	...
2693	Struct.non-refractory clay; ceramic products		24	142	368	97		...	...	...	...		...	...
2694	Cement, lime and plaster		126	1717	3061	2637		...	...	...	...		...	...
2695	Articles of concrete, cement and plaster		165	1961	2905	2998		...	...	...	...		...	...
2696	Cutting, shaping & finishing of stone		...	...	...	...		...	...	...	...		...	...
2699	Other non-metallic mineral products n.e.c.		...	...	...	...		...	...	...	...		...	...
2710	Basic iron and steel		1236	20698	35136	40230		...	...	...	...		...	...
2720	Basic precious and non-ferrous metals		2875	41031	76109	84937		...	...	...	...		...	...
273	Casting of metals		...	...	...	...		...	...	...	...		...	...
2731	Casting of iron and steel		...	...	...	...		...	...	...	...		...	...
2732	Casting of non-ferrous metals		...	...	...	...		...	...	...	...		...	...
281	Struct.metal products;tanks;steam generators		218	2706	5108	5445		...	...	...	...		...	...
2811	Structural metal products		193	2255	4002	4063		...	...	...	...		...	...
2812	Tanks, reservoirs and containers of metal		21	383	1097	1134		...	...	...	...		...	...
2813	Steam generators		4	68	9	248		...	...	...	...		...	...
289	Other metal products; metal working services		...	...	...	...		...	...	...	...		...	...
2891	Metal forging/pressing/stamping/roll-forming		...	...	...	...		...	...	...	...		...	...
2892	Treatment & coating of metals		...	...	...	...		...	...	...	...		...	...
2893	Cutlery, hand tools and general hardware		23	248	272	199		...	...	...	...		...	...
2899	Other fabricated metal products n.e.c.		62	599	1140	1659		...	...	...	...		...	...
291	General purpose machinery		...	...	...	...		...	...	...	...		...	...
2911	Engines & turbines(not for transport equip.)		11	81	211	-		...	...	...	...		...	...
2912	Pumps, compressors, taps and valves		7	68	212	186		...	...	...	...		...	...
2913	Bearings, gears, gearing & driving elements		34	863	2092	2844		...	...	...	...		...	...
2914	Ovens, furnaces and furnace burners		4	33	29	67		...	...	...	...		...	...
2915	Lifting and handling equipment		1	12	35	20		...	...	...	...		...	...
2919	Other general purpose machinery		...	...	...	...		...	...	...	...		...	...

292	Special purpose machinery	...	...	...	...	...	...	...	...	...	...
2921	Agricultural and forestry machinery	203	1477	2962	2657	...	...	...	...	...	...
2922	Machine tools	16	170	225	177	...	...	...	...	...	...
2923	Machinery for metallurgy	21	383	1097	1134	...	...	...	...	...	...
2924	Machinery for mining & construction	98	1520	2330	2118	...	...	...	...	...	...
2925	Food/beverage/tobacco processing machinery	4	36	114	121	...	...	...	...	...	...
2926	Machinery for textile, apparel and leather	1	1	...	...	...	...	...	...	...	...
2927	Weapons and ammunition	...	...	...	...	...	...	...	...	...	...
2929	Other special purpose machinery	166	2269	3993	3009	...	...	...	...	...	...
2930	Domestic appliances n.e.c.	7	178	190	120	...	...	...	...	...	...
3000	Office, accounting and computing machinery	...	...	...	...	...	...	...	...	...	...
3110	Electric motors, generators and transformers	...	...	...	...	...	...	...	...	...	...
3120	Electricity distribution & control apparatus	...	...	...	...	...	...	...	...	...	...
3130	Insulated wire and cable	24	183	276	572	...	...	...	...	...	...
3140	Accumulators, primary cells and batteries	78	762	1643	1505	...	...	...	...	...	...
3150	Lighting equipment and electric lamps	...	...	...	...	...	...	...	...	...	...
3190	Other electrical equipment n.e.c.	41	425	778	861	...	...	...	...	...	...
3210	Electronic valves, tubes, etc.	...	...	...	...	...	...	...	...	...	...
3220	TV/radio transmitters; line comm. apparatus	...	...	...	...	...	...	...	...	...	...
3230	TV and radio receivers and associated goods	...	...	...	...	...	...	...	...	...	...
331	Medical, measuring, testing appliances, etc.	50	562	755	500	...	...	...	...	...	...
3311	Medical, surgical and orthopaedic equipment	6	85	237	-	...	...	...	...	...	...
3312	Measuring/testing/navigating appliances,etc.	38	442	478	359	...	...	...	...	...	...
3313	Industrial process control equipment	6	35	40	141	...	...	...	...	...	...
3320	Optical instruments & photographic equipment	...	...	...	...	...	...	...	...	...	...
3330	Watches and clocks	...	...	...	...	...	...	...	...	...	...
3410	Motor vehicles	27	248	391	228	...	...	...	...	...	...
3420	Automobile bodies, trailers & semi-trailers	...	...	...	...	...	...	...	...	...	...
3430	Parts/accessories for automobiles	...	...	...	...	...	...	...	...	...	...
351	Building and repairing of ships and boats	...	...	...	...	...	...	...	...	...	...
3511	Building and repairing of ships	2	42	69	55	...	...	...	...	...	...
3512	Building/repairing of pleasure/sport. boats	...	...	...	...	...	...	...	...	...	...
3520	Railway/tramway locomotives & rolling stock	...	...	...	...	...	...	...	...	...	...
3530	Aircraft and spacecraft	...	...	...	...	...	...	...	...	...	...
359	Transport equipment n.e.c.	...	...	...	...	...	...	...	...	...	...
3591	Motorcycles	...	...	...	...	...	...	...	...	...	...
3592	Bicycles and invalid carriages	...	...	...	...	...	...	...	...	...	...
3599	Other transport equipment n.e.c.	...	...	...	...	...	...	...	...	...	...
3610	Furniture	121	1332	1952	1863	...	...	...	...	...	...
369	Manufacturing n.e.c.	...	...	...	...	...	...	...	...	...	...
3691	Jewellery and related articles	2	49	16	35	...	...	...	...	...	...
3692	Musical instruments	-	3	1	...	...	...	...	...	...	...
3693	Sports goods	...	...	...	...	...	...	...	...	...	...
3694	Games and toys	5	14	15	16	...	...	...	...	...	...
3699	Other manufacturing n.e.c.	26	233	588	523	...	...	...	...	...	...
3710	Recycling of metal waste and scrap	...	...	...	...	...	...	...	...	...	...
3720	Recycling of non-metal waste and scrap	...	...	...	...	...	...	...	...	...	...
D	Total manufacturing	19054	260904	447428	482338	...	...	...	...	...	...

Kazakhstan

ISIC Revision 3			Index numbers of industrial production (1990=100)											
ISIC	Industry	Note	1985	1986	1987	1988	1989	1990	1991	1992	1993	1994	1995	1996
15	Food and beverages		...	...	...	...	...	...	...	...	...	...	...	...
16	Tobacco products		...	...	...	...	...	...	...	...	...	...	...	...
17	Textiles		...	...	...	...	...	...	...	...	...	...	...	...
18	Wearing apparel, fur		...	...	...	...	...	...	...	...	...	...	...	...
19	Leather, leather products and footwear		...	...	...	...	...	...	...	...	...	...	...	...
20	Wood products (excl. furniture)		...	...	...	...	...	...	...	...	...	...	...	...
21	Paper and paper products		...	...	...	...	...	...	...	...	...	...	...	...
22	Printing and publishing		...	...	...	...	...	...	...	...	...	...	...	...
23	Coke,refined petroleum products,nuclear fuel		...	...	...	...	...	...	...	...	...	...	...	...
24	Chemicals and chemical products		...	...	...	...	...	...	...	...	...	...	...	...
25	Rubber and plastics products		...	...	...	...	...	...	...	...	...	...	...	...
26	Non-metallic mineral products		...	...	...	...	...	...	...	...	...	...	...	...
27	Basic metals		...	...	...	...	...	...	...	...	...	...	...	...
28	Fabricated metal products		...	...	...	...	...	...	...	...	...	...	...	...
29	Machinery and equipment n.e.c.		...	...	...	...	...	...	...	...	...	...	...	...
30	Office, accounting and computing machinery		...	...	...	...	...	...	...	...	...	...	...	...
31	Electrical machinery and apparatus		...	...	...	...	...	...	...	...	...	...	...	...
32	Radio,television and communication equipment		...	...	...	...	...	...	...	...	...	...	...	...
33	Medical, precision and optical instruments		...	...	...	...	...	...	...	...	...	...	...	...
34	Motor vehicles, trailers, semi-trailers		...	...	...	...	...	...	...	...	...	...	...	...
35	Other transport equipment		...	...	...	...	...	...	...	...	...	...	...	...
36	Furniture; manufacturing n.e.c.		...	...	...	...	...	...	...	...	...	...	...	...
37	Recycling		...	...	...	...	...	...	...	...	...	...	...	...
D	Total manufacturing		...	...	...	...	...	...	...	...	...	...	...	...

KENYA

Supplier of information:
Central Bureau of Statistics, Ministry of Planning and National Development, Nairobi.

Basic source of data:
Annual survey of industrial production and, every five years, census of industrial production.

Major deviations from ISIC (Revision 2):
Manufacture of metal furniture and fixtures (part of ISIC 381) is classified under ISIC 332, and ISIC 384 includes repair of motor vehicles (part of ISIC major division 9).

Reference period (if not calendar year):

Scope:
All establishments.

Method of enumeration:
The survey is conducted by mail.

Adjusted for non-response:
Yes.

Concepts and definitions of variables:
Number of employees is the average of the numbers at the beginning and end of the reference year.
Wages and salaries is compensation of employees. It is computed as 12 times the value of wages and salaries for June of the reference year.
Output is gross output and includes gross revenues from goods shipped in the same condition as received.
All value data presented are in Kenya pounds (1 Kenya pound = 20 Kenya shillings).

Related national publications:
Statistical Abstract (annual), published by the Central Bureau of Statistics, Ministry of Planning and National Development, Nairobi.

Kenya

ISIC Revision 2	Number of establishments					Number of employees					Wages and salaries paid to employees				
		(numbers)					(numbers)					(thousand POUNDS)			
ISIC Industry	Note	1993	1994	1995	1996	Note	1993	1994	1995	1996	Note	1993	1994	1995	1996
311/2 Food products		647	746	748	...		55429	57660	60583	...		107692.9	132729.2	177466.9	...
3111 Slaughtering, preparing & preserving meat		1	2	2	...		3790	3898	4469	...		9676.2	11093.2	15497.4	...
3112 Dairy products		37	52	52	...		4099	4185	4268	...		14328.9	16604.0	21636.3	...
3113 Canning, preserving of fruits & vegetables		9	9	9	...		4126	4157	4216	...		7938.9	8887.8	11485.6	...
3114 Canning, preserving and processing of fish		1	1	3	...		198	195	197	...		329.8	435.0	580.9	...
3115 Vegetable and animal oils and fats		33	37	37	...		1616	1703	1807	...		6956.9	7910.2	10852.4	...
3116 Grain mill products		159	172	172	...		4466	4852	5256	...		9821.7	13331.1	18422.7	...
3117 Bakery products		88	104	104	...		2340	2436	2552	...		5216.3	6978.7	9537.3	...
3118 Sugar factories and refineries		23	27	27	...		12869	12961	13000	...		22524.0	26865.9	35321.6	...
3119 Cocoa, chocolate and sugar confectionery		19	19	19	...		686	745	814	...		1939.4	2740.1	3649.6	...
3121 Other food products		276	321	321	...		20391	21600	23009	...		27159.8	35491.7	47158.9	...
3122 Prepared animal feeds		1	2	2	...		848	928	995	...		1801.0	2391.5	3324.2	...
313 Beverages		38a/	50a/	50a/	...		8225a/	8511a/	8806a/	...		39453.3a/	47167.3a/	64311.7a/	...
3131 Distilling, rectifying and blending spirits		...	...	...	...		...	...	...	...		...	...	...	...
3132 Wine industries		...	...	...	...		...	...	...	...		...	...	...	...
3133 Malt liquors and malt		...	...	...	...		...	...	...	...		...	...	...	...
3134 Soft drinks and carbonated waters		16	27	27	...		2308	2330	2359	...		8712.8	10639.9	13929.5	...
314 Tobacco		...a/	...a/	...a/	...		...a/	...a/	...a/	...		...a/	...a/	...a/	...
321 Textiles		92	101	101	...		25137	24787	24968	...		44457.3	52351.4	66648.6	...
3211 Spinning, weaving and finishing textiles		29	31	31	...		12664	12176	12030	...		20323.9	23405.5	29687.0	...
3212 Made-up textile goods excl. wearing apparel		36	36	36	...		2661	2623	2625	...		4420.7	5058.9	6392.8	...
3213 Knitting mills		15	22	22	...		7249	7447	7720	...		15401.2	19048.0	24472.6	...
3214 Carpets and rugs		-	-	-	...		-	-	-	...		-	-	-	...
3215 Cordage, rope and twine		7	7	7	...		2181	2159	2199	...		3862.3	4263.5	5312.9	...
3219 Other textiles		5	5	5	...		382	382	394	...		449.2	575.5	783.3	...
322 Wearing apparel, except footwear		533	557	557	...		6820	6976	7114	...		10320.0	13749.2	17124.6	...
323 Leather and fur products		23	26	26	...		1564	1613	1673	...		3394.4	3613.9	4429.1	...
3231 Tanneries and leather finishing		20	22	22	...		1222	1259	1304	...		2749.5	2875.5	3512.3	...
3232 Fur dressing and dyeing industries		-	-	-	...		-	-	-	...		-	-	-	...
3233 Leather prods. excl. wearing apparel		3	4	4	...		342	354	369	...		644.9	738.4	916.8	...
324 Footwear, except rubber or plastic		15	15	15	...		2296	2350	2419	...		5971.0	7785.1	10211.8	...
331 Wood products, except furniture		177	223	223	...		8672	8840	9160	...		12515.7	15314.8	19663.1	...
3311 Sawmills, planing and other wood mills		175	220	220	...		8528	8695	9012	...		12304.7	15066.0	19329.4	...
3312 Wooden and cane containers		2	3	3	...		22	23	24	...		43.3	46.7	66.2	...
3319 Other wood and cork products		...	...	...	...		122	122	124	...		167.7	202.1	267.5	...
332 Furniture and fixtures, excl. metal		270	292	292	...		3830	3907	4050	...		7429.4	9502.8	12209.2	...
341 Paper and products		48	60	60	...		7378	7547	7759	...		19613.1	25459.6	31041.3	...
3411 Pulp, paper and paperboard articles		1	1	1	...		3726	3828	3945	...		8073.5	10641.0	12319.2	...
3412 Containers of paper and paperboard		-	-	-	...		-	-	-	...		-	-	-	...
3419 Other pulp, paper and paperboard articles		47	59	59	...		3652	3719	3814	...		11539.6	14818.6	18722.1	...
342 Printing and publishing		338	367	367	...		6063	6284	6575	...		20385.5	23477.1	29371.4	...
351 Industrial chemicals		31	38	38	...		3612	3671	3839	...		10604.5	14162.4	19405.9	...
3511 Basic chemicals excl. fertilizers		21	28	28	...		2551	2574	2708	...		7748.5	10032.7	13436.7	...
3512 Fertilizers and pesticides		10	10	10	...		1061	1097	1131	...		2856.0	4129.7	5969.2	...
3513 Synthetic resins and plastic materials		-	-	-	...		-	-	-	...		-	-	-	...
352 Other chemicals		134	148	148	...		9355	9693	10051	...		40368.0	46266.8	59664.2	...
3521 Paints, varnishes and lacquers		10	10	10	...		987	994	1024	...		3498.1	3925.6	5035.0	...
3522 Drugs and medicines		23	29	29	...		1987	2218	2412	...		9730.5	12283.7	15543.7	...
3523 Soap, cleaning preps., perfumes, cosmetics		58	66	66	...		4191	4313	4428	...		20137.8	22318.7	29494.9	...
3529 Other chemical products		43	43	43	...		2190	2168	2187	...		7001.6	7738.8	9590.6	...
353 Petroleum refineries		1	2	2	...		264	264	266	...		2889.5	4020.3	6111.8	...

354	Misc. petroleum and coal products	-	-	-	...	-	-	-	...	-	-	-	...
355	Rubber products	56	67	67	...	2334	2398	2440	...	10136.6	10950.3	15393.6	...
3551	Tyres and tubes	...	...	...	...	...	...	...	...	...	...	...	...
3559	Other rubber products	...	...	...	...	...	...	...	...	...	...	...	...
356	Plastic products	48	64	64	...	4051	4217	4465	...	9969.5	11938.1	16865.8	...
361	Pottery, china, earthenware	1	1	1	...	221	228	237	...	500.5	583.7	770.5	...
362	Glass and products	3	3	3	...	1487	1472	1516	...	3436.5	3645.3	5011.5	...
369	Other non-metallic mineral products	47	48	48	...	5703	5640	6037	...	21234.9	23341.9	31525.9	...
3691	Structural clay products	1	2	2	...	955	916	898	...	1668.6	1914.4	2574.8	...
3692	Cement, lime and plaster	1	1	1	...	3507	3466	3861	...	15505.7	16542.8	22035.1	...
3699	Other non-metallic mineral products	45	45	45	...	1241	1258	1278	...	4060.6	4884.7	6916.0	...
371	Iron and steel	29b/	42b/	42b/	...	5614b/	5684b/	5774b/	...	12910.0b/	14861.4b/	17208.5b/	...
372	Non-ferrous metals	...b/	...b/	...b/	...	...b/	...b/	...b/	...	...b/	...b/	...b/	...
381	Fabricated metal products	330	377	377	...	12201	12462	13173	...	34586.0	39743.4	49835.5	...
3811	Cutlery, hand tools and general hardware	22	26	26	...	850	893	950	...	2319.6	2575.1	3473.6	...
3812	Furniture and fixtures primarily of metal	26	26	26	...	911	901	918	...	2455.2	2715.3	3792.1	...
3813	Structural metal products	53	69	69	...	3252	3264	3295	...	9579.1	9821.3	12138.1	...
3819	Other fabricated metal products	229	256	256	...	7188	7404	8010	...	20232.1	24631.7	30431.7	...
382	Non-electrical machinery	61	67	67	...	1492	1506	1502	...	3347.6	4676.6	5601.6	...
3821	Engines and turbines	...	...	...	...	...	...	...	...	...	...	...	...
3822	Agricultural machinery and equipment	...	...	...	...	...	...	...	...	...	...	...	...
3823	Metal and wood working machinery	...	...	...	...	...	...	...	...	...	...	...	...
3824	Other special industrial machinery	...	...	...	...	...	...	...	...	...	...	...	...
3825	Office, computing and accounting machinery	...	...	...	...	...	...	...	...	...	...	...	...
3829	Other non-electrical machinery & equipment	...	...	...	...	...	...	...	...	...	...	...	...
383	Electrical machinery	39	47	47	...	2799	2834	3218	...	11614.2	15440.1	22079.9	...
3831	Electrical industrial machinery	...	...	...	...	...	...	...	...	...	...	...	...
3832	Radio, television and communication equipm.	...	...	...	...	...	...	...	...	...	...	...	...
3833	Electrical appliances and housewares	...	...	...	...	...	...	...	...	...	...	...	...
3839	Other electrical apparatus and supplies	...	...	...	...	...	...	...	...	...	...	...	...
384	Transport equipment	60	72	72	...	15348	15370	15297	...	44543.2	52378.7	70330.7	...
3841	Shipbuilding and repairing	4	4	4	...	499	521	547	...	2593.5	3266.5	4485.8	...
3842	Railroad equipment	1	1	1	...	11209	11432	11320	...	28520.7	32092.4	44375.9	...
3843	Motor vehicles	52	61	61	...	3487	3265	3275	...	12791.0	16168.1	20397.4	...
3844	Motorcycles and bicycles	1	4	4	...	2	3	3	...	3.8	5.9	8.7	...
3845	Aircraft	2	2	2	...	151	149	152	...	634.2	845.8	1062.9	...
3849	Other transport equipment	...	...	...	...	...	...	...	...	...	...	...	...
385	Professional and scientific equipment	1	1	6	...	244	266	292	...	497.8	661.5	900.7	...
3851	Prof. and scientific equipment n.e.c.	...	...	...	...	...	...	...	...	...	...	...	...
3852	Photographic and optical goods	...	...	...	...	...	...	...	...	...	...	...	...
3853	Watches and clocks	...	...	...	...	...	...	...	...	...	...	...	...
390	Other manufacturing industries	231	264	264	...	3398	3469	3579	...	8309.8	8764.8	12165.8	...
3901	Jewellery and related articles	...	...	...	...	...	...	...	...	...	...	...	...
3902	Musical instruments	...	...	...	...	...	...	...	...	...	...	...	...
3903	Sporting and athletic goods	...	...	...	...	...	...	...	...	...	...	...	...
3909	Manufacturing industries, n.e.c.	...	...	...	...	...	...	...	...	...	...	...	...
3	Total manufacturing	3253	3678	3685	...	193537	197649	204793	...	486181.2	582585.7	765349.6	958150.0

a/ 313 includes 314.
b/ 371 includes 372.

Kenya

ISIC Revision 2	Output in factor values					Value added in factor values					Gross fixed capital formation		
		(million POUNDS)					(million POUNDS)					(million POUNDS)	
ISIC Industry	Note	1993	1994	1995	1996	Note	1993	1994	1995	1996	Note	1995	1996
311/2 Food products		7310	8463	9960	...		480	639	847	...		...	...
313 Beverages		427	456	564	...		149	190	216	...		...	...
314 Tobacco		283	327	438	...		22	30	33	...		...	...
321 Textiles		221	284	387	...		87	112	94	...		...	...
322 Wearing apparel, except footwear		365	434	151	...		24	35	36	...		...	...
323 Leather and fur products		26	26	27	...		7	8	8	...		...	...
324 Footwear, except rubber or plastic		65	86	102	...		14	20	22	...		...	...
331 Wood products, except furniture		92	101	194	...		27	35	38	...		...	...
332 Furniture and fixtures, excl. metal	a/	70	80	38	...	a/	12	16	17	...		...	...
341 Paper and products		237	277	459	...		62	87	86	...		...	...
342 Printing and publishing		267	275	129	...		41	51	53	...		...	...
351 Industrial chemicals		301	359	473	...		26	38	42	...		...	...
352 Other chemicals		1720	1751	2244	...		100	130	139	...		...	...
353 Petroleum refineries		1412	1755	1431	...		11	16	20	...		...	...
354 Misc. petroleum and coal products		-	-	-	...		-	-	-	...		...	...
355 Rubber products		158	166	190	...		50	58	68	...		...	...
356 Plastic products		215	230	345	...		50	65	75	...		...	...
361 Pottery, china, earthenware		2	2	2	...		1	2	2	...		...	...
362 Glass and products		11	11	13	...		7	8	10	...		...	...
369 Other non-metallic mineral products		251	262	309	...		63	72	82	...		...	...
371 Iron and steel		221b/	...	...	...		...	...	...	...		...	...
372 Non-ferrous metals		...b/	...	...	...		...	...	...	...		...	...
381 Fabricated metal products	a/	590	626	770	...	a/	101	125	131	...		...	...
382 Non-electrical machinery		33	42	134	...		8	12	12	...		...	...
383 Electrical machinery		1063	1281	348	...		78	112	133	...		...	...
384 Transport equipment		856	1654	3504	...		56	73	81	...		...	...
385 Professional and scientific equipment		17	19	16	...		32c/	36c/	1	...		...	...
390 Other manufacturing industries		98	94	50	...		...c/	...c/	41	...		...	...
3 Total manufacturing		16311	19061	22278	28820		1508	1970	2287	2552		...	...

a/ 332 includes metal furniture and fixtures.
b/ 371 includes 372.
c/ 385 includes 390.

Kenya

ISIC Revision 2		Index numbers of industrial production											
		(1990=100)											
ISIC Industry	Note	1985	1986	1987	1988	1989	1990	1991	1992	1993	1994	1995	1996
311/2 Food products		79	84	92	98	98	100	102	98	98	98	114	114
313 Beverages		67	79	93	96	96	100	100	117	116	107	112	98
314 Tobacco		85	88	96	100	100	100	97	108	109	110	119	126
321 Textiles		86	93	95	97	97	100	108	108	125	92	68	62
322 Wearing apparel, except footwear		93	93	94	97	97	100	86	85	77	49	40	40
323 Leather and fur products	a/	84	86	88	93	93	100	107	103	93	102	69	73
324 Footwear, except rubber or plastic	a/	...	...	...	...	...	...	...	...	...	...	...	...
331 Wood products, except furniture		97	99	99	97	97	100	107	109	108	112	108	110
332 Furniture and fixtures, excl. metal		98	100	101	100	100	100	97	64	68	69	72	80
341 Paper and products		74	80	86	95	95	100	108	130	91	79	77	97
342 Printing and publishing		84	89	95	99	99	100	103	105	105	108	115	124
351 Industrial chemicals		83	84	85	92	92	100	118	118	124	108	106	102
352 Other chemicals		65	70	76	87	87	100	129	122	119	115	124	134
353 Petroleum refineries	b/	65	70	76	87	87	100	129	122	119	115	124	136
354 Misc. petroleum and coal products	b/	...	...	...	...	...	...	...	...	...	...	...	...
355 Rubber products		80	85	90	93	93	100	104	204	202	199	201	204
356 Plastic products		91	94	97	93	93	100	125	148	163	166	176	181
361 Pottery, china, earthenware		...	...	...	...	...	...	...	...	...	...	...	...
362 Glass and products		85	85	86	90	63	100	77	170	355	524	621	703
369 Other non-metallic mineral products		82	92	98	96	98	100	119	140	137	144	143	149
371 Iron and steel		...	...	...	...	...	...	...	...	...	...	...	...
372 Non-ferrous metals		...	...	...	...	...	...	...	...	...	...	...	...
381 Fabricated metal products		61	68	75	86	85	100	131	119	119	133	134	159
382 Non-electrical machinery		83	89	96	104	104	100	76	72	71	76	59	86
383 Electrical machinery		80	84	87	98	98	100	134	130	116	117	131	138
384 Transport equipment		105	93	86	96	96	100	104	95	79	85	83	112
385 Professional and scientific equipment		...	...	...	...	...	...	...	...	...	...	...	...
390 Other manufacturing industries		54	70	90	96	100	100	118	118	118	118	126	152
3 Total manufacturing		78	83	89	95	95	100	110	115	114	112	117	123

a/ 323 includes 324.
b/ 353 includes 354.

KUWAIT

Supplier of information:
Central Statistical Office, Ministry of Planning, Safat.

Basic source of data:
Annual industrial survey.

Major deviations from ISIC (Revision 2):
None reported.

Reference period (if not calendar year):
The reference period is the calendar year, but data reported for the financial year are accepted and incorporated in the calendar year in which the major part of the financial year falls. For establishments in the petroleum sector, estimates for the calendar year are made on the basis of the average of the two fiscal years.

Scope:
All industrial establishments in the private and public sectors, including establishments with joint private and public ownership.

Method of enumeration:
Establishments are covered on a census-cum-sample basis as follows: a) census coverage of all establishments with 10 or more employees as well as establishments in those activities (as defined by a 5-digit code based on the ISIC) containing less than 20 establishments; b) sample coverage of all establishments not covered by the census. These establishments are divided into two groups according to employment levels 1-4 and 5-9 and samples are taken from both groups. Data are collected by trained field enumerators using specially designed questionnaires.

Adjusted for non-response:
Not reported.

Concepts and definitions of variables:
No deviations from the standard UN concepts and definitions are reported.

Related national publications:
Annual Survey of Establishments (Industry) and Statistical Abstract (annual), both published by the Central Statistical Office, Ministry of Planning, Safat.

Kuwait

ISIC Revision 2	Number of establishments					Number of employees					Wages and salaries paid to employees				
		(numbers)					(numbers)					(thousand DINARS)			
ISIC Industry	Note	1992	1993	1994	1995	Note	1992	1993	1994	1995	Note	1992	1993	1994	1995
311/2 Food products		300	305	296	295		5953	6744	6689	7604		13001	14167	14067	16556
3111 Slaughtering, preparing & preserving meat		-	-	4	4		-	-	267	254		-	-	607	580
3112 Dairy products		4	5	5	5		857	1012	1092	1199		2084	2764	2911	3002
3113 Canning, preserving of fruits & vegetables		-	-	-	-		-	-	-	-		-	-	-	-
3114 Canning, preserving and processing of fish		-	-	4	4		-	-	554	533		-	-	801	965
3115 Vegetable and animal oils and fats		-	-	-	-		-	-	-	-		-	-	-	-
3116 Grain mill products		-	-	-	-		-	-	-	-		-	-	-	-
3117 Bakery products		271	274	265	264		3828	3958	3805	4463		7923	7497	7265	8451
3118 Sugar factories and refineries		-	-	-	-		-	-	-	-		-	-	-	-
3119 Cocoa, chocolate and sugar confectionery		-	-	-	-		-	-	-	-		-	-	-	-
3121 Other food products		23	24	16	16		1253	1757	957	1136		2969	3875	2459	3521
3122 Prepared animal feeds		2	2	2	2		15	17	14	19		25	31	24	37
313 Beverages		5	6	5	5		1761	2204	2050	2316		3357	4315	4596	4813
3131 Distilling, rectifying and blending spirits		-	-	-	-		-	-	-	-		-	-	-	-
3132 Wine industries		-	-	-	-		-	-	-	-		-	-	-	-
3133 Malt liquors and malt		-	-	-	-		-	-	-	-		-	-	-	-
3134 Soft drinks and carbonated waters		5	6	5	5		1761	2204	2050	2316		3357	4315	4596	4813
314 Tobacco		-	-	-	-		-	-	-	-		-	-	-	-
321 Textiles		260	264	263	262		1568	1341	1437	1370		3471	2911	2827	2614
3211 Spinning, weaving and finishing textiles		-	-	-	-		-	-	-	-		-	-	-	-
3212 Made-up textile goods excl. wearing apparel		260	264	263	262		1568	1341	1437	1370		3471	2911	2827	2614
3213 Knitting mills		-	-	-	-		-	-	-	-		-	-	-	-
3214 Carpets and rugs		-	-	-	-		-	-	-	-		-	-	-	-
3215 Cordage, rope and twine		-	-	-	-		-	-	-	-		-	-	-	-
3219 Other textiles		-	-	-	-		-	-	-	-		-	-	-	-
322 Wearing apparel, except footwear		1912	1905	1899	1896		10254	10853	9856	10720		14749	16350	14766	14871
323 Leather and fur products		1	2	2	1		112	132	125	137		208	307	231	186
3231 Tanneries and leather finishing		1	2	2	1		112	132	125	137		208	307	231	186
3232 Fur dressing and dyeing industries		-	-	-	-		-	-	-	-		-	-	-	-
3233 Leather prods. excl. wearing apparel		-	-	-	-		-	-	-	-		-	-	-	-
324 Footwear, except rubber or plastic		-	-	2	3		-	-	61	87		-	-	82	98
331 Wood products, except furniture		109	103	103	106		1193	1163	1095	1345		2240	2005	2010	2431
3311 Sawmills, planing and other wood mills		73	67	67	70		1080	1091	1023	1255		2015	1878	1924	2267
3312 Wooden and cane containers		-	-	-	-		-	-	-	-		-	-	-	-
3319 Other wood and cork products		36	36	36	36		113	72	72	90		225	127	86	164
332 Furniture and fixtures, excl. metal		345	334	326	326		3327	3576	3542	3272		6244	6472	5797	6079
341 Paper and products		13	13	12	13		834	874	912	982		1861	2258	2358	2543
3411 Pulp, paper and paperboard articles		-	-	-	-		-	-	-	-		-	-	-	-
3412 Containers of paper and paperboard		6	6	4	5		331	413	378	420		763	909	913	982
3419 Other pulp, paper and paperboard articles		7	7	8	8		503	461	534	562		1098	1349	1445	1561
342 Printing and publishing		54	55	57	58		3213	3384	3691	3535		8877	9442	11147	12697
351 Industrial chemicals		7	7	7	7		1186	1276	1287	1304		12014	13878	13861	12719
3511 Basic chemicals excl. fertilizers		6	6	6	6		225	227	219	224		615	635	702	686
3512 Fertilizers and pesticides		1	1	1	1		961	1049	1068	1080		11399	13243	13159	12033
3513 Synthetic resins and plastic materials		-	-	-	-		-	-	-	-		-	-	-	-
352 Other chemicals		15	16	15	15		507	517	552	583		1358	1477	1550	1745
3521 Paints, varnishes and lacquers		6	7	7	7		261	252	294	289		885	890	929	1047
3522 Drugs and medicines		-	-	-	-		-	-	-	-		-	-	-	-
3523 Soap, cleaning preps., perfumes, cosmetics		3	3	6	7		150	159	219	271		253	317	503	621
3529 Other chemical products		6	6	2	1		96	106	39	23		220	270	118	77
353 Petroleum refineries		1	1	1	1		4133	4753	5065	5277		56784	63312	66335	68725

354	Misc. petroleum and coal products	6	6	6	6	148	177	225	248	372	481	645	547
355	Rubber products	2	2	3	3	114	106	127	130	104	145	228	249
3551	Tyres and tubes	-	-	-	-	-	-	-	-	-	-	-	-
3559	Other rubber products	2	2	3	3	114	106	127	130	104	145	228	249
356	Plastic products	21	22	24	23	1252	1492	1615	1562	2630	2931	3200	3455
361	Pottery, china, earthenware	-	-	-	-	-	-	-	-	-	-	-	-
362	Glass and products	13	16	15	15	432	463	480	552	1119	1218	1492	1567
369	Other non-metallic mineral products	85	90	102	105	3381	3912	4824	5204	8146	9472	11706	12191
3691	Structural clay products	-	-	-	-	-	-	-	-	-	-	-	-
3692	Cement, lime and plaster	6	6	6	6	368	436	511	493	1534	1368	1784	1623
3699	Other non-metallic mineral products	79	84	96	99	3013	3476	4313	4711	6612	8104	9922	10568
371	Iron and steel	6	6	6	6	541	696	740	767	921	1429	1652	1700
372	Non-ferrous metals	-	-	-	-	-	-	-	-	-	-	-	-
381	Fabricated metal products	608	606	600	602	5495	5833	5876	6068	10992	12028	12444	13337
3811	Cutlery, hand tools and general hardware	2	1	-	-	6	4	-	-	10	8	-	-
3812	Furniture and fixtures primarily of metal	16	15	13	15	627	468	601	745	1073	930	1072	1424
3813	Structural metal products	455	454	454	455	3933	4005	4070	4001	7583	7466	8360	8700
3819	Other fabricated metal products	135	136	133	132	929	1356	1205	1322	2326	3624	3012	3213
382	Non-electrical machinery	23	24	24	23	4120	4504	4698	5130	7536	9621	11882	7998
3821	Engines and turbines	-	-	-	-	-	-	-	-	-	-	-	-
3822	Agricultural machinery and equipment	-	-	-	-	-	-	-	-	-	-	-	-
3823	Metal and wood working machinery	-	-	-	-	-	-	-	-	-	-	-	-
3824	Other special industrial machinery	13	13	11	11	3639	4130	4021	4215	6518	8675	10283	6096
3825	Office, computing and accounting machinery	-	1	-	-	-	27	-	-	-	84	-	-
3829	Other non-electrical machinery & equipment	10	10	13	12	481	347	677	915	1018	862	1599	1902
383	Electrical machinery	36	36	36	35	966	1150	1353	1312	2587	3160	3669	3388
3831	Electrical industrial machinery	31	31	31	31	546	719	874	926	1288	1781	2203	2112
3832	Radio, television and communication equipm.	-	-	-	-	-	-	-	-	-	-	-	-
3833	Electrical appliances and housewares	-	-	-	-	-	-	-	-	-	-	-	-
3839	Other electrical apparatus and supplies	5	5	5	4	420	431	479	386	1299	1379	1466	1276
384	Transport equipment	14	14	15	18	2614	2768	1009	1463	10540	10729	3744	3610
3841	Shipbuilding and repairing	6	7	8	10	2402	2541	736	1193	9800	9973	2995	2941
3842	Railroad equipment	-	-	-	-	-	-	-	-	-	-	-	-
3843	Motor vehicles	8	7	7	8	212	227	273	270	740	756	749	669
3844	Motorcycles and bicycles	-	-	-	-	-	-	-	-	-	-	-	-
3845	Aircraft	-	-	-	-	-	-	-	-	-	-	-	-
3849	Other transport equipment	-	-	-	-	-	-	-	-	-	-	-	-
385	Professional and scientific equipment	-	-	-	-	-	-	-	-	-	-	-	-
3851	Prof. and scientific equipment n.e.c.	-	-	-	-	-	-	-	-	-	-	-	-
3852	Photographic and optical goods	-	-	-	-	-	-	-	-	-	-	-	-
3853	Watches and clocks	-	-	-	-	-	-	-	-	-	-	-	-
390	Other manufacturing industries	190	190	190	189	1204	1051	1181	1169	2428	2436	2557	2503
3901	Jewellery and related articles	174	173	174	173	997	930	1036	1027	2008	2194	2295	2263
3902	Musical instruments	-	-	-	-	-	-	-	-	-	-	-	-
3903	Sporting and athletic goods	-	-	-	-	-	-	-	-	-	-	-	-
3909	Manufacturing industries, n.e.c.	16	17	16	16	207	121	145	142	420	242	262	240
3	Total manufacturing	4026	4023	4009	4013	54308	58969	58490	62137	171539	190544	192846	196622

Kuwait

ISIC Revision 2 ISIC Industry	Note	Output in producers' prices (thousand DINARS) 1992	1993	1994	1995	Note	Value added in producers' prices (thousand DINARS) 1992	1993	1994	1995	Note	Gross fixed capital formation (thousand DINARS) 1994	1995
311/2 Food products		69742	81000	88793	100535		33629	35610	37283	40662		3822	5856
3111 Slaughtering, preparing & preserving meat		-	-	6559	6953		-	-	2243	1618		108	304
3112 Dairy products		18409	23174	26945	27240		8411	10033	11392	11700		1919	2688
3113 Canning, preserving of fruits & vegetables		-	-	-	-		-	-	-	-		-	-
3114 Canning, preserving and processing of fish		-	-	4883	3722		-	-	1368	748		292	518
3115 Vegetable and animal oils and fats		-	-	-	-		-	-	-	-		-	-
3116 Grain mill products		-	-	-	-		-	-	-	-		-	-
3117 Bakery products		31710	31988	32555	38237		17139	17721	17314	20818		1353	750
3118 Sugar factories and refineries		-	-	-	-		-	-	-	-		-	-
3119 Cocoa, chocolate and sugar confectionery		-	-	-	-		-	-	-	-		-	-
3121 Other food products		19322	25453	17483	23825		7998	7756	4869	5660		145	1592
3122 Prepared animal feeds		301	385	368	558		81	100	97	118		5	4
313 Beverages		19377	26714	28088	28459		8941	12619	12094	13256		2686	2317
3131 Distilling, rectifying and blending spirits		-	-	-	-		-	-	-	-		-	-
3132 Wine industries		-	-	-	-		-	-	-	-		-	-
3133 Malt liquors and malt		-	-	-	-		-	-	-	-		-	-
3134 Soft drinks and carbonated waters		19377	26714	28088	28459		8941	12619	12094	13256		2686	2317
314 Tobacco		-	-	-	-		-	-	-	-		-	-
321 Textiles		13206	13016	11511	11926		7220	7363	6248	6486		101	61
3211 Spinning, weaving and finishing textiles		-	-	-	-		-	-	-	-		-	-
3212 Made-up textile goods excl. wearing apparel		13206	13016	11511	11926		7220	7363	6248	6486		101	61
3213 Knitting mills		-	-	-	-		-	-	-	-		-	-
3214 Carpets and rugs		-	-	-	-		-	-	-	-		-	-
3215 Cordage, rope and twine		-	-	-	-		-	-	-	-		-	-
3219 Other textiles		-	-	-	-		-	-	-	-		-	-
322 Wearing apparel, except footwear		38392	49905	45749	45169		30015	35722	32926	34553		328	-3
323 Leather and fur products		1865	2030	2083	2195		1267	1169	988	922		28	1
3231 Tanneries and leather finishing		1865	2030	2083	2195		1267	1169	988	922		28	1
3232 Fur dressing and dyeing industries		-	-	-	-		-	-	-	-		-	-
3233 Leather prods. excl. wearing apparel		-	-	-	-		-	-	-	-		-	-
324 Footwear, except rubber or plastic		-	-	544	250		-	-	280	109		28	35
331 Wood products, except furniture		11343	9405	9324	16867		4525	3584	4244	6361		61	357
3311 Sawmills, planing and other wood mills		10244	8644	8752	16302		3899	3243	3903	5927		61	357
3312 Wooden and cane containers		-	-	-	-		-	-	-	-		-	-
3319 Other wood and cork products		1099	761	572	565		626	341	341	434		-	-
332 Furniture and fixtures, excl. metal		27454	29674	26642	28034		13627	15103	13319	14125		879	1186
341 Paper and products		14435	17816	20356	25411		4970	7326	8039	8996		882	605
3411 Pulp, paper and paperboard articles		-	-	-	-		-	-	-	-		-	-
3412 Containers of paper and paperboard		7264	8911	9657	12152		2272	3422	3406	3984		467	88
3419 Other pulp, paper and paperboard articles		7171	8905	10699	13259		2698	3904	4633	5012		415	517
342 Printing and publishing		20365	19894	22993	22177		10824	6962	7616	6271		2245	2619
351 Industrial chemicals		17810	29291	39669	56372		8416	19065	29158	44370		3883	4645
3511 Basic chemicals excl. fertilizers		3417	4186	3843	3973		2398	2917	2741	2694		146	153
3512 Fertilizers and pesticides		14393	25105	35826	52399		6018	16148	26417	41676		3737	4492
3513 Synthetic resins and plastic materials		-	-	-	-		-	-	-	-		-	-
352 Other chemicals		11605	14154	14339	15471		4963	6419	6354	5968		293	436
3521 Paints, varnishes and lacquers		7970	9435	9207	9682		3639	4323	4088	3546		145	121
3522 Drugs and medicines		-	-	-	-		-	-	-	-		-	-
3523 Soap, cleaning preps., perfumes, cosmetics		2270	2520*	3773	4561		872	1204	1679	1919		83	307
3529 Other chemical products		1365	2199	1359	1228		452	892	587	503		65	8
353 Petroleum refineries		776403	954352	1299163	1527950		306947	383525	522091	614037		44181	26735

354 Misc. petroleum and coal products	2735	2975	4826	4003	1042	1470	2029	1844	332	39
355 Rubber products	1262	1414	2174	2586	238	272	883	718	608	123
3551 Tyres and tubes	-	-	-	-	-	-	-	-	-	-
3559 Other rubber products	1262	1414	2174	2586	238	272	883	718	608	123
356 Plastic products	17082	24037	30895	33138	8663	11525	14278	13819	3608	2589
361 Pottery, china, earthenware	-	-	-	-	-	-	-	-	-	-
362 Glass and products	6393	7343	7488	7933	3487	4106	4352	4484	358	839
369 Other non-metallic mineral products	53033	83353	106588	112831	24596	31302	45946	44736	8939	9179
3691 Structural clay products	-	-	-	-	-	-	-	-	-	-
3692 Cement, lime and plaster	12889	25086	34338	35971	5895	6183	10759	10507	218	484
3699 Other non-metallic mineral products	40144	58267	72250	76860	18701	25119	35187	34229	8721	8695
371 Iron and steel	7547	12617	14923	14625	5045	7251	8599	6680	960	710
372 Non-ferrous metals	-	-	-	-	-	-	-	-	-	-
381 Fabricated metal products	64021	71473	68128	71557	28925	33343	31314	32939	2239	767
3811 Cutlery, hand tools and general hardware	42	17	-	-	23	11	-	-	-	-
3812 Furniture and fixtures primarily of metal	4972	3907	4749	6620	2556	2179	2397	3009	34	34
3813 Structural metal products	45231	44433	47694	47809	19102	19867	20392	20953	1385	499
3819 Other fabricated metal products	13776	23116	15685	17128	7244	11286	8525	8977	820	234
382 Non-electrical machinery	18158	24603	26531	22524	13200	17804	18572	14006	1526	1611
3821 Engines and turbines	-	-	-	-	-	-	-	-	-	-
3822 Agricultural machinery and equipment	-	-	-	-	-	-	-	-	-	-
3823 Metal and wood working machinery	-	-	-	-	-	-	-	-	-	-
3824 Other special industrial machinery	13004	17975	19798	13531	10982	14703	15038	9258	952	1292
3825 Office, computing and accounting machinery	-	165	-	-	-	157	-	-	-	-
3829 Other non-electrical machinery & equipment	5154	6463	6733	8993	2218	2944	3534	4748	574	319
383 Electrical machinery	20743	27951	33645	34143	7837	10230	12017	11772	1063	519
3831 Electrical industrial machinery	7126	8119	13633	11537	3416	3894	5319	5107	923	441
3832 Radio, television and communication equipm.	-	-	-	-	-	-	-	-	-	-
3833 Electrical appliances and housewares	-	-	-	-	-	-	-	-	-	-
3839 Other electrical apparatus and supplies	13617	19832	20012	22606	4421	6336	6698	6665	140	78
384 Transport equipment	19721	23991	14295	18367	15036	15572	7005	6495	230	1470
3841 Shipbuilding and repairing	16415	20668	11260	15709	13599	14272	5619	5460	226	1461
3842 Railroad equipment	-	-	-	-	-	-	-	-	-	-
3843 Motor vehicles	3306	3323	3035	2658	1437	1300	1386	1035	4	9
3844 Motorcycles and bicycles	-	-	-	-	-	-	-	-	-	-
3845 Aircraft	-	-	-	-	-	-	-	-	-	-
3849 Other transport equipment	-	-	-	-	-	-	-	-	-	-
385 Professional and scientific equipment	-	-	-	-	-	-	-	-	-	-
3851 Prof. and scientific equipment n.e.c.	-	-	-	-	-	-	-	-	-	-
3852 Photographic and optical goods	-	-	-	-	-	-	-	-	-	-
3853 Watches and clocks	-	-	-	-	-	-	-	-	-	-
390 Other manufacturing industries	10173	20142	8939	32403	5614	6069	5180	5947	106	26
3901 Jewellery and related articles	8452	18992	7903	31404	4706	5517	4642	5384	1	17
3902 Musical instruments	-	-	-	-	-	-	-	-	-	-
3903 Sporting and athletic goods	-	-	-	-	-	-	-	-	-	-
3909 Manufacturing industries, n.e.c.	1721	1150	1036	999	908	552	538	563	105	9
3 Total manufacturing	1242865	1547150	1927686	2234926	549027	673411	830815	939556	79386	62722

Kuwait

ISIC Revision 2		Index numbers of industrial production											
		(1990=100)											
ISIC Industry	Note	1985	1986	1987	1988	1989	1990	1991	1992	1993	1994	1995	1996
311/2 Food products		...	...	...	...	...	...	...	...	...	...	...	...
313 Beverages		...	...	...	...	...	...	...	...	...	...	...	...
314 Tobacco		...	...	...	...	...	...	...	...	...	...	...	...
321 Textiles		...	...	...	...	...	...	...	...	...	...	...	...
322 Wearing apparel, except footwear		...	...	...	...	...	...	...	...	...	...	...	...
323 Leather and fur products		...	...	...	...	...	...	...	...	...	...	...	...
324 Footwear, except rubber or plastic		...	...	...	...	...	...	...	...	...	...	...	...
331 Wood products, except furniture		...	...	...	...	...	...	...	...	...	...	...	...
332 Furniture and fixtures, excl. metal		...	...	...	...	...	...	...	...	...	...	...	...
341 Paper and products		...	...	...	...	...	...	...	...	...	...	...	...
342 Printing and publishing		...	...	...	...	...	...	...	...	...	...	...	...
351 Industrial chemicals		...	...	...	...	...	...	...	...	...	...	...	...
352 Other chemicals		...	...	...	...	...	...	...	...	...	...	...	...
353 Petroleum refineries		101	108	108	118	124	100	18	58	73	120	133	...
354 Misc. petroleum and coal products		...	...	...	...	...	...	...	...	...	...	...	...
355 Rubber products		...	...	...	...	...	...	...	...	...	...	...	...
356 Plastic products		...	...	...	...	...	...	...	...	...	...	...	...
361 Pottery, china, earthenware		...	...	...	...	...	...	...	...	...	...	...	...
362 Glass and products		...	...	...	...	...	...	...	...	...	...	...	...
369 Other non-metallic mineral products		...	...	...	...	...	...	...	...	...	...	...	...
371 Iron and steel		...	...	...	...	...	...	...	...	...	...	...	...
372 Non-ferrous metals		...	...	...	...	...	...	...	...	...	...	...	...
381 Fabricated metal products		...	...	...	...	...	...	...	...	...	...	...	...
382 Non-electrical machinery		...	...	...	...	...	...	...	...	...	...	...	...
383 Electrical machinery		...	...	...	...	...	...	...	...	...	...	...	...
384 Transport equipment		...	...	...	...	...	...	...	...	...	...	...	...
385 Professional and scientific equipment		...	...	...	...	...	...	...	...	...	...	...	...
390 Other manufacturing industries		...	...	...	...	...	...	...	...	...	...	...	...
3 Total manufacturing		...	...	...	...	...	...	...	...	...	...	...	...

KYRGYZSTAN

Supplier of information:
National Statistical Commission of the Kyrgyz Republic, Bishkek City.

Basic source of data:
Annual industrial survey.

Major deviations from ISIC (Revision 3):
Data collected under the national classification system have been reclassified by the national authorities to correspond with ISIC (Rev. 3).

Reference period (if not calendar year):

Scope:
All enterprises operating under an independent regime and enterprises operating under a non-industrial organization regime.

Method of enumeration:
Not reported.

Adjusted for non-response:
Data refer to all surveyed enterprises.

Concepts and definitions of variables:
No deviations from the standard UN concepts and definitions are reported.

Related national publications:

Kyrgyzstan

ISIC Revision 3	Number of establishments					Number of employees					Wages and salaries paid to employees				
		(numbers)					(numbers)					(thousand SOMS)			
ISIC Industry	Note	1993	1994	1995	1996	Note	1993	1994	1995	1996	Note	1993	1994	1995	1996
151 Processed meat,fish,fruit,vegetables,fats		256	270	207	200		7754	5929	3723	2474		7788.9	14887.1	13677.7	11323.2
1511 Processing/preserving of meat		158	182	117	121		4169	3446	1917	1186		4349.7	9830.2	8425.1	6538.1
1512 Processing/preserving of fish		12	10	8	6		229	208	278	131		219.2	539.0	499.8	507.4
1513 Processing/preserving of fruit & vegetables		51	33	26	23		2700	1776	1127	784		2791.4	3182.7	3268.1	2924.5
1514 Vegetable and animal oils and fats		35	45	56	50		656	499	401	373		428.6	1335.2	1484.7	1353.2
1520 Dairy products		39	54	48	51		2641	2344	1988	1376		4102.3	10465.2	11388.2	7998.7
153 Grain mill products; starches; animal feeds		404	385	314	552		4215	4971	4180	4497		5598.8	17736.2	28562.5	33734.2
1531 Grain mill products		305	328	268	504		3494	4390	3736	4010		4978.7	16252.8	26859.5	31427.7
1532 Starches and starch products		1	1	1	1		459	409	341	343		538.2	1181.5	1366.9	1830.3
1533 Prepared animal feeds		98	56	45	47		262	172	103	144		81.9	301.9	336.1	476.2
154 Other food products		156	169	161	132		9987	8233	6150	5435		14400.1	35790.0	36510.3	42399.8
1541 Bakery products		135	146	139	113		6446	5745	4106	3339		7910.2	22727.2	24003.2	20978.2
1542 Sugar		3	3	3	3		1585	980	878	1140		2361.4	5073.4	5148.0	16053.2
1543 Cocoa, chocolate and sugar confectionery		18	17	13	9		1956	1448	1089	882		4128.5	7888.7	6941.9	4946.0
1544 Macaroni, noodles & similar products		-	3	6	7		-	60	77	74		...	100.7	417.2	422.4
1549 Other food products n.e.c.		-	-	-	-		-	-	-	-		-	-	-	-
155 Beverages		37	29	29	31		2582	2284	2181	2195		2879.3	7464.6	11505.3	16938.1
1551 Distilling, rectifying & blending of spirits		1	1	4	3		166	161	192	199		336.2	979.0	1543.2	1905.2
1552 Wines		15	13	13	12		1151	976	907	834		1307.9	2941.6	4429.5	5839.2
1553 Malt liquors and malt		8	7	7	7		981	898	845	847		987.8	2745.9	4703.0	7484.0
1554 Soft drinks; mineral waters		13	8	5	9		284	249	237	315		247.4	798.1	829.6	1709.7
1600 Tobacco products		6	6	6	6		1444	1294	1220	960		2439.5	6664.5	7341.5	6864.4
171 Spinning, weaving and finishing of textiles		18	18	20	16		30772	24488	15939	12772		47315.3	99903.1	108373.8	97748.6
1711 Textile fibre preparation; textile weaving		...	...	...	...		...	...	...	...		...	...	...	...
1712 Finishing of textiles		...	...	...	...		...	...	...	...		...	...	...	...
172 Other textiles		...	...	...	...		...	...	...	...		...	...	...	...
1721 Made-up textile articles, except apparel		...	...	...	...		...	...	...	...		...	...	...	...
1722 Carpets and rugs		...	...	...	...		...	...	...	...		...	...	...	...
1723 Cordage, rope, twine and netting		...	...	...	...		...	...	...	...		...	...	...	...
1729 Other textiles n.e.c.		-	-	-	-		-	-	-	-		-	-	-	-
1730 Knitted and crocheted fabrics and articles		13	11	8	9		6409	5751	2578	1581		10740.5	21183.0	19945.0	16787.9
1810 Wearing apparel, except fur apparel		73	63	63	61		12242	8505	5053	3932		14485.4	21102.1	16711.3	18520.2
1820 Dressing & dyeing of fur; processing of fur		19	11	9	4		1063	819	640	354		1960.3	3158.0	3803.9	2641.0
191 Tanning, dressing and processing of leather		3	3	3	3		1263	1061	887	912		2658.6	6208.2	6483.3	7910.3
1911 Tanning and dressing of leather		3	2	2	2		1263	821	667	687		2658.6	5287.0	5154.0	6111.3
1912 Luggage, handbags, etc.; saddlery & harness		-	1	1	1		-	240	220	225		-	921.2	1329.3	1799.0
1920 Footwear		20	18	16	16		3332	2296	1520	990		4005.3	6975.4	5756.3	4866.9
2010 Sawmilling and planing of wood		150	94	67	51		458	210	124	120		397.1	421.6	369.2	400.4
202 Products of wood, cork, straw, etc.		170	109	97	80		3403	2185	1445	1148		2924.1	4122.5	3748.1	3942.8
2021 Veneer sheets, plywood, particle board, etc.		-	-	-	-		-	-	-	-		-	-	-	-
2022 Builders' carpentry and joinery		134	88	79	58		1321	904	538	491		1488.8	2541.7	2209.5	2393.1
2023 Wooden containers		14	9	6	3		445	85	55	46		502.8	243.3	200.6	207.3
2029 Other wood products; articles of cork/straw		22	12	12	19		1637	1196	852	611		932.5	1337.5	1338.0	1342.4
210 Paper and paper products		2	1	1	1		102	82	83	78		114.9	235.8	358.8	442.0
2101 Pulp, paper and paperboard		-	-	-	-		-	-	-	-		-	-	-	-
2102 Corrugated paper and paperboard		2	1	1	1		102	82	83	78		114.9	235.8	358.8	442.0
2109 Other articles of paper and paperboard		-	-	-	-		-	-	-	-		-	-	-	-
221 Publishing		26	21	18	18		1787	1415	1302	1250		2526.3	7071.3	11427.6	12009.7
2211 Publishing of books and other publications		...	...	...	...		...	...	...	...		...	...	...	...
2212 Publishing of newspapers, journals, etc.		...	...	...	...		...	...	...	...		...	...	...	...
2213 Publishing of recorded media		...	...	...	...		...	...	...	...		...	...	...	...
2219 Other publishing		...	...	...	...		...	...	...	...		...	...	...	...

222 Printing and related service activities	...	...	...	...	...	...	...	...	...	...	...	...
2221 Printing	...	...	...	...	...	...	...	...	...	...	...	...
2222 Service activities related to printing	...	...	...	...	...	...	...	...	...	...	...	...
2230 Reproduction of recorded media	1	1	1	1	14	20	12	5	5.7	33.4	29.3	34.5
2310 Coke oven products	-	-	-	-	-	-	-	-	-	-	-	-
2320 Refined petroleum products	-	-	-	-	-	-	-	-	-	-	-	-
2330 Processing of nuclear fuel	-	-	-	-	-	-	-	-	-	-	-	-
241 Basic chemicals	-	-	-	-	-	-	-	-	-	-	-	-
2411 Basic chemicals, except fertilizers	-	-	-	-	-	-	-	-	-	-	-	-
2412 Fertilizers and nitrogen compounds	-	-	-	-	-	-	-	-	-	-	-	-
2413 Plastics in primary forms; synthetic rubber	-	-	-	-	-	-	-	-	-	-	-	-
242 Other chemicals	9	6	6	6	622	429	402	294	1019.6	2880.3	3475.1	3001.5
2421 Pesticides and other agro-chemical products	-	-	-	-	-	-	-	-	-	-	-	-
2422 Paints, varnishes, printing ink and mastics	4	2	2	2	116	92	69	77	316.6	937.5	833.9	826.2
2423 Pharmaceuticals, medicinal chemicals, etc.	3	3	3	3	420	272	278	170	577.7	1615.2	2300.8	1852.0
2424 Soap, cleaning & cosmetic preparations	1	-	-	-	-	-	-	-	-	-	-	-
2429 Other chemical products n.e.c.	1	1	1	1	86	65	55	47	125.3	327.6	340.4	323.3
2430 Man-made fibres	-	-	-	-	-	-	-	-	-	-	-	-
251 Rubber products	1	1	1	1	216	144	151	135	236.2	592.7	615.3	786.4
2511 Rubber tyres and tubes	-	-	-	-	-	-	-	-	-	-	-	-
2519 Other rubber products	1	1	1	1	216	144	151	135	236.2	592.7	615.3	786.4
2520 Plastic products	3	4	4	4	892	468	419	381	1154.8	2230.8	2412.2	2900.6
2610 Glass and glass products	2	2	2	1	2027	1838	1532	1061	4443.0	12850.1	11271.7	12345.1
269 Non-metallic mineral products n.e.c.	172	144	114	92	17937	12119	9695	8899	21766.5	50947.8	60557.4	70910.6
2691 Pottery, china and earthenware	1	1	1	1	599	377	225	204	801.9	1154.1	1063.3	1024.8
2692 Refractory ceramic products	-	-	-	-	-	-	-	-	-	-	-	-
2693 Struct.non-refractory clay; ceramic products	46	29	17	16	4262	2751	2370	2196	4238.1	9417.2	12824.8	15378.6
2694 Cement, lime and plaster	6	6	6	5	2089	1926	1547	1420	3457.1	12442.9	11323.2	14985.3
2695 Articles of concrete, cement and plaster	100	87	75	55	10121	6342	5048	4550	12008.9	24418.7	31165.5	34561.0
2696 Cutting, shaping & finishing of stone	2	4	2	2	338	236	151	143	445.3	878.9	1112.9	961.2
2699 Other non-metallic mineral products n.e.c.	17	17	13	13	528	487	354	386	815.2	2636.0	3067.7	3999.7
2710 Basic iron and steel	-	-	-	-	-	-	-	-	-	-	-	-
2720 Basic precious and non-ferrous metals	4	5	7	7	9720	8098	6817	6028	23272.0	69268.8	79128.3	85497.3
273 Casting of metals	-	-	-	-	-	-	-	-	-	-	-	-
2731 Casting of iron and steel	-	-	-	-	-	-	-	-	-	-	-	-
2732 Casting of non-ferrous metals	-	-	-	-	-	-	-	-	-	-	-	-
281 Struct.metal products;tanks;steam generators	14	5	6	8	601	330	119	233	1309.5	2042.6	1089.6	2350.2
2811 Structural metal products	14	5	6	8	601	330	119	233	1309.5	2042.6	1089.6	2350.2
2812 Tanks, reservoirs and containers of metal	-	-	-	-	-	-	-	-	-	-	-	-
2813 Steam generators	-	-	-	-	-	-	-	-	-	-	-	-
289 Other metal products; metal working services	29	25	18	19	3704	2454	1286	1074	5726.3	9113.8	7911.5	7398.4
2891 Metal forging/pressing/stamping/roll-forming	-	-	-	-	-	-	-	-	-	-	-	-
2892 Treatment & coating of metals	-	-	-	-	-	-	-	-	-	-	-	-
2893 Cutlery, hand tools and general hardware	2	4	2	2	2195	1522	692	466	3767.7	5626.7	4053.5	3341.5
2899 Other fabricated metal products n.e.c.	27	21	16	17	1509	932	594	608	1958.6	3487.1	3858.0	4056.9
291 General purpose machinery	2	2	2	2	1614	1327	970	770	2397.0	5449.4	4277.5	6160.6
2911 Engines & turbines(not for transport equip.)	-	-	-	-	-	-	-	-	-	-	-	-
2912 Pumps, compressors, taps and valves	1	1	1	1	1026	917	660	564	1916.2	4537.7	3347.8	4649.1
2913 Bearings, gears, gearing & driving elements	1	1	1	1	588	410	310	206	480.8	911.7	929.7	1511.5
2914 Ovens, furnaces and furnace burners	-	-	-	-	-	-	-	-	-	-	-	-
2915 Lifting and handling equipment	-	-	-	-	-	-	-	-	-	-	-	-
2919 Other general purpose machinery	-	-	-	-	-	-	-	-	-	-	-	-
292 Special purpose machinery	329	316	280	229	32395	22566	13959	9845	31374.6	64068.3	67290.3	59397.2
2921 Agricultural and forestry machinery	308	297	261	197	13459	10302	6308	3660	9763.1	25575.5	20198.2	14249.2
2922 Machine tools	7	5	5	7	9029	5856	4825	3773	9697.8	21568.9	25094.1	23902.0
2923 Machinery for metallurgy	-	-	-	-	-	-	-	-	-	-	-	-
2924 Machinery for mining & construction	1	1	1	1	87	51	54	61	129.6	319.5	435.3	618.3
2925 Food/beverage/tobacco processing machinery	4	5	5	4	1536	864	540	478	2107.0	3974.9	3814.4	1835.0
2926 Machinery for textile, apparel and leather	-	-	-	-	-	-	-	-	-	-	-	-
2927 Weapons and ammunition	-	-	-	-	-	-	-	-	-	-	-	-
2929 Other special purpose machinery	9	8	8	20	8284	5493	2232	1873	9677.1	12629.5	17748.3	18792.7
2930 Domestic appliances n.e.c.	1	1	1	1	984	781	738	546	2018.3	5833.3	6158.9	5918.9

continued

Kyrgyzstan

ISIC Revision 3		Number of establishments					Number of employees					Wages and salaries paid to employees			
		(numbers)					(numbers)					(thousand SOMS)			
ISIC Industry	Note	1993	1994	1995	1996	Note	1993	1994	1995	1996	Note	1993	1994	1995	1996
3000 Office, accounting and computing machinery		3	3	3	3		1836	868	149	139		2246.1	2461.9	652.3	643.9
3110 Electric motors, generators and transformers		11	14	12	13		6102	3989	3488	2906		8687.5	14607.5	15085.8	14802.0
3120 Electricity distribution & control apparatus		-	-	-	-		-	-	-	-		-	-	-	-
3130 Insulated wire and cable		1	1	1	1		1292	1000	884	674		1475.3	3006.9	4080.9	4477.6
3140 Accumulators, primary cells and batteries		-	-	-	-		-	-	-	-		-	-	-	-
3150 Lighting equipment and electric lamps		1	1	2	2		6209	3360	3221	2891		12152.8	11903.8	15774.2	24104.5
3190 Other electrical equipment n.e.c.		...	...	...	...		...	...	...	...		...	...	...	...
3210 Electronic valves, tubes, etc.		-	-	-	-		-	-	-	-		-	-	-	-
3220 TV/radio transmitters; line comm. apparatus		-	-	-	-		-	-	-	-		-	-	-	-
3230 TV and radio receivers and associated goods		...	...	...	...		...	...	...	...		...	...	...	...
331 Medical, measuring, testing appliances, etc.		3	3	2	2		5516	2389	2059	1711		8113.7	14177.6	17218.0	15306.1
3311 Medical, surgical and orthopaedic equipment		-	-	-	-		-	-	-	-		-	-	-	-
3312 Measuring/testing/navigating appliances,etc.		-	-	-	-		-	-	-	-		-	-	-	-
3313 Industrial process control equipment		3	3	2	2		5516	2389	2059	1711		8113.7	14177.6	17218.0	15306.1
3320 Optical instruments & photographic equipment		-	-	-	-		-	-	-	-		-	-	-	-
3330 Watches and clocks		-	-	-	-		-	-	-	-		-	-	-	-
3410 Motor vehicles		3	3	3	3		3934	2140	1860	1390		9068.6	12305.8	13130.0	13515.3
3420 Automobile bodies, trailers & semi-trailers		...	...	...	...		...	...	...	...		...	...	...	...
3430 Parts/accessories for automobiles		...	...	...	...		...	...	...	...		...	...	...	...
351 Building and repairing of ships and boats		1	1	1	1		43	33	35	42		56.3	135.6	247.1	365.2
3511 Building and repairing of ships		1	1	1	1		43	33	35	42		56.3	135.6	247.1	365.2
3512 Building/repairing of pleasure/sport. boats		-	-	-	-		-	-	-	-		-	-	-	-
3520 Railway/tramway locomotives & rolling stock		1	1	1	1		106	25	25	28		198.3	198.0	222.0	308.0
3530 Aircraft and spacecraft		-	-	-	-		-	-	-	-		-	-	-	-
359 Transport equipment n.e.c.		-	-	-	-		-	-	-	-		-	-	-	-
3591 Motorcycles		-	-	-	-		-	-	-	-		-	-	-	-
3592 Bicycles and invalid carriages		-	-	-	-		-	-	-	-		-	-	-	-
3599 Other transport equipment n.e.c.		-	-	-	-		-	-	-	-		-	-	-	-
3610 Furniture		8	8	7	8		2638	1765	1424	1018		4632.0	8010.2	8171.5	6577.8
369 Manufacturing n.e.c.		55	51	25	52		937	725	554	422		1286.0	3923.5	3758.4	3091.8
3691 Jewellery and related articles		-	-	1	1		-	-	-	-		-	-	-	-
3692 Musical instruments		-	-	-	-		-	-	-	-		-	-	-	-
3693 Sports goods		-	-	-	-		-	-	-	-		-	-	-	-
3694 Games and toys		-	-	-	-		-	-	-	-		-	-	-	-
3699 Other manufacturing n.e.c.		55	51	24	51		937	725	554	422		1286.0	3923.5	3758.4	3091.8
3710 Recycling of metal waste and scrap		1	1	1	1		95	89	60	59		232.8	581.6	489.2	554.0
3720 Recycling of non-metal waste and scrap		-	-	-	-		-	-	-	-		-	-	-	-
D Total manufacturing		2047	1861	1567	1689		188888	138824	98872	80625		267209.6	560012.3	609009.3	624975.7

ISIC Revision 3	Output in producers' prices					Value added					Gross fixed capital formation		
		(thousand SOMS)					(million SOMS)					(million SOMS)	
ISIC Industry	Note	1993	1994	1995	1996	Note	1993	1994	1995	1996	Note	1995	1996
151 Processed meat,fish,fruit,vegetables,fats		208130	211815	178027	132071		...	...	...	...		...	...
1511 Processing/preserving of meat		135235	167740	135584	88473		...	...	...	...		...	...
1512 Processing/preserving of fish		911	1627	1724	1734		...	...	...	...		...	...
1513 Processing/preserving of fruit & vegetables		69004	32602	16892	28459		...	...	...	...		...	...
1514 Vegetable and animal oils and fats		2980	9846	23827	13405		...	...	...	...		...	...
1520 Dairy products		76812	148372	139295	139063		...	...	...	...		...	...
153 Grain mill products; starches; animal feeds		28341	386181	558483	975085		...	...	...	...		...	...
1531 Grain mill products		15737	362645	516619	911908		...	...	...	...		...	...
1532 Starches and starch products		7887	11235	32204	45862		...	...	...	...		...	...
1533 Prepared animal feeds		4728	12302	9660	17315		...	...	...	...		...	...
154 Other food products		146696	310981	308304	540132		...	...	...	...		...	...
1541 Bakery products		66934	174661	159191	162444		...	...	...	...		...	...
1542 Sugar		15844	27285	47451	293417		...	...	...	...		...	...
1543 Cocoa, chocolate and sugar confectionery		63918	108094	97408	78568		...	...	...	...		...	...
1544 Macaroni, noodles & similar products		-	941	4254	5703		...	...	...	...		...	...
1549 Other food products n.e.c.		-	-	-	-		...	...	...	...		...	...
155 Beverages		30921	78638	153574	245891		...	...	...	...		...	...
1551 Distilling, rectifying & blending of spirits		4506	19038	39766	50804		...	...	...	...		...	...
1552 Wines		16518	30943	60199	108341		...	...	...	...		...	...
1553 Malt liquors and malt		6698	21493	34666	59499		...	...	...	...		...	...
1554 Soft drinks; mineral waters		3199	7164	18943	27247		...	...	...	...		...	...
1600 Tobacco products		157620	189025	128950	143639		...	...	...	...		...	...
171 Spinning, weaving and finishing of textiles		703425	1009286	1041450	844079		...	...	...	...		...	...
1711 Textile fibre preparation; textile weaving		...	...	...	...		...	...	...	...		...	...
1712 Finishing of textiles		...	...	...	...		...	...	...	...		...	...
172 Other textiles		...	...	...	...		...	...	...	...		...	...
1721 Made-up textile articles, except apparel		...	...	...	...		...	...	...	...		...	...
1722 Carpets and rugs		...	...	...	...		...	...	...	...		...	...
1723 Cordage, rope, twine and netting		...	...	...	...		...	...	...	...		...	...
1729 Other textiles n.e.c.		-	-	-	-		...	...	...	...		...	...
1730 Knitted and crocheted fabrics and articles		81208	106954	59856	68200		...	...	...	...		...	...
1810 Wearing apparel, except fur apparel		108231	114956	76358	82396		...	...	...	...		...	...
1820 Dressing & dyeing of fur; processing of fur		15018	15531	14697	8767		...	...	...	...		...	...
191 Tanning, dressing and processing of leather		17772	36535	44656	56233		...	...	...	...		...	...
1911 Tanning and dressing of leather		17772	27013	31700	36975		...	...	...	...		...	...
1912 Luggage, handbags, etc.; saddlery & harness		-	9522	12956	19258		...	...	...	...		...	...
1920 Footwear		22718	37212	18676	21928		...	...	...	...		...	...
2010 Sawmilling and planing of wood		1785	1812	1895	1824		...	...	...	...		...	...
202 Products of wood, cork, straw, etc.		17223	16712	13366	13164		...	...	...	...		...	...
2021 Veneer sheets, plywood, particle board, etc.		-	-	-	-		...	...	...	...		...	...
2022 Builders' carpentry and joinery		10111	10478	8588	8173		...	...	...	...		...	...
2023 Wooden containers		3326	643	350	508		...	...	...	...		...	...
2029 Other wood products; articles of cork/straw		3786	5591	4428	4483		...	...	...	...		...	...
210 Paper and paper products		889	1490	2024	2450		...	...	...	...		...	...
2101 Pulp, paper and paperboard		-	-	-	-		...	...	...	...		...	...
2102 Corrugated paper and paperboard		889	1490	2024	2450		...	...	...	...		...	...
2109 Other articles of paper and paperboard		-	-	-	-		...	...	...	...		...	...
221 Publishing		6707	20963	37359	47578		...	...	...	...		...	...
2211 Publishing of books and other publications		...	...	...	...		...	...	...	...		...	...
2212 Publishing of newspapers, journals, etc.		...	...	...	...		...	...	...	...		...	...
2213 Publishing of recorded media		...	...	...	...		...	...	...	...		...	...
2219 Other publishing		...	...	...	...		...	...	...	...		...	...

continued

Kyrgyzstan

ISIC Revision 3		Output in producers' prices (thousand SOMS)					Value added (million SOMS)					Gross fixed capital formation (million SOMS)	
ISIC Industry	Note	1993	1994	1995	1996	Note	1993	1994	1995	1996	Note	1995	1996
222 Printing and related service activities		...	...	...	...		...	...	...	...		...	...
2221 Printing		...	...	...	...		...	...	...	...		...	...
2222 Service activities related to printing		...	...	...	...		...	...	...	...		...	...
2230 Reproduction of recorded media		22	99	47	81		...	...	...	...		...	...
2310 Coke oven products		-	-	-	-		...	...	...	...		...	...
2320 Refined petroleum products		-	-	-	-		...	...	...	...		...	...
2330 Processing of nuclear fuel		-	-	-	-		...	...	...	...		...	...
241 Basic chemicals		-	-	-	-		...	...	...	...		...	...
2411 Basic chemicals, except fertilizers		-	-	-	-		...	...	...	...		...	...
2412 Fertilizers and nitrogen compounds		-	-	-	-		...	...	...	...		...	...
2413 Plastics in primary forms; synthetic rubber		-	-	-	-		...	...	...	...		...	...
242 Other chemicals		6598	14007	12262	11169		...	...	...	...		...	...
2421 Pesticides and other agro-chemical products		-	-	-	-		...	...	...	...		...	...
2422 Paints, varnishes, printing ink and mastics		2353	5799	6106	7389		...	...	...	...		...	...
2423 Pharmaceuticals, medicinal chemicals, etc.		2473	5334	5201	3491		...	...	...	...		...	...
2424 Soap, cleaning & cosmetic preparations		2	-	-	-		...	...	...	...		...	...
2429 Other chemical products n.e.c.		1770	2874	955	289		...	...	...	...		...	...
2430 Man-made fibres		-	-	-	-		...	...	...	...		...	...
251 Rubber products		1566	2521	2940	3752		...	...	...	...		...	...
2511 Rubber tyres and tubes		-	-	-	-		...	...	...	...		...	...
2519 Other rubber products		1566	2521	2940	3752		...	...	...	...		...	...
2520 Plastic products		6218	6894	8070	10133		...	...	...	...		...	...
2610 Glass and glass products		55625	126652	84196	131205		...	...	...	...		...	...
269 Non-metallic mineral products n.e.c.		141072	271670	281973	454770		...	...	...	...		...	...
2691 Pottery, china and earthenware		3071	8025	9654	9701		...	...	...	...		...	...
2692 Refractory ceramic products		-	-	-	-		...	...	...	...		...	...
2693 Struct.non-refractory clay; ceramic products		22714	43948	48389	64637		...	...	...	...		...	...
2694 Cement, lime and plaster		52080	130001	117509	252410		...	...	...	...		...	...
2695 Articles of concrete, cement and plaster		54428	69850	85383	97850		...	...	...	...		...	...
2696 Cutting, shaping & finishing of stone		1500	2615	2180	3075		...	...	...	...		...	...
2699 Other non-metallic mineral products n.e.c.		7279	17231	18858	27097		...	...	...	...		...	...
2710 Basic iron and steel		-	-	-	-		...	...	...	...		...	...
2720 Basic precious and non-ferrous metals		129623	376531	379838	484428		...	...	...	...		...	...
273 Casting of metals		-	-	-	-		...	...	...	...		...	...
2731 Casting of iron and steel		-	-	-	-		...	...	...	...		...	...
2732 Casting of non-ferrous metals		-	-	-	-		...	...	...	...		...	...
281 Struct.metal products;tanks;steam generators		6335	10437	7833	11246		...	...	...	...		...	...
2811 Structural metal products		6335	10437	7833	11246		...	...	...	...		...	...
2812 Tanks, reservoirs and containers of metal		-	-	-	-		...	...	...	...		...	...
2813 Steam generators		-	-	-	-		...	...	...	...		...	...
289 Other metal products; metal working services		12878	25911	19785	20468		...	...	...	...		...	...
2891 Metal forging/pressing/stamping/roll-forming		-	-	-	-		...	...	...	...		...	...
2892 Treatment & coating of metals		-	-	-	-		...	...	...	...		...	...
2893 Cutlery, hand tools and general hardware		4366	14207	9470	9958		...	...	...	...		...	...
2899 Other fabricated metal products n.e.c.		8512	11704	10315	10510		...	...	...	...		...	...
291 General purpose machinery		19338	31990	23133	33031		...	...	...	...		...	...
2911 Engines & turbines(not for transport equip.)		-	-	-	-		...	...	...	...		...	...
2912 Pumps, compressors, taps and valves		17289	29215	21604	30064		...	...	...	...		...	...
2913 Bearings, gears, gearing & driving elements		2049	2775	1529	2967		...	...	...	...		...	...
2914 Ovens, furnaces and furnace burners		-	-	-	-		...	...	...	...		...	...
2915 Lifting and handling equipment		-	-	-	-		...	...	...	...		...	...
2919 Other general purpose machinery		-	-	-	-		...	...	...	...		...	...

292 Special purpose machinery	158199	295957	238840	245205	...	...	...	...	...	...
2921 Agricultural and forestry machinery	75845	73132	60357	63366	...	...	...	...	...	...
2922 Machine tools	42199	62071	127544	109610	...	...	...	...	...	...
2923 Machinery for metallurgy	-	-	-	-	...	...	...	...	...	...
2924 Machinery for mining & construction	414	731	1170	1937	...	...	...	...	...	...
2925 Food/beverage/tobacco processing machinery	9374	12789	11728	10269	...	...	...	...	...	...
2926 Machinery for textile, apparel and leather	-	-	-	-	...	...	...	...	...	...
2927 Weapons and ammunition	-	-	-	-	...	...	...	...	...	...
2929 Other special purpose machinery	30367	147234	38041	60023	...	...	...	...	...	...
2930 Domestic appliances n.e.c.	12995	26961	25712	29150	...	...	...	...	...	...
3000 Office, accounting and computing machinery	7732	2507	6889	9153	...	...	...	...	...	...
3110 Electric motors, generators and transformers	56139	50046	51042	63051	...	...	...	...	...	...
3120 Electricity distribution & control apparatus	-	-	-	-	...	...	...	...	...	...
3130 Insulated wire and cable	31432	25693	37940	40818	...	...	...	...	...	...
3140 Accumulators, primary cells and batteries	-	-	-	-	...	...	...	...	...	...
3150 Lighting equipment and electric lamps	81689	73234	131607	190640	...	...	...	...	...	...
3190 Other electrical equipment n.e.c.	...	...	...	...	...	...	...	...	...	...
3210 Electronic valves, tubes, etc.	-	-	-	-	...	...	...	...	...	...
3220 TV/radio transmitters; line comm. apparatus	-	-	-	-	...	...	...	...	...	...
3230 TV and radio receivers and associated goods	...	...	...	...	...	...	...	...	...	...
331 Medical, measuring, testing appliances, etc.	30101	40410	41447	42900	...	...	...	...	...	...
3311 Medical, surgical and orthopaedic equipment	-	-	-	-	...	...	...	...	...	...
3312 Measuring/testing/navigating appliances,etc.	-	-	-	-	...	...	...	...	...	...
3313 Industrial process control equipment	30101	40410	41447	42900	...	...	...	...	...	...
3320 Optical instruments & photographic equipment	-	-	-	-	...	...	...	...	...	...
3330 Watches and clocks	-	-	-	-	...	...	...	...	...	...
3410 Motor vehicles	99437	54607	55626	47536	...	...	...	...	...	...
3420 Automobile bodies, trailers & semi-trailers	...	...	...	...	...	...	...	...	...	...
3430 Parts/accessories for automobiles	...	...	...	...	...	...	...	...	...	...
351 Building and repairing of ships and boats	74	147	394	613	...	...	...	...	...	...
3511 Building and repairing of ships	74	147	394	613	...	...	...	...	...	...
3512 Building/repairing of pleasure/sport. boats	-	-	-	-	...	...	...	...	...	...
3520 Railway/tramway locomotives & rolling stock	160	852	924	2006	...	...	...	...	...	...
3530 Aircraft and spacecraft	-	-	-	-	...	...	...	...	...	...
359 Transport equipment n.e.c.	-	-	-	-	...	...	...	...	...	...
3591 Motorcycles	-	-	-	-	...	...	...	...	...	...
3592 Bicycles and invalid carriages	-	-	-	-	...	...	...	...	...	...
3599 Other transport equipment n.e.c.	-	-	-	-	...	...	...	...	...	...
3610 Furniture	22811	31180	30593	24958	...	...	...	...	...	...
369 Manufacturing n.e.c.	5911	20926	26795	44179	...	...	...	...	...	...
3691 Jewellery and related articles	-	-	1270	3280	...	...	...	...	...	...
3692 Musical instruments	-	-	-	-	...	...	...	...	...	...
3693 Sports goods	-	-	-	-	...	...	...	...	...	...
3694 Games and toys	-	-	-	-	...	...	...	...	...	...
3699 Other manufacturing n.e.c.	5911	20926	25525	40899	...	...	...	...	...	...
3710 Recycling of metal waste and scrap	1983	1928	2418	4350	...	...	...	...	...	...
3720 Recycling of non-metal waste and scrap	-	-	-	-	...	...	...	...	...	...
D Total manufacturing	2511434	4177623	4247274	5227342	...	...	...	...	...	...

Kyrgyzstan

ISIC Revision 3			Index numbers of industrial production											
			(1990=100)											
ISIC	Industry	Note	1985	1986	1987	1988	1989	1990	1991	1992	1993	1994	1995	1996
15	Food and beverages		...	...	...	...	...	...	...	...	...	...	...	...
16	Tobacco products		...	...	...	...	...	...	...	...	...	...	...	...
17	Textiles		...	...	...	...	...	...	...	...	...	...	...	...
18	Wearing apparel, fur		...	...	...	...	...	...	...	...	...	...	...	...
19	Leather, leather products and footwear		...	...	...	...	...	...	...	...	...	...	...	...
20	Wood products (excl. furniture)		...	...	...	...	...	...	...	...	...	...	...	...
21	Paper and paper products		...	...	...	...	...	...	...	...	...	...	...	...
22	Printing and publishing		...	...	...	...	...	...	...	...	...	...	...	...
23	Coke,refined petroleum products,nuclear fuel		...	...	...	...	...	...	...	...	...	...	...	...
24	Chemicals and chemical products		...	...	...	...	...	...	...	...	...	...	...	...
25	Rubber and plastics products		...	...	...	...	...	...	...	...	...	...	...	...
26	Non-metallic mineral products		...	...	...	...	...	...	...	...	...	...	...	...
27	Basic metals		...	...	...	...	...	...	...	...	...	...	...	...
28	Fabricated metal products		...	...	...	...	...	...	...	...	...	...	...	...
29	Machinery and equipment n.e.c.		...	...	...	...	...	...	...	...	...	...	...	...
30	Office, accounting and computing machinery		...	...	...	...	...	...	...	...	...	...	...	...
31	Electrical machinery and apparatus		...	...	...	...	...	...	...	...	...	...	...	...
32	Radio,television and communication equipment		...	...	...	...	...	...	...	...	...	...	...	...
33	Medical, precision and optical instruments		...	...	...	...	...	...	...	...	...	...	...	...
34	Motor vehicles, trailers, semi-trailers		...	...	...	...	...	...	...	...	...	...	...	...
35	Other transport equipment		...	...	...	...	...	...	...	...	...	...	...	...
36	Furniture; manufacturing n.e.c.		...	...	...	...	...	...	...	...	...	...	...	...
37	Recycling		...	...	...	...	...	...	...	...	...	...	...	...
D	Total manufacturing		...	...	...	...	...	...	...	...	...	...	...	...

LATVIA

Supplier of information:
State Committee for Statistics of the Republic of Latvia, Riga.

Basic source of data:
Annual survey of all enterprises with industrial activity.

Major deviations from ISIC (Revision 3):
None reported.

Reference period (if not calendar year):

Scope:
All establishments with industrial production, excluding individual producers.

Method of enumeration:
Not reported.

Adjusted for non-response:
No.

Concepts and definitions of variables:
Number of establishments: Beginning 1992, all industrial activities of a non-industrial enterprise are classified as belonging to the single industrial branch that accounts for the largest share of such activities.
Output excludes VAT.

Related national publications:

Latvia

ISIC Revision 3 ISIC Industry	Note	Number of establishments (numbers) 1993	1994a/	1995	1996	Note	Number of employees (numbers) 1993	1994	1995	1996	Note	Wages and salaries paid to employees (thousand LATS) 1993	1994	1995	1996
151 Processed meat,fish,fruit,vegetables,fats		303	211	227	274		16921	13686	12905	13605		10351.6	14059.9	16432.2	21473.5
1511 Processing/preserving of meat		224	137	134	162		8107	5611	5358	4183		4783.5	5525.9	6185.9	6089.4
1512 Processing/preserving of fish		37	34	52	77		6884	6406	6184	8268		4459.2	7266.7	8884.9	14179.8
1513 Processing/preserving of fruit & vegetables		40	37	39	33		1740	1503	1255	1067		842.9	...	...	1135.9
1514 Vegetable and animal oils and fats		2	3	2	2		...	...	...	...		133.3	...	...	68.3
1520 Dairy products		81	74	74	68		6961	6200	5796	6061		3831.6	5662.6	6640.1	8350.6
153 Grain mill products; starches; animal feeds		224	63	44	56		3574	2200	1938	1951		2840.5	2824.5	3243.5	3855.9
1531 Grain mill products		187	45	23	37		2055	1435	1228	1367		1663.8	...	...	...
1532 Starches and starch products		1	1	1	2		...	...	...	...		31.8	...	...	...
1533 Prepared animal feeds		36	17	20	17		1480	713	654	514		1163.4	...	...	805.4
154 Other food products		153	112	192	320		8879	9420	9798	10173		7213.3	11700.8	13406.0	15707.0
1541 Bakery products		127	94	163	269		6045	6690	7106	7069		4794.9	...	...	...
1542 Sugar		3	3	6	3		1517	1237	1166	1233		919.8	...	...	...
1543 Cocoa, chocolate and sugar confectionery		13	9	9	9		1043	1135	1184	1431		1393.5	...	...	...
1544 Macaroni, noodles & similar products		-	-	-	-		-	-	-	-		-	...	...	...
1549 Other food products n.e.c.		10	6	14	39		274	358	342	440		189.8	...	...	...
155 Beverages		37	36	36	49		3142	2947	3073	3247		2690.2	4625.3	5772.6	7175.1
1551 Distilling, rectifying & blending of spirits		6	7	7	11		677	761	852	1076		500.2	...	...	3062.7
1552 Wines		3	3	2	3		235	290	274	285		226.3	...	...	1447.3
1553 Malt liquors and malt		19	18	17	19		1625	1621	1575	1688		1433.4	...	...	2493.4
1554 Soft drinks; mineral waters		9	8	10	16		605	275	372	198		411.7	...	...	171.6
1600 Tobacco products		1	1	1	1		...	...	...	...		309.3	404.1	536.7	738.4
171 Spinning, weaving and finishing of textiles		48	23	32	23		4862	3586	3223	2989		2302.8	2820.3	3311.1	4014.0
1711 Textile fibre preparation; textile weaving		48	23	32	23		4862	3586	3223	2989		2313.3	...	...	...
1712 Finishing of textiles		-	-	-	-		-	-	-	-		2.1	...	...	...
172 Other textiles		37	28	44	60		3542	4013	3847	3942		2248.9	3833.2	5151.9	5220.2
1721 Made-up textile articles, except apparel		16	20	28	42		185	993	1035	1299		141.0	...	...	1314.5
1722 Carpets and rugs		-	-	-	-		-	-	-	-		-	...	...	...
1723 Cordage, rope, twine and netting		3	-	6	5		6	-	21	33		6.2	...	...	...
1729 Other textiles n.e.c.		18	8	10	13		3351	3020	2791	2610		2122.4	...	...	...
1730 Knitted and crocheted fabrics and articles		68	34	63	52		9719	7201	6214	5129		4506.5	5755.9	5838.7	6483.5
1810 Wearing apparel, except fur apparel		150	80	178	243		9018	7884	8456	9717		4099.2	5410.6	6705.3	9672.3
1820 Dressing & dyeing of fur; processing of fur		19	17	24	20		519	486	366	263		264.4	329.0	243.8	161.7
191 Tanning, dressing and processing of leather		35	22	34	42		1512	1232	921	978		850.6	771.9	763.7	779.3
1911 Tanning and dressing of leather		11	5	12	8		798	493	443	411		557.4	...	...	432.8
1912 Luggage, handbags, etc.; saddlery & harness		24	17	22	34		714	739	478	567		292.7	...	...	346.5
1920 Footwear		40	24	32	38		6671	4469	3262	2850		3389.4	3048.2	2469.2	2388.0
2010 Sawmilling and planing of wood		284	205	439	619		5518	8309	9531	11858		2219.6	...	...	9184.6
202 Products of wood, cork, straw, etc.		141	60	170	220		7102	5639	6167	6374		4061.8	...	...	9953.1
2021 Veneer sheets, plywood, particle board, etc.		5	8	9	11		2363	3363	3745	4103		1761.1	...	...	8370.5
2022 Builders' carpentry and joinery		89	41	144	167		2918	1794	2018	1724		1739.9	...	...	1195.7
2023 Wooden containers		22	9	7	12		362	245	146	145		155.6	...	...	102.6
2029 Other wood products; articles of cork/straw		25	2	10	30		1459	237	258	402		429.3	...	...	284.3
210 Paper and paper products		24	27	27	39		2418	1887	1637	1810		1029.8	1232.1	1573.1	2128.2
2101 Pulp, paper and paperboard		7	4	4	8		1761	1089	961	830		708.1	...	...	...
2102 Corrugated paper and paperboard		5	12	12	20		118	312	167	484		52.2	...	...	...
2109 Other articles of paper and paperboard		12	11	11	11		539	486	509	496		274.5	...	...	...
221 Publishing		122	61	209	256		1440	1527	2846	3478		1241.2	...	...	6994.2
2211 Publishing of books and other publications		53	11	77	83		527	300	526	742		342.2	...	...	...
2212 Publishing of newspapers, journals, etc.		64	46	118	148		887	1153	2221	2651		843.0	...	...	...
2213 Publishing of recorded media		-	-	4	-		-	-	7	-		-	...	...	...
2219 Other publishing		5	4	10	25		26	74	92	85		22.7	...	...	...

222 Printing and related service activities	55	35	99	122	2676	2531	2468	2797	1656.7	...	...	4291.8
2221 Printing	53	31	95	101	2635	2357	2421	2680	1655.0	...	...	...
2222 Service activities related to printing	2	4	4	21	41	174	47	117	11.3	...	...	...
2230 Reproduction of recorded media	4	1	3	5	178	103	64	78	73.9	...	...	34.9
2310 Coke oven products	-	-	-	-	-	-	-	-	-	...	...	...
2320 Refined petroleum products	2	1	2	3	396	86	88	107	522.2	...	...	...
2330 Processing of nuclear fuel	-	-	-	-	-	-	-	-	-	...	...	...
241 Basic chemicals	12	6	12	16	697	254	306	357	346.3	...	...	...
2411 Basic chemicals, except fertilizers	11	6	10	16	632	254	276	357	314.0	...	...	...
2412 Fertilizers and nitrogen compounds	1	-	1	-	65	-	29	-	...	...	...	...
2413 Plastics in primary forms; synthetic rubber	-	-	1	-	-	-	1	-	-	...	...	...
242 Other chemicals	69	42	52	70	6024	5216	4235	4026	3951.3	...	...	6590.7
2421 Pesticides and other agro-chemical products	-	-	-	1	-	-	-	...	-	...	...	2.2
2422 Paints, varnishes, printing ink and mastics	8	5	7	12	462	687	592	556	302.4	...	...	970.3
2423 Pharmaceuticals, medicinal chemicals, etc.	19	15	23	23	2484	2325	2251	2183	1751.2	...	...	3763.3
2424 Soap, cleaning & cosmetic preparations	34	15	18	19	2876	1944	1247	1101	1761.8	...	...	1510.3
2429 Other chemical products n.e.c.	8	7	4	15	202	260	145	182	48.8	...	...	344.5
2430 Man-made fibres	1	2	2	1	...	...	...	...	2120.1	...	...	4367.5
251 Rubber products	8	7	12	11	163	149	197	154	111.0	...	...	155.6
2511 Rubber tyres and tubes	2	2	2	3	22	37	66	25	16.5	...	...	...
2519 Other rubber products	6	5	10	8	141	112	131	129	95.3	...	...	...
2520 Plastic products	53	20	50	46	1462	1622	1521	1273	887.9	...	...	1425.2
2610 Glass and glass products	15	17	22	20	2786	1210	1149	1027	1323.2	689.1	663.8	754.9
269 Non-metallic mineral products n.e.c.	96	76	104	108	8373	6282	5467	4534	4630.9	4984.4	5108.6	5123.5
2691 Pottery, china and earthenware	9	11	12	17	2089	1668	1380	1247	1048.1	1132.5	1128.1	963.8
2692 Refractory ceramic products	4	2	3	2	31	40	25	19	6.4	...	...	...
2693 Struct.non-refractory clay; ceramic products	5	6	9	10	77	633	715	1007	30.0	...	...	814.6
2694 Cement, lime and plaster	5	3	4	4	1096	997	990	362	708.8	...	...	983.8
2695 Articles of concrete, cement and plaster	58	47	68	49	4838	2696	2067	1769	2717.0	...	...	1367.6
2696 Cutting, shaping & finishing of stone	3	2	2	24	39	45	27	126	21.7	...	...	128.4
2699 Other non-metallic mineral products n.e.c.	12	5	6	2	203	203	263	4	59.3	...	...	3.7
2710 Basic iron and steel	1	1	1	1	...	...	...	...	1827.6	...	...	3654.9
2720 Basic precious and non-ferrous metals	-	-	-	-	-	-	-	-	-	...	...	...
273 Casting of metals	3	2	2	5	88	67	75	105	57.1	...	...	...
2731 Casting of iron and steel	-	1	1	1	-	-	4	-	-	...	...	...
2732 Casting of non-ferrous metals	3	1	1	4	88	67	71	105	57.1	...	...	...
281 Struct.metal products;tanks;steam generators	37	19	29	50	1315	772	796	829	689.4	...	...	677.6
2811 Structural metal products	28	14	22	36	918	620	633	527	363.4	...	...	425.8
2812 Tanks, reservoirs and containers of metal	2	1	3	4	81	41	37	63	43.3	...	...	90.2
2813 Steam generators	7	4	4	10	316	111	126	239	224.4	...	...	161.5
289 Other metal products; metal working services	119	49	131	153	3431	3275	3290	4543	1654.7	...	...	4591.1
2891 Metal forging/pressing/stamping/roll-forming	2	-	7	2	...	-	...	...	61.9	...	...	9.8
2892 Treatment & coating of metals	1	2	2	24	78	43	33	283	24.7	...	...	254.7
2893 Cutlery, hand tools and general hardware	12	8	25	19	703	518	599	1414	334.6	...	...	760.3
2899 Other fabricated metal products n.e.c.	104	39	97	108	2532	2714	2641	2833	1240.9	...	...	3566.3
291 General purpose machinery	45	34	51	60	5079	4236	3819	3558	2469.0	...	...	...
2911 Engines & turbines(not for transport equip.)	10	8	16	8	718	816	816	713	355.4	...	...	3832.9
2912 Pumps, compressors, taps and valves	8	5	6	11	855	557	408	498	427.3	...	...	...
2913 Bearings, gears, gearing & driving elements	2	1	1	2	...	...	...	...	828.0	...	...	...
2914 Ovens, furnaces and furnace burners	1	-	-	-	-	-	-	-	-	...	...	...
2915 Lifting and handling equipment	7	6	10	9	107	692	518	257	65.1	...	...	...
2919 Other general purpose machinery	17	14	18	30	1712	928	805	783	798.5	...	...	1112.4
292 Special purpose machinery	199	83	141	155	11967	8289	8163	7551	5831.8	...	...	...
2921 Agricultural and forestry machinery	160	51	94	99	5234	3337	3401	2757	2279.9	...	...	2467.4
2922 Machine tools	11	15	24	27	4172	3933	3874	4005	2399.6	...	...	5041.1
2923 Machinery for metallurgy	1	1	1	2	...	...	...	...	269.1	...	...	...
2924 Machinery for mining & construction	6	4	3	3	693	229	157	106	284.2	...	...	...
2925 Food/beverage/tobacco processing machinery	8	6	4	13	398	221	149	234	157.6	...	...	...
2926 Machinery for textile, apparel and leather	3	1	1	-	102	-	62	-	20.7	...	...	...
2927 Weapons and ammunition	-	-	-	-	-	23	-	-	-	...	...	...
2929 Other special purpose machinery	10	5	14	11	782	140	163	114	356.0	...	...	710.1
2930 Domestic appliances n.e.c.	8	3	5	11	885	267	83	97	460.9	...	...	135.4

continued

Latvia

ISIC Revision 3	Number of establishments					Number of employees					Wages and salaries paid to employees				
		(numbers)					(numbers)					(thousand LATS)			
ISIC Industry	Note	1993	1994a/	1995	1996	Note	1993	1994	1995	1996	Note	1993	1994	1995	1996
3000 Office, accounting and computing machinery		12	3	6	8		146	27	65	92		99.3	21.1	55.7	96.3
3110 Electric motors, generators and transformers		19	6	14	18		3747	3193	2736	2691		2056.2	...	...	...
3120 Electricity distribution & control apparatus		6	9	9	12		1548	2274	1660	1488		677.5	...	...	...
3130 Insulated wire and cable		2	1	1	1		...	...	...	...		6.8	...	...	...
3140 Accumulators, primary cells and batteries		-	-	-	-		-	-	-	-		-	...	...	...
3150 Lighting equipment and electric lamps		4	9	11	18		663	1410	1129	1007		320.7	...	...	...
3190 Other electrical equipment n.e.c.		19	3	6	7		2172	108	79	68		1495.6	...	...	6402.4
3210 Electronic valves, tubes, etc.		5	4	3	4		3721	1191	593	425		1506.6	...	...	...
3220 TV/radio transmitters; line comm. apparatus		22	11	24	33		10074	7377	5386	4312		3875.7	...	...	...
3230 TV and radio receivers and associated goods		22	7	16	21		4245	2187	1628	1273		1692.7	...	...	...
331 Medical, measuring, testing appliances, etc.		29	19	48	73		545	628	526	606		258.3	...	...	...
3311 Medical, surgical and orthopaedic equipment		14	11	26	36		310	353	376	414		180.5	...	...	...
3312 Measuring/testing/navigating appliances,etc.		13	5	18	37		156	200	146	192		62.7	...	...	...
3313 Industrial process control equipment		2	3	4	-		79	75	4	-		16.1	...	...	...
3320 Optical instruments & photographic equipment		3	3	3	6		134	124	106	113		57.5	...	...	...
3330 Watches and clocks		3	1	1	1		...	...	...	...		13.1	...	...	...
3410 Motor vehicles		6	3	4	5		4362	3717	2770	2096		2653.3	...	...	...
3420 Automobile bodies, trailers & semi-trailers		5	8	10	13		73	132	142	210		91.1	...	...	...
3430 Parts/accessories for automobiles		8	4	7	7		126	49	54	51		56.4	...	...	...
351 Building and repairing of ships and boats		22	19	26	34		3163	3181	3708	3263		3232.3	...	...	4479.8
3511 Building and repairing of ships		15	16	21	20		3047	3125	3677	3148		3203.0	...	...	...
3512 Building/repairing of pleasure/sport. boats		7	3	5	14		116	56	31	115		45.7	...	...	...
3520 Railway/tramway locomotives & rolling stock		6	5	7	9		5586	5594	5972	5832		3156.5	...	...	7527.7
3530 Aircraft and spacecraft		4	2	1	2		350	31	3	3		156.2	...	...	16.4
359 Transport equipment n.e.c.		2	2	3	5		1260	851	523	363		484.3	...	...	...
3591 Motorcycles		2	1	1	2		...	...	...	...		484.3	...	...	...
3592 Bicycles and invalid carriages		-	1	1	2		...	...	...	...		-	...	...	...
3599 Other transport equipment n.e.c.		-	-	1	1		...	...	...	...		-	...	...	...
3610 Furniture		104	67	130	169		7716	6687	6080	5380		4303.7	5307.3	5213.0	4644.9
369 Manufacturing n.e.c.		55	29	66	69		1832	2984	2420	1811		973.5	1968.4	2085.1	1896.7
3691 Jewellery and related articles		6	5	10	17		333	1174	509	249		171.5	...	...	276.1
3692 Musical instruments		2	1	1	5		216	152	70	90		79.6	...	...	93.2
3693 Sports goods		7	4	8	5		129	109	61	45		30.8	...	...	16.8
3694 Games and toys		7	4	2	16		76	215	192	345		21.0	...	...	329.3
3699 Other manufacturing n.e.c.		33	15	45	26		1078	1334	1588	1082		626.5	...	...	1181.4
3710 Recycling of metal waste and scrap		8	11	17	21		321	430	447	378		334.1	...	...	...
3720 Recycling of non-metal waste and scrap		-	1	2	10		-	4	5	54		6.0	...	...	...
D Total manufacturing		2860	1703	2959	3763		196293	164294	154252	153005		109743.5	145360.8	169239.1	195882.7

a/ Data cover all state, local government and other enterprises with 20 employees and more at the beginning of the year.

Latvia

ISIC Revision 3 ISIC Industry	Note	Output in producers' prices (million LATS) 1993	1994	1995	1996	Note	Value added in factor values (million LATS) 1993	1994	1995	1996	Note	Gross fixed capital formation (thousand LATS) 1995	1996
151 Processed meat,fish,fruit,vegetables,fats		106.3	111.5	120.8	173.7		29.3	34.2	35.6	61.2		10851.8	9379.7
1511 Processing/preserving of meat		76.7	70.9	61.8	67.4		19.3	16.3	15.3	19.5		6159.5	4095.5
1512 Processing/preserving of fish		25.1	36.3	48.2	81.2		7.6	16.0	16.9	32.8		3091.9	4553.2
1513 Processing/preserving of fruit & vegetables		2.7	4.1	10.6	24.9		1.3	1.8	3.3	8.8		1595.0	726.4
1514 Vegetable and animal oils and fats		...	...	...	...		...	...	...	...		...	...
1520 Dairy products		66.4	64.6	72.6	88.1		20.8	22.1	22.4	26.9		4498.4	4215.9
153 Grain mill products; starches; animal feeds		34.1	34.6	36.1	48.7		9.5	11.0	13.4	10.9		6301.6	4851.3
1531 Grain mill products		21.3	25.9	26.0	40.6		5.4	8.4	11.2	12.9		5465.4	4158.4
1532 Starches and starch products		...	...	...	...		...	...	...	...		...	...
1533 Prepared animal feeds		12.4	8.5	9.7	6.4		3.9	2.5	1.9	-2.4		759.8	585.9
154 Other food products		71.9	79.8	89.9	112.4		34.3	40.6	41.7	44.9		4382.0	10017.4
1541 Bakery products		47.9	48.2	51.7	59.2		19.7	24.3	25.6	26.4		2489.5	3145.9
1542 Sugar		10.5	8.0	12.7	17.1		6.7	3.0	5.2	5.0		102.6	880.9
1543 Cocoa, chocolate and sugar confectionery		11.5	20.9	22.4	28.2		6.6	11.8	9.7	11.0		1739.5	2522.0
1544 Macaroni, noodles & similar products		-	-	-	-		-	-	-	-		-	-
1549 Other food products n.e.c.		2.0	2.8	3.2	8.0		1.3	1.5	1.3	2.5		50.4	3468.6
155 Beverages		29.1	43.9	59.8	67.8		26.5	42.3	57.3	59.8		5684.1	4686.7
1551 Distilling, rectifying & blending of spirits		10.1	17.5	23.0	28.9		14.0	21.0	28.4	28.2		1856.5	751.6
1552 Wines		5.9	8.7	11.8	15.9		3.5	7.1	11.1	14.7		1627.5	1121.3
1553 Malt liquors and malt		10.1	13.2	18.9	20.3		6.6	11.6	13.9	15.9		1921.6	2735.6
1554 Soft drinks; mineral waters		3.1	4.6	6.1	2.7		2.3	2.7	3.8	1.1		278.5	78.2
1600 Tobacco products		...	...	...	...		...	...	...	...		...	...
171 Spinning, weaving and finishing of textiles		15.5	11.5	14.7	19.9		5.4	3.6	6.6	8.7		53.6	722.5
1711 Textile fibre preparation; textile weaving		15.5	11.5	14.7	19.9		5.4	3.6	6.6	8.7		53.6	722.5
1712 Finishing of textiles		-	-	-	-		-	-	-	-		-	-
172 Other textiles		18.8	21.8	23.9	32.6		8.1	11.0	7.9	13.6		1090.1	2046.7
1721 Made-up textile articles, except apparel		2.4	6.0	6.2	9.3		1.2	2.8	0.7	3.3		179.6	826.1
1722 Carpets and rugs		-	-	-	-		-	-	-	-		-	-
1723 Cordage, rope, twine and netting		-	-	0.1	0.1		-	-	0.1	-		-	-
1729 Other textiles n.e.c.		16.4	15.8	17.5	23.2		6.9	8.1	7.2	10.3		910.5	1220.6
1730 Knitted and crocheted fabrics and articles		21.0	20.0	20.1	28.6		8.5	8.4	6.6	10.4		407.0	401.7
1810 Wearing apparel, except fur apparel		11.7	14.8	18.8	31.7		7.6	11.8	13.4	20.5		811.0	1399.5
1820 Dressing & dyeing of fur; processing of fur		1.4	1.3	0.6	0.8		1.0	0.9	0.3	0.6		13.2	27.5
191 Tanning, dressing and processing of leather		5.3	4.0	4.0	3.8		2.0	1.5	1.4	1.2		105.4	64.2
1911 Tanning and dressing of leather		4.2	2.9	3.1	2.4		1.5	0.8	0.9	0.5		86.3	8.0
1912 Luggage, handbags, etc.; saddlery & harness		1.1	1.1	0.9	1.3		0.5	0.7	0.5	0.8		19.1	56.2
1920 Footwear		21.0	12.3	7.6	10.0		8.0	5.1	3.6	4.9		311.1	203.9
2010 Sawmilling and planing of wood		15.4	30.2	52.8	74.4		7.4	13.2	22.6	23.3		7559.3	7453.2
202 Products of wood, cork, straw, etc.		26.8	36.6	49.2	58.8		12.4	18.1	18.9	24.1		2965.7	4829.7
2021 Veneer sheets, plywood, particle board, etc.		22.7	30.9	42.7	50.7		10.1	15.4	16.0	20.5		2016.7	4006.6
2022 Builders' carpentry and joinery		3.3	4.0	5.4	5.6		1.8	2.1	2.3	2.7		914.5	744.4
2023 Wooden containers		0.7	1.3	0.7	1.0		0.4	0.5	0.4	0.3		13.2	7.3
2029 Other wood products; articles of cork/straw		0.1	0.3	0.4	1.4		0.1	0.1	0.3	0.7		21.3	71.4
210 Paper and paper products		5.9	4.7	6.1	14.2		2.2	2.0	1.5	5.1		197.1	3810.3
2101 Pulp, paper and paperboard		2.6	0.8	1.4	2.0		0.1	0.3	-	0.9		121.9	350.2
2102 Corrugated paper and paperboard		0.7	0.9	0.6	6.0		0.4	0.5	0.2	1.6		5.1	2888.2
2109 Other articles of paper and paperboard		2.6	2.9	4.0	6.3		1.7	1.2	1.3	2.6		70.1	571.9
221 Publishing		6.3	10.5	25.6	33.2		3.8	6.1	15.4	17.9		1389.0	906.8
2211 Publishing of books and other publications		2.1	3.1	6.4	8.7		1.3	1.8	3.1	3.9		220.7	290.0
2212 Publishing of newspapers, journals, etc.		3.7	7.1	18.6	23.3		2.0	4.1	12.0	13.5		1137.2	579.0
2213 Publishing of recorded media		-	-	0.2	-		-	-	-	-		20.2	-
2219 Other publishing		0.6	0.3	0.4	1.2		0.4	0.1	0.3	0.6		10.9	37.8

continued

Latvia

ISIC Revision 3	Output in producers' prices					Value added in factor values					Gross fixed capital formation		
		(million LATS)					(million LATS)					(thousand LATS)	
ISIC Industry	Note	1993	1994	1995	1996	Note	1993	1994	1995	1996	Note	1995	1996
222 Printing and related service activities		5.6	9.6	12.0	17.9		4.2	7.5	7.8	10.4		3444.3	1839.8
2221 Printing		5.5	8.9	11.7	17.5		4.0	7.0	7.6	10.2		3402.0	1816.2
2222 Service activities related to printing		0.2	0.7	0.3	0.4		0.1	0.5	0.2	0.2		42.3	23.6
2230 Reproduction of recorded media		0.4	0.2	0.2	0.3		-	0.1	0.1	0.1		299.8	20.0
2310 Coke oven products		-	-	-	-		-	-	-	-		-	-
2320 Refined petroleum products		0.4	0.4	1.0	1.2		0.1	0.4	0.3	0.5		65.5	18.1
2330 Processing of nuclear fuel		-	-	-	-		-	-	-	-		-	-
241 Basic chemicals		0.4	0.7	1.1	1.1		-	0.1	0.5	0.4		234.7	23.7
2411 Basic chemicals, except fertilizers		0.4	0.7	1.0	1.1		-	0.1	0.5	0.4		233.5	23.7
2412 Fertilizers and nitrogen compounds		-	-	0.1	-		-	-	-	-		-	-
2413 Plastics in primary forms; synthetic rubber		-	-	-	-		-	-	-	-		1.2	-
242 Other chemicals		34.7	33.1	35.8	40.7		18.3	11.7	16.4	19.3		4405.1	2253.5
2421 Pesticides and other agro-chemical products		-	-	-	...		-	-	-	...		-	-
2422 Paints, varnishes, printing ink and mastics		4.9	6.9	9.7	12.1		1.7	2.1	3.2	4.2		63.4	334.2
2423 Pharmaceuticals, medicinal chemicals, etc.		11.8	12.5	16.3	19.4		6.1	3.9	8.8	11.6		1728.6	737.1
2424 Soap, cleaning & cosmetic preparations		16.9	12.5	9.1	7.7		9.8	5.3	4.0	2.9		2562.4	999.9
2429 Other chemical products n.e.c.		1.0	1.2	0.7	1.6		0.5	0.5	0.5	0.6		50.7	182.3
2430 Man-made fibres		...	...	...	...		...	...	...	...		...	...
251 Rubber products		0.6	0.6	1.0	0.5		0.3	0.2	0.6	0.2		54.5	5.2
2511 Rubber tyres and tubes		0.1	0.3	0.6	0.1		-	0.1	0.3	-		37.0	4.9
2519 Other rubber products		0.4	0.3	0.4	0.4		0.3	0.1	0.3	0.2		17.5	0.3
2520 Plastic products		3.3	5.5	7.3	8.8		2.1	3.4	3.4	4.0		263.9	561.7
2610 Glass and glass products		3.8	3.9	5.0	6.3		2.4	2.0	1.6	2.1		618.0	388.5
269 Non-metallic mineral products n.e.c.		17.6	22.9	21.1	23.6		8.8	12.3	10.6	11.0		2095.4	2440.2
2691 Pottery, china and earthenware		3.4	3.9	2.7	2.1		1.9	2.8	1.6	1.3		28.7	32.7
2692 Refractory ceramic products		-	-	-	-		-	-	-	-		9.0	-
2693 Struct.non-refractory clay; ceramic products		1.1	1.8	2.3	2.6		0.3	1.0	1.3	1.6		33.7	234.2
2694 Cement, lime and plaster		4.6	6.6	7.2	8.9		2.5	3.5	3.9	4.0		255.6	1706.9
2695 Articles of concrete, cement and plaster		7.6	7.6	6.6	9.6		3.6	4.0	3.3	3.9		1713.0	460.8
2696 Cutting, shaping & finishing of stone		0.1	0.1	0.1	0.4		-	0.1	-	0.3		0.2	5.6
2699 Other non-metallic mineral products n.e.c.		0.9	2.8	2.0	-		0.5	0.9	0.5	-		55.2	-
2710 Basic iron and steel		...	...	...	...		...	...	...	...		...	...
2720 Basic precious and non-ferrous metals		-	-	-	-		-	-	-	-		-	-
273 Casting of metals		0.4	0.6	1.4	1.0		0.3	0.2	0.3	0.3		0.3	0.5
2731 Casting of iron and steel		-	-	...	...		-	-	...	...		...	...
2732 Casting of non-ferrous metals		0.4	0.6	1.4	1.0		0.3	0.2	0.3	0.3		-	0.4
281 Struct.metal products;tanks;steam generators		1.5	2.8	3.2	5.0		0.8	1.9	1.4	3.0		388.6	154.2
2811 Structural metal products		1.2	2.2	2.6	3.5		0.5	1.4	0.9	2.2		124.4	97.6
2812 Tanks, reservoirs and containers of metal		0.1	0.1	0.1	0.2		0.1	0.1	0.1	0.1		-	12.0
2813 Steam generators		0.3	0.6	0.5	1.3		0.2	0.4	0.3	0.7		264.2	44.6
289 Other metal products; metal working services		6.9	9.5	17.8	28.9		...	5.5	9.0	13.2		2523.5	2387.0
2891 Metal forging/pressing/stamping/roll-forming		...	-	...	...		...	-	...	...		...	...
2892 Treatment & coating of metals		-	0.1	0.2	1.1		-	-	0.1	0.7		7.0	227.2
2893 Cutlery, hand tools and general hardware		0.8	1.7	1.9	3.1		0.4	1.0	1.0	1.9		215.4	135.6
2899 Other fabricated metal products n.e.c.		6.1	7.8	15.7	24.6		3.8	4.4	8.0	10.6		2283.5	2001.1
291 General purpose machinery		16.0	14.5	18.9	18.2		...	9.7	12.8	11.4		327.5	550.9
2911 Engines & turbines(not for transport equip.)		1.6	3.4	3.1	3.0		0.9	1.8	2.0	1.9		28.7	69.4
2912 Pumps, compressors, taps and valves		2.0	1.8	1.3	1.9		1.2	1.1	0.9	1.4		13.4	106.8
2913 Bearings, gears, gearing & driving elements		...	...	...	...		...	...	...	...		...	...
2914 Ovens, furnaces and furnace burners		-	-	-	-		...	-	-	-		-	-
2915 Lifting and handling equipment		2.5	1.0	1.7	1.5		1.8	0.3	1.1	0.9		19.6	33.2
2919 Other general purpose machinery		2.9	2.2	3.5	3.7		2.3	1.5	2.5	2.1		93.2	99.7

Code	Description		col 1	col 2	col 3	col 4	col 5	col 6	col 7	col 8	col 9	col 10
292	Special purpose machinery		24.9	25.4	29.6	32.9	...	11.4	14.7	15.3	945.3	1185.0
2921	Agricultural and forestry machinery		6.6	8.4	7.7	7.9	3.5	4.9	3.9	3.7	633.9	139.0
2922	Machine tools		16.0	14.5	19.2	22.1	8.7	4.9	9.4	9.5	292.4	805.1
2923	Machinery for metallurgy		...	...	...	...	...	...	...	...	...	...
2924	Machinery for mining & construction		0.5	0.9	0.7	0.9	0.3	0.6	0.4	0.8	0.3	45.7
2925	Food/beverage/tobacco processing machinery		0.4	0.3	0.4	1.1	0.4	0.3	0.2	0.7	-	181.0
2926	Machinery for textile, apparel and leather		-	-	-	-	...	-	-	-	-	-
2927	Weapons and ammunition		-	-	-	-	-	-	-	-	-	-
2929	Other special purpose machinery		0.4	0.6	0.6	0.2	0.1	0.3	0.3	0.2	2.0	10.2
2930	Domestic appliances n.e.c.		1.5	0.2	0.1	0.8	0.9	-	-	0.3	1.9	-
3000	Office, accounting and computing machinery		1.4	2.6	4.1	4.8	0.3	0.7	1.6	1.0	43.7	43.6
3110	Electric motors, generators and transformers		7.1	9.5	11.2	11.3	4.6	6.9	7.0	6.9	246.5	457.1
3120	Electricity distribution & control apparatus		13.4	8.5	6.9	7.9	7.9	5.4	3.5	3.4	95.5	254.6
3130	Insulated wire and cable		...	...	...	...	...	...	...	...	-	-
3140	Accumulators, primary cells and batteries		-	-	-	-	-	-	-	-	-	-
3150	Lighting equipment and electric lamps		5.7	4.6	4.1	4.2	2.5	2.0	1.7	1.7	194.5	149.7
3190	Other electrical equipment n.e.c.		0.3	0.2	0.1	0.1	0.1	0.1	0.1	0.1	18.0	9.5
3210	Electronic valves, tubes, etc.		2.5	1.3	1.0	1.0	1.7	0.8	0.6	0.6	1.4	12.2
3220	TV/radio transmitters; line comm. apparatus		12.1	13.6	12.0	12.3	5.1	7.9	6.6	6.5	133.2	357.3
3230	TV and radio receivers and associated goods		2.9	3.1	3.0	7.4	1.4	0.6	-2.6	0.7	297.1	27.0
331	Medical, measuring, testing appliances, etc.		1.6	2.4	3.7	3.4	1.1	1.3	2.6	1.7	121.9	85.3
3311	Medical, surgical and orthopaedic equipment		1.3	1.8	3.3	2.9	0.8	1.0	2.3	1.4	97.2	39.7
3312	Measuring/testing/navigating appliances,etc.		0.2	0.4	0.4	0.5	0.1	0.2	0.2	0.4	17.1	45.6
3313	Industrial process control equipment		0.1	0.1	-	-	0.1	0.1	-	-	7.6	-
3320	Optical instruments & photographic equipment		0.2	0.3	0.2	0.4	0.1	0.2	0.2	0.3	0.1	23.5
3330	Watches and clocks		...	...	...	...	...	...	...	...	...	-
3410	Motor vehicles		41.5	24.6	17.1	5.8	9.5	7.4	4.8	0.9	596.4	408.7
3420	Automobile bodies, trailers & semi-trailers		0.9	1.0	2.4	2.7	0.3	0.4	1.6	1.2	57.1	83.5
3430	Parts/accessories for automobiles		0.6	0.2	0.1	0.2	0.4	0.1	0.1	0.1	2.4	-
351	Building and repairing of ships and boats		9.9	12.9	13.1	18.0	7.2	8.9	7.3	11.5	2891.5	1563.6
3511	Building and repairing of ships		9.9	12.9	13.0	17.5	7.1	9.0	7.3	11.3	2889.2	1526.5
3512	Building/repairing of pleasure/sport. boats		0.1	-	0.1	0.5	0.1	-	-	0.1	2.3	37.1
3520	Railway/tramway locomotives & rolling stock		12.6	26.6	32.6	30.2	7.5	15.2	19.0	14.5	251.2	578.0
3530	Aircraft and spacecraft		0.4	0.1	0.1	-	0.3	-	0.1	-	9.0	-
359	Transport equipment n.e.c.		2.9	1.8	1.7	0.9	0.8	0.9	0.9	0.1	-	0.9
3591	Motorcycles		...	...	...	...	...	...	...	...	...	...
3592	Bicycles and invalid carriages		...	...	...	...	...	...	...	...	...	...
3599	Other transport equipment n.e.c.		...	...	...	...	...	...	...	...	...	...
3610	Furniture		24.3	24.3	24.3	23.9	10.8	11.8	10.8	11.8	2601.9	1620.5
369	Manufacturing n.e.c.		7.7	8.4	9.1	10.0	4.4	5.5	4.7	4.5	202.0	240.5
3691	Jewellery and related articles		2.2	2.6	2.6	1.9	1.7	2.2	2.0	0.8	99.5	42.6
3692	Musical instruments		0.2	-	0.1	0.1	0.2	-	-	-	34.0	14.0
3693	Sports goods		0.2	0.2	0.2	0.2	0.1	-	0.1	0.1	-	5.3
3694	Games and toys		0.8	0.8	0.7	1.4	0.4	0.5	0.4	0.7	6.4	85.3
3699	Other manufacturing n.e.c.		4.3	4.7	5.5	6.4	2.1	2.8	2.2	2.9	62.1	93.3
3710	Recycling of metal waste and scrap		7.8	9.1	6.2	5.0	4.1	4.9	3.2	2.6	50.2	88.9
3720	Recycling of non-metal waste and scrap		-	-	-	0.1	-	-	-	0.1	-	6.1
D	Total manufacturing		809.4	860.1	983.5	1208.7	340.4	399.9	440.3	522.0	105634.8	111591.2

Latvia

ISIC Revision 3			Index numbers of industrial production (1990=100)											
ISIC	Industry	Note	1985	1986	1987	1988	1989	1990	1991	1992	1993	1994	1995	1996
15	Food and beverages		...	...	...	...	...	...	...	...	...	...	...	...
16	Tobacco products		...	...	...	...	...	...	...	...	...	...	...	...
17	Textiles		...	...	...	...	...	...	...	...	...	...	...	...
18	Wearing apparel, fur		...	...	...	...	...	...	...	...	...	...	...	...
19	Leather, leather products and footwear		...	...	...	...	...	...	...	...	...	...	...	...
20	Wood products (excl. furniture)		...	...	...	...	...	...	...	...	...	...	...	...
21	Paper and paper products		...	...	...	...	...	...	...	...	...	...	...	...
22	Printing and publishing		...	...	...	...	...	...	...	...	...	...	...	...
23	Coke,refined petroleum products,nuclear fuel		...	...	...	...	...	...	...	...	...	...	...	...
24	Chemicals and chemical products		...	...	...	...	...	...	...	...	...	...	...	...
25	Rubber and plastics products		...	...	...	...	...	...	...	...	...	...	...	...
26	Non-metallic mineral products		...	...	...	...	...	...	...	...	...	...	...	...
27	Basic metals		...	...	...	...	...	...	...	...	...	...	...	...
28	Fabricated metal products		...	...	...	...	...	...	...	...	...	...	...	...
29	Machinery and equipment n.e.c.		...	...	...	...	...	...	...	...	...	...	...	...
30	Office, accounting and computing machinery		...	...	...	...	...	...	...	...	...	...	...	...
31	Electrical machinery and apparatus		...	...	...	...	...	...	...	...	...	...	...	...
32	Radio,television and communication equipment		...	...	...	...	...	...	...	...	...	...	...	...
33	Medical, precision and optical instruments		...	...	...	...	...	...	...	...	...	...	...	...
34	Motor vehicles, trailers, semi-trailers		...	...	...	...	...	...	...	...	...	...	...	...
35	Other transport equipment		...	...	...	...	...	...	...	...	...	...	...	...
36	Furniture; manufacturing n.e.c.		...	...	...	...	...	...	...	...	...	...	...	...
37	Recycling		...	...	...	...	...	...	...	...	...	...	...	...
D	Total manufacturing		...	...	...	...	...	100	99	64	42	37	35	38

LEBANON

Supplier of information:
General Directorate of Industry, Ministry of Industry, Beirut.

Basic source of data:
Not reported.

Major deviations from ISIC (Revision 3):
None reported.

Reference period (if not calendar year):

Scope:
Not reported.

Method of enumeration:
Not reported.

Adjusted for non-response:
Not reported.

Concepts and definitions of variables:
No deviations from the standard UN concepts and definitions are reported.

Related national publications:

Lebanon

ISIC Revision 3	Number of establishments (numbers)					Number of employees a/ (numbers)					Wages and salaries paid to employees (million POUNDS)				
ISIC Industry	Note	1993	1994	1995	1996	Note	1993	1994	1995	1996	Note	1993	1994	1995	1996
151 Processed meat,fish,fruit,vegetables,fats		...	...	...	57		...	...	...	473		...	...	...	...
1511 Processing/preserving of meat		...	...	...	47		...	...	...	211		...	...	...	...
1512 Processing/preserving of fish		...	...	...	8		...	...	...	234		...	...	...	...
1513 Processing/preserving of fruit & vegetables		...	...	...	2		...	...	...	28		...	...	...	...
1514 Vegetable and animal oils and fats		...	...	...	-		...	...	...	-		...	...	...	...
1520 Dairy products		...	...	...	3		...	...	...	44		...	...	...	...
153 Grain mill products; starches; animal feeds		...	...	...	186		...	...	...	1334		...	...	...	...
1531 Grain mill products		...	...	...	11		...	...	...	61		...	...	...	...
1532 Starches and starch products		...	...	...	9		...	...	...	97		...	...	...	...
1533 Prepared animal feeds		...	...	...	166		...	...	...	1176		...	...	...	...
154 Other food products		...	...	...	229		...	...	...	876		...	...	...	...
1541 Bakery products		...	...	...	58		...	...	...	229		...	...	...	...
1542 Sugar		...	...	...	171		...	...	...	647		...	...	...	...
1543 Cocoa, chocolate and sugar confectionery		...	...	...	-		...	...	...	-		...	...	...	...
1544 Macaroni, noodles & similar products		...	...	...	-		...	...	...	-		...	...	...	...
1549 Other food products n.e.c.		...	...	...	-		...	...	...	-		...	...	...	...
155 Beverages		...	...	...	387		...	...	...	2038		...	...	...	...
1551 Distilling, rectifying & blending of spirits		...	...	...	257		...	...	...	1432		...	...	...	...
1552 Wines		...	...	...	130		...	...	...	606		...	...	...	...
1553 Malt liquors and malt		...	...	...	-		...	...	...	-		...	...	...	...
1554 Soft drinks; mineral waters		...	...	...	-		...	...	...	-		...	...	...	...
1600 Tobacco products		...	...	...	10		...	...	...	2050		...	...	...	...
171 Spinning, weaving and finishing of textiles		...	...	...	-		...	...	...	-		...	...	...	...
1711 Textile fibre preparation; textile weaving		...	...	...	-		...	...	...	-		...	...	...	...
1712 Finishing of textiles		...	...	...	-		...	...	...	-		...	...	...	...
172 Other textiles		...	...	...	-		...	...	...	-		...	...	...	...
1721 Made-up textile articles, except apparel		...	...	...	-		...	...	...	-		...	...	...	...
1722 Carpets and rugs		...	...	...	-		...	...	...	-		...	...	...	...
1723 Cordage, rope, twine and netting		...	...	...	-		...	...	...	-		...	...	...	...
1729 Other textiles n.e.c.		...	...	...	-		...	...	...	-		...	...	...	...
1730 Knitted and crocheted fabrics and articles		...	...	...	14		...	...	...	141		...	...	...	...
1810 Wearing apparel, except fur apparel		...	...	...	3		...	...	...	4		...	...	...	...
1820 Dressing & dyeing of fur; processing of fur		...	...	...	-		...	...	...	-		...	...	...	...
191 Tanning, dressing and processing of leather		...	...	...	-		...	...	...	-		...	...	...	...
1911 Tanning and dressing of leather		...	...	...	-		...	...	...	-		...	...	...	...
1912 Luggage, handbags, etc.; saddlery & harness		...	...	...	-		...	...	...	-		...	...	...	...
1920 Footwear		...	...	...	167		...	...	...	412		...	...	...	...
2010 Sawmilling and planing of wood		...	...	...	25		...	...	...	12		...	...	...	...
202 Products of wood, cork, straw, etc.		...	...	...	-		...	...	...	-		...	...	...	...
2021 Veneer sheets, plywood, particle board, etc.		...	...	...	-		...	...	...	-		...	...	...	...
2022 Builders' carpentry and joinery		...	...	...	-		...	...	...	-		...	...	...	...
2023 Wooden containers		...	...	...	-		...	...	...	-		...	...	...	...
2029 Other wood products; articles of cork/straw		...	...	...	-		...	...	...	-		...	...	...	...
210 Paper and paper products		...	...	...	-		...	...	...	-		...	...	...	...
2101 Pulp, paper and paperboard		...	...	...	-		...	...	...	-		...	...	...	...
2102 Corrugated paper and paperboard		...	...	...	-		...	...	...	-		...	...	...	...
2109 Other articles of paper and paperboard		...	...	...	-		...	...	...	-		...	...	...	...
221 Publishing		...	...	...	150		...	...	...	1609		...	...	...	...
2211 Publishing of books and other publications		...	...	...	130		...	...	...	1243		...	...	...	...
2212 Publishing of newspapers, journals, etc.		...	...	...	14		...	...	...	344		...	...	...	...
2213 Publishing of recorded media		...	...	...	6		...	...	...	22		...	...	...	...
2219 Other publishing		...	...	...	-		...	...	...	-		...	...	...	...

222 Printing and related service activities	...	...	...	245	...	...	...	1179	...	...	...	...
2221 Printing	...	...	...	2	...	...	...	12	...	...	...	...
2222 Service activities related to printing	...	...	...	243	...	...	...	1167	...	...	...	...
2230 Reproduction of recorded media	...	...	...	-	...	...	...	-	...	...	...	...
2310 Coke oven products	...	...	...	-	...	...	...	-	...	...	...	...
2320 Refined petroleum products	...	...	...	24	...	...	...	128	...	...	...	...
2330 Processing of nuclear fuel	...	...	...	-	...	...	...	-	...	...	...	...
241 Basic chemicals	...	...	...	6	...	...	...	69	...	...	...	...
2411 Basic chemicals, except fertilizers	...	...	...	4	...	...	...	60	...	...	...	...
2412 Fertilizers and nitrogen compounds	...	...	...	2	...	...	...	9	...	...	...	...
2413 Plastics in primary forms; synthetic rubber	...	...	...	-	...	...	...	-	...	...	...	...
242 Other chemicals	...	...	...	-	...	...	...	-	...	...	...	...
2421 Pesticides and other agro-chemical products	...	...	...	-	...	...	...	-	...	...	...	...
2422 Paints, varnishes, printing ink and mastics	...	...	...	-	...	...	...	-	...	...	...	...
2423 Pharmaceuticals, medicinal chemicals, etc.	...	...	...	-	...	...	...	-	...	...	...	...
2424 Soap, cleaning & cosmetic preparations	...	...	...	-	...	...	...	-	...	...	...	...
2429 Other chemical products n.e.c.	...	...	...	-	...	...	...	-	...	...	...	...
2430 Man-made fibres	...	...	...	101	...	...	...	536	...	...	...	...
251 Rubber products	...	...	...	3	...	...	...	3	...	...	...	...
2511 Rubber tyres and tubes	...	...	...	3	...	...	...	3	...	...	...	...
2519 Other rubber products	...	...	...	-	...	...	...	-	...	...	...	...
2520 Plastic products	...	...	...	-	...	...	...	-	...	...	...	...
2610 Glass and glass products	...	...	...	-	...	...	...	-	...	...	...	...
269 Non-metallic mineral products n.e.c.	...	...	...	-	...	...	...	-	...	...	...	...
2691 Pottery, china and earthenware	...	...	...	-	...	...	...	-	...	...	...	...
2692 Refractory ceramic products	...	...	...	-	...	...	...	-	...	...	...	...
2693 Struct.non-refractory clay; ceramic products	...	...	...	-	...	...	...	-	...	...	...	...
2694 Cement, lime and plaster	...	...	...	-	...	...	...	-	...	...	...	...
2695 Articles of concrete, cement and plaster	...	...	...	-	...	...	...	-	...	...	...	...
2696 Cutting, shaping & finishing of stone	...	...	...	-	...	...	...	-	...	...	...	...
2699 Other non-metallic mineral products n.e.c.	...	...	...	-	...	...	...	-	...	...	...	...
2710 Basic iron and steel	...	...	...	34	...	...	...	214	...	...	...	...
2720 Basic precious and non-ferrous metals	...	...	...	-	...	...	...	-	...	...	...	...
273 Casting of metals	...	...	...	23	...	...	...	59	...	...	...	...
2731 Casting of iron and steel	...	...	...	20	...	...	...	58	...	...	...	...
2732 Casting of non-ferrous metals	...	...	...	3	...	...	...	1	...	...	...	...
281 Struct.metal products;tanks;steam generators	...	...	...	2775	...	...	...	8792	...	...	...	...
2811 Structural metal products	...	...	...	45	...	...	...	209	...	...	...	...
2812 Tanks, reservoirs and containers of metal	...	...	...	2730	...	...	...	8583	...	...	...	...
2813 Steam generators	...	...	...	-	...	...	...	-	...	...	...	...
289 Other metal products; metal working services	...	...	...	-	...	...	...	-	...	...	...	...
2891 Metal forging/pressing/stamping/roll-forming	...	...	...	-	...	...	...	-	...	...	...	...
2892 Treatment & coating of metals	...	...	...	-	...	...	...	-	...	...	...	...
2893 Cutlery, hand tools and general hardware	...	...	...	-	...	...	...	-	...	...	...	...
2899 Other fabricated metal products n.e.c.	...	...	...	-	...	...	...	-	...	...	...	...
291 General purpose machinery	...	...	...	35	...	...	...	691	...	...	...	...
2911 Engines & turbines(not for transport equip.)	...	...	...	13	...	...	...	47	...	...	...	...
2912 Pumps, compressors, taps and valves	...	...	...	17	...	...	...	42	...	...	...	...
2913 Bearings, gears, gearing & driving elements	...	...	...	3	...	...	...	595	...	...	...	...
2914 Ovens, furnaces and furnace burners	...	...	...	2	...	...	...	7	...	...	...	...
2915 Lifting and handling equipment	...	...	...	-	...	...	...	-	...	...	...	...
2919 Other general purpose machinery	...	...	...	-	...	...	...	-	...	...	...	...
292 Special purpose machinery	...	...	...	104	...	...	...	739	...	...	...	...
2921 Agricultural and forestry machinery	...	...	...	26	...	...	...	250	...	...	...	...
2922 Machine tools	...	...	...	29	...	...	...	362	...	...	...	...
2923 Machinery for metallurgy	...	...	...	37	...	...	...	107	...	...	...	...
2924 Machinery for mining & construction	...	...	...	12	...	...	...	20	...	...	...	...
2925 Food/beverage/tobacco processing machinery	...	...	...	-	...	...	...	-	...	...	...	...
2926 Machinery for textile, apparel and leather	...	...	...	-	...	...	...	-	...	...	...	...
2927 Weapons and ammunition	...	...	...	-	...	...	...	-	...	...	...	...
2929 Other special purpose machinery	...	...	...	-	...	...	...	-	...	...	...	...
2930 Domestic appliances n.e.c.	...	...	...	-	...	...	...	-	...	...	...	...

continued

Lebanon

ISIC Revision 3	Number of establishments					Number of employees a/					Wages and salaries paid to employees				
		(numbers)					(numbers)					(million POUNDS)			
ISIC Industry	Note	1993	1994	1995	1996	Note	1993	1994	1995	1996	Note	1993	1994	1995	1996
3000 Office, accounting and computing machinery		...	...	...	-		...	...	...	-		...	...	...	...
3110 Electric motors, generators and transformers		...	...	...	204		...	...	...	862		...	...	...	...
3120 Electricity distribution & control apparatus		...	...	...	80		...	...	...	301		...	...	...	...
3130 Insulated wire and cable		...	...	...	5		...	...	...	511		...	...	...	...
3140 Accumulators, primary cells and batteries		...	...	...	6		...	...	...	-		...	...	...	...
3150 Lighting equipment and electric lamps		...	...	...	17		...	...	...	20		...	...	...	...
3190 Other electrical equipment n.e.c.		...	...	...	-		...	...	...	-		...	...	...	...
3210 Electronic valves, tubes, etc.		...	...	...	15		...	...	...	59		...	...	...	...
3220 TV/radio transmitters; line comm. apparatus		...	...	...	-		...	...	...	-		...	...	...	...
3230 TV and radio receivers and associated goods		...	...	...	2		...	...	...	7		...	...	...	...
331 Medical, measuring, testing appliances, etc.		...	...	...	-		...	...	...	-		...	...	...	...
3311 Medical, surgical and orthopaedic equipment		...	...	...	-		...	...	...	-		...	...	...	...
3312 Measuring/testing/navigating appliances,etc.		...	...	...	-		...	...	...	-		...	...	...	...
3313 Industrial process control equipment		...	...	...	-		...	...	...	-		...	...	...	...
3320 Optical instruments & photographic equipment		...	...	...	-		...	...	...	-		...	...	...	...
3330 Watches and clocks		...	...	...	-		...	...	...	-		...	...	...	...
3410 Motor vehicles		...	...	...	-		...	...	...	-		...	...	...	...
3420 Automobile bodies, trailers & semi-trailers		...	...	...	63		...	...	...	509		...	...	...	...
3430 Parts/accessories for automobiles		...	...	...	292		...	...	...	666		...	...	...	...
351 Building and repairing of ships and boats		...	...	...	19		...	...	...	71		...	...	...	...
3511 Building and repairing of ships		...	...	...	19		...	...	...	71		...	...	...	...
3512 Building/repairing of pleasure/sport. boats		...	...	...	-		...	...	...	-		...	...	...	...
3520 Railway/tramway locomotives & rolling stock		...	...	...	-		...	...	...	-		...	...	...	...
3530 Aircraft and spacecraft		...	...	...	-		...	...	...	-		...	...	...	...
359 Transport equipment n.e.c.		...	...	...	-		...	...	...	-		...	...	...	...
3591 Motorcycles		...	...	...	-		...	...	...	-		...	...	...	...
3592 Bicycles and invalid carriages		...	...	...	-		...	...	...	-		...	...	...	...
3599 Other transport equipment n.e.c.		...	...	...	-		...	...	...	-		...	...	...	...
3610 Furniture		...	...	...	-		...	...	...	-		...	...	...	...
369 Manufacturing n.e.c.		...	...	...	-		...	...	...	-		...	...	...	...
3691 Jewellery and related articles		...	...	...	-		...	...	...	-		...	...	...	...
3692 Musical instruments		...	...	...	-		...	...	...	-		...	...	...	...
3693 Sports goods		...	...	...	-		...	...	...	-		...	...	...	...
3694 Games and toys		...	...	...	-		...	...	...	-		...	...	...	...
3699 Other manufacturing n.e.c.		...	...	...	-		...	...	...	-		...	...	...	...
3710 Recycling of metal waste and scrap		...	...	...	-		...	...	...	-		...	...	...	...
3720 Recycling of non-metal waste and scrap		...	...	...	-		...	...	...	-		...	...	...	...
D Total manufacturing		...	...	...	5284		...	...	...	24409		...	...	...	...

a/ Incomplete coverage in certain industries.

LITHUANIA

Supplier of information:
Lithuanian Department of Statistics, Vilnius.

Basic source of data:
Annual survey of industrial enterprises.

Major deviations from ISIC (Revision 3):
Data collected under the national classification system have been reclassified by the national authorities to correspond approximately with ISIC (Rev. 3).

Reference period (if not calendar year):

Scope:
Data relate to all operating industrial establishments as well as non-industrial enterprises with industrial production. For the years 1995 and 1996, the figures relate to all operating industrial enterprises.

Method of enumeration:
Not reported.

Adjusted for non-response:
No.

Concepts and definitions of variables:
No deviations from the standard UN concepts and definitions are reported.

Related national publications:
Lithuanian Statistics Yearbook 1993. Industry 1996.

Lithuania

ISIC Revision 3 ISIC Industry	Number of enterprises Note	(numbers) 1993	1994	1995	1996	Number of employees Note	(numbers) 1993	1994	1995	1996	Wages and salaries paid to employees Note	(thousand LITA) 1993	1994	1995	1996
151 Processed meat, fish, fruit, vegetables, fats		42	62	...	154		27552	21580	...	11947		72052	98636	...	103210
1511 Processing/preserving of meat		19	36	...	103		12286	9840	...	8200		34204	47114	...	61863
1512 Processing/preserving of fish		9	13	...	26		11730	9259	...	2151		30826	41554	...	28799
1513 Processing/preserving of fruit & vegetables		13	11	...	21		3260	2266	...	1255		5985	7478	...	8108
1514 Vegetable and animal oils and fats		1	2	...	4		276	215	...	341		1037	2490	...	4440
1520 Dairy products		47	52	...	59		17174	14811	...	10668		43072	68427	...	93596
153 Grain mill products; starches; animal feeds		24	31	...	44		5362	4713	...	4369		15763	27818	...	46880
1531 Grain mill products		9	14	...	29		1616	1308	...	2296		5255	7723	...	20691
1532 Starches and starch products		1	1	...	1		62	54	...	...		75	69	...	...
1533 Prepared animal feeds		14	16	...	14		3684	3351	...	2039		10433	20026	...	25997
154 Other food products		66	80	...	152		13205	12073	...	12152		44663	78499	...	119789
1541 Bakery products		56	68	...	134		7872	7962	...	8002		25033	48154	...	62463
1542 Sugar		4	4	...	4		2713	1984	...	1737		9344	11404	...	22948
1543 Cocoa, chocolate and sugar confectionery		5	6	...	7		2568	2070	...	2292		10108	18555	...	33686
1544 Macaroni, noodles & similar products		-	-	...	1		-	-	...	2		-	-	...	3
1549 Other food products n.e.c.		1	2	...	6		52	57	...	119		178	386	...	689
155 Beverages		24	32	...	47		6307	5523	...	5218		23310	38988	...	66454
1551 Distilling, rectifying & blending of spirits		4	5	...	4		1698	1482	...	1534		5970	10830	...	20893
1552 Wines		2	2	...	2		1308	1000	...	950		4473	6312	...	13450
1553 Malt liquors and malt		15	16	...	19		3237	2855	...	2393		12702	20796	...	29430
1554 Soft drinks; mineral waters		3	9	...	22		64	186	...	341		165	1050	...	2681
1600 Tobacco products		2	2	...	1		568	570	...	...		2406	4965	...	...
171 Spinning, weaving and finishing of textiles		36	43	...	47		28690	24397	...	16269		65757	...	...	132040
1711 Textile fibre preparation; textile weaving		36	42	...	45		28690	24395	...	16094		65757	98946	...	131918
1712 Finishing of textiles		-	1	...	2		-	2	...	175		-	...	...	122
172 Other textiles		8	14	...	17		3182	2345	...	1138		8356	9949	...	9411
1721 Made-up textile articles, except apparel		5	9	...	4		2323	1670	...	325		5018	5892	...	2351
1722 Carpets and rugs		1	1	...	1		714	518	...	...		3179	3729	...	...
1723 Cordage, rope, twine and netting		-	1	...	3		-	21	...	64		-	18	...	3139
1729 Other textiles n.e.c.		2	3	...	9		145	136	...	460		159	310	...	1368
1730 Knitted and crocheted fabrics and articles		59	54	...	55		23128	19058	...	9615		49124	67923	...	68266
1810 Wearing apparel, except fur apparel		111	135	...	219		24779	22339	...	18552		54415	76399	...	124699
1820 Dressing & dyeing of fur; processing of fur		4	8	...	6		3021	2861	...	1575		7903	12394	...	12933
191 Tanning, dressing and processing of leather		18	18	...	16		3019	2448	...	1714		6791	9014	...	11513
1911 Tanning and dressing of leather		6	7	...	5		1329	1061	...	965		3445	4736	...	7178
1912 Luggage, handbags, etc.; saddlery & harness		12	11	...	11		1690	1387	...	749		3346	4278	...	4335
1920 Footwear		19	17	...	22		8353	6352	...	4158		15837	21648	...	28563
2010 Sawmilling and planing of wood		63	92	...	239		2400	3457	...	4290		4090	8504	...	21260
202 Products of wood, cork, straw, etc.		99	149	...	245		15720	15143	...	9573		34021	56320	...	55627
2021 Veneer sheets, plywood, particle board, etc.		23	40	...	56		4697	4580	...	2898		11160	18686	...	19876
2022 Builders' carpentry and joinery		46	68	...	111		4642	4942	...	3909		10639	19333	...	22213
2023 Wooden containers		5	3	...	5		2540	1768	...	833		6553	8083	...	5437
2029 Other wood products; articles of cork/straw		25	38	...	73		3841	3853	...	1933		5669	10218	...	8101
210 Paper and paper products		16	13	...	17		5905	5000	...	4225		14580	24640	...	41658
2101 Pulp, paper and paperboard		6	6	...	8		4625	3806	...	3284		10322	16807	...	29862
2102 Corrugated paper and paperboard		4	3	...	4		618	599	...	619		2136	4227	...	7820
2109 Other articles of paper and paperboard		6	4	...	5		662	595	...	322		2122	3606	...	3976
221 Publishing		78	82	...	122		1871	2457	...	2551		4941	17006	...	31176
2211 Publishing of books and other publications		15	15	...	34		1354	1203	...	949		3461	7088	...	10148
2212 Publishing of newspapers, journals, etc.		60	58	...	77		451	1152	...	1459		1256	9276	...	18624
2213 Publishing of recorded media		-	1	...	-		-	25	...	-		-	11	...	-
2219 Other publishing		3	8	...	11		66	77	...	143		224	631	...	2404

222 Printing and related service activities	25	60	...	86	2206	2933	...	3331	6433	20695	...	34131
2221 Printing	25	52	...	75	2206	2857	...	3179	6433	20433	...	33043
2222 Service activities related to printing	-	8	...	11	-	76	...	152	-	262	...	1088
2230 Reproduction of recorded media	-	2	...	5	-	10	...	54	-	15	...	191
2310 Coke oven products	-	-	...	-	-	-	...	-	-	-	...	-
2320 Refined petroleum products	2	2	...	3	3089	3200	...	3211	17237	30720	...	65710
2330 Processing of nuclear fuel	-	-	...	-	-	-	...	-	-	-	...	-
241 Basic chemicals	5	8	...	11	4162	3699	...	3252	11559	22452	...	57347
2411 Basic chemicals, except fertilizers	3	5	...	8	33	55	...	133	163	320	...	1258
2412 Fertilizers and nitrogen compounds	2	2	...	2	4129	3637	...	3119	11396	22110	...	56089
2413 Plastics in primary forms; synthetic rubber	-	1	...	1	-	7	...	...	-	22	...	...
242 Other chemicals	24	29	...	44	4065	3435	...	3272	8652	16104	...	30369
2421 Pesticides and other agro-chemical products	-	-	...	-	-	-	...	-	-	-	...	-
2422 Paints, varnishes, printing ink and mastics	1	4	...	6	20	20	...	38	80	80	...	236
2423 Pharmaceuticals, medicinal chemicals, etc.	10	10	...	14	2277	1994	...	2004	4700	9571	...	19611
2424 Soap, cleaning & cosmetic preparations	10	11	...	13	1587	1199	...	843	3314	5137	...	6720
2429 Other chemical products n.e.c.	3	4	...	11	181	222	...	387	558	1316	...	3802
2430 Man-made fibres	1	1	...	1	1793	1486	...	...	3679	6651	...	...
251 Rubber products	7	11	...	14	267	331	...	363	439	875	...	2127
2511 Rubber tyres and tubes	5	6	...	8	117	132	...	143	241	619	...	749
2519 Other rubber products	2	5	...	6	150	199	...	220	198	256	...	1378
2520 Plastic products	35	49	...	96	2633	2359	...	3180	5972	9666	...	22534
2610 Glass and glass products	5	5	...	12	1884	2134	...	1964	4974	11319	...	19636
269 Non-metallic mineral products n.e.c.	139	152	...	177	23121	21514	...	11936	61425	97022	...	88800
2691 Pottery, china and earthenware	9	7	...	13	1024	1377	...	780	2430	3910	...	5345
2692 Refractory ceramic products	5	1	...	1	435	98	...	...	1305	294	...	...
2693 Struct.non-refractory clay; ceramic products	9	24	...	29	1554	2214	...	3540	2910	7652	...	25616
2694 Cement, lime and plaster	1	1	...	2	1925	1767	...	1177	5568	9285	...	11461
2695 Articles of concrete, cement and plaster	83	81	...	82	17606	15202	...	5827	48170	73517	...	43659
2696 Cutting, shaping & finishing of stone	24	22	...	38	205	407	...	325	246	918	...	1271
2699 Other non-metallic mineral products n.e.c.	8	16	...	12	372	449	...	284	796	1446	...	1431
2710 Basic iron and steel	1	1	...	1	36	31	...	...	49	44	...	...
2720 Basic precious and non-ferrous metals	-	-	...	2	-	-	...	24	-	-	...	228
273 Casting of metals	5	6	...	10	2564	1769	...	1200	7374	8377	...	9499
2731 Casting of iron and steel	4	3	...	8	2552	1737	...	1162	7350	8317	...	9265
2732 Casting of non-ferrous metals	1	3	...	2	12	32	...	38	24	60	...	234
281 Struct.metal products;tanks;steam generators	19	45	...	45	2672	3182	...	1607	5535	10149	...	10448
2811 Structural metal products	14	37	...	40	1630	2022	...	1208	3677	7473	...	7325
2812 Tanks, reservoirs and containers of metal	4	7	...	4	1010	1112	...	376	1776	2464	...	2893
2813 Steam generators	1	1	...	1	32	48	...	...	82	212	...	...
289 Other metal products; metal working services	50	56	...	92	9338	7418	...	4126	18049	25013	...	30448
2891 Metal forging/pressing/stamping/roll-forming	-	2	...	4	-	257	...	130	-	318	...	796
2892 Treatment & coating of metals	4	2	...	5	347	384	...	62	428	1092	...	552
2893 Cutlery, hand tools and general hardware	8	9	...	9	3699	2119	...	624	5682	6052	...	4388
2899 Other fabricated metal products n.e.c.	38	43	...	74	5292	4658	...	3310	11939	17551	...	24712
291 General purpose machinery	34	41	...	52	10973	11002	...	6709	22874	41598	...	51525
2911 Engines & turbines(not for transport equip.)	2	5	...	5	15	1194	...	136	150	7150	...	643
2912 Pumps, compressors, taps and valves	4	3	...	5	5825	4669	...	3018	13001	17033	...	24864
2913 Bearings, gears, gearing & driving elements	-	-	...	1	-	-	...	...	-	-	...	...
2914 Ovens, furnaces and furnace burners	4	3	...	4	517	501	...	180	1128	1894	...	1333
2915 Lifting and handling equipment	7	14	...	20	56	869	...	867	168	3264	...	7585
2919 Other general purpose machinery	17	16	...	17	4560	3769	...	2490	8427	12257	...	17038
292 Special purpose machinery	55	66	...	61	14086	11154	...	6564	24000	35550	...	40826
2921 Agricultural and forestry machinery	35	40	...	28	5620	4485	...	2816	9711	15016	...	18454
2922 Machine tools	16	18	...	19	6449	5156	...	2754	10912	15592	...	18390
2923 Machinery for metallurgy	-	-	...	-	-	-	...	-	-	-	...	-
2924 Machinery for mining & construction	1	1	...	1	195	190	...	...	512	725	...	...
2925 Food/beverage/tobacco processing machinery	2	5	...	6	1727	1237	...	772	2694	3874	...	2616
2926 Machinery for textile, apparel and leather	-	-	...	-	-	-	...	-	-	-	...	-
2927 Weapons and ammunition	-	-	...	1	-	-	...	...	-	-	...	...
2929 Other special purpose machinery	1	2	...	6	95	86	...	115	171	343	...	726
2930 Domestic appliances n.e.c.	18	15	...	15	9241	8094	...	4738	32713	40697	...	43363

continued

Lithuania

ISIC Revision 3 — ISIC Industry	Note	Number of enterprises (numbers) 1993	1994	1995	1996	Note	Number of employees (numbers) 1993	1994	1995	1996	Note	Wages and salaries paid to employees (thousand LITA) 1993	1994	1995	1996
3000 Office, accounting and computing machinery		10	12	...	13		4373	3006	...	1375		4828	7034	...	7918
3110 Electric motors, generators and transformers		10	14	...	18		6547	5089	...	2348		12570	17893	...	16873
3120 Electricity distribution & control apparatus		2	4	...	4		115	211	...	1256		278	1257	...	13118
3130 Insulated wire and cable		4	5	...	5		851	1072	...	1311		2807	3372	...	12437
3140 Accumulators, primary cells and batteries		1	2	...	3		1077	816	...	483		2644	3868	...	3795
3150 Lighting equipment and electric lamps		3	2	...	5		289	218	...	183		485	460	...	1121
3190 Other electrical equipment n.e.c.		2	5	...	6		161	194	...	167		386	934	...	1499
3210 Electronic valves, tubes, etc.		4	4	...	8		7898	7077	...	6734		20566	27855	...	57943
3220 TV/radio transmitters; line comm. apparatus		-	4	...	8		-	130	...	346		-	994	...	4623
3230 TV and radio receivers and associated goods		10	8	...	15		18142	13793	...	4211		43541	40386	...	31139
331 Medical, measuring, testing appliances, etc.		14	31	...	42		8672	9081	...	2809		14523	25869	...	21824
3311 Medical, surgical and orthopaedic equipment		5	10	...	15		338	473	...	506		922	2318	...	5616
3312 Measuring/testing/navigating appliances,etc.		9	21	...	25		8334	8608	...	2294		13601	23551	...	16183
3313 Industrial process control equipment		-	-	...	2		-	-	...	9		-	-	...	25
3320 Optical instruments & photographic equipment		2	4	...	4		25	19	...	20		30	23	...	84
3330 Watches and clocks		-	-	...	-		-	-	...	-		-	-	...	-
3410 Motor vehicles		-	-	...	1		-	-	...	...		-	-	...	...
3420 Automobile bodies, trailers & semi-trailers		2	2	...	2		120	99	...	41		260	405	...	358
3430 Parts/accessories for automobiles		8	8	...	11		2674	2201	...	2332		4719	5811	...	12075
351 Building and repairing of ships and boats		16	24	...	30		7546	7806	...	4912		18907	34553	...	45200
3511 Building and repairing of ships		15	23	...	29		7519	7786	...	4897		18858	34476	...	45200
3512 Building/repairing of pleasure/sport. boats		1	1	...	1		27	20	...	...		49	77	...	...
3520 Railway/tramway locomotives & rolling stock		-	-	...	2		-	-	...	3		-	-	...	16
3530 Aircraft and spacecraft		1	3	...	2		680	645	...	207		1428	1989	...	1687
359 Transport equipment n.e.c.		3	2	...	3		1974	2099	...	1098		3558	8561	...	10734
3591 Motorcycles		1	1	...	1		1416	1014	...	...		2056	3054	...	...
3592 Bicycles and invalid carriages		1	1	...	2		476	1085	...	901		1342	5507	...	9382
3599 Other transport equipment n.e.c.		1	-	...	-		82	-	...	-		160	-	...	-
3610 Furniture		62	77	...	125		12626	11002	...	8890		33333	44888	...	62535
369 Manufacturing n.e.c.		25	40	...	39		3574	3098	...	1476		6039	7981	...	8598
3691 Jewellery and related articles		4	6	...	5		1230	803	...	324		1697	1494	...	1453
3692 Musical instruments		1	2	...	1		14	148	...	...		25	550	...	...
3693 Sports goods		1	1	...	2		227	198	...	116		462	669	...	...
3694 Games and toys		5	8	...	7		696	777	...	154		1474	1850	...	597
3699 Other manufacturing n.e.c.		14	23	...	24		1407	1172	...	871		2381	3418	...	6495
3710 Recycling of metal waste and scrap		7	9	...	9		368	476	...	382		1951	4890	...	5636
3720 Recycling of non-metal waste and scrap		5	7	...	2		112	173	...	21		218	511	...	36
D Total manufacturing		1333	1700	1979	2546		360190	317183	265276	215883		871116	1336557	1569843	1817773

Lithuania

ISIC Revision 3		Output in producers' prices					Value added					Gross fixed capital formation		
			(thousand LITA)					(thousand LITA)					(thousand LITA)	
ISIC	Industry	Note	1993	1994	1995	1996	Note	1993	1994	1995	1996	Note	1995	1996
151	Processed meat,fish,fruit,vegetables,fats		1005183	792215	768070	887289		...	...	...	...		...	...
1511	Processing/preserving of meat		769976	657716	631343	715123		...	...	...	...		...	...
1512	Processing/preserving of fish		177400	86917	68150	101648		...	...	...	...		...	...
1513	Processing/preserving of fruit & vegetables		46275	26641	38237	33381		...	...	...	...		...	...
1514	Vegetable and animal oils and fats		11532	20941	30340	37137		...	...	...	...		...	...
1520	Dairy products		766887	822742	1093936	1368259		...	...	...	...		...	...
153	Grain mill products; starches; animal feeds		309103	421784	476744	650024		...	...	...	...		...	...
1531	Grain mill products		102165	122442	241060	338742		...	...	...	...		...	...
1532	Starches and starch products		1001	995	...	...		...	...	...	...		...	...
1533	Prepared animal feeds		205937	298347	234551	309798		...	...	...	...		...	...
154	Other food products		429411	621296	733283	962494		...	...	...	...		...	...
1541	Bakery products		190932	286146	314590	379653		...	...	...	...		...	...
1542	Sugar		156437	128474	176539	268169		...	...	...	...		...	...
1543	Cocoa, chocolate and sugar confectionery		80979	202674	237326	288249		...	...	...	...		...	...
1544	Macaroni, noodles & similar products		-	-	-	...		...	...	...	...		...	...
1549	Other food products n.e.c.		1063	4002	4828	26377		...	...	...	...		...	...
155	Beverages		443691	630811	516956	598403		...	...	...	...		...	...
1551	Distilling, rectifying & blending of spirits		217749	328933	199480	229711		...	...	...	...		...	...
1552	Wines		111565	125586	147476	155610		...	...	...	...		...	...
1553	Malt liquors and malt		112661	171232	156018	196933		...	...	...	...		...	...
1554	Soft drinks; mineral waters		1716	5060	13982	16149		...	...	...	...		...	...
1600	Tobacco products		48081	133162	111137	...		...	...	...	...		...	...
171	Spinning, weaving and finishing of textiles		530126	532454	599734	673137		...	...	...	...		...	...
1711	Textile fibre preparation; textile weaving		530126	530740	595012	670721		...	...	...	...		...	...
1712	Finishing of textiles		-	1714	4722	2416		...	...	...	...		...	...
172	Other textiles		70057	51459	42466	45986		...	...	...	...		...	...
1721	Made-up textile articles, except apparel		37973	25061	7985	9191		...	...	...	...		...	...
1722	Carpets and rugs		31671	25198	9297	...		...	...	...	...		...	...
1723	Cordage, rope, twine and netting		-	210	1110	1720		...	...	...	...		...	...
1729	Other textiles n.e.c.		413	990	24074	27788		...	...	...	...		...	...
1730	Knitted and crocheted fabrics and articles		225960	265742	290244	326484		...	...	...	...		...	...
1810	Wearing apparel, except fur apparel		237871	313633	527816	820789		...	...	...	...		...	...
1820	Dressing & dyeing of fur; processing of fur		59523	60942	52038	63205		...	...	...	...		...	...
191	Tanning, dressing and processing of leather		64512	60263	59490	66992		...	...	...	...		...	...
1911	Tanning and dressing of leather		48865	47821	48987	55181		...	...	...	...		...	...
1912	Luggage, handbags, etc.; saddlery & harness		15647	12442	10503	11811		...	...	...	...		...	...
1920	Footwear		98460	114859	119118	127179		...	...	...	...		...	...
2010	Sawmilling and planing of wood		33908	44645	57948	131164		...	...	...	...		...	...
202	Products of wood, cork, straw, etc.		230429	375136	203103	272737		...	...	...	...		...	...
2021	Veneer sheets, plywood, particle board, etc.		111133	138768	82390	114751		...	...	...	...		...	...
2022	Builders' carpentry and joinery		62441	128021	77622	96958		...	...	...	...		...	...
2023	Wooden containers		24006	40456	26007	31330		...	...	...	...		...	...
2029	Other wood products; articles of cork/straw		32849	67891	17084	29698		...	...	...	...		...	...
210	Paper and paper products		88272	143210	206796	210748		...	...	...	...		...	...
2101	Pulp, paper and paperboard		55100	93486	130556	139899		...	...	...	...		...	...
2102	Corrugated paper and paperboard		23248	35526	57819	43788		...	...	...	...		...	...
2109	Other articles of paper and paperboard		9924	14198	18421	27061		...	...	...	...		...	...
221	Publishing		29578	67022	84979	126600		...	...	...	...		...	...
2211	Publishing of books and other publications		10288	27967	35826	53185		...	...	...	...		...	...
2212	Publishing of newspapers, journals, etc.		16574	35115	42705	61975		...	...	...	...		...	...
2213	Publishing of recorded media		-	258	-	-		...	...	...	...		...	...
2219	Other publishing		2716	3682	6448	11440		...	...	...	...		...	...

continued

Lithuania

ISIC Revision 3		Output in producers' prices					Value added					Gross fixed capital formation	
		(thousand LITA)					(thousand LITA)					(thousand LITA)	
ISIC Industry	Note	1993	1994	1995	1996	Note	1993	1994	1995	1996	Note	1995	1996
222 Printing and related service activities		19065	78045	116352	159049		...	...	...	...		...	...
2221 Printing		19065	77119	113891	155593		...	...	...	...		...	...
2222 Service activities related to printing		-	926	2461	3456		...	...	...	...		...	...
2230 Reproduction of recorded media		-	47	606	1152		...	...	...	...		...	...
2310 Coke oven products		-	-	-	-		...	...	...	...		...	...
2320 Refined petroleum products		2541628	2084191	1788249	2579579		...	...	...	...		...	...
2330 Processing of nuclear fuel		-	-	-	-		...	...	...	...		...	...
241 Basic chemicals		279390	380151	731656	827604		...	...	...	...		...	...
2411 Basic chemicals, except fertilizers		947	9623	21959	11463		...	...	...	...		...	...
2412 Fertilizers and nitrogen compounds		278443	370463	709697	816141		...	...	...	...		...	...
2413 Plastics in primary forms; synthetic rubber		-	65	-	...		...	...	...	...		...	...
242 Other chemicals		69897	99993	136799	173856		...	...	...	...		...	...
2421 Pesticides and other agro-chemical products		-	-	-	-		...	...	...	...		...	...
2422 Paints, varnishes, printing ink and mastics		107	848	1534	2906		...	...	...	...		...	...
2423 Pharmaceuticals, medicinal chemicals, etc.		35789	60563	85620	114198		...	...	...	...		...	...
2424 Soap, cleaning & cosmetic preparations		32090	32649	35030	37350		...	...	...	...		...	...
2429 Other chemical products n.e.c.		1911	5933	14615	19402		...	...	...	...		...	...
2430 Man-made fibres		37212	63319	...	...		...	...	...	...		...	...
251 Rubber products		2002	3684	9995	12712		...	...	...	...		...	...
2511 Rubber tyres and tubes		1682	2808	2975	4501		...	...	...	...		...	...
2519 Other rubber products		320	876	7020	8211		...	...	...	...		...	...
2520 Plastic products		26360	47048	71092	124131		...	...	...	...		...	...
2610 Glass and glass products		34010	45280	93281	137689		...	...	...	...		...	...
269 Non-metallic mineral products n.e.c.		362899	443063	379194	372096		...	...	...	...		...	...
2691 Pottery, china and earthenware		8600	9615	9962	8920		...	...	...	...		...	...
2692 Refractory ceramic products		833	849	...	...		...	...	...	...		...	...
2693 Struct.non-refractory clay; ceramic products		20475	84215	87595	79178		...	...	...	...		...	...
2694 Cement, lime and plaster		92328	110248	87178	101240		...	...	...	...		...	...
2695 Articles of concrete, cement and plaster		230292	232169	186847	169954		...	...	...	...		...	...
2696 Cutting, shaping & finishing of stone		1303	1382	2646	4018		...	...	...	...		...	...
2699 Other non-metallic mineral products n.e.c.		9068	4585	4963	8779		...	...	...	...		...	...
2710 Basic iron and steel		220	48	...	...		...	...	...	...		...	...
2720 Basic precious and non-ferrous metals		-	-	317	4750		...	...	...	...		...	...
273 Casting of metals		39580	43475	25225	28289		...	...	...	...		...	...
2731 Casting of iron and steel		39527	43215	24605	27428		...	...	...	...		...	...
2732 Casting of non-ferrous metals		53	260	620	861		...	...	...	...		...	...
281 Struct.metal products;tanks;steam generators		30034	37588	41342	54191		...	...	...	...		...	...
2811 Structural metal products		23708	27263	29067	35705		...	...	...	...		...	...
2812 Tanks, reservoirs and containers of metal		6211	10192	11998	17967		...	...	...	...		...	...
2813 Steam generators		115	133	...	...		...	...	...	...		...	...
289 Other metal products; metal working services		84390	96802	105726	145205		...	...	...	...		...	...
2891 Metal forging/pressing/stamping/roll-forming		-	9109	16827	19401		...	...	...	...		...	...
2892 Treatment & coating of metals		2722	403	657	2384		...	...	...	...		...	...
2893 Cutlery, hand tools and general hardware		24536	17725	22294	16434		...	...	...	...		...	...
2899 Other fabricated metal products n.e.c.		57132	69565	65948	106986		...	...	...	...		...	...
291 General purpose machinery		130291	153762	150581	165288		...	...	...	...		...	...
2911 Engines & turbines(not for transport equip.)		420	19050	1830	2338		...	...	...	...		...	...
2912 Pumps, compressors, taps and valves		76165	79696	64607	87673		...	...	...	...		...	...
2913 Bearings, gears, gearing & driving elements		-	-	...	...		...	...	...	...		...	...
2914 Ovens, furnaces and furnace burners		6361	6932	4563	3248		...	...	...	...		...	...
2915 Lifting and handling equipment		5113	5627	26581	19967		...	...	...	...		...	...
2919 Other general purpose machinery		42232	42457	53000	52062		...	...	...	...		...	...

292 Special purpose machinery		97763	98709	92491	108253		...	...	...	...		...	...
2921 Agricultural and forestry machinery		39175	49415	45144	55974		...	...	...	...		...	...
2922 Machine tools		49610	32816	28626	29313		...	...	...	...		...	...
2923 Machinery for metallurgy		-	-	-	-		...	...	...	...		...	...
2924 Machinery for mining & construction		1805	3353	...	...		...	...	...	...		...	...
2925 Food/beverage/tobacco processing machinery		6964	10857	13971	15730		...	...	...	...		...	...
2926 Machinery for textile, apparel and leather		-	-	-	-		...	...	...	...		...	...
2927 Weapons and ammunition		-	-	...	...		...	...	...	...		...	...
2929 Other special purpose machinery		209	2268	2101	4663		...	...	...	...		...	...
2930 Domestic appliances n.e.c.		302878	281028	265908	197432		...	...	...	...		...	...
3000 Office, accounting and computing machinery		13795	15539	12511	16181		...	...	...	...		...	...
3110 Electric motors, generators and transformers		85455	64018	42353	44678		...	...	...	...		...	...
3120 Electricity distribution & control apparatus		1369	6032	27843	38232		...	...	...	...		...	...
3130 Insulated wire and cable		31564	20573	75624	151499		...	...	...	...		...	...
3140 Accumulators, primary cells and batteries		19416	19221	15160	7427		...	...	...	...		...	...
3150 Lighting equipment and electric lamps		3405	1371	3204	3779		...	...	...	...		...	...
3190 Other electrical equipment n.e.c.		2636	3816	8504	5825		...	...	...	...		...	...
3210 Electronic valves, tubes, etc.		162562	180539	288547	331062		...	...	...	...		...	...
3220 TV/radio transmitters; line comm. apparatus		-	10570	26211	33165		...	...	...	...		...	...
3230 TV and radio receivers and associated goods		325426	160775	92811	110147		...	...	...	...		...	...
331 Medical, measuring, testing appliances, etc.		91870	119805	75392	86852		...	...	...	...		...	...
3311 Medical, surgical and orthopaedic equipment		3380	9412	19990	26031		...	...	...	...		...	...
3312 Measuring/testing/navigating appliances,etc.		88490	110393	55273	60775		...	...	...	...		...	...
3313 Industrial process control equipment		-	-	129	46		...	...	...	...		...	...
3320 Optical instruments & photographic equipment		31	158	700	1183		...	...	...	...		...	...
3330 Watches and clocks		-	-	-	-		...	...	...	...		...	...
3410 Motor vehicles		-	-	-	...		...	...	...	...		...	...
3420 Automobile bodies, trailers & semi-trailers		2531	1602	1109	2865		...	...	...	...		...	...
3430 Parts/accessories for automobiles		32395	19708	19585	23454		...	...	...	...		...	...
351 Building and repairing of ships and boats		120120	178759	128264	203243		...	...	...	...		...	...
3511 Building and repairing of ships		120119	178754	127579	202831		...	...	...	...		...	...
3512 Building/repairing of pleasure/sport. boats		1	5	...	...		...	...	...	...		...	...
3520 Railway/tramway locomotives & rolling stock		-	-	-	45		...	...	...	...		...	...
3530 Aircraft and spacecraft		634	29554	1002	1818		...	...	...	...		...	...
359 Transport equipment n.e.c.		23240	64076	62064	82111		...	...	...	...		...	...
3591 Motorcycles		16589	17044	...	...		...	...	...	...		...	...
3592 Bicycles and invalid carriages		5018	47032	58122	78942		...	...	...	...		...	...
3599 Other transport equipment n.e.c.		1633	-	-	-		...	...	...	...		...	...
3610 Furniture		215720	211682	252146	311439		...	...	...	...		...	...
369 Manufacturing n.e.c.		30949	45113	45678	45360		...	...	...	...		...	...
3691 Jewellery and related articles		7596	2828	2911	1533		...	...	...	...		...	...
3692 Musical instruments		85	1029	...	...		...	...	...	...		...	...
3693 Sports goods		1134	1205	1019	1344		...	...	...	...		...	...
3694 Games and toys		6837	5650	1706	995		...	...	...	...		...	...
3699 Other manufacturing n.e.c.		15297	34401	39844	41242		...	...	...	...		...	...
3710 Recycling of metal waste and scrap		18265	46742	48312	39359		...	...	...	...		...	...
3720 Recycling of non-metal waste and scrap		1498	947	49	68		...	...	...	...		...	...
D Total manufacturing		9908552	10608208	11338876	14361249		...	...	...	...		...	...

Lithuania

ISIC Revision 3			Index numbers of industrial production											
			(1990=100)											
ISIC	Industry	Note	1985	1986	1987	1988	1989	1990	1991	1992	1993	1994	1995	1996
15	Food and beverages		...	...	...	...	...	...	...	...	...	...	...	...
16	Tobacco products		...	...	...	...	...	...	...	...	...	...	...	...
17	Textiles		...	...	...	...	...	...	...	...	...	...	...	...
18	Wearing apparel, fur		...	...	...	...	...	...	...	...	...	...	...	...
19	Leather, leather products and footwear		...	...	...	...	...	...	...	...	...	...	...	...
20	Wood products (excl. furniture)		...	...	...	...	...	...	...	...	...	...	...	...
21	Paper and paper products		...	...	...	...	...	...	...	...	...	...	...	...
22	Printing and publishing		...	...	...	...	...	...	...	...	...	...	...	...
23	Coke,refined petroleum products,nuclear fuel		...	...	...	...	...	...	...	...	...	...	...	...
24	Chemicals and chemical products		...	...	...	...	...	...	...	...	...	...	...	...
25	Rubber and plastics products		...	...	...	...	...	...	...	...	...	...	...	...
26	Non-metallic mineral products		...	...	...	...	...	...	...	...	...	...	...	...
27	Basic metals		...	...	...	...	...	...	...	...	...	...	...	...
28	Fabricated metal products		...	...	...	...	...	...	...	...	...	...	...	...
29	Machinery and equipment n.e.c.		...	...	...	...	...	...	...	...	...	...	...	...
30	Office, accounting and computing machinery		...	...	...	...	...	...	...	...	...	...	...	...
31	Electrical machinery and apparatus		...	...	...	...	...	...	...	...	...	...	...	...
32	Radio,television and communication equipment		...	...	...	...	...	...	...	...	...	...	...	...
33	Medical, precision and optical instruments		...	...	...	...	...	...	...	...	...	...	...	...
34	Motor vehicles, trailers, semi-trailers		...	...	...	...	...	...	...	...	...	...	...	...
35	Other transport equipment		...	...	...	...	...	...	...	...	...	...	...	...
36	Furniture; manufacturing n.e.c.		...	...	...	...	...	...	...	...	...	...	...	...
37	Recycling		...	...	...	...	...	...	...	...	...	...	...	...
D	Total manufacturing		...	...	...	...	...	...	...	...	...	...	...	...

MACAU

Supplier of information:
Direcçao de Serviços de Estatística e Censos, Macau.

Basic source of data:
Annual industrial census.

Major deviations from ISIC (Revision 2):
ISIC 383 includes manufacture of electrical office computing and accounting equipment, which is not shown on the detailed industry level. ISIC 390 includes manufacture of toys, which is not shown on the detailed industry level.

Reference period (if not calendar year):

Scope:
All legal establishments.

Method of enumeration:
The inquiry is carried out through field interviews by enumerators, mail returns and through respondents personal delivery of questionnaires.

Adjusted for non-response:
No.

Concepts and definitions of variables:
Number of employees is the average of the quarterly numbers.

Related national publications:
Inquerito Industrial (annual), published by the Direcçao de Serviços de Estatística e Censos, Macau.

Macau

ISIC Revision 2 ISIC Industry	Note	Number of establishments (numbers) 1993	1994	1995	1996	Note	Number of employees (numbers) 1993	1994	1995	1996	Note	Wages and salaries paid to employees (thousand PATACAS) 1993	1994	1995	1996
311/2 Food products		126	129	119	130		828	958	856	960		35217	46340	47523	53722
3111 Slaughtering, preparing & preserving meat		9	8	9	8		112	105	112	104		5549	5958	6639	6545
3112 Dairy products		3	3	4	5		25	19	22	33		1049	1018	1220	2115
3113 Canning, preserving of fruits & vegetables		3	3	4	4		43	37	30	27		1435	1406	1505	1484
3114 Canning, preserving and processing of fish		5	4	4	3		90	78	61	40		3533	3390	2901	2080
3115 Vegetable and animal oils and fats		1	1	-	-		6	5	-	-		221	247	-	-
3116 Grain mill products		-	-	-	-		-	-	-	-		-	-	-	-
3117 Bakery products		95	101	90	100		505	668	600	723		21621	32477	33939	40227
3118 Sugar factories and refineries		-	-	-	-		-	-	-	-		-	-	-	-
3119 Cocoa, chocolate and sugar confectionery		1	1	1	1		1	1	1	1		55	60	60	62
3121 Other food products		9	8	7	9		46	45	30	32		1754	1784	1259	1209
3122 Prepared animal feeds		-	-	-	-		-	-	-	-		-	-	-	-
313 Beverages		6	5	3	3		190	193	179	176		12071	12508	14017	16059
3131 Distilling, rectifying and blending spirits		4	3	2	2		17	16	19	18		556	482	562	704
3132 Wine industries		-	-	-	-		-	-	-	-		-	-	-	-
3133 Malt liquors and malt		-	-	-	-		-	-	-	-		-	-	-	-
3134 Soft drinks and carbonated waters		2	2	1	1		173	177	160	158		11514	12026	13455	15355
314 Tobacco		2	2	2	2		75	82	...a/	...a/		2425	3728	...a/	...a/
321 Textiles		227	179	165	147		8884	8247	6835	6399		372753	379303	332953	324991
3211 Spinning, weaving and finishing textiles		66	54	50	47		1404	1054	792	985		61245	54598	37502	47687
3212 Made-up textile goods excl. wearing apparel		32	27	23	21		398	322	209	161		17161	15105	10078	7248
3213 Knitting mills		117	86	82	70		6879	6656	5751	5177		286613	300764	281676	266404
3214 Carpets and rugs		-	-	-	-		-	-	-	-		-	-	-	-
3215 Cordage, rope and twine		4	4	4	4		23	33	35	33		657	901	1240	1281
3219 Other textiles		8	8	6	5		180	182	48	43		7077	7935	2457	2372
322 Wearing apparel, except footwear		588	512	422	449		28184	26256	25073	24762		1154398	1120763	1131473	1169940
323 Leather and fur products		5	2	1	2		328	184	3	26		15677	11133	138	1866
3231 Tanneries and leather finishing		1	1	1	1		3	3	3	3		114	117	138	152
3232 Fur dressing and dyeing industries		1	1	-	-		265	181	-	-		13466	11016	-	-
3233 Leather prods. excl. wearing apparel		3	-	-	1		60	-	-	23		2097	-	-	1714
324 Footwear, except rubber or plastic		19	19	17	11		504	833	1033	768		20702	27399	28495	28224
331 Wood products, except furniture		29	27	18	17		81	119	54	42		3560	4018	2455	1791
3311 Sawmills, planing and other wood mills		12	11	7	6		66	114	40	31		2995	3760	1825	1237
3312 Wooden and cane containers		8	7	4	4		10	5	8	5		385	258	338	225
3319 Other wood and cork products		9	9	7	7		5	-	6	6		180	-	291	329
332 Furniture and fixtures, excl. metal		145	129	105	111		406	298	190	264		20594	17232	11204	13957
341 Paper and products		37	35	28	24		269	216	183	140		11495	9179	7687	6368
3411 Pulp, paper and paperboard articles		-	-	-	-		-	-	-	-		-	-	-	-
3412 Containers of paper and paperboard		29	29	22	18		248	199	167	124		10506	8304	6999	5539
3419 Other pulp, paper and paperboard articles		8	6	6	6		21	17	16	16		989	875	688	829
342 Printing and publishing		97	103	92	98		1241	1278	1139	1077		65920	73547	78976	75840
351 Industrial chemicals		-	-	-	-		-	-	-	-		-	-	-	-
3511 Basic chemicals excl. fertilizers		-	-	-	-		-	-	-	-		-	-	-	-
3512 Fertilizers and pesticides		-	-	-	-		-	-	-	-		-	-	-	-
3513 Synthetic resins and plastic materials		-	-	-	-		-	-	-	-		-	-	-	-
352 Other chemicals		10	10	10	11		261	262	246	250		17029	19901	19250	21137
3521 Paints, varnishes and lacquers		1	1	1	1		22	26	11	10		1208	1452	664	813
3522 Drugs and medicines		5	5	5	5		91	91	99	99		8733	9614	9851	10518
3523 Soap, cleaning preps., perfumes, cosmetics		1	1	1	2		-	-	-	2		-	-	-	253
3529 Other chemical products		3	3	3	3		148	145	136	139		7088	8835	8735	9554
353 Petroleum refineries		-	-	-	-		-	-	-	-		-	-	-	-

354	Misc. petroleum and coal products		-	-	-	-		-	-	-	-		-	-	-	-
355	Rubber products		1	1	1	1		9	...a/	...a/	...a/		338	...a/	...a/	...a/
3551	Tyres and tubes		-	-	-	-		-	-	-	-		-	-	-	-
3559	Other rubber products		1	1	1	1		9	...a/	...a/	...a/		338	...a/	...a/	...a/
356	Plastic products		24	21	18	14		405	223	142	110		19902	9576	6016	4856
361	Pottery, china, earthenware		1	...a/	-	-		83	...a/	-	-		3705	...a/	-	-
362	Glass and products		13	...a/	7	7		20	...a/	9	6		1297	...a/	494	470
369	Other non-metallic mineral products		14	13	16	15		245	444	491	422		20035	38716	37420	35298
3691	Structural clay products		-	-	1	1		-	-	36	37		-	-	2124	1944
3692	Cement, lime and plaster		1	1	1	1		...a/	166	183	166		...a/	14502	15288	14890
3699	Other non-metallic mineral products		13	12	14	13		245	278	272	219		20035	24214	20008	18464
371	Iron and steel		-	-	-	-		-	-	-	-		-	-	-	-
372	Non-ferrous metals		-	-	-	-		-	-	-	-		-	-	-	-
381	Fabricated metal products		243	225	206	197		698	765	525	544		35872	41478	29366	32509
3811	Cutlery, hand tools and general hardware		12	33	25	14		29	73	35	31		1523	3959	1640	2080
3812	Furniture and fixtures primarily of metal		1	1	1	1		12	10	8	7		500	521	495	444
3813	Structural metal products		200	164	159	166		498	567	382	400		24865	30152	21219	23331
3819	Other fabricated metal products		30	27	21	16		159	115	100	106		8983	6846	6011	6654
382	Non-electrical machinery		31	24	23	27		99	55	80	104		6997	2431	4456	5452
3821	Engines and turbines		-	-	-	-		-	-	-	-		-	-	-	-
3822	Agricultural machinery and equipment		-	-	-	-		-	-	-	-		-	-	-	-
3823	Metal and wood working machinery		1	2	3	3		4	5	26	4		94	145	1129	123
3824	Other special industrial machinery		22	18	16	20		74	41	30	43		5767	1888	1774	2486
3825	Office, computing and accounting machinery		1	-	-	-		-	-	-	-		-	-	-	-
3829	Other non-electrical machinery & equipment		7	4	4	4		21	9	24	57		1136	398	1553	2843
383	Electrical machinery	b/	31	27	21	19	b/	660	904	1341	1151	b/	26628	45878	67674	63050
3831	Electrical industrial machinery		4	7	9	10		6	53	53	62		320	7632	8727	8268
3832	Radio, television and communication equipm.		3	2	...a/	-		38	28	...a/	-		1200	1058	...a/	-
3833	Electrical appliances and housewares		3	2	-	-		4	-	-	-		170	-	-	-
3839	Other electrical apparatus and supplies		18	10	7	6		330	260	599	553		13899	10638	22651	25850
384	Transport equipment		53	43	45	40		294	275	268	278		26734	28161	24174	27608
3841	Shipbuilding and repairing		51	41	...a/	39		293	274	...a/	278		26675	28106	...a/	27608
3842	Railroad equipment		-	-	-	-		-	-	-	-		-	-	-	-
3843	Motor vehicles		-	-	-	-		-	-	-	-		-	-	-	-
3844	Motorcycles and bicycles		-	-	-	-		-	-	-	-		-	-	-	-
3845	Aircraft		-	-	-	-		-	-	-	-		-	-	-	-
3849	Other transport equipment		2	2	...a/	1		1	1	...a/	-		59	55	...a/	-
385	Professional and scientific equipment		2	-	-	-		393	-	-	-		38400	-	-	-
3851	Prof. and scientific equipment n.e.c.		-	-	-	-		-	-	-	-		-	-	-	-
3852	Photographic and optical goods		2	-	-	-		393	-	-	-		38400	-	-	-
3853	Watches and clocks		-	-	-	-		-	-	-	-		-	-	-	-
390	Other manufacturing industries	c/	83	67	65	60	c/	3705	3814	3300	2255	c/	139565	152029	131242	94062
3901	Jewellery and related articles		11	11	13	9		27	32	37	35		1189	1213	2439	3043
3902	Musical instruments		1	1	...a/	1		35	35	...a/	36		5502	1744	...a/	1429
3903	Sporting and athletic goods		3	2	...a/	1		175	133	...a/	...a/		6662	5691	...a/	...a/
3909	Manufacturing industries, n.e.c.		45	34	32	36		238	182	235	241		9636	9168	8830	10137
3	Total manufacturing		1787	1584	1385	1385		47862	45475	42034	39821		2051313	2047302	1979607	1982396

a/ Data suppressed due to confidentiality rules.
b/ Including data not shown at the detailed industry level, i.e. manufacture of electrical office computing and accounting equipment.
c/ Including data not shown at the detailed industry level, i.e. manufacture of toys.

Macau

ISIC Revision 2	Output in producers' prices					Value added in producers' prices					Gross fixed capital formation		
		(thousand PATACAS)					(thousand PATACAS)					(thousand PATACAS)	
ISIC Industry	Note	1993	1994	1995	1996	Note	1993	1994	1995	1996	Note	1995	1996
311/2 Food products		155330	194520	183086	189849		60495	78363	77855	89091		5128	5158
3111 Slaughtering, preparing & preserving meat		16650	16672	17630	18191		9758	10186	10557	10761		118	113
3112 Dairy products		3070	2979	3650	8451		1623	1631	2241	5170		16	1061
3113 Canning, preserving of fruits & vegetables		9475	8103	8218	8379		2407	2152	2104	2280		-	-
3114 Canning, preserving and processing of fish		36113	37815	26890	22061		3671	3431	2846	1830		2	10
3115 Vegetable and animal oils and fats		603	771	-	-		282	360	-	-		-	-
3116 Grain mill products		-	-	-	-		-	-	-	-		-	-
3117 Bakery products		84841	122442	121561	127274		40848	58000	57174	66089		4557	3082
3118 Sugar factories and refineries		-	-	-	-		-	-	-	-		-	-
3119 Cocoa, chocolate and sugar confectionery		461	541	441	414		206	212	145	143		-	12
3121 Other food products		4117	5197	4696	5078		1701	2391	2788	2818		435	880
3122 Prepared animal feeds		-	-	-	-		-	-	-	-		-	-
313 Beverages		72281	77569	81143	78351		22680	22657	28553	30916		943	1132
3131 Distilling, rectifying and blending spirits		3249	2897	2837	3167		1111	795	452	509		-13	31
3132 Wine industries		-	-	-	-		-	-	-	-		-	-
3133 Malt liquors and malt		-	-	-	-		-	-	-	-		-	-
3134 Soft drinks and carbonated waters		69032	74672	78306	75185		21569	21862	28101	30407		956	1101
314 Tobacco		48126	54051	...a/	...a/		9289	11507	...a/	...a/	a/	...	...
321 Textiles		2585347	2468180	2424231	2578206		694322	673677	586967	578718		38958	40621
3211 Spinning, weaving and finishing textiles		385159	360992	258376	340235		125351	103135	84328	85745		4757	8523
3212 Made-up textile goods excl. wearing apparel		39959	48888	23482	18857		26790	27277	15573	11686		122	935
3213 Knitting mills		2131881	2026655	2128782	2204994		530949	530060	480987	474704		34044	31096
3214 Carpets and rugs		-	-	-	-		-	-	-	-		-	-
3215 Cordage, rope and twine		3739	3954	4447	4580		1437	1742	1859	2188		-	-
3219 Other textiles		24609	27691	9144	9540		9795	11463	4220	4395		35	67
322 Wearing apparel, except footwear		7197354	7216615	7651034	8148215		1931692	1857941	1953173	2049564		126873	108379
323 Leather and fur products		78858	34617	1850	11760		25005	15540	533	6206		-	-
3231 Tanneries and leather finishing		1640	1627	1850	1663		423	455	533	267		-	-
3232 Fur dressing and dyeing industries		72129	32990	-	-		21890	15085	-	-		-	-
3233 Leather prods. excl. wearing apparel		5089	-	-	10098		2692	-	-	5939		-	-
324 Footwear, except rubber or plastic		123463	258776	231063	212762		38922	68192	50330	30319		-260	1107
331 Wood products, except furniture		12672	11201	8825	5574		4401	5289	3745	2957		3	-
3311 Sawmills, planing and other wood mills		9906	8924	6804	3644		3307	4448	2745	1986		-	-
3312 Wooden and cane containers		1057	1316	893	636		485	630	460	340		3	-
3319 Other wood and cork products		1709	961	1128	1294		609	211	540	631		-	-
332 Furniture and fixtures, excl. metal		67538	51326	41662	47958		32084	26481	17789	23922		539	1064
341 Paper and products		71875	63708	51544	44072		19413	18168	15458	11357		7	1
3411 Pulp, paper and paperboard articles		-	-	-	-		-	-	-	-		-	-
3412 Containers of paper and paperboard		64782	59837	48234	40498		17282	16617	14192	9915		7	1
3419 Other pulp, paper and paperboard articles		7093	3871	3309	3574		2131	1551	1266	1441		-	-
342 Printing and publishing		236851	248047	261148	203906		117841	111241	115251	76867		16270	29263
351 Industrial chemicals		-	-	-	-		-	-	-	-		-	-
3511 Basic chemicals excl. fertilizers		-	-	-	-		-	-	-	-		-	-
3512 Fertilizers and pesticides		-	-	-	-		-	-	-	-		-	-
3513 Synthetic resins and plastic materials		-	-	-	-		-	-	-	-		-	-
352 Other chemicals		126368	127899	145723	132677		36616	32739	41500	41892		2587	17447
3521 Paints, varnishes and lacquers		4036	3026	3435	3094		1685	1488	2266	646		5	2
3522 Drugs and medicines		63971	62736	89425	77311		13688	13941	22050	26728		1524	16090
3523 Soap, cleaning preps., perfumes, cosmetics		200	630	260	1365		82	234	167	631		-	500
3529 Other chemical products		58161	61507	52603	50908		21161	17076	17017	13886		1058	855
353 Petroleum refineries		-	-	-	-		-	-	-	-		-	-

354	Misc. petroleum and coal products		-	-	-	-		-	-	-	-		-	-
355	Rubber products		1533	...a/	...a/	...a/		607	...a/	...a/	...a/	a/	...	...
3551	Tyres and tubes		-	-	-	-		-	-	-	-		-	-
3559	Other rubber products		1533	...a/	...a/	...a/		607	...a/	...a/	...a/	a/	...	...
356	Plastic products		311242	62064	45955	37768		54102	17398	13270	11348		44	1868
361	Pottery, china, earthenware		5910	...a/	-	-		5239	...a/	-	-		-	-
362	Glass and products		8154	...a/	4959	4168		3313	...a/	1870	1236		10	122
369	Other non-metallic mineral products		273525	692888	512180	482269		58910	152774	110658	101070		30756	11116
3691	Structural clay products		-	-	1270	4524		-	-	341	2774		13055	-
3692	Cement, lime and plaster		...a/	319730	290373	309094		...a/	67350	55400	68012		13442	10754
3699	Other non-metallic mineral products		273525	373158	220537	168603		58910	85424	54917	30285		4259	362
371	Iron and steel		-	-	-	-		-	-	-	-		-	-
372	Non-ferrous metals		-	-	-	-		-	-	-	-		-	-
381	Fabricated metal products		153608	164542	139924	163357		64008	70370	53472	69261		1530	618
3811	Cutlery, hand tools and general hardware		4455	11148	4345	5967		2746	6614	2077	2383		-	-
3812	Furniture and fixtures primarily of metal		965	846	789	651		786	630	592	512		-	-
3813	Structural metal products		90427	94627	73031	83787		44963	47676	35303	42587		758	418
3819	Other fabricated metal products		57761	57921	61759	72952		15513	15450	15500	23778		772	200
382	Non-electrical machinery		16970	9916	12171	15414		10345	4349	6373	8765		120	74
3821	Engines and turbines		-	-	-	-		-	-	-	-		-	-
3822	Agricultural machinery and equipment		-	-	-	-		-	-	-	-		-	-
3823	Metal and wood working machinery		188	286	2823	349		165	231	1646	289		120	-
3824	Other special industrial machinery		12462	5946	4919	7045		8250	3245	3085	3980		-	-
3825	Office, computing and accounting machinery		24	-	-	-		19	-	-	-		-	-
3829	Other non-electrical machinery & equipment		4296	3684	4428	8020		1911	873	1642	4497		-	74
383	Electrical machinery	b/	295286	411042	458437	369102	b/	46900	82255	116280	111981		58672	36450
3831	Electrical industrial machinery		802	20101	31346	35204		501	11178	7229	11262		4434	1346
3832	Radio, television and communication equipm.		1870	2330	...a/	-		1419	1236	...a/	-		...a/	-
3833	Electrical appliances and housewares		737	288	-	-		153	148	-	-		-	-
3839	Other electrical apparatus and supplies		136147	65961	181651	236964		26177	19364	38944	53482		29520	26696
384	Transport equipment		50438	53538	63088	78012		29186	28026	28965	40864		2858	598
3841	Shipbuilding and repairing		49919	53011	...a/	77678		29007	27851	...a/	40797		...a/	598
3842	Railroad equipment		-	-	-	-		-	-	-	-		-	-
3843	Motor vehicles		-	-	-	-		-	-	-	-		-	-
3844	Motorcycles and bicycles		-	-	-	-		-	-	-	-		-	-
3845	Aircraft		-	-	-	-		-	-	-	-		-	-
3849	Other transport equipment		519	527	...a/	334		179	175	...a/	67		...a/	...
385	Professional and scientific equipment		43650	-	-	-		15309	-	-	-		-	-
3851	Prof. and scientific equipment n.e.c.		-	-	-	-		-	-	-	-		-	-
3852	Photographic and optical goods		43650	-	-	-		15309	-	-	-		-	-
3853	Watches and clocks		-	-	-	-		-	-	-	-		-	-
390	Other manufacturing industries	c/	952011	1066395	761791	470529	c/	285532	281732	197337	125072		-8290	4302
3901	Jewellery and related articles		2149	2328	4808	13109		1888	1931	3586	4997		133	152
3902	Musical instruments		19905	18530	...a/	15140		5565	5166	...a/	3411		...a/	192
3903	Sporting and athletic goods		51846	43860	...a/	...a/		12628	12926	...a/	...a/	a/	...	...
3909	Manufacturing industries, n.e.c.		56453	46376	65784	73827		19157	17577	17096	20083		2075	641
3	Total manufacturing		12888390	13279300	13147320	13352720		3566212	3565619	3437081	3425402		290974	262962

a/ Data suppressed due to confidentiality rules.
b/ Including data not shown at the detailed industry level, i.e. manufacture of electrical office computing and accounting equipment.
c/ Including data not shown at the detailed industry level, i.e. manufacture of toys.

Macau

ISIC Revision 2		Index numbers of industrial production											
		(1990=100)											
ISIC Industry	Note	1985	1986	1987	1988	1989	1990	1991	1992	1993	1994	1995	1996
311/2 Food products		...	...	...	...	...	...	...	...	...	...	...	...
313 Beverages		...	...	...	...	...	...	...	...	...	...	...	...
314 Tobacco		...	...	...	...	...	...	...	...	...	...	...	...
321 Textiles		...	...	...	...	...	...	...	...	...	...	...	...
322 Wearing apparel, except footwear		...	...	...	...	...	...	...	...	...	...	...	...
323 Leather and fur products		...	...	...	...	...	...	...	...	...	...	...	...
324 Footwear, except rubber or plastic		...	...	...	...	...	...	...	...	...	...	...	...
331 Wood products, except furniture		...	...	...	...	...	...	...	...	...	...	...	...
332 Furniture and fixtures, excl. metal		...	...	...	...	...	...	...	...	...	...	...	...
341 Paper and products		...	...	...	...	...	...	...	...	...	...	...	...
342 Printing and publishing		...	...	...	...	...	...	...	...	...	...	...	...
351 Industrial chemicals		...	...	...	...	...	...	...	...	...	...	...	...
352 Other chemicals		...	...	...	...	...	...	...	...	...	...	...	...
353 Petroleum refineries		...	...	...	...	...	...	...	...	...	...	...	...
354 Misc. petroleum and coal products		...	...	...	...	...	...	...	...	...	...	...	...
355 Rubber products		...	...	...	...	...	...	...	...	...	...	...	...
356 Plastic products		...	...	...	...	...	...	...	...	...	...	...	...
361 Pottery, china, earthenware		...	...	...	...	...	...	...	...	...	...	...	...
362 Glass and products		...	...	...	...	...	...	...	...	...	...	...	...
369 Other non-metallic mineral products		...	...	...	...	...	...	...	...	...	...	...	...
371 Iron and steel		...	...	...	...	...	...	...	...	...	...	...	...
372 Non-ferrous metals		...	...	...	...	...	...	...	...	...	...	...	...
381 Fabricated metal products		...	...	...	...	...	...	...	...	...	...	...	...
382 Non-electrical machinery		...	...	...	...	...	...	...	...	...	...	...	...
383 Electrical machinery		...	...	...	...	...	...	...	...	...	...	...	...
384 Transport equipment		...	...	...	...	...	...	...	...	...	...	...	...
385 Professional and scientific equipment		...	...	...	...	...	...	...	...	...	...	...	...
390 Other manufacturing industries		...	...	...	...	...	...	...	...	...	...	...	...
3 Total manufacturing		...	...	...	...	...	...	...	...	...	...	...	...

MALAYSIA

Supplier of information:
Jabatan Perangkaan (Department of Statistics), Kuala Lumpur.

Basic source of data:
Annual Survey of Manufacturing Industries.

Major deviations from ISIC (Revision 2):
Data collected under the national classification system have been reclassified by the national authorities to correspond approximately with ISIC (Rev. 2).

Reference period (if not calendar year):
Basically, the calendar year. Some establishments, however, report for accounting years not coinciding with the calendar year.

Scope:
All establishments registered under the Industrial Coordination Act (I.C.A.) 1975.

Method of enumeration:
Establishments are completely enumerated. The annual survey is reviewed after each census to ensure that it covers about the same percentage of manufacturing output, value added and employment in each year. The annual survey is conducted both by mail and through field contacts. For 1995, data refer to overall estimates of the manufacturing sector based on a sample survey.

Adjusted for non-response:
Yes.

Concepts and definitions of variables:
Number of employees includes workers paid through labour contractors.
Wages and salaries excludes payment in kind.
Output includes gross revenues from goods shipped in the same condition as received.

Related national publications:
Survey of Manufacturing Industries (annual); Industrial Surveys, Malaysia (annual); Annual Statistical Bulletin, Malaysia; Monthly Statistical Bulletin, all published by the Jabatan Perangkaan (Department of Statistics), Kuala Lumpur.

Malaysia

ISIC Revision 2	Number of establishments					Number of employees					Wages and salaries paid to employees				
		(numbers)					(thousands)					(million RINGGITS)			
ISIC Industry	Note	1992	1993	1994	1995	Note	1992	1993	1994	1995	Note	1992	1993	1994	1995
311/2 Food products		1297	1400	1406	3172		77.6	81.1	82.6	92.0		710.4	808.7	899.3	1083.7
3111 Slaughtering, preparing & preserving meat		18	19	22	52		2.5	2.8	3.0	3.7		22.3	23.6	29.7	39.0
3112 Dairy products		33	35	34	61		3.5	3.9	3.8	3.4		59.5	68.3	71.4	71.2
3113 Canning, preserving of fruits & vegetables		81	93	85	212		3.9	4.3	4.2	3.9		31.9	36.3	37.1	37.6
3114 Canning, preserving and processing of fish		57	54	58	120		7.2	6.9	7.3	7.6		38.6	41.8	48.9	53.0
3115 Vegetable and animal oils and fats		170	173	175	243		17.2	18.6	18.3	23.3		188.4	219.1	236.1	299.4
3116 Grain mill products		146	160	155	391		6.8	6.7	6.4	7.3		60.8	68.3	73.0	92.1
3117 Bakery products		317	367	379	1082		15.5	16.0	17.4	18.9		93.6	114.0	135.1	170.4
3118 Sugar factories and refineries		7	7	6	5		2.9	2.8	2.8	2.7		39.0	40.5	50.8	51.8
3119 Cocoa, chocolate and sugar confectionery		44	42	41	67		5.0	4.7	4.4	5.0		48.6	52.7	49.5	65.6
3121 Other food products		364	384	387	851		10.0	11.1	11.6	12.7		88.3	101.2	118.1	149.1
3122 Prepared animal feeds		60	66	64	88		3.1	3.3	3.4	3.5		39.3	43.1	49.6	54.5
313 Beverages		56	53	53	104		4.4	4.3	4.2	4.9		69.9	71.6	75.2	87.0
3131 Distilling, rectifying and blending spirits	a/	14	14	14	20	a/	1.6	1.4	1.2	1.3	a/	36.2	31.9	33.5	34.9
3132 Wine industries		-	-	-	-		-	-	-	-		-	-	-	-
3133 Malt liquors and malt	a/	...	...	...	...	a/	...	...	...	...	a/	...	...	...	...
3134 Soft drinks and carbonated waters		42	39	39	84		2.8	2.9	3.0	3.6		33.7	39.7	41.7	52.1
314 Tobacco		33	29	26	289		4.7	4.1	4.6	15.8		63.5	59.2	63.3	90.0
321 Textiles		269	327	318	673		42.8	44.5	43.6	46.4		374.2	426.1	457.3	537.0
3211 Spinning, weaving and finishing textiles		113	147	150	310		25.2	26.7	25.3	27.7		233.6	262.7	274.2	330.7
3212 Made-up textile goods excl. wearing apparel		54	65	61	198		3.3	3.6	3.0	3.6		23.5	27.5	26.0	30.7
3213 Knitting mills		78	86	77	136		12.2	11.8	12.9	12.6		102.1	111.9	130.6	146.6
3214 Carpets and rugs		10	10	10	11		0.9	0.9	1.1	1.1		8.1	11.5	13.8	14.2
3215 Cordage, rope and twine		11	13	14	14		1.2	1.2	1.1	1.2		6.5	8.8	10.4	12.1
3219 Other textiles		3	6	6	4		-	0.3	0.2	0.2		0.4	3.5	2.3	2.7
322 Wearing apparel, except footwear		363	377	352	3606		71.5	70.7	65.5	72.8		514.5	535.7	555.9	648.0
323 Leather and fur products		38	47	49	100		3.0	3.3	3.5	2.9		19.8	23.9	29.2	29.4
3231 Tanneries and leather finishing		6	8	9	9		0.8	0.9	0.7	0.3		5.3	6.0	5.2	6.1
3232 Fur dressing and dyeing industries		-	-	-	-		-	-	-	-		-	-	-	-
3233 Leather prods. excl. wearing apparel		32	39	40	91		2.2	2.4	2.8	2.6		14.5	17.9	24.0	23.3
324 Footwear, except rubber or plastic		16	26	20	144		1.9	2.1	1.7	2.5		12.1	19.3	15.8	24.0
331 Wood products, except furniture		806	893	917	1493		109.3	127.9	137.2	145.2		813.2	1008.8	1110.4	1205.9
3311 Sawmills, planing and other wood mills		723	804	836	1176		105.2	123.2	133.1	139.7		788.0	979.0	1077.8	1158.8
3312 Wooden and cane containers		30	35	32	103		1.1	1.3	1.0	1.1		6.0	7.8	8.2	8.8
3319 Other wood and cork products		53	54	49	214		3.0	3.4	3.1	4.4		19.2	22.0	24.4	38.3
332 Furniture and fixtures, excl. metal		406	507	495	1620		24.1	30.5	32.8	41.7		169.2	233.7	270.2	375.6
341 Paper and products		153	171	175	285		17.6	19.1	19.5	22.6		184.6	217.2	243.2	292.4
3411 Pulp, paper and paperboard articles		12	15	16	27		3.0	3.1	2.9	4.2		47.2	50.1	51.8	62.9
3412 Containers of paper and paperboard		76	91	94	134		9.4	10.5	10.8	11.7		93.4	114.6	131.0	152.3
3419 Other pulp, paper and paperboard articles		65	65	65	124		5.2	5.5	5.8	6.6		44.0	52.5	60.4	77.2
342 Printing and publishing		258	290	291	889		25.5	27.9	30.1	34.5		341.7	393.8	461.8	558.5
351 Industrial chemicals		116	126	120	150		12.4	13.3	12.3	12.7		256.5	301.2	307.7	351.0
3511 Basic chemicals excl fertilizers		59	65	66	75		6.9	7.4	6.4	6.9		144.2	169.4	160.2	194.8
3512 Fertilizers and pesticides		30	30	25	30		2.5	2.2	2.1	2.2		56.7	58.1	63.6	67.1
3513 Synthetic resins and plastic materials		27	31	29	45		3.0	3.7	3.8	3.6		55.7	73.7	83.9	89.1
352 Other chemicals		155	164	164	415		14.4	15.3	15.9	18.7		190.5	231.2	265.5	313.0
3521 Paints, varnishes and lacquers		26	27	30	64		2.3	2.3	2.6	3.5		42.8	48.9	57.5	75.8
3522 Drugs and medicines		41	37	33	97		3.1	3.2	3.5	4.3		34.9	39.4	43.7	54.5
3523 Soap, cleaning preps., perfumes, cosmetics		28	32	32	67		4.0	3.9	3.9	4.1		61.1	71.6	83.3	85.5
3529 Other chemical products		60	68	69	187		5.0	5.9	5.9	6.8		51.7	71.2	81.0	97.2
353 Petroleum refineries		8	8	6	6		1.2	1.3	2.7	2.7		50.3	53.5	109.6	121.0

ISIC	Industry														
354	Misc. petroleum and coal products		32	30	35	39		1.0	1.0	1.2	1.4		13.2	14.4	23.7	28.7
355	Rubber products		381	379	366	526		64.9	68.8	69.0	74.6		540.5	628.6	664.1	806.6
3551	Tyres and tubes		57	58	57	70		7.2	7.0	6.6	7.9		108.7	116.8	117.4	141.4
3559	Other rubber products		324	321	309	456		57.7	61.8	62.4	66.7		431.8	511.8	546.7	665.2
356	Plastic products		403	476	509	1224		49.1	54.2	62.3	71.1		382.9	468.9	614.5	757.0
361	Pottery, china, earthenware		44	48	48	87		7.7	8.3	8.1	7.6		53.4	58.1	69.6	77.8
362	Glass and products		27	28	29	76		3.7	4.2	5.2	5.8		57.1	62.1	84.3	100.0
369	Other non-metallic mineral products		357	373	376	730		28.9	29.8	31.5	37.5		327.5	376.7	428.1	555.3
3691	Structural clay products		164	164	165	222		12.8	13.0	13.4	13.7		107.2	122.5	135.1	148.9
3692	Cement, lime and plaster		31	31	32	49		4.0	3.9	4.1	4.6		76.4	81.7	96.1	109.0
3699	Other non-metallic mineral products		162	178	179	459		12.1	12.9	14.0	19.2		143.9	172.5	196.9	297.4
371	Iron and steel		140	157	159	397		16.0	17.2	18.4	21.9		236.8	269.5	303.7	372.4
372	Non-ferrous metals		36	40	42	58		6.4	7.3	7.3	8.6		76.8	97.4	112.3	139.0
381	Fabricated metal products		578	652	642	2820		44.1	46.7	49.1	71.4		462.6	521.9	605.0	881.6
3811	Cutlery, hand tools and general hardware		34	45	39	502		2.2	2.7	2.3	3.7		14.3	21.4	19.9	33.9
3812	Furniture and fixtures primarily of metal		40	47	45	99		3.4	3.5	3.8	4.3		27.3	32.7	35.3	45.4
3813	Structural metal products		195	233	220	1418		8.1	9.3	8.9	18.3		110.9	124.3	129.2	228.0
3819	Other fabricated metal products		309	327	338	801		30.4	31.2	34.1	45.1		310.1	343.5	420.6	574.3
382	Non-electrical machinery		433	506	512	1376		35.7	45.2	46.6	62.6		419.1	537.2	606.8	824.6
3821	Engines and turbines	b/	20	19	20	38	b/	1.1	1.2	1.1	1.2	b/	14.6	18.2	16.2	20.7
3822	Agricultural machinery and equipment	b/	...	...	...	...	b/	...	...	...	...	b/	...	...	...	...
3823	Metal and wood working machinery		17	20	23	43		0.5	0.8	1.0	1.4		5.0	9.5	11.7	17.3
3824	Other special industrial machinery		35	39	33	79		2.0	1.8	1.6	2.4		25.4	26.0	24.1	40.6
3825	Office, computing and accounting machinery		24	28	28	25		9.3	13.2	11.6	14.9		75.4	100.3	113.1	127.9
3829	Other non-electrical machinery & equipment		337	400	408	1191		22.8	28.1	31.3	42.7		298.7	383.2	441.7	618.1
383	Electrical machinery		530	594	609	851		282.1	332.9	370.3	397.5		2737.4	3393.2	4185.4	4955.0
3831	Electrical industrial machinery		52	68	63	116		13.3	15.2	15.2	18.3		110.6	134.3	157.3	201.1
3832	Radio, television and communication equipm.		316	342	359	509		241.1	285.9	319.4	341.2		2356.9	2929.0	3611.1	4270.4
3833	Electrical appliances and housewares		14	17	17	34		2.7	3.0	3.3	3.8		40.3	46.0	53.9	69.0
3839	Other electrical apparatus and supplies		148	167	170	192		25.0	28.8	32.4	34.2		229.6	283.9	363.1	414.5
384	Transport equipment		282	321	330	501		33.3	38.3	43.5	50.0		426.3	507.1	611.4	752.1
3841	Shipbuilding and repairing		76	83	84	148		6.8	7.4	7.6	8.2		106.1	121.9	126.1	145.1
3842	Railroad equipment	c/	9	8	8	7	c/	1.3	1.2	1.5	1.4	c/	21.3	22.3	25.4	32.8
3843	Motor vehicles		144	171	180	274		18.8	22.3	26.4	31.3		237.6	286.9	366.4	458.7
3844	Motorcycles and bicycles		53	59	58	72		6.4	7.4	8.0	9.1		61.3	76.0	93.5	115.5
3845	Aircraft	c/	...	...	...	...	c/	...	...	...	...	c/	...	...	...	...
3849	Other transport equipment	c/	...	...	...	...	c/	...	...	...	...	c/	...	...	...	...
385	Professional and scientific equipment		37	34	37	48		18.5	19.9	22.4	24.1		177.9	200.4	248.0	309.3
3851	Prof. and scientific equipment n.e.c.		13	12	12	17		4.5	4.2	4.5	4.5		47.1	50.7	59.4	71.7
3852	Photographic and optical goods		13	11	13	19		6.0	6.0	6.8	7.8		60.8	66.4	76.8	98.5
3853	Watches and clocks		11	11	12	12		8.0	9.7	11.1	11.8		69.9	83.3	111.8	139.1
390	Other manufacturing industries		207	250	242	772		20.8	20.2	20.2	19.4		148.1	168.4	182.0	189.9
3901	Jewellery and related articles		72	95	90	340		3.8	4.3	4.8	5.7		29.5	39.2	48.2	62.9
3902	Musical instruments	d/	25	28	26	23	d/	3.0	2.7	2.7	2.7	d/	17.9	19.3	22.2	25.7
3903	Sporting and athletic goods	d/	...	...	...	...	d/	...	...	...	...	d/	...	...	...	...
3909	Manufacturing industries, n.e.c.		110	127	126	409		14.0	13.2	12.7	11.0		100.6	109.9	111.6	101.3
3	Total manufacturing		7461	8306	8328	22453		1022.7	1140.0	1211.3	1369.0		9830.0	11687.8	13603.3	16465.8

a/ 3131 includes 3133.
b/ 3821 includes 3822.
c/ 3842 includes 3845 and 3849.
d/ 3902 includes 3903.

Malaysia

ISIC Revision 2 ISIC Industry	Note	Output in factor values (million RINGGITS) 1992	1993	1994	1995	Note	Value added in factor values (million RINGGITS) 1992	1993	1994	1995	Note	Gross fixed capital formation (million RINGGITS) 1994	1995
311/2 Food products		19346.0	20240.0	25658.7	34164.9		2996.0	3362.4	3706.6	4998.9		659	796
3111 Slaughtering, preparing & preserving meat		293.0	334.3	449.6	558.3		75.6	84.7	134.3	154.6		16	17
3112 Dairy products		1299.1	1413.0	1418.4	1274.5		278.4	291.9	298.9	322.7		16	43
3113 Canning, preserving of fruits & vegetables		304.8	357.5	341.0	361.2		80.6	93.0	77.7	86.1		16	2
3114 Canning, preserving and processing of fish		597.7	602.2	750.2	827.7		111.0	147.4	180.7	209.1		24	35
3115 Vegetable and animal oils and fats		10942.5	11242.3	15675.9	22505.1		1167.2	1321.8	1495.8	2449.2		181	277
3116 Grain mill products		1209.9	1380.2	1398.9	1670.4		206.0	221.1	253.6	260.0		73	85
3117 Bakery products		738.9	837.0	1008.9	1329.8		262.7	298.3	362.3	461.3		78	142
3118 Sugar factories and refineries		969.4	941.4	1053.8	1150.8		218.6	238.0	207.4	195.4		34	25
3119 Cocoa, chocolate and sugar confectionery		665.2	653.6	736.0	881.7		154.9	149.6	170.3	197.5		71	39
3121 Other food products		850.8	984.5	1183.9	1726.9		260.3	315.6	309.5	401.1		99	90
3122 Prepared animal feeds		1474.7	1494.0	1642.1	1878.5		180.1	200.9	216.1	261.9		51	41
313 Beverages		987.0	953.5	1105.7	1313.1		382.0	379.8	431.9	467.6		42	97
3131 Distilling, rectifying and blending spirits	a/	373.2	309.1	389.5	452.1	a/	198.7	171.8	229.2	249.8	a/	7	37
3132 Wine industries		-	-	-	-		-	-	-	-		-	-
3133 Malt liquors and malt	a/	...	...	...	...	a/	...	...	...	...	a/	...	...
3134 Soft drinks and carbonated waters		613.7	644.5	716.2	861.0		183.1	208.0	202.7	217.8		35	60
314 Tobacco		1003.0	1115.6	1257.3	1462.1		380.0	435.6	487.7	698.1		19	33
321 Textiles		3576.0	3890.4	4741.2	5779.8		1096.0	1283.3	1595.4	1771.9		872	1430
3211 Spinning, weaving and finishing textiles		2427.8	2719.5	3280.5	4109.1		734.8	897.3	1067.9	1185.5		679	1335
3212 Made-up textile goods excl. wearing apparel		115.0	134.5	131.4	148.8		52.6	62.3	59.9	66.9		13	13
3213 Knitting mills		911.7	854.4	1108.3	1282.6		259.4	248.7	379.2	421.2		166	56
3214 Carpets and rugs		67.4	89.4	110.8	119.2		24.9	32.4	39.6	42.5		6	8
3215 Cordage, rope and twine		47.3	47.6	69.5	80.3		23.0	22.6	29.4	35.0		10	17
3219 Other textiles		6.7	45.0	40.7	39.8		1.0	20.0	19.4	20.8		-2	1
322 Wearing apparel, except footwear		2981.0	2986.3	3164.6	3386.4		938.0	968.3	979.8	1195.8		104	119
323 Leather and fur products		128.0	140.0	218.4	186.8		35.0	45.2	65.3	63.1		13	17
3231 Tanneries and leather finishing		43.7	42.4	47.8	52.2		9.1	12.8	12.0	13.0		1	2
3232 Fur dressing and dyeing industries		-	-	-	-		-	-	-	-		-	-
3233 Leather prods. excl. wearing apparel		84.0	97.6	170.6	134.6		25.6	32.4	53.3	50.1		12	15
324 Footwear, except rubber or plastic		69.0	89.3	72.6	136.0		30.0	38.8	27.4	54.6		7	7
331 Wood products, except furniture		6766.0	9761.2	10787.0	11227.2		1930.0	3171.7	3229.4	3383.5		1584	1383
3311 Sawmills, planing and other wood mills		6602.4	9542.6	10529.3	10841.0		1880.8	3106.4	3152.0	3277.7		1567	1341
3312 Wooden and cane containers		41.2	59.3	67.4	70.0		13.6	17.4	21.0	16.0		3	1
3319 Other wood and cork products		122.4	159.3	190.3	316.2		35.6	47.9	56.4	89.8		14	41
332 Furniture and fixtures, excl. metal		1028.0	1497.9	1800.1	2655.5		355.0	517.9	646.5	873.5		188	219
341 Paper and products		1730.0	1958.1	2455.4	3308.8		593.0	649.4	826.0	1057.9		241	397
3411 Pulp, paper and paperboard articles		336.6	301.5	441.0	672.6		125.9	79.9	138.4	231.1		48	99
3412 Containers of paper and paperboard		870.4	1077.3	1376.2	1824.9		280.4	360.6	455.1	561.5		111	241
3419 Other pulp, paper and paperboard articles		523.0	579.3	638.2	811.3		186.9	208.9	232.5	265.3		82	57
342 Printing and publishing		1948.0	2230.4	2579.2	3418.0		1005.0	1132.0	1325.1	1640.2		255	273
351 Industrial chemicals		6865.0	7758.7	8290.2	10709.5		2985.0	3372.8	2958.6	3418.0		514	1070
3511 Basic chemicals excl. fertilizers		4801.1	5336.7	5040.0	6910.9		2427.0	2786.4	2148.8	2454.5		283	831
3512 Fertilizers and pesticides		1020.4	1029.7	1126.6	1225.7		317.7	257.9	329.7	442.7		107	18
3513 Synthetic resins and plastic materials		1043.8	1392.3	2123.6	2572.9		240.6	328.5	480.1	520.8		124	221
352 Other chemicals		2443.0	2601.7	3158.0	3824.7		918.0	940.1	1088.1	1353.1		220	268
3521 Paints, varnishes and lacquers		586.8	630.9	793.2	1020.8		199.3	213.3	268.5	309.4		55	43
3522 Drugs and medicines		298.9	312.2	336.2	419.9		121.6	139.1	161.0	204.9		31	74
3523 Soap, cleaning preps., perfumes, cosmetics		954.5	903.6	1072.9	1167.1		384.9	317.4	354.9	481.7		48	52
3529 Other chemical products		603.3	755.0	955.7	1216.9		211.8	270.2	303.7	357.1		86	98
353 Petroleum refineries		4476.0	4250.4	5010.7	5745.7		493.0	482.5	1221.9	1711.9		1041	840

ISIC	Industry													
354	Misc. petroleum and coal products		315.0	332.5	520.7	518.2		119.0	144.9	241.7	219.6		29	12
355	Rubber products		5954.0	6214.2	7299.3	9674.4		1709.0	1896.5	2091.2	2768.5		476	577
3551	Tyres and tubes		958.2	950.9	922.2	1135.7		414.7	392.2	388.2	436.7		89	113
3559	Other rubber products		4996.3	5263.3	6377.1	8538.7		1294.3	1504.3	1703.0	2331.8		387	464
356	Plastic products		3070.0	3668.2	4998.1	6338.3		1170.0	1444.2	1886.3	2273.3		681	769
361	Pottery, china, earthenware		212.0	256.7	285.4	339.7		115.0	137.9	158.7	173.6		36	47
362	Glass and products		450.0	494.9	967.4	1441.1		228.0	234.5	370.9	553.0		395	503
369	Other non-metallic mineral products		3523.0	3831.6	4835.3	6273.0		1602.0	1620.5	2318.4	2580.9		999	1046
3691	Structural clay products		684.5	766.9	827.6	972.8		381.4	399.2	454.6	519.9		172	286
3692	Cement, lime and plaster		1428.7	1487.6	2097.1	2048.1		740.2	732.6	1261.5	1078.8		698	277
3699	Other non-metallic mineral products		1409.6	1577.1	1910.6	3252.1		480.7	488.6	602.3	982.2		129	483
371	Iron and steel		5098.0	5927.3	7008.0	8321.7		970.0	1219.2	923.1	864.1		757	535
372	Non-ferrous metals		1498.0	1555.9	1970.0	2819.0		302.0	303.6	423.1	573.4		269	303
381	Fabricated metal products		5053.0	5501.5	6421.5	8545.5		1521.0	1790.4	2005.8	2500.7		514	724
3811	Cutlery, hand tools and general hardware		145.0	165.8	148.9	250.9		46.8	55.5	49.4	92.1		9	23
3812	Furniture and fixtures primarily of metal		181.7	208.6	230.2	293.7		66.4	77.9	79.0	102.2		19	24
3813	Structural metal products		1262.1	1465.2	1392.6	1795.8		445.0	570.1	510.3	532.8		77	123
3819	Other fabricated metal products		3463.9	3661.9	4649.8	6205.1		962.6	1086.8	1367.1	1773.6		409	554
382	Non-electrical machinery		5468.0	6913.7	8636.0	11587.7		1558.0	2059.9	2356.9	2990.7		606	933
3821	Engines and turbines	b/	96.0	87.2	114.4	202.3	b/	34.6	31.5	34.0	44.9	b/	6	6
3822	Agricultural machinery and equipment	b/	...	...	...	...	b/	...	...	...	...	b/	...	...
3823	Metal and wood working machinery		29.3	43.2	67.3	171.9		11.9	18.7	28.3	48.2		14	21
3824	Other special industrial machinery		133.2	171.0	181.0	314.6		40.2	60.4	56.2	117.1		9	15
3825	Office, computing and accounting machinery		1328.7	2051.4	2398.7	3596.8		235.5	373.6	342.2	413.6		106	272
3829	Other non-electrical machinery & equipment		3881.0	4560.9	5874.6	7302.1		1235.5	1575.7	1896.2	2366.9		471	619
383	Electrical machinery		40851.0	51546.7	69910.8	85498.7		9161.0	11393.0	14757.1	17253.9		5230	7647
3831	Electrical industrial machinery		1094.2	1393.0	1709.0	1939.7		331.1	502.6	582.8	678.0		135	137
3832	Radio, television and communication equipm.		36169.8	45889.6	62652.9	77030.5		7830.1	9581.5	12549.9	14833.7		4565	6958
3833	Electrical appliances and housewares		631.7	663.0	807.1	988.6		178.3	176.5	201.9	228.3		49	62
3839	Other electrical apparatus and supplies		2955.5	3601.1	4741.8	5539.9		821.8	1132.3	1422.5	1513.0		481	490
384	Transport equipment		6232.0	7620.3	9750.2	13201.1		1610.0	1966.9	2360.2	3009.0		952	817
3841	Shipbuilding and repairing		644.4	809.2	1056.8	1333.2		258.7	386.1	365.3	479.2		213	179
3842	Railroad equipment	c/	131.0	122.1	87.8	106.1	c/	56.2	56.5	56.6	74.5	c/	6	14
3843	Motor vehicles		4226.7	5204.7	6933.2	9732.5		1035.6	1194.9	1590.9	2000.2		579	520
3844	Motorcycles and bicycles		1229.7	1484.3	1672.4	2029.3		259.9	329.3	347.4	455.1		154	104
3845	Aircraft	c/	...	...	...	...	c/	...	...	...	...	c/	...	...
3849	Other transport equipment	c/	...	...	...	...	c/	...	...	...	...	c/	...	...
385	Professional and scientific equipment		1530.0	1857.7	2570.8	3279.2		413.0	476.3	616.3	715.6		145	217
3851	Prof. and scientific equipment n.e.c.		281.3	287.1	330.2	396.9		125.0	133.9	149.2	174.1		24	40
3852	Photographic and optical goods		772.7	952.4	1237.7	1777.4		148.6	155.0	184.0	219.7		30	79
3853	Watches and clocks		475.8	618.2	1002.9	1104.9		139.4	187.4	283.1	321.8		91	98
390	Other manufacturing industries		1550.0	1516.6	1439.8	1767.2		485.0	457.0	432.6	464.7		86	113
3901	Jewellery and related articles		791.5	673.3	784.5	1048.2		215.3	94.0	153.9	163.6		20	23
3902	Musical instruments	d/	104.5	123.6	139.8	157.5	d/	34.6	43.1	55.9	65.1	d/	23	31
3903	Sporting and athletic goods	d/	...	...	...	...	d/	...	...	...	...	d/	...	...
3909	Manufacturing industries, n.e.c.		653.7	719.7	515.5	561.5		234.8	319.9	222.8	236.0		43	59
3	Total manufacturing		134150.0	156711.6	196912.4	246923.3		35099.0	41924.7	49532.0	59629.1		16934	21191

a/ 3131 includes 3133.
b/ 3821 includes 3822.
c/ 3842 includes 3845 and 3849.
d/ 3902 includes 3903.

Malaysia

ISIC Revision 2		Index numbers of industrial production											
		(1990=100)											
ISIC Industry	Note	1985	1986	1987	1988	1989	1990	1991	1992	1993	1994	1995	1996
311/2 Food products	a/	...	...	...	82	94	100	97	103	109	118	125	137
313 Beverages	a/	...	...	...	...	...	...	...	...	...	...	...	...
314 Tobacco		100	80	80	92	94	100	101	96	90	89	90	97
321 Textiles		56	63	72	74	90	100	106	123	161	192	210	214
322 Wearing apparel, except footwear		56	63	75	83	96	100	100	105	106	102	101	98
323 Leather and fur products	b/	...	...	...	...	...	100	96	92	83	102	80	80
324 Footwear, except rubber or plastic	b/	...	...	...	...	...	...	...	...	...	...	...	...
331 Wood products, except furniture		57	55	66	75	88	100	105	117	140	146	155	173
332 Furniture and fixtures, excl. metal		...	...	...	...	...	...	...	...	...	...	...	...
341 Paper and products		...	...	...	...	...	100	98	93	85	99	108	103
342 Printing and publishing		...	...	...	...	...	...	...	...	...	...	...	...
351 Industrial chemicals	c/	...	...	...	89	96	100	114	121	131	145	159	195
352 Other chemicals	c/	...	...	...	...	...	...	...	...	...	...	...	...
353 Petroleum refineries		62	76	79	84	88	100	106	110	119	135	153	172
354 Misc. petroleum and coal products		...	...	...	...	...	...	...	...	...	...	...	...
355 Rubber products	d/	...	...	...	85	90	100	111	126	150	174	198	219
356 Plastic products	d/	...	...	...	...	...	...	...	...	...	...	...	...
361 Pottery, china, earthenware	e/	...	...	...	80	105	100	149	163	171	193	214	266
362 Glass and products	e/	...	...	...	...	...	...	...	...	...	...	...	...
369 Other non-metallic mineral products	e/	...	...	...	...	...	...	...	...	...	...	...	...
371 Iron and steel	f/	...	...	...	76	89	100	111	131	148	170	192	225
372 Non-ferrous metals	f/	...	...	...	...	...	...	...	...	...	...	...	...
381 Fabricated metal products		73	71	82	87	84	100	119	170	268	314	342	421
382 Non-electrical machinery		...	...	...	...	87	100	165	220	206	276	323	310
383 Electrical machinery		28	40	49	59	79	100	139	154	174	204	237	265
384 Transport equipment		41	30	31	54	76	100	117	110	114	136	185	227
385 Professional and scientific equipment		...	...	...	...	...	...	...	...	...	...	...	...
390 Other manufacturing industries		...	...	...	...	...	...	...	...	...	...	...	...
3 Total manufacturing		...	...	...	...	...	...	...	...	...	...	...	...

a/ 311/2 includes 313.
b/ 323 includes 324.
c/ 351 includes 352.
d/ 355 includes 356.
e/ 361 includes 362 and 369.
f/ 371 includes 372.

MONGOLIA

Supplier of information:
State Statistical Office of Mongolia, Ulan-Bator.

Basic source of data:
For 1994, Census of industrial establishments.

Major deviations from ISIC (Revision 3):
None reported.

Reference period (if not calendar year):

Scope:
All establishments covered by the report.

Method of enumeration:
The inquiry is carried out through questionnaires.

Adjusted for non-response:
Yes.

Concepts and definitions of variables:
Output is different from the standard definition in the accounting of the value of the shipments and receipt from the sale of products. In the present accounting practice, products are shipped out, but not paid off from the stock of shipped products. Therefore, the calculation of the value of goods produced during the reference period on the shipment basis requires two types of stock adjustments: change in stock of shipped goods and change in stock of finished goods.

Related national publications:
Report on the Census of Industrial Establishments, 1994, published by the State Statistical Office of Mongolia, Ulan-Bator, in co-operation with UNIDO.

Mongolia

ISIC Revision 3	Number of establishments					Number of persons engaged					Wages and salaries paid to employees				
		(numbers)					(numbers)					(million TUGRIKS)			
ISIC Industry	Note	1993	1994	1995	1996	Note	1993	1994	1995	1996	Note	1993	1994	1995	1996
151 Processed meat,fish,fruit,vegetables,fats		6	7	7	13		...	...	3957	1849		212.6	356.3	486.2	715.2
1511 Processing/preserving of meat		5	6	7	11		2242	3865	3957	1809		211.8	348.5	486.2	702.6
1512 Processing/preserving of fish		-	-	-	-		-	-	-	-		-	-	-	-
1513 Processing/preserving of fruit & vegetables		1	1	-	1		...	...	-	20		0.8	7.8	-	7.3
1514 Vegetable and animal oils and fats		-	-	-	1		-	-	-	20		-	-	-	5.3
1520 Dairy products		2	1	2	3		...	...	...	160		15.9	3.2	32.8	58.0
153 Grain mill products; starches; animal feeds		12	14	12	32		2307	2848	2063	2201		133.6	303.4	461.2	649.7
1531 Grain mill products		10	10	10	28		2179	2687	2011	2113		129.2	287.4	455.2	641.7
1532 Starches and starch products		-	-	-	-		-	-	-	-		-	-	-	-
1533 Prepared animal feeds		2	4	2	4		128	161	52	88		4.4	16.0	6.0	8.0
154 Other food products		38	67	91	67		4684	5670	4155	4197		329.8	540.9	941.5	1070.8
1541 Bakery products		38	66	88	62		4684	5514	4092	4117		329.8	539.4	921.3	1040.9
1542 Sugar		-	-	-	-		-	-	-	-		-	-	-	-
1543 Cocoa, chocolate and sugar confectionery		-	-	-	-		-	-	-	-		-	-	-	-
1544 Macaroni, noodles & similar products		-	-	-	2		-	-	-	20		-	-	-	3.4
1549 Other food products n.e.c.		-	1	3	3		-	156	63	60		-	1.5	20.0	26.5
155 Beverages		3	3	3	16		...	...	...	1126		69.6	101.1	268.1	515.2
1551 Distilling, rectifying & blending of spirits		2	2	2	13		...	...	...	1104		68.9	100.0	268.0	511.6
1552 Wines		-	-	-	-		-	-	-	-		-	-	-	-
1553 Malt liquors and malt		-	-	-	1		-	-	-	13		-	-	-	...
1554 Soft drinks; mineral waters		1	1	1	2		...	...	...	9		0.7	1.1	0.1	1.6
1600 Tobacco products		-	-	-	-		-	-	-	-		-	-	-	-
171 Spinning, weaving and finishing of textiles		6	6	6	6		1442	1591	1157	1158		90.8	163.8	318.6	159.0
1711 Textile fibre preparation; textile weaving		6	6	6	6		1442	1591	1157	1158		90.8	163.8	318.6	159.0
1712 Finishing of textiles		-	-	-	-		-	-	-	-		-	-	-	-
172 Other textiles		6	6	8	10		2653	2202	1951	2374		202.7	349.9	758.7	722.9
1721 Made-up textile articles, except apparel		-	-	-	-		-	-	-	-		-	-	-	-
1722 Carpets and rugs		4	3	5	6		...	...	...	2227		164.8	298.8	647.7	641.2
1723 Cordage, rope, twine and netting		-	-	-	-		-	-	-	-		-	-	-	-
1729 Other textiles n.e.c.		2	3	3	4		...	...	...	147		37.9	51.1	111.0	81.7
1730 Knitted and crocheted fabrics and articles		8	16	11	8		1051	1722	1606	2089		150.9	304.8	616.2	996.9
1810 Wearing apparel, except fur apparel		34	43	42	31		3409	4273	5976	4138		521.4	1158.5	1216.6	1050.8
1820 Dressing & dyeing of fur; processing of fur		2	2	2	2		950	1005	990	1002		129.1	194.0	270.6	459.0
191 Tanning, dressing and processing of leather		8	10	8	7		3415	3524	2347	559		71.9	68.0	44.0	109.9
1911 Tanning and dressing of leather		6	9	7	5		...	...	...	390		50.4	58.9	37.6	95.2
1912 Luggage, handbags, etc.; saddlery & harness		2	1	1	2		...	...	...	169		21.5	9.1	6.4	14.7
1920 Footwear		4	14	16	12		1615	2653	2506	562		35.7	216.8	228.3	85.6
2010 Sawmilling and planing of wood		26	32	26	23		3325	6015	4940	3892		177.1	328.6	334.4	208.7
202 Products of wood, cork, straw, etc.		8	13	14	16		497	540	675	334		15.1	54.6	55.3	42.9
2021 Veneer sheets, plywood, particle board, etc.		-	-	-	-		-	-	-	-		-	-	-	-
2022 Builders' carpentry and joinery		2	1	1	-		...	...	...	-		4.8	5.4	4.2	-
2023 Wooden containers		1	2	1	2		...	...	...	40		1.2	8.1	9.6	2.3
2029 Other wood products; articles of cork/straw		5	10	12	14		...	...	...	294		9.1	41.1	41.5	40.6
210 Paper and paper products		-	-	-	-		-	-	-	-		-	-	-	-
2101 Pulp, paper and paperboard		-	-	-	-		-	-	-	-		-	-	-	-
2102 Corrugated paper and paperboard		-	-	-	-		-	-	-	-		-	-	-	-
2109 Other articles of paper and paperboard		-	-	-	-		-	-	-	-		-	-	-	-
221 Publishing		-	-	-	-		-	-	-	-		-	-	-	-
2211 Publishing of books and other publications		-	-	-	-		-	-	-	-		-	-	-	-
2212 Publishing of newspapers, journals, etc.		-	-	-	-		-	-	-	-		-	-	-	-
2213 Publishing of recorded media		-	-	-	-		-	-	-	-		-	-	-	-
2219 Other publishing		-	-	-	-		-	-	-	-		-	-	-	-

222 Printing and related service activities	34	40	38	41	783	1038	868	845	185.4	128.5	165.0	380.9
2221 Printing	34	40	38	41	783	1038	868	845	185.4	128.5	165.0	380.9
2222 Service activities related to printing	-	-	-	-	-	-	-	-	-	-	-	-
2230 Reproduction of recorded media	-	-	-	-	-	-	-	-	-	-	-	-
2310 Coke oven products	-	-	-	-	-	-	-	-	-	-	-	-
2320 Refined petroleum products	-	-	-	-	-	-	-	-	-	-	-	-
2330 Processing of nuclear fuel	-	-	-	-	-	-	-	-	-	-	-	-
241 Basic chemicals	-	-	-	-	-	-	-	-	-	-	-	-
2411 Basic chemicals, except fertilizers	-	-	-	-	-	-	-	-	-	-	-	-
2412 Fertilizers and nitrogen compounds	-	-	-	-	-	-	-	-	-	-	-	-
2413 Plastics in primary forms; synthetic rubber	-	-	-	-	-	-	-	-	-	-	-	-
242 Other chemicals	9	8	12	14	508	519	551	709	41.5	95.6	249.1	213.5
2421 Pesticides and other agro-chemical products	-	-	-	-	-	-	-	-	-	-	-	-
2422 Paints, varnishes, printing ink and mastics	2	2	1	1	...	...	...	16	1.1	4.1	7.0	6.5
2423 Pharmaceuticals, medicinal chemicals, etc.	5	4	7	7	...	...	...	512	28.9	69.0	198.1	142.4
2424 Soap, cleaning & cosmetic preparations	2	2	4	6	...	...	...	181	11.5	22.5	44.0	64.6
2429 Other chemical products n.e.c.	-	-	-	-	-	-	-	-	-	-	-	-
2430 Man-made fibres	-	-	-	-	-	-	-	-	-	-	-	-
251 Rubber products	-	-	-	1	-	-	-	12	-	-	-	0.6
2511 Rubber tyres and tubes	-	-	-	-	-	-	-	-	-	-	-	-
2519 Other rubber products	-	-	-	1	-	-	-	12	-	-	-	0.6
2520 Plastic products	-	-	-	-	-	-	-	-	-	-	-	-
2610 Glass and glass products	-	-	2	-	-	-	...	-	-	-	0.5	-
269 Non-metallic mineral products n.e.c.	37	44	33	29	2176	4310	3631	3726	204.9	1097.4	1133.7	614.9
2691 Pottery, china and earthenware	2	2	2	2	...	...	...	112	10.2	16.5	11.7	15.8
2692 Refractory ceramic products	-	1	-	-	-	...	-	-	-	0.2	-	-
2693 Struct.non-refractory clay; ceramic products	17	23	16	6	...	...	...	676	44.3	571.0	486.2	262.4
2694 Cement, lime and plaster	4	4	4	5	...	...	...	1779	86.8	235.8	419.3	166.4
2695 Articles of concrete, cement and plaster	10	8	7	12	...	...	...	806	58.7	238.7	183.1	137.1
2696 Cutting, shaping & finishing of stone	3	3	3	3	...	...	...	231	2.3	8.5	20.6	8.1
2699 Other non-metallic mineral products n.e.c.	1	3	1	1	...	...	...	122	2.5	25.7	12.9	25.1
2710 Basic iron and steel	1	1	2	2	93	560	564	495	3.3	30.5	108.4	94.2
2720 Basic precious and non-ferrous metals	-	-	-	-	-	-	-	-	-	-	-	-
273 Casting of metals	-	-	-	1	-	-	-	20	-	-	-	8.5
2731 Casting of iron and steel	-	-	-	1	-	-	-	20	-	-	-	8.5
2732 Casting of non-ferrous metals	-	-	-	-	-	-	-	-	-	-	-	-
281 Struct.metal products;tanks;steam generators	1	2	2	3	157	160	149	142	5.9	17.9	22.1	40.6
2811 Structural metal products	1	2	2	3	157	160	149	142	5.9	17.9	22.1	40.6
2812 Tanks, reservoirs and containers of metal	-	-	-	-	-	-	-	-	-	-	-	-
2813 Steam generators	-	-	-	-	-	-	-	-	-	-	-	-
289 Other metal products; metal working services	4	18	4	1	89	250	90	18	15.0	44.4	28.7	4.0
2891 Metal forging/pressing/stamping/roll-forming	-	-	-	-	-	-	-	-	-	-	-	-
2892 Treatment & coating of metals	-	1	1	1	-	...	...	18	-	2.0	2.5	4.0
2893 Cutlery, hand tools and general hardware	-	-	-	-	-	-	-	-	-	-	-	-
2899 Other fabricated metal products n.e.c.	4	17	3	-	...	...	...	-	15.0	42.4	26.2	-
291 General purpose machinery	-	-	-	-	-	-	-	-	-	-	-	-
2911 Engines & turbines(not for transport equip.)	-	-	-	-	-	-	-	-	-	-	-	-
2912 Pumps, compressors, taps and valves	-	-	-	-	-	-	-	-	-	-	-	-
2913 Bearings, gears, gearing & driving elements	-	-	-	-	-	-	-	-	-	-	-	-
2914 Ovens, furnaces and furnace burners	-	-	-	-	-	-	-	-	-	-	-	-
2915 Lifting and handling equipment	-	-	-	-	-	-	-	-	-	-	-	-
2919 Other general purpose machinery	-	-	-	-	-	-	-	-	-	-	-	-
292 Special purpose machinery	2	2	1	2	...	...	...	127	11.8	19.2	14.8	4.9
2921 Agricultural and forestry machinery	-	-	-	-	-	-	-	-	-	-	-	-
2922 Machine tools	-	-	-	-	-	-	-	-	-	-	-	-
2923 Machinery for metallurgy	-	-	-	-	-	-	-	-	-	-	-	-
2924 Machinery for mining & construction	-	-	-	-	-	-	-	-	-	-	-	-
2925 Food/beverage/tobacco processing machinery	2	2	1	2	...	...	...	127	11.8	19.2	14.8	4.9
2926 Machinery for textile, apparel and leather	-	-	-	-	-	-	-	-	-	-	-	-
2927 Weapons and ammunition	-	-	-	-	-	-	-	-	-	-	-	-
2929 Other special purpose machinery	-	-	-	-	-	-	-	-	-	-	-	-
2930 Domestic appliances n.e.c.	-	-	-	-	-	-	-	-	-	-	-	-

continued

Mongolia

ISIC Revision 3	Number of establishments					Number of persons engaged					Wages and salaries paid to employees				
		(numbers)					(numbers)					(million TUGRIKS)			
ISIC Industry	Note	1993	1994	1995	1996	Note	1993	1994	1995	1996	Note	1993	1994	1995	1996
3000 Office, accounting and computing machinery		-	-	-	-		-	-	-	-		-	-	-	-
3110 Electric motors, generators and transformers		1	1	1	2		140	144	142	142		3.9	7.7	11.3	11.6
3120 Electricity distribution & control apparatus		-	-	-	-		-	-	-	-		-	-	-	-
3130 Insulated wire and cable		-	-	-	-		-	-	-	-		-	-	-	-
3140 Accumulators, primary cells and batteries		-	-	-	-		-	-	-	-		-	-	-	-
3150 Lighting equipment and electric lamps		1	1	-	1		...	...	-	30		4.3	11.7	-	14.3
3190 Other electrical equipment n.e.c.		-	-	-	-		-	-	-	-		-	-	-	-
3210 Electronic valves, tubes, etc.		-	-	-	-		-	-	-	-		-	-	-	-
3220 TV/radio transmitters; line comm. apparatus		1	4	5	8		...	...	...	200		8.0	16.6	38.2	60.8
3230 TV and radio receivers and associated goods		-	-	-	-		-	-	-	-		-	-	-	-
331 Medical, measuring, testing appliances, etc.		2	4	2	3		105	167	120	147		3.5	13.5	10.4	27.9
3311 Medical, surgical and orthopaedic equipment		1	1	1	2		...	...	...	117		2.9	6.3	8.6	21.4
3312 Measuring/testing/navigating appliances,etc.		1	3	1	1		...	...	...	30		0.6	7.2	1.8	6.5
3313 Industrial process control equipment		-	-	-	-		-	-	-	-		-	-	-	-
3320 Optical instruments & photographic equipment		1	1	1	1		9	9	7	7		0.8	1.8	1.2	1.6
3330 Watches and clocks		-	-	-	-		-	-	-	-		-	-	-	-
3410 Motor vehicles		-	-	-	-		-	-	-	-		-	-	-	-
3420 Automobile bodies, trailers & semi-trailers		...	...	...	...		11	12	10	10		...	...	...	...
3430 Parts/accessories for automobiles		7	8	18	6		350	347	345	346		3.0	44.2	88.1	52.2
351 Building and repairing of ships and boats		-	-	-	-		-	-	-	-		-	-	-	-
3511 Building and repairing of ships		-	-	-	-		-	-	-	-		-	-	-	-
3512 Building/repairing of pleasure/sport. boats		-	-	-	-		-	-	-	-		-	-	-	-
3520 Railway/tramway locomotives & rolling stock		1	1	1	1		91	94	90	87		8.9	17.8	34.9	52.2
3530 Aircraft and spacecraft		-	-	-	-		-	-	-	-		-	-	-	-
359 Transport equipment n.e.c.		-	-	-	-		-	-	-	-		-	-	-	-
3591 Motorcycles		-	-	-	-		-	-	-	-		-	-	-	-
3592 Bicycles and invalid carriages		-	-	-	-		-	-	-	-		-	-	-	-
3599 Other transport equipment n.e.c.		-	-	-	-		-	-	-	-		-	-	-	-
3610 Furniture		11	16	11	14		498	440	456	428		48.0	90.0	58.3	15.6
369 Manufacturing n.e.c.		157	231	76	10		...	...	...	532		2788.0	3524.7	390.2	113.5
3691 Jewellery and related articles		1	1	1	1		150	145	149	135		5.2	23.8	36.8	66.6
3692 Musical instruments		-	2	1	-		-	...	...	-		-	20.6	31.7	-
3693 Sports goods		-	-	-	-		-	-	-	-		-	-	-	-
3694 Games and toys		-	-	-	-		-	-	-	-		-	-	-	-
3699 Other manufacturing n.e.c.		156	228	74	9		...	...	...	397		2782.8	3480.3	321.7	46.9
3710 Recycling of metal waste and scrap		-	-	-	-		-	-	-	-		-	-	-	-
3720 Recycling of non-metal waste and scrap		-	-	-	-		-	-	-	-		-	-	-	-
D Total manufacturing		433	616	457	387		36945	47815	45551	33664		5592.4	9304.7	8387.4	8554.4

Mongolia

ISIC Revision 3	Output in producers' prices					Value added in producers' prices					Gross fixed capital formation		
		(million TUGRIKS)					(million TUGRIKS)					(million TUGRIKS)	
ISIC Industry	Note	1993	1994	1995	1996	Note	1993	1994	1995	1996	Note	1995	1996
151 Processed meat,fish,fruit,vegetables,fats		5144.3	7379.6	10746.0	16174.2		1619.3	2700.6	1324.8	1858.6		5202.2	7700.0
1511 Processing/preserving of meat		5063.8	7327.3	10746.0	14993.7		1560.7	2683.3	1324.8	1789.5		5202.2	7605.1
1512 Processing/preserving of fish		-	-	-	-		-	-	-	-		-	-
1513 Processing/preserving of fruit & vegetables		80.5	52.3	-	31.8		58.6	17.3	-	21.0		-	55.3
1514 Vegetable and animal oils and fats		-	-	-	1148.7		-	-	-	48.1		-	40.0
1520 Dairy products		566.2	107.1	299.6	857.3		-17.7	30.6	44.7	-17.6		1918.1	3711.3
153 Grain mill products; starches; animal feeds		6398.0	10715.0	16975.3	17821.6		2140.9	1755.2	2672.9	3972.1		2869.0	4759.1
1531 Grain mill products		6319.6	10533.5	16905.2	17643.4		2118.7	1725.4	2667.6	3912.7		2869.0	2973.9
1532 Starches and starch products		-	-	-	-		-	-	-	-		-	-
1533 Prepared animal feeds		78.3	181.5	70.1	178.2		22.2	29.8	5.3	59.4		-	1785.2
154 Other food products		7354.4	9935.0	14127.8	17017.2		2567.2	3361.7	4482.9	4448.2		3659.1	5356.5
1541 Bakery products		7354.4	9929.6	13994.7	16378.8		2567.2	3357.3	4412.9	4347.3		3659.1	5109.6
1542 Sugar		-	-	-	-		-	-	-	-		-	-
1543 Cocoa, chocolate and sugar confectionery		-	-	-	-		-	-	-	-		-	-
1544 Macaroni, noodles & similar products		-	-	-	25.6		-	-	-	8.3		-	55.7
1549 Other food products n.e.c.		-	5.4	133.1	612.8		-	4.4	70.0	92.6		-	191.2
155 Beverages		3850.5	2367.6	3735.3	9379.5		2930.1	951.5	1641.6	3316.6		1054.3	1197.9
1551 Distilling, rectifying & blending of spirits		3845.5	2357.7	3734.7	9358.8		2927.4	944.4	1642.4	3314.0		1054.3	1103.1
1552 Wines		-	-	-	-		-	-	-	-		-	-
1553 Malt liquors and malt		-	-	-	12.7		-	-	-	-0.6		-	92.9
1554 Soft drinks; mineral waters		5.0	9.9	0.6	8.0		2.7	7.1	-0.8	3.2		-	1.9
1600 Tobacco products		-	-	-	-		-	-	-	-		-	-
171 Spinning, weaving and finishing of textiles		1325.4	2903.0	1171.8	3811.0		478.6	854.0	1171.8	759.1		389.1	490.4
1711 Textile fibre preparation; textile weaving		1325.4	2903.0	1171.8	3811.0		478.6	854.0	1171.8	759.1		389.1	490.4
1712 Finishing of textiles		-	-	-	-		-	-	-	-		-	-
172 Other textiles		3487.2	3709.2	4079.1	6501.0		619.9	579.8	1122.1	1852.8		659.5	832.4
1721 Made-up textile articles, except apparel		-	-	-	-		-	-	-	-		-	-
1722 Carpets and rugs		3119.7	3394.0	3408.4	5856.5		469.5	429.7	772.7	1522.2		561.1	708.6
1723 Cordage, rope, twine and netting		-	-	-	-		-	-	-	-		-	-
1729 Other textiles n.e.c.		367.5	315.2	670.7	644.5		150.4	150.1	349.4	330.6		98.4	123.8
1730 Knitted and crocheted fabrics and articles		4377.0	9673.0	26199.2	20077.8		3752.0	8081.8	22487.2	3910.9		2403.0	3033.2
1810 Wearing apparel, except fur apparel		3438.9	4243.4	5291.3	3657.3		1397.3	1792.4	1936.2	1720.6		3942.8	2796.6
1820 Dressing & dyeing of fur; processing of fur		1844.3	2778.8	2017.2	1981.1		470.2	454.4	402.5	1062.0		...	141.4
191 Tanning, dressing and processing of leather		2444.0	1208.3	960.5	697.7		442.5	337.5	80.3	224.5		...	235.1
1911 Tanning and dressing of leather		1301.5	1135.2	879.4	613.8		350.0	305.3	114.2	208.6		...	212.0
1912 Luggage, handbags, etc.; saddlery & harness		1142.5	73.1	81.1	83.9		92.5	32.2	-33.9	15.9		...	23.1
1920 Footwear		1889.9	1852.6	1825.4	1512.1		917.0	1000.1	788.2	1149.6		...	921.3
2010 Sawmilling and planing of wood		1659.9	2105.4	2169.5	2102.1		501.9	715.0	702.0	734.5		...	1249.2
202 Products of wood, cork, straw, etc.		108.1	545.0	463.9	280.5		31.5	322.1	141.5	112.5		...	172.7
2021 Veneer sheets, plywood, particle board, etc.		-	-	-	-		-	-	-	-		-	-
2022 Builders' carpentry and joinery		43.5	44.6	31.9	-		10.9	18.3	14.9	-		-	-
2023 Wooden containers		5.5	62.6	91.5	106.8		2.9	38.0	31.2	37.2		...	6.9
2029 Other wood products; articles of cork/straw		59.1	437.8	340.5	173.7		17.7	265.8	95.4	75.3		...	165.8
210 Paper and paper products		-	-	-	-		-	-	-	-		-	-
2101 Pulp, paper and paperboard		-	-	-	-		-	-	-	-		-	-
2102 Corrugated paper and paperboard		-	-	-	-		-	-	-	-		-	-
2109 Other articles of paper and paperboard		-	-	-	-		-	-	-	-		-	-
221 Publishing		-	-	-	-		-	-	-	-		-	-
2211 Publishing of books and other publications		-	-	-	-		-	-	-	-		-	-
2212 Publishing of newspapers, journals, etc.		-	-	-	-		-	-	-	-		-	-
2213 Publishing of recorded media		-	-	-	-		-	-	-	-		-	-
2219 Other publishing		-	-	-	-		-	-	-	-		-	-

continued

Mongolia

ISIC Revision 3 ISIC Industry	Note	Output in producers' prices (million TUGRIKS) 1993	1994	1995	1996	Note	Value added in producers' prices (million TUGRIKS) 1993	1994	1995	1996	Note	Gross fixed capital formation (million TUGRIKS) 1995	1996
222 Printing and related service activities		354.7	812.8	1160.0	2782.0		354.7	342.7	326.6	834.2		657.8	1088.8
2221 Printing		354.7	812.8	1160.0	2782.0		354.7	342.7	326.6	834.2		657.8	1088.8
2222 Service activities related to printing		-	-	-	-		-	-	-	-		-	-
2230 Reproduction of recorded media		-	-	-	-		-	-	-	-		-	-
2310 Coke oven products		-	-	-	-		-	-	-	-		-	-
2320 Refined petroleum products		-	-	-	-		-	-	-	-		-	-
2330 Processing of nuclear fuel		-	-	-	-		-	-	-	-		-	-
241 Basic chemicals		-	-	-	-		-	-	-	-		-	-
2411 Basic chemicals, except fertilizers		-	-	-	-		-	-	-	-		-	-
2412 Fertilizers and nitrogen compounds		-	-	-	-		-	-	-	-		-	-
2413 Plastics in primary forms; synthetic rubber		-	-	-	-		-	-	-	-		-	-
242 Other chemicals		518.9	1109.3	1696.5	2187.7		201.4	521.2	658.8	724.9		1612.5	2706.4
2421 Pesticides and other agro-chemical products		-	-	-	-		-	-	-	-		-	-
2422 Paints, varnishes, printing ink and mastics		41.3	84.9	98.7	78.9		11.8	20.1	44.5	36.6		...	25.7
2423 Pharmaceuticals, medicinal chemicals, etc.		275.1	656.0	997.1	1150.4		93.6	271.1	457.9	495.2		...	1491.6
2424 Soap, cleaning & cosmetic preparations		202.6	368.4	600.7	958.5		96.0	230.0	156.4	193.1		...	1189.1
2429 Other chemical products n.e.c.		-	-	-	-		-	-	-	-		-	-
2430 Man-made fibres		-	-	-	-		-	-	-	-		-	-
251 Rubber products		-	-	-	6.5		-	-	-	1.1		-	353.0
2511 Rubber tyres and tubes		-	-	-	-		-	-	-	-		-	-
2519 Other rubber products		-	-	-	6.5		-	-	-	1.1		-	-
2520 Plastic products		-	-	-	-		-	-	-	-		-	-
2610 Glass and glass products		-	-	7.4	-		-	-	0.5	-		...	-
269 Non-metallic mineral products n.e.c.		2097.5	6754.8	7689.8	7937.8		485.7	2015.0	2229.8	1708.8		3635.1	6372.4
2691 Pottery, china and earthenware		77.0	77.8	71.0	72.3		21.7	30.4	24.8	24.5		...	18.7
2692 Refractory ceramic products		-	2.7	-	-		-	2.7	-	-		-	-
2693 Struct.non-refractory clay; ceramic products		501.1	2899.8	2785.9	1418.7		140.7	1052.1	798.8	590.2		...	642.1
2694 Cement, lime and plaster		893.9	1751.2	3186.0	3814.2		183.7	477.9	976.3	240.6		...	2806.1
2695 Articles of concrete, cement and plaster		587.7	1708.5	1434.7	2286.6		128.9	352.2	383.7	764.2		...	2478.6
2696 Cutting, shaping & finishing of stone		21.1	69.1	151.3	221.8		2.2	24.3	31.5	49.2		...	49.2
2699 Other non-metallic mineral products n.e.c.		16.7	245.8	60.9	124.2		8.4	78.1	14.7	40.1		...	40.1
2710 Basic iron and steel		12.2	643.8	2233.1	1633.7		4.7	71.6	74.6	-461.7		15413.3	27826.5
2720 Basic precious and non-ferrous metals		-	-	-	-		-	-	-	-		-	-
273 Casting of metals		-	-	-	42.1		-	-	-	15.7		-	11.1
2731 Casting of iron and steel		-	-	-	42.1		-	-	-	15.7		-	11.1
2732 Casting of non-ferrous metals		-	-	-	-		-	-	-	-		-	-
281 Struct.metal products;tanks;steam generators		13.6	65.1	60.5	118.8		39.9	36.8	26.1	-27.5		1013.6	671.9
2811 Structural metal products		13.6	65.1	60.5	118.8		39.9	36.8	26.1	-27.5		-	671.9
2812 Tanks, reservoirs and containers of metal		-	-	-	-		-	-	-	-		-	-
2813 Steam generators		-	-	-	-		-	-	-	-		-	-
289 Other metal products; metal working services		98.5	768.5	302.4	15.6		31.2	517.6	84.1	7.6		...	15.1
2891 Metal forging/pressing/stamping/roll-forming		-	-	-	-		-	-	-	-		-	-
2892 Treatment & coating of metals		-	16.3	11.7	15.6		-	1.6	5.1	7.6		...	15.1
2893 Cutlery, hand tools and general hardware		-	-	-	-		-	-	-	-		-	-
2899 Other fabricated metal products n.e.c.		98.5	752.2	290.7	-		31.2	516.0	79.0	-		-	-
291 General purpose machinery		-	-	-	-		-	-	-	-		-	-
2911 Engines & turbines(not for transport equip.)		-	-	-	-		-	-	-	-		-	-
2912 Pumps, compressors, taps and valves		-	-	-	-		-	-	-	-		-	-
2913 Bearings, gears, gearing & driving elements		-	-	-	-		-	-	-	-		-	-
2914 Ovens, furnaces and furnace burners		-	-	-	-		-	-	-	-		-	-
2915 Lifting and handling equipment		-	-	-	-		-	-	-	-		-	-
2919 Other general purpose machinery		-	-	-	-		-	-	-	-		-	-

ISIC	Industry	(1)	(2)	(3)	(4)	(5)	(6)	(7)	(8)	(9)	(10)
292	Special purpose machinery	73.3	79.9	72.1	229.1	33.1	33.5	35.8	34.1	...	368.1
2921	Agricultural and forestry machinery	-	-	-	-	-	-	-	-	-	-
2922	Machine tools	-	-	-	-	-	-	-	-	-	-
2923	Machinery for metallurgy	-	-	-	-	-	-	-	-	-	-
2924	Machinery for mining & construction	-	-	-	-	-	-	-	-	-	-
2925	Food/beverage/tobacco processing machinery	73.3	79.9	72.1	229.1	33.1	33.5	35.8	34.1	...	368.1
2926	Machinery for textile, apparel and leather	-	-	-	-	-	-	-	-	-	-
2927	Weapons and ammunition	-	-	-	-	-	-	-	-	-	-
2929	Other special purpose machinery	-	-	-	-	-	-	-	-	-	-
2930	Domestic appliances n.e.c.	-	-	-	-	-	-	-	-	-	-
3000	Office, accounting and computing machinery	-	-	-	-	-	-	-	-	-	-
3110	Electric motors, generators and transformers	32.1	71.0	106.6	215.2	6.9	20.3	34.5	98.7	-	338.7
3120	Electricity distribution & control apparatus	-	-	-	-	-	-	-	-	-	-
3130	Insulated wire and cable	-	-	-	-	-	-	-	-	-	-
3140	Accumulators, primary cells and batteries	-	-	-	-	-	-	-	-	-	-
3150	Lighting equipment and electric lamps	30.1	63.2	-	87.3	7.1	32.6	-	98.7	...	37.4
3190	Other electrical equipment n.e.c.	-	-	-	-	-	-	-	-	-	-
3210	Electronic valves, tubes, etc.	-	-	-	-	-	-	-	-	-	-
3220	TV/radio transmitters; line comm. apparatus	24.6	61.5	353.4	1555.4	11.8	31.9	123.5	582.9	...	3190.5
3230	TV and radio receivers and associated goods	-	-	-	-	-	-	-	-	-	-
331	Medical, measuring, testing appliances, etc.	17.6	61.3	287.2	598.0	8.0	29.4	39.5	190.1	...	1799.4
3311	Medical, surgical and orthopaedic equipment	10.2	18.9	270.1	551.7	4.7	9.5	34.7	179.9	...	1784.2
3312	Measuring/testing/navigating appliances,etc.	7.4	42.4	17.1	46.3	3.3	19.9	4.8	10.2	...	15.2
3313	Industrial process control equipment	-	-	-	-	-	-	-	-	-	-
3320	Optical instruments & photographic equipment	7.6	8.1	6.2	6.7	1.8	2.4	1.6	2.8	-	0.2
3330	Watches and clocks	-	-	-	-	-	-	-	-	-	-
3410	Motor vehicles	-	-	-	-	-	-	-	-	-	-
3420	Automobile bodies, trailers & semi-trailers	...	...	...	...	...	...	...	3.8	...	46.1
3430	Parts/accessories for automobiles	63.4	233.5	605.7	347.0	27.2	115.8	275.2	96.7	...	575.0
351	Building and repairing of ships and boats	-	-	-	-	-	-	-	-	-	-
3511	Building and repairing of ships	-	-	-	-	-	-	-	-	-	-
3512	Building/repairing of pleasure/sport. boats	-	-	-	-	-	-	-	-	-	-
3520	Railway/tramway locomotives & rolling stock	59.5	113.4	163.7	282.6	16.5	40.6	...	96.3	...	68.5
3530	Aircraft and spacecraft	-	-	-	-	-	-	-	-	-	-
359	Transport equipment n.e.c.	-	-	-	-	-	-	-	-	-	-
3591	Motorcycles	-	-	-	-	-	-	-	-	-	-
3592	Bicycles and invalid carriages	-	-	-	-	-	-	-	-	-	-
3599	Other transport equipment n.e.c.	-	-	-	-	-	-	-	-	-	-
3610	Furniture	249.7	433.6	304.9	398.2	91.1	155.8	133.4	86.5	...	825.6
369	Manufacturing n.e.c.	21504.8	17733.3	4461.2	1239.9	8639.7	7903.6	1738.1	284.1	209.3	286.3
3691	Jewellery and related articles	461.4	666.3	1034.0	895.3	238.3	253.2	555.7	166.1	...	205.6
3692	Musical instruments	-	276.2	333.5	-	-	144.9	183.6	-	...	-
3693	Sports goods	-	-	-	-	-	-	-	-	-	-
3694	Games and toys	-	-	-	-	-	-	-	-	-	-
3699	Other manufacturing n.e.c.	21043.4	16790.8	3093.7	344.6	8401.4	7505.5	998.8	118.0	...	80.7
3710	Recycling of metal waste and scrap	-	-	-	-	-	-	-	-	-	-
3720	Recycling of non-metal waste and scrap	-	-	-	-	-	-	-	-	-	-
D	Total manufacturing	69046.1	88536.1	111752.3	121565.8	27811.5	34807.5	44838.5	29406.3	44638.7	...

Mongolia

ISIC Revision 3			Index numbers of industrial production											
			(1990=100)											
ISIC	Industry	Note	1985	1986	1987	1988	1989	1990	1991	1992	1993	1994	1995	1996
15	Food and beverages		99	102	104	107	110	100	75	48	41	36	41	31
16	Tobacco products		...	...	...	...	...	...	...	...	...	...	...	...
17	Textiles		92	85	100	99	112	100	84	76	54	38	51	58
18	Wearing apparel, fur		95	100	97	98	111	100	89	39	19	17	21	14
19	Leather, leather products and footwear		82	82	89	92	96	100	66	48	31	27	13	6
20	Wood products (excl. furniture)		117	122	121	120	122	100	72	46	41	32	39	44
21	Paper and paper products		...	...	...	...	...	...	...	...	...	...	...	...
22	Printing and publishing		88	101	107	112	116	100	102	70	71	79	100	57
23	Coke,refined petroleum products,nuclear fuel		...	...	...	...	...	...	...	...	...	...	...	...
24	Chemicals and chemical products		69	80	87	103	106	100	89	83	74	68	92	100
25	Rubber and plastics products		...	...	...	...	...	...	...	...	...	...	...	...
26	Non-metallic mineral products		64	89	100	105	105	100	66	50	39	48	46	48
27	Basic metals		101	105	117	119	118	100	77	101	34	50	102	95
28	Fabricated metal products		...	...	...	...	...	...	...	...	...	...	...	...
29	Machinery and equipment n.e.c.		...	...	...	...	...	...	...	...	...	...	...	...
30	Office, accounting and computing machinery		...	...	...	...	...	...	...	...	...	...	...	...
31	Electrical machinery and apparatus		...	...	...	...	...	...	...	...	...	...	...	...
32	Radio,television and communication equipment		...	...	...	...	...	...	...	...	...	...	...	...
33	Medical, precision and optical instruments		...	...	...	...	...	...	...	...	...	...	...	...
34	Motor vehicles, trailers, semi-trailers		...	...	...	...	...	...	...	...	...	...	...	...
35	Other transport equipment		...	...	...	...	...	...	...	...	...	...	...	...
36	Furniture; manufacturing n.e.c.		...	...	...	...	...	...	...	...	...	...	...	...
37	Recycling		...	...	...	...	...	...	...	...	...	...	...	...
D	Total manufacturing		89	96	100	103	107	100	76	55	42	37	41	37

MOROCCO

Supplier of information:
Direction de la statistique, Ministère de la Prévision Economique et du Plan, Rabat.

Basic source of data:
Industrial survey.

Major deviations from ISIC (Revision 2):
None reported.

Reference period (if not calendar year):

Scope:
All establishments.

Method of enumeration:
Not reported.

Adjusted for non-response:
Not reported.

Concepts and definitions of variables:
Wages and salaries is compensation of employees.

Related national publications:
Situation des Industries de transformation, published by the Direction des études et de la planification, Ministère du Commerce et de l'Industrie (MCI), Rabat.

ISIC Revision 2	Number of establishments					Number of persons engaged					Wages and salaries paid to employees				
		(numbers)					(numbers)					(million DIRHAMS)			
ISIC Industry	Note	1993	1994	1995	1996	Note	1993	1994	1995	1996	Note	1993	1994	1995	1996
311/2 Food products		1505	1502	1571	1558		91568	88845	90989	90912		2468	2865	2865	3046
3111 Slaughtering, preparing & preserving meat		...	...	...	18		...	...	...	418		...	...	...	8
3112 Dairy products		...	...	...	37		...	...	...	8101		...	...	...	346
3113 Canning, preserving of fruits & vegetables		...	...	...	165		...	...	...	19340		...	...	...	424
3114 Canning, preserving and processing of fish		...	...	...	103		...	...	...	17312		...	...	...	380
3115 Vegetable and animal oils and fats		...	...	...	108		...	...	...	7954		...	...	...	302
3116 Grain mill products		...	...	...	171		...	...	...	8642		...	...	...	283
3117 Bakery products		...	...	...	739		...	...	...	8036		...	...	...	163
3118 Sugar factories and refineries		...	...	...	15		...	...	...	11487		...	...	...	669
3119 Cocoa, chocolate and sugar confectionery		...	...	...	19		...	...	...	1644		...	...	...	60
3121 Other food products		...	...	...	88		...	...	...	4239		...	...	...	282
3122 Prepared animal feeds		...	...	...	95		...	...	...	3739		...	...	...	128
313 Beverages		37	38	37	39		6060	8915	7328	7417		381	677a/	454	425
3131 Distilling, rectifying and blending spirits		...	...	...	2		...	...	...	27		...	...	...	-
3132 Wine industries		...	...	...	12		...	...	...	1389		...	...	...	57
3133 Malt liquors and malt		...	...	...	7		...	...	...	2365		...	...	...	150
3134 Soft drinks and carbonated waters		...	...	...	18		...	...	...	3636		...	...	...	218
314 Tobacco		6	6	6	6		2872	2872	2872	2380		242	...a/	266	316
321 Textiles		774	760	738	734		72165	71269	70390	70052		1741	2120	2262	2349
3211 Spinning, weaving and finishing textiles		...	...	...	256		...	...	...	29484		...	...	...	1055
3212 Made-up textile goods excl. wearing apparel		...	...	...	143		...	...	...	6353		...	...	...	169
3213 Knitting mills		...	...	...	293		...	...	...	25065		...	...	...	613
3214 Carpets and rugs		...	...	...	36		...	...	...	7815		...	...	...	412
3215 Cordage, rope and twine		...	...	...	-		...	...	...	-		...	...	...	-
3219 Other textiles		...	...	...	6		...	...	...	1335		...	...	...	100
322 Wearing apparel, except footwear		786	781	742	724		95102	100725	101788	106469		1834	1952	2111	2301
323 Leather and fur products		178	168	139	137		8392	8175	7079	6642		173	381b/	157	161
3231 Tanneries and leather finishing		...	...	...	54		...	...	...	3205		...	...	...	84
3232 Fur dressing and dyeing industries		...	...	...	3		...	...	...	406		...	...	...	15
3233 Leather prods. excl. wearing apparel		...	...	...	80		...	...	...	3031		...	...	...	62
324 Footwear, except rubber or plastic		124	128	128	138		7129	8100	8505	8287		195	...b/	214	226
331 Wood products, except furniture		201	214	268	242		9505	8558	10101	8523		250	396c/	266	249
3311 Sawmills, planing and other wood mills		...	...	...	35		...	...	...	686		...	...	...	19
3312 Wooden and cane containers		...	...	...	21		...	...	...	1655		...	...	...	57
3319 Other wood and cork products		...	...	...	186		...	...	...	6182		...	...	...	172
332 Furniture and fixtures, excl. metal		58	59	28	62		2990	3001	2709	2899		124	...c/	127	136
341 Paper and products		91	89	92	94		8410	8193	9607	9126		348	662d/	399	390
3411 Pulp, paper and paperboard articles		...	...	...	12		...	...	...	2771		...	...	...	187
3412 Containers of paper and paperboard		...	...	...	82		...	...	...	6355		...	...	...	203
3419 Other pulp, paper and paperboard articles		...	...	...	-		...	...	...	-		...	...	...	-
342 Printing and publishing		322	343	350	355		6702	6581	7217	7405		259	...d/	305	320
351 Industrial chemicals		60	59	63	60		12193	13661	15100	13688		817	1849e/	987	1129
3511 Basic chemicals excl. fertilizers		...	...	...	22		...	...	...	9184		...	...	...	809
3512 Fertilizers and pesticides		...	...	...	20		...	...	...	2032		...	...	...	171
3513 Synthetic resins and plastic materials		...	...	...	18		...	...	...	2472		...	...	...	149
352 Other chemicals		330	332	337	342		13934	14039	16352	21363		895	...e/	1010	1099
3521 Paints, varnishes and lacquers		...	...	...	36		...	...	...	2384		...	...	...	196
3522 Drugs and medicines		...	...	...	21		...	...	...	6020		...	...	...	443
3523 Soap, cleaning preps., perfumes, cosmetics		...	...	...	49		...	...	...	9268		...	...	...	295
3529 Other chemical products		...	...	...	236		...	...	...	3691		...	...	...	165
353 Petroleum refineries		...	...	...	...		...	...	...	...		...	...	...	...

354 Misc. petroleum and coal products		...	...	...	...		...	...	...	...		...	...	...	...
355 Rubber products		28	30	31	29		2646	2803	2878	2487		199	476f/	232	240
3551 Tyres and tubes		...	...	...	6		...	...	...	1439		...	...	...	201
3559 Other rubber products		...	...	...	23		...	...	...	1048		...	...	...	39
356 Plastic products		258	249	252	261		9021	9218	9524	10067		237	...f/	273	299
361 Pottery, china, earthenware		20	23	26	26		4220	4794	5001	5253		149	1303g/	195	212
362 Glass and products		21	21	22	23		1840	1299	1618	1657		68	...g/	66	65
369 Other non-metallic mineral products		374	389	386	408		29928	27734	26173	30904		971	...g/	1014	1504
3691 Structural clay products		...	...	...	86		...	...	...	4704		...	...	...	125
3692 Cement, lime and plaster		...	...	...	23		...	...	...	4452		...	...	...	447
3699 Other non-metallic mineral products		...	...	...	299		...	...	...	21748		...	...	...	932
371 Iron and steel		3	5	4	5		806	953	982	997		60	113h/	64	68
372 Non-ferrous metals		8	8	8	9		656	782	951	1001		42	...h/	53	60
381 Fabricated metal products		457	440	456	445		26813	23310	24271	23535		1040	991	1053	986
3811 Cutlery, hand tools and general hardware		...	...	...	33		...	...	...	1326		...	...	...	38
3812 Furniture and fixtures primarily of metal		...	...	...	22		...	...	...	1427		...	...	...	60
3813 Structural metal products		...	...	...	210		...	...	...	11757		...	...	...	484
3819 Other fabricated metal products		...	...	...	180		...	...	...	9025		...	...	...	403
382 Non-electrical machinery	i/	290	296	296	300	i/	7394	7987	7374	7219	i/	308	356	325	322
3821 Engines and turbines		...	...	...	2		...	...	...	127		...	...	...	10
3822 Agricultural machinery and equipment		...	...	...	5		...	...	...	500		...	...	...	29
3823 Metal and wood working machinery		...	...	...	8		...	...	...	147		...	...	...	4
3824 Other special industrial machinery		...	...	...	26		...	...	...	923		...	...	...	48
3825 Office, computing and accounting machinery		...	...	...	35		...	...	...	2187		...	...	...	112
3829 Other non-electrical machinery & equipment		...	...	...	224		...	...	...	3335		...	...	...	119
383 Electrical machinery		113	111	108	116		10493	9956	10658	11276		534	548	604	590
3831 Electrical industrial machinery		...	...	...	19		...	...	...	750		...	...	...	35
3832 Radio, television and communication equipm.		...	...	...	5		...	...	...	2830		...	...	...	187
3833 Electrical appliances and housewares		...	...	...	6		...	...	...	387		...	...	...	11
3839 Other electrical apparatus and supplies		...	...	...	86		...	...	...	7309		...	...	...	357
384 Transport equipment		102	110	112	116		11706	11779	12490	11547		592	652	689	685
3841 Shipbuilding and repairing		...	...	...	35		...	...	...	757		...	...	...	51
3842 Railroad equipment		...	...	...	1		...	...	...	147		...	...	...	7
3843 Motor vehicles		...	...	...	65		...	...	...	9911		...	...	...	591
3844 Motorcycles and bicycles		...	...	...	12		...	...	...	666		...	...	...	34
3845 Aircraft		...	...	...	3		...	...	...	66		...	...	...	2
3849 Other transport equipment		...	...	...	-		...	...	...	-		...	...	...	-
385 Professional and scientific equipment	i/	29	35	34	35	i/	853	1046	967	1637	i/	26	34	34	54
3851 Prof. and scientific equipment n.e.c.		...	...	...	25		...	...	...	1285		...	...	...	43
3852 Photographic and optical goods		...	...	...	8		...	...	...	258		...	...	...	9
3853 Watches and clocks		...	...	...	2		...	...	...	94		...	...	...	2
390 Other manufacturing industries		27	27	25	18		663	634	651	494		25	27	26	21
3901 Jewellery and related articles		...	...	...	10		...	...	...	118		...	...	...	3
3902 Musical instruments		...	...	...	8		...	...	...	376		...	...	...	18
3903 Sporting and athletic goods		...	...	...	-		...	...	...	-		...	...	...	-
3909 Manufacturing industries, n.e.c.		...	...	...	-		...	...	...	-		...	...	...	-
3 Total manufacturing		6202	6223	6259	6282		444061	445227	453575	463237		13977	15402	16052	17253

a/ 313 includes 314.
b/ 323 includes 324.
c/ 331 includes 332.
d/ 341 includes 342.
e/ 351 includes 352.
f/ 355 includes 356.
g/ 361 includes 362 and 369.
h/ 371 includes 372.
i/ ISIC 385 includes office machines (ISIC 3825).

Morocco

ISIC Revision 2	Output					Value added					Gross fixed capital formation		
		(million DIRHAMS)					(million DIRHAMS)					(million DIRHAMS)	
ISIC Industry	Note	1993	1994	1995	1996	Note	1993	1994	1995	1996	Note	1995	1996
311/2 Food products		33032	34742	36359	39280		5970	6493	7153	7910		1464	1535
3111 Slaughtering, preparing & preserving meat		...	...	...	76		...	...	...	12		...	11
3112 Dairy products		...	...	...	4938		...	...	...	837		...	149
3113 Canning, preserving of fruits & vegetables		...	...	...	4020		...	...	...	865		...	237
3114 Canning, preserving and processing of fish		...	...	...	2678		...	...	...	747		...	102
3115 Vegetable and animal oils and fats		...	...	...	4973		...	...	...	1370		...	128
3116 Grain mill products		...	...	...	9303		...	...	...	893		...	273
3117 Bakery products		...	...	...	1247		...	...	...	319		...	144
3118 Sugar factories and refineries		...	...	...	5897		...	...	...	1635		...	197
3119 Cocoa, chocolate and sugar confectionery		...	...	...	501		...	...	...	106		...	24
3121 Other food products		...	...	...	2248		...	...	...	764		...	139
3122 Prepared animal feeds		...	...	...	3399		...	...	...	362		...	131
313 Beverages		3748	3951	4123	4501		2011	1953	1866	2001		386	520
3131 Distilling, rectifying and blending spirits		...	...	...	17		...	...	...	4		...	-
3132 Wine industries		...	...	...	886		...	...	...	260		...	34
3133 Malt liquors and malt		...	...	...	1912		...	...	...	975		...	171
3134 Soft drinks and carbonated waters		...	...	...	1686		...	...	...	762		...	315
314 Tobacco		3701	4134	4754	4345		5005	5606	6406	6046		250	183
321 Textiles		11219	11953	12160	12392		3528	4107	4165	4098		1035	1110
3211 Spinning, weaving and finishing textiles		...	...	...	7236		...	...	...	2158		...	728
3212 Made-up textile goods excl. wearing apparel		...	...	...	1083		...	...	...	296		...	60
3213 Knitting mills		...	...	...	3206		...	...	...	1034		...	242
3214 Carpets and rugs		...	...	...	346		...	...	...	451		...	40
3215 Cordage, rope and twine		...	...	...	-		...	...	...	-		...	-
3219 Other textiles		...	...	...	521		...	...	...	159		...	40
322 Wearing apparel, except footwear		7359	7699	8105	8787		2785	2966	3285	3575		586	752
323 Leather and fur products		1074	1140	1101	1337		264	255	265	262		21	19
3231 Tanneries and leather finishing		...	...	...	937		...	...	...	136		...	11
3232 Fur dressing and dyeing industries		...	...	...	95		...	...	...	26		...	1
3233 Leather prods. excl. wearing apparel		...	...	...	305		...	...	...	100		...	7
324 Footwear, except rubber or plastic		1015	1047	1080	1020		272	292	330	352		66	37
331 Wood products, except furniture		1986	2170	1652	2151		564	488	411	503		63	51
3311 Sawmills, planing and other wood mills		...	...	...	478		...	...	...	74		...	8
3312 Wooden and cane containers		...	...	...	439		...	...	...	100		...	4
3319 Other wood and cork products		...	...	...	1234		...	...	...	329		...	39
332 Furniture and fixtures, excl. metal		514	605	498	503		166	221	157	184		13	14
341 Paper and products		3833	3956	4350	4315		748	934	1431	1136		714	169
3411 Pulp, paper and paperboard articles		...	...	...	2019		...	...	...	600		...	85
3412 Containers of paper and paperboard		...	...	...	2296		...	...	...	536		...	84
3419 Other pulp, paper and paperboard articles		...	...	...	-		...	...	...	-		...	-
342 Printing and publishing		1383	1479	1487	1625		519	560	604	564		119	124
351 Industrial chemicals		11849	12442	14395	13508		2028	3897	4459	5025		281	343
3511 Basic chemicals excl fertilizers		...	...	...	10518		...	...	...	4146		...	193
3512 Fertilizers and pesticides		...	...	...	1588		...	...	...	451		...	34
3513 Synthetic resins and plastic materials		...	...	...	1402		...	...	...	428		...	116
352 Other chemicals		6964	7324	7058	7181		1624	2054	2091	2252		365	439
3521 Paints, varnishes and lacquers		...	...	...	1617		...	...	...	502		...	56
3522 Drugs and medicines		...	...	...	2409		...	...	...	895		...	217
3523 Soap, cleaning preps., perfumes, cosmetics		...	...	...	2197		...	...	...	547		...	91
3529 Other chemical products		...	...	...	958		...	...	...	308		...	75
353 Petroleum refineries		...	...	...	...		...	...	...	...		...	...

ISIC	Industry													
354	Misc. petroleum and coal products		...	...	...	...		...	...	...	...		...	...
355	Rubber products		945	917	1000	1192		504	524	473	477		47	70
3551	Tyres and tubes		...	...	...	980		...	...	...	399		...	39
3559	Other rubber products		...	...	...	212		...	...	...	78		...	31
356	Plastic products		1890	1976	2157	2566		509	525	623	684		233	250
361	Pottery, china, earthenware		1073	1059	1317	1448		328	351	469	499		598	521
362	Glass and products		379	371	405	375		139	84	146	164		50	69
369	Other non-metallic mineral products		6874	7020	7024	7712		2886	3269	3497	4311		535	885
3691	Structural clay products		...	...	...	568		...	...	...	213		...	188
3692	Cement, lime and plaster		...	...	...	3985		...	...	...	2518		...	179
3699	Other non-metallic mineral products		...	...	...	3159		...	...	...	1580		...	518
371	Iron and steel		1754	1994	2240	2186		401	474	530	553		8	11
372	Non-ferrous metals		672	594	578	754		136	128	132	133		12	10
381	Fabricated metal products		6889	7261	8165	7335		1865	1823	1879	1788		393	390
3811	Cutlery, hand tools and general hardware		...	...	...	251		...	...	...	73		...	15
3812	Furniture and fixtures primarily of metal		...	...	...	228		...	...	...	89		...	3
3813	Structural metal products		...	...	...	2915		...	...	...	841		...	185
3819	Other fabricated metal products		...	...	...	3941		...	...	...	785		...	187
382	Non-electrical machinery	a/	1541	1924	1786	1743	a/	569	702	579	637	a/	100	105
3821	Engines and turbines		...	...	...	68		...	...	...	27		...	-
3822	Agricultural machinery and equipment		...	...	...	236		...	...	...	72		...	3
3823	Metal and wood working machinery		...	...	...	22		...	...	...	10		...	7
3824	Other special industrial machinery		...	...	...	166		...	...	...	80		...	25
3825	Office, computing and accounting machinery		...	...	...	775		...	...	...	247		...	40
3829	Other non-electrical machinery & equipment		...	...	...	476		...	...	...	201		...	30
383	Electrical machinery		3051	3196	3197	3282		1054	1148	1178	1331		276	313
3831	Electrical industrial machinery		...	...	...	173		...	...	...	67		...	14
3832	Radio, television and communication equipm.		...	...	...	560		...	...	...	355		...	140
3833	Electrical appliances and housewares		...	...	...	104		...	...	...	28		...	3
3839	Other electrical apparatus and supplies		...	...	...	2445		...	...	...	881		...	156
384	Transport equipment		4390	4761	4726	4925		1393	1428	1470	1540		226	146
3841	Shipbuilding and repairing		...	...	...	158		...	...	...	75		...	3
3842	Railroad equipment		...	...	...	7		...	...	...	14		...	-
3843	Motor vehicles		...	...	...	4480		...	...	...	1397		...	135
3844	Motorcycles and bicycles		...	...	...	269		...	...	...	51		...	8
3845	Aircraft		...	...	...	11		...	...	...	3		...	-
3849	Other transport equipment		...	...	...	-		...	...	...	-		...	-
385	Professional and scientific equipment	a/	220	230	215	271	a/	65	65	63	100	a/	17	44
3851	Prof. and scientific equipment n.e.c.		...	...	...	221		...	...	...	73		...	25
3852	Photographic and optical goods		...	...	...	43		...	...	...	20		...	19
3853	Watches and clocks		...	...	...	7		...	...	...	7		...	-
390	Other manufacturing industries		109	117	104	85		38	42	37	28		2	3
3901	Jewellery and related articles		...	...	...	13		...	...	...	5		...	1
3902	Musical instruments		...	...	...	72		...	...	...	23		...	2
3903	Sporting and athletic goods		...	...	...	-		...	...	...	-		...	-
3909	Manufacturing industries, n.e.c.		...	...	...	-		...	...	...	-		...	-
3	Total manufacturing		117464	124062	130036	134819		35371	40386	43700	46153		7860	8113

a/ ISIC 385 includes office machines (ISIC 3825).

Morocco

ISIC Revision 2		Index numbers of industrial production (1990=100)											
ISIC Industry	Note	1985	1986	1987	1988	1989	1990	1991	1992	1993	1994	1995	1996
311/2 Food products		108	113	94	99	98	100	104	104	115	120	119	121
313 Beverages		62	66	77	90	98	100	116	113	95	101	112	119
314 Tobacco		106	105	105	108	97	100	95	91	90	102	104	110
321 Textiles		75	82	91	97	96	100	104	106	103	97	99	97
322 Wearing apparel, except footwear		100	111	107	100	101	100	93	103	108	116	127	135
323 Leather and fur products	a/b/	105	93	89	97	102	100	112	112	111	124	120	132
324 Footwear, except rubber or plastic	a/	...	...	...	...	...	...	...	...	...	...	...	...
331 Wood products, except furniture		97	92	91	98	100	100	108	102	108	117	105	127
332 Furniture and fixtures, excl. metal	c/	...	...	...	...	...	...	...	...	...	...	...	...
341 Paper and products		97	101	96	103	100	100	92	99	94	104	114	120
342 Printing and publishing		78	80	68	86	90	100	97	81	77	89	84	82
351 Industrial chemicals		105	113	95	101	85	100	91	93	98	87	85	100
352 Other chemicals		90	93	89	98	100	100	102	111	109	129	145	149
353 Petroleum refineries		106	95	79	87	94	100	94	105	107	114	105	102
354 Misc. petroleum and coal products		...	...	...	...	...	...	...	...	...	...	...	...
355 Rubber products		85	80	85	92	92	100	104	95	97	104	113	97
356 Plastic products		57	63	80	81	84	100	101	96	98	100	99	105
361 Pottery, china, earthenware	d/	68	63	67	75	85	100	112	114	95	116	120	119
362 Glass and products	d/	...	...	...	...	...	...	...	...	...	...	...	...
369 Other non-metallic mineral products	d/	...	...	...	...	...	...	...	...	...	...	...	...
371 Iron and steel	e/	66	64	67	83	101	100	107	104	100	101	115	113
372 Non-ferrous metals	e/	...	...	...	...	...	...	...	...	...	...	...	...
381 Fabricated metal products		80	66	85	89	94	100	107	122	113	117	123	123
382 Non-electrical machinery		112	128	125	111	94	100	105	109	104	113	110	106
383 Electrical machinery		78	90	86	82	92	100	95	85	96	90	94	94
384 Transport equipment		48	55	78	84	93	100	103	85	83	94	92	91
385 Professional and scientific equipment		82	78	75	59	89	100	117	145	137	134	135	119
390 Other manufacturing industries	c/	81	95	107	108	112	100	101	101	124	136	119	118
3 Total manufacturing		89	91	89	94	95	100	102	103	101	108	110	113

a/ 323 includes 324.
b/ Excluding fur and fur products.
c/ 390 includes 332.
d/ 361 includes 362 and 369.
e/ 371 includes 372.

MOZAMBIQUE

Supplier of information:
Direcçao Nacional de Estatística, Maputo.

Basic source of data:
Annual inquiries undertaken by government agencies: for peeling and whitening of rice, the Cereals Institute of Mozambique and, for other industrial activities and saltern operations, the Direcçao Nacional de Estatística, Maputo.

Major deviations from ISIC (Revision 2):
The following activities are not included in manufacturing: poultry slaughtering, copra drying, tailoring, dressmaking, upholstering, manufacture of underclothes and embroidering.

Reference period (if not calendar year):

Scope:
All registered establishments.

Method of enumeration:
Questionnaires are distributed by mail.

Adjusted for non-response:
Yes.

Concepts and definitions of variables:
Number of establishments refers to those in operation on 31 December of the reference year.
Number of persons engaged is as of 31 December of the reference year.

Related national publications:
Estatistica Industriais (annual), published by the Direcçao Nacional de Estatística, Maputo.

Mozambique

ISIC Revision 2	Number of establishments					Number of employees					Wages and salaries paid to employees				
		(numbers)					(numbers)					(million METICAIS)			
ISIC Industry	Note	1993	1994	1995	1996	Note	1993	1994	1995	1996	Note	1993	1994	1995	1996
311/2 Food products		100	104	125	126		20780	18598	17003	12763		25313	33535	14214	21926
3111 Slaughtering, preparing & preserving meat		1	1	1	-		-	-	-	-		-	-	-	-
3112 Dairy products		2	2	2	1		521	492	525	153		600	918	876	736
3113 Canning, preserving of fruits & vegetables		3	4	4	4		66	72	105	...		93	115	240	...
3114 Canning, preserving and processing of fish		21	19	17	16		534	470	439	406		3177	3563	2953	4099
3115 Vegetable and animal oils and fats		5	6	5	5		1472	1519	1339	1162		2367	2470	1015	1915
3116 Grain mill products		18	21	36	44		2053	2124	2323	1584		2522	6637	4516	2152
3117 Bakery products		25	32	39	39		672	909	1172	272		1515	2192	1146	2512
3118 Sugar factories and refineries		1	2	2	2		9179	8906	10084	3843		8201	12549	2212	3570
3119 Cocoa, chocolate and sugar confectionery		7	5	5	5		-	26	48	...		-	30	230	...
3121 Other food products		16	10	10	9		6283	4080	968	5042		6838	5061	...	4668
3122 Prepared animal feeds		1	2	4	1		-	-	...	301		-	-	1026	2274
313 Beverages		16	16	17	19		1101	1398	1853	1442		1906	5369	11667	8848
3131 Distilling, rectifying and blending spirits		6	5	6	8		59	64	57	...		85	181	368	...
3132 Wine industries		-	1	1	1		-	-	54	-		-	-	4157	-
3133 Malt liquors and malt		3	3	3	3		886	956	1420	1442		1511	4203	5723	1848
3134 Soft drinks and carbonated waters		7	7	7	7		156	344	322	...		310	984	1419	...
314 Tobacco		3	2	1	3		274	275	389	232		349	815	1689	2931
321 Textiles		20	16	14	13		7191	5947	4969	4748		8875	11063	3185	3611
3211 Spinning, weaving and finishing textiles		9	8	8	8		580	398	337	304		693	544	931	1621
3212 Made-up textile goods excl. wearing apparel		7	5	3	3		178	178	162	155		190	314	238	1949
3213 Knitting mills		4	3	3	2		79	75	63	-		116	127	133	-
3214 Carpets and rugs		...	...	...	...		...	...	...	...		...	...	...	...
3215 Cordage, rope and twine		...	...	...	...		...	...	...	...		...	...	...	...
3219 Other textiles		...	...	...	...		...	...	...	...		...	...	...	...
322 Wearing apparel, except footwear		21	17	12	14		2769	1818	1489	1260		2785	2561	2604	1120
323 Leather and fur products		1	3	3	3		46	59	71	...		62	145	460	...
3231 Tanneries and leather finishing		-	1	1	1		-	-	-	-		-	-	-	-
3232 Fur dressing and dyeing industries		-	-	-	-		-	-	-	-		-	-	-	-
3233 Leather prods. excl. wearing apparel		1	2	2	2		46	59	71	...		62	145	460	...
324 Footwear, except rubber or plastic		5	6	5	6		502	391	444	445		573	338	333	1362
331 Wood products, except furniture		17	18	16	16		1890	2208	2480	2910		2696	3551	3099	3720
3311 Sawmills, planing and other wood mills		17	18	16	16		1890	2208	2480	2910		2696	3551	3099	3720
3312 Wooden and cane containers		-	-	-	-		-	-	-	-		-	-	-	-
3319 Other wood and cork products		-	-	-	-		-	-	-	-		-	-	-	-
332 Furniture and fixtures, excl. metal		33	32	41	40		750	790	1683	3021		600	1063	802	1722
341 Paper and products		4	4	4	3		584	514	504	383		1271	1848	1827	1945
3411 Pulp, paper and paperboard articles		3	3	3	2		520	448	423	383		1135	1631	1493	1945
3412 Containers of paper and paperboard		1	1	1	1		64	66	81	...		136	217	334	...
3419 Other pulp, paper and paperboard articles		-	-	-	-		-	-	-	-		-	-	-	-
342 Printing and publishing		30	28	27	26		1945	2027	1828	1469		3855	6824	6548	3189
351 Industrial chemicals		5	5	5	5		285	281	293	160		1480	1516	1770	1249
3511 Basic chemicals excl. fertilizers		4	4	4	4		...	...	...	...		...	...	...	...
3512 Fertilizers and pesticides		1	1	1	1		...	...	...	...		...	...	...	...
3513 Synthetic resins and plastic materials		-	-	-	-		...	...	...	...		...	...	...	...
352 Other chemicals		23	24	23	22		1751	1738	1613	1281		3022	4632	2871	3859
3521 Paints, varnishes and lacquers		5	6	6	5		180	184	203	...		442	556	651	...
3522 Drugs and medicines		1	1	1	1		304	313	336	283		814	1365	609	2222
3523 Soap, cleaning preps., perfumes, cosmetics		13	12	11	13		1176	1109	998	998		1608	2452	1348	1637
3529 Other chemical products		4	5	5	4		91	132	76	...		159	260	263	...
353 Petroleum refineries		2	3	1	1		460	745	458	469		2336	8920	4072	7400

354	Misc. petroleum and coal products	...	...	...	...	...	...	...	...	...	...	...	...
355	Rubber products	8	6	6	5	870	805	770	674	3905	5912	2901	5694
3551	Tyres and tubes	6	5	5	5	...	...	...	...	...	...	...	...
3559	Other rubber products	2	1	1	...	...	...	...	...	...	...	...	...
356	Plastic products	10	9	9	8	860	726	385	362	1670	2047	632	2169
361	Pottery, china, earthenware	...	...	...	...	...	...	...	...	...	...	...	...
362	Glass and products	1	1	1	1	854	680	660	...	2723	2675	4476	...
369	Other non-metallic mineral products	12	10	10	11	1345	1208	1202	1251	3715	7229	4965	5509
3691	Structural clay products	5	3	4	4	72	80	225	255	58	97	225	332
3692	Cement, lime and plaster	3	3	3	3	994	852	721	694	3332	6643	4395	4633
3699	Other non-metallic mineral products	4	4	3	4	279	276	256	302	325	489	345	542
371	Iron and steel	4	5	4	4	1350	1026	996	820	2727	3865	1301	2267
372	Non-ferrous metals	2	3	2	1	...	36	29	...	...	48	242	...
381	Fabricated metal products	31	34	34	33	2245	2204	1827	1052	4033	6154	3298	3603
3811	Cutlery, hand tools and general hardware	8	10	9	10	575	511	34	...	907	1069	1161	...
3812	Furniture and fixtures primarily of metal	4	4	4	4	703	684	724	514	1507	2234	1075	1613
3813	Structural metal products	3	4	5	5	263	214	...	...	446	960	...	...
3819	Other fabricated metal products	16	16	16	14	704	795	1069	538	1174	1890	1062	1990
382	Non-electrical machinery	7	7	7	8	801	754	632	142	1139	2222	1746	1478
3821	Engines and turbines	-	-	-	-	-	-	-	-	-	-	-	-
3822	Agricultural machinery and equipment	...	...	...	...	-	-	-	-	-	-	-	-
3823	Metal and wood working machinery	-	-	-	-	-	-	-	-	-	-	-	-
3824	Other special industrial machinery	1	1	1	1	242	148	232	...	337	386	760	...
3825	Office, computing and accounting machinery	1	1	1	1	32	28	35	...	81	121	336	...
3829	Other non-electrical machinery & equipment	6	6	6	7	527	578	365	142	721	1715	650	1478
383	Electrical machinery	11	10	11	10	780	562	585	465	2235	1999	1082	2743
3831	Electrical industrial machinery	3	2	3	3	...	...	...	...	...	...	...	...
3832	Radio, television and communication equipm.	-	-	-	-	...	...	...	...	...	...	...	...
3833	Electrical appliances and housewares	4	4	4	4	...	...	36	...	...	...	657	...
3839	Other electrical apparatus and supplies	4	4	4	3	116	101	97	...	217	272	397	...
384	Transport equipment	11	10	11	10	1138	1049	446	911	2483	5284	1616	3694
3841	Shipbuilding and repairing	2	2	2	1	116	277	216	207	198	2053	706	2187
3842	Railroad equipment	1	1	1	1	698	533	...	587	1871	2470	...	1184
3843	Motor vehicles	6	5	7	7	206	112	107	-	248	332	491	-
3844	Motorcycles and bicycles	2	2	1	1	118	127	123	117	167	429	419	323
3845	Aircraft	-	-	-	-	-	-	-	-	-	-	-	-
3849	Other transport equipment	-	-	-	-	-	-	-	-	-	-	-	-
385	Professional and scientific equipment	1	1	1	1	88	86	70	...	190	302	477	...
3851	Prof. and scientific equipment n.e.c.	-	-	-	-	-	-	-	-	-	-	-	-
3852	Photographic and optical goods	-	-	-	-	-	-	-	-	-	-	-	-
3853	Watches and clocks	1	1	1	1	88	86	70	...	190	302	477	...
390	Other manufacturing industries	1	1	1	1	75	144	66	...	93	248	242	...
3901	Jewellery and related articles	-	1	-	-	-	74	-	-	-	139	-	-
3902	Musical instruments	-	-	-	-	-	-	-	-	-	-	-	-
3903	Sporting and athletic goods	-	-	-	-	-	-	-	-	-	-	-	-
3909	Manufacturing industries, n.e.c.	1	1	1	1	75	70	66	...	93	109	242	...
3	Total manufacturing	379	375	391	390	50734	46069	42745	36260	80036	120165	78119	90039

Mozambique

ISIC Revision 2	Output					Value added					Gross fixed capital formation		
		(million METICAIS)					(million METICAIS)					(million METICAIS)	
ISIC Industry	Note	1993	1994	1995	1996	Note	1993	1994	1995	1996	Note	1995	1996
311/2 Food products		175913	267071	549151	744732		...	...	...	...		...	...
313 Beverages		79179	155592	421195	858158		...	...	...	...		...	...
314 Tobacco		11628	14041	32661	50958		...	...	...	...		...	...
321 Textiles		66774	74413	74052	105808		...	...	...	...		...	...
322 Wearing apparel, except footwear		13801	9068	11029	10303		...	...	...	...		...	...
323 Leather and fur products		346	1079	1405	1910		...	...	...	...		...	...
324 Footwear, except rubber or plastic		2180	2829	1465	1518		...	...	...	...		...	...
331 Wood products, except furniture		5457	5710	14236	12370		...	...	...	...		...	...
332 Furniture and fixtures, excl. metal		4861	7359	14967	15912		...	...	...	...		...	...
341 Paper and products		17598	18802	20937	29119		...	...	...	...		...	...
342 Printing and publishing		19043	30907	52588	68947		...	...	...	...		...	...
351 Industrial chemicals		10343	19740	30305	43044		...	...	...	...		...	...
352 Other chemicals		66512	81664	121775	163029		...	...	...	...		...	...
353 Petroleum refineries		4047	3978	5347	6863		...	...	...	...		...	...
354 Misc. petroleum and coal products		...	...	...	...		...	...	...	...		...	...
355 Rubber products		11667	15609	35765	72466		...	...	...	...		...	...
356 Plastic products		6783	7818	14363	46337		...	...	...	...		...	...
361 Pottery, china, earthenware		12	17	49	71		...	...	...	...		...	...
362 Glass and products		11112	19463	17973	8233		...	...	...	...		...	...
369 Other non-metallic mineral products		56498	86057	266096	368257		...	...	...	...		...	...
371 Iron and steel		26430	26614	54400	22316		...	...	...	...		...	...
372 Non-ferrous metals		6345	9673	10669	12731		...	...	...	...		...	...
381 Fabricated metal products		22081	25368	44312	61679		...	...	...	...		...	...
382 Non-electrical machinery		2532	3686	6009	6374		...	...	...	...		...	...
383 Electrical machinery		13305	13517	13290	20138		...	...	...	...		...	...
384 Transport equipment		7999	15810	19669	40002		...	...	...	...		...	...
385 Professional and scientific equipment		24	24	35	44		...	...	...	...		...	...
390 Other manufacturing industries		447	593	1187	1794		...	...	...	...		...	...
3 Total manufacturing		642917	916502	1870695	2773118		...	...	...	...		...	...

MYANMAR

Supplier of information:
Ministry of National Planning and Economic Development, Central Statistical Organization, Yangon.

Basic source of data:
Not reported.

Major deviations from ISIC (Revision 2):
None reported.

Reference period (if not calendar year):

Scope:
Not reported.

Method of enumeration:
Not reported.

Adjusted for non-response:
Not reported.

Concepts and definitions of variables:
No deviations from the standard UN concepts and definitions are reported.

Related national publications:

Myanmar

ISIC Revision 2	Number of establishments					Number of employees					Wages and salaries paid to employees				
		(numbers)					(numbers)					(million KYATS)			
ISIC Industry	Note	1993	1994	1995	1996	Note	1993	1994	1995	1996	Note	1993	1994	1995	1996
311/2 Food products		...	...	...	...		...	...	...	...		...	...	...	...
3111 Slaughtering, preparing & preserving meat		...	...	...	...		...	...	...	...		...	...	...	...
3112 Dairy products		...	...	...	...		...	...	...	...		...	...	...	...
3113 Canning, preserving of fruits & vegetables		...	...	...	...		...	...	...	...		...	...	...	...
3114 Canning, preserving and processing of fish		...	...	...	...		...	...	...	...		...	...	...	...
3115 Vegetable and animal oils and fats		...	...	...	...		...	...	...	...		...	...	...	...
3116 Grain mill products		...	...	6	6		...	...	927	912		...	...	1.4	1.5
3117 Bakery products		...	...	7	7		...	...	77	78		...	...	8.8	8.7
3118 Sugar factories and refineries		7	-	...	...		2591	-	...	...		38.3	-	...	...
3119 Cocoa, chocolate and sugar confectionery		...	...	...	...		...	...	...	...		...	...	...	...
3121 Other food products		7	4	2	2		1220	1330	326	294		18.1	17.5	4.2	3.6
3122 Prepared animal feeds		...	...	...	...		...	...	...	...		...	...	...	...
313 Beverages		...	...	...	...		...	...	...	...		...	...	...	...
3131 Distilling, rectifying and blending spirits		...	...	4	4		...	...	392	370		...	...	13.4	15.4
3132 Wine industries		4a/	4a/	...	...		729a/	735a/	...	...		10.8a/	11.6a/	...	...
3133 Malt liquors and malt		...a/	...a/	1	1		...a/	...a/	343	325		...a/	...a/	1.3	3.2
3134 Soft drinks and carbonated waters		11	10	9	9		998	1108	1108	1114		14.8	15.8	21.3	20.9
314 Tobacco		3	3	4	4		1675	1541	1541	1829		24.8	13.3	19.4	36.5
321 Textiles		...	...	...	...		...	...	...	...		...	...	...	...
3211 Spinning, weaving and finishing textiles		23	17	17	17		13814	13125	13335	11505		175.6	190.0	14.9	14.0
3212 Made-up textile goods excl. wearing apparel		4	4	3	3		1964	1717	1625	1787		28.7	21.7	23.5	27.9
3213 Knitting mills		1	1	1	1		735	604	504	315		7.4	...	...	...
3214 Carpets and rugs		...	...	...	...		...	...	...	...		...	...	...	...
3215 Cordage, rope and twine		...	...	...	...		...	...	...	...		...	...	...	...
3219 Other textiles		1	1	1	1		804	448	411	448		17.1	8.4	10.6	11.1
322 Wearing apparel, except footwear		...	...	...	...		...	...	...	...		...	...	...	...
323 Leather and fur products		3	2	2	2		357	346	350	350		4.6	4.2	3.9	4.4
3231 Tanneries and leather finishing		...	...	...	...		...	...	...	...		...	...	...	...
3232 Fur dressing and dyeing industries		...	...	...	...		...	...	...	...		...	...	...	...
3233 Leather prods. excl. wearing apparel		...	...	...	...		...	...	...	...		...	...	...	...
324 Footwear, except rubber or plastic		2	2	2	2		1010	1045	1054	1128		13.7	11.0	7.7	9.1
331 Wood products, except furniture		97	100	111	111		14397	14660	16253	16174		162.4	148.9	199.4	210.1
3311 Sawmills, planing and other wood mills		91	93	102	102		12391	12654	13520	13493		148.5	125.2	171.9	181.8
3312 Wooden and cane containers		1	1	2	2		41	41	85	43		0.3	0.3	1.9	1.0
3319 Other wood and cork products		5	5	7	7		1965	1965	2648	2638		13.7	23.4	25.7	27.3
332 Furniture and fixtures, excl. metal		6	7	7	7		1623	1623	1623	1623		26.0	19.9	23.2	25.0
341 Paper and products		...	...	...	...		...	...	...	...		...	...	...	...
3411 Pulp, paper and paperboard articles		5	4	4	4		2505	2534	2673	2792		34.9	45.9	65.9	53.1
3412 Containers of paper and paperboard		...	...	1	1		...	...	318	238		...	...	4.4	4.6
3419 Other pulp, paper and paperboard articles		...	...	...	...		...	...	...	...		...	...	...	...
342 Printing and publishing		...	15	14	14		...	639	830	770		...	24.3	24.1	23.1
351 Industrial chemicals		...	...	...	...		...	...	...	...		...	...	...	...
3511 Basic chemicals excl. fertilizers		2	2	2	2		149	145	137	139		2.4	2.7	2.5	2.7
3512 Fertilizers and pesticides		3	3	3	3		1979	3156	2250	2164		...	...	20.2	27.7
3513 Synthetic resins and plastic materials		...	...	...	...		...	...	...	...		...	...	...	...
352 Other chemicals		10	10	11	10		3576	3587	3954	3844		48.2	58.5	71.2	75.7
3521 Paints, varnishes and lacquers		2	2	2	1		540	543	532	316		7.5	7.6	9.0	8.2
3522 Drugs and medicines		2	2	3	3		1728	1748	1885	2048		23.1	28.4	33.2	39.5
3523 Soap, cleaning preps., perfumes, cosmetics		5	5	5	5		1258	1248	1317	1309		16.7	21.5	23.4	24.7
3529 Other chemical products		1	1	1	1		50	48	220	171		0.8	1.0	5.6	3.4
353 Petroleum refineries		3	3	3	3		4434	3804	4471	4479		...	...	57.6	58.0

354 Misc. petroleum and coal products	...	...	...	...	...	...	...	...	...	...	...	...
355 Rubber products	3	2	2	2	1583	1430	1423	1522	16.8	16.2	15.5	16.0
3551 Tyres and tubes	1	1	1	1	...	...	1138	1209	...	...	12.5	13.0
3559 Other rubber products	2	1	1	1	...	...	285	313	...	...	3.0	3.0
356 Plastic products	3	3	5	5	...	...	417	416	4.5	6.1	7.6	9.2
361 Pottery, china, earthenware	...	...	2	2	...	...	596	588	...	...	7.8	8.7
362 Glass and products	2	2	2	2	1459	1465	1464	1571	14.5	16.0	16.9	24.9
369 Other non-metallic mineral products	...	...	12	12	...	...	6643	6918	...	...	90.6	97.6
3691 Structural clay products	4	4	4	4	1063	1055	1057	1149	12.0	13.2	16.0	18.5
3692 Cement, lime and plaster	3	3	4	4	4273	4291	4465	4627	30.9	37.9	58.9	60.0
3699 Other non-metallic mineral products	...	...	4	4	...	...	1121	1142	...	...	15.7	19.2
371 Iron and steel	2	2	2	2	2002	1465	1573	1473	24.4	25.6	23.7	23.9
372 Non-ferrous metals	15	...	...	...	12578	...	...	...	195.5	...	...	...
381 Fabricated metal products	4	4	4	4	1271	1268	1261	1212	13.3	13.7	13.4	14.7
3811 Cutlery, hand tools and general hardware	...	...	...	...	...	...	...	...	...	...	...	...
3812 Furniture and fixtures primarily of metal	...	...	...	...	...	...	...	...	...	...	...	...
3813 Structural metal products	...	...	...	...	...	...	...	...	...	...	...	...
3819 Other fabricated metal products	...	...	...	...	...	...	...	...	...	...	...	...
382 Non-electrical machinery	...	...	...	...	...	...	...	...	...	...	...	...
3821 Engines and turbines	...	...	...	...	...	...	...	...	...	...	...	...
3822 Agricultural machinery and equipment	...	...	...	...	...	...	...	...	...	...	...	...
3823 Metal and wood working machinery	...	...	...	...	...	...	...	...	...	...	...	...
3824 Other special industrial machinery	...	...	...	...	...	...	...	...	...	...	...	...
3825 Office, computing and accounting machinery	...	...	...	...	...	...	...	...	...	...	...	...
3829 Other non-electrical machinery & equipment	...	...	...	...	...	...	...	...	...	...	...	...
383 Electrical machinery	12	12	12	12	...	...	...	...	...	...	...	...
3831 Electrical industrial machinery	9	9	9	9	1520	1299	1186	1195	17.8	16.2	15.3	15.0
3832 Radio, television and communication equipm.	1	1	1	1	...	...	...	...	...	...	...	...
3833 Electrical appliances and housewares	1	1	1	1	714	677	655	655	9.8	9.5	13.0	13.0
3839 Other electrical apparatus and supplies	1	1	1	1	399	372	318	313	4.6	4.7	3.5	3.4
384 Transport equipment	...	...	...	...	...	...	...	...	...	...	...	...
3841 Shipbuilding and repairing	...	...	...	...	...	...	...	...	...	...	...	...
3842 Railroad equipment	...	...	...	...	...	...	...	...	...	...	...	...
3843 Motor vehicles	2	2	2	2	2529	2226	1726	1590	30.6	28.1	13.7	13.6
3844 Motorcycles and bicycles	1	1	1	1	...	...	...	...	...	...	...	...
3845 Aircraft	...	...	...	...	...	...	...	...	...	...	...	...
3849 Other transport equipment	...	...	...	...	...	...	...	...	...	...	...	...
385 Professional and scientific equipment	...	...	...	...	...	...	...	...	...	...	...	...
3851 Prof. and scientific equipment n.e.c.	...	...	...	...	...	...	...	...	...	...	...	...
3852 Photographic and optical goods	...	...	...	...	...	...	...	...	...	...	...	...
3853 Watches and clocks	...	...	...	...	...	...	...	...	...	...	...	...
390 Other manufacturing industries	2	2	2	2	3446	3386	3300	3660	41.0	43.1	45.7	42.1
3901 Jewellery and related articles	...	...	...	...	...	...	...	...	...	...	...	...
3902 Musical instruments	...	...	...	...	...	...	...	...	...	...	...	...
3903 Sporting and athletic goods	...	...	...	...	...	...	...	...	...	...	...	...
3909 Manufacturing industries, n.e.c.	...	...	...	...	...	...	...	...	...	...	...	...
3 Total manufacturing	...	...	...	...	...	...	...	...	...	...	...	...

a/ 3132 includes 3133.

Myanmar

ISIC	Industry	Note	Output in producers' prices (million KYATS) 1993	1994	1995	1996	Note	Value added (million KYATS) 1993	1994	1995	1996	Note	Gross fixed capital formation (million KYATS) 1995	1996
311/2	Food products		...	...	...	...		...	...	...	...		...	...
3111	Slaughtering, preparing & preserving meat		...	...	...	...		...	...	...	...		...	...
3112	Dairy products		...	...	...	...		...	...	...	...		...	...
3113	Canning, preserving of fruits & vegetables		2.4	...	...	...		4.1	...	...	...		...	...
3114	Canning, preserving and processing of fish		...	...	...	...		...	...	...	...		...	...
3115	Vegetable and animal oils and fats		...	...	...	...		...	...	...	...		...	...
3116	Grain mill products		...	...	173.7a/	243.1a/		...	...	...	...		28.1	27.3
3117	Bakery products		...	...	...a/	...a/		...	...	...	...		35.0	35.2
3118	Sugar factories and refineries		714.3	-	...	...		535.0	-	...	...		...	...
3119	Cocoa, chocolate and sugar confectionery		...	...	...	...		...	...	...	...		...	...
3121	Other food products		199.9	233.0	58.4	197.5		244.8	257.0	...	...		246.8	250.1
3122	Prepared animal feeds		...	...	...	...		...	...	...	...		...	...
313	Beverages		...	...	...	...		...	...	...	...		...	...
3131	Distilling, rectifying and blending spirits		...	...	1206.5	1382.9		...	...	...	...		338.1	335.8
3132	Wine industries		616.2b/	835.0b/	...	...		883.5b/	1238.0b/	...	...		...	...
3133	Malt liquors and malt		...b/	...b/	241.2	373.7		...b/	...b/	...	...		250.7	444.7
3134	Soft drinks and carbonated waters		146.9	210.0	266.7	332.5		196.1	283.0	...	...		109.8	201.8
314	Tobacco		175.7	402.0	441.9	1105.8		241.6	550.0	...	...		93.3	149.6
321	Textiles		...	...	...	...		...	...	...	...		...	...
3211	Spinning, weaving and finishing textiles		1083.9	1417.0	2152.2	1994.6		1032.9	1140.0	1065.2	1141.1		77.3	90.2
3212	Made-up textile goods excl. wearing apparel		126.8	100.0	199.3	263.2		102.1	66.0	150.5	187.8		...	131.2
3213	Knitting mills		22.5	...	...	...		22.5	...	-	-		...	...
3214	Carpets and rugs		...	...	...	...		...	...	...	...		...	...
3215	Cordage, rope and twine		...	...	...	...		...	...	...	...		...	...
3219	Other textiles		211.8	...	...	...		237.6	124.0	623.9	654.8		49.8	73.1
322	Wearing apparel, except footwear		...	...	...	...		...	...	...	...		...	...
323	Leather and fur products		28.0	45.0	55.1	59.3		13.0	26.0	12.7	13.3		69.5	75.0
3231	Tanneries and leather finishing		...	...	...	...		...	...	...	...		...	...
3232	Fur dressing and dyeing industries		...	...	...	...		...	...	...	...		...	...
3233	Leather prods. excl. wearing apparel		...	...	...	...		...	...	...	...		...	...
324	Footwear, except rubber or plastic		57.0	69.0	91.2	93.9		21.0	31.0	22.2	31.7		64.1	65.3
331	Wood products, except furniture		177.6	336.0	354.2	318.3		97.6	149.0	957.0	1173.4		145.1	159.2
3311	Sawmills, planing and other wood mills		141.7	211.0	205.7	191.5		83.0	118.0	926.2	1148.1		17.5	36.0
3312	Wooden and cane containers		1.5	1.0	11.0	3.8		0.5	-	5.6	2.6		15.5	8.6
3319	Other wood and cork products		34.4	124.0	137.5	123.0		14.1	31.0	25.2	22.6		112.1	114.6
332	Furniture and fixtures, excl. metal		72.0	95.0	112.4	108.7		34.0	40.0	3.8	10.0		6.2	6.2
341	Paper and products		...	...	...	...		...	...	...	...		...	...
3411	Pulp, paper and paperboard articles		408.3	545.0	713.5	800.8		303.3	169.0	145.9	129.3		1426.2	1499.6
3412	Containers of paper and paperboard		...	...	96.9	95.7		...	...	27.5	36.6		85.6	89.8
3419	Other pulp, paper and paperboard articles		...	...	...	...		...	...	...	...		...	...
342	Printing and publishing		...	85.0	83.7	112.0		...	...	...	...		367.0	373.4
351	Industrial chemicals		...	...	...	...		...	...	...	...		...	...
3511	Basic chemicals excl. fertilizers		16.4	17.0	17.1	22.0		10.1	4.0	4.5	4.3		55.5	59.6
3512	Fertilizers and pesticides		300.9	589.7	571.1	400.5		...	...	...	...		1090.0	998.7
3513	Synthetic resins and plastic materials		...	...	...	...		...	...	...	...		...	...
352	Other chemicals		538.0	1016.0	1505.7	1523.6		191.0	567.0	663.7	612.4		629.9	705.1
3521	Paints, varnishes and lacquers		60.6	47.0	90.6	72.9		22.9	8.0	8.8	13.0		49.3	50.4
3522	Drugs and medicines		154.1	185.0	280.5	313.0		86.3	105.0	152.4	189.3		303.8	391.7
3523	Soap, cleaning preps., perfumes, cosmetics		319.0	779.0	993.6	1038.6		78.8	451.0	462.1	383.1		200.4	223.2
3529	Other chemical products		4.3	5.0	141.0	99.2		3.0	3.0	40.4	27.0		76.4	39.7
353	Petroleum refineries		1832.7	3.1	2021.0	3269.3		...	...	...	...		1187.9	1128.9

354 Misc. petroleum and coal products		...	...	...	...		...	...	...	...		...	...
355 Rubber products		43.6	91.3	460.4	577.1		22.3	35.0	193.9	200.7		...	...
3551 Tyres and tubes		...	...	425.5	537.4		...	...	165.3	167.6		...	...
3559 Other rubber products		...	...	34.9	39.7		...	...	28.6	33.1		29.9	28.5
356 Plastic products		25.6	74.0	191.6	167.9		13.1	5.0	55.2	76.8		80.8	106.9
361 Pottery, china, earthenware		...	...	28.4	29.4		...	...	23.1	27.4		...	...
362 Glass and products		159.0	275.0	293.2	396.4		131.0	197.0	199.2	234.4		50.5	16.8
369 Other non-metallic mineral products		...	...	866.4	865.1		...	...	799.8	815.0		36.6	45.8
3691 Structural clay products		58.0	58.0	70.1	71.0		54.0	41.0	59.1	67.3		7.8	5.8
3692 Cement, lime and plaster		466.0	578.0	685.9	657.6		411.0	574.0	681.0	667.3		22.6	26.9
3699 Other non-metallic mineral products		...	...	110.3	136.5		...	...	59.7	80.3		6.2	13.1
371 Iron and steel		391.3	587.0	983.3	947.5		322.3	529.0	396.3	593.9		446.2	411.7
372 Non-ferrous metals		318.6	616.0	...	...		370.0	485.0	...	...		...	...
381 Fabricated metal products		35.9	39.7	38.8	48.3		11.3	13.4	10.0	13.9		...	...
3811 Cutlery, hand tools and general hardware		...	...	...	...		...	...	...	...		...	...
3812 Furniture and fixtures primarily of metal		...	...	...	...		...	...	...	...		...	...
3813 Structural metal products		...	...	...	...		...	...	...	...		...	...
3819 Other fabricated metal products		...	...	...	...		...	...	...	...		...	...
382 Non-electrical machinery		...	...	...	...		...	...	...	...		...	...
3821 Engines and turbines		...	...	...	...		...	...	...	...		...	...
3822 Agricultural machinery and equipment		...	...	...	...		...	...	...	...		...	...
3823 Metal and wood working machinery		...	...	...	...		...	...	...	...		...	...
3824 Other special industrial machinery		...	...	...	...		...	...	...	...		...	...
3825 Office, computing and accounting machinery		...	...	...	...		...	...	...	...		...	...
3829 Other non-electrical machinery & equipment		...	...	...	...		...	...	...	...		...	...
383 Electrical machinery		...	...	...	...		...	...	...	...		...	...
3831 Electrical industrial machinery		65.0	24.7	51.0	64.3		24.9	13.0	24.9	32.0		...	...
3832 Radio, television and communication equipm.		0.2	0.3	...	...		0.1	0.2	...	...		...	...
3833 Electrical appliances and housewares		24.6	6.3	15.1	34.9		10.2	2.2	6.5	14.2		...	...
3839 Other electrical apparatus and supplies		1.8	10.7	4.6	5.0		0.6	-	2.5	3.0		...	...
384 Transport equipment		...	...	...	...		...	...	...	...		...	...
3841 Shipbuilding and repairing		...	...	...	...		...	...	...	...		...	...
3842 Railroad equipment		...	...	...	...		...	...	...	...		...	...
3843 Motor vehicles		283.6	273.8	310.9	242.5		77.8	61.0	118.9	103.8		...	...
3844 Motorcycles and bicycles		...	...	...	...		...	...	...	...		...	...
3845 Aircraft		...	...	...	...		...	...	...	...		...	...
3849 Other transport equipment		...	...	...	...		...	...	...	...		...	...
385 Professional and scientific equipment		...	...	...	...		...	...	...	...		...	...
3851 Prof. and scientific equipment n.e.c.		...	...	...	...		...	...	...	...		...	...
3852 Photographic and optical goods		...	...	...	...		...	...	...	...		...	...
3853 Watches and clocks		...	...	...	...		...	...	...	...		...	...
390 Other manufacturing industries		621.8	540.0	332.0	295.3		262.9	204.8	181.0	125.1		...	...
3901 Jewellery and related articles		...	...	...	...		...	...	...	...		...	...
3902 Musical instruments		...	...	...	...		...	...	...	...		...	...
3903 Sporting and athletic goods		...	...	...	...		...	...	...	...		...	...
3909 Manufacturing industries, n.e.c.		...	...	...	...		...	...	...	...		...	...
3 Total manufacturing		...	...	...	...		...	...	...	...		...	...

a/ 3116 includes 3117.
b/ 3132 includes 3133.

Myanmar

ISIC Revision 2		Index numbers of industrial production											
		(1990=100)											
ISIC Industry	Note	1985	1986	1987	1988	1989	1990	1991	1992	1993	1994	1995	1996
311/2 Food products		...	...	...	...	99	100	94	106	118	123	129	133
313 Beverages		...	...	...	...	...	...	...	...	...	...	...	...
314 Tobacco		358	161	56	97	81	100	70	41	44	45	77	176
321 Textiles	a/	...	...	...	...	93	100	99	129	116	161	176	175
322 Wearing apparel, except footwear	a/	...	...	...	...	...	...	...	...	...	...	...	...
323 Leather and fur products	a/	...	...	...	...	...	...	...	...	...	...	...	...
324 Footwear, except rubber or plastic	a/	...	...	...	...	...	...	...	...	...	...	...	...
331 Wood products, except furniture		209	193	133	96	127	100	81	95	104	104	104	...
332 Furniture and fixtures, excl. metal		...	...	...	...	...	...	...	...	...	...	...	...
341 Paper and products		...	...	...	...	...	...	...	...	...	...	...	...
342 Printing and publishing		193	297	116	104	130	100	104	106	120	124	185	233
351 Industrial chemicals		...	...	...	...	...	...	...	...	...	...	...	...
352 Other chemicals		...	...	...	...	...	...	...	...	...	...	...	...
353 Petroleum refineries		157	129	110	93	97	100	98	98	97	128	182	173
354 Misc. petroleum and coal products		...	...	...	...	...	...	...	...	...	...	...	...
355 Rubber products		114	114	100	108	97	100	101	101	101	...	...	...
356 Plastic products		...	...	...	...	...	...	...	...	...	...	...	...
361 Pottery, china, earthenware		...	...	...	...	...	...	...	...	...	...	...	...
362 Glass and products		...	...	...	...	...	...	...	...	...	...	...	...
369 Other non-metallic mineral products	b/	...	...	...	...	78	100	98	103	114	104	107	113
371 Iron and steel	b/	...	...	...	...	...	...	...	...	...	...	...	...
372 Non-ferrous metals	b/	...	...	...	...	...	...	...	...	...	...	...	...
381 Fabricated metal products		...	...	...	...	...	...	...	...	...	...	...	...
382 Non-electrical machinery		...	...	...	...	...	...	...	...	...	...	...	...
383 Electrical machinery		...	...	...	...	88	100	154	116	41	51	80	97
384 Transport equipment		...	...	...	...	120	100	77	93	93	140	223	264
385 Professional and scientific equipment		...	...	...	...	...	...	...	...	...	...	...	...
390 Other manufacturing industries		...	...	...	...	...	...	...	...	...	...	...	...
3 Total manufacturing		...	...	...	...	...	...	...	...	...	...	...	...

a/ 321 includes 322, 323 and 324.
b/ 369 includes 371 and 372.

NEPAL

Supplier of information:
Central Bureau of Statistics, National Planning Commission, Kathmandu.

Basic source of data:
Census of Manufacturing Establishments.

Major deviations from ISIC (Revision 3):
None reported.

Reference period (if not calendar year):
Fiscal year beginning 15 July of the year indicated.

Scope:
Establishments with 10 or more persons engaged.

Method of enumeration:
The inquiry is carried out through questionnaires, with follow-up telephone calls and site visits as required. The enumeration of establishments is based on the 1991/1992 Census of Manufacturing Establishments.

Adjusted for non-response:
Yes.

Concepts and definitions of variables:
Number of employees is as of 15 January of the reference year. It includes workers paid through labor contractors.
Wages and salaries is compensation of employees.
Output includes gross revenues from goods shipped in the same condition as received.
... denotes data suppressed because of confidentiality rules (1996).

Related national publications:
Census of Manufacturing Establishments 1996-1997, published by the Central Bureau of Statistics, Kathmandu.

Nepal

ISIC Revision 3	Number of establishments					Number of employees					Wages and salaries paid to employees				
		(numbers)					(numbers)					(thousand RUPEES)			
ISIC Industry	Note	1993	1994	1995	1996	Note	1993	1994	1995	1996	Note	1993	1994	1995	1996
151 Processed meat,fish,fruit,vegetables,fats		...	...	...	51		...	...	...	...		...	...	...	...
1511 Processing/preserving of meat		...	...	...	2		...	...	...	...		...	...	...	...
1512 Processing/preserving of fish		...	...	...	-		...	...	...	-		...	...	...	-
1513 Processing/preserving of fruit & vegetables		...	...	...	2		...	...	...	...		...	...	...	...
1514 Vegetable and animal oils and fats		...	...	...	47		...	...	...	1767		...	...	...	51133
1520 Dairy products		...	...	...	26		...	...	...	1760		...	...	...	64934
153 Grain mill products; starches; animal feeds		...	...	...	328		...	...	...	...		...	...	...	...
1531 Grain mill products		...	...	...	286		...	...	...	4329		...	...	...	82373
1532 Starches and starch products		...	...	...	2		...	...	...	...		...	...	...	...
1533 Prepared animal feeds		...	...	...	40		...	...	...	663		...	...	...	19487
154 Other food products		...	...	...	229		...	...	...	11722		...	...	...	278851
1541 Bakery products		...	...	...	113		...	...	...	2619		...	...	...	59998
1542 Sugar		...	...	...	30		...	...	...	6343		...	...	...	162415
1543 Cocoa, chocolate and sugar confectionery		...	...	...	26		...	...	...	363		...	...	...	6591
1544 Macaroni, noodles & similar products		...	...	...	17		...	...	...	613		...	...	...	18541
1549 Other food products n.e.c.		...	...	...	43		...	...	...	1784		...	...	...	31306
155 Beverages		...	...	...	27		...	...	...	1920		...	...	...	60750
1551 Distilling, rectifying & blending of spirits		...	...	...	16		...	...	...	691		...	...	...	19414
1552 Wines		...	...	...	-		...	...	...	-		...	...	...	-
1553 Malt liquors and malt		...	...	...	4		...	...	...	694		...	...	...	21189
1554 Soft drinks; mineral waters		...	...	...	7		...	...	...	535		...	...	...	20147
1600 Tobacco products		...	...	...	38		...	...	...	3142		...	...	...	101939
171 Spinning, weaving and finishing of textiles		...	...	...	223		...	...	...	13733		...	...	...	365685
1711 Textile fibre preparation; textile weaving		...	...	...	134		...	...	...	7090		...	...	...	182576
1712 Finishing of textiles		...	...	...	89		...	...	...	6643		...	...	...	183109
172 Other textiles		...	...	...	558		...	...	...	58077		...	...	...	1234033
1721 Made-up textile articles, except apparel		...	...	...	19		...	...	...	882		...	...	...	12652
1722 Carpets and rugs		...	...	...	532		...	...	...	52729		...	...	...	1130234
1723 Cordage, rope, twine and netting		...	...	...	-		...	...	...	-		...	...	...	-
1729 Other textiles n.e.c.		...	...	...	7		...	...	...	4466		...	...	...	91147
1730 Knitted and crocheted fabrics and articles		...	...	...	47		...	...	...	749		...	...	...	14576
1810 Wearing apparel, except fur apparel		...	...	...	136		...	...	...	14848		...	...	...	374818
1820 Dressing & dyeing of fur; processing of fur		...	...	...	-		...	...	...	-		...	...	...	-
191 Tanning, dressing and processing of leather		...	...	...	13		...	...	...	621		...	...	...	17540
1911 Tanning and dressing of leather		...	...	...	13		...	...	...	621		...	...	...	17540
1912 Luggage, handbags, etc.; saddlery & harness		...	...	...	-		...	...	...	-		...	...	...	-
1920 Footwear		...	...	...	64		...	...	...	1343		...	...	...	28721
2010 Sawmilling and planing of wood		...	...	...	137		...	...	...	1891		...	...	...	46552
202 Products of wood, cork, straw, etc.		...	...	...	61		...	...	...	1468		...	...	...	29483
2021 Veneer sheets, plywood, particle board, etc.		...	...	...	30		...	...	...	995		...	...	...	18190
2022 Builders' carpentry and joinery		...	...	...	13		...	...	...	123		...	...	...	3720
2023 Wooden containers		...	...	...	-		...	...	...	-		...	...	...	-
2029 Other wood products; articles of cork/straw		...	...	...	18		...	...	...	350		...	...	...	7573
210 Paper and paper products		...	...	...	118		...	...	...	3269		...	...	...	76894
2101 Pulp, paper and paperboard		...	...	...	60		...	...	...	2035		...	...	...	46492
2102 Corrugated paper and paperboard		...	...	...	26		...	...	...	657		...	...	...	17496
2109 Other articles of paper and paperboard		...	...	...	32		...	...	...	577		...	...	...	12906
221 Publishing		...	...	...	14		...	...	...	...		...	...	...	...
2211 Publishing of books and other publications		...	...	...	1		...	...	...	...		...	...	...	...
2212 Publishing of newspapers, journals, etc.		...	...	...	13		...	...	...	1449		...	...	...	41245
2213 Publishing of recorded media		...	...	...	-		...	...	...	-		...	...	...	-
2219 Other publishing		...	...	...	-		...	...	...	-		...	...	...	-

222 Printing and related service activities	...	...	...	65	...	...	...	736	...	...	...	17918
2221 Printing	...	...	...	58	...	...	...	655	...	...	...	15956
2222 Service activities related to printing	...	...	...	7	...	...	...	81	...	...	...	1962
2230 Reproduction of recorded media	...	...	...	-	...	...	...	-	...	...	...	-
2310 Coke oven products	...	...	...	-	...	...	...	-	...	...	...	-
2320 Refined petroleum products	...	...	...	3	...	...	...	148	...	...	...	5652
2330 Processing of nuclear fuel	...	...	...	...	...	...	...	...	...	...	...	...
241 Basic chemicals	...	...	...	2	...	...	...	...	...	...	...	...
2411 Basic chemicals, except fertilizers	...	...	...	-	...	...	...	-	...	...	...	-
2412 Fertilizers and nitrogen compounds	...	...	...	-	...	...	...	-	...	...	...	-
2413 Plastics in primary forms; synthetic rubber	...	...	...	2	...	...	...	...	...	...	...	...
242 Other chemicals	...	...	...	90	...	...	...	...	...	...	...	...
2421 Pesticides and other agro-chemical products	...	...	...	2	...	...	...	...	...	...	...	...
2422 Paints, varnishes, printing ink and mastics	...	...	...	11	...	...	...	289	...	...	...	9884
2423 Pharmaceuticals, medicinal chemicals, etc.	...	...	...	36	...	...	...	2978	...	...	...	107202
2424 Soap, cleaning & cosmetic preparations	...	...	...	35	...	...	...	1418	...	...	...	35497
2429 Other chemical products n.e.c.	...	...	...	6	...	...	...	140	...	...	...	4114
2430 Man-made fibres	...	...	...	-	...	...	...	-	...	...	...	-
251 Rubber products	...	...	...	12	...	...	...	584	...	...	...	20691
2511 Rubber tyres and tubes	...	...	...	3	...	...	...	459	...	...	...	17496
2519 Other rubber products	...	...	...	9	...	...	...	125	...	...	...	3195
2520 Plastic products	...	...	...	134	...	...	...	2492	...	...	...	56506
2610 Glass and glass products	...	...	...	4	...	...	...	48	...	...	...	1279
269 Non-metallic mineral products n.e.c.	...	...	...	619	...	...	...	...	...	...	...	...
2691 Pottery, china and earthenware	...	...	...	-	...	...	...	-	...	...	...	-
2692 Refractory ceramic products	...	...	...	1	...	...	...	...	...	...	...	...
2693 Struct.non-refractory clay; ceramic products	...	...	...	475	...	...	...	36804	...	...	...	358442
2694 Cement, lime and plaster	...	...	...	11	...	...	...	2911	...	...	...	108985
2695 Articles of concrete, cement and plaster	...	...	...	60	...	...	...	977	...	...	...	22332
2696 Cutting, shaping & finishing of stone	...	...	...	69	...	...	...	1623	...	...	...	39511
2699 Other non-metallic mineral products n.e.c.	...	...	...	3	...	...	...	276	...	...	...	11891
2710 Basic iron and steel	...	...	...	9	...	...	...	513	...	...	...	14038
2720 Basic precious and non-ferrous metals	...	...	...	4	...	...	...	191	...	...	...	5772
273 Casting of metals	...	...	...	9	...	...	...	...	...	...	...	...
2731 Casting of iron and steel	...	...	...	8	...	...	...	474	...	...	...	13404
2732 Casting of non-ferrous metals	...	...	...	1	...	...	...	...	...	...	...	...
281 Struct.metal products;tanks;steam generators	...	...	...	75	...	...	...	1358	...	...	...	38451
2811 Structural metal products	...	...	...	68	...	...	...	1268	...	...	...	35580
2812 Tanks, reservoirs and containers of metal	...	...	...	7	...	...	...	90	...	...	...	2871
2813 Steam generators	...	...	...	-	...	...	...	-	...	...	...	-
289 Other metal products; metal working services	...	...	...	108	...	...	...	...	...	...	...	...
2891 Metal forging/pressing/stamping/roll-forming	...	...	...	78	...	...	...	2967	...	...	...	90867
2892 Treatment & coating of metals	...	...	...	1	...	...	...	...	...	...	...	...
2893 Cutlery, hand tools and general hardware	...	...	...	7	...	...	...	70	...	...	...	1493
2899 Other fabricated metal products n.e.c.	...	...	...	22	...	...	...	356	...	...	...	9479
291 General purpose machinery	...	...	...	10	...	...	...	...	...	...	...	...
2911 Engines & turbines(not for transport equip.)	...	...	...	5	...	...	...	69	...	...	...	1459
2912 Pumps, compressors, taps and valves	...	...	...	1	...	...	...	...	...	...	...	...
2913 Bearings, gears, gearing & driving elements	...	...	...	-	...	...	...	-	...	...	...	-
2914 Ovens, furnaces and furnace burners	...	...	...	1	...	...	...	...	...	...	...	...
2915 Lifting and handling equipment	...	...	...	-	...	...	...	-	...	...	...	-
2919 Other general purpose machinery	...	...	...	3	...	...	...	25	...	...	...	525
292 Special purpose machinery	...	...	...	6	...	...	...	...	...	...	...	...
2921 Agricultural and forestry machinery	...	...	...	4	...	...	...	82	...	...	...	2193
2922 Machine tools	...	...	...	-	...	...	...	-	...	...	...	-
2923 Machinery for metallurgy	...	...	...	-	...	...	...	-	...	...	...	-
2924 Machinery for mining & construction	...	...	...	-	...	...	...	-	...	...	...	-
2925 Food/beverage/tobacco processing machinery	...	...	...	-	...	...	...	-	...	...	...	-
2926 Machinery for textile, apparel and leather	...	...	...	-	...	...	...	-	...	...	...	-
2927 Weapons and ammunition	...	...	...	-	...	...	...	-	...	...	...	-
2929 Other special purpose machinery	...	...	...	2	...	...	...	...	...	...	...	...
2930 Domestic appliances n.e.c.	...	...	...	3	...	...	...	30	...	...	...	704

continued

Nepal

ISIC Revision 3	Number of establishments					Number of employees					Wages and salaries paid to employees				
		(numbers)					(numbers)					(thousand RUPEES)			
ISIC Industry	Note	1993	1994	1995	1996	Note	1993	1994	1995	1996	Note	1993	1994	1995	1996
3000 Office, accounting and computing machinery		...	...	...	-		...	...	...	-		...	...	...	-
3110 Electric motors, generators and transformers		...	...	...	3		...	...	...	142		...	...	...	4980
3120 Electricity distribution & control apparatus		...	...	...	3		...	...	...	98		...	...	...	2452
3130 Insulated wire and cable		...	...	...	17		...	...	...	995		...	...	...	30526
3140 Accumulators, primary cells and batteries		...	...	...	4		...	...	...	257		...	...	...	7529
3150 Lighting equipment and electric lamps		...	...	...	2		...	...	...	...		...	...	...	...
3190 Other electrical equipment n.e.c.		...	...	...	-		...	...	...	-		...	...	...	-
3210 Electronic valves, tubes, etc.		...	...	...	-		...	...	...	-		...	...	...	-
3220 TV/radio transmitters; line comm. apparatus		...	...	...	-		...	...	...	-		...	...	...	-
3230 TV and radio receivers and associated goods		...	...	...	5		...	...	...	266		...	...	...	7386
331 Medical, measuring, testing appliances, etc.		...	...	...	-		...	...	...	-		...	...	...	-
3311 Medical, surgical and orthopaedic equipment		...	...	...	-		...	...	...	-		...	...	...	-
3312 Measuring/testing/navigating appliances,etc.		...	...	...	-		...	...	...	-		...	...	...	-
3313 Industrial process control equipment		...	...	...	-		...	...	...	-		...	...	...	-
3320 Optical instruments & photographic equipment		...	...	...	-		...	...	...	-		...	...	...	-
3330 Watches and clocks		...	...	...	-		...	...	...	-		...	...	...	-
3410 Motor vehicles		...	...	...	-		...	...	...	-		...	...	...	-
3420 Automobile bodies, trailers & semi-trailers		...	...	...	4		...	...	...	55		...	...	...	1907
3430 Parts/accessories for automobiles		...	...	...	1		...	...	...	...		...	...	...	...
351 Building and repairing of ships and boats		...	...	...	-		...	...	...	-		...	...	...	-
3511 Building and repairing of ships		...	...	...	-		...	...	...	-		...	...	...	-
3512 Building/repairing of pleasure/sport. boats		...	...	...	-		...	...	...	-		...	...	...	-
3520 Railway/tramway locomotives & rolling stock		...	...	...	-		...	...	...	-		...	...	...	-
3530 Aircraft and spacecraft		...	...	...	-		...	...	...	-		...	...	...	-
359 Transport equipment n.e.c.		...	...	...	-		...	...	...	-		...	...	...	-
3591 Motorcycles		...	...	...	-		...	...	...	-		...	...	...	-
3592 Bicycles and invalid carriages		...	...	...	-		...	...	...	-		...	...	...	-
3599 Other transport equipment n.e.c.		...	...	...	-		...	...	...	-		...	...	...	-
3610 Furniture		...	...	...	273		...	...	...	3349		...	...	...	84879
369 Manufacturing n.e.c.		...	...	...	22		...	...	...	1126		...	...	...	28854
3691 Jewellery and related articles		...	...	...	-		...	...	...	-		...	...	...	-
3692 Musical instruments		...	...	...	-		...	...	...	-		...	...	...	-
3693 Sports goods		...	...	...	-		...	...	...	-		...	...	...	-
3694 Games and toys		...	...	...	-		...	...	...	-		...	...	...	-
3699 Other manufacturing n.e.c.		...	...	...	22		...	...	...	1126		...	...	...	28854
3710 Recycling of metal waste and scrap		...	...	...	...		...	...	...	...		...	...	...	...
3720 Recycling of non-metal waste and scrap		...	...	...	...		...	...	...	...		...	...	...	...
D Total manufacturing		...	...	...	3557		...	...	...	187316		...	...	...	4058069

Nepal

ISIC Revision 3 ISIC Industry	Output in producers' prices Note	(thousand RUPEES) 1993	1994	1995	1996	Value added in producers' prices Note	(thousand RUPEES) 1993	1994	1995	1996	Gross fixed capital formation Note	(thousand RUPEES) 1995	1996
151 Processed meat,fish,fruit,vegetables,fats		...	...	...	...		...	...	...	...		...	...
1511 Processing/preserving of meat		...	...	...	...		...	...	...	...		...	...
1512 Processing/preserving of fish		...	...	...	-		...	...	...	-		...	-
1513 Processing/preserving of fruit & vegetables		...	...	...	...		...	...	...	...		...	...
1514 Vegetable and animal oils and fats		...	...	...	2918741		...	...	...	489981		...	22295
1520 Dairy products		...	...	...	1466197		...	...	...	567458		...	24136
153 Grain mill products; starches; animal feeds		...	...	...	...		...	...	...	...		...	...
1531 Grain mill products		...	...	...	3633909		...	...	...	640981		...	19352
1532 Starches and starch products		...	...	...	...		...	...	...	...		...	...
1533 Prepared animal feeds		...	...	...	488054		...	...	...	136158		...	-1971
154 Other food products		...	...	...	3137672		...	...	...	1138507		...	724889
1541 Bakery products		...	...	...	593762		...	...	...	176460		...	18347
1542 Sugar		...	...	...	1748040		...	...	...	642391		...	679141
1543 Cocoa, chocolate and sugar confectionery		...	...	...	69829		...	...	...	19700		...	1326
1544 Macaroni, noodles & similar products		...	...	...	415121		...	...	...	172343		...	8324
1549 Other food products n.e.c.		...	...	...	310920		...	...	...	127613		...	17751
155 Beverages		...	...	...	2861780		...	...	...	1992105		...	112491
1551 Distilling, rectifying & blending of spirits		...	...	...	739806		...	...	...	594669		...	7318
1552 Wines		...	...	...	-		...	...	...	-		...	-
1553 Malt liquors and malt		...	...	...	1499931		...	...	...	1066487		...	10370
1554 Soft drinks; mineral waters		...	...	...	622043		...	...	...	330949		...	94803
1600 Tobacco products		...	...	...	3665159		...	...	...	2624063		...	31133
171 Spinning, weaving and finishing of textiles		...	...	...	3826814		...	...	...	1365642		...	131472
1711 Textile fibre preparation; textile weaving		...	...	...	2177660		...	...	...	742610		...	65317
1712 Finishing of textiles		...	...	...	1649154		...	...	...	623032		...	66155
172 Other textiles		...	...	...	8579002		...	...	...	4270577		...	283843
1721 Made-up textile articles, except apparel		...	...	...	140067		...	...	...	50322		...	4410
1722 Carpets and rugs		...	...	...	7745650		...	...	...	3890332		...	33802
1723 Cordage, rope, twine and netting		...	...	...	-		...	...	...	-		...	-
1729 Other textiles n.e.c.		...	...	...	693285		...	...	...	329923		...	245631
1730 Knitted and crocheted fabrics and articles		...	...	...	103222		...	...	...	36741		...	1886
1810 Wearing apparel, except fur apparel		...	...	...	3801673		...	...	...	1376123		...	37879
1820 Dressing & dyeing of fur; processing of fur		...	...	...	-		...	...	...	-		...	-
191 Tanning, dressing and processing of leather		...	...	...	531231		...	...	...	185963		...	2060
1911 Tanning and dressing of leather		...	...	...	531231		...	...	...	185963		...	2060
1912 Luggage, handbags, etc.; saddlery & harness		...	...	...	-		...	...	...	-		...	-
1920 Footwear		...	...	...	285202		...	...	...	101811		...	8679
2010 Sawmilling and planing of wood		...	...	...	613470		...	...	...	222880		...	3529
202 Products of wood, cork, straw, etc.		...	...	...	195011		...	...	...	86298		...	1872
2021 Veneer sheets, plywood, particle board, etc.		...	...	...	115167		...	...	...	51364		...	1146
2022 Builders' carpentry and joinery		...	...	...	29742		...	...	...	9926		...	285
2023 Wooden containers		...	...	...	-		...	...	...	-		...	-
2029 Other wood products; articles of cork/straw		...	...	...	50102		...	...	...	25008		...	441
210 Paper and paper products		...	...	...	1049740		...	...	...	369750		...	799671
2101 Pulp, paper and paperboard		...	...	...	649652		...	...	...	228972		...	795973
2102 Corrugated paper and paperboard		...	...	...	244465		...	...	...	86274		...	2394
2109 Other articles of paper and paperboard		...	...	...	155623		...	...	...	54504		...	1304
221 Publishing		...	...	...	...		...	...	...	...		...	...
2211 Publishing of books and other publications		...	...	...	...		...	...	...	...		...	...
2212 Publishing of newspapers, journals, etc.		...	...	...	361891		...	...	...	223978		...	-5523
2213 Publishing of recorded media		...	...	...	-		...	...	...	-		...	-
2219 Other publishing		...	...	...	-		...	...	...	-		...	-

continued

Nepal

ISIC Revision 3		Output in producers' prices					Value added in producers' prices					Gross fixed capital formation		
		Note	(thousand RUPEES)				Note	(thousand RUPEES)				Note	(thousand RUPEES)	
ISIC	Industry		1993	1994	1995	1996		1993	1994	1995	1996		1995	1996
222	Printing and related service activities		...	...	...	153525		...	...	...	62081		...	9271
2221	Printing		...	...	...	117802		...	...	...	53050		...	9169
2222	Service activities related to printing		...	...	...	35723		...	...	...	9031		...	102
2230	Reproduction of recorded media		...	...	...	-		...	...	...	-		...	-
2310	Coke oven products		...	...	...	-		...	...	...	-		...	-
2320	Refined petroleum products		...	...	...	136429		...	...	...	33040		...	1825
2330	Processing of nuclear fuel		...	...	...	...		...	...	...	...		...	...
241	Basic chemicals		...	...	...	...		...	...	...	...		...	...
2411	Basic chemicals, except fertilizers		...	...	...	-		...	...	...	-		...	-
2412	Fertilizers and nitrogen compounds		...	...	...	-		...	...	...	-		...	-
2413	Plastics in primary forms; synthetic rubber		...	...	...	...		...	...	...	...		...	...
242	Other chemicals		...	...	...	...		...	...	...	...		...	...
2421	Pesticides and other agro-chemical products		...	...	...	...		...	...	...	...		...	...
2422	Paints, varnishes, printing ink and mastics		...	...	...	287609		...	...	...	99608		...	13755
2423	Pharmaceuticals, medicinal chemicals, etc.		...	...	...	1550451		...	...	...	531652		...	157368
2424	Soap, cleaning & cosmetic preparations		...	...	...	1715848		...	...	...	630869		...	11103
2429	Other chemical products n.e.c.		...	...	...	68509		...	...	...	22839		...	211
2430	Man-made fibres		...	...	...	-		...	...	...	-		...	-
251	Rubber products		...	...	...	622528		...	...	...	287406		...	10015
2511	Rubber tyres and tubes		...	...	...	571572		...	...	...	267087		...	8000
2519	Other rubber products		...	...	...	50956		...	...	...	20319		...	2015
2520	Plastic products		...	...	...	1277436		...	...	...	361164		...	22663
2610	Glass and glass products		...	...	...	36412		...	...	...	15761		...	31
269	Non-metallic mineral products n.e.c.		...	...	...	...		...	...	...	...		...	...
2691	Pottery, china and earthenware		...	...	...	-		...	...	...	-		...	-
2692	Refractory ceramic products		...	...	...	...		...	...	...	...		...	...
2693	Struct.non-refractory clay; ceramic products		...	...	...	1067361		...	...	...	630063		...	7154
2694	Cement, lime and plaster		...	...	...	1347320		...	...	...	700298		...	25023
2695	Articles of concrete, cement and plaster		...	...	...	162571		...	...	...	76393		...	5054
2696	Cutting, shaping & finishing of stone		...	...	...	282235		...	...	...	154756		...	7820
2699	Other non-metallic mineral products n.e.c.		...	...	...	15026		...	...	...	6755		...	7674
2710	Basic iron and steel		...	...	...	697179		...	...	...	101827		...	60237
2720	Basic precious and non-ferrous metals		...	...	...	192528		...	...	...	25903		...	6918
273	Casting of metals		...	...	...	...		...	...	...	...		...	...
2731	Casting of iron and steel		...	...	...	1102255		...	...	...	258317		...	22152
2732	Casting of non-ferrous metals		...	...	...	...		...	...	...	...		...	...
281	Struct.metal products;tanks;steam generators		...	...	...	305350		...	...	...	123651		...	7946
2811	Structural metal products		...	...	...	296858		...	...	...	119804		...	7530
2812	Tanks, reservoirs and containers of metal		...	...	...	8492		...	...	...	3847		...	416
2813	Steam generators		...	...	...	-		...	...	...	-		...	-
289	Other metal products; metal working services		...	...	...	...		...	...	...	...		...	...
2891	Metal forging/pressing/stamping/roll-forming		...	...	...	3229685		...	...	...	919001		...	176632
2892	Treatment & coating of metals		...	...	...	...		...	...	...	...		...	...
2893	Cutlery, hand tools and general hardware		...	...	...	18025		...	...	...	5757		...	30
2899	Other fabricated metal products n.e.c.		...	...	...	190687		...	...	...	45223		...	884
291	General purpose machinery		...	...	...	...		...	...	...	...		...	...
2911	Engines & turbines(not for transport equip.)		...	...	...	14061		...	...	...	5769		...	70
2912	Pumps, compressors, taps and valves		...	...	...	...		...	...	...	...		...	...
2913	Bearings, gears, gearing & driving elements		...	...	...	-		...	...	...	-		...	-
2914	Ovens, furnaces and furnace burners		...	...	...	...		...	...	...	...		...	...
2915	Lifting and handling equipment		...	...	...	-		...	...	...	-		...	-
2919	Other general purpose machinery		...	...	...	3093		...	...	...	1482		...	-

292 Special purpose machinery	...	...	...	...	...	...	...	...	...	...
2921 Agricultural and forestry machinery	...	...	...	12686	...	...	...	5973	...	1951
2922 Machine tools	...	...	...	-	...	...	...	-	...	-
2923 Machinery for metallurgy	...	...	...	-	...	...	...	-	...	-
2924 Machinery for mining & construction	...	...	...	-	...	...	...	-	...	-
2925 Food/beverage/tobacco processing machinery	...	...	...	-	...	...	...	-	...	-
2926 Machinery for textile, apparel and leather	...	...	...	-	...	...	...	-	...	-
2927 Weapons and ammunition	...	...	...	-	...	...	...	-	...	-
2929 Other special purpose machinery	...	...	...	...	...	...	...	...	...	...
2930 Domestic appliances n.e.c.	...	...	...	9022	...	...	...	1589	...	22
3000 Office, accounting and computing machinery	...	...	...	-	...	...	...	-	...	-
3110 Electric motors, generators and transformers	...	...	...	123519	...	...	...	58439	...	3300
3120 Electricity distribution & control apparatus	...	...	...	19771	...	...	...	5316	...	120
3130 Insulated wire and cable	...	...	...	1357881	...	...	...	337040	...	22330
3140 Accumulators, primary cells and batteries	...	...	...	223179	...	...	...	81315	...	4989
3150 Lighting equipment and electric lamps	...	...	...	...	...	...	...	...	...	...
3190 Other electrical equipment n.e.c.	...	...	...	-	...	...	...	-	...	-
3210 Electronic valves, tubes, etc.	...	...	...	-	...	...	...	-	...	-
3220 TV/radio transmitters; line comm. apparatus	...	...	...	-	...	...	...	-	...	-
3230 TV and radio receivers and associated goods	...	...	...	145578	...	...	...	59431	...	14294
331 Medical, measuring, testing appliances, etc.	...	...	...	-	...	...	...	-	...	-
3311 Medical, surgical and orthopaedic equipment	...	...	...	-	...	...	...	-	...	-
3312 Measuring/testing/navigating appliances,etc.	...	...	...	-	...	...	...	-	...	-
3313 Industrial process control equipment	...	...	...	-	...	...	...	-	...	-
3320 Optical instruments & photographic equipment	...	...	...	-	...	...	...	-	...	-
3330 Watches and clocks	...	...	...	-	...	...	...	-	...	-
3410 Motor vehicles	...	...	...	-	...	...	...	-	...	-
3420 Automobile bodies, trailers & semi-trailers	...	...	...	12195	...	...	...	3172	...	-
3430 Parts/accessories for automobiles	...	...	...	...	...	...	...	...	...	...
351 Building and repairing of ships and boats	...	...	...	-	...	...	...	-	...	-
3511 Building and repairing of ships	...	...	...	-	...	...	...	-	...	-
3512 Building/repairing of pleasure/sport. boats	...	...	...	-	...	...	...	-	...	-
3520 Railway/tramway locomotives & rolling stock	...	...	...	-	...	...	...	-	...	-
3530 Aircraft and spacecraft	...	...	...	-	...	...	...	-	...	-
359 Transport equipment n.e.c.	...	...	...	-	...	...	...	-	...	-
3591 Motorcycles	...	...	...	-	...	...	...	-	...	-
3592 Bicycles and invalid carriages	...	...	...	-	...	...	...	-	...	-
3599 Other transport equipment n.e.c.	...	...	...	-	...	...	...	-	...	-
3610 Furniture	...	...	...	444100	...	...	...	190820	...	7807
369 Manufacturing n.e.c.	...	...	...	233482	...	...	...	101218	...	15334
3691 Jewellery and related articles	...	...	...	-	...	...	...	-	...	-
3692 Musical instruments	...	...	...	-	...	...	...	-	...	-
3693 Sports goods	...	...	...	-	...	...	...	-	...	-
3694 Games and toys	...	...	...	-	...	...	...	-	...	-
3699 Other manufacturing n.e.c.	...	...	...	233482	...	...	...	101218	...	15334
3710 Recycling of metal waste and scrap	...	...	...	...	...	...	...	...	...	...
3720 Recycling of non-metal waste and scrap	...	...	...	...	...	...	...	...	...	...
D Total manufacturing	...	...	...	54927092	...	...	...	21875315	...	2826384

Nepal

ISIC Revision 3		Index numbers of industrial production											
		(1990=100)											
ISIC Industry	Note	1985	1986	1987	1988	1989	1990	1991	1992	1993	1994	1995	1996
15 Food and beverages		...	...	...	...	...	...	...	...	...	...	...	...
16 Tobacco products		...	...	...	...	...	...	...	...	...	...	...	...
17 Textiles		...	...	...	...	...	...	...	...	...	...	...	...
18 Wearing apparel, fur		...	...	...	...	...	...	...	...	...	...	...	...
19 Leather, leather products and footwear		...	...	...	...	...	...	...	...	...	...	...	...
20 Wood products (excl. furniture)		...	...	...	...	...	...	...	...	...	...	...	...
21 Paper and paper products		...	...	...	...	...	...	...	...	...	...	...	...
22 Printing and publishing		...	...	...	...	...	...	...	...	...	...	...	...
23 Coke,refined petroleum products,nuclear fuel		...	...	...	...	...	...	...	...	...	...	...	...
24 Chemicals and chemical products		...	...	...	...	...	...	...	...	...	...	...	...
25 Rubber and plastics products		...	...	...	...	...	...	...	...	...	...	...	...
26 Non-metallic mineral products		...	...	...	...	...	...	...	...	...	...	...	...
27 Basic metals		...	...	...	...	...	...	...	...	...	...	...	...
28 Fabricated metal products		...	...	...	...	...	...	...	...	...	...	...	...
29 Machinery and equipment n.e.c.		...	...	...	...	...	...	...	...	...	...	...	...
30 Office, accounting and computing machinery		...	...	...	...	...	...	...	...	...	...	...	...
31 Electrical machinery and apparatus		...	...	...	...	...	...	...	...	...	...	...	...
32 Radio,television and communication equipment		...	...	...	...	...	...	...	...	...	...	...	...
33 Medical, precision and optical instruments		...	...	...	...	...	...	...	...	...	...	...	...
34 Motor vehicles, trailers, semi-trailers		...	...	...	...	...	...	...	...	...	...	...	...
35 Other transport equipment		...	...	...	...	...	...	...	...	...	...	...	...
36 Furniture; manufacturing n.e.c.		...	...	...	...	...	...	...	...	...	...	...	...
37 Recycling		...	...	...	...	...	...	...	...	...	...	...	...
D Total manufacturing		...	...	...	...	...	...	...	...	...	...	...	...

NETHERLANDS ANTILLES

Supplier of information:
Central Bureau of Statistics, Willemstad.

Basic source of data:
National Accounts Survey Establishment Census, March 1993; Labour Force Sample Surveys 1989-1996.

Major deviations from ISIC (Revision 3):
Data do not include petroleum refineries.

Reference period (if not calendar year):
Not reported.

Scope:
All establishments.

Method of enumeration:
For the National Accounts Survey, establishments with 10 or more employees are completely enumerated and establishments with less than 10 employees are sampled. All establishments are completely enumerated for the Business Census. The survey is carried out by mail and personal visits.

Adjusted for non-response:
Yes.

Concepts and definitions of variables:
Output is gross output.
Value added is total value added.

Related national publications:
1995 National Accounts; Bedrijventelling 1993, Nederlandse Antillen; both published by the Central Bureau of Statistics, Willemstad.

Netherlands Antilles

ISIC Revision 3	Number of establishments					Number of employees					Wages and salaries paid to employees				
		(numbers)					(numbers)					(million GUILDERS)			
ISIC Industry	Note	1992	1993	1994	1995	Note	1992	1993	1994	1995	Note	1992	1993	1994	1995
D Total manufacturing		...	403	...	...		4774	5041	5187	5119		119.0	114.4	126.0	146.4

ISIC Revision 3	Output in producers' prices					Value added					Gross fixed capital formation		
		(million GUILDERS)					(million GUILDERS)					(million GUILDERS)	
ISIC Industry	Note	1992	1993	1994	1995	Note	1992	1993	1994	1995	Note	1994	1995
D Total manufacturing		602.9	616.9	724.1	659.5		220.8	196.1	229.5	217.5		35.4	27.5

ISIC Revision 3	Index numbers of industrial production												
		(1990=100)											
ISIC Industry	Note	1985	1986	1987	1988	1989	1990	1991	1992	1993	1994	1995	1996
D Total manufacturing		...	...	...	...	...	...	...	...	...	...	...	...

NIGER

Supplier of information:
Direction de la statistique et des comptes nationaux, Ministère du plan, Niamey.

Basic source of data:
Annual accounts survey.

Major deviations from ISIC (Revision 2):
None reported.

Reference period (if not calendar year):

Scope:
All industrial enterprises in the modern sector.

Method of enumeration:
Questionnaires are distributed by mail with follow-up site visits as required.

Adjusted for non-response:
Yes.

Concepts and definitions of variables:
No deviations from the standard UN concepts and definitions are reported.

Related national publications:
Rapport sur les statistiques des entreprises, 1990-96, published by the Direction de la statistique et des comptes nationaux, Ministere du plan, Niamey.

Niger

ISIC Revision 2		Number of enterprises					Number of employees					Wages and salaries paid to employees			
		(numbers)					(numbers)					(million CFA FRANCS)			
ISIC Industry	Note	1993	1994	1995	1996	Note	1993	1994	1995	1996	Note	1993	1994	1995	1996
311/2 Food products	a/	11	13	13	14		...	...	...	...		...	...	...	...
313 Beverages	a/	...	...	...	...		...	...	...	...		...	...	...	...
314 Tobacco	a/	...	...	...	...		...	...	...	...		...	...	...	...
321 Textiles	b/	3	3	4	4		...	...	...	...		...	...	...	...
322 Wearing apparel, except footwear	b/	...	...	...	...		...	...	...	...		...	...	...	...
323 Leather and fur products	b/	...	...	...	...		...	...	...	...		...	...	...	...
324 Footwear, except rubber or plastic	b/	...	...	...	...		...	...	...	...		...	...	...	...
331 Wood products, except furniture	c/	3	3	3	3		...	...	...	...		...	...	...	...
332 Furniture and fixtures, excl. metal	c/	...	...	...	...		...	...	...	...		...	...	...	...
341 Paper and products	d/	12	13	14	15		...	...	...	...		...	...	...	...
342 Printing and publishing	d/	...	...	...	...		...	...	...	...		...	...	...	...
351 Industrial chemicals	e/	3	3	3	3		...	...	...	...		...	...	...	...
352 Other chemicals	e/	...	...	...	...		...	...	...	...		...	...	...	...
353 Petroleum refineries	e/	...	...	...	...		...	...	...	...		...	...	...	...
354 Misc. petroleum and coal products	e/	...	...	...	...		...	...	...	...		...	...	...	...
355 Rubber products	e/	...	...	...	...		...	...	...	...		...	...	...	...
356 Plastic products	e/	...	...	...	...		...	...	...	...		...	...	...	...
361 Pottery, china, earthenware	f/	2	3	3	3		...	...	...	...		...	...	...	...
362 Glass and products	f/	...	...	...	...		...	...	...	...		...	...	...	...
369 Other non-metallic mineral products	f/	...	...	...	...		...	...	...	...		...	...	...	...
371 Iron and steel		...	...	...	...		...	...	...	...		...	...	...	...
372 Non-ferrous metals		...	...	...	...		...	...	...	...		...	...	...	...
381 Fabricated metal products	g/	6	7	7	7		...	...	...	...		...	...	...	...
382 Non-electrical machinery	g/	...	...	...	...		...	...	...	...		...	...	...	...
383 Electrical machinery	g/	...	...	...	...		...	...	...	...		...	...	...	...
384 Transport equipment	g/	...	...	...	...		...	...	...	...		...	...	...	...
385 Professional and scientific equipment	g/	...	...	...	...		...	...	...	...		...	...	...	...
390 Other manufacturing industries		...	...	...	...		...	...	...	...		...	...	...	...
3 Total manufacturing		40	45	47	49		...	...	...	...		...	...	...	...

a/ 311/2 includes 313 and 314.
b/ 321 includes 322, 323 and 324.
c/ 331 includes 332.
d/ 341 includes 342.
e/ 351 includes 352, 353, 354, 355 and 356.
f/ 361 includes 362 and 369.
g/ 381 includes 382, 383, 384 and 385.

Niger

ISIC Revision 2	Output in producers' prices					Value added in producers' prices					Gross fixed capital formation		
		(million CFA FRANCS)					(million CFA FRANCS)					(million CFA FRANCS)	
ISIC Industry	Note	1993	1994	1995	1996	Note	1993	1994	1995	1996	Note	1995	1996
311/2 Food products	a/	7566	9846	9178	9186	a/	2280	2644	1485	1162	a/	126	319
313 Beverages	a/	...	...	...	...	a/	...	...	...	...	a/	...	...
314 Tobacco	a/	...	...	...	...	a/	...	...	...	...	a/	...	...
321 Textiles	b/	2343	2288	2295	1932	b/	403	103	50	58	b/	36	3
322 Wearing apparel, except footwear	b/	...	...	...	...	b/	...	...	...	...	b/	...	...
323 Leather and fur products	b/	...	...	...	...	b/	...	...	...	...	b/	...	...
324 Footwear, except rubber or plastic	b/	...	...	...	...	b/	...	...	...	...	b/	...	...
331 Wood products, except furniture	c/	102	118	130	117	c/	30	28	24	26	c/	-	-
332 Furniture and fixtures, excl. metal	c/	...	...	...	...	c/	...	...	...	...	c/	...	...
341 Paper and products	d/	1747	2631	2534	3362	d/	712	1037	1125	1779	d/	58	91
342 Printing and publishing	d/	...	...	...	...	d/	...	...	...	...	d/	...	...
351 Industrial chemicals	e/	2398	3439	3756	3794	e/	887	1049	788	1091	e/	12	49
352 Other chemicals	e/	...	...	...	...	e/	...	...	...	...	e/	...	...
353 Petroleum refineries	e/	...	...	...	...	e/	...	...	...	...	e/	...	...
354 Misc. petroleum and coal products	e/	...	...	...	...	e/	...	...	...	...	e/	...	...
355 Rubber products	e/	...	...	...	...	e/	...	...	...	...	e/	...	...
356 Plastic products	e/	...	...	...	...	e/	...	...	...	...	e/	...	...
361 Pottery, china, earthenware	f/	1337	1818	2033	1982	f/	381	331	485	519	f/	102	430
362 Glass and products	f/	...	...	...	...	f/	...	...	...	...	f/	...	...
369 Other non-metallic mineral products	f/	...	...	...	...	f/	...	...	...	...	f/	...	...
371 Iron and steel		...	...	...	...		...	...	...	...		...	...
372 Non-ferrous metals		...	...	...	...		...	...	...	...		...	...
381 Fabricated metal products	g/	1119	1645	1811	1313	g/	388	501	506	381	g/	50	70
382 Non-electrical machinery	g/	...	...	...	...	g/	...	...	...	...	g/	...	...
383 Electrical machinery	g/	...	...	...	...	g/	...	...	...	...	g/	...	...
384 Transport equipment	g/	...	...	...	...	g/	...	...	...	...	g/	...	...
385 Professional and scientific equipment	g/	...	...	...	...	g/	...	...	...	...	g/	...	...
390 Other manufacturing industries		...	...	...	...		...	...	...	...		...	...
3 Total manufacturing		16612	21785	21737	21686		5081	5693	4463	5016		384	962

a/ 311/2 includes 313 and 314.
b/ 321 includes 322, 323 and 324.
c/ 331 includes 332.
d/ 341 includes 342.
e/ 351 includes 352, 353, 354, 355 and 356.
f/ 361 includes 362 and 369.
g/ 381 includes 382, 383, 384 and 385.

Niger

ISIC Revision 2		Index numbers of industrial production											
		(1990=100)											
ISIC Industry	Note	1985	1986	1987	1988	1989	1990	1991	1992	1993	1994	1995	1996
311/2 Food products		...	...	...	...	...	...	...	...	...	...	...	...
313 Beverages		...	...	...	...	...	...	...	...	...	...	...	...
314 Tobacco		...	...	...	...	...	...	...	...	...	...	...	...
321 Textiles		...	...	...	...	...	...	...	...	...	...	...	...
322 Wearing apparel, except footwear		...	...	...	...	...	...	...	...	...	...	...	...
323 Leather and fur products		...	...	...	...	...	...	...	...	...	...	...	...
324 Footwear, except rubber or plastic		...	...	...	...	...	...	...	...	...	...	...	...
331 Wood products, except furniture		...	...	...	...	...	...	...	...	...	...	...	...
332 Furniture and fixtures, excl. metal		...	...	...	...	...	...	...	...	...	...	...	...
341 Paper and products		...	...	...	...	...	...	...	...	...	...	...	...
342 Printing and publishing		...	...	...	...	...	...	...	...	...	...	...	...
351 Industrial chemicals		...	...	...	...	...	...	...	...	...	...	...	...
352 Other chemicals		...	...	...	...	...	...	...	...	...	...	...	...
353 Petroleum refineries		...	...	...	...	...	...	...	...	...	...	...	...
354 Misc. petroleum and coal products		...	...	...	...	...	...	...	...	...	...	...	...
355 Rubber products		...	...	...	...	...	...	...	...	...	...	...	...
356 Plastic products		...	...	...	...	...	...	...	...	...	...	...	...
361 Pottery, china, earthenware		...	...	...	...	...	...	...	...	...	...	...	...
362 Glass and products		...	...	...	...	...	...	...	...	...	...	...	...
369 Other non-metallic mineral products		...	...	...	...	...	...	...	...	...	...	...	...
371 Iron and steel		...	...	...	...	...	...	...	...	...	...	...	...
372 Non-ferrous metals		...	...	...	...	...	...	...	...	...	...	...	...
381 Fabricated metal products		...	...	...	...	...	...	...	...	...	...	...	...
382 Non-electrical machinery		...	...	...	...	...	...	...	...	...	...	...	...
383 Electrical machinery		...	...	...	...	...	...	...	...	...	...	...	...
384 Transport equipment		...	...	...	...	...	...	...	...	...	...	...	...
385 Professional and scientific equipment		...	...	...	...	...	...	...	...	...	...	...	...
390 Other manufacturing industries		...	...	...	...	...	...	...	...	...	...	...	...
3 Total manufacturing		...	...	...	...	...	...	...	...	...	...	...	...

NIGERIA

Supplier of information:
Federal Office of Statistics, Lagos.

Basic source of data:
Annual survey of manufacturing industries.

Major deviations from ISIC (Revision 2):
None reported.

Reference period (if not calendar year):

Scope:
Establishments with 10 or more persons engaged.

Method of enumeration:
The survey is carried out through personal interviews.

Adjusted for non-response:
Not reported.

Concepts and definitions of variables:
No deviations from the standard UN concepts and definitions are reported.

Related national publications:

Nigeria

ISIC Revision 2	Number of establishments					Number of employees					Wages and salaries paid to employees				
		(numbers)					(numbers)					(million NAIRAS)			
ISIC Industry	Note	1991	1992	1993	1994	Note	1991	1992	1993	1994	Note	1991	1992	1993	1994
311/2 Food products		652	647	...	...		41454	42399	...	...		401.6	444.0	...	...
3111 Slaughtering, preparing & preserving meat		2	2	...	...		341	341	...	...		2.7	2.9	...	...
3112 Dairy products		6	6	...	...		139	139	...	...		1.1	1.1	...	...
3113 Canning, preserving of fruits & vegetables		5	5	...	...		412	490	...	...		3.3	4.0	...	...
3114 Canning, preserving and processing of fish		-	-	...	...		-	-	...	...		-	-	...	...
3115 Vegetable and animal oils and fats		102	102	...	...		9595	10149	...	...		101.5	107.6	...	...
3116 Grain mill products		37	37	...	...		2596	2775	...	...		29.0	42.5	...	...
3117 Bakery products		467	460	...	...		11867	11684	...	...		102.8	104.3	...	...
3118 Sugar factories and refineries		-	-	...	...		-	-	...	...		-	-	...	...
3119 Cocoa, chocolate and sugar confectionery		23	24	...	...		16236	16576	...	...		159.2	179.8	...	...
3121 Other food products		4	4	...	...		43	41	...	...		0.4	0.4	...	...
3122 Prepared animal feeds		6	7	...	...		225	204	...	...		1.6	1.5	...	...
313 Beverages		278	282	...	...		25808	27874	...	...		180.9	210.3	...	...
3131 Distilling, rectifying and blending spirits		208	208	...	...		15029	15496	...	...		103.3	107.1	...	...
3132 Wine industries		22	22	...	...		734	2080	...	...		6.0	19.0	...	...
3133 Malt liquors and malt		12	12	...	...		4458	4424	...	...		28.8	30.0	...	...
3134 Soft drinks and carbonated waters		36	40	...	...		5587	5874	...	...		42.8	54.3	...	...
314 Tobacco		3	3	...	...		1605	1527	...	...		49.2	64.1	...	...
321 Textiles		114	115	...	...		17122	18401	...	...		194.3	320.8	...	...
3211 Spinning, weaving and finishing textiles		42	44	...	...		4180	4388	...	...		42.7	86.4	...	...
3212 Made-up textile goods excl. wearing apparel		28	27	...	...		6907	8062	...	...		91.0	146.2	...	...
3213 Knitting mills		12	12	...	...		487	728	...	...		4.1	9.8	...	...
3214 Carpets and rugs		11	11	...	...		903	1172	...	...		7.1	9.8	...	...
3215 Cordage, rope and twine		9	9	...	...		2890	2452	...	...		37.2	54.2	...	...
3219 Other textiles		12	12	...	...		1755	1599	...	...		12.2	14.5	...	...
322 Wearing apparel, except footwear		1263	1262	...	...		9486	9952	...	...		99.3	105.4	...	...
323 Leather and fur products		26	27	...	...		1573	1858	...	...		12.7	14.2	...	...
3231 Tanneries and leather finishing		7	8	...	...		1092	1433	...	...		8.5	10.8	...	...
3232 Fur dressing and dyeing industries		-	-	...	...		-	-	...	...		-	-	...	...
3233 Leather prods. excl. wearing apparel		19	19	...	...		481	425	...	...		4.2	3.4	...	...
324 Footwear, except rubber or plastic		92	91	...	...		5462	5452	...	...		54.9	58.3	...	...
331 Wood products, except furniture		191	193	...	...		4729	4450	...	...		48.4	52.0	...	...
3311 Sawmills, planing and other wood mills		170	172	...	...		4459	4180	...	...		45.3	48.8	...	...
3312 Wooden and cane containers		8	8	...	...		109	109	...	...		0.7	0.7	...	...
3319 Other wood and cork products		13	13	...	...		161	161	...	...		2.4	2.4	...	...
332 Furniture and fixtures, excl. metal		829	829	...	...		13767	13970	...	...		194.4	239.3	...	...
341 Paper and products		73	72	...	...		5311	5413	...	...		60.5	73.8	...	...
3411 Pulp, paper and paperboard articles		4	4	...	...		862	922	...	...		7.8	13.0	...	...
3412 Containers of paper and paperboard		15	15	...	...		2194	2281	...	...		27.6	34.8	...	...
3419 Other pulp, paper and paperboard articles		54	53	...	...		2255	2210	...	...		25.1	26.1	...	...
342 Printing and publishing		283	284	...	...		7595	8011	...	...		90.7	87.5	...	...
351 Industrial chemicals		36	40	...	...		2438	4176	...	...		24.8	98.8	...	...
3511 Basic chemicals excl. fertilizers		11	16	...	...		1339	3002	...	...		10.6	84.1	...	...
3512 Fertilizers and pesticides		23	22	...	...		1048	1123	...	...		13.3	14.1	...	...
3513 Synthetic resins and plastic materials		2	2	...	...		51	51	...	...		0.8	0.6	...	...
352 Other chemicals		205	205	...	...		23760	25179	...	...		241.2	256.7	...	...
3521 Paints, varnishes and lacquers		25	25	...	...		1051	1365	...	...		7.9	10.9	...	...
3522 Drugs and medicines		94	95	...	...		17841	18615	...	...		189.6	193.4	...	...
3523 Soap, cleaning preps., perfumes, cosmetics		73	72	...	...		4267	4587	...	...		37.8	44.9	...	...
3529 Other chemical products		13	13	...	...		601	612	...	...		5.9	7.5	...	...
353 Petroleum refineries		3	3	...	...		50	47	...	...		0.4	0.3	...	...

354 Misc. petroleum and coal products	1	1	...	...	131	159	...	...	2.0	2.8	...	...
355 Rubber products	10	11	...	...	2237	2698	...	...	19.9	24.8	...	...
3551 Tyres and tubes	1	1	...	...	49	44	...	...	0.5	0.5	...	...
3559 Other rubber products	9	10	...	...	2188	2654	...	...	19.4	24.3	...	...
356 Plastic products	204	208	...	...	12402	13841	...	...	266.8	265.0	...	...
361 Pottery, china, earthenware	2	2	...	...	422	463	...	...	2.7	3.2	...	...
362 Glass and products	20	20	...	...	3724	3919	...	...	41.4	43.9	...	...
369 Other non-metallic mineral products	293	296	...	...	7698	7782	...	...	63.5	62.8	...	...
3691 Structural clay products	21	23	...	...	987	1129	...	...	7.8	10.5	...	...
3692 Cement, lime and plaster	47	48	...	...	3460	3394	...	...	24.2	22.2	...	...
3699 Other non-metallic mineral products	225	225	...	...	3251	3259	...	...	31.5	30.1	...	...
371 Iron and steel	135	144	...	...	10559	17356	...	...	93.6	147.5	...	...
372 Non-ferrous metals	61	61	...	...	2454	2574	...	...	38.3	50.4	...	...
381 Fabricated metal products	240	232	...	...	10116	10275	...	...	111.0	147.3	...	...
3811 Cutlery, hand tools and general hardware	74	65	...	...	586	505	...	...	4.9	4.3	...	...
3812 Furniture and fixtures primarily of metal	7	7	...	...	129	134	...	...	1.0	1.0	...	...
3813 Structural metal products	63	64	...	...	2495	2398	...	...	21.1	23.7	...	...
3819 Other fabricated metal products	96	96	...	...	6906	7238	...	...	84.0	118.3	...	...
382 Non-electrical machinery	52	52	...	...	913	874	...	...	11.0	10.8	...	...
3821 Engines and turbines	-	-	...	...	-	-	...	...	-	-	...	...
3822 Agricultural machinery and equipment	22	22	...	...	449	421	...	...	6.4	6.8	...	...
3823 Metal and wood working machinery	6	6	...	...	205	205	...	...	2.4	1.8	...	...
3824 Other special industrial machinery	-	-	...	...	-	-	...	...	-	-	...	...
3825 Office, computing and accounting machinery	-	-	...	...	-	-	...	...	-	-	...	...
3829 Other non-electrical machinery & equipment	24	24	...	...	259	248	...	...	2.2	2.1	...	...
383 Electrical machinery	65	65	...	...	10052	11093	...	...	92.4	107.7	...	...
3831 Electrical industrial machinery	18	18	...	...	628	634	...	...	9.3	9.4	...	...
3832 Radio, television and communication equipm.	8	8	...	...	442	651	...	...	5.1	7.0	...	...
3833 Electrical appliances and housewares	22	22	...	...	5997	5904	...	...	55.0	60.9	...	...
3839 Other electrical apparatus and supplies	17	17	...	...	2985	3904	...	...	22.9	30.3	...	...
384 Transport equipment	10	10	...	...	2248	2318	...	...	19.1	21.6	...	...
3841 Shipbuilding and repairing	-	-	...	...	-	-	...	...	-	-	...	...
3842 Railroad equipment	-	-	...	...	-	-	...	...	-	-	...	...
3843 Motor vehicles	10	10	...	...	2248	2318	...	...	19.1	21.6	...	...
3844 Motorcycles and bicycles	-	-	...	...	-	-	...	...	-	-	...	...
3845 Aircraft	-	-	...	...	-	-	...	...	-	-	...	...
3849 Other transport equipment	-	-	...	...	-	-	...	...	-	-	...	...
385 Professional and scientific equipment	-	-	...	...	-	-	...	...	-	-	...	...
3851 Prof. and scientific equipment n.e.c.	-	-	...	...	-	-	...	...	-	-	...	...
3852 Photographic and optical goods	-	-	...	...	-	-	...	...	-	-	...	...
3853 Watches and clocks	-	-	...	...	-	-	...	...	-	-	...	...
390 Other manufacturing industries	48	48	...	...	2399	2496	...	...	28.2	28.9	...	...
3901 Jewellery and related articles	12	12	...	...	91	107	...	...	1.9	1.2	...	...
3902 Musical instruments	-	-	...	...	-	-	...	...	-	-	...	...
3903 Sporting and athletic goods	-	-	...	...	-	-	...	...	-	-	...	...
3909 Manufacturing industries, n.e.c.	36	36	...	...	2308	2389	...	...	26.3	27.7	...	...
3 Total manufacturing	5189	5203	...	...	225515	244557	...	...	2443.2	2942.1	...	...

Nigeria

ISIC Revision 2	Output in producers' prices					Value added					Gross fixed capital formation		
		(million NAIRAS)					(million NAIRAS)					(million NAIRAS)	
ISIC Industry	Note	1991	1992	1993	1994	Note	1991	1992	1993	1994	Note	1991	1992
311/2 Food products		12696.0	16461.6	...	...		...	...	...	...		325.0	473.5
3111 Slaughtering, preparing & preserving meat		10.2	13.4	...	...		...	...	...	...		-	-
3112 Dairy products		6.3	3.7	...	...		...	...	...	...		-	-
3113 Canning, preserving of fruits & vegetables		252.5	311.3	...	...		...	...	...	...		0.6	0.2
3114 Canning, preserving and processing of fish		-	-	...	...		...	...	...	...		-	-
3115 Vegetable and animal oils and fats		6046.4	6817.7	...	...		...	...	...	...		2.6	1.6
3116 Grain mill products		697.4	1084.6	...	...		...	...	...	...		10.5	3.3
3117 Bakery products		4162.9	5849.7	...	...		...	...	...	...		260.0	253.7
3118 Sugar factories and refineries		-	-	...	...		...	...	...	...		-	-
3119 Cocoa, chocolate and sugar confectionery		1460.6	2329.7	...	...		...	...	...	...		49.2	212.9
3121 Other food products		1.0	0.7	...	...		...	...	...	...		-	-
3122 Prepared animal feeds		58.7	50.7	...	...		...	...	...	...		2.1	1.9
313 Beverages		6330.3	9261.7	...	...		...	...	...	...		125.0	1819.7
3131 Distilling, rectifying and blending spirits		3507.1	7294.9	...	...		...	...	...	...		32.0	1739.4
3132 Wine industries		36.4	183.8	...	...		...	...	...	...		7.1	10.2
3133 Malt liquors and malt		1216.0	1237.7	...	...		...	...	...	...		20.8	33.2
3134 Soft drinks and carbonated waters		1570.8	545.3	...	...		...	...	...	...		65.1	36.9
314 Tobacco		196.7	302.8	...	...		...	...	...	...		1.8	0.9
321 Textiles		33004.9	52595.5	...	...		...	...	...	...		203.2	264.8
3211 Spinning, weaving and finishing textiles		341.8	394.9	...	...		...	...	...	...		24.7	7.3
3212 Made-up textile goods excl. wearing apparel		31832.7	51312.1	...	...		...	...	...	...		170.9	216.4
3213 Knitting mills		15.3	41.8	...	...		...	...	...	...		-	-
3214 Carpets and rugs		272.9	265.2	...	...		...	...	...	...		5.3	21.2
3215 Cordage, rope and twine		463.9	566.2	...	...		...	...	...	...		1.7	18.5
3219 Other textiles		78.3	15.4	...	...		...	...	...	...		0.6	1.4
322 Wearing apparel, except footwear		4850.7	5444.9	...	...		...	...	...	...		821.4	466.8
323 Leather and fur products		174.8	250.5	...	...		...	...	...	...		64.2	93.1
3231 Tanneries and leather finishing		164.0	237.3	...	...		...	...	...	...		64.2	93.1
3232 Fur dressing and dyeing industries		-	-	...	...		...	...	...	...		-	-
3233 Leather prods. excl. wearing apparel		10.8	13.1	...	...		...	...	...	...		-	-
324 Footwear, except rubber or plastic		848.1	553.6	...	...		...	...	...	...		33.9	10.2
331 Wood products, except furniture		117.5	116.0	...	...		...	...	...	...		6.8	9.5
3311 Sawmills, planing and other wood mills		107.4	104.0	...	...		...	...	...	...		6.8	8.0
3312 Wooden and cane containers		6.1	6.5	...	...		...	...	...	...		-	-
3319 Other wood and cork products		4.0	5.5	...	...		...	...	...	...		-	1.5
332 Furniture and fixtures, excl. metal		4606.4	6408.7	...	...		...	...	...	...		80.5	63.2
341 Paper and products		816.8	1145.1	...	...		...	...	...	...		13.8	164.7
3411 Pulp, paper and paperboard articles		170.7	143.7	...	...		...	...	...	...		1.7	139.0
3412 Containers of paper and paperboard		196.6	518.3	...	...		...	...	...	...		3.0	19.4
3419 Other pulp, paper and paperboard articles		449.5	483.1	...	...		...	...	...	...		9.0	6.3
342 Printing and publishing		956.1	1346.9	...	...		...	...	...	...		155.7	152.5
351 Industrial chemicals		533.9	1636.5	...	...		...	...	...	...		99.4	223.9
3511 Basic chemicals excl. fertilizers		355.3	1065.2	...	...		...	...	...	...		7.7	81.2
3512 Fertilizers and pesticides		174.2	562.2	...	...		...	...	...	...		91.1	138.1
3513 Synthetic resins and plastic materials		4.5	9.2	...	...		...	...	...	...		0.7	4.6
352 Other chemicals		6667.8	9835.0	...	...		...	...	...	...		142.4	177.8
3521 Paints, varnishes and lacquers		426.4	493.9	...	...		...	...	...	...		5.5	7.8
3522 Drugs and medicines		4794.1	7634.9	...	...		...	...	...	...		91.0	123.2
3523 Soap, cleaning preps., perfumes, cosmetics		1373.4	1620.4	...	...		...	...	...	...		43.4	46.6
3529 Other chemical products		73.9	85.8	...	...		...	...	...	...		2.6	0.1
353 Petroleum refineries		1.6	1.4	...	...		...	...	...	...		-	0.4

ISIC	Industry										
354	Misc. petroleum and coal products	10.6	14.6	...	...	...	...	...	...	-	-
355	Rubber products	364.2	733.8	...	...	...	...	...	...	2.1	3.8
3551	Tyres and tubes	2.4	2.7	...	...	...	...	...	...	-	-
3559	Other rubber products	361.8	731.0	...	...	...	...	...	...	2.1	3.8
356	Plastic products	2143.7	6116.0	...	...	...	...	...	...	215.0	139.8
361	Pottery, china, earthenware	33.8	52.0	...	...	...	...	...	...	-	-
362	Glass and products	632.4	862.1	...	...	...	...	...	...	249.3	146.1
369	Other non-metallic mineral products	3585.2	4946.6	...	...	...	...	...	...	6511.3	273.7
3691	Structural clay products	64.5	215.4	...	...	...	...	...	...	0.3	2.4
3692	Cement, lime and plaster	3134.2	4312.7	...	...	...	...	...	...	6500.9	259.9
3699	Other non-metallic mineral products	386.5	418.5	...	...	...	...	...	...	10.1	11.4
371	Iron and steel	4980.5	3616.6	...	...	...	...	...	...	150.5	82.6
372	Non-ferrous metals	974.6	1419.6	...	...	...	...	...	...	5.9	14.0
381	Fabricated metal products	3393.2	4399.2	...	...	...	...	...	...	181.6	299.0
3811	Cutlery, hand tools and general hardware	34.4	49.1	...	...	...	...	...	...	1.2	1.2
3812	Furniture and fixtures primarily of metal	10.0	12.2	...	...	...	...	...	...	-	-
3813	Structural metal products	98.6	101.5	...	...	...	...	...	...	19.7	20.4
3819	Other fabricated metal products	3250.1	4236.5	...	...	...	...	...	...	160.7	277.4
382	Non-electrical machinery	2648.9	3918.2	...	...	...	...	...	...	0.8	1.1
3821	Engines and turbines	-	-	...	...	...	...	...	...	-	-
3822	Agricultural machinery and equipment	2613.6	3886.7	...	...	...	...	...	...	-	0.1
3823	Metal and wood working machinery	20.0	17.4	...	...	...	...	...	...	0.8	0.9
3824	Other special industrial machinery	-	-	...	...	...	...	...	...	-	-
3825	Office, computing and accounting machinery	-	-	...	...	...	...	...	...	-	-
3829	Other non-electrical machinery & equipment	15.2	14.2	...	...	...	...	...	...	-	-
383	Electrical machinery	8119.1	7697.2	...	...	...	...	...	...	71.8	101.1
3831	Electrical industrial machinery	3490.7	3504.0	...	...	...	...	...	...	0.3	0.3
3832	Radio, television and communication equipm.	115.7	136.0	...	...	...	...	...	...	5.1	6.0
3833	Electrical appliances and housewares	1369.7	1679.6	...	...	...	...	...	...	50.3	58.5
3839	Other electrical apparatus and supplies	3142.9	2377.6	...	...	...	...	...	...	16.2	36.3
384	Transport equipment	85.4	441.1	...	...	...	...	...	...	12.3	24.4
3841	Shipbuilding and repairing	-	-	...	...	...	...	...	...	-	-
3842	Railroad equipment	-	-	...	...	...	...	...	...	-	-
3843	Motor vehicles	85.4	441.1	...	...	...	...	...	...	12.3	24.4
3844	Motorcycles and bicycles	-	-	...	...	...	...	...	...	-	-
3845	Aircraft	-	-	...	...	...	...	...	...	-	-
3849	Other transport equipment	-	-	...	...	...	...	...	...	-	-
385	Professional and scientific equipment	-	-	...	...	...	...	...	...	-	-
3851	Prof. and scientific equipment n.e.c.	-	-	...	...	...	...	...	...	-	-
3852	Photographic and optical goods	-	-	...	...	...	...	...	...	-	-
3853	Watches and clocks	-	-	...	...	...	...	...	...	-	-
390	Other manufacturing industries	313.3	508.0	...	...	...	...	...	...	13.1	19.4
3901	Jewellery and related articles	4.9	6.2	...	...	...	...	...	...	0.7	-
3902	Musical instruments	-	-	...	...	...	...	...	...	-	-
3903	Sporting and athletic goods	-	-	...	...	...	...	...	...	-	-
3909	Manufacturing industries, n.e.c.	308.4	501.8	...	...	...	...	...	...	12.4	19.4
3	Total manufacturing	99086.7	140085.5	...	...	...	...	...	...	9486.9	5025.9

Nigeria

ISIC Revision 2		Index numbers of industrial production											
		(1990=100)											
ISIC Industry	Note	1985	1986	1987	1988	1989	1990	1991	1992	1993	1994	1995	1996
311/2 Food products		...	...	...	...	...	...	...	...	...	...	...	...
313 Beverages		102	129	85	114	104	100	103	145	214	304	412	...
314 Tobacco		...	...	...	...	...	...	...	...	...	...	...	...
321 Textiles		...	...	...	...	...	...	...	...	...	...	...	...
322 Wearing apparel, except footwear		...	...	...	...	...	...	...	...	...	...	...	...
323 Leather and fur products		...	...	...	...	...	...	...	...	...	...	...	...
324 Footwear, except rubber or plastic		...	...	...	...	...	...	...	...	...	...	...	...
331 Wood products, except furniture		...	...	...	...	...	...	...	...	...	...	...	...
332 Furniture and fixtures, excl. metal		...	...	...	...	...	...	...	...	...	...	...	...
341 Paper and products		...	...	...	...	...	...	...	...	...	...	...	...
342 Printing and publishing		...	...	...	...	...	...	...	...	...	...	...	...
351 Industrial chemicals		...	...	...	...	...	...	...	...	...	...	...	...
352 Other chemicals		...	...	...	...	...	...	...	...	...	...	...	...
353 Petroleum refineries		...	...	...	...	...	...	...	...	...	...	...	...
354 Misc. petroleum and coal products		...	...	...	...	...	...	...	...	...	...	...	...
355 Rubber products		...	...	...	...	...	...	...	...	...	...	...	...
356 Plastic products		...	...	...	...	...	...	...	...	...	...	...	...
361 Pottery, china, earthenware		...	...	...	...	...	...	...	...	...	...	...	...
362 Glass and products		...	...	...	...	...	...	...	...	...	...	...	...
369 Other non-metallic mineral products		113	122	104	135	143	100	115	118	118	87	101	101
371 Iron and steel		...	...	...	...	...	...	...	...	...	...	...	...
372 Non-ferrous metals		...	...	...	...	...	...	...	...	...	...	...	...
381 Fabricated metal products		...	...	...	...	...	...	...	...	...	...	...	...
382 Non-electrical machinery		...	...	...	...	...	...	...	...	...	...	...	...
383 Electrical machinery		...	...	...	...	...	...	...	...	...	...	...	...
384 Transport equipment		...	...	...	...	...	...	...	...	...	...	...	...
385 Professional and scientific equipment		...	...	...	...	...	...	...	...	...	...	...	...
390 Other manufacturing industries		...	...	...	...	...	...	...	...	...	...	...	...
3 Total manufacturing		...	...	...	...	...	...	...	...	...	...	...	...

NORWAY

Supplier of information:
Statistisk sentralbyra (Statistics Norway), Oslo.
Industrial statistics for the OECD countries are compiled by the OECD secretariat, which supplies them to UNIDO.

Basic source of data:
Annual industrial inquiry, National Accounts estimates.

Major deviations from ISIC (Revision 3):
Data presented in ISIC (Rev. 3), were originally classified according to the NACE (Revision 1).

Reference period (if not calendar year):

Scope:
Up to 1994, all establishments with 10 or more persons engaged are covered.

Method of enumeration:
Not reported.

Adjusted for non-response:
Not reported.

Concepts and definitions of variables:
Number of employees is calculated as the average number of employees throughout the year, whether full- or part-time; homeworkers are not included.
Wages and salaries includes regular and overtime payments, bonuses, cost-of-living allowances, vacation and sick leave pay. allowances (e.g., travelling, clothing expenses), payments in kind and supplements. Supplements are social expenses levied by law.
Output refers to gross output and is valued in producers' prices, excluding all subsidies, and including all indirect taxes but VAT. Included is the value of all products, work done on own account, services rendered, fixed assets produced for own use, waste products and goods produced by homeworkers. Net changes in work in progress and stocks are allowed for.
Value added refers to census value added (1992-1994). The cost of materials, fuels and other supplies, contract and commission work done by others, repair and maintenance work done by others and electricity purchased are deducted from gross output. Cost of non-industrial services and receipts for non-industrial services are included. Input estimates are made on a consumed basis. For 1995, value added refers to total value added derived from National Accounts estimates.
Gross fixed capital formation is the value of purchases of fixed assets plus own-account construction, less the value of sales. Fixed assets covered are those with a productive life of at least one year, and include new and used assets, those made by a unit's labour force for its own use, and additions, alterations and improvements to existing assets. Valuation is at full cost incurred, including the delivered price, the cost of installation, and the investment levy. Assets produced by the unit cover the cost of labour, materials and other supplies. The actual amount realized is taken for sales of used assets.

Related national publications: Industristatistikk (annual); National Accounts Statistics (annual), both published by Statistics Norway, Oslo.

Norway

ISIC Revision 3	Number of establishments					Number of employees					Wages and salaries paid to employees				
		(numbers)					(numbers)					(million KRONER)			
ISIC Industry	Note	1992	1993	1994	1995	Note	1992	1993	1994	1995a/b/	Note	1992	1993	1994	1995b/
151 Processed meat,fish,fruit,vegetables,fats		454	466	485	...		21372	22505	23431	47700c/		3865	4193	4576	10673c/
1511 Processing/preserving of meat		156	155	157	...		9938	10057	10338	...		1927	2009	2226	...
1512 Processing/preserving of fish		258	274	295	...		9437	10430	11176	...		1540	1762	1935	...
1513 Processing/preserving of fruit & vegetables		26	25	20	...		1285	1335	1229	...		232	246	244	...
1514 Vegetable and animal oils and fats		14	12	13	...		712	683	688	...		167	176	171	...
1520 Dairy products		122	116	113	...		5709	5625	5754	...c/		1213	1245	1272	...c/
153 Grain mill products; starches; animal feeds		59	57	59	...		1940	1831	1908	...c/		447	466	509	...c/
1531 Grain mill products		17	18	18	...		506	463	471	...		...	...	...	...
1532 Starches and starch products		2	2	2	...		47	59	49	...		...	...	...	...
1533 Prepared animal feeds		40	37	39	...		1387	1309	1388	...		330	345	386	...
154 Other food products		227	220	229	...		9536	9669	9663	...c/		1708	1791	1885	...c/
1541 Bakery products		198	189	198	...		5011	5082	5361	...		816	852	915	...
1542 Sugar		-	-	-	...		-	-	-	...		-	-	-	...
1543 Cocoa, chocolate and sugar confectionery		4	4	4	...		2491	2517	2226	...		471	488	503	...
1544 Macaroni, noodles & similar products		2	2	2	...		152	154	156	...		...	...	...	...
1549 Other food products n.e.c.		23	25	25	...		1882	1916	1920	...		...	...	...	...
155 Beverages		42d/	36d/	34d/	...		5045d/	4913d/	5336d/	5600		1196d/	1248d/	1430d/	1516
1551 Distilling, rectifying & blending of spirits		3	2	2	...		143	46	45	...		...	...	...	...
1552 Wines		...	...	...	...		...	...	...	...		...	...	...	...
1553 Malt liquors and malt		...	...	...	...		...	...	...	...		...	...	...	...
1554 Soft drinks; mineral waters		...	...	...	...		...	...	...	...		...	...	...	...
1600 Tobacco products		...d/	...d/	...d/	...		...d/	...d/	...d/	600		...d/	...d/	...d/	153
171 Spinning, weaving and finishing of textiles		26	24	22	...		1454	1452	1376	...		259	259	256	...
1711 Textile fibre preparation; textile weaving		22	20	19	...		1232	1239	1175	...		219	219	220	...
1712 Finishing of textiles		4	4	3	...		222	213	201	...		40	40	36	...
172 Other textiles		70	68	73	...		2155	2005	2047	...		355	347	385	...
1721 Made-up textile articles, except apparel		33	32	32	...		827	764	805	...		127	123	137	...
1722 Carpets and rugs		1	-	-	...		12	-	-	...		...	...	...	...
1723 Cordage, rope, twine and netting		26	27	31	...		672	687	757	...		112	120	140	...
1729 Other textiles n.e.c.		10	9	10	...		644	554	485	...		...	...	...	...
1730 Knitted and crocheted fabrics and articles		24	23	22	...		1160	1147	1265	...		173	175	200	...
1810 Wearing apparel, except fur apparel		56	53	51	...		1621	1549	1503	...		225	217	222	...
1820 Dressing & dyeing of fur; processing of fur		5	5	5	...		103	95	90	...		13	15	16	...
191 Tanning, dressing and processing of leather		10	9	9	...		382	366	387	...		59	62	66	...
1911 Tanning and dressing of leather		2	2	2	...		183	181	192	...		...	...	...	...
1912 Luggage, handbags, etc.; saddlery & harness		8	7	7	...		199	185	195	...		...	...	...	...
1920 Footwear		9	9	9	...		371	360	383	...		53	55	59	...
2010 Sawmilling and planing of wood		125	122	125	...		4660	4432	4551	6200		864	845	903	1222
202 Products of wood, cork, straw, etc.		178	164	172	...		5955	5857	6491	10400		1055	1070	1263	2062
2021 Veneer sheets, plywood, particle board, etc.		16	17	17	...		1169	1381	1467	...		220	263	311	...
2022 Builders' carpentry and joinery		138	129	136	...		4362	4129	4649	...		765	744	878	...
2023 Wooden containers		16	12	12	...		292	243	253	...		48	43	50	...
2029 Other wood products; articles of cork/straw		8	6	7	...		132	104	122	...		23	19	23	...
210 Paper and paper products		84	82	80	...		10421	10150	10166	11300		2226	2253	2378	3073
2101 Pulp, paper and paperboard		40	39	38	...		7128	6876	6820	7500		1537	1541	1604	2026
2102 Corrugated paper and paperboard		25	24	24	...		2404	2365	2470	...		505	517	579	...
2109 Other articles of paper and paperboard		19	19	18	...		889	909	876	...		184	196	196	...
221 Publishing		204	207	224	...		22376	22553	23337	25300		3943	4179	4394	5895
2211 Publishing of books and other publications		36	39	41	...		1729	1767	1875	...		438	470	519	...
2212 Publishing of newspapers, journals, etc.		162	162	176	...		20455	20621	21266	...		3460	3671	3835	...
2213 Publishing of recorded media		-	-	2	...		-	-	33	...		-	-	...	...
2219 Other publishing		6	6	5	...		192	165	163	...		45	38	...	...

222 Printing and related service activities	244	240	257	...	6545	6539	6719	13500	1613	1643	1732	2964
2221 Printing	196	193	205	...	5653	5657	5762	...	1407	1435	1500	...
2222 Service activities related to printing	48	47	52	...	892	882	957	...	206	209	232	...
2230 Reproduction of recorded media	5	5	10	...	137	137	202	600	37	37	54	124
2310 Coke oven products	-	-	-	...	-	-	-	...	-	-	-	...
2320 Refined petroleum products	11	59	65	...	1315	1574	1639	1900	434	520	557	653
2330 Processing of nuclear fuel	-	-	-	...	-	-	-	...	-	-	-	...
241 Basic chemicals	47	50	52	...	8198	8231	8324	9400	2322	2359	2481	3073
2411 Basic chemicals, except fertilizers	32	35	36	...	4059	4088	4207	...	...	...	...	...
2412 Fertilizers and nitrogen compounds	2	2	2	...	2146	2106	2075	2400	...	...	...	795
2413 Plastics in primary forms; synthetic rubber	13	13	14	...	1993	2037	2042	...	...	...	...	...
242 Other chemicals	53	49	50	...	5089	4983	4929	6400	1261	1338	1359	1906
2421 Pesticides and other agro-chemical products	1	-	-	...	15	-	-	...	-	-	-	...
2422 Paints, varnishes, printing ink and mastics	17	15	16	...	1384	1337	1342	...	333	353	355	...
2423 Pharmaceuticals, medicinal chemicals, etc.	15	14	14	...	2170	2255	2402	3100	567	644	711	931
2424 Soap, cleaning & cosmetic preparations	9	8	9	...	729	713	572	...	175	167	134	...
2429 Other chemical products n.e.c.	11	12	11	...	791	678	613	...	186	174	158	...
2430 Man-made fibres	-	-	-	...	-	-	-	...	-	-	-	...
251 Rubber products	15	16	24	...	590	630	720	...	116	129	159	...
2511 Rubber tyres and tubes	8	8	10	...	332	329	155	...	...	...	28	...
2519 Other rubber products	7	8	14	...	258	301	565	...	...	...	131	...
2520 Plastic products	101	110	120	...	4283	4384	4750	...	849	909	1016	...
2610 Glass and glass products	29	30	27	...	1576	1522	1597	1600	...	320	346	457
269 Non-metallic mineral products n.e.c.	114	147	146	...	5180	4993	5078	6900	...	1148	1217	1865
2691 Pottery, china and earthenware	5	7	6	...	707	731	731	...	...	...	...	...
2692 Refractory ceramic products	1	1	1	...	47	47	47	...	...	...	...	...
2693 Struct.non-refractory clay; ceramic products	4	4	4	...	203	179	187	...	...	36	41	...
2694 Cement, lime and plaster	4	4	4	...	600	650	619	...	184	211	206	...
2695 Articles of concrete, cement and plaster	76	107	105	...	2458	2284	2330	...	551	499	531	...
2696 Cutting, shaping & finishing of stone	14	14	17	...	422	361	414	...	91	79	91	...
2699 Other non-metallic mineral products n.e.c.	10	10	9	...	743	741	750	...	174	173	193	...
2710 Basic iron and steel	33	37	35	...	4497	4444	4194	4600	1105	...	1113	1335
2720 Basic precious and non-ferrous metals	28	28	26	...	9216	8790	8615	10100	2457	2461	2553	2997
273 Casting of metals	4	2	22	...	150	23	1792	1900	32	...	400	530
2731 Casting of iron and steel	-	-	13	...	-	-	1401	...	-	-	317	...
2732 Casting of non-ferrous metals	4	2	9	...	150	23	391	...	32	...	82	...
281 Struct.metal products;tanks;steam generators	206	193	180	...	6525	6240	6165	...	...	...	1376	...
2811 Structural metal products	190	179	170	...	6008	5759	5783	...	1244	1232	1287	...
2812 Tanks, reservoirs and containers of metal	15	12	8	...	431	370	265	...	...	...	...	...
2813 Steam generators	1	2	2	...	86	111	117	...	...	...	...	...
289 Other metal products; metal working services	204	196	187	...	6526	6465	6335	...	1311	1329	1376	...
2891 Metal forging/pressing/stamping/roll-forming	-	-	6	...	-	-	160	...	-	-	32	...
2892 Treatment & coating of metals	31	35	39	...	606	960	1056	...	131	205	236	...
2893 Cutlery, hand tools and general hardware	29	26	26	...	1416	1370	1455	...	273	269	313	...
2899 Other fabricated metal products n.e.c.	144	135	116	...	4504	4135	3664	...	907	855	795	...
291 General purpose machinery	196	187	199	...	10715	10268	10492	14100	2585	2556	2726	3826
2911 Engines & turbines(not for transport equip.)	16	15	17	...	1669	1726	2338	...	445	464	677	...
2912 Pumps, compressors, taps and valves	39	34	35	...	2595	2306	2151	...	637	615	542	...
2913 Bearings, gears, gearing & driving elements	14	13	12	...	765	734	640	...	177	158	149	...
2914 Ovens, furnaces and furnace burners	8	8	10	...	317	280	313	...	92	75	78	...
2915 Lifting and handling equipment	60	59	60	...	3217	3084	3063	...	759	742	774	...
2919 Other general purpose machinery	59	58	65	...	2152	2138	1987	...	475	502	505	...
292 Special purpose machinery	91	94	104	...	6470	6744	6765	9300	1463	1602	1683	2456
2921 Agricultural and forestry machinery	17	17	17	...	1400	1339	1329	...	274	289	314	...
2922 Machine tools	13	12	17	...	389	325	478	...	81	68	105	...
2923 Machinery for metallurgy	3	3	3	...	126	117	104	...	29	25	24	...
2924 Machinery for mining & construction	22	22	26	...	788	813	891	...	170	187	205	...
2925 Food/beverage/tobacco processing machinery	7	7	12	...	369	367	514	...	81	83	131	...
2926 Machinery for textile, apparel and leather	2	2	3	...	50	48	60	...	...	...	12	...
2927 Weapons and ammunition	8	7	8	...	2266	2533	2383	...	556	630	611	...
2929 Other special purpose machinery	19	24	18	...	1082	1202	1006	...	...	...	280	...
2930 Domestic appliances n.e.c.	13	13	14	...	1100	1099	1101	1100	215	218	243	307

continued

Norway

ISIC Revision 3		Number of establishments					Number of employees					Wages and salaries paid to employees			
		(numbers)					(numbers)					(million KRONER)			
ISIC Industry	Note	1992	1993	1994	1995	Note	1992	1993	1994	1995a/b/	Note	1992	1993	1994	1995b/
3000 Office, accounting and computing machinery		6	6	6	...		918	774	764	1000		226	226	250	277
3110 Electric motors, generators and transformers		31	31	29	...		2493	2662	2217	6100e/		613	695	601	1747e/
3120 Electricity distribution & control apparatus		31	33	38	...		2128	2176	2289	...e/		500	533	591	...e/
3130 Insulated wire and cable		12	14	14	...		1329	1376	1398	2000		439	420	459	573
3140 Accumulators, primary cells and batteries		2	2	2	...		141	125	136	2300f/		...	...	...	628f/
3150 Lighting equipment and electric lamps		16	15	13	...		1318	1157	1191	...f/		255	249	250	...f/
3190 Other electrical equipment n.e.c.		35	24	21	...		1193	775	780	...f/		...	...	...	...f/
3210 Electronic valves, tubes, etc.		13	15	16	...		668	687	759	4700g/		137	137	160	1330g/
3220 TV/radio transmitters; line comm. apparatus		15	14	15	...		2418	2508	2728	...g/		656	709	812	...g/
3230 TV and radio receivers and associated goods		14	15	13	...		524	661	606	400		109	144	145	108
331 Medical, measuring, testing appliances, etc.		52	52	52	...		3162	3310	3450	6100		...	...	1063	1686
3311 Medical, surgical and orthopaedic equipment		22	22	24	...		950	1009	1102	...		231	258	292	...
3312 Measuring/testing/navigating appliances,etc.		28	28	25	...		1974	2069	2136	...		597	637	696	...
3313 Industrial process control equipment		2	2	3	...		238	232	212	...		...	...	75	...
3320 Optical instruments & photographic equipment		3	3	3	...		94	99	109	100h/		...	...	26	35h/
3330 Watches and clocks		-	-	-	...		-	-	-	...h/		-	-	-	...h/
3410 Motor vehicles		2	2	2	...		167	165	184	...		...	...	...	...
3420 Automobile bodies, trailers & semi-trailers		20	20	23	...		846	826	907	...		...	...	...	...
3430 Parts/accessories for automobiles		35	30	29	...		2137	2208	2140	...		432	476	486	...
351 Building and repairing of ships and boats		255	268	263	...		28343	29408	29046	33500		6612	7257	7238	9313
3511 Building and repairing of ships		230	246	243	...		27859	28994	28630	...		6524	7180	7152	...
3512 Building/repairing of pleasure/sport. boats		25	22	20	...		484	414	416	...		87	77	86	...
3520 Railway/tramway locomotives & rolling stock		9	9	8	...		1987	1959	1971	1800		409	426	445	520
3530 Aircraft and spacecraft		13	14	12	...		2668	2623	2438	2800		719	733	800	801
359 Transport equipment n.e.c.		6	9	9	...		517	574	615	500		94	109	122	126
3591 Motorcycles		-	-	-	...		-	-	-	...		...	...	...	...
3592 Bicycles and invalid carriages		3	6	6	...		398	454	476	...		...	...	...	...
3599 Other transport equipment n.e.c.		3	3	3	...		119	120	139	...		21	23	26	...
3610 Furniture		165	169	178	...		6372	6405	6833	8700		1108	1142	1291	1772
369 Manufacturing n.e.c.		67	51	51	...		2877	2547	2569	4100		548	531	547	811
3691 Jewellery and related articles		21	20	21	...		814	815	814	...		...	...	...	...
3692 Musical instruments		1	1	1	...		11	12	14	...		...	...	...	...
3693 Sports goods		12	12	12	...		804	819	880	...		166	173	193	...
3694 Games and toys		-	-	-	...		-	-	-	...		...	...	...	...
3699 Other manufacturing n.e.c.		33	18	17	...		1248	901	861	...		219	190	183	...
3710 Recycling of metal waste and scrap		1	1	6	...		11	11	103	200		...	...	25	43
3720 Recycling of non-metal waste and scrap		2	2	4	...		59	59	64	200		...	...	14	52
D Total manufacturing		3900	3916	4037	...		234742	234670	240402	299600		50574	52688	55982	75780

a/ Number of persons engaged.
b/ National accounts estimates.
c/ 151 includes 1520, 153 and 154.
d/ 155 includes 1600.
e/ 3110 includes 3120.
f/ 3140 includes 3150 and 3190.
g/ 3210 includes 3220.
h/ 3320 includes 3330.

Norway

ISIC Revision 3 ISIC Industry	Note	Output (million KRONER) 1992	1993	1994	1995a/	Note	Value added (million KRONER) 1992	1993	1994	1995a/	Note	Gross fixed capital formation (million KRONER) 1994	1995a/
151 Processed meat,fish,fruit,vegetables,fats		36895	37302	39350	80247b/		5983	5975	5939	15763b/		1097	2339b/
1511 Processing/preserving of meat		21868	21655	21676	...		2669	2324	1944	...		483	...
1512 Processing/preserving of fish		11390	12234	13968	...		2421	2766	3086	...		483	...
1513 Processing/preserving of fruit & vegetables		1873	1941	1782	...		477	454	462	...		71	...
1514 Vegetable and animal oils and fats		1765	1473	1924	...		416	431	447	...		60	...
1520 Dairy products		13478	13624	13674	...b/		-453	239	229	...b/		420	...b/
153 Grain mill products; starches; animal feeds		9161	8895	9338	...b/		1834	1814	1795	...b/		190	...b/
1531 Grain mill products		...	...	...	...		...	...	...	...		...	...
1532 Starches and starch products		...	...	...	...		...	...	...	...		...	...
1533 Prepared animal feeds		7088	6941	7437	...		948	1024	1085	...		144	...
154 Other food products		8985	9506	10066	...b/		3370	3530	3725	...b/		403	...b/
1541 Bakery products		3361	3441	3713	...		1316	1381	1484	...		156	...
1542 Sugar		-	-	-	...		-	-	-	...		-	...
1543 Cocoa, chocolate and sugar confectionery		2119	2291	2306	...		1119	1159	1183	...		117	...
1544 Macaroni, noodles & similar products		...	...	...	...		...	...	...	...		...	...
1549 Other food products n.e.c.		...	...	...	...		...	...	...	...		...	...
155 Beverages		11224c/	11187c/	12305c/	5030		8450c/	8407c/	8880c/	...		443c/	360
1551 Distilling, rectifying & blending of spirits		...	...	...	...		...	...	...	...		...	...
1552 Wines		...	...	...	...		...	...	...	...		...	...
1553 Malt liquors and malt		...	...	...	...		...	...	...	...		...	...
1554 Soft drinks; mineral waters		...	...	...	...		...	...	...	...		...	...
1600 Tobacco products		...c/	...c/	...c/	788		...c/	...c/	...c/	293		...c/	14
171 Spinning, weaving and finishing of textiles		1039	989	1050	...		409	391	404	...		57	...
1711 Textile fibre preparation; textile weaving		858	842	926	...		339	337	353	...		47	...
1712 Finishing of textiles		181	147	124	...		70	54	51	...		9	...
172 Other textiles		1598	1586	1694	...		609	582	557	...		60	...
1721 Made-up textile articles, except apparel		609	577	640	...		202	191	225	...		8	...
1722 Carpets and rugs		...	...	...	...		...	...	...	...		...	...
1723 Cordage, rope, twine and netting		461	519	615	...		187	201	225	...		22	...
1729 Other textiles n.e.c.		...	...	...	...		...	...	...	...		...	...
1730 Knitted and crocheted fabrics and articles		611	630	657	...		276	279	280	...		27	...
1810 Wearing apparel, except fur apparel		906	983	1122	...		355	389	403	...		25	...
1820 Dressing & dyeing of fur; processing of fur		58	51	48	...		23	20	20	...		1	...
191 Tanning, dressing and processing of leather		336	340	378	...		92	96	103	...		7	...
1911 Tanning and dressing of leather		...	...	...	...		...	...	...	...		...	...
1912 Luggage, handbags, etc.; saddlery & harness		...	...	...	...		...	...	...	...		...	...
1920 Footwear		169	176	177	...		75	76	81	...		8	...
2010 Sawmilling and planing of wood		4800	4541	6005	7011		1286	1366	1750	1587		332	399
202 Products of wood, cork, straw, etc.		4605	4865	5843	8095		1524	1549	1932	2655		225	357
2021 Veneer sheets, plywood, particle board, etc.		1031	1182	1514	...		319	403	487	...		96	...
2022 Builders' carpentry and joinery		3284	3435	4009	...		1090	1046	1337	...		114	...
2023 Wooden containers		223	187	234	...		81	70	73	...		11	...
2029 Other wood products; articles of cork/straw		67	61	86	...		34	30	35	...		4	...
210 Paper and paper products		15364	15028	16849	23344		3634	3906	4527	7223		623	1482
2101 Pulp, paper and paperboard		12128	11739	13417	18900		2530	2729	3286	5783		506	1239
2102 Corrugated paper and paperboard		2365	2352	2506	...		819	862	927	...		93	...
2109 Other articles of paper and paperboard		871	937	926	...		284	315	314	...		24	...
221 Publishing		13329	13725	14716	17644		6038	6435	6860	7853		543	511
2211 Publishing of books and other publications		2471	2582	2848	...		768	827	880	...		28	...
2212 Publishing of newspapers, journals, etc.		10710	11010	11724	...		5211	5555	5920	...		510	...
2213 Publishing of recorded media		-	-	...	...		-	-	...	...		...	...
2219 Other publishing		148	133	...	...		58	53	...	...		...	...

continued

Norway

ISIC Revision 3

ISIC Industry	Output Note	Output (million KRONER) 1992	1993	1994	1995a/	Value added Note	Value added (million KRONER) 1992	1993	1994	1995a/	Gross fixed capital formation Note	Gross fixed capital formation (million KRONER) 1994	1995a/
222 Printing and related service activities		5443	5486	5720	...		2380	2428	2484	3827		349	734
2221 Printing		4913	4932	5094	...		2072	2112	2138	...		326	...
2222 Service activities related to printing		530	554	626	9175		308	316	347	...		23	...
2230 Reproduction of recorded media		85	85	165	383		48	48	94	218		3	22
2310 Coke oven products		-	-	-	...		-	-	-	...		-	...
2320 Refined petroleum products		14766	16518	15698	13398		940	1806	1561	839		261	477
2330 Processing of nuclear fuel		-	-	-	...		-	-	-	...		-	...
241 Basic chemicals		15331	16340	18924	20938		4316	4772	5824	7267		756	2538
2411 Basic chemicals, except fertilizers		...	...	...	...		...	...	...	...		...	...
2412 Fertilizers and nitrogen compounds		...	...	...	4798		...	...	...	1958		...	207
2413 Plastics in primary forms; synthetic rubber		...	...	...	...		...	...	...	...		...	...
242 Other chemicals		7443	7979	8042	8876		2828	3062	2893	3492		416	267
2421 Pesticides and other agro-chemical products		-	-	-	...		-	-	-	...		-	...
2422 Paints, varnishes, printing ink and mastics		1612	1656	1754	...		487	486	502	...		48	...
2423 Pharmaceuticals, medicinal chemicals, etc.		3667	4204	4422	4388		1601	1786	1727	2168		249	156
2424 Soap, cleaning & cosmetic preparations		1190	1217	992	...		479	495	364	...		45	...
2429 Other chemical products n.e.c.		974	902	874	...		261	295	301	...		74	...
2430 Man-made fibres		-	-	-	...		-	-	-	...		-	...
251 Rubber products		428	409	534	...		176	180	209	...		14	...
2511 Rubber tyres and tubes		...	...	141	...		...	...	43	...		3	...
2519 Other rubber products		...	...	393	...		...	...	166	...		10	...
2520 Plastic products		3905	4023	4611	...		1505	1521	1667	...		256	...
2610 Glass and glass products		...	1189	1372	1519		...	501	567	653		35	80
269 Non-metallic mineral products n.e.c.		...	5483	6203	8453		...	2254	2451	3240		437	727
2691 Pottery, china and earthenware		...	...	...	...		...	...	...	...		...	...
2692 Refractory ceramic products		...	...	...	...		...	...	...	...		...	...
2693 Struct.non-refractory clay; ceramic products		...	143	152	...		...	58	62	...		6	...
2694 Cement, lime and plaster		1168	1487	1578	...		352	733	701	...		277	...
2695 Articles of concrete, cement and plaster		2261	2288	2734	...		780	836	980	...		100	...
2696 Cutting, shaping & finishing of stone		606	287	345	...		256	121	154	...		12	...
2699 Other non-metallic mineral products n.e.c.		861	918	1005	...		290	295	342	...		28	...
2710 Basic iron and steel		6722	...	7655	8908		1528	...	1884	2405		303	422
2720 Basic precious and non-ferrous metals		18350	18429	22894	26538		3978	4182	5122	6819		554	636
273 Casting of metals		145	...	1164	1396		54	...	542	634		39	67
2731 Casting of iron and steel		-	-	885	...		-	-	422	...		26	...
2732 Casting of non-ferrous metals		145	...	280	...		54	...	121	...		13	...
281 Struct.metal products;tanks;steam generators		...	...	4866	...		...	...	1803	...		52	...
2811 Structural metal products		4594	4385	4610	...		1684	1643	1691	...		49	...
2812 Tanks, reservoirs and containers of metal		...	...	...	...		...	...	...	...		...	...
2813 Steam generators		...	...	...	...		...	...	...	...		...	...
289 Other metal products; metal working services		4648	4766	5126	...		1987	2122	2240	...		180	...
2891 Metal forging/pressing/stamping/roll-forming		-	-	89	...		-	-	44	...		1	...
2892 Treatment & coating of metals		427	874	886	...		212	440	465	...		65	...
2893 Cutlery, hand tools and general hardware		814	856	1055	...		409	433	512	...		22	...
2899 Other fabricated metal products n.e.c.		3407	3036	3096	...		1366	1249	1220	...		92	...
291 General purpose machinery		10444	9954	11343	14766		3534	3341	3615	4843		204	323
2911 Engines & turbines(not for transport equip.)		1801	1939	3277	...		576	590	776	...		75	...
2912 Pumps, compressors, taps and valves		2383	2446	1909	...		833	782	772	...		44	...
2913 Bearings, gears, gearing & driving elements		796	572	638	...		261	215	200	...		10	...
2914 Ovens, furnaces and furnace burners		305	266	285	...		83	84	92	...		3	...
2915 Lifting and handling equipment		3151	2831	3081	...		1083	1009	1008	...		51	...
2919 Other general purpose machinery		2008	1899	2153	...		698	660	768	...		20	...

ISIC	Industry													
292	Special purpose machinery		5298	5623	6253	8582		2132	2223	2321	3092		156	314
2921	Agricultural and forestry machinery		1061	1062	1298	...		445	455	510	...		16	...
2922	Machine tools		205	196	499	...		109	109	158	...		-10	...
2923	Machinery for metallurgy		51	110	72	...		25	25	28	...		7	...
2924	Machinery for mining & construction		625	631	816	...		252	267	316	...		13	...
2925	Food/beverage/tobacco processing machinery		235	292	448	...		113	119	165	...		7	...
2926	Machinery for textile, apparel and leather		...	...	30	...		...	...	16	...		-	...
2927	Weapons and ammunition		1953	2052	1852	...		828	825	754	...		89	...
2929	Other special purpose machinery		...	...	1238	...		...	...	374	...		33	...
2930	Domestic appliances n.e.c.		856	886	975	974		322	348	388	353		32	41
3000	Office, accounting and computing machinery		1005	928	1398	1299		334	283	390	359		27	58
3110	Electric motors, generators and transformers		2545	2986	3021	5783d/		859	1018	905	2206d/		32	141d/
3120	Electricity distribution & control apparatus		1770	1924	2218	...d/		710	736	849	...d/		56	...d/
3130	Insulated wire and cable		2451	1939	2195	2608		802	848	854	905		93	106
3140	Accumulators, primary cells and batteries		...	...	...	2323e/		...	...	...	785e/		...	29e/
3150	Lighting equipment and electric lamps		968	914	909	...e/		365	359	363	...e/		12	...e/
3190	Other electrical equipment n.e.c.		...	...	...	...e/		...	...	...	...e/		...	...e/
3210	Electronic valves, tubes, etc.		526	570	610	5312f/		214	203	230	1887f/		26	173f/
3220	TV/radio transmitters; line comm. apparatus		2764	2583	3407	...f/		956	1030	1216	...f/		135	...f/
3230	TV and radio receivers and associated goods		411	612	537	384		169	244	215	125		8	6
331	Medical, measuring, testing appliances, etc.		...	...	4047	5671		...	...	1526	2125		172	267
3311	Medical, surgical and orthopaedic equipment		768	906	1030	...		371	420	454	...		50	...
3312	Measuring/testing/navigating appliances,etc.		2350	2517	2685	...		830	881	977	...		120	...
3313	Industrial process control equipment		...	...	332	...		...	...	95	...		2	...
3320	Optical instruments & photographic equipment		...	...	174	230g/		...	...	69	54g/		2	10g/
3330	Watches and clocks		-	-	-	...g/		-	-	-	...g/		-	...g/
3410	Motor vehicles		...	...	...	...		...	...	...	...		...	...
3420	Automobile bodies, trailers & semi-trailers		...	...	...	...		...	...	...	...		...	...
3430	Parts/accessories for automobiles		1690	1771	2023	...		598	686	748	...		118	...
351	Building and repairing of ships and boats		28093	29445	28747	31365		8735	9951	9418	10804		664	687
3511	Building and repairing of ships		27706	29113	28377	...		8626	9857	9302	...		660	...
3512	Building/repairing of pleasure/sport. boats		387	332	370	...		109	94	116	...		4	...
3520	Railway/tramway locomotives & rolling stock		1352	1449	1335	1155		520	566	507	431		57	21
3530	Aircraft and spacecraft		2180	2041	3052	3152		896	928	1040	914		54	119
359	Transport equipment n.e.c.		391	393	469	485		144	124	161	166		10	7
3591	Motorcycles		...	...	...	...		...	...	...	...		...	...
3592	Bicycles and invalid carriages		...	...	...	...		...	...	...	...		...	...
3599	Other transport equipment n.e.c.		71	77	89	...		26	23	27	...		1	...
3610	Furniture		4663	4667	5521	6810		1634	1649	1974	2392		189	265
369	Manufacturing n.e.c.		1798	1740	1731	2307		802	804	778	980		56	78
3691	Jewellery and related articles		...	...	...	...		...	...	...	...		...	...
3692	Musical instruments		...	...	...	...		...	...	...	...		...	...
3693	Sports goods		478	528	611	...		246	274	316	...		21	...
3694	Games and toys		...	...	...	...		...	...	...	...		...	...
3699	Other manufacturing n.e.c.		742	629	616	...		316	287	257	...		26	...
3710	Recycling of metal waste and scrap		...	...	157	264		...	...	58	117		8	15
3720	Recycling of non-metal waste and scrap		...	...	62	223		...	...	26	66		4	3
D	Total manufacturing		286087	291964	318506	366194		84969	88899	95167	111072		10255	15316

a/ National accounts estimates.
b/ 151 includes 1520, 153 and 154.
c/ 155 includes 1600.
d/ 3110 includes 3120.
e/ 3140 includes 3150 and 3190.
f/ 3210 includes 3220.
g/ 3320 includes 3330.

Norway

ISIC Revision 3			Index numbers of industrial production											
			(1990=100)											
ISIC	Industry	Note	1985	1986	1987	1988	1989	1990	1991	1992	1993	1994	1995	1996
15	Food and beverages	a/	...	102	102	101	102	100	103	103	104	109	110	112
16	Tobacco products	a/	...	...	...	...	...	...	...	...	...	...	...	...
17	Textiles		...	130	122	106	97	100	100	95	93	104	100	101
18	Wearing apparel, fur		...	180	157	125	102	100	98	94	90	94	93	101
19	Leather, leather products and footwear		...	132	128	113	101	100	99	100	102	110	101	87
20	Wood products (excl. furniture)		...	113	112	106	104	100	91	91	92	101	103	105
21	Paper and paper products		...	95	95	95	101	100	99	97	104	113	118	111
22	Printing and publishing		...	99	100	100	101	100	100	100	100	104	108	111
23	Coke,refined petroleum products,nuclear fuel		...	68	75	70	75	100	95	105	105	108	98	108
24	Chemicals and chemical products		...	85	88	89	95	100	95	95	100	104	107	108
25	Rubber and plastics products		...	101	102	100	100	100	93	84	88	93	94	94
26	Non-metallic mineral products		...	117	120	113	103	100	89	91	92	104	116	122
27	Basic metals		...	84	89	97	99	100	99	100	102	110	109	112
28	Fabricated metal products		...	107	107	103	100	100	98	101	106	111	118	128
29	Machinery and equipment n.e.c.		...	108	106	99	100	100	97	100	101	109	118	123
30	Office, accounting and computing machinery		...	109	112	107	98	100	59	59	50	53	56	61
31	Electrical machinery and apparatus		...	102	104	100	101	100	98	100	110	113	122	126
32	Radio,television and communication equipment		...	82	89	95	100	100	90	89	92	103	112	120
33	Medical, precision and optical instruments		...	88	92	94	97	100	96	97	107	127	137	143
34	Motor vehicles, trailers, semi-trailers		...	106	108	104	103	100	98	101	102	116	130	135
35	Other transport equipment		...	105	103	96	98	100	105	117	120	122	124	127
36	Furniture; manufacturing n.e.c.		...	123	118	110	103	100	98	94	94	101	102	107
37	Recycling		...	123	118	110	103	100	98	94	97	106	105	110
D	Total manufacturing		99	100	101	99	100	100	98	100	102	108	112	115

a/ 15 includes 16.

OMAN

Supplier of information:
Industrial Statistics Center, Ministry of Commerce and Industry, Muscat.

Basic source of data:
Industrial Census.

Major deviations from ISIC (Revision 3):
None reported.

Reference period (if not calendar year):

Scope:
All registered establishments.

Method of enumeration:
Individual sites are visited by enumerators..

Adjusted for non-response:
Yes.

Concepts and definitions of variables:
No deviations from the standard UN concepts and definitions are reported.

Related national publications:

Oman

ISIC Revision 3 ISIC Industry	Number of establishments Note	(numbers) 1993	1994	1995	1996	Number of employees Note	(numbers) 1993	1994	1995	1996	Wages and salaries paid to employees Note	(thousand RIALS) 1993	1994	1995	1996
151 Processed meat,fish,fruit,vegetables,fats		12	14	17	...		580	775	878	...		1141.6	1631.0	1695.4	...
1511 Processing/preserving of meat		1	2	2	...		1	76	82	...		0.6	130.0	150.2	...
1512 Processing/preserving of fish		7	8	11	...		263	287	312	...		574.2	644.5	658.7	...
1513 Processing/preserving of fruit & vegetables		2	2	2	...		117	204	213	...		201.5	385.8	366.3	...
1514 Vegetable and animal oils and fats		2	2	2	...		199	208	271	...		365.3	470.7	520.2	...
1520 Dairy products		10	8	9	...		605	648	664	...		1331.2	1573.3	1608.2	...
153 Grain mill products; starches; animal feeds		20	15	15	...		281	276	291	...		1334.3	1383.9	1454.0	...
1531 Grain mill products		18	13	13	...		141	135	152	...		856.7	920.8	970.0	...
1532 Starches and starch products		-	-	-	...		-	-	-	...		-	-	-	...
1533 Prepared animal feeds		2	2	2	...		140	141	139	...		477.6	463.2	484.0	...
154 Other food products		87	92	96	...		1675	1698	1804	...		2760.4	2859.7	3012.1	...
1541 Bakery products		66	68	73	...		1197	1477	1576	...		1682.4	2416.4	2545.8	...
1542 Sugar		-	-	-	...		-	-	-	...		-	-	-	...
1543 Cocoa, chocolate and sugar confectionery		1	1	1	...		54	56	47	...		102.5	113.4	109.6	...
1544 Macaroni, noodles & similar products		-	-	-	...		-	-	-	...		-	-	-	...
1549 Other food products n.e.c.		20	23	22	...		424	165	181	...		975.6	329.9	356.7	...
155 Beverages		15	19	18	...		893	998	1007	...		1451.0	1871.7	2011.7	...
1551 Distilling, rectifying & blending of spirits		-	-	-	...		-	-	-	...		-	-	-	...
1552 Wines		-	-	-	...		-	-	-	...		-	-	-	...
1553 Malt liquors and malt		-	-	-	...		-	-	-	...		-	-	-	...
1554 Soft drinks; mineral waters		15	19	18	...		893	998	1007	...		1451.0	1871.7	2011.7	...
1600 Tobacco products		-	-	-	...		-	-	-	...		-	-	-	...
171 Spinning, weaving and finishing of textiles		1	1	1	...		210	220	249	...		568.8	749.7	909.0	...
1711 Textile fibre preparation; textile weaving		1	1	1	...		210	220	249	...		568.8	749.7	909.0	...
1712 Finishing of textiles		-	-	-	...		-	-	-	...		-	-	-	...
172 Other textiles		2	2	2	...		21	26	26	...		19.7	28.6	30.0	...
1721 Made-up textile articles, except apparel		2	2	2	...		21	26	26	...		19.7	28.6	30.0	...
1722 Carpets and rugs		-	-	-	...		-	-	-	...		-	-	-	...
1723 Cordage, rope, twine and netting		-	-	-	...		-	-	-	...		-	-	-	...
1729 Other textiles n.e.c.		-	-	-	...		-	-	-	...		-	-	-	...
1730 Knitted and crocheted fabrics and articles		-	-	-	...		-	-	-	...		-	-	-	...
1810 Wearing apparel, except fur apparel		21	24	25	...		4722	5707	5851	...		4142.0	5471.3	5620.4	...
1820 Dressing & dyeing of fur; processing of fur		-	-	-	...		-	-	-	...		-	-	-	...
191 Tanning, dressing and processing of leather		-	-	-	...		-	-	-	...		-	-	-	...
1911 Tanning and dressing of leather		-	-	-	...		-	-	-	...		-	-	-	...
1912 Luggage, handbags, etc.; saddlery & harness		-	-	-	...		-	-	-	...		-	-	-	...
1920 Footwear		1	1	3	...		61	22	99	...		88.4	41.4	147.7	...
2010 Sawmilling and planing of wood		-	-	-	...		-	-	-	...		-	-	-	...
202 Products of wood, cork, straw, etc.		215	192	179	...		1077	1236	1383	...		1091.0	1340.5	2062.3	...
2021 Veneer sheets, plywood, particle board, etc.		-	-	-	...		-	-	-	...		-	-	-	...
2022 Builders' carpentry and joinery		207	190	178	...		1010	1231	1381	...		1025.3	1336.3	2060.5	...
2023 Wooden containers		3	2	1	...		31	5	2	...		32.1	4.1	1.8	...
2029 Other wood products; articles of cork/straw		5	-	-	...		36	-	-	...		33.6	-	-	...
210 Paper and paper products		4	6	10	...		247	172	458	...		462.2	521.3	1096.3	...
2101 Pulp, paper and paperboard		1	2	3	...		30	91	184	...		47.0	372.7	348.7	...
2102 Corrugated paper and paperboard		2	1	3	...		159	8	136	...		236.2	7.9	271.0	...
2109 Other articles of paper and paperboard		1	3	4	...		58	73	138	...		179.0	140.7	476.7	...
221 Publishing		9	13	12	...		469	711	635	...		894.1	1696.9	1463.7	...
2211 Publishing of books and other publications		8	9	7	...		368	397	341	...		684.3	900.4	823.4	...
2212 Publishing of newspapers, journals, etc.		-	2	3	...		-	192	277	...		-	495.1	612.0	...
2213 Publishing of recorded media		-	1	1	...		-	14	14	...		-	25.7	25.7	...
2219 Other publishing		1	1	1	...		101	108	3	...		209.8	275.6	2.5	...

222 Printing and related service activities	17	17	17	...	430	444	417	...	780.3	678.3	643.5	...
2221 Printing	17	17	17	...	430	444	417	...	780.3	678.3	643.5	...
2222 Service activities related to printing	-	-	-	...	-	-	-	...	-	-	-	...
2230 Reproduction of recorded media	-	-	-	...	-	-	-	...	-	-	-	...
2310 Coke oven products	-	-	1	...	-	-	9	...	-	-	10.1	...
2320 Refined petroleum products	8	8	8	...	584	509	493	...	2779.9	3599.9	4134.4	...
2330 Processing of nuclear fuel	-	-	-	...	-	-	-	...	-	-	-	...
241 Basic chemicals	7	8	8	...	111	152	143	...	227.8	356.4	373.4	...
2411 Basic chemicals, except fertilizers	6	8	8	...	100	152	143	...	185.3	356.4	373.4	...
2412 Fertilizers and nitrogen compounds	-	-	-	...	-	-	-	...	-	-	-	...
2413 Plastics in primary forms; synthetic rubber	1	-	-	...	11	-	-	...	42.5	-	-	...
242 Other chemicals	16	14	17	...	644	728	675	...	1633.8	1747.1	1965.4	...
2421 Pesticides and other agro-chemical products	1	1	2	...	12	10	32	...	14.8	15.7	75.4	...
2422 Paints, varnishes, printing ink and mastics	4	4	4	...	177	185	189	...	557.8	669.4	702.3	...
2423 Pharmaceuticals, medicinal chemicals, etc.	1	1	1	...	86	151	113	...	117.4	172.7	194.8	...
2424 Soap, cleaning & cosmetic preparations	8	7	8	...	333	365	314	...	866.8	855.8	943.5	...
2429 Other chemical products n.e.c.	2	1	2	...	36	17	27	...	77.0	33.5	49.4	...
2430 Man-made fibres	-	-	-	...	-	-	-	...	-	-	-	...
251 Rubber products	-	2	1	...	-	11	10	...	-	15.2	17.6	...
2511 Rubber tyres and tubes	-	2	1	...	-	11	10	...	-	15.2	17.6	...
2519 Other rubber products	-	-	-	...	-	-	-	...	-	-	-	...
2520 Plastic products	15	12	16	...	567	473	579	...	981.4	927.3	1047.9	...
2610 Glass and glass products	11	14	14	...	388	503	564	...	746.3	1003.6	1110.3	...
269 Non-metallic mineral products n.e.c.	570	501	454	...	5452	5254	4925	...	8681.9	9073.9	8771.0	...
2691 Pottery, china and earthenware	-	-	-	...	-	-	-	...	-	-	-	...
2692 Refractory ceramic products	1	1	1	...	77	51	54	...	114.8	93.3	99.7	...
2693 Struct.non-refractory clay; ceramic products	-	-	-	...	-	-	-	...	-	-	-	...
2694 Cement, lime and plaster	4	4	6	...	609	655	688	...	2415.1	2784.9	2948.2	...
2695 Articles of concrete, cement and plaster	521	445	396	...	3634	3381	2808	...	4415.9	4033.9	3370.5	...
2696 Cutting, shaping & finishing of stone	5	8	5	...	281	189	249	...	367.2	309.9	373.9	...
2699 Other non-metallic mineral products n.e.c.	39	43	46	...	851	978	1126	...	1368.8	1851.9	1978.8	...
2710 Basic iron and steel	-	-	-	...	-	-	-	...	-	-	-	...
2720 Basic precious and non-ferrous metals	3	4	4	...	1011	837	699	...	4477.1	3947.4	3339.7	...
273 Casting of metals	-	-	-	...	-	-	-	...	-	-	-	...
2731 Casting of iron and steel	-	-	-	...	-	-	-	...	-	-	-	...
2732 Casting of non-ferrous metals	-	-	-	...	-	-	-	...	-	-	-	...
281 Struct.metal products;tanks;steam generators	325	285	275	...	2393	2132	2379	...	3799.5	3584.0	5077.1	...
2811 Structural metal products	289	284	275	...	2141	2129	2379	...	3491.4	3581.6	5077.1	...
2812 Tanks, reservoirs and containers of metal	36	1	-	...	252	3	-	...	308.1	2.4	-	...
2813 Steam generators	-	-	-	...	-	-	-	...	-	-	-	...
289 Other metal products; metal working services	28	52	54	...	229	392	417	...	402.0	736.5	657.5	...
2891 Metal forging/pressing/stamping/roll-forming	-	-	1	...	-	-	6	...	-	-	12.6	...
2892 Treatment & coating of metals	1	3	2	...	5	43	14	...	6.2	60.0	26.3	...
2893 Cutlery, hand tools and general hardware	2	-	1	...	8	-	2	...	5.8	-	2.4	...
2899 Other fabricated metal products n.e.c.	25	49	50	...	216	349	395	...	390.0	676.5	616.2	...
291 General purpose machinery	4	3	6	...	88	87	178	...	202.7	260.6	410.8	...
2911 Engines & turbines(not for transport equip.)	1	-	1	...	15	-	2	...	12.6	-	1.4	...
2912 Pumps, compressors, taps and valves	1	1	3	...	41	40	121	...	112.2	137.2	277.3	...
2913 Bearings, gears, gearing & driving elements	-	-	-	...	-	-	-	...	-	-	-	...
2914 Ovens, furnaces and furnace burners	-	-	-	...	-	-	-	...	-	-	-	...
2915 Lifting and handling equipment	1	-	-	...	8	-	-	...	11.1	-	-	...
2919 Other general purpose machinery	1	2	2	...	24	47	55	...	66.8	123.4	132.0	...
292 Special purpose machinery	1	2	2	...	6	69	69	...	5.0	117.7	122.0	...
2921 Agricultural and forestry machinery	-	-	-	...	-	-	-	...	-	-	-	...
2922 Machine tools	1	-	-	...	6	-	-	...	5.0	-	-	...
2923 Machinery for metallurgy	-	-	-	...	-	-	-	...	-	-	-	...
2924 Machinery for mining & construction	-	-	-	...	-	-	-	...	-	-	-	...
2925 Food/beverage/tobacco processing machinery	-	-	-	...	-	-	-	...	-	-	-	...
2926 Machinery for textile, apparel and leather	-	-	-	...	-	-	-	...	-	-	-	...
2927 Weapons and ammunition	-	1	1	...	-	59	59	...	-	102.1	106.4	...
2929 Other special purpose machinery	-	1	1	...	-	10	10	...	-	15.6	15.6	...
2930 Domestic appliances n.e.c.	1	1	1	...	67	76	96	...	116.1	170.1	188.0	...

continued

Oman

ISIC Revision 3 ISIC Industry	Number of establishments (numbers) Note	1993	1994	1995	1996	Number of employees (numbers) Note	1993	1994	1995	1996	Wages and salaries paid to employees (thousand RIALS) Note	1993	1994	1995	1996
3000 Office, accounting and computing machinery		-	-	2	...		-	-	18	...		-	-	34.6	...
3110 Electric motors, generators and transformers		-	-	-	...		-	-	-	...		-	-	-	...
3120 Electricity distribution & control apparatus		-	2	2	...		-	55	56	...		-	119.0	138.8	...
3130 Insulated wire and cable		-	2	2	...		-	119	184	...		-	209.4	485.0	...
3140 Accumulators, primary cells and batteries		-	2	2	...		-	162	188	...		-	280.4	313.3	...
3150 Lighting equipment and electric lamps		-	1	1	...		-	31	31	...		-	40.6	40.6	...
3190 Other electrical equipment n.e.c.		-	-	-	...		-	-	-	...		-	-	-	...
3210 Electronic valves, tubes, etc.		-	-	-	...		-	-	-	...		-	-	-	...
3220 TV/radio transmitters; line comm. apparatus		-	-	-	...		-	-	-	...		-	-	-	...
3230 TV and radio receivers and associated goods		-	-	-	...		-	-	-	...		-	-	-	...
331 Medical, measuring, testing appliances, etc.		-	-	-	...		-	-	-	...		-	-	-	...
3311 Medical, surgical and orthopaedic equipment		-	-	-	...		-	-	-	...		-	-	-	...
3312 Measuring/testing/navigating appliances,etc.		-	-	-	...		-	-	-	...		-	-	-	...
3313 Industrial process control equipment		-	-	-	...		-	-	-	...		-	-	-	...
3320 Optical instruments & photographic equipment		-	-	1	...		-	-	14	...		-	-	30.4	...
3330 Watches and clocks		-	-	-	...		-	-	-	...		-	-	-	...
3410 Motor vehicles		-	1	-	...		-	4	-	...		-	2.4	-	...
3420 Automobile bodies, trailers & semi-trailers		1	2	1	...		23	2	1	...		59.9	1.9	1.2	...
3430 Parts/accessories for automobiles		10	2	3	...		275	39	48	...		415.6	59.8	120.3	...
351 Building and repairing of ships and boats		9	9	9	...		73	53	61	...		118.4	50.9	83.0	...
3511 Building and repairing of ships		9	9	9	...		73	53	61	...		118.4	50.9	83.0	...
3512 Building/repairing of pleasure/sport. boats		-	-	-	...		-	-	-	...		-	-	-	...
3520 Railway/tramway locomotives & rolling stock		-	-	-	...		-	-	-	...		-	-	-	...
3530 Aircraft and spacecraft		-	-	-	...		-	-	-	...		-	-	-	...
359 Transport equipment n.e.c.		-	-	-	...		-	-	-	...		-	-	-	...
3591 Motorcycles		-	-	-	...		-	-	-	...		-	-	-	...
3592 Bicycles and invalid carriages		-	-	-	...		-	-	-	...		-	-	-	...
3599 Other transport equipment n.e.c.		-	-	-	...		-	-	-	...		-	-	-	...
3610 Furniture		90	76	62	...		1956	1638	1195	...		3073.8	2824.2	2042.2	...
369 Manufacturing n.e.c.		6	7	3	...		124	121	96	...		244.6	249.0	200.6	...
3691 Jewellery and related articles		2	2	-	...		14	9	-	...		31.8	24.6	-	...
3692 Musical instruments		-	-	-	...		-	-	-	...		-	-	-	...
3693 Sports goods		-	-	-	...		-	-	-	...		-	-	-	...
3694 Games and toys		-	-	-	...		-	-	-	...		-	-	-	...
3699 Other manufacturing n.e.c.		4	5	3	...		110	112	96	...		212.9	224.4	200.6	...
3710 Recycling of metal waste and scrap		1	2	2	...		13	28	26	...		45.1	68.8	80.4	...
3720 Recycling of non-metal waste and scrap		-	-	-	...		-	-	-	...		-	-	-	...
D Total manufacturing		1520	1416	1355	...		25275	26408	26916	...		44076.0	49293.9	52549.9	...

Oman

ISIC Revision 3		Output					Value added					Gross fixed capital formation		
			(thousand RIALS)					(thousand RIALS)					(thousand RIALS)	
ISIC	Industry	Note	1993	1994	1995	1996	Note	1993	1994	1995	1996	Note	1994	1995
151	Processed meat,fish,fruit,vegetables,fats		16573.7	25813.8	31913.2	...		4048.5	7653.0	7925.8	...		8717.2	18597.8
1511	Processing/preserving of meat		5.4	2271.3	3175.8	...		3.2	614.8	701.8	...		469.0	6259.8
1512	Processing/preserving of fish		4400.4	8128.4	9143.5	...		1711.9	3412.4	3170.0	...		3799.8	4263.0
1513	Processing/preserving of fruit & vegetables		1729.7	1970.1	1995.7	...		903.4	1000.9	1142.5	...		2879.7	3382.0
1514	Vegetable and animal oils and fats		10438.2	13444.0	17598.2	...		1430.0	2624.9	2911.5	...		1568.8	4693.0
1520	Dairy products		11651.4	10248.7	14208.6	...		4052.2	4063.9	5030.6	...		8920.3	7941.9
153	Grain mill products; starches; animal feeds		29152.9	31903.8	32397.3	...		8979.1	10412.4	10028.9	...		15990.4	15639.7
1531	Grain mill products		16338.5	17740.3	18847.9	...		5461.4	6097.0	5929.2	...		8746.7	9527.3
1532	Starches and starch products		-	-	-	...		-	-	-	...		-	-
1533	Prepared animal feeds		12814.4	14163.5	13549.5	...		3517.6	4315.4	4099.8	...		7243.7	6112.4
154	Other food products		18682.1	18951.3	19637.2	...		8871.4	7907.1	7508.1	...		8863.5	7450.9
1541	Bakery products		10614.4	16482.5	17051.3	...		6115.8	6904.0	6421.8	...		6888.2	6084.3
1542	Sugar		-	-	-	...		-	-	-	...		-	-
1543	Cocoa, chocolate and sugar confectionery		465.9	764.0	572.7	...		219.4	360.6	230.1	...		725.5	584.8
1544	Macaroni, noodles & similar products		-	-	-	...		-	-	-	...		-	-
1549	Other food products n.e.c.		7601.8	1704.8	2013.3	...		2536.2	642.5	856.2	...		1249.8	781.9
155	Beverages		12642.6	15361.0	24874.4	...		1223.2	3816.7	7684.9	...		14030.9	15283.7
1551	Distilling, rectifying & blending of spirits		-	-	-	...		-	-	-	...		-	-
1552	Wines		-	-	-	...		-	-	-	...		-	-
1553	Malt liquors and malt		-	-	-	...		-	-	-	...		-	-
1554	Soft drinks; mineral waters		12642.6	15361.0	24874.4	...		1223.2	3816.7	7684.9	...		14030.9	15283.7
1600	Tobacco products		-	-	-	...		-	-	-	...		-	-
171	Spinning, weaving and finishing of textiles		6868.8	7286.6	8428.5	...		4376.3	4556.8	5108.1	...		6899.3	7188.6
1711	Textile fibre preparation; textile weaving		6868.8	7286.6	8428.5	...		4376.3	4556.8	5108.1	...		6899.3	7188.6
1712	Finishing of textiles		-	-	-	...		-	-	-	...		-	-
172	Other textiles		30.8	201.1	236.8	...		18.3	143.5	83.9	...		13.1	85.0
1721	Made-up textile articles, except apparel		30.8	201.1	236.8	...		18.3	143.5	83.9	...		13.1	85.0
1722	Carpets and rugs		-	-	-	...		-	-	-	...		-	-
1723	Cordage, rope, twine and netting		-	-	-	...		-	-	-	...		-	-
1729	Other textiles n.e.c.		-	-	-	...		-	-	-	...		-	-
1730	Knitted and crocheted fabrics and articles		-	-	-	...		-	-	-	...		-	-
1810	Wearing apparel, except fur apparel		24625.7	35014.5	38196.3	...		7531.2	16947.5	15771.1	...		6738.5	7474.7
1820	Dressing & dyeing of fur; processing of fur		-	-	-	...		-	-	-	...		-	-
191	Tanning, dressing and processing of leather		-	-	-	...		-	-	-	...		-	-
1911	Tanning and dressing of leather		-	-	-	...		-	-	-	...		-	-
1912	Luggage, handbags, etc.; saddlery & harness		-	-	-	...		-	-	-	...		-	-
1920	Footwear		593.1	182.2	669.0	...		334.0	74.1	294.9	...		34.3	125.6
2010	Sawmilling and planing of wood		-	-	-	...		-	-	-	...		-	-
202	Products of wood, cork, straw, etc.		6211.9	7563.2	11157.8	...		2973.0	4015.0	5834.7	...		3233.6	4812.1
2021	Veneer sheets, plywood, particle board, etc.		-	-	-	...		-	-	-	...		-	-
2022	Builders' carpentry and joinery		5927.6	7547.7	11079.6	...		2914.3	4008.0	5830.4	...		3233.1	4806.7
2023	Wooden containers		125.8	15.4	78.2	...		26.9	7.0	4.3	...		0.5	5.4
2029	Other wood products; articles of cork/straw		158.5	-	-	...		31.7	-	-	...		-	-
210	Paper and paper products		5687.4	4213.2	9516.1	...		2606.5	1984.2	3254.4	...		1456.8	5209.1
2101	Pulp, paper and paperboard		442.3	2772.1	2811.0	...		154.6	1457.1	801.7	...		688.9	1424.1
2102	Corrugated paper and paperboard		2827.6	18.7	2015.0	...		1200.8	9.4	407.9	...		103.7	2590.7
2109	Other articles of paper and paperboard		2417.4	1422.4	4690.1	...		1251.1	517.8	2044.9	...		664.2	1194.3
221	Publishing		4710.6	7523.2	7468.1	...		2186.2	4223.7	4348.7	...		10283.6	15413.1
2211	Publishing of books and other publications		3300.7	3629.2	3780.8	...		1439.0	1529.8	1953.4	...		6075.5	6374.9
2212	Publishing of newspapers, journals, etc.		-	2386.2	3464.0	...		-	1790.4	2224.8	...		2497.8	8804.5
2213	Publishing of recorded media		-	213.0	213.0	...		-	165.7	165.7	...		219.6	219.6
2219	Other publishing		1409.9	1294.7	10.4	...		747.2	737.9	4.8	...		1490.7	14.0

continued

Oman

ISIC	ISIC Revision 3 Industry	Note	Output (thousand RIALS) 1993	1994	1995	1996	Note	Value added (thousand RIALS) 1993	1994	1995	1996	Note	Gross fixed capital formation (thousand RIALS) 1994	1995
222	Printing and related service activities		3837.6	3354.4	3546.1	...		1734.3	1588.7	1655.6	...		3817.6	3645.5
2221	Printing		3837.6	3354.4	3546.1	...		1734.3	1588.7	1655.6	...		3817.6	3645.5
2222	Service activities related to printing		-	-	-	...		-	-	-	...		-	-
2230	Reproduction of recorded media		-	-	-	...		-	-	-	...		-	-
2310	Coke oven products		-	-	11.2	...		-	-	6.5	...		-	25.3
2320	Refined petroleum products		239703.7	226642.3	202238.0	...		89463.3	45367.2	70649.4	...		12997.7	95604.2
2330	Processing of nuclear fuel		-	-	-	...		-	-	-	...		-	-
241	Basic chemicals		1557.0	2232.9	2591.2	...		739.7	1605.7	1952.8	...		1748.8	1657.4
2411	Basic chemicals, except fertilizers		856.7	2232.9	2591.2	...		498.6	1605.7	1952.8	...		1748.8	1657.4
2412	Fertilizers and nitrogen compounds		-	-	-	...		-	-	-	...		-	-
2413	Plastics in primary forms; synthetic rubber		700.3	-	-	...		241.1	-	-	...		-	-
242	Other chemicals		28841.9	29714.3	36028.9	...		10286.8	12059.3	12563.5	...		7189.2	8163.6
2421	Pesticides and other agro-chemical products		347.5	399.3	709.5	...		81.4	82.1	209.8	...		150.3	264.5
2422	Paints, varnishes, printing ink and mastics		7897.3	7855.5	8653.2	...		3913.3	3742.3	3333.0	...		1532.6	2023.0
2423	Pharmaceuticals, medicinal chemicals, etc.		6948.0	9122.4	13175.4	...		656.5	2701.0	3354.1	...		2318.5	2542.9
2424	Soap, cleaning & cosmetic preparations		13037.8	12137.1	13138.3	...		5348.7	5403.9	5470.1	...		3082.5	2930.1
2429	Other chemical products n.e.c.		611.3	200.1	352.5	...		286.9	130.0	196.5	...		105.2	403.2
2430	Man-made fibres		-	-	-	...		-	-	-	...		-	-
251	Rubber products		-	46.2	76.3	...		-	16.5	40.8	...		211.9	97.7
2511	Rubber tyres and tubes		-	46.2	76.3	...		-	16.5	40.8	...		211.9	97.7
2519	Other rubber products		-	-	-	...		-	-	-	...		-	-
2520	Plastic products		9342.4	8753.4	10265.9	...		4647.4	4178.3	3922.7	...		6485.3	5731.2
2610	Glass and glass products		6958.2	8390.4	8362.3	...		3291.6	3842.8	3643.7	...		5544.6	5513.2
269	Non-metallic mineral products n.e.c.		72799.3	77567.9	77074.1	...		36293.7	42981.1	42072.3	...		80240.7	85056.7
2691	Pottery, china and earthenware		-	-	-	...		-	-	-	...		-	-
2692	Refractory ceramic products		1979.3	562.0	394.5	...		734.8	411.2	268.8	...		1578.3	1501.0
2693	Struct.non-refractory clay; ceramic products		-	-	-	...		-	-	-	...		-	-
2694	Cement, lime and plaster		27931.6	28898.3	31784.0	...		15385.7	16689.2	18656.8	...		49847.7	55361.6
2695	Articles of concrete, cement and plaster		30059.0	27811.5	23313.2	...		13503.6	13814.1	10685.3	...		18735.2	14989.2
2696	Cutting, shaping & finishing of stone		1700.4	2140.6	2397.4	...		1088.6	1024.0	1287.2	...		1037.4	3950.0
2699	Other non-metallic mineral products n.e.c.		11129.1	18155.3	19185.0	...		5580.9	11042.6	11174.2	...		9042.1	9254.9
2710	Basic iron and steel		-	-	-	...		-	-	-	...		-	-
2720	Basic precious and non-ferrous metals		25859.5	23617.0	27385.7	...		9781.2	10723.6	15242.9	...		45129.8	27129.2
273	Casting of metals		-	-	-	...		-	-	-	...		-	-
2731	Casting of iron and steel		-	-	-	...		-	-	-	...		-	-
2732	Casting of non-ferrous metals		-	-	-	...		-	-	-	...		-	-
281	Struct.metal products;tanks;steam generators		20916.4	23019.9	24442.1	...		12300.6	11843.1	12802.8	...		13493.9	9494.9
2811	Structural metal products		18927.8	23008.3	24442.1	...		11248.2	11837.4	12802.8	...		13489.9	9494.9
2812	Tanks, reservoirs and containers of metal		1988.6	11.6	-	...		1052.4	5.7	-	...		4.0	-
2813	Steam generators		-	-	-	...		-	-	-	...		-	-
289	Other metal products; metal working services		5966.0	5888.7	6038.2	...		1561.6	2206.4	1847.3	...		3077.7	4725.1
2891	Metal forging/pressing/stamping/roll-forming		-	-	75.0	...		-	-	66.3	...		-	8.9
2892	Treatment & coating of metals		10.9	565.2	162.5	...		6.5	254.0	58.7	...		245.4	16.5
2893	Cutlery, hand tools and general hardware		34.0	-	9.0	...		24.5	-	8.2	...		-	4.0
2899	Other fabricated metal products n.e.c.		5921.1	5323.6	5791.7	...		1530.6	1952.4	1714.2	...		2832.2	4695.7
291	General purpose machinery		4712.4	4443.4	6839.7	...		2428.9	1633.9	2308.5	...		639.0	1334.0
2911	Engines & turbines(not for transport equip.)		89.6	-	3.9	...		74.2	-	2.4	...		-	0.1
2912	Pumps, compressors, taps and valves		1992.8	2271.9	4823.2	...		803.2	813.1	1515.4	...		236.9	828.8
2913	Bearings, gears, gearing & driving elements		-	-	-	...		-	-	-	...		-	-
2914	Ovens, furnaces and furnace burners		-	-	-	...		-	-	-	...		-	-
2915	Lifting and handling equipment		71.8	-	-	...		23.8	-	-	...		-	-
2919	Other general purpose machinery		2558.3	2171.4	2012.7	...		1527.8	820.9	790.7	...		402.1	505.1

ISIC	Description													
292	Special purpose machinery		31.8	461.1	400.5	...		27.6	311.8	279.6	...		99.9	83.0
2921	Agricultural and forestry machinery		-	-	-	...		-	-	-	...		-	-
2922	Machine tools		31.8	-	-	...		27.6	-	-	...		-	-
2923	Machinery for metallurgy		-	-	-	...		-	-	-	...		-	-
2924	Machinery for mining & construction		-	-	-	...		-	-	-	...		-	-
2925	Food/beverage/tobacco processing machinery		-	-	-	...		-	-	-	...		-	-
2926	Machinery for textile, apparel and leather		-	-	-	...		-	-	-	...		-	-
2927	Weapons and ammunition		-	426.1	365.5	...		-	290.2	258.0	...		35.5	25.3
2929	Other special purpose machinery		-	35.0	35.0	...		-	21.6	21.6	...		64.4	57.6
2930	Domestic appliances n.e.c.		1734.4	1979.4	1860.8	...		400.7	419.2	818.4	...		112.9	-
3000	Office, accounting and computing machinery		-	-	522.4	...		-	-	121.4	...		-	288.1
3110	Electric motors, generators and transformers		-	-	-	...		-	-	-	...		-	-
3120	Electricity distribution & control apparatus		-	1094.5	1265.9	...		-	399.9	528.5	...		304.6	131.6
3130	Insulated wire and cable		-	1583.5	5046.1	...		-	466.2	1830.2	...		3164.3	9537.2
3140	Accumulators, primary cells and batteries		-	3921.3	4416.3	...		-	1955.9	1714.4	...		1638.6	2397.0
3150	Lighting equipment and electric lamps		-	162.9	162.9	...		-	55.6	55.6	...		42.2	86.8
3190	Other electrical equipment n.e.c.		-	-	-	...		-	-	-	...		-	-
3210	Electronic valves, tubes, etc.		-	-	-	...		-	-	-	...		-	-
3220	TV/radio transmitters; line comm. apparatus		-	-	-	...		-	-	-	...		-	-
3230	TV and radio receivers and associated goods		-	-	-	...		-	-	-	...		-	-
331	Medical, measuring, testing appliances, etc.		-	-	-	...		-	-	-	...		-	-
3311	Medical, surgical and orthopaedic equipment		-	-	-	...		-	-	-	...		-	-
3312	Measuring/testing/navigating appliances,etc.		-	-	-	...		-	-	-	...		-	-
3313	Industrial process control equipment		-	-	-	...		-	-	-	...		-	-
3320	Optical instruments & photographic equipment		-	-	48.7	...		-	-	20.5	...		-	197.7
3330	Watches and clocks		-	-	-	...		-	-	-	...		-	-
3410	Motor vehicles		-	4.8	-	...		-	2.5	-	...		2.0	-
3420	Automobile bodies, trailers & semi-trailers		531.7	10.3	8.4	...		262.3	5.7	1.9	...		2.8	2.3
3430	Parts/accessories for automobiles		3580.7	202.7	364.5	...		1527.1	113.7	219.2	...		28.7	90.7
351	Building and repairing of ships and boats		451.0	284.2	314.1	...		225.9	139.8	148.4	...		348.6	343.2
3511	Building and repairing of ships		451.0	284.2	314.1	...		225.9	139.8	148.4	...		348.6	343.2
3512	Building/repairing of pleasure/sport. boats		-	-	-	...		-	-	-	...		-	-
3520	Railway/tramway locomotives & rolling stock		-	-	-	...		-	-	-	...		-	-
3530	Aircraft and spacecraft		-	-	-	...		-	-	-	...		-	-
359	Transport equipment n.e.c.		-	-	-	...		-	-	-	...		-	-
3591	Motorcycles		-	-	-	...		-	-	-	...		-	-
3592	Bicycles and invalid carriages		-	-	-	...		-	-	-	...		-	-
3599	Other transport equipment n.e.c.		-	-	-	...		-	-	-	...		-	-
3610	Furniture		16054.2	13690.0	11815.9	...		8476.4	7087.8	5281.9	...		6648.2	7351.9
369	Manufacturing n.e.c.		1550.3	1746.4	1461.7	...		596.4	656.5	743.0	...		818.9	865.5
3691	Jewellery and related articles		102.3	35.8	-	...		20.5	-5.9	-	...		46.2	-
3692	Musical instruments		-	-	-	...		-	-	-	...		-	-
3693	Sports goods		-	-	-	...		-	-	-	...		-	-
3694	Games and toys		-	-	-	...		-	-	-	...		-	-
3699	Other manufacturing n.e.c.		1448.0	1710.7	1461.7	...		575.9	662.4	743.0	...		772.7	865.5
3710	Recycling of metal waste and scrap		348.4	561.5	696.4	...		117.4	197.0	316.9	...		78.7	60.4
3720	Recycling of non-metal waste and scrap		-	-	-	...		-	-	-	...		-	-
D	Total manufacturing		582208.0	603635.9	631987.7	...		231362.7	215656.0	253662.9	...		279048.1	374835.4

Oman

ISIC Revision 3		Index numbers of industrial production											
		(1990=100)											
ISIC Industry	Note	1985	1986	1987	1988	1989	1990	1991	1992	1993	1994	1995	1996
15 Food and beverages		...	...	...	...	...	...	...	...	...	...	...	...
16 Tobacco products		...	...	...	...	...	...	...	...	...	...	...	...
17 Textiles		...	...	...	...	...	...	...	...	...	...	...	...
18 Wearing apparel, fur		...	...	...	...	...	...	...	...	...	...	...	...
19 Leather, leather products and footwear		...	...	...	...	...	...	...	...	...	...	...	...
20 Wood products (excl. furniture)		...	...	...	...	...	...	...	...	...	...	...	...
21 Paper and paper products		...	...	...	...	...	...	...	...	...	...	...	...
22 Printing and publishing		...	...	...	...	...	...	...	...	...	...	...	...
23 Coke,refined petroleum products,nuclear fuel		...	...	...	...	...	...	...	...	...	...	...	...
24 Chemicals and chemical products		...	...	...	...	...	...	...	...	...	...	...	...
25 Rubber and plastics products		...	...	...	...	...	...	...	...	...	...	...	...
26 Non-metallic mineral products		...	...	...	...	...	...	...	...	...	...	...	...
27 Basic metals		...	...	...	...	...	...	...	...	...	...	...	...
28 Fabricated metal products		...	...	...	...	...	...	...	...	...	...	...	...
29 Machinery and equipment n.e.c.		...	...	...	...	...	...	...	...	...	...	...	...
30 Office, accounting and computing machinery		...	...	...	...	...	...	...	...	...	...	...	...
31 Electrical machinery and apparatus		...	...	...	...	...	...	...	...	...	...	...	...
32 Radio,television and communication equipment		...	...	...	...	...	...	...	...	...	...	...	...
33 Medical, precision and optical instruments		...	...	...	...	...	...	...	...	...	...	...	...
34 Motor vehicles, trailers, semi-trailers		...	...	...	...	...	...	...	...	...	...	...	...
35 Other transport equipment		...	...	...	...	...	...	...	...	...	...	...	...
36 Furniture; manufacturing n.e.c.		...	...	...	...	...	...	...	...	...	...	...	...
37 Recycling		...	...	...	...	...	...	...	...	...	...	...	...
D Total manufacturing		...	...	...	...	...	...	...	...	...	...	...	...

PANAMA

Supplier of information:
Dirección de Estadística y Censo, Contraloría General de la República, Panama.

Basic source of data:
National Economic Census.

Major deviations from ISIC (Revision 3):
None reported.

Reference period (if not calendar year):

Scope:
Establishments with five or more persons engaged.

Method of enumeration:
Individual sites are visited by enumerators.

Adjusted for non-response:
Not reported.

Concepts and definitions of variables:

Related national publications:
Fourth Censos Económicos Nacionales, Volúmen I, estructura productiva y financiera de las industrias manufactureras, published by the Dirección de Estadística y Censo, Panama.

Panama

ISIC Revision 3	Number of establishments					Number of employees					Wages and salaries paid to employees				
		(numbers)					(numbers)					(thousand BALBOAS)			
ISIC Industry	Note	1992	1993	1994	1995	Note	1992	1993	1994	1995	Note	1992	1993	1994	1995
151 Processed meat,fish,fruit,vegetables,fats		67	62	61	...		5006	4394	4106	...		23010	31324	30184	...
1511 Processing/preserving of meat		33	31	31	...		1870	1856	1802	...		7162	9823	10310	...
1512 Processing/preserving of fish		23	20	20	...		1145	971	1053	...		4586	4927	5282	...
1513 Processing/preserving of fruit & vegetables		8	8	7	...		1242	812	536	...		6517	8075	6430	...
1514 Vegetable and animal oils and fats		3	3	3	...		749	755	715	...		4745	8499	8162	...
1520 Dairy products		27	25	25	...		1641	1467	1557	...		9817	21538	23708	...
153 Grain mill products; starches; animal feeds		75	71	71	...		1501	1847	1983	...		5925	14795	15531	...
1531 Grain mill products		62	58	58	...		1138	1473	1473	...		4476	12535	12971	...
1532 Starches and starch products		-	-	-	...		-	-	-	...		-	-	-	...
1533 Prepared animal feeds		13	13	13	...		363	374	510	...		1449	2260	2740	...
154 Other food products		258	252	252	...		7632	6734	7236	...		33524	41875	40641	...
1541 Bakery products		182	179	179	...		3508	3323	3426	...		10472	15509	16355	...
1542 Sugar		4	4	4	...		2306	1645	1930	...		15631	16009	13723	...
1543 Cocoa, chocolate and sugar confectionery		8	5	5	...		180	131	146	...		610	690	737	...
1544 Macaroni, noodles & similar products		9	9	9	...		229	231	230	...		1040	1345	1382	...
1549 Other food products n.e.c.		55	55	55	...		1409	1404	1504	...		5771	8322	8444	...
155 Beverages		19	19	18	...		1773	1899	2003	...		10921	18075	17114	...
1551 Distilling, rectifying & blending of spirits		9	8	8	...		519	536	545	...		2740	4540	4503	...
1552 Wines		-	-	-	...		-	-	-	...		-	-	-	...
1553 Malt liquors and malt		4	4	4	...		793	844	943	...		5324	8811	8463	...
1554 Soft drinks; mineral waters		6	7	6	...		461	519	515	...		2857	4724	4148	...
1600 Tobacco products		2	2	2	...		374	307	232	...		3594	5368	4399	...
171 Spinning, weaving and finishing of textiles		-	-	-	...		-	-	-	...		-	-	-	...
1711 Textile fibre preparation; textile weaving		-	-	-	...		-	-	-	...		-	-	-	...
1712 Finishing of textiles		-	-	-	...		-	-	-	...		-	-	-	...
172 Other textiles		10	5	5	...		194	96	106	...		662	509	531	...
1721 Made-up textile articles, except apparel		7	5a/	5a/	...		117	96a/	106a/	...		323	509a/	531a/	...
1722 Carpets and rugs		-	...a/	...a/	...		-	...a/	...a/	...		-	...a/	...a/	...
1723 Cordage, rope, twine and netting		...b/	...a/	...a/	...		...b/	...a/	...a/	...		...b/	...a/	...a/	...
1729 Other textiles n.e.c.		3b/	-	-	...		77b/	-	-	...		339b/	-	-	...
1730 Knitted and crocheted fabrics and articles		3	3	3	...		287	315	296	...		868	1514	1557	...
1810 Wearing apparel, except fur apparel		79	72	72	...		5485	5028	5208	...		16641	20085	19132	...
1820 Dressing & dyeing of fur; processing of fur		-	-	-	...		-	-	-	...		-	-	-	...
191 Tanning, dressing and processing of leather		12	8	8	...		317	330	283	...		1237	1565	1840	...
1911 Tanning and dressing of leather		7	8c/	8c/	...		291	330c/	283c/	...		1187	1565c/	1840c/	...
1912 Luggage, handbags, etc.; saddlery & harness		5	...c/	...c/	...		26	...c/	...c/	...		50	...c/	...c/	...
1920 Footwear		21	20	20	...		855	729	704	...		2854	3513	3343	...
2010 Sawmilling and planing of wood		9	8	8	...		390	387	385	...		1144	1747	1743	...
202 Products of wood, cork, straw, etc.		31	26	26	...		546	590	659	...		1518	2424	2734	...
2021 Veneer sheets, plywood, particle board, etc.		4	4	4	...		314	314	316	...		824	1239	1546	...
2022 Builders' carpentry and joinery		19	16	16	...		171	225	285	...		523	995	991	...
2023 Wooden containers		4	6d/	6d/	...		23	51d/	58d/	...		47	190d/	197d/	...
2029 Other wood products; articles of cork/straw		4	...d/	...d/	...		38	...d/	...d/	...		124	...d/	...d/	...
210 Paper and paper products		29	23	23	...		1280	1277	1474	...		8410	12568	13316	...
2101 Pulp, paper and paperboard		3	3	3	...		191	190	190	...		1459	2266	1976	...
2102 Corrugated paper and paperboard		10	9	9	...		685	694	811	...		4393	6538	7040	...
2109 Other articles of paper and paperboard		16	11	11	...		404	393	473	...		2558	3764	4300	...
221 Publishing		16	14	14	...		887	933	975	...		5357	8628	8991	...
2211 Publishing of books and other publications		-	-	-	...		-	-	-	...		-	-	-	...
2212 Publishing of newspapers, journals, etc.		7	5	5	...		793	815	856	...		4925	7998	8276	...
2213 Publishing of recorded media		-	-	-	...		-	-	-	...		-	-	-	...
2219 Other publishing		9	9	9	...		94	118	119	...		432	630	715	...

222 Printing and related service activities	64	66	66	...	1110	1127	1155	...	5460	6377	6359	...
2221 Printing	64	66	66	...	1110	1127	1155	...	5460	6377	6359	...
2222 Service activities related to printing	-	-	-	...	-	-	-	...	-	-	-	...
2230 Reproduction of recorded media	-	-	-	...	-	-	-	...	-	-	-	...
2310 Coke oven products	-	-	-	...	-	-	-	...	-	-	-	...
2320 Refined petroleum products	6	6	6	...	439	443	434	...	12041	15685	16384	...
2330 Processing of nuclear fuel	-	-	-	...	-	-	-	...	-	-	-	...
241 Basic chemicals	...	...	...	...	...	...	...	...	...	...	...	...
2411 Basic chemicals, except fertilizers	6	6	6	...	135	190	183	...	900	1621	1546	...
2412 Fertilizers and nitrogen compounds	...e/	...e/	...e/	...	...e/	...e/	...e/	...	...e/	...e/	...e/	...
2413 Plastics in primary forms; synthetic rubber	-	-	-	...	-	-	-	...	-	-	-	...
242 Other chemicals	...	...	...	...	...	...	...	...	...	...	...	...
2421 Pesticides and other agro-chemical products	...e/	...e/	...e/	...	...e/	...e/	...e/	...	...e/	...e/	...e/	...
2422 Paints, varnishes, printing ink and mastics	8	8	8	...	305	355	391	...	1568	3225	3446	...
2423 Pharmaceuticals, medicinal chemicals, etc.	9	7	7	...	286	261	310	...	1471	2143	2337	...
2424 Soap, cleaning & cosmetic preparations	23	18	18	...	845	781	827	...	3716	5962	6563	...
2429 Other chemical products n.e.c.	5e/	4e/	4e/	...	122e/	63e/	72e/	...	416e/	301e/	371e/	...
2430 Man-made fibres	-	-	-	...	-	-	-	...	-	-	-	...
251 Rubber products	7	6	6	...	170	187	192	...	565	1040	1150	...
2511 Rubber tyres and tubes	7	6	6	...	170	187	192	...	565	1040	1150	...
2519 Other rubber products	-	-	-	...	-	-	-	...	-	-	-	...
2520 Plastic products	40	42	42	...	1973	2018	2159	...	9176	14016	14921	...
2610 Glass and glass products	7	5	5	...	321	269	364	...	1136	1531	1883	...
269 Non-metallic mineral products n.e.c.	...	...	...	...	...	...	...	...	...	...	...	...
2691 Pottery, china and earthenware	7	5	5	...	154	241	235	...	739	1759	1766	...
2692 Refractory ceramic products	-	-	-	...	-	-	-	...	-	-	-	...
2693 Struct.non-refractory clay; ceramic products	3	-	-	...	108	-	-	...	401	-	-	...
2694 Cement, lime and plaster	4	4	4	...	720	651	620	...	4125	5444	5422	...
2695 Articles of concrete, cement and plaster	62f/	52f/	52f/	...	1161f/	1623f/	1628f/	...	4673f/	8061f/	8569f/	...
2696 Cutting, shaping & finishing of stone	...f/g/	...f/g/	...f/g/	...	...f/g/	...f/g/	...f/g/	...	...f/g/	...f/g/	...f/g/	...
2699 Other non-metallic mineral products n.e.c.	-	-	-	...	-	-	-	...	-	-	-	...
2710 Basic iron and steel	5	5h/	5h/	...	355	555h/	511h/	...	1825	2458h/	2584h/	...
2720 Basic precious and non-ferrous metals	5	...h/	...h/	...	190	...h/	...h/	...	715	...h/	...h/	...
273 Casting of metals	-	-	-	...	-	-	-	...	-	-	-	...
2731 Casting of iron and steel	-	-	-	...	-	-	-	...	-	-	-	...
2732 Casting of non-ferrous metals	-	-	-	...	-	-	-	...	-	-	-	...
281 Struct.metal products;tanks;steam generators	46	53	53	...	645	1021	1019	...	2937	8225	9256	...
2811 Structural metal products	40	48	48	...	533	906	875	...	2335	7435	8257	...
2812 Tanks, reservoirs and containers of metal	6	5	5	...	112	115	144	...	602	790	999	...
2813 Steam generators	-	-	-	...	-	-	-	...	-	-	-	...
289 Other metal products; metal working services	...	...	...	...	...	...	...	...	...	...	...	...
2891 Metal forging/pressing/stamping/roll-forming	-	-	-	...	-	-	-	...	-	-	-	...
2892 Treatment & coating of metals	3	3	3	...	30	66	68	...	319	450	503	...
2893 Cutlery, hand tools and general hardware	...i/g/	...i/g/	...i/g/	...	...i/g/	...i/g/	...i/g/	...	...i/g/	...i/g/	...i/g/	...
2899 Other fabricated metal products n.e.c.	22i/	23i/	21i/	...	324i/	302i/	293i/	...	1201i/	1578i/	1739i/	...
291 General purpose machinery	5	4	4	...	60	58	35	...	199	237	239	...
2911 Engines & turbines(not for transport equip.)	-	-	-	...	-	-	-	...	-	-	-	...
2912 Pumps, compressors, taps and valves	-	-	-	...	-	-	-	...	-	-	-	...
2913 Bearings, gears, gearing & driving elements	-	-	-	...	-	-	-	...	-	-	-	...
2914 Ovens, furnaces and furnace burners	-	-	-	...	-	-	-	...	-	-	-	...
2915 Lifting and handling equipment	-	-	-	...	-	-	-	...	-	-	-	...
2919 Other general purpose machinery	5j/	4j/	4j/	...	60j/	58j/	35j/	...	199j/	237j/	239j/	...
292 Special purpose machinery	...	...	...	...	...	...	...	...	...	...	...	...
2921 Agricultural and forestry machinery	-	-	-	...	-	-	-	...	-	-	-	...
2922 Machine tools	-	-	-	...	-	-	-	...	-	-	-	...
2923 Machinery for metallurgy	-	-	-	...	-	-	-	...	-	-	-	...
2924 Machinery for mining & construction	-	-	-	...	-	-	-	...	-	-	-	...
2925 Food/beverage/tobacco processing machinery	...g/	...g/	...g/	...	...g/	...g/	...g/	...	...g/	...g/	...g/	...
2926 Machinery for textile, apparel and leather	-	-	-	...	-	-	-	...	-	-	-	...
2927 Weapons and ammunition	-	-	-	...	-	-	-	...	-	-	-	...
2929 Other special purpose machinery	...j/g/	...j/g/	...j/g/	...	...j/g/	...j/g/	...j/g/	...	...j/g/	...j/g/	...j/g/	...
2930 Domestic appliances n.e.c.	3	3	3	...	67	65	51	...	308	470	428	...

continued

ISIC Revision 3	Number of establishments					Number of employees					Wages and salaries paid to employees				
		(numbers)					(numbers)					(thousand BALBOAS)			
ISIC Industry	Note	1992	1993	1994	1995	Note	1992	1993	1994	1995	Note	1992	1993	1994	1995
3000 Office, accounting and computing machinery		-	-	-	...		-	-	-	...		-	-	-	...
3110 Electric motors, generators and transformers		5	4	4	...		46	49	53	...		197	228	187	...
3120 Electricity distribution & control apparatus		-	-	-	...		-	-	-	...		-	-	-	...
3130 Insulated wire and cable		...k/g/	...k/g/	...k/g/	...		...k/g/	...k/g/	...k/g/	...		...k/g/	...k/g/	...k/g/	...
3140 Accumulators, primary cells and batteries		...k/	...k/	...k/	...		...k/	...k/	...k/	...		...k/	...k/	...k/	...
3150 Lighting equipment and electric lamps		8k/	10k/	10k/	...		100k/	252k/	276k/	...		595k/	1843k/	2000k/	...
3190 Other electrical equipment n.e.c.		-	-	-	...		-	-	-	...		-	-	-	...
3210 Electronic valves, tubes, etc.		-	-	-	...		-	-	-	...		-	-	-	...
3220 TV/radio transmitters; line comm. apparatus		-	-	-	...		-	-	-	...		-	-	-	...
3230 TV and radio receivers and associated goods		3	-	-	...		37	-	-	...		288	-	-	...
331 Medical, measuring, testing appliances, etc.		9	8	8	...		71	58	62	...		319	361	383	...
3311 Medical, surgical and orthopaedic equipment		9	8	8	...		71	58	62	...		319	361	383	...
3312 Measuring/testing/navigating appliances,etc.		-	-	-	...		-	-	-	...		-	-	-	...
3313 Industrial process control equipment		-	-	-	...		-	-	-	...		-	-	-	...
3320 Optical instruments & photographic equipment		4	3	3	...		32	28	26	...		119	145	125	...
3330 Watches and clocks		-	-	-	...		-	-	-	...		-	-	-	...
3410 Motor vehicles		-	-	-	...		-	-	-	...		-	-	-	...
3420 Automobile bodies, trailers & semi-trailers		4	3	3	...		68	76	91	...		207	296	367	...
3430 Parts/accessories for automobiles		11	11	11	...		132	140	137	...		614	722	802	...
351 Building and repairing of ships and boats		9	8	8	...		554	459	369	...		1856	3507	4789	...
3511 Building and repairing of ships		9	8	8	...		554	459	369	...		1856	3507	4789	...
3512 Building/repairing of pleasure/sport. boats		-	-	-	...		-	-	-	...		-	-	-	...
3520 Railway/tramway locomotives & rolling stock		-	-	-	...		-	-	-	...		-	-	-	...
3530 Aircraft and spacecraft		4	3	3	...		40	31	28	...		235	266	234	...
359 Transport equipment n.e.c.		-	-	-	...		-	-	-	...		-	-	-	...
3591 Motorcycles		-	-	-	...		-	-	-	...		-	-	-	...
3592 Bicycles and invalid carriages		-	-	-	...		-	-	-	...		-	-	-	...
3599 Other transport equipment n.e.c.		-	-	-	...		-	-	-	...		-	-	-	...
3610 Furniture		85	69	69	...		1596	1553	1635	...		4911	6734	7120	...
369 Manufacturing n.e.c.		22	16	16	...		618	827	1001	...		2315	3286	4100	...
3691 Jewellery and related articles		7	5	5	...		97	100	94	...		474	644	731	...
3692 Musical instruments		-	-	-	...		-	-	-	...		-	-	-	...
3693 Sports goods		-	-	-	...		-	-	-	...		-	-	-	...
3694 Games and toys		-	-	-	...		-	-	-	...		-	-	-	...
3699 Other manufacturing n.e.c.		15g/	11g/	11g/	...		521g/	727g/	907g/	...		1841g/	2642g/	3369g/	...
3710 Recycling of metal waste and scrap		-	-	-	...		-	-	-	...		-	-	-	...
3720 Recycling of non-metal waste and scrap		-	-	-	...		-	-	-	...		-	-	-	...
D Total manufacturing		1162	1065	1061	...		40982	40082	41432	...		191029	283483	290357	...

a/ 1721 includes 1722 and 1723.
b/ 1729 includes 1723.
c/ 1911 includes 1912.
d/ 2023 includes 2029.
e/ 2429 includes 2412 and 2421.
f/ 2695 includes 2696.
g/ 3699 includes 2696, 2893, 2925, 2929 and 3130.
h/ 2710 includes 2720.
i/ 2899 includes 2893.
j/ 2919 includes 2929.
k/ 3150 includes 3130 and 3140.

Panama

ISIC Revision 3 ISIC Industry	Output in producers' prices (thousand BALBOAS) Note	1992	1993	1994	1995	Value added in producers' prices (thousand BALBOAS) Note	1992	1993	1994	1995	Gross fixed capital formation (thousand BALBOAS) Note	1993	1994
151 Processed meat,fish,fruit,vegetables,fats		276609	294194	317412	...		76538	62558	70270	...		12407	11720
1511 Processing/preserving of meat		93468	90651	105319	...		15032	16582	17142	...		6123	1464
1512 Processing/preserving of fish		56966	58867	67743	...		15308	7743	12028	...		333	1138
1513 Processing/preserving of fruit & vegetables		58468	67360	65261	...		23795	18199	19805	...		4248	6828
1514 Vegetable and animal oils and fats		67707	77316	79089	...		22403	20034	21295	...		1703	2290
1520 Dairy products		115699	119737	131491	...		39906	37903	42472	...		12353	7091
153 Grain mill products; starches; animal feeds		147837	162268	172323	...		27813	31354	34503	...		7049	6261
1531 Grain mill products		90325	98730	105465	...		20901	23803	26275	...		2233	4233
1532 Starches and starch products		-	-	-	...		-	-	-	...		-	-
1533 Prepared animal feeds		57512	63538	66858	...		6912	7551	8228	...		4816	2028
154 Other food products		245600	250430	259566	...		106895	80545	81477	...		11503	11816
1541 Bakery products		65801	73461	75443	...		25289	22532	24262	...		2094	4225
1542 Sugar		89008	80592	79134	...		50707	37847	33839	...		4453	2392
1543 Cocoa, chocolate and sugar confectionery		5514	3622	4308	...		2495	1020	1267	...		101	80
1544 Macaroni, noodles & similar products		8034	7910	8951	...		2761	1912	2176	...		382	281
1549 Other food products n.e.c.		77243	84845	91730	...		25643	17234	19933	...		4473	4838
155 Beverages		154567	184059	191780	...		82366	72680	75369	...		11506	18701
1551 Distilling, rectifying & blending of spirits		36870	44261	44599	...		23752	21774	20888	...		386	2025
1552 Wines		-	-	-	...		-	-	-	...		-	-
1553 Malt liquors and malt		81624	83986	87143	...		47701	39135	43105	...		10203	14183
1554 Soft drinks; mineral waters		36073	55812	60038	...		10913	11771	11367	...		917	2493
1600 Tobacco products		40767	42094	37621	...		30575	22871	19585	...		985	-5857
171 Spinning, weaving and finishing of textiles		-	-	-	...		-	-	-	...		-	-
1711 Textile fibre preparation; textile weaving		-	-	-	...		-	-	-	...		-	-
1712 Finishing of textiles		-	-	-	...		-	-	-	...		-	-
172 Other textiles		4496	2648	3693	...		1448	804	322	...		173	346
1721 Made-up textile articles, except apparel		2851	2648a/	3693a/	...		950	804a/	322a/	...	a/	173	346
1722 Carpets and rugs		-	...a/	...a/	...		-	...a/	...a/	...	a/	...	...
1723 Cordage, rope, twine and netting		...b/	...a/	...a/	...		...b/	...a/	...a/	...	a/	...	...
1729 Other textiles n.e.c.		1645b/	-	-	...		498b/	-	-	...		-	-
1730 Knitted and crocheted fabrics and articles		7623	8414	8642	...		2969	2908	2993	...		1054	1542
1810 Wearing apparel, except fur apparel		82487	73353	74541	...		36374	25669	26337	...		1448	1281
1820 Dressing & dyeing of fur; processing of fur		-	-	-	...		-	-	-	...		-	-
191 Tanning, dressing and processing of leather		10671	14183	17064	...		2911	3706	3658	...		5	98
1911 Tanning and dressing of leather		10389	14183c/	17064c/	...		2804	3706c/	3658c/	...	c/	5	98
1912 Luggage, handbags, etc.; saddlery & harness		282	...c/	...c/	...		107	...c/	...c/	...	c/	...	...
1920 Footwear		19814	20230	18491	...		6474	4814	4939	...		-523	1033
2010 Sawmilling and planing of wood		8572	10662	11527	...		1855	2306	2361	...		234	289
202 Products of wood, cork, straw, etc.		9224	13154	14514	...		3789	3116	3569	...		458	818
2021 Veneer sheets, plywood, particle board, etc.		4971	5455	6865	...		2057	1379	1818	...		162	480
2022 Builders' carpentry and joinery		3284	6570	6512	...		1363	1413	1374	...		275	339
2023 Wooden containers		245	1129d/	1137d/	...		74	324d/	377d/	...	d/	21	-1
2029 Other wood products; articles of cork/straw		724	...d/	...d/	...		295	...d/	...d/	...	d/	...	...
210 Paper and paper products		117950	121484	132400	...		35557	29746	31911	...		12654	5720
2101 Pulp, paper and paperboard		22013	24579	24730	...		6429	6350	6548	...		345	46
2102 Corrugated paper and paperboard		64630	65788	73732	...		15964	13708	14446	...		5574	3707
2109 Other articles of paper and paperboard		31307	31117	33938	...		13164	9688	10917	...		6735	1967
221 Publishing		26682	34273	37765	...		13751	13259	15866	...		2169	6781
2211 Publishing of books and other publications		-	-	-	...		-	-	-	...		-	-
2212 Publishing of newspapers, journals, etc.		24981	32348	35625	...		12780	12471	14918	...		1890	6627
2213 Publishing of recorded media		-	-	-	...		-	-	-	...		-	-
2219 Other publishing		1701	1925	2140	...		971	788	948	...		279	154

continued

Panama

ISIC Revision 3	Output in producers' prices					Value added in producers' prices					Gross fixed capital formation		
		(thousand BALBOAS)					(thousand BALBOAS)					(thousand BALBOAS)	
ISIC Industry	Note	1992	1993	1994	1995	Note	1992	1993	1994	1995	Note	1993	1994
222 Printing and related service activities		30773	30145	32257	...		14113	9452	10497	...		1517	1605
2221 Printing		30773	30145	32257	...		14113	9452	10497	...		1517	1605
2222 Service activities related to printing		-	-	-	...		-	-	-	...		-	-
2230 Reproduction of recorded media		-	-	-	...		-	-	-	...		-	-
2310 Coke oven products		-	-	-	...		-	-	-	...		-	-
2320 Refined petroleum products		297319	285938	257975	...		33510	8879	6325	...		9980	47950
2330 Processing of nuclear fuel		-	-	-	...		-	-	-	...		-	-
241 Basic chemicals		...	...	...	...		...	...	...	...		...	...
2411 Basic chemicals, except fertilizers		11278	19113	22544	...		4787	5444	5731	...		1131	604
2412 Fertilizers and nitrogen compounds		...e/	...e/	...e/	...		...e/	...e/	...e/	...	e/	...	...
2413 Plastics in primary forms; synthetic rubber		-	-	-	...		-	-	-	...		-	-
242 Other chemicals		...	...	...	...		...	...	...	...		...	...
2421 Pesticides and other agro-chemical products		...e/	...e/	...e/	...		...e/	...e/	...e/	...	e/	...	...
2422 Paints, varnishes, printing ink and mastics		25739	31796	33057	...		7343	6316	6401	...		704	809
2423 Pharmaceuticals, medicinal chemicals, etc.		18689	18848	20833	...		9470	6733	7824	...		1426	1101
2424 Soap, cleaning & cosmetic preparations		48925	49512	46966	...		22992	15324	15171	...		4012	1930
2429 Other chemical products n.e.c.		13281e/	5345e/	5299e/	...		3233e/	869e/	847e/	...	e/	90	116
2430 Man-made fibres		-	-	-	...		-	-	-	...		-	-
251 Rubber products		5708	6764	7578	...		1553	1580	1406	...		308	366
2511 Rubber tyres and tubes		5708	6764	7578	...		1553	1580	1406	...		308	366
2519 Other rubber products		-	-	-	...		-	-	-	...		-	-
2520 Plastic products		76799	82850	88622	...		32077	27322	28259	...		7228	7708
2610 Glass and glass products		14905	16297	19916	...		7468	6777	8265	...		802	797
269 Non-metallic mineral products n.e.c.		...	...	...	...		...	...	...	...		...	...
2691 Pottery, china and earthenware		5363	6128	6115	...		3577	2306	3080	...		77	1018
2692 Refractory ceramic products		-	-	-	...		-	-	-	...		-	-
2693 Struct.non-refractory clay; ceramic products		2214	-	-	...		1303	-	-	...		-	-
2694 Cement, lime and plaster		43924	59404	65670	...		21148	21882	23042	...		1999	3177
2695 Articles of concrete, cement and plaster		49015f/	72888f/	83987f/	...		18152f/	16855f/	17671f/	...	f/	3563	5094
2696 Cutting, shaping & finishing of stone		...f/g/	...f/g/	...f/g/	...		...f/g/	...f/g/	...f/g/	...	f/g/	...	...
2699 Other non-metallic mineral products n.e.c.		-	-	-	...		-	-	-	...		-	-
2710 Basic iron and steel		33496	30972h/	25108h/	...		9876	7142h/	4596h/	...	h/	4497	1740
2720 Basic precious and non-ferrous metals		9809	...h/	...h/	...		2547	...h/	...h/	...	h/	...	...
273 Casting of metals		-	-	-	...		-	-	-	...		-	-
2731 Casting of iron and steel		-	-	-	...		-	-	-	...		-	-
2732 Casting of non-ferrous metals		-	-	-	...		-	-	-	...		-	-
281 Struct.metal products;tanks;steam generators		34972	62800	63838	...		10839	16442	17455	...		2055	1474
2811 Structural metal products		26869	55183	56136	...		8095	14843	15328	...		1515	733
2812 Tanks, reservoirs and containers of metal		8103	7617	7702	...		2744	1599	2127	...		540	741
2813 Steam generators		-	-	-	...		-	-	-	...		-	-
289 Other metal products; metal working services		...	...	...	...		...	...	...	...		...	...
2891 Metal forging/pressing/stamping/roll-forming		-	-	-	...		-	-	-	...		-	-
2892 Treatment & coating of metals		1416	1660	1914	...		880	730	720	...		142	139
2893 Cutlery, hand tools and general hardware		...i/g/	...i/g/	...i/g/	...		...i/g/	...i/g/	...i/g/	...	i/g/	...	...
2899 Other fabricated metal products n.e.c.		10713i/	11573i/	10814i/	...		3641i/	2909i/	2951i/	...	i/	170	103
291 General purpose machinery		565	821	637	...		391	428	280	...		118	2
2911 Engines & turbines(not for transport equip.)		-	-	-	...		-	-	-	...		-	-
2912 Pumps, compressors, taps and valves		-	-	-	...		-	-	-	...		-	-
2913 Bearings, gears, gearing & driving elements		-	-	-	...		-	-	-	...		-	-
2914 Ovens, furnaces and furnace burners		-	-	-	...		-	-	-	...		-	-
2915 Lifting and handling equipment		-	-	-	...		-	-	-	...		-	-
2919 Other general purpose machinery		565j/	821j/	637j/	...		391j/	428j/	280j/	...	j/	118	2

292 Special purpose machinery		...	...	...	...		...	...	...	...		...	...
2921 Agricultural and forestry machinery		-	-	-	...		-	-	-	...		-	-
2922 Machine tools		-	-	-	...		-	-	-	...		-	-
2923 Machinery for metallurgy		-	-	-	...		-	-	-	...		-	-
2924 Machinery for mining & construction		-	-	-	...		-	-	-	...		-	-
2925 Food/beverage/tobacco processing machinery		...g/	...g/	...g/	...		...g/	...g/	...g/	...	g/	...	...
2926 Machinery for textile, apparel and leather		-	-	-	...		-	-	-	...		-	-
2927 Weapons and ammunition		-	-	-	...		-	-	-	...		-	-
2929 Other special purpose machinery		...j/g/	...j/g/	...j/g/	...		...j/g/	...j/g/	...j/g/	...	j/g/	...	...
2930 Domestic appliances n.e.c.		3941	4149	4589	...		1131	752	972	...		206	-116
3000 Office, accounting and computing machinery		-	-	-	...		-	-	-	...		-	-
3110 Electric motors, generators and transformers		956	980	966	...		642	299	234	...		11	10
3120 Electricity distribution & control apparatus		-	-	-	...		-	-	-	...		-	-
3130 Insulated wire and cable		...k/g/	...k/g/	...k/g/	...		...k/g/	...k/g/	...k/g/	...	k/g/	...	...
3140 Accumulators, primary cells and batteries		...k/	...k/	...k/	...		...k/	...k/	...k/	...	k/	...	...
3150 Lighting equipment and electric lamps		2740k/	14797k/	17193k/	...		1063k/	3950k/	5203k/	...	k/	296	626
3190 Other electrical equipment n.e.c.		-	-	-	...		-	-	-	...		-	-
3210 Electronic valves, tubes, etc.		-	-	-	...		-	-	-	...		-	-
3220 TV/radio transmitters; line comm. apparatus		-	-	-	...		-	-	-	...		-	-
3230 TV and radio receivers and associated goods		706	-	-	...		465	-	-	...		-	-
331 Medical, measuring, testing appliances, etc.		989	926	1034	...		645	478	536	...		7	17
3311 Medical, surgical and orthopaedic equipment		989	926	1034	...		645	478	536	...		7	17
3312 Measuring/testing/navigating appliances,etc.		-	-	-	...		-	-	-	...		-	-
3313 Industrial process control equipment		-	-	-	...		-	-	-	...		-	-
3320 Optical instruments & photographic equipment		1410	1342	1409	...		771	365	379	...		142	-84
3330 Watches and clocks		-	-	-	...		-	-	-	...		-	-
3410 Motor vehicles		-	-	-	...		-	-	-	...		-	-
3420 Automobile bodies, trailers & semi-trailers		2110	1771	2079	...		887	487	566	...		10	82
3430 Parts/accessories for automobiles		3995	4084	4288	...		2291	1408	1372	...		272	354
351 Building and repairing of ships and boats		15520	12016	14928	...		12124	2779	5523	...		110	-33
3511 Building and repairing of ships		15520	12016	14928	...		12124	2779	5523	...		110	-33
3512 Building/repairing of pleasure/sport. boats		-	-	-	...		-	-	-	...		-	-
3520 Railway/tramway locomotives & rolling stock		-	-	-	...		-	-	-	...		-	-
3530 Aircraft and spacecraft		459	559	664	...		394	287	277	...		58	5
359 Transport equipment n.e.c.		-	-	-	...		-	-	-	...		-	-
3591 Motorcycles		-	-	-	...		-	-	-	...		-	-
3592 Bicycles and invalid carriages		-	-	-	...		-	-	-	...		-	-
3599 Other transport equipment n.e.c.		-	-	-	...		-	-	-	...		-	-
3610 Furniture		29415	29623	30039	...		10651	8913	9738	...		793	1287
369 Manufacturing n.e.c.		20033	19933	29105	...		8041	4839	7767	...		735	1452
3691 Jewellery and related articles		2410	3291	9567	...		1322	982	1520	...		324	15
3692 Musical instruments		-	-	-	...		-	-	-	...		-	-
3693 Sports goods		-	-	-	...		-	-	-	...		-	-
3694 Games and toys		-	-	-	...		-	-	-	...		-	-
3699 Other manufacturing n.e.c.		17623g/	16642g/	19538g/	...		6719g/	3857g/	6247g/	...	g/	411	1437
3710 Recycling of metal waste and scrap		-	-	-	...		-	-	-	...		-	-
3720 Recycling of non-metal waste and scrap		-	-	-	...		-	-	-	...		-	-
D Total manufacturing		2085775	2234217	2328263	...		717226	576186	608720	...		116434	146943

a/ 1721 includes 1722 and 1723.
b/ 1729 includes 1723.
c/ 1911 includes 1912.
d/ 2023 includes 2029.
e/ 2429 includes 2412 and 2421.
f/ 2695 includes 2696.
g/ 3699 includes 2696, 2893, 2925, 2929 and 3130.
h/ 2710 includes 2720.
i/ 2899 includes 2893.
j/ 2919 includes 2929.
k/ 3150 includes 3130 and 3140.

Panama

ISIC Revision 3		Note	Index numbers of industrial production (1990=100)											
ISIC	Industry		1985	1986	1987	1988	1989	1990	1991	1992	1993	1994	1995	1996
15	Food and beverages		99	97	104	90	97	100	105	111	115	118	118	121
16	Tobacco products		107	107	102	82	77	100	95	99	129	171	162	179
17	Textiles		85	88	88	62	86	100	102	90	101	101	93	94
18	Wearing apparel, fur		122	123	120	87	90	100	121	131	128	114	109	99
19	Leather, leather products and footwear		152	185	171	119	97	100	106	110	116	127	144	118
20	Wood products (excl. furniture)		145	127	126	65	89	100	98	118	116	133	114	101
21	Paper and paper products		87	84	93	88	94	100	103	105	104	124	125	114
22	Printing and publishing		135	127	103	75	80	100	103	120	127	135	140	127
23	Coke,refined petroleum products,nuclear fuel		106	82	120	85	80	100	97	150	136	97	112	184
24	Chemicals and chemical products		98	105	111	89	95	100	110	122	126	135	140	131
25	Rubber and plastics products		78	80	99	76	89	100	110	126	130	141	141	131
26	Non-metallic mineral products		138	166	178	73	73	100	156	178	238	255	232	211
27	Basic metals		106	121	185	62	58	100	146	169	196	170	202	227
28	Fabricated metal products		125	131	161	71	76	100	116	127	134	149	155	156
29	Machinery and equipment n.e.c.		58	84	151	71	40	100	47	31	32	39	45	33
30	Office, accounting and computing machinery		...	...	...	...	...	...	...	...	...	...	...	...
31	Electrical machinery and apparatus		139	130	138	68	64	100	127	149	194	219	213	253
32	Radio,television and communication equipment		...	...	...	...	...	...	...	...	...	...	...	...
33	Medical, precision and optical instruments		100	105	84	80	90	100	101	109	105	121	125	119
34	Motor vehicles, trailers, semi-trailers		...	...	...	...	...	100	63	60	74	77	76	73
35	Other transport equipment		...	...	...	...	...	100	60	61	71	61	93	96
36	Furniture; manufacturing n.e.c.		139	158	140	64	78	100	110	115	125	131	116	110
37	Recycling		...	...	...	...	...	...	...	...	...	...	...	...
D	Total manufacturing		101	103	111	84	89	100	108	118	126	130	130	131

PERU

Supplier of information:
Oficina General de Informàtica, Estadística y Racionalizaciòn. Ministerio de Industria, Turismo, Integración y Negociaciones Comerciales Internacionales, Lima.

Basic source of data:
Survey of the manufacturing industry.

Major deviations from ISIC (Revision 2):
The following industries are not included in manufacturing: canning, preserving and processing of fish and crustacea; extraction of fish and other marine animal oils; and production of fish meal.

Reference period (if not calendar year):

Scope:
Establishments with 5 or more persons engaged.

Method of enumeration:
Not reported.

Adjusted for non-response:
Yes.

Concepts and definitions of variables:
Output is gross output.
Value added is total value added.

Related national publications:

Peru

ISIC Revision 2	Number of establishments					Number of persons engaged					Wages and salaries paid to employees				
		(numbers)					(numbers)					(thousand NEW SOLES)			
ISIC Industry	Note	1991	1992	1993	1994	Note	1991	1992	1993	1994	Note	1991	1992	1993	1994
311/2 Food products	a/	2853	2736	...	3130	a/	42557	43192	...	48023	a/	128879	196400	...	409871
3111 Slaughtering, preparing & preserving meat		85	74	...	89		1367	1352	...	1741		3962	5072	...	13736
3112 Dairy products		152	106	...	144		2587	2402	...	2569		16470	24434	...	46786
3113 Canning, preserving of fruits & vegetables		139	147	...	173		4519	4922	...	4827		10538	15502	...	29687
3114 Canning, preserving and processing of fish		...	...	...	...		...	...	...	...		...	...	...	...
3115 Vegetable and animal oils and fats		46	49	...	57		2308	2008	...	2144		15315	22964	...	37235
3116 Grain mill products		287	290	...	346		4689	4451	...	5616		18801	25767	...	57890
3117 Bakery products		1500	1457	...	1654		13156	14232	...	17133		24591	40668	...	89066
3118 Sugar factories and refineries		41	41	...	40		5505	5194	...	5062		9828	18004	...	50039
3119 Cocoa, chocolate and sugar confectionery		113	99	...	92		2587	2353	...	1965		9941	13074	...	20812
3121 Other food products		383	365	...	403		4334	4500	...	4773		14297	22556	...	48093
3122 Prepared animal feeds		107	108	...	132		1505	1778	...	2193		5136	8359	...	16527
313 Beverages		571	501	...	571		11909	11696	...	12029		62696	115097	...	213914
3131 Distilling, rectifying and blending spirits		282	258	...	268		1962	1656	...	1690		2684	5054	...	7725
3132 Wine industries		121	122	...	124		1222	1168	...	1313		1425	2379	...	5009
3133 Malt liquors and malt		12	12	...	12		3838	4176	...	3308		40448	76133	...	130244
3134 Soft drinks and carbonated waters		156	109	...	167		4887	4696	...	5718		18139	31531	...	70936
314 Tobacco		11	11	...	3		820	814	...	470		5474	10238	...	13771
321 Textiles		1262	1226	...	1292		35059	32487	...	31023		111188	154067	...	245674
3211 Spinning, weaving and finishing textiles		578	562	...	607		24498	23093	...	20610		86541	120328	...	183156
3212 Made-up textile goods excl. wearing apparel		87	71	...	72		581	555	...	504		1203	1027	...	1594
3213 Knitting mills		532	535	...	557		9199	8074	...	9205		21697	29602	...	54058
3214 Carpets and rugs		21	18	...	16		221	269	...	250		263	538	...	2418
3215 Cordage, rope and twine		15	13	...	13		233	226	...	217		842	1421	...	3155
3219 Other textiles		29	27	...	27		327	270	...	237		642	1151	...	1293
322 Wearing apparel, except footwear		1968	1177	...	1262		15619	13784	...	16751		20303	26239	...	59042
323 Leather and fur products		288	269	...	281		3816	3450	...	3389		5884	9940	...	19118
3231 Tanneries and leather finishing		142	137	...	138		2446	2291	...	2072		4641	7590	...	12678
3232 Fur dressing and dyeing industries		40	29	...	29		211	183	...	161		217	272	...	728
3233 Leather prods. excl. wearing apparel		106	103	...	114		1159	976	...	1156		1026	2078	...	5712
324 Footwear, except rubber or plastic		650	283	...	345		3645	3532	...	3675		6496	8297	...	11895
331 Wood products, except furniture		723	512	...	659		4543	5476	...	6961		5540	11830	...	26381
3311 Sawmills, planing and other wood mills		579	409	...	566		4015	4828	...	6276		4893	10632	...	23763
3312 Wooden and cane containers		51	19	...	22		133	119	...	126		148	231	...	381
3319 Other wood and cork products		93	84	...	71		395	529	...	559		499	966	...	2237
332 Furniture and fixtures, excl. metal		788	563	...	604		6136	4448	...	4891		10778	11471	...	20771
341 Paper and products		207	195	...	196		5815	5209	...	4793		22740	24368	...	48780
3411 Pulp, paper and paperboard articles		22	23	...	16		2783	2137	...	1553		12829	8229	...	19382
3412 Containers of paper and paperboard		109	96	...	94		1650	1454	...	1649		5509	7961	...	14000
3419 Other pulp, paper and paperboard articles		76	76	...	86		1382	1618	...	1591		4402	8178	...	15399
342 Printing and publishing		909	676	...	862		11222	9534	...	10936		43474	59446	...	132741
351 Industrial chemicals		322	304	...	322		7302	6210	...	5791		37399	52913	...	87553
3511 Basic chemicals excl. fertilizers		232	218	...	240		3624	3529	...	3563		17508	28691	...	46985
3512 Fertilizers and pesticides		44	43	...	39		1132	1041	...	800		7395	9694	...	11880
3513 Synthetic resins and plastic materials		46	43	...	43		2546	1640	...	1428		12496	14528	...	28688
352 Other chemicals		787	701	...	781		14018	12832	...	13644		69428	119365	...	232182
3521 Paints, varnishes and lacquers		90	89	...	101		1709	1624	...	1707		6421	11254	...	23159
3522 Drugs and medicines		170	164	...	176		5084	4909	...	4868		30304	55020	...	99349
3523 Soap, cleaning preps., perfumes, cosmetics		197	151	...	201		2974	2485	...	3187		17158	27554	...	58441
3529 Other chemical products		330	297	...	303		4251	3814	...	3882		15545	25536	...	51234
353 Petroleum refineries		26	27	...	29		3780	2989	...	2553		36056	35009	...	83717

354	Misc. petroleum and coal products		12	11	...	11		66	62	...	66		209	309	...	745
355	Rubber products		121	93	...	107		2222	1650	...	2033		14140	16911	...	34249
3551	Tyres and tubes		8	8	...	9		833	596	...	621		8763	11836	...	24516
3559	Other rubber products		113	85	...	98		1389	1054	...	1412		5377	5075	...	9733
356	Plastic products		585	544	...	588		9520	9342	...	9750		26971	47835	...	110687
361	Pottery, china, earthenware		67	69	...	75		1175	1148	...	1025		2929	4894	...	8684
362	Glass and products		136	121	...	124		2986	2527	...	2301		8422	8597	...	25212
369	Other non-metallic mineral products		687	628	...	580		10584	9155	...	9182		27885	42036	...	89137
3691	Structural clay products		326	291	...	228		5162	4281	...	4053		9549	15402	...	34379
3692	Cement, lime and plaster		57	57	...	64		2163	2015	...	1808		11286	17223	...	35713
3699	Other non-metallic mineral products		304	280	...	288		3259	2859	...	3321		7050	9411	...	19046
371	Iron and steel		86	82	...	90		7035	6293	...	5338		29507	35364	...	92700
372	Non-ferrous metals		123	115	...	125		9072	8623	...	9021		48315	63164	...	200218
381	Fabricated metal products		1612	1326	...	1442		13980	14042	...	15315		35581	58743	...	113439
3811	Cutlery, hand tools and general hardware		121	80	...	94		1052	767	...	829		2750	3104	...	5060
3812	Furniture and fixtures primarily of metal		210	114	...	107		1929	1396	...	1328		3380	4477	...	7721
3813	Structural metal products		350	269	...	331		1406	2333	...	3082		1968	5575	...	15738
3819	Other fabricated metal products		931	863	...	910		9593	9546	...	10076		27483	45587	...	84920
382	Non-electrical machinery		711	585	...	612		9307	8098	...	8008		26433	37939	...	76197
3821	Engines and turbines		20	18	...	25		146	144	...	221		280	442	...	1399
3822	Agricultural machinery and equipment		64	59	...	63		1475	1012	...	893		3369	3719	...	6380
3823	Metal and wood working machinery		65	48	...	56		305	399	...	485		677	1758	...	4444
3824	Other special industrial machinery		130	124	...	120		1629	1365	...	1628		4745	5560	...	15132
3825	Office, computing and accounting machinery		42	40	...	44		539	379	...	431		1247	1110	...	2625
3829	Other non-electrical machinery & equipment		390	296	...	304		5213	4799	...	4350		16115	25351	...	46219
383	Electrical machinery		540	437	...	452		7251	7131	...	7057		25393	39800	...	67496
3831	Electrical industrial machinery		129	122	...	127		2056	1853	...	2090		7265	9970	...	25005
3832	Radio, television and communication equipm.		170	89	...	91		1274	870	...	893		2630	4751	...	5615
3833	Electrical appliances and housewares		67	65	...	67		848	1789	...	1379		2698	6965	...	5634
3839	Other electrical apparatus and supplies		174	161	...	167		3073	2619	...	2695		12800	18113	...	31242
384	Transport equipment		500	382	...	424		8601	7328	...	6703		26486	41779	...	73512
3841	Shipbuilding and repairing		84	71	...	82		2636	2280	...	2127		7658	9863	...	23247
3842	Railroad equipment		2	-	...	1		63	-	...	...		134	-	...	...
3843	Motor vehicles		362	273	...	304		5356	4551	...	4139		17113	28787	...	45419
3844	Motorcycles and bicycles		37	27	...	26		463	418	...	354		1437	2975	...	4608
3845	Aircraft		1	1	...	1		15	12	...	...		30	22	...	...
3849	Other transport equipment		14	10	...	10		68	67	...	83		114	131	...	238
385	Professional and scientific equipment		104	91	...	106		1181	1273	...	1551		3569	7211	...	13903
3851	Prof. and scientific equipment n.e.c.		51	50	...	59		950	1027	...	1205		3025	6167	...	10994
3852	Photographic and optical goods		44	32	...	39		226	217	...	341		539	927	...	2897
3853	Watches and clocks		9	9	...	8		5	29	...	5		5	116	...	13
390	Other manufacturing industries		497	460	...	439		5417	5174	...	5021		11764	22501	...	37493
3901	Jewellery and related articles		181	165	...	163		2640	2150	...	2190		4851	11753	...	14447
3902	Musical instruments		15	6	...	8		25	33	...	27		44	140	...	54
3903	Sporting and athletic goods		18	12	...	10		80	65	...	50		62	281	...	182
3909	Manufacturing industries, n.e.c.		283	277	...	258		2672	2926	...	2754		6806	10328	...	22810
3	Total manufacturing	a/	17146	14125	...	15512	a/	254638	237499	...	247300	a/	853940	1261763	...	2549084

a/ Excluding canning, preserving and processing of fish and crustacea, extraction of fish and other marine animal oils, production of fish meal.

ISIC Revision 2	Output in producers' prices					Value added in producers' prices					Gross fixed capital formation		
		(million NEW SOLES)					(million NEW SOLES)					(million NEW SOLES)	
ISIC Industry	Note	1991	1992	1993	1994	Note	1991	1992	1993	1994	Note	1993	1994
311/2 Food products	a/	2251.2	3555.7	...	6553.4	a/	780.6	1135.9	...	1820.6	a/	...	244.9
3111 Slaughtering, preparing & preserving meat		56.2	65.7	...	160.1		13.6	24.6	...	47.2		...	5.6
3112 Dairy products		241.7	474.5	...	814.2		68.6	178.4	...	200.8		...	55.3
3113 Canning, preserving of fruits & vegetables		116.0	218.4	...	304.9		35.4	69.5	...	90.3		...	53.9
3114 Canning, preserving and processing of fish		...	...	...	...		...	...	...	...		...	...
3115 Vegetable and animal oils and fats		221.5	369.9	...	849.5		60.1	103.5	...	261.4		...	37.7
3116 Grain mill products		410.2	540.2	...	1151.4		137.8	101.6	...	266.9		...	35.5
3117 Bakery products		313.4	556.5	...	1067.5		103.1	197.1	...	376.4		...	15.9
3118 Sugar factories and refineries		255.7	339.9	...	641.5		110.1	97.0	...	156.8		...	4.7
3119 Cocoa, chocolate and sugar confectionery		105.3	187.8	...	266.1		42.8	61.8	...	79.3		...	5.4
3121 Other food products		212.6	445.7	...	667.9		79.1	171.4	...	252.2		...	20.9
3122 Prepared animal feeds		318.5	357.2	...	630.4		129.9	130.9	...	89.3		...	10.1
313 Beverages		837.0	1517.8	...	3117.2		471.5	871.4	...	1729.1		...	386.1
3131 Distilling, rectifying and blending spirits		38.3	48.1	...	123.1		18.3	21.0	...	35.9		...	0.4
3132 Wine industries		17.1	30.2	...	80.5		7.2	13.4	...	28.8		...	0.6
3133 Malt liquors and malt		541.3	971.9	...	1742.2		349.9	642.1	...	1241.4		...	214.5
3134 Soft drinks and carbonated waters		240.3	467.6	...	1171.4		96.1	194.9	...	422.9		...	170.6
314 Tobacco		64.8	105.5	...	169.7		39.4	64.9	...	106.6		...	3.9
321 Textiles		959.8	1557.2	...	2864.1		366.2	567.3	...	726.0		...	235.3
3211 Spinning, weaving and finishing textiles		684.8	1088.7	...	2005.7		276.1	404.7	...	530.2		...	137.4
3212 Made-up textile goods excl. wearing apparel		7.0	14.2	...	27.7		2.8	6.6	...	7.6		...	0.1
3213 Knitting mills		241.3	403.4	...	710.3		79.9	137.9	...	158.8		...	82.8
3214 Carpets and rugs		3.6	7.2	...	18.8		1.1	2.1	...	4.1		...	5.6
3215 Cordage, rope and twine		17.9	34.7	...	89.6		4.2	13.4	...	20.7		...	8.8
3219 Other textiles		5.3	9.0	...	12.0		2.0	2.6	...	4.6		...	0.6
322 Wearing apparel, except footwear		228.3	301.0	...	932.9		68.9	91.5	...	232.6		...	11.7
323 Leather and fur products		53.0	84.0	...	227.7		20.4	25.4	...	63.7		...	5.6
3231 Tanneries and leather finishing		41.0	63.5	...	151.9		15.7	17.9	...	36.5		...	3.2
3232 Fur dressing and dyeing industries		3.9	3.9	...	16.0		1.4	1.0	...	4.4		...	-
3233 Leather prods. excl. wearing apparel		8.2	16.5	...	59.8		3.3	6.6	...	22.9		...	2.4
324 Footwear, except rubber or plastic		55.5	111.8	...	219.0		24.9	34.2	...	50.0		...	3.0
331 Wood products, except furniture		61.1	136.7	...	328.2		19.3	45.3	...	106.1		...	11.1
3311 Sawmills, planing and other wood mills		55.9	128.3	...	299.1		17.3	41.8	...	96.9		...	10.5
3312 Wooden and cane containers		1.0	2.4	...	6.4		0.4	0.9	...	1.1		...	0.2
3319 Other wood and cork products		4.2	5.9	...	22.7		1.6	2.6	...	8.1		...	0.4
332 Furniture and fixtures, excl. metal		81.3	111.0	...	261.5		32.7	43.2	...	79.9		...	10.5
341 Paper and products		188.0	256.1	...	677.3		52.0	76.1	...	171.0		...	42.0
3411 Pulp, paper and paperboard articles		69.4	65.9	...	192.9		13.7	15.5	...	52.8		...	5.4
3412 Containers of paper and paperboard		55.0	83.1	...	188.9		19.7	24.1	...	42.9		...	20.2
3419 Other pulp, paper and paperboard articles		63.6	107.1	...	295.5		18.6	36.6	...	75.3		...	16.4
342 Printing and publishing		360.5	491.1	...	1126.6		160.2	210.1	...	490.0		...	50.2
351 Industrial chemicals		328.2	512.4	...	898.4		138.0	208.3	...	303.8		...	43.9
3511 Basic chemicals excl. fertilizers		167.8	289.8	...	483.7		74.1	121.9	...	171.6		...	21.7
3512 Fertilizers and pesticides		50.8	68.8	...	80.4		25.7	27.5	...	23.6		...	1.6
3513 Synthetic resins and plastic materials		109.7	153.7	...	334.3		38.2	58.9	...	108.6		...	20.6
352 Other chemicals		782.8	1314.2	...	2525.7		314.7	507.1	...	934.8		...	115.6
3521 Paints, varnishes and lacquers		79.0	127.9	...	255.9		29.1	41.0	...	72.6		...	8.7
3522 Drugs and medicines		312.7	564.7	...	910.5		142.1	257.2	...	395.5		...	50.5
3523 Soap, cleaning preps., perfumes, cosmetics		254.3	373.9	...	901.3		91.0	121.1	...	302.9		...	43.5
3529 Other chemical products		136.8	247.7	...	458.0		52.5	87.7	...	163.9		...	12.9
353 Petroleum refineries		1731.9	2575.1	...	5094.1		1516.1	1474.3	...	2985.4		...	99.8

354	Misc. petroleum and coal products		3.5	4.9	...	12.6		1.7	2.3	...	3.6		...	0.3
355	Rubber products		88.3	142.9	...	331.2		36.0	53.5	...	126.7		...	11.8
3551	Tyres and tubes		58.3	94.0	...	230.7		23.4	38.7	...	91.2		...	3.1
3559	Other rubber products		30.0	48.9	...	100.4		12.6	14.7	...	35.5		...	8.8
356	Plastic products		251.3	446.0	...	1216.2		95.5	151.7	...	372.1		...	114.0
361	Pottery, china, earthenware		12.7	26.1	...	63.2		7.4	13.0	...	26.1		...	23.9
362	Glass and products		117.4	147.2	...	246.3		38.9	58.2	...	90.9		...	54.6
369	Other non-metallic mineral products		301.2	534.5	...	1281.3		127.1	270.2	...	595.8		...	46.9
3691	Structural clay products		60.8	110.9	...	274.0		27.0	56.5	...	120.0		...	10.2
3692	Cement, lime and plaster		152.6	231.8	...	748.8		60.6	87.1	...	387.9		...	30.9
3699	Other non-metallic mineral products		87.9	191.7	...	258.5		39.6	126.6	...	87.9		...	5.8
371	Iron and steel		238.2	329.5	...	769.6		83.6	127.7	...	250.7		...	14.5
372	Non-ferrous metals		1018.0	1577.0	...	3397.3		461.0	578.2	...	1389.2		...	198.2
381	Fabricated metal products		335.2	614.8	...	1344.2		127.9	208.4	...	450.7		...	49.7
3811	Cutlery, hand tools and general hardware		20.6	23.0	...	64.5		7.6	11.3	...	21.8		...	0.5
3812	Furniture and fixtures primarily of metal		27.5	43.5	...	69.3		8.8	12.3	...	26.1		...	0.4
3813	Structural metal products		22.3	67.0	...	225.2		7.6	21.6	...	78.8		...	2.0
3819	Other fabricated metal products		264.8	481.3	...	985.2		103.9	163.2	...	323.9		...	46.9
382	Non-electrical machinery		229.5	318.1	...	810.7		90.2	131.3	...	312.4		...	55.8
3821	Engines and turbines		3.2	3.7	...	18.3		1.0	1.5	...	7.6		...	0.2
3822	Agricultural machinery and equipment		21.0	19.6	...	63.6		8.8	10.1	...	30.8		...	1.2
3823	Metal and wood working machinery		6.0	8.4	...	22.3		3.0	4.4	...	13.2		...	0.2
3824	Other special industrial machinery		33.5	67.0	...	183.7		12.7	28.0	...	64.2		...	20.2
3825	Office, computing and accounting machinery		27.6	8.1	...	28.8		6.3	2.4	...	8.5		...	0.2
3829	Other non-electrical machinery & equipment		138.1	211.2	...	494.0		58.5	84.9	...	188.1		...	33.8
383	Electrical machinery		274.3	501.4	...	704.5		109.9	155.1	...	221.3		...	36.6
3831	Electrical industrial machinery		50.8	81.2	...	191.1		22.0	35.1	...	68.2		...	2.7
3832	Radio, television and communication equipm.		74.5	189.3	...	49.3		30.1	38.1	...	13.3		...	0.1
3833	Electrical appliances and housewares		30.5	68.9	...	63.9		14.0	20.9	...	18.6		...	1.3
3839	Other electrical apparatus and supplies		118.5	162.0	...	400.1		43.8	61.0	...	121.2		...	32.4
384	Transport equipment		293.5	401.6	...	947.6		122.8	168.3	...	352.4		...	61.5
3841	Shipbuilding and repairing		57.5	65.0	...	194.2		29.1	28.8	...	65.5		...	11.3
3842	Railroad equipment		0.6	-	...	...		0.1	-	...	...		...	...
3843	Motor vehicles		217.3	295.8	...	661.3		87.6	123.8	...	260.9		...	46.4
3844	Motorcycles and bicycles		17.4	39.9	...	85.6		5.5	15.3	...	25.0		...	3.7
3845	Aircraft		0.2	0.2	...	...		0.1	0.1	...	...		...	...
3849	Other transport equipment		0.5	0.8	...	6.6		0.3	0.3	...	0.9		...	-
385	Professional and scientific equipment		28.3	52.8	...	167.8		12.7	20.4	...	76.7		...	6.0
3851	Prof. and scientific equipment n.e.c.		26.4	46.8	...	133.9		11.5	18.2	...	59.0		...	4.4
3852	Photographic and optical goods		1.9	5.3	...	33.6		1.1	1.8	...	17.6		...	1.6
3853	Watches and clocks		0.1	0.7	...	0.3		-	0.3	...	0.1		...	-
390	Other manufacturing industries		136.1	283.9	...	479.3		44.1	120.6	...	170.2		...	15.4
3901	Jewellery and related articles		78.4	188.1	...	165.2		20.6	73.8	...	51.0		...	2.2
3902	Musical instruments		0.4	0.6	...	0.3		0.1	0.3	...	0.1		...	-
3903	Sporting and athletic goods		0.6	1.0	...	1.9		0.1	0.5	...	0.6		...	-
3909	Manufacturing industries, n.e.c.		56.8	94.3	...	311.8		23.3	46.0	...	118.4		...	13.2
3	Total manufacturing	a/	11311.1	18010.3	...	36767.5	a/	5363.6	7413.8	...	14238.7	a/	...	1952.7

a/ Excluding canning, preserving and processing of fish and crustacea, extraction of fish and other marine animal oils, production of fish meal.

Peru

ISIC Revision 2		Index numbers of industrial production											
		(1990=100)											
ISIC Industry	Note	1985	1986	1987	1988	1989	1990	1991	1992	1993	1994	1995	1996
311/2 Food products		99	111	125	118	99	100	97	101	101	121	128	128
313 Beverages		97	144	177	140	99	100	129	123	123	138	143	137
314 Tobacco		117	139	127	96	90	100	104	95	95	105	113	127
321 Textiles		109	116	129	121	112	100	97	90	86	120	132	141
322 Wearing apparel, except footwear		112	123	137	135	102	100	112	104	105	147	151	143
323 Leather and fur products		126	157	172	147	109	100	85	90	87	83	85	85
324 Footwear, except rubber or plastic		136	146	154	146	97	100	132	112	121	113	139	130
331 Wood products, except furniture		137	167	212	208	106	100	125	102	125	150	143	110
332 Furniture and fixtures, excl. metal		...	...	...	...	...	...	...	...	...	...	...	...
341 Paper and products		114	138	168	164	86	100	76	46	49	96	132	130
342 Printing and publishing		123	127	149	163	91	100	101	111	108	188	231	232
351 Industrial chemicals		116	138	153	140	103	100	101	88	99	107	113	127
352 Other chemicals		97	132	173	150	96	100	109	114	122	143	186	168
353 Petroleum refineries		111	114	126	123	104	100	102	103	107	111	109	108
354 Misc. petroleum and coal products		...	...	...	...	...	...	...	...	...	...	...	...
355 Rubber products		117	135	147	121	103	100	86	79	87	89	95	92
356 Plastic products		160	217	245	183	116	100	118	121	166	216	219	240
361 Pottery, china, earthenware		92	122	138	162	105	100	125	142	169	244	315	379
362 Glass and products		107	153	190	174	103	100	91	76	71	86	128	170
369 Other non-metallic mineral products		82	101	117	115	98	100	103	99	123	154	178	178
371 Iron and steel		132	162	195	156	115	100	112	113	126	171	179	188
372 Non-ferrous metals		127	115	112	86	110	100	119	119	123	136	148	172
381 Fabricated metal products		151	214	305	192	105	100	108	99	133	158	220	226
382 Non-electrical machinery		96	170	185	134	81	100	114	98	80	110	144	97
383 Electrical machinery		120	160	197	143	94	100	103	84	75	75	109	103
384 Transport equipment		115	177	226	149	85	100	112	83	68	118	108	68
385 Professional and scientific equipment		...	...	...	...	...	...	...	...	...	...	...	...
390 Other manufacturing industries		100	131	178	154	93	100	110	121	124	183	185	170
3 Total manufacturing		112	130	149	129	102	100	106	103	107	128	140	141

PHILIPPINES

Supplier of information:
National Statistics Office, Manila.

Basic source of data:
Annual survey of establishments and census of establishments.

Major deviations from ISIC (Revision 2):
None reported.

Reference period (if not calendar year):

Scope:
Establishments with 10 or more persons engaged.

Method of enumeration:
For 1992 and 1993, establishments with 50 or more persons engaged are completely enumerated, and those with less than 50 persons engaged are sampled. For 1994, establishments with 10 or more persons engaged are completely enumerated. For 1995, establishments with 100 or more persons engaged are completely enumerated, and those with less than 100 persons engaged are sampled.

Adjusted for non-response:
Yes.

Concepts and definitions of variables:
Wages and salaries includes severance pay.

Related national publications:
Census of Establishments, 1994; Annual Survey of Establishments, 1995, both published by the National Statistics Office, Manila.

Philippines

ISIC Revision 2	Number of establishments					Number of employees					Wages and salaries paid to employees				
		(numbers)					(thousands)					(million PESOS)			
ISIC Industry	Note	1992	1993	1994	1995	Note	1992	1993	1994	1995	Note	1992	1993	1994	1995
311/2 Food products		2824	2689	2630	2508		158.6	163.8	159.1	159.7		10050	10919	11210	11907
3111 Slaughtering, preparing & preserving meat		65	57	71	73		8.3	8.5	11.5	11.2		668	642	607	969
3112 Dairy products		42	44	42	38		7.7	7.9	7.3	7.1		1180	1460	1388	1547
3113 Canning, preserving of fruits & vegetables		98	97	96	86		17.6	17.9	18.5	17.5		1524	1735	1839	1679
3114 Canning, preserving and processing of fish		114	108	100	104		21.4	21.9	18.8	22.0		810	907	743	792
3115 Vegetable and animal oils and fats		96	89	85	83		6.1	6.9	7.0	6.6		450	482	482	496
3116 Grain mill products		408	379	364	336		9.2	10.1	8.5	8.1		397	512	478	467
3117 Bakery products		1535	1457	1409	1318		30.1	31.3	30.8	31.1		928	1027	1206	1329
3118 Sugar factories and refineries		47	44	39	46		25.6	24.9	24.5	23.5		1833	1775	1890	1898
3119 Cocoa, chocolate and sugar confectionery		100	99	96	84		5.6	6.5	6.3	5.9		415	409	459	461
3121 Other food products		214	213	223	233		20.8	21.5	19.8	20.3		1332	1511	1623	1757
3122 Prepared animal feeds		105	102	105	107		6.4	6.4	6.0	6.4		514	460	495	515
313 Beverages		97	86	86	88		28.1	26.4	25.1	24.9		2986	2866	3231	3264
3131 Distilling, rectifying and blending spirits		40	36	34	32		4.4	4.9	3.4	3.4		385	382	239	289
3132 Wine industries		4	9a/	4	6		0.1	4.3a/	0.2	0.2		4	522a/	8	10
3133 Malt liquors and malt		7	...a/	7	8		4.2	...a/	4.2	3.8		521	...a/	604	690
3134 Soft drinks and carbonated waters		46	41	41	42		19.4	17.2	17.3	17.5		2075	1962	2381	2275
314 Tobacco		25	22	21	20		14.1	12.7	11.7	11.1		953	826	906	968
321 Textiles		592	575	537	491		79.1	66.6	63.5	55.7		3890	3339	3673	3547
3211 Spinning, weaving and finishing textiles		218	194	184	169		47.8	38.2	38.9	30.1		2484	2147	2437	2098
3212 Made-up textile goods excl. wearing apparel		61	57	53	57		8.3	4.5	5.0	5.0		323	191	231	257
3213 Knitting mills		153	145	128	114		14.5	14.2	12.1	13.6		703	642	637	766
3214 Carpets and rugs		11	12	11	12		1.5	1.8	1.4	1.5		79	96	93	131
3215 Cordage, rope and twine		136	155	151	129		5.9	7.1	5.6	4.8		248	234	247	251
3219 Other textiles		13	12	10	10		1.1	0.7	0.5	0.7		54	31	29	44
322 Wearing apparel, except footwear		1861	1722	1612	1495		176.0	160.3	144.6	143.4		8434	7523	7518	8072
323 Leather and fur products		99	83	84	84		7.7	5.4	6.2	8.0		365	266	308	418
3231 Tanneries and leather finishing		29b/	21b/	17	16		3.0b/	1.3b/	1.3	1.6		126b/	51b/	53	85
3232 Fur dressing and dyeing industries		...b/	...b/	-	-		...b/	...b/	-	-		...b/	...b/	-	-
3233 Leather prods. excl. wearing apparel		70	62	67	68		4.7	4.1	4.9	6.4		239	215	255	334
324 Footwear, except rubber or plastic		348	363	384	370		15.4	15.1	15.1	14.1		437	470	579	593
331 Wood products, except furniture		539	454	401	351		35.1	29.6	23.9	23.5		1409	1159	1049	1085
3311 Sawmills, planing and other wood mills		210	227	184	164		23.9	23.8	19.0	18.7		986	975	869	906
3312 Wooden and cane containers		99	84	67	52		3.7	2.4	1.4	1.3		146	98	63	64
3319 Other wood and cork products		230	143	150	135		7.5	3.3	3.5	3.5		277	85	118	116
332 Furniture and fixtures, excl. metal		638	557	497	435		30.0	23.1	23.9	20.8		1080	858	971	940
341 Paper and products		197	200	215	205		18.1	15.7	17.7	18.9		1235	1050	1449	1637
3411 Pulp, paper and paperboard articles		48	46	47	54		8.7	7.1	8.2	10.7		601	600	776	994
3412 Containers of paper and paperboard		84	80	93	83		6.4	5.4	6.0	5.0		436	264	430	408
3419 Other pulp, paper and paperboard articles		65	74	75	68		3.0	3.2	3.5	3.2		193	186	243	236
342 Printing and publishing		644	630	637	632		23.2	26.2	21.9	22.8		1491	1794	1646	1844
351 Industrial chemicals		149	148	171	189		12.4	11.6	11.5	11.9		1353	1384	1292	1511
3511 Basic chemicals excl. fertilizers		82	76	76	77		5.4	4.9	4.6	4.7		596	622	518	602
3512 Fertilizers and pesticides		26	25	23	24		3.6	3.3	3.0	2.8		418	432	417	436
3513 Synthetic resins and plastic materials		41	47	72	88		3.4	3.4	3.9	4.4		339	329	357	473
352 Other chemicals		328	291	288	293		31.1	30.9	30.9	32.2		5256	5334	5770	6448
3521 Paints, varnishes and lacquers		46	41	48	49		2.8	2.9	3.5	3.8		203	242	296	352
3522 Drugs and medicines		107	93	86	85		13.9	14.0	13.4	13.6		2687	2785	2869	3128
3523 Soap, cleaning preps., perfumes, cosmetics		69	62	69	67		9.5	8.6	9.3	9.7		1897	1758	2059	2233
3529 Other chemical products		106	95	85	92		4.9	5.4	4.7	5.1		469	549	547	736
353 Petroleum refineries		4	4	4	4		2.5	2.6	2.7	2.6		909	1005	1400	1234

Code	Industry														
354	Misc. petroleum and coal products	17	16	14	16		0.7	0.8	0.8	0.6		48	46	44	83
355	Rubber products	186	178	187	175		29.5	22.6	23.8	20.0		2018	1871	1692	1378
3551	Tyres and tubes	47	48	43	44		4.9	5.1	3.9	4.1		870	874	531	496
3559	Other rubber products	139	130	144	131		24.6	17.4	19.9	15.9		1148	996	1162	882
356	Plastic products	372	377	377	359		24.9	23.6	25.8	24.8		1375	1256	1685	1823
361	Pottery, china, earthenware	73	61	68	59		11.8	9.4	10.2	8.3		652	538	638	605
362	Glass and products	49	53	53	46		7.2	5.8	5.1	5.2		729	521	521	601
369	Other non-metallic mineral products	417	340	322	267		23.2	19.8	20.9	19.2		1723	1540	1705	1921
3691	Structural clay products	23	22	23	26		3.4	3.3	3.7	3.3		292	296	270	287
3692	Cement, lime and plaster	19	18	42	18		7.2	6.7	8.0	7.1		729	747	914	1020
3699	Other non-metallic mineral products	375	300	257	223		12.6	9.7	9.2	8.8		701	497	521	614
371	Iron and steel	180	178	191	196		19.8	18.8	21.5	22.9		1789	1723	1985	2112
372	Non-ferrous metals	26	30	34	40		3.2	3.4	3.6	4.1		250	353	421	479
381	Fabricated metal products	633	600	589	583		28.4	30.8	30.8	35.5		1465	1555	1841	2115
3811	Cutlery, hand tools and general hardware	64	51	58	46		1.1	1.1	1.5	1.3		52	41	74	62
3812	Furniture and fixtures primarily of metal	41	35	34	35		1.5	1.4	1.8	2.3		79	55	108	96
3813	Structural metal products	268	269	255	263		9.6	11.0	11.0	13.1		453	523	593	744
3819	Other fabricated metal products	260	245	242	239		16.2	17.3	16.5	18.8		881	936	1067	1213
382	Non-electrical machinery	540	488	464	451		20.7	19.6	21.6	28.8		1261	910	1496	2225
3821	Engines and turbines	4	4	-	-		0.2	0.4	-	-		13	21	-	-
3822	Agricultural machinery and equipment	34	34	37	33		1.0	1.0	1.2	1.1		43	43	55	52
3823	Metal and wood working machinery	25	24	20	22		1.2	1.5	0.9	0.9		71	86	59	59
3824	Other special industrial machinery	28	24	23	23		0.9	0.9	1.1	1.2		59	62	71	94
3825	Office, computing and accounting machinery	37	21	28	37		2.3	3.7	9.0	16.5		120	155	825	1454
3829	Other non-electrical machinery & equipment	412	381	356	336		15.1	12.1	9.4	9.1		955	542	487	565
383	Electrical machinery	296	265	271	287		102.0	98.6	107.8	126.9		7517	7766	9424	10775
3831	Electrical industrial machinery	46	42	36	43		4.0	4.0	3.8	3.1		370	313	339	314
3832	Radio, television and communication equipm.	134	118	113	126		70.3	67.5	73.8	94.4		5315	5427	6441	7738
3833	Electrical appliances and housewares	17	20	32	27		3.0	6.0	6.3	6.5		212	600	760	808
3839	Other electrical apparatus and supplies	99	85	90	91		24.7	21.1	23.9	22.9		1621	1426	1883	1915
384	Transport equipment	266	257	264	253		24.8	23.8	24.1	24.9		1807	1834	2304	2436
3841	Shipbuilding and repairing	49	46	44	39		5.2	3.9	3.3	3.6		332	263	239	276
3842	Railroad equipment	-	-	3	-		-	-	0.1	-		-	-	1	-
3843	Motor vehicles	191	185	190	184		16.6	17.6	17.9	17.9		1259	1396	1836	1884
3844	Motorcycles and bicycles	19	19	20	24		2.6	1.8	2.2	2.8		175	127	180	228
3845	Aircraft	7c/	7c/	6	5	c/	0.4	0.5	0.6	0.6	c/	40	48	48	47
3849	Other transport equipment	...c/	...c/	1	1	c/	...	...	...	...	c/	...	...	...	...
385	Professional and scientific equipment	16	19	13	18		3.4	7.4	6.6	6.9		285	386	523	557
3851	Prof. and scientific equipment n.e.c.	11	14	6	7		0.7	2.6	0.5	0.5		52	128	35	50
3852	Photographic and optical goods	5d/	5d/	5	9		2.8d/	4.8d/	1.2	1.9		233d/	257d/	62	98
3853	Watches and clocks	...d/	...d/	2	2		...d/	...d/	4.9	4.5		...d/	...d/	426	409
390	Other manufacturing industries	348	319	312	304		27.9	26.0	26.7	25.7		1208	1208	1460	1530
3901	Jewellery and related articles	33	32	35	35		2.6	2.7	3.1	2.7		117	183	224	220
3902	Musical instruments	12	7	9	7		0.5	0.2	0.3	0.3		17	5	12	9
3903	Sporting and athletic goods	10	14	20	21		2.8	2.9	3.8	4.1		138	142	202	236
3909	Manufacturing industries, n.e.c.	293	266	248	241		22.0	20.2	19.5	18.6		937	879	1022	1064
3	Total manufacturing	11764	11005	10726	10219		958.8	900.6	887.1	903.4		61974	60347	66742	72108

a/ 3132 includes 3133.
b/ 3231 includes 3232.
c/ 3845 includes 3849.
d/ 3852 includes 3853.

ISIC Revision 2 ISIC Industry	Output in producers' prices Note	(million PESOS) 1992	1993	1994	1995	Value added in producers' prices Note	(million PESOS) 1992	1993	1994	1995	Gross fixed capital formation Note	(million PESOS) 1994	1995
311/2 Food products		148144	161083	169191	208632		46147	56247	58066	74448		8691	9156
3111 Slaughtering, preparing & preserving meat		10096	13211	13927	23913		2700	4773	4252	7436		380	515
3112 Dairy products		18002	17979	19301	20932		6030	6268	8042	8418		1114	831
3113 Canning, preserving of fruits & vegetables		9069	9949	10889	12348		3206	5357	6273	6061		386	991
3114 Canning, preserving and processing of fish		11803	14452	11564	15486		3301	4659	2594	3729		421	459
3115 Vegetable and animal oils and fats		19047	15880	21285	24122		3225	3495	4708	6878		630	1162
3116 Grain mill products		10949	13595	15004	18929		2585	3522	3064	3613		1065	735
3117 Bakery products		8054	14022	9011	11654		2911	6555	3617	4649		610	731
3118 Sugar factories and refineries		29771	23442	26181	24576		12779	8439	9049	9284		2214	2653
3119 Cocoa, chocolate and sugar confectionery		4343	3882	4600	4840		1091	1276	1712	1542		133	78
3121 Other food products		16318	19890	22596	30411		6650	9084	11079	16655		1437	597
3122 Prepared animal feeds		10694	14781	14834	21420		1669	2820	3678	6182		302	405
313 Beverages		42533	55139	47678	53008		24586	32773	28835	33132		2631	7729
3131 Distilling, rectifying and blending spirits		6520	7564	5106	5651		3185	3519	1506	2380		302	276
3132 Wine industries		21	15841a/	13	40		6	9435a/	7	20		2	2
3133 Malt liquors and malt		17390	...a/	18829	21953		10938	...a/	12342	16333		974	6061
3134 Soft drinks and carbonated waters		18602	31734	23729	25363		10456	19820	14980	14398		1352	1391
314 Tobacco		22153	22804	26937	27573		13571	14796	17968	18563		149	453
321 Textiles		29238	26071	26639	32381		9464	10147	10069	12394		1640	2398
3211 Spinning, weaving and finishing textiles		19997	18122	19043	22344		6425	7152	6909	8958		1369	1850
3212 Made-up textile goods excl. wearing apparel		2257	1363	1579	1687		548	468	609	515		66	62
3213 Knitting mills		4331	4183	3493	5138		1454	1526	1316	1788		153	242
3214 Carpets and rugs		387	422	405	443		211	266	303	296		12	24
3215 Cordage, rope and twine		1964	1792	2004	2309		683	607	869	678		40	161
3219 Other textiles		302	190	116	460		142	127	62	159		1	59
322 Wearing apparel, except footwear		32523	36848	36536	36036		15558	17410	20344	18632		645	741
323 Leather and fur products		1500	1142	1202	1697		653	487	500	739		14	23
3231 Tanneries and leather finishing		409b/	205b/	190	361		214b/	108b/	109	162		2	3
3232 Fur dressing and dyeing industries		...b/	...b/	-	-		...b/	...b/	-	-		-	-
3233 Leather prods. excl. wearing apparel		1092	937	1012	1336		438	379	391	577		12	20
324 Footwear, except rubber or plastic		2630	3877	3604	3019		1019	2427	1121	1060		43	43
331 Wood products, except furniture		9962	10571	9166	8251		3568	3740	3240	2871		800	245
3311 Sawmills, planing and other wood mills		6709	8918	7956	7108		2434	3158	2753	2445		766	227
3312 Wooden and cane containers		1261	1162	637	562		376	321	193	166		4	8
3319 Other wood and cork products		1992	491	574	581		759	261	293	260		30	10
332 Furniture and fixtures, excl. metal		5022	5900	5650	5140		2131	2200	2402	1999		154	143
341 Paper and products		18958	14375	17266	23030		6562	5115	6663	8003		1140	3582
3411 Pulp, paper and paperboard articles		11871	8884	10416	15746		4721	3445	4237	5916		719	3231
3412 Containers of paper and paperboard		4903	3769	4877	5060		1255	1168	1720	1493		368	245
3419 Other pulp, paper and paperboard articles		2184	1722	1974	2225		586	502	705	594		54	106
342 Printing and publishing		9305	14770	10980	13130		3753	5955	4803	5420		606	468
351 Industrial chemicals		24140	21836	22749	27851		9793	9765	8550	9724		1028	1272
3511 Basic chemicals excl. fertilizers		10718	8723	8806	10810		3250	3229	3631	4046		683	666
3512 Fertilizers and pesticides		8925	8347	9016	11086		4899	4709	3214	3351		152	197
3513 Synthetic resins and plastic materials		4497	4766	4927	5955		1645	1827	1704	2327		193	409
352 Other chemicals		57244	60375	63292	68741		30750	32123	33820	36417		3310	4129
3521 Paints, varnishes and lacquers		4068	5252	5542	6456		1055	1348	1428	1559		143	119
3522 Drugs and medicines		23014	23451	24409	26213		13734	13659	13330	15741		1541	996
3523 Soap, cleaning preps., perfumes, cosmetics		25015	25931	27748	28300		13817	14272	16249	15272		1374	1922
3529 Other chemical products		5149	5742	5593	7773		2144	2844	2814	3844		252	1093
353 Petroleum refineries		86765	91567	111690	123116		19869	13303	26241	40819		7740	3672

ISIC	Industry													
354	Misc. petroleum and coal products		951	1110	849	1617		335	373	169	467		3	20
355	Rubber products		13891	11210	9848	10375		6308	5428	4489	5149		389	1566
3551	Tyres and tubes		8420	7078	4354	4599		3971	3537	2248	2376		184	1197
3559	Other rubber products		5471	4132	5494	5777		2338	1891	2241	2774		205	369
356	Plastic products		14065	13206	15583	20262		4827	5085	6423	7269		1182	2563
361	Pottery, china, earthenware		2319	2358	2498	2339		1272	1308	1521	1387		167	142
362	Glass and products		4769	4933	5733	6309		2397	2434	3418	3848		341	1157
369	Other non-metallic mineral products		18773	18561	22147	26191		8502	8602	10149	12880		6281	7973
3691	Structural clay products		1886	1674	2026	2134		1128	1041	1162	1295		371	948
3692	Cement, lime and plaster		12091	13325	16379	19452		5134	5773	7153	9502		5747	6733
3699	Other non-metallic mineral products		4796	3562	3742	4606		2239	1789	1834	2084		162	292
371	Iron and steel		33935	38962	35408	48657		9784	9455	14877	14101		13326	2320
372	Non-ferrous metals		11745	15912	17565	24407		1933	7106	3476	6496		175	549
381	Fabricated metal products		12634	14316	16418	18995		4209	4788	6189	6320		788	993
3811	Cutlery, hand tools and general hardware		437	263	549	345		180	94	203	160		48	14
3812	Furniture and fixtures primarily of metal		449	397	584	764		215	101	171	242		28	22
3813	Structural metal products		2920	4493	4088	4957		1098	1711	1587	2358		230	398
3819	Other fabricated metal products		8828	9163	11198	12928		2716	2881	4228	3560		482	559
382	Non-electrical machinery		6843	10484	11535	21519		3226	2975	3712	8075		1118	1960
3821	Engines and turbines		33	76	-	-		23	33	-	-		-	-
3822	Agricultural machinery and equipment		190	248	271	298		86	86	110	128		28	24
3823	Metal and wood working machinery		346	336	285	427		221	190	154	262		376	100
3824	Other special industrial machinery		293	429	307	444		132	161	152	239		7	22
3825	Office, computing and accounting machinery		810	6216	8381	16099		301	1147	2204	5245		617	1663
3829	Other non-electrical machinery & equipment		5171	3179	2291	4251		2464	1357	1092	2201		90	151
383	Electrical machinery		80459	81397	102221	125955		25801	28278	32241	43504		10488	13387
3831	Electrical industrial machinery		2165	2305	2143	2163		890	981	1074	652		59	74
3832	Radio, television and communication equipm.		55122	55703	70230	94499		17638	18549	21714	31192		8640	12387
3833	Electrical appliances and housewares		2535	3998	7037	7167		1164	1635	2765	2989		527	288
3839	Other electrical apparatus and supplies		20636	19391	22811	22126		6109	7113	6688	8671		1262	638
384	Transport equipment		37861	45405	51060	60049		9949	12579	11579	15626		1310	1686
3841	Shipbuilding and repairing		1622	3096	1148	1407		1004	1609	524	873		146	72
3842	Railroad equipment		-	-	20	-		-	-	3	-		-	-
3843	Motor vehicles		32464	37424	41919	50667		7918	8819	7589	12555		1023	1225
3844	Motorcycles and bicycles		3567	4590	7623	7573		917	1981	3318	2091		96	380
3845	Aircraft	c/	208	294	351	401	c/	110	170	145	107	c/	45	9
3849	Other transport equipment	c/	...	...	...	...	c/	...	...	...	...	c/	...	...
385	Professional and scientific equipment		819	2408	1686	2011		461	1064	972	990		171	261
3851	Prof. and scientific equipment n.e.c.		388	902	502	537		176	363	209	167		25	18
3852	Photographic and optical goods		431d/	1507d/	525	765		285d/	701d/	200	215		75	184
3853	Watches and clocks		...d/	...d/	659	708		...d/	...d/	563	608		71	59
390	Other manufacturing industries		5696	6664	7434	7868		2674	3186	3250	3689		506	431
3901	Jewellery and related articles		278	948	1059	926		200	375	405	450		78	82
3902	Musical instruments		80	23	46	112		46	11	22	79		-	-
3903	Sporting and athletic goods		874	1174	1798	1805		292	491	679	578		108	132
3909	Manufacturing industries, n.e.c.		4462	4518	4530	5025		2136	2308	2143	2583		320	217
3	Total manufacturing		734877	793282	852565	1008158		269101	299148	325084	394020		64833	69061

a/ 3132 includes 3133.
b/ 3231 includes 3232.
c/ 3845 includes 3849.
d/ 3852 includes 3853.

Philippines

ISIC Revision 2		Index numbers of industrial production											
		(1990=100)											
ISIC Industry	Note	1985	1986	1987	1988	1989	1990	1991	1992	1993	1994	1995	1996
311/2 Food products		57	56	76	86	93	100	110	120	120	134	133	154
313 Beverages		51	52	66	72	82	100	122	132	131	149	150	182
314 Tobacco		123	91	88	97	102	100	106	110	122	136	140	152
321 Textiles		51	68	79	93	97	100	108	104	86	83	96	88
322 Wearing apparel, except footwear		...	53	69	77	101	100	99	110	120	133	138	100
323 Leather and fur products		65	61	70	82	91	100	122	128	137	141	162	189
324 Footwear, except rubber or plastic		...	...	...	...	...	...	...	...	...	...	...	...
331 Wood products, except furniture		62	46	55	67	74	100	118	84	107	97	87	83
332 Furniture and fixtures, excl. metal		41	44	50	60	76	100	92	91	76	71	88	181
341 Paper and products		78	91	104	110	157	100	153	143	146	172	210	210
342 Printing and publishing		54	61	70	80	92	100	120	131	139	155	171	193
351 Industrial chemicals	a/	...	74	74	83	96	100	118	142	176	194	240	226
352 Other chemicals	a/	...	...	...	...	...	...	...	...	...	...	...	...
353 Petroleum refineries	b/	...	67	69	64	70	100	133	142	135	126	173	202
354 Misc. petroleum and coal products	b/	...	...	...	...	...	...	...	...	...	...	...	...
355 Rubber products	a/	...	...	...	...	...	...	...	...	...	...	...	...
356 Plastic products		...	64	76	78	92	100	115	118	108	98	89	70
361 Pottery, china, earthenware	c/	48	50	61	75	85	100	125	133	137	148	175	193
362 Glass and products	c/	...	...	...	...	...	...	...	...	...	...	...	...
369 Other non-metallic mineral products	c/	...	...	...	...	...	...	...	...	...	...	...	...
371 Iron and steel	d/	...	40	50	73	105	100	127	108	115	123	156	162
372 Non-ferrous metals	d/	...	...	...	...	...	...	...	...	...	...	...	...
381 Fabricated metal products		39	70	69	69	84	100	108	117	127	130	141	164
382 Non-electrical machinery	e/	...	56	69	90	88	100	141	151	197	265	320	419
383 Electrical machinery	e/	...	...	...	...	...	...	...	...	...	...	...	...
384 Transport equipment		6	15	27	55	94	100	121	148	230	273	335	344
385 Professional and scientific equipment		...	...	...	...	...	...	...	...	...	...	...	...
390 Other manufacturing industries		132	215	181	80	88	100	144	148	293	363	521	562
3 Total manufacturing		...	61	72	81	92	100	119	127	141	159	182	200

a/ 351 includes 352 and 355.
b/ 353 includes 354.
c/ 361 includes 362 and 369.
d/ 371 includes 372.
e/ 382 includes 383.

POLAND

Supplier of information:
Central Statistical Office of Poland, Warsaw.

Basic source of data:
Annual statistical reports.

Major deviations from ISIC (Revision 3):
Data presented in accordance with ISIC (Rev. 3), were originally classified according to the NACE (Revision 1) at a 2-digit level.

Reference period (if not calendar year):

Scope:
Data cover all economic units.

Method of enumeration:
Data are compiled according to the enterprise and self-financing establishment method.

Adjusted for non-response:
Not reported.

Concepts and definitions of variables:
Number of establishments is as of 31 December of the reference year.
Number of employees includes part-time employees expressed in terms of full-time equivalents.
Gross fixed capital formation includes outlays on productive and non-productive investment, outlays on capital repairs are excluded. The value of sales of fixed assets is not deducted.

Related national publications:
Rocznik Statystyczny Przemyslu (Statistical Yearbook of Industry); Rocznik Statystyczny (Statistical Yearbook); Concise Statistical Yearbook of Poland; Zatrudnienie w gospodarce narodowej (Employment in National Economy); Zatrudniene i wynagrodzenia w gospodarce narodowej (Employment and Earnings in National Economy), all published by the Central Statistical Office.

Poland

ISIC Revision 3	Number of establishments					Number of employees					Wages and salaries paid to employees				
		(numbers)					(thousands)					(million NEW ZLOTYS)			
ISIC Industry	Note	1993	1994	1995	1996	Note	1993	1994	1995	1996	Note	1993	1994	1995	1996
151 Processed meat,fish,fruit,vegetables,fats		...	...	...	...	a/	467	454	484	486	a/	1967	2516	3535	4535
1511 Processing/preserving of meat		...	...	...	...		...	...	...	...		...	...	...	...
1512 Processing/preserving of fish		...	...	...	...		...	...	...	...		...	...	...	...
1513 Processing/preserving of fruit & vegetables		...	...	...	...		...	...	...	...		...	...	...	...
1514 Vegetable and animal oils and fats		...	...	...	...		...	...	...	...		...	...	...	...
1520 Dairy products		...	...	...	...		...	...	...	...		...	...	...	...
153 Grain mill products; starches; animal feeds		...	...	...	...	a/	...	...	...	...	a/	...	...	...	...
1531 Grain mill products		...	...	...	...	a/	...	...	...	...	a/	...	...	...	...
1532 Starches and starch products		...	...	...	...		...	...	...	...		...	...	...	...
1533 Prepared animal feeds		...	...	...	...		...	...	...	...		...	...	...	...
154 Other food products		...	...	...	...	a/	...	...	...	...	a/	...	...	...	...
1541 Bakery products		...	...	...	...		...	...	...	...		...	...	...	...
1542 Sugar		...	...	...	...		...	...	...	...		...	...	...	...
1543 Cocoa, chocolate and sugar confectionery		...	...	...	...		...	...	...	...		...	...	...	...
1544 Macaroni, noodles & similar products		...	...	...	...		...	...	...	...		...	...	...	...
1549 Other food products n.e.c.		...	...	...	...		...	...	...	...		...	...	...	...
155 Beverages		...	...	...	...	a/	...	...	...	...	a/	...	...	...	...
1551 Distilling, rectifying & blending of spirits		...	...	...	...		...	...	...	...		...	...	...	...
1552 Wines		...	...	...	...		...	...	...	...		...	...	...	...
1553 Malt liquors and malt		...	...	...	...		...	...	...	...		...	...	...	...
1554 Soft drinks; mineral waters		...	...	...	...		...	...	...	...		...	...	...	...
1600 Tobacco products		...	...	...	...		12	12	12	12		72	107	147	230
171 Spinning, weaving and finishing of textiles		...	...	...	...	b/	172	171	165	153	b/	635	861	1073	1235
1711 Textile fibre preparation; textile weaving		...	...	...	...		...	...	...	...		...	...	...	...
1712 Finishing of textiles		...	...	...	...		...	...	...	...		...	...	...	...
172 Other textiles		...	...	...	...	b/	...	...	...	...	b/	...	...	...	...
1721 Made-up textile articles, except apparel		...	...	...	...		...	...	...	...		...	...	...	...
1722 Carpets and rugs		...	...	...	...		...	...	...	...		...	...	...	...
1723 Cordage, rope, twine and netting		...	...	...	...		...	...	...	...		...	...	...	...
1729 Other textiles n.e.c.		...	...	...	...		...	...	...	...		...	...	...	...
1730 Knitted and crocheted fabrics and articles		...	...	...	...	b/	...	...	...	...	b/	...	...	...	...
1810 Wearing apparel, except fur apparel		...	...	...	...	c/	229	238	274	260	c/	768	1024	1461	1676
1820 Dressing & dyeing of fur; processing of fur		...	...	...	...	c/	...	...	...	...	c/	...	...	...	...
191 Tanning, dressing and processing of leather		...	...	...	...	d/	80	77	76	76	d/	265	332	436	551
1911 Tanning and dressing of leather		...	...	...	...		...	...	...	...		...	...	...	...
1912 Luggage, handbags, etc.; saddlery & harness		...	...	...	...		...	...	...	...		...	...	...	...
1920 Footwear		...	...	...	...	d/	...	...	...	...	d/	...	...	...	...
2010 Sawmilling and planing of wood		...	...	...	...	e/	95	96	109	116	e/	349	492	714	914
202 Products of wood, cork, straw, etc.		...	...	...	...	e/	...	...	...	...	e/	...	...	...	...
2021 Veneer sheets, plywood, particle board, etc.		...	...	...	...		...	...	...	...		...	...	...	...
2022 Builders' carpentry and joinery		...	...	...	...		...	...	...	...		...	...	...	...
2023 Wooden containers		...	...	...	...		...	...	...	...		...	...	...	...
2029 Other wood products; articles of cork/straw		...	...	...	...		...	...	...	...		...	...	...	...
210 Paper and paper products		...	...	...	...		36	40	38	39		172	258	372	485
2101 Pulp, paper and paperboard		...	...	...	...		...	...	...	...		...	...	...	...
2102 Corrugated paper and paperboard		...	...	...	...		...	...	...	...		...	...	...	...
2109 Other articles of paper and paperboard		...	...	...	...		...	...	...	...		...	...	...	...
221 Publishing		...	...	...	...	f/	58	59	66	69	f/	312	433	648	856
2211 Publishing of books and other publications		...	...	...	...		...	...	...	...		...	...	...	...
2212 Publishing of newspapers, journals, etc.		...	...	...	...		...	...	...	...		...	...	...	...
2213 Publishing of recorded media		...	...	...	...		...	...	...	...		...	...	...	...
2219 Other publishing		...	...	...	...		...	...	...	...		...	...	...	...

222 Printing and related service activities	...	...	...	...	f/	...	...	...	...	f/	...	...	...	...
2221 Printing	...	...	...	...		...	...	...	...		...	...	...	...
2222 Service activities related to printing	...	...	...	...		...	...	...	...		...	...	...	...
2230 Reproduction of recorded media	...	...	...	...	f/	...	...	...	...	f/	...	...	...	...
2310 Coke oven products	...	...	...	...	g/	23	24	23	23	g/	203	289	390	462
2320 Refined petroleum products	...	...	...	...	g/	...	...	...	...	g/	...	...	...	...
2330 Processing of nuclear fuel	...	...	...	...	g/	...	...	...	...	g/	...	...	...	...
241 Basic chemicals	...	...	...	...	h/	136	141	141	140	h/	706	1064	1512	1943
2411 Basic chemicals, except fertilizers	...	...	...	...		...	...	...	...		...	...	...	...
2412 Fertilizers and nitrogen compounds	...	...	...	...		...	...	...	...		...	...	...	...
2413 Plastics in primary forms; synthetic rubber	...	...	...	...		...	...	...	...		...	...	...	...
242 Other chemicals	...	...	...	...	h/	...	...	...	...	h/	...	...	...	...
2421 Pesticides and other agro-chemical products	...	...	...	...		...	...	...	...		...	...	...	...
2422 Paints, varnishes, printing ink and mastics	...	...	...	...		...	...	...	...		...	...	...	...
2423 Pharmaceuticals, medicinal chemicals, etc.	...	...	...	...		...	...	...	...		...	...	...	...
2424 Soap, cleaning & cosmetic preparations	...	...	...	...		...	...	...	...		...	...	...	...
2429 Other chemical products n.e.c.	...	...	...	...		...	...	...	...		...	...	...	...
2430 Man-made fibres	...	...	...	...	h/	...	...	...	...	h/	...	...	...	...
251 Rubber products	...	...	...	...	i/	77	85	89	95	i/	357	539	766	996
2511 Rubber tyres and tubes	...	...	...	...		...	...	...	...		...	...	...	...
2519 Other rubber products	...	...	...	...		...	...	...	...		...	...	...	...
2520 Plastic products	...	...	...	...	i/	...	...	...	...	i/	...	...	...	...
2610 Glass and glass products	...	...	...	...	j/	168	160	166	166	j/	689	932	1302	1642
269 Non-metallic mineral products n.e.c.	...	...	...	...	j/	...	...	...	...	j/	...	...	...	...
2691 Pottery, china and earthenware	...	...	...	...		...	...	...	...		...	...	...	...
2692 Refractory ceramic products	...	...	...	...		...	...	...	...		...	...	...	...
2693 Struct.non-refractory clay; ceramic products	...	...	...	...		...	...	...	...		...	...	...	...
2694 Cement, lime and plaster	...	...	...	...		...	...	...	...		...	...	...	...
2695 Articles of concrete, cement and plaster	...	...	...	...		...	...	...	...		...	...	...	...
2696 Cutting, shaping & finishing of stone	...	...	...	...		...	...	...	...		...	...	...	...
2699 Other non-metallic mineral products n.e.c.	...	...	...	...		...	...	...	...		...	...	...	...
2710 Basic iron and steel	...	...	...	...	k/	165	154	150	154	k/	860	1173	1594	2092
2720 Basic precious and non-ferrous metals	...	...	...	...	k/	...	...	...	...	k/	...	...	...	...
273 Casting of metals	...	...	...	...	k/	...	...	...	...	k/	...	...	...	...
2731 Casting of iron and steel	...	...	...	...		...	...	...	...		...	...	...	...
2732 Casting of non-ferrous metals	...	...	...	...		...	...	...	...		...	...	...	...
281 Struct.metal products;tanks;steam generators	...	...	...	...	m/	141	146	161	174	m/	594	829	1208	1655
2811 Structural metal products	...	...	...	...		...	...	...	...		...	...	...	...
2812 Tanks, reservoirs and containers of metal	...	...	...	...		...	...	...	...		...	...	...	...
2813 Steam generators	...	...	...	...		...	...	...	...		...	...	...	...
289 Other metal products; metal working services	...	...	...	...	m/	...	...	...	...	m/	...	...	...	...
2891 Metal forging/pressing/stamping/roll-forming	...	...	...	...		...	...	...	...		...	...	...	...
2892 Treatment & coating of metals	...	...	...	...		...	...	...	...		...	...	...	...
2893 Cutlery, hand tools and general hardware	...	...	...	...		...	...	...	...		...	...	...	...
2899 Other fabricated metal products n.e.c.	...	...	...	...		...	...	...	...		...	...	...	...
291 General purpose machinery	...	...	...	...	n/	312	298	300	287	n/	1368	1795	2425	2994
2911 Engines & turbines(not for transport equip.)	...	...	...	...		...	...	...	...		...	...	...	...
2912 Pumps, compressors, taps and valves	...	...	...	...		...	...	...	...		...	...	...	...
2913 Bearings, gears, gearing & driving elements	...	...	...	...		...	...	...	...		...	...	...	...
2914 Ovens, furnaces and furnace burners	...	...	...	...		...	...	...	...		...	...	...	...
2915 Lifting and handling equipment	...	...	...	...		...	...	...	...		...	...	...	...
2919 Other general purpose machinery	...	...	...	...		...	...	...	...		...	...	...	...
292 Special purpose machinery	...	...	...	...	n/	...	...	...	...	n/	...	...	...	...
2921 Agricultural and forestry machinery	...	...	...	...		...	...	...	...		...	...	...	...
2922 Machine tools	...	...	...	...		...	...	...	...		...	...	...	...
2923 Machinery for metallurgy	...	...	...	...		...	...	...	...		...	...	...	...
2924 Machinery for mining & construction	...	...	...	...		...	...	...	...		...	...	...	...
2925 Food/beverage/tobacco processing machinery	...	...	...	...		...	...	...	...		...	...	...	...
2926 Machinery for textile, apparel and leather	...	...	...	...		...	...	...	...		...	...	...	...
2927 Weapons and ammunition	...	...	...	...		...	...	...	...		...	...	...	...
2929 Other special purpose machinery	...	...	...	...		...	...	...	...		...	...	...	...
2930 Domestic appliances n.e.c.	...	...	...	...	n/	...	...	...	...	n/	...	...	...	...

continued

Poland

ISIC Revision 3	Number of establishments					Number of employees					Wages and salaries paid to employees				
		(numbers)					(thousands)					(million NEW ZLOTYS)			
ISIC Industry	Note	1993	1994	1995	1996	Note	1993	1994	1995	1996	Note	1993	1994	1995	1996
3000 Office, accounting and computing machinery		...	...	...	...		5	4	4	4		27	28	38	49
3110 Electric motors, generators and transformers		...	...	...	...	p/	85	88	90	91	p/	406	580	789	1023
3120 Electricity distribution & control apparatus		...	...	...	...	p/	...	...	...	...	p/	...	...	...	...
3130 Insulated wire and cable		...	...	...	...	p/	...	...	...	...	p/	...	...	...	...
3140 Accumulators, primary cells and batteries		...	...	...	...	p/	...	...	...	...	p/	...	...	...	...
3150 Lighting equipment and electric lamps		...	...	...	...	p/	...	...	...	...	p/	...	...	...	...
3190 Other electrical equipment n.e.c.		...	...	...	...	p/	...	...	...	...	p/	...	...	...	...
3210 Electronic valves, tubes, etc.		...	...	...	...	q/	53	49	45	42	q/	244	310	399	480
3220 TV/radio transmitters; line comm. apparatus		...	...	...	...	q/	...	...	...	...	q/	...	...	...	...
3230 TV and radio receivers and associated goods		...	...	...	...	q/	...	...	...	...	q/	...	...	...	...
331 Medical, measuring, testing appliances, etc.		...	...	...	...	r/	40	41	42	43	r/	186	268	373	473
3311 Medical, surgical and orthopaedic equipment		...	...	...	...		...	...	...	...		...	...	...	...
3312 Measuring/testing/navigating appliances,etc.		...	...	...	...		...	...	...	...		...	...	...	...
3313 Industrial process control equipment		...	...	...	...		...	...	...	...		...	...	...	...
3320 Optical instruments & photographic equipment		...	...	...	...	r/	...	...	...	...	r/	...	...	...	...
3330 Watches and clocks		...	...	...	...	r/	...	...	...	...	r/	...	...	...	...
3410 Motor vehicles		...	...	...	...	s/	97	102	99	101	s/	459	656	855	1159
3420 Automobile bodies, trailers & semi-trailers		...	...	...	...	s/	...	...	...	...	s/	...	...	...	...
3430 Parts/accessories for automobiles		...	...	...	...	s/	...	...	...	...	s/	...	...	...	...
351 Building and repairing of ships and boats		...	...	...	...	t/	117	116	114	108	t/	567	781	1009	1207
3511 Building and repairing of ships		...	...	...	...		...	...	...	...		...	...	...	...
3512 Building/repairing of pleasure/sport. boats		...	...	...	...		...	...	...	...		...	...	...	...
3520 Railway/tramway locomotives & rolling stock		...	...	...	...		...	...	...	...		...	...	...	...
3530 Aircraft and spacecraft		...	...	...	...	t/	...	...	...	...	t/	...	...	...	...
359 Transport equipment n.e.c.		...	...	...	...	t/	...	...	...	...	t/	...	...	...	...
3591 Motorcycles		...	...	...	...	t/	...	...	...	...	t/	...	...	...	...
3592 Bicycles and invalid carriages		...	...	...	...		...	...	...	...		...	...	...	...
3599 Other transport equipment n.e.c.		...	...	...	...		...	...	...	...		...	...	...	...
3610 Furniture		...	...	...	...	u/	127	132	153	157	u/	473	647	987	1230
369 Manufacturing n.e.c.		...	...	...	...	u/	...	...	...	...	u/	...	...	...	...
3691 Jewellery and related articles		...	...	...	...		...	...	...	...		...	...	...	...
3692 Musical instruments		...	...	...	...		...	...	...	...		...	...	...	...
3693 Sports goods		...	...	...	...		...	...	...	...		...	...	...	...
3694 Games and toys		...	...	...	...		...	...	...	...		...	...	...	...
3699 Other manufacturing n.e.c.		...	...	...	...		...	...	...	...		...	...	...	...
3710 Recycling of metal waste and scrap		...	...	...	...	v/	5	7	6	6	v/	31	59	66	81
3720 Recycling of non-metal waste and scrap		...	...	...	...	v/	...	...	...	...	v/	...	...	...	...
D Total manufacturing		249705	214260	...	...		2700	2693	2809	2803		11709	15970	22097	27970

a/ 151 includes 1520, 153, 154 and 155.
b/ 171 includes 172 and 1730.
c/ 1810 includes 1820.
d/ 191 includes 1920.
e/ 2010 includes 202.
f/ 221 includes 222 and 2230.
g/ 2310 includes 2320 and 2330.
h/ 241 includes 242 and 2430.
i/ 251 includes 2520.
j/ 2610 includes 269.
k/ 2710 includes 2720 and 273.
m/ 281 includes 289.
n/ 291 includes 292 and 2930.
p/ 3110 includes 3120, 3130, 3140, 3150 and 3190.
q/ 3210 includes 3220 and 3230.
r/ 331 includes 3320 and 3330.
s/ 3410 includes 3420 and 3430.
t/ 351 includes 3520, 3530 and 359.
u/ 3610 includes 369.
v/ 3710 includes 3720.

Poland

ISIC Revision 3	Output					Value added					Gross fixed capital formation		
		(million NEW ZLOTYS)					(million NEW ZLOTYS)					(million NEW ZLOTYS)	
ISIC Industry	Note	1993	1994	1995	1996	Note	1993	1994	1995	1996	Note	1995	1996
151 Processed meat,fish,fruit,vegetables,fats	a/	26293	36539	46658	59861	a/	9660	10562	10950	11733	a/	2695	3731
1511 Processing/preserving of meat		...	...	...	...		...	...	...	...		...	...
1512 Processing/preserving of fish		...	...	...	...		...	...	...	...		...	...
1513 Processing/preserving of fruit & vegetables		...	...	...	...		...	...	...	...		...	...
1514 Vegetable and animal oils and fats		...	...	...	...		...	...	...	...		...	...
1520 Dairy products	a/	...	...	...	...	a/	...	...	...	...	a/	...	...
153 Grain mill products; starches; animal feeds	a/	...	...	...	...	a/	...	...	...	...	a/	...	...
1531 Grain mill products		...	...	...	...		...	...	...	...		...	...
1532 Starches and starch products		...	...	...	...		...	...	...	...		...	...
1533 Prepared animal feeds		...	...	...	...		...	...	...	...		...	...
154 Other food products	a/	...	...	...	...	a/	...	...	...	...	a/	...	...
1541 Bakery products		...	...	...	...		...	...	...	...		...	...
1542 Sugar		...	...	...	...		...	...	...	...		...	...
1543 Cocoa, chocolate and sugar confectionery		...	...	...	...		...	...	...	...		...	...
1544 Macaroni, noodles & similar products		...	...	...	...		...	...	...	...		...	...
1549 Other food products n.e.c.		...	...	...	...		...	...	...	...		...	...
155 Beverages	a/	...	...	...	...	a/	...	...	...	...	a/	...	...
1551 Distilling, rectifying & blending of spirits		...	...	...	...		...	...	...	...		...	...
1552 Wines		...	...	...	...		...	...	...	...		...	...
1553 Malt liquors and malt		...	...	...	...		...	...	...	...		...	...
1554 Soft drinks; mineral waters		...	...	...	...		...	...	...	...		...	...
1600 Tobacco products		2200	3042	1816	2228		1459	1936	453	596		122	322
171 Spinning, weaving and finishing of textiles	b/	3486	5203	6399	6890	b/	1334	1901	2285	2685	b/	327	385
1711 Textile fibre preparation; textile weaving		...	...	...	...		...	...	...	...		...	...
1712 Finishing of textiles		...	...	...	...		...	...	...	...		...	...
172 Other textiles	b/	...	...	...	...	b/	...	...	...	...	b/	...	...
1721 Made-up textile articles, except apparel		...	...	...	...		...	...	...	...		...	...
1722 Carpets and rugs		...	...	...	...		...	...	...	...		...	...
1723 Cordage, rope, twine and netting		...	...	...	...		...	...	...	...		...	...
1729 Other textiles n.e.c.		...	...	...	...		...	...	...	...		...	...
1730 Knitted and crocheted fabrics and articles	b/	...	...	...	...	b/	...	...	...	...	b/	...	...
1810 Wearing apparel, except fur apparel	c/	4026	5250	6330	6714	c/	1981	2335	3222	3338	c/	233	258
1820 Dressing & dyeing of fur; processing of fur	c/	...	...	...	...	c/	...	...	...	...	c/	...	...
191 Tanning, dressing and processing of leather	d/	1501	2071	2679	3239	d/	594	852	1002	1239	d/	80	98
1911 Tanning and dressing of leather		...	...	...	...		...	...	...	...		...	...
1912 Luggage, handbags, etc.; saddlery & harness		...	...	...	...		...	...	...	...		...	...
1920 Footwear	d/	...	...	...	...	d/	...	...	...	...	d/	...	...
2010 Sawmilling and planing of wood	e/	2916	4654	6813	7846	e/	1075	1830	2078	2714	e/	510	562
202 Products of wood, cork, straw, etc.	e/	...	...	...	...	e/	...	...	...	...	e/	...	...
2021 Veneer sheets, plywood, particle board, etc.		...	...	...	...		...	...	...	...		...	...
2022 Builders' carpentry and joinery		...	...	...	...		...	...	...	...		...	...
2023 Wooden containers		...	...	...	...		...	...	...	...		...	...
2029 Other wood products; articles of cork/straw		...	...	...	...		...	...	...	...		...	...
210 Paper and paper products		1644	2723	5403	5354		493	798	1761	1468		489	687
2101 Pulp, paper and paperboard		...	...	...	...		...	...	...	...		...	...
2102 Corrugated paper and paperboard		...	...	...	...		...	...	...	...		...	...
2109 Other articles of paper and paperboard		...	...	...	...		...	...	...	...		...	...
221 Publishing	f/	2928	4350	6473	7879	f/	1092	1857	2747	3512	f/	255	421
2211 Publishing of books and other publications		...	...	...	...		...	...	...	...		...	...
2212 Publishing of newspapers, journals, etc.		...	...	...	...		...	...	...	...		...	...
2213 Publishing of recorded media		...	...	...	...		...	...	...	...		...	...
2219 Other publishing		...	...	...	...		...	...	...	...		...	...

continued

ISIC Revision 3		Output					Value added					Gross fixed capital formation	
		(million NEW ZLOTYS)					(million NEW ZLOTYS)					(million NEW ZLOTYS)	
ISIC Industry	Note	1993	1994	1995	1996	Note	1993	1994	1995	1996	Note	1995	1996
222 Printing and related service activities	f/	...	...	...	...	f/	...	...	...	...	f/	...	...
2221 Printing		...	...	...	...		...	...	...	...		...	...
2222 Service activities related to printing		...	...	...	...		...	...	...	...		...	...
2230 Reproduction of recorded media	f/	...	...	...	...	f/	...	...	...	...	f/	...	...
2310 Coke oven products	g/	8987	10914	10137	11295	g/	3411	3971	1737	1370	g/	709	1254
2320 Refined petroleum products	g/	...	...	...	...	g/	...	...	...	...	g/	...	...
2330 Processing of nuclear fuel	g/	...	...	...	...	g/	...	...	...	...	g/	...	...
241 Basic chemicals	h/	7290	11071	16692	18415	h/	2325	3371	5395	6115	h/	1181	1554
2411 Basic chemicals, except fertilizers		...	...	...	...		...	...	...	...		...	...
2412 Fertilizers and nitrogen compounds		...	...	...	...		...	...	...	...		...	...
2413 Plastics in primary forms; synthetic rubber		...	...	...	...		...	...	...	...		...	...
242 Other chemicals	h/	...	...	...	...	h/	...	...	...	...	h/	...	...
2421 Pesticides and other agro-chemical products		...	...	...	...		...	...	...	...		...	...
2422 Paints, varnishes, printing ink and mastics		...	...	...	...		...	...	...	...		...	...
2423 Pharmaceuticals, medicinal chemicals, etc.		...	...	...	...		...	...	...	...		...	...
2424 Soap, cleaning & cosmetic preparations		...	...	...	...		...	...	...	...		...	...
2429 Other chemical products n.e.c.		...	...	...	...		...	...	...	...		...	...
2430 Man-made fibres	h/	...	...	...	...	h/	...	...	...	...	h/	...	...
251 Rubber products	i/	3417	5231	7770	8908	i/	1365	1933	2953	3306	i/	543	855
2511 Rubber tyres and tubes		...	...	...	...		...	...	...	...		...	...
2519 Other rubber products		...	...	...	...		...	...	...	...		...	...
2520 Plastic products	i/	...	...	...	...	i/	...	...	...	...	i/	...	...
2610 Glass and glass products	j/	4622	6918	9090	11189	j/	1807	2731	3550	4566	j/	845	1279
269 Non-metallic mineral products n.e.c.	j/	...	...	...	...	j/	...	...	...	...	j/	...	...
2691 Pottery, china and earthenware		...	...	...	...		...	...	...	...		...	...
2692 Refractory ceramic products		...	...	...	...		...	...	...	...		...	...
2693 Struct.non-refractory clay; ceramic products		...	...	...	...		...	...	...	...		...	...
2694 Cement, lime and plaster		...	...	...	...		...	...	...	...		...	...
2695 Articles of concrete, cement and plaster		...	...	...	...		...	...	...	...		...	...
2696 Cutting, shaping & finishing of stone		...	...	...	...		...	...	...	...		...	...
2699 Other non-metallic mineral products n.e.c.		...	...	...	...		...	...	...	...		...	...
2710 Basic iron and steel	k/	7511	11277	16057	17106	k/	1743	2572	4092	4037	k/	1101	1913
2720 Basic precious and non-ferrous metals	k/	...	...	...	...	k/	...	...	...	...	k/	...	...
273 Casting of metals	k/	...	...	...	...	k/	...	...	...	...	k/	...	...
2731 Casting of iron and steel		...	...	...	...		...	...	...	...		...	...
2732 Casting of non-ferrous metals		...	...	...	...		...	...	...	...		...	...
281 Struct.metal products;tanks;steam generators	m/	4615	6581	9367	10441	m/	2049	2602	3733	4927	m/	326	580
2811 Structural metal products		...	...	...	...		...	...	...	...		...	...
2812 Tanks, reservoirs and containers of metal		...	...	...	...		...	...	...	...		...	...
2813 Steam generators		...	...	...	...		...	...	...	...		...	...
289 Other metal products; metal working services	m/	...	...	...	...	m/	...	...	...	...	m/	...	...
2891 Metal forging/pressing/stamping/roll-forming		...	...	...	...		...	...	...	...		...	...
2892 Treatment & coating of metals		...	...	...	...		...	...	...	...		...	...
2893 Cutlery, hand tools and general hardware		...	...	...	...		...	...	...	...		...	...
2899 Other fabricated metal products n.e.c.		...	...	...	...		...	...	...	...		...	...
291 General purpose machinery	n/	6575	9343	13689	16345	n/	2817	3721	5367	6674	n/	584	773
2911 Engines & turbines(not for transport equip.)		...	...	...	...		...	...	...	...		...	...
2912 Pumps, compressors, taps and valves		...	...	...	...		...	...	...	...		...	...
2913 Bearings, gears, gearing & driving elements		...	...	...	...		...	...	...	...		...	...
2914 Ovens, furnaces and furnace burners		...	...	...	...		...	...	...	...		...	...
2915 Lifting and handling equipment		...	...	...	...		...	...	...	...		...	...
2919 Other general purpose machinery		...	...	...	...		...	...	...	...		...	...

292	Special purpose machinery	n/	...	...	...	...	n/	...	...	...	...	n/	...	...
2921	Agricultural and forestry machinery		...	...	...	...		...	...	...	...		...	...
2922	Machine tools		...	...	...	...		...	...	...	...		...	...
2923	Machinery for metallurgy		...	...	...	...		...	...	...	...		...	...
2924	Machinery for mining & construction		...	...	...	...		...	...	...	...		...	...
2925	Food/beverage/tobacco processing machinery		...	...	...	...		...	...	...	...		...	...
2926	Machinery for textile, apparel and leather		...	...	...	...		...	...	...	...		...	...
2927	Weapons and ammunition		...	...	...	...		...	...	...	...		...	...
2929	Other special purpose machinery		...	...	...	...		...	...	...	...		...	...
2930	Domestic appliances n.e.c.	n/	...	...	...	...	n/	...	...	...	...	n/	...	...
3000	Office, accounting and computing machinery		179	172	479	716		65	115	188	247		16	17
3110	Electric motors, generators and transformers	p/	2993	4056	6179	7574	p/	1156	1401	2167	2921	p/	381	557
3120	Electricity distribution & control apparatus	p/	...	...	...	...	p/	...	...	...	...	p/	...	...
3130	Insulated wire and cable	p/	...	...	...	...	p/	...	...	...	...	p/	...	...
3140	Accumulators, primary cells and batteries	p/	...	...	...	...	p/	...	...	...	...	p/	...	...
3150	Lighting equipment and electric lamps	p/	...	...	...	...	p/	...	...	...	...	p/	...	...
3190	Other electrical equipment n.e.c.	p/	...	...	...	...	p/	...	...	...	...	p/	...	...
3210	Electronic valves, tubes, etc.	q/	1546	2356	3347	4082	q/	561	758	1125	1327	q/	151	327
3220	TV/radio transmitters; line comm. apparatus	q/	...	...	...	...	q/	...	...	...	...	q/	...	...
3230	TV and radio receivers and associated goods	q/	...	...	...	...	q/	...	...	...	...	q/	...	...
331	Medical, measuring, testing appliances, etc.	r/	1042	1452	2197	2665	r/	580	630	964	1386	r/	91	133
3311	Medical, surgical and orthopaedic equipment		...	...	...	...		...	...	...	...		...	...
3312	Measuring/testing/navigating appliances,etc.		...	...	...	...		...	...	...	...		...	...
3313	Industrial process control equipment		...	...	...	...		...	...	...	...		...	...
3320	Optical instruments & photographic equipment	r/	...	...	...	...	r/	...	...	...	...	r/	...	...
3330	Watches and clocks	r/	...	...	...	...	r/	...	...	...	...	r/	...	...
3410	Motor vehicles	s/	4153	5819	8704	13694	s/	1370	1450	2023	3105	s/	494	808
3420	Automobile bodies, trailers & semi-trailers	s/	...	...	...	...	s/	...	...	...	...	s/	...	...
3430	Parts/accessories for automobiles	s/	...	...	...	...	s/	...	...	...	...	s/	...	...
351	Building and repairing of ships and boats	t/	2985	4534	5679	6299	t/	881	1798	1869	2228	t/	197	247
3511	Building and repairing of ships		...	...	...	...		...	...	...	...		...	...
3512	Building/repairing of pleasure/sport. boats		...	...	...	...		...	...	...	...		...	...
3520	Railway/tramway locomotives & rolling stock	t/	...	...	...	...	t/	...	...	...	...	t/	...	...
3530	Aircraft and spacecraft	t/	...	...	...	...	t/	...	...	...	...	t/	...	...
359	Transport equipment n.e.c.	t/	...	...	...	...	t/	...	...	...	...	t/	...	...
3591	Motorcycles		...	...	...	...		...	...	...	...		...	...
3592	Bicycles and invalid carriages		...	...	...	...		...	...	...	...		...	...
3599	Other transport equipment n.e.c.		...	...	...	...		...	...	...	...		...	...
3610	Furniture	u/	3204	4991	7609	8858	u/	1368	1908	2668	3200	u/	378	423
369	Manufacturing n.e.c.	u/	...	...	...	...	u/	...	...	...	...	u/	...	...
3691	Jewellery and related articles		...	...	...	...		...	...	...	...		...	...
3692	Musical instruments		...	...	...	...		...	...	...	...		...	...
3693	Sports goods		...	...	...	...		...	...	...	...		...	...
3694	Games and toys		...	...	...	...		...	...	...	...		...	...
3699	Other manufacturing n.e.c.		...	...	...	...		...	...	...	...		...	...
3710	Recycling of metal waste and scrap	v/	329	483	780	782	v/	109	148	244	187	v/	27	31
3720	Recycling of non-metal waste and scrap	v/	...	...	...	...	v/	...	...	...	...	v/	...	...
D	Total manufacturing		104441	149028	200348	238379		39294	51179	62575	72880		11733	17215

a/ 151 includes 1520, 153, 154 and 155.
b/ 171 includes 172 and 1730.
c/ 1810 includes 1820.
d/ 191 includes 1920.
e/ 2010 includes 202.
f/ 221 includes 222 and 2230.
g/ 2310 includes 2320 and 2330.
h/ 241 includes 242 and 2430.
i/ 251 includes 2520.
j/ 2610 includes 269.
k/ 2710 includes 2720 and 273.
m/ 281 includes 289.
n/ 291 includes 292 and 2930.
p/ 3110 includes 3120, 3130, 3140, 3150 and 3190.
q/ 3210 includes 3220 and 3230.
r/ 331 includes 3320 and 3330.
s/ 3410 includes 3420 and 3430.
t/ 351 includes 3520, 3530 and 359.
u/ 3610 includes 369.
v/ 3710 includes 3720.

Poland

ISIC Revision 3		Note	Index numbers of industrial production (1990=100)											
ISIC Industry			1985	1986	1987	1988	1989	1990	1991	1992	1993	1994	1995	1996
15	Food and beverages		149	155	160	163	146	100	97	109	118	133	146	160
16	Tobacco products		94	100	103	92	106	100	95	101	117	129	128	122
17	Textiles		146	147	149	162	168	100	81	79	86	99	98	101
18	Wearing apparel, fur		125	132	137	151	146	100	89	99	107	119	121	127
19	Leather, leather products and footwear		136	143	151	162	151	100	82	70	69	77	84	94
20	Wood products (excl. furniture)		125	129	130	135	136	100	164	204	212	234	258	291
21	Paper and paper products		114	122	127	135	131	100	97	106	113	141	167	183
22	Printing and publishing		95	107	118	130	134	100	87	91	126	134	158	180
23	Coke,refined petroleum products,nuclear fuel		133	135	137	142	132	100	86	100	112	120	127	130
24	Chemicals and chemical products		127	134	141	149	141	100	110	97	103	121	137	144
25	Rubber and plastics products		99	104	109	121	128	100	125	140	168	195	228	267
26	Non-metallic mineral products		121	126	131	138	138	100	91	101	111	128	134	147
27	Basic metals		130	135	132	131	121	100	76	73	75	87	101	101
28	Fabricated metal products		121	128	134	140	144	100	86	92	98	113	131	158
29	Machinery and equipment n.e.c.		102	111	119	129	128	100	76	68	75	86	104	114
30	Office, accounting and computing machinery		...	...	...	...	...	...	...	...	...	...	...	...
31	Electrical machinery and apparatus		...	...	...	...	...	100	81	68	76	83	96	108
32	Radio,television and communication equipment		...	...	...	...	...	100	77	70	89	112	132	157
33	Medical, precision and optical instruments		95	106	116	128	126	100	82	82	95	106	134	153
34	Motor vehicles, trailers, semi-trailers		...	...	...	...	...	100	65	84	107	122	139	186
35	Other transport equipment		...	...	...	...	...	100	60	64	71	87	90	86
36	Furniture; manufacturing n.e.c.		118	125	131	146	149	100	98	104	115	132	164	187
37	Recycling		...	...	...	...	...	...	...	...	...	...	...	...
D	Total manufacturing		121	128	131	139	135	100	90	94	104	118	132	147

PORTUGAL

Supplier of information:
National Statistical Institute, Lisbon.
Industrial statistics for the OECD countries are compiled by the OECD secretariat, which supplies them to UNIDO. The notes appearing here are based on information in the OECD publication *Industrial Structure Statistics* (annual), OECD, Paris.

Basic source of data:
Annual inquiry of 65000 enterprises in the mining, manufacturing and utilities sectors.

Major deviations from ISIC (Revision 2):
None reported.

Reference period (if not calendar year):

Scope:
Wages and salaries paid to employees relate to enterprises with 100 or more persons engaged, while all other variables cover all enterprises.

Method of enumeration:
Not reported.

Adjusted for non-response:
Not reported.

Concepts and definitions of variables:
Number of persons engaged covers all persons working, on vacation or sick leave, or on strike, during the last week of the year.
Output is gross output, defined as the total value of finished goods produced (intermediate goods sold as such are considered as finished products), plus the value of fixed assets produced for own use, industrial work done for others, electricity sold, waste products sold to third persons, less the value of work in progress at the beginning of the year.
Value added is gross output, plus the value of work done in the capacity of sub-contractor, less the value of materials, lubricants and energy consumed, hiring of machinery and contract work done by others, the value of industrial, repair and maintenance work done by others and non-industrial services received, and the value of duties paid for utilisation of manufacturing processes.

Related national publications:
Industrial Statistics (Volume I and Volume II), published by the National Statistical Institute, Lisbon.

Portugal

ISIC Revision 2	Number of enterprises					Number of persons engaged					Wages and salaries paid a/ to employees				
		(numbers)					(thousands)					(million ESCUDOS)			
ISIC Industry	Note	1992	1993	1994	1995	Note	1992	1993	1994	1995	Note	1992	1993	1994	1995
311/2 Food products		6830	6773	7475	6956		97.2	97.9	103.4	95.9		65183	65510	66789	65732
3111 Slaughtering, preparing & preserving meat		398	449	461	447		14.5	15.3	15.7	15.8		8042	9215	11440	10850
3112 Dairy products		242	247	275	255		13.4	11.9	11.3	10.6		15135	14336	12781	...
3113 Canning, preserving of fruits & vegetables		91	87	97	100		3.8	4.7	4.2	4.5		3317	5075	4401	5854
3114 Canning, preserving and processing of fish		103	109	139	122		6.4	6.4	7.1	6.7		3608	3563	3853	4126
3115 Vegetable and animal oils and fats		696	636	495	537		5.0	4.2	4.2	3.7		5852	4990	4920	3940
3116 Grain mill products		674	548	915	590		4.0	3.6	4.1	3.5		2357	2004	2359	1984
3117 Bakery products		4196	4299	4595	4472		34.5	37.8	41.8	37.0		7148	7846	8131	8135
3118 Sugar factories and refineries		5	4	4	4		1.2	1.0	1.1	1.0		2290	...	2379	2209
3119 Cocoa, chocolate and sugar confectionery		109	86	111	110		2.7	2.0	2.2	2.2		2913	...	1397	1427
3121 Other food products		212	189	265	203		5.8	5.7	6.4	6.0		8739	9911	10367	9359
3122 Prepared animal feeds		104	119	118	116		5.9	5.4	5.2	5.0		5782	4755	4761	4745
313 Beverages		653	770	652	726		17.6	17.4	17.4	16.6		18532	19994	21415	21026
3131 Distilling, rectifying and blending spirits		329	428	317	384		0.9	1.0	1.0	1.2		-	-	...	...
3132 Wine industries		255	270	275	274		8.1	8.4	8.9	7.9		5708	6601	7278	6304
3133 Malt liquors and malt		5	5	6	5		3.7	3.3	3.5	3.4		7699	7792	8697	9078
3134 Soft drinks and carbonated waters		64	67	54	63		5.0	4.8	4.1	4.0		5125	5601	...	...
314 Tobacco		4	5	5	4		1.5	1.5	1.4	1.3		3128	3634	2801	2903
321 Textiles		4056	4241	3945	4027		140.4	134.0	127.6	122.3		90618	90831	88176	87837
3211 Spinning, weaving and finishing textiles		1162	1098	1105	1023		78.3	72.4	64.9	61.4		62669	61985	55954	54850
3212 Made-up textile goods excl. wearing apparel		1041	1013	1100	1054		12.3	12.3	15.1	15.2		3651	3679	6469	7086
3213 Knitting mills		1414	1662	1275	1477		38.4	38.0	36.4	34.8		17431	18700	17661	17473
3214 Carpets and rugs		239	232	223	245		4.3	3.6	3.3	3.2		2008	1399	1503	1466
3215 Cordage, rope and twine		47	52	54	53		4.4	4.2	5.4	5.4		3723	3719	5471	5718
3219 Other textiles		153	184	188	175		2.7	3.5	2.6	2.3		1136	1349	1118	1244
322 Wearing apparel, except footwear		8405	8471	8481	7929		151.4	146.2	149.0	141.0		50508	50398	52622	53550
323 Leather and fur products		746	786	802	807		8.9	9.3	8.3	8.1		2515	2548	2463	2470
3231 Tanneries and leather finishing		195	204	167	177		4.5	4.6	3.9	3.6		...	...	...	...
3232 Fur dressing and dyeing industries		18	22	21	21		0.1	0.2	0.4	0.5		-	-	-	...
3233 Leather prods. excl. wearing apparel		533	560	614	609		4.3	4.6	4.0	4.1		...	...	...	...
324 Footwear, except rubber or plastic		2102	2134	2163	1939		62.1	65.7	65.1	62.5		25405	29315	29044	29621
331 Wood products, except furniture		7345	7654	7477	7571		51.7	51.3	51.1	50.6		13367	13300	15076	15755
3311 Sawmills, planing and other wood mills		5305	5662	5442	5635		33.3	32.5	32.3	31.7		6292	6137	7724	7465
3312 Wooden and cane containers		483	463	443	414		1.6	1.5	1.5	1.5		...	...	...	...
3319 Other wood and cork products		1557	1529	1592	1522		16.9	17.3	17.3	17.4		...	...	...	...
332 Furniture and fixtures, excl. metal		6560	6450	6715	6598		51.4	40.2	40.5	41.0		3554	4674	4672	4752
341 Paper and products		419	442	452	448		16.8	17.1	14.8	14.4		26191	23520	21735	24367
3411 Pulp, paper and paperboard articles		100	101	84	78		10.4	10.2	7.8	7.8		22222	18949	17574	19835
3412 Containers of paper and paperboard		191	189	213	226		4.0	4.6	4.9	4.8		2699	3319	...	...
3419 Other pulp, paper and paperboard articles		128	152	155	144		2.4	2.2	2.0	1.9		1270	1252	...	...
342 Printing and publishing		2549	2923	2960	2953		34.2	35.5	35.0	34.5		20891	22517	23621	25428
351 Industrial chemicals		185	208	201	196		9.7	8.9	7.4	7.2		17228	16900	14586	15592
3511 Basic chemicals excl. fertilizers		87	96	94	94		4.2	3.9	3.4	3.3		7379	7647	6708	6995
3512 Fertilizers and pesticides		28	21	19	15		2.5	2.1	1.6	1.5		...	...	...	...
3513 Synthetic resins and plastic materials		70	91	88	87		3.0	2.9	2.5	2.4		...	...	...	...
352 Other chemicals		729	707	701	692		23.3	22.2	21.1	21.0		32205	33629	34399	36722
3521 Paints, varnishes and lacquers		126	140	135	134		4.6	4.6	4.4	4.3		5219	5166	5129	4912
3522 Drugs and medicines		111	121	125	121		9.7	9.0	8.8	8.8		16741	18295	19402	21619
3523 Soap, cleaning preps., perfumes, cosmetics		151	154	168	159		4.0	4.2	4.0	3.9		5894	6313	6292	6445
3529 Other chemical products		341	292	273	278		5.0	4.4	3.9	4.0		...	3855	3576	3746
353 Petroleum refineries		2	1	1	1		...	3.7	3.6	3.5		...	14853	15320	15317

354	Misc. petroleum and coal products	23	25	23	18	...	0.3	0.3	0.3	...	...	...	...
355	Rubber products	252	243	243	233	6.4	5.9	5.8	5.9	...	4545	4480	4683
3551	Tyres and tubes	147	136	131	137	3.4	3.1	3.1	3.2	3469	3045	3353	3664
3559	Other rubber products	105	107	112	96	3.0	2.8	2.8	2.7	...	1500	1127	1019
356	Plastic products	672	795	874	827	16.3	16.0	15.9	16.4	8482	7876	7512	8337
361	Pottery, china, earthenware	977	954	973	1026	24.8	24.6	25.5	26.6	16478	17629	19208	20850
362	Glass and products	484	504	461	467	9.2	8.9	9.0	9.3	12253	11774	11723	12413
369	Other non-metallic mineral products	2456	2605	2670	2516	35.1	36.5	35.1	34.0	19357	19079	20742	21487
3691	Structural clay products	349	347	339	293	10.9	10.3	9.2	8.8	4570	4638	4033	4314
3692	Cement, lime and plaster	59	66	65	64	3.1	2.5	2.5	2.4	6414	5270	6224	6897
3699	Other non-metallic mineral products	2048	2192	2266	2159	21.1	23.7	23.3	22.7	8373	9171	10485	10276
371	Iron and steel	258	335	295	285	12.0	12.0	8.0	9.4	14462	14891	8089	13260
372	Non-ferrous metals	346	358	368	322	5.6	5.6	5.6	4.7	3088	3223	4178	3299
381	Fabricated metal products	11742	11473	11521	11271	83.6	80.4	77.7	78.7	28505	29521	29680	30855
3811	Cutlery, hand tools and general hardware	8877	6727	6476	5740	40.0	32.4	26.9	25.8	5603	5395	3946	3833
3812	Furniture and fixtures primarily of metal	194	220	166	178	5.5	6.0	4.0	4.1	3295	3759	2072	2278
3813	Structural metal products	859	2649	2952	3333	12.4	16.4	20.6	20.6	5808	5958	8741	8025
3819	Other fabricated metal products	1812	1877	1927	2020	25.8	25.6	26.1	28.1	13799	14409	14921	16719
382	Non-electrical machinery	2515	2795	2945	2813	38.2	38.7	38.6	38.5	24235	23606	19669	20749
3821	Engines and turbines	36	50	51	50	1.7	1.0	0.2	0.3	...	...	-	...
3822	Agricultural machinery and equipment	406	420	419	435	4.0	3.6	3.5	3.6	1723	1396	1280	1261
3823	Metal and wood working machinery	92	117	116	110	2.5	2.3	2.2	2.1	1354	1175	...	...
3824	Other special industrial machinery	569	890	1024	950	11.7	13.0	14.7	14.7	7255	7315	5761	6047
3825	Office, computing and accounting machinery	88	125	173	171	0.8	1.0	1.2	1.0	...	...	...	...
3829	Other non-electrical machinery & equipment	1324	1193	1162	1097	17.3	17.9	16.8	16.9	9735	10628	10678	11366
383	Electrical machinery	1104	1227	1312	1187	44.8	45.2	45.9	46.6	61327	67256	67951	73873
3831	Electrical industrial machinery	366	396	403	380	9.2	8.3	5.3	5.0	18079	11587	7588	7319
3832	Radio, television and communication equipm.	307	356	392	312	16.1	15.6	16.3	14.9	27674	30667	30433	32109
3833	Electrical appliances and housewares	82	89	80	71	3.1	3.4	2.2	2.5	3374	3548	1780	2575
3839	Other electrical apparatus and supplies	349	386	437	424	16.4	17.9	22.2	24.2	12200	21454	28150	31870
384	Transport equipment	772	800	831	862	33.5	32.7	36.2	39.8	47052	46640	59686	71759
3841	Shipbuilding and repairing	303	295	267	314	11.6	10.9	7.5	9.1	19173	17921	12527	15930
3842	Railroad equipment	1	1	4	4	0.2	0.1	3.1	3.0	281	213	6654	7558
3843	Motor vehicles	389	418	464	461	19.0	19.0	20.9	23.6	25742	26961	34476	42659
3844	Motorcycles and bicycles	56	56	63	54	2.6	2.5	2.4	2.4	1856	1545	...	...
3845	Aircraft	12	15	16	14	0.1	0.2	2.3	1.4	-	-	...	...
3849	Other transport equipment	11	15	17	15	-	0.1	0.1	0.4	-	-	-	...
385	Professional and scientific equipment	315	336	409	418	4.8	5.0	5.3	5.5	3873	4357	4884	5226
3851	Prof. and scientific equipment n.e.c.	260	276	345	359	2.9	3.2	3.1	3.3	2090	2487	2287	2360
3852	Photographic and optical goods	28	28	35	34	1.6	1.5	1.8	1.9	...	...	...	...
3853	Watches and clocks	27	32	29	25	0.4	0.3	0.4	0.3	...	...	...	...
390	Other manufacturing industries	1966	1979	1988	2009	13.5	14.1	14.4	13.2	4296	4091	4280	3762
3901	Jewellery and related articles	...	1026	914	972	4.0	4.4	4.5	4.4	1175	1057	1064	1154
3902	Musical instruments	10	13	18	17	-	-	0.1	0.1	-	-	-	...
3903	Sporting and athletic goods	52	46	58	55	0.4	0.4	0.6	0.6	-	-	-	...
3909	Manufacturing industries, n.e.c.	1007	894	998	965	9.0	9.3	9.4	8.2	3121	3034	3216	2608
3	Total manufacturing	64467	65994	66943	65101	998.6	977.1	969.1	948.8	631900	646111	654801	691625

a/ Wages and salaries paid to employees relate to enterprises with 100 or more persons engaged.

Portugal

ISIC Revision 2 ISIC Industry	Note	Output in producers' prices (billion ESCUDOS) 1992	1993	1994	1995	Note	Value added in producers' prices (billion ESCUDOS) 1992	1993	1994	1995	Note	Gross fixed capital formation (billion ESCUDOS) 1994	1995
311/2 Food products		1195.7	1191.3	1341.2	1320.1		228.2	220.6	232.2	231.8		80.4	43.0
3111 Slaughtering, preparing & preserving meat		214.3	225.1	260.9	240.3		28.3	30.9	36.6	37.3		13.6	7.2
3112 Dairy products		222.6	208.0	193.1	214.5		42.6	39.1	31.4	35.1		16.0	7.7
3113 Canning, preserving of fruits & vegetables		35.4	49.0	66.5	70.6		5.6	7.6	8.8	12.4		4.2	2.7
3114 Canning, preserving and processing of fish		62.9	65.9	85.5	82.9		10.0	12.1	11.6	13.2		7.4	5.5
3115 Vegetable and animal oils and fats		81.0	73.4	84.7	93.7		10.2	8.5	8.1	9.0		2.0	1.4
3116 Grain mill products		85.3	83.5	96.2	93.0		13.8	13.2	12.6	11.3		4.7	-2.9
3117 Bakery products		130.5	148.5	161.4	149.5		43.8	48.7	55.3	52.8		14.1	8.6
3118 Sugar factories and refineries		41.9	44.2	45.4	46.2		9.7	9.2	9.0	9.6		2.4	0.9
3119 Cocoa, chocolate and sugar confectionery		22.2	13.2	16.0	16.4		7.3	4.2	5.3	4.6		1.7	0.6
3121 Other food products		93.9	89.5	114.7	107.7		26.9	23.3	26.0	22.1		8.7	9.7
3122 Prepared animal feeds		205.6	191.0	216.8	205.3		30.0	23.8	27.5	24.5		5.5	1.7
313 Beverages		224.1	240.5	269.6	308.2		61.7	65.5	70.2	81.0		27.5	21.4
3131 Distilling, rectifying and blending spirits		8.5	7.5	10.4	15.4		-0.2	-0.7	1.4	3.6		-0.5	0.6
3132 Wine industries		106.3	114.4	135.8	154.6		20.8	21.8	25.3	29.8		5.9	5.1
3133 Malt liquors and malt		64.0	65.2	70.2	80.5		27.4	27.1	28.7	33.9		15.2	9.9
3134 Soft drinks and carbonated waters		45.3	53.2	53.2	57.8		13.7	17.3	14.7	13.7		6.9	5.7
314 Tobacco		132.6	149.0	145.1	141.9		117.7	135.3	132.6	130.0		0.7	-0.4
321 Textiles		735.0	745.0	823.7	853.1		224.5	241.2	273.7	262.1		58.3	49.4
3211 Spinning, weaving and finishing textiles		410.3	398.2	414.4	421.3		133.2	139.7	149.9	140.9		31.7	28.1
3212 Made-up textile goods excl. wearing apparel		57.7	62.6	90.4	99.6		16.5	17.8	29.4	31.9		5.1	6.5
3213 Knitting mills		212.8	229.0	250.3	255.0		57.0	64.6	71.4	66.5		18.8	11.4
3214 Carpets and rugs		16.3	13.7	15.4	15.8		5.5	4.7	5.2	4.9		0.6	0.3
3215 Cordage, rope and twine		21.3	22.2	33.9	40.0		7.6	8.3	12.7	12.9		1.9	2.6
3219 Other textiles		16.6	19.3	19.3	21.4		4.8	6.1	5.1	4.9		0.2	0.5
322 Wearing apparel, except footwear		529.0	531.8	561.3	573.3		162.0	178.5	197.2	200.2		30.4	21.8
323 Leather and fur products		70.6	78.0	87.9	77.8		16.7	18.4	21.3	17.6		3.8	2.0
3231 Tanneries and leather finishing		53.7	59.4	66.7	52.6		11.0	12.6	14.6	10.5		2.6	1.2
3232 Fur dressing and dyeing industries		0.2	3.8	7.4	8.0		0.1	0.8	1.7	1.2		0.7	0.3
3233 Leather prods. excl. wearing apparel		16.6	14.8	13.9	17.2		5.6	5.0	5.0	5.9		0.5	0.5
324 Footwear, except rubber or plastic		265.7	330.1	392.0	369.3		71.4	94.6	104.8	102.8		17.9	14.1
331 Wood products, except furniture		336.8	355.2	402.0	444.8		84.3	89.9	102.4	107.4		21.0	19.4
3311 Sawmills, planing and other wood mills		184.4	178.8	207.5	233.3		53.9	50.4	58.3	62.6		13.6	12.9
3312 Wooden and cane containers		4.7	4.8	5.6	8.4		1.6	1.3	1.8	2.6		0.5	0.4
3319 Other wood and cork products		147.8	171.6	189.0	203.1		28.9	38.3	42.2	42.3		6.8	6.1
332 Furniture and fixtures, excl. metal		148.9	141.7	144.2	154.9		50.2	46.8	49.9	53.0		21.4	8.1
341 Paper and products		271.9	254.3	322.9	440.2		71.5	59.1	101.8	152.2		8.7	15.1
3411 Pulp, paper and paperboard articles		200.8	171.8	224.8	322.9		57.5	43.6	77.7	126.3		3.6	8.7
3412 Containers of paper and paperboard		37.3	41.8	79.3	95.5		10.3	12.2	19.0	21.0		3.5	4.1
3419 Other pulp, paper and paperboard articles		33.8	40.7	18.8	21.9		3.7	3.3	5.1	4.9		1.6	2.3
342 Printing and publishing		261.1	279.7	283.7	325.9		97.2	106.6	114.8	133.7		27.0	21.9
351 Industrial chemicals		192.6	184.7	200.7	244.5		45.0	45.9	48.9	60.6		8.2	10.5
3511 Basic chemicals excl. fertilizers		75.1	71.6	61.6	63.7		23.1	22.8	20.3	21.2		4.5	5.9
3512 Fertilizers and pesticides		32.6	29.1	33.0	39.1		9.2	9.7	8.7	11.1		1.6	0.5
3513 Synthetic resins and plastic materials		84.9	84.0	106.1	141.7		12.7	13.4	19.9	28.4		2.1	4.2
352 Other chemicals		322.3	316.7	319.9	357.7		96.8	92.3	95.7	102.9		16.8	14.6
3521 Paints, varnishes and lacquers		60.6	63.2	65.6	77.8		20.7	21.1	22.5	23.1		3.0	3.6
3522 Drugs and medicines		115.2	115.8	128.7	139.7		40.3	38.5	41.3	49.0		7.4	7.3
3523 Soap, cleaning preps., perfumes, cosmetics		76.4	78.9	77.6	78.6		18.8	17.5	16.9	16.7		2.9	2.2
3529 Other chemical products		70.1	58.8	48.0	61.6		17.0	15.3	14.9	14.1		3.5	1.5
353 Petroleum refineries		...	592.2	694.9	755.9		...	313.8	361.5	424.7		-5.5	8.4

354	Misc. petroleum and coal products	...	5.7	6.0	6.4	...	1.4	1.5	1.6	0.2	0.3
355	Rubber products	36.8	39.0	49.2	57.9	11.5	14.2	16.2	19.1	7.4	3.8
3551	Tyres and tubes	20.8	21.7	30.0	37.6	5.4	8.2	9.7	12.4	6.0	2.8
3559	Other rubber products	16.0	17.2	19.2	20.3	6.1	5.9	6.5	6.7	1.4	1.0
356	Plastic products	126.8	126.8	145.6	179.8	39.4	40.6	43.0	52.8	22.1	10.4
361	Pottery, china, earthenware	99.5	111.8	127.8	135.9	48.2	54.1	63.5	67.0	12.3	22.8
362	Glass and products	76.2	74.3	83.0	95.7	30.4	29.7	36.9	40.5	4.5	10.4
369	Other non-metallic mineral products	309.3	329.5	360.0	385.8	122.7	133.4	148.3	157.2	29.9	30.0
3691	Structural clay products	51.4	53.8	53.0	63.5	23.0	22.7	23.6	28.5	8.8	8.9
3692	Cement, lime and plaster	90.6	82.7	103.9	109.5	49.4	45.1	58.2	59.0	6.9	6.1
3699	Other non-metallic mineral products	167.3	193.0	203.2	212.8	50.3	65.6	66.4	69.7	14.3	15.0
371	Iron and steel	103.3	114.4	107.6	167.2	25.0	29.7	23.3	31.6	2.0	4.9
372	Non-ferrous metals	44.6	42.8	51.5	55.5	12.6	12.7	15.1	15.2	3.3	2.6
381	Fabricated metal products	448.9	449.5	475.4	542.7	153.6	157.4	170.8	188.2	36.3	31.9
3811	Cutlery, hand tools and general hardware	166.3	138.0	127.2	135.9	56.4	50.1	47.4	48.4	10.4	9.2
3812	Furniture and fixtures primarily of metal	32.1	35.1	22.3	29.9	12.2	12.9	8.5	10.9	1.7	2.5
3813	Structural metal products	78.1	101.6	137.3	145.7	24.8	32.0	44.7	47.5	14.4	6.3
3819	Other fabricated metal products	172.4	174.8	188.6	231.2	60.2	62.5	70.3	81.4	9.8	13.8
382	Non-electrical machinery	246.8	270.8	285.2	311.3	81.7	91.5	98.5	102.7	16.2	20.5
3821	Engines and turbines	14.4	11.5	2.0	2.3	6.8	5.5	0.5	0.8	0.1	0.1
3822	Agricultural machinery and equipment	25.7	22.0	26.2	27.6	7.3	6.9	8.2	8.8	1.7	0.5
3823	Metal and wood working machinery	12.7	12.3	12.7	13.1	5.1	5.0	5.6	6.1	0.9	0.9
3824	Other special industrial machinery	59.1	74.0	94.2	106.3	20.6	28.3	38.5	44.0	8.1	13.9
3825	Office, computing and accounting machinery	5.8	8.6	12.9	11.8	2.2	2.6	3.2	3.2	-0.8	0.3
3829	Other non-electrical machinery & equipment	129.2	142.5	137.3	150.2	39.8	43.2	42.5	39.8	6.3	4.8
383	Electrical machinery	430.6	467.9	517.7	585.0	138.3	149.2	161.1	164.1	15.8	23.7
3831	Electrical industrial machinery	74.8	79.5	49.7	46.8	29.3	25.8	18.7	15.8	1.8	1.7
3832	Radio, television and communication equipm.	201.8	217.7	251.6	272.8	58.6	67.9	68.0	63.2	-0.5	8.8
3833	Electrical appliances and housewares	29.1	31.7	20.8	29.3	5.6	6.7	4.5	7.0	1.6	1.4
3839	Other electrical apparatus and supplies	124.8	139.0	195.6	236.2	44.8	48.8	69.9	78.2	13.0	11.8
384	Transport equipment	347.8	325.3	382.6	608.0	78.1	69.9	97.3	145.5	91.1	45.7
3841	Shipbuilding and repairing	63.1	55.7	49.8	78.1	21.9	23.4	19.3	24.7	1.8	-3.5
3842	Railroad equipment	1.8	1.8	23.3	26.9	0.7	0.5	12.2	14.8	0.9	-5.7
3843	Motor vehicles	266.0	253.0	278.9	470.7	49.8	41.2	52.6	95.3	85.7	52.8
3844	Motorcycles and bicycles	16.1	14.0	15.8	18.7	5.4	4.4	4.9	4.6	1.7	1.4
3845	Aircraft	0.6	0.7	14.3	11.4	0.2	0.3	8.2	5.5	1.0	0.6
3849	Other transport equipment	0.2	0.2	0.3	2.3	0.1	0.1	0.1	0.6	-	-
385	Professional and scientific equipment	25.0	28.8	34.7	37.8	10.9	12.4	15.0	16.7	1.6	8.2
3851	Prof. and scientific equipment n.e.c.	16.7	20.0	21.5	23.6	7.1	8.5	9.6	10.8	1.2	6.9
3852	Photographic and optical goods	6.7	7.3	11.7	13.0	3.2	3.4	4.9	5.3	0.5	1.3
3853	Watches and clocks	1.6	1.5	1.4	1.2	0.5	0.4	0.5	0.6	-0.1	-
390	Other manufacturing industries	76.4	91.7	99.1	110.0	21.9	25.4	28.6	31.1	7.5	4.6
3901	Jewellery and related articles	30.1	37.0	39.1	47.2	7.1	8.2	9.2	11.3	1.7	1.2
3902	Musical instruments	1.0	1.1	0.2	0.1	0.1	0.1	0.1	0.1	-	-
3903	Sporting and athletic goods	1.9	1.9	3.5	3.9	0.5	0.5	1.0	1.2	0.1	0.2
3909	Manufacturing industries, n.e.c.	43.4	51.6	56.3	58.8	14.1	16.6	18.3	18.6	5.6	3.2
3	Total manufacturing	7586.9	7868.6	8714.7	9646.5	2399.0	2530.2	2826.0	3093.5	566.8	469.0

Portugal

ISIC Revision 2 ISIC Industry	Note	Index numbers of industrial production (1990=100) 1985	1986	1987	1988	1989	1990	1991	1992	1993	1994	1995	1996
311/2 Food products	a/	...	...	...	...	...	100	102	97	98	95	98	101
313 Beverages	a/	...	...	...	...	...	...	...	...	...	...	...	...
314 Tobacco		93	91	98	94	100	100	102	98	95	87	82	78
321 Textiles		92	99	97	97	97	100	105	98	86	90	89	83
322 Wearing apparel, except footwear		92	99	97	97	97	100	101	99	89	79	86	85
323 Leather and fur products	b/	...	...	...	...	...	100	98	97	94	91	91	92
324 Footwear, except rubber or plastic	b/	...	...	...	...	...	...	...	...	...	...	...	...
331 Wood products, except furniture		101	96	103	112	104	100	109	111	114	97	104	110
332 Furniture and fixtures, excl. metal		...	...	...	...	...	...	...	...	...	...	...	...
341 Paper and products		87	92	92	96	99	100	111	108	100	106	111	109
342 Printing and publishing		...	...	...	...	...	...	...	...	...	...	...	...
351 Industrial chemicals	c/	75	83	85	91	93	100	88	82	74	75	73	74
352 Other chemicals	c/	...	...	...	...	...	...	...	...	...	...	...	...
353 Petroleum refineries	d/	62	78	71	79	92	100	93	98	93	113	120	108
354 Misc. petroleum and coal products	d/	...	...	...	...	...	...	...	...	...	...	...	...
355 Rubber products	e/	...	...	...	...	...	100	100	96	90	97	104	116
356 Plastic products	e/	...	...	...	...	...	...	...	...	...	...	...	...
361 Pottery, china, earthenware	f/	67	73	82	90	93	100	98	102	106	107	111	114
362 Glass and products	f/	...	...	...	...	...	...	...	...	...	...	...	...
369 Other non-metallic mineral products	f/	...	...	...	...	...	...	...	...	...	...	...	...
371 Iron and steel	g/	87	88	94	101	99	100	93	100	96	98	104	100
372 Non-ferrous metals	g/	...	...	...	...	...	...	...	...	...	...	...	...
381 Fabricated metal products		78	92	88	91	91	100	102	96	89	94	94	103
382 Non-electrical machinery		80	81	86	91	92	100	97	91	82	87	88	96
383 Electrical machinery		94	76	80	87	89	100	103	108	103	105	124	130
384 Transport equipment		85	89	99	104	101	100	99	92	78	71	75	88
385 Professional and scientific equipment		...	...	...	...	...	...	...	...	...	...	...	...
390 Other manufacturing industries		...	...	...	...	...	...	...	...	...	...	...	...
3 Total manufacturing		82	86	89	93	95	100	100	98	93	93	97	98

a/ 311/2 includes 313.
b/ 323 includes 324.
c/ 351 includes 352.
d/ 353 includes 354.
e/ 355 includes 356.
f/ 361 includes 362 and 369.
g/ 371 includes 372.

REPUBLIC OF MOLDOVA

Supplier of information:
State Department of Statistics of the Republic of Moldova, Chisinau.

Basic source of data:
Not reported.

Major deviations from ISIC (Revision 2) and ISIC (Revision 3):
None reported.

Reference period (if not calendar year):

Scope:
All self-sustained establishments. Data for 1993 to 1996 exclude the area of the left bank of the Dniester and the town of Bender.

Method of enumeration:
Not reported.

Adjusted for non-response:
Not reported.

Concepts and definitions of variables:
No deviations from the standard UN concepts and definitions are reported.

Related national publications:

Republic of Moldova

ISIC Revision 2	Number of establishments					Number of employees					Wages and salaries paid to employees				
		(numbers)					(numbers)					(thousand LEI)			
ISIC Industry	Note	1993	1994	1995	1996	Note	1993	1994	1995	1996	Note	1993	1994	1995	1996
311/2 Food products		85	83	85	81		52157	48636	47623	...		24345	112713	145703	...
313 Beverages		86	100	105	108		12699	10863	11684	...		11910	27111	38571	...
314 Tobacco		8	8	8	8		2182	2341	2293	...		2626	9006	11162	...
321 Textiles		12	12	12	12		13725	15939	12616	...		6085	16352	14417	...
322 Wearing apparel, except footwear		23	24	25	23		14746	14895	12786	...		4688	12539	12325	...
323 Leather and fur products		4	4	4	3		3103	3110	2601	...		1044	3456	3927	...
324 Footwear, except rubber or plastic		3	3	3	3		4626	4808	3644	...		2179	4266	4215	...
331 Wood products, except furniture		9	9	13	10		3815	1504	1501	...		...	2677	2785	...
332 Furniture and fixtures, excl. metal		9	9	9	9		5733	5445	4898	...		4700	9827	10648	...
341 Paper and products		2	2	2	4		1470	1348	1338	...		652	2684	3510	...
342 Printing and publishing		16	17	17	29		2498	2410	2099	...		1389	5838	7474	...
351 Industrial chemicals		2	2	2	3		288	311	322	...		92	357	750	...
352 Other chemicals		11	10	8	5		1829	1654	1545	...		857	3657	4309	...
353 Petroleum refineries		-	-	-	-		-	-	-	...		-	-	-	...
354 Misc. petroleum and coal products		1	1	1	1		644	...	530	...		...	...	1075	...
355 Rubber products		-	-	-	-		-	-	-	...		-	-	-	...
356 Plastic products		1	1	1	5		1751	1607	1217	...		517	1187	514	...
361 Pottery, china, earthenware		-	-	-	-		-	-	-	...		-	-	-	...
362 Glass and products		3	3	3	3		2389	2470	2341	...		...	5153	8033	...
369 Other non-metallic mineral products		37	37	35	37		13832	5918	5728	...		3854	8160	8616	...
371 Iron and steel		...	...	1	4		...	218	178	...		100	340	341	...
372 Non-ferrous metals		-	-	-	-		-	-	-	...		-	-	-	...
381 Fabricated metal products		20	19	20	18		17165	4138	4941	...		...	7785	11384	...
382 Non-electrical machinery		...	...	...	...		...	...	...	...		...	...	...	...
383 Electrical machinery		...	...	...	...		...	...	...	...		...	...	...	...
384 Transport equipment		1	1	1	1		412	...	...	...		...	...	...	...
385 Professional and scientific equipment		-	-	-	-		-	-	-	...		-	-	-	...
390 Other manufacturing industries		...	...	...	...		...	1465	...	...		223	2948	...	...
3 Total manufacturing		393	405	400	421		210832	129080	119355	...		65261	236056	288684	...

Republic of Moldova

ISIC Revision 2		Output in producers' prices					Value added					Gross fixed capital formation		
			(thousand LEI)					(thousand LEI)					(thousand LEI)	
ISIC	Industry	Note	1993	1994	1995	1996	Note	1993	1994	1995	1996	Note	1995	1996
311/2	Food products		482081	1461944	1719825	1834453		...	...	...	...		...	...
313	Beverages		89319	302893	529707	708291		...	...	...	...		...	...
314	Tobacco		63908	149805	162979	246587		...	...	...	...		...	...
321	Textiles		44139	121345	118467	109165		...	...	...	...		...	...
322	Wearing apparel, except footwear		24501	55126	48133	60372		...	...	...	...		...	...
323	Leather and fur products		14635	34093	41251	46797		...	...	...	...		...	...
324	Footwear, except rubber or plastic		10405	21184	20765	28019		...	...	...	...		...	...
331	Wood products, except furniture		7733	28437	27599	24218		...	...	...	...		...	...
332	Furniture and fixtures, excl. metal		31202	78579	90131	73907		...	...	...	...		...	...
341	Paper and products		11730	47892	51977	55082		...	...	...	...		...	...
342	Printing and publishing		6555	29264	42665	48721		...	...	...	...		...	...
351	Industrial chemicals		740	2283	5459	4411		...	...	...	...		...	...
352	Other chemicals		13266	30460	30620	36829		...	...	...	...		...	...
353	Petroleum refineries		-	-	-	-		...	...	...	...		...	...
354	Misc. petroleum and coal products		4793	18779	20288	38255		...	...	...	...		...	...
355	Rubber products		-	-	-	-		...	...	...	...		...	...
356	Plastic products		2224	4631	2729	11929		...	...	...	...		...	...
361	Pottery, china, earthenware		-	-	-	-		...	...	...	...		...	...
362	Glass and products		17913	79697	104929	100050		...	...	...	...		...	...
369	Other non-metallic mineral products		38289	139650	129425	146432		...	...	...	...		...	...
371	Iron and steel		...	...	1714	2561		...	...	...	...		...	...
372	Non-ferrous metals		-	-	-	-		...	...	...	...		...	...
381	Fabricated metal products		48469	94420	105246	91215		...	...	...	...		...	...
382	Non-electrical machinery		...	...	...	...		...	...	...	...		...	...
383	Electrical machinery		...	...	...	...		...	...	...	...		...	...
384	Transport equipment		600	...	...	...		...	...	...	...		...	...
385	Professional and scientific equipment		-	-	-	-		...	...	...	...		...	...
390	Other manufacturing industries		...	...	...	...		...	...	...	...		...	...
3	Total manufacturing		1050815	3051935	3609670	3970562		629055	1354801	1476732	1783904		...	...

Republic of Moldova

ISIC Revision 3	Number of establishments					Number of employees					Wages and salaries paid to employees				
		(numbers)					(numbers)					(thousand LEI)			
ISIC Industry	Note	1993	1994	1995	1996	Note	1993	1994	1995	1996	Note	1993	1994	1995	1996
151 Processed meat,fish,fruit,vegetables,fats		...	...	...	34		...	...	...	20887		...	...	...	48400
1511 Processing/preserving of meat		...	...	...	10		...	...	...	...		...	...	...	...
1512 Processing/preserving of fish		...	...	...	...		...	...	...	...		...	...	...	...
1513 Processing/preserving of fruit & vegetables		...	...	...	22		...	...	...	...		...	...	...	...
1514 Vegetable and animal oils and fats		...	...	...	2		...	...	...	...		...	...	...	...
1520 Dairy products		...	...	...	22		...	...	...	2651		...	...	...	11037
153 Grain mill products; starches; animal feeds		...	...	...	14		...	...	...	6850		...	...	...	23633
1531 Grain mill products		...	...	...	7		...	...	...	...		...	...	...	...
1532 Starches and starch products		...	...	...	-		...	...	...	...		...	...	...	...
1533 Prepared animal feeds		...	...	...	7		...	...	...	...		...	...	...	...
154 Other food products		...	...	...	17		...	...	...	15432		...	...	...	65187
1541 Bakery products		...	...	...	6		...	...	...	...		...	...	...	...
1542 Sugar		...	...	...	9		...	...	...	...		...	...	...	...
1543 Cocoa, chocolate and sugar confectionery		...	...	...	1		...	...	...	...		...	...	...	...
1544 Macaroni, noodles & similar products		...	...	...	...		...	...	...	...		...	...	...	...
1549 Other food products n.e.c.		...	...	...	1		...	...	...	...		...	...	...	...
155 Beverages		...	...	...	101		...	...	...	14183		...	...	...	54510
1551 Distilling, rectifying & blending of spirits		...	...	...	3		...	...	...	...		...	...	...	...
1552 Wines		...	...	...	93		...	...	...	...		...	...	...	...
1553 Malt liquors and malt		...	...	...	4		...	...	...	...		...	...	...	...
1554 Soft drinks; mineral waters		...	...	...	1		...	...	...	...		...	...	...	...
1600 Tobacco products		...	...	...	8		...	...	...	2306		...	...	...	18909
171 Spinning, weaving and finishing of textiles		...	...	...	-		...	...	...	-		...	...	...	-
1711 Textile fibre preparation; textile weaving		...	...	...	-		...	...	...	...		...	...	...	...
1712 Finishing of textiles		...	...	...	-		...	...	...	...		...	...	...	...
172 Other textiles		...	...	...	11		...	...	...	...		...	...	...	...
1721 Made-up textile articles, except apparel		...	...	...	2		...	...	...	...		...	...	...	...
1722 Carpets and rugs		...	...	...	5		...	...	...	...		...	...	...	...
1723 Cordage, rope, twine and netting		...	...	...	-		...	...	...	...		...	...	...	...
1729 Other textiles n.e.c.		...	...	...	4		...	...	...	...		...	...	...	...
1730 Knitted and crocheted fabrics and articles		...	...	...	3		...	...	...	...		...	...	...	...
1810 Wearing apparel, except fur apparel		...	...	...	21		...	...	...	...		...	...	...	...
1820 Dressing & dyeing of fur; processing of fur		...	...	...	1		...	...	...	...		...	...	...	...
191 Tanning, dressing and processing of leather		...	...	...	3		...	...	...	...		...	...	...	...
1911 Tanning and dressing of leather		...	...	...	2		...	...	...	...		...	...	...	...
1912 Luggage, handbags, etc.; saddlery & harness		...	...	...	1		...	...	...	...		...	...	...	...
1920 Footwear		...	...	...	3		...	...	...	...		...	...	...	...
2010 Sawmilling and planing of wood		...	...	...	...		...	...	...	...		...	...	...	...
202 Products of wood, cork, straw, etc.		...	...	...	10		...	...	...	...		...	...	...	...
2021 Veneer sheets, plywood, particle board, etc.		...	...	...	-		...	...	...	...		...	...	...	...
2022 Builders' carpentry and joinery		...	...	...	8		...	...	...	...		...	...	...	...
2023 Wooden containers		...	...	...	2		...	...	...	...		...	...	...	...
2029 Other wood products; articles of cork/straw		...	...	...	...		...	...	...	...		...	...	...	...
210 Paper and paper products		...	...	...	6		...	...	...	2027		...	...	...	8003
2101 Pulp, paper and paperboard		...	...	...	-		...	...	...	...		...	...	...	...
2102 Corrugated paper and paperboard		...	...	...	4		...	...	...	...		...	...	...	...
2109 Other articles of paper and paperboard		...	...	...	2		...	...	...	...		...	...	...	...
221 Publishing		...	...	...	-		...	...	...	-		...	...	...	-
2211 Publishing of books and other publications		...	...	...	-		...	...	...	-		...	...	...	-
2212 Publishing of newspapers, journals, etc.		...	...	...	-		...	...	...	-		...	...	...	-
2213 Publishing of recorded media		...	...	...	-		...	...	...	-		...	...	...	-
2219 Other publishing		...	...	...	-		...	...	...	-		...	...	...	-

222 Printing and related service activities	...	...	...	27	...	...	...	...	...	...	...	...
2221 Printing	...	...	...	27	...	...	...	...	...	...	...	...
2222 Service activities related to printing	...	...	...	-	...	...	...	...	...	...	...	...
2230 Reproduction of recorded media	...	...	...	-	...	...	...	-	...	...	...	-
2310 Coke oven products	...	...	...	-	...	...	...	-	...	...	...	-
2320 Refined petroleum products	...	...	...	-	...	...	...	-	...	...	...	-
2330 Processing of nuclear fuel	...	...	...	-	...	...	...	-	...	...	...	-
241 Basic chemicals	...	...	...	...	...	...	...	...	...	...	...	...
2411 Basic chemicals, except fertilizers	...	...	...	...	...	...	...	...	...	...	...	...
2412 Fertilizers and nitrogen compounds	...	...	...	...	...	...	...	...	...	...	...	...
2413 Plastics in primary forms; synthetic rubber	...	...	...	...	...	...	...	...	...	...	...	...
242 Other chemicals	...	...	...	8	...	...	...	...	...	...	...	...
2421 Pesticides and other agro-chemical products	...	...	...	-	...	...	...	...	...	...	...	...
2422 Paints, varnishes, printing ink and mastics	...	...	...	...	...	...	...	...	...	...	...	...
2423 Pharmaceuticals, medicinal chemicals, etc.	...	...	...	4	...	...	...	...	...	...	...	...
2424 Soap, cleaning & cosmetic preparations	...	...	...	3	...	...	...	...	...	...	...	...
2429 Other chemical products n.e.c.	...	...	...	1	...	...	...	...	...	...	...	...
2430 Man-made fibres	...	...	...	-	...	...	...	-	...	...	...	-
251 Rubber products	...	...	...	...	...	...	...	...	...	...	...	...
2511 Rubber tyres and tubes	...	...	...	-	...	...	...	...	...	...	...	...
2519 Other rubber products	...	...	...	...	...	...	...	...	...	...	...	...
2520 Plastic products	...	...	...	5	...	...	...	...	...	...	...	...
2610 Glass and glass products	...	...	...	3	...	...	...	...	...	...	...	...
269 Non-metallic mineral products n.e.c.	...	...	...	37	...	...	...	...	...	...	...	...
2691 Pottery, china and earthenware	...	...	...	1	...	...	...	...	...	...	...	...
2692 Refractory ceramic products	...	...	...	-	...	...	...	...	...	...	...	...
2693 Struct.non-refractory clay; ceramic products	...	...	...	8	...	...	...	...	...	...	...	...
2694 Cement, lime and plaster	...	...	...	3	...	...	...	...	...	...	...	...
2695 Articles of concrete, cement and plaster	...	...	...	16	...	...	...	...	...	...	...	...
2696 Cutting, shaping & finishing of stone	...	...	...	9	...	...	...	...	...	...	...	...
2699 Other non-metallic mineral products n.e.c.	...	...	...	-	...	...	...	...	...	...	...	...
2710 Basic iron and steel	...	...	...	...	...	...	...	...	...	...	...	...
2720 Basic precious and non-ferrous metals	...	...	...	-	...	...	...	-	...	...	...	-
273 Casting of metals	...	...	...	4	...	...	...	...	...	...	...	...
2731 Casting of iron and steel	...	...	...	4	...	...	...	...	...	...	...	...
2732 Casting of non-ferrous metals	...	...	...	...	...	...	...	...	...	...	...	...
281 Struct.metal products;tanks;steam generators	...	...	...	1	...	...	...	...	...	...	...	...
2811 Structural metal products	...	...	...	1	...	...	...	...	...	...	...	...
2812 Tanks, reservoirs and containers of metal	...	...	...	-	...	...	...	...	...	...	...	...
2813 Steam generators	...	...	...	-	...	...	...	...	...	...	...	...
289 Other metal products; metal working services	...	...	...	11	...	...	...	...	...	...	...	...
2891 Metal forging/pressing/stamping/roll-forming	...	...	...	-	...	...	...	...	...	...	...	...
2892 Treatment & coating of metals	...	...	...	-	...	...	...	...	...	...	...	...
2893 Cutlery, hand tools and general hardware	...	...	...	2	...	...	...	...	...	...	...	...
2899 Other fabricated metal products n.e.c.	...	...	...	9	...	...	...	...	...	...	...	...
291 General purpose machinery	...	...	...	9	...	...	...	...	...	...	...	...
2911 Engines & turbines(not for transport equip.)	...	...	...	4	...	...	...	...	...	...	...	...
2912 Pumps, compressors, taps and valves	...	...	...	2	...	...	...	...	...	...	...	...
2913 Bearings, gears, gearing & driving elements	...	...	...	-	...	...	...	...	...	...	...	...
2914 Ovens, furnaces and furnace burners	...	...	...	1	...	...	...	...	...	...	...	...
2915 Lifting and handling equipment	...	...	...	1	...	...	...	...	...	...	...	...
2919 Other general purpose machinery	...	...	...	1	...	...	...	...	...	...	...	...
292 Special purpose machinery	...	...	...	22	...	...	...	...	...	...	...	...
2921 Agricultural and forestry machinery	...	...	...	7	...	...	...	...	...	...	...	...
2922 Machine tools	...	...	...	5	...	...	...	...	...	...	...	...
2923 Machinery for metallurgy	...	...	...	-	...	...	...	...	...	...	...	...
2924 Machinery for mining & construction	...	...	...	2	...	...	...	...	...	...	...	...
2925 Food/beverage/tobacco processing machinery	...	...	...	4	...	...	...	...	...	...	...	...
2926 Machinery for textile, apparel and leather	...	...	...	...	...	...	...	...	...	...	...	...
2927 Weapons and ammunition	...	...	...	-	...	...	...	...	...	...	...	...
2929 Other special purpose machinery	...	...	...	4	...	...	...	...	...	...	...	...
2930 Domestic appliances n.e.c.	...	...	...	4	...	...	...	...	...	...	...	...

continued

Republic of Moldova

ISIC Revision 3 ISIC Industry	Note	Number of establishments (numbers) 1993	1994	1995	1996	Note	Number of employees (numbers) 1993	1994	1995	1996	Note	Wages and salaries paid to employees (thousand LEI) 1993	1994	1995	1996
3000 Office, accounting and computing machinery		...	...	...	2		...	...	...	2225		...	...	...	2560
3110 Electric motors, generators and transformers		...	...	...	1		...	...	...	...		...	...	...	...
3120 Electricity distribution & control apparatus		...	...	...	-		...	...	...	-		...	...	...	-
3130 Insulated wire and cable		...	...	...	-		...	...	...	-		...	...	...	-
3140 Accumulators, primary cells and batteries		...	...	...	-		...	...	...	-		...	...	...	-
3150 Lighting equipment and electric lamps		...	...	...	1		...	...	...	...		...	...	...	...
3190 Other electrical equipment n.e.c.		...	...	...	8		...	...	...	...		...	...	...	...
3210 Electronic valves, tubes, etc.		...	...	...	-		...	...	...	-		...	...	...	-
3220 TV/radio transmitters; line comm. apparatus		...	...	...	-		...	...	...	-		...	...	...	-
3230 TV and radio receivers and associated goods		...	...	...	6		...	...	...	...		...	...	...	...
331 Medical, measuring, testing appliances, etc.		...	...	...	6		...	...	...	...		...	...	...	...
3311 Medical, surgical and orthopaedic equipment		...	...	...	...		...	...	...	...		...	...	...	...
3312 Measuring/testing/navigating appliances,etc.		...	...	...	4		...	...	...	...		...	...	...	...
3313 Industrial process control equipment		...	...	...	2		...	...	...	...		...	...	...	...
3320 Optical instruments & photographic equipment		...	...	...	...		...	...	...	...		...	...	...	...
3330 Watches and clocks		...	...	...	-		...	...	...	-		...	...	...	-
3410 Motor vehicles		...	...	...	-		...	...	...	-		...	...	...	-
3420 Automobile bodies, trailers & semi-trailers		...	...	...	-		...	...	...	-		...	...	...	-
3430 Parts/accessories for automobiles		...	...	...	...		...	...	...	...		...	...	...	...
351 Building and repairing of ships and boats		...	...	...	-		...	...	...	-		...	...	...	-
3511 Building and repairing of ships		...	...	...	-		...	...	...	-		...	...	...	-
3512 Building/repairing of pleasure/sport. boats		...	...	...	-		...	...	...	-		...	...	...	-
3520 Railway/tramway locomotives & rolling stock		...	...	...	...		...	...	...	...		...	...	...	...
3530 Aircraft and spacecraft		...	...	...	-		...	...	...	-		...	...	...	-
359 Transport equipment n.e.c.		...	...	...	1		...	...	...	...		...	...	...	...
3591 Motorcycles		...	...	...	-		...	...	...	...		...	...	...	...
3592 Bicycles and invalid carriages		...	...	...	-		...	...	...	...		...	...	...	...
3599 Other transport equipment n.e.c.		...	...	...	1		...	...	...	...		...	...	...	...
3610 Furniture		...	...	...	9		...	...	...	...		...	...	...	...
369 Manufacturing n.e.c.		...	...	...	2		...	...	...	...		...	...	...	...
3691 Jewellery and related articles		...	...	...	1		...	...	...	...		...	...	...	...
3692 Musical instruments		...	...	...	-		...	...	...	...		...	...	...	...
3693 Sports goods		...	...	...	-		...	...	...	...		...	...	...	...
3694 Games and toys		...	...	...	...		...	...	...	...		...	...	...	...
3699 Other manufacturing n.e.c.		...	...	...	1		...	...	...	...		...	...	...	...
3710 Recycling of metal waste and scrap		...	...	...	-		...	...	...	-		...	...	...	-
3720 Recycling of non-metal waste and scrap		...	...	...	-		...	...	...	-		...	...	...	-
D Total manufacturing		...	...	...	421		...	...	...	161214		...	...	...	417239

Republic of Moldova

ISIC Revision 3	Output in producers' prices					Value added					Gross fixed capital formation		
		(thousand LEI)					(thousand LEI)					(thousand LEI)	
ISIC Industry	Note	1993	1994	1995	1996	Note	1993	1994	1995	1996	Note	1995	1996
151 Processed meat,fish,fruit,vegetables,fats		...	...	...	675549		...	...	...	...		...	...
1511 Processing/preserving of meat		...	...	...	330345		...	...	...	...		...	...
1512 Processing/preserving of fish		...	...	...	6168		...	...	...	...		...	...
1513 Processing/preserving of fruit & vegetables		...	...	...	296578		...	...	...	...		...	...
1514 Vegetable and animal oils and fats		...	...	...	42458		...	...	...	...		...	...
1520 Dairy products		...	...	...	137368		...	...	...	...		...	...
153 Grain mill products; starches; animal feeds		...	...	...	368284		...	...	...	...		...	...
1531 Grain mill products		...	...	...	265115		...	...	...	...		...	...
1532 Starches and starch products		...	...	...	-		...	...	...	...		...	...
1533 Prepared animal feeds		...	...	...	103169		...	...	...	...		...	...
154 Other food products		...	...	...	654149		...	...	...	...		...	...
1541 Bakery products		...	...	...	282536		...	...	...	...		...	...
1542 Sugar		...	...	...	287510		...	...	...	...		...	...
1543 Cocoa, chocolate and sugar confectionery		...	...	...	75251		...	...	...	...		...	...
1544 Macaroni, noodles & similar products		...	...	...	65		...	...	...	...		...	...
1549 Other food products n.e.c.		...	...	...	8787		...	...	...	...		...	...
155 Beverages		...	...	...	708291		...	...	...	...		...	...
1551 Distilling, rectifying & blending of spirits		...	...	...	62697		...	...	...	...		...	...
1552 Wines		...	...	...	587234		...	...	...	...		...	...
1553 Malt liquors and malt		...	...	...	39847		...	...	...	...		...	...
1554 Soft drinks; mineral waters		...	...	...	18513		...	...	...	...		...	...
1600 Tobacco products		...	...	...	246587		...	...	...	...		...	...
171 Spinning, weaving and finishing of textiles		...	...	...	-		...	...	...	...		...	...
1711 Textile fibre preparation; textile weaving		...	...	...	-		...	...	...	...		...	...
1712 Finishing of textiles		...	...	...	-		...	...	...	...		...	...
172 Other textiles		...	...	...	90756		...	...	...	...		...	...
1721 Made-up textile articles, except apparel		...	...	...	4416		...	...	...	...		...	...
1722 Carpets and rugs		...	...	...	79017		...	...	...	...		...	...
1723 Cordage, rope, twine and netting		...	...	...	-		...	...	...	...		...	...
1729 Other textiles n.e.c.		...	...	...	7323		...	...	...	...		...	...
1730 Knitted and crocheted fabrics and articles		...	...	...	23096		...	...	...	...		...	...
1810 Wearing apparel, except fur apparel		...	...	...	55685		...	...	...	...		...	...
1820 Dressing & dyeing of fur; processing of fur		...	...	...	16729		...	...	...	...		...	...
191 Tanning, dressing and processing of leather		...	...	...	51098		...	...	...	...		...	...
1911 Tanning and dressing of leather		...	...	...	48451		...	...	...	...		...	...
1912 Luggage, handbags, etc.; saddlery & harness		...	...	...	2647		...	...	...	...		...	...
1920 Footwear		...	...	...	28027		...	...	...	...		...	...
2010 Sawmilling and planing of wood		...	...	...	13182		...	...	...	...		...	...
202 Products of wood, cork, straw, etc.		...	...	...	17076		...	...	...	...		...	...
2021 Veneer sheets, plywood, particle board, etc.		...	...	...	-		...	...	...	...		...	...
2022 Builders' carpentry and joinery		...	...	...	13967		...	...	...	...		...	...
2023 Wooden containers		...	...	...	2471		...	...	...	...		...	...
2029 Other wood products; articles of cork/straw		...	...	...	638		...	...	...	...		...	...
210 Paper and paper products		...	...	...	82069		...	...	...	...		...	...
2101 Pulp, paper and paperboard		...	...	...	-		...	...	...	...		...	...
2102 Corrugated paper and paperboard		...	...	...	55047		...	...	...	...		...	...
2109 Other articles of paper and paperboard		...	...	...	27022		...	...	...	...		...	...
221 Publishing		...	...	...	-		...	...	...	...		...	...
2211 Publishing of books and other publications		...	...	...	-		...	...	...	...		...	...
2212 Publishing of newspapers, journals, etc.		...	...	...	-		...	...	...	...		...	...
2213 Publishing of recorded media		...	...	...	-		...	...	...	...		...	...
2219 Other publishing		...	...	...	-		...	...	...	...		...	...

continued

Republic of Moldova

ISIC Revision 3	Output in producers' prices					Value added					Gross fixed capital formation		
		(thousand LEI)					(thousand LEI)					(thousand LEI)	
ISIC Industry	Note	1993	1994	1995	1996	Note	1993	1994	1995	1996	Note	1995	1996
222 Printing and related service activities		...	...	...	21734		...	...	...	...		...	...
2221 Printing		...	...	...	21734		...	...	...	...		...	...
2222 Service activities related to printing		...	...	...	-		...	...	...	...		...	...
2230 Reproduction of recorded media		...	...	...	-		...	...	...	...		...	...
2310 Coke oven products		...	...	...	-		...	...	...	...		...	...
2320 Refined petroleum products		...	...	...	-		...	...	...	...		...	...
2330 Processing of nuclear fuel		...	...	...	-		...	...	...	...		...	...
241 Basic chemicals		...	...	...	764		...	...	...	...		...	...
2411 Basic chemicals, except fertilizers		...	...	...	-		...	...	...	...		...	...
2412 Fertilizers and nitrogen compounds		...	...	...	-		...	...	...	...		...	...
2413 Plastics in primary forms; synthetic rubber		...	...	...	764		...	...	...	...		...	...
242 Other chemicals		...	...	...	39579		...	...	...	...		...	...
2421 Pesticides and other agro-chemical products		...	...	...	-		...	...	...	...		...	...
2422 Paints, varnishes, printing ink and mastics		...	...	...	1209		...	...	...	...		...	...
2423 Pharmaceuticals, medicinal chemicals, etc.		...	...	...	18474		...	...	...	...		...	...
2424 Soap, cleaning & cosmetic preparations		...	...	...	19116		...	...	...	...		...	...
2429 Other chemical products n.e.c.		...	...	...	780		...	...	...	...		...	...
2430 Man-made fibres		...	...	...	-		...	...	...	...		...	...
251 Rubber products		...	...	...	1780		...	...	...	...		...	...
2511 Rubber tyres and tubes		...	...	...	-		...	...	...	...		...	...
2519 Other rubber products		...	...	...	1780		...	...	...	...		...	...
2520 Plastic products		...	...	...	11929		...	...	...	...		...	...
2610 Glass and glass products		...	...	...	100050		...	...	...	...		...	...
269 Non-metallic mineral products n.e.c.		...	...	...	146358		...	...	...	...		...	...
2691 Pottery, china and earthenware		...	...	...	1369		...	...	...	...		...	...
2692 Refractory ceramic products		...	...	...	-		...	...	...	...		...	...
2693 Struct.non-refractory clay; ceramic products		...	...	...	24151		...	...	...	...		...	...
2694 Cement, lime and plaster		...	...	...	11520		...	...	...	...		...	...
2695 Articles of concrete, cement and plaster		...	...	...	95110		...	...	...	...		...	...
2696 Cutting, shaping & finishing of stone		...	...	...	14208		...	...	...	...		...	...
2699 Other non-metallic mineral products n.e.c.		...	...	...	-		...	...	...	...		...	...
2710 Basic iron and steel		...	...	...	27		...	...	...	...		...	...
2720 Basic precious and non-ferrous metals		...	...	...	-		...	...	...	...		...	...
273 Casting of metals		...	...	...	6741		...	...	...	...		...	...
2731 Casting of iron and steel		...	...	...	4071		...	...	...	...		...	...
2732 Casting of non-ferrous metals		...	...	...	2670		...	...	...	...		...	...
281 Struct.metal products;tanks;steam generators		...	...	...	9298		...	...	...	...		...	...
2811 Structural metal products		...	...	...	9298		...	...	...	...		...	...
2812 Tanks, reservoirs and containers of metal		...	...	...	-		...	...	...	...		...	...
2813 Steam generators		...	...	...	-		...	...	...	...		...	...
289 Other metal products; metal working services		...	...	...	22310		...	...	...	...		...	...
2891 Metal forging/pressing/stamping/roll-forming		...	...	...	-		...	...	...	...		...	...
2892 Treatment & coating of metals		...	...	...	-		...	...	...	...		...	...
2893 Cutlery, hand tools and general hardware		...	...	...	4702		...	...	...	...		...	...
2899 Other fabricated metal products n.e.c.		...	...	...	17608		...	...	...	...		...	...
291 General purpose machinery		...	...	...	69924		...	...	...	...		...	...
2911 Engines & turbines(not for transport equip.)		...	...	...	11870		...	...	...	...		...	...
2912 Pumps, compressors, taps and valves		...	...	...	51678		...	...	...	...		...	...
2913 Bearings, gears, gearing & driving elements		...	...	...	-		...	...	...	...		...	...
2914 Ovens, furnaces and furnace burners		...	...	...	1160		...	...	...	...		...	...
2915 Lifting and handling equipment		...	...	...	2064		...	...	...	...		...	...
2919 Other general purpose machinery		...	...	...	3152		...	...	...	...		...	...

ISIC	Industry										
292	Special purpose machinery	...	...	...	122850	...	...	...	...	...	...
2921	Agricultural and forestry machinery	...	...	...	88038	...	...	...	...	...	...
2922	Machine tools	...	...	...	6401	...	...	...	...	...	...
2923	Machinery for metallurgy	...	...	...	-	...	...	...	...	...	...
2924	Machinery for mining & construction	...	...	...	5493	...	...	...	...	...	...
2925	Food/beverage/tobacco processing machinery	...	...	...	13513	...	...	...	...	...	...
2926	Machinery for textile, apparel and leather	...	...	...	9	...	...	...	...	...	...
2927	Weapons and ammunition	...	...	...	-	...	...	...	...	...	...
2929	Other special purpose machinery	...	...	...	9396	...	...	...	...	...	...
2930	Domestic appliances n.e.c.	...	...	...	33821	...	...	...	...	...	...
3000	Office, accounting and computing machinery	...	...	...	4114	...	...	...	...	...	...
3110	Electric motors, generators and transformers	...	...	...	4737	...	...	...	...	...	...
3120	Electricity distribution & control apparatus	...	...	...	-	...	...	...	...	...	...
3130	Insulated wire and cable	...	...	...	-	...	...	...	...	...	...
3140	Accumulators, primary cells and batteries	...	...	...	-	...	...	...	...	...	...
3150	Lighting equipment and electric lamps	...	...	...	10623	...	...	...	...	...	...
3190	Other electrical equipment n.e.c.	...	...	...	6218	...	...	...	...	...	...
3210	Electronic valves, tubes, etc.	...	...	...	-	...	...	...	...	...	...
3220	TV/radio transmitters; line comm. apparatus	...	...	...	-	...	...	...	...	...	...
3230	TV and radio receivers and associated goods	...	...	...	50640	...	...	...	...	...	...
331	Medical, measuring, testing appliances, etc.	...	...	...	28152	...	...	...	...	...	...
3311	Medical, surgical and orthopaedic equipment	...	...	...	2984	...	...	...	...	...	...
3312	Measuring/testing/navigating appliances,etc.	...	...	...	23780	...	...	...	...	...	...
3313	Industrial process control equipment	...	...	...	1388	...	...	...	...	...	...
3320	Optical instruments & photographic equipment	...	...	...	801	...	...	...	...	...	...
3330	Watches and clocks	...	...	...	-	...	...	...	...	...	...
3410	Motor vehicles	...	...	...	-	...	...	...	...	...	...
3420	Automobile bodies, trailers & semi-trailers	...	...	...	-	...	...	...	...	...	...
3430	Parts/accessories for automobiles	...	...	...	317	...	...	...	...	...	...
351	Building and repairing of ships and boats	...	...	...	-	...	...	...	...	...	...
3511	Building and repairing of ships	...	...	...	-	...	...	...	...	...	...
3512	Building/repairing of pleasure/sport. boats	...	...	...	-	...	...	...	...	...	...
3520	Railway/tramway locomotives & rolling stock	...	...	...	3575	...	...	...	...	...	...
3530	Aircraft and spacecraft	...	...	...	-	...	...	...	...	...	...
359	Transport equipment n.e.c.	...	...	...	2015	...	...	...	...	...	...
3591	Motorcycles	...	...	...	-	...	...	...	...	...	...
3592	Bicycles and invalid carriages	...	...	...	-	...	...	...	...	...	...
3599	Other transport equipment n.e.c.	...	...	...	2015	...	...	...	...	...	...
3610	Furniture	...	...	...	73907	...	...	...	...	...	...
369	Manufacturing n.e.c.	...	...	...	30352	...	...	...	...	...	...
3691	Jewellery and related articles	...	...	...	13616	...	...	...	...	...	...
3692	Musical instruments	...	...	...	-	...	...	...	...	...	...
3693	Sports goods	...	...	...	-	...	...	...	...	...	...
3694	Games and toys	...	...	...	36	...	...	...	...	...	...
3699	Other manufacturing n.e.c.	...	...	...	16700	...	...	...	...	...	...
3710	Recycling of metal waste and scrap	...	...	...	-	...	...	...	...	...	...
3720	Recycling of non-metal waste and scrap	...	...	...	-	...	...	...	...	...	...
D	Total manufacturing	...	...	...	3970562	629055	1354801	1476732	1783904	...	...

Republic of Moldova

ISIC Revision 3			Index numbers of industrial production											
			(1990=100)											
ISIC	Industry	Note	1985	1986	1987	1988	1989	1990	1991	1992	1993	1994	1995	1996
15	Food and beverages		...	...	...	...	...	...	...	...	...	...	...	...
16	Tobacco products		...	...	...	...	...	...	...	...	...	...	...	...
17	Textiles		...	...	...	...	...	...	...	...	...	...	...	...
18	Wearing apparel, fur		...	...	...	...	...	...	...	...	...	...	...	...
19	Leather, leather products and footwear		...	...	...	...	...	...	...	...	...	...	...	...
20	Wood products (excl. furniture)		...	...	...	...	...	...	...	...	...	...	...	...
21	Paper and paper products		...	...	...	...	...	...	...	...	...	...	...	...
22	Printing and publishing		...	...	...	...	...	...	...	...	...	...	...	...
23	Coke,refined petroleum products,nuclear fuel		...	...	...	...	...	...	...	...	...	...	...	...
24	Chemicals and chemical products		...	...	...	...	...	...	...	...	...	...	...	...
25	Rubber and plastics products		...	...	...	...	...	...	...	...	...	...	...	...
26	Non-metallic mineral products		...	...	...	...	...	...	...	...	...	...	...	...
27	Basic metals		...	...	...	...	...	...	...	...	...	...	...	...
28	Fabricated metal products		...	...	...	...	...	...	...	...	...	...	...	...
29	Machinery and equipment n.e.c.		...	...	...	...	...	...	...	...	...	...	...	...
30	Office, accounting and computing machinery		...	...	...	...	...	...	...	...	...	...	...	...
31	Electrical machinery and apparatus		...	...	...	...	...	...	...	...	...	...	...	...
32	Radio,television and communication equipment		...	...	...	...	...	...	...	...	...	...	...	...
33	Medical, precision and optical instruments		...	...	...	...	...	...	...	...	...	...	...	...
34	Motor vehicles, trailers, semi-trailers		...	...	...	...	...	...	...	...	...	...	...	...
35	Other transport equipment		...	...	...	...	...	...	...	...	...	...	...	...
36	Furniture; manufacturing n.e.c.		...	...	...	...	...	...	...	...	...	...	...	...
37	Recycling		...	...	...	...	...	...	...	...	...	...	...	...
D	Total manufacturing		...	...	...	...	...	...	...	...	...	...	...	...

ROMANIA

Supplier of information:
National Commission for Statistics, Bucharest.

Basic source of data:
Statistical reports on industrial production.

Major deviations from ISIC (Revision 3):
The concepts, definitions and classification by branches of industry are in accordance with the standards of the new National Activities Classification.

Reference period (if not calendar year):

Scope:
State enterprises under the direction of the central government. These enterprises account for about 80 per cent of all industrial enterprises and about the same percentage of industrial output.

Method of enumeration:
Not reported.

Adjusted for non-response:
Not reported.

Concepts and definitions of variables:
Figures for wages and salaries are computed by UNIDO from reported wages and salaries per employee.

Related national publications:
Anuarul Statistic al Romaniei, published by the National Commission for Statistics, Bucharest.

Romania

ISIC Revision 3	Number of establishments					Number of employees					Wages and salaries paid to employees				
		(numbers)					(thousands)					(billion LEI)			
ISIC Industry	Note	1993	1994	1995	1996	Note	1993	1994	1995	1996	Note	1993	1994	1995	1996
151 Processed meat,fish,fruit,vegetables,fats		1127	1898	2213	2489	a/	255.2	243.9	231.2	218.8	a/	180.4	402.0	582.8	848.6
1511 Processing/preserving of meat		...	1280	1528	1862		...	...	...	...		...	...	...	...
1512 Processing/preserving of fish		...	17	28	23		...	...	...	...		...	...	...	...
1513 Processing/preserving of fruit & vegetables		...	506	472	406		...	...	...	...		...	...	...	...
1514 Vegetable and animal oils and fats		...	95	185	198		...	...	...	...		...	...	...	...
1520 Dairy products		276	441	592	683	a/	...	...	...	...	a/	...	...	...	...
153 Grain mill products; starches; animal feeds		484	986	1292	1051	a/	...	...	...	...	a/	...	...	...	...
1531 Grain mill products		...	905	1211	968		...	...	...	...		...	...	...	...
1532 Starches and starch products		...	10	10	11		...	...	...	...		...	...	...	...
1533 Prepared animal feeds		...	71	71	72		...	...	...	...		...	...	...	...
154 Other food products		1722	2979	3602	3419	a/	...	...	...	...	a/	...	...	...	...
1541 Bakery products		...	2002	2448	2584		...	...	...	...		...	...	...	...
1542 Sugar		...	35	35	35		...	...	...	...		...	...	...	...
1543 Cocoa, chocolate and sugar confectionery		...	74	96	114		...	...	...	...		...	...	...	...
1544 Macaroni, noodles & similar products		...	32	32	79		...	...	...	...		...	...	...	...
1549 Other food products n.e.c.		...	836	991	607		...	...	...	...		...	...	...	...
155 Beverages		852	965	1183	994	a/	...	...	...	...	a/	...	...	...	...
1551 Distilling, rectifying & blending of spirits		...	364	364	359		...	...	...	...		...	...	...	...
1552 Wines		...	65	64	53		...	...	...	...		...	...	...	...
1553 Malt liquors and malt		...	88	90	115		...	...	...	...		...	...	...	...
1554 Soft drinks; mineral waters		...	448	665	467		...	...	...	...		...	...	...	...
1600 Tobacco products		1	14	16	15		5.8	7.5	7.0	5.1		5.2	17.7	24.0	36.2
171 Spinning, weaving and finishing of textiles		508	519	568	622	b/	273.2	221.4	185.5	189.1	b/	142.0	269.6	335.6	538.4
1711 Textile fibre preparation; textile weaving		...	468	520	593		...	...	...	...		...	...	...	...
1712 Finishing of textiles		...	51	48	29		...	...	...	...		...	...	...	...
172 Other textiles		745	861	988	906	b/	...	...	...	...	b/	...	...	...	...
1721 Made-up textile articles, except apparel		...	456	591	582		...	...	...	...		...	...	...	...
1722 Carpets and rugs		...	71	59	50		...	...	...	...		...	...	...	...
1723 Cordage, rope, twine and netting		...	30	30	43		...	...	...	...		...	...	...	...
1729 Other textiles n.e.c.		...	304	308	231		...	...	...	...		...	...	...	...
1730 Knitted and crocheted fabrics and articles		906	1188	1103	935	b/	...	...	...	...	b/	...	...	...	...
1810 Wearing apparel, except fur apparel		2245	3963	3590	3349	c/	200.0	208.1	188.8	202.9	c/	108.0	262.6	356.0	573.3
1820 Dressing & dyeing of fur; processing of fur		153	147	109	132	c/	...	...	...	...	c/	...	...	...	...
191 Tanning, dressing and processing of leather		357	729	523	520	d/	96.3	98.3	83.2	83.4	d/	53.9	121.6	153.3	240.0
1911 Tanning and dressing of leather		...	196	149	202		...	...	...	...		...	...	...	...
1912 Luggage, handbags, etc.; saddlery & harness		...	533	374	318		...	...	...	...		...	...	...	...
1920 Footwear		376	665	583	616	d/	...	...	...	...	d/	...	...	...	...
2010 Sawmilling and planing of wood		295	1067	1483	1516	e/	79.5	82.5	76.6	65.5	e/	48.4	109.1	157.1	208.1
202 Products of wood, cork, straw, etc.		1063	2338	1961	1911	e/	...	...	...	...	e/	...	...	...	...
2021 Veneer sheets, plywood, particle board, etc.		...	135	115	102		...	...	...	...		...	...	...	...
2022 Builders' carpentry and joinery		...	868	841	1029		...	...	...	...		...	...	...	...
2023 Wooden containers		...	155	134	107		...	...	...	...		...	...	...	...
2029 Other wood products; articles of cork/straw		...	1180	871	673		...	...	...	...		...	...	...	...
210 Paper and paper products		103	223	261	282		32.1	28.3	27.0	28.0		21.7	43.3	67.9	105.8
2101 Pulp, paper and paperboard		...	25	19	25		...	...	...	...		...	...	...	...
2102 Corrugated paper and paperboard		...	89	93	106		...	...	...	...		...	...	...	...
2109 Other articles of paper and paperboard		...	109	149	151		...	...	...	...		...	...	...	...
221 Publishing		191	1332	1385	1171	f/	32.0	28.0	21.9	20.5	f/	22.8	50.7	61.4	81.5
2211 Publishing of books and other publications		...	1009	1017	824		...	...	...	...		...	...	...	...
2212 Publishing of newspapers, journals, etc.		...	184	204	212		...	...	...	...		...	...	...	...
2213 Publishing of recorded media		...	64	64	40		...	...	...	...		...	...	...	...
2219 Other publishing		...	75	100	95		...	...	...	...		...	...	...	...

ISIC	Industry														
222	Printing and related service activities	105	340	427	537	f/	...	...	...	...	f/	...	...	...	...
2221	Printing	...	307	387	501		...	...	...	...		...	...	...	...
2222	Service activities related to printing	...	33	40	36		...	...	...	...		...	...	...	...
2230	Reproduction of recorded media	54	244	250	105	f/	...	...	...	...	f/	...	...	...	...
2310	Coke oven products	1	-	-	-	g/	35.2	35.5	35.8	35.4	g/	35.5	97.1	143.4	224.5
2320	Refined petroleum products	11	14	17	15	g/	...	...	...	...	g/	...	...	...	...
2330	Processing of nuclear fuel	-	-	...	...	g/	...	...	...	...	g/	...	...	...	...
241	Basic chemicals	163	209	162	187	h/	151.2	142.8	126.0	126.3	h/	122.5	269.2	388.3	596.7
2411	Basic chemicals, except fertilizers	...	125	100	123		...	...	...	...		...	...	...	...
2412	Fertilizers and nitrogen compounds	...	14	8	9		...	...	...	...		...	...	...	...
2413	Plastics in primary forms; synthetic rubber	...	70	54	55		...	...	...	...		...	...	...	...
242	Other chemicals	314	795	576	605	h/	...	...	...	...	h/	...	...	...	...
2421	Pesticides and other agro-chemical products	...	10	8	7		...	...	...	...		...	...	...	...
2422	Paints, varnishes, printing ink and mastics	...	123	112	118		...	...	...	...		...	...	...	...
2423	Pharmaceuticals, medicinal chemicals, etc.	...	199	144	131		...	...	...	...		...	...	...	...
2424	Soap, cleaning & cosmetic preparations	...	146	122	158		...	...	...	...		...	...	...	...
2429	Other chemical products n.e.c.	...	317	190	191		...	...	...	...		...	...	...	...
2430	Man-made fibres	16	35	17	21	h/	...	...	...	...	h/	...	...	...	...
251	Rubber products	440	572	423	431	i/	54.6	54.4	49.2	48.5	i/	41.7	92.9	139.6	206.0
2511	Rubber tyres and tubes	...	69	55	81		...	...	...	...		...	...	...	...
2519	Other rubber products	...	503	368	350		...	...	...	...		...	...	...	...
2520	Plastic products	771	971	768	777	i/	...	...	...	...	i/	...	...	...	...
2610	Glass and glass products	149	115	191	234	j/	137.7	135.5	123.0	118.6	j/	97.3	232.7	319.9	473.6
269	Non-metallic mineral products n.e.c.	501	590	863	747	j/	...	...	...	...	j/	...	...	...	...
2691	Pottery, china and earthenware	...	75	136	135		...	...	...	...		...	...	...	...
2692	Refractory ceramic products	...	18	23	25		...	...	...	...		...	...	...	...
2693	Struct.non-refractory clay; ceramic products	...	223	308	221		...	...	...	...		...	...	...	...
2694	Cement, lime and plaster	...	19	20	26		...	...	...	...		...	...	...	...
2695	Articles of concrete, cement and plaster	...	167	237	214		...	...	...	...		...	...	...	...
2696	Cutting, shaping & finishing of stone	...	63	98	91		...	...	...	...		...	...	...	...
2699	Other non-metallic mineral products n.e.c.	...	25	41	35		...	...	...	...		...	...	...	...
2710	Basic iron and steel	47	101	81	75	k/	164.3	164.3	146.9	148.9	k/	143.0	344.5	485.8	769.5
2720	Basic precious and non-ferrous metals	39	61	39	47	k/	...	...	...	...	k/	...	...	...	...
273	Casting of metals	137	211	144	203	k/	...	...	...	...	k/	...	...	...	...
2731	Casting of iron and steel	...	75	53	72		...	...	...	...		...	...	...	...
2732	Casting of non-ferrous metals	...	136	91	131		...	...	...	...		...	...	...	...
281	Struct.metal products;tanks;steam generators	443	1389	1715	1675	m/	153.4	136.3	122.9	109.9	m/	97.5	205.8	303.1	408.3
2811	Structural metal products	...	1343	1668	1618		...	...	...	...		...	...	...	...
2812	Tanks, reservoirs and containers of metal	...	32	32	42		...	...	...	...		...	...	...	...
2813	Steam generators	...	14	15	15		...	...	...	...		...	...	...	...
289	Other metal products; metal working services	1064	1095	1167	914	m/	...	...	...	...	m/	...	...	...	...
2891	Metal forging/pressing/stamping/roll-forming	...	27	28	22		...	...	...	...		...	...	...	...
2892	Treatment & coating of metals	...	34	31	39		...	...	...	...		...	...	...	...
2893	Cutlery, hand tools and general hardware	...	236	235	185		...	...	...	...		...	...	...	...
2899	Other fabricated metal products n.e.c.	...	798	873	668		...	...	...	...		...	...	...	...
291	General purpose machinery	197	214	184	233	n/	391.4	362.1	323.3	292.6	n/	276.9	580.1	823.1	1234.2
2911	Engines & turbines(not for transport equip.)	...	24	22	26		...	...	...	...		...	...	...	...
2912	Pumps, compressors, taps and valves	...	41	35	51		...	...	...	...		...	...	...	...
2913	Bearings, gears, gearing & driving elements	...	26	19	25		...	...	...	...		...	...	...	...
2914	Ovens, furnaces and furnace burners	...	3	2	2		...	...	...	...		...	...	...	...
2915	Lifting and handling equipment	...	35	27	46		...	...	...	...		...	...	...	...
2919	Other general purpose machinery	...	85	79	83		...	...	...	...		...	...	...	...
292	Special purpose machinery	196	334	297	340	n/	...	...	...	...	n/	...	...	...	...
2921	Agricultural and forestry machinery	...	67	54	64		...	...	...	...		...	...	...	...
2922	Machine tools	...	69	59	65		...	...	...	...		...	...	...	...
2923	Machinery for metallurgy	...	20	15	14		...	...	...	...		...	...	...	...
2924	Machinery for mining & construction	...	60	45	39		...	...	...	...		...	...	...	...
2925	Food/beverage/tobacco processing machinery	...	38	33	42		...	...	...	...		...	...	...	...
2926	Machinery for textile, apparel and leather	...	31	21	25		...	...	...	...		...	...	...	...
2927	Weapons and ammunition	...	3	17	20		...	...	...	...		...	...	...	...
2929	Other special purpose machinery	...	46	53	71		...	...	...	...		...	...	...	...
2930	Domestic appliances n.e.c.	151	179	144	120	n/	...	...	...	...	n/	...	...	...	...

continued

Romania

ISIC Revision 3	Number of establishments					Number of employees					Wages and salaries paid to employees				
		(numbers)					(thousands)					(billion LEI)			
ISIC Industry	Note	1993	1994	1995	1996	Note	1993	1994	1995	1996	Note	1993	1994	1995	1996
3000 Office, accounting and computing machinery		131	240	201	174	p/	114.1	102.3	96.1	91.3	p/	73.4	155.8	265.8	366.8
3110 Electric motors, generators and transformers		24	98	64	82	p/	...	...	...	...	p/	...	...	...	...
3120 Electricity distribution & control apparatus		31	79	67	64	p/	...	...	...	...	p/	...	...	...	...
3130 Insulated wire and cable		8	15	15	21	p/	...	...	...	...	p/	...	...	...	...
3140 Accumulators, primary cells and batteries		6	22	15	28	p/	...	...	...	...	p/	...	...	...	...
3150 Lighting equipment and electric lamps		26	47	38	48	p/	...	...	...	...	p/	...	...	...	...
3190 Other electrical equipment n.e.c.		89	181	162	140	p/	...	...	...	...	p/	...	...	...	...
3210 Electronic valves, tubes, etc.		44	135	57	47	p/	...	...	...	...	p/	...	...	...	...
3220 TV/radio transmitters; line comm. apparatus		24	94	56	66	p/	...	...	...	...	p/	...	...	...	...
3230 TV and radio receivers and associated goods		27	124	64	61	p/	...	...	...	...	p/	...	...	...	...
331 Medical, measuring, testing appliances, etc.		110	172	188	196	q/	24.6	25.5	19.5	18.2	q/	15.6	38.0	45.6	69.8
3311 Medical, surgical and orthopaedic equipment		...	76	80	78		...	...	...	...		...	...	...	...
3312 Measuring/testing/navigating appliances,etc.		...	45	51	50		...	...	...	...		...	...	...	...
3313 Industrial process control equipment		...	51	57	68		...	...	...	...		...	...	...	...
3320 Optical instruments & photographic equipment		8	25	24	26	q/	...	...	...	...	q/	...	...	...	...
3330 Watches and clocks		4	12	6	3	q/	...	...	...	...	q/	...	...	...	...
3410 Motor vehicles		5	22	10	10	r/	219.6	191.5	180.5	189.8	r/	162.4	337.4	519.4	858.6
3420 Automobile bodies, trailers & semi-trailers		13	20	14	24	r/	...	...	...	...	r/	...	...	...	...
3430 Parts/accessories for automobiles		136	154	96	125	r/	...	...	...	...	r/	...	...	...	...
351 Building and repairing of ships and boats		24	85	84	132	r/	...	...	...	...	r/	...	...	...	...
3511 Building and repairing of ships		...	75	81	119		...	...	...	...		...	...	...	...
3512 Building/repairing of pleasure/sport. boats		...	10	3	13		...	...	...	...		...	...	...	...
3520 Railway/tramway locomotives & rolling stock		21	39	25	27	r/	...	...	...	...	r/	...	...	...	...
3530 Aircraft and spacecraft		8	7	7	7	r/	...	...	...	...	r/	...	...	...	...
359 Transport equipment n.e.c.		10	16	12	10	r/	...	...	...	...	r/	...	...	...	...
3591 Motorcycles		...	4	1	-		...	...	...	...		...	...	...	...
3592 Bicycles and invalid carriages		...	2	2	4		...	...	...	...		...	...	...	...
3599 Other transport equipment n.e.c.		...	10	9	6		...	...	...	...		...	...	...	...
3610 Furniture		2337	1731	2360	1186	s/	162.8	150.1	140.7	148.1	s/	102.0	203.9	300.5	467.4
369 Manufacturing n.e.c.		3901	1417	1642	1568	s/	...	...	...	...	s/	...	...	...	...
3691 Jewellery and related articles		...	145	179	69		...	...	...	...		...	...	...	...
3692 Musical instruments		...	21	18	7		...	...	...	...		...	...	...	...
3693 Sports goods		...	52	58	19		...	...	...	...		...	...	...	...
3694 Games and toys		...	220	211	78		...	...	...	...		...	...	...	...
3699 Other manufacturing n.e.c.		...	979	1176	1395		...	...	...	...		...	...	...	...
3710 Recycling of metal waste and scrap		134	559	269	228	t/	7.5	7.3	6.6	6.7	t/	5.4	11.2	16.2	23.9
3720 Recycling of non-metal waste and scrap		28	87	42	54	t/	...	...	...	...	t/	...	...	...	...
D Total manufacturing		23352	33165	34435	32200		2590.5	2425.6	2191.7	2147.6		1755.9	3840.7	5469.0	8332.8

a/ 151 includes 1520, 153, 154 and 155.
b/ 171 includes 172 and 1730.
c/ 1810 includes 1820.
d/ 191 includes 1920.
e/ 2010 includes 202.
f/ 221 includes 222 and 2230.
g/ 2310 includes 2320 and 2330.
h/ 241 includes 242 and 2430.
i/ 251 includes 2520.
j/ 2610 includes 269.
k/ 2710 includes 2720 and 273.
m/ 281 includes 289.
n/ 291 includes 292 and 2930.
p/ 3000 includes 3110, 3120, 3130, 3140, 3150, 3190, 3210, 3220 and 3230.
q/ 331 includes 3320 and 3330.
r/ 3410 includes 3420, 3430, 351, 3520, 3530 and 359
s/ 3610 includes 369.
t/ 3710 includes 3720.

Romania

ISIC Revision 3	Output					Value added					Gross fixed capital formation		
		(billion LEI)					(billion LEI)					(billion LEI)	
ISIC Industry	Note	1993	1994	1995	1996	Note	1993	1994	1995	1996	Note	1995	1996
151 Processed meat,fish,fruit,vegetables,fats		1733.0	4230.0	6685.1	...		513.7	1359.7	2133.9	...		156.5	334.3
1511 Processing/preserving of meat		1199.2	2469.5	3956.1	...		366.2	823.5	1332.2	...		83.8	204.3
1512 Processing/preserving of fish		37.7	121.9	106.2	...		11.0	36.6	37.8	...		0.7	2.2
1513 Processing/preserving of fruit & vegetables		322.4	1099.4	1826.5	...		86.0	329.4	512.5	...		20.7	36.5
1514 Vegetable and animal oils and fats		173.7	539.2	796.3	...		50.5	170.2	251.4	...		51.2	91.3
1520 Dairy products		360.6	1017.4	1334.2	...		107.9	321.6	418.3	...		58.3	92.7
153 Grain mill products; starches; animal feeds		620.8	1272.1	1515.2	...		149.8	376.0	335.5	...		54.6	126.8
1531 Grain mill products		83.8a/	276.7a/	435.3a/	...		35.8a/	131.8a/	194.7a/	...		45.9	95.1
1532 Starches and starch products		...a/	...a/	...a/	...		...a/	...a/	...a/	...		1.1	1.9
1533 Prepared animal feeds		537.0	995.4	1079.9	...		114.0	244.2	140.8	...		7.6	29.7
154 Other food products		682.7	1434.9	1877.9	...		248.3	562.0	694.9	...		94.7	227.8
1541 Bakery products		...	...	...	...		...	...	...	...		56.3	119.6
1542 Sugar		...	...	...	...		...	...	...	...		8.0	22.2
1543 Cocoa, chocolate and sugar confectionery		...	...	...	...		...	...	...	...		15.7	31.8
1544 Macaroni, noodles & similar products		...	...	...	...		...	...	...	...		2.0	14.9
1549 Other food products n.e.c.		...	...	...	...		...	...	...	...		12.7	39.3
155 Beverages		867.6	2268.8	4148.8	...		343.3	930.0	1697.2	...		525.3	678.1
1551 Distilling, rectifying & blending of spirits		...	...	...	...		...	...	...	...		22.3	93.3
1552 Wines		...	...	...	...		...	...	...	...		14.8	34.0
1553 Malt liquors and malt		...	...	...	...		...	...	...	...		120.4	269.1
1554 Soft drinks; mineral waters		...	...	...	...		...	...	...	...		367.7	281.7
1600 Tobacco products		86.8	246.4	269.9	...		46.8	131.3	141.8	...		3.7	45.6
171 Spinning, weaving and finishing of textiles		1003.0b/	1897.2b/	2557.8b/	...		320.3b/	663.8b/	840.0b/	...		88.2	125.8
1711 Textile fibre preparation; textile weaving		...	...	...	...		...	...	...	...		84.0	125.8
1712 Finishing of textiles		...	...	...	...		...	...	...	...		4.1	-
172 Other textiles		...b/	...b/	...b/	...		...b/	...b/	...b/	...		11.4	31.6
1721 Made-up textile articles, except apparel		...	...	...	...		...	...	...	...		3.8	10.2
1722 Carpets and rugs		...	...	...	...		...	...	...	...		1.8	2.3
1723 Cordage, rope, twine and netting		...	...	...	...		...	...	...	...		0.4	0.4
1729 Other textiles n.e.c.		...	...	...	...		...	...	...	...		5.5	18.7
1730 Knitted and crocheted fabrics and articles		...b/	...b/	...b/	...		...b/	...b/	...b/	...		23.7	161.8
1810 Wearing apparel, except fur apparel		421.2	1503.1	2215.3	...		201.2	836.8	1176.4	...		132.6	255.7
1820 Dressing & dyeing of fur; processing of fur		34.9	93.8	126.2	...		18.4	59.2	75.9	...		0.8	2.9
191 Tanning, dressing and processing of leather		297.1c/	611.8c/	825.5c/	...		118.5c/	268.9c/	334.0c/	...		5.6	13.6
1911 Tanning and dressing of leather		...	...	...	...		...	...	...	...		4.7	10.0
1912 Luggage, handbags, etc.; saddlery & harness		...	...	...	...		...	...	...	...		0.9	3.6
1920 Footwear		...c/	...c/	...c/	...		...c/	...c/	...c/	...		13.0	50.0
2010 Sawmilling and planing of wood		348.7d/	937.9d/	1244.0d/	...		168.5d/	489.0d/	625.0d/	...		29.7	71.8
202 Products of wood, cork, straw, etc.		...d/	...d/	...d/	...		...d/	...d/	...d/	...		42.8	114.8
2021 Veneer sheets, plywood, particle board, etc.		...	...	...	...		...	...	...	...		8.8	67.7
2022 Builders' carpentry and joinery		...	...	...	...		...	...	...	...		5.9	18.0
2023 Wooden containers		...	...	...	...		...	...	...	...		1.2	2.9
2029 Other wood products; articles of cork/straw		...	...	...	...		...	...	...	...		26.8	26.3
210 Paper and paper products		202.8	445.5	750.4	...		59.2	152.2	244.4	...		59.7	168.1
2101 Pulp, paper and paperboard		...	...	...	...		...	...	...	...		47.6	87.0
2102 Corrugated paper and paperboard		...	...	...	...		...	...	...	...		7.9	59.2
2109 Other articles of paper and paperboard		...	...	...	...		...	...	...	...		4.2	21.9
221 Publishing		133.7e/	407.2e/	657.7e/	...		38.4e/	138.8e/	211.4e/	...		9.4	33.1
2211 Publishing of books and other publications		...	...	...	...		...	...	...	...		3.2	11.8
2212 Publishing of newspapers, journals, etc.		...	...	...	...		...	...	...	...		5.4	14.9
2213 Publishing of recorded media		...	...	...	...		...	...	...	...		-	5.5
2219 Other publishing		...	...	...	...		...	...	...	...		0.8	0.8

continued

Romania

ISIC Revision 3	Output					Value added					Gross fixed capital formation		
		(billion LEI)					(billion LEI)					(billion LEI)	
ISIC Industry	Note	1993	1994	1995	1996	Note	1993	1994	1995	1996	Note	1995	1996
222 Printing and related service activities		...e/	...e/	...e/	...		...e/	...e/	...e/	...		53.4	73.3
2221 Printing		...	...	...	...		...	...	...	...		52.8	72.5
2222 Service activities related to printing		...	...	...	...		...	...	...	...		0.6	0.8
2230 Reproduction of recorded media		...e/	...e/	...e/	...		...e/	...e/	...e/	...		0.1	0.6
2310 Coke oven products		275.0	531.3	678.5	...		87.3	180.1	80.0	...		17.4	8.4
2320 Refined petroleum products		1247.8	3123.7	4361.6	...		237.9	455.9	348.4	...		82.5	106.0
2330 Processing of nuclear fuel		-	-	-	...		-	-	-	...		1.0	0.7
241 Basic chemicals		611.0	1464.7	2772.0	...		63.3	218.8	417.4	...		187.8	751.1
2411 Basic chemicals, except fertilizers		...	...	...	...		...	...	...	...		143.9	680.3
2412 Fertilizers and nitrogen compounds		...	...	...	...		...	...	...	...		42.6	68.1
2413 Plastics in primary forms; synthetic rubber		...	...	...	...		...	...	...	...		1.3	2.7
242 Other chemicals		743.9	1821.9	2456.6	...		265.2	745.7	936.1	...		98.3	206.3
2421 Pesticides and other agro-chemical products		206.4	435.6	653.0	...		39.9	99.9	131.4	...		-	0.7
2422 Paints, varnishes, printing ink and mastics		119.9	351.0	434.1	...		45.6	149.7	183.5	...		9.5	18.7
2423 Pharmaceuticals, medicinal chemicals, etc.		186.5	437.2	594.6	...		103.5	270.9	351.4	...		13.8	67.7
2424 Soap, cleaning & cosmetic preparations		78.2	308.8	363.0	...		29.0	130.7	140.4	...		40.2	62.1
2429 Other chemical products n.e.c.		152.9	289.3	411.9	...		47.2	94.5	129.4	...		34.7	57.1
2430 Man-made fibres		119.6	253.7	430.5	...		31.0	74.2	113.4	...		26.6	46.6
251 Rubber products		246.8	458.7	784.8	...		101.2	184.4	264.9	...		47.2	83.0
2511 Rubber tyres and tubes		...	...	...	...		...	...	...	...		20.7	32.4
2519 Other rubber products		...	...	...	...		...	...	...	...		26.5	50.6
2520 Plastic products		231.7	387.7	554.0	...		79.3	147.1	184.4	...		52.9	88.9
2610 Glass and glass products		106.0	245.8	434.6	...		51.2	122.0	202.6	...		15.9	43.4
269 Non-metallic mineral products n.e.c.		763.4	1548.3	2015.7	...		301.0	672.9	816.8	...		93.1	225.9
2691 Pottery, china and earthenware		...	...	...	...		...	...	...	...		8.9	44.7
2692 Refractory ceramic products		...	...	...	...		...	...	...	...		4.6	28.8
2693 Struct.non-refractory clay; ceramic products		...	...	...	...		...	...	...	...		12.8	27.2
2694 Cement, lime and plaster		...	...	...	...		...	...	...	...		21.0	34.6
2695 Articles of concrete, cement and plaster		...	...	...	...		...	...	...	...		10.6	43.0
2696 Cutting, shaping & finishing of stone		...	...	...	...		...	...	...	...		10.5	10.2
2699 Other non-metallic mineral products n.e.c.		...	...	...	...		...	...	...	...		24.7	37.5
2710 Basic iron and steel		1085.6	2981.8	4008.6	...		226.1	732.0	908.0	...		206.5	459.3
2720 Basic precious and non-ferrous metals		306.1	794.8	1403.1	...		33.3	118.9	204.7	...		57.2	88.8
273 Casting of metals		168.3	435.4	650.9	...		45.7	140.1	204.2	...		15.9	20.7
2731 Casting of iron and steel		...	...	...	...		...	...	...	...		12.5	14.0
2732 Casting of non-ferrous metals		...	...	...	...		...	...	...	...		3.4	6.7
281 Struct.metal products;tanks;steam generators		666.4f/	1745.0f/	2095.1f/	...		235.2f/	693.5f/	802.6f/	...		34.3	96.6
2811 Structural metal products		...	...	...	...		...	...	...	...		23.4	83.2
2812 Tanks, reservoirs and containers of metal		...	...	...	...		...	...	...	...		5.3	5.3
2813 Steam generators		...	...	...	...		...	...	...	...		5.5	8.1
289 Other metal products; metal working services		...f/	...f/	...f/	...		...f/	...f/	...f/	...		53.5	80.2
2891 Metal forging/pressing/stamping/roll-forming		...	...	...	...		...	...	...	...		9.6	14.2
2892 Treatment & coating of metals		...	...	...	...		...	...	...	...		0.8	2.9
2893 Cutlery, hand tools and general hardware		...	...	...	...		...	...	...	...		7.1	25.4
2899 Other fabricated metal products n.e.c.		...	...	...	...		...	...	...	...		36.0	37.7
291 General purpose machinery		448.5	947.5	1280.0	...		166.1	413.8	485.8	...		49.2	210.7
2911 Engines & turbines(not for transport equip.)		...	...	...	...		...	...	...	...		6.0	8.5
2912 Pumps, compressors, taps and valves		...	...	...	...		...	...	...	...		5.4	98.4
2913 Bearings, gears, gearing & driving elements		...	...	...	...		...	...	...	...		29.4	90.1
2914 Ovens, furnaces and furnace burners		...	...	...	...		...	...	...	...		-	0.2
2915 Lifting and handling equipment		...	...	...	...		...	...	...	...		2.6	3.4
2919 Other general purpose machinery		...	...	...	...		...	...	...	...		5.9	10.0

292 Special purpose machinery	790.4	1837.2	2383.9	...	274.3	784.5	969.7	...	61.7	104.4
2921 Agricultural and forestry machinery	237.1	520.7	655.8	...	78.7	205.3	250.4	...	13.5	9.1
2922 Machine tools	100.0	220.6	252.7	...	36.7	84.7	87.1	...	4.1	13.5
2923 Machinery for metallurgy	453.3g/	1095.9g/	1475.4g/	...	158.9g/	494.5g/	632.2g/	...	12.1	11.9
2924 Machinery for mining & construction	...g/	...g/	...g/	...	...g/	...g/	...g/	...	13.8	28.9
2925 Food/beverage/tobacco processing machinery	...g/	...g/	...g/	...	...g/	...g/	...g/	...	1.2	3.5
2926 Machinery for textile, apparel and leather	...g/	...g/	...g/	...	...g/	...g/	...g/	...	2.0	1.4
2927 Weapons and ammunition	...g/	...g/	...g/	...	...g/	...g/	...g/	...	6.8	11.8
2929 Other special purpose machinery	...g/	...g/	...g/	...	...g/	...g/	...g/	...	8.2	24.3
2930 Domestic appliances n.e.c.	60.3	190.3	381.8	...	25.8	90.1	162.1	...	11.1	25.7
3000 Office, accounting and computing machinery	48.7	115.7	182.3	...	11.2	26.2	40.4	...	6.4	16.7
3110 Electric motors, generators and transformers	272.0h/	779.1h/	1339.6h/	...	85.0h/	322.1h/	548.9h/	...	9.0	25.0
3120 Electricity distribution & control apparatus	...h/	...h/	...h/	...	...h/	...h/	...h/	...	8.0	19.2
3130 Insulated wire and cable	...h/	...h/	...h/	...	...h/	...h/	...h/	...	4.9	25.1
3140 Accumulators, primary cells and batteries	...h/	...h/	...h/	...	...h/	...h/	...h/	...	2.7	5.6
3150 Lighting equipment and electric lamps	...h/	...h/	...h/	...	...h/	...h/	...h/	...	8.2	13.5
3190 Other electrical equipment n.e.c.	...h/	...h/	...h/	...	...h/	...h/	...h/	...	16.2	21.7
3210 Electronic valves, tubes, etc.	257.4i/	725.4i/	919.5i/	...	98.4i/	327.7i/	415.7i/	...	0.8	3.3
3220 TV/radio transmitters; line comm. apparatus	...i/	...i/	...i/	...	...i/	...i/	...i/	...	12.1	23.8
3230 TV and radio receivers and associated goods	...i/	...i/	...i/	...	...i/	...i/	...i/	...	4.6	35.7
331 Medical, measuring, testing appliances, etc.	157.9j/	386.3j/	519.6j/	...	74.1j/	204.7j/	271.1j/	...	14.3	18.3
3311 Medical, surgical and orthopaedic equipment	...	...	...	...	...	...	...	...	7.0	3.9
3312 Measuring/testing/navigating appliances,etc.	...	...	...	...	...	...	...	...	4.5	5.3
3313 Industrial process control equipment	...	...	...	...	...	...	...	...	2.8	9.1
3320 Optical instruments & photographic equipment	...j/	...j/	...j/	...	...j/	...j/	...j/	...	0.6	0.5
3330 Watches and clocks	...j/	...j/	...j/	...	...j/	...j/	...j/	...	0.1	0.1
3410 Motor vehicles	602.1k/	1383.4k/	2017.9k/	...	160.2k/	451.8k/	657.4k/	...	281.9	114.3
3420 Automobile bodies, trailers & semi-trailers	...k/	...k/	...k/	...	...k/	...k/	...k/	...	3.9	16.0
3430 Parts/accessories for automobiles	...k/	...k/	...k/	...	...k/	...k/	...k/	...	24.5	46.8
351 Building and repairing of ships and boats	108.2	276.8	485.9	...	34.8	96.6	163.1	...	17.5	28.7
3511 Building and repairing of ships	...	...	...	...	...	...	...	...	17.5	28.5
3512 Building/repairing of pleasure/sport. boats	...	...	...	...	...	...	...	...	-	0.2
3520 Railway/tramway locomotives & rolling stock	228.1	272.1	292.8	...	64.8	85.4	84.9	...	8.0	14.5
3530 Aircraft and spacecraft	64.7	73.4	69.9	...	24.0	29.3	27.7	...	2.9	2.5
359 Transport equipment n.e.c.	37.8	64.8	44.4	...	12.2	38.4	27.3	...	2.7	0.2
3591 Motorcycles	...	...	...	...	...	...	...	...	-	-
3592 Bicycles and invalid carriages	...	...	...	...	...	...	...	...	-	-
3599 Other transport equipment n.e.c.	...	...	...	...	...	...	...	...	2.6	0.2
3610 Furniture	510.9	1224.8	1867.3	...	186.6	509.2	639.8	...	76.7	153.3
369 Manufacturing n.e.c.	79.1	259.2	370.3	...	28.9	132.8	180.4	...	3.5	10.4
3691 Jewellery and related articles	...	...	...	...	...	...	...	...	1.2	1.0
3692 Musical instruments	...	...	...	...	...	...	...	...	0.3	1.1
3693 Sports goods	...	...	...	...	...	...	...	...	0.4	0.1
3694 Games and toys	...	...	...	...	...	...	...	...	0.5	1.6
3699 Other manufacturing n.e.c.	...	...	...	...	...	...	...	...	1.1	6.6
3710 Recycling of metal waste and scrap	...	...	...	...	...	...	...	...	3.8	7.4
3720 Recycling of non-metal waste and scrap	...	...	...	...	...	...	...	...	0.5	0.7
D Total manufacturing	17030.6	40694.9	59009.2	...	5338.4	14287.5	19086.5	...	2989.1	5858.4

a/ 1531 includes 1532.
b/ 171 includes 172 and 1730.
c/ 191 includes 1920.
d/ 2010 includes 202.
e/ 221 includes 222 and 2230.
f/ 281 includes 289.
g/ 2923 includes 2924, 2925, 2926, 2927 and 2929.
h/ 3110 includes 3120, 3130, 3140, 3150 and 3190.
i/ 3210 includes 3220 and 3230.
j/ 331 includes 3320 and 3330.
k/ 3410 includes 3420 and 3430.

Romania

ISIC Revision 3			Index numbers of industrial production											
			(1990=100)											
ISIC	Industry	Note	1985	1986	1987	1988	1989	1990	1991	1992	1993	1994	1995	1996
15	Food and beverages		102	106	114	114	114	100	83	68	59	67	69	67
16	Tobacco products		...	...	...	...	118	100	102	102	89	84	89	96
17	Textiles		108	114	116	119	118	100	87	61	59	59	59	48
18	Wearing apparel, fur		106	114	113	120	124	100	93	65	62	88	110	150
19	Leather, leather products and footwear		102	109	110	109	113	100	88	63	61	68	74	67
20	Wood products (excl. furniture)		113	117	118	123	127	100	79	65	59	49	49	51
21	Paper and paper products		121	136	132	136	139	100	69	52	47	47	62	57
22	Printing and publishing		127	119	119	120	118	100	83	84	122	211	264	340
23	Coke,refined petroleum products,nuclear fuel		104	113	125	132	130	100	64	57	56	65	66	60
24	Chemicals and chemical products		122	132	126	131	126	100	65	57	59	54	59	56
25	Rubber and plastics products		...	...	...	...	126	100	75	53	56	45	48	50
26	Non-metallic mineral products		107	119	124	129	131	100	76	52	52	47	53	55
27	Basic metals		124	134	128	132	128	100	74	52	55	57	67	66
28	Fabricated metal products		124	141	145	148	147	100	87	61	56	48	58	58
29	Machinery and equipment n.e.c.		104	108	111	114	102	100	72	54	55	51	63	81
30	Office, accounting and computing machinery		...	...	...	...	124	100	63	47	34	37	40	53
31	Electrical machinery and apparatus		76	85	91	95	91	100	75	49	53	81	103	129
32	Radio,television and communication equipment		...	...	...	...	137	100	100	61	72	144	184	332
33	Medical, precision and optical instruments		...	...	...	...	138	100	89	63	62	54	73	102
34	Motor vehicles, trailers, semi-trailers		...	...	...	...	123	100	80	57	70	63	64	79
35	Other transport equipment		...	...	...	...	130	100	85	67	75	56	68	80
36	Furniture; manufacturing n.e.c.		...	...	...	...	104	100	99	81	104	116	152	227
37	Recycling		...	...	...	...	...	...	...	...	...	...	...	...
D	Total manufacturing		139	142	138	137	129	100	76	54	54	56	63	70

RUSSIAN FEDERATION

Supplier of information:
Russian Federation State Committee on Statistics, Moscow.

Basic source of data:
Not reported.

Major deviations from ISIC (Revision 2):
None reported.

Reference period (if not calendar year):

Scope:
All enterprises having independent financial accounts.

Method of enumeration:
Not reported.

Adjusted for non-response:
Yes.

Concepts and definitions of variables:
Figures for wages and salaries are computed by UNIDO from reported wages and salaries per employee.

Related national publications:

ISIC Revision 2		Number of enterprises					Number of employees					Wages and salaries paid to employees			
		(numbers)					(thousands)					(billion ROUBLES)			
ISIC Industry	Note	1993	1994	1995	1996	Note	1993	1994	1995	1996	Note	1993	1994	1995	1996
311/2 Food products		8473	9396	13200	16960		1533	1475	1468	1415		1464.5	4722.9	9783.7	15451.1
3111 Slaughtering, preparing & preserving meat		1187	1294	1963	2838		258	256	247	243		222.2	758.5	1371.5	2280.8
3112 Dairy products		1783	1849	2054	2335		225	218	214	206		183.0	588.6	1205.6	1811.6
3113 Canning, preserving of fruits & vegetables		568	431	539	560		87	72	65	57		44.3	107.2	203.8	274.0
3114 Canning, preserving and processing of fish		719	778	1611	1858		252	224	220	200		339.2	1101.3	2460.5	3338.0
3115 Vegetable and animal oils and fats		160	363	544	811		34	37	42	47		38.9	111.5	283.7	503.5
3116 Grain mill products		408	468	604	562		89	87	96	82		76.1	284.6	653.4	986.5
3117 Bakery products		2190	2771	4139	5719		332	330	345	354		344.5	1096.5	2240.2	4010.0
3118 Sugar factories and refineries		103	101	165	178		59	57	54	55		57.0	130.3	266.2	465.3
3119 Cocoa, chocolate and sugar confectionery		569	630	793	1034		103	102	99	98		89.3	307.8	647.1	1159.3
3121 Other food products		414	385	372	605		24	26	26	24		18.7	64.3	129.4	193.1
3122 Prepared animal feeds		372	326	416	460		71	66	60	51		51.3	172.3	319.4	429.1
313 Beverages		744	946	1255	1682		141	144	153	160		132.6	431.9	944.4	1759.6
3131 Distilling, rectifying and blending spirits		183	230	276	307		49	50	57	57		58.0	160.0	363.7	559.4
3132 Wine industries		131	161	244	283		31	31	28	25		26.1	88.0	153.5	263.1
3133 Malt liquors and malt		264	298	361	504		45	45	47	50		37.7	139.4	318.6	675.4
3134 Soft drinks and carbonated waters		166	257	374	588		16	17	21	29		10.8	44.5	108.4	261.7
314 Tobacco		35	36	52	47		16	15	13	15		21.2	67.0	119.4	257.7
321 Textiles		2777	2690	3965	3950		821	700	606	517		433.1	1033.5	1973.0	2699.8
3211 Spinning, weaving and finishing textiles		636	667	970	963		477	404	348	304		237.9	568.3	1112.1	1562.7
3212 Made-up textile goods excl. wearing apparel		131	116	122	133		30	23	18	13		13.0	30.2	48.0	63.1
3213 Knitting mills		1535	1430	2169	2109		180	160	138	109		92.8	217.7	370.9	486.5
3214 Carpets and rugs		74	86	137	104		63	52	45	37		42.9	75.9	131.1	167.4
3215 Cordage, rope and twine		41	50	49	53		13	10	9	8		6.9	22.4	50.9	65.9
3219 Other textiles		360	341	518	588		59	51	49	45		39.6	119.0	260.5	354.1
322 Wearing apparel, except footwear		9051	7921	12673	12958		630	547	502	425		343.4	706.0	1244.9	1723.7
323 Leather and fur products		979	1080	1717	1861		96	89	86	71		60.2	163.7	372.9	391.6
3231 Tanneries and leather finishing		163	167	240	235		33	31	27	19		22.5	60.0	166.1	116.5
3232 Fur dressing and dyeing industries		577	616	1063	1128		36	37	38	35		22.6	70.5	141.0	192.8
3233 Leather prods. excl. wearing apparel		239	297	474	498		27	22	21	17		15.1	33.2	65.1	82.3
324 Footwear, except rubber or plastic		1548	1341	1676	1774		168	142	119	102		92.4	211.7	364.8	518.1
331 Wood products, except furniture		5144	5002	7396	9005		515	470	452	424		317.1	1017.5	2199.9	3144.5
3311 Sawmills, planing and other wood mills		3528	3954	5838	7373		414	394	385	368		266.5	881.3	1928.0	2785.5
3312 Wooden and cane containers		265	284	453	433		28	22	18	15		12.0	35.6	64.2	84.0
3319 Other wood and cork products		1351	764	1105	1199		74	54	48	41		38.6	100.6	203.6	274.9
332 Furniture and fixtures, excl. metal		2947	3076	4816	6010		271	261	237	203		176.3	493.2	927.9	1240.4
341 Paper and products		378	383	502	598		185	165	172	166		145.9	499.8	1584.3	2139.3
3411 Pulp, paper and paperboard articles		126	130	144	152		161	143	150	146		132.6	451.8	1456.8	1950.2
3412 Containers of paper and paperboard		95	100	143	179		12	11	12	10		7.2	26.8	77.1	104.9
3419 Other pulp, paper and paperboard articles		157	153	215	267		12	10	10	9		6.1	21.2	50.7	84.2
342 Printing and publishing		3058	4730	3874	4235		132	132	123	111		84.3	331.5	702.2	1142.1
351 Industrial chemicals		584	607	750	856		696	641	579	539		518.7	1635.3	3709.6	5480.5
3511 Basic chemicals excl. fertilizers		425	416	514	568		459	428	379	349		347.9	1165.6	2540.3	3726.3
3512 Fertilizers and pesticides		32	40	81	97		49	46	44	41		33.5	107.3	262.9	387.7
3513 Synthetic resins and plastic materials		127	151	155	191		189	166	155	149		137.3	362.4	906.5	1366.5
352 Other chemicals		1305	1610	2169	2587		198	169	194	190		136.3	436.2	1159.2	2027.8
3521 Paints, varnishes and lacquers		205	256	329	393		32	29	34	36		23.4	74.7	190.5	380.6
3522 Drugs and medicines		438	635	852	910		90	83	83	81		57.5	210.2	472.3	805.4
3523 Soap, cleaning preps., perfumes, cosmetics		155	189	296	490		19	17	17	16		14.1	46.2	115.5	183.1
3529 Other chemical products		507	530	692	794		57	40	61	58		41.3	105.1	382.7	658.7
353 Petroleum refineries		122	133	171	272		108	112	117	132		155.1	611.2	1519.2	2716.1

ISIC	Industry															
354	Misc. petroleum and coal products		122	196	339	354		78	80	83	75		97.7	382.7	757.2	1240.7
355	Rubber products		488	444	642	750		175	151	142	138		117.8	314.6	744.4	1357.0
3551	Tyres and tubes		210	106	143	151		68	59	55	55		54.1	131.2	352.0	652.5
3559	Other rubber products		278	338	499	599		107	92	87	83		63.7	183.4	392.5	704.5
356	Plastic products		1157	1239	1866	2337		83	73	81	82		43.4	140.8	364.0	598.8
361	Pottery, china, earthenware		320	431	739	846		98	90	35	31		67.4	187.1	138.0	204.6
362	Glass and products		542	549	727	821		114	101	96	88		64.8	187.7	448.3	684.8
369	Other non-metallic mineral products		5980	4964	6698	8038		995	901	870	775		801.6	2640.5	5386.0	7573.5
3691	Structural clay products		179	157	195	470		57	51	52	50		40.1	134.4	314.0	546.5
3692	Cement, lime and plaster		239	246	307	318		77	74	72	70		60.9	199.6	472.0	727.1
3699	Other non-metallic mineral products		5562	4561	6196	7250		861	777	745	655		700.6	2306.5	4599.4	6299.9
371	Iron and steel		636	798	1115	1602		691	643	644	625		629.5	1844.8	4627.7	8230.1
372	Non-ferrous metals		416	531	832	1147		331	389	221	223		536.7	2254.2	3763.3	5848.8
381	Fabricated metal products		5834	4172	6927	8000		421	351	321	310		256.7	774.7	1545.2	2462.9
3811	Cutlery, hand tools and general hardware		1891	1514	2727	3056		99	87	90	84		52.1	187.0	384.3	577.9
3812	Furniture and fixtures primarily of metal		2114	1156	1927	2164		137	106	76	69		75.5	206.1	308.3	420.4
3813	Structural metal products		695	986	1534	1887		107	104	103	107		88.8	287.5	664.6	1175.3
3819	Other fabricated metal products		1134	516	739	893		78	55	52	51		40.3	94.1	188.1	289.3
382	Non-electrical machinery		6904	9707	14960	18899		3090	2622	2331	2118		1761.4	5383.9	10602.3	16173.5
3821	Engines and turbines		123	137	173	204		150	135	125	120		99.0	304.0	653.8	1072.0
3822	Agricultural machinery and equipment		541	629	974	1015		600	533	453	405		276.3	912.5	1493.5	2171.6
3823	Metal and wood working machinery		638	707	951	1225		217	182	156	136		108.3	312.8	680.2	912.7
3824	Other special industrial machinery		2411	2827	4323	4501		661	540	482	454		460.5	1360.4	2800.0	4681.8
3825	Office, computing and accounting machinery		780	2925	4529	6995		110	94	98	89		41.5	133.0	365.6	513.8
3829	Other non-electrical machinery & equipment		2681	2482	4010	4959		1353	1139	1018	914		773.1	2354.4	4609.1	6821.7
383	Electrical machinery		1764	1883	2808	3630		644	516	471	440		334.5	924.4	1710.9	3188.6
3831	Electrical industrial machinery		1275	1343	1885	2547		494	384	341	319		232.0	641.1	1402.3	2164.8
3832	Radio, television and communication equipm.	a/	...	...	...	...	a/	...	...	...	...	a/	...	...	...	...
3833	Electrical appliances and housewares		112	185	465	483		22	17	18	16		14.3	32.5	70.3	86.5
3839	Other electrical apparatus and supplies		377	355	458	600		128	115	112	105		88.2	250.8	579.8	937.3
384	Transport equipment		4170	2850	4204	5118		1415	1263	1181	1080		1115.4	3641.7	7283.4	11032.1
3841	Shipbuilding and repairing	a/	...	...	...	...	a/	...	...	...	...	a/	...	...	...	...
3842	Railroad equipment		160	209	268	322		217	200	196	169		162.3	557.8	1256.7	1664.4
3843	Motor vehicles		2636	2267	3609	4470		910	814	778	731		764.7	2521.1	5515.7	7943.5
3844	Motorcycles and bicycles		17	19	28	28		19	18	19	17		13.1	28.9	60.6	80.5
3845	Aircraft	a/	...	...	...	...	a/	...	...	...	...	a/	...	...	...	...
3849	Other transport equipment		1357	355	299	298		270	231	188	164		175.3	533.9	988.6	1343.7
385	Professional and scientific equipment		1967	1879	2643	3034		394	307	265	263		185.5	553.7	967.3	1301.3
3851	Prof. and scientific equipment n.e.c.		1883	1689	2437	2766		211	161	157	155		99.9	308.9	571.2	905.2
3852	Photographic and optical goods		61	141	151	200		115	91	66	66		54.1	166.7	284.2	276.3
3853	Watches and clocks		23	49	55	68		67	55	42	42		31.5	78.1	119.9	119.9
390	Other manufacturing industries		17997	7217	10598	8770		385	236	260	231		186.8	460.8	1112.0	1560.1
3901	Jewellery and related articles		213	232	369	430		21	20	23	21		20.7	59.1	127.2	213.3
3902	Musical instruments		50	86	155	102		12	9	7	5		4.7	10.7	19.7	22.2
3903	Sporting and athletic goods		33	87	122	165		2	2	2	3		1.3	3.1	9.9	20.0
3909	Manufacturing industries, n.e.c.		17701	6812	9952	8073		350	204	228	203		160.0	387.8	955.2	1304.6
3	Total manufacturing	b/	87548	78420	112496	129359	b/	16372	14353	13181	12139	b/	11316.3	34602.2	72980.6	110562.0

a/ Data suppressed due to confidentiality rules.
b/ Including ISIC 3832,3841 and 3845.

ISIC Revision 2		Output in producers' prices					Value added					Gross fixed capital formation	
		(billion ROUBLES)					(billion ROUBLES)					(million ROUBLES)	
ISIC Industry	Note	1993	1994	1995	1996	Note	1993	1994	1995	1996	Note	1995	1996
311/2 Food products		16445	47546	125539	163512		5603	18299	39992	...		...	...
3111 Slaughtering, preparing & preserving meat		4711	13041	29555	37048		1223	4056	6906	...		...	...
3112 Dairy products		2337	6872	22226	25838		648	2333	5416	...		...	...
3113 Canning, preserving of fruits & vegetables		430	895	1821	2158		227	461	755	...		...	...
3114 Canning, preserving and processing of fish		1704	4570	13790	15527		849	2485	6179	...		...	...
3115 Vegetable and animal oils and fats		656	1896	4890	5655		229	729	1872	...		...	...
3116 Grain mill products		1545	4868	14243	22713		379	1444	4472	...		...	...
3117 Bakery products		1614	7137	19465	29325		683	3467	7270	...		...	...
3118 Sugar factories and refineries		1039	1162	3370	4377		469	564	1296	...		...	...
3119 Cocoa, chocolate and sugar confectionery		1038	3221	8333	11376		509	1612	3316	...		...	...
3121 Other food products		295	758	1313	1409		145	342	762	...		...	...
3122 Prepared animal feeds		1076	3126	6533	8086		242	806	1748	...		...	...
313 Beverages		973	2778	8407	14037		517	1504	4002	...		...	...
3131 Distilling, rectifying and blending spirits		474	1080	3339	4269		231	498	1447	...		...	...
3132 Wine industries		210	606	1244	1983		116	323	554	...		...	...
3133 Malt liquors and malt		225	863	2699	5177		137	546	1468	...		...	...
3134 Soft drinks and carbonated waters		64	229	1125	2608		33	137	533	...		...	...
314 Tobacco		371	673	1847	2767		160	315	845	...		...	...
321 Textiles		3611	5910	13904	13237		1549	2824	5541	...		...	...
3211 Spinning, weaving and finishing textiles		2223	3280	8031	7255		796	1481	3225	...		...	...
3212 Made-up textile goods excl. wearing apparel		74	150	308	290		58	90	233	...		...	...
3213 Knitting mills		557	1030	1825	1795		381	620	886	...		...	...
3214 Carpets and rugs		334	470	921	848		116	192	301	...		...	...
3215 Cordage, rope and twine		38	85	251	330		20	43	100	...		...	...
3219 Other textiles		385	895	2568	2719		178	398	796	...		...	...
322 Wearing apparel, except footwear		1339	3028	6167	7390		926	1794	3158	...		...	...
323 Leather and fur products		439	963	2018	2203		256	495	964	...		...	...
3231 Tanneries and leather finishing		192	391	818	733		117	196	360	...		...	...
3232 Fur dressing and dyeing industries		163	425	876	1073		81	210	425	...		...	...
3233 Leather prods. excl. wearing apparel		84	147	324	397		58	89	179	...		...	...
324 Footwear, except rubber or plastic		666	1169	2114	2843		454	646	924	...		...	...
331 Wood products, except furniture		1525	4780	11718	14255		843	1996	4386	...		...	...
3311 Sawmills, planing and other wood mills		1286	4201	10251	12609		738	1758	3801	...		...	...
3312 Wooden and cane containers		46	136	366	367		25	59	135	...		...	...
3319 Other wood and cork products		193	443	1101	1279		80	179	450	...		...	...
332 Furniture and fixtures, excl. metal		1095	2852	6419	7024		615	1226	2364	...		...	...
341 Paper and products		1191	4706	20925	16577		524	1871	8360	...		...	...
3411 Pulp, paper and paperboard articles		1077	4224	19164	14821		453	1626	7617	...		...	...
3412 Containers of paper and paperboard		58	272	1186	1086		35	126	434	...		...	...
3419 Other pulp, paper and paperboard articles		56	210	572	670		36	119	309	...		...	...
342 Printing and publishing		332	1310	3404	5346		254	900	1956	...		...	...
351 Industrial chemicals		5962	18457	53093	54187		2670	8210	16421	...		...	...
3511 Basic chemicals excl. fertilizers		3752	12948	34944	34714		1876	6240	11650	...		...	...
3512 Fertilizers and pesticides		440	1242	3510	3546		162	422	713	...		...	...
3513 Synthetic resins and plastic materials		1770	4267	14639	15927		632	1548	4058	...		...	...
352 Other chemicals		1422	4448	13692	21465		687	2501	6238	...		...	...
3521 Paints, varnishes and lacquers		356	1049	3494	4264		195	592	1463	...		...	...
3522 Drugs and medicines		471	1895	4629	6311		236	1062	2201	...		...	...
3523 Soap, cleaning preps., perfumes, cosmetics		180	527	1626	5221		92	265	726	...		...	...
3529 Other chemical products		415	977	3943	5669		164	582	1848	...		...	...
353 Petroleum refineries		8388	18836	49016	58969		1800	4599	14965	...		...	...

ISIC	Industry												
354	Misc. petroleum and coal products		1274	3937	12746	17000		475	1501	4419	...	...	...
355	Rubber products		1260	3019	10277	15754		480	1407	3675	...	...	...
3551	Tyres and tubes		749	1661	5960	9778		206	665	1956	...	...	...
3559	Other rubber products		511	1358	4317	5976		274	742	1719	...	...	...
356	Plastic products		332	982	3245	4242		181	588	1360	...	...	...
361	Pottery, china, earthenware		338	920	2665	2992		217	536	1259	...	...	...
362	Glass and products		367	1110	3382	4140		187	512	1584	...	...	...
369	Other non-metallic mineral products		4539	14712	41241	49933		2283	7340	16091	...	...	...
3691	Structural clay products		271	855	2870	2033		182	586	1565	...	...	...
3692	Cement, lime and plaster		519	1864	5722	7433		207	776	1949	...	...	...
3699	Other non-metallic mineral products		3749	11993	32649	40467		1894	5978	12577	...	...	...
371	Iron and steel		8657	25539	79991	91941		4194	10227	23534	...	...	...
372	Non-ferrous metals		6421	16865	48295	50617		3571	9439	24676	...	...	...
381	Fabricated metal products		1236	3352	10024	14563		746	2000	4698	...	...	...
3811	Cutlery, hand tools and general hardware		215	715	2226	3100		164	420	1112	...	...	...
3812	Furniture and fixtures primarily of metal		308	750	2163	2659		163	458	979	...	...	...
3813	Structural metal products		457	1317	4163	7052		305	756	1950	...	...	...
3819	Other fabricated metal products		256	570	1472	1752		114	366	657	...	...	...
382	Non-electrical machinery		7615	23069	61473	95790		4844	15187	34611	...	...	...
3821	Engines and turbines		498	1733	4576	6725		264	1034	2308	...	...	...
3822	Agricultural machinery and equipment		824	2390	5401	7445		551	1532	2812	...	...	...
3823	Metal and wood working machinery		377	1058	2546	3126		236	692	1712	...	...	...
3824	Other special industrial machinery		1920	6162	15932	20816		1155	4396	9604	...	...	...
3825	Office, computing and accounting machinery		275	1049	2526	4505		199	680	1364	...	...	...
3829	Other non-electrical machinery & equipment		3721	10677	30492	53173		2439	6853	16811	...	...	...
383	Electrical machinery		2312	5514	16257	18913		1313	3093	8398	...	...	...
3831	Electrical industrial machinery		1061	2874	8516	10661		671	1877	5487	...	...	...
3832	Radio, television and communication equipm.	a/	...	...	...	...		...a/	...a/	...a/	...	...	...
3833	Electrical appliances and housewares		180	284	506	467		63	94	212	...	...	...
3839	Other electrical apparatus and supplies		1071	2356	7235	7785		579	1122	2699	...	...	...
384	Transport equipment		8868	23426	53522	72121		4338	11267	9458	...	...	...
3841	Shipbuilding and repairing	a/	...	...	...	...		...a/	...a/	...a/	...	...	...
3842	Railroad equipment		812	3191	8832	11891		544	2099	4455	...	...	...
3843	Motor vehicles		6522	16232	43367	58442		3534	7722	3993	...	...	...
3844	Motorcycles and bicycles		89	180	296	356		46	64	75	...	...	...
3845	Aircraft	a/	...	...	...	...		...a/	...a/	...a/	...	...	...
3849	Other transport equipment		1445	3823	1027	1432		214	1382	935	...	...	...
385	Professional and scientific equipment		946	2443	4130	5642		670	1853	2591	...	...	...
3851	Prof. and scientific equipment n.e.c.		606	1702	2755	4157		463	1382	1705	...	...	...
3852	Photographic and optical goods		162	462	931	1086		106	303	628	...	...	...
3853	Watches and clocks		178	279	444	399		101	168	258	...	...	...
390	Other manufacturing industries		1265	3730	9521	11411		600	1802	4154	...	...	...
3901	Jewellery and related articles		445	1396	2408	2631		104	314	484	...	...	...
3902	Musical instruments		18	33	69	77		16	21	41	...	...	...
3903	Sporting and athletic goods		4	15	44	85		3	12	19	...	...	...
3909	Manufacturing industries, n.e.c.		798	2286	7000	8618		477	1455	3610	...	...	...
3	Total manufacturing	b/	92820	256611	697497	871806	b/	43171	119436	266232	...	...	...

a/ Data suppressed due to confidentiality rules.
b/ Including ISIC 3832,3841 and 3845.

Russian Federation

ISIC Revision 2		Index numbers of industrial production											
		(1990=100)											
ISIC Industry	Note	1985	1986	1987	1988	1989	1990	1991	1992	1993	1994	1995	1996
311/2 Food products	a/	...	...	...	...	...	100	93	86	82	67	58	52
313 Beverages	a/	...	...	...	...	...	...	...	...	...	...	...	...
314 Tobacco		...	...	...	...	...	100	93	86	82	80	83	81
321 Textiles		...	...	...	...	...	100	82	63	48	25	18	14
322 Wearing apparel, except footwear		...	...	...	...	...	100	85	70	59	28	19	16
323 Leather and fur products	b/	...	...	...	...	...	100	85	70	55	26	18	13
324 Footwear, except rubber or plastic	b/	...	...	...	...	...	...	...	...	...	...	...	...
331 Wood products, except furniture		...	...	...	...	...	100	89	78	63	40	44	36
332 Furniture and fixtures, excl. metal		...	...	...	...	...	...	...	...	...	...	...	...
341 Paper and products		...	...	...	...	...	100	89	78	63	47	58	47
342 Printing and publishing		...	...	...	...	...	...	...	...	...	...	...	...
351 Industrial chemicals	c/	...	...	...	...	...	100	86	71	57	42	44	39
352 Other chemicals	c/	...	...	...	...	...	...	...	...	...	...	...	...
353 Petroleum refineries	d/	...	...	...	...	...	100	89	78	59	51	52	52
354 Misc. petroleum and coal products	d/	...	...	...	...	...	...	...	...	...	...	...	...
355 Rubber products		...	...	...	...	...	...	...	...	...	...	...	...
356 Plastic products		...	...	...	...	...	...	...	...	...	...	...	...
361 Pottery, china, earthenware		...	...	...	...	...	...	...	...	...	...	...	...
362 Glass and products		...	...	...	...	...	...	...	...	...	...	...	...
369 Other non-metallic mineral products		...	...	...	...	...	...	...	...	...	...	...	...
371 Iron and steel	e/	...	...	...	...	...	100	88	77	65	56	60	59
372 Non-ferrous metals	e/	...	...	...	...	...	...	...	...	...	...	...	...
381 Fabricated metal products		...	...	...	...	...	...	...	...	...	...	...	...
382 Non-electrical machinery		...	...	...	...	...	100	85	75	63	46	32	24
383 Electrical machinery		...	...	...	...	...	...	...	...	...	...	...	...
384 Transport equipment		...	...	...	...	...	...	...	...	...	...	...	...
385 Professional and scientific equipment		...	...	...	...	...	...	...	...	...	...	...	...
390 Other manufacturing industries		...	...	...	...	...	...	...	...	...	...	...	...
3 Total manufacturing		...	...	...	...	...	...	...	...	...	...	...	...

a/ 311/2 includes 313.
b/ 323 includes 324.
c/ 351 includes 352.
d/ 353 includes 354.
e/ 371 includes 372.

SENEGAL

Supplier of information:
Direction de la statistique, Ministère de l'économie et des finances, Dakar.

Basic source of data:
Survey of industrial activities.

Major deviations from ISIC (Revision 2):
Data collected under the national classification system have been reclassified by the national authorities to correspond with ISIC (Rev. 2). Lack of detail in national data, however, results in several cases where exact correspondence with the ISIC cannot be achieved. Data for food products (ISIC 311/2) exclude the processing of fish.

Reference period (if not calendar year):

Scope:
All establishments excluding handicrafts.

Method of enumeration:
Not reported.

Adjusted for non-response:
Not reported.

Concepts and definitions of variables:
No deviations from the standard UN concepts and definitions are reported.

Related national publications:
Comptes économiques (annual) published by the Direction de la statistique, Ministère de l'économie et des finances, Dakar.

Senegal

ISIC Revision 2	Number of establishments					Number of persons engaged					Wages and salaries paid to employees				
		(numbers)					(numbers)					(million CFA FRANCS)			
ISIC Industry	Note	1993	1994	1995	1996	Note	1993	1994	1995	1996	Note	1993	1994	1995	1996
311/2 Food products		44	53	64	63		13557	15505	17045	17714		19337	20687	...	25462
3111 Slaughtering, preparing & preserving meat		2	4	4	3		31	259	1299	296		...	225	675	538
3112 Dairy products		3	3	3	3		329	292	289	262		...	1335	1039	1293
3113 Canning, preserving of fruits & vegetables		2	2	1	2		501	249	454	217		...	113	202	44
3114 Canning, preserving and processing of fish		8	12	16	15		2713	5216	4793	4961		...	3924	3456	3297
3115 Vegetable and animal oils and fats		1	1	1	2		2250	2175	2271	2355		...	4107	4287	4701
3116 Grain mill products		2	2	3	2		621	448	1447	1417		...	989	1189	2109
3117 Bakery products		15	19	22	19		481	478	566	308		...	518	634	372
3118 Sugar factories and refineries		1	1	1	1		6252	6119	5556	7456		...	9339	...	12406
3119 Cocoa, chocolate and sugar confectionery		2	1	1	2		227	132	97	245		...	19	250	444
3121 Other food products		6	6	9	12		103	115	205	173		...	94	297	205
3122 Prepared animal feeds		2	2	3	2		49	22	68	24		...	24	121	53
313 Beverages		3	4	5	5		381	359	348	362		1100	1300	1223	1295
3131 Distilling, rectifying and blending spirits		-	-	-	-		-	-	-	-		...	-	-	-
3132 Wine industries		-	-	-	-		-	-	-	-		...	-	-	-
3133 Malt liquors and malt	a/	3	4	5	5	a/	381	359	348	362		...	1300a/	1223a/	1295a/
3134 Soft drinks and carbonated waters	a/	...	...	...	...	a/	...	...	...	...		...	...a/	...a/	...a/
314 Tobacco		2	1	1	1		321	321	321	286		1066	1317	1533	1580
321 Textiles		7	10	11	12		1775	2340	2433	1912		2279	5307	2605	1134
3211 Spinning, weaving and finishing textiles		5	9	9	8		1690	2250	2353	1795		...	5187	2586	1038
3212 Made-up textile goods excl. wearing apparel		-	-	-	1		-	-	-	...		...	-	-	...
3213 Knitting mills		1	-	1	2		...	-	80	20		...	-	19	41
3214 Carpets and rugs		1	1	1	-		85	90	...	-		...	120	...	-
3215 Cordage, rope and twine		-	-	-	-		-	-	-	-		...	-	-	-
3219 Other textiles		-	-	-	1		-	-	-	97		...	-	-	55
322 Wearing apparel, except footwear		2	-	2	2		621	-	621	621		465	-	...	...
323 Leather and fur products		-	-	1	1		-	-	...	3		-	-	...	2
3231 Tanneries and leather finishing		...	...	1	1		...	...	...	3		...	...	...	2
3232 Fur dressing and dyeing industries		...	...	-	-		...	...	-	-		...	...	-	-
3233 Leather prods. excl. wearing apparel		...	...	-	-		...	...	-	-		...	...	-	-
324 Footwear, except rubber or plastic		-	-	-	2		-	-	...	81		-	-	...	78
331 Wood products, except furniture		3	2	3	2		171	68	88	68		114	110	171	156
3311 Sawmills, planing and other wood mills		...	2	3	2		...	68	88	68		...	110	171	156
3312 Wooden and cane containers		...	-	-	-		...	-	-	-		...	-	-	-
3319 Other wood and cork products		...	-	-	-		...	-	-	-		...	-	-	-
332 Furniture and fixtures, excl. metal		4	5	6	4		63	87	98	77		54	65	71	54
341 Paper and products		4	3	6	7		291	278	743	1452		600	605	1016	969
3411 Pulp, paper and paperboard articles		...	-	-	-		...	-	-	-		...	-	-	-
3412 Containers of paper and paperboard		...	2	4	5		...	271	730	1435		...	596	1001	964
3419 Other pulp, paper and paperboard articles		...	1	2	2		...	7	13	17		...	9	15	5
342 Printing and publishing		16	18	24	24		672	870	683	466		1391	1182	1868	1165
351 Industrial chemicals		10	10	8	9		1311	1362	1375	2839		3118	3629	3680	8082
3511 Basic chemicals excl. fertilizers		...	6	4	5		...	1120	1087	2611		...	2978	2906	7398
3512 Fertilizers and pesticides		...	2	2	2		...	135	141	120		...	471	597	527
3513 Synthetic resins and plastic materials		...	2	2	2		...	107	147	108		...	180	177	157
352 Other chemicals		11	15	16	16		759	909	1338	1975		1603	3137	2968	3195
3521 Paints, varnishes and lacquers		...	4	5	3		...	120	189	247		...	257	454	350
3522 Drugs and medicines		...	3	3	3		...	237	246	191		...	1260	871	334
3523 Soap, cleaning preps., perfumes, cosmetics		...	4	4	6		...	415	764	1364		...	1329	1369	2236
3529 Other chemical products		...	4	4	4		...	137	139	173		...	291	274	275
353 Petroleum refineries		1	1	1	1		299	228	228	229		1008	1143	1179	1245

ISIC												
354 Misc. petroleum and coal products	2	2	-	-	32	28	-	-	72	53	-	-
355 Rubber products	1	1	1	1	9	6	6	...	8	5	...	...
3551 Tyres and tubes	...	1	1	1	...	6	6	...	...	5	...	...
3559 Other rubber products	...	-	-	-	...	-	-	-	...	-	-	-
356 Plastic products	14	16	20	19	855	2545	1558	787	898	1286	995	901
361 Pottery, china, earthenware	-	-	-	-	-	-	-	-	-	-	-	-
362 Glass and products	-	-	-	-	-	-	-	-	-	-	-	-
369 Other non-metallic mineral products	4	2	4	4	735	725	380	436	1204	1308	15	1815
3691 Structural clay products	...	-	-	-	...	-	-	-	...	-	-	-
3692 Cement, lime and plaster	...	1	1	1	...	301	296	303	...	979	1	1496
3699 Other non-metallic mineral products	...	1	3	3	...	424	84	133	...	329	14	319
371 Iron and steel	-	-	-	-	-	-	-	-	-	-	-	-
372 Non-ferrous metals	-	-	-	-	-	-	-	-	-	-	-	-
381 Fabricated metal products	11	12	19	17	545	583	942	769	1132	1386	1508	1745
3811 Cutlery, hand tools and general hardware	...	-	1	1	...	-	7	7	...	-	16	16
3812 Furniture and fixtures primarily of metal	...	4	5	3	...	121	213	55	...	96	200	92
3813 Structural metal products	...	4	7	9	...	140	294	377	...	253	202	698
3819 Other fabricated metal products	...	4	6	4	...	322	428	330	...	1037	1090	939
382 Non-electrical machinery	1	1	4	4	216	116	167	227	314	168	2	352
3821 Engines and turbines	...	-	-	1	...	-	-	1	...	-	-	14
3822 Agricultural machinery and equipment	...	1	3	2	...	116	161	225	...	168	...	335
3823 Metal and wood working machinery	...	-	-	-	...	-	-	-	...	-	-	-
3824 Other special industrial machinery	...	-	-	1	...	-	-	1	...	-	-	3
3825 Office, computing and accounting machinery	...	-	-	-	...	-	-	-	...	-	-	-
3829 Other non-electrical machinery & equipment	...	-	1	-	...	-	6	-	...	-	2	-
383 Electrical machinery	1	1	3	3	251	173	169	200	482	515	508	420
3831 Electrical industrial machinery	...	-	-	-	...	-	-	-	...	-	-	-
3832 Radio, television and communication equipm.	...	-	-	-	...	-	-	-	...	-	-	-
3833 Electrical appliances and housewares	...	-	-	-	...	-	-	-	...	-	-	-
3839 Other electrical apparatus and supplies	...	1	3	3	...	173	169	200	...	515	508	420
384 Transport equipment	8	10	10	8	375	1548	1094	259	1141	2715	1324	548
3841 Shipbuilding and repairing	...	4	4	3	...	1213	669	44	...	1944	561	120
3842 Railroad equipment	...	1	1	1	...	25	27	28	...	36	20	63
3843 Motor vehicles	...	4	5	4	...	292	398	187	...	689	743	365
3844 Motorcycles and bicycles	...	1	-	-	...	18	-	-	...	46	-	-
3845 Aircraft	...	-	-	-	...	-	-	-	...	-	-	-
3849 Other transport equipment	...	-	-	-	...	-	-	-	...	-	-	-
385 Professional and scientific equipment	-	-	-	1	-	-	-	23	-	-	-	8
3851 Prof. and scientific equipment n.e.c.	...	-	-	1	...	-	-	23	...	-	-	8
3852 Photographic and optical goods	...	-	-	-	...	-	-	-	...	-	-	-
3853 Watches and clocks	...	-	-	-	...	-	-	-	...	-	-	-
390 Other manufacturing industries	1	2	1	-	2	3	1	-	1	3	1	-
3901 Jewellery and related articles	...	2	1	-	...	3	1	-	...	3	1	-
3902 Musical instruments	...	-	-	-	...	-	-	-	...	-	-	-
3903 Sporting and athletic goods	...	-	-	-	...	-	-	-	...	-	-	-
3909 Manufacturing industries, n.e.c.	...	-	-	-	...	-	-	-	...	-	-	-
3 Total manufacturing	150	169	210	206	23241	28054	29638	30786	37387	45921	32817	50206

a/ 3133 includes 3134.

Senegal

ISIC Revision 2		Output					Value added in producers' prices					Gross fixed capital formation	
		(million CFA FRANCS)					(million CFA FRANCS)					(million CFA FRANCS)	
ISIC Industry	Note	1993	1994	1995	1996	Note	1993	1994	1995	1996	Note	1995	1996
311/2 Food products		...	...	273390	264368		47037	71606	64464	57026		...	...
3111 Slaughtering, preparing & preserving meat		...	...	5404	4323		...	1475	1966	1329		...	...
3112 Dairy products		...	...	17249	20068		...	3558	4184	4489		...	...
3113 Canning, preserving of fruits & vegetables		...	...	3876	6781		...	1176	870	638		...	...
3114 Canning, preserving and processing of fish		...	...	39249	54889		...	11199	8385	8154		...	...
3115 Vegetable and animal oils and fats		...	...	105198	96945		...	15270	14931	18620		...	...
3116 Grain mill products		...	...	34997	8620		...	7160	9261	8574		...	...
3117 Bakery products		...	...	5584	9376		...	1193	1565	1582		...	...
3118 Sugar factories and refineries		...	...	51215	46892		...	29626	20994	10803		...	...
3119 Cocoa, chocolate and sugar confectionery		...	...	1778	6090		...	722	670	1068		...	...
3121 Other food products		...	...	6144	6697		...	169	1418	1514		...	...
3122 Prepared animal feeds		...	...	2696	3687		...	58	220	255		...	...
313 Beverages		...	...	18071	21562		4693	4997	1077	6064		...	...
3131 Distilling, rectifying and blending spirits		...	...	-	-		...	-	-	-		...	...
3132 Wine industries		...	...	-	-		...	-	-	-		...	...
3133 Malt liquors and malt		...	...	18071a/	21562a/		...	4997a/	1077a/	6064a/		...	...
3134 Soft drinks and carbonated waters		...	...	...a/	...a/		...	...a/	...a/	...a/		...	...
314 Tobacco		...	...	16940	18355		4197	6533	6148	6143		...	...
321 Textiles		...	...	29817	19760		906	8733	7964	5054		...	...
3211 Spinning, weaving and finishing textiles		...	...	29630	18047		...	8518	7880	4614		...	...
3212 Made-up textile goods excl. wearing apparel		...	...	-	69		...	-	-	24		...	...
3213 Knitting mills		...	...	77	142		...	-	40	25		...	...
3214 Carpets and rugs		...	...	110	-		...	215	44	-		...	...
3215 Cordage, rope and twine		...	...	-	-		...	-	-	-		...	...
3219 Other textiles		...	...	-	1502		...	-	-	391		...	...
322 Wearing apparel, except footwear		...	...	141	191		1382	-	6	3		...	...
323 Leather and fur products		...	...	88	172		-	-	5	50		...	...
3231 Tanneries and leather finishing		...	...	88	172		...	...	5	50		...	...
3232 Fur dressing and dyeing industries		...	...	-	-		...	...	-	-		...	...
3233 Leather prods. excl. wearing apparel		...	...	-	-		...	...	-	-		...	...
324 Footwear, except rubber or plastic		...	...	-	742		-	-	-	222		...	...
331 Wood products, except furniture		...	...	4604	4486		227	400	579	503		...	...
3311 Sawmills, planing and other wood mills		...	...	4604	4486		...	400	579	503		...	...
3312 Wooden and cane containers		...	...	-	-		...	-	-	-		...	...
3319 Other wood and cork products		...	...	-	-		...	-	-	-		...	...
332 Furniture and fixtures, excl. metal		...	...	474	570		59	151	92	97		...	...
341 Paper and products		...	...	13900	15931		1499	2068	2356	2076		...	...
3411 Pulp, paper and paperboard articles		...	...	-	-		...	-	-	-		...	...
3412 Containers of paper and paperboard		...	...	13724	15728		...	2040	2312	2056		...	...
3419 Other pulp, paper and paperboard articles		...	...	176	203		...	28	44	20		...	...
342 Printing and publishing		...	...	10375	9017		2366	2630	3664	2996		...	...
351 Industrial chemicals		...	...	91729	116064		7745	28775	25972	33313		...	...
3511 Basic chemicals excl. fertilizers		...	...	81521	105538		...	25964	23656	31432		...	...
3512 Fertilizers and pesticides		...	...	8367	8400		...	2402	1851	1646		...	...
3513 Synthetic resins and plastic materials		...	...	1841	2126		...	409	465	235		...	...
352 Other chemicals		...	...	45534	44190		5309	11154	13284	14854		...	...
3521 Paints, varnishes and lacquers		...	...	6428	4768		...	1357	1431	744		...	...
3522 Drugs and medicines		...	...	8466	9495		...	3002	3212	5378		...	...
3523 Soap, cleaning preps., perfumes, cosmetics		...	...	28001	27328		...	6027	7857	8215		...	...
3529 Other chemical products		...	...	2639	2599		...	768	784	517		...	...
353 Petroleum refineries		...	...	84795	100976		3700	9247	6324	5795		...	...

ISIC	Industry										
354	Misc. petroleum and coal products	...	...	-	-	65	137	-	-	...	...
355	Rubber products	...	...	109	75	-3	25	43	13	...	...
3551	Tyres and tubes	...	...	109	75	...	25	43	13	...	...
3559	Other rubber products	...	...	-	-	...	-	-	-	...	...
356	Plastic products	...	...	12151	13465	2155	3711	2551	2542	...	...
361	Pottery, china, earthenware	...	...	-	-	-	-	-	-	...	...
362	Glass and products	...	...	-	-	-	-	-	-	...	...
369	Other non-metallic mineral products	...	...	27420	34787	8410	11156	9632	11627	...	...
3691	Structural clay products	...	...	-	-	...	-	-	-	...	...
3692	Cement, lime and plaster	...	...	25654	32736	...	10306	8767	10668	...	...
3699	Other non-metallic mineral products	...	...	1766	2051	...	850	865	959	...	...
371	Iron and steel	...	...	-	-	-	-	-	-	...	...
372	Non-ferrous metals	...	...	-	-	-	-	-	-	...	...
381	Fabricated metal products	...	...	25713	22252	3232	6062	6237	6507	...	...
3811	Cutlery, hand tools and general hardware	...	...	53	50	...	-	7	11	...	...
3812	Furniture and fixtures primarily of metal	...	...	1724	947	...	157	514	300	...	...
3813	Structural metal products	...	...	8411	9396	...	1170	1024	1323	...	...
3819	Other fabricated metal products	...	...	15525	11859	...	4735	4692	4873	...	...
382	Non-electrical machinery	...	...	2231	4022	378	394	569	791	...	...
3821	Engines and turbines	...	...	-	1435	...	-	-	21	...	...
3822	Agricultural machinery and equipment	...	...	2227	2531	...	394	567	763	...	...
3823	Metal and wood working machinery	...	...	-	-	...	-	-	-	...	...
3824	Other special industrial machinery	...	...	-	49	...	-	-	7	...	...
3825	Office, computing and accounting machinery	...	...	-	-	...	-	-	-	...	...
3829	Other non-electrical machinery & equipment	...	...	4	7	...	-	2	-	...	...
383	Electrical machinery	...	...	5021	5516	717	57	750	-98	...	...
3831	Electrical industrial machinery	...	...	-	-	...	-	-	-	...	...
3832	Radio, television and communication equipm.	...	...	-	-	...	-	-	-	...	...
3833	Electrical appliances and housewares	...	...	-	-	...	-	-	-	...	...
3839	Other electrical apparatus and supplies	...	...	5021	5516	...	57	750	-98	...	...
384	Transport equipment	...	...	14136	5859	2209	4033	5372	2521	...	...
3841	Shipbuilding and repairing	...	...	5508	3087	...	2451	3209	1593	...	...
3842	Railroad equipment	...	...	174	316	...	66	31	146	...	...
3843	Motor vehicles	...	...	8454	2456	...	1420	2132	782	...	...
3844	Motorcycles and bicycles	...	...	-	-	...	96	-	-	...	...
3845	Aircraft	...	...	-	-	...	-	-	-	...	...
3849	Other transport equipment	...	...	-	-	...	-	-	-	...	...
385	Professional and scientific equipment	...	...	-	105	-	-	-	17	...	...
3851	Prof. and scientific equipment n.e.c.	...	...	-	105	...	-	-	17	...	...
3852	Photographic and optical goods	...	...	-	-	...	-	-	-	...	...
3853	Watches and clocks	...	...	-	-	...	-	-	-	...	...
390	Other manufacturing industries	...	...	5	-	-4	2	-3	-	...	...
3901	Jewellery and related articles	...	...	5	-	...	2	-3	-	...	...
3902	Musical instruments	...	...	-	-	...	-	-	-	...	...
3903	Sporting and athletic goods	...	...	-	-	...	-	-	-	...	...
3909	Manufacturing industries, n.e.c.	...	...	-	-	...	-	-	-	...	...
3	Total manufacturing	...	...	676644	702465	96279	171871	157086	158116	...	...

a/ 3133 includes 3134.

Senegal

ISIC Revision 2		Index numbers of industrial production (1990=100)											
ISIC Industry	Note	1985	1986	1987	1988	1989	1990	1991	1992	1993	1994	1995	1996
311/2 Food products	a/	92	74	98	93	97	100	82	86	86	90	99	91
313 Beverages	a/	...	...	...	...	...	...	...	...	...	...	...	...
314 Tobacco		133	126	90	61	78	100	89	78	76	72	94	63
321 Textiles		169	102	139	157	82	100	91	92	81	84	70	75
322 Wearing apparel, except footwear		...	...	...	...	...	...	...	...	...	...	...	...
323 Leather and fur products		...	...	...	...	...	...	...	...	...	...	...	...
324 Footwear, except rubber or plastic		...	...	...	...	...	...	...	...	...	...	...	...
331 Wood products, except furniture		125	106	136	91	70	100	110	108	106	90	103	105
332 Furniture and fixtures, excl. metal		...	...	...	...	...	...	...	...	...	...	...	...
341 Paper and products		93	137	92	91	93	100	100	82	75	85	77	77
342 Printing and publishing		...	...	...	...	...	...	...	...	...	...	...	...
351 Industrial chemicals	b/	90	88	104	101	85	100	113	105	106	92	121	115
352 Other chemicals	b/	...	...	...	...	...	...	...	...	...	...	...	...
353 Petroleum refineries	b/	...	...	...	...	...	...	...	...	...	...	...	...
354 Misc. petroleum and coal products	b/	...	...	...	...	...	...	...	...	...	...	...	...
355 Rubber products	b/	...	...	...	...	...	...	...	...	...	...	...	...
356 Plastic products	b/	...	...	...	...	...	...	...	...	...	...	...	...
361 Pottery, china, earthenware		...	...	...	...	...	...	...	...	...	...	...	...
362 Glass and products		...	...	...	...	...	...	...	...	...	...	...	...
369 Other non-metallic mineral products		86	79	72	81	77	100	101	117	116	139	140	159
371 Iron and steel		...	...	...	...	...	...	...	...	...	...	...	...
372 Non-ferrous metals		...	...	...	...	...	...	...	...	...	...	...	...
381 Fabricated metal products		67	77	79	64	51	100	103	90	98	89	96	92
382 Non-electrical machinery		...	...	77	79	65	100	118	88	84	74	113	103
383 Electrical machinery		369	286	231	241	276	100	29	21	26	25	38	37
384 Transport equipment		69	37	100	81	52	100	81	91	92	80	129	125
385 Professional and scientific equipment		...	...	...	...	...	...	...	...	...	...	...	...
390 Other manufacturing industries		...	...	...	...	...	...	...	...	...	...	...	...
3 Total manufacturing		...	...	...	...	...	...	...	...	...	...	...	...

a/ 311/2 includes 313.
b/ 351 includes 352, 353, 354, 355 and 356.

SINGAPORE

Supplier of information:
Research and Statistics Unit, Economic Development Board, Singapore.

Basic source of data:
Annual census of industrial production.

Major deviations from ISIC (Revision 3):
Data collected under the national classification system have been reclassified by the national authorities to correspond approximately with ISIC (Rev. 3).

Reference period (if not calendar year):
Establishments with financial years ending on or before 31 March are allowed to report on a financial year basis.

Scope:
All establishments in the private sector with 10 or more persons engaged.

Method of enumeration:
The census is conducted primarily by mail.

Adjusted for non-response:
Yes.

Concepts and definitions of variables:
Persons engaged is as of the pay period nearest to 30 June of the reference year.
Wages and salaries is compensation of employees.
Output does not include net revenues from goods shipped in the same condition as received.

Related national publications:
Report on the Census of Industrial Production (annual), published by the Economic Development Board, Singapore. Yearbook of Statistics, Singapore, published by the Department of Statistics, Singapore.

Singapore

ISIC Revision 3 ISIC Industry	Number of establishments Note	(numbers) 1993	1994	1995	1996	Number of persons engaged Note	(numbers) 1993	1994	1995	1996	Wages and salaries paid to employees Note	(million DOLLARS) 1993	1994	1995	1996
151 Processed meat,fish,fruit,vegetables,fats		62	64	68	72		2429	2468	2564	2601		55.2	58.4	65.1	69.5
1511 Processing/preserving of meat		19	24	25	26		764	1003	1070	1058		14.2	20.3	24.0	25.9
1512 Processing/preserving of fish		24	22	24	27		742	648	607	684		14.6	13.8	14.1	16.4
1513 Processing/preserving of fruit & vegetables		6	6	6	6		158	194	208	163		3.3	4.0	4.3	3.7
1514 Vegetable and animal oils and fats		13	12	13	13		765	623	679	696		23.1	20.2	22.7	23.4
1520 Dairy products		8	9	9	8		1296	1349	1306	1332		36.3	38.9	40.4	40.8
153 Grain mill products; starches; animal feeds		8	9	8	6		432	413	328	303		12.5	13.0	9.7	11.5
1531 Grain mill products		-	-	-	-		-	-	-	-		-	-	-	-
1532 Starches and starch products		-	-	-	-		-	-	-	-		-	-	-	-
1533 Prepared animal feeds		8	9	8	6		432	413	328	303		12.5	13.0	9.7	11.5
154 Other food products		211	216	212	216		7504	7444	7341	8315		167.3	181.3	191.5	244.8
1541 Bakery products		67	69	65	61		2548	2654	2619	2554		51.5	58.3	59.8	62.6
1542 Sugar		-	-	-	-		-	-	-	-		-	-	-	-
1543 Cocoa, chocolate and sugar confectionery		7	7	7	7		684	422	441	444		20.1	15.1	17.3	18.7
1544 Macaroni, noodles & similar products		27	28	28	29		752	740	737	796		13.9	16.1	16.4	18.3
1549 Other food products n.e.c.		110	112	112	119		3520	3628	3544	4521		81.9	91.9	98.0	145.3
155 Beverages		13	11	12	11		2190	2156	1687	1664		67.8	68.4	62.2	68.4
1551 Distilling, rectifying & blending of spirits		4	4	4	-		87	87	91	-		2.0	2.3	2.5	-
1552 Wines		-	-	-	-		-	-	-	-		-	-	-	-
1553 Malt liquors and malt		-	-	-	-		-	-	-	-		-	-	-	-
1554 Soft drinks; mineral waters		9	7	8	11		2103	2069	1596	1664		65.8	66.1	59.7	68.4
1600 Tobacco products		3	3	3	-		762	843	770	-		33.6	40.0	37.5	-
171 Spinning, weaving and finishing of textiles		23	20	18	15		1706	1396	1128	799		34.4	30.5	26.1	20.0
1711 Textile fibre preparation; textile weaving		17	15	13	15		1238	975	715	799		25.3	20.8	16.6	20.0
1712 Finishing of textiles		6	5	5	-		468	421	413	-		9.1	9.7	9.5	-
172 Other textiles		18	18	20	20		551	551	557	550		11.1	11.6	13.1	14.2
1721 Made-up textile articles, except apparel		13	14	16	20		357	373	381	550		5.9	7.3	8.7	14.2
1722 Carpets and rugs		-	-	-	-		-	-	-	-		-	-	-	-
1723 Cordage, rope, twine and netting		-	-	-	-		-	-	-	-		-	-	-	-
1729 Other textiles n.e.c.		5	4	4	-		194	178	176	-		5.2	4.3	4.4	-
1730 Knitted and crocheted fabrics and articles		24	21	20	18		844	666	553	399		17.0	14.7	13.2	9.6
1810 Wearing apparel, except fur apparel		310	274	231	193		20751	18143	14684	10309		281.0	263.8	224.6	176.5
1820 Dressing & dyeing of fur; processing of fur		-	-	-	-		-	-	-	-		-	-	-	-
191 Tanning, dressing and processing of leather		20	20	20	16		826	768	708	682		17.0	17.3	17.2	16.7
1911 Tanning and dressing of leather		-	-	-	-		-	-	-	-		-	-	-	-
1912 Luggage, handbags, etc.; saddlery & harness		20	20	20	16		826	768	708	682		17.0	17.3	17.2	16.7
1920 Footwear		24	19	13	11		459	419	368	316		8.0	8.6	8.1	8.1
2010 Sawmilling and planing of wood		11	11	10	9		152	159	150	130		5.1	5.7	6.0	4.9
202 Products of wood, cork, straw, etc.		64	58	54	48		1751	1590	1476	1320		34.3	34.8	32.8	30.2
2021 Veneer sheets, plywood, particle board, etc.		13	10	10	8		497	421	378	178		10.5	9.5	8.7	4.8
2022 Builders' carpentry and joinery		26	25	22	21		675	628	575	607		13.5	13.8	13.3	14.1
2023 Wooden containers		17	18	16	19		486	480	449	535		8.8	10.0	9.1	11.2
2029 Other wood products; articles of cork/straw		8	5	6	-		93	61	74	-		1.5	1.4	1.8	-
210 Paper and paper products		103	106	110	104		5198	5475	5730	5474		137.5	153.0	167.5	171.7
2101 Pulp, paper and paperboard		-	-	-	-		-	-	-	-		-	-	-	-
2102 Corrugated paper and paperboard		69	74	76	74		3738	3973	4119	4064		102.5	116.8	128.3	131.3
2109 Other articles of paper and paperboard		34	32	34	30		1460	1502	1611	1410		35.0	36.2	39.3	40.4
221 Publishing		58	57	65	73		4673	4593	4723	4880		210.3	229.6	253.2	267.0
2211 Publishing of books and other publications		19	19	23	30		701	704	721	821		21.6	22.5	26.0	30.7
2212 Publishing of newspapers, journals, etc.		39	38	42	43		3972	3889	4002	4059		188.7	207.1	227.3	236.3
2213 Publishing of recorded media		-	-	-	-		-	-	-	-		-	-	-	-
2219 Other publishing		-	-	-	-		-	-	-	-		-	-	-	-

Code	Description												
222	Printing and related service activities	325	323	334	334	13425	13308	13600	13678	323.7	352.0	382.9	392.7
2221	Printing	265	267	273	272	10555	10701	11028	11266	261.6	288.3	315.2	326.2
2222	Service activities related to printing	60	56	61	62	2870	2607	2572	2412	62.0	63.8	67.6	66.6
2230	Reproduction of recorded media	4	6	8	8	132	214	328	374	3.3	5.9	11.8	11.4
2310	Coke oven products	-	-	-	-	-	-	-	-	-	-	-	-
2320	Refined petroleum products	16	18	20	18	3713	3752	3700	3531	282.7	280.8	277.2	301.8
2330	Processing of nuclear fuel	-	-	-	-	-	-	-	-	-	-	-	-
241	Basic chemicals	50	52	50	49	3178	3330	3393	3707	149.5	159.8	165.7	181.1
2411	Basic chemicals, except fertilizers	31	32	31	29	1726	1779	1759	1717	83.1	86.7	82.4	78.4
2412	Fertilizers and nitrogen compounds	-	-	-	-	-	-	-	-	-	-	-	-
2413	Plastics in primary forms; synthetic rubber	19	20	19	20	1452	1551	1634	1990	66.4	73.2	83.3	102.7
242	Other chemicals	124	133	137	146	7991	8665	9337	9914	339.0	394.6	462.2	495.2
2421	Pesticides and other agro-chemical products	-	-	-	-	-	-	-	-	-	-	-	-
2422	Paints, varnishes, printing ink and mastics	23	25	26	26	1679	1728	1960	1934	65.7	76.7	82.2	81.9
2423	Pharmaceuticals, medicinal chemicals, etc.	18	18	18	17	1649	1700	1855	1758	60.0	65.7	82.6	83.3
2424	Soap, cleaning & cosmetic preparations	31	33	33	35	1105	1367	1440	1567	34.3	51.1	66.9	72.6
2429	Other chemical products n.e.c.	52	57	60	68	3558	3870	4082	4655	179.1	201.0	230.6	257.4
2430	Man-made fibres	-	-	-	-	-	-	-	-	-	-	-	-
251	Rubber products	29	31	30	30	1760	1867	1878	1751	42.7	47.4	53.5	53.2
2511	Rubber tyres and tubes	-	-	-	-	-	-	-	-	-	-	-	-
2519	Other rubber products	29	31	30	30	1760	1867	1878	1751	42.7	47.4	53.5	53.2
2520	Plastic products	304	306	316	325	16867	17388	18669	19794	365.3	397.4	451.6	485.8
2610	Glass and glass products	11	10	10	11	946	882	1268	1302	25.7	31.9	37.8	40.6
269	Non-metallic mineral products n.e.c.	81	83	75	84	5355	5707	4244	5203	144.1	163.6	145.1	170.0
2691	Pottery, china and earthenware	-	-	-	-	-	-	-	-	-	-	-	-
2692	Refractory ceramic products	-	-	-	-	-	-	-	-	-	-	-	-
2693	Struct.non-refractory clay; ceramic products	7	7	7	7	300	278	277	289	8.0	9.0	8.5	9.1
2694	Cement, lime and plaster	5	5	5	6	465	484	490	528	24.8	27.5	29.2	30.9
2695	Articles of concrete, cement and plaster	35	37	23	22	2836	3083	1471	1632	65.5	76.6	48.3	56.2
2696	Cutting, shaping & finishing of stone	4	...	6	10	88	...	150	469	1.4	...	4.1	16.1
2699	Other non-metallic mineral products n.e.c.	30	34	34	39	1666	1862	1856	2285	44.3	50.5	55.0	57.6
2710	Basic iron and steel	18	18	18	17	1639	1819	1769	1660	66.1	70.9	67.8	73.6
2720	Basic precious and non-ferrous metals	-	-	-	-	-	-	-	-	-	-	-	-
273	Casting of metals	11	9	7	8	578	482	446	445	14.1	13.4	14.3	13.4
2731	Casting of iron and steel	-	-	-	-	-	-	-	-	-	-	-	-
2732	Casting of non-ferrous metals	11	9	7	8	578	482	446	445	14.1	13.4	14.3	13.4
281	Struct.metal products;tanks;steam generators	181	187	199	209	7531	8764	8978	9567	194.4	217.5	247.1	251.3
2811	Structural metal products	165	171	180	189	6885	8174	8316	8850	166.3	192.0	218.3	224.9
2812	Tanks, reservoirs and containers of metal	11	11	13	13	397	385	453	526	16.5	16.0	18.2	18.4
2813	Steam generators	5	5	6	7	249	205	209	191	11.6	9.5	10.6	7.9
289	Other metal products; metal working services	352	372	385	396	23072	23686	24656	25198	559.3	628.0	698.5	754.8
2891	Metal forging/pressing/stamping/roll-forming	93	91	92	86	7222	7458	8143	8138	160.3	187.5	206.4	220.9
2892	Treatment & coating of metals	61	64	66	76	2748	2639	2671	3095	66.0	67.3	75.1	91.5
2893	Cutlery, hand tools and general hardware	10	9	9	10	1260	1070	1229	1215	27.8	26.2	30.7	31.5
2899	Other fabricated metal products n.e.c.	188	208	218	224	11842	12519	12613	12750	305.2	346.9	386.3	410.9
291	General purpose machinery	143	155	154	154	12667	13172	13567	13815	357.0	390.3	428.6	451.4
2911	Engines & turbines(not for transport equip.)	7	7	6	5	329	358	259	142	13.4	17.7	12.8	5.7
2912	Pumps, compressors, taps and valves	8	7	7	8	447	392	367	357	14.2	13.7	15.2	15.3
2913	Bearings, gears, gearing & driving elements	8	8	9	9	2306	2148	2158	2109	61.4	62.0	65.8	63.5
2914	Ovens, furnaces and furnace burners	-	-	-	-	-	-	-	-	-	-	-	-
2915	Lifting and handling equipment	37	43	45	45	3140	3324	3586	3907	98.8	114.1	129.7	146.4
2919	Other general purpose machinery	83	90	87	87	6445	6950	7197	7300	169.2	182.9	205.1	220.5
292	Special purpose machinery	324	339	357	406	14479	15586	17629	19664	445.4	507.1	590.9	675.0
2921	Agricultural and forestry machinery	-	-	-	-	-	-	-	-	-	-	-	-
2922	Machine tools	161	175	189	211	5046	5537	6311	6852	141.3	167.2	200.1	226.7
2923	Machinery for metallurgy	-	-	-	-	-	-	-	-	-	-	-	-
2924	Machinery for mining & construction	44	46	46	46	4563	4519	4750	5311	164.1	175.6	181.3	192.5
2925	Food/beverage/tobacco processing machinery	-	-	-	-	-	-	-	-	-	-	-	-
2926	Machinery for textile, apparel and leather	4	4	4	-	222	226	224	-	7.1	7.6	8.4	-
2927	Weapons and ammunition	-	-	-	-	-	-	-	-	-	-	-	-
2929	Other special purpose machinery	115	114	118	149	4648	5304	6344	7501	132.9	156.6	201.0	255.8
2930	Domestic appliances n.e.c.	6	5	4	5	3068	2942	1740	1666	73.5	70.0	58.9	57.3

continued

Singapore

ISIC Revision 3	Number of establishments					Number of persons engaged					Wages and salaries paid to employees				
		(numbers)					(numbers)					(million DOLLARS)			
ISIC Industry	Note	1993	1994	1995	1996	Note	1993	1994	1995	1996	Note	1993	1994	1995	1996
3000 Office, accounting and computing machinery		50	49	46	45		43733	46529	50447	57703		914.3	984.8	1159.2	1293.5
3110 Electric motors, generators and transformers		28	25	28	29		4111	5111	5303	4361		94.3	120.1	129.1	131.4
3120 Electricity distribution & control apparatus		39	37	41	41		2523	2097	2903	2426		61.0	55.6	81.7	70.2
3130 Insulated wire and cable		51	54	51	50		6135	6471	6668	6362		163.9	179.3	191.8	194.7
3140 Accumulators, primary cells and batteries		6	9	9	10		2224	2431	2130	1869		54.4	63.4	64.7	66.2
3150 Lighting equipment and electric lamps		13	14	16	14		330	792	818	312		8.7	21.6	24.7	8.9
3190 Other electrical equipment n.e.c.		5	6	5	8		266	268	229	322		7.8	9.1	9.2	13.5
3210 Electronic valves, tubes, etc.		159	157	161	163		44781	48097	51370	51940		1115.2	1296.9	1471.0	1670.0
3220 TV/radio transmitters; line comm. apparatus		8	8	11	11		5635	4902	5646	4219		142.4	148.0	168.4	158.7
3230 TV and radio receivers and associated goods		24	23	21	19		22899	22852	19428	14593		467.9	523.7	481.5	400.4
331 Medical, measuring, testing appliances, etc.		40	40	44	44		5539	6194	6190	6281		134.7	160.1	172.0	197.1
3311 Medical, surgical and orthopaedic equipment		14	15	16	15		2968	3159	3404	3612		62.3	70.3	85.3	96.1
3312 Measuring/testing/navigating appliances,etc.		18	16	18	18		1157	952	957	785		26.7	22.0	22.8	20.9
3313 Industrial process control equipment		8	9	10	11		1414	2083	1829	1884		45.7	67.7	63.9	80.2
3320 Optical instruments & photographic equipment		14	10	10	10		1949	1681	1735	1797		42.5	41.8	45.5	49.0
3330 Watches and clocks		6	7	8	8		1278	1391	1307	1213		33.6	39.0	40.9	42.7
3410 Motor vehicles		-	-	-	-		-	-	-	-		-	-	-	-
3420 Automobile bodies, trailers & semi-trailers		11	11	12	13		1034	836	1066	1023		23.6	33.0	27.4	40.2
3430 Parts/accessories for automobiles		10	12	12	10		504	488	473	437		13.2	15.9	16.3	16.3
351 Building and repairing of ships and boats		224	226	234	239		21771	23826	24967	23749		574.9	614.4	629.0	634.1
3511 Building and repairing of ships		153	157	161	153		18179	19847	21053	19561		454.3	477.6	488.7	485.9
3512 Building/repairing of pleasure/sport. boats		71	69	73	86		3592	3979	3914	4188		120.6	136.8	140.3	148.2
3520 Railway/tramway locomotives & rolling stock		-	-	-	-		-	-	-	-		-	-	-	-
3530 Aircraft and spacecraft		33	36	39	39		9093	9037	9214	9012		359.5	390.4	431.3	452.5
359 Transport equipment n.e.c.		7	9	8	6		832	777	900	671		24.3	28.3	28.7	21.8
3591 Motorcycles		-	-	-	-		-	-	-	-		-	-	-	-
3592 Bicycles and invalid carriages		-	-	-	-		-	-	-	-		-	-	-	-
3599 Other transport equipment n.e.c.		7	9	8	6		832	777	900	671		24.3	28.3	28.7	21.8
3610 Furniture		159	153	153	152		6763	6350	5590	5499		126.9	128.1	127.6	128.9
369 Manufacturing n.e.c.		160	157	142	127		5739	5342	4495	3748		114.9	123.9	115.2	95.0
3691 Jewellery and related articles		65	62	54	51		1342	1199	1006	931		29.1	27.8	24.4	23.1
3692 Musical instruments		-	-	-	-		-	-	-	-		-	-	-	-
3693 Sports goods		-	-	-	-		-	-	-	-		-	-	-	-
3694 Games and toys		16	14	10	6		1480	1183	682	443		22.3	18.0	11.8	8.9
3699 Other manufacturing n.e.c.		79	81	78	70		2917	2960	2807	2374		63.4	78.2	79.0	63.1
3710 Recycling of metal waste and scrap		7	7	8	10		111	119	127	175		3.0	3.6	4.6	5.4
3720 Recycling of non-metal waste and scrap		-	-	-	-		-	-	-	-		-	-	-	-
D Total manufacturing		3993	4013	4036	4068		355175	365588	370281	368055		8995.4	9881.0	10681.7	11252.8

Singapore

ISIC Revision 3	Output in factor values					Value added in factor values					Gross fixed capital formation		
		(million DOLLARS)					(million DOLLARS)					(million DOLLARS)	
ISIC Industry	Note	1993	1994	1995	1996	Note	1993	1994	1995	1996	Note	1995	1996
151 Processed meat,fish,fruit,vegetables,fats		674.8	745.4	899.8	851.6		122.6	136.6	146.6	157.8		62.0	35.1
1511 Processing/preserving of meat		92.7	164.0	178.2	196.2		35.8	47.3	52.1	57.4		20.9	5.3
1512 Processing/preserving of fish		120.3	122.8	102.8	154.6		25.2	26.5	22.5	32.3		10.5	8.9
1513 Processing/preserving of fruit & vegetables		13.6	17.2	17.6	17.0		3.7	6.0	5.8	5.9		2.4	3.4
1514 Vegetable and animal oils and fats		448.2	441.4	601.2	483.8		58.0	56.8	66.2	62.2		28.1	17.5
1520 Dairy products		320.4	323.0	326.1	310.4		130.6	142.2	156.3	132.0		15.9	14.1
153 Grain mill products; starches; animal feeds		106.2	109.2	96.1	98.2		20.6	27.3	22.4	25.1		4.3	0.9
1531 Grain mill products		-	-	-	-		-	-	-	-		-	-
1532 Starches and starch products		-	-	-	-		-	-	-	-		-	-
1533 Prepared animal feeds		106.2	109.2	96.1	98.2		20.6	27.3	22.4	25.1		4.3	0.9
154 Other food products		1091.4	1261.6	1359.9	1852.5		415.7	458.8	471.2	709.3		105.3	165.8
1541 Bakery products		228.9	248.1	252.3	270.5		119.7	131.5	131.7	142.6		37.9	24.1
1542 Sugar		-	-	-	-		-	-	-	-		-	-
1543 Cocoa, chocolate and sugar confectionery		142.0	169.4	176.2	189.4		49.2	47.6	48.4	54.9		11.2	8.3
1544 Macaroni, noodles & similar products		68.7	70.9	66.1	79.9		29.0	31.5	27.7	33.9		4.7	5.2
1549 Other food products n.e.c.		651.8	773.1	865.3	1312.7		217.7	248.2	263.4	477.8		51.5	128.2
155 Beverages		558.1	555.7	537.9	537.6		290.1	305.0	291.8	287.2		31.5	21.3
1551 Distilling, rectifying & blending of spirits		9.2	10.5	9.1	-		4.2	6.9	5.1	-		0.2	-
1552 Wines		-	-	-	-		-	-	-	-		-	-
1553 Malt liquors and malt		-	-	-	-		-	-	-	-		-	-
1554 Soft drinks; mineral waters		548.9	545.2	528.8	537.6		285.8	298.1	286.7	287.2		31.3	21.3
1600 Tobacco products		384.6	462.5	387.9	-		181.6	210.4	181.4	-		30.1	-
171 Spinning, weaving and finishing of textiles		166.3	159.2	140.1	114.4		62.9	59.4	48.1	38.7		16.0	8.6
1711 Textile fibre preparation; textile weaving		116.3	95.0	69.1	114.4		48.6	42.7	32.9	38.7		10.1	8.6
1712 Finishing of textiles		50.0	64.2	71.1	-		14.3	16.7	15.3	-		6.0	-
172 Other textiles		52.0	54.6	54.1	55.9		21.6	23.0	25.2	24.8		1.9	1.6
1721 Made-up textile articles, except apparel		25.0	29.1	28.1	55.9		10.5	13.4	15.2	24.8		1.7	1.6
1722 Carpets and rugs		-	-	-	-		-	-	-	-		-	-
1723 Cordage, rope, twine and netting		-	-	-	-		-	-	-	-		-	-
1729 Other textiles n.e.c.		27.0	25.5	26.0	-		11.1	9.6	10.0	-		0.1	-
1730 Knitted and crocheted fabrics and articles		149.7	106.9	100.2	67.3		32.2	27.5	18.9	16.1		6.1	3.2
1810 Wearing apparel, except fur apparel		1323.4	1205.8	973.7	801.6		427.1	365.9	304.2	242.5		19.3	35.6
1820 Dressing & dyeing of fur; processing of fur		-	-	-	-		-	-	-	-		-	-
191 Tanning, dressing and processing of leather		78.1	82.2	78.8	75.1		32.8	32.9	31.3	28.2		1.2	0.9
1911 Tanning and dressing of leather		-	-	-	-		-	-	-	-		-	-
1912 Luggage, handbags, etc.; saddlery & harness		78.1	82.2	78.8	75.1		32.8	32.9	31.3	28.2		1.2	0.9
1920 Footwear		45.5	39.3	37.7	36.9		15.7	14.6	14.1	14.9		0.6	0.4
2010 Sawmilling and planing of wood		25.8	26.5	24.0	21.8		8.7	10.5	12.1	9.6		0.9	1.0
202 Products of wood, cork, straw, etc.		269.3	256.8	265.6	248.4		71.8	71.1	71.0	71.5		21.7	14.4
2021 Veneer sheets, plywood, particle board, etc.		87.2	60.9	52.4	38.6		23.0	13.9	11.4	10.8		3.1	0.3
2022 Builders' carpentry and joinery		109.8	115.7	128.6	134.8		28.4	34.2	37.4	39.4		13.9	10.3
2023 Wooden containers		60.6	71.9	75.3	75.0		17.5	20.5	19.0	21.4		4.5	3.8
2029 Other wood products; articles of cork/straw		11.7	8.4	9.3	-		2.9	2.4	3.3	-		0.2	-
210 Paper and paper products		855.5	950.4	1056.9	1021.9		402.5	464.5	469.8	471.9		91.0	103.7
2101 Pulp, paper and paperboard		-	-	-	-		-	-	-	-		-	-
2102 Corrugated paper and paperboard		666.3	750.5	841.5	809.9		329.2	384.9	385.7	394.4		71.5	81.6
2109 Other articles of paper and paperboard		189.3	199.9	215.4	212.0		73.3	79.6	84.1	77.4		19.5	22.1
221 Publishing		981.2	965.7	1028.9	1114.3		695.7	767.6	800.7	819.6		28.9	26.4
2211 Publishing of books and other publications		74.4	80.0	97.1	110.7		44.3	48.5	53.5	62.3		5.1	8.5
2212 Publishing of newspapers, journals, etc.		906.9	885.7	931.8	1003.7		651.4	719.0	747.1	757.3		23.8	17.9
2213 Publishing of recorded media		-	-	-	-		-	-	-	-		-	-
2219 Other publishing		-	-	-	-		-	-	-	-		-	-

continued

Singapore

ISIC Revision 3	Output in factor values					Value added in factor values					Gross fixed capital formation		
		(million DOLLARS)					(million DOLLARS)					(million DOLLARS)	
ISIC Industry	Note	1993	1994	1995	1996	Note	1993	1994	1995	1996	Note	1995	1996
222 Printing and related service activities		1325.6	1426.1	1571.0	1568.3		657.3	723.6	769.1	771.2		166.3	214.5
2221 Printing		1169.4	1265.8	1406.1	1402.5		548.6	608.2	652.7	653.0		150.2	198.0
2222 Service activities related to printing		156.3	160.3	164.9	165.8		108.7	115.5	116.5	118.2		16.0	16.5
2230 Reproduction of recorded media		23.3	54.6	61.0	72.7		12.4	32.0	36.8	49.6		37.2	22.0
2310 Coke oven products		-	-	-	-		-	-	-	-		-	-
2320 Refined petroleum products		11154.4	10909.5	10653.8	13746.5		1937.5	1899.2	1721.6	2042.0		461.3	616.3
2330 Processing of nuclear fuel		-	-	-	-		-	-	-	-		-	-
241 Basic chemicals		1370.6	1609.2	1891.1	1836.8		457.2	546.7	664.7	598.6		134.7	183.9
2411 Basic chemicals, except fertilizers		445.1	461.5	514.5	420.0		199.7	217.7	245.6	180.6		51.3	55.5
2412 Fertilizers and nitrogen compounds		-	-	-	-		-	-	-	-		-	-
2413 Plastics in primary forms; synthetic rubber		925.5	1147.8	1376.6	1416.8		257.5	329.0	419.1	418.0		83.4	128.4
242 Other chemicals		3783.8	4309.5	4974.0	5326.3		2050.8	2217.0	2518.5	2821.8		302.7	272.9
2421 Pesticides and other agro-chemical products		-	-	-	-		-	-	-	-		-	-
2422 Paints, varnishes, printing ink and mastics		435.1	498.6	558.2	554.2		161.1	188.2	190.2	200.0		30.3	49.0
2423 Pharmaceuticals, medicinal chemicals, etc.		1426.5	1324.3	1339.0	1695.8		1208.5	1112.9	1129.3	1492.6		132.5	57.4
2424 Soap, cleaning & cosmetic preparations		200.9	229.4	310.2	418.1		82.8	102.4	132.3	160.1		31.0	32.1
2429 Other chemical products n.e.c.		1721.4	2257.2	2766.5	2658.2		598.4	813.6	1066.6	969.1		108.8	134.4
2430 Man-made fibres		-	-	-	-		-	-	-	-		-	-
251 Rubber products		167.7	196.6	243.1	231.9		86.6	93.4	107.3	104.6		24.0	22.8
2511 Rubber tyres and tubes		-	-	-	-		-	-	-	-		-	-
2519 Other rubber products		167.7	196.6	243.1	231.9		86.6	93.4	107.3	104.6		24.0	22.8
2520 Plastic products		1851.3	2079.2	2345.4	2369.1		761.5	843.8	906.5	939.4		217.0	237.0
2610 Glass and glass products		236.6	272.1	376.0	390.0		106.2	117.2	161.8	187.8		264.4	52.2
269 Non-metallic mineral products n.e.c.		1593.5	1729.8	1679.1	1982.0		491.1	543.6	519.8	566.7		65.2	141.9
2691 Pottery, china and earthenware		-	-	-	-		-	-	-	-		-	-
2692 Refractory ceramic products		-	-	-	-		-	-	-	-		-	-
2693 Struct.non-refractory clay; ceramic products		39.9	39.0	37.6	32.0		22.0	22.8	22.3	17.6		2.9	1.1
2694 Cement, lime and plaster		426.8	454.8	485.7	477.5		170.9	180.9	194.6	168.1		8.5	58.7
2695 Articles of concrete, cement and plaster		883.7	974.8	859.9	1080.0		188.9	222.4	164.7	195.6		35.9	57.9
2696 Cutting, shaping & finishing of stone		8.7	...	27.8	110.5		3.0	...	12.3	51.0		1.5	12.4
2699 Other non-metallic mineral products n.e.c.		234.3	261.2	268.2	282.2		106.2	117.5	125.9	134.4		16.4	11.7
2710 Basic iron and steel		655.4	647.5	591.7	567.6		181.7	174.2	154.3	144.4		47.9	15.8
2720 Basic precious and non-ferrous metals		-	-	-	-		-	-	-	-		-	-
273 Casting of metals		78.8	73.3	71.0	69.2		36.6	39.4	37.5	33.9		2.3	1.9
2731 Casting of iron and steel		-	-	-	-		-	-	-	-		-	-
2732 Casting of non-ferrous metals		78.8	73.3	71.0	69.2		36.6	39.4	37.5	33.9		2.3	1.9
281 Struct.metal products;tanks;steam generators		1185.2	1524.7	1688.9	1546.7		397.6	511.1	594.4	506.8		54.8	106.7
2811 Structural metal products		1064.7	1418.6	1564.1	1406.8		351.1	470.8	542.6	456.8		51.5	101.4
2812 Tanks, reservoirs and containers of metal		87.6	79.7	88.8	103.5		31.4	23.8	30.6	33.0		2.1	4.2
2813 Steam generators		32.9	26.5	36.0	36.4		15.2	16.5	21.2	17.1		1.2	1.1
289 Other metal products; metal working services		3483.6	4082.7	4624.3	4751.1		1302.9	1450.6	1603.7	1675.2		429.1	467.9
2891 Metal forging/pressing/stamping/roll-forming		941.1	1142.7	1269.8	1286.2		362.4	411.7	451.3	475.9		115.3	132.9
2892 Treatment & coating of metals		294.7	329.2	372.2	399.7		143.6	161.7	182.0	209.0		43.6	54.8
2893 Cutlery, hand tools and general hardware		148.0	132.7	159.8	135.8		93.6	84.5	100.4	81.2		9.9	6.7
2899 Other fabricated metal products n.e.c.		2099.8	2478.1	2822.5	2929.3		703.2	792.7	869.9	909.1		260.4	273.5
291 General purpose machinery		1966.9	2215.0	2585.7	2684.1		769.5	824.5	953.8	997.8		146.2	146.9
2911 Engines & turbines(not for transport equip.)		60.7	53.0	60.7	31.6		18.3	17.5	19.3	11.9		1.6	0.1
2912 Pumps, compressors, taps and valves		75.9	75.1	91.1	92.0		23.6	18.5	23.8	25.6		4.5	4.1
2913 Bearings, gears, gearing & driving elements		293.8	301.5	376.6	372.4		167.6	172.9	215.0	206.0		39.5	31.0
2914 Ovens, furnaces and furnace burners		-	-	-	-		-	-	-	-		-	-
2915 Lifting and handling equipment		397.9	459.3	549.6	608.5		142.9	156.8	186.7	219.4		21.3	41.9
2919 Other general purpose machinery		1138.6	1326.2	1507.7	1579.6		417.1	458.9	509.0	534.9		79.3	69.8

292	Special purpose machinery	1971.3	2300.8	2834.8	3334.0	885.3	1011.9	1212.2	1343.2	252.8	305.3
2921	Agricultural and forestry machinery	-	-	-	-	-	-	-	-	-	-
2922	Machine tools	472.6	599.0	788.0	850.3	249.6	307.0	395.7	418.2	90.4	97.1
2923	Machinery for metallurgy	-	-	-	-	-	-	-	-	-	-
2924	Machinery for mining & construction	813.1	890.4	970.8	1237.9	335.6	346.0	348.8	399.3	87.9	110.9
2925	Food/beverage/tobacco processing machinery	-	-	-	-	-	-	-	-	-	-
2926	Machinery for textile, apparel and leather	36.8	37.5	39.0	-	22.7	22.3	21.8	-	2.0	-
2927	Weapons and ammunition	-	-	-	-	-	-	-	-	-	-
2929	Other special purpose machinery	648.9	773.8	1037.0	1245.8	277.4	336.6	445.8	525.7	72.6	97.4
2930	Domestic appliances n.e.c.	456.9	449.3	428.8	434.1	182.0	157.5	137.2	145.0	11.0	11.4
3000	Office, accounting and computing machinery	21096.7	26090.1	31657.6	37231.7	5848.8	6566.7	7413.9	9450.7	1004.7	1090.9
3110	Electric motors, generators and transformers	667.4	851.9	867.3	788.4	205.5	268.3	259.3	223.9	39.3	38.6
3120	Electricity distribution & control apparatus	300.5	252.0	452.0	444.2	114.6	89.7	152.0	171.4	40.4	24.2
3130	Insulated wire and cable	995.8	1234.2	1485.9	1407.3	358.7	427.6	479.1	483.4	141.2	107.7
3140	Accumulators, primary cells and batteries	237.3	293.2	334.2	348.1	120.0	139.0	157.0	163.0	32.6	19.4
3150	Lighting equipment and electric lamps	30.2	138.3	174.1	35.9	10.3	58.8	58.1	13.1	3.6	0.5
3190	Other electrical equipment n.e.c.	24.0	27.6	31.4	86.9	13.1	14.0	16.7	26.7	2.2	1.3
3210	Electronic valves, tubes, etc.	10698.2	13628.2	18071.6	17598.8	2965.5	4093.2	5563.6	5294.3	1970.6	2725.6
3220	TV/radio transmitters; line comm. apparatus	1846.7	1653.7	1914.2	1683.7	928.1	723.4	1000.1	721.7	115.1	77.4
3230	TV and radio receivers and associated goods	6065.0	7353.3	6229.4	4398.6	1291.4	1434.4	1184.9	963.8	242.2	104.5
331	Medical, measuring, testing appliances, etc.	825.7	899.0	1156.4	1221.6	441.2	473.5	559.1	616.2	48.4	51.1
3311	Medical, surgical and orthopaedic equipment	484.4	542.6	641.8	722.4	304.6	336.8	367.9	422.9	21.5	25.4
3312	Measuring/testing/navigating appliances,etc.	123.8	119.1	122.7	120.2	44.2	44.5	40.8	39.6	6.3	2.0
3313	Industrial process control equipment	217.4	237.3	392.0	379.0	92.3	92.2	150.4	153.6	20.6	23.6
3320	Optical instruments & photographic equipment	113.9	105.0	118.9	130.1	79.2	69.9	77.0	85.4	10.9	12.3
3330	Watches and clocks	197.4	180.8	197.8	195.3	64.5	67.7	64.9	64.0	15.9	44.3
3410	Motor vehicles	-	-	-	-	-	-	-	-	-	-
3420	Automobile bodies, trailers & semi-trailers	142.3	145.9	168.8	204.8	41.5	55.4	46.0	64.3	7.7	25.6
3430	Parts/accessories for automobiles	66.2	70.4	88.5	77.5	27.1	28.3	36.2	31.6	2.9	5.2
351	Building and repairing of ships and boats	2655.2	3048.1	3101.8	2714.3	1174.6	1287.3	1253.9	1096.7	169.6	338.4
3511	Building and repairing of ships	2254.1	2548.2	2660.6	2278.0	983.3	1052.9	1040.5	875.2	136.0	298.1
3512	Building/repairing of pleasure/sport. boats	401.1	499.9	441.3	436.4	191.2	234.4	213.4	221.5	33.7	40.3
3520	Railway/tramway locomotives & rolling stock	-	-	-	-	-	-	-	-	-	-
3530	Aircraft and spacecraft	1310.8	1387.9	1433.5	1574.8	749.2	787.5	818.0	902.3	110.2	86.2
359	Transport equipment n.e.c.	447.9	419.4	399.0	256.5	171.2	133.2	154.3	116.3	15.0	11.2
3591	Motorcycles	-	-	-	-	-	-	-	-	-	-
3592	Bicycles and invalid carriages	-	-	-	-	-	-	-	-	-	-
3599	Other transport equipment n.e.c.	447.9	419.4	399.0	256.5	171.2	133.2	154.3	116.3	15.0	11.2
3610	Furniture	663.4	674.2	646.4	649.7	218.2	221.5	220.7	228.2	33.8	45.3
369	Manufacturing n.e.c.	850.6	965.0	816.9	665.3	209.7	203.4	194.9	174.2	72.2	20.1
3691	Jewellery and related articles	340.6	427.5	319.7	288.5	42.2	41.1	35.6	31.2	4.2	3.0
3692	Musical instruments	-	-	-	-	-	-	-	-	-	-
3693	Sports goods	-	-	-	-	-	-	-	-	-	-
3694	Games and toys	185.1	191.6	135.0	55.9	38.0	32.9	24.4	5.7	3.8	2.1
3699	Other manufacturing n.e.c.	324.9	345.9	362.2	320.9	129.5	129.4	134.9	137.3	64.1	15.0
3710	Recycling of metal waste and scrap	16.5	19.4	25.0	36.7	6.5	8.1	8.3	12.9	3.5	5.7
3720	Recycling of non-metal waste and scrap	-	-	-	-	-	-	-	-	-	-
D	Total manufacturing	87639.0	100622.1	113358.0	119869.0	28287.2	31453.9	34882.4	36881.3	7135.6	8087.9

Singapore

ISIC Revision 3			Index numbers of industrial production (1990=100)											
ISIC	Industry	Note	1985	1986	1987	1988	1989	1990	1991	1992	1993	1994	1995	1996
15	Food and beverages		77	84	89	99	99	100	104	110	112	112	113	115
16	Tobacco products		39	31	26	47	68	100	111	126	130	182	180	173
17	Textiles		82	83	95	102	107	100	107	94	83	80	58	43
18	Wearing apparel, fur		73	84	99	105	107	100	100	90	71	62	51	42
19	Leather, leather products and footwear		89	93	107	113	100	100	111	107	104	97	90	76
20	Wood products (excl. furniture)		143	107	115	115	107	100	85	86	79	73	71	74
21	Paper and paper products		58	64	85	93	95	100	104	92	93	99	107	102
22	Printing and publishing		65	68	74	82	91	100	109	116	126	135	141	141
23	Coke,refined petroleum products,nuclear fuel		74	80	74	78	88	100	103	104	120	122	119	126
24	Chemicals and chemical products		62	64	71	75	83	100	115	107	112	126	127	136
25	Rubber and plastics products		82	74	90	102	102	100	111	108	115	128	141	130
26	Non-metallic mineral products		59	49	63	68	94	100	107	116	125	124	143	151
27	Basic metals		84	82	87	91	91	100	98	103	109	111	101	101
28	Fabricated metal products		66	73	83	98	102	100	101	107	111	124	143	140
29	Machinery and equipment n.e.c.		65	57	66	79	93	100	113	111	105	127	143	150
30	Office, accounting and computing machinery		...	...	...	...	...	...	...	...	...	...	...	...
31	Electrical machinery and apparatus	a/	55	60	79	95	108	100	109	109	113	125	131	130
32	Radio,television and communication equipment	a/	...	...	...	...	...	...	...	...	...	...	...	...
33	Medical, precision and optical instruments	a/	...	...	...	...	...	...	...	...	...	...	...	...
34	Motor vehicles, trailers, semi-trailers	b/	52	57	61	74	90	100	105	105	104	112	113	107
35	Other transport equipment	b/	...	...	...	...	...	...	...	...	...	...	...	...
36	Furniture; manufacturing n.e.c.		72	84	116	124	96	100	102	88	83	87	68	65
37	Recycling		...	...	...	...	...	...	...	...	...	...	...	...
D	Total manufacturing		55	59	70	83	91	100	105	108	119	134	148	153

a/ 31 includes 32 and 33.
b/ 34 includes 35.

SLOVAKIA

Supplier of information:
Statistical Office of the Slovak Republic, Bratislava.

Basic source of data:
Not reported.

Major deviations from ISIC (Revision 3):
None reported.

Reference period (if not calendar year):

Scope:
Not reported.

Method of enumeration:
Not reported.

Adjusted for non-response:
Not reported.

Concepts and definitions of variables:
No deviations from the standard UN concepts and definitions are reported.

Related national publications:

Slovakia

ISIC Revision 3 ISIC Industry	Number of establishments Note	(numbers) 1993	1994	1995	1996	Number of employees Note	(numbers) 1993	1994	1995	1996	Wages and salaries paid to employees Note	(million KORUNAS) 1993	1994	1995	1996
151 Processed meat, fish, fruit, vegetables, fats		69	70	76	85		...	...	14325	14348		...	...	1142	1350
1511 Processing/preserving of meat		49	51	52	55		11578	10993	10339	9954		682	771	829	959
1512 Processing/preserving of fish		4	3	5	5		460	412	632	639		32	35	54	61
1513 Processing/preserving of fruit & vegetables		15	15	16	20		2574	2476	2404	2659		142	155	163	207
1514 Vegetable and animal oils and fats		1	1	3	5		...	...	950	1096		...	...	96	123
1520 Dairy products		36	33	34	38		5144	4943	4923	5129		320	364	424	509
153 Grain mill products; starches; animal feeds		44	46	46	48		5628	5642	5539	5399		385	467	521	586
1531 Grain mill products		11	11	10	11		2437	2393	2377	2166		169	207	234	250
1532 Starches and starch products		5	6	6	6		660	669	653	690		46	55	59	73
1533 Prepared animal feeds		28	29	30	31		2531	2580	2509	2543		170	205	228	263
154 Other food products		70	78	82	102		...	...	14544	...		...	...	1194	...
1541 Bakery products		51	56	61	79		8189	8837	9314	10773		471	600	699	904
1542 Sugar		8	7	8	8		3355	2236	2513	2632		196	167	231	275
1543 Cocoa, chocolate and sugar confectionery		1	3	3	4		...	1916	1691	1492		...	156	164	162
1544 Macaroni, noodles & similar products		1	1	-	1		...	...	-	...		...	...	-	...
1549 Other food products n.e.c.		9	11	10	10		1655	1725	1026	1422		100	127	100	136
155 Beverages		35	39	41	53		8845	9237	9362	9043		577	729	830	905
1551 Distilling, rectifying & blending of spirits		5	7	7	8		1612	1860	1881	1775		104	136	151	162
1552 Wines		6	9	9	13		1553	1494	1642	1510		106	124	154	153
1553 Malt liquors and malt		12	13	13	15		4434	4495	4326	4398		285	360	395	458
1554 Soft drinks; mineral waters		12	10	12	17		1246	1388	1513	1360		82	109	130	132
1600 Tobacco products		1	1	1	1		...	...	...	...		...	...	...	...
171 Spinning, weaving and finishing of textiles		17	17	20	27		...	...	...	...		...	...	...	...
1711 Textile fibre preparation; textile weaving		16	16	19	26		13242	11459	10576	10669		647	637	648	757
1712 Finishing of textiles		1	1	1	1		...	...	...	...		...	...	...	...
172 Other textiles		15	22	24	22		...	...	...	1788		...	...	...	111
1721 Made-up textile articles, except apparel		9	14	16	16		2222	1552	1302	1448		94	76	75	91
1722 Carpets and rugs		2	2	1	-		...	...	...	-		...	...	...	-
1723 Cordage, rope, twine and netting		-	-	-	-		-	-	-	-		-	-	-	-
1729 Other textiles n.e.c.		4	6	7	6		284	534	595	340		18	34	46	20
1730 Knitted and crocheted fabrics and articles		17	21	25	35		12372	12178	9603	9827		533	594	522	601
1810 Wearing apparel, except fur apparel		69	83	103	132		23465	26159	29746	29078		1167	1438	1795	1915
1820 Dressing & dyeing of fur; processing of fur		1	1	2	1		...	...	...	...		...	...	...	...
191 Tanning, dressing and processing of leather		16	16	18	19		5576	5084	4688	4203		296	301	319	315
1911 Tanning and dressing of leather		5	5	6	9		3816	3358	2943	2607		215	220	218	206
1912 Luggage, handbags, etc.; saddlery & harness		11	11	12	10		1760	1726	1745	1596		81	81	101	109
1920 Footwear		21	37	51	51		17388	15405	17496	17691		835	853	1010	1103
2010 Sawmilling and planing of wood		17	28	33	60		5877	6595	6869	6145		332	445	534	512
202 Products of wood, cork, straw, etc.		46	48	53	61		...	...	8137	8552		...	...	604	707
2021 Veneer sheets, plywood, particle board, etc.		10	10	10	12		4808	4428	4490	4090		275	287	350	353
2022 Builders' carpentry and joinery		21	25	25	25		2838	2633	2566	2616		153	164	183	212
2023 Wooden containers		2	2	3	4		...	...	187	323		...	...	13	23
2029 Other wood products; articles of cork/straw		13	11	15	20		911	1146	894	1523		43	60	58	119
210 Paper and paper products		17	19	23	28		...	14026	13956	13555		...	1022	1281	1470
2101 Pulp, paper and paperboard		5	5	5	8		10601	10090	10065	9417		640	715	919	1006
2102 Corrugated paper and paperboard		2	3	4	4		...	1001	1040	924		...	84	107	115
2109 Other articles of paper and paperboard		10	11	14	16		3024	2935	2851	3214		200	223	255	349
221 Publishing		36	37	36	38		2581	2330	2403	2375		232	260	326	...
2211 Publishing of books and other publications		11	8	8	13		670	458	388	476		53	40	45	70
2212 Publishing of newspapers, journals, etc.		22	24	23	23		1606	1583	1742	1763		156	196	255	330
2213 Publishing of recorded media		-	-	-	-		-	-	-	-		-	-	-	-
2219 Other publishing		3	5	5	2		305	289	273	136		23	24	26	...

222 Printing and related service activities	30	31	35	42	5842	6030	6082	6140	444	542	607	718
2221 Printing	23	27	31	35	4476	4706	4637	4569	351	420	465	534
2222 Service activities related to printing	7	4	4	7	1366	1324	1445	1571	93	122	142	184
2230 Reproduction of recorded media	1	1	1	1	...	...	...	...	...	...	...	...
2310 Coke oven products	1	1	1	1	...	...	...	...	...	...	...	...
2320 Refined petroleum products	3	3	3	3	7510	6468	6044	5716	689	795	870	895
2330 Processing of nuclear fuel	-	-	-	-	-	-	-	-	-	-	-	-
241 Basic chemicals	10	10	10	18	...	...	...	11213	...	...	...	1355
2411 Basic chemicals, except fertilizers	8	7	7	12	6102	5625	5560	5741	434	473	555	670
2412 Fertilizers and nitrogen compounds	1	2	2	3	...	...	...	2821	...	...	...	305
2413 Plastics in primary forms; synthetic rubber	1	1	1	3	...	...	...	2651	...	...	...	380
242 Other chemicals	19	19	20	22	...	...	...	7657	...	...	...	965
2421 Pesticides and other agro-chemical products	-	-	-	-	-	-	-	-	-	-	-	-
2422 Paints, varnishes, printing ink and mastics	2	2	3	4	...	...	1068	1112	...	...	118	134
2423 Pharmaceuticals, medicinal chemicals, etc.	7	7	8	9	5055	4971	5214	5302	406	486	574	686
2424 Soap, cleaning & cosmetic preparations	8	8	7	6	1269	1390	1407	987	99	124	141	119
2429 Other chemical products n.e.c.	2	2	2	3	...	...	...	256	...	...	...	26
2430 Man-made fibres	3	3	3	3	9892	8846	8143	7585	717	732	797	860
251 Rubber products	9	10	12	11	6338	6454	7321	7424	532	650	847	989
2511 Rubber tyres and tubes	4	4	4	4	4147	4206	4765	4898	372	451	592	717
2519 Other rubber products	5	6	8	7	2191	2248	2556	2526	160	199	255	272
2520 Plastic products	24	29	37	52	7078	7594	7736	7963	474	576	698	848
2610 Glass and glass products	14	14	17	24	8774	8524	8739	8526	575	654	792	885
269 Non-metallic mineral products n.e.c.	80	84	79	109	...	...	...	...	...	...	...	...
2691 Pottery, china and earthenware	4	4	4	5	659	578	610	786	40	44	52	76
2692 Refractory ceramic products	5	6	6	6	4520	4378	4356	4459	325	329	408	438
2693 Struct.non-refractory clay; ceramic products	17	17	16	38	4346	3805	3124	2978	282	275	266	271
2694 Cement, lime and plaster	12	12	11	12	4376	4307	4100	3819	358	426	459	480
2695 Articles of concrete, cement and plaster	35	38	36	41	6026	5075	4718	4478	371	373	411	471
2696 Cutting, shaping & finishing of stone	6	6	5	6	376	433	365	321	24	32	28	31
2699 Other non-metallic mineral products n.e.c.	1	1	1	1	...	...	...	...	...	...	...	...
2710 Basic iron and steel	13	15	15	18	21169	21019	21397	23150	1972	2385	2907	3543
2720 Basic precious and non-ferrous metals	7	7	6	7	7692	6231	6172	6451	616	590	704	819
273 Casting of metals	5	4	5	6	...	...	...	...	...	...	...	...
2731 Casting of iron and steel	3	3	3	4	1605	1161	1148	1498	110	105	120	161
2732 Casting of non-ferrous metals	2	1	2	2	...	...	...	...	...	...	...	...
281 Struct.metal products;tanks;steam generators	44	58	70	77	12774	13729	...	14260	...	...	...	...
2811 Structural metal products	27	34	44	51	4704	5125	5990	6777	317	393	535	617
2812 Tanks, reservoirs and containers of metal	15	22	24	23	2835	3745	3984	3074	205	308	372	300
2813 Steam generators	2	2	2	3	5235	4859	...	4409	...	...	...	...
289 Other metal products; metal working services	77	100	129	73	10733	...	...	...	722	...	...	...
2891 Metal forging/pressing/stamping/roll-forming	-	1	1	2	-	...	...	...	-	...	...	...
2892 Treatment & coating of metals	7	16	24	30	626	1013	1651	2152	37	78	141	209
2893 Cutlery, hand tools and general hardware	24	27	38	41	2827	3368	4136	3979	202	269	373	366
2899 Other fabricated metal products n.e.c.	46	56	66	-	7280	7550	7794	-	483	560	690	-
291 General purpose machinery	60	76	82	94	...	...	25346	26538	...	...	2168	2522
2911 Engines & turbines(not for transport equip.)	8	9	7	9	2893	2377	1929	1705	172	178	161	173
2912 Pumps, compressors, taps and valves	6	7	7	13	4934	4852	4503	4538	355	395	396	462
2913 Bearings, gears, gearing & driving elements	11	16	15	16	9784	8884	9728	10875	519	587	796	1004
2914 Ovens, furnaces and furnace burners	1	1	-	-	...	...	-	-	...	...	-	-
2915 Lifting and handling equipment	10	13	16	16	4509	2850	2910	2757	246	194	228	248
2919 Other general purpose machinery	24	30	37	40	5230	5043	6276	6663	330	397	587	635
292 Special purpose machinery	97	99	100	129	46473	42486	...	...	...	...	...	...
2921 Agricultural and forestry machinery	16	16	15	37	6539	6168	5580	3892	375	403	412	337
2922 Machine tools	13	14	13	17	6439	5959	5847	6693	401	428	480	612
2923 Machinery for metallurgy	2	2	2	1	885	1677	...	...	...	...	...	...
2924 Machinery for mining & construction	13	15	13	16	7494	6178	6092	5665	455	444	507	525
2925 Food/beverage/tobacco processing machinery	7	5	7	6	1296	1160	903	763	72	75	69	67
2926 Machinery for textile, apparel and leather	6	7	7	4	1649	1516	1544	1179	82	91	110	83
2927 Weapons and ammunition	-	-	1	-	-	-	...	-	-	-	...	-
2929 Other special purpose machinery	40	40	42	48	22171	19828	18806	19149	1339	1371	1549	1820
2930 Domestic appliances n.e.c.	7	7	8	7	6373	5631	5376	4969	406	413	435	479

continued

Slovakia

ISIC Revision 3	Number of establishments					Number of employees					Wages and salaries paid to employees				
		(numbers)					(numbers)					(million KORUNAS)			
ISIC Industry	Note	1993	1994	1995	1996	Note	1993	1994	1995	1996	Note	1993	1994	1995	1996
3000 Office, accounting and computing machinery		4	6	8	10		1734	1368	1238	1336		94	110	120	139
3110 Electric motors, generators and transformers		7	9	10	12		2139	2138	3351	4155		127	164	291	389
3120 Electricity distribution & control apparatus		10	12	14	17		3750	3247	3175	2692		223	224	256	236
3130 Insulated wire and cable		5	5	7	12		1457	1932	2457	3040		96	142	212	297
3140 Accumulators, primary cells and batteries		3	3	2	1		235	214	...	...		15	17	...	...
3150 Lighting equipment and electric lamps		4	4	7	12		4875	3737	3552	3123		264	220	218	227
3190 Other electrical equipment n.e.c.		12	17	20	27		3601	3857	5114	6261		253	320	438	600
3210 Electronic valves, tubes, etc.		7	11	11	10		3092	1815	1623	1524		168	147	164	167
3220 TV/radio transmitters; line comm. apparatus		5	6	8	6		4461	3927	3894	3119		235	253	281	267
3230 TV and radio receivers and associated goods		6	3	2	3		4650	4233	...	3788		287	311	...	313
331 Medical, measuring, testing appliances, etc.		18	18	20	24		9704	8680	8488	7607		623	622	707	790
3311 Medical, surgical and orthopaedic equipment		4	4	4	7		3574	3910	3943	3978		224	287	333	389
3312 Measuring/testing/navigating appliances,etc.		9	8	9	9		5164	3933	3789	2882		332	265	289	270
3313 Industrial process control equipment		5	6	7	8		966	837	756	747		67	70	85	131
3320 Optical instruments & photographic equipment		1	1	1	2		...	...	...	...		...	...	...	...
3330 Watches and clocks		-	-	-	-		-	-	-	-		-	-	-	-
3410 Motor vehicles		6	6	6	6		7832	7298	7632	7531		463	582	714	848
3420 Automobile bodies, trailers & semi-trailers		5	4	3	8		453	497	348	1145		27	36	32	86
3430 Parts/accessories for automobiles		13	17	19	19		6076	5374	4689	4431		399	403	419	460
351 Building and repairing of ships and boats		2	2	3	3		...	...	3068	2912		...	...	278	294
3511 Building and repairing of ships		2	2	3	3		...	...	3068	2912		...	...	278	294
3512 Building/repairing of pleasure/sport. boats		-	-	-	-		-	-	-	-		-	-	-	-
3520 Railway/tramway locomotives & rolling stock		2	4	6	7		...	3728	6367	6353		...	307	621	690
3530 Aircraft and spacecraft		1	1	1	6		...	...	...	3189		...	...	...	294
359 Transport equipment n.e.c.		3	6	6	7		...	...	...	...		...	...	...	...
3591 Motorcycles		2	4	2	2		...	816	...	...		...	50	...	...
3592 Bicycles and invalid carriages		-	-	1	2		-	-	...	...		-	-	...	...
3599 Other transport equipment n.e.c.		1	2	3	3		...	...	1621	1484		...	...	162	232
3610 Furniture		61	60	71	77		15713	13628	12831	11156		840	847	906	883
369 Manufacturing n.e.c.		25	26	25	34		...	...	...	...		...	...	...	...
3691 Jewellery and related articles		6	6	5	6		1132	1027	849	863		69	73	69	77
3692 Musical instruments		-	-	-	-		-	-	-	-		-	-	-	-
3693 Sports goods		1	1	1	2		...	...	...	...		...	...	...	...
3694 Games and toys		2	1	4	4		...	...	190	253		...	...	9	14
3699 Other manufacturing n.e.c.		16	18	15	22		1920	2072	1696	2021		101	120	116	167
3710 Recycling of metal waste and scrap		5	5	4	5		727	708	594	587		60	73	72	65
3720 Recycling of non-metal waste and scrap		3	4	5	19		1129	1074	1136	1118		59	68	96	95
D Total manufacturing		1286	1390	1560	1825		538988	446477	452078	446266		35707	33336	39160	43905

Slovakia

ISIC Revision 3	Output					Value added					Gross fixed capital formation		
		(million KORUNAS)					(million KORUNAS)					(million KORUNAS)	
ISIC Industry	Note	1993	1994	1995	1996	Note	1993	1994	1995	1996	Note	1995	1996
151 Processed meat,fish,fruit,vegetables,fats		...	...	16937	20651		...	...	3265	3611		961.7	...
1511 Processing/preserving of meat		10956	10902	12111	14578		1688	1867	2069	2347		608.9	...
1512 Processing/preserving of fish		432	571	733	784		167	159	209	115		33.1	...
1513 Processing/preserving of fruit & vegetables		1283	1254	1121	1612		496	351	267	318		179.3	...
1514 Vegetable and animal oils and fats		...	...	2972	3676		...	...	720	831		140.5	...
1520 Dairy products		8474	8946	9511	10581		1190	1125	1229	1272		604.4	...
153 Grain mill products; starches; animal feeds		6758	7522	7519	9006		1409	1646	1692	1642		494.1	...
1531 Grain mill products		3573	3636	3357	3562		573	688	590	593		189.6	...
1532 Starches and starch products		456	630	882	965		81	206	399	275		111.1	...
1533 Prepared animal feeds		2729	3256	3280	4479		755	752	703	774		193.4	...
154 Other food products		...	...	11231	...		...	...	3778	...		1144.7	...
1541 Bakery products		3712	4543	4624	5728		1306	1701	1786	1976		858.8	...
1542 Sugar		2674	2086	2775	4411		776	614	1034	975		146.4	...
1543 Cocoa, chocolate and sugar confectionery		...	2271	2008	2227		...	510	417	518		13.5	...
1544 Macaroni, noodles & similar products		...	...	-	...		...	...	-	...		-	...
1549 Other food products n.e.c.		1329	1700	1824	2503		358	442	541	602		126.0	...
155 Beverages		6999	8360	9385	10417		2351	2647	2825	2891		728.6	...
1551 Distilling, rectifying & blending of spirits		1236	1656	1826	1916		402	561	477	604		118.5	...
1552 Wines		1461	1673	2040	2572		464	389	473	501		116.1	...
1553 Malt liquors and malt		3514	3925	4402	4669		1109	1253	1549	1377		431.8	...
1554 Soft drinks; mineral waters		788	1106	1117	1261		376	444	326	409		62.3	...
1600 Tobacco products		...	...	...	...		...	...	...	...		332.8	...
171 Spinning, weaving and finishing of textiles		...	...	...	...		...	...	...	...		207.1	...
1711 Textile fibre preparation; textile weaving		4504	4346	4086	6349		1515	1386	1180	1301		128.6	...
1712 Finishing of textiles		...	...	...	...		...	...	...	...		78.4	...
172 Other textiles		...	...	...	644		...	...	...	172		178.2	...
1721 Made-up textile articles, except apparel		454	476	514	558		203	136	142	132		67.0	...
1722 Carpets and rugs		...	...	...	-		...	...	...	-		7.8	...
1723 Cordage, rope, twine and netting		-	-	-	-		-	-	-	-		-0.2	...
1729 Other textiles n.e.c.		182	468	740	86		65	84	201	40		103.5	...
1730 Knitted and crocheted fabrics and articles		2377	2624	2103	2665		1041	1116	806	913		112.1	...
1810 Wearing apparel, except fur apparel		4922	5744	6422	7793		2496	3028	3334	3276		683.9	...
1820 Dressing & dyeing of fur; processing of fur		...	...	...	...		...	...	...	...		2.2	...
191 Tanning, dressing and processing of leather		1726	1774	1730	2023		778	534	521	380		146.0	...
1911 Tanning and dressing of leather		1468	1544	1423	1667		663	429	372	238		159.0	...
1912 Luggage, handbags, etc.; saddlery & harness		258	230	307	356		115	105	149	143		-13.0	...
1920 Footwear		3767	3323	4183	4757		1376	1301	1430	1182		314.0	...
2010 Sawmilling and planing of wood		1835	2511	3184	3033		718	830	921	646		159.5	...
202 Products of wood, cork, straw, etc.		...	...	3626	4601		...	...	1398	1228		738.1	...
2021 Veneer sheets, plywood, particle board, etc.		2147	2129	2486	2560		909	846	952	694		381.0	...
2022 Builders' carpentry and joinery		729	575	799	1022		269	227	336	276		134.0	...
2023 Wooden containers		...	...	69	130		...	...	11	31		21.1	...
2029 Other wood products; articles of cork/straw		155	212	272	889		71	79	99	226		202.1	...
210 Paper and paper products		...	12757	17473	19123		...	3935	6761	4890		1827.0	...
2101 Pulp, paper and paperboard		7261	9253	13087	11572		1568	3178	5592	3084		1173.7	...
2102 Corrugated paper and paperboard		...	902	1130	1162		...	234	244	111		90.1	...
2109 Other articles of paper and paperboard		1876	2602	3256	6389		516	523	925	1695		563.2	...
221 Publishing		1217	1308	1504	...		...	715	524	...		126.9	...
2211 Publishing of books and other publications		293	241	211	560		141	73	74	159		47.2	...
2212 Publishing of newspapers, journals, etc.		801	984	1185	2269		352	615	408	672		56.9	...
2213 Publishing of recorded media		-	-	-	-		-	-	-	-		0.8	...
2219 Other publishing		123	83	108	...		...	27	42	...		22.0	...

continued

Slovakia

ISIC Revision 3 ISIC Industry	Output (million KORUNAS) Note	1993	1994	1995	1996	Value added (million KORUNAS) Note	1993	1994	1995	1996	Gross fixed capital formation (million KORUNAS) Note	1995	1996
222 Printing and related service activities		3341	4050	4781	5965		1257	1480	1581	1885		580.8	...
2221 Printing		2562	3175	3701	4574		971	1191	1225	1456		379.5	...
2222 Service activities related to printing		779	875	1080	1391		286	289	356	429		201.3	...
2230 Reproduction of recorded media		...	...	...	...		...	...	...	...		10.3	...
2310 Coke oven products		...	...	...	...		...	...	...	...		0.2	...
2320 Refined petroleum products		24580	27053	29664	37025		5803	5871	6030	5408		2239.5	...
2330 Processing of nuclear fuel		-	-	-	-		-	-	-	-		-	...
241 Basic chemicals		...	...	...	17827		...	...	...	4434		720.1	...
2411 Basic chemicals, except fertilizers		5244	6510	9091	10451		1296	1847	2560	2730		428.3	...
2412 Fertilizers and nitrogen compounds		...	...	...	3825		...	179	...	726		50.4	...
2413 Plastics in primary forms; synthetic rubber		...	...	...	3551		...	...	...	978		241.3	...
242 Other chemicals		...	...	...	12905		...	3134	...	3821		2019.4	...
2421 Pesticides and other agro-chemical products		-	-	-	-		-	-	-	-		-	...
2422 Paints, varnishes, printing ink and mastics		...	...	1843	1867		402	415	490	310		208.0	...
2423 Pharmaceuticals, medicinal chemicals, etc.		4786	5050	6619	8962		2031	2081	2716	2956		1710.4	...
2424 Soap, cleaning & cosmetic preparations		2118	1924	1972	1780		557	604	587	496		72.2	...
2429 Other chemical products n.e.c.		...	...	...	296		...	34	...	59		28.8	...
2430 Man-made fibres		6766	8309	9422	9403		1918	2403	2346	2307		264.8	...
251 Rubber products		5809	6545	9239	10246		1850	1866	2545	2410		561.4	...
2511 Rubber tyres and tubes		4649	5161	7365	8062		1558	1495	2053	1929		436.9	...
2519 Other rubber products		1160	1384	1874	2184		292	371	492	481		124.4	...
2520 Plastic products		4380	5367	6671	9398		1433	1717	2247	2268		1011.0	...
2610 Glass and glass products		3773	4258	5076	6232		1967	2063	2070	2088		456.0	...
269 Non-metallic mineral products n.e.c.		9303	9298	...	...		3406	3494	...	...		1484.9	...
2691 Pottery, china and earthenware		189	213	249	355		82	78	68	113		181.8	...
2692 Refractory ceramic products		1895	1765	2461	2603		662	580	944	884		257.4	...
2693 Struct.non-refractory clay; ceramic products		1623	1449	1539	1992		711	625	699	859		320.1	...
2694 Cement, lime and plaster		3649	3962	4576	4862		1210	1428	1704	1325		467.4	...
2695 Articles of concrete, cement and plaster		1831	1747	1682	3161		696	752	771	950		216.2	...
2696 Cutting, shaping & finishing of stone		116	162	139	253		45	31	43	57		34.3	...
2699 Other non-metallic mineral products n.e.c.		-	-	...	...		-	-	...	...		7.7	...
2710 Basic iron and steel		35615	41241	49837	61521		5907	8119	10637	8888		393.8	...
2720 Basic precious and non-ferrous metals		6662	6547	8494	12988		1482	1289	2660	3569		2170.2	...
273 Casting of metals		...	...	...	...		...	...	...	...		102.5	...
2731 Casting of iron and steel		472	462	581	739		129	182	176	199		100.3	...
2732 Casting of non-ferrous metals		...	...	...	...		...	...	...	...		2.1	...
281 Struct.metal products;tanks;steam generators		...	...	...	...		...	...	...	...		1092.0	...
2811 Structural metal products		1660	1977	2932	3439		636	746	1079	992		693.8	...
2812 Tanks, reservoirs and containers of metal		1586	2481	2884	1791		660	673	491	311		314.0	...
2813 Steam generators		...	...	...	...		...	...	...	...		84.3	...
289 Other metal products; metal working services		3264	...	...	...		1411	...	...	...		560.4	...
2891 Metal forging/pressing/stamping/roll-forming		-	...	...	...		-	...	...	...		10.7	...
2892 Treatment & coating of metals		138	405	692	947		66	143	275	351		100.6	...
2893 Cutlery, hand tools and general hardware		712	966	1461	1633		361	445	697	691		6.0	...
2899 Other fabricated metal products n.e.c.		2414	2786	4159	-		984	1216	1452	-		443.1	...
291 General purpose machinery		...	...	8953	14628		...	...	4044	4802		841.7	...
2911 Engines & turbines(not for transport equip.)		665	545	624	938		250	191	225	279		71.8	...
2912 Pumps, compressors, taps and valves		2186	2024	1699	2706		1128	1112	870	875		225.4	...
2913 Bearings, gears, gearing & driving elements		1603	2227	3675	5794		678	777	1654	1886		420.4	...
2914 Ovens, furnaces and furnace burners		...	...	-	-		...	...	-	-		28.3	...
2915 Lifting and handling equipment		845	734	827	1538		385	338	284	390		-15.5	...
2919 Other general purpose machinery		1247	1499	2128	3652		581	614	1011	1373		111.3	...

Code	Industry												
292	Special purpose machinery		...	...	...	...		...	...	...	...		822.9	...
2921	Agricultural and forestry machinery		1242	1292	1472	1417		542	597	693	450		111.9	...
2922	Machine tools		1372	1593	2134	2726		666	702	987	620		246.6	...
2923	Machinery for metallurgy		...	...	...	...		...	...	...	...		47.5	...
2924	Machinery for mining & construction		1787	1614	1974	2705		722	581	844	717		178.4	...
2925	Food/beverage/tobacco processing machinery		256	243	224	298		110	109	116	124		0.3	...
2926	Machinery for textile, apparel and leather		225	312	459	371		115	143	182	131		13.4	...
2927	Weapons and ammunition		-	-	...	-		-	-	...	-		4.7	...
2929	Other special purpose machinery		5495	4708	5600	8968		2432	1731	2093	1686		220.1	...
2930	Domestic appliances n.e.c.		5182	4800	5514	5286		1537	1336	849	769		338.1	...
3000	Office, accounting and computing machinery		387	376	398	845		150	207	314	291		59.4	...
3110	Electric motors, generators and transformers		990	1782	1825	3744		215	419	577	669		387.5	...
3120	Electricity distribution & control apparatus		1270	1131	1344	1193		546	435	446	392		75.3	...
3130	Insulated wire and cable		1310	1874	2793	3606		211	172	420	561		317.3	...
3140	Accumulators, primary cells and batteries		161	137	...	...		49	43	...	...		12.4	...
3150	Lighting equipment and electric lamps		1280	1004	941	1128		309	390	318	271		26.0	...
3190	Other electrical equipment n.e.c.		1218	1250	1804	3062		624	745	1019	1164		232.1	...
3210	Electronic valves, tubes, etc.		1708	1216	1952	2831		232	300	508	553		62.1	...
3220	TV/radio transmitters; line comm. apparatus		600	843	909	1098		353	482	489	519		94.4	...
3230	TV and radio receivers and associated goods		1933	1850	...	1790		585	528	...	365		78.4	...
331	Medical, measuring, testing appliances, etc.		3291	3267	3702	5876		1599	1517	1543	1662		218.0	...
3311	Medical, surgical and orthopaedic equipment		1120	1438	1513	2348		482	743	785	845		194.6	...
3312	Measuring/testing/navigating appliances,etc.		2044	1618	1809	2956		1012	632	558	565		-12.9	...
3313	Industrial process control equipment		127	211	380	572		105	142	200	253		36.2	...
3320	Optical instruments & photographic equipment		...	...	...	...		...	...	...	...		16.0	...
3330	Watches and clocks		-	-	-	-		-	-	-	-		1.9	...
3410	Motor vehicles		4132	5939	16571	21341		1269	1148	1925	2477		2141.2	...
3420	Automobile bodies, trailers & semi-trailers		130	230	292	648		40	67	124	173		-7.9	...
3430	Parts/accessories for automobiles		2352	2095	2325	3115		971	908	843	929		-76.1	...
351	Building and repairing of ships and boats		...	...	2561	2979		...	...	989	479		196.5	...
3511	Building and repairing of ships		...	...	2561	2979		...	...	989	479		197.3	...
3512	Building/repairing of pleasure/sport. boats		-	-	-	-		-	-	-	-		-0.8	...
3520	Railway/tramway locomotives & rolling stock		...	2835	4132	4817		...	883	1363	1257		121.1	...
3530	Aircraft and spacecraft		...	...	...	3235		...	...	...	384		31.7	...
359	Transport equipment n.e.c.		...	...	...	...		...	177	...	...		67.3	...
3591	Motorcycles		...	249	...	...		...	53	...	...		6.8	...
3592	Bicycles and invalid carriages		-	-	...	...		-	-	...	...		9.5	...
3599	Other transport equipment n.e.c.		...	...	894	1729		...	124	353	533		51.0	...
3610	Furniture		5091	4805	5555	6236		1561	1466	1574	1573		184.3	...
369	Manufacturing n.e.c.		...	...	...	...		...	...	...	...		162.2	...
3691	Jewellery and related articles		477	459	385	772		160	147	144	174		17.8	...
3692	Musical instruments		-	-	-	-		-	-	-	-		-0.3	...
3693	Sports goods		...	...	...	...		...	...	...	...		11.7	...
3694	Games and toys		...	...	40	60		...	...	24	29		3.9	...
3699	Other manufacturing n.e.c.		449	452	599	779		204	239	271	262		129.2	...
3710	Recycling of metal waste and scrap		868	1150	1104	1075		257	257	272	144		94.2	...
3720	Recycling of non-metal waste and scrap		422	515	830	704		115	182	259	165		49.9	...
D	Total manufacturing		316389	295356	362936	447104		77950	87156	104417	100456		29026.4	...

Slovakia

ISIC Revision 3			Index numbers of industrial production											
			(1990=100)											
ISIC	Industry	Note	1985	1986	1987	1988	1989	1990	1991	1992	1993	1994	1995	1996
15	Food and beverages		...	...	...	...	...	...	...	...	...	...	...	...
16	Tobacco products		...	...	...	...	...	...	...	...	...	...	...	...
17	Textiles		...	...	...	...	...	...	...	...	...	...	...	...
18	Wearing apparel, fur		...	...	...	...	...	...	...	...	...	...	...	...
19	Leather, leather products and footwear		...	...	...	...	...	...	...	...	...	...	...	...
20	Wood products (excl. furniture)		...	...	...	...	...	...	...	...	...	...	...	...
21	Paper and paper products		...	...	...	...	...	...	...	...	...	...	...	...
22	Printing and publishing		...	...	...	...	...	...	...	...	...	...	...	...
23	Coke,refined petroleum products,nuclear fuel		...	...	...	...	...	...	...	...	...	...	...	...
24	Chemicals and chemical products		...	...	...	...	...	...	...	...	...	...	...	...
25	Rubber and plastics products		...	...	...	...	...	...	...	...	...	...	...	...
26	Non-metallic mineral products		...	...	...	...	...	...	...	...	...	...	...	...
27	Basic metals		...	...	...	...	...	...	...	...	...	...	...	...
28	Fabricated metal products		...	...	...	...	...	...	...	...	...	...	...	...
29	Machinery and equipment n.e.c.		...	...	...	...	...	...	...	...	...	...	...	...
30	Office, accounting and computing machinery		...	...	...	...	...	...	...	...	...	...	...	...
31	Electrical machinery and apparatus		...	...	...	...	...	...	...	...	...	...	...	...
32	Radio,television and communication equipment		...	...	...	...	...	...	...	...	...	...	...	...
33	Medical, precision and optical instruments		...	...	...	...	...	...	...	...	...	...	...	...
34	Motor vehicles, trailers, semi-trailers		...	...	...	...	...	...	...	...	...	...	...	...
35	Other transport equipment		...	...	...	...	...	...	...	...	...	...	...	...
36	Furniture; manufacturing n.e.c.		...	...	...	...	...	...	...	...	...	...	...	...
37	Recycling		...	...	...	...	...	...	...	...	...	...	...	...
D	Total manufacturing		...	...	...	...	...	100	86	72	68	71	78	80

SLOVENIA

Supplier of information:
Statistical Office of the Republic of Slovenia, Ljubljana.

Basic source of data:
Administrative data, Final statements.
Financial data were collected by the Agency for Payments. The Statistical Office of the Republic of Slovenia is a user of these data.

Major deviations from ISIC (Revision 2):
Data are based on the Standard Classification of Economic Activities, in accordance with NACE (Revision 1).

Reference period (if not calendar year):

Scope:
All registered establishments.

Method of enumeration:
Individual sites are visited by enumerators.

Adjusted for non-response:
Yes.

Concepts and definitions of variables:
For the year 1996, output and value added are valued in basic values, before 1996 they are valued in producers' prices.

Related national publications: Statistical Yearbook and Rapid Report on National Account, both published by Statistical Office of the Republic of Slovenia, Ljubljana.

Slovenia

ISIC Revision 2	Number of enterprises					Number of employees					Wages and salaries paid to employees				
		(numbers)					(numbers)					(million TOLARS)			
ISIC Industry	Note	1993	1994	1995	1996	Note	1993	1994	1995	1996	Note	1993	1994	1995	1996
311/2 Food products		853	1083	837	933a/	a/	21050	22383	21006	21408	a/	21379	27848	28703	33365
313 Beverages		40	45	69	...a/	a/	...	...	...	...	a/	...	...	...	...
314 Tobacco		1	1	1	...a/	a/	...	...	...	...	a/	...	...	...	...
321 Textiles		181	186	649	2964b/	b/	47201	43437	39064	35190	b/	30211	33924	32457	33551
322 Wearing apparel, except footwear		2560	2927	1826	...b/	b/	...	...	...	...	b/	...	...	...	...
323 Leather and fur products		409	572	298	773c/	c/	12018	12153	10750	10227	c/	7785	10080	9825	9714
324 Footwear, except rubber or plastic		46	38	271	...c/	c/	...	...	...	...	c/	...	...	...	...
331 Wood products, except furniture		2932	3668	1536	2368		13905	12595	11919	13168		8654	10591	11743	13852
332 Furniture and fixtures, excl. metal		250	277	1754	...d/	d/	...	...	...	...	d/	...	...	...	...
341 Paper and products		325	323	264	1832e/	e/	16670	16783	17103	17079	e/	16880	21215	22436	24061
342 Printing and publishing		813	880	1235	...e/	e/	...	...	...	...	e/	...	...	...	...
351 Industrial chemicals		27	27	73	272f/	f/	11432	13595	13559	14294	f/	13910	21394	24465	29247
352 Other chemicals		95	108	166	...f/	f/	...	...	...	...	f/	...	...	...	...
353 Petroleum refineries		5	4	11	13g/	g/	1126	880	852	345	g/	1290	1117	1374	1516
354 Misc. petroleum and coal products		...	...	-	...g/	g/	...	...	...	...	g/	...	...	...	...
355 Rubber products		86	254	213	1745h/	h/	10105	10573	11495	11132	h/	8787	12146	13447	14471
356 Plastic products		1076	1254	1084	...h/	h/	...	...	...	...	h/	...	...	...	...
361 Pottery, china, earthenware		34	82	60	519i/	i/	13235	12517	12420	11658	i/	11235	13356	14714	15514
362 Glass and products		60	68	67	...i/	i/	...	...	...	...	i/	...	...	...	...
369 Other non-metallic mineral products		326	451	289	...i/	i/	...	...	...	...	i/	...	...	...	...
371 Iron and steel		14	16	15	6118j/	j/	39963	36718	34621	33759	j/	28244	35976	37283	40575
372 Non-ferrous metals		65	63	114	...j/	j/	...	...	...	...	j/	...	...	...	...
381 Fabricated metal products		5632	6338	4813	...j/	j/	...	...	...	...	j/	...	...	...	...
382 Non-electrical machinery		314	350	1134	1369k/	k/	27470	23953	29078	23336	k/	19289	24111	26708	28290
383 Electrical machinery		1182	1459	1723	2575		29952	27482	27592	26637		22716	29422	31774	35108
384 Transport equipment		97	104	117	129		15254	14907	12632	10982		11148	14718	13815	14001
385 Professional and scientific equipment		...	...	474	...k/	k/	...	...	...	...	k/	...	...	...	...
390 Other manufacturing industries		2317	2902	768	3038d/	d/	20387	17154	15289	14626	d/	13397	14539	14937	15314
3 Total manufacturing		19740	23480	19861	24648		279768	265130	257380	244350		214925	270437	283681	308577

a/ 311/2 includes 313 and 314.
b/ 321 includes 322.
c/ 323 includes 324.
d/ 390 includes 332.
e/ 341 includes 342.
f/ 351 includes 352.
g/ 353 includes 354.
h/ 355 includes 356.
i/ 361 includes 362 and 369.
j/ 371 includes 372 and 381.
k/ 382 includes 385.

Slovenia

ISIC Revision 2 ISIC Industry	Note	Output in producers' prices (million TOLARS) 1993	1994	1995	1996a/	Note	Value added in producers' prices (million TOLARS) 1993	1994	1995	1996b/	Note	Gross fixed capital formation (million TOLARS) 1995	1996
311/2 Food products		133342	153091	159899	250505c/		54430	52185	58306	76476d/		7682	18473c/
313 Beverages		27487	34006	40874	...c/		11341	13158	16003	...d/		8662	...c/
314 Tobacco		15461	7968	8624	...c/		11775	3187	3935	...		574	...c/
321 Textiles		60912	66602	76105	134756e/		30734	22677	23666	57178e/	e/	5813	3722
322 Wearing apparel, except footwear		41978	43951	51356	...e/		24096	24974	28479	...e/	e/	...	...
323 Leather and fur products		31539	42098	38800	39438f/		11724	15533	13936	15324f/		375	904f/
324 Footwear, except rubber or plastic		19461	22113	21456	...f/		8178	8436	8932	...f/		629	...f/
331 Wood products, except furniture		52083	65045	71629	82997		14693	18927	19066	24450		662	2288
332 Furniture and fixtures, excl. metal		77284	82866	77526	...g/		27854	15510	20739	...g/		3270	...g/
341 Paper and products		94160	126532	147683	156846h/		30800	38542	42476	53215h/		1253	9395h/
342 Printing and publishing		48435	57151	71498	...h/		20488	24520	29668	...h/		3227	...h/
351 Industrial chemicals		87693	139745	161416	186049i/		30310	50158	54297	66261i/		7259	17311i/
352 Other chemicals		43163	109894	126382	...i/		19476	27853	44564	...i/		13218	...i/
353 Petroleum refineries	j/	15105	12639	19802	19810	j/	1366	1716	3104	395	j/	527	148
354 Misc. petroleum and coal products	j/	...	...	...	...	j/	...	...	...	...	j/	...	...
355 Rubber products		23396	28490	33732	38866k/		8965	10196	11195	33996k/		3511	5343k/
356 Plastic products		23373	31734	51337	...k/		7384	10286	16756	...k/		3139	...k/
361 Pottery, china, earthenware	m/	50905	63065	66621	79461	m/	18789	25294	25861	30358	m/	2299	5229
362 Glass and products	m/	...	...	...	...	m/	...	...	...	...	m/	...	...
369 Other non-metallic mineral products	m/	...	...	...	...	m/	...	...	...	...	m/	...	...
371 Iron and steel		169563	205309	235339	256293n/		48652	60439	70807	78714n/		1743	11103n/
372 Non-ferrous metals		14638	16778	50245	...n/		2888	1816	10947	...n/		1475	...n/
381 Fabricated metal products		65718	88338	136821	...n/		22393	29604	50653	...n/		5020	...n/
382 Non-electrical machinery		99899	125014	147275	167384p/		28825	37405	40662	50161p/	p/	1904	8286
383 Electrical machinery		110568	142517	164792	193400		39095	51119	55092	68364		12998	9542
384 Transport equipment		102816	137134	160556	183532		19785	24123	26866	23221		3948	4048
385 Professional and scientific equipment		21262	27307	36699	...p/		7403	10941	13636	...p/	p/	...	...
390 Other manufacturing industries		7803	8900	11779	87776g/		3038	3605	4546	30799g/		134	3610g/
3 Total manufacturing		1438044	1838287	2168246	1877113		504482	582204	694192	609415		89322	99402

a/ Output (in basic values).
b/ Value added (in basic values).
c/ 311/2 includes 313 and 314.
d/ 311/2 includes 313.
e/ 321 includes 322.
f/ 323 includes 324.
g/ 390 includes 332.
h/ 341 includes 342.
i/ 351 includes 352.
j/ 353 includes 354.
k/ 355 includes 356.
m/ 361 includes 362 and 369.
n/ 371 includes 372 and 381.
p/ 382 includes 385.

Slovenia

ISIC Revision 2		Index numbers of industrial production											
		(1990=100)											
ISIC Industry	Note	1985	1986	1987	1988	1989	1990	1991	1992	1993	1994	1995	1996
311/2 Food products		98	101	105	103	99	100	96	78	76	79	80	...
313 Beverages		96	101	99	96	89	100	96	86	82	81	78	...
314 Tobacco		139	123	129	138	124	100	93	102	94	91	83	...
321 Textiles		138	137	130	126	119	100	81	70	70	70	80	...
322 Wearing apparel, except footwear		98	104	111	100	108	100	91	79	80	74	68	...
323 Leather and fur products		115	116	113	114	118	100	86	87	79	77	72	...
324 Footwear, except rubber or plastic		131	135	136	120	120	100	75	75	74	71	60	...
331 Wood products, except furniture		129	128	117	115	111	100	86	75	74	79	78	...
332 Furniture and fixtures, excl. metal		125	141	124	128	119	100	95	88	92	95	104	...
341 Paper and products		106	105	106	111	105	100	88	77	72	80	78	...
342 Printing and publishing		66	71	75	81	105	100	104	88	96	99	82	...
351 Industrial chemicals		122	122	118	127	125	100	82	79	73	87	91	...
352 Other chemicals		100	103	117	113	108	100	90	61	61	71	71	...
353 Petroleum refineries		70	76	78	84	88	100	111	111	110	71	108	...
354 Misc. petroleum and coal products		101	115	120	119	111	100	85	87	94	121	110	...
355 Rubber products		93	95	96	96	101	100	101	101	100	106	111	...
356 Plastic products		134	132	99	103	106	100	89	67	72	78	83	...
361 Pottery, china, earthenware		138	139	135	138	135	100	106	94	93	92	94	...
362 Glass and products		76	81	82	88	105	100	85	80	81	98	104	...
369 Other non-metallic mineral products		109	108	111	113	107	100	86	79	72	79	79	...
371 Iron and steel		126	125	121	117	115	100	70	68	62	71	72	...
372 Non-ferrous metals		86	87	86	97	103	100	88	81	79	82	89	...
381 Fabricated metal products		121	121	120	115	118	100	94	80	76	76	70	...
382 Non-electrical machinery		100	99	103	99	109	100	79	64	61	72	76	...
383 Electrical machinery		135	142	129	126	133	100	84	68	70	86	100	...
384 Transport equipment		118	125	120	107	107	100	82	68	56	55	57	...
385 Professional and scientific equipment		100	105	106	106	102	100	101	95	97	106	125	...
390 Other manufacturing industries		141	161	192	165	143	100	77	84	97	93	91	...
3 Total manufacturing		116	118	116	114	114	100	87	75	73	78	81	...

SOLOMON ISLANDS

Supplier of information:
Statistical Office of the Solomon Islands, Honiara.

Basic source of data:
Not reported.

Major deviations from ISIC (Revision 2):
None reported.

Reference period (if not calendar year):

Scope:
Not reported.

Method of enumeration:
Not reported.

Adjusted for non-response:
Not reported.

Concepts and definitions of variables:
No deviations from the standard UN concepts and definitions are reported.

Related national publications:

Solomon Islands

ISIC Revision 2	Number of establishments					Number of employees					Wages and salaries paid to employees				
		(numbers)					(numbers)					(DOLLARS)			
ISIC Industry	Note	1993	1994	1995	1996	Note	1993	1994	1995	1996	Note	1993	1994	1995	1996
311/2 Food products		51	51	51	51		...	...	...	...		...	...	...	...
313 Beverages		4	4	4	4		...	...	...	...		...	...	...	...
314 Tobacco		1	1	1	1		...	...	...	...		...	...	...	...
321 Textiles		-	-	-	-		...	...	...	...		...	...	...	...
322 Wearing apparel, except footwear		25	25	25	25		...	...	...	...		...	...	...	...
323 Leather and fur products		1	1	1	1		...	...	...	...		...	...	...	...
324 Footwear, except rubber or plastic		1	1	1	1		...	...	...	...		...	...	...	...
331 Wood products, except furniture		44	44	44	44		...	...	...	...		...	...	...	...
332 Furniture and fixtures, excl. metal		29	29	29	29		...	...	...	...		...	...	...	...
341 Paper and products		6	6	6	6		...	...	...	...		...	...	...	...
342 Printing and publishing		31	31	31	31		...	...	...	...		...	...	...	...
351 Industrial chemicals		-	-	-	-		...	...	...	...		...	...	...	...
352 Other chemicals		3	3	3	3		...	...	...	...		...	...	...	...
353 Petroleum refineries		-	-	-	-		...	...	...	...		...	...	...	...
354 Misc. petroleum and coal products		-	-	-	-		...	...	...	...		...	...	...	...
355 Rubber products		1	1	1	1		...	...	...	...		...	...	...	...
356 Plastic products		5	5	5	5		...	...	...	...		...	...	...	...
361 Pottery, china, earthenware		-	-	-	-		...	...	...	...		...	...	...	...
362 Glass and products		7	7	7	7		...	...	...	...		...	...	...	...
369 Other non-metallic mineral products		9	9	9	9		...	...	...	...		...	...	...	...
371 Iron and steel		-	-	-	-		...	...	...	...		...	...	...	...
372 Non-ferrous metals		...	-	-	-		...	...	...	...		...	...	...	...
381 Fabricated metal products		18	18	18	18		...	...	...	...		...	...	...	...
382 Non-electrical machinery		1	1	1	1		...	...	...	...		...	...	...	...
383 Electrical machinery		-	-	-	-		...	...	...	...		...	...	...	...
384 Transport equipment		12	12	12	12		...	...	...	...		...	...	...	...
385 Professional and scientific equipment		-	-	-	-		...	...	...	...		...	...	...	...
390 Other manufacturing industries		8	8	8	8		...	...	...	...		...	...	...	...
3 Total manufacturing		257	257	257	257		...	...	...	...		...	...	...	...

SOUTH AFRICA

Supplier of information:
Central Statistical Service, Pretoria.

Basic source of data:
Monthly surveys and periodic censuses.

Major deviations from ISIC (Revision 3):
Manufacture mainly for consumption on premises, grain mills and sawmills operated by farmers for and at their own convenience, and custom milling by retail stores are excluded from manufacturing. The classification is based on the system described in the national publication Standard Industrial Classification of All Economic Activities, 5th Edition, 1993.

Reference period (if not calendar year):

Scope:
All private manufacturing establishments. For the number of establishments and wages and salaries, some government establishments are included.

Method of enumeration:
For the monthly surveys establishments were sampled.

Adjusted for non-response:
Yes.

Concepts and definitions of variables:
Number of employees is as of 30 June of the reference year.
Wages and salaries includes some employers' contributions to pension, holiday and medical aid funds. Employers' contributions to unemployment insurance and workmen's compensation are excluded. Payments in kind are also excluded.
Output is gross output.
Value added is total value added.
Gross fixed capital formation was derived from national accounts calculations.

Related national publications:

South Africa

ISIC Revision 3	Number of establishments					Number of employees					Wages and salaries paid to employees				
		(numbers)					(thousands)					(million RAND)			
ISIC Industry	Note	1993	1994	1995	1996	Note	1993	1994	1995	1996	Note	1993	1994	1995	1996
151 Processed meat,fish,fruit,vegetables,fats		505	...	...	...		69.6	...	...	...		1465	1437	1560	1660
1511 Processing/preserving of meat		260	...	...	...		25.6	...	...	...		...	...	...	...
1512 Processing/preserving of fish		61	...	...	...		13.4	...	...	...		...	...	...	...
1513 Processing/preserving of fruit & vegetables		159	...	...	...		23.6	...	...	...		...	...	...	...
1514 Vegetable and animal oils and fats		25	...	...	...		7.0	...	...	...		...	...	...	...
1520 Dairy products		143	...	...	...		18.5	...	...	...		742	879	938	962
153 Grain mill products; starches; animal feeds		317	...	...	...		26.9	...	...	...		...	690	720	775
1531 Grain mill products		230	...	...	...		18.8	...	...	...		...	...	...	...
1532 Starches and starch products		-	...	...	...		-	...	...	...		...	...	...	...
1533 Prepared animal feeds		87	...	...	...		8.1	...	...	...		...	...	...	...
154 Other food products		827	...	...	...		67.5	...	...	...		1801	1920	2071	2377
1541 Bakery products		553	...	...	...		26.9	...	...	...		...	...	...	...
1542 Sugar		22	...	...	...		12.7	...	...	...		...	...	...	...
1543 Cocoa, chocolate and sugar confectionery		63	...	...	...		10.2	...	...	...		...	...	...	...
1544 Macaroni, noodles & similar products		189a/	...	...	...		17.7a/	...	...	...		...	...	...	...
1549 Other food products n.e.c.		...a/	...	...	...		...a/	...	...	...		...	...	...	...
155 Beverages		236	...	...	...		35.5	...	...	...		1114	1189	1278	1386
1551 Distilling, rectifying & blending of spirits		118b/	...	...	...		10.3b/	...	...	...		...	...	...	...
1552 Wines		...b/	...	...	...		...b/	...	...	...		...	...	...	...
1553 Malt liquors and malt		56	...	...	...		13.5	...	...	...		...	...	...	...
1554 Soft drinks; mineral waters		62	...	...	...		11.7	...	...	...		...	...	...	...
1600 Tobacco products		12	...	...	...		4.3	...	...	...		143	137	140	145
171 Spinning, weaving and finishing of textiles		157	...	...	...		37.0	...	...	...		770	867	905	1180
1711 Textile fibre preparation; textile weaving		122	...	...	...		33.0	...	...	...		...	...	...	...
1712 Finishing of textiles		35	...	...	...		4.0	...	...	...		...	...	...	...
172 Other textiles		490	...	...	...		29.8	...	...	...		586	699	798	875
1721 Made-up textile articles, except apparel		400	...	...	...		21.4	...	...	...		...	...	...	...
1722 Carpets and rugs		36	...	...	...		3.9	...	...	...		...	...	...	...
1723 Cordage, rope, twine and netting		11	...	...	...		1.1	...	...	...		...	...	...	...
1729 Other textiles n.e.c.		43	...	...	...		3.3	...	...	...		...	...	...	...
1730 Knitted and crocheted fabrics and articles		198	...	...	...		19.2	...	...	...		253	252	265	327
1810 Wearing apparel, except fur apparel		1392c/	...	...	...		118.2c/	...	...	...	c/	1755	1818	2140	2446
1820 Dressing & dyeing of fur; processing of fur		...c/	...	...	...		...c/	...	...	...	c/	...	...	...	...
191 Tanning, dressing and processing of leather		157	...	...	...		8.6	...	...	...		168	170	183	187
1911 Tanning and dressing of leather		28	...	...	...		4.0	...	...	...		...	...	...	...
1912 Luggage, handbags, etc.; saddlery & harness		129	...	...	...		4.6	...	...	...		...	...	...	...
1920 Footwear		253	...	...	...		32.8	...	...	...		441	477	538	532
2010 Sawmilling and planing of wood		178	...	...	...		24.4	...	...	...		330	424	437	429
202 Products of wood, cork, straw, etc.		793	...	...	...		25.7	...	...	...		482	541	562	592
2021 Veneer sheets, plywood, particle board, etc.		33	...	...	...		6.5	...	...	...		...	...	...	...
2022 Builders' carpentry and joinery		269	...	...	...		9.2	...	...	...		...	...	...	...
2023 Wooden containers		84	...	...	...		3.4	...	...	...		...	...	...	...
2029 Other wood products; articles of cork/straw		407	...	...	...		6.6	...	...	...		...	...	...	...
210 Paper and paper products		392	...	...	...		45.1	...	...	...		1738	1895	2129	2335
2101 Pulp, paper and paperboard		38	...	...	...		13.3	...	...	...		...	...	...	...
2102 Corrugated paper and paperboard		201	...	...	...		20.7	...	...	...		...	...	...	...
2109 Other articles of paper and paperboard		153	...	...	...		11.0	...	...	...		...	...	...	...
221 Publishing		264	...	...	...		14.8	...	...	...		376	399	466	750
2211 Publishing of books and other publications		165	...	...	...		4.0	...	...	...		...	...	...	...
2212 Publishing of newspapers, journals, etc.		99d/	...	...	...		10.9d/	...	...	...		...	...	...	...
2213 Publishing of recorded media		...d/	...	...	...		...d/	...	...	...		...	...	...	...
2219 Other publishing		...	...	...	...		...	...	...	...		...	...	...	...

ISIC	Industry													
222	Printing and related service activities	1342	...	...	...	34.9	...	...	...		2068	1835	1980	1740
2221	Printing	1180	...	...	...	31.5	...	...	...		...	...	...	...
2222	Service activities related to printing	162e/	...	...	...	3.4e/	...	...	...		...	...	...	...
2230	Reproduction of recorded media	...e/	...	...	...	...e/	...	...	...		2	4	5	13
2310	Coke oven products	37	...	...	...	2.5	...	...	...		79	80	93	102
2320	Refined petroleum products	47f/	...	...	...	18.2f/	...	...	...	f/	1082	1325	1347	1473
2330	Processing of nuclear fuel	...f/	...	...	...	...f/	...	...	...	f/	...	...	...	...
241	Basic chemicals	228	...	...	...	32.4	...	...	...		1521	1654	1781	1870
2411	Basic chemicals, except fertilizers	149	...	...	...	17.3	...	...	...		...	...	...	...
2412	Fertilizers and nitrogen compounds	37	...	...	...	5.3	...	...	...		...	...	...	...
2413	Plastics in primary forms; synthetic rubber	42	...	...	...	9.8	...	...	...		...	...	...	...
242	Other chemicals	664	...	...	...	50.6	...	...	...		2895	3013	3365	3685
2421	Pesticides and other agro-chemical products	20	...	...	...	1.8	...	...	...		...	...	...	...
2422	Paints, varnishes, printing ink and mastics	156	...	...	...	8.3	...	...	...		...	...	...	...
2423	Pharmaceuticals, medicinal chemicals, etc.	90	...	...	...	12.5	...	...	...		...	...	...	...
2424	Soap, cleaning & cosmetic preparations	239	...	...	...	14.2	...	...	...		...	...	...	...
2429	Other chemical products n.e.c.	159g/	...	...	...	13.9g/	...	...	...		...	...	...	...
2430	Man-made fibres	...g/	...	...	...	...g/	...	...	...		...	...	...	...
251	Rubber products	178	...	...	...	18.7	...	...	...		598	660	725	752
2511	Rubber tyres and tubes	55	...	...	...	11.8	...	...	...		...	...	...	...
2519	Other rubber products	123	...	...	...	6.8	...	...	...		...	...	...	...
2520	Plastic products	885	...	...	...	43.0	...	...	...		1182	1187	1389	1462
2610	Glass and glass products	75	...	...	...	8.4	...	...	...		390	434	493	593
269	Non-metallic mineral products n.e.c.	1183	...	...	...	61.1	...	...	...		1714	1796	1968	2117
2691	Pottery, china and earthenware	119	...	...	...	4.2	...	...	...		...	...	...	...
2692	Refractory ceramic products	16	...	...	...	0.5	...	...	...		...	...	...	...
2693	Struct.non-refractory clay; ceramic products	251	...	...	...	20.8	...	...	...		...	...	...	...
2694	Cement, lime and plaster	24	...	...	...	5.0	...	...	...		...	...	...	...
2695	Articles of concrete, cement and plaster	611	...	...	...	24.4	...	...	...		...	...	...	...
2696	Cutting, shaping & finishing of stone	100	...	...	...	3.2	...	...	...		...	...	...	...
2699	Other non-metallic mineral products n.e.c.	62	...	...	...	3.2	...	...	...		...	...	...	...
2710	Basic iron and steel	142	...	...	...	69.9	...	...	...		3072	3224	3671	3957
2720	Basic precious and non-ferrous metals	98	...	...	...	18.5	...	...	...		686	759	885	895
273	Casting of metals	16	...	...	...	0.7	...	...	...		...	...	...	...
2731	Casting of iron and steel	11	...	...	...	0.5	...	...	...		...	...	...	...
2732	Casting of non-ferrous metals	5	...	...	...	0.2	...	...	...		...	...	...	...
281	Struct.metal products;tanks;steam generators	1300	...	...	...	35.6	...	...	...		1270	1444	1671	1828
2811	Structural metal products	999	...	...	...	26.9	...	...	...		...	...	...	...
2812	Tanks, reservoirs and containers of metal	196	...	...	...	5.3	...	...	...		...	...	...	...
2813	Steam generators	105	...	...	...	3.3	...	...	...		...	...	...	...
289	Other metal products; metal working services	2259	...	...	...	67.7	...	...	...		2020	2219	2352	2834
2891	Metal forging/pressing/stamping/roll-forming	11	...	...	...	0.4	...	...	...		...	...	...	...
2892	Treatment & coating of metals	1159	...	...	...	13.8	...	...	...		...	...	...	...
2893	Cutlery, hand tools and general hardware	173	...	...	...	8.2	...	...	...		...	...	...	...
2899	Other fabricated metal products n.e.c.	916	...	...	...	45.2	...	...	...		...	...	...	...
291	General purpose machinery	1090	...	...	...	28.4	...	...	...		973	1135	1179	1358
2911	Engines & turbines(not for transport equip.)	24	...	...	...	2.2	...	...	...		...	...	...	...
2912	Pumps, compressors, taps and valves	113	...	...	...	2.4	...	...	...		...	...	...	...
2913	Bearings, gears, gearing & driving elements	44	...	...	...	2.1	...	...	...		...	...	...	...
2914	Ovens, furnaces and furnace burners	13	...	...	...	0.1	...	...	...		...	...	...	...
2915	Lifting and handling equipment	104	...	...	...	3.2	...	...	...		...	...	...	...
2919	Other general purpose machinery	792	...	...	...	18.3	...	...	...		...	...	...	...
292	Special purpose machinery	1209	...	...	...	41.2	...	...	...		1224	1399	1731	2000
2921	Agricultural and forestry machinery	128	...	...	...	2.9	...	...	...		...	...	...	...
2922	Machine tools	158	...	...	...	3.8	...	...	...		...	...	...	...
2923	Machinery for metallurgy	6	...	...	...	0.2	...	...	...		...	...	...	...
2924	Machinery for mining & construction	137	...	...	...	6.4	...	...	...		...	...	...	...
2925	Food/beverage/tobacco processing machinery	30	...	...	...	1.2	...	...	...		...	...	...	...
2926	Machinery for textile, apparel and leather	6	...	...	...	-	...	...	...		...	...	...	...
2927	Weapons and ammunition	744h/	...	...	...	26.7h/	...	...	...		...	...	...	...
2929	Other special purpose machinery	...h/	...	...	...	...h/	...	...	...		...	...	...	...
2930	Domestic appliances n.e.c.	124	...	...	...	11.0	...	...	...		246	242	267	312

continued

South Africa

ISIC Revision 3	Number of establishments					Number of employees					Wages and salaries paid to employees				
		(numbers)					(thousands)					(million RAND)			
ISIC Industry	Note	1993	1994	1995	1996	Note	1993	1994	1995	1996	Note	1993	1994	1995	1996
3000 Office, accounting and computing machinery		38	...	...	...		1.3	...	...	...		50	33	45	42
3110 Electric motors, generators and transformers		...i/	...	...	...		2.0	...	...	...		...	1056	1422	428
3120 Electricity distribution & control apparatus		...i/	...	...	...		5.1	...	...	...		175	185	191	254
3130 Insulated wire and cable		37	...	...	...		8.7	...	...	...		347	371	435	442
3140 Accumulators, primary cells and batteries		15	...	...	...		4.1	...	...	...		146	164	180	172
3150 Lighting equipment and electric lamps		64	...	...	...		3.0	...	...	...		63	52	55	62
3190 Other electrical equipment n.e.c.		714i/	...	...	...		19.6	...	...	...		1654	1969	1886	2521
3210 Electronic valves, tubes, etc.		9	...	...	...		0.6	...	...	...		...	...	...	...
3220 TV/radio transmitters; line comm. apparatus		13	...	...	...		0.2	...	...	...		...	...	...	...
3230 TV and radio receivers and associated goods		148	...	...	...		13.8	...	...	...		...	577	627	660
331 Medical, measuring, testing appliances, etc.		233	...	...	...		6.2	...	...	...		182	199	198	189
3311 Medical, surgical and orthopaedic equipment		107	...	...	...		3.0	...	...	...		...	...	...	...
3312 Measuring/testing/navigating appliances,etc.		115	...	...	...		2.9	...	...	...		...	...	...	...
3313 Industrial process control equipment		11	...	...	...		0.2	...	...	...		...	...	...	...
3320 Optical instruments & photographic equipment		60	...	...	...		1.5	...	...	...		31	32	33	40
3330 Watches and clocks		5	...	...	...		-	...	...	...		...	...	...	...
3410 Motor vehicles		48	...	...	...		33.2	...	...	...		1325	1414	1749	1874
3420 Automobile bodies, trailers & semi-trailers		194	...	...	...		8.7	...	...	...		276	283	330	400
3430 Parts/accessories for automobiles		726	...	...	...		37.2	...	...	...		946	1050	1280	1366
351 Building and repairing of ships and boats		149	...	...	...		5.0	...	...	...		125	118	111	118
3511 Building and repairing of ships		131	...	...	...		4.8	...	...	...		...	...	...	...
3512 Building/repairing of pleasure/sport. boats		18	...	...	...		0.2	...	...	...		...	...	...	...
3520 Railway/tramway locomotives & rolling stock		33	...	...	...		1.8	...	...	...		129	134	156	188
3530 Aircraft and spacecraft		...j/	...	...	...		...j/	...	...	...		348	327	327	231
359 Transport equipment n.e.c.		85	...	...	...		5.8	...	...	...		17	18	21	18
3591 Motorcycles		14k/	...	...	...		0.3k/	...	...	...		...	...	...	...
3592 Bicycles and invalid carriages		...k/	...	...	...		...k/	...	...	...		...	...	...	...
3599 Other transport equipment n.e.c.		71j/	...	...	...		5.5j/	...	...	...		...	...	...	...
3610 Furniture		1460	...	...	...		42.2	...	...	...		921	997	1099	1141
369 Manufacturing n.e.c.		999	...	...	...		19.8	...	...	...		458	503	498	577
3691 Jewellery and related articles		386	...	...	...		5.7	...	...	...		...	...	...	...
3692 Musical instruments		9	...	...	...		-	...	...	...		...	...	...	...
3693 Sports goods		75	...	...	...		1.6	...	...	...		...	...	...	...
3694 Games and toys		50	...	...	...		1.0	...	...	...		...	...	...	...
3699 Other manufacturing n.e.c.		479m/	...	...	...		11.5m/	...	...	...		...	...	...	...
3710 Recycling of metal waste and scrap		...m/	...	...	...		...m/	...	...	...		...	...	...	...
3720 Recycling of non-metal waste and scrap		...m/	...	...	...		...m/	...	...	...		...	...	...	...
D Total manufacturing		22385	...	...	...		1340.6	...	...	...		40378	45687	50675	54668

a/ 1544 includes 1549.
b/ 1551 includes 1552.
c/ 1810 includes 1820.
d/ 2212 includes 2213.
e/ 2222 includes 2230.
f/ 2320 includes 2330.
g/ 2429 includes 2430.
h/ 2927 includes 2929.
i/ 3190 includes 3110 and 3120.
j/ 3599 includes 3530.
k/ 3591 includes 3592.
m/ 3699 includes 3710 and 3720.

South Africa

ISIC Revision 3		Output					Value added					Gross fixed capital formation	
		(million RAND)					(million RAND)					(million RAND)	
ISIC Industry	Note	1993	1994	1995	1996	Note	1993	1994	1995	1996	Note	1995	1996
151 Processed meat,fish,fruit,vegetables,fats		10129	11012	12337	13865		3493	...	...	...		...	...
1511 Processing/preserving of meat		3346	3898	4219	4534		1069	...	...	...		...	...
1512 Processing/preserving of fish		1283	1117	1286	1556		528	...	...	...		...	...
1513 Processing/preserving of fruit & vegetables		2733	2905	3126	3899		1148	...	...	...		...	...
1514 Vegetable and animal oils and fats		2767	3092	3705	3875		748	...	...	...		...	...
1520 Dairy products		4579	5007	5426	5730		1448	...	...	...		...	...
153 Grain mill products; starches; animal feeds		9935	10642	12325	14394		2535	...	...	...		...	...
1531 Grain mill products		6965	7546	8709	10087		1941	...	...	...		...	...
1532 Starches and starch products		-	-	-	-		-	...	...	...		...	...
1533 Prepared animal feeds		2969	3096	3616	4307		594	...	...	...		...	...
154 Other food products		11803	13298	14394	17317		4598	...	...	...		...	...
1541 Bakery products		3664	4266	4651	5164		1271	...	...	...		...	...
1542 Sugar		2541	2820	2921	4034		770	...	...	...		...	...
1543 Cocoa, chocolate and sugar confectionery		1552	1809	1980	2402		655	...	...	...		...	...
1544 Macaroni, noodles & similar products	a/	4046	4403	4842	5718		1902a/	...	...	...		...	...
1549 Other food products n.e.c.	a/	...	...	...	...		...a/	...	...	...		...	...
155 Beverages		11556	13179	15131	16248		4646	...	...	...		...	...
1551 Distilling, rectifying & blending of spirits	b/	3270	4115	4724	5520		1019b/	...	...	...		...	...
1552 Wines	b/	...	...	...	...		...b/	...	...	...		...	...
1553 Malt liquors and malt		5235	5732	6675	6754		2325	...	...	...		...	...
1554 Soft drinks; mineral waters		3051	3332	3731	3974		1303	...	...	...		...	...
1600 Tobacco products	c/	...	...	...	...		463	...	...	...		...	...
171 Spinning, weaving and finishing of textiles		4589	5281	6038	6181		1567	...	...	...		...	...
1711 Textile fibre preparation; textile weaving		243	270	302	308		1391	...	...	...		...	...
1712 Finishing of textiles		4346	5011	5736	5874		176	...	...	...		...	...
172 Other textiles		2401	2507	2735	2883		1102	...	...	...		...	...
1721 Made-up textile articles, except apparel		907	974	1023	1077		725	...	...	...		...	...
1722 Carpets and rugs		605	595	617	671		164	...	...	...		...	...
1723 Cordage, rope, twine and netting	d/	...	...	...	...		41	...	...	...		...	...
1729 Other textiles n.e.c.	d/	889	938	1094	1135		173	...	...	...		...	...
1730 Knitted and crocheted fabrics and articles		1324	1377	1504	1453		572	...	...	...		...	...
1810 Wearing apparel, except fur apparel	e/	5761	6375	7522	7384		2594e/	...	...	...		...	...
1820 Dressing & dyeing of fur; processing of fur	e/	...	...	...	...		...e/	...	...	...		...	...
191 Tanning, dressing and processing of leather		1039	1341	1573	1645		340	...	...	...		...	...
1911 Tanning and dressing of leather		...	...	...	...		226	...	...	...		...	...
1912 Luggage, handbags, etc.; saddlery & harness		...	...	...	...		114	...	...	...		...	...
1920 Footwear		2126	2332	2637	2457		962	...	...	...		...	...
2010 Sawmilling and planing of wood		1192	1294	1399	1534		654	...	...	...		...	...
202 Products of wood, cork, straw, etc.		2586	2966	3345	3730		910	...	...	...		...	...
2021 Veneer sheets, plywood, particle board, etc.		975	1186	1314	1413		376	...	...	...		...	...
2022 Builders' carpentry and joinery	f/	1610	1780	2031	2317		264	...	...	...		...	...
2023 Wooden containers	f/	...	...	...	...		68	...	...	...		...	...
2029 Other wood products; articles of cork/straw	f/	...	...	...	...		202	...	...	...		...	...
210 Paper and paper products		10659	12091	16058	16180		4441	...	...	...		...	...
2101 Pulp, paper and paperboard		5015	5937	8351	7500		2281	...	...	...		...	...
2102 Corrugated paper and paperboard		3703	4052	4942	5530		1319	...	...	...		...	...
2109 Other articles of paper and paperboard		1941	2102	2766	3150		841	...	...	...		...	...
221 Publishing		2608	2866	3296	3605		1432	...	...	...		...	...
2211 Publishing of books and other publications		...	...	...	...		394	...	...	...		...	...
2212 Publishing of newspapers, journals, etc.		...	...	...	...		1038g/	...	...	...		...	...
2213 Publishing of recorded media		...	...	...	...		...g/	...	...	...		...	...
2219 Other publishing		...	...	...	...		...	...	...	...		...	...

continued

South Africa

ISIC Revision 3	Output					Value added					Gross fixed capital formation		
		(million RAND)					(million RAND)					(million RAND)	
ISIC Industry	Note	1993	1994	1995	1996	Note	1993	1994	1995	1996	Note	1995	1996
222 Printing and related service activities	h/	4385	4817	5541	5825		2087	...	...	...		...	...
2221 Printing		...	...	...	...		1803	...	...	...		...	...
2222 Service activities related to printing		...	...	...	...		283i/	...	...	...		...	...
2230 Reproduction of recorded media	h/	...	...	...	...		...i/	...	...	...		...	...
2310 Coke oven products		576	569	667	779		205	...	...	...		...	...
2320 Refined petroleum products	j/	14399	13759	15528	17776		5266j/	...	...	...		...	...
2330 Processing of nuclear fuel	j/	...	...	...	...		...j/	...	...	...		...	...
241 Basic chemicals		10019	11115	13263	15552		3995	...	...	...		...	...
2411 Basic chemicals, except fertilizers		3543	3745	4104	4706		1971	...	...	...		...	...
2412 Fertilizers and nitrogen compounds		2284	2464	3166	4005		546	...	...	...		...	...
2413 Plastics in primary forms; synthetic rubber		4192	4906	5994	6841		1478	...	...	...		...	...
242 Other chemicals		13408	14683	17268	19310		6137	...	...	...		...	...
2421 Pesticides and other agro-chemical products		814	972	1096	1291		335	...	...	...		...	...
2422 Paints, varnishes, printing ink and mastics		1721	2002	2759	3057		671	...	...	...		...	...
2423 Pharmaceuticals, medicinal chemicals, etc.		3403	3673	4561	5184		1878	...	...	...		...	...
2424 Soap, cleaning & cosmetic preparations		3911	4398	4949	5429		1886	...	...	...		...	...
2429 Other chemical products n.e.c.	k/	3558	3638	3903	4349		1367k/	...	...	...		...	...
2430 Man-made fibres	k/	...	...	...	...		...k/	...	...	...		...	...
251 Rubber products		2926	3229	3805	3963		1376	...	...	...		...	...
2511 Rubber tyres and tubes		2099	2331	2841	2970		1023	...	...	...		...	...
2519 Other rubber products		827	898	963	993		354	...	...	...		...	...
2520 Plastic products		5902	6928	8316	8883		2617	...	...	...		...	...
2610 Glass and glass products		1619	2013	2283	2292		806	...	...	...		...	...
269 Non-metallic mineral products n.e.c.		6152	6627	7747	8454		2924	...	...	...		...	...
2691 Pottery, china and earthenware		225	261	297	285		117	...	...	...		...	...
2692 Refractory ceramic products	m/	1575	1639	1796	2068		22	...	...	...		...	...
2693 Struct.non-refractory clay; ceramic products	m/	...	...	...	...		669	...	...	...		...	...
2694 Cement, lime and plaster		1623	1782	2039	2145		796	...	...	...		...	...
2695 Articles of concrete, cement and plaster	n/	...	...	...	...		988	...	...	...		...	...
2696 Cutting, shaping & finishing of stone	n/	...	...	...	...		94	...	...	...		...	...
2699 Other non-metallic mineral products n.e.c.	n/	2729	2945	3615	3956		238	...	...	...		...	...
2710 Basic iron and steel		14845	16810	21149	22279		5208	...	...	...		...	...
2720 Basic precious and non-ferrous metals		4574	5491	7322	10842		1680	...	...	...		...	...
273 Casting of metals		...	...	...	...		31	...	...	...		...	...
2731 Casting of iron and steel		...	...	...	...		22	...	...	...		...	...
2732 Casting of non-ferrous metals		...	...	...	...		9	...	...	...		...	...
281 Struct.metal products;tanks;steam generators		4168	5433	6326	7494		1691	...	...	...		...	...
2811 Structural metal products		1637	2134	2491	3182		1091	...	...	...		...	...
2812 Tanks, reservoirs and containers of metal	p/	2531	3300	3835	4313		284	...	...	...		...	...
2813 Steam generators	p/	...	...	...	...		316	...	...	...		...	...
289 Other metal products; metal working services		9931	10319	11520	12195		4176	...	...	...		...	...
2891 Metal forging/pressing/stamping/roll-forming	q/	1517	1547	1658	1773		28	...	...	...		...	...
2892 Treatment & coating of metals	q/	...	...	...	...		727	...	...	...		...	...
2893 Cutlery, hand tools and general hardware		955	974	1080	1193		481	...	...	...		...	...
2899 Other fabricated metal products n.e.c.		7458	7798	8783	9229		2940	...	...	...		...	...
291 General purpose machinery		5384	5575	6585	7436		2110	...	...	...		...	...
2911 Engines & turbines(not for transport equip.)		...	...	...	...		195	...	...	...		...	...
2912 Pumps, compressors, taps and valves		...	...	...	...		231	...	...	...		...	...
2913 Bearings, gears, gearing & driving elements		...	...	...	...		163	...	...	...		...	...
2914 Ovens, furnaces and furnace burners		...	...	...	...		8	...	...	...		...	...
2915 Lifting and handling equipment		...	...	...	...		302	...	...	...		...	...
2919 Other general purpose machinery		...	...	...	...		1211	...	...	...		...	...

292	Special purpose machinery		6785	7025	8233	9088		2803	...	...	...		...	...
2921	Agricultural and forestry machinery		...	...	...	...		153	...	...	...		...	...
2922	Machine tools		...	...	...	...		257	...	...	...		...	...
2923	Machinery for metallurgy		...	...	...	...		12	...	...	...		...	...
2924	Machinery for mining & construction		...	...	...	...		412	...	...	...		...	...
2925	Food/beverage/tobacco processing machinery		...	...	...	...		55	...	...	...		...	...
2926	Machinery for textile, apparel and leather		...	...	...	...		1	...	...	...		...	...
2927	Weapons and ammunition		...	...	...	...		1913r/	...	...	...		...	...
2929	Other special purpose machinery		...	...	...	...		...r/	...	...	...		...	...
2930	Domestic appliances n.e.c.		1374	1422	1651	1813		466	...	...	...		...	...
3000	Office, accounting and computing machinery		...	...	...	...		121	...	...	...		...	...
3110	Electric motors, generators and transformers		353	382	469	528		123	...	...	...		...	...
3120	Electricity distribution & control apparatus		717	770	816	835		312	...	...	...		...	...
3130	Insulated wire and cable		1705	2158	2949	2591		584	...	...	...		...	...
3140	Accumulators, primary cells and batteries		727	860	1013	1132		407	...	...	...		...	...
3150	Lighting equipment and electric lamps		361	387	443	418		167	...	...	...		...	...
3190	Other electrical equipment n.e.c.		2764	2996	3736	4097		1199	...	...	...		...	...
3210	Electronic valves, tubes, etc.	s/	2650	3051	2981	2903		30	...	...	...		...	...
3220	TV/radio transmitters; line comm. apparatus	s/	...	...	...	...		16	...	...	...		...	...
3230	TV and radio receivers and associated goods	s/	...	...	...	...		989	...	...	...		...	...
331	Medical, measuring, testing appliances, etc.	t/	905	982	1030	1056		526	...	...	...		...	...
3311	Medical, surgical and orthopaedic equipment		...	...	...	...		285	...	...	...		...	...
3312	Measuring/testing/navigating appliances,etc.		...	...	...	...		227	...	...	...		...	...
3313	Industrial process control equipment		...	...	...	...		14	...	...	...		...	...
3320	Optical instruments & photographic equipment	t/	...	...	...	...		86	...	...	...		...	...
3330	Watches and clocks	t/	...	...	...	...		1	...	...	...		...	...
3410	Motor vehicles		14222	17514	23878	24881		3169	...	...	...		...	...
3420	Automobile bodies, trailers & semi-trailers		1324	1430	1892	1801		432	...	...	...		...	...
3430	Parts/accessories for automobiles		5143	5770	7225	7477		2215	...	...	...		...	...
351	Building and repairing of ships and boats		...	...	...	...		267	...	...	...		...	...
3511	Building and repairing of ships		...	...	...	...		261	...	...	...		...	...
3512	Building/repairing of pleasure/sport. boats		...	...	...	...		6	...	...	...		...	...
3520	Railway/tramway locomotives & rolling stock		...	...	...	...		130	...	...	...		...	...
3530	Aircraft and spacecraft		...	...	...	...		...u/	...	...	...		...	...
359	Transport equipment n.e.c.		1617	1755	1556	1842		466	...	...	...		...	...
3591	Motorcycles		...	...	...	...		7v/	...	...	...		...	...
3592	Bicycles and invalid carriages		...	...	...	...		...v/	...	...	...		...	...
3599	Other transport equipment n.e.c.		...	...	...	...		458u/	...	...	...		...	...
3610	Furniture		3469	3826	4485	4905		1556	...	...	...		...	...
369	Manufacturing n.e.c.		7017	7290	7988	8805		839	...	...	...		...	...
3691	Jewellery and related articles		1614	1784	1753	2174		215	...	...	...		...	...
3692	Musical instruments		...	...	...	...		2	...	...	...		...	...
3693	Sports goods		...	...	...	...		70	...	...	...		...	...
3694	Games and toys		...	...	...	...		36	...	...	...		...	...
3699	Other manufacturing n.e.c.	c/	5403	5505	6235	6631		516w/	...	...	...		...	...
3710	Recycling of metal waste and scrap	c/	...	...	...	...		...w/	...	...	...		...	...
3720	Recycling of non-metal waste and scrap	c/	...	...	...	...		...w/	...	...	...		...	...
D	Total manufacturing		231705	256554	303385	331858		88968	...	...	...		...	...

a/ 1544 includes 1549.
b/ 1551 includes 1552.
c/ 3699 includes 1600, 3710 and 3720.
d/ 1729 includes 1723.
e/ 1810 includes 1820.
f/ 2022 includes 2023 and 2029.
g/ 2212 includes 2213.
h/ 222 includes 2230.
i/ 2222 includes 2230.
j/ 2320 includes 2330.
k/ 2429 includes 2430.
m/ 2692 includes 2693.
n/ 2699 includes 2695 and 2696.
p/ 2812 includes 2813.
q/ 2891 includes 2892.
r/ 2927 includes 2929.
s/ 3210 includes 3220 and 3230.
t/ 331 includes 3320 and 3330.
u/ 3599 includes 3530.
v/ 3591 includes 3592.
w/ 3699 includes 3710 and 3720.

South Africa

ISIC Revision 3		Index numbers of industrial production											
		(1990=100)											
ISIC Industry	Note	1985	1986	1987	1988	1989	1990	1991	1992	1993	1994	1995	1996
15 Food and beverages		...	...	...	...	...	...	...	...	...	...	...	...
16 Tobacco products		...	...	...	...	...	...	...	...	...	...	...	...
17 Textiles		117	121	113	112	111	100	100	99	101	105	107	104
18 Wearing apparel, fur		85	85	89	91	98	100	95	87	90	92	101	91
19 Leather, leather products and footwear		...	...	...	...	...	...	...	...	...	...	...	...
20 Wood products (excl. furniture)		99	96	100	108	103	100	100	95	95	103	107	109
21 Paper and paper products		92	103	103	112	111	100	96	97	95	99	110	98
22 Printing and publishing		99	99	100	104	105	100	101	91	96	94	91	88
23 Coke,refined petroleum products,nuclear fuel		...	...	...	...	...	...	...	...	...	...	...	...
24 Chemicals and chemical products		...	...	...	...	...	...	...	...	...	...	...	...
25 Rubber and plastics products		...	...	...	...	...	...	...	...	...	...	...	...
26 Non-metallic mineral products		...	...	...	...	...	...	...	...	...	...	...	...
27 Basic metals		...	...	...	...	...	...	...	...	...	...	...	...
28 Fabricated metal products		129	114	93	94	100	100	94	89	82	83	86	88
29 Machinery and equipment n.e.c.	a/	92	90	82	90	97	100	94	90	89	86	93	98
30 Office, accounting and computing machinery	a/	...	...	...	...	...	...	...	...	...	...	...	...
31 Electrical machinery and apparatus		85	81	95	102	101	100	99	94	92	100	111	106
32 Radio,television and communication equipment		...	...	...	...	...	100	88	76	76	84	72	60
33 Medical, precision and optical instruments		97	100	108	109	106	100	112	128	119	108	100	97
34 Motor vehicles, trailers, semi-trailers		74	75	89	115	112	100	98	87	89	93	112	107
35 Other transport equipment		110	91	102	112	106	100	96	87	66	60	50	65
36 Furniture; manufacturing n.e.c.		...	...	...	...	...	...	...	...	...	...	...	...
37 Recycling		...	...	...	...	...	...	...	...	...	...	...	...
D Total manufacturing		94	93	96	98	100	100	96	93	94	96	102	103

a/ 29 includes 30.

ST. VINCENT AND THE GRENADINES

Supplier of information:
Statistical Office, Kingstown.

Basic source of data:
National accounts survey of establishments.

Major deviations from ISIC (Revision 2):
None reported.

Reference period (if not calendar year):

Scope:
Not reported.

Method of enumeration:
Questionnaires were distributed by mail.

Adjusted for non-response:
Not reported.

Concepts and definitions of variables:
No deviations from the Standard UN concepts and definitions are reported.

Related national publications:

St. Vincent and the Grenadines

ISIC Revision 2	Number of establishments					Number of employees					Wages and salaries paid to employees				
		(numbers)					(numbers)					(thousand DOLLARS)			
ISIC Industry	Note	1993	1994	1995	1996	Note	1993	1994	1995	1996	Note	1993	1994	1995	1996
311/2 Food products		17	19	21	21		251	256	233	235		4509.0	4659.9	...	...
3111 Slaughtering, preparing & preserving meat		...	...	...	...		...	...	...	...		...	...	...	...
3112 Dairy products		...	...	...	...		...	...	...	...		...	...	...	...
3113 Canning, preserving of fruits & vegetables		...	...	...	...		...	...	...	...		...	...	...	...
3114 Canning, preserving and processing of fish		...	...	1	1		...	...	...	...		...	...	...	...
3115 Vegetable and animal oils and fats		1	1	1	1		24	24	20	22		164.9	273.7	...	...
3116 Grain mill products		...	...	...	...		...	...	...	...		...	...	...	...
3117 Bakery products		14	16	17	17		17	20	...	...		131.1	167.6	...	...
3118 Sugar factories and refineries		...	...	...	...		...	...	...	...		...	...	...	...
3119 Cocoa, chocolate and sugar confectionery		...	...	...	...		...	...	...	...		...	...	...	...
3121 Other food products		1	1	1	1		192	194	196	196		3506.0	3511.6	...	...
3122 Prepared animal feeds		1	1	1	1		18	18	17	17		707.0	707.0	...	...
313 Beverages		4	4	5	5		105	109	108	119		265.6	265.6	...	...
3131 Distilling, rectifying and blending spirits		1	1	1	2		27	27	27	39		265.6	265.6	...	...
3132 Wine industries		...	...	...	...		...	...	...	...		...	...	...	...
3133 Malt liquors and malt		1	1	1	1		78	82	81	80		...	...	...	...
3134 Soft drinks and carbonated waters		2	2	3	2		...	...	...	...		...	...	...	...
314 Tobacco		1	1	1	1		24	24	24	24		273.7	273.7	...	...
321 Textiles		...	...	...	...		...	...	...	...		...	...	...	...
3211 Spinning, weaving and finishing textiles		...	...	...	...		...	...	...	...		...	...	...	...
3212 Made-up textile goods excl. wearing apparel		...	...	...	...		...	...	...	...		...	...	...	...
3213 Knitting mills		...	...	...	...		...	...	...	...		...	...	...	...
3214 Carpets and rugs		...	...	...	...		...	...	...	...		...	...	...	...
3215 Cordage, rope and twine		...	...	...	...		...	...	...	...		...	...	...	...
3219 Other textiles		...	...	...	...		...	...	...	...		...	...	...	...
322 Wearing apparel, except footwear		3	3	4	4		296	289	301	298		1642.8	1503.8	...	...
323 Leather and fur products		...	...	...	...		...	...	...	...		...	...	...	...
3231 Tanneries and leather finishing		...	...	...	...		...	...	...	...		...	...	...	...
3232 Fur dressing and dyeing industries		...	...	...	...		...	...	...	...		...	...	...	...
3233 Leather prods. excl. wearing apparel		...	...	...	...		...	...	...	...		...	...	...	...
324 Footwear, except rubber or plastic		...	...	...	...		...	...	...	...		...	...	...	...
331 Wood products, except furniture		...	...	...	...		...	...	...	...		...	...	...	...
3311 Sawmills, planing and other wood mills		...	...	...	...		...	...	...	...		...	...	...	...
3312 Wooden and cane containers		...	...	...	...		...	...	...	...		...	...	...	...
3319 Other wood and cork products		...	...	...	...		...	...	...	...		...	...	...	...
332 Furniture and fixtures, excl. metal		...	...	...	...		...	...	...	...		...	...	...	...
341 Paper and products		1	1	2	2		87	87	102	102		1098.7	1292.4	...	...
3411 Pulp, paper and paperboard articles		1	1	1	1		87	87	94	94		1098.7	1292.4	...	...
3412 Containers of paper and paperboard		...	...	...	...		...	...	...	...		...	...	...	...
3419 Other pulp, paper and paperboard articles		...	...	1	1		...	...	8	8		...	...	...	...
342 Printing and publishing		...	...	...	...		...	...	...	...		...	...	...	...
351 Industrial chemicals		...	...	1	1		...	...	7	8		...	...	...	...
3511 Basic chemicals excl. fertilizers		...	...	...	...		...	...	...	...		...	...	...	...
3512 Fertilizers and pesticides		...	...	...	...		...	...	...	...		...	...	...	...
3513 Synthetic resins and plastic materials		...	...	...	...		...	...	...	...		...	...	...	...
352 Other chemicals		...	...	1	1		...	...	10	10		...	...	...	...
3521 Paints, varnishes and lacquers		...	...	...	...		...	...	...	...		...	...	...	...
3522 Drugs and medicines		...	...	...	...		...	...	...	...		...	...	...	...
3523 Soap, cleaning preps., perfumes, cosmetics		...	...	1	1		...	...	10	10		...	...	...	...
3529 Other chemical products		...	...	...	...		...	...	...	...		...	...	...	...
353 Petroleum refineries		...	...	...	...		...	...	...	...		...	...	...	...

ISIC	Industry														
354	Misc. petroleum and coal products		...	...	...	...		...	...	...	...		...	...	...	...
355	Rubber products		...	...	...	...		...	...	...	...		...	...	...	...
3551	Tyres and tubes		...	...	...	...		...	...	...	...		...	...	...	...
3559	Other rubber products		...	...	...	...		...	...	...	...		...	...	...	...
356	Plastic products		1	1	2	2		...	...	...	...		...	...	...	...
361	Pottery, china, earthenware		...	...	...	...		...	...	...	...		...	...	...	...
362	Glass and products		...	...	...	...		...	...	...	...		...	...	...	...
369	Other non-metallic mineral products		...	...	...	...		...	...	...	...		...	...	...	...
3691	Structural clay products		...	...	...	...		...	...	...	...		...	...	...	...
3692	Cement, lime and plaster		...	...	...	...		...	...	...	...		...	...	...	...
3699	Other non-metallic mineral products		...	...	...	...		...	...	...	...		...	...	...	...
371	Iron and steel		...	...	...	...		...	...	...	...		...	...	...	...
372	Non-ferrous metals		...	...	...	...		...	...	...	...		...	...	...	...
381	Fabricated metal products		1	1	1	1		...	...	61	61		...	...	...	...
3811	Cutlery, hand tools and general hardware		...	...	...	...		...	...	...	...		...	...	...	...
3812	Furniture and fixtures primarily of metal		...	...	...	...		...	...	...	...		...	...	...	...
3813	Structural metal products		...	...	...	...		...	...	...	...		...	...	...	...
3819	Other fabricated metal products		1	1	1	1		...	...	61	61		...	...	...	...
382	Non-electrical machinery		...	...	...	...		...	...	...	...		...	...	...	...
3821	Engines and turbines		...	...	...	...		...	...	...	...		...	...	...	...
3822	Agricultural machinery and equipment		...	...	...	...		...	...	...	...		...	...	...	...
3823	Metal and wood working machinery		...	...	...	...		...	...	...	...		...	...	...	...
3824	Other special industrial machinery		...	...	...	...		...	...	...	...		...	...	...	...
3825	Office, computing and accounting machinery		...	...	...	...		...	...	...	...		...	...	...	...
3829	Other non-electrical machinery & equipment		...	...	...	...		...	...	...	...		...	...	...	...
383	Electrical machinery		1	1	1	1		...	...	...	...		...	...	...	...
3831	Electrical industrial machinery		...	...	...	...		...	...	...	...		...	...	...	...
3832	Radio, television and communication equipm.		...	...	...	...		...	...	...	...		...	...	...	...
3833	Electrical appliances and housewares		...	...	...	...		...	...	...	...		...	...	...	...
3839	Other electrical apparatus and supplies		1	1	1	1		...	...	...	...		...	...	...	...
384	Transport equipment		...	...	...	...		...	...	...	...		...	...	...	...
3841	Shipbuilding and repairing		...	...	...	...		...	...	...	...		...	...	...	...
3842	Railroad equipment		...	...	...	...		...	...	...	...		...	...	...	...
3843	Motor vehicles		...	...	...	...		...	...	...	...		...	...	...	...
3844	Motorcycles and bicycles		...	...	...	...		...	...	...	...		...	...	...	...
3845	Aircraft		...	...	...	...		...	...	...	...		...	...	...	...
3849	Other transport equipment		...	...	...	...		...	...	...	...		...	...	...	...
385	Professional and scientific equipment		...	...	...	...		...	...	...	...		...	...	...	...
3851	Prof. and scientific equipment n.e.c.		...	...	...	...		...	...	...	...		...	...	...	...
3852	Photographic and optical goods		...	...	...	...		...	...	...	...		...	...	...	...
3853	Watches and clocks		...	...	...	...		...	...	...	...		...	...	...	...
390	Other manufacturing industries		...	...	...	...		...	...	...	...		...	...	...	...
3901	Jewellery and related articles		...	...	...	...		...	...	...	...		...	...	...	...
3902	Musical instruments		...	...	...	...		...	...	...	...		...	...	...	...
3903	Sporting and athletic goods		...	...	...	...		...	...	...	...		...	...	...	...
3909	Manufacturing industries, n.e.c.		...	...	...	...		...	...	...	...		...	...	...	...
3	Total manufacturing	a/	29	31	39	39	a/	763	765	846	857	a/	7789.8	7995.4	...	...

a/ Sum of available data.

St. Vincent and the Grenadines

ISIC Revision 2	Output					Value added					Gross fixed capital formation		
		(DOLLARS)					(DOLLARS)						
ISIC Industry	Note	1993	1994	1995	1996	Note	1993	1994	1995	1996	Note	1995	1996
311/2 Food products		...	...	...	...		...	...	...	...		...	...
313 Beverages		...	...	...	...		...	...	...	...		...	...
314 Tobacco		...	...	...	...		...	...	...	...		...	...
321 Textiles		...	...	...	...		...	...	...	...		...	...
322 Wearing apparel, except footwear		...	...	...	...		...	...	...	...		...	...
323 Leather and fur products		...	...	...	...		...	...	...	...		...	...
324 Footwear, except rubber or plastic		...	...	...	...		...	...	...	...		...	...
331 Wood products, except furniture		...	...	...	...		...	...	...	...		...	...
332 Furniture and fixtures, excl. metal		...	...	...	...		...	...	...	...		...	...
341 Paper and products		...	...	...	...		...	...	...	...		...	...
342 Printing and publishing		...	...	...	...		...	...	...	...		...	...
351 Industrial chemicals		...	...	...	...		...	...	...	...		...	...
352 Other chemicals		...	...	...	...		...	...	...	...		...	...
353 Petroleum refineries		...	...	...	...		...	...	...	...		...	...
354 Misc. petroleum and coal products		...	...	...	...		...	...	...	...		...	...
355 Rubber products		...	...	...	...		...	...	...	...		...	...
356 Plastic products		...	...	...	...		...	...	...	...		...	...
361 Pottery, china, earthenware		...	...	...	...		...	...	...	...		...	...
362 Glass and products		...	...	...	...		...	...	...	...		...	...
369 Other non-metallic mineral products		...	...	...	...		...	...	...	...		...	...
371 Iron and steel		...	...	...	...		...	...	...	...		...	...
372 Non-ferrous metals		...	...	...	...		...	...	...	...		...	...
381 Fabricated metal products		...	...	...	...		...	...	...	...		...	...
382 Non-electrical machinery		...	...	...	...		...	...	...	...		...	...
383 Electrical machinery		...	...	...	...		...	...	...	...		...	...
384 Transport equipment		...	...	...	...		...	...	...	...		...	...
385 Professional and scientific equipment		...	...	...	...		...	...	...	...		...	...
390 Other manufacturing industries		...	...	...	...		...	...	...	...		...	...
3 Total manufacturing		...	...	...	...		...	...	...	...		...	...

SWAZILAND

Supplier of information:
Central Statistical Office, Mbabane.

Basic source of data:
Annual industrial census.

Major deviations from ISIC (Revision 2):
None reported.

Reference period (if not calendar year):

Scope:
Establishments with 10 or more persons engaged and establishments with less than 10 persons engaged whose structure and accounting practices allow them to complete the questionnaire without difficulty.

Method of enumeration:
Questionnaires were distributed by mail with follow-up site visits as required.

Adjusted for non-response:
No.

Concepts and definitions of variables:
Wages and salaries is compensation of employees.
Output is gross output and value added is total value added.

Related national publications:
Census of Industrial Production (annual); Annual Statistical Bulletin, both published by the Central Statistical Office, Mbabane.

Swaziland

ISIC Revision 2	Number of establishments					Number of employees					Wages and salaries paid to employees				
		(numbers)					(numbers)					(thousand EMALANGENI)			
ISIC Industry	Note	1992	1993	1994	1995	Note	1992	1993	1994	1995	Note	1992	1993	1994	1995
311/2 Food products		...	...	...	...		...	...	...	...		...	...	...	...
3111 Slaughtering, preparing & preserving meat		1	1	1	1		...	...	154	154		...	...	2336	2596
3112 Dairy products		2	2	3	3		243	233	270	270		3361	3601	5371	6524
3113 Canning, preserving of fruits & vegetables		5	5	5	5		1751	1493	1534	1774		9089	12548	18299	18155
3114 Canning, preserving and processing of fish		...	...	...	...		...	...	...	...		...	...	...	...
3115 Vegetable and animal oils and fats		...	...	...	...		...	...	...	...		...	...	...	...
3116 Grain mill products		3	3	3	4		412	388	460	528		4596	5338	5866	5883
3117 Bakery products		6	6	2	3		355	446	374	410		7488	8208	9187	10689
3118 Sugar factories and refineries		3	3	3	3		5620	5590	4875	4751		37196	28303	86976	97798
3119 Cocoa, chocolate and sugar confectionery		...	...	...	...		...	...	...	...		...	...	...	...
3121 Other food products		...	...	...	...		...	...	...	...		...	...	...	...
3122 Prepared animal feeds		...	...	...	...		...	...	...	...		...	...	...	...
313 Beverages		...	...	...	...		...	...	...	...		...	...	...	...
3131 Distilling, rectifying and blending spirits		...	...	...	...		...	...	...	...		...	...	...	...
3132 Wine industries		...	...	...	...		...	...	...	...		...	...	...	...
3133 Malt liquors and malt		...	...	...	...		...	...	...	...		...	...	...	...
3134 Soft drinks and carbonated waters		3	3	3	3		486	479	494	470		12231	12903	15131	17287
314 Tobacco		...	...	...	...		...	...	...	...		...	...	...	...
321 Textiles		...	...	...	...		...	...	...	...		...	...	...	...
3211 Spinning, weaving and finishing textiles		3	3	2	2		216	192	142	189		1901	2215	1728	1803
3212 Made-up textile goods excl. wearing apparel		...	...	...	...		...	...	77	92		...	...	604	746
3213 Knitting mills		...	...	...	...		...	...	...	...		...	...	...	...
3214 Carpets and rugs		4	4	4	4		2	8	34	36		2	4	207	246
3215 Cordage, rope and twine		...	...	...	...		...	...	...	...		...	...	...	...
3219 Other textiles		...	...	...	...		...	...	...	...		...	...	...	...
322 Wearing apparel, except footwear		14	14	14	14		2343	2056	2482	2537		25260	19273	32714	36574
323 Leather and fur products		1	1	1	1		...	...	...	...		...	...	...	...
3231 Tanneries and leather finishing		-	-	-	-		-	-	-	-		-	-	-	-
3232 Fur dressing and dyeing industries		-	-	-	-		-	-	-	-		-	-	-	-
3233 Leather prods. excl. wearing apparel		1	1	1	1		...	...	...	...		...	...	...	...
324 Footwear, except rubber or plastic		1	1	1	1		431	422	308	308		3201	3800	4040	...
331 Wood products, except furniture		...	...	...	...		...	...	...	...		...	...	...	...
3311 Sawmills, planing and other wood mills		4	3	3	3		550	562	729	777		5686	6421	7837	9208
3312 Wooden and cane containers		...	...	...	...		...	...	...	...		...	...	...	...
3319 Other wood and cork products		...	...	...	...		...	...	...	...		...	...	...	...
332 Furniture and fixtures, excl. metal		7	3	6	6		309	326	801	589		2116	2624	2826	4699
341 Paper and products		5	5	5	5		3313	3432	3360	3562		68116	68577	85112	81379
3411 Pulp, paper and paperboard articles		4	4	4	4		3166	3290	3240	3422		64690	65390	81677	77668
3412 Containers of paper and paperboard		1	1	1	1		147	142	120	140		3426	3187	3435	3711
3419 Other pulp, paper and paperboard articles		-	-	-	-		-	-	-	-		-	-	-	-
342 Printing and publishing		19	19	20	20		396	406	482	505		4857	12082	15510	11443
351 Industrial chemicals		1	1	1	1		6	6	6	7		35	50	56	62
3511 Basic chemicals excl. fertilizers		1	1	1	1		6	6	6	7		35	50	56	62
3512 Fertilizers and pesticides		-	-	-	-		-	-	-	-		-	-	-	-
3513 Synthetic resins and plastic materials		-	-	-	-		-	-	-	-		-	-	-	-
352 Other chemicals		...	...	...	...		...	...	...	...		...	...	...	...
3521 Paints, varnishes and lacquers		7	6	6	6		52	38	48	51		609	833	806	892
3522 Drugs and medicines		...	...	...	...		...	...	...	...		...	...	...	...
3523 Soap, cleaning preps., perfumes, cosmetics		3	3	2	2		3	3	6	9		3	513	42	75
3529 Other chemical products		3	3	3	3		121	128	112	111		1350	1692	1887	1885
353 Petroleum refineries		...	...	...	...		...	...	...	...		...	...	...	...

354	Misc. petroleum and coal products	...	...	...	...	...	...	...	...	...	...	...	...
355	Rubber products	...	...	...	...	...	...	...	...	...	...	...	...
3551	Tyres and tubes	...	...	...	...	...	...	...	...	...	42	...	...
3559	Other rubber products	...	...	...	...	...	...	...	...	...	...	...	...
356	Plastic products	4	4	2	2	248	251	32	39	1670	2670	745	922
361	Pottery, china, earthenware	...	...	...	...	...	...	...	...	...	...	...	...
362	Glass and products	1	1	1	1	48	57	49	64	396	479	1243	809
369	Other non-metallic mineral products	10	9	9	7	299	258	494	365	4795	2816	3868	5200
3691	Structural clay products	-	-	-	-	-	-	...	...	-	-	-	-
3692	Cement, lime and plaster	-	-	-	-	-	-	...	...	-	-	-	-
3699	Other non-metallic mineral products	10	9	9	7	299	258	494	365	4795	2816	3868	5200
371	Iron and steel	...	...	...	...	...	...	...	...	...	...	...	...
372	Non-ferrous metals	...	...	...	...	...	...	...	...	...	...	...	...
381	Fabricated metal products	17	15	17	17	401	493	668	618	8033	9161	10955	15471
3811	Cutlery, hand tools and general hardware	-	-	-	-	-	-	-	-	-	-	-	-
3812	Furniture and fixtures primarily of metal	1	1	1	1	15	32	21	21	216	203	160	135
3813	Structural metal products	5	5	7	7	79	128	279	242	1446	1715	2107	5690
3819	Other fabricated metal products	11	9	9	9	307	333	368	355	6371	7243	8688	9646
382	Non-electrical machinery	...	...	...	...	...	...	...	...	...	...	...	...
3821	Engines and turbines	...	...	...	...	...	...	...	...	...	...	...	...
3822	Agricultural machinery and equipment	...	...	...	...	...	...	...	...	...	...	...	...
3823	Metal and wood working machinery	1	1	2	2	15	15	28	19	80	84	256	202
3824	Other special industrial machinery	2	2	2	2	...	...	4	5	...	...	43	29
3825	Office, computing and accounting machinery	...	...	1	1	...	...	9	...	...	...	...	...
3829	Other non-electrical machinery & equipment	4	4	4	4	660	660	670	710	6392	8429	12565	13822
383	Electrical machinery	...	...	...	...	...	...	...	...	...	...	...	...
3831	Electrical industrial machinery	...	...	...	...	...	...	...	...	...	...	...	...
3832	Radio, television and communication equipm.	...	...	...	...	...	...	...	...	...	...	...	...
3833	Electrical appliances and housewares	...	...	...	...	...	...	...	...	...	...	...	...
3839	Other electrical apparatus and supplies	...	...	...	...	...	...	...	...	...	...	...	...
384	Transport equipment	...	...	...	...	...	...	...	...	...	...	...	...
3841	Shipbuilding and repairing	...	...	...	...	...	...	...	...	...	...	...	...
3842	Railroad equipment	...	...	...	...	...	...	...	...	...	...	...	...
3843	Motor vehicles	...	...	1	1	270	300	345	278	4142	4602	798	887
3844	Motorcycles and bicycles	...	...	...	...	...	...	...	...	...	...	...	...
3845	Aircraft	...	...	...	...	...	...	...	...	...	...	...	...
3849	Other transport equipment	...	...	...	...	...	...	...	...	...	...	...	...
385	Professional and scientific equipment	...	...	...	...	...	...	...	...	...	...	...	...
3851	Prof. and scientific equipment n.e.c.	...	...	...	...	...	...	...	...	...	...	...	...
3852	Photographic and optical goods	...	...	...	...	...	...	...	...	...	...	...	...
3853	Watches and clocks	...	...	...	...	...	...	...	...	...	...	...	...
390	Other manufacturing industries	5	4	4	4	30	14	22	14	206	190	231	104
3901	Jewellery and related articles	1	-	-	-	...	-	-	-	...	-	...	...
3902	Musical instruments	-	-	-	-	-	-	-	-	-	-	...	...
3903	Sporting and athletic goods	-	-	-	-	-	-	-	-	-	-	...	...
3909	Manufacturing industries, n.e.c.	4	4	4	4	30	14	22	14	206	190	231	104
3	Total manufacturing	139	129	131	131	18580	18256	19069	19242	212811	217458	327239	345390

Swaziland

ISIC Revision 2	Output in factor values					Value added in factor values					Gross fixed capital formation		
		(thousand EMALANGENI)					(thousand EMALANGENI)					(thousand EMALANGENI)	
ISIC Industry	Note	1992	1993	1994	1995	Note	1992	1993	1994	1995	Note	1994	1995
311/2 Food products		...	...	...	...		...	...	...	...		...	...
3111 Slaughtering, preparing & preserving meat		...	...	41064	41292		...	...	2676	...		651	682
3112 Dairy products		38608	31625	51150	56125		6748	7415	10576	10199		-	962
3113 Canning, preserving of fruits & vegetables		101176	169333	192365	209479		11784	46884	50665	53893		327	1540
3114 Canning, preserving and processing of fish		...	...	...	...		...	...	...	...		...	...
3115 Vegetable and animal oils and fats		...	...	...	...		...	...	...	...		...	...
3116 Grain mill products		115816	137529	137770	147169		19910	22345	21662	17609		387	3305
3117 Bakery products		42250	48402	61353	75582		9704	10362	11846	13414		2348	380
3118 Sugar factories and refineries		502073	596085	688495	749375		133048	140632	235693	238869		6168	61569
3119 Cocoa, chocolate and sugar confectionery		...	...	...	...		...	...	...	...		...	...
3121 Other food products		...	...	...	...		...	...	...	...		...	...
3122 Prepared animal feeds		...	...	...	...		...	...	...	...		...	...
313 Beverages		...	...	...	...		...	...	...	...		...	...
3131 Distilling, rectifying and blending spirits		...	...	...	...		...	...	...	...		...	...
3132 Wine industries		...	...	...	...		...	...	...	...		...	...
3133 Malt liquors and malt		...	...	...	...		...	...	...	...		...	...
3134 Soft drinks and carbonated waters		441783	589496	695075	1198494		307751	338881	432929	510673		14096	13534
314 Tobacco		...	...	...	...		...	...	...	...		...	...
321 Textiles		...	...	...	...		...	...	...	...		...	...
3211 Spinning, weaving and finishing textiles		17278	17219	16759	17701		1765	-623	2986	3341		129	120
3212 Made-up textile goods excl. wearing apparel		...	...	6239	9254		...	...	825	965		-	99
3213 Knitting mills		...	...	...	...		...	...	...	...		...	...
3214 Carpets and rugs		374	296	589	782		6	-27	144	275		-	-
3215 Cordage, rope and twine		...	...	...	...		...	...	...	...		...	...
3219 Other textiles		...	...	...	...		...	...	...	...		...	...
322 Wearing apparel, except footwear		110764	87003	179776	173148		21484	19650	57480	36244		2878	2858
323 Leather and fur products		...	...	...	...		...	...	...	...		...	...
3231 Tanneries and leather finishing		-	-	-	-		-	-	-	-		...	...
3232 Fur dressing and dyeing industries		-	-	-	-		-	-	-	-		...	...
3233 Leather prods. excl. wearing apparel		...	...	...	...		...	...	...	...		...	...
324 Footwear, except rubber or plastic		22368	25526	24740	...		8375	9042	7789	...		935	...
331 Wood products, except furniture		...	...	...	...		...	...	...	...		...	...
3311 Sawmills, planing and other wood mills		35244	36377	56145	61304		8883	9518	15321	14961		404	-2118
3312 Wooden and cane containers		...	...	...	...		...	...	...	...		...	...
3319 Other wood and cork products		...	...	...	...		...	...	...	...		...	...
332 Furniture and fixtures, excl. metal		14069	12309	15265	37590		12589	2889	4069	9380		4875	2404
341 Paper and products		312642	323076	415866	426389		146931	92266	176489	217179		136146	250323
3411 Pulp, paper and paperboard articles		296318	303337	388134	398745		146222	87008	171373	210664		136017	244061
3412 Containers of paper and paperboard		16324	19739	27732	27644		709	5258	5116	6515		129	6262
3419 Other pulp, paper and paperboard articles		-	-	-	-		-	-	-	-		...	...
342 Printing and publishing		20961	31964	52158	73668		4861	16487	22629	13340		1327	1435
351 Industrial chemicals		326	373	557	522		46	65	78	84		-	-
3511 Basic chemicals excl. fertilizers		326	373	557	522		46	65	78	84		-	-
3512 Fertilizers and pesticides		-	-	-	-		-	-	-	-		-	-
3513 Synthetic resins and plastic materials		-	-	-	-		-	-	-	-		...	-
352 Other chemicals		...	...	...	...		...	...	...	...		...	...
3521 Paints, varnishes and lacquers		5419	8257	6562	8489		1612	1631	1743	2037		129	18
3522 Drugs and medicines		...	...	...	...		...	...	...	...		...	...
3523 Soap, cleaning preps., perfumes, cosmetics		191	2244	292	897		13	1427	11	49		-	-
3529 Other chemical products		5831	6184	6360	1788		2635	3098	2200	328		-444	-
353 Petroleum refineries		...	...	...	...		...	...	...	...		...	...

354	Misc. petroleum and coal products	...	...	...	...	...	...	...	...	...	...
355	Rubber products	...	...	...	...	...	...	...	...	...	...
3551	Tyres and tubes	...	500	...	...	...	...	...	...	...	...
3559	Other rubber products	...	...	...	...	...	...	...	...	...	...
356	Plastic products	28081	22858	7477	8714	7513	4665	1976	1897	859	479
361	Pottery, china, earthenware	...	...	...	...	...	...	...	...	...	...
362	Glass and products	2735	2624	3602	3417	786	315	1854	1460	173	429
369	Other non-metallic mineral products	21610	15605	19919	14408	6582	4306	5545	5711	493	472
3691	Structural clay products	-	-	...	...	-	-	-	-	...	...
3692	Cement, lime and plaster	-	-	...	...	-	-	-	-	...	...
3699	Other non-metallic mineral products	21610	15605	19919	14408	6582	4306	5545	5711	493	472
371	Iron and steel	...	...	...	...	...	...	...	...	...	...
372	Non-ferrous metals	...	...	...	...	...	...	...	...	...	...
381	Fabricated metal products	52275	59839	69880	75117	16219	17336	19085	26623	5187	1751
3811	Cutlery, hand tools and general hardware	-	-	-	-	-	-	-	-	-	-
3812	Furniture and fixtures primarily of metal	1542	1269	1290	...	413	250	185	...	-	51
3813	Structural metal products	5426	6775	9137	8106	1723	1877	2120	2416	160	273
3819	Other fabricated metal products	45307	51795	59453	67011	14083	15209	16780	24207	5027	1427
382	Non-electrical machinery	...	...	...	...	...	...	...	...	...	...
3821	Engines and turbines	...	...	...	...	...	...	...	...	...	...
3822	Agricultural machinery and equipment	...	...	...	...	...	...	...	...	...	...
3823	Metal and wood working machinery	370	406	1232	613	65	128	362	260	-	-
3824	Other special industrial machinery	...	...	174	406	...	...	9	175	-	48
3825	Office, computing and accounting machinery	...	...	917	...	...	...	206	...	-66	...
3829	Other non-electrical machinery & equipment	93329	111688	184421	224227	22098	30896	27980	33662	3387	8777
383	Electrical machinery	...	...	...	...	...	...	...	...	...	...
3831	Electrical industrial machinery	...	...	...	...	...	...	...	...	...	...
3832	Radio, television and communication equipm.	...	...	...	...	...	...	...	...	...	...
3833	Electrical appliances and housewares	...	...	...	...	...	...	...	...	...	...
3839	Other electrical apparatus and supplies	...	...	...	...	...	...	...	...	...	...
384	Transport equipment	...	...	...	...	...	...	...	...	...	...
3841	Shipbuilding and repairing	...	...	...	...	...	...	...	...	...	...
3842	Railroad equipment	...	...	...	...	...	...	...	...	...	...
3843	Motor vehicles	17022	17548	28595	27675	2854	3097	2401	2413	820	-
3844	Motorcycles and bicycles	...	...	...	...	...	...	...	...	...	...
3845	Aircraft	...	...	...	...	...	...	...	...	...	...
3849	Other transport equipment	...	...	...	...	...	...	...	...	...	...
385	Professional and scientific equipment	...	...	...	...	...	...	...	...	...	...
3851	Prof. and scientific equipment n.e.c.	...	...	...	...	...	...	...	...	...	...
3852	Photographic and optical goods	...	...	...	...	...	...	...	...	...	...
3853	Watches and clocks	...	...	...	...	...	...	...	...	...	...
390	Other manufacturing industries	688	875	867	434	145	262	179	125	-	-
3901	Jewellery and related articles	...	-	-	-	...	-	-	-	...	...
3902	Musical instruments	-	-	-	-	-	-	-	-	...	...
3903	Sporting and athletic goods	-	-	-	-	-	-	-	-	...	...
3909	Manufacturing industries, n.e.c.	688	875	867	434	145	262	179	125	-	-
3	Total manufacturing	2003283	2355241	2965664	3644059	754407	782947	1117408	1215166	181209	349067

Swaziland

ISIC Revision 2		Index numbers of industrial production											
		(1990=100)											
ISIC Industry	Note	1985	1986	1987	1988	1989	1990	1991	1992	1993	1994	1995	1996
311/2 Food products		...	...	...	...	...	...	...	...	...	...	...	...
313 Beverages		...	...	...	...	...	...	...	...	...	...	...	...
314 Tobacco		...	...	...	...	...	...	...	...	...	...	...	...
321 Textiles		...	...	...	...	...	...	...	...	...	...	...	...
322 Wearing apparel, except footwear		...	...	...	...	...	...	...	...	...	...	...	...
323 Leather and fur products		...	...	...	...	...	...	...	...	...	...	...	...
324 Footwear, except rubber or plastic		...	...	...	...	...	...	...	...	...	...	...	...
331 Wood products, except furniture		...	...	...	...	...	...	...	...	...	...	...	...
332 Furniture and fixtures, excl. metal		...	...	...	...	...	...	...	...	...	...	...	...
341 Paper and products		...	...	...	...	...	...	...	...	...	...	...	...
342 Printing and publishing		...	...	...	...	...	...	...	...	...	...	...	...
351 Industrial chemicals		...	...	...	...	...	...	...	...	...	...	...	...
352 Other chemicals		...	...	...	...	...	...	...	...	...	...	...	...
353 Petroleum refineries		...	...	...	...	...	...	...	...	...	...	...	...
354 Misc. petroleum and coal products		...	...	...	...	...	...	...	...	...	...	...	...
355 Rubber products		...	...	...	...	...	...	...	...	...	...	...	...
356 Plastic products		...	...	...	...	...	...	...	...	...	...	...	...
361 Pottery, china, earthenware		...	...	...	...	...	...	...	...	...	...	...	...
362 Glass and products		...	...	...	...	...	...	...	...	...	...	...	...
369 Other non-metallic mineral products		...	...	...	...	...	...	...	...	...	...	...	...
371 Iron and steel		...	...	...	...	...	...	...	...	...	...	...	...
372 Non-ferrous metals		...	...	...	...	...	...	...	...	...	...	...	...
381 Fabricated metal products		...	...	...	...	...	...	...	...	...	...	...	...
382 Non-electrical machinery		...	...	...	...	...	...	...	...	...	...	...	...
383 Electrical machinery		...	...	...	...	...	...	...	...	...	...	...	...
384 Transport equipment		...	...	...	...	...	...	...	...	...	...	...	...
385 Professional and scientific equipment		...	...	...	...	...	...	...	...	...	...	...	...
390 Other manufacturing industries		...	...	...	...	...	...	...	...	...	...	...	...
3 Total manufacturing		...	...	...	...	...	...	...	...	...	...	...	...

SWITZERLAND

Supplier of information:
Office fédéral de la statistique (OFS), Berne. Industrial statistics for the OECD countries are compiled by the OECD secretariat, which supplies them to UNIDO. The notes appearing here are based on information in the OECD publication *Industrial Structure Statistics* (annual), OECD, Paris.

Basic source of data:
Annual survey of manufacturing.

Major deviations from ISIC (Revision 2):
Data were converted from the national classification system to ISIC (Rev. 2). However, the following should be noted: (a) ISIC 3213 (knitting mills) is included in ISIC 322-324 (wearing apparel, leather and footwear) combined; (b) ISIC 33 (wood products and furniture) includes ISIC 39 (other manufacturing) except ISIC 3901 (jewellery); (c) ISIC 36 (non-metallic mineral products) includes ISIC 2 (mining and quarrying); (d) ISIC 37 (basic metal industries) includes ISIC 3813 (structural metal products); (e) ISIC 382 (non-electrical machinery) includes ISIC 384 (transport equipment) and ISIC 3851 (professional equipment); (f) ISIC 383 (electrical machinery) includes ISIC 3852 (photographic and optical goods); (g) ISIC 3853 (watches and clocks) includes ISIC 3901 (jewellery).

Reference period (if not calendar year):

Scope:
All establishments.

Method of enumeration:
Not reported.

Adjusted for non-response:
Not reported.

Concepts and definitions of variables:
Number of persons engaged refers to the average number throughout the year. It includes working proprietors, active business partners, unpaid family workers, salaried employees, wage-earners, and full- and part-time employees.
Output is production measured in producers' prices. It refers to the value of all products.
Value added, also in producers' prices, uses the national accounting concept of value added.

Related national publications:
(i) H.G. Graf, F. Kneschaurek, Y. Wang, Vorleistungen, Wertschöpfung und Produktivität in Industrie- und Dienstleistungsbranchen der Schweiz, 1989;
(ii) H.G. Graf, Das St. Galler Branchenmodell: Stand der Revisionsarbeiten, in: Mitteilungen des SGZZ, Ziff. 2.3, Nr. 27, 1990.

Switzerland

ISIC Revision 2	Number of establishments					Number of persons engaged					Wages and salaries paid to employees				
		(numbers)					(thousands)					(thousand FRANCS)			
ISIC Industry	Note	1993	1994	1995	1996	Note	1993	1994	1995	1996	Note	1993	1994	1995	1996
311/2 Food products		...	...	...	...	a/	69.1	70.7	70.3	68.2		...	...	...	...
313 Beverages		...	...	...	...	a/	...	...	...	...		...	...	...	...
314 Tobacco		...	...	...	...	a/	...	...	...	...		...	...	...	...
321 Textiles		...	...	...	...		24.3	23.8	22.3	19.8		...	...	...	...
322 Wearing apparel, except footwear		...	...	...	...	b/c/	15.9	16.4	15.3	14.3		...	...	...	...
323 Leather and fur products		...	...	...	...	b/	...	...	...	...		...	...	...	...
324 Footwear, except rubber or plastic		...	...	...	...	b/	...	...	...	...		...	...	...	...
331 Wood products, except furniture		...	...	...	...	d/e/	78.1	79.5	79.0	75.3		...	...	...	...
332 Furniture and fixtures, excl. metal		...	...	...	...	d/	...	...	...	...		...	...	...	...
341 Paper and products		...	...	...	...		15.7	15.2	15.3	14.9		...	...	...	...
342 Printing and publishing		...	...	...	...		62.0	62.4	61.6	59.0		...	...	...	...
351 Industrial chemicals		...	...	...	...	f/	72.9	74.6	74.5	73.0		...	...	...	...
352 Other chemicals		...	...	...	...	f/	...	...	...	...		...	...	...	...
353 Petroleum refineries		...	...	...	...	f/	...	...	...	...		...	...	...	...
354 Misc. petroleum and coal products		...	...	...	...	f/	...	...	...	...		...	...	...	...
355 Rubber products		...	...	...	...	g/	27.9	28.5	28.2	26.4		...	...	...	...
356 Plastic products		...	...	...	...	g/	...	...	...	...		...	...	...	...
361 Pottery, china, earthenware		...	...	...	...	h/i/	29.7	30.3	30.1	27.9		...	...	...	...
362 Glass and products		...	...	...	...	h/	...	...	...	...		...	...	...	...
369 Other non-metallic mineral products		...	...	...	...	h/	...	...	...	...		...	...	...	...
371 Iron and steel		...	...	...	...	j/	94.4	94.4	93.8	88.6		...	...	...	...
372 Non-ferrous metals		...	...	...	...	j/	...	...	...	...		...	...	...	...
381 Fabricated metal products		...	...	...	...	j/	...	...	...	...		...	...	...	...
382 Non-electrical machinery		...	...	...	...	k/m/	142.6	136.9	136.9	132.3		...	...	...	...
383 Electrical machinery		...	...	...	...	n/	115.4	114.5	113.2	112.7		...	...	...	...
384 Transport equipment		...	...	...	...	k/	...	...	...	...		...	...	...	...
385 Professional and scientific equipment		...	...	...	...	p/	35.0	36.5	36.9	35.4		...	...	...	...
390 Other manufacturing industries		...	...	...	...	d/	...	...	...	...		...	...	...	...
3 Total manufacturing		...	...	...	...		783.0	783.7	777.4	747.8		...	...	...	...

a/ 311/2 includes 313 and 314.
b/ 322 includes 323 and 324.
c/ Including knitting mills (ISIC 3213).
d/ 331 includes 332 and 390.
e/ Excluding jewellery (ISIC 3901).
f/ 351 includes 352, 353 and 354.
g/ 355 includes 356.
h/ 361 includes 362 and 369.
i/ Including mining and quarrying (ISIC 2).
j/ 371 includes 372 and 381.
k/ 382 includes 384.
m/ Including professional and scientific equipment (ISIC 3851).
n/ Including photographic and optical goods (ISIC 3852).
p/ 385 refers to watches and clocks (ISIC 3853) and jewellery (ISIC 3901).

Switzerland

ISIC Revision 2	Note	Output in producers' prices (million FRANCS)				Note	Value added in producers' prices (million FRANCS)				Note	Gross fixed capital formation (million FRANCS)	
ISIC Industry		1993	1994	1995	1996		1993	1994	1995	1996		1995	1996
311/2 Food products	a/	26901	28395	29162	28851	a/	7737	8003	8384	8266		...	...
313 Beverages	a/	...	...	...	...	a/	...	...	...	...		...	...
314 Tobacco	a/	...	...	...	...	a/	...	...	...	...		...	...
321 Textiles		3705	3798	3897	3657		1579	1579	1623	1516		...	...
322 Wearing apparel, except footwear	b/c/	2127	1948	2903	3152	b/c/	813	782	1132	1229		...	...
323 Leather and fur products	b/	...	...	...	...	b/	...	...	...	...		...	...
324 Footwear, except rubber or plastic	b/	...	...	...	...	b/	...	...	...	...		...	...
331 Wood products, except furniture	d/e/	13096	14224	14939	13946	d/e/	5551	6025	6289	5857		...	...
332 Furniture and fixtures, excl. metal	d/	...	...	...	...	d/	...	...	...	...		...	...
341 Paper and products		3832	4019	4535	3860		1433	1437	1692	1447		...	...
342 Printing and publishing		9788	9862	10535	10789		4932	4916	5188	5330		...	...
351 Industrial chemicals	f/	30662	34442	37910	40319	f/	11108	12723	13149	13953		...	...
352 Other chemicals	f/	...	...	...	...	f/	...	...	...	...		...	...
353 Petroleum refineries	f/	...	...	...	...	f/	...	...	...	...		...	...
354 Misc. petroleum and coal products	f/	...	...	...	...	f/	...	...	...	...		...	...
355 Rubber products	g/	5395	5963	6836	6398	g/	2217	2558	2858	2655		...	...
356 Plastic products	g/	...	...	...	...	g/	...	...	...	...		...	...
361 Pottery, china, earthenware	h/i/	6515	7294	7164	6841	h/i/	3055	3317	3353	3215		...	...
362 Glass and products	h/	...	...	...	...	h/	...	...	...	...		...	...
369 Other non-metallic mineral products	h/	...	...	...	...	h/	...	...	...	...		...	...
371 Iron and steel	j/	20248	21069	23482	21127	j/	7880	8011	9111	8239		...	...
372 Non-ferrous metals	j/	...	...	...	...	j/	...	...	...	...		...	...
381 Fabricated metal products	j/	...	...	...	...	j/	...	...	...	...		...	...
382 Non-electrical machinery	k/m/	26497	28678	27525	26463	k/m/	12063	13192	12373	11710		...	...
383 Electrical machinery	n/	27634	29908	30226	31336	n/	10849	11963	11788	12158		...	...
384 Transport equipment	k/	...	...	...	...	k/	...	...	...	...		...	...
385 Professional and scientific equipment	p/	10689	11558	13152	13843	p/	3869	4233	4840	5108		...	...
390 Other manufacturing industries	d/	...	...	...	...	d/	...	...	...	...		...	...
3 Total manufacturing		187090	201158	212266	210582		73086	78739	81780	80683		...	...

a/ 311/2 includes 313 and 314.
b/ 322 includes 323 and 324.
c/ Including knitting mills (ISIC 3213).
d/ 331 includes 332 and 390.
e/ Excluding jewellery (ISIC 3901).
f/ 351 includes 352, 353 and 354.
g/ 355 includes 356.
h/ 361 includes 362 and 369.
i/ Including mining and quarrying (ISIC 2).
j/ 371 includes 372 and 381.
k/ 382 includes 384.
m/ Including professional and scientific equipment (ISIC 3851).
n/ Including photographic and optical goods (ISIC 3852).
p/ 385 refers to watches and clocks (ISIC 3853) and jewellery (ISIC 3901).

Switzerland

ISIC Revision 2		Index numbers of industrial production (1990=100)											
ISIC Industry	Note	1985	1986	1987	1988	1989	1990	1991	1992	1993	1994	1995	1996
311/2 Food products	a/	91	93	94	95	98	100	100	99	101	100	102	103
313 Beverages	a/	...	...	...	...	...	...	...	...	...	...	...	...
314 Tobacco	a/	...	...	...	...	...	...	...	...	...	...	...	...
321 Textiles		106	108	106	107	105	100	97	94	90	92	96	90
322 Wearing apparel, except footwear		116	120	111	101	97	100	103	91	86	82	82	85
323 Leather and fur products	b/	80	81	83	91	94	100	91	86	85	80	84	81
324 Footwear, except rubber or plastic		...	...	...	...	...	...	...	...	...	...	...	...
331 Wood products, except furniture		80	86	87	88	93	100	94	92	86	94	91	89
332 Furniture and fixtures, excl. metal		...	...	...	...	...	...	...	...	...	...	...	...
341 Paper and products		83	89	93	96	99	100	100	102	101	104	104	99
342 Printing and publishing		84	89	94	99	99	100	98	95	93	102	105	107
351 Industrial chemicals	c/	72	73	75	85	99	100	101	106	113	130	143	157
352 Other chemicals	c/	...	...	...	...	...	...	...	...	...	...	...	...
353 Petroleum refineries		...	...	...	...	...	...	...	...	...	...	...	...
354 Misc. petroleum and coal products		...	...	...	...	...	...	...	...	...	...	...	...
355 Rubber products	b/	...	...	...	...	...	...	...	...	...	...	...	...
356 Plastic products		...	...	...	...	...	...	...	...	...	...	...	...
361 Pottery, china, earthenware	d/	103	96	98	100	102	100	87	83	77	85	81	77
362 Glass and products	d/	...	...	...	...	...	...	...	...	...	...	...	...
369 Other non-metallic mineral products	d/	...	...	...	...	...	...	...	...	...	...	...	...
371 Iron and steel	e/	86	88	90	98	100	100	90	90	83	83	86	85
372 Non-ferrous metals	e/	...	...	...	...	...	...	...	...	...	...	...	...
381 Fabricated metal products	f/	82	87	87	93	93	100	105	104	100	102	104	102
382 Non-electrical machinery	f/	...	...	...	...	...	...	...	...	...	...	...	...
383 Electrical machinery	f/	...	...	...	...	...	...	...	...	...	...	...	...
384 Transport equipment	f/	...	...	...	...	...	...	...	...	...	...	...	...
385 Professional and scientific equipment	g/	91	101	95	96	101	100	96	111	117	105	100	93
390 Other manufacturing industries	g/	...	...	...	...	...	...	...	...	...	...	...	...
3 Total manufacturing		84	88	89	94	96	100	101	101	100	103	106	106

a/ 311/2 includes 313 and 314.
b/ 323 includes 355.
c/ 351 includes 352.
d/ 361 includes 362 and 369.
e/ 371 includes 372.
f/ 381 includes 382, 383 and 384.
g/ 385 includes 390.

TAJIKISTAN

Supplier of information:
State Statistical Agency, Dushanbe.

Basic source of data:
Not reported.

Major deviations from ISIC (Revision 3):
None reported.

Reference period (if not calendar year):

Scope:
Not reported.

Method of enumeration:
Not reported.

Adjusted for non-response:
Not reported.

Concepts and definitions of variables:
No deviations from the standard UN concepts and definitions are reported.

In May 1995, the national currency was changed from roubles to the tajik roubles (1 tajik rouble = 100 roubles). All data reported in terms of national currency are in tajik roubles.

Related national publications:

Tajikistan

ISIC Revision 3		Number of establishments					Number of employees					Wages and salaries paid to employees				
			(numbers)					(numbers)					(million T.ROUBLES)			
ISIC	Industry	Note	1993	1994	1995	1996	Note	1993	1994	1995	1996	Note	1993	1994	1995	1996
151	Processed meat,fish,fruit,vegetables,fats		241	133	132	100		10264	8793	9256	6024		...	...	...	...
1511	Processing/preserving of meat		99	22	27	21		1660	1378	1388	762		...	...	...	...
1512	Processing/preserving of fish		6	5	5	5		328	315	319	285		...	...	...	...
1513	Processing/preserving of fruit & vegetables		47	34	33	16		6405	5063	4332	3049		...	...	...	...
1514	Vegetable and animal oils and fats		89	72	67	58		1871	2037	3217	1928		...	...	...	...
1520	Dairy products		12	15	13	23		982	1007	912	690		...	...	...	...
153	Grain mill products; starches; animal feeds		...	...	...	...		...	...	...	...		...	...	...	...
1531	Grain mill products		194	204	192	269		3480	2913	3343	2733		...	...	...	...
1532	Starches and starch products		...	...	...	...		...	...	...	...		...	...	...	...
1533	Prepared animal feeds		38	9	10	1		147	87	89	25		...	...	...	...
154	Other food products		...	...	...	...		...	...	...	...		...	...	...	...
1541	Bakery products		40	43	43	42		6714	6908	6940	5439		...	...	...	...
1542	Sugar		...	...	...	...		...	...	...	...		...	...	...	...
1543	Cocoa, chocolate and sugar confectionery		5	6	6	4		889	906	790	376		...	...	...	...
1544	Macaroni, noodles & similar products		...	...	...	...		...	...	...	...		...	...	...	...
1549	Other food products n.e.c.		2	2	2	3		383	398	437	484		...	...	...	...
155	Beverages		...	...	...	...		...	...	...	...		...	...	...	...
1551	Distilling, rectifying & blending of spirits		1	1	1	-		121	156	137	-		...	...	...	...
1552	Wines		14	7	8	17		879	761	725	839		...	...	...	...
1553	Malt liquors and malt		...	...	...	...		...	...	...	...		...	...	...	...
1554	Soft drinks; mineral waters		3	4	4	5		477	484	436	397		...	...	...	...
1600	Tobacco products		3	3	3	3		572	588	531	404		...	...	...	...
171	Spinning, weaving and finishing of textiles		...	...	...	...		...	...	...	...		...	...	...	...
1711	Textile fibre preparation; textile weaving		44	45	47	50		30666	30228	28227	22413		...	...	...	...
1712	Finishing of textiles		...	...	...	...		...	...	...	...		...	...	...	...
172	Other textiles		...	...	...	...		...	...	...	...		...	...	...	...
1721	Made-up textile articles, except apparel		...	...	...	...		...	...	...	...		...	...	...	...
1722	Carpets and rugs		5	5	5	4		6883	6166	4679	2046		...	...	...	...
1723	Cordage, rope, twine and netting		...	...	...	...		...	...	...	...		...	...	...	...
1729	Other textiles n.e.c.		1	1	1	1		437	470	450	330		...	...	...	...
1730	Knitted and crocheted fabrics and articles		8	8	8	7		7207	6970	5815	4028		...	...	...	...
1810	Wearing apparel, except fur apparel		49	33	42	18		14016	12694	8825	4511		...	...	...	...
1820	Dressing & dyeing of fur; processing of fur		1	1	1	1		118	92	74	50		...	...	...	...
191	Tanning, dressing and processing of leather		...	...	...	...		...	...	...	...		...	...	...	...
1911	Tanning and dressing of leather		...	...	...	...		...	...	...	...		...	...	...	...
1912	Luggage, handbags, etc.; saddlery & harness		1	1	1	1		106	59	76	68		...	...	...	...
1920	Footwear		17	7	8	5		5853	4488	3578	1101		...	...	...	...
2010	Sawmilling and planing of wood		37	18	19	13		86	33	40	13		...	...	...	...
202	Products of wood, cork, straw, etc.		...	...	...	...		...	...	...	...		...	...	...	...
2021	Veneer sheets, plywood, particle board, etc.		...	...	...	...		...	...	...	...		...	...	...	...
2022	Builders' carpentry and joinery		54	36	41	5		831	713	730	225		...	...	...	...
2023	Wooden containers		17	6	8	4		595	391	295	175		...	...	...	...
2029	Other wood products; articles of cork/straw		1	-	-	-		8	-	-	-		...	...	...	...
210	Paper and paper products		...	...	...	...		...	...	...	...		...	...	...	...
2101	Pulp, paper and paperboard		1	1	1	1		81	81	63	52		...	...	...	...
2102	Corrugated paper and paperboard		...	...	...	...		...	...	...	...		...	...	...	...
2109	Other articles of paper and paperboard		...	...	...	...		...	...	...	...		...	...	...	...
221	Publishing		...	...	...	...		...	...	...	...		...	...	...	...
2211	Publishing of books and other publications		...	...	...	...		...	...	...	...		...	...	...	...
2212	Publishing of newspapers, journals, etc.		...	...	...	...		...	...	...	...		...	...	...	...
2213	Publishing of recorded media		...	...	...	...		...	...	...	...		...	...	...	...
2219	Other publishing		...	...	...	...		...	...	...	...		...	...	...	...

ISIC												
222 Printing and related service activities	...	...	...	...	...	...	...	...	...	...	...	...
2221 Printing	37	34	34	32	1759	1967	1559	1081	...	...	...	...
2222 Service activities related to printing	...	...	...	...	...	...	...	...	...	...	...	...
2230 Reproduction of recorded media	...	...	...	...	...	...	...	...	...	...	...	...
2310 Coke oven products	...	...	...	...	...	...	...	...	...	...	...	...
2320 Refined petroleum products	...	...	...	...	...	...	...	...	...	...	...	...
2330 Processing of nuclear fuel	...	...	...	...	...	...	...	...	...	...	...	...
241 Basic chemicals	...	...	...	...	...	...	...	...	...	...	...	...
2411 Basic chemicals, except fertilizers	6	4	4	3	7323	6976	5594	4097	...	...	...	...
2412 Fertilizers and nitrogen compounds	1	1	1	1	871	735	745	787	...	...	...	...
2413 Plastics in primary forms; synthetic rubber	...	...	...	...	...	...	...	...	...	...	...	...
242 Other chemicals	...	...	...	...	...	...	...	...	...	...	...	...
2421 Pesticides and other agro-chemical products	...	...	...	...	...	...	...	...	...	...	...	...
2422 Paints, varnishes, printing ink and mastics	2	2	2	2	419	428	530	268	...	...	...	...
2423 Pharmaceuticals, medicinal chemicals, etc.	...	...	...	...	...	...	...	...	...	...	...	...
2424 Soap, cleaning & cosmetic preparations	3	2	2	-	48	45	42	-	...	...	...	...
2429 Other chemical products n.e.c.	1	1	1	1	158	155	...	...	...	...	...	...
2430 Man-made fibres	...	...	...	...	...	...	...	...	...	...	...	...
251 Rubber products	...	...	...	...	...	...	...	...	...	...	...	...
2511 Rubber tyres and tubes	1	1	1	1	125	116	124	105	...	...	...	...
2519 Other rubber products	...	...	...	...	...	...	...	...	...	...	...	...
2520 Plastic products	1	1	1	1	126	127	127	124	...	...	...	...
2610 Glass and glass products	2	2	2	2	1906	1842	1634	1358	...	...	...	...
269 Non-metallic mineral products n.e.c.	...	...	...	...	...	...	...	...	...	...	...	...
2691 Pottery, china and earthenware	...	...	...	...	...	...	...	...	...	...	...	...
2692 Refractory ceramic products	...	...	...	...	...	...	...	...	...	...	...	...
2693 Struct.non-refractory clay; ceramic products	...	...	...	...	...	...	...	...	...	...	...	...
2694 Cement, lime and plaster	5	5	5	5	1010	1048	968	931	...	...	...	...
2695 Articles of concrete, cement and plaster	133	117	115	63	8815	8278	7487	4307	...	...	...	...
2696 Cutting, shaping & finishing of stone	30	20	29	20	399	373	361	584	...	...	...	...
2699 Other non-metallic mineral products n.e.c.	...	...	...	...	...	...	...	...	...	...	...	...
2710 Basic iron and steel	...	...	...	...	...	...	...	...	...	...	...	...
2720 Basic precious and non-ferrous metals	5	5	5	5	13141	13882	15852	14411	...	...	...	...
273 Casting of metals	...	...	...	...	...	...	...	...	...	...	...	...
2731 Casting of iron and steel	...	...	...	...	...	...	...	...	...	...	...	...
2732 Casting of non-ferrous metals	...	...	...	...	...	...	...	...	...	...	...	...
281 Struct.metal products;tanks;steam generators	...	...	...	...	...	...	...	...	...	...	...	...
2811 Structural metal products	21	20	13	9	370	294	170	55	...	...	...	...
2812 Tanks, reservoirs and containers of metal	...	...	...	...	...	...	...	...	...	...	...	...
2813 Steam generators	...	...	...	...	...	...	...	...	...	...	...	...
289 Other metal products; metal working services	...	...	...	...	...	...	...	...	...	...	...	...
2891 Metal forging/pressing/stamping/roll-forming	...	...	...	...	...	...	...	...	...	...	...	...
2892 Treatment & coating of metals	...	...	...	...	...	...	...	...	...	...	...	...
2893 Cutlery, hand tools and general hardware	...	...	...	...	...	...	...	...	...	...	...	...
2899 Other fabricated metal products n.e.c.	...	...	...	...	...	...	...	...	...	...	...	...
291 General purpose machinery	...	...	...	...	...	...	...	...	...	...	...	...
2911 Engines & turbines(not for transport equip.)	...	...	...	...	...	...	...	...	...	...	...	...
2912 Pumps, compressors, taps and valves	...	...	...	...	...	...	...	...	...	...	...	...
2913 Bearings, gears, gearing & driving elements	...	...	...	...	...	...	...	...	...	...	...	...
2914 Ovens, furnaces and furnace burners	...	...	...	...	...	...	...	...	...	...	...	...
2915 Lifting and handling equipment	...	...	...	...	...	...	...	...	...	...	...	...
2919 Other general purpose machinery	2	3	3	4	1172	1170	1038	769	...	...	...	...
292 Special purpose machinery	...	...	...	...	...	...	...	...	...	...	...	...
2921 Agricultural and forestry machinery	4	4	4	4	2751	2572	2307	1516	...	...	...	...
2922 Machine tools	2	2	2	2	610	601	499	313	...	...	...	...
2923 Machinery for metallurgy	...	...	...	...	...	...	...	...	...	...	...	...
2924 Machinery for mining & construction	...	...	...	...	...	...	...	...	...	...	...	...
2925 Food/beverage/tobacco processing machinery	...	...	...	...	...	...	...	...	...	...	...	...
2926 Machinery for textile, apparel and leather	1	2	2	2	1130	2387	2146	1721	...	...	...	...
2927 Weapons and ammunition	...	...	...	...	...	...	...	...	...	...	...	...
2929 Other special purpose machinery	...	...	...	...	...	...	...	...	...	...	...	...
2930 Domestic appliances n.e.c.	1	1	1	2	746	714	683	781	...	...	...	...

continued

Tajikistan

ISIC Revision 3	Number of establishments					Number of employees					Wages and salaries paid to employees				
		(numbers)					(numbers)					(million T.ROUBLES)			
ISIC Industry	Note	1993	1994	1995	1996	Note	1993	1994	1995	1996	Note	1993	1994	1995	1996
3000 Office, accounting and computing machinery		...	...	...	...		...	...	...	...		...	...	...	...
3110 Electric motors, generators and transformers		4	3	3	-		1748	1635	1517	-		...	...	...	...
3120 Electricity distribution & control apparatus		...	...	...	...		...	...	...	...		...	...	...	...
3130 Insulated wire and cable		2	2	2	1		333	329	348	...		...	...	...	...
3140 Accumulators, primary cells and batteries		...	...	...	...		...	...	...	...		...	...	...	...
3150 Lighting equipment and electric lamps		...	...	...	...		...	...	...	...		...	...	...	...
3190 Other electrical equipment n.e.c.		...	...	...	...		...	...	...	...		...	...	...	...
3210 Electronic valves, tubes, etc.		...	...	...	...		...	...	...	...		...	...	...	...
3220 TV/radio transmitters; line comm. apparatus		...	...	...	...		...	...	...	...		...	...	...	...
3230 TV and radio receivers and associated goods		...	...	...	...		...	...	...	...		...	...	...	...
331 Medical, measuring, testing appliances, etc.		...	...	...	...		...	...	...	...		...	...	...	...
3311 Medical, surgical and orthopaedic equipment		...	...	...	...		...	...	...	...		...	...	...	...
3312 Measuring/testing/navigating appliances,etc.		...	...	...	...		...	...	...	...		...	...	...	...
3313 Industrial process control equipment		...	...	...	...		...	...	...	...		...	...	...	...
3320 Optical instruments & photographic equipment		...	...	...	...		...	...	...	...		...	...	...	...
3330 Watches and clocks		...	...	...	...		...	...	...	...		...	...	...	...
3410 Motor vehicles		...	...	...	...		...	...	...	...		...	...	...	...
3420 Automobile bodies, trailers & semi-trailers		...	...	...	...		...	...	...	...		...	...	...	...
3430 Parts/accessories for automobiles		3	3	3	3		2063	2119	1939	1769		...	...	...	...
351 Building and repairing of ships and boats		...	...	...	...		...	...	...	...		...	...	...	...
3511 Building and repairing of ships		...	...	...	...		...	...	...	...		...	...	...	...
3512 Building/repairing of pleasure/sport. boats		...	...	...	...		...	...	...	...		...	...	...	...
3520 Railway/tramway locomotives & rolling stock		...	...	...	...		...	...	...	...		...	...	...	...
3530 Aircraft and spacecraft		...	...	...	...		...	...	...	...		...	...	...	...
359 Transport equipment n.e.c.		...	...	...	...		...	...	...	...		...	...	...	...
3591 Motorcycles		...	...	...	...		...	...	...	...		...	...	...	...
3592 Bicycles and invalid carriages		...	...	...	...		...	...	...	...		...	...	...	...
3599 Other transport equipment n.e.c.		...	...	...	...		...	...	...	...		...	...	...	...
3610 Furniture		13	10	10	6		1493	1306	946	769		...	...	...	...
369 Manufacturing n.e.c.		...	...	...	...		...	...	...	...		...	...	...	...
3691 Jewellery and related articles		1	1	2	2		765	628	1551	1131		...	...	...	...
3692 Musical instruments		...	...	...	...		...	...	...	...		...	...	...	...
3693 Sports goods		...	...	...	...		...	...	...	...		...	...	...	...
3694 Games and toys		...	...	...	...		...	...	...	...		...	...	...	...
3699 Other manufacturing n.e.c.		...	...	...	...		...	...	...	...		...	...	...	...
3710 Recycling of metal waste and scrap		1	1	1	1		96	91	78	61		...	...	...	...
3720 Recycling of non-metal waste and scrap		...	...	...	...		...	...	...	...		...	...	...	...
D Total manufacturing		1566	1129	1125	1261		165505	157855	142130	108197		...	...	...	...

Tajikistan

ISIC Revision 3	Output					Value added					Gross fixed capital formation		
		(million T.ROUBLES)					(million T.ROUBLES)					(million T.ROUBLES)	
ISIC Industry	Note	1993	1994	1995	1996	Note	1993	1994	1995	1996	Note	1995	1996
151 Processed meat,fish,fruit,vegetables,fats		381.1	722.6	2040.0	4765.0		...	...	...	...		255.0	3164.0
1511 Processing/preserving of meat		108.0	244.2	407.0	483.0		...	...	...	...		68.0	755.0
1512 Processing/preserving of fish		9.4	15.0	19.0	27.0		...	...	...	...		14.0	177.0
1513 Processing/preserving of fruit & vegetables		187.2	245.3	828.0	2339.0		...	...	...	...		122.0	1428.0
1514 Vegetable and animal oils and fats		76.5	218.1	786.0	1916.0		...	...	...	...		51.0	804.0
1520 Dairy products		47.7	196.5	298.0	385.0		...	...	...	...		30.0	625.0
153 Grain mill products; starches; animal feeds		...	...	...	...		...	...	...	...		...	...
1531 Grain mill products		734.7	1967.7	6373.0	23526.0		...	...	...	...		102.0	1661.0
1532 Starches and starch products		...	...	...	...		...	...	...	...		...	...
1533 Prepared animal feeds		5.9	10.6	39.0	58.0		...	...	...	...		2.8	2.4
154 Other food products		...	...	...	...		...	...	...	...		...	...
1541 Bakery products		233.7	683.5	2516.0	16908.0		...	...	...	...		111.0	813.0
1542 Sugar		...	...	...	...		...	...	...	...		...	...
1543 Cocoa, chocolate and sugar confectionery		37.4	58.2	127.0	109.0		...	...	...	...		71.0	380.0
1544 Macaroni, noodles & similar products		...	...	...	...		...	...	...	...		...	...
1549 Other food products n.e.c.		6.4	27.3	79.0	363.0		...	...	...	...		3.0	38.0
155 Beverages		...	...	...	...		...	...	...	...		...	...
1551 Distilling, rectifying & blending of spirits		11.8	61.6	167.0	-		...	...	...	...		0.6	-
1552 Wines		42.5	96.3	130.0	309.0		...	...	...	...		26.0	506.0
1553 Malt liquors and malt		...	...	...	...		...	...	...	...		...	...
1554 Soft drinks; mineral waters		9.3	26.3	35.0	129.0		...	...	...	...		9.4	333.0
1600 Tobacco products		115.3	199.3	364.0	1104.0		...	...	...	...		27.0	208.0
171 Spinning, weaving and finishing of textiles		...	...	...	...		...	...	...	...		...	...
1711 Textile fibre preparation; textile weaving		1912.0	4629.9	14758.0	35023.0		...	...	...	...		568.0	9967.0
1712 Finishing of textiles		...	...	...	...		...	...	...	...		...	...
172 Other textiles		...	...	...	...		...	...	...	...		...	...
1721 Made-up textile articles, except apparel		...	...	...	...		...	...	...	...		...	...
1722 Carpets and rugs		332.2	372.0	359.0	986.0		...	...	...	...		74.0	2095.0
1723 Cordage, rope, twine and netting		...	...	...	...		...	...	...	...		...	...
1729 Other textiles n.e.c.		6.0	12.9	21.0	28.0		...	...	...	...		7.8	33.0
1730 Knitted and crocheted fabrics and articles		103.2	182.6	250.0	576.0		...	...	...	...		463.0	1278.0
1810 Wearing apparel, except fur apparel		166.3	332.5	462.0	998.0		...	...	...	...		121.0	855.0
1820 Dressing & dyeing of fur; processing of fur		0.9	2.9	1.4	2.1		...	...	...	...		4.7	161.0
191 Tanning, dressing and processing of leather		...	...	...	...		...	...	...	...		...	...
1911 Tanning and dressing of leather		...	...	...	...		...	...	...	...		...	...
1912 Luggage, handbags, etc.; saddlery & harness		1.0	1.5	6.4	2.6		...	...	...	...		0.5	0.5
1920 Footwear		78.3	57.6	146.0	228.0		...	...	...	...		49.0	598.0
2010 Sawmilling and planing of wood		0.7	2.1	47.0	0.2		...	...	...	...		0.3	1.3
202 Products of wood, cork, straw, etc.		...	...	...	...		...	...	...	...		...	...
2021 Veneer sheets, plywood, particle board, etc.		...	...	...	...		...	...	...	...		...	...
2022 Builders' carpentry and joinery		18.2	39.4	61.0	10.0		...	...	...	...		304.0	210.0
2023 Wooden containers		5.3	6.4	10.0	20.0		...	...	...	...		4.6	64.0
2029 Other wood products; articles of cork/straw		0.1	-	-	-		...	...	...	...		-	-
210 Paper and paper products		...	...	...	...		...	...	...	...		...	...
2101 Pulp, paper and paperboard		0.8	2.3	13.0	29.0		...	...	...	...		1.3	37.0
2102 Corrugated paper and paperboard		...	...	...	...		...	...	...	...		...	...
2109 Other articles of paper and paperboard		...	...	...	...		...	...	...	...		...	...
221 Publishing		...	...	...	...		...	...	...	...		...	...
2211 Publishing of books and other publications		...	...	...	...		...	...	...	...		...	...
2212 Publishing of newspapers, journals, etc.		...	...	...	...		...	...	...	...		...	...
2213 Publishing of recorded media		...	...	...	...		...	...	...	...		...	...
2219 Other publishing		...	...	...	...		...	...	...	...		...	...

continued

Tajikistan

ISIC Revision 3 ISIC Industry	Output Note	(million T.ROUBLES) 1993	1994	1995	1996	Value added Note	(million T.ROUBLES) 1993	1994	1995	1996	Gross fixed capital formation Note	(million T.ROUBLES) 1995	1996
222 Printing and related service activities		...	...	...	...		...	...	...	...		...	...
2221 Printing		8.1	38.7	59.0	202.0		...	...	...	...		58.0	983.0
2222 Service activities related to printing		...	...	...	...		...	...	...	...		...	...
2230 Reproduction of recorded media		...	...	...	...		...	...	...	...		...	...
2310 Coke oven products		...	...	...	...		...	...	...	...		...	...
2320 Refined petroleum products		...	...	...	...		...	...	...	...		...	...
2330 Processing of nuclear fuel		...	...	...	...		...	...	...	...		...	...
241 Basic chemicals		...	...	...	...		...	...	...	...		...	...
2411 Basic chemicals, except fertilizers		203.0	572.2	3321.0	7586.0		...	...	...	...		264.0	4875.0
2412 Fertilizers and nitrogen compounds		21.7	61.5	790.0	1547.0		...	...	...	...		452.0	452.0
2413 Plastics in primary forms; synthetic rubber		...	...	...	...		...	...	...	...		...	...
242 Other chemicals		...	...	...	...		...	...	...	...		...	...
2421 Pesticides and other agro-chemical products		...	...	...	...		...	...	...	...		...	...
2422 Paints, varnishes, printing ink and mastics		5.2	31.3	139.0	213.0		...	...	...	...		3.4	36.0
2423 Pharmaceuticals, medicinal chemicals, etc.		...	...	...	...		...	...	...	...		...	...
2424 Soap, cleaning & cosmetic preparations		9.9	10.6	8.9	-		...	...	...	...		4.2	-
2429 Other chemical products n.e.c.		2.8	3.6	...	...		...	...	...	...		1.3	1.3
2430 Man-made fibres		...	...	...	...		...	...	...	...		...	...
251 Rubber products		...	...	...	...		...	...	...	...		...	...
2511 Rubber tyres and tubes		2.3	16.0	33.0	56.0		...	...	...	...		0.4	16.0
2519 Other rubber products		...	...	...	...		...	...	...	...		...	...
2520 Plastic products		1.7	4.3	11.0	29.0		...	...	...	...		4.6	149.0
2610 Glass and glass products		34.4	65.4	228.0	599.0		...	...	...	...		243.0	800.0
269 Non-metallic mineral products n.e.c.		...	...	...	...		...	...	...	...		...	...
2691 Pottery, china and earthenware		...	...	...	...		...	...	...	...		...	...
2692 Refractory ceramic products		...	...	...	...		...	...	...	...		...	...
2693 Struct.non-refractory clay; ceramic products		...	...	...	...		...	...	...	...		...	...
2694 Cement, lime and plaster		53.3	167.2	358.0	742.0		...	...	...	...		57.0	398.0
2695 Articles of concrete, cement and plaster		215.2	740.8	1741.0	1780.0		...	...	...	...		373.0	3651.0
2696 Cutting, shaping & finishing of stone		8.0	34.2	84.0	130.0		...	...	...	...		35.0	602.0
2699 Other non-metallic mineral products n.e.c.		...	...	...	...		...	...	...	...		...	...
2710 Basic iron and steel		...	...	...	...		...	...	...	...		...	...
2720 Basic precious and non-ferrous metals		1666.0	6007.6	32427.0	80333.0		...	...	...	...		1011.0	24302.0
273 Casting of metals		...	...	...	...		...	...	...	...		...	...
2731 Casting of iron and steel		...	...	...	...		...	...	...	...		...	...
2732 Casting of non-ferrous metals		...	...	...	...		...	...	...	...		...	...
281 Struct.metal products;tanks;steam generators		...	...	...	...		...	...	...	...		...	...
2811 Structural metal products		8.8	40.8	215.0	44.0		...	...	...	...		22.0	39.0
2812 Tanks, reservoirs and containers of metal		...	...	...	...		...	...	...	...		...	...
2813 Steam generators		...	...	...	...		...	...	...	...		...	...
289 Other metal products; metal working services		...	...	...	...		...	...	...	...		...	...
2891 Metal forging/pressing/stamping/roll-forming		...	...	...	...		...	...	...	...		...	...
2892 Treatment & coating of metals		...	...	...	...		...	...	...	...		...	...
2893 Cutlery, hand tools and general hardware		...	...	...	...		...	...	...	...		...	...
2899 Other fabricated metal products n.e.c.		...	...	...	...		...	...	...	...		...	...
291 General purpose machinery		...	...	...	...		...	...	...	...		...	...
2911 Engines & turbines(not for transport equip.)		...	...	...	...		...	...	...	...		...	...
2912 Pumps, compressors, taps and valves		...	...	...	...		...	...	...	...		...	...
2913 Bearings, gears, gearing & driving elements		...	...	...	...		...	...	...	...		...	...
2914 Ovens, furnaces and furnace burners		...	...	...	...		...	...	...	...		...	...
2915 Lifting and handling equipment		...	...	...	...		...	...	...	...		...	...
2919 Other general purpose machinery		21.0	49.4	139.0	267.0		...	...	...	...		20.0	521.0

Code	Industry										
292	Special purpose machinery	...	...	...	...	...	...	...	...	...	...
2921	Agricultural and forestry machinery	34.9	41.5	149.0	406.0	...	...	...	...	190.0	1065.0
2922	Machine tools	4.7	13.8	28.0	45.0	...	...	...	...	6.2	161.0
2923	Machinery for metallurgy	...	...	...	...	...	...	...	...	...	...
2924	Machinery for mining & construction	...	...	...	...	...	...	...	...	...	...
2925	Food/beverage/tobacco processing machinery	...	...	...	...	...	...	...	...	...	...
2926	Machinery for textile, apparel and leather	12.2	67.5	186.0	574.0	...	...	...	...	38.0	763.0
2927	Weapons and ammunition	...	...	...	...	...	...	...	...	...	...
2929	Other special purpose machinery	...	...	...	...	...	...	...	...	...	...
2930	Domestic appliances n.e.c.	17.7	9.3	9.0	113.0	...	...	...	...	16.0	239.0
3000	Office, accounting and computing machinery	...	...	...	...	...	...	...	...	...	...
3110	Electric motors, generators and transformers	21.3	26.2	116.0	-	...	...	...	...	25.0	-
3120	Electricity distribution & control apparatus	...	...	...	...	...	...	...	...	...	...
3130	Insulated wire and cable	59.9	154.8	686.0	...	...	...	...	...	17.0	...
3140	Accumulators, primary cells and batteries	...	...	...	...	...	...	...	...	...	...
3150	Lighting equipment and electric lamps	...	...	...	...	...	...	...	...	...	...
3190	Other electrical equipment n.e.c.	...	...	...	...	...	...	...	...	...	...
3210	Electronic valves, tubes, etc.	...	...	...	...	...	...	...	...	...	...
3220	TV/radio transmitters; line comm. apparatus	...	...	...	...	...	...	...	...	...	...
3230	TV and radio receivers and associated goods	...	...	...	...	...	...	...	...	...	...
331	Medical, measuring, testing appliances, etc.	...	...	...	...	...	...	...	...	...	...
3311	Medical, surgical and orthopaedic equipment	...	...	...	...	...	...	...	...	...	...
3312	Measuring/testing/navigating appliances,etc.	...	...	...	...	...	...	...	...	...	...
3313	Industrial process control equipment	...	...	...	...	...	...	...	...	...	...
3320	Optical instruments & photographic equipment	...	...	...	...	...	...	...	...	...	...
3330	Watches and clocks	...	...	...	...	...	...	...	...	...	...
3410	Motor vehicles	...	...	...	...	...	...	...	...	...	...
3420	Automobile bodies, trailers & semi-trailers	...	...	...	...	...	...	...	...	...	...
3430	Parts/accessories for automobiles	60.1	109.5	267.0	681.0	...	...	...	...	30.0	765.0
351	Building and repairing of ships and boats	...	...	...	...	...	...	...	...	...	...
3511	Building and repairing of ships	...	...	...	...	...	...	...	...	...	...
3512	Building/repairing of pleasure/sport. boats	...	...	...	...	...	...	...	...	...	...
3520	Railway/tramway locomotives & rolling stock	...	...	...	...	...	...	...	...	...	...
3530	Aircraft and spacecraft	...	...	...	...	...	...	...	...	...	...
359	Transport equipment n.e.c.	...	...	...	...	...	...	...	...	...	...
3591	Motorcycles	...	...	...	...	...	...	...	...	...	...
3592	Bicycles and invalid carriages	...	...	...	...	...	...	...	...	...	...
3599	Other transport equipment n.e.c.	...	...	...	...	...	...	...	...	...	...
3610	Furniture	27.7	46.5	56.0	106.0	...	...	...	...	26.0	356.0
369	Manufacturing n.e.c.	...	...	...	...	...	...	...	...	...	...
3691	Jewellery and related articles	2.5	10.3	21.0	3552.0	...	...	...	...	32.0	2915.0
3692	Musical instruments	...	...	...	...	...	...	...	...	...	...
3693	Sports goods	...	...	...	...	...	...	...	...	...	...
3694	Games and toys	...	...	...	...	...	...	...	...	...	...
3699	Other manufacturing n.e.c.	...	...	...	...	...	...	...	...	...	...
3710	Recycling of metal waste and scrap	2.6	2.5	5.1	0.3	...	...	...	...	4.5	130.0
3720	Recycling of non-metal waste and scrap	...	...	...	...	...	...	...	...	...	...
D	Total manufacturing	7074.2	18884.9	71618.0	193297.0	...	...	...	...	7140.0	83221.0

Tajikistan

ISIC Revision 3		Index numbers of industrial production											
		(1990=100)											
ISIC Industry	Note	1985	1986	1987	1988	1989	1990	1991	1992	1993	1994	1995	1996
15 Food and beverages		...	...	...	...	...	...	...	...	...	...	...	...
16 Tobacco products		...	...	...	...	...	...	...	...	...	...	...	...
17 Textiles		...	...	...	...	...	...	...	...	...	...	...	...
18 Wearing apparel, fur		...	...	...	...	...	...	...	...	...	...	...	...
19 Leather, leather products and footwear		...	...	...	...	...	...	...	...	...	...	...	...
20 Wood products (excl. furniture)		...	...	...	...	...	...	...	...	...	...	...	...
21 Paper and paper products		...	...	...	...	...	...	...	...	...	...	...	...
22 Printing and publishing		...	...	...	...	...	...	...	...	...	...	...	...
23 Coke,refined petroleum products,nuclear fuel		...	...	...	...	...	...	...	...	...	...	...	...
24 Chemicals and chemical products		...	...	...	...	...	...	...	...	...	...	...	...
25 Rubber and plastics products		...	...	...	...	...	...	...	...	...	...	...	...
26 Non-metallic mineral products		...	...	...	...	...	...	...	...	...	...	...	...
27 Basic metals		...	...	...	...	...	...	...	...	...	...	...	...
28 Fabricated metal products		...	...	...	...	...	...	...	...	...	...	...	...
29 Machinery and equipment n.e.c.		...	...	...	...	...	...	...	...	...	...	...	...
30 Office, accounting and computing machinery		...	...	...	...	...	...	...	...	...	...	...	...
31 Electrical machinery and apparatus		...	...	...	...	...	...	...	...	...	...	...	...
32 Radio,television and communication equipment		...	...	...	...	...	...	...	...	...	...	...	...
33 Medical, precision and optical instruments		...	...	...	...	...	...	...	...	...	...	...	...
34 Motor vehicles, trailers, semi-trailers		...	...	...	...	...	...	...	...	...	...	...	...
35 Other transport equipment		...	...	...	...	...	...	...	...	...	...	...	...
36 Furniture; manufacturing n.e.c.		...	...	...	...	...	...	...	...	...	...	...	...
37 Recycling		...	...	...	...	...	...	...	...	...	...	...	...
D Total manufacturing		...	...	...	...	...	100	96	73	66	48	40	32

THAILAND

Supplier of information:
National Statistical Office, Bangkok, Metropolis.

Basic source of data:
Annual survey.

Major deviations from ISIC (Revision 2):
Data collected under the national classification system have been reclassified by the national authorities to correspond approximately with ISIC (Rev. 2). In cases where the exact correspondance of the national classification to the ISIC could not be achieved, it can result in differences between the data on the 3-digit level and the sum of the respective data on the 4-digit level.

Reference period (if not calendar year):

Scope:
All establishments with 10 and more persons engaged.

Method of enumeration:
Questionnaires are distributed by mail with follow-up site visits as required.

Adjusted for non-response:
No.

Concepts and definitions of variables:
Number of employees is as of 31 December or the last pay period of the reference year.
Output includes gross revenues from goods shipped in the same condition as received.

Related national publications:
Report of the Industrial Survey (annual), published by the National Statistical Office, Bangkok, Metropolis.

Thailand

ISIC Revision 2 ISIC Industry	Note	Number of establishments (numbers) 1991	1992	1993	1994	Note	Number of employees (thousands) 1991	1992	1993	1994	Note	Wages and salaries paid to employees (million BAHT) 1991	1992	1993	1994
311/2 Food products		2726	...	3208	3427		219.3	...	287.8	285.1		11375	...	17955	18971
3111 Slaughtering, preparing & preserving meat		63	...	42	52		24.7	...	34.5	12.3		1031	...	1775	696
3112 Dairy products		54	...	62	63		7.6	...	6.6	9.7		826	...	1068	963
3113 Canning, preserving of fruits & vegetables		179	...	177	186		27.3	...	34.3	35.2		1142	...	1577	2053
3114 Canning, preserving and processing of fish		243	...	242	247		48.0	...	106.4	99.2		2110	...	6091	5261
3115 Vegetable and animal oils and fats		65	...	39	60		8.5	...	9.1	7.7		863	...	1313	1184
3116 Grain mill products		1125	...	1221	1543		28.4	...	21.7	34.5		958	...	849	2078
3117 Bakery products		252	...	237	243		18.7	...	14.7	14.0		896	...	787	896
3118 Sugar factories and refineries		60	...	61	61		20.8	...	19.1	36.3		1558	...	1816	2990
3119 Cocoa, chocolate and sugar confectionery		72	...	66	52		3.3	...	9.6	5.6		136	...	573	369
3121 Other food products		295	...	314	294		7.0	...	7.9	8.5		279	...	446	525
3122 Prepared animal feeds		140	...	181	153		8.5	...	9.8	9.8		520	...	934	103
313 Beverages		79	...	72	67		20.9	...	45.2	21.4		2351	...	4883	1640
3131 Distilling, rectifying and blending spirits		15	...	7	3		6.3	...	4.9	0.3		843	...	852	12
3132 Wine industries		2	...	1	4		...	...	...	0.4		...	...	...	48
3133 Malt liquors and malt		3	...	2	3		3.5	...	...	6.5		818	...	...	404
3134 Soft drinks and carbonated waters		58	...	61	42		10.6	...	37.8	13.6		667	...	3860	1112
314 Tobacco		164	...	141	137		22.5	...	23.9	24.0		3804	...	2427	2779
321 Textiles		1464	...	1529	1821		276.5	...	335.3	377.3		13359	...	18192	27610
3211 Spinning, weaving and finishing textiles		1006	...	924	1103		233.3	...	279.9	290.8		11363	...	14902	20540
3212 Made-up textile goods excl. wearing apparel		77	...	55	103		17.3	...	1.2	10.1		895	...	42	829
3213 Knitting mills		151	...	171	198		17.6	...	19.6	50.1		783	...	1357	3408
3214 Carpets and rugs		37	...	15	12		1.6	...	1.7	5.5		54	...	63	785
3215 Cordage, rope and twine		30	...	41	47		3.5	...	21.0	12.0		161	...	1162	1512
3219 Other textiles		9	...	10	16		0.3	...	0.2	0.6		10	...	9	21
322 Wearing apparel, except footwear		1327	...	1459	1505		227.3	...	546.6	659.4		17519	...	39413	60475
323 Leather and fur products		206	...	142	232		13.4	...	16.6	21.7		769	...	920	1070
3231 Tanneries and leather finishing		68	...	5	35		4.8	...	0.9	4.7		257	...	20	214
3232 Fur dressing and dyeing industries		...	...	...	...		...	...	...	...		...	...	...	...
3233 Leather prods. excl. wearing apparel		92	...	110	160		7.7	...	12.7	16.5		331	...	730	835
324 Footwear, except rubber or plastic		257	...	158	158		63.3	...	55.1	21.0		2820	...	3678	1214
331 Wood products, except furniture		858	...	922	910		42.0	...	48.2	47.3		2004	...	2673	2733
3311 Sawmills, planing and other wood mills		576	...	551	656		31.7	...	34.5	33.8		1658	...	2075	2154
3312 Wooden and cane containers		102	...	72	65		2.4	...	4.4	7.2		51	...	194	293
3319 Other wood and cork products		81	...	66	97		5.2	...	2.9	5.3		209	...	110	250
332 Furniture and fixtures, excl. metal		333	...	497	517		29.0	...	30.3	29.1		1433	...	1411	1541
341 Paper and products		124	...	254	267		17.4	...	21.5	18.4		887	...	2153	2332
3411 Pulp, paper and paperboard articles		19	...	25	26		5.5	...	6.2	4.8		248	...	496	629
3412 Containers of paper and paperboard		62	...	147	159		6.5	...	9.6	8.7		341	...	1131	1152
3419 Other pulp, paper and paperboard articles		40	...	73	72		4.5	...	5.5	4.8		259	...	504	529
342 Printing and publishing		420	...	411	429		32.4	...	24.0	29.7		3853	...	2851	4245
351 Industrial chemicals		245	...	273	282		18.9	...	19.8	10.9		3923	...	2221	1639
3511 Basic chemicals excl. fertilizers		118	...	144	147		6.3	...	8.0	4.9		671	...	1256	548
3512 Fertilizers and pesticides		45	...	41	41		3.3	...	3.4	1.9		654	...	725	340
3513 Synthetic resins and plastic materials		49	...	39	53		9.8	...	6.4	3.6		2630	...	171	742
352 Other chemicals		312	...	341	329		33.6	...	38.1	24.5		3487	...	5208	3129
3521 Paints, varnishes and lacquers		56	...	32	37		3.6	...	3.6	4.8		147	...	267	426
3522 Drugs and medicines		141	...	129	128		13.5	...	11.9	11.0		1505	...	1500	1618
3523 Soap, cleaning preps., perfumes, cosmetics		60	...	49	29		10.0	...	6.0	2.1		1347	...	972	173
3529 Other chemical products		57	...	77	51		6.6	...	15.9	4.0		489	...	2383	669
353 Petroleum refineries		10	...	10	13		2.4	...	13.7	5.6		702	...	5927	2732

Industry												
354 Misc. petroleum and coal products	5	...	4	4	0.2	...	0.2	0.4	15	...	11	37
355 Rubber products	377	...	394	405	54.6	...	60.6	53.3	3333	...	4780	3524
3551 Tyres and tubes	53	...	78	87	19.9	...	17.1	12.1	1903	...	2578	1486
3559 Other rubber products	256	...	279	262	33.5	...	42.8	41.1	1370	...	2144	2034
356 Plastic products	490	...	579	651	26.3	...	40.2	52.0	1191	...	2225	3415
361 Pottery, china, earthenware	198	...	233	245	18.3	...	20.8	28.3	849	...	1076	1478
362 Glass and products	27	...	29	33	17.7	...	9.2	11.3	1775	...	890	1580
369 Other non-metallic mineral products	1049	...	1180	1233	62.8	...	56.7	71.1	7775	...	9174	7874
3691 Structural clay products	310	...	331	323	10.0	...	9.5	9.7	500	...	646	814
3692 Cement, lime and plaster	51	...	51	51	16.7	...	15.4	14.6	4544	...	5496	2552
3699 Other non-metallic mineral products	662	...	687	851	30.2	...	30.4	44.8	1786	...	2956	4056
371 Iron and steel	258	...	238	252	34.7	...	54.2	27.4	3263	...	2978	2299
372 Non-ferrous metals	123	...	90	215	12.1	...	6.3	35.4	1757	...	325	3188
381 Fabricated metal products	890	...	972	1046	64.6	...	74.1	129.9	4340	...	4940	9307
3811 Cutlery, hand tools and general hardware	55	...	46	48	2.9	...	3.2	2.4	115	...	239	107
3812 Furniture and fixtures primarily of metal	52	...	54	108	3.0	...	3.4	8.2	127	...	195	770
3813 Structural metal products	53	...	100	207	1.0	...	3.2	7.1	37	...	180	452
3819 Other fabricated metal products	428	...	551	586	51.2	...	61.8	111.0	3782	...	4171	7908
382 Non-electrical machinery	419	...	457	485	59.0	...	64.6	33.4	5786	...	6513	2743
3821 Engines and turbines	15	...	11	27	0.2	...	0.1	1.0	4	...	10	153
3822 Agricultural machinery and equipment	102	...	93	122	4.7	...	2.3	4.0	531	...	77	208
3823 Metal and wood working machinery	19	...	73	75	0.9	...	2.3	2.7	52	...	110	192
3824 Other special industrial machinery	53	...	41	44	1.7	...	2.8	6.4	98	...	178	648
3825 Office, computing and accounting machinery	19	...	24	24	1.3	...	2.1	0.4	104	...	188	22
3829 Other non-electrical machinery & equipment	85	...	95	92	46.2	...	52.9	15.9	4580	...	5782	1302
383 Electrical machinery	276	...	388	409	73.6	...	125.6	119.8	8054	...	9284	11135
3831 Electrical industrial machinery	53	...	48	52	17.4	...	7.1	9.5	1497	...	867	1248
3832 Radio, television and communication equipm.	86	...	126	134	35.4	...	86.2	53.8	4743	...	5599	4696
3833 Electrical appliances and housewares	19	...	22	29	2.2	...	4.3	16.8	63	...	245	1752
3839 Other electrical apparatus and supplies	103	...	100	112	16.5	...	19.5	34.1	1321	...	1944	3048
384 Transport equipment	697	...	756	779	78.1	...	83.7	71.9	7608	...	8220	8061
3841 Shipbuilding and repairing	36	...	10	34	1.9	...	0.6	1.2	111	...	34	90
3842 Railroad equipment	...	...	3	3	...	...	0.2	0.2	...	...	47	49
3843 Motor vehicles	447	...	377	498	68.4	...	53.3	47.9	6934	...	5897	5669
3844 Motorcycles and bicycles	77	...	66	99	3.9	...	22.7	19.7	215	...	1982	2116
3845 Aircraft	...	...	...	...	...	...	...	...	...	...	...	...
3849 Other transport equipment	3	...	5	6	-	...	0.1	0.1	1	...	4	5
385 Professional and scientific equipment	30	...	32	39	10.4	...	7.1	8.7	671	...	667	1327
3851 Prof. and scientific equipment n.e.c.	...	...	...	...	...	...	...	...	...	...	...	...
3852 Photographic and optical goods	...	...	...	...	...	...	...	...	...	...	...	...
3853 Watches and clocks	...	...	...	...	...	...	...	...	...	...	...	...
390 Other manufacturing industries	562	...	376	1002	65.6	...	59.7	63.3	3660	...	3423	3804
3901 Jewellery and related articles	218	...	137	151	33.4	...	24.0	25.4	1876	...	1456	1595
3902 Musical instruments	...	...	...	...	...	...	...	...	...	...	...	...
3903 Sporting and athletic goods	20	...	21	20	2.3	...	2.3	3.3	83	...	86	163
3909 Manufacturing industries, n.e.c.	298	...	211	303	28.9	...	32.5	29.5	1665	...	1853	1806
3 Total manufacturing	13926	...	15145	16892	1596.7	...	2169.2	2281.6	118348	...	164468	191880

Thailand

ISIC Revision 2		Output in producers' prices (million BAHT)					Value added in producers' prices (million BAHT)					Gross fixed capital formation (million BAHT)	
ISIC Industry	Note	1991	1992	1993	1994	Note	1991	1992	1993	1994	Note	1993	1994
311/2 Food products		253693	...	380843	329100		69025	...	112047	88933		17712	14736
3111 Slaughtering, preparing & preserving meat		18259	...	29576	7376		2341	...	157	718		-468	33
3112 Dairy products		22214	...	21639	22904		7457	...	5730	9003		1024	2492
3113 Canning, preserving of fruits & vegetables		13185	...	14564	17682		5208	...	6088	7771		555	2720
3114 Canning, preserving and processing of fish		40106	...	85655	72718		10560	...	16747	21970		4328	-5968
3115 Vegetable and animal oils and fats		24994	...	40978	30129		4587	...	3109	3082		1448	910
3116 Grain mill products		39523	...	15615	53687		8052	...	4983	10684		2753	1193
3117 Bakery products		8090	...	5577	5488		2924	...	1624	1972		2336	396
3118 Sugar factories and refineries		25429	...	74071	51810		8041	...	56300	14813		1892	7626
3119 Cocoa, chocolate and sugar confectionery		1177	...	7574	6528		466	...	4215	3737		577	310
3121 Other food products		2837	...	4448	5401		1221	...	1243	1875		97	2679
3122 Prepared animal feeds		30922	...	53870	40489		7833	...	9612	9806		1365	967
313 Beverages		49025	...	70734	52571		37610	...	44144	37516		7120	4588
3131 Distilling, rectifying and blending spirits		19351	...	18997	166		15882	...	10094	73		4808	1
3132 Wine industries		...	...	...	682		...	...	...	384		-	46
3133 Malt liquors and malt		23274	...	...	42340		18719	...	...	32072		...	1777
3134 Soft drinks and carbonated waters		5860	...	30411	7920		2838	...	17994	3856		1206	2718
314 Tobacco		57378	...	32893	37097		47883	...	25465	27921		1495	464
321 Textiles		134885	...	200701	213985		51372	...	84085	76677		19493	41001
3211 Spinning, weaving and finishing textiles		124109	...	150945	164747		46634	...	45225	50339		17700	26408
3212 Made-up textile goods excl. wearing apparel		4363	...	268	8125		1519	...	170	3983		108	7600
3213 Knitting mills		3622	...	29255	16446		2187	...	25952	8963		246	1548
3214 Carpets and rugs		762	...	1616	4079		274	...	551	3547		8	4026
3215 Cordage, rope and twine		944	...	6769	16924		392	...	2213	8263		348	1285
3219 Other textiles		200	...	38	131		95	...	26	69		14	14
322 Wearing apparel, except footwear		165090	...	233520	314659		84142	...	67127	89886		8190	14380
323 Leather and fur products		30033	...	10773	6817		15425	...	3324	3049		3061	3638
3231 Tanneries and leather finishing		14048	...	309	2210		7147	...	79	570		1	1304
3232 Fur dressing and dyeing industries		...	...	...	...		...	...	...	...		-	-
3233 Leather prods. excl. wearing apparel		2610	...	8379	4445		1580	...	2577	2396		2459	2315
324 Footwear, except rubber or plastic		15973	...	16406	6320		7317	...	7422	2805		412	670
331 Wood products, except furniture		22939	...	21597	27584		10053	...	7544	12248		1535	7515
3311 Sawmills, planing and other wood mills		19246	...	15853	25429		9176	...	6409	11282		916	7323
3312 Wooden and cane containers		222	...	542	541		75	...	267	300		114	24
3319 Other wood and cork products		1949	...	609	1274		455	...	283	501		234	101
332 Furniture and fixtures, excl. metal		13920	...	10537	9880		7065	...	3771	4201		852	2204
341 Paper and products		14605	...	61400	48328		4098	...	18932	16050		5881	8273
3411 Pulp, paper and paperboard articles		6066	...	16464	19920		1286	...	3690	4097		746	279
3412 Containers of paper and paperboard		3417	...	36402	20478		1191	...	12640	7828		4269	6922
3419 Other pulp, paper and paperboard articles		3768	...	8307	7699		1440	...	2519	4041		867	1069
342 Printing and publishing		571209	...	55155	56553		565470	...	42073	44451		1129	2522
351 Industrial chemicals		61837	...	47561	31206		25853	...	16681	8867		1524	2079
3511 Basic chemicals excl. fertilizers		5440	...	25570	4965		2293	...	10166	2048		640	220
3512 Fertilizers and pesticides		18096	...	19874	11496		5777	...	5507	3595		833	80
3513 Synthetic resins and plastic materials		38852	...	1511	14678		17919	...	942	3203		28	1744
352 Other chemicals		59848	...	55334	37496		20461	...	1690	13289		4194	4469
3521 Paints, varnishes and lacquers		794	...	6170	11483		321	...	2131	3125		451	1265
3522 Drugs and medicines		18890	...	17273	16410		9583	...	7479	6808		396	457
3523 Soap, cleaning preps., perfumes, cosmetics		33872	...	18355	1203		8400	...	3985	654		1006	25
3529 Other chemical products		6245	...	12905	6764		2141	...	-12081	1959		2290	2634
353 Petroleum refineries		133029	...	479432	270755		131145	...	134100	109864		44599	10789

Code	Industry													
354	Misc. petroleum and coal products		836	...	3056	1294		326	...	664	651		-	780
355	Rubber products		69774	...	83747	76573		26049	...	26634	16178		1998	2536
3551	Tyres and tubes		41713	...	33103	19095		17853	...	9145	4134		1154	226
3559	Other rubber products		27665	...	50047	57455		8014	...	17433	12035		818	2291
356	Plastic products		11564	...	21753	34876		5439	...	6810	11165		5605	4103
361	Pottery, china, earthenware		8081	...	6374	6497		4900	...	3696	3909		982	1821
362	Glass and products		17791	...	5083	11613		10919	...	1866	5997		1328	1950
369	Other non-metallic mineral products		122688	...	124689	75938		57759	...	55778	35421		17305	9985
3691	Structural clay products		5405	...	6733	6263		2933	...	1748	2881		811	565
3692	Cement, lime and plaster		89611	...	69438	28918		40074	...	38196	16613		12380	7750
3699	Other non-metallic mineral products		14645	...	47875	36538		6805	...	15663	13614		4073	1539
371	Iron and steel		84056	...	175125	68273		29108	...	45703	28302		11407	28190
372	Non-ferrous metals		41880	...	2354	17925		7785	...	670	4184		481	1312
381	Fabricated metal products		56325	...	53757	82271		27714	...	13759	30515		6140	8403
3811	Cutlery, hand tools and general hardware		492	...	801	589		194	...	422	316		290	53
3812	Furniture and fixtures primarily of metal		1678	...	1206	4349		494	...	259	2312		95	2211
3813	Structural metal products		189	...	1338	3311		106	...	774	2362		75	2597
3819	Other fabricated metal products		51556	...	49972	73709		26092	...	12089	25357		4881	3417
382	Non-electrical machinery		259899	...	128245	208132		174242	...	74727	166475		8862	2541
3821	Engines and turbines		45	...	34	1994		10	...	26	700		-	35
3822	Agricultural machinery and equipment		14042	...	386	1082		3884	...	271	499		16	165
3823	Metal and wood working machinery		44186	...	12968	13416		10115	...	3219	3355		207	353
3824	Other special industrial machinery		676	...	2443	3841		182	...	532	1511		269	451
3825	Office, computing and accounting machinery		1964	...	3140	380		1564	...	2915	110		5	6
3829	Other non-electrical machinery & equipment		187805	...	107869	185963		156034	...	67523	159419		8321	1436
383	Electrical machinery		217126	...	202713	175643		118439	...	49191	52279		27123	15011
3831	Electrical industrial machinery		16509	...	7156	20186		6904	...	1859	5167		510	2934
3832	Radio, television and communication equipm.		162441	...	158135	95029		93418	...	33267	29383		22230	7799
3833	Electrical appliances and housewares		1628	...	4450	12590		313	...	1141	4268		269	975
3839	Other electrical apparatus and supplies		19493	...	18513	39738		7316	...	12977	10967		2070	3272
384	Transport equipment		150122	...	198244	142209		100499	...	45194	51900		15806	5822
3841	Shipbuilding and repairing		576	...	240	397		182	...	130	195		38	15
3842	Railroad equipment		...	...	286	327		...	...	63	107		-	-
3843	Motor vehicles		138607	...	78869	70503		96699	...	29768	35843		8836	3007
3844	Motorcycles and bicycles		8571	...	115761	69435		2653	...	14257	15396		5882	2400
3845	Aircraft		...	...	...	...		...	...	...	...		-	-
3849	Other transport equipment		11	...	43	57		1	...	7	13		5	-
385	Professional and scientific equipment		5712	...	3785	8374		3219	...	789	3312		1398	630
3851	Prof. and scientific equipment n.e.c.		...	...	...	...		...	...	...	...		...	...
3852	Photographic and optical goods		...	...	...	...		...	...	...	...		...	...
3853	Watches and clocks		...	...	...	...		...	...	...	...		...	...
390	Other manufacturing industries		52046	...	36747	30562		25818	...	16300	12734		2707	809
3901	Jewellery and related articles		28948	...	18220	20425		12304	...	9814	8265		1439	354
3902	Musical instruments		...	...	...	...		...	...	...	...		-	-
3903	Sporting and athletic goods		894	...	921	1204		160	...	153	533		222	9
3909	Manufacturing industries, n.e.c.		21429	...	17369	7674		13225	...	6262	3409		1019	439
3	Total manufacturing		2681362	...	2717563	2382533		1669136	...	910196	958780		218338	201220

Thailand

ISIC Revision 2		Index numbers of industrial production											
		(1990=100)											
ISIC Industry	Note	1985	1986	1987	1988	1989	1990	1991	1992	1993	1994	1995	1996
311/2 Food products		96	98	92	89	103	100	84	99	97	90	103	...
313 Beverages		...	...	...	...	...	...	...	...	...	...	...	...
314 Tobacco		...	...	...	...	...	...	...	...	...	...	...	...
321 Textiles		...	...	...	...	...	...	...	...	...	...	...	...
322 Wearing apparel, except footwear		...	...	...	...	...	...	...	...	...	...	...	...
323 Leather and fur products		...	...	...	...	...	...	...	...	...	...	...	...
324 Footwear, except rubber or plastic		...	...	...	...	...	...	...	...	...	...	...	...
331 Wood products, except furniture		...	...	...	...	...	...	...	...	...	...	...	...
332 Furniture and fixtures, excl. metal		...	...	...	...	...	...	...	...	...	...	...	...
341 Paper and products		47	47	49	50	50	100	98	61	...	...	...	...
342 Printing and publishing		...	...	...	...	...	...	...	...	...	...	...	...
351 Industrial chemicals		...	...	...	...	...	...	...	...	...	...	...	...
352 Other chemicals		...	...	...	...	...	...	...	...	...	...	...	...
353 Petroleum refineries		...	...	...	...	...	...	...	...	...	...	...	...
354 Misc. petroleum and coal products		...	...	...	...	...	...	...	...	...	...	...	...
355 Rubber products		...	...	...	...	...	...	...	...	...	...	...	...
356 Plastic products		...	...	...	...	...	...	...	...	...	...	...	...
361 Pottery, china, earthenware		...	...	...	...	...	...	...	...	...	...	...	...
362 Glass and products		...	...	...	...	...	...	...	...	...	...	...	...
369 Other non-metallic mineral products		44	44	55	64	83	100	106	120	146	166	190	...
371 Iron and steel		...	...	...	...	...	...	...	...	...	...	...	...
372 Non-ferrous metals		...	...	...	...	...	...	...	...	...	...	...	...
381 Fabricated metal products		...	...	...	...	...	...	...	...	...	...	...	...
382 Non-electrical machinery		...	...	...	...	...	...	...	...	...	...	...	...
383 Electrical machinery		...	...	...	...	...	...	...	...	...	...	...	...
384 Transport equipment		...	...	...	...	...	...	...	...	...	...	...	...
385 Professional and scientific equipment		...	...	...	...	...	...	...	...	...	...	...	...
390 Other manufacturing industries		...	...	...	...	...	...	...	...	...	...	...	...
3 Total manufacturing		...	...	...	...	...	...	...	...	...	...	...	...

THE FORMER YUGOSLAV REPUBLIC OF MACEDONIA

Supplier of information:
Statistical Office of the former Yugoslav Republic of Macedonia, Skopje.

Basic source of data:
Annual report on industrial activity.

Major deviations from ISIC (Revision 2):
None reported.

Reference period (if not calendar year):

Scope:
Not reported.

Method of enumeration:
Not reported.

Adjusted for non-response:
Not reported.

Concepts and definitions of variables:
Wages and salaries is compensation of employees.
Output is gross output valued in basic values.
For the period 1990-1994, value added refers to social product and is calculated as the difference between the value of production, including turnover tax, and material expenditure by establishment.
Data for the years 1995 and 1996 refer to value added by enterprises according to the national accounts system and are valued in basic values.

Related national publications:

The former Yugoslav Republic of Macedonia

ISIC Revision 2	Number of enterprises					Number of employees					Wages and salaries paid to employees				
		(numbers)					(numbers)					(million NEW DENARS)			
ISIC Industry	Note	1993	1994	1995	1996	Note	1993	1994	1995	1996	Note	1993	1994	1995	1996
311/2 Food products		287	388	588	663		14257	13346	15884	15825		967.9	1986.0	3081.0	3465.0
313 Beverages		67	157	146	137		1894	2895	1881	1823		154.1	571.0	559.0	578.0
314 Tobacco		26	25	25	25		7130	5758	6200	5604		525.8	951.0	1120.0	1308.0
321 Textiles		73	85	97	109		21733	16131	15977	15276		748.8	1291.0	1732.0	1519.0
322 Wearing apparel, except footwear		307	367	444	482		25675	26933	20533	19174		1067.8	2239.0	2211.0	1926.0
323 Leather and fur products		26	41	47	51		4324	3893	3726	3718		250.7	419.0	289.0	500.0
324 Footwear, except rubber or plastic		43	28	87	111		2803	2890	1330	3846		133.0	418.0	127.0	324.0
331 Wood products, except furniture		35	56	70	99		1392	1456	1463	1079		60.7	142.0	116.0	116.0
332 Furniture and fixtures, excl. metal		236	292	352	416		6141	6360	4979	4711		265.5	452.0	571.0	456.0
341 Paper and products		39	65	101	118		1541	1694	1750	1208		98.3	225.0	300.0	169.0
342 Printing and publishing		217	171	373	437		3946	3856	4452	4533		304.6	283.0	673.0	805.0
351 Industrial chemicals		43	67	78	89		6559	5964	5614	5475		436.1	966.0	777.0	959.0
352 Other chemicals		46	60	69	77		2537	2043	2958	3036		236.4	409.0	928.0	987.0
353 Petroleum refineries		2	1	3	6		1318	552	1310	1316		148.4	123.0	439.0	401.0
354 Misc. petroleum and coal products		-	-	-	-		-	-	-	-		-	-	-	-
355 Rubber products		8	11	14	15		8	13	29	44		3.7	3.0	4.0	8.0
356 Plastic products		107	145	177	170		1732	2683	1589	1385		104.6	302.0	219.0	254.0
361 Pottery, china, earthenware		23	26	28	31		2246	2323	1834	1828		96.5	214.0	214.0	192.0
362 Glass and products		4	9	12	14		183	728	232	256		18.7	94.0	41.0	39.0
369 Other non-metallic mineral products		7	8	9	10		1366	1399	1115	1042		64.2	154.0	203.0	155.0
371 Iron and steel		5	4	7	8		11360	9708	8146	7828		657.7	1007.0	1343.0	1246.0
372 Non-ferrous metals		17	24	21	21		1817	1087	1201	69		118.9	147.0	272.0	8.0
381 Fabricated metal products		332	461	585	620		9886	10957	7368	8206		466.1	1051.0	1074.0	1185.0
382 Non-electrical machinery		62	77	84	93		3092	2728	1774	1803		179.6	273.0	284.0	333.0
383 Electrical machinery		384	527	621	693		10841	9550	12671	11687		570.8	1171.0	1477.0	1770.0
384 Transport equipment		154	229	288	333		8980	8460	8817	7929		484.5	992.0	1257.0	1015.0
385 Professional and scientific equipment		54	79	94	109		350	449	389	403		21.5	57.0	52.0	46.0
390 Other manufacturing industries		78	107	134	154		1455	1400	2058	1840		87.8	156.0	247.0	230.0
3 Total manufacturing		2682	3510	4554	5091		154566	145256	135280	130944		8272.7	16096.0	19610.0	19994.0

The former Yugoslav Republic of Macedonia

ISIC Revision 2	Output					Value added					Gross fixed capital formation		
		(million NEW DENARS)					(million NEW DENARS)					(million NEW DENARS)	
ISIC Industry	Note	1993	1994	1995	1996	Note	1993	1994	1995	1996	Note	1995	1996
311/2 Food products		7903	13909	14695	15594		3455	734	4956	4745		411.9	231.0
313 Beverages		1474	5688	3094	3533		673	2915	649	1156		21.4	64.9
314 Tobacco		5451	8556	7276	6684		2780	4230	2382	1802		137.0	68.6
321 Textiles		4085	4685	4667	5119		2246	2273	1322	1420		77.7	21.5
322 Wearing apparel, except footwear		3407	6801	4440	4608		1971	3867	1982	1930		29.2	20.2
323 Leather and fur products		1739	2377	2171	2473		855	823	31	447		29.6	9.1
324 Footwear, except rubber or plastic		706	833	393	1452		327	354	189	487		3.8	-
331 Wood products, except furniture		288	594	434	317		123	260	66	49		16.8	11.3
332 Furniture and fixtures, excl. metal		1318	2055	1736	1731		614	956	582	516		10.8	4.1
341 Paper and products		602	1283	1338	695		225	435	401	208		48.5	4.5
342 Printing and publishing		912	1039	2846	2793		556	484	1170	1104		146.9	92.7
351 Industrial chemicals		2336	5116	4213	4620		105	1950	408	1321		77.4	106.4
352 Other chemicals		1332	2385	3297	3286		804	1234	1089	1227		322.2	97.7
353 Petroleum refineries		2335	1729	910	3626		1299	1545	257	91		12.8	2.6
354 Misc. petroleum and coal products		-	-	-	-		-	-	-	-		-	-
355 Rubber products		11	63	52	52		5	42	19	26		1.5	-
356 Plastic products		401	1321	784	727		223	622	264	296		17.5	15.2
361 Pottery, china, earthenware		511	801	320	305		289	405	130	179		-	0.9
362 Glass and products		46	474	71	56		32	156	10	16		-	-
369 Other non-metallic mineral products		350	616	361	344		175	336	133	141		1.7	2.9
371 Iron and steel		4371	4726	5535	7400		1469	1136	1474	1484		102.1	39.5
372 Non-ferrous metals		601	610	761	31		268	272	201	7		15.1	-
381 Fabricated metal products		1973	4035	3596	3587		1110	2240	1776	1301		37.4	35.4
382 Non-electrical machinery		763	980	1437	717		607	596	876	258		5.2	3.2
383 Electrical machinery		4096	6229	7302	8217		1588	2426	1498	2293		77.9	106.3
384 Transport equipment		2080	3715	3188	2596		1293	2330	1765	1122		45.8	32.9
385 Professional and scientific equipment		94	210	179	198		56	113	49	69		3.6	0.9
390 Other manufacturing industries		368	690	702	712		271	469	335	403		20.0	8.3
3 Total manufacturing		49553	81520	75798	81473		23419	33203	24014	24098		1673.8	980.1

The former Yugoslav Republic of Macedonia

ISIC Revision 2			Index numbers of industrial production											
			(1990=100)											
ISIC	Industry	Note	1985	1986	1987	1988	1989	1990	1991	1992	1993	1994	1995	1996
311/2	Food products		...	...	...	...	...	...	...	...	...	...	...	...
313	Beverages		...	...	...	...	...	...	...	...	...	...	...	...
314	Tobacco		...	...	...	...	...	...	...	...	...	...	...	...
321	Textiles		...	...	...	...	...	...	...	...	...	...	...	...
322	Wearing apparel, except footwear		...	...	...	...	...	...	...	...	...	...	...	...
323	Leather and fur products		...	...	...	...	...	...	...	...	...	...	...	...
324	Footwear, except rubber or plastic		...	...	...	...	...	...	...	...	...	...	...	...
331	Wood products, except furniture		...	...	...	...	...	...	...	...	...	...	...	...
332	Furniture and fixtures, excl. metal		...	...	...	...	...	...	...	...	...	...	...	...
341	Paper and products		...	...	...	...	...	...	...	...	...	...	...	...
342	Printing and publishing		...	...	...	...	...	...	...	...	...	...	...	...
351	Industrial chemicals		...	...	...	...	...	...	...	...	...	...	...	...
352	Other chemicals		...	...	...	...	...	...	...	...	...	...	...	...
353	Petroleum refineries		...	...	...	...	...	...	...	...	...	...	...	...
354	Misc. petroleum and coal products		...	...	...	...	...	...	...	...	...	...	...	...
355	Rubber products		...	...	...	...	...	...	...	...	...	...	...	...
356	Plastic products		...	...	...	...	...	...	...	...	...	...	...	...
361	Pottery, china, earthenware		...	...	...	...	...	...	...	...	...	...	...	...
362	Glass and products		...	...	...	...	...	...	...	...	...	...	...	...
369	Other non-metallic mineral products		...	...	...	...	...	...	...	...	...	...	...	...
371	Iron and steel		...	...	...	...	...	...	...	...	...	...	...	...
372	Non-ferrous metals		...	...	...	...	...	...	...	...	...	...	...	...
381	Fabricated metal products		...	...	...	...	...	...	...	...	...	...	...	...
382	Non-electrical machinery		...	...	...	...	...	...	...	...	...	...	...	...
383	Electrical machinery		...	...	...	...	...	...	...	...	...	...	...	...
384	Transport equipment		...	...	...	...	...	...	...	...	...	...	...	...
385	Professional and scientific equipment		...	...	...	...	...	...	...	...	...	...	...	...
390	Other manufacturing industries		...	...	...	...	...	...	...	...	...	...	...	...
3	Total manufacturing		...	...	...	...	...	...	...	...	...	...	...	...

TRINIDAD AND TOBAGO

Supplier of information:
Central Statistical Office, Port-of-Spain.

Basic source of data:
Annual survey of establishments.

Major deviations from ISIC (Revision 2):
Data collected under the national classification system have been reclassified by the national authorities to correspond approximately with ISIC (Rev. 2).

Reference period (if not calendar year):
The reference period is the calendar year, but data reported for the financial year are accepted and incorporated in the calendar year in which the major part of the financial year falls.

Scope:
For industries dominated by one or two establishments, the survey covers all activity; for those with several establishments, the coverage accounts for about 70 per cent of employment.

Method of enumeration:
Questionnaires were distributed by mail with follow-up site visits as required. Some questionnaires are hand delivered.

Adjusted for non-response:
Yes.

Concepts and definitions of variables:
Number of establishments refers to both producing and distributing units.
Number of employees is as of the last week in November of the reference year.
Wages and salaries includes employers' contributions to pension funds.

Related national publications:
Quarterly Economic Report; Annual Statistical Digest; Business Surveys (annual), all published by the Central Statistical Office, Port-of-Spain.

Trinidad and Tobago

ISIC Revision 2 ISIC Industry	Note	Number of establishments (numbers) 1992	1993	1994	1995	Note	Number of employees (numbers) 1992	1993	1994	1995	Note	Wages and salaries paid to employees (million DOLLARS) 1992	1993	1994	1995
311/2 Food products		388	406	480	480		14639	16613	16708	16454		318.8	321.4	332.5	322.3
3111 Slaughtering, preparing & preserving meat		29	33	32	32		1006	1034	748	748		22.9	8.8	13.1	8.7
3112 Dairy products		13	18	24	24		808	725	855	855		37.8	40.1	42.5	38.5
3113 Canning, preserving of fruits & vegetables		22	24	27	27		376	368	509	509		13.3	13.9	15.6	16.3
3114 Canning, preserving and processing of fish		17	17	25	25		267	312	282	282		3.1	2.2	0.4	2.1
3115 Vegetable and animal oils and fats		3	3	4	4		796	796	736	709		49.5	51.0	56.7	52.3
3116 Grain mill products		7	7	9	9		507	507	734	734		24.8	30.4	26.2	28.3
3117 Bakery products		172	174	193	193		1169	1169	1083	1083		24.7	28.1	29.7	23.5
3118 Sugar factories and refineries		1	1	1	1		7592	9085	8112	7885		77.2	72.5	74.4	81.8
3119 Cocoa, chocolate and sugar confectionery		21	21	24	24		598	953	1471	1471		18.2	22.3	22.6	23.2
3121 Other food products		84	89	124	124		960	1104	1479	1479		33.6	37.4	39.3	35.8
3122 Prepared animal feeds		19	19	17	17		560	560	699	699		13.6	14.7	12.0	11.8
313 Beverages		19	19	21	21		1041	1501	2202	2235		60.6	70.4	102.4	66.4
3131 Distilling, rectifying and blending spirits		2	2	2	2		226	222	226	259		13.2	16.5	14.9	15.7
3132 Wine industries	a/	6	6	7	7	a/	120	584	848	848	a/	27.8	34.4	62.0	26.4
3133 Malt liquors and malt	a/	...	...	...	...	a/	...	...	...	...	a/	...	...	...	...
3134 Soft drinks and carbonated waters		11	11	12	12		695	695	1128	1128		19.6	19.5	25.5	24.3
314 Tobacco		1	1	1	1		267	233	189	166		20.2	18.1	21.5	18.4
321 Textiles		15	16	18	17		323	198	214	177		7.8	4.5	5.2	4.6
3211 Spinning, weaving and finishing textiles	b/	12	11	11	11	b/	254	127	146	107	b/	5.6	2.6	3.1	2.6
3212 Made-up textile goods excl. wearing apparel	b/	...	...	...	...	b/	...	...	...	...	b/	...	...	...	...
3213 Knitting mills		3	5	7	6		69	71	68	70		2.2	1.9	2.1	2.0
3214 Carpets and rugs	b/	...	...	...	...	b/	...	...	...	...	b/	...	...	...	...
3215 Cordage, rope and twine	b/	...	...	...	...	b/	...	...	...	...	b/	...	...	...	...
3219 Other textiles	b/	...	...	...	...	b/	...	...	...	...	b/	...	...	...	...
322 Wearing apparel, except footwear		131	130	189	175		2596	2418	2270	2256		28.7	26.7	28.0	26.2
323 Leather and fur products		6	6	7	8		109	96	95	120		1.2	0.9	1.1	1.9
3231 Tanneries and leather finishing	c/	...	...	...	...	c/	...	...	...	...	c/	...	...	...	...
3232 Fur dressing and dyeing industries		-	-	-	-		-	-	-	-		-	-	-	-
3233 Leather prods. excl. wearing apparel	c/	6	6	7	8	c/	109	96	95	120	c/	1.2	0.9	1.1	1.9
324 Footwear, except rubber or plastic		14	17	21	21		405	334	373	330	d/	5.8	4.5	4.9	4.6
331 Wood products, except furniture		73	74	65	62		686	735	745	666		11.9	13.0	14.6	14.2
3311 Sawmills, planing and other wood mills		67	63	61	58		616	583	668	591		10.5	9.9	13.1	13.0
3312 Wooden and cane containers		1	1	1	4		39	39	36	75		0.8	0.8	0.8	1.2
3319 Other wood and cork products		5	10	3	-		31	113	41	-		0.6	2.3	0.7	-
332 Furniture and fixtures, excl. metal		257	204	206	204		1439	1565	1660	1513		28.8	23.3	29.3	31.8
341 Paper and products		27	26	29	31		1093	988	1106	1361		34.6	25.6	26.7	30.7
3411 Pulp, paper and paperboard articles		...	...	...	...		...	...	...	...		...	...	...	...
3412 Containers of paper and paperboard		...	...	...	...		...	...	...	...		...	...	...	...
3419 Other pulp, paper and paperboard articles		...	...	...	...		...	...	...	...		...	...	...	...
342 Printing and publishing		175	187	247	246		1942	2087	2107	1883		59.6	48.2	57.3	52.6
351 Industrial chemicals		11	13	12	11		1354	1150	1096	1121		99.0	93.5	96.3	101.7
3511 Basic chemicals excl. fertilizers		9	11	10	11e/		1302	1099	1047	1121e/		92.4	85.6	86.2	101.7e/
3512 Fertilizers and pesticides		2	2	2	...e/		52	51	49	...e/	f/	6.6	7.9	10.1	...e/
3513 Synthetic resins and plastic materials		...	...	...	...		...	...	...	...		...	...	...	...
352 Other chemicals		65	68	58	60		1323	1425	1393	1387		38.1	40.5	37.2	40.0
3521 Paints, varnishes and lacquers		11	13	13	12		680	681	726	585		22.5	23.0	22.8	20.6
3522 Drugs and medicines		6	6	2	2		89	98	46	50		3.6	4.2	1.3	1.6
3523 Soap, cleaning preps., perfumes, cosmetics		15	15	13	14		207	204	161	188		4.0	3.9	3.7	3.5
3529 Other chemical products		33	34	30	32		347	442	460	564		8.0	9.4	9.4	14.3
353 Petroleum refineries	g/	2	2	2	2	g/	2608	2608	2942	3105	g/	237.4	259.6	243.2	380.1

ISIC	Industry														
354	Misc. petroleum and coal products	g/	...	...	...	...	g/	...	...	...	...	g/	...	...	...	...
355	Rubber products		30	35	33	35		506	451	170	219		20.8	17.2	4.5	10.1
3551	Tyres and tubes		23	28	27	27		478	422	143	174		20.0	16.9	4.1	3.8
3559	Other rubber products		7	7	6	8		28	29	27	45		0.8	0.3	0.4	6.3
356	Plastic products		2	2	2	2		250	239	302	259		6.6	11.2	10.8	8.1
361	Pottery, china, earthenware		10	11	10	9		73	79	81	92		1.4	1.4	1.7	1.8
362	Glass and products		1	1	1	1		516	490	437	462		25.3	27.4	24.7	25.7
369	Other non-metallic mineral products		40	43	39	42		1107	1211	1344	1552		43.9	50.7	58.3	56.6
3691	Structural clay products		5	5	5	5		212	217	336	439		5.8	6.0	9.3	10.7
3692	Cement, lime and plaster		1	1	1	1		387	406	377	378		25.7	31.1	32.3	26.4
3699	Other non-metallic mineral products		34	37	33	36		508	588	631	735		12.4	13.6	16.7	19.5
371	Iron and steel		14	12	10	12		1460	1462	1457	1505		83.4	81.6	88.8	88.7
372	Non-ferrous metals		-	-	-	-		-	-	-	-		-	-	-	-
381	Fabricated metal products		181	183	177	182		1505	1351	1415	1484		32.4	45.8	31.2	33.0
3811	Cutlery, hand tools and general hardware		...	...	...	...		...	...	...	...		...	...	...	...
3812	Furniture and fixtures primarily of metal		6	6	5	4		196	195	219	158		4.3	4.6	4.4	3.5
3813	Structural metal products		15	17	13	14		262	323	332	356		7.7	10.1	8.7	8.6
3819	Other fabricated metal products		160	160	159	164		1047	833	864	970		20.4	31.1	18.1	20.9
382	Non-electrical machinery		14	18	15	15		230	268	295	587		4.8	5.7	7.0	11.9
3821	Engines and turbines	h/	...	...	...	...	h/	...	...	...	...	h/	...	...	...	...
3822	Agricultural machinery and equipment	h/	...	...	...	...	h/	...	...	...	...	h/	...	...	...	...
3823	Metal and wood working machinery	h/	...	...	...	...	h/	...	...	...	...	h/	...	...	...	...
3824	Other special industrial machinery	h/	...	...	...	...	h/	...	...	...	...	h/	...	...	...	...
3825	Office, computing and accounting machinery		1	1	1	1		7	7	5	5		0.3	0.3	0.4	0.4
3829	Other non-electrical machinery & equipment	h/	13	17	14	14	h/	223	261	290	582	h/	4.5	5.4	6.6	11.5
383	Electrical machinery		26	25	23	22		1401	1196	1065	1134		38.4	30.4	31.9	32.3
3831	Electrical industrial machinery		...	...	...	...		...	...	...	...		...	...	...	...
3832	Radio, television and communication equipm.		10	8	7	5		217	213	177	171		4.7	5.0	4.3	4.0
3833	Electrical appliances and housewares		5	6	4	3		480	320	118	132		16.9	10.8	6.4	5.3
3839	Other electrical apparatus and supplies		11	11	12	14		704	663	770	831		16.8	14.6	21.2	23.0
384	Transport equipment		43	43	38	40		865	712	275	268		21.2	16.7	5.6	5.0
3841	Shipbuilding and repairing		10	11	11	12		79	79	78	67		2.4	2.3	2.4	1.8
3842	Railroad equipment		-	-	-	-		-	-	-	-		-	-	-	-
3843	Motor vehicles	i/	33	32	27	28	i/	786	633	197	201	i/	18.8	14.4	3.2	3.2
3844	Motorcycles and bicycles	i/	...	...	...	...	i/	...	...	...	...	i/	...	...	...	...
3845	Aircraft		-	-	-	-		-	-	-	-		-	-	-	-
3849	Other transport equipment	i/	...	...	...	...	i/	...	...	...	...	i/	...	...	...	...
385	Professional and scientific equipment		...	...	...	...		...	...	...	...		...	...	...	...
3851	Prof. and scientific equipment n.e.c.		...	...	...	...		...	...	...	...		...	...	...	...
3852	Photographic and optical goods	j/	...	...	...	...	j/	...	...	...	...	j/	...	...	...	...
3853	Watches and clocks	j/	...	...	...	...	j/	...	...	...	...	j/	...	...	...	...
390	Other manufacturing industries	k/	68	67	64	64	k/	1807	2016	2004	1626	k/	60.3	49.7	58.3	50.3
3901	Jewellery and related articles		15	15	14	14		425	445	317	302		9.2	8.1	7.2	6.5
3902	Musical instruments		...	...	...	...		...	...	...	...		...	...	...	...
3903	Sporting and athletic goods		...	...	...	...		...	...	...	...		...	...	...	...
3909	Manufacturing industries, n.e.c.	j/	53	52	50	50	j/	1382	1571	1687	1324	j/	51.1	41.6	51.1	43.8
3	Total manufacturing		1613	1609	1768	1763		39545	41426	41945	41962		1291.1	1288.0	1323.0	1419.0

a/ 3132 includes 3133.
b/ 3211 includes 3212, 3214, 3215 and 3219.
c/ 3233 includes 3231.
d/ 324 includes rubber and plastic footwear.
e/ 3511 includes 3512.
f/ 3512 refers only to fertilizers.
g/ 353 includes 354.
h/ 3829 includes 3821, 3822, 3823 and 3824.
i/ 3843 includes 3844 and 3849.
j/ 3909 includes 3852 and 3853.
k/ 390 includes photographic and optical goods (ISIC 3852) as well as watches and clocks (ISIC 3853).

Trinidad and Tobago

ISIC Revision 2		Output					Value added					Gross fixed capital formation	
		(million DOLLARS)					(million DOLLARS)					(million DOLLARS)	
ISIC Industry	Note	1992	1993	1994	1995	Note	1992	1993	1994	1995	Note	1994	1995
311/2 Food products		2394.6	2673.5	2862.1	3119.0		617.6	547.1	560.5	616.4		41.7	86.1
3111 Slaughtering, preparing & preserving meat		104.5	133.8	155.7	209.9		18.3	11.9	12.5	15.0		0.4	1.7
3112 Dairy products		265.6	289.6	312.2	288.8		86.8	53.1	75.2	102.4		7.6	35.8
3113 Canning, preserving of fruits & vegetables		95.5	107.9	117.3	122.1		33.7	25.5	25.4	25.9		2.2	4.7
3114 Canning, preserving and processing of fish		22.6	12.0	1.8	17.9		6.2	3.4	0.7	3.6		-	28.0
3115 Vegetable and animal oils and fats		378.9	471.9	520.6	533.3		130.8	125.5	85.0	98.6		8.2	2.6
3116 Grain mill products		348.4	380.5	407.1	427.5		70.3	71.8	72.3	85.0		3.1	-
3117 Bakery products		187.4	190.2	244.5	289.9		43.2	4.5	85.5	99.3		11.7	0.1
3118 Sugar factories and refineries		294.8	329.3	383.7	414.1		-6.6	-12.4	4.2	-6.8		3.1	3.6
3119 Cocoa, chocolate and sugar confectionery		130.3	116.0	169.6	229.3		44.9	28.0	60.0	57.0		1.7	5.8
3121 Other food products		302.8	314.9	235.4	264.0		150.0	184.8	88.7	93.3		3.3	3.3
3122 Prepared animal feeds		263.9	327.4	314.2	322.2		39.8	51.0	51.0	43.1		0.4	0.5
313 Beverages		559.4	662.1	715.6	1068.1		264.4	304.5	301.4	464.1		74.7	101.8
3131 Distilling, rectifying and blending spirits		74.3	99.8	104.9	189.5		32.3	40.5	48.4	134.4		5.8	32.9
3132 Wine industries	a/	274.1	308.6	326.7	463.1	a/	174.7	198.8	199.3	276.5	a/	46.0	46.0
3133 Malt liquors and malt	a/	...	...	...	...	a/	...	...	...	...	a/	...	...
3134 Soft drinks and carbonated waters		211.0	253.7	284.0	415.5		57.4	65.2	53.7	53.2		22.9	22.9
314 Tobacco		237.9	244.7	242.6	217.6		192.9	196.9	196.9	168.2		4.9	4.9
321 Textiles		48.6	27.4	32.7	34.0		22.0	10.6	10.7	11.2		1.3	1.1
3211 Spinning, weaving and finishing textiles	b/	37.8	17.2	19.2	19.9	b/	18.6	6.3	6.3	5.5	b/	1.3	0.6
3212 Made-up textile goods excl. wearing apparel	b/	...	...	...	...	b/	...	...	...	...	b/	...	...
3213 Knitting mills		10.8	10.2	13.5	14.1		3.4	4.3	4.4	5.7		-	0.5
3214 Carpets and rugs	b/	...	...	...	...	b/	...	...	...	...	b/	...	...
3215 Cordage, rope and twine	b/	...	...	...	...	b/	...	...	...	...	b/	...	...
3219 Other textiles	b/	...	...	...	...	b/	...	...	...	...	b/	...	...
322 Wearing apparel, except footwear		125.3	133.5	142.5	131.1		38.4	47.3	46.1	43.7		6.7	5.3
323 Leather and fur products		5.9	5.4	7.4	8.4		2.0	1.3	2.3	3.3		0.2	0.5
3231 Tanneries and leather finishing	c/	...	...	...	...	c/	...	...	...	...	c/	...	...
3232 Fur dressing and dyeing industries		-	-	-	-		-	-	-	-		...	...
3233 Leather prods. excl. wearing apparel	c/	5.9	5.4	7.4	8.4	c/	2.0	1.3	2.3	3.3	c/	0.2	0.5
324 Footwear, except rubber or plastic	d/	35.4	29.5	31.6	28.7	d/	10.9	9.6	9.6	7.9	d/	1.0	0.2
331 Wood products, except furniture		30.6	33.2	44.1	37.5		14.1	16.7	26.3	20.1		-	62.6
3311 Sawmills, planing and other wood mills		26.3	24.9	36.1	33.1		12.3	12.2	23.2	17.4		...	62.6
3312 Wooden and cane containers		2.3	2.1	2.4	4.4		1.0	1.0	1.4	2.7		-	-
3319 Other wood and cork products		2.0	6.2	5.6	-		0.8	3.5	1.7	-		...	...
332 Furniture and fixtures, excl. metal		123.1	142.0	173.0	178.6		35.5	49.8	57.2	53.5		...	5.2
341 Paper and products		229.0	251.9	326.1	416.0		70.8	71.7	75.4	143.1		10.5	23.8
3411 Pulp, paper and paperboard articles		...	...	...	...		...	...	...	...		...	...
3412 Containers of paper and paperboard		...	...	...	...		...	...	...	...		...	...
3419 Other pulp, paper and paperboard articles		...	...	...	...		...	...	...	...		...	...
342 Printing and publishing		240.3	255.0	288.5	297.9		111.2	114.3	120.9	126.7		14.6	28.1
351 Industrial chemicals		1326.2	1844.4	3417.9	3769.2		367.1	676.8	1601.4	1868.9		1170.3	563.4
3511 Basic chemicals excl. fertilizers		1054.4	1503.1	3004.6	3769.2e/		315.8	611.4	1505.1	1868.9e/		1161.9	563.4e/
3512 Fertilizers and pesticides	f/	271.8	341.3	413.3	...e/	f/	51.3	65.4	96.3	...e/	f/	8.4	...e/
3513 Synthetic resins and plastic materials		...	...	...	...		...	...	...	...		...	...
352 Other chemicals		240.9	296.7	319.9	352.1		69.0	91.1	79.0	75.4		15.9	16.5
3521 Paints, varnishes and lacquers		143.4	153.9	167.9	171.4		41.6	43.1	43.8	28.8		6.8	6.4
3522 Drugs and medicines		16.4	18.0	7.7	15.9		2.9	4.7	1.6	4.1		0.5	0.5
3523 Soap, cleaning preps., perfumes, cosmetics		22.2	24.3	30.1	39.1		5.3	6.1	5.5	8.0		2.2	0.4
3529 Other chemical products		58.9	100.5	114.2	125.7		19.1	37.2	28.1	34.5		6.4	9.2
353 Petroleum refineries	g/	2495.6	2941.7	3524.1	3960.2	g/	386.5	347.7	666.3	540.4	g/	328.3	1116.3

ISIC	Industry													
354	Misc. petroleum and coal products	g/	...	...	...	...	g/	...	...	...	...	g/	...	...
355	Rubber products		60.7	57.7	20.1	25.5		26.3	17.9	6.8	10.7		1.2	0.7
3551	Tyres and tubes		57.9	55.5	17.4	19.2		25.0	17.2	5.7	8.6		1.2	0.6
3559	Other rubber products		2.8	2.2	2.7	6.3		1.3	0.7	1.1	2.1		-	0.1
356	Plastic products		38.1	38.7	63.4	61.9		16.8	17.8	23.5	26.4		0.1	2.1
361	Pottery, china, earthenware		6.1	6.6	7.3	5.6		2.1	3.3	2.8	-0.5		2.5	0.4
362	Glass and products		84.5	110.4	116.4	126.3		47.1	55.6	51.1	59.7		4.3	8.6
369	Other non-metallic mineral products		251.6	301.7	407.4	435.4		118.1	135.4	164.5	183.6		66.0	145.0
3691	Structural clay products		31.8	35.5	65.3	59.7		11.0	10.1	25.2	30.9		1.1	1.1
3692	Cement, lime and plaster		148.1	184.3	218.0	235.0		83.7	102.5	106.2	119.9		49.6	133.3
3699	Other non-metallic mineral products		71.8	81.9	124.1	140.7		23.3	22.8	33.1	32.8		15.3	10.6
371	Iron and steel		920.8	1123.0	1440.8	1721.3		165.6	239.2	310.6	422.8		475.3	94.4
372	Non-ferrous metals		-	-	-	-		-	-	-	-		-	-
381	Fabricated metal products		186.9	208.8	207.9	239.8		60.5	81.0	68.8	69.8		6.8	13.7
3811	Cutlery, hand tools and general hardware		...	...	...	...		...	...	...	...		...	...
3812	Furniture and fixtures primarily of metal		25.1	28.1	31.3	22.7		10.5	11.4	10.2	-0.6		0.4	1.1
3813	Structural metal products		59.7	77.5	71.8	74.4		13.1	18.4	23.4	29.0		2.3	2.5
3819	Other fabricated metal products		102.1	103.2	104.8	142.7		36.9	51.2	35.2	41.4		4.1	10.1
382	Non-electrical machinery		22.8	27.9	29.7	34.4		10.2	12.4	14.0	15.2		4.2	5.8
3821	Engines and turbines	h/	...	...	...	...	h/	...	...	...	...		...	...
3822	Agricultural machinery and equipment	h/	...	...	...	...	h/	...	...	...	...		...	...
3823	Metal and wood working machinery	h/	...	...	...	...	h/	...	...	...	...		...	...
3824	Other special industrial machinery	h/	...	...	...	...	h/	...	...	...	...		...	...
3825	Office, computing and accounting machinery		2.0	2.0	1.6	1.6		0.7	0.7	0.5	0.5		0.5	-
3829	Other non-electrical machinery & equipment	h/	20.8	25.9	28.1	32.8	h/	9.5	11.7	13.5	14.7		3.7	5.8
383	Electrical machinery		268.3	195.3	242.4	246.6		84.3	75.7	49.3	87.5		6.9	4.6
3831	Electrical industrial machinery		...	...	...	...		...	...	...	...		...	...
3832	Radio, television and communication equipm.		51.5	51.4	52.9	40.7		14.6	16.6	11.7	13.6		0.4	0.3
3833	Electrical appliances and housewares		88.1	70.4	45.7	37.9		19.4	13.5	1.5	-1.0		0.4	-
3839	Other electrical apparatus and supplies		128.7	73.5	143.8	168.0		50.3	45.6	36.1	74.9		6.1	4.3
384	Transport equipment		192.7	174.3	65.3	45.3		66.0	38.0	11.8	11.7		1.2	1.0
3841	Shipbuilding and repairing		20.6	37.7	39.4	21.9		0.9	8.4	4.7	4.5		1.0	0.6
3842	Railroad equipment		-	-	-	-		-	-	-	-		-	-
3843	Motor vehicles	i/	172.1	136.6	25.9	23.4	i/	65.1	29.6	7.1	7.2	i/	0.2	0.4
3844	Motorcycles and bicycles	i/	...	...	...	...	i/	...	...	...	...	i/	...	...
3845	Aircraft		-	-	-	-		...	...	...	...		...	...
3849	Other transport equipment	i/	...	...	...	...	i/	...	...	...	...	i/	...	...
385	Professional and scientific equipment		...	...	...	...		...	...	...	...		...	...
3851	Prof. and scientific equipment n.e.c.		...	...	...	...		...	...	...	...		...	...
3852	Photographic and optical goods	j/	...	...	...	...	j/	...	...	...	...	j/	...	...
3853	Watches and clocks	j/	...	...	...	...	j/	...	...	...	...	j/	...	...
390	Other manufacturing industries	k/	228.1	253.5	290.7	271.5	k/	82.7	89.5	106.9	97.3	k/	14.6	9.4
3901	Jewellery and related articles		30.3	25.1	18.6	16.4		8.3	7.3	9.4	5.5		0.9	0.5
3902	Musical instruments		...	...	...	...		...	...	...	...		...	...
3903	Sporting and athletic goods		...	...	...	...		...	...	...	...		...	...
3909	Manufacturing industries, n.e.c.	j/	197.8	228.4	272.1	255.1	j/	74.4	82.2	97.5	91.8	j/	13.7	8.9
3	Total manufacturing		10353.5	12038.9	15019.5	16832.0		2882.1	3251.2	4564.1	5127.1		2253.2	2301.5

a/ 3132 includes 3133.
b/ 3211 includes 3212, 3214, 3215 and 3219.
c/ 3233 includes 3231.
d/ 324 includes rubber and plastic footwear.
e/ 3511 includes 3512.
f/ 3512 refers only to fertilizers.
g/ 353 includes 354.
h/ 3829 includes 3821, 3822, 3823 and 3824.
i/ 3843 includes 3844 and 3849.
j/ 3909 includes 3852 and 3853.
k/ 390 includes photographic and optical goods (ISIC 3852) as well as watches and clocks (ISIC 3853).

Trinidad and Tobago

ISIC Revision 2		Index numbers of industrial production											
		(1990=100)											
ISIC Industry	Note	1985	1986	1987	1988	1989	1990	1991	1992	1993	1994	1995	1996
311/2 Food products		98	102	101	99	101	100	103	107	99	106	108	109
313 Beverages		72	73	85	73	91	100	96	89	84	89	88	89
314 Tobacco		133	126	117	126	101	100	101	95	92	88	96	115
321 Textiles		102	126	90	69	79	100	91	93	59	52	51	48
322 Wearing apparel, except footwear		...	...	...	...	...	...	...	...	...	...	...	...
323 Leather and fur products	a/	...	...	...	...	...	...	...	...	...	...	...	...
324 Footwear, except rubber or plastic		112	143	208	118	106	100	97	67	51	41	37	25
331 Wood products, except furniture		142	136	72	58	75	100	59	69	91	66	67	59
332 Furniture and fixtures, excl. metal		1350	1400	1200	250	150	100	97	58	68	32	68	50
341 Paper and products		137	290	171	100	83	100	93	89	134	118	137	128
342 Printing and publishing		140	131	112	108	105	100	111	120	126	115	125	142
351 Industrial chemicals		71	83	80	95	99	100	104	98	101	105	117	121
352 Other chemicals		87	109	105	100	103	100	99	95	82	83	75	76
353 Petroleum refineries		111	108	118	108	100	100	92	105	99	97	88	99
354 Misc. petroleum and coal products		...	...	...	...	...	...	...	...	...	...	...	...
355 Rubber products		...	...	...	...	...	...	...	...	...	...	...	...
356 Plastic products	a/	...	...	...	...	...	...	...	...	...	...	...	...
361 Pottery, china, earthenware		...	...	...	...	...	...	...	...	...	...	...	...
362 Glass and products		...	...	...	...	...	...	...	...	...	...	...	...
369 Other non-metallic mineral products		114	115	117	112	100	100	114	119	116	124	140	149
371 Iron and steel		...	...	...	...	...	...	...	...	...	...	...	...
372 Non-ferrous metals		...	...	...	...	...	...	...	...	...	...	...	...
381 Fabricated metal products		53	89	104	95	96	100	126	156	138	179	199	184
382 Non-electrical machinery		...	...	...	...	...	...	...	...	...	...	...	...
383 Electrical machinery		158	118	120	98	80	100	131	132	128	117	156	131
384 Transport equipment		291	274	161	152	117	100	163	134	94	81	31	21
385 Professional and scientific equipment		...	...	...	...	...	...	...	...	...	...	...	...
390 Other manufacturing industries	a/	79	100	102	100	98	100	111	114	131	148	148	126
3 Total manufacturing		...	...	...	...	...	...	...	...	...	...	...	...

a/ 390 includes 323 and 356.

TUNISIA

Supplier of information:
Institut national de la statistique, Ministère du développement économique, Tunis.

Basic source of data:
Not reported.

Major deviations from ISIC (Revision 2):
Data collected under the national classification system (NAP 50) have been reclassified by the national authorities to achieve the best possible correspondence with ISIC (Rev. 2).

Reference period (if not calendar year):

Scope:
Number of establishments and employees relate to enterprises, with at least one employee registered under the social security scheme. Other variables relate to all enterprises.

Method of enumeration:
Not reported.

Adjusted for non-response:
Not reported.

Concepts and definitions of variables:
Wages and salaries, output, value added and gross fixed capital formation were derived from national accounts data.

Related national publications:

Tunisia

ISIC Revision 2	Number of establishments a/					Number of employees a/					Wages and salaries paid to employees				
		(numbers)					(numbers)					(million DINARS)			
ISIC Industry	Note	1993	1994	1995	1996	Note	1993	1994	1995	1996	Note	1993	1994	1995	1996
311/2 Food products		3121	2628	2541	2782		41896	34546	33732	34676		146.4	153.0	181.7	203.1
3111 Slaughtering, preparing & preserving meat		15	15	19	18		238	312	790	764		13.1	13.9	16.5	17.2
3112 Dairy products		27	29	34	36		2485	2833	3312	3613		19.1	20.4	24.2	27.6
3113 Canning, preserving of fruits & vegetables		56	61	61	64		1843	4090	2690	2868	b/	8.5	8.6	10.2	12.6
3114 Canning, preserving and processing of fish		34	33	37	35		2045	1598	1564	1275	b/	...	...	...	...
3115 Vegetable and animal oils and fats		971	439	347	412		15670	4654	3789	4720		9.8	10.5	12.5	13.7
3116 Grain mill products		106	111	120	131		4298	4942	4372	4319	c/	71.4	75.9	90.1	100.5
3117 Bakery products		1789	1810	1791	1942		11852	11135	11796	12264	c/	...	...	...	...
3118 Sugar factories and refineries		3	4	4	3		1046	2222	1786	1019	d/	12.9	12.8	15.2	17.5
3119 Cocoa, chocolate and sugar confectionery		29	28	25	28		873	906	982	1087	d/	...	...	...	...
3121 Other food products		46	43	43	44		1122	982	1730	1547	e/	11.7	10.9	12.9	14.0
3122 Prepared animal feeds		45	55	60	69		424	872	921	1200	e/	...	...	...	...
313 Beverages		51	53	53	52		3076	3296	3636	3541		25.1	25.4	30.1	31.6
3131 Distilling, rectifying and blending spirits		6	6	5	6		98	93	92	89		...	...	...	...
3132 Wine industries		16	16	16	16		929	903	926	850		...	...	...	...
3133 Malt liquors and malt		1	1	1	1		868	897	884	842		...	...	...	...
3134 Soft drinks and carbonated waters		28	30	31	29		1181	1403	1734	1760		...	...	...	...
314 Tobacco		2	2	10	9		2710	2500	2669	2510		19.2	19.2	22.8	24.5
321 Textiles		525	448	562	625		19761	15187	17899	18519		138.2	129.5	159.3	141.6
3211 Spinning, weaving and finishing textiles		190	192	154	168		9285	9074	7951	8187	f/	87.3	77.4	95.1	75.0
3212 Made-up textile goods excl. wearing apparel		77	22	86	98		2388	706	1854	2085	f/	...	...	...	...
3213 Knitting mills		138	144	149	173		2911	2905	2945	3079		40.8	41.6	51.1	54.0
3214 Carpets and rugs		59	21	65	71		3304	733	1113	981		10.1	10.6	13.0	12.7
3215 Cordage, rope and twine		7	6	43	40		347	395	2841	2759	g/	...	...	...	...
3219 Other textiles		54	63	65	75		1526	1374	1195	1428		...	...	...	...
322 Wearing apparel, except footwear		1609	1716	1687	2021		77938	88454	94274	102655		250.5	254.6	313.1	347.7
323 Leather and fur products		89	88	93	110		3080	3096	3496	3430	h/	42.4	43.7	53.7	59.1
3231 Tanneries and leather finishing		29	26	26	32		860	715	961	982		...	...	...	...
3232 Fur dressing and dyeing industries		2	2	2	2		54	60	69	79		...	...	...	...
3233 Leather prods. excl. wearing apparel		58	60	65	76		2166	2321	2466	2369		...	...	...	...
324 Footwear, except rubber or plastic		312	318	294	400		6652	8213	7976	9047	h/	...	...	...	...
331 Wood products, except furniture		168	178	158	166		2184	2288	2089	1977	i/	49.2	51.7	56.4	62.9
3311 Sawmills, planing and other wood mills		115	119	108	107		859	915	960	1033		...	...	...	...
3312 Wooden and cane containers		10	14	8	10		499	611	284	262		...	...	...	...
3319 Other wood and cork products		43	45	42	49		826	762	845	682		...	...	...	...
332 Furniture and fixtures, excl. metal		1463	1511	1732	1983		8071	8346	8642	9639	i/	...	...	...	...
341 Paper and products		75	79	89	106		3710	4488	4907	4740	j/	37.1	39.1	42.7	43.1
3411 Pulp, paper and paperboard articles		56	61	60	71		2890	3562	3532	3510		...	...	...	...
3412 Containers of paper and paperboard		13	14	20	24		762	900	1313	1138		...	...	...	...
3419 Other pulp, paper and paperboard articles		6	4	9	11		58	26	62	92		...	...	...	...
342 Printing and publishing		254	268	274	309		4059	4057	4238	4441	j/	...	...	...	...
351 Industrial chemicals		53	64	47	50		4949	5388	5283	5021		46.1	45.9	62.3	80.2
3511 Basic chemicals excl. fertilizers		6	22	20	22		283	876	1609	1386		4.4	4.4	5.9	7.9
3512 Fertilizers and pesticides		18	18	14	14		3969	3969	3244	3213		41.7	41.6	56.4	72.3
3513 Synthetic resins and plastic materials		29	24	13	14		697	543	430	422		...	...	...	...
352 Other chemicals		193	221	211	246		3894	4822	5384	6266		39.6	40.8	55.4	61.7
3521 Paints, varnishes and lacquers		23	28	31	34		728	858	748	843	k/	32.7	33.4	45.3	50.8
3522 Drugs and medicines		19	24	20	28		550	926	903	1177		6.9	7.4	10.1	10.9
3523 Soap, cleaning preps., perfumes, cosmetics		117	131	132	153		1698	2089	2909	3357	k/	...	...	...	...
3529 Other chemical products		34	38	28	31		918	949	824	889	k/	...	...	...	...
353 Petroleum refineries		1	1	1	1		484	484	484	767	m/	34.7	50.1	37.6	44.2

354	Misc. petroleum and coal products	2	6	2	3	48	91	44	48	m/	...	...	...	...
355	Rubber products	93	97	105	133	2465	2670	2633	2505		12.9	14.1	19.1	20.0
3551	Tyres and tubes	66	71	78	103	1312	1355	1337	1234		...	...	...	...
3559	Other rubber products	27	26	27	30	1153	1315	1296	1271		...	...	...	...
356	Plastic products	141	172	176	197	4400	5858	6314	6725	n/	13.6	13.9	15.2	18.6
361	Pottery, china, earthenware	70	74	87	160	4647	5023	5142	4331		42.8	45.1	46.5	48.2
362	Glass and products	33	37	41	42	970	1107	1090	1258		6.4	6.7	6.9	7.7
369	Other non-metallic mineral products	340	349	359	378	15524	15485	15858	16351		126.4	130.6	142.0	160.7
3691	Structural clay products	106	106	113	142	5043	4942	5937	6437		...	...	...	...
3692	Cement, lime and plaster	20	26	23	24	4014	4341	4131	4112		53.2	57.9	59.7	59.0
3699	Other non-metallic mineral products	214	217	223	212	6467	6202	5790	5802	p/	73.2	72.7	82.3	101.7
371	Iron and steel	4	6	8	8	2805	2768	2979	2789		38.8	39.9	42.0	41.7
372	Non-ferrous metals	105	113	112	120	6555	6490	6212	5670	q/	46.0	49.8	52.5	54.3
381	Fabricated metal products	497	507	502	564	8951	9429	10818	10640	q/	...	...	...	...
3811	Cutlery, hand tools and general hardware	127	119	109	120	2806	2723	3154	2846		...	...	...	...
3812	Furniture and fixtures primarily of metal	21	25	24	27	530	625	796	1086		...	...	...	...
3813	Structural metal products	135	136	142	159	1451	1618	2793	2617		...	...	...	...
3819	Other fabricated metal products	214	227	227	258	4164	4463	4075	4091		...	...	...	...
382	Non-electrical machinery	755	755	781	887	5988	6362	5679	5615		11.5	11.5	12.1	13.2
3821	Engines and turbines	9	13	26	34	38	49	245	244		...	...	...	...
3822	Agricultural machinery and equipment	38	35	10	13	674	557	561	568		...	...	...	...
3823	Metal and wood working machinery	658	651	680	768	4110	3972	3341	3581		...	...	...	...
3824	Other special industrial machinery	50	56	65	72	1166	1784	1532	1222		...	...	...	...
3825	Office, computing and accounting machinery	-	-	-	-	-	-	-	-		...	...	...	...
3829	Other non-electrical machinery & equipment	-	-	-	-	-	-	-	-		...	...	...	...
383	Electrical machinery	199	227	225	267	6475	8558	10683	12309		56.4	57.9	61.0	66.9
3831	Electrical industrial machinery	60	67	71	97	1117	1321	2345	2689	r/	28.4	29.4	31.0	34.4
3832	Radio, television and communication equipm.	24	26	32	33	1023	1497	2018	1882	s/	20.1	20.4	21.5	22.9
3833	Electrical appliances and housewares	-	-	-	-	-	-	-	-		8.0	8.1	8.6	9.6
3839	Other electrical apparatus and supplies	115	134	122	137	4335	5740	6320	7738	r/	...	...	...	...
384	Transport equipment	514	543	567	727	6553	7377	8316	8462		35.6	36.8	38.8	43.0
3841	Shipbuilding and repairing	58	60	52	59	1376	1498	1458	1488	t/	10.7	11.0	11.6	11.6
3842	Railroad equipment	1	1	1	1	367	367	566	438	t/	...	...	...	...
3843	Motor vehicles	422	450	476	622	4547	5265	6046	6288	u/	24.8	25.9	27.2	31.5
3844	Motorcycles and bicycles	32	32	37	44	261	247	244	246	u/	...	...	...	...
3845	Aircraft	-	-	-	-	-	-	-	-	t/	...	...	...	...
3849	Other transport equipment	1	-	1	1	2	-	2	2	u/	...	...	...	...
385	Professional and scientific equipment	86	79	89	104	591	481	682	791		...	...	...	...
3851	Prof. and scientific equipment n.e.c.	61	59	66	85	370	279	423	531	s/	...	...	...	...
3852	Photographic and optical goods	10	9	10	6	173	176	237	230	g/	...	...	...	...
3853	Watches and clocks	15	11	13	13	48	26	22	30	g/	...	...	...	...
390	Other manufacturing industries	165	175	179	217	2784	2519	2429	2674	g/	11.1	11.3	12.3	14.7
3901	Jewellery and related articles	51	57	57	70	423	461	464	448		...	...	...	...
3902	Musical instruments	8	8	9	15	154	154	158	208		...	...	...	...
3903	Sporting and athletic goods	29	28	29	32	740	670	700	859		...	...	...	...
3909	Manufacturing industries, n.e.c.	77	82	84	100	1467	1234	1107	1159		...	...	...	...
3	Total manufacturing	10920	10715	10985	12667	251220	259383	273588	287397		1229.9	1270.7	1463.6	1588.8

a/ Data derived from social security records.
b/ 3113 includes 3114.
c/ 3116 includes 3117.
d/ 3118 includes 3119.
e/ 3121 includes 3122.
f/ 3211 includes 3212.
g/ 390 includes 3215, 3852 and 3853.
h/ 323 includes 324.
i/ 331 includes 332.
j/ 341 includes 342.
k/ 3521 includes 3523 and 3529.
m/ 353 includes 354 and production of crude petroleum and natural gas.
n/ 356 includes 3513.
p/ 3699 includes 290.
q/ 372 includes 381.
r/ 3831 includes 3839.
s/ 3832 includes 3851.
t/ 3841 includes 3842 and 3845.
u/ 3843 includes 3844 and 3849.

Tunisia

ISIC Revision 2	Output in producers' prices					Value added in producers' prices					Gross fixed capital formation		
		(million DINARS)					(million DINARS)					(million DINARS)	
ISIC Industry	Note	1993	1994	1995	1996	Note	1993	1994	1995	1996	Note	1995	1996
311/2 Food products		2219.8	2499.2	2511.2	2731.3		362.5	422.2	430.8	478.5		112	123
3111 Slaughtering, preparing & preserving meat		592.0	605.2	636.3	675.5		63.9	69.2	73.8	77.0		1	1
3112 Dairy products		201.1	211.0	230.1	251.0		11.4	14.2	15.9	18.2		14	20
3113 Canning, preserving of fruits & vegetables	a/	167.8	182.4	207.6	252.6	a/	30.7	34.4	39.2	48.1	a/	14	17
3114 Canning, preserving and processing of fish	a/	...	...	...	...	a/	...	...	...	...	a/	...	...
3115 Vegetable and animal oils and fats		283.5	385.3	236.0	245.7		44.7	60.6	37.3	40.9		25	26
3116 Grain mill products	b/	566.1	655.3	699.6	759.7	b/	132.9	154.5	165.0	184.0	b/	24	25
3117 Bakery products	b/	...	...	...	...	b/	...	...	...	...	b/	...	...
3118 Sugar factories and refineries	c/	133.0	142.8	159.5	175.2	c/	31.1	32.4	35.3	40.6	c/	13	14
3119 Cocoa, chocolate and sugar confectionery	c/	...	...	...	...	c/	...	...	...	...	c/	...	...
3121 Other food products	d/	276.3	317.4	342.1	371.6	d/	47.8	56.9	64.2	69.7	d/	21	20
3122 Prepared animal feeds	d/	...	...	...	...	d/	...	...	...	...	d/	...	...
313 Beverages		254.6	280.5	288.4	301.7		123.8	136.3	140.5	147.6		16	15
3131 Distilling, rectifying and blending spirits		...	...	...	...		...	...	...	...		...	...
3132 Wine industries		...	...	...	...		...	...	...	...		...	...
3133 Malt liquors and malt		...	...	...	...		...	...	...	...		...	...
3134 Soft drinks and carbonated waters		...	...	...	...		...	...	...	...		...	...
314 Tobacco		330.4	367.4	405.3	439.5		240.7	275.8	305.6	328.8		2	2
321 Textiles		856.4	954.6	1064.0	1084.5		261.8	292.5	316.1	356.5		42	43
3211 Spinning, weaving and finishing textiles	e/	578.4	634.0	685.6	720.0	e/	183.5	200.5	209.9	228.2	e/	29	35
3212 Made-up textile goods excl. wearing apparel	e/	...	...	...	...	e/	...	...	...	...	e/	...	...
3213 Knitting mills		208.3	245.2	295.0	278.2		44.1	55.1	64.4	83.9		11	5
3214 Carpets and rugs		69.7	75.3	83.4	86.3		34.2	36.9	41.8	44.4		2	3
3215 Cordage, rope and twine	f/	...	...	...	...	f/	...	...	...	...	f/	...	...
3219 Other textiles		...	...	...	...		...	...	...	...		...	...
322 Wearing apparel, except footwear		1613.3	1949.4	2257.2	2214.0		485.4	590.5	681.4	756.6		72	83
323 Leather and fur products	g/	336.3	410.7	485.9	531.9	g/	126.7	155.5	183.4	201.8	g/	26	30
3231 Tanneries and leather finishing		...	...	...	...		...	...	...	...		...	...
3232 Fur dressing and dyeing industries		...	...	...	...		...	...	...	...		...	...
3233 Leather prods. excl. wearing apparel		...	...	...	...		...	...	...	...		...	...
324 Footwear, except rubber or plastic	g/	...	...	...	...	g/	...	...	...	...	g/	...	...
331 Wood products, except furniture	h/	449.1	481.2	520.4	570.3	h/	187.6	201.1	218.2	243.1	h/	12	15
3311 Sawmills, planing and other wood mills		...	...	...	...		...	...	...	...		...	...
3312 Wooden and cane containers		...	...	...	...		...	...	...	...		...	...
3319 Other wood and cork products		...	...	...	...		...	...	...	...		...	..
332 Furniture and fixtures, excl. metal	h/	...	...	...	...	h/	...	...	...	...	h/	...	...
341 Paper and products	i/	314.9	333.3	392.3	381.4	i/	82.1	93.1	111.3	112.5	i/	24	25
3411 Pulp, paper and paperboard articles		...	...	...	...		...	...	...	...		...	...
3412 Containers of paper and paperboard		...	...	...	...		...	...	...	...		...	...
3419 Other pulp, paper and paperboard articles		...	...	...	...		...	...	...	...		...	...
342 Printing and publishing	i/	...	...	...	...	i/	...	...	...	...	i/	...	...
351 Industrial chemicals		881.6	1067.4	1221.8	1382.3		96.8	148.3	188.0	241.9		34	30
3511 Basic chemicals excl. fertilizers		48.5	46.6	53.1	71.3		16.8	16.1	18.9	25.3		5	5
3512 Fertilizers and pesticides		833.1	1020.8	1168.7	1311.0		80.0	132.1	169.0	216.6		29	25
3513 Synthetic resins and plastic materials		...	...	...	...		...	...	...	...		...	...
352 Other chemicals		367.0	437.5	472.5	501.8		118.3	142.2	152.9	170.5		24	30
3521 Paints, varnishes and lacquers	j/	326.1	377.2	408.7	434.3	j/	100.9	116.6	125.8	141.2	j/	13	15
3522 Drugs and medicines		40.9	60.3	63.7	67.5		17.4	25.6	27.1	29.3		11	15
3523 Soap, cleaning preps., perfumes, cosmetics	j/	...	...	...	...	j/	...	...	...	...	j/	...	...
3529 Other chemical products	j/	...	...	...	...	j/	...	...	...	...	j/	...	...
353 Petroleum refineries	k/	1201.2	1244.1	1213.6	1374.6	k/	748.6	734.5	725.3	852.3	k/	316	151

354 Misc. petroleum and coal products	k/	...	...	...	...	k/	...	...	...	...	k/	...	...
355 Rubber products		77.5	82.4	91.2	94.2		34.5	36.7	41.0	42.9		7	10
3551 Tyres and tubes		...	...	...	...		...	...	...	...		...	...
3559 Other rubber products		...	...	...	...		...	...	...	...		...	...
356 Plastic products	m/	155.3	172.8	194.9	220.9	m/	48.2	51.1	58.5	71.6	m/	20	23
361 Pottery, china, earthenware		208.3	224.7	243.3	243.9		88.8	96.6	103.5	107.3		45	48
362 Glass and products		44.2	51.1	45.6	49.7		18.6	21.3	19.0	21.1		2	2
369 Other non-metallic mineral products		677.5	741.6	827.6	903.8		236.6	267.1	299.6	352.5		73	87
3691 Structural clay products		...	...	...	...		...	...	...	...		...	...
3692 Cement, lime and plaster		528.9	581.3	640.4	638.8		168.2	187.5	207.6	205.3		46	54
3699 Other non-metallic mineral products	n/	148.6	160.2	187.2	265.0	n/	68.4	79.6	92.0	147.2	n/	27	33
371 Iron and steel		322.4	339.3	365.0	368.1		60.7	64.6	75.9	75.3		12	13
372 Non-ferrous metals	p/	381.6	411.8	323.0	448.0	p/	124.2	137.0	145.2	150.3	p/	13	15
381 Fabricated metal products	p/	...	...	...	...	p/	...	...	...	...	p/	...	...
3811 Cutlery, hand tools and general hardware		...	...	...	...		...	...	...	...		...	...
3812 Furniture and fixtures primarily of metal		...	...	...	...		...	...	...	...		...	...
3813 Structural metal products		...	...	...	...		...	...	...	...		...	...
3819 Other fabricated metal products		...	...	...	...		...	...	...	...		...	...
382 Non-electrical machinery		98.3	104.3	108.9	116.2		14.8	16.8	18.0	19.6		7	8
3821 Engines and turbines		...	...	...	...		...	...	...	...		...	...
3822 Agricultural machinery and equipment		...	...	...	...		...	...	...	...		...	...
3823 Metal and wood working machinery		...	...	...	...		...	...	...	...		...	...
3824 Other special industrial machinery		...	...	...	...		...	...	...	...		...	...
3825 Office, computing and accounting machinery		...	...	...	...		...	...	...	...		...	...
3829 Other non-electrical machinery & equipment		...	...	...	...		...	...	...	...		...	...
383 Electrical machinery		526.5	583.2	643.9	712.9		132.1	147.6	168.5	186.2		34	37
3831 Electrical industrial machinery	q/	264.3	303.0	346.4	384.2	q/	86.0	98.2	113.4	125.9	q/	17	19
3832 Radio, television and communication equipm.	r/	181.7	190.4	204.4	224.5	r/	27.6	28.9	33.3	34.2	r/	11	13
3833 Electrical appliances and housewares		80.5	89.8	93.0	104.2		18.5	20.5	21.7	26.1		6	6
3839 Other electrical apparatus and supplies	q/	...	...	...	...	q/	...	...	...	...	q/	...	...
384 Transport equipment		261.9	293.1	308.9	342.8		77.4	87.8	89.9	102.5		10	12
3841 Shipbuilding and repairing	s/	15.5	19.2	21.0	20.1	s/	6.3	7.8	8.7	8.7	s/	2	2
3842 Railroad equipment	s/	...	...	...	...	s/	...	...	...	...	s/	...	...
3843 Motor vehicles	t/	246.4	273.9	287.8	322.7	t/	71.1	80.0	81.2	93.8	t/	8	10
3844 Motorcycles and bicycles	t/	...	...	...	...	t/	...	...	...	...	t/	...	...
3845 Aircraft	s/	...	...	...	...	s/	...	...	...	...	s/	...	...
3849 Other transport equipment	t/	...	...	...	...	t/	...	...	...	...	t/	...	...
385 Professional and scientific equipment		...	...	...	...		...	...	...	...		...	...
3851 Prof. and scientific equipment n.e.c.	r/	...	...	...	...	r/	...	...	...	...	r/	...	...
3852 Photographic and optical goods	f/	...	...	...	...	f/	...	...	...	...	f/	...	...
3853 Watches and clocks	f/	...	...	...	...	f/	...	...	...	...	f/	...	...
390 Other manufacturing industries	f/	131.8	140.1	160.0	170.0	f/	39.6	41.9	48.6	57.9	f/	14	18
3901 Jewellery and related articles		...	...	...	...		...	...	...	...		...	...
3902 Musical instruments		...	...	...	...		...	...	...	...		...	...
3903 Sporting and athletic goods		...	...	...	...		...	...	...	...		...	...
3909 Manufacturing industries, n.e.c.		...	...	...	...		...	...	...	...		...	...
3 Total manufacturing		11709.9	13169.5	14145.2	15183.8		3709.8	4160.6	4521.4	5077.3		917	817

a/ 3113 includes 3114.
b/ 3116 includes 3117.
c/ 3118 includes 3119.
d/ 3121 includes 3122.
e/ 3211 includes 3212.
f/ 390 includes 3215, 3852 and 3853.
g/ 323 includes 324.
h/ 331 includes 332.
i/ 341 includes 342.
j/ 3521 includes 3523 and 3529.
k/ 353 includes 354 and production of crude petroleum and natural gas.
m/ 356 includes 3513.

n/ 3699 includes 290.
p/ 372 includes 381.
q/ 3831 includes 3839.
r/ 3832 includes 3851.
s/ 3841 includes 3842 and 3845.
t/ 3843 includes 3844 and 3849.

Tunisia

ISIC Revision 2		Index numbers of industrial production											
		(1990=100)											
ISIC Industry	Note	1985	1986	1987	1988	1989	1990	1991	1992	1993	1994	1995	1996
311/2 Food products	a/	...	...	...	...	...	100	109	117	114	120	118	123
313 Beverages	a/	...	...	...	...	...	...	...	...	...	...	...	...
314 Tobacco		...	...	...	...	...	100	114	113	100	103	106	104
321 Textiles		92	88	99	105	105	100	103	108	121	130	149	135
322 Wearing apparel, except footwear		...	...	...	...	...	100	110	123	135	149	156	160
323 Leather and fur products	b/	...	...	...	...	...	100	108	117	137	167	179	190
324 Footwear, except rubber or plastic	b/	...	...	...	...	...	...	...	...	...	...	...	...
331 Wood products, except furniture		...	...	...	...	...	100	95	98	102	110	112	94
332 Furniture and fixtures, excl. metal	c/	...	...	...	...	...	...	...	...	...	...	...	...
341 Paper and products		86	90	89	92	85	100	100	161	99	101	107	98
342 Printing and publishing		...	...	...	...	...	100	107	102	102	106	113	110
351 Industrial chemicals	d/	66	77	81	92	97	100	107	114	113	128	136	143
352 Other chemicals	d/	...	...	...	...	...	...	...	...	...	...	...	...
353 Petroleum refineries	e/	...	...	...	...	...	100	98	97	95	99	109	108
354 Misc. petroleum and coal products	e/	...	...	...	...	...	...	...	...	...	...	...	...
355 Rubber products	f/	...	...	...	...	...	100	100	101	113	121	124	134
356 Plastic products	f/	...	...	...	...	...	...	...	...	...	...	...	...
361 Pottery, china, earthenware	g/	...	...	...	...	...	100	105	104	112	113	118	115
362 Glass and products	g/	...	...	...	...	...	...	...	...	...	...	...	...
369 Other non-metallic mineral products	g/	...	...	...	...	...	...	...	...	...	...	...	...
371 Iron and steel	h/	89	104	99	99	97	100	103	98	99	97	96	97
372 Non-ferrous metals	h/	...	...	...	...	...	...	...	...	...	...	...	...
381 Fabricated metal products		106	97	87	92	97	100	100	98	97	106	102	103
382 Non-electrical machinery		225	189	108	106	89	100	144	157	150	166	168	156
383 Electrical machinery		69	58	61	73	81	100	108	119	110	119	117	125
384 Transport equipment		229	106	83	72	78	100	101	106	115	119	107	115
385 Professional and scientific equipment		...	...	...	...	...	100	93	98	102	98	103	124
390 Other manufacturing industries	c/	...	...	...	...	...	100	111	113	123	128	119	134
3 Total manufacturing		...	...	...	...	...	...	...	...	...	...	...	...

a/ 311/2 includes 313.
b/ 323 includes 324.
c/ 390 includes 332.
d/ 351 includes 352.
e/ 353 includes 354.
f/ 355 includes 356.
g/ 361 includes 362 and 369.
h/ 371 includes 372.

UKRAINE

Supplier of information:
Ministry of Statistics of the Ukraine, Kiev.

Basic source of data:
Annual statistical reports of enterprises.

Major deviations from ISIC (Revision 2):
Data collected under the national classification system have been reclassified by the national authorities to correspond approximately to ISIC (Rev. 2).

Reference period (if not calendar year):

Scope:
All establishments.

Method of enumeration:
Not reported.

Adjusted for non-response:
Not reported.

Concepts and definitions of variables:
No deviations from the standard UN concepts and definitions are reported.

In September 1996, the national currency was changed from karbovanets to hryvnias (1 hryvnia = 100,000 karbovanets). All data reported in terms of national currency are in hryvnias.

Related national publications:

Ukraine

ISIC Revision 2	Number of establishments					Number of employees					Wages and salaries paid to employees				
		(numbers)					(thousands)					(thousand HRYVNIAS)			
ISIC Industry	Note	1993	1994	1995	1996	Note	1993	1994	1995	1996	Note	1993	1994	1995	1996
311/2 Food products		23426	26178	29802	30944		606	586	556	532		12064	102735	535895	980855
3111 Slaughtering, preparing & preserving meat		5946	6082	6795	6931		95	91	86	75		1880	16142	70362	116179
3112 Dairy products		801	1220	1207	1352		74	96	91	70		1459	16638	82785	131425
3113 Canning, preserving of fruits & vegetables		995	1034	1033	975		63	59	49	41		1073	7232	24132	32634
3114 Canning, preserving and processing of fish		16	14	6	5		2	2	2	7		40	389	1752	7679
3115 Vegetable and animal oils and fats		1659	2257	2739	3099		14	15	16	16		404	3237	21231	47808
3116 Grain mill products		7877	8860	10851	11633		24	30	29	26		512	4352	23445	78227
3117 Bakery products		1433	2044	2663	3221		115	112	104	100		3321	18528	106292	208505
3118 Sugar factories and refineries		204	196	196	196		99	98	106	103		2309	21532	133585	190800
3119 Cocoa, chocolate and sugar confectionery		218	196	196	196		39	49	48	33		864	8920	42394	69394
3121 Other food products		8	11	11	11		78	31	22	58		1603	6082	21503	126345
3122 Prepared animal feeds		16	16	17	16		3	3	3	3		42	354	2620	6183
313 Beverages		836	821	857	803		63	61	61	63		1240	11651	75520	182604
3131 Distilling, rectifying and blending spirits		132	140	146	134		20	21	22	23		442	3667	31556	86778
3132 Wine industries		310	318	322	310		15	14	14	14		320	2653	15589	34615
3133 Malt liquors and malt		...	...	...	...		18	17	17	17		326	3921	21891	46737
3134 Soft drinks and carbonated waters		306	274	297	266		10	9	8	9		150	1319	6492	14475
314 Tobacco		17	14	14	19		5	3	3	7		119	623	3424	31539
321 Textiles		653	637	563	503		201	175	151	133		3908	24595	82482	114073
3211 Spinning, weaving and finishing textiles		485	452	393	351		104	96	83	75		2043	14351	50517	69981
3212 Made-up textile goods excl. wearing apparel		36	33	34	33		16	13	11	9		289	1538	5141	7938
3213 Knitting mills		61	64	68	73		67	57	48	40		1449	7356	20425	25133
3214 Carpets and rugs		...	...	...	...		...	...	...	...		...	...	...	...
3215 Cordage, rope and twine		48	64	44	23		2	2	2	2		42	369	1664	3779
3219 Other textiles		23	24	24	23		12	7	7	4		2617	1014	4817	3709
322 Wearing apparel, except footwear		1291	1265	1162	1015		168	143	120	115		2655	15167	58882	94713
323 Leather and fur products		77	76	75	72		13	18	16	15		281	2784	10339	16356
3231 Tanneries and leather finishing		...	...	...	...		...	...	...	...		...	...	...	...
3232 Fur dressing and dyeing industries		...	...	...	...		...	...	...	...		...	...	...	...
3233 Leather prods. excl. wearing apparel		26	26	24	24		...	...	...	...		...	...	...	...
324 Footwear, except rubber or plastic		75	104	95	101		82	70	58	48		1562	9880	27715	35078
331 Wood products, except furniture		14378	14114	13753	12949		68	61	52	48		1037	8365	31549	46219
3311 Sawmills, planing and other wood mills		13075	13040	12883	12122		27	39	32	23		441	5505	19860	23216
3312 Wooden and cane containers		881	749	674	456		8	6	5	4		105	770	3080	4092
3319 Other wood and cork products		422	325	196	371		33	16	15	21		490	2096	8545	18885
332 Furniture and fixtures, excl. metal		342	342	335	324		112	101	92	79		2075	14374	48057	63785
341 Paper and products		92	88	80	69		26	24	23	23		378	3806	22386	41763
3411 Pulp, paper and paperboard articles		22	22	23	23		20	18	18	17		303	2970	18356	34296
3412 Containers of paper and paperboard		56	51	42	31		3	3	2	3		32	389	1249	3094
3419 Other pulp, paper and paperboard articles		14	15	15	15		3	3	3	3		44	441	2953	4373
342 Printing and publishing		548	547	554	553		32	30	30	28		530	5206	30132	59731
351 Industrial chemicals		102	85	88	84		182	170	164	161		3040	29570	156613	303202
3511 Basic chemicals excl. fertilizers		...	...	...	...		...	...	48	46		...	...	46581	80652
3512 Fertilizers and pesticides		17	13	13	15		65	96	93	94		1175	16761	90117	190317
3513 Synthetic resins and plastic materials		11	9	10	10		27	24	23	21		401	3826	19872	32233
352 Other chemicals		153	159	154	166		49	44	43	44		833	8493	42100	92960
3521 Paints, varnishes and lacquers		57	60	55	52		12	11	11	11		220	2380	13555	27375
3522 Drugs and medicines		47	48	49	49		15	14	14	14		293	3404	16469	41162
3523 Soap, cleaning preps., perfumes, cosmetics		21	22	22	24		4	3	3	3		83	618	2751	4516
3529 Other chemical products		...	...	...	...		18	16	15	16		...	2098	9576	18908
353 Petroleum refineries		10	10	10	12		15	16	17	17		337	3428	35678	69457

354	Misc. petroleum and coal products	729	707	670	720	48	48	47	48	1260	9678	63388	126266
355	Rubber products	38	37	37	38	43	37	35	32	805	6991	35133	68863
3551	Tyres and tubes	13	13	13	13	20	18	18	17	391	3674	21012	46407
3559	Other rubber products	25	24	24	25	23	19	17	15	414	3327	14272	22456
356	Plastic products	77	75	64	75	17	15	12	11	243	2027	6676	11469
361	Pottery, china, earthenware	35	32	28	34	24	24	23	23	536	5148	17650	29015
362	Glass and products	65	65	63	62	61	54	50	46	936	8331	37380	64675
369	Other non-metallic mineral products	4141	4151	4108	3595	345	291	268	235	6228	53833	249626	342461
3691	Structural clay products	50	36	35	41	11	10	10	9	181	1924	10039	14296
3692	Cement, lime and plaster	14	15	15	15	15	16	16	15	431	3384	22216	30678
3699	Other non-metallic mineral products	...	...	...	...	...	...	242	211	...	...	217539	297487
371	Iron and steel	52	58	61	69	294	279	271	277	8378	56368	371606	783258
372	Non-ferrous metals	26	29	28	37	47	25	24	41	1161	4842	30531	109206
381	Fabricated metal products	14672	14610	14405	14181	427	354	320	285	8248	58908	273830	447903
3811	Cutlery, hand tools and general hardware	656	610	536	480	65	59	55	51	1142	9483	46675	67419
3812	Furniture and fixtures primarily of metal	60	60	61	59	27	23	19	18	457	3033	11320	20640
3813	Structural metal products	313	317	315	310	26	23	22	21	602	4604	19673	35632
3819	Other fabricated metal products	13643	13623	13493	13332	309	249	224	195	6047	41765	196278	324213
382	Non-electrical machinery	654	637	635	652	618	542	487	444	10361	79528	346958	578682
3821	Engines and turbines	4	5	5	5	12	11	10	13	205	1553	6449	21732
3822	Agricultural machinery and equipment	118	121	119	119	181	158	137	124	2689	19670	83285	146478
3823	Metal and wood working machinery	144	119	112	123	80	64	57	48	1343	9591	38755	61052
3824	Other special industrial machinery	331	341	346	351	265	214	197	183	4881	36607	166473	269997
3825	Office, computing and accounting machinery	24	17	17	17	35	29	23	19	475	3245	11600	13502
3829	Other non-electrical machinery & equipment	33	34	36	37	45	66	63	57	766	8874	40393	65922
383	Electrical machinery	187	191	196	205	217	191	168	152	3335	25331	111767	180555
3831	Electrical industrial machinery	169	172	176	181	185	164	147	136	2882	22800	104235	168941
3832	Radio, television and communication equipm.	...	...	...	...	...	...	...	...	...	...	...	...
3833	Electrical appliances and housewares	18	19	20	24	32	27	21	16	453	2522	7600	11614
3839	Other electrical apparatus and supplies	...	...	...	...	...	...	...	...	...	...	...	...
384	Transport equipment	154	147	140	145	381	342	298	276	7654	59837	256006	407522
3841	Shipbuilding and repairing	73	60	54	55	129	118	97	96	2581	23249	95995	175897
3842	Railroad equipment	16	19	17	18	63	56	53	49	1094	9009	49462	77847
3843	Motor vehicles	41	45	46	48	92	85	76	67	2070	15994	63658	65509
3844	Motorcycles and bicycles	3	3	3	4	12	9	7	4	206	1155	2585	3117
3845	Aircraft	21	20	20	20	85	74	65	60	1702	10455	44585	85152
3849	Other transport equipment	...	...	...	...	...	...	...	...	...	...	...	...
385	Professional and scientific equipment	110	120	121	123	157	138	117	94	2112	14167	53436	78769
3851	Prof and scientific equipment n.e.c.	91	102	104	106	107	98	84	67	1507	10045	38072	53591
3852	Photographic and optical goods	19	18	17	17	50	40	33	27	605	4122	15361	25177
3853	Watches and clocks	...	...	...	...	...	...	...	...	...	...	...	...
390	Other manufacturing industries	...	...	...	...	131	116	113	107	2212	18669	96547	172835
3901	Jewellery and related articles	6	6	6	6	8	7	7	7	190	1689	8826	16580
3902	Musical instruments	10	12	12	14	3	3	2	2	36	311	1065	1689
3903	Sporting and athletic goods	...	...	...	...	...	...	...	...	...	...	...	...
3909	Manufacturing industries, n.e.c.	...	...	...	...	...	...	...	...	...	...	...	...
3	Total manufacturing	63338	65771	68583	68037	4432	3958	3619	3384	89691	692479	3284815	5786816

Ukraine

ISIC Revision 2 ISIC Industry	Note	Output in factor values (million HRYVNIAS) 1993	1994	1995	1996	Note	Value added (million HRYVNIAS) 1993	1994	1995	1996	Note	Gross fixed capital formation (thousand HRYVNIAS) 1995	1996
311/2 Food products		356.7	2275.2	9140.1	12126.2		...	...	...	...		82425	685057
3111 Slaughtering, preparing & preserving meat		70.2	560.3	1962.3	2590.0		...	...	...	...		-6263	108336
3112 Dairy products		39.1	323.2	1555.3	1780.6		...	...	...	...		20891	58704
3113 Canning, preserving of fruits & vegetables		15.7	100.6	274.6	253.7		...	...	...	...		-13517	-3315
3114 Canning, preserving and processing of fish		0.6	4.0	15.6	44.7		...	...	...	...		47	-1864
3115 Vegetable and animal oils and fats		24.8	122.1	479.7	606.6		...	...	...	...		6127	-20974
3116 Grain mill products		30.4	200.2	1166.0	1920.7		...	...	...	...		-16879	46849
3117 Bakery products		26.7	215.8	1314.0	2018.9		...	...	...	...		10202	66603
3118 Sugar factories and refineries		101.3	457.1	1135.1	1073.9		...	...	...	...		78341	123545
3119 Cocoa, chocolate and sugar confectionery		17.7	114.2	479.9	679.5		...	...	...	...		8542	21364
3121 Other food products		1.0	7.4	26.3	35.1		...	...	...	...		533	-3251
3122 Prepared animal feeds		1.4	8.4	53.3	79.7		...	...	...	...		2893	158
313 Beverages		24.7	165.0	869.5	1690.8		...	...	...	...		11491	184357
3131 Distilling, rectifying and blending spirits		13.1	61.8	380.7	797.1		...	...	...	...		19936	42637
3132 Wine industries		6.7	47.3	212.4	390.9		...	...	...	...		-30510	99444
3133 Malt liquors and malt		...	...	...	...		...	...	...	...		...	...
3134 Soft drinks and carbonated waters		1.5	13.6	51.9	107.8		...	...	...	...		6550	16014
314 Tobacco		3.2	8.6	41.0	304.0		...	...	...	...		4442	31281
321 Textiles		54.8	296.2	835.4	721.5		...	...	...	...		1956	-56798
3211 Spinning, weaving and finishing textiles		37.0	212.4	597.6	501.6		...	...	...	...		1804	-39377
3212 Made-up textile goods excl. wearing apparel		2.4	10.9	30.1	31.9		...	...	...	...		257	-3036
3213 Knitting mills		12.0	54.4	135.1	113.8		...	...	...	...		1155	-12469
3214 Carpets and rugs		...	...	...	...		...	...	...	...		...	...
3215 Cordage, rope and twine		0.5	3.2	14.2	18.9		...	...	...	...		98	2465
3219 Other textiles		2.9	15.2	58.4	55.3		...	...	...	...		-1358	-4381
322 Wearing apparel, except footwear		20.8	86.8	286.6	314.5		...	...	...	...		1579	-9245
323 Leather and fur products		7.4	47.7	125.3	140.9		...	...	...	...		12694	7398
3231 Tanneries and leather finishing		...	...	...	...		...	...	...	...		...	...
3232 Fur dressing and dyeing industries		...	...	...	...		...	...	...	...		...	...
3233 Leather prods. excl. wearing apparel		1.0	4.0	8.5	6.1		...	...	...	...		15	-616
324 Footwear, except rubber or plastic		14.4	84.9	192.5	173.9		...	...	...	...		1558	-11982
331 Wood products, except furniture		10.4	68.8	264.2	355.4		...	...	...	...		-20347	100349
3311 Sawmills, planing and other wood mills		8.1	52.6	198.2	298.3		...	...	...	...		-17660	75164
3312 Wooden and cane containers		0.7	5.7	23.5	20.5		...	...	...	...		-351	3250
3319 Other wood and cork products		1.7	10.4	42.5	36.6		...	...	...	...		-2336	21935
332 Furniture and fixtures, excl. metal		19.0	109.3	338.3	329.3		...	...	...	...		2277	16702
341 Paper and products		8.3	58.6	353.8	435.9		...	...	...	...		3337	7489
3411 Pulp, paper and paperboard articles		7.1	50.7	306.3	382.2		...	...	...	...		3433	5473
3412 Containers of paper and paperboard		0.5	3.2	19.2	22.3		...	...	...	...		-57	976
3419 Other pulp, paper and paperboard articles		0.7	4.7	28.4	31.4		...	...	...	...		-39	1040
342 Printing and publishing		3.1	26.4	154.6	223.0		...	...	...	...		1639	-2615
351 Industrial chemicals		64.4	588.1	2685.8	3111.0		...	...	...	...		65968	47199
3511 Basic chemicals excl. fertilizers		...	...	...	...		...	...	...	...		...	...
3512 Fertilizers and pesticides		30.1	313.7	1544.7	2139.4		...	...	...	...		38902	10453
3513 Synthetic resins and plastic materials		7.2	49.6	156.4	165.7		...	...	...	...		861	3262
352 Other chemicals		17.1	144.2	638.8	885.8		...	...	...	...		6389	34678
3521 Paints, varnishes and lacquers		7.4	60.0	293.5	333.1		...	...	...	...		2841	17305
3522 Drugs and medicines		4.7	47.7	216.9	396.9		...	...	...	...		2907	9100
3523 Soap, cleaning preps., perfumes, cosmetics		1.8	11.0	33.7	40.4		...	...	...	...		144	3343
3529 Other chemical products		...	...	...	...		...	...	...	...		...	...
353 Petroleum refineries		66.7	272.3	996.8	1180.4		...	...	...	...		65345	136121

Code	Industry										
354	Misc. petroleum and coal products	42.9	432.4	1366.8	1241.5	...	...	...	...	10780	66963
355	Rubber products	17.7	107.8	749.6	1110.3	...	...	...	...	5487	20651
3551	Tyres and tubes	11.7	69.6	593.1	933.6	...	...	...	...	4035	21094
3559	Other rubber products	6.0	38.2	156.4	176.7	...	...	...	...	1452	-443
356	Plastic products	2.4	16.3	59.1	66.1	...	...	...	...	9081	80041
361	Pottery, china, earthenware	2.9	21.2	85.3	108.8	...	...	...	...	806	2641
362	Glass and products	8.8	65.7	300.6	408.3	...	...	...	...	27402	45698
369	Other non-metallic mineral products	74.6	475.9	2196.7	2321.7	...	...	...	...	24763	386743
3691	Structural clay products	1.8	13.3	56.7	72.0	...	...	...	...	-2746	3135
3692	Cement, lime and plaster	9.2	63.9	322.0	332.4	...	...	...	...	-340	2565
3699	Other non-metallic mineral products	...	...	...	...	...	...	...	...	...	...
371	Iron and steel	199.2	1735.0	8995.4	11867.4	...	...	...	...	112136	1755642
372	Non-ferrous metals	21.3	121.1	725.7	807.6	...	...	...	...	6007	-1506
381	Fabricated metal products	58.5	435.1	1991.2	2615.1	...	...	...	...	24597	97490
3811	Cutlery, hand tools and general hardware	16.1	116.2	488.6	534.4	...	...	...	...	12777	31180
3812	Furniture and fixtures primarily of metal	2.3	15.2	54.4	74.5	...	...	...	...	1757	867
3813	Structural metal products	5.3	32.5	151.3	180.4	...	...	...	...	46	19400
3819	Other fabricated metal products	34.7	271.2	1296.9	1825.8	...	...	...	...	10017	920043
382	Non-electrical machinery	91.0	557.8	2351.0	2881.1	...	...	...	...	18371	38904
3821	Engines and turbines	1.9	20.2	101.9	162.7	...	...	...	...	1174	5119
3822	Agricultural machinery and equipment	32.7	168.6	623.1	791.3	...	...	...	...	-761	22283
3823	Metal and wood working machinery	7.2	41.8	158.8	187.0	...	...	...	...	2337	24427
3824	Other special industrial machinery	36.3	246.9	1168.5	1417.9	...	...	...	...	15990	2261
3825	Office, computing and accounting machinery	2.8	19.5	55.0	44.8	...	...	...	...	-3817	-3476
3829	Other non-electrical machinery & equipment	10.2	60.7	243.7	277.5	...	...	...	...	3447	-11710
383	Electrical machinery	30.7	199.1	873.3	1037.4	...	...	...	...	18741	50000
3831	Electrical industrial machinery	27.9	186.0	840.6	985.9	...	...	...	...	13125	59887
3832	Radio, television and communication equipm.	...	...	...	...	...	...	...	...	...	...
3833	Electrical appliances and housewares	2.8	13.1	32.7	51.5	...	...	...	...	5615	-9887
3839	Other electrical apparatus and supplies	...	...	...	...	...	...	...	...	...	...
384	Transport equipment	83.4	501.7	2109.1	1834.7	...	...	...	...	35725	69
3841	Shipbuilding and repairing	16.3	130.8	516.3	559.5	...	...	...	...	5896	2338
3842	Railroad equipment	16.8	108.4	533.0	586.5	...	...	...	...	8260	22359
3843	Motor vehicles	35.7	185.1	741.2	386.5	...	...	...	...	5209	-26167
3844	Motorcycles and bicycles	2.3	8.4	12.7	14.6	...	...	...	...	-78	-11
3845	Aircraft	12.3	69.0	305.9	287.6	...	...	...	...	16438	1550
3849	Other transport equipment	...	...	...	...	...	...	...	...	...	...
385	Professional and scientific equipment	9.5	61.9	230.4	296.2	...	...	...	...	-523	-62678
3851	Prof. and scientific equipment n.e.c.	7.1	47.7	180.4	225.3	...	...	...	...	451	-46680
3852	Photographic and optical goods	2.4	14.3	50.0	70.9	...	...	...	...	-974	-15998
3853	Watches and clocks	...	...	...	...	...	...	...	...	...	...
390	Other manufacturing industries	...	...	...	...	...	...	...	...	...	...
3901	Jewellery and related articles	5.1	36.2	71.5	60.0	...	...	...	...	1122	339
3902	Musical instruments	0.3	1.6	4.8	6.1	...	...	...	...	67	-962
3903	Sporting and athletic goods	...	...	...	...	...	...	...	...	...	...
3909	Manufacturing industries, n.e.c.	...	...	...	...	...	...	...	...	...	...
3	Total manufacturing	1387.9	9375.6	40505.3	50326.3	...	...	...	...	835705	4239895

Ukraine

ISIC Revision 2		Index numbers of industrial production (1990=100)											
ISIC Industry	Note	1985	1986	1987	1988	1989	1990	1991	1992	1993	1994	1995	1996
311/2 Food products	a/	...	...	94	94	97	100	88	77	72	61	54	...
313 Beverages	a/	...	...	...	...	...	...	...	...	...	...	...	...
314 Tobacco		...	...	109	113	110	100	104	102	64	64	61	...
321 Textiles		...	...	92	97	101	100	97	100	82	43	28	...
322 Wearing apparel, except footwear		...	...	95	96	98	100	105	118	108	80	52	...
323 Leather and fur products	b/	...	...	67	93	96	100	100	117	107	52	30	...
324 Footwear, except rubber or plastic	b/	...	...	...	...	...	...	...	...	...	...	...	...
331 Wood products, except furniture		...	...	93	97	101	100	93	83	86	64	49	...
332 Furniture and fixtures, excl. metal		...	...	...	...	...	...	...	...	...	...	...	...
341 Paper and products		...	...	84	89	93	100	111	110	84	48	43	...
342 Printing and publishing		...	...	80	86	94	100	157	235	363	298	281	...
351 Industrial chemicals	c/	...	...	96	100	102	100	93	84	66	51	45	...
352 Other chemicals	c/	...	...	...	...	...	...	...	...	...	...	...	...
353 Petroleum refineries	d/	...	...	102	103	103	100	89	73	53	38	37	...
354 Misc. petroleum and coal products	d/	...	...	...	...	...	...	...	...	...	...	...	...
355 Rubber products	e/	...	...	91	95	99	100	85	85	71	40	34	...
356 Plastic products	e/	...	...	...	...	...	...	...	...	...	...	...	...
361 Pottery, china, earthenware	f/	...	...	92	97	103	100	102	100	86	57	46	...
362 Glass and products	f/	...	...	...	...	...	...	...	...	...	...	...	...
369 Other non-metallic mineral products	f/	...	...	...	...	...	...	...	...	...	...	...	...
371 Iron and steel	g/	...	...	102	104	104	100	92	83	65	42	39	...
372 Non-ferrous metals	g/	...	...	...	...	...	...	...	...	...	...	...	...
381 Fabricated metal products		...	...	95	99	100	100	110	120	123	67	48	...
382 Non-electrical machinery		...	...	84	84	90	100	100	119	127	104	85	...
383 Electrical machinery		...	...	84	92	97	100	104	97	100	58	47	...
384 Transport equipment		...	...	91	96	98	100	102	98	104	72	57	...
385 Professional and scientific equipment		...	...	81	86	96	100	106	113	119	81	59	...
390 Other manufacturing industries		...	...	...	...	...	...	...	...	...	...	...	...
3 Total manufacturing		...	...	93	95	99	100	96	94	87	63	52	...

a/ 311/2 includes 313.
b/ 323 includes 324.
c/ 351 includes 352.
d/ 353 includes 354.
e/ 355 includes 356.
f/ 361 includes 362 and 369.
g/ 371 includes 372.

UNITED KINGDOM

Supplier of information:
Department of Trade and Industry, London
Industrial statistics for the OECD countries are compiled by the OECD secretariat, which supplies them to UNIDO.

Basic source of data:
Annual census of production.

Major deviations from ISIC (Revision 3):
None reported.

Reference period (if not calendar year):

Scope:
Establishments employing 20 or more persons.

Method of enumeration:

Adjusted for non-response:
Yes.

Concepts and definitions of variables:
Wages and salaries includes all overtime payments, bonuses, commissions, holiday pay and redundancy payments less any amounts reimbursed from government sources. No deduction is made for income tax, insurance, contributory pensions, etc. Payments in kind, travelling expenses, lodging allowances, etc. are excluded.
Output relates to gross output and is calculated by adjusting the value of total sales, work done and services rendered, by the net changes during the year of work in progress and stocks of finished goods. Total sales represents deliveries on sale of goods produced by establishments and includes sales of goods made from materials given out by them to other organizations or to outworkers. The value of sales is the amount charged to customers. Where products attract excise duty, the value is inclusive of duty if goods are sold "duty-paid", and exclusive of duty if goods are sold in bond or exported. Sales of fixed assets are excluded.
Value added represents gross value added in factor values and is defined as the value of gross output less the cost of purchases of materials for use in production and packaging, fuels, goods for merchanting or factoring and the cost of industrial and non-industrial services received. The value of purchases is adjusted for changes in stocks of materials, stores and fuel.
Gross fixed capital formation is the value of purchases of fixed assets less the value of sales of such assets. Valuation is at full cost incurred, including the cost of installation and certain fees and taxes (namely legal fees, stamp duty, agents' commissions, etc.), and is inclusive of any amounts received or expected to be received in grants and/or allowances from government sources, statutory bodies or local authorities. The value of capital goods produced for own use are included. The value of any assets acquired in taking over an existing business are excluded. The figures include non-deductible VAT but exclude deductible VAT.

Related national publications:

United Kingdom

ISIC Revision 3	Number of establishments					Number of employees					Wages and salaries paid to employees				
		(numbers)					(thousands)					(million POUNDS)			
ISIC Industry	Note	1992	1993	1994	1995	Note	1992	1993	1994	1995	Note	1992	1993	1994	1995
151 Processed meat,fish,fruit,vegetables,fats		...	2900	3112	2906		...	185	191	185		...	2188	2292	2238
1511 Processing/preserving of meat		...	1460	1459	1396		...	111	116	115		...	1250	1334	1347
1512 Processing/preserving of fish		...	222	220	347		...	19	21	21		...	184	217	212
1513 Processing/preserving of fruit & vegetables		...	1169	1392	1100		...	50	49	46		...	641	632	616
1514 Vegetable and animal oils and fats		...	49	41	63		...	6	5	3		...	114	108	63
1520 Dairy products		...	743	749	830		...	48	46	42		...	699	679	599
153 Grain mill products; starches; animal feeds		...	725	828	801		...	35	33	33		...	625	615	590
1531 Grain mill products		...	145	165	154		...	14	13	12		...	240	236	225
1532 Starches and starch products		...	8	8	11		...	1	1	1		...	30	33	29
1533 Prepared animal feeds		...	572	655	636		...	20	19	20		...	355	346	336
154 Other food products		...	4372	4425	3509		...	220	213	195		...	2442	2514	2434
1541 Bakery products		...	3846	3872	2725		...	154	146	126		...	1454	1456	1351
1542 Sugar		...	5	11	14		...	5	4	4		...	105	104	90
1543 Cocoa, chocolate and sugar confectionery		...	315	311	310		...	37	37	35		...	506	541	506
1544 Macaroni, noodles & similar products		...	14	14	32		...	2	1	1		...	19	17	16
1549 Other food products n.e.c.		...	192	217	428		...	23	25	29		...	358	396	471
155 Beverages		...	655	683	682		...	57	56	55		...	948	1045	1077
1551 Distilling, rectifying & blending of spirits		...	181	97	86		...	12	12	11		...	212	209	213
1552 Wines		...	95	125	111		...	4	3	3		...	62	64	68
1553 Malt liquors and malt		...	213	256	260		...	29	28	28		...	462	548	565
1554 Soft drinks; mineral waters		...	166	205	225		...	13	13	13		...	212	225	231
1600 Tobacco products		...	41	23	19		...	9	9	8		...	232	244	235
171 Spinning, weaving and finishing of textiles		...	2593	2685	1555		...	71	71	61		...	810	842	752
1711 Textile fibre preparation; textile weaving		...	2063	2131	777		...	53	53	44		...	587	610	536
1712 Finishing of textiles		...	530	554	778		...	19	18	17		...	223	232	216
172 Other textiles		...	3581	2244	3684		...	73	69	68		...	805	797	787
1721 Made-up textile articles, except apparel		...	2756	1401	1620		...	36	34	28		...	329	313	261
1722 Carpets and rugs		...	825a/	843a/	397		...	37a/	36a/	18		...	476a/	484a/	258
1723 Cordage, rope, twine and netting		...	...a/	...a/	111		...	...a/	...a/	2		...	...a/	...a/	16
1729 Other textiles n.e.c.		...	...a/	...a/	1556		...	...a/	...a/	20		...	...a/	...a/	251
1730 Knitted and crocheted fabrics and articles		...	1082	1081	1067		...	54	51	63		...	505	508	669
1810 Wearing apparel, except fur apparel		...	7444	7855	8338		...	181	168	180		...	1387	1402	1449
1820 Dressing & dyeing of fur; processing of fur		...	55	62	61		...	1	1	1		...	8	8	7
191 Tanning, dressing and processing of leather		...	1536	1101	1014		...	17	16	14		...	233	174	161
1911 Tanning and dressing of leather		...	635	706	497		...	7	6	7		...	85	79	74
1912 Luggage, handbags, etc.; saddlery & harness		...	901	395	517		...	10	10	7		...	148	95	88
1920 Footwear		...	620	582	525		...	40	41	38		...	376	405	378
2010 Sawmilling and planing of wood		...	1976	1924	1471		...	15	16	16		...	172	216	167
202 Products of wood, cork, straw, etc.		...	5791	5254	6798		...	55	62	58		...	681	776	765
2021 Veneer sheets, plywood, particle board, etc.		...	92	111	159		...	5	6	6		...	81	89	98
2022 Builders' carpentry and joinery		...	1882	1488	3737		...	30	31	35		...	378	381	462
2023 Wooden containers		...	501	488	610		...	8	8	7		...	85	105	78
2029 Other wood products; articles of cork/straw		...	3316	3167	2292		...	12	17	10		...	138	201	126
210 Paper and paper products		...	3094	3269	3190		...	125	126	122		...	1960	2029	2036
2101 Pulp, paper and paperboard		...	442	419	531		...	26	26	26		...	431	448	489
2102 Corrugated paper and paperboard		...	1216	1268	1130		...	51	50	49		...	749	766	783
2109 Other articles of paper and paperboard		...	1436	1582	1529		...	49	50	47		...	779	815	764
221 Publishing		...	7925	6677	7441		...	137	145	142		...	2326	2592	2552
2211 Publishing of books and other publications		...	4200	2868	2992		...	35	34	33		...	567	593	543
2212 Publishing of newspapers, journals, etc.		...	3099	3379	3504		...	95	104	100		...	1657	1899	1904
2213 Publishing of recorded media		...	394	296	513		...	1	1	2		...	29	18	14
2219 Other publishing		...	232	134	432		...	6	6	7		...	73	82	91

Code	Description												
222	Printing and related service activities	...	15752	18673	18876	...	168	181	166	...	2667	3109	2652
2221	Printing	...	14216	16757	16112	...	150	154	139	...	2385	2658	2240
2222	Service activities related to printing	...	1536	1916	2764	...	18	27	27	...	282	451	412
2230	Reproduction of recorded media	...	54	68	218	...	4	4	6	...	77	67	111
2310	Coke oven products	...	22	37	32	...	1	1	...	...	17	22	...
2320	Refined petroleum products	...	148	174	366	...	13	12	13	...	317	315	332
2330	Processing of nuclear fuel	...	29	10	43	...	16	14	14	...	335	335	...
241	Basic chemicals	...	1620	1567	1529	...	84	79	81	...	1739	1702	1665
2411	Basic chemicals, except fertilizers	...	848	772	722	...	61	55	54	...	1285	1227	1197
2412	Fertilizers and nitrogen compounds	...	112	119	130	...	3	2	3	...	55	45	55
2413	Plastics in primary forms; synthetic rubber	...	660	676	677	...	20	22	25	...	399	430	413
242	Other chemicals	...	2145	2232	2968	...	179	178	188	...	3284	3353	3802
2421	Pesticides and other agro-chemical products	...	31	37	48	...	6	7	7	...	122	140	162
2422	Paints, varnishes, printing ink and mastics	...	473	390	651	...	28	27	28	...	460	441	481
2423	Pharmaceuticals, medicinal chemicals, etc.	...	334	414	581	...	69	69	76	...	1431	1465	1782
2424	Soap, cleaning & cosmetic preparations	...	824	984	608	...	46	45	44	...	710	727	753
2429	Other chemical products n.e.c.	...	483	407	1080	...	30	31	33	...	561	580	624
2430	Man-made fibres	...	44	57	64	...	8	7	7	...	157	184	158
251	Rubber products	...	577	649	873	...	51	50	50	...	788	806	814
2511	Rubber tyres and tubes	...	94	78	97	...	22	21	21	...	392	392	401
2519	Other rubber products	...	483	571	776	...	29	28	29	...	397	413	413
2520	Plastic products	...	4526	5033	6039	...	179	183	185	...	2408	2560	2629
2610	Glass and glass products	...	899	1083	1712	...	37	40	43	...	542	568	582
269	Non-metallic mineral products n.e.c.	...	4047b/	3412b/	3540	...	183b/	186b/	116	...	2780b/	2939b/	1737
2691	Pottery, china and earthenware	...	765	758	754	...	37	37	34	...	425	448	421
2692	Refractory ceramic products	...	139	105	140	...	8	7	8	...	113	113	123
2693	Struct.non-refractory clay; ceramic products	...	229	304	421	...	15	16	16	...	226	243	262
2694	Cement, lime and plaster	...	183	171	124	...	7	7	6	...	131	131	131
2695	Articles of concrete, cement and plaster	...	539	569	874	...	29	33	33	...	408	496	497
2696	Cutting, shaping & finishing of stone	...	122	150	551	...	3	3	5	...	37	42	73
2699	Other non-metallic mineral products n.e.c.	...	2070c/	1355c/	676	...	85c/	83c/	14	...	1441c/	1465c/	230
2710	Basic iron and steel	...	...c/	...c/	890	...	...c/	...c/	64	...	...c/	...c/	1268
2720	Basic precious and non-ferrous metals	...	1415	1072	1071	...	37	33	33	...	587	542	559
273	Casting of metals	...	654	675	827	...	37	36	37	...	505	540	575
2731	Casting of iron and steel	...	374	382	438	...	22	20	20	...	301	311	321
2732	Casting of non-ferrous metals	...	280	293	389	...	15	16	17	...	204	229	254
281	Struct.metal products;tanks;steam generators	...	3687	3645	4493	...	93	90	81	...	1474	1465	1257
2811	Structural metal products	...	3090	3262	3802	...	63	64	54	...	970	1004	781
2812	Tanks, reservoirs and containers of metal	...	187	191	309	...	14	12	13	...	204	189	202
2813	Steam generators	...	410	192	382	...	17	14	14	...	301	273	273
289	Other metal products; metal working services	...	22483	24084	24362	...	269	290	309	...	3785	4040	4196
2891	Metal forging/pressing/stamping/roll-forming	...	958	815	1252	...	36	37	37	...	486	524	554
2892	Treatment & coating of metals	...	11247	12078	13901	...	92	108	121	...	1425	1521	1635
2893	Cutlery, hand tools and general hardware	...	2152	2196	2681	...	42	46	45	...	553	627	650
2899	Other fabricated metal products n.e.c.	...	8126	8995	6528	...	99	100	106	...	1321	1368	1358
291	General purpose machinery	...	5340	5924	6997	...	209	215	216	...	3341	3527	3642
2911	Engines & turbines(not for transport equip.)	...	215	257	433	...	22	20	21	...	372	358	377
2912	Pumps, compressors, taps and valves	...	986	1035	988	...	51	53	52	...	834	878	904
2913	Bearings, gears, gearing & driving elements	...	276	285	389	...	24	24	25	...	398	398	425
2914	Ovens, furnaces and furnace burners	...	221	140	202	...	5	5	5	...	69	79	86
2915	Lifting and handling equipment	...	1399	1465	1633	...	40	39	40	...	631	668	674
2919	Other general purpose machinery	...	2243	2742	3352	...	68	74	73	...	1036	1147	1176
292	Special purpose machinery	...	5753	6246	7807	...	138	137	148	...	2250	2368	2508
2921	Agricultural and forestry machinery	...	1199	1275	1612	...	17	17	19	...	272	280	295
2922	Machine tools	...	2646	2892	2705	...	32	36	35	...	492	583	544
2923	Machinery for metallurgy	...	...	49	68	...	...	3	2	...	...	46	42
2924	Machinery for mining & construction	...	402	451	590	...	17	16	18	...	292	298	342
2925	Food/beverage/tobacco processing machinery	...	204	264	523	...	12	12	13	...	205	215	212
2926	Machinery for textile, apparel and leather	...	427	442	431	...	9	9	10	...	137	132	164
2927	Weapons and ammunition	...	...	126	176	...	...	16	15	...	...	287	301
2929	Other special purpose machinery	...	686	747	1702	...	28	29	35	...	468	527	608
2930	Domestic appliances n.e.c.	...	543	646	766	...	39	40	35	...	480	520	479

continued

United Kingdom

ISIC Revision 3	Number of establishments					Number of employees					Wages and salaries paid to employees				
		(numbers)					(thousands)					(million POUNDS)			
ISIC Industry	Note	1992	1993	1994	1995	Note	1992	1993	1994	1995	Note	1992	1993	1994	1995
3000 Office, accounting and computing machinery		...	1626	1678	2146		...	70	68	63		...	1508	1332	1155
3110 Electric motors, generators and transformers		...	1688	1489	1233		...	35	36	34		...	481	515	490
3120 Electricity distribution & control apparatus		...	516	660	884		...	49	52	51		...	697	757	788
3130 Insulated wire and cable		...	382	359	377		...	22	24	25		...	325	347	350
3140 Accumulators, primary cells and batteries		...	49	61	93		...	7	8	7		...	111	116	112
3150 Lighting equipment and electric lamps		...	320	325	450		...	23	23	19		...	305	305	251
3190 Other electrical equipment n.e.c.		...	2574	3209	2653		...	49	52	47		...	699	710	677
3210 Electronic valves, tubes, etc.		...	570	609	1104		...	46	51	58		...	637	750	891
3220 TV/radio transmitters; line comm. apparatus		...	1147	1248	1051		...	39	46	43		...	682	888	854
3230 TV and radio receivers and associated goods		...	1354	1568	1078		...	33	35	36		...	436	522	504
331 Medical, measuring, testing appliances, etc.		...	3289	3826	5758		...	126	117	117		...	1963	1877	1873
3311 Medical, surgical and orthopaedic equipment		...	613	841	2725		...	29	30	35		...	403	453	493
3312 Measuring/testing/navigating appliances,etc.		...	2561	2855	2723		...	92	82	77		...	1464	1342	1282
3313 Industrial process control equipment		...	115	130	310		...	5	5	6		...	95	81	98
3320 Optical instruments & photographic equipment		...	268	321	608		...	15	14	14		...	202	203	215
3330 Watches and clocks		...	119	134	160		...	2	2	2		...	24	33	35
3410 Motor vehicles		...	427	530	859		...	115	114	117		...	2191	2312	2462
3420 Automobile bodies, trailers & semi-trailers		...	422	579	857		...	24	28	28		...	336	407	424
3430 Parts/accessories for automobiles		...	640	647	2042		...	81	86	95		...	1170	1313	1431
351 Building and repairing of ships and boats		...	1479	1754	1600		...	48	42	39		...	838	678	641
3511 Building and repairing of ships		...	1374	1619	1258		...	45	38	33		...	791	620	560
3512 Building/repairing of pleasure/sport. boats		...	105	135	342		...	3	4	6		...	47	58	82
3520 Railway/tramway locomotives & rolling stock		...	79	89	113		...	17	15	12		...	270	260	215
3530 Aircraft and spacecraft		...	502	572	1146		...	126	114	109		...	2307	2144	2115
359 Transport equipment n.e.c.		...	155	185	249		...	6	6	7		...	69	74	85
3591 Motorcycles		...	72	97	90		...	1	1	1		...	6	8	12
3592 Bicycles and invalid carriages		...	44	49	116		...	4	4	5		...	50	53	60
3599 Other transport equipment n.e.c.		...	39	39	43		...	1	1	1		...	13	13	13
3610 Furniture		...	6403	7624	7187		...	119	128	115		...	1515	1665	1494
369 Manufacturing n.e.c.		...	8669	11513	10707		...	64	79	72		...	689	962	833
3691 Jewellery and related articles		...	1381	1395	1513		...	9	8	13		...	106	120	139
3692 Musical instruments		...	216	215	238		...	2	2	2		...	22	27	31
3693 Sports goods		...	166	187	400		...	6	6	6		...	59	72	83
3694 Games and toys		...	661	925	1042		...	9	14	12		...	94	165	154
3699 Other manufacturing n.e.c.		...	6245	8791	7514		...	38	50	39		...	408	578	427
3710 Recycling of metal waste and scrap		...	...	90	338		...	...	3	4		...	...	39	58
3720 Recycling of non-metal waste and scrap		...	...	30	226		...	...	1	3		...	...	6	32
D Total manufacturing		...	161625	156941	170283		...	4184	4233	4188		...	61384	64313	64173

a/ 1722 includes 1723 and 1729.
b/ 269 includes 2710.
c/ 2699 includes 2710.

United Kingdom

ISIC Revision 3		Output in producers' prices					Value added in factor values					Gross fixed capital formation		
			(million POUNDS)					(million POUNDS)					(million POUNDS)	
ISIC	Industry	Note	1992	1993	1994	1995	Note	1992	1993	1994	1995	Note	1994	1995
151	Processed meat,fish,fruit,vegetables,fats		...	17064	17680	18511		...	5558	5728	4314		556	639
1511	Processing/preserving of meat		...	9611	10160	11028		...	2707	2847	2352		313	373
1512	Processing/preserving of fish		...	1395	1531	1648		...	450	466	342		45	48
1513	Processing/preserving of fruit & vegetables		...	4416	4186	4331		...	1999	1976	1497		156	186
1514	Vegetable and animal oils and fats		...	1642	1804	1504		...	403	438	123		42	31
1520	Dairy products		...	7628	7675	8502		...	2004	2214	1409		179	195
153	Grain mill products; starches; animal feeds		...	8284	8048	7814		...	2468	2564	1587		234	247
1531	Grain mill products		...	3139	2898	2702		...	1155	1085	731		82	83
1532	Starches and starch products		...	451	456	398		...	172	166	84		28	36
1533	Prepared animal feeds		...	4694	4694	4714		...	1141	1313	772		124	128
154	Other food products		...	14151	15256	15251		...	6548	7074	5239		659	632
1541	Bakery products		...	6171	6303	6074		...	2981	3027	2306		275	289
1542	Sugar		...	1577	1523	1460		...	506	504	386		58	43
1543	Cocoa, chocolate and sugar confectionery		...	3349	3618	3516		...	1695	1740	1276		171	130
1544	Macaroni, noodles & similar products		...	162	102	75		...	62	47	29		5	2
1549	Other food products n.e.c.		...	2892	3710	4127		...	1304	1757	1242		148	168
155	Beverages		...	10596	11019	12145		...	3877	3804	3161		507	570
1551	Distilling, rectifying & blending of spirits		...	2419	2233	2471		...	1155	1080	884		83	116
1552	Wines		...	642	613	749		...	265	206	170		40	32
1553	Malt liquors and malt		...	5412	5944	6441		...	1503	1524	1457		295	324
1554	Soft drinks; mineral waters		...	2123	2229	2483		...	954	994	651		89	98
1600	Tobacco products		...	7601	7543	8260		...	1620	1660	1428		85	88
171	Spinning, weaving and finishing of textiles		...	3684	4104	3655		...	1627	1771	1289		174	139
1711	Textile fibre preparation; textile weaving		...	2818	3190	2842		...	1167	1279	918		121	82
1712	Finishing of textiles		...	865	914	813		...	461	492	371		53	57
172	Other textiles		...	3548	3669	4035		...	1706	1719	1444		102	116
1721	Made-up textile articles, except apparel		...	1327	1333	1172		...	656	646	472		30	22
1722	Carpets and rugs		...	2221a/	2336a/	1277		...	1050a/	1073a/	426		72a/	48
1723	Cordage, rope, twine and netting		...	...a/	...a/	72		...	...a/	...a/	28		...a/	4
1729	Other textiles n.e.c.		...	...a/	...a/	1514		...	...a/	...a/	517		...a/	41
1730	Knitted and crocheted fabrics and articles		...	1984	1984	2656		...	997	997	1114		81	88
1810	Wearing apparel, except fur apparel		...	5267	5760	6258		...	2586	2964	2377		104	113
1820	Dressing & dyeing of fur; processing of fur		...	45	24	32		...	19	14	15		1	-
191	Tanning, dressing and processing of leather		...	947	944	806		...	411	371	244		20	12
1911	Tanning and dressing of leather		...	622	579	489		...	207	190	123		13	7
1912	Luggage, handbags, etc.; saddlery & harness		...	325	364	316		...	204	181	121		7	4
1920	Footwear		...	1556	1740	1368		...	762	829	510		44	46
2010	Sawmilling and planing of wood		...	1220	1660	1317		...	393	504	272		33	39
202	Products of wood, cork, straw, etc.		...	3203	3633	3701		...	1468	1625	1289		92	102
2021	Veneer sheets, plywood, particle board, etc.		...	632	697	776		...	249	277	280		38	38
2022	Builders' carpentry and joinery		...	1553	1693	1982		...	693	771	714		20	43
2023	Wooden containers		...	459	555	423		...	195	226	117		8	6
2029	Other wood products; articles of cork/straw		...	558	687	519		...	331	351	178		26	14
210	Paper and paper products		...	10333	11619	13117		...	4710	5216	4373		669	775
2101	Pulp, paper and paperboard		...	2819	3277	4026		...	1208	1440	1327		293	349
2102	Corrugated paper and paperboard		...	3646	3940	4566		...	1600	1762	1491		217	289
2109	Other articles of paper and paperboard		...	3869	4402	4525		...	1902	2014	1554		159	136
221	Publishing		...	11002	11806	12469		...	7240	8044	5603		358	452
2211	Publishing of books and other publications		...	3206	3307	3476		...	1952	2140	1481		62	170
2212	Publishing of newspapers, journals, etc.		...	7282	8029	8487		...	4957	5640	3913		273	248
2213	Publishing of recorded media		...	140	68	72		...	114	42	20		4	8
2219	Other publishing		...	374	402	434		...	217	222	189		19	26

continued

United Kingdom

ISIC Revision 3	Output in producers' prices					Value added in factor values					Gross fixed capital formation		
		(million POUNDS)					(million POUNDS)					(million POUNDS)	
ISIC Industry	Note	1992	1993	1994	1995	Note	1992	1993	1994	1995	Note	1994	1995
222 Printing and related service activities		...	9515	10724	9719		...	5534	6067	4553		664	645
2221 Printing		...	8682	9444	8511		...	4933	5235	3862		569	556
2222 Service activities related to printing		...	833	1280	1207		...	601	832	691		94	89
2230 Reproduction of recorded media		...	595	593	743		...	375	363	364		28	64
2310 Coke oven products		...	109	130	55		...	42	47	15		3	1
2320 Refined petroleum products		...	20595	20338	19557		...	1893	1925	1685		316	348
2330 Processing of nuclear fuel		...	1389	1364	1935		...	1173	1153	1145		260	390
241 Basic chemicals		...	14259	15080	17580		...	5052	5642	5412		662	821
2411 Basic chemicals, except fertilizers		...	9764	9676	10598		...	3548	3747	3199		471	579
2412 Fertilizers and nitrogen compounds		...	610	636	829		...	176	175	203		12	18
2413 Plastics in primary forms; synthetic rubber		...	3885	4768	6153		...	1327	1719	2010		179	224
242 Other chemicals		...	22109	23821	24966		...	11499	12112	9279		1139	1362
2421 Pesticides and other agro-chemical products		...	1526	1791	1531		...	742	741	762		35	35
2422 Paints, varnishes, printing ink and mastics		...	2659	2656	2911		...	1208	1238	895		91	111
2423 Pharmaceuticals, medicinal chemicals, etc.		...	8225	9296	9823		...	5104	5590	4331		652	765
2424 Soap, cleaning & cosmetic preparations		...	5696	5903	5971		...	2725	2781	1704		232	269
2429 Other chemical products n.e.c.		...	4003	4176	4730		...	1719	1761	1586		130	182
2430 Man-made fibres		...	1099	963	1144		...	443	356	431		56	91
251 Rubber products		...	3151	3368	3778		...	1643	1744	1473		112	129
2511 Rubber tyres and tubes		...	1564	1655	2029		...	792	818	805		65	60
2519 Other rubber products		...	1586	1713	1749		...	852	926	668		48	69
2520 Plastic products		...	11517	12933	13467		...	5628	6250	4771		637	777
2610 Glass and glass products		...	2197	2465	2856		...	1165	1313	1096		133	173
269 Non-metallic mineral products n.e.c.		...	15133b/	17657b/	8571		...	6772b/	8071b/	3663		486b/	404
2691 Pottery, china and earthenware		...	1124	1290	1228		...	740	856	663		49	51
2692 Refractory ceramic products		...	517	529	545		...	243	242	210		17	26
2693 Struct.non-refractory clay; ceramic products		...	710	872	917		...	482	586	492		35	67
2694 Cement, lime and plaster		...	888	1134	1012		...	564	741	520		50	55
2695 Articles of concrete, cement and plaster		...	2450	3116	3476		...	1185	1582	1197		94	148
2696 Cutting, shaping & finishing of stone		...	127	130	182		...	62	86	95		5	4
2699 Other non-metallic mineral products n.e.c.		...	9317c/	10585c/	1211		...	3498c/	3977c/	487		238c/	53
2710 Basic iron and steel		...	...c/	...c/	10498		...	...c/	...c/	3173		...c/	273
2720 Basic precious and non-ferrous metals		...	4916	5077	6319		...	1371	1499	1469		91	116
273 Casting of metals		...	1671	1996	2055		...	922	1027	867		83	113
2731 Casting of iron and steel		...	961	1064	1090		...	541	559	491		35	53
2732 Casting of non-ferrous metals		...	710	932	965		...	381	468	375		48	60
281 Struct.metal products;tanks;steam generators		...	5636	6059	5209		...	2654	2722	1943		107	134
2811 Structural metal products		...	3696	4256	3333		...	1782	1936	1264		73	85
2812 Tanks, reservoirs and containers of metal		...	859	836	856		...	413	396	320		23	32
2813 Steam generators		...	1082	968	1020		...	459	389	359		11	17
289 Other metal products; metal working services		...	12518	14408	15976		...	7006	7735	7055		607	627
2891 Metal forging/pressing/stamping/roll-forming		...	1719	1937	2079		...	890	1000	841		79	66
2892 Treatment & coating of metals		...	3834	4552	5269		...	2312	2649	2701		222	209
2893 Cutlery, hand tools and general hardware		...	1856	2229	2337		...	1116	1286	1158		84	121
2899 Other fabricated metal products n.e.c.		...	5109	5690	6291		...	2688	2800	2355		222	231
291 General purpose machinery		...	13461	14969	16738		...	6390	7098	6205		438	542
2911 Engines & turbines(not for transport equip.)		...	2104	2161	2190		...	860	777	720		45	66
2912 Pumps, compressors, taps and valves		...	3345	3564	4049		...	1699	1845	1664		133	151
2913 Bearings, gears, gearing & driving elements		...	1313	1437	1747		...	651	718	711		59	110
2914 Ovens, furnaces and furnace burners		...	275	337	379		...	136	170	140		7	7
2915 Lifting and handling equipment		...	2538	2962	3543		...	1106	1257	1099		87	87
2919 Other general purpose machinery		...	3886	4509	4830		...	1939	2331	1872		108	121

ISIC Revision 3														
292 Special purpose machinery		...	10034	10785	12985		...	4396	4703	4438		311	386
2921 Agricultural and forestry machinery		...	1833	2191	2548		...	616	749	723		36	59
2922 Machine tools		...	1875	2424	2511		...	1015	1161	861		114	87
2923 Machinery for metallurgy		...	...	112	157		...	...	32	65		3	2
2924 Machinery for mining & construction		...	1427	1588	1991		...	599	656	680		34	57
2925 Food/beverage/tobacco processing machinery		...	805	795	997		...	411	432	305		16	47
2926 Machinery for textile, apparel and leather		...	561	510	652		...	275	248	300		18	19
2927 Weapons and ammunition		...	...	1208	1511		...	...	406	503		26	27
2929 Other special purpose machinery		...	1765	1958	2617		...	878	1019	1001		65	88
2930 Domestic appliances n.e.c.		...	2267	2475	2412		...	1027	1116	749		96	98
3000 Office, accounting and computing machinery		...	11150	10714	12678		...	3100	3271	2873		313	363
3110 Electric motors, generators and transformers		...	1951	1907	2070		...	823	910	794		57	46
3120 Electricity distribution & control apparatus		...	2706	3022	3372		...	1348	1519	1322		75	100
3130 Insulated wire and cable		...	1670	1891	2000		...	776	898	702		57	53
3140 Accumulators, primary cells and batteries		...	567	636	538		...	272	312	205		24	28
3150 Lighting equipment and electric lamps		...	1313	1394	1153		...	620	639	387		35	35
3190 Other electrical equipment n.e.c.		...	2975	3132	2881		...	1295	1497	1187		92	120
3210 Electronic valves, tubes, etc.		...	3284	4186	5328		...	1597	2018	2127		394	848
3220 TV/radio transmitters; line comm. apparatus		...	3374	4701	5508		...	1589	2118	1815		194	258
3230 TV and radio receivers and associated goods		...	2965	3502	4081		...	935	1086	1007		150	164
331 Medical, measuring, testing appliances, etc.		...	7425	7514	8171		...	3924	4132	3302		318	252
3311 Medical, surgical and orthopaedic equipment		...	1874	1986	2727		...	984	1114	994		89	68
3312 Measuring/testing/navigating appliances,etc.		...	5171	5227	5092		...	2758	2876	2168		225	172
3313 Industrial process control equipment		...	380	302	352		...	182	142	140		4	12
3320 Optical instruments & photographic equipment		...	813	914	981		...	456	499	470		31	63
3330 Watches and clocks		...	99	151	123		...	50	71	50		4	8
3410 Motor vehicles		...	20029	22971	24212		...	6288	5966	4964		970	1576
3420 Automobile bodies, trailers & semi-trailers		...	1608	2054	2242		...	591	773	736		38	25
3430 Parts/accessories for automobiles		...	5078	5964	7121		...	2215	2637	2612		250	336
351 Building and repairing of ships and boats		...	2940	2804	2427		...	1595	1652	1110		26	32
3511 Building and repairing of ships		...	2749	2555	2067		...	1514	1535	1015		22	23
3512 Building/repairing of pleasure/sport. boats		...	191	249	359		...	81	117	95		5	10
3520 Railway/tramway locomotives & rolling stock		...	1117	1184	925		...	383	435	236		-21	63
3530 Aircraft and spacecraft		...	9130	9952	9459		...	4716	5180	3531		230	249
359 Transport equipment n.e.c.		...	352	317	434		...	151	147	167		8	20
3591 Motorcycles		...	27	29	92		...	14	15	53		1	8
3592 Bicycles and invalid carriages		...	248	238	285		...	106	108	94		6	10
3599 Other transport equipment n.e.c.		...	77	49	58		...	31	24	19		1	3
3610 Furniture		...	6245	7003	6576		...	3030	3372	2370		166	152
369 Manufacturing n.e.c.		...	3216	4186	4208		...	1611	2239	1518		129	165
3691 Jewellery and related articles		...	...	585	683		...	251	266	276		9	14
3692 Musical instruments		...	...	83	95		...	35	196	41		5	1
3693 Sports goods		...	292	291	448		...	150	151	136		10	9
3694 Games and toys		...	494	895	868		...	253	391	340		25	18
3699 Other manufacturing n.e.c.		...	1791	2332	2114		...	923	1236	725		80	123
3710 Recycling of metal waste and scrap		...	...	806	1016		...	...	211	170		22	43
3720 Recycling of non-metal waste and scrap		...	...	32	236		...	...	19	78		1	18
D Total manufacturing		...	350293	380304	404200		...	146346	159591	129186		13691	16768

a/ 1722 includes 1723 and 1729.
b/ 269 includes 2710.
c/ 2699 includes 2710.

United Kingdom

ISIC Revision 3		Note	Index numbers of industrial production (1990=100)											
ISIC	Industry		1985	1986	1987	1988	1989	1990	1991	1992	1993	1994	1995	1996
15	Food and beverages		...	...	...	...	...	...	...	...	...	...	...	...
16	Tobacco products		97	88	96	99	96	100	102	107	100	108	103	107
17	Textiles		125	99	104	105	102	100	90	90	90	90	88	85
18	Wearing apparel, fur		103	103	104	103	99	100	90	93	93	97	94	96
19	Leather, leather products and footwear		...	...	...	...	...	...	...	...	...	...	...	...
20	Wood products (excl. furniture)		...	...	...	...	...	...	...	...	...	...	...	...
21	Paper and paper products		84	87	90	94	96	100	98	100	102	106	107	105
22	Printing and publishing		71	75	84	93	99	100	94	95	99	101	101	100
23	Coke,refined petroleum products,nuclear fuel		...	...	...	...	...	...	...	...	...	...	...	...
24	Chemicals and chemical products		...	...	...	...	...	...	...	...	...	...	...	...
25	Rubber and plastics products		...	...	...	...	...	...	...	...	...	...	...	...
26	Non-metallic mineral products		...	...	...	...	...	...	...	...	...	...	...	...
27	Basic metals		...	...	...	...	...	...	...	...	...	...	...	...
28	Fabricated metal products		102	84	87	95	100	100	91	86	84	86	88	87
29	Machinery and equipment n.e.c.	a/	94	81	85	94	99	100	93	94	96	108	112	112
30	Office, accounting and computing machinery	a/	...	...	...	...	...	...	...	...	...	...	...	...
31	Electrical machinery and apparatus	b/	136	84	85	93	100	100	93	90	92	104	107	109
32	Radio,television and communication equipment	b/	...	...	...	...	...	...	...	...	...	...	...	...
33	Medical, precision and optical instruments		94	87	91	97	100	100	96	96	100	97	98	102
34	Motor vehicles, trailers, semi-trailers	c/	76	80	83	91	102	100	94	92	91	93	92	96
35	Other transport equipment	c/	...	...	...	...	...	...	...	...	...	...	...	...
36	Furniture; manufacturing n.e.c.		...	...	...	...	...	...	...	...	...	...	...	...
37	Recycling		...	...	...	...	...	...	...	...	...	...	...	...
D	Total manufacturing		85	86	90	96	100	100	95	95	96	101	103	103

a/ 29 includes 30.
b/ 31 includes 32.
c/ 34 includes 35.

URUGUAY

Supplier of information:
Instituto Nacional de Estadística, Oficina de Planeamiento y Presupuesto, Montevideo.

Basic source of data:
Annual survey of the manufacturing industry.

Major deviations from ISIC (Revision 2):
None reported.

Reference period (if not calendar year):

Scope:
Establishments with 5 or more persons engaged.

Method of enumeration:
Not reported.

Adjusted for non-response:
Yes.

Concepts and definitions of variables:
Value added is total value added.

Related national publications:
Encuesta Anual de Producción, Sector Industrial (annual), published by the Instituto Nacional de Estadística, Montevideo.

Uruguay

ISIC Revision 2	Number of establishments					Number of persons engaged					Wages and salaries paid to employees				
		(numbers)					(numbers)					(million PESOS)			
ISIC Industry	Note	1992	1993	1994	1995	Note	1992	1993	1994	1995	Note	1992	1993	1994	1995
311/2 Food products		...	...	...	...		42867	39397	39086	36818		542.6	764.5	1151.0	1439.2
3111 Slaughtering, preparing & preserving meat		...	...	...	...		10478	9558	10380	9280		...	...	...	...
3112 Dairy products		...	...	...	...		4666	4661	4588	4491		...	...	...	...
3113 Canning, preserving of fruits & vegetables		...	...	...	...		939	676	587	556		...	...	...	...
3114 Canning, preserving and processing of fish		...	...	...	...		3845	2719	2402	2495		...	...	...	...
3115 Vegetable and animal oils and fats		...	...	...	...		703	602	461	442		...	...	...	...
3116 Grain mill products		...	...	...	...		3087	2534	2159	2186		...	...	...	...
3117 Bakery products		...	...	...	...		14163	14174	13977	12743		...	...	...	...
3118 Sugar factories and refineries		...	...	...	...		1390	695	655	639		...	...	...	...
3119 Cocoa, chocolate and sugar confectionery		...	...	...	...		1170	1026	996	809		...	...	...	...
3121 Other food products		...	...	...	...		2140	2424	2555	2979		...	...	...	...
3122 Prepared animal feeds		...	...	...	...		286	328	326	198		...	...	...	...
313 Beverages		...	...	...	...		4998	5071	4620	4232		110.9	184.1	243.5	336.2
3131 Distilling, rectifying and blending spirits		...	...	...	...		843	926	742	658		...	...	...	...
3132 Wine industries		...	...	...	...		1082	1265	1227	1135		...	...	...	...
3133 Malt liquors and malt		...	...	...	...		1473	1159	1076	965		...	...	...	...
3134 Soft drinks and carbonated waters		...	...	...	...		1600	1721	1575	1474		...	...	...	...
314 Tobacco		...	...	...	...		520	514	489	468		18.6	27.8	38.7	55.0
321 Textiles		...	...	...	...		16378	13615	11438	9659		232.9	301.2	363.3	430.8
3211 Spinning, weaving and finishing textiles		...	...	...	...		11154	8880	7671	6419		...	...	...	...
3212 Made-up textile goods excl. wearing apparel		...	...	...	...		568	446	415	256		...	...	...	...
3213 Knitting mills		...	...	...	...		3840	3515	2742	2333		...	...	...	...
3214 Carpets and rugs		...	...	...	...		85	82	63	30		...	...	...	...
3215 Cordage, rope and twine		...	...	...	...		41	40	43	44		...	...	...	...
3219 Other textiles		...	...	...	...		690	652	504	577		...	...	...	...
322 Wearing apparel, except footwear		...	...	...	...		14888	13092	11774	9919		132.9	153.6	185.9	215.4
323 Leather and fur products		...	...	...	...		4138	3761	2921	2756		71.9	78.8	102.3	130.6
3231 Tanneries and leather finishing		...	...	...	...		3445	2460	2259	2111		...	...	...	...
3232 Fur dressing and dyeing industries		...	...	...	...		-	-	-	-		...	...	...	...
3233 Leather prods. excl. wearing apparel		...	...	...	...		693	1301	662	645		...	...	...	...
324 Footwear, except rubber or plastic		...	...	...	...		4307	3156	3047	2329		28.8	35.1	48.2	45.4
331 Wood products, except furniture		...	...	...	...		2536	2249	1490	1318		21.1	30.4	27.6	35.0
3311 Sawmills, planing and other wood mills		...	...	...	...		2108	1865	1229	1077		...	...	...	...
3312 Wooden and cane containers		...	...	...	...		125	132	96	96		...	...	...	...
3319 Other wood and cork products		...	...	...	...		303	252	165	145		...	...	...	...
332 Furniture and fixtures, excl. metal		...	...	...	...		2391	2197	2061	1586		16.5	21.5	27.9	35.7
341 Paper and products		...	...	...	...		3169	3034	2510	2290		58.4	85.6	102.1	151.0
3411 Pulp, paper and paperboard articles		...	...	...	...		1614	1537	1234	1154		...	...	...	...
3412 Containers of paper and paperboard		...	...	...	...		1029	1045	937	820		...	...	...	...
3419 Other pulp, paper and paperboard articles		...	...	...	...		526	452	339	316		...	...	...	...
342 Printing and publishing		...	...	...	...		6378	6769	5960	5809		97.6	181.1	216.9	288.2
351 Industrial chemicals		...	...	...	...		1259	1223	1158	1152		37.4	56.7	82.8	117.1
3511 Basic chemicals excl. fertilizers		...	...	...	...		654	634	633	583		...	...	...	...
3512 Fertilizers and pesticides		...	...	...	...		381	379	368	334		...	...	...	...
3513 Synthetic resins and plastic materials		...	...	...	...		224	210	157	235		...	...	...	...
352 Other chemicals		...	...	...	...		5771	5681	5313	4800		154.0	245.8	332.5	444.2
3521 Paints, varnishes and lacquers		...	...	...	...		819	915	792	741		...	...	...	...
3522 Drugs and medicines		...	...	...	...		2131	2203	1988	2327		...	...	...	...
3523 Soap, cleaning preps., perfumes, cosmetics		...	...	...	...		2358	2232	2163	1404		...	...	...	...
3529 Other chemical products		...	...	...	...		463	331	370	328		...	...	...	...
353 Petroleum refineries		...	...	...	...		1486	615	100	976	a/	38.3	24.6	7.7	90.0

ISIC	Industry													
354	Misc. petroleum and coal products	...	...	...	...	81	78	94	101	a/	...	...	...	...
355	Rubber products	...	...	...	...	2100	2051	1707	1555		32.8	51.3	53.2	73.4
3551	Tyres and tubes	...	...	...	...	1193	1169	985	962		...	...	...	...
3559	Other rubber products	...	...	...	...	907	882	722	593		...	...	...	...
356	Plastic products	...	...	...	...	4801	4352	4410	4178		66.4	98.2	149.9	188.8
361	Pottery, china, earthenware	...	...	...	...	2121	2063	1843	1522		33.9	48.4	61.6	71.6
362	Glass and products	...	...	...	...	939	938	792	585		17.3	29.6	36.3	36.9
369	Other non-metallic mineral products	...	...	...	...	4610	4377	4194	3675		58.3	85.2	127.2	154.2
3691	Structural clay products	...	...	...	...	986	1015	1067	818		...	...	...	...
3692	Cement, lime and plaster	...	...	...	...	1282	1246	1139	996		...	...	...	...
3699	Other non-metallic mineral products	...	...	...	...	2342	2116	1988	1861		...	...	...	...
371	Iron and steel	...	...	...	...	767	849	817	859		11.1	25.9	34.6	50.8
372	Non-ferrous metals	...	...	...	...	444	414	350	296		8.6	11.2	15.6	19.4
381	Fabricated metal products	...	...	...	...	7125	6862	6315	6374		101.6	158.0	204.7	277.8
3811	Cutlery, hand tools and general hardware	...	...	...	...	590	569	510	492		...	...	...	...
3812	Furniture and fixtures primarily of metal	...	...	...	...	357	423	374	335		...	...	...	...
3813	Structural metal products	...	...	...	...	1741	1746	1508	1664		...	...	...	...
3819	Other fabricated metal products	...	...	...	...	4437	4124	3923	3883		...	...	...	...
382	Non-electrical machinery	...	...	...	...	2588	2807	2370	2018		31.3	55.6	69.9	81.7
3821	Engines and turbines	...	...	...	...	-	-	-	-		...	...	...	...
3822	Agricultural machinery and equipment	...	...	...	...	538	563	529	418		...	...	...	...
3823	Metal and wood working machinery	...	...	...	...	21	19	18	14		...	...	...	...
3824	Other special industrial machinery	...	...	...	...	904	1060	814	666		...	...	...	...
3825	Office, computing and accounting machinery	...	...	...	...	319	266	227	207		...	...	...	...
3829	Other non-electrical machinery & equipment	...	...	...	...	806	899	782	713		...	...	...	...
383	Electrical machinery	...	...	...	...	4051	3709	3044	2661		65.7	86.7	93.7	117.3
3831	Electrical industrial machinery	...	...	...	...	698	762	703	567		...	...	...	...
3832	Radio, television and communication equipm.	...	...	...	...	310	283	248	165		...	...	...	...
3833	Electrical appliances and housewares	...	...	...	...	1512	1568	969	788		...	...	...	...
3839	Other electrical apparatus and supplies	...	...	...	...	1531	1096	1124	1141		...	...	...	...
384	Transport equipment	...	...	...	...	4023	3546	2987	2643		75.6	100.6	112.5	131.5
3841	Shipbuilding and repairing	...	...	...	...	1104	972	861	877		...	...	...	...
3842	Railroad equipment	...	...	...	...	-	-	-	-		...	...	...	...
3843	Motor vehicles	...	...	...	...	2478	2044	1563	1201		...	...	...	...
3844	Motorcycles and bicycles	...	...	...	...	441	530	563	565		...	...	...	...
3845	Aircraft	...	...	...	...	-	-	-	-		...	...	...	...
3849	Other transport equipment	...	...	...	...	-	-	-	-		...	...	...	...
385	Professional and scientific equipment	...	...	...	...	642	652	794	742		8.9	14.0	21.2	29.9
3851	Prof. and scientific equipment n.e.c.	...	...	...	...	430	432	577	530		...	...	...	...
3852	Photographic and optical goods	...	...	...	...	212	220	217	212		...	...	...	...
3853	Watches and clocks	...	...	...	...	-	-	-	-		...	...	...	...
390	Other manufacturing industries	...	...	...	...	2039	1257	1149	1176		17.5	17.5	23.0	37.2
3901	Jewellery and related articles	...	...	...	...	238	216	205	182		...	...	...	...
3902	Musical instruments	...	...	...	...	-	-	-	-		...	...	...	...
3903	Sporting and athletic goods	...	...	...	...	77	77	30	27		...	...	...	...
3909	Manufacturing industries, n.e.c.	...	...	...	...	1724	964	914	967		...	...	...	...
3	Total manufacturing	...	...	...	...	147417	134329	122833	112497		2091.0	2973.1	3933.7	5084.2

a/ 353 includes 354.

Uruguay

ISIC Revision 2		Output in producers' prices					Value added in producers' prices					Gross fixed capital formation	
		(million PESOS)					(million PESOS)					(million PESOS)	
ISIC Industry	Note	1992	1993	1994	1995	Note	1992	1993	1994	1995	Note	1994	1995
311/2 Food products		5510.7	7586.6	11325.4	15959.4		1883.9	2808.7	4101.4	5751.4		365.7	502.8
313 Beverages		1559.6	2285.2	3074.5	4085.6		989.1	1472.6	1992.3	2603.8		74.4	138.3
314 Tobacco		548.2	777.3	1041.2	1220.9		449.1	653.5	914.6	996.4		19.1	10.0
321 Textiles		1825.0	2092.9	2798.3	3829.3		824.6	966.6	1290.7	1707.1		87.1	135.1
322 Wearing apparel, except footwear		1237.6	1266.2	1282.0	1457.7		367.6	437.4	633.3	750.6		19.0	8.5
323 Leather and fur products		657.9	757.5	1276.8	1618.6		252.4	251.0	411.1	426.1		33.2	37.7
324 Footwear, except rubber or plastic		199.0	241.9	322.5	327.9		70.8	57.5	93.3	55.4		2.8	1.4
331 Wood products, except furniture		91.7	127.9	146.7	179.4		47.1	68.6	72.7	87.5		3.8	1.8
332 Furniture and fixtures, excl. metal		102.7	168.0	228.0	245.8		56.7	75.1	131.7	121.8		12.1	-0.7
341 Paper and products		454.7	555.1	781.5	1136.6		224.9	251.1	377.5	498.5		18.0	207.5
342 Printing and publishing		570.4	1090.4	1246.0	1563.2		289.8	578.6	711.2	974.5		55.1	56.9
351 Industrial chemicals		355.6	496.9	629.4	928.0		152.3	218.2	276.5	423.8		18.2	32.6
352 Other chemicals		1205.2	1884.7	2534.5	3508.8		624.6	984.8	1323.9	1936.3		70.8	134.0
353 Petroleum refineries		1756.7	652.4	110.8	4200.5		844.1	339.4	56.4	2819.6		33.2	770.1
354 Misc. petroleum and coal products		8.2	16.2	28.6	29.8		2.8	6.5	13.1	9.3		-1.5	0.8
355 Rubber products		200.9	290.9	278.2	375.8		108.1	140.1	128.7	179.1		5.6	7.2
356 Plastic products		531.3	686.5	1085.0	1306.6		258.0	339.3	516.3	612.7		62.4	56.3
361 Pottery, china, earthenware		144.3	172.7	241.5	285.8		95.4	99.8	151.7	167.1		3.0	4.0
362 Glass and products		83.5	152.3	144.9	160.9		41.9	81.3	76.8	91.3		9.9	4.0
369 Other non-metallic mineral products		400.9	599.8	906.2	1007.4		193.8	263.5	414.0	555.6		38.3	0.9
371 Iron and steel		116.4	264.1	396.1	610.9		39.5	109.4	185.1	288.9		58.4	95.3
372 Non-ferrous metals		55.1	72.1	110.2	165.4		29.5	41.5	64.1	70.8		1.3	-2.6
381 Fabricated metal products		563.1	817.4	1163.7	1429.9		302.3	424.3	633.9	730.5		30.5	44.5
382 Non-electrical machinery		138.2	237.4	291.2	350.3		79.2	136.9	165.1	208.5		6.7	4.0
383 Electrical machinery		521.6	590.5	651.3	715.3		264.7	325.3	321.4	363.2		24.8	8.6
384 Transport equipment		731.7	850.6	975.1	916.9		401.0	409.7	485.0	564.7		19.5	41.1
385 Professional and scientific equipment		77.7	124.6	159.2	209.4		41.5	76.5	97.1	115.4		9.0	6.5
390 Other manufacturing industries		201.1	173.0	209.6	294.1		61.1	75.9	103.3	127.7		1.5	0.7
3 Total manufacturing		19848.9	25031.0	33438.5	48120.1		8995.9	11693.2	15742.5	23237.7		1082.2	2307.2

Uruguay

ISIC Revision 2		Index numbers of industrial production (1990=100)											
ISIC Industry	Note	1985	1986	1987	1988	1989	1990	1991	1992	1993	1994	1995	1996
311/2 Food products		96	95	93	99	102	100	101	104	100	108	110	120
313 Beverages		82	93	101	97	100	100	99	106	108	108	108	106
314 Tobacco		87	87	97	99	106	100	103	123	112	112	100	111
321 Textiles		85	99	106	101	96	100	108	109	99	99	79	77
322 Wearing apparel, except footwear	a/	113	128	139	117	130	100	101	96	95	93	77	85
323 Leather and fur products		98	104	109	94	112	100	100	84	99	126	126	157
324 Footwear, except rubber or plastic	a/	...	...	...	...	...	...	...	...	...	...	...	...
331 Wood products, except furniture		32	51	74	81	88	100	91	122	122	122	122	...
332 Furniture and fixtures, excl. metal		...	...	...	...	...	...	...	...	...	...	...	...
341 Paper and products		85	105	109	105	100	100	114	122	120	130	112	135
342 Printing and publishing		109	112	127	109	103	100	119	114	117	113	102	107
351 Industrial chemicals	b/	66	82	97	99	100	100	97	97	98	105	97	97
352 Other chemicals	b/	...	...	...	...	...	...	...	...	...	...	...	...
353 Petroleum refineries		89	81	94	95	93	100	102	91	30	2	94	109
354 Misc. petroleum and coal products		...	...	...	...	...	...	...	...	...	...	...	...
355 Rubber products		73	92	105	106	94	100	83	82	82	83	86	73
356 Plastic products		92	109	125	104	103	100	104	106	104	117	125	119
361 Pottery, china, earthenware	c/	55	70	92	89	95	100	96	139	143	144	139	118
362 Glass and products	c/	...	...	...	...	...	...	...	...	...	...	...	...
369 Other non-metallic mineral products	c/	...	...	...	...	...	...	...	...	...	...	...	...
371 Iron and steel		90	95	113	110	110	100	104	98	86	78	74	73
372 Non-ferrous metals		85	89	96	94	92	100	83	95	80	...	...	...
381 Fabricated metal products		80	100	120	106	100	100	91	89	79	89	65	61
382 Non-electrical machinery		...	...	...	...	...	...	...	...	...	...	...	...
383 Electrical machinery		85	106	131	115	108	100	84	84	69	72	70	87
384 Transport equipment		60	81	125	110	97	100	110	99	99	133	67	30
385 Professional and scientific equipment		...	...	...	...	...	...	...	...	...	...	...	...
390 Other manufacturing industries		...	...	...	...	...	...	...	...	...	...	...	...
3 Total manufacturing		...	...	...	...	...	...	...	...	...	...	...	...

a/ 322 includes 324.
b/ 351 includes 352.
c/ 361 includes 362 and 369.

VENEZUELA

Supplier of information:
Oficina Central de Estadística e Informática (OCEI), Presidencia de la República, Caracas.

Basic source of data:
Annual industrial survey.

Major deviations from ISIC (Revision 2):
None reported.

Reference period (if not calendar year):

Scope:
Establishments with 5 or more persons engaged.

Method of enumeration:
Establishments with more than 50 persons engaged are completely enumerated, and smaller establishments are sampled. Individual sites are visited by enumerators.

Adjusted for non-response:
Yes.

Concepts and definitions of variables:
Both output and value added exclude net revenues from goods shipped in the same condition as received.

Related national publications:
Anuario Estadístico; Encuesta Industrial (annual), both published by the Oficina Central de Estadística e Informática (OCEI), Presidencia de la República, Caracas.

Venezuela

ISIC Revision 2	Number of establishments					Number of employees					Wages and salaries paid to employees				
		(numbers)					(numbers)					(million BOLIVARES)			
ISIC Industry	Note	1993	1994	1995	1996a/	Note	1993	1994	1995	1996a/	Note	1993	1994	1995	1996a/
311/2 Food products		2111	2139	2223	3297		82742	86627	87193	87278		28032	43659	65327	95869
3111 Slaughtering, preparing & preserving meat		91	85	96	121		11683	11458	11062	10856		3253	4564	7084	10069
3112 Dairy products		81	71	76	129		9066	8641	7312	7347		3668	4586	5641	7224
3113 Canning, preserving of fruits & vegetables		31	33	30	43		5540	4898	2977	3416		2329	3669	3271	5095
3114 Canning, preserving and processing of fish		14	18	19	18		2909	5127	6225	5527		923	1444	3366	5026
3115 Vegetable and animal oils and fats		11	13	12	11		3094	3380	3440	3294		1245	2340	3348	4940
3116 Grain mill products		86	74	79	74		8417	7123	7996	7715		4359	5758	10936	10424
3117 Bakery products		1535	1589	1653	2554		22205	26216	25589	28559		4887	9599	13922	25220
3118 Sugar factories and refineries		51	53	54	50		7618	6565	7450	7099		2078	2982	3950	9581
3119 Cocoa, chocolate and sugar confectionery		28	28	33	37		3899	4234	3944	1973		1955	2252	3870	2869
3121 Other food products		151	150	146	226		5311	5486	6015	6471		1961	4528	6425	10256
3122 Prepared animal feeds		32	25	25	34		3000	3499	5183	5021		1374	1937	3514	5165
313 Beverages		100	85	93	106		16916	17282	14597	15162		10941	13354	17517	22884
3131 Distilling, rectifying and blending spirits		36	27	31	43		2887	2406	2321	2617		1191	1635	2056	3127
3132 Wine industries		2	2	4	5		...b/	105	172	188		...b/	91	217	348
3133 Malt liquors and malt		6	6	6	6		5470	5796	4349	5509		5794	6278	6170	12464
3134 Soft drinks and carbonated waters		56	50	52	52		8460	8975	7755	6848		3872	5350	9074	6945
314 Tobacco		22	15	21	23		3702	3034	2861	2581		3428	3565	3290	3871
321 Textiles		175	190	198	341		20517	19495	18968	20650		8481	10795	13851	20504
3211 Spinning, weaving and finishing textiles		123	143	145	158		17436	16606	15943	15551		7701	9372	11680	15819
3212 Made-up textile goods excl. wearing apparel		25	29	32	163		603	1288	1187	3251		174	652	980	2432
3213 Knitting mills		3	-	1	-		61	-	117	-		22	-	37	-
3214 Carpets and rugs		14	10	9	2		1040	494	455	428		309	280	356	538
3215 Cordage, rope and twine		6	4	5	8		1233	786	834	1002		220	357	450	906
3219 Other textiles		4	4	6	10		144	321	432	418		55	134	348	809
322 Wearing apparel, except footwear		871	840	771	823		27661	22456	19995	20539		7034	9158	13867	18333
323 Leather and fur products		93	89	77	108		4418	3267	3367	3412		1197	1277	2265	3091
3231 Tanneries and leather finishing		-	-	-	-		-	-	-	-		-	-	-	-
3232 Fur dressing and dyeing industries		20	18	21	27		2994	2134	2230	2405		848	939	1643	2172
3233 Leather prods. excl. wearing apparel		73	71	56	81		1424	1133	1137	1007		349	338	622	919
324 Footwear, except rubber or plastic		497	471	450	476		15772	14436	13992	13308		4307	5038	8290	11775
331 Wood products, except furniture		248	198	249	660		6428	6545	6494	10100		1569	2451	3596	7704
3311 Sawmills, planing and other wood mills		213	181	219	574		5783	6159	6069	9290		1420	2325	3407	6976
3312 Wooden and cane containers		1	3	4	24		...b/	74	83	222		...b/	16	34	94
3319 Other wood and cork products		34	14	26	62		636	312	342	588		148	110	155	634
332 Furniture and fixtures, excl. metal		732	779	688	969		14721	16316	11863	12352		4115	6449	7772	10256
341 Paper and products		83	93	97	129		11782	12167	11881	11918		5991	9338	12510	17981
3411 Pulp, paper and paperboard articles		19	35	39	42		6984	8028	7483	7094		3733	6488	8202	10329
3412 Containers of paper and paperboard		45	49	50	46		3680	3523	3682	3708		1856	2655	3704	5913
3419 Other pulp, paper and paperboard articles		19	9	8	41		1118	616	716	1116		402	195	604	1739
342 Printing and publishing		529	518	522	650		17598	15991	15474	14977		7168	10410	15735	20484
351 Industrial chemicals		113	92	91	183		12862	11675	11194	12516		14049	17567	24610	43540
3511 Basic chemicals excl. fertilizers		78	68	61	106		6844	6554	6101	6389		7525	9210	11225	17683
3512 Fertilizers and pesticides		11	8	8	9		3283	3126	2734	2467		3976	5330	8231	15598
3513 Synthetic resins and plastic materials		24	16	22	68		2735	1995	2359	3660		2548	3027	5154	10259
352 Other chemicals		268	253	278	361		28899	26886	24972	24582		18809	24622	35045	45477
3521 Paints, varnishes and lacquers		44	39	48	78		3152	3010	2704	3282		2190	2844	3927	5454
3522 Drugs and medicines		61	59	55	69		8864	9331	8143	6995		6281	9548	13293	16694
3523 Soap, cleaning preps., perfumes, cosmetics		77	74	83	117		11216	9437	8996	8982		7228	8402	11836	14099
3529 Other chemical products		86	81	92	97		5667	5108	5129	5323		3110	3828	5989	9230
353 Petroleum refineries		10	10	9	13		6592	6476	7743	7744		10023	11170	12260	19344

354 Misc. petroleum and coal products	23	24	22	35	1361	1007	1117	1452	494	594	740	1729
355 Rubber products	69	65	64	88	6656	6633	6690	6848	2967	4748	8205	17747
3551 Tyres and tubes	21	20	15	19	4111	4121	4283	4502	2248	3502	6548	15443
3559 Other rubber products	48	45	49	69	2545	2512	2407	2346	719	1246	1657	2304
356 Plastic products	420	396	398	277	21766	20840	20998	17467	7744	11089	17379	23152
361 Pottery, china, earthenware	29	19	44	140	3498	2435	5229	5046	1568	1993	4729	6157
362 Glass and products	62	63	58	98	6174	7040	6883	6926	2547	4635	6740	10435
369 Other non-metallic mineral products	446	468	477	725	20400	21390	16520	19257	9315	12374	15991	23778
3691 Structural clay products	79	85	82	85	7042	8602	5128	4801	2431	3920	3567	6062
3692 Cement, lime and plaster	28	29	32	45	5268	4961	4237	4549	4066	4911	6639	7040
3699 Other non-metallic mineral products	339	354	363	595	8090	7827	7155	9907	2818	3543	5785	10676
371 Iron and steel	142	171	192	189	22915	22041	23683	23371	12117	14912	59174	96565
372 Non-ferrous metals	65	81	68	80	12675	12093	12214	13908	9703	8191	13548	38862
381 Fabricated metal products	984	1007	902	1425	31268	28350	26280	30007	11009	14067	22790	38358
3811 Cutlery, hand tools and general hardware	98	96	91	125	5310	4608	3933	3853	1600	1914	2924	4132
3812 Furniture and fixtures primarily of metal	99	98	88	168	2413	1816	1724	2905	748	905	1368	3657
3813 Structural metal products	667	677	621	903	12622	11515	12289	13400	4192	4837	10177	16752
3819 Other fabricated metal products	120	136	102	229	10923	10411	8334	9849	4469	6411	8321	13817
382 Non-electrical machinery	253	247	278	602	16236	14195	14021	17274	5582	7929	10886	20516
3821 Engines and turbines	1	-	1	3	...b/	-	70	254	...b/	-	61	416
3822 Agricultural machinery and equipment	26	22	26	56	954	495	558	716	197	195	362	630
3823 Metal and wood working machinery	3	8	5	160	149	106	89	1904	50	32	61	1685
3824 Other special industrial machinery	49	31	51	76	2060	1091	1689	1941	621	844	1654	3217
3825 Office, computing and accounting machinery	9	1	1	7	322	22	23	102	153	9	10	94
3829 Other non-electrical machinery & equipment	165	185	194	300	12735	12481	11592	12357	4549	6849	8738	14474
383 Electrical machinery	204	164	190	276	16422	11959	11309	12019	7743	8445	11948	19301
3831 Electrical industrial machinery	92	69	80	133	7568	5711	5244	6191	3941	4316	5085	9332
3832 Radio, television and communication equipm.	21	14	14	34	1817	931	790	931	628	479	903	1700
3833 Electrical appliances and housewares	8	3	4	10	1083	376	430	599	424	295	465	632
3839 Other electrical apparatus and supplies	83	78	92	99	5954	4941	4845	4298	2750	3355	5495	7637
384 Transport equipment	234	217	215	383	19906	18333	18213	20138	10154	15651	18974	30142
3841 Shipbuilding and repairing	17	13	17	43	831	616	1005	1052	293	214	738	1262
3842 Railroad equipment	-	-	-	1	-	-	-	6	-	-	-	7
3843 Motor vehicles	206	195	183	308	18805	17530	16818	18426	9799	15366	17994	28257
3844 Motorcycles and bicycles	10	8	11	21	261	180	231	398	61	69	158	356
3845 Aircraft	-	-	-	-	-	-	-	-	-	-	-	-
3849 Other transport equipment	1	1	4	10	...b/	7	159	256	...b/	2	84	260
385 Professional and scientific equipment	43	44	47	68	2604	2286	2370	2664	1437	2193	3019	3303
3851 Prof. and scientific equipment n.e.c.	37	38	40	65	2306	2010	1972	2088	1354	2070	2767	2732
3852 Photographic and optical goods	5	5	7	3	277	255	398	576	75	109	252	571
3853 Watches and clocks	1	1	-	-	...b/	21	-	-	...b/	14	-	-
390 Other manufacturing industries	148	153	127	216	5800	4920	4675	5263	2140	2299	3750	5824
3901 Jewellery and related articles	18	19	18	13	297	272	202	107	117	193	274	133
3902 Musical instruments	1	2	2	9	...b/	24	30	38	...b/	5	11	14
3903 Sporting and athletic goods	8	9	9	19	130	135	189	254	40	67	122	399
3909 Manufacturing industries, n.e.c.	121	123	98	175	5363	4489	4254	4864	1981	2034	3343	5278
3 Total manufacturing	8974	8891	8849	12741	458291	436175	420796	438759	209664	277973	433808	676982

a/ Data are provisional.
b/ Data suppressed due to confidentiality rules.

Venezuela

ISIC Revision 2		Output in producers' prices					Value added in producers' prices					Gross fixed capital formation	
		(million BOLIVARES)					(million BOLIVARES)					(million BOLIVARES)	
ISIC Industry	Note	1993	1994	1995	1996a/	Note	1993	1994	1995	1996a/	Note	1995	1996a/
311/2 Food products		437330	674844	1239484	2217328		121258	209437	376347	734339		33386	74385
3111 Slaughtering, preparing & preserving meat		65542	97905	163777	299634		10519	18805	48705	70583		...	7994
3112 Dairy products		65276	79159	134966	249457		16488	18023	34901	63869		...	4556
3113 Canning, preserving of fruits & vegetables		30887	44548	44097	89886		11118	18431	17031	31909		...	3629
3114 Canning, preserving and processing of fish		11762	16405	26482	49449		4462	6531	9079	15650		...	2707
3115 Vegetable and animal oils and fats		39480	59134	101608	221740		10512	25228	31802	66385		...	6027
3116 Grain mill products		87311	122107	254841	452961		26477	38307	78681	152322		...	10304
3117 Bakery products		39531	82359	131079	298003		10909	27395	40565	117595		...	10188
3118 Sugar factories and refineries		18698	37614	65839	118488		6255	11719	22780	44007		...	7504
3119 Cocoa, chocolate and sugar confectionery		18122	24787	46935	39441		9129	11439	22995	15810		...	2303
3121 Other food products		20838	59258	175940	178988		6340	24430	36409	71536		...	12374
3122 Prepared animal feeds		39883	51568	93920	219281		9049	9129	33399	84673		...	6799
313 Beverages		139029	170858	287973	467483		73095	82381	137636	262556		17297	29469
3131 Distilling, rectifying and blending spirits		21612	24851	39998	74939		8047	7439	13646	33799		...	2038
3132 Wine industries		...b/	531	2698	2991		...b/	85	1443	857		...	252
3133 Malt liquors and malt		81308	92563	154161	281198		49037	52733	77526	179368		...	20621
3134 Soft drinks and carbonated waters		35595	52913	91116	108355		15837	22124	45021	48532		...	6558
314 Tobacco		51904	61615	99723	857903		34872	39393	65243	829609		209	3393
321 Textiles		51126	84795	150344	272766		17475	30841	59553	115926		3609	6621
3211 Spinning, weaving and finishing textiles		46266	74130	130210	220040		15745	26721	50978	90557		...	4937
3212 Made-up textile goods excl. wearing apparel		1066	4026	8186	31703		401	1667	3833	15645		...	333
3213 Knitting mills		122	-	185	-		45	-	108	-		...	-
3214 Carpets and rugs		1927	1836	2644	3416		747	668	1094	1764		...	489
3215 Cordage, rope and twine		1102	1546	3535	6456		418	916	1846	3386		...	463
3219 Other textiles		643	3257	5584	11151		119	869	1694	4574		...	399
322 Wearing apparel, except footwear		40479	62624	90431	242933		-13339	22307	34538	126252		637	2588
323 Leather and fur products		10776	15132	26032	34649		2653	5550	8860	11113		457	395
3231 Tanneries and leather finishing		-	-	-	-		-	-	-	-		...	-
3232 Fur dressing and dyeing industries		8608	12854	19421	27325		2022	4823	6754	8774		...	314
3233 Leather prods. excl. wearing apparel		2168	2278	6611	7324		631	727	2106	2339		...	81
324 Footwear, except rubber or plastic		45301	33575	60646	106222		18652	11051	22714	44817		700	1438
331 Wood products, except furniture		9377	12247	22827	61107		3313	4960	9047	25098		523	1296
3311 Sawmills, planing and other wood mills		8416	11500	21689	56565		2937	4636	8586	23278		...	1236
3312 Wooden and cane containers		...b/	213	245	1098		...b/	125	137	482		...	-
3319 Other wood and cork products		947	534	893	3444		372	199	324	1338		...	60
332 Furniture and fixtures, excl. metal		24146	36780	45389	74593		8592	12902	15681	33406		910	713
341 Paper and products		67277	111600	180065	286119		23682	38760	62338	107780		4606	14551
3411 Pulp, paper and paperboard articles		44787	80352	116199	167089		16496	28499	40213	58590		...	12198
3412 Containers of paper and paperboard		18243	28942	58402	107792		6245	9561	20987	45002		...	2275
3419 Other pulp, paper and paperboard articles		4247	2306	5464	11238		941	700	1138	4188		...	78
342 Printing and publishing		62536	78791	120690	195201		28463	35313	58204	98404		4502	7936
351 Industrial chemicals		132487	227305	426431	981005		51684	83531	191886	505972		32092	78756
3511 Basic chemicals excl. fertilizers		62965	126409	235439	551224		26771	46797	119422	332858		...	37394
3512 Fertilizers and pesticides		30492	41392	75671	152939		10915	19080	34324	83978		...	18162
3513 Synthetic resins and plastic materials		39030	59504	115321	276842		13998	17654	38140	89136		...	23200
352 Other chemicals		154119	195624	350186	625802		61138	76839	157662	301614		7648	13364
3521 Paints, varnishes and lacquers		24005	34157	67959	142794		9071	14168	28390	78979		...	1707
3522 Drugs and medicines		49438	67942	100633	162786		24198	28240	45675	82816		...	2837
3523 Soap, cleaning preps., perfumes, cosmetics		60074	62546	124104	226269		20655	21734	61608	103956		...	6597
3529 Other chemical products		20602	30979	57490	93953		7214	12697	21989	35863		...	2223
353 Petroleum refineries		357784	405662	777717	1353696		268549	293983	556708	1021470		10213	20634

354 Misc. petroleum and coal products	5657	5468	8767	31138	1236	1704	2939	11354	111	1636
355 Rubber products	36126	62953	96925	226281	16575	29461	44883	141482	5558	9055
3551 Tyres and tubes	30530	54193	81810	198428	14713	26504	39492	131435	...	8512
3559 Other rubber products	5596	8760	15115	27853	1862	2957	5391	10047	...	543
356 Plastic products	60261	88900	159102	231380	19298	34486	59902	105358	3277	11209
361 Pottery, china, earthenware	6790	8505	29006	45891	3557	4620	14813	24901	854	812
362 Glass and products	29981	45024	82366	189898	14975	29140	54372	124932	2622	32143
369 Other non-metallic mineral products	74244	100924	186247	359886	32321	46082	104145	191861	13502	12983
3691 Structural clay products	17153	25411	21964	44358	8630	12147	10416	23439	...	1591
3692 Cement, lime and plaster	36195	51938	110680	182256	17163	24349	67729	104047	...	7364
3699 Other non-metallic mineral products	20896	23575	53603	133272	6528	9586	26000	64375	...	4028
371 Iron and steel	133318	231459	402239	938847	44390	100351	190621	458901	22531	773755
372 Non-ferrous metals	125953	207019	334203	752753	39899	99234	197028	397525	9526	22951
381 Fabricated metal products	100721	132775	220993	424705	37586	52071	94929	177758	9949	15642
3811 Cutlery, hand tools and general hardware	11930	14879	24581	43349	5141	5704	9868	18439	...	1259
3812 Furniture and fixtures primarily of metal	4556	5119	7480	25409	1398	1844	3203	10035	...	207
3813 Structural metal products	26220	33142	54815	121310	10565	15684	26882	58065	...	2485
3819 Other fabricated metal products	58015	79635	134117	234637	20482	28839	54976	91219	...	11691
382 Non-electrical machinery	52798	72835	99202	233509	19417	32290	41529	113046	4084	7571
3821 Engines and turbines	...b/	-	216	8297	...b/	-	162	2297	...	1492
3822 Agricultural machinery and equipment	1373	1104	2885	3111	470	494	1755	1499	...	76
3823 Metal and wood working machinery	289	362	332	5734	123	174	123	3688	...	164
3824 Other special industrial machinery	6041	7243	15780	44589	2415	3101	7205	23001	...	894
3825 Office, computing and accounting machinery	1389	14	20	280	993	10	11	162	...	6
3829 Other non-electrical machinery & equipment	43642	64112	79969	171498	15394	28511	32273	82399	...	4939
383 Electrical machinery	65429	72128	120023	220735	22253	27912	50474	111989	3285	4677
3831 Electrical industrial machinery	23023	25807	40612	100893	8912	10489	18129	61077	...	2867
3832 Radio, television and communication equipm.	11148	5730	5033	12653	3408	2112	1527	3657	...	22
3833 Electrical appliances and housewares	5363	3598	6698	14187	2581	1396	2803	5856	...	32
3839 Other electrical apparatus and supplies	25895	36993	67680	93002	7352	13915	28015	41399	...	1756
384 Transport equipment	174977	239939	475836	937675	65635	95133	205159	401808	6858	17628
3841 Shipbuilding and repairing	1584	1327	4231	21015	552	831	2104	17896	...	13
3842 Railroad equipment	-	-	-	501	-	-	-	25	...	38
3843 Motor vehicles	172827	238139	470161	910279	64912	94165	202513	382478	...	17600
3844 Motorcycles and bicycles	541	458	1111	4220	166	127	367	704	...	26
3845 Aircraft	-	-	-	-	-	-	-	-	...	-
3849 Other transport equipment	...b/	15	333	1660	...b/	10	175	705	...	-49
385 Professional and scientific equipment	13665	31814	43282	37188	4009	16565	13037	18006	284	1293
3851 Prof. and scientific equipment n.e.c.	13236	31047	41605	30460	3847	16217	12195	13606	...	341
3852 Photographic and optical goods	404	693	1677	6728	150	320	842	4400	...	952
3853 Watches and clocks	...b/	74	-	-	...b/	28	-	-	...	-
390 Other manufacturing industries	11373	14918	24752	45874	4341	5869	11738	21841	588	1600
3901 Jewellery and related articles	1209	1169	1556	603	354	204	711	180	...	81
3902 Musical instruments	...b/	12	27	65	...b/	10	21	233	...	1
3903 Sporting and athletic goods	297	369	1258	3868	114	173	565	742	...	67
3909 Manufacturing industries, n.e.c.	9863	13368	21911	41338	3870	5482	10441	20686	...	1451
3 Total manufacturing	2474964	3486113	6160881	12452570	1025579	1522166	2841986	6519118	199818	1168494

a/ Data are provisional.
b/ Data suppressed due to confidentiality rules.

Venezuela

ISIC Revision 2		Index numbers of industrial production											
		(1990=100)											
ISIC Industry	Note	1985	1986	1987	1988	1989	1990	1991	1992	1993	1994	1995	1996
311/2 Food products		...	...	...	...	...	...	...	...	...	...	...	...
313 Beverages		...	...	...	...	...	...	...	...	...	...	...	...
314 Tobacco		...	...	...	...	...	...	...	...	...	...	...	...
321 Textiles		...	...	...	...	...	...	...	...	...	...	...	...
322 Wearing apparel, except footwear		...	...	...	...	...	...	...	...	...	...	...	...
323 Leather and fur products		...	...	...	...	...	...	...	...	...	...	...	...
324 Footwear, except rubber or plastic		...	...	...	...	...	...	...	...	...	...	...	...
331 Wood products, except furniture		...	...	...	...	...	...	...	...	...	...	...	...
332 Furniture and fixtures, excl. metal		...	...	...	...	...	...	...	...	...	...	...	...
341 Paper and products		...	...	...	...	...	...	...	...	...	...	...	...
342 Printing and publishing		...	...	...	...	...	...	...	...	...	...	...	...
351 Industrial chemicals		...	...	...	...	...	...	...	...	...	...	...	...
352 Other chemicals		...	...	...	...	...	...	...	...	...	...	...	...
353 Petroleum refineries		...	...	...	...	...	...	...	...	...	...	...	...
354 Misc. petroleum and coal products		...	...	...	...	...	...	...	...	...	...	...	...
355 Rubber products		...	...	...	...	...	...	...	...	...	...	...	...
356 Plastic products		...	...	...	...	...	...	...	...	...	...	...	...
361 Pottery, china, earthenware		...	...	...	...	...	...	...	...	...	...	...	...
362 Glass and products		...	...	...	...	...	...	...	...	...	...	...	...
369 Other non-metallic mineral products		...	...	...	...	...	...	...	...	...	...	...	...
371 Iron and steel		...	...	...	...	...	...	...	...	...	...	...	...
372 Non-ferrous metals		...	...	...	...	...	...	...	...	...	...	...	...
381 Fabricated metal products		...	...	...	...	...	...	...	...	...	...	...	...
382 Non-electrical machinery		...	...	...	...	...	...	...	...	...	...	...	...
383 Electrical machinery		...	...	...	...	...	...	...	...	...	...	...	...
384 Transport equipment		...	...	...	...	...	...	...	...	...	...	...	...
385 Professional and scientific equipment		...	...	...	...	...	...	...	...	...	...	...	...
390 Other manufacturing industries		...	...	...	...	...	...	...	...	...	...	...	...
3 Total manufacturing		...	...	...	...	...	...	...	...	...	...	...	...

YEMEN

Supplier of information:
Ministry of Planning and Development, Central Statistical Organisation, Republic of Yemen, Sana'a.

Basic source of data:
Industrial survey.

Major deviations from ISIC (Revision 2):
None reported.

Reference period (if not calendar year):

Scope:
Complete coverage of the establishments with 10 or more persons engaged. Small and medium-scale industry is not included.

Method of enumeration:
Not reported.

Adjusted for non-response:
Not reported.

Concepts and definitions of variables:
No deviations from the standard UN concepts and definitions are reported.

Related national publications:
Statistical Yearbook, Ministry of Planning and Development, Central Statistical Organization, Republic of Yemen, Sana'a.

Yemen

ISIC Revision 2	Number of establishments					Number of employees					Wages and salaries paid to employees				
		(numbers)					(numbers)					(thousand RIALS)			
ISIC Industry	Note	1993	1994	1995	1996	Note	1993	1994	1995	1996	Note	1993	1994	1995	1996
311/2 Food products		59a/	57a/	59	61		12407a/	11760a/	9466	9495		...	...	...	...
3111 Slaughtering, preparing & preserving meat		...	...	1	1		...	...	111	111		...	...	...	...
3112 Dairy products		...	...	6	6		...	...	2059	2059		...	...	...	...
3113 Canning, preserving of fruits & vegetables		...	...	3	3		...	...	529	529		...	...	...	...
3114 Canning, preserving and processing of fish		...	...	9	9		...	...	1608	1608		...	...	...	...
3115 Vegetable and animal oils and fats		...	...	4	4		...	...	1258	1258		...	...	...	...
3116 Grain mill products		...	...	4	4		...	...	816	816		...	...	...	...
3117 Bakery products		...	...	14	15		...	...	411	426		...	...	...	...
3118 Sugar factories and refineries		...	...	-	-		...	...	-	-		...	...	...	...
3119 Cocoa, chocolate and sugar confectionery		...	...	9	10		...	...	2435	2449		...	...	...	...
3121 Other food products		...	...	9	9		...	...	239	239		...	...	...	...
3122 Prepared animal feeds		...	...	-	-		...	...	-	-		...	...	...	...
313 Beverages		...a/	...a/	8	9		...a/	...a/	1715	1795		...	...	...	...
3131 Distilling, rectifying and blending spirits		...	...	-	-		...	...	-	-		...	...	...	...
3132 Wine industries		...	...	-	-		...	...	-	-		...	...	...	...
3133 Malt liquors and malt		...	...	-	-		...	...	-	-		...	...	...	...
3134 Soft drinks and carbonated waters		...	...	8	9		...	...	1715	1795		...	...	...	...
314 Tobacco		...a/	...a/	3	3		...a/	...a/	961	961		...	...	...	...
321 Textiles		27b/	11b/	15	15		3989b/	3205b/	2248	2248		...	...	...	...
3211 Spinning, weaving and finishing textiles		...	...	2	2		...	...	1791	1791		...	...	...	...
3212 Made-up textile goods excl. wearing apparel		...	...	-	-		...	...	-	-		...	...	...	...
3213 Knitting mills		...	...	9	9		...	...	209	209		...	...	...	...
3214 Carpets and rugs		...	...	1	1		...	...	21	21		...	...	...	...
3215 Cordage, rope and twine		...	...	-	-		...	...	-	-		...	...	...	...
3219 Other textiles		...	...	3	3		...	...	227	227		...	...	...	...
322 Wearing apparel, except footwear		...b/	...b/	5	8		...b/	...b/	336	367		...	...	...	...
323 Leather and fur products		...b/	...b/	2	3		...b/	...b/	228	238		...	...	...	...
3231 Tanneries and leather finishing		...	...	1	2		...	...	212	222		...	...	...	...
3232 Fur dressing and dyeing industries		...	...	-	-		...	...	-	-		...	...	...	...
3233 Leather prods. excl. wearing apparel		...	...	1	1		...	...	16	16		...	...	...	...
324 Footwear, except rubber or plastic		...b/	...b/	7	8		...b/	...b/	380	400		...	...	...	...
331 Wood products, except furniture		6c/	5c/	9	9		1015c/	216c/	339	339		...	...	...	...
3311 Sawmills, planing and other wood mills		...	...	...	...		...	...	...	...		...	...	...	...
3312 Wooden and cane containers		...	...	...	...		...	...	...	...		...	...	...	...
3319 Other wood and cork products		...	...	...	...		...	...	...	...		...	...	...	...
332 Furniture and fixtures, excl. metal		...c/	...c/	8	8		...c/	...c/	754	764		...	...	...	...
341 Paper and products		10d/	7d/	9	9		1309d/	991d/	617	617		...	...	...	...
3411 Pulp, paper and paperboard articles		...	...	8	8		...	...	546	546		...	...	...	...
3412 Containers of paper and paperboard		...	...	1	1		...	...	71	71		...	...	...	...
3419 Other pulp, paper and paperboard articles		...	...	-	-		...	...	-	-		...	...	...	...
342 Printing and publishing		...d/	...d/	16	17		...d/	...d/	1066	1181		...	...	...	...
351 Industrial chemicals		48e/	43e/	22	22		7196e/	7150e/	2820	2820		...	...	...	...
3511 Basic chemicals excl. fertilizers		...	...	-	-		...	...	-	-		...	...	...	...
3512 Fertilizers and pesticides		...	...	1	1		...	...	17	17		...	...	...	...
3513 Synthetic resins and plastic materials		...	...	21	21		...	...	2803	2803		...	...	...	...
352 Other chemicals		...e/	...e/	13	13		...e/	...e/	2342	2342		...	...	...	...
3521 Paints, varnishes and lacquers		...	...	4	4		...	...	500	500		...	...	...	...
3522 Drugs and medicines		...	...	2	2		...	...	218	218		...	...	...	...
3523 Soap, cleaning preps., perfumes, cosmetics		...	...	7	7		...	...	1624	1624		...	...	...	...
3529 Other chemical products		...	...	-	-		...	...	-	-		...	...	...	...
353 Petroleum refineries		...e/	...e/	2	2		...e/	...e/	2596	2596		...	...	...	...

ISIC	Industry												
354	Misc. petroleum and coal products	...e/	...e/	-	-	...e/	...e/	-	-	...	...	...	...
355	Rubber products	...e/	...e/	1	1	...e/	...e/	40	40	...	...	...	...
3551	Tyres and tubes	...	...	-	-	...	...	-	-	...	...	...	...
3559	Other rubber products	...	...	1	1	...	...	40	40	...	...	...	...
356	Plastic products	...e/	...e/	-	-	...e/	...e/	-	-	...	...	...	...
361	Pottery, china, earthenware	18f/	18f/	-	-	2549f/	2386f/	-	-	...	...	...	...
362	Glass and products	...f/	...f/	-	-	...f/	...f/	-	-	...	...	...	...
369	Other non-metallic mineral products	...f/	...f/	36	39	...f/	...f/	2785	2851	...	...	...	...
3691	Structural clay products	...	...	2	5	...	...	61	127	...	...	...	...
3692	Cement, lime and plaster	...	...	4	4	...	...	1814	1814	...	...	...	...
3699	Other non-metallic mineral products	...	...	30	30	...	...	910	910	...	...	...	...
371	Iron and steel	27g/	19g/	-	-	1834g/	1155g/	-	-	...	...	...	...
372	Non-ferrous metals	...g/	...g/	-	-	...g/	...g/	-	-	...	...	...	...
381	Fabricated metal products	...g/	...g/	47	48	...g/	...g/	1766	1766	...	...	...	...
3811	Cutlery, hand tools and general hardware	...	...	7	7	...	...	559	559	...	...	...	...
3812	Furniture and fixtures primarily of metal	...	...	10	10	...	...	325	325	...	...	...	...
3813	Structural metal products	...	...	-	-	...	...	-	-	...	...	...	...
3819	Other fabricated metal products	...	...	30	31	...	...	882	882	...	...	...	...
382	Non-electrical machinery	...g/	...g/	-	-	...g/	...g/	-	-	...	...	...	...
3821	Engines and turbines	...	...	-	-	...	...	-	-	...	...	...	...
3822	Agricultural machinery and equipment	...	...	-	-	...	...	-	-	...	...	...	...
3823	Metal and wood working machinery	...	...	-	-	...	...	-	-	...	...	...	...
3824	Other special industrial machinery	...	...	-	-	...	...	-	-	...	...	...	...
3825	Office, computing and accounting machinery	...	...	-	-	...	...	-	-	...	...	...	...
3829	Other non-electrical machinery & equipment	...	...	-	-	...	...	-	-	...	...	...	...
383	Electrical machinery	...g/	...g/	-	-	...g/	...g/	-	-	...	...	...	...
3831	Electrical industrial machinery	...	...	-	-	...	...	-	-	...	...	...	...
3832	Radio, television and communication equipm.	...	...	-	-	...	...	-	-	...	...	...	...
3833	Electrical appliances and housewares	...	...	-	-	...	...	-	-	...	...	...	...
3839	Other electrical apparatus and supplies	...	...	-	-	...	...	-	-	...	...	...	...
384	Transport equipment	...g/	...g/	-	-	...g/	...g/	-	-	...	...	...	...
3841	Shipbuilding and repairing	...	...	-	-	...	...	-	-	...	...	...	...
3842	Railroad equipment	...	...	-	-	...	...	-	-	...	...	...	...
3843	Motor vehicles	...	...	-	-	...	...	-	-	...	...	...	...
3844	Motorcycles and bicycles	...	...	-	-	...	...	-	-	...	...	...	...
3845	Aircraft	...	...	-	-	...	...	-	-	...	...	...	...
3849	Other transport equipment	...	...	-	-	...	...	-	-	...	...	...	...
385	Professional and scientific equipment	...g/	...g/	-	-	...g/	...g/	-	-	...	...	...	...
3851	Prof. and scientific equipment n.e.c.	...	...	-	-	...	...	-	-	...	...	...	...
3852	Photographic and optical goods	...	...	-	-	...	...	-	-	...	...	...	...
3853	Watches and clocks	...	...	-	-	...	...	-	-	...	...	...	...
390	Other manufacturing industries	...	...	-	-	...	...	-	-	...	...	...	...
3901	Jewellery and related articles	...	...	-	-	...	...	-	-	...	...	...	...
3902	Musical instruments	...	...	-	-	...	...	-	-	...	...	...	...
3903	Sporting and athletic goods	...	...	-	-	...	...	-	-	...	...	...	...
3909	Manufacturing industries, n.e.c.	...	...	-	-	...	...	-	-	...	...	...	...
3	Total manufacturing	195	160	262	275	30299	26863	30459	30820	...	...	...	...

a/ 311/2 includes 313 and 314.
b/ 321 includes 322, 323 and 324.
c/ 331 includes 332.
d/ 341 includes 342.
e/ 351 includes 352, 353, 354, 355 and 356.
f/ 361 includes 362 and 369.
g/ 371 includes 372, 381, 382, 383, 384 and 385.

Yemen

ISIC Revision 2	Output					Value added					Gross fixed capital formation		
		(million RIALS)					(million RIALS)					(million RIALS)	
ISIC Industry	Note	1993	1994	1995	1996	Note	1993	1994	1995	1996	Note	1995	1996
311/2 Food products		20328.8a/	27225.5a/	...	...		...	...	...	...		...	...
313 Beverages		...a/	...a/	...	...		...	...	...	...		...	...
314 Tobacco		...a/	...a/	...	...		...	...	...	...		...	...
321 Textiles		540.4b/	723.5b/	...	...		...	...	...	...		...	...
322 Wearing apparel, except footwear		...b/	...b/	...	...		...	...	...	...		...	...
323 Leather and fur products		...b/	...b/	...	...		...	...	...	...		...	...
324 Footwear, except rubber or plastic		...b/	...b/	...	...		...	...	...	...		...	...
331 Wood products, except furniture		195.7c/	242.4c/	...	...		...	...	...	...		...	...
332 Furniture and fixtures, excl. metal		...c/	...c/	...	...		...	...	...	...		...	...
341 Paper and products		2581.0d/	3599.3d/	...	...		...	...	...	...		...	...
342 Printing and publishing		...d/	...d/	...	...		...	...	...	...		...	...
351 Industrial chemicals		9509.0e/	5618.6e/	...	...		...	...	...	...		...	...
352 Other chemicals		...e/	...e/	...	...		...	...	...	...		...	...
353 Petroleum refineries		...e/	...e/	...	...		...	...	...	...		...	...
354 Misc. petroleum and coal products		...e/	...e/	...	...		...	...	...	...		...	...
355 Rubber products		...e/	...e/	...	...		...	...	...	...		...	...
356 Plastic products		...e/	...e/	...	...		...	...	...	...		...	...
361 Pottery, china, earthenware		2791.0f/	4481.7f/	...	...		...	...	...	...		...	...
362 Glass and products		...f/	...f/	...	...		...	...	...	...		...	...
369 Other non-metallic mineral products		...f/	...f/	...	...		...	...	...	...		...	...
371 Iron and steel		533.0g/	632.2g/	...	...		...	...	...	...		...	...
372 Non-ferrous metals		...g/	...g/	...	...		...	...	...	...		...	...
381 Fabricated metal products		...g/	...g/	...	...		...	...	...	...		...	...
382 Non-electrical machinery		...g/	...g/	...	...		...	...	...	...		...	...
383 Electrical machinery		...g/	...g/	...	...		...	...	...	...		...	...
384 Transport equipment		...g/	...g/	...	...		...	...	...	...		...	...
385 Professional and scientific equipment		...g/	...g/	...	...		...	...	...	...		...	...
390 Other manufacturing industries		...	...	...	...		...	...	...	...		...	...
3 Total manufacturing		36478.9	42523.2	...	...		...	...	...	...		...	...

a/ 311/2 includes 313 and 314.
b/ 321 includes 322, 323 and 324.
c/ 331 includes 332.
d/ 341 includes 342.
e/ 351 includes 352, 353, 354, 355 and 356.
f/ 361 includes 362 and 369.
g/ 371 includes 372, 381, 382, 383, 384 and 385.

Yemen

ISIC Revision 2		Index numbers of industrial production											
		(1990=100)											
ISIC Industry	Note	1985	1986	1987	1988	1989	1990	1991	1992	1993	1994	1995	1996
311/2 Food products		...	...	...	...	...	...	...	...	...	...	...	...
313 Beverages		...	...	...	...	...	...	...	...	...	...	...	...
314 Tobacco		...	...	...	...	...	...	...	...	...	...	...	...
321 Textiles		...	...	...	...	...	...	...	...	...	...	...	...
322 Wearing apparel, except footwear		...	...	...	...	...	...	...	...	...	...	...	...
323 Leather and fur products		...	...	...	...	...	...	...	...	...	...	...	...
324 Footwear, except rubber or plastic		...	...	...	...	...	...	...	...	...	...	...	...
331 Wood products, except furniture		...	...	...	...	...	...	...	...	...	...	...	...
332 Furniture and fixtures, excl. metal		...	...	...	...	...	...	...	...	...	...	...	...
341 Paper and products		...	...	...	...	...	...	...	...	...	...	...	...
342 Printing and publishing		...	...	...	...	...	...	...	...	...	...	...	...
351 Industrial chemicals		...	...	...	...	...	...	...	...	...	...	...	...
352 Other chemicals		...	...	...	...	...	...	...	...	...	...	...	...
353 Petroleum refineries		78	74	77	78	79	100	107	113	124	77	108	...
354 Misc. petroleum and coal products		...	...	...	...	...	...	...	...	...	...	...	...
355 Rubber products		...	...	...	...	...	...	...	...	...	...	...	...
356 Plastic products		...	...	...	...	...	...	...	...	...	...	...	...
361 Pottery, china, earthenware		...	...	...	...	...	...	...	...	...	...	...	...
362 Glass and products		...	...	...	...	...	...	...	...	...	...	...	...
369 Other non-metallic mineral products		...	...	...	...	...	...	...	...	...	...	...	...
371 Iron and steel		...	...	...	...	...	...	...	...	...	...	...	...
372 Non-ferrous metals		...	...	...	...	...	...	...	...	...	...	...	...
381 Fabricated metal products		...	...	...	...	...	...	...	...	...	...	...	...
382 Non-electrical machinery		...	...	...	...	...	...	...	...	...	...	...	...
383 Electrical machinery		...	...	...	...	...	...	...	...	...	...	...	...
384 Transport equipment		...	...	...	...	...	...	...	...	...	...	...	...
385 Professional and scientific equipment		...	...	...	...	...	...	...	...	...	...	...	...
390 Other manufacturing industries		...	...	...	...	...	...	...	...	...	...	...	...
3 Total manufacturing		...	...	...	...	...	...	...	...	...	...	...	...

YUGOSLAVIA

Supplier of information:
Federal Statistical Office, Federal Republic of Yugoslavia, Belgrade.

Basic source of data:
Not reported.

Major deviations from ISIC (Revision 2):
None reported.

Reference period (if not calendar year):

Scope:
Not reported.

Method of enumeration:
Not reported.

Adjusted for non-response:
Not reported.

Concepts and definitions of variables:
Figures for wages and salaries are computed by UNIDO from reported monthly wages and salaries per employee.

Related national publications:

Yugoslavia

ISIC Revision 2	Number of establishments					Number of employees					Wages and salaries paid to employees				
		(numbers)					(thousands)					(million DINARS)			
ISIC Industry	Note	1993	1994	1995	1996	Note	1993	1994	1995	1996	Note	1993	1994	1995	1996
311/2 Food products		2585	2629	2895	3007		94.7	93.3	92.8	93.3		...	323.6	486.6	889.0
313 Beverages		641	709	748	626		17.5	18.2	19.2	19.5		...	70.3	111.5	223.9
314 Tobacco		23	21	22	21		4.8	5.0	4.8	5.1		...	17.9	50.3	58.7
321 Textiles		1227	1275	1301	1361		78.3	74.6	73.7	69.9		...	124.4	173.3	253.3
322 Wearing apparel, except footwear		1204	1232	1229	1260		72.6	68.9	67.0	65.2		...	91.8	125.4	207.3
323 Leather and fur products		305	308	523	526		12.8	12.4	11.5	10.4		...	21.0	33.1	45.4
324 Footwear, except rubber or plastic		192	204	215	283		28.7	27.2	26.2	24.3		...	41.1	57.9	77.6
331 Wood products, except furniture		2851	2982	3881	3649		19.7	19.3	19.4	19.6		...	37.3	62.2	91.7
332 Furniture and fixtures, excl. metal		641	664	672	692		21.2	20.5	19.4	19.1		...	42.1	67.0	108.6
341 Paper and products		829	863	904	901		12.9	12.6	13.1	13.4		...	39.3	62.7	91.8
342 Printing and publishing		1503	1536	1587	1590		27.1	24.1	26.1	26.0		...	70.6	122.5	255.5
351 Industrial chemicals		263	276	283	293		24.7	24.5	24.3	23.2		...	73.2	106.7	248.6
352 Other chemicals		705	763	819	815		17.0	17.2	17.3	17.9		...	77.6	120.6	227.3
353 Petroleum refineries		4	5	6	8		4.6	4.5	4.4	4.5		...	17.9	37.0	79.3
354 Misc. petroleum and coal products		2	2	4	3		0.9	0.9	1.0	1.0		...	2.8	5.2	10.5
355 Rubber products		132	135	133	136		17.5	17.2	15.8	15.4		...	41.9	56.7	95.7
356 Plastic products		1172	1215	799	1310		10.2	9.5	9.7	10.4		...	27.2	42.5	87.2
361 Pottery, china, earthenware		65	64	65	87		6.1	6.3	6.6	6.4		...	17.7	22.1	25.9
362 Glass and products		57	58	56	74		9.5	9.0	8.2	8.1		...	18.1	36.4	47.5
369 Other non-metallic mineral products		511	521	524	590		33.2	31.7	31.0	31.8		...	98.9	144.7	299.9
371 Iron and steel		30	31	32	33		18.2	17.5	15.9	17.1		...	44.3	72.7	113.9
372 Non-ferrous metals		105	104	121	123		17.8	17.7	17.3	17.5		...	43.1	99.0	191.7
381 Fabricated metal products		4272	4352	4280	4323		94.7	90.7	87.5	83.0		...	209.0	306.6	417.3
382 Non-electrical machinery		439	454	612	493		58.5	57.0	55.9	52.1		...	130.6	203.3	257.6
383 Electrical machinery		2253	2278	2332	2495		55.5	51.6	50.8	49.7		...	109.6	180.4	315.5
384 Transport equipment		338	346	348	364		81.0	80.1	76.1	73.0		...	149.0	202.7	309.2
385 Professional and scientific equipment		152	154	157	165		4.1	3.9	3.8	3.8		...	11.9	15.5	17.7
390 Other manufacturing industries		338	356	355	356		9.5	9.3	9.1	8.7		...	23.3	36.7	48.3
3 Total manufacturing		22839	23537	24903	25584		853.3	824.7	807.9	789.4		...	1975.5	3041.4	5096.2

Yugoslavia

ISIC Revision 2	Output					Value added					Gross fixed capital formation		
	Note	(million DINARS)				Note	(million DINARS)				Note	(million DINARS)	
ISIC Industry		1993	1994	1995	1996		1993	1994	1995	1996		1995	1996
311/2 Food products		...	3849	7605	14862		...	1432	2597	4355		158.4	367.5
313 Beverages		...	714	1421	2880		...	372	723	1509		51.2	177.0
314 Tobacco		...	267	739	742		...	129	542	406		57.5	104.0
321 Textiles		...	378	1257	1944		...	388	686	909		13.4	69.0
322 Wearing apparel, except footwear		...	389	663	1120		...	178	331	581		26.2	15.7
323 Leather and fur products		...	159	285	472		...	75	126	203		8.3	10.2
324 Footwear, except rubber or plastic		...	243	310	484		...	100	142	228		1.5	1.9
331 Wood products, except furniture		...	300	575	1037		...	111	221	383		6.0	8.5
332 Furniture and fixtures, excl. metal		...	310	548	949		...	125	240	387		7.3	11.8
341 Paper and products		...	375	946	1330		...	151	387	423		13.0	15.8
342 Printing and publishing		...	631	1352	2462		...	315	658	1125		30.0	35.1
351 Industrial chemicals		...	548	899	2489		...	244	324	460		22.5	36.0
352 Other chemicals		...	991	2709	3871		...	529	1009	2037		173.5	200.3
353 Petroleum refineries		...	359	613	1074		...	214	287	175		15.2	50.6
354 Misc. petroleum and coal products		...	14	29	62		...	8	14	30		1.9	3.1
355 Rubber products		...	274	408	1064		...	145	204	430		54.5	28.0
356 Plastic products		...	281	626	924		...	133	282	382		10.5	18.0
361 Pottery, china, earthenware		...	65	120	252		...	38	72	144		1.7	12.4
362 Glass and products		...	120	223	364		...	38	109	161		4.4	6.2
369 Other non-metallic mineral products		...	580	1124	2377		...	248	492	1064		28.5	66.5
371 Iron and steel		...	357	615	1867		...	150	178	348		9.5	18.0
372 Non-ferrous metals		...	659	1332	2500		...	205	461	572		11.7	149.8
381 Fabricated metal products		...	1235	2358	3903		...	597	1148	1706		40.1	35.5
382 Non-electrical machinery		...	606	1054	1897		...	330	579	975		9.4	12.5
383 Electrical machinery		...	997	1993	3993		...	456	840	1382		17.0	26.9
384 Transport equipment		...	663	1195	2246		...	357	673	1221		35.2	51.0
385 Professional and scientific equipment		...	42	82	170		...	25	49	99		1.1	7.3
390 Other manufacturing industries		...	79	115	151		...	37	60	82		3.5	4.2
3 Total manufacturing		...	15485	31193	57486		...	7130	13434	21777		813.0	1542.8

Yugoslavia

ISIC Revision 2		Index numbers of industrial production (1990=100)											
ISIC Industry	Note	1985	1986	1987	1988	1989	1990	1991	1992	1993	1994	1995	1996
311/2 Food products	a/	...	...	...	...	...	100	95	79	57	58	62	64
313 Beverages	a/	...	...	...	...	...	...	...	...	...	...	...	...
314 Tobacco		...	...	...	...	...	100	103	101	87	83	77	73
321 Textiles		...	...	...	...	...	100	81	62	35	36	33	33
322 Wearing apparel, except footwear		...	...	...	...	...	100	87	62	28	30	24	26
323 Leather and fur products	b/	...	...	...	...	...	100	71	60	40	34	25	29
324 Footwear, except rubber or plastic	b/	...	...	...	...	...	...	...	...	...	...	...	...
331 Wood products, except furniture		...	...	...	...	...	100	84	79	57	48	50	48
332 Furniture and fixtures, excl. metal	c/	...	...	...	...	...	...	...	...	...	...	...	...
341 Paper and products		...	...	...	...	...	100	86	69	34	35	39	37
342 Printing and publishing		...	...	...	...	...	100	91	67	43	41	43	51
351 Industrial chemicals	d/	...	...	...	...	...	100	85	70	32	36	41	56
352 Other chemicals	d/	...	...	...	...	...	...	...	...	...	...	...	...
353 Petroleum refineries	e/	...	...	...	...	...	100	75	50	22	20	22	32
354 Misc. petroleum and coal products	e/	...	...	...	...	...	...	...	...	...	...	...	...
355 Rubber products	f/	...	...	...	...	...	100	86	64	21	27	28	36
356 Plastic products	f/	...	...	...	...	...	...	...	...	...	...	...	...
361 Pottery, china, earthenware	g/	...	...	...	...	...	100	87	72	37	41	44	55
362 Glass and products	g/	...	...	...	...	...	...	...	...	...	...	...	...
369 Other non-metallic mineral products	g/	...	...	...	...	...	...	...	...	...	...	...	...
371 Iron and steel	h/	...	...	...	...	...	100	79	55	22	23	28	40
372 Non-ferrous metals	h/	...	...	...	...	...	...	...	...	...	...	...	...
381 Fabricated metal products		...	...	...	...	...	100	79	58	30	24	24	24
382 Non-electrical machinery		...	...	...	...	...	100	49	33	16	11	11	11
383 Electrical machinery		...	...	...	...	...	100	65	43	16	21	23	25
384 Transport equipment		...	...	...	...	...	100	69	40	16	15	15	17
385 Professional and scientific equipment		...	...	...	...	...	100	67	47	19	25	32	29
390 Other manufacturing industries	c/	...	...	...	...	...	100	87	67	42	41	40	39
3 Total manufacturing		...	...	...	...	...	100	81	61	34	34	35	39

a/ 311/2 includes 313.
b/ 323 includes 324.
c/ 390 includes 332.
d/ 351 includes 352.
e/ 353 includes 354.
f/ 355 includes 356.
g/ 361 includes 362 and 369.
h/ 371 includes 372.

ZIMBABWE

Supplier of information:
Central Statistical Office, Harare.

Basic source of data:
Annual census of production.

Major deviations from ISIC (Revision 2):
Data collected under the national classification system have been reclassified by the national authorities to correspond approximately with ISIC (Rev. 2). Footwear made of vulcanized or moulded rubber (part of ISIC 355) and footwear made of plastic (part of ISIC 356) are included in ISIC 324.

Reference period (if not calendar year):
Fiscal year beginning 1 April of the year indicated.

Scope:
All public and private establishments engaged in manufacturing. Establishments with an annual output of less than 2,000 dollars are excluded. Also excluded are establishments that are mainly in the nature of self-employed, such as dressmakers, tailors, and cabinet makers.

Method of enumeration:
Questionnaires were distributed by mail with follow-up site visits as required.

Adjusted for non-response:
Yes.

Concepts and definitions of variables:
Number of employees includes working proprietors and family members if they are paid a definite wage or salary.
Wages and salaries is compensation of employees.
Output includes gross revenues from goods shipped in the same condition as received.
Gross fixed capital formation includes progress payments for fixed assets on order.

Related national publications:
The Census of Production (annual); Monthly Digest of Statistics, both published by the Central Statistical Office, Harare.

Zimbabwe

ISIC Revision 2	Number of establishments					Number of employees					Wages and salaries paid to employees				
		(numbers)					(numbers)					(million DOLLARS)			
ISIC Industry	Note	1992	1993	1994	1995	Note	1992	1993	1994	1995	Note	1992	1993	1994	1995
311/2 Food products		100	95	100	97		26560	24700	24100	24000		428.9	402.7	508.8	665.1
3111 Slaughtering, preparing & preserving meat		7	7	6	5		4800	4500	4200	3600		86.4	99.8	109.9	135.8
3112 Dairy products	a/	17	15	19	16	a/	8700	7500	7500	6900	a/	141.2	124.0	182.5	243.7
3113 Canning, preserving of fruits & vegetables	a/	...	...	...	...	a/	...	...	...	...	a/	...	...	...	...
3114 Canning, preserving and processing of fish	a/	...	...	...	...	a/	...	...	...	...	a/	...	...	...	...
3115 Vegetable and animal oils and fats	a/	...	...	...	...	a/	...	...	...	...	a/	...	...	...	...
3116 Grain mill products	b/	10	7	6	7	b/	6860	6200	6600	6600	b/	103.7	110.1	133.3	157.9
3117 Bakery products		60	60	63	63		4900	5200	4400	5500		87.5	55.8	67.3	108.3
3118 Sugar factories and refineries	a/	...	...	...	...	a/	...	...	...	...	a/	...	...	...	...
3119 Cocoa, chocolate and sugar confectionery		6	6	6	6		1300	1300	1400	1400		10.1	13.0	15.8	19.4
3121 Other food products	a/	...	...	...	...	a/	...	...	...	...	a/	...	...	...	...
3122 Prepared animal feeds	b/	...	...	...	...	b/	...	...	...	...	b/	...	...	...	...
313 Beverages		17	19	19	20		6000	6900	7000	7500		120.3	149.0	189.1	266.8
3131 Distilling, rectifying and blending spirits	c/	9	11	10	10	c/	3500	4300	4300	4800	c/	72.9	93.7	116.0	161.6
3132 Wine industries	c/	...	...	...	...	c/	...	...	...	...	c/	...	...	...	...
3133 Malt liquors and malt	c/	...	...	...	...	c/	...	...	...	...	c/	...	...	...	...
3134 Soft drinks and carbonated waters		8	8	9	10		2500	2600	2700	2700		47.4	55.3	73.1	105.2
314 Tobacco		8	7	5	5		6400	5800	2800	4400		84.7	93.2	95.9	117.5
321 Textiles		50	50	48	45		23700	20800	17400	17700		236.8	282.7	273.6	308.8
3211 Spinning, weaving and finishing textiles	d/	25	25	23	23	d/	19300	16100	12400	13300	d/	193.6	228.0	198.8	226.7
3212 Made-up textile goods excl. wearing apparel		-	-	-	-		-	-	-	-		-	-	-	-
3213 Knitting mills	e/	14	14	14	13	e/	2400	2400	2600	2500	e/	20.0	25.6	34.9	38.6
3214 Carpets and rugs	d/	...	...	...	...	d/	...	...	...	...	d/	...	...	...	...
3215 Cordage, rope and twine	e/	...	...	...	...	e/	...	...	...	...	e/	...	...	...	...
3219 Other textiles		11	11	11	9		2000	2300	2400	1900		23.2	29.1	39.9	43.5
322 Wearing apparel, except footwear		106	96	96	91		56700	17200	17800	16500		142.0	155.5	211.7	209.6
323 Leather and fur products		15	14	15	16		2300	2600	2700	1700		16.3	21.1	21.9	32.8
3231 Tanneries and leather finishing		...	...	...	...		...	...	...	...		...	...	...	...
3232 Fur dressing and dyeing industries		...	...	...	...		...	...	...	...		...	...	...	...
3233 Leather prods. excl. wearing apparel		...	...	...	...		...	...	...	...		...	...	...	...
324 Footwear, except rubber or plastic		15	14	15	14		5900	6200	6400	6100		67.9	76.9	95.2	115.3
331 Wood products, except furniture		26	24	27	26		5600	5800	6800	6800		65.8	70.7	198.2	114.8
3311 Sawmills, planing and other wood mills		...	...	...	...		...	...	...	...		...	...	...	...
3312 Wooden and cane containers		...	...	...	...		...	...	...	...		...	...	...	...
3319 Other wood and cork products		...	...	...	...		...	...	...	...		...	...	...	...
332 Furniture and fixtures, excl. metal		45	45	47	45		4900	5100	5700	5900		44.6	45.1	59.7	87.9
341 Paper and products		12	12	12	13		3700	4000	3600	4600		66.5	82.1	100.8	137.6
3411 Pulp, paper and paperboard articles	f/	12	12	12	13	f/	3700	4000	3600	4600	f/	66.5	82.1	100.8	137.6
3412 Containers of paper and paperboard		-	-	-	-		-	-	-	-		-	-	-	-
3419 Other pulp, paper and paperboard articles	f/	...	...	...	...	f/	...	...	...	...	f/	...	...	...	...
342 Printing and publishing		68	68	73	70		5000	5000	5500	5100		122.7	130.7	169.5	208.5
351 Industrial chemicals	g/	10	12	15	11	g/	2700	2700	2900	2900	g/	68.2	89.7	109.6	143.1
3511 Basic chemicals excl. fertilizers	h/	6	8	11	7	h/	400	400	600	500	h/	10.5	16.2	20.4	27.2
3512 Fertilizers and pesticides		4	4	4	4		2300	2300	2300	2400		57.7	73.5	89.2	115.9
3513 Synthetic resins and plastic materials	h/	...	...	...	...	h/	...	...	...	...	h/	...	...	...	...
352 Other chemicals		51	49	46	45		5500	5300	5300	5100		150.4	102.4	195.4	273.4
3521 Paints, varnishes and lacquers		5	5	5	4		700	800	700	600		14.3	16.6	26.4	78.5
3522 Drugs and medicines	i/	33	33	30	28	i/	3700	3500	3500	3200	i/	109.6	60.9	135.3	145.9
3523 Soap, cleaning preps., perfumes, cosmetics	i/	...	...	...	...	i/	...	...	...	...	i/	...	...	...	...
3529 Other chemical products		13	11	11	13		1100	1000	1100	1300		26.5	24.9	33.7	49.0
353 Petroleum refineries	g/h/	...	...	...	...	g/h/	...	...	...	...	g/h/	...	...	...	...

354 Misc. petroleum and coal products	g/h/	...	...	...	...	g/h/	...	...	...	...	g/h/	...	...	...	...
355 Rubber products		13	13	14	14		3100	3000	3100	3100		50.4	58.1	83.1	111.7
3551 Tyres and tubes		...	...	...	...		...	...	...	...		...	...	...	...
3559 Other rubber products		...	...	...	...		...	...	...	...		...	...	...	...
356 Plastic products		22	20	21	20		3800	3400	3500	3800		59.7	56.9	65.6	94.9
361 Pottery, china, earthenware		5	6	5	4		900	800	300	400		5.9	5.3	4.0	4.8
362 Glass and products		5	5	5	5		900	900	900	900		17.1	20.7	27.8	28.7
369 Other non-metallic mineral products		30	31	32	35		7000	6700	7100	7400		86.8	105.0	142.8	187.3
3691 Structural clay products		...	...	...	...		...	...	...	...		...	...	...	...
3692 Cement, lime and plaster		...	...	...	...		...	...	...	...		...	...	...	...
3699 Other non-metallic mineral products		...	...	...	...		...	...	...	...		...	...	...	...
371 Iron and steel		23	23	21	19		17100	14600	11900	12100		299.9	317.1	380.5	364.3
372 Non-ferrous metals		6	5	6	6		1400	1300	1200	1200		16.7	17.7	22.6	29.3
381 Fabricated metal products		171	161	178	175		14500	13200	15100	13400		186.5	214.2	297.3	387.9
3811 Cutlery, hand tools and general hardware		...	...	...	...		...	...	...	...		...	...	...	...
3812 Furniture and fixtures primarily of metal		...	...	...	...		...	...	...	...		...	...	...	...
3813 Structural metal products		...	...	...	...		...	...	...	...		...	...	...	...
3819 Other fabricated metal products		...	...	...	...		...	...	...	...		...	...	...	...
382 Non-electrical machinery		43	40	38	36		2500	2300	2400	2500		34.2	35.7	41.9	67.4
3821 Engines and turbines		...	...	...	...		...	...	...	...		...	...	...	...
3822 Agricultural machinery and equipment		...	...	...	...		...	...	...	...		...	...	...	...
3823 Metal and wood working machinery		...	...	...	...		...	...	...	...		...	...	...	...
3824 Other special industrial machinery		...	...	...	...		...	...	...	...		...	...	...	...
3825 Office, computing and accounting machinery		...	...	...	...		...	...	...	...		...	...	...	...
3829 Other non-electrical machinery & equipment		...	...	...	...		...	...	...	...		...	...	...	...
383 Electrical machinery		60	49	54	53		6200	5500	5500	5900		91.2	96.8	112.2	163.3
3831 Electrical industrial machinery		-	-	-	-		-	-	-	-		-	-	-	-
3832 Radio, television and communication equipm.		9	6	5	5		1200	800	800	1000		15.3	11.7	15.0	22.4
3833 Electrical appliances and housewares		-	-	-	-		-	-	-	-		-	-	-	-
3839 Other electrical apparatus and supplies		51	43	49	48		5000	4700	4700	4900		75.9	85.1	97.2	140.9
384 Transport equipment		56	54	53	50		6200	5900	5700	5300		111.5	124.2	141.9	174.0
3841 Shipbuilding and repairing		-	-	-	-		-	-	-	-		-	-	-	-
3842 Railroad equipment	j/	12	11	12	11	j/	1100	1100	800	500	j/	31.3	37.7	14.8	16.7
3843 Motor vehicles		44	43	41	39		5100	4800	4900	4800		80.2	86.5	127.1	157.3
3844 Motorcycles and bicycles	j/	...	...	...	...	j/	...	...	...	...	j/	...	...	...	...
3845 Aircraft	j/	...	...	...	...	j/	...	...	...	...	j/	...	...	...	...
3849 Other transport equipment	j/	...	...	...	...	j/	...	...	...	...	j/	...	...	...	...
385 Professional and scientific equipment		11	10	10	9		100	100	200	200		1.9	2.4	3.5	4.6
3851 Prof. and scientific equipment n.e.c.		...	...	...	...		...	...	...	-		...	...	...	...
3852 Photographic and optical goods		...	...	...	...		...	...	...	-		...	...	...	...
3853 Watches and clocks		...	...	...	...		...	...	...	-		...	...	...	...
390 Other manufacturing industries		46	44	44	42		1800	2900	2600	2700		17.2	22.6	30.4	39.2
3901 Jewellery and related articles		...	...	...	...		...	...	...	...		...	...	...	...
3902 Musical instruments		...	...	...	...		...	...	...	...		...	...	...	...
3903 Sporting and athletic goods		...	...	...	...		...	...	...	...		...	...	...	...
3909 Manufacturing industries, n.e.c.		...	...	...	...		...	...	...	...		...	...	...	...
3 Total manufacturing		1014	966	999	966		220460	172700	167500	167200		2594.1	2778.5	3583.0	4338.6

a/ 3112 includes 3113, 3114, 3115, 3118 and 3121.
b/ 3116 includes 3122.
c/ 3131 includes 3132 and 3133.
d/ 3211 includes 3214.
e/ 3213 includes 3215.
f/ 3411 includes 3419.
g/ 351 includes 353 and 354.
h/ 3511 includes 3513, 353 and 354.
i/ 3522 includes 3523.
j/ 3842 includes 3844, 3845 and 3849.

Zimbabwe

ISIC Revision 2	Output in factor values					Value added in factor values					Gross fixed capital formation		
		(million DOLLARS)					(million DOLLARS)					(million DOLLARS)	
ISIC Industry	Note	1992	1993	1994	1995	Note	1992	1993	1994	1995	Note	1994	1995
311/2 Food products		5106	5329	6746	7901		1833	2376	1962	2167		451	334
3111 Slaughtering, preparing & preserving meat		705	1047	1195	1480		276	478	427	241		...	...
3112 Dairy products	a/	1777	2047	2609	3034	a/	725	1044	528	811		...	...
3113 Canning, preserving of fruits & vegetables	a/	...	...	...	...	a/	...	...	...	...		...	...
3114 Canning, preserving and processing of fish	a/	...	...	...	...	a/	...	...	...	...		...	...
3115 Vegetable and animal oils and fats	a/	...	...	...	...	a/	...	...	...	...		...	...
3116 Grain mill products	b/	2004	1535	2050	2241	b/	595	596	568	544		...	...
3117 Bakery products		520	548	693	880		191	195	368	474		...	...
3118 Sugar factories and refineries	a/	...	...	...	...	a/	...	...	...	...		...	...
3119 Cocoa, chocolate and sugar confectionery		100	152	199	266		46	63	72	98		...	...
3121 Other food products	a/	...	...	...	...	a/	...	...	...	...		...	...
3122 Prepared animal feeds	b/	...	...	...	...	b/	...	...	...	...		...	...
313 Beverages		1516	1875	2237	2755		1098	1327	1555	2024		82	116
3131 Distilling, rectifying and blending spirits	c/	1078	1348	1518	1898	c/	828	1031	1113	1530		...	...
3132 Wine industries	c/	...	...	...	...	c/	...	...	...	...		...	...
3133 Malt liquors and malt	c/	...	...	...	...	c/	...	...	...	...		...	...
3134 Soft drinks and carbonated waters		438	527	719	857		270	296	442	494		...	...
314 Tobacco		608	649	972	1603		480	477	496	628		55	15
321 Textiles		1772	2584	2607	2792		804	857	944	1320		239	433
3211 Spinning, weaving and finishing textiles	d/	1434	2116	1981	2230	d/	680	712	703	1124		...	...
3212 Made-up textile goods excl. wearing apparel		-	-	-	-		-	-	-	-		...	...
3213 Knitting mills	e/	93	129	203	235	e/	42	62	97	111		...	...
3214 Carpets and rugs	d/	...	...	...	...	d/	...	...	...	...		...	...
3215 Cordage, rope and twine	e/	...	...	...	...	e/	...	...	...	...		...	...
3219 Other textiles		245	339	423	327		82	83	144	85		...	...
322 Wearing apparel, except footwear		694	853	1085	1096		301	320	429	443		18	27
323 Leather and fur products		124	133	155	201		50	42	47	61	f/	...	...
3231 Tanneries and leather finishing		...	...	...	...		...	...	...	...		...	...
3232 Fur dressing and dyeing industries		...	...	...	...		...	...	...	...		...	...
3233 Leather prods. excl. wearing apparel		...	...	...	...		...	...	...	...		...	...
324 Footwear, except rubber or plastic		482	541	647	672		220	248	238	300		18	6
331 Wood products, except furniture		335	395	738	591		199	237	384	374		275	164
3311 Sawmills, planing and other wood mills		...	...	...	...		...	...	...	...		...	...
3312 Wooden and cane containers		...	...	...	...		...	...	...	...		...	...
3319 Other wood and cork products		...	...	...	...		...	...	...	...		...	...
332 Furniture and fixtures, excl. metal		235	297	398	507		100	102	165	256		39	22
341 Paper and products		572	621	840	1056		267	258	276	328		48	68
3411 Pulp, paper and paperboard articles	g/	572	621	840	1056	g/	267	258	276	328		...	...
3412 Containers of paper and paperboard		-	-	-	-		-	-	-	-		...	...
3419 Other pulp, paper and paperboard articles	g/	...	...	...	...	g/	...	...	...	...		...	...
342 Printing and publishing		448	512	714	826		279	354	283	443		75	102
351 Industrial chemicals	h/	852	1318	1639	1943	h/	456	411	365	574	h/	14	30
3511 Basic chemicals excl. fertilizers	i/	101	145	169	241	i/	54	65	64	125		...	...
3512 Fertilizers and pesticides		751	1173	1470	1702		402	346	301	449		...	...
3513 Synthetic resins and plastic materials	i/	...	...	...	...	i/	...	...	...	...		...	...
352 Other chemicals		999	813	1676	1847		433	307	707	724		258	306
3521 Paints, varnishes and lacquers		185	187	291	193		65	60	91	66		...	...
3522 Drugs and medicines	j/	680	475	1136	1214	j/	292	175	499	419		...	...
3523 Soap, cleaning preps., perfumes, cosmetics	j/	...	...	...	...	j/	...	...	...	...		...	...
3529 Other chemical products		134	151	249	440		76	72	117	240		...	...
353 Petroleum refineries	h/i/	...	...	...	...	h/i/	...	...	...	...	h/	...	...

354 Misc. petroleum and coal products	h/i/	...	...	...	...	h/i/	...	...	...	...	h/	...	...
355 Rubber products		543	594	872	1031		193	238	340	400		24	50
3551 Tyres and tubes		...	...	...	...		...	...	...	...		...	...
3559 Other rubber products		...	...	...	...		...	...	...	...		...	...
356 Plastic products		430	429	527	572		140	132	244	191		76	44
361 Pottery, china, earthenware		22	17	14	15		16	9	8	10	k/	214	305
362 Glass and products		86	121	158	155		39	52	40	42	k/	...	...
369 Other non-metallic mineral products		532	602	905	1227		313	250	515	769	k/	...	...
3691 Structural clay products		...	...	...	...		...	...	...	...		...	...
3692 Cement, lime and plaster		...	...	...	...		...	...	...	...		...	...
3699 Other non-metallic mineral products		...	...	...	...		...	...	...	...		...	...
371 Iron and steel		2559	1894	2651	2750		1601	963	1433	1225	m/	312	442
372 Non-ferrous metals		176	159	208	252		80	58	71	114	m/	...	...
381 Fabricated metal products		1142	1223	1609	2046		542	519	682	912	n/	109	128
3811 Cutlery, hand tools and general hardware		...	...	...	...		...	...	...	...		...	...
3812 Furniture and fixtures primarily of metal		...	...	...	...		...	...	...	...		...	...
3813 Structural metal products		...	...	...	...		...	...	...	...		...	...
3819 Other fabricated metal products		...	...	...	...		...	...	...	...		...	...
382 Non-electrical machinery		208	196	235	352		113	103	117	176	n/	...	...
3821 Engines and turbines		...	...	...	...		...	...	...	...		...	...
3822 Agricultural machinery and equipment		...	...	...	...		...	...	...	...		...	...
3823 Metal and wood working machinery		...	...	...	...		...	...	...	...		...	...
3824 Other special industrial machinery		...	...	...	...		...	...	...	...		...	...
3825 Office, computing and accounting machinery		...	...	...	...		...	...	...	...		...	...
3829 Other non-electrical machinery & equipment		...	...	...	...		...	...	...	...		...	...
383 Electrical machinery		590	634	897	1127		307	325	390	524		62	29
3831 Electrical industrial machinery		-	-	-	-		-	-	-	-		...	...
3832 Radio, television and communication equipm.		69	69	105	127		30	30	18	32		...	...
3833 Electrical appliances and housewares		-	-	-	-		-	-	-	-		...	...
3839 Other electrical apparatus and supplies		521	565	792	1000		277	296	372	491		...	...
384 Transport equipment		1315	1387	1454	1805		324	473	385	422		33	77
3841 Shipbuilding and repairing		-	-	-	-		-	-	-	-		...	...
3842 Railroad equipment	p/	169	182	144	162	p/	78	41	30	39		...	...
3843 Motor vehicles		1146	1205	1310	1643		246	433	356	383		...	...
3844 Motorcycles and bicycles	p/	...	...	...	...	p/	...	...	...	...		...	...
3845 Aircraft	p/	...	...	...	...	p/	...	...	...	...		...	...
3849 Other transport equipment	p/	...	...	...	...	p/	...	...	...	...		...	...
385 Professional and scientific equipment		17	24	33	39		10	13	17	22	f/	17	1
3851 Prof. and scientific equipment n.e.c.		...	...	...	...		...	...	...	...		...	...
3852 Photographic and optical goods		...	...	...	...		...	...	...	...		...	...
3853 Watches and clocks		...	...	...	...		...	...	...	...		...	...
390 Other manufacturing industries		88	104	134	177		45	51	79	96	f/	...	...
3901 Jewellery and related articles		...	...	...	...		...	...	...	...		...	...
3902 Musical instruments		...	...	...	...		...	...	...	...		...	...
3903 Sporting and athletic goods		...	...	...	...		...	...	...	...		...	...
3909 Manufacturing industries, n.e.c.		...	...	...	...		...	...	...	...		...	...
3 Total manufacturing		21451	23305	30151	35338		10240	10503	12171	14546		2415	2699

a/ 3112 includes 3113, 3114, 3115, 3118 and 3121.
b/ 3116 includes 3122.
c/ 3131 includes 3132 and 3133.
d/ 3211 includes 3214.
e/ 3213 includes 3215.
f/ 385 includes 390 and 323.
g/ 3411 includes 3419.
h/ 351 includes 353 and 354.
i/ 3511 includes 3513, 353 and 354.
j/ 3522 includes 3523.
k/ 361 includes 362 and 369.
m/ 371 includes 372.
n/ 381 includes 382.

p/ 3842 includes 3844, 3845 and 3849.

Zimbabwe

ISIC Revision 2		Index numbers of industrial production											
		(1990=100)											
ISIC Industry	Note	1985	1986	1987	1988	1989	1990	1991	1992	1993	1994	1995	1996
311/2 Food products		79	88	91	90	92	100	102	104	85	90	99	89
313 Beverages	a/	73	74	83	90	88	100	103	103	97	98	92	101
314 Tobacco	a/	...	...	...	...	...	...	...	...	...	...	...	...
321 Textiles		81	88	90	94	96	100	104	82	89	95	37	37
322 Wearing apparel, except footwear	b/	77	74	83	83	95	100	103	86	88	86	69	70
323 Leather and fur products		...	...	...	...	...	...	...	...	...	...	...	...
324 Footwear, except rubber or plastic	b/	...	...	...	...	...	...	...	...	...	...	...	...
331 Wood products, except furniture	c/	91	97	90	106	94	100	113	118	106	118	128	178
332 Furniture and fixtures, excl. metal	c/	...	...	...	...	...	...	...	...	...	...	...	...
341 Paper and products	d/	82	82	87	88	96	100	105	105	109	124	114	112
342 Printing and publishing	d/	...	...	...	...	...	...	...	...	...	...	...	...
351 Industrial chemicals	e/	77	77	75	82	92	100	100	87	82	94	84	86
352 Other chemicals	e/	...	...	...	...	...	...	...	...	...	...	...	...
353 Petroleum refineries	e/	...	...	...	...	...	...	...	...	...	...	...	...
354 Misc. petroleum and coal products		...	...	...	...	...	...	...	...	...	...	...	...
355 Rubber products		...	...	...	...	...	...	...	...	...	...	...	...
356 Plastic products		...	...	...	...	...	...	...	...	...	...	...	...
361 Pottery, china, earthenware	f/	65	78	88	88	94	100	106	98	81	105	97	113
362 Glass and products	f/	...	...	...	...	...	...	...	...	...	...	...	...
369 Other non-metallic mineral products	f/	...	...	...	...	...	...	...	...	...	...	...	...
371 Iron and steel	g/	91	88	86	90	95	100	102	90	74	83	79	80
372 Non-ferrous metals	g/	...	...	...	...	...	...	...	...	...	...	...	...
381 Fabricated metal products	g/	...	...	...	...	...	...	...	...	...	...	...	...
382 Non-electrical machinery	g/	...	...	...	...	...	...	...	...	...	...	...	...
383 Electrical machinery	g/	...	...	...	...	...	...	...	...	...	...	...	...
384 Transport equipment		66	67	57	71	100	100	97	96	56	91	95	137
385 Professional and scientific equipment		...	...	...	...	...	...	...	...	...	...	...	...
390 Other manufacturing industries		131	129	122	151	169	100	98	75	194	173	109	112
3 Total manufacturing		80	82	84	89	94	100	103	95	87	95	84	89

a/ 313 includes 314.
b/ 322 includes 324.
c/ 331 includes 332.
d/ 341 includes 342.
e/ 351 includes 352 and 353.
f/ 361 includes 362 and 369.
g/ 371 includes 372, 381, 382 and 383.